D1366862

A32?5?

abnormal psychology

AN EXPERIMENTAL CLINICAL APPROACH

abnormal psychology

Third Edition

AN EXPERIMENTAL CLINICAL APPROACH

Gerald C. Davison
John M. Neale

175 YEARS OF PUBLISHING

1807 · 1982

John Wiley & Sons, Inc.
New York
Chichester
Brisbane
Toronto
Singapore

Cover: Paul Jenkins, "Phenomena After Image."
        Courtesy of the artist.

Credits: Production Supervisor: Cathy Starnella
                Development Editor: Priscilla Todd
                Design: Edward A. Burke/Ann Renzi
                Photo Researcher: Flavia Rando—Picturebook
                Photo Editor: Stella Kupferberg
                Basic Book Coordinator: Edward Starr

Copyright © 1974, 1978, 1982 by John Wiley & Sons, Inc.

All rights reserved. Published simultaneously in Canada.

Reproduction or translation of any part of this work beyond
that permitted by Sections 107 and 108 of the 1976 United
States Copyright Act without the permission of the copyright
owner is unlawful. Requests for permission or further information should be addressed to the Permissions Department,
John Wiley & Sons.

Library of Congress Cataloging in Publication Data
Davison, Gerald C.
    Abnormal psychology.

    Bibliography: p.
    Includes index.
    1. Psychology, Pathological. I. Neale, John M.,
1943-   . II. Title. [DNLM: 1. Psychopathology.
WM 100 D265a]
RC454. D3   1982   616.89   81-13150
ISBN 0-471-06159-X   AACR2

Printed in the United States of America

10 9 8 7 6

To Eve and Asher

GCD

To Gail and Sean

JMN

Gerald C. Davison is Professor of Psychology and Director of Clinical Training at the University of Southern California. From 1966 to 1979, he was on the psychology faculty at the State University of New York at Stony Brook. In the 1969-1970 academic year he was visiting associate professor at Stanford University, where he received his Ph.D. in 1965, and in 1975-1976, a National Institute of Mental Health Special Fellow at Harvard, where he obtained his B.A. in 1961. He has published widely in the general area of behavior therapy and personality, with particular emphasis on theoretical and philosophical issues, and is co-author of *Clinical Behavior Therapy* (1976). He is a Fellow of the American Psychological Association and has served on the Executive Committee of the Division of Clinical Psychology, on the Board of Scientific Affairs, on the Committee on Scientific Awards, and on the Council of Representatives. He is also a past-president of the Association for Advancement of Behavior Therapy. He has been on the editorial board of several professional journals, including the *Journal of Consulting and Clinical Psychology, Behavior Therapy,* and *Cognitive Therapy and Research.* His current research program focuses on the relations between cognition and stress. In addition to his teaching and research, he is a practicing clinical psychologist.

John M. Neale, a Canadian, received his B.A. from the University of Toronto in 1965 and his Ph.D. from Vanderbilt University in 1969. Thereafter he spent a year as Fellow in Medical Psychology at Langley Porter Neuropsychiatric Institute and since then has been at the State University of New York at Stony Brook, where he is Professor of Psychology. His major research interests are cognitive processes in schizophrenia, the study of children at high risk for the disorder, and the effects of life stress on health. In 1974 he won the American Psychological Association's Early Career Award for his research in schizophrenia. He is a consulting editor for the *Journal of Abnormal Psychology.* In addition to being a reviewer and an active contributor to professional journals such as the *Journal of Abnormal Psychology,* he has coauthored four books, *Science and Behavior: An Introduction to Methods of Research, The Early Window: Effects of Television on Children and Youth, Psychology,* and *Schizophrenia.* And in addition to his research and teaching activities, he is involved in clinical supervision and training.

Preface

Contemporary abnormal psychology is a field in which there are few hard and fast answers. Indeed, the very way the field should be conceptualized and the kinds of questions that should be asked are hotly debated issues. In this book we have tried to present what glimpses there are of answers to two primary questions: what causes deviant behavior and which treatments are most effective in reducing psychological suffering.

It has become commonplace in psychology to recognize the selective nature of perception. Certainly the writing of a textbook is guided by biases on the part of the authors, and our effort is no exception. We share a strong commitment to a scientific approach but at the same time appreciate the often uncontrollable nature of the subject matter and the importance of clinical findings. Rather than pretend that we are unbiased and objective, we have tried to alert readers to our assumptions. Forewarned in this manner, they may consider on their own the merits of our point of view. At the same time, we attempt as best we can to represent fairly and comprehensively the major alternative conceptualizations in contemporary psychopathology. A recurrent theme in the book is the importance of points of view or, to use Kuhn's (1962) phrase, paradigms. Our experience in teaching undergraduates has made us very much aware of the importance of making explicit the unspoken assumptions underlying any quest for knowledge. In our handling of the paradigms, we have tried to make their premises clear. Long after specific facts are forgotten, the student should retain a grasp of the basic problems in the field of psychopathology.

A related issue is the use of more than one model in studying abnormal psychology. Rather than force an entire field into, for example, a social-learning paradigm, we argue, from the available information, that different problems in psychopathology are amenable to analyses within different frameworks. For instance, physiological processes must be considered when examining mental retardation and schizophrenia, but for many disorders a cognitive behavioral theory seems the most helpful.

Preparing this third edition has given us an opportunity to strengthen many parts of the book and to include significant new material that has appeared since completion of the second edition. Those familiar with our earlier efforts will find that our basic orientation has not changed. Our intent is to communicate to students our own excitement about our discipline, particularly the puzzles that challenge researchers in their search for the causes of psychopathology and for ways to prevent and ameliorate it. We try to encourage readers to participate with us in a process of discovery as we sift through the evidence on the origin of abnormal behavior and the effectiveness of specific treatments.

Any abnormal psychology textbook written in the 1980s must attend to the third edition of the *Diagnostic and Statistical Manual of Mental Disorders,* and ours does. It has been gratifying to note that many of the changes introduced into DSM-III—recategorizing affective disorders, better definitions of each category, omission of homosexuality from the list of mental disorders, a narrower definition of schizophrenia—were anticipated and advocated in our two earlier editions. To help readers find their way through DSM-III, a summary table on the back end-papers of the book compares DSM-III with DSM-II.

We do not accept DSM-III uncritically; those responsible for its compilation are themselves aware of our incomplete and evolving understanding of human suffering. Many times throughout the book we comment critically on this diagnostic scheme. We have every expectation that there will be a DSM-IV one day, and we hope to make some contribution, along with other colleagues, to the continuing refinement of the manual.

A major organizational change in the textbook was made in response to suggestions from users of the previous editions. Treatments of specific disorders are now discussed in the chapters reviewing them. The final section on treatment is retained, however, for we continue to believe that only a separate and extended consideration of interventions allows us to explore with the reader the many perplexing and intriguing problems encountered by mental health professionals. Chapter 2, the pivotal chapter devoted to paradigms, now covers their implications for treatment. This heavily rewritten chapter lays the foundation for Chapters 5 through 17, which describe the various disorders and give what is known about their etiologies and about treating and preventing them.

Part Five, entitled Developmental Disorders, is almost entirely new. Chapters 15 and 16 cover childhood disorders; Chapter 17 considers the clinical problems of older people, in what we believe is the most comprehensive review of this important subject in a textbook on abnormal psychology. The brain dysfunctions delirium and dementia are described in this new chapter on aging. Other brain dysfunctions are discussed in the Appendix.

Chapters 11 and 12 still cover sexual problems, but with different emphases. Chapter 11 is now devoted to what DSM-III calls the paraphilias, with an extended discussion of rape and its aftermath. Chapter 12 of the first two editions discussed homosexuality, but because it is not a psychological disorder, we have now eliminated most of this material. In Chapter 11 a few critical points about how people have regarded and studied homosexuality are retained. The new Chapter 12 is an extensive review of the psychosexual dysfunctions and their treatment.

In the second edition we dealt at length with modern psychodynamic theories and their relation to behavior therapy; in this edition we continue to investigate a rapprochement of therapeutic interventions. More space is now given to the several humanistic and existential points of view and to their influence on the thinking and practices of contemporary behavior therapists. The cognitive enthusiasts within the behavioral camp in particular seem to be consorting with their insight-oriented counterparts, without always realizing it.

It is a pleasure to acknowledge the contributions of a number of students and colleagues to this revision. Helpful library research was done at Stony Brook by Robert Emery, Arthur C. Houts, and Bruce Reed, and at the University of Southern California by Curt Hileman, Sam Popkin, and Carl Osborn. Robert Emery also drafted a considerable portion of Chapter 15. We continued to enjoy and benefit from the skills and dedication of our "Wiley family," Jack Burton, Stella Kupferberg, Cathy Starnella, Ann Renzi, and Connie Rende. As before, our deepest appreciation goes to Priscilla Todd, who lent her writing talents to what we have striven mightily to make a readable and engaging text, without sacrificing scientific accuracy or professional responsibility. We wish to thank as well the secretarial work of Fran Goldstein at Stony Brook and of Gertrude Langerud at the University of Southern California. Finally, our loving thanks to our respective families, who once again have had to put up with "lost weekends" and occasional grumpiness: Gail and Sean Neale and Carol, Eve, and Asher Davison.

September 1981

Gerald C. Davison
John M. Neale

Santa Monica, California
Stony Brook, New York

Contents

Pablo Picasso, "Man With A Hat" (December 1912). Collection, The
Museum of Modern Art, New York. Purchase.

part one
introduction and basic issues

1

chapter 1

INTRODUCTION: HISTORICAL AND SCIENTIFIC CONSIDERATIONS

The Mental Health Professions
History of Psychopathology
Science: A Human Enterprise

Slumping in a comfortable leather chair, Ernest H., a thirty-five-year-old city policeman, looked skeptically at his therapist as he struggled to relate a series of problems. His recent inability to maintain an erection when making love to his wife was the immediate reason for his seeking therapy, but after gentle prodding from the therapist, Ernest recounted a host of other difficulties, some of them dating from his childhood but most of them originating during the previous several years.

Ernest's childhood had not been a happy one. His mother, whom he had loved dearly, died suddenly when he was only six, and for the next ten years he lived either with his father or with a maternal aunt. His father drank so heavily that he seldom managed to get through any day without some alcohol. Moreover, the man's moods were extremely variable; he had even spent several months in a state hospital with a diagnosis of "manic-depressive psychosis." The father's income was irregular and never enough to pay bills on time or to allow his son and himself to live in any but the most run-down neighborhoods. At times the father was totally incapable of caring for himself, let alone his son. Ernest would then spend weeks, sometimes months, with his aunt in a nearby suburb.

Despite these apparent handicaps, Ernest completed high school and entered the tuition-free city university. He earned his miscellaneous living expenses by waiting table at a small restaurant. During these college years his psychological problems began to concern him. He often became profoundly depressed, for no apparent reason, and these bouts of sadness were sometimes followed by periods of manic elation. His lack of control over these mood swings troubled him greatly, for he had observed this same pattern in his alcoholic father. He also felt an acute self-consciousness with people who he felt had authority over him—his boss, his professors, and even some of his class-

mates, with whom he compared himself unfavorably. He was especially sensitive about his clothes, which were old and worn compared to those of his peers; their families had more money than his.

It was on the opening day of classes in his junior year that he first saw his future wife. When the tall, slender young woman moved to her seat with grace and self-assurance, his were not the only eyes that followed her. He spent the rest of that semester watching her from afar, taking care to sit where he could glance over at her without being conspicuous. Then one day, as they and the other students were leaving class, they bumped into each other quite by accident, and her warmth and charm emboldened him to ask her to join him for some coffee. When she said yes, he almost wished she had not.

Amazingly enough, as he saw it, they soon fell in love, and before the end of his senior year they were married. Ernest could never quite believe that his wife, as intelligent a woman as she was beautiful, really cared for him. As the years wore on, his doubts about himself, and about her feelings toward him, would continue to grow.

He had hoped to enter law school, and both his grades and law school boards made these plans a possibility, but he decided instead to enter the police academy. His reasons, as he related them to his therapist, had to do with doubts about his intellectual abilities, as well as his increasing uneasiness in situations in which he felt himself being evaluated. Seminars had become unbearable for him in his last year in college, and he had hopes that the badge and uniform of a police officer would give him the instant recognition and respect that he seemed incapable of earning on his own.

To help him get through the academy, his wife quit college at the end of her junior year, against Ernest's pleas, and sought a secretarial job. He felt she was far brighter than he and saw no reason why she should sacrifice her potential to help him make his way in life. But at the same time he recognized the fiscal realities and grudgingly accepted her financial support.

The police academy proved to be even more stressful than college. Ernest's mood swings, although less frequent, still troubled him. And like his father, who was now confined to a state mental hospital, he drank to ease his psychological pain. He felt that his instructors considered him a fool when he had difficulty standing up in front of the class to give an answer that he himself knew was correct. But he made it through the physical, intellectual, and social rigors of the academy, and he was assigned to foot patrol in one of the wealthier sections of the city.

Several years later, when it seemed that life should be getting easier, he found himself in ever greater turmoil. Now thirty-two years of age, with a fairly secure job which paid reasonably well, he began to think of starting a family. His wife wanted this as well, and it was at this time that his problems with impotence began. He thought at first it was the alcohol—he was drinking at least six ounces of bourbon every night, except when on the swing shift. Soon, though, he began to wonder whether he was actually avoiding the responsibility of having a child, and later he began to doubt that his wife really found him attractive and desirable. The more understanding and patient she was about his sometimes frantic efforts to consummate sex with her, the less "manly" he felt himself to be. He was unable to accept help from his wife, for he did not believe that this was the "right" way to maintain a sexual relationship. The problems in bed spread to other areas of their lives. The less often they made love, the more suspicious he was of his wife, for she had become even more beautiful and vibrant as she entered her thirties. In addition, she had been promoted to the position of administrative assistant at the law firm where she worked. She would mention—perhaps to taunt him—long, martini-filled lunches with her boss at a posh uptown restaurant.

The impetus for his contacting the therapist was an ugly argument with his wife one evening when she came home from work after ten. Ernest had been elated and agitated for several days. To combat his fear that he was losing control, he had consumed almost a full bottle of bourbon each night. By the time that his wife walked in the door on that final evening, Ernest was already very drunk, and he attacked her both verbally and physically about her alleged infidelity. In her own anger and fear, she questioned his masculinity in striking a woman and taunted him with the disappointments of their lovemaking. Ernest stormed out of the house, spent the night at a local bar, and the next day somehow pulled himself together enough to seek professional help.

Every day of our lives we must try to understand the behavior of people with whom we come in contact. Determining why another person does or feels something is a difficult task. Indeed, we do not always understand why we ourselves feel and behave as we do. Acquiring insight into what we consider the normal range of expected behavior is arduous enough, but human behavior beyond the normal range, such as that of the policeman just described, is even more perplexing.

When we refer to strange behavior, we frequently use phrases such as "He's out of his mind," "He's all screwed up," "He's a maniac," "She's a hysteric," or "She's really paranoid." Such terms indicate that as observers we have found a person's behavior inexplicable and can attribute it only to an unbalanced mind. These minds are very often much sounder than such phrases and adjectives imply. Terrifying instances of unusual behavior, however, although not personally observed by most of us, are very much in the public eye. Hardly a week passes that a violent act, such as an ugly axe murder or multiple slayings, is not reported. The assailant is diagnosed by a police officer or mental health authority as a "mental case" and is found to have had a history of mental instability. Sometimes we learn that the person has previously been confined in a mental hospital.

This book is concerned with the whole range of abnormal behavior and with the various explanations for it, both past and present. There are, however, numerous pitfalls in seeking valid explanations. To study abnormal psychology, we must have what might be called "great tolerance for ambiguity," an ability to be comfortable with very tentative, often conflicting pieces of information. Much less is known with certainty about the field than we might hope, presenting problems both for the professional and for the beginning student. Indeed, as already indicated, precious little is known of why human beings behave in a normal fashion, to say nothing of their abnormal behavior. In approaching the study of psychopathology, we do well to keep in mind that the subject offers few hard and fast answers. Although we shall report such findings as there are, many of the facts that will be introduced will undoubtedly be outdated in a matter of years. And yet, as will become evident when we discuss our orientation to scientific inquiry, the study of abnormal behavior is no less worthwhile because of its ambiguities. The kinds of questions asked rather than the specific answers available at any particular time constitute the very essence of the field.

Another problem that professionals share with laypeople is the closeness of any human being to the subject matter of behavior. Physicists, for example, would seem better able to detach themselves emotionally from their subject matter than psychologists, particularly those who specialize in the study of abnormal behavior. The pervasiveness and disturbing effects of abnormal behavior intrude on our lives. Who, for example, has not experienced irrational thoughts and feelings? Or who has not known someone, a friend or perhaps a relative, whose behavior was impossible to fathom? If you have, you realize how frustrating and frightening it is to try to understand and help a person suffering psychological difficulties.

Our closeness to the subject matter, of course, adds to its intrinsic fascination; no wonder that undergraduate courses in abnormal psychology are among the most popular in psychology departments and indeed in the entire college curriculum. Familiarity with the subject matter encourages people to study abnormal psychology, but it has one distinct disadvantage. All of us have already developed certain ways of thinking and talking about behavior, certain words and concepts that somehow seem to *fit*. For example, some may assert that the study of fear should concentrate on the immediate experience of fear; this is technically known as a _phenomenological_ approach and is one formal way of setting about the study of human behavior. As behavioral scientists, we ourselves have had to grapple with the difference between what we may *feel* is the appropriate way to talk about human behavior and experience, and what we have learned to be more fruitful means of discussing behavior. Where most people would speak of a "feeling of terror," we might be more inclined to use a phrase such as "fear-response of great magnitude." In doing so we would not be merely playing verbal games. The word "games" does in-

deed apply in the sense that our procedures have rules, but it does not apply in the sense that we are engaging in activities that do not mean very much or that could just as well be carried out in another fashion. The crucial point is that the concepts and verbal labels we use in the serious study of abnormal behavior must be free of the subjective feelings of appropriateness ordinarily attached to certain human phenomena. We may be asking you, then, to adopt frames of reference different from those you are accustomed to, and indeed different from those we ourselves employ when we are not wearing our professional hats.

The case study with which this chapter began is open to a wide range of interpretations. No doubt you have some ideas about how Ernest's problems developed, what his primary difficulties are, and perhaps even how you might try to help him. We know of no greater intellectual or emotional challenge than deciding both how to conceptualize the life of a person with psychological problems and how best to treat him or her. At the end of the next chapter we refer back to the case of Ernest H. to illustrate how workers from different theoretical orientations might describe him and seek to help.

The Mental Health Professions

The training of clinicians, the various professionals who are regarded as legitimate purveyors of psychological services, takes different forms. A _psychiatrist_ is a physician who holds an M.D. degree and has taken postgraduate training, called a residency, wherein he or she has received supervision in psychotherapy. By virtue of the M.D. degree, the psychiatrist can also continue functioning as a physician—giving physical examinations, diagnosing medical problems, and the like. In actuality, however, the only aspect of medical practice that most psychiatrists engage in is prescribing _psychoactive drugs,_ chemical compounds which are able to change how people feel and think.

The term _psychoanalyst_ is reserved for those individuals who have received specialized training at a psychoanalytic institute; the program usually involves several years of clinical training as well as an in-depth psychoanalysis of the trainee. Although Sigmund Freud held that psychoanalysts do _not_ require medical training, until recently most psychoanalytic institutes required of their graduates an M.D. and a psychiatric residency. After the B.A., then, it can take up to ten years to become a psychoanalyst. Psychoanalysts are usually in private practice, and their fees are extremely high.

To practice _clinical psychology_ (the profession of the authors of this textbook) requires a Ph.D. degree, which usually entails four to five years of graduate study. Training is much like that for the other special fields of psychology—experimental, physiological, social, developmental—with a heavy emphasis on laboratory work, research design, statistics, and the empirically based study of human and animal behavior. As with these other fields of psychology, the degree is basically a research one, and candidates are required to write a lengthy dissertation on a specialized topic. In addition, however, clinical psychologists learn how to practice psychotherapy, much as a psychiatrist in training does. They take courses in which they master specific techniques under close professional supervision; then, during an intensive internship or postdoctoral training, clinicians gradually assume increasing responsibility for the care of patients.

Other graduate programs prepare people for psychotherapeutic practice. Some schools have initiated Psy.D. (Doctor of Psychology) programs for training in clinical psychology. The curriculum offered candidates for this new degree is generally the same as that available to Ph.D. students, but there is less emphasis on research and more on clinical training. The assumption is that clinical psychology has advanced to a level of knowledge that justifies—and even requires—intensive training in specific techniques of therapeutic intervention. A _psychiatric social worker_ obtains a Master of Social Work degree. There are also master's and doctoral-level programs in _counseling psychology,_ somewhat similar to graduate training in clinical psychology but usually with less emphasis on research. Recent years have seen a movement to _paraprofessional training,_ in which workers without advanced degrees learn to conduct various forms of therapy under the close supervision of professionals.

The actual therapy conducted by any of these individuals depends for the most part on the orientation of the school attended. By and large, except for the administration of drugs, specific therapies relate very little to the therapist's academic degree.

In addition to professionals who offer therapeutic services to the public, there is a highly diverse group who can be called _psychopathologists._ These people conduct research into the nature and development of the various disorders that their therapist colleagues try to treat. Psychopathologists may come from any number of disciplines; some are clinicians, but the educational backgrounds of others may range from biochemistry to developmental psychology, and their academic degrees are at virtually any level. What unites them is their commitment to the study of how abnormal behavior develops. Since relatively little is known about psychopathology, the diversity of backgrounds and interests is an advantage, for it is too soon to be certain where major advances will be made. The work of both psychopathologists and clinicians provides the subject matter of this book.

History of Psychopathology

Some General Remarks on Historical Analysis

Before we present a brief history of psychopathology in order to place contemporary developments in perspective, it may be useful to comment on the manner in which historians go about reconstructing the past. Let us consider what archaeologists conjecture about *trephining,* a crude surgical practice believed to have been prevalent in the Stone Age. They have assumed that people of very early periods chipped away holes in the skulls of troubled comrades to allow the escape of evil spirits who were supposedly causing deviant behavior. But on what is this supposition based, since there are no known recorded interviews with people who practiced this primitive surgical art? First of all, skulls with circular holes in them have been found by ar-

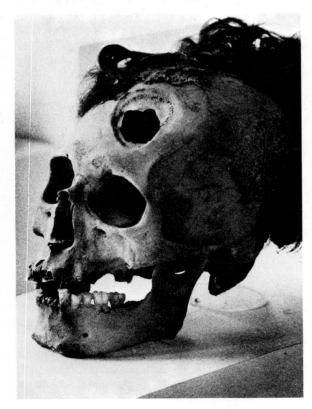

A trephined skull with some healing of the bone, indicating that the disturbed patient sometimes survived this crude Stone Age operation.

chaeologists in Britain, France, and other parts of Europe and in Peru. The holes in these skulls seem to have been intentionally created by repeated impacts with sharp stones. Because bone had grown back at the edges of the circle in a number of these skulls, it is clear that at least some people survived these crude operations. But why do historians conclude that these holes were made for the purposes just mentioned rather than, for example, inflicted in the heat of combat?

The currently popular interpretation of trephining as a practice to facilitate the exit of evil spirits from a person's mind and body is closely linked to what historians have been able to learn and conjecture about the nature of Stone Age man's social order and beliefs. Even before the trephined skulls were found, historians had anticipated that such practices were in vogue. Finding skulls with holes in them strengthened this supposition, although it is unclear how prehistoric man determined that the spirits were located in the head. Conjecture seems a reasonable means for trying to find out what happened in the preliterate past, but we must be mindful of the amount of inference resorted to.

Even when historians can rely on written records, they still have difficulty making generalizations. We often hear phrases such as "The Renaissance *began* with the . . ." What in fact does this mean? Consider a recent event that is likely to be discussed in future history books. When did the so-called drug culture begin? The onset of this important phenomenon might be traced to the visit of Dr. Timothy Leary to Mexico, where he was first exposed to the "magic mushrooms." We could look earlier to the publication of a fascinating little book by Aldous Huxley, entitled *Doors of Perception.* Or perhaps the drug culture "began" when Leary and his colleague Richard Alpert (who became known as Baba Ram Dass) left Harvard in 1962, for up until that time it seems reasonable to assert that only among graduate students at Harvard was psilocybin being used for the deliberate induction of "psychedelic" states. Not until the two men went out into the world could their work have had a more general influence. Consider also the migration of the "flower people" to the Haight-Ashbury district of San Francisco in the 1960s. No doubt

The drug culture is often thought of as a modern phenomenon. But in earlier centuries opium dens were common in Asian cultures.

any adequate history of this period would have to include all these events and many more. But what brought about the phenomenon of taking psychedelic drugs? What are the dimensions of the phenomenon? How far back in time must we go to trace and *explain* the initial urge? These are formidable questions indeed, and perhaps in the course of this book some light may be shed on these issues; our point here is merely to indicate the difficulties inherent in making generalizations about the sweep of human events.

Historical Overview

As psychopathologists, our interest is in the causes of deviant behavior. The search for these causes has gone on for a considerable period of time. Before the age of scientific inquiry, all good and bad manifestations of power beyond the control of humankind—eclipses, earthquakes, storms, lightning and thunder, fire, serious and disabling disease, darkness and light, the passing of the seasons—were regarded as supernatural. Any behavior seemingly beyond the control of the individual was subject to similar interpretation. The earliest writings of the philosophers, theologians, and physicians who studied the troubled mind found its deviancy to reflect the displeasure of the gods or possession by demons.

Early demonology

The doctrine that a semiautonomous or completely autonomous evil being, such as the devil, may dwell within a person and control his or her mind and body is called *demonology.* We have already presented the current suppositions about Stone Age trephining. Thousands of years later the ancient Babylonians had in their religion a specific demon for each disease. Idta was the demon who caused insanity. Similar examples of demonological thinking can be found in the records of early Chinese, Egyptians, and Greeks. Among the Hebrews as well, deviancy was attributed to possession of the person by bad spirits, after God in his wrath had withdrawn protection. Christ is reported to have cured a man with an "unclean spirit" by casting out the devils from within him and hurling them onto a herd of swine. The animals were then said to have become possessed and to have run "violently down a steep place into the sea" (Mark 5: 8-13). Treatment to combat and exorcise demons typically took the form of elaborate prayer rites, noise making, forcing the afflicted to drink terrible-tasting brews, and on occasion more extreme measures such as flogging and starvation in order to render the body uninhabitable to the devils.

Even in these early times, however, priests learned to temper their incantations with kindness. Imhotep, a third-dynasty Egyptian priest of great wisdom and accomplishment, became a demigod soon after his death and many centuries later, in Ptolemaic times, the deity of healing. Many shrines and temples were erected to him. The Imhotep temple in Memphis, Egypt, became a hospital and medical school. Sleeping in the temple was a principal means of therapy. Patients were also urged to engage in artistic endeavors, to take excursions on the Nile, and to attend concerts and dances. The Greek god of medicine, Asclepius, is similarly thought to have

lived as a human physician, in about 1200 B.C., and then been deified in later times. The temples erected to him were near healing springs or on high mountains. And again the priests of this sect relied on sleep within the sanctuaries; in their dreams patients were supposedly visited and advised by Asclepius or one of his priests. In the morning they departed cured or began the regimens revealed to them in their dreams. Baths, diet, and walking, riding, and other exercise all played a part in treatment. But those whose erratic behavior lay beyond these healing measures might be chased from the temples by stoning.

Somatogenesis

In the fifth century B.C. Hippocrates (460–370 B.C.) received his early medical training at the famous temple of Asclepius at Cos. Often regarded as the father of modern medicine and operating outside the *Zeitgeist* or intellectual and emotional orientation of the times, he separated medicine from religion, magic, and superstition and rejected the prevailing Greek belief that the gods sent serious physical diseases and mental disturbances as punishment. He insisted instead that such illnesses had natural causes and hence should be treated like other more common maladies such as colds and constipation. Hippocrates regarded the brain as the organ of consciousness, of intellectual life and emotion, and it followed that if someone's thinking and behavior were deviant, there was some kind of brain pathology. He is often considered one of the very earliest proponents of a *somatogenic* hypothesis to explain disordered behavior—that something wrong with the *soma* or physical body disturbs thought and action. He also recognized that environmental and emotional stress can damage the body and mind. Hippocrates classified mental disorders into three categories, mania, melancholia, and phrenitis or brain fever. Through his teachings the phenomena of abnormal behavior became more clearly the province of physicians than of priests.

In treating patients, Hippocrates tried to find natural remedies for what he regarded as natural phenomena. For melancholia he prescribed tranquility, sobriety, care in choosing food and drink, and abstinence from sexual activity. Such a regi-

The Greek physician Hippocrates held a somatogenic view of abnormal behavior, considering insanity a disease of the brain.

men was assumed to have a healthful effect on the brain and the body. Because Hippocrates believed in natural causes rather than supernatural, he depended on his own keen observations and made a valuable contribution as a clinician. Remarkably detailed records describing many of the symptoms now recognized in epilepsy, alcoholic delusion, stroke, and paranoia have come down to us from him.

Hippocrates' physiology was rather crude, however, for he conceived of normal brain functioning, and therefore of mental health, as dependent on a delicate balance among four "humors" or fluids of the body, namely blood, black bile, yellow bile, and phlegm. An imbalance produced disorders. If a person was sluggish and dull, for example, the body supposedly contained a preponderance of phlegm. A preponderance of black bile was the explanation for melancholia, too much yellow bile explained irascibility and anxiousness, and too much blood changeable temperament. Hippocrates' humoral pathology has not, of course, withstood later scientific scrutiny. His basic premise, however, that human behavior is directly determined by bodily structures or substances, and that abnormal behavior is produced by some kind of imbalance or even damage, foreshadowed aspects of contemporary thought. In the seven centuries before and after the birth of Christ, Hippocrates' naturalistic approach to disorder was generally accepted by other Greeks, such as Plato, Aristotle, and Galen, as well as by the Romans, who adopted the medicine of the Greeks after their city became the seat of power in the ancient world.

Asclepiades, a Greek physician who practiced in Rome around 100 B.C., held to a somatogenic premise with a different physiology. He considered the body to be made up of attracting and repelling atoms, between which were pores. If the pores grew too large or too small, the individual became ill. Therapy consisted of restoring atoms to proper harmonious motility through massage, baths, soothing music, fresh air, corrective diet, and soporifics such as wine. But Asclepiades was a clinical observer of mental disorders, just as Hippocrates had been. He distinguished between acute deleria and chronic disorders, between delusional conditions and those in which hallucinations were experienced. He did much to win the Romans over to Greek medical practices, vehemently opposing restraints for the mentally disturbed and their confinement in dungeons.

Aretaeus, another Greek physician practicing in Rome two centuries later, considered certain mental disorders to be extensions of normal personality traits. He theorized that individuals whose natures are irritable, violent, and too easily elated may give way to manic excitement. Those overly serious in temperament may be overcome by melancholia. He also understood, correctly, that mania and melancholia could be phases of one and the same illness, with periods of lucidity between them.

Galen, the last major physician of the classical era (A.D. 130–200), was a prolific writer who codified the medicine of antiquity, covering the seven centuries from Hippocrates to his own time. He accepted and elaborated on the doctrine of the humors, although he was also the first experimental physiologist. The dissection of the human body was illegal in his day, but Galen was an avid explorer of the anatomy of the Barbary ape and pigs. Through his scientific examination of the nervous system, he was able to draw attention to the role of the brain in mental functioning.

Medieval woodcuts of the four temperaments thought by Hippocrates to result from excesses of the four humors. From left to right: the man with changeable temperament, who has plenty of blood; the melancholy man, full of dark bile; the hot-tempered man, who has a surplus of choler or yellow bile; and the sluggish man with too much phlegm.

The Dark Ages

In a massive generalization, historians have often suggested that the death of Galen in the third century A.D. marked the beginning of the Dark Ages for all medicine and for the treatment and investigation of abnormal behavior in particular. During the third century the imperial power of Rome became invested in the military as it wholly absorbed civil administration. The emperors were successful generals, chosen by the troops. The one aim of the armies was to preserve the frontiers of the overextended empire against the Germans and Persians. The economy collapsed under the burden, and intellectual life was greatly diminished. In 285 the empire was divided into eastern and western sectors.

A few decades later, in 313, Constantine I was converted to Christianity. The churches, which had gained some influence but were until then weak and divided, grew in strength. Then, toward the end of the fifth century (476), the last Roman emperor of the west was deposed by a German, who was also a Christian. After several centuries of decay, Greek and Roman civilization had finally ceased to be. Soon thereafter the pa-

pacy was declared independent of the state. With the disintegration of the empire into barbaric kingdoms, the papacy became the important element of unity in the west.

Moreover, monasticism had already started to spread westward from the eastern empire. Monasticism is a way of life that expresses the separation of the church from the world. Through its missionary and educational work it became a dominant world force, replacing classical culture. To lead a life of the spirit that would allow the soul to be reunited with God after death was the accepted goal. Nature was regarded as a reflection of divine will and beyond the reach of human reason. The principles of systematic observation established by the Greeks were not applicable in such a scheme.

The monasteries, however, provided infinite care and nursing of the sick, and a few were repositories for the classic Greek medical manuscripts, even though the knowledge within them might not be applied. When monks cared for the mentally disordered, they prayed over them and touched them with relics, or they concocted fantastic potions for them to drink in the waning

After the fall of Greco-Roman civilization, care of the sick, including the mentally ill, was entrusted to the monks.

phase of the moon. The families of the deranged might take them to shrines, or they sometimes disavowed them through fear and superstition. Many of the mentally ill roamed the countryside, becoming more and more bedraggled and losing more and more of their faculties.

The Middle Ages and demonology

The early church was both skeptical about *witchcraft* and disapproving of any effort to practice it.[1] In 906, however, a canonist described wicked women converted to Satan who claimed to ride by night on the backs of beasts. These claims were still denounced as false, since God alone was viewed as powerful, and clergy were urged to preach against such fantasies. In 1140 such a paragraph became part of canon law.

The dualistic heresy, which ascribed real power to the devil, and the sermons preached against witchcraft were to bring it much greater attention in the next few centuries. The numbers

[1] Much of the following material on witchcraft is based on the article on this subject in the *Encyclopaedia Britannica*, 1973, volume 23, pages 604–605.

of some heretical groups were increasing to such an extent that the state as well as the church seemed threatened. After an ecclesiastical trial, if heretics did not recant, it was decided that they should be turned over to civil authorities for punishment. About 1197 the practice of burning all heretics alive after condemnation was introduced in Spain and became the established punishment. Pope Gregory IX began sending members of the Dominican order as papal inquisitors to the threatened bishoprics. In 1252 Pope Innocent IV authorized inquisitors to use torture as a means of obtaining confessions and the names of other heretics.

In this atmosphere of heresy and the strenuous efforts to rout it, of accusations and denunciations, a populace already suffering from social unrest and recurrent famines and plagues became obsessed with the devil. Witchcraft, now viewed as instigated by the powerful Satan of the heretics, was itself a heresy and denial of God. The reputed practices of witches—attending sabbats, having intercourse with the devil, turning themselves into animals, rendering men impotent, causing a neighbor's wheat to rot, his cattle to sicken, and making people die by melting wax images of them—were no longer regarded as fantasies but believed to take place in fact. Such evil was clearly within the scope of the Inquisition, and so witches began to be hunted and burned throughout Europe, especially in Germany.

In 1484 Pope Innocent VIII, in a papal bull, exhorted the clergy of Europe to leave no stone unturned in the search for witches. He sent two Dominicans, Jakob Sprenger and Henricus Institoris, to northern Germany as inquisitors. Two years later they issued a comprehensive and explicit manual, *Malleus Maleficarum* ("the witches' hammer") to guide the witch hunts. It was a legal and theological document which came to be regarded by Catholics and Protestants alike as a textbook on witchcraft. "Carnal lust," insatiable in some women, was the reason they consorted "even with devils" and became witches. Various signs by which witches could be detected, such as red spots or areas of insensitivity on the skin, supposedly made by the claw of the devil when touching the person to seal a pact, were described. And the manual

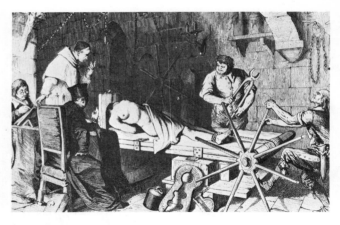

Pope Innocent VIII, whose 1484 decree launched a witch hunt that extended throughout Europe and lasted through three centuries.

Tortures by which confessions were extracted from accused witches.

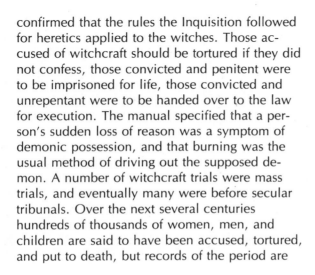

confirmed that the rules the Inquisition followed for heretics applied to the witches. Those accused of witchcraft should be tortured if they did not confess, those convicted and penitent were to be imprisoned for life, those convicted and unrepentant were to be handed over to the law for execution. The manual specified that a person's sudden loss of reason was a symptom of demonic possession, and that burning was the usual method of driving out the supposed demon. A number of witchcraft trials were mass trials, and eventually many were before secular tribunals. Over the next several centuries hundreds of thousands of women, men, and children are said to have been accused, tortured, and put to death, but records of the period are not reliable.

The first abatement in witch hunting came in Spain, in 1610, when the inquisitor Alonso Salanger y Frías concluded that most of the accusations in Lograno, Navarre, had been false. He ordained that accusations must be accompanied by independent evidence, that torture could not be used, and that the property of the convicted would not be confiscated. Thereafter accusations of witchcraft dropped sharply in Spain. Although there was to be an episode of witch hunting twenty years later, during a succeeding reign, Queen Christina of Sweden wrote a letter to one of her ministers on February 16, 1649, ordering him to free all prisoners accused of witchcraft except those clearly guilty of murder. In France

Witch burning.

The dunking test. If the woman did not drown, she was thought to be in league with the devil.

witchcraft trials declined after an edict was issued by Louis XIV in 1682. The last execution of a witch was in Switzerland, in the year 1782.[2]

The prevailing interpretation is that all the

[2] Even during the early frenzy of witch hunting, some men spoke out against this practice which so convulsed western Europe. A German physician, Henrich Agrippa, attacked the belief in witches in a book published in 1531. Paracelsus, a physician born in Switzerland, had already written his *The Diseases That Deprive Man of His Reason* around 1525, although it was not published until 1567, a good quarter century after his death. Paracelsus advocated treating diseases with minerals and metals rather than the medicines derived from plants. The second part of his book on mental diseases contains such prescriptions for them. Francois Rabelais, the great French comic writer (1494–1553), mocked those who hunted witches in his bawdy tales. In 1563 Johann Weyer (1515–1588), a student of Agrippa, published *The Deception of Demons*, a refutation of the *Malleus*, in which he asserted that many if not all "witches" were really sick mentally or bodily, and that the barbarous acts perpetrated against these people were terrible wrongs. Reginald Scot's *The Discovery of Witchcraft*, published in England in 1584, was another attack on the persecution of "aged, melancholly, and superstitious" people by the "searchers and witch-tryers."

mentally ill of the later Middle Ages were considered witches (Zilboorg and Henry, 1941). In their confessions the accused sometimes reported having had intercourse with the devil and having flown to sabbats, the secret meetings of their cults. These reports are interpreted as delusions or hallucinations and thus are taken to indicate that some witches were psychotic. Moreover, to identify people with the "Devil's mark," areas of insensitivity to pain, professional witch prickers went from town to town sticking pins into the bodies of the accused. Because anesthesia is regarded as a symptom of hysteria, the fact that some "witches" did indeed not respond to the prickings is considered evidence of their disturbed natures.

In this painting a priest is conducting an exorcism, trying to get the evil spirit to leave the woman's body.

More careful analyses of the witch hunts, however, reveal that although some accused witches were mentally disturbed, many more sane than insane people were tried. The delusionlike confessions were typically obtained during brutal torture; words were put on the lips of the tortured by their accusers and by the beliefs of the times. Indeed, in England, where torture was not allowed, the confessions did not usually contain descriptions indicative of delusions or hallucinations. Similarly, insensitivity to pain is subject to many interpretations, including organic dysfunctions. More important, there are documented cases of deliberate trickery. A needle was attached to a hollow shaft so that it did not actually puncture the skin, although to observers it appeared to be penetrating deeply (Schoeneman, 1977; Spanos, 1978).

Evaluations of other sources of information indicate that witchcraft was not the prevailing interpretation of mental illness. From the thirteenth century onward, as the cities of Europe grew larger, hospitals began to come under secular jurisdiction. Municipal authorities, when they grew powerful, tended to supplement or take over some of the activities of the church, one of these of course being the care of the ill. The foundation deed for the Holy Trinity Hospital in Salisbury, England, dating from the mid-fourteenth century, specified the purposes of the hospital. Among them was that "the mad are kept safe until they are restored of reason." British laws during this period allowed both the dangerously insane and the incompetent to be confined in a hospital. Notably, the people to be confined were not described as being possessed (Allderidge, 1979).

Neugebauer (1979) has examined the records from lunacy trials in Britain during the Middle Ages. Beginning in the thirteenth century, these trials were held to determine a person's sanity. The trials were conducted under the Crown's right to protect the mentally impaired, and a judgment of insanity allowed the Crown to become guardian of the lunatic's estate. The defendant's orientation, memory, intellect, daily life, and habits were at issue in the trial. Explanations for strange behavior typically linked it to physical illness or injury or to some emotional shock. Of all the cases that Neugebauer examines, in only *one* was demonological possession referred to. Thus it appears that this explanation of mental disturbance was not as dominant during the Middle Ages as had once been thought (see Box 1.1).

Development of asylums

Until the end of the Crusades, in the fifteenth century, there were virtually no mental hospitals in Europe. Earlier than this, however, there were thousands of hospitals for lepers. In the twelfth century, for example, England and Scotland had 220 for a population of a million and a half. After the principal Crusades had been waged, leprosy gradually disappeared from Europe, probably because of the break with the eastern sources of the infection. With leprosy no longer of such great social concern, attention seems to have focused on the mad. Towns generally drove them outside their limits or turned them over to boatmen, who would try to unload them in another city. But ports became alert to this practice and soon made it difficult to leave the insane behind. So they remained permanently on their ''ship of fools,'' traveling the rivers of Europe (Foucault, 1965).

Confinement of the mentally ill began in earnest in the fifteenth and sixteenth centuries, sometimes in what had been leprosariums. Some of these _asylums_ took in a mixed lot, beggars as well as disturbed people. Beggars were regarded as a great social problem at the time. Indeed, in

THE COMMONWEALTH OF MASSACHUSETTS

In the Year One Thousand Nine Hundred and Fifty-seven

RESOLVE RELATIVE TO THE INDICTMENT, TRIAL, CONVICTION AND EXECUTION OF ANN PUDEATOR AND CERTAIN OTHER PERSONS FOR "WITCHCRAFT" IN THE YEAR SIXTEEN HUNDRED AND NINETY-TWO.

Whereas, One Ann Pudeator and certain other persons were indicted, tried, found guilty, sentenced to death and executed in the year sixteen hundred and ninety-two for "Witchcraft"; and

Whereas, Said persons may have been illegally tried, convicted and sentenced by a possibly illegal court of oyer and terminer created by the then governor of the Province without authority under the Province Charter of Massachusetts Bay; and

Whereas, Although there was a public repentance by Judge Sewall, one of the judges of the so-called "Witchcraft Court", and by all the members of the "Witchcraft" jury, and a public Fast Day proclaimed and observed in repentance for the proceedings, but no other action taken in regard to them; and

Whereas, The General Court of Massachusetts is informed that certain descendants of said Ann Pudeator and said other persons are still distressed by the record of said proceedings; therefore be it

Resolved, That in order to alleviate such distress and although the facts of such proceedings cannot be obliterated, the General Court of Massachusetts declares its belief that such proceedings, even if lawful under the Province Charter and the law of Massachusetts as it then was, were and are shocking, and the result of a wave of popular hysterical fear of the Devil in the community, and further declares that, as all the laws under which said proceedings, even if then legally conducted, have been long since abandoned and superseded by our more civilized laws no disgrace or cause for distress attaches to the said descendants or any of them by reason of said proceedings; and be it further

Resolved, That the passage of this resolve shall not bestow on the commonwealth or any of its subdivisions, or on any person any right which did not exist prior to said passage, shall not authorize any suit or other proceeding nor deprive any party to a suit or other proceeding of any defense which he hitherto had, shall not affect in any way whatever the title to or rights in any real or personal property, nor shall it require or permit the remission of any penalty, fine or forfeiture hitherto imposed or incurred.

House of Representatives, August 26 1957.

Passed, *[signature]* Speaker.

A bill passed in 1957 by the Massachusetts legislature exonerating a woman who had been executed for witchcraft in 1692.

BOX 1.1 The Salem Incident: Witchcraft or Poisoning?

In December 1691 eight girls who lived in or near Salem Village were afflicted with "distempers," which called for medical attention. Physicians, however, could find no cause for their disorderly speech, strange postures and gestures, and their convulsive fits. One of the girls was the daughter of the minister, Samuel Parris, another his niece. A neighbor soon took it upon herself to have Parris's Barbados slave, Tituba, concoct a "witch cake" of rye meal and the urine of the afflicted, and to feed it to a dog to determine whether witchcraft was indicated. Shortly thereafter, in February 1692, the girls accused Tituba and two elderly women of witchcraft, and the three were taken into custody. In his church records Parris denounced his neighbor's action and stated that until a community member had gone "to the Devil for help against the Devil," there had been no suspicion of witchcraft and no reports of torture by apparitions.

But now the accusations began to spew from the young girls and from other residents of the village. The jails of Salem, of surrounding towns, and even of faraway Boston filled with prisoners awaiting trial. By the end of September, nineteen people had been sent to the gallows, and one man had been pressed to death. The convictions were all obtained on the bases of "spectral evidence"—an apparition of the accused had appeared to the accuser; and the test of touch—an accuser's fit ceased after he or she was touched by the accused. The afflicted girls were present at the trials and often disturbed the proceedings with their violent fits, convulsions, and apparent hallucinations of specters and "familiars."

Even before the last execution the witchcraft trials were adjourned until November. But the special court appointed earlier by Governor Phips never met again for this purpose. In January 1693 a superior court convened and received the fifty indictments for witchcraft that had already been made by a grand jury. It tried twenty persons, acquitted seventeen, and condemned three, although they were never executed. In May of 1693 Governor Phips ordered a general reprieve; about 150 persons still being held on charges of witchcraft were released, ending the strange episode.

Salem is usually discussed as an illustration of

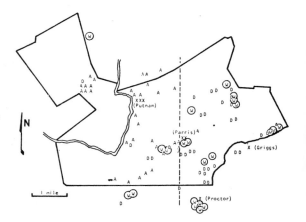

Residence patterns in Salem, 1692. The names in parenthesis indicate the homes where the "possessed" girls lived. Residents are labeled as follows: X, afflicted girl; W, accused witch; D, defender of an accused witch; and A, accuser. Thirty of the thirty-two adult accusers lived in the western section of the village and twelve of the fourteen accused witches in the eastern section.

how the hapless mentally ill of the era were mistreated through the widespread belief in possession, although the accused witches were for the most part persons of good reputation in the community. The accusers are sometimes proposed to have been schizophrenic, on the basis of their hallucinations. But schizophrenia is not likely to occur simultaneously in a group of young women. Or the episode is sometimes seen as an instance of "mass hysteria"; the witchcraft accusation, once made, mushroomed for some reason. Earlier accusations of witchcraft in Puritan communities of New England had never had such an outcome, however. Linnda Caporael (1976) has recently proposed a new theory, that the accusers were suffering from ergot poisoning.

Ergot, a parasitic fungus, grows on cereal grains, principally rye, and its development is fostered by warm, rainy growing seasons. Several of the alkaloids* of ergot contain as their

---

* Alkaloids are organic substances that are found for the most part in seed plants, usually not singly but as mixtures of similar alkaloids. They all contain nitrogen and are the active agents that give a number of natural drugs their medicinal and also their toxic properties.

Lithograph of the Salem witch trials. The powers of evil have caused the accused witch's handcuffs to fly from her hands and frighten the others present at the trial.

basis lysergic acid, from which LSD is synthesized. Ingestion of food made from flour contaminated with ergot can cause crawling sensations on the skin, tingling in the fingers, vertigo, headache, hallucinations, vomiting, diarrhea, and convulsions. The alkaloids of ergot can also induce delirium and mood changes such as mania and depression.

Could ergot poisoning account for the events in question? First, the behavior of the initial accusers is indeed similar to the known effects of ergot poisoning. The girls did report having hallucinations; they also vomited, had convulsions, and said that they felt as though they were being choked and pricked with pins. Second, rye was a well-established crop in Salem, and there had been heavy rains in 1691, which would facilitate the growth of the fungus. Rye was usually harvested in August and threshed in the late autumn. The onset of the girls' strange behavior occurred at about the time they would be beginning to eat food made from the new grain. The accumulating accusations of witchcraft appar-

ently came to an abrupt halt in the following autumn, when a new supply of grain, grown during a dry 1692, became available. After that time the afflictions of the girls and those of others in Salem are not mentioned.

What can account, though, for the fact that only some people felt that their bodies had been possessed? Caporael argues that the western portion of Salem Village, where the ground is lower and the meadows are swampy, would be the most likely source of contaminated grain. The pattern of residence of the young girls and of the other accusers fits this hypothesis; they were more likely to reside in or to eat grain grown in the western fields. Most of the accused witches and their defenders lived in the eastern section of the village.

Caporael has presented a compelling set of arguments for her ergot poisoning theory. Of course, it remains a theory, but it is interesting to speculate how many wichcraft persecutions throughout the later Middle Ages may have had ergotism as a root cause.

the sixteenth century, Paris had 30,000 beggars in its population of fewer than 100,000. These institutions had no specific regimen for their inmates other than to get them to work. But during the same period hospitals geared more specifically for the confinement of the mentally ill also appeared. The Priory of St. Mary of Bethlehem was founded in 1243. In 1403 it housed six insane men, and in 1547 Henry VIII handed it over to the city of London, thereafter to be a hospital devoted solely to the confinement of the mentally ill. The city retained the hospital until 1948. The conditions in Bethlehem were deplorable. Over the years the word "bedlam," a contraction and popular name for this hospital, became a descriptive term for a place or scene of wild uproar and confusion. Bethlehem was eventually one of London's great tourist attractions, by the eighteenth century rivaling both Westminster Abbey and the Tower of London. Even as late as the nineteenth century, viewing the violent patients and their antics was considered entertainment, and tickets of admission to Bedlam were sold. In the Lunatics' Tower, constructed in Vienna in 1784, patients were confined in the spaces between inner square rooms and the outer walls. There they could be looked at from below by passersby. The first mental hospital in the United States was founded in Williamsburg, Virginia, in 1773.

A tour of St. Mary's of Bethlehem (Bedlam) provides amusement for these two upper-class ladies. Hogarth captures the poignancy of the scene in this eighteenth-century painting.

At the Lunatics' Tower (e, center) in Vienna, a remarkable collection of strange instruments and fetters were employed in the treatment of the insane. A lunatic in hood and straightjacket (a), padlocked to a cell wall. The machine (b) in which lunatics were swung until they were in a state of stupefaction and therefore remained quiet. A maniac strapped to a chair (c), in a position sometimes held for weeks. The "English coffin" (d) in which the lunatic was kept, his face at the hole for discipline. The face and the box together resembled a standing clock. A cell door (f) with its iron "spy-hole." An enormous wheel (g), which turned each time the lunatic inside it moved. A maniac's hands in padlocked handcuffs (h). Another straightjacketed lunatic (i).

It should not be assumed, however, that the inclusion of abnormal behavior within the domain of hospitals and medicine necessarily led to more humane and effective treatment. Benjamin Rush, who practiced medicine in the United States at the end of the eighteenth century and into the early nineteenth and is considered the father of American psychiatry, believed that mental disorder was caused by an excess of blood in the brain. Consequently, his favored treatment was to draw from "the insane" great quantities of blood, as much as six quarts over a period of a few months. Little wonder that patients so treated became less agitated (Farina, 1976)! Rush entertained another hypothesis, namely that many "lunatics" could be cured by frightening them. In one such recommended procedure the physician was to convince the patient of his impending death. A New England doctor of the nineteenth century implemented this prescription in an ingenious manner. "On his premises stood a tank of water, into which a patient, packed into a coffin-like box pierced with holes, was lowered. . . . He was kept under water until the bubbles of air ceased to rise, after which he was taken out, rubbed, and revived—if he had not already passed beyond reviving!" (Deutsch, 1949, p. 82).

The padded cell.

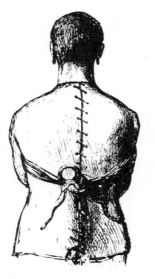

The straightjacket.

The crib, an early method for restraining mental patients.

Pinel releasing the patients at La Bicêtre.

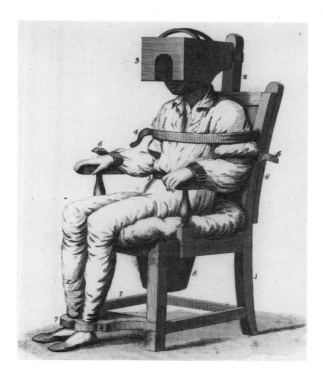

The "tranquilizing chair," used by Benjamin Rush as a means of treating mental disorders.

Moral treatment

A primary figure in the movement for humanitarian treatment of those in asylums was Philippe Pinel. In 1793, while the French Revolution raged, he was put in charge of a large asylum in Paris known as La Bicêtre. A historian has written of the conditions at this particular hospital.

[The patients were] shackled to the walls of their cells, by iron collars which held them flat against the wall and permitted little movement. . . . They could not lie down at night, as a rule. . . . Oftentimes there was a hoop of iron around the waist of the patient and in addition . . . chains on both the hands and the feet. . . . These chains [were] sufficiently long so that the patient could feed himself out of a bowl, the food usually being a mushy gruel—bread soaked in a weak soup. Since little was known

about dietetics, [no attention] was paid to the type of diet given the patients. They were presumed to be animals . . . and not to care whether the food was good or bad (Selling, 1940, p. 54).

Pinel was reluctantly allowed to remove the chains of the people imprisoned in La Bicêtre and to treat them as sick human beings rather than as beasts. Many who had been excited and completely unmanageable became calm and much easier to handle. Formerly considered dangerous, they strolled through the hospital and grounds with no inclination to create disturbances or to harm anyone. Light and airy rooms replaced their dungeons. Some who had been incarcerated for years were soon restored to health and were eventually discharged from the hospital.

Freeing the patients of their restraints was not the only humanitarian reform advocated by Pinel.[3] He believed that the mental patients in his care were essentially normal people who should be approached with compassion and understanding and treated as individual human beings with dignity. Their reason supposedly having left them because of severe personal and social problems, it might be restored to them through comforting counsel and purposeful activity.

About the time Pinel began reforming La Bicêtre, a prominent merchant and Quaker, William Tuke, had occasion to be shocked by the conditions at York Asylum in England. He proposed to the Society of Friends that they found their own institution. In 1796 York Retreat was established on a country estate. It provided the mentally ill with a quiet and religious atmosphere in which to live, work, and rest. They discussed their difficulties with attendants, worked in the garden, and took walks through the countryside. In the United States the Friends' Asylum, founded in 1817 in Pennsylvania, and the Hartford Retreat, founded in 1824 in Connecticut, were patterned after the York Retreat. A number of other American hospitals were influ-

[3] Not all scholars agree that Pinel deserves as much adulation as he enjoys. Thomas Szasz (1974), whose influential writings on involuntary hospitalization are reviewed in Chapter 21, points to sections of Pinel's famous *A Treatise on Insanity* (1801). They indicate that he relied on terror and coercion in dealing with patients of the lower classes.

Some early mental hospitals were pleasant sanctuaries located in the country. Pictured here is the retreat founded by William Tuke.

Scenes from some earlier asylums. Inmates gathered in a day room, Mattewan Insane Hospital, New York, early in this century. The painting by Silvio surveys patients in the yard of an asylum near Rome.

enced by the sympathetic and attentive treatment provided by Pinel and Tuke. Of course not all asylums adopted their so-called _moral practices,_ but the smaller ones that did achieved remarkable successes. Unfortunately, this personal attention to the patients was no longer possible when the large mental hospitals that are prevalent today began to be built (Bockhoven, 1963).

The beginning of contemporary thought

Somatogenesis Earlier Hippocrates was described as the first to enunciate a somatogenic hypothesis of mental illness. His view was revived in Europe in the middle of the nineteenth century by a German physician, Wilhelm Griesinger, who insisted that any diagnosis of mental disorder specify a physiological cause. A textbook of psychiatry, written by his well-known follower, Emil Kraepelin, and first published in 1883, furnished a classification system to help establish the organic nature of mental illnesses. Kraepelin discerned among mental disorders a tendency for a certain group of _symptoms,_ called a _syndrome,_ to appear together regularly enough to be regarded as having an underlying physical cause, much as a particular medical disease and its syndrome may be attributed to a physiological dysfunction. He regarded each mental illness as distinct from all others, having its own genesis, symptoms, course, and outcome. Even though cures had not been worked out, at least the course of the disease could be predicted. Kraepelin proposed that there were two major groups of severe mental diseases: dementia praecox, an early term for schizophrenia, and manic-depressive psychosis. He postulated a chemical imbalance as the cause of schizophrenia and an irregularity in metabolism as the explanation of manic-depressive psychosis. Kraepelin's scheme for classifying these and other mental illnesses became the basis for the present psychiatric categories, which will be described more fully in Chapter 3.

Much was being learned about the nervous system in the second half of the nineteenth century but not enough yet to reveal all the expected abnormalities in structure that might underlie mental disorders. Degenerative changes in the brain cells associated with senile and presenile psychoses and some structural pathologies that accompany mental retardation were identified, however. Pellagra and the serious disorientation brought on by it were traced to a vitamin deficiency. Perhaps the most striking medical success was the discovery of the full nature and origin of _syphilis._ The venereal disease syphilis had been recognized for several centuries, and since 1798 it had been known that a number of mental patients manifested a similar and steady deterioration of both physical and mental abilities. These patients were observed to suffer multiple impairments, including delusions of grandeur and progressive paralysis. Soon after these symptoms were recognized, it was realized that these patients never recovered. In 1825 this deterioration in mental and physical health was designated a disease, _general paresis._ Although in 1857 it was established that some patients with paresis had earlier had syphilis, there were many competing theories of the origin of paresis. For example, in attempting to account for the high rate of the disorder among sailors, some supposed that sea water might be the cause. And Griesinger, in trying to explain the higher incidence among men, speculated whether liquor, tobacco, and coffee were implicated. Then in the 1860s and 1870s Louis Pasteur established the _germ theory of disease._ It thus became possible to demonstrate the relation between syphilis and general paresis. In 1897 Richard von Krafft-

Ebing inoculated paretic patients with matter from syphilitic sores. The patients did not develop syphilis, indicating that they had been infected earlier. Finally, in 1905, the specific microorganism causing syphilis was discovered. Fortunately, measures that can detect the presence of syphilis and prevent its spread were developed soon after the discovery of the spirochete that causes it.

Psychogenesis The search for somatogenic causes dominated psychiatry until well into the twentieth century, no doubt partly because of the stunning discoveries made about general paresis. But in other parts of western Europe, in the late eighteenth century and throughout the nineteenth, mental illnesses were considered to have an entirely different genesis. Various _psychogenic_ points of view, attributing mental disorders to psychic malfunctions, were fashionable in France and Austria. For reasons that are not clear to us even today, many people in western Europe were at that time subject to hysterical states (in contemporary terms, conversion disorders): they suffered from physical incapacities that made absolutely no anatomical sense (see page 179). For example, in "glove anesthesia" the person had no feeling in his or her hand, but sensation was present just beyond the wrist and on up into the arm. Since the nerves run continuously from the shoulder down to the fingertips, there is no known physiological explanation for such an anesthesia.

Franz Anton Mesmer, an Austrian physician practicing in Vienna and Paris in the late eighteenth century, believed that hysterical disorders were caused by a particular distribution of a universal magnetic fluid in the body. Moreover, he felt that one person could influence the fluid of another to bring about a change in the person's behavior. He conducted meetings cloaked in mystery and mysticism, during which afflicted patients sat around a covered _baquet_ or tub with iron rods protruding through the cover from the bottles of various chemicals that were beneath. Mesmer would enter a room, clothed in rather outlandish garments, and take various of the rods from the tub and touch afflicted parts of his patients' bodies. The rods were believed to transmit "animal magnetism" and adjust the distribution of the universal magnetic fluid, thereby removing

Two portrayals of Franz Anton Mesmer's procedure for transmitting animal magnetism from the *baquet* to his patients. The caricature shows the process as a form of exorcism. Ordered to leave Austria, Mesmer took up practice in Paris. Benjamin Franklin was a member of the French commission that investigated his activities in 1784.

the hysterical anesthesias and paralyses. Whatever we may think of what seems today to be a questionable theoretical explanation and procedure, the fact remains that Mesmer seemingly helped quite a number of people overcome their hysterical problems. Our discussion of Mesmer's work under the rubric of psychogenic causes is rather arbitrary, since Mesmer regarded the hysterical disorders as strictly physical. Because of the setting in which Mesmer worked with his patients, however, he is generally considered one of the earlier practitioners of *hypnosis* (see Box 1.2). (The familiar word mesmerize is the older term for hypnotize.)

Although Mesmer was regarded as a quack by his contemporaries, the study of hypnosis gradually became respectable. A great Parisian neurologist, Jean Martin Charcot, also studied hysterical states, not only anesthesia and paralysis, but blindness, deafness, convulsive attacks, and gaps in memory brought about by hysteria. Practicing in the second half of the nineteenth century, Charcot initially espoused a somatogenic point of view. One day, however, some of his enterprising students hypnotized a normal woman and suggested to her certain hysterical symptoms. Charcot was deceived into believing that she was an actual hysterical patient. When the students showed him how readily they could remove the symptoms by waking the woman, Charcot changed his mind about hysteria and became interested in nonphysiological interpretations of these very puzzling phenomena. Further psychological theorizing and research was done by Pierre Janet, one of Charcot's pupils. He believed that in hysteria part of the organized system of thoughts, emotions, and sensations broke loose from the rest through a weakness of the nervous system.

In Vienna, toward the end of the century, a physician named Josef Breuer treated a young woman who had become bedridden with a number of hysterical symptoms. Her legs and right arm were paralyzed, her sight and hearing impaired, and she often had difficulty speaking. She also sometimes went into a dreamlike state or "absence," during which she mumbled to herself, seemingly preoccupied with troubling thoughts. Perhaps not knowing what else to do, Breuer hypnotized her and repeated some of her

BOX **1.2** Hypnosis

A discussion of hypnosis could appear in several chapters of this book; inasmuch as it played a central role in the development of psychogenic theories of psychopathology, we include it here.

An initial question to be asked is what exactly is hypnosis. In view of how often psychologists and psychiatrists employ the term, it is sobering to realize how much heated controversy there is about its very nature. Hilgard (1965) suggests the following characteristics.

1. *Increased suggestibility.* Hypnotized subjects seem much more open to suggestions from the hypnotist than they would be in a waking state. Indeed, many hypnotized subjects show annoyance when the hypnotist directs them to do some planning of their own while they are hypnotized. Many theorists believe that hypnosis is nothing more than a state of heightened suggestibility.

2. *Redistribution of attention.* Hypnotized subjects appear extremely attentive to what the hypnotist is saying, thereby becoming less aware of other stimulation, such as noises in an adjacent room.

3. *Heightened ability to fantasize.* Clinical evidence suggests that visual images are more vivid under hypnosis, although there is a notable lack of controlled experimental data on this point

4. *Increased tolerance for persistent distortion of reality.* Many hypnotized subjects readily accept all kinds of perceptual distortions that they would not tolerate when awake. Thus hypnotized subjects may accept suggestions that an animal is talking to them or that someone is present in the room when no one is actually there. The logic that operates during a hypnotic trance, allowing a person to perceive the world in a way remarkably different from how he or she regards it when awake, has been called "trance logic" (Orne, 1959).

5. *Role behavior.* Subjects have a greater ability to assume a particular role when hypnotized than when awake. Indeed, Sarbin (1950) has constructed an entire theory about the nature of hypnosis in terms of role taking.

These, then, are what many workers regard as characteristics of hypnotized subjects. As in all aspects of human behavior, not all people manifest all these characteristics in the same way, and it is indeed possible for subjects who otherwise appear to be deeply hypnotized not to give all these noticeable indications at any one time.

Our historical review mentioned Mesmer's therapy for hysterical disabilities and subsequent work by Charcot, Janet, and Breuer. During the same period of time surgeons were "mesmerizing" patients to block pain. For example, in 1842 a British physician, W. S. Ward, amputated the leg of a patient after hypnotizing him. Apparently the patient felt nothing during what would otherwise have been an excruciatingly painful operation. And in 1849 a mesmeric infirmary was opened in London. Hundreds of apparently painless operations were performed while the patients were in hypnotic trances. In the same decade, however, ether was proved to produce insensibility to pain. The term anesthesia had heretofore been applied to the numbness felt in hysterical states and paralysis. Oliver Wendell Holmes is credited with suggesting that it be applied to the effects of this new agent and others like it, and that the agents be called anesthetics. The availability of these chemicals for surgical operations forestalled the continuing use of hypnosis as an alleviator of pain.

The person who coined the modern term hypnotism is usually considered to be James Braid (1795–1860), a British physician who was also hypnotizing people to reduce pain. Unlike Mesmer, however, Braid did not break with his profession, describing what happened in terms that were more consistent with the *Zeitgeist*. He characterized the trance as a "nervous sleep," from which came the name "neurohypnology," later shortened to hypnotism. Braid rejected the mystical orientation of Mesmer and yet continued to experiment with the phenomenon as he saw it. He sought a physiological cause and felt he had found one in his discovery that trances could be readily induced by having people stare at a bright object located somewhat above the line of vision. The object was placed in front of a person in such a way that the levator muscles of the eyelids had to be strained in order to keep it in view. Braid suggested that the muscles were markedly affected by having them remain fixed in this position for a given period of time and that somehow this led to nervous sleep or hypnosis. He therefore placed the cause of the sleep inside the subject rather than external to him, as Mesmer had suggested with his concept of animal magnetism. In this way he was able to perform many public demonstrations without incurring the disapproval of his medical colleagues.

As already indicated, the discovery of drugs for anesthesia discouraged the use of hypnosis in medicine, for drugs are clearly more reliable, although more dangerous as well, than hypnotic inductions. In clinical work many practitioners have employed hypnotic procedures for psychotherapeutic purposes, especially during World War II. To relieve shell shock, doctors hypnotized the frightened soldier and encouraged him to relive traumatic events in his imagination.

The scientific study of hypnosis had to await the development of relatively objective measures in the 1950s. Perhaps the principal device is that developed at Stanford University by Weitzenhoffer and Hilgard (1959), the Stanford Hypnotic Susceptibility Scale. In the application of this scale, or, more properly, scales, since there are a number of them, the subject is hypnotized and then asked to undertake a series of tasks. For example, the hypnotist may suggest to a subject that his right hand is so heavy that it is doubtful whether he can raise it. Then the hypnotist will ask the subject to try to lift the heavy hand even though he probably will not be able to do so. The hypnotist observes the degree to which the subject can or cannot raise the hand and gives a plus or minus score. After the subject has been observed at a number of tasks, he is given a score ranging from zero to twelve, and this score is regarded as a measure of how deeply hypnotized he is.

Most of these scales, however, do not measure the more subjective aspects of hypnosis. For example, many hypnotized subjects, even though they have not been specifically told that it may happen, experience sensations such as floating or spinning. Many hypnotists consider such subjective experiences at least as important as the more observable performances tapped by the various scales. As we might expect, this divergence of interests contributes to the controversy within the field, with the more clinically oriented hypnotists rejecting the validity of such scales as the Stanford. They instead content themselves with what subjects report of their subjective reactions.

Stanford psychologist Ernest Hilgard, who pioneered the development of a reliable method of assessing hypnotic susceptibility.

Josef Breuer (1842–1925), the Austrian physician and physiologist whose collaboration with Freud was important in the early development of psychoanalysis. He treated only Anna O. by the cathartic method he originated. Becoming alarmed by her what would later be called transference and his own countertransference, he described his procedures to Freud and turned her treatment over to him.

mumbled words. He succeeded in getting her to talk more freely and ultimately with considerable emotion about some very troubling past events. Upon awakening from these hypnotic sessions, she would frequently feel much better. With this young woman and other hysterical patients Breuer found that the relief and cure of their symptoms seemed to last longer if, under hypnosis, they were able to recall the original precipitating event for the symptom and if, furthermore, their original emotion was expressed. This reliving of an earlier emotional catastrophe and the release of the emotional tension produced by previously forgotten thoughts about the event was called abreaction or catharsis. Breuer's method became known as the _cathartic method_. In 1895 one of his colleagues joined him in the publication of *Studies in Hysteria,* a book considered to be a milestone in abnormal psychology. Breuer's collaborator was Sigmund Freud, whose thinking we examine in the next chapter.[4]

[4] Anna O., the young woman treated by Breuer with the cathartic method or *"talking cure,"* has become one of the best-known clinical cases in all psychotherapy literature, and, as indicated above, the report of this case and four others in 1895 formed the basis of Freud's important later contributions. But historical investigations by Ellenberger (1972) cast serious doubt on how accurate Breuer's reporting was. Indeed, Anna O.—in reality Bertha Pappenheim, member of a well-to-do Viennese family—was apparently helped only temporarily by Breuer's talking cure! Carl Jung, Freud's renowned colleague, is quoted as saying that, during a conference in 1925, Freud told him that Anna O. had never been cured. Hospital records discovered by Ellenberger confirmed that she continued to rely on morphine to ease the "hysterical" problems that Breuer is reputed to have removed by catharsis. In fact, evidence suggests that some of her problems were organic, not psychological. It is fascinating and ironic to consider that psychoanalysis traces its roots back to an improperly reported clinical case.

Science: A Human Enterprise

In space exploration highly sophisticated satellites are sent aloft to make observations. Astronauts have also been catapulted to the moon, where they use their human senses as well as man-made machines to carry out still more observations. It is possible, however, that certain phenomena are being missed because our instruments do not have sensing devices capable of recording the presence or absence of such phenomena, and because people are not trained to look for them. When the Viking 1 and Viking 2 Mars landers began to forage for life in July and September of 1976, space scientists repeatedly cautioned against concluding that there was no life on Mars just because instruments failed to detect any. Scientists are sophisticated enough by training to know that they are in a bind. Life on another planet can be looked for only with the instruments they themselves have developed, but these devices are limited by their own preconceptions. The tests run on Mars make assumptions about the nature of living matter that may not match what has evolved on this distant planet. Carl Sagan, renowned Cornell space scientist, has cautioned that we may simply be asking the wrong questions. The Viking experiments can determine only whether the Martian soil samples contain earthlike life, but life on Mars could be based on an entirely different chemistry (*Time*, August 2, 1976, p. 23).

This discursion on outer space exploration is one way of pointing out that scientific observation is a human endeavor, reflecting both the strengths of human ingenuity and scholarship as well as our intrinsic incapacity to be fully knowledgeable about the nature of our universe. Scientists are able to design instruments to make only the kinds of observations about which they have some initial idea. They realize that certain observations are not being made because our knowledge about the general nature of the universe is limited. Thomas Kuhn, a well-known philosopher of science, has put the problem this way: "The decision to employ a particular piece of apparatus and to use it in a particular way carries an assumption that only certain sorts of circumstances will arise" (1962, p. 59). Robert Pirsig, in *Zen and the Art of Motorcycle Maintenance* (1974), expressed the issue somewhat more poetically: "We take a handful of sand from the endless landscape of awareness around us and call that handful of sand the world" (p. 75).

Subjectivity in Science: The Role of Paradigms

We believe that every effort should be made to study abnormal behavior according to scientific principles. It should be clear at this point, however, that science is *not* a completely objective and certain enterprise. Rather, as we can infer from the comment by Kuhn, subjective factors, as well as limitations in our perspective on the universe, enter into the conduct of scientific inquiry. Central to any application of scientific principles, in Kuhn's view, is the concept of _paradigm,_ which may be defined as a conceptual framework within which a scientist works. A paradigm, according to Kuhn, is a set of basic assumptions that outline the *particular* universe of scientific inquiry, specifying both the kinds of concepts that will be regarded as legitimate as well as methods that may be used to collect and interpret data. Indeed, every decision about what constitutes a datum, or scientific observation, is made within a paradigm. A paradigm has profound implications for how scientists operate at any given time, for "Men whose research is based on shared paradigms are committed to the same rules and standards for scientific practice" (Kuhn, 1962, p. 11). Paradigms specify what problems scientists will investigate and how they will go about the investigation.

Although made explicit only when scientists address themselves to philosophy, paradigms are nonetheless an intrinsic part of a science, serving the vital function of indicating how the game is to be played. In perceptual terms a paradigm may be likened to a general _set,_ a tendency to see certain factors and not to see others.

In addition to injecting inevitable biases into the definition and collection of data, a paradigm may also affect the interpretation of facts. In other words, the meaning or import attributed to data may depend to a considerable extent on a

An early book in astronomy depicted the relationship between the earth and the planets according to the Ptolemaic paradigm.

paradigm. Let us look briefly at the classic example of how for nearly 1400 years a particular paradigm influenced the interpretation of data about the heavens. From the second until the sixteenth century A.D., astronomy was dominated by the Ptolemaic paradigm. The earth was viewed as the center of the universe and the various planets and stars were considered to revolve around it. Although such a point of view seems rather absurd when examined in the light of current scientific knowledge, it was in fact, with some embellishments, able to provide relatively good predictions of the positions of the planets, the sun, and the moon and of such phenomena as eclipses.

Fairly accurate observations and measurements of planetary positions and motions had been made by Hipparchus, 300 years earlier, and Ptolemy had extended this work. The astronomical data to be encompassed by any paradigm interpreting the heavens were therefore considerable. To explain the retrograde, or westward, motion of planets and other orbital eccentricities—changes of position actually reflecting the revolution of the earth about the sun—the Ptolemaic

system postulated a number of complicated concepts. A planet was thought to move in a small circle, the epicycle, the center of which was at the same time traveling an orbit, the planet's deferent, around the earth. The earth was not located in the exact center of the diameter of the deferent but a little to the side, at the eccentric (Figure 1.1). The equant was yet another position on the diameter of the deferent, the same distance from the center as the eccentric. Around this point the center of each planet's epicycle appeared to move with uniform speed. To the proponents of the Ptolemaic system, who were certainly no fools, such motions seemed eminently reasonable because they explained a universe of which the earth was the immovable center. Although some minor discrepancies between the predictions and the actual observations of planetary motions remained unexplained, these discrepancies did not lead people to doubt the basic assumption, that the earth was the center of the universe. The task of astronomy for fourteen centuries was the refinement of the Ptolemaic system in order to improve its predictions.

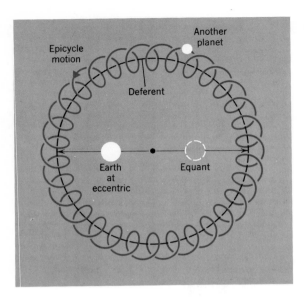

FIGURE **1.1**
Planetary movements in the Ptolemaic system, showing the epicycle, deferent, eccentric, and equant.

Kuhn (1959) has labeled such a period "normal science." Astronomers during these centuries shared a common view of the phenomena in which they were interested. Because this shared view, that the earth was the center of the universe, was so strongly held, it was never questioned when contradictory evidence was discovered. Instead, scientists attempted to readjust aspects of the paradigm. To bring the Ptolemaic system more in line with any new observations of the positions and movements of the planets, astronomers elaborated the arrangement of deferents and epicycles.

In 1543 Copernicus proposed a radically different paradigm as a theoretical basis for astronomy. Specifically, he suggested that the sun rather than the earth be considered the center of the universe. Moreover, orbits should be regarded as perfectly circular and uniform and not be subject to complexities such as the equant. *It is important to note that the Copernican revolution was not based on the acquisition of new data.* Rather, the data available to Copernicus were but little different from those available to Ptolemy over 1400 years earlier. What, then, led to the revolution in thought, the paradigm shift?

Two points seem to have been particularly important to Copernicus in his rejection of the Ptol-emaic system. First, he recognized its great complexity and lack of elegance. The Ptolemaic view of the universe had become inordinately flexible and complex—encompassing additional and eccentric epicycles—in order to avoid being disproved. Second, based on religious-cosmological considerations, Copernicus believed that planetary orbits "ought to be" circular since the circle was the most perfect form in nature. Thus we see that the postulation of a paradigm to interpret observed data can depend heavily on *subjective,* nonscientific views held by the theorist. In fact, when the Copernican system was initially proposed, it provided no increment in predictive power over what could be obtained by adhering to the Ptolemaic system. At least initially, the adoption of the Copernican paradigm was based on factors other than the adequacy with which it could account for the available data.

Subjective factors such as those we have discussed in relation to the Copernican revolution have also greatly affected theorizing about psychopathology. We have already examined several instances of what might be called "paradigm clashes" in the history of thinking about the problems of abnormal behavior (see Box 1.3). Hippocrates' revolt against demonology and the treatment reforms of Pinel can both be considered attempts to change radically the way in which abnormal behavior was viewed. Moreover, at the time these men proposed what we consider more rational approaches to abnormal behavior, they had no definitive proof that their new visions would be better than the old.

An Example of Paradigms in Abnormal Psychology

We have been examining Kuhn's concept of paradigm—a set of assumptions which are shared by investigators and determine not only what they will consider "legitimately" scientific but also how they will perceive data. A striking demonstration of this "I'll see it when I believe it" feature of science is provided in an experiment by Langer and Abelson (1974). They were interested in how different theoretical orientations might affect the ways in which trained clinicians view the "adjustment" of a person.

BOX 1.3 Paradigm Clash in the Study of Hypnosis

Box 1.2 reviewed some of the history of hypnosis and its generally accepted characteristics. There is an interesting paradigm clash about hypnosis, for the very idea that we should talk at *all* about a state called hypnosis has been challenged. Probably the most outspoken critic of "state theories" of hypnosis—conceptions of hypnosis that assume a separate state underlying the phenomena—is an experimental psychologist, Theodore X. Barber. Barber's line of reasoning, presented in scores of theoretical papers and experiments (for example, Barber, 1969), is essentially as follows.

1. "Hypnosis," as a state, is inferred solely on the basis of behavioral phenomena that it is alleged to cause. A subject's inability to lift his or her hand when extreme heaviness is suggested is, at the same time, interpreted both as a sign of hypnosis and as a result of hypnosis. To say that the heaviness indicates the person has been hypnotized and then to conclude the heaviness is caused by hypnosis is to engage in circular reasoning. Nothing has really been explained.

2. Behavior generally regarded as caused by hypnosis can be readily produced in subjects who are not given a hypnotic induction. Barber and Calverley (1964b) found that subjects will report a variety of vivid auditory and visual hallucinations, seeing and hearing things that are not really present, when they are simply urged to try very hard to hallucinate.

3. Therefore it is not scientifically useful nor is it necessary to employ a state concept of "hypnosis."

Not surprisingly, Barber's position has been attacked, sometimes vehemently, by investigators who operate under the assumption that we can talk meaningfully of a state of hypnosis. Spanos (1970), one of Barber's associates, has reviewed and replied to the principal criticisms. State theorists have suggested that the subjects in Barber's experiments, although not given a formal hypnotic induction, nonetheless slip into a hypnotic trance and *therefore* shows signs of hypnosis. Spanos points out that this is a purely *post hoc* argument, an "explanation" offered only after the data are in, and therefore impossible to refute. If nonhypnotized subjects do something hypnotic, they can be said to have slipped into a trance; but if, like many subjects, they fail to "look hypnotized," they can always be said *afterward* not to have been in a trance.

Barber's critics (for example, Conn and Conn, 1967) have also proposed that subjects' verbal reports of being hypnotized are evidence of the state. Spanos replies that scientists do not always believe what subjects tell them. For example, suppose a subject tells a hypnotist that she cannot lift her arm because the devil is holding it down. How many present-day scientists would conclude that hypnosis is the devil's doing? Moreover, an investigator who does not initially believe in a separate state of hypnosis will not be swayed by a subject's reporting that he or she has been in one.

Some of Barber's research has questioned the very existence of behavioral phenomena that state theorists have accepted on the basis of self-report. For instance, some hypnotized subjects report deafness after it has been suggested to them that they may not be able to hear. Barber and Calverley (1964a) decided to assess deafness in a less obvious fashion, one that would not rely on self-report. Delayed auditory feedback is a procedure whereby subjects hear what they are saying through headphones, although it is delayed by a given period of time, say one second. Numerous studies have shown that such delayed feedback of speech invariably causes stuttering in otherwise fluent people. Barber and Calverley reasoned that if people could truly be rendered deaf by hypnotic suggestion, they would not stutter when their words were fed back to them. In a carefully controlled experiment subjects who were, according to objective measures, deeply hypnotized were given a suggestion of deafness. They then claimed that they could not hear, but their speech was nonetheless markedly affected by delayed auditory feedback.

The authors of this book are sympathetic to the arguments of Barber and his colleagues. At the same time it seems quite reasonable to study the phenomena called hypnosis, as indeed Barber himself has done for many years. In our own clinical work we occasionally make use of hypnotic inductions to achieve certain specific ends, for example, helping people to relax. It seems possible to do this without affirming allegiance to either a state or a nonstate theory of hypnosis. The expectations a person has about being hypnotized may be the important factor. Whether a hypnotic induction *really* produces a *state* in which a person imagines more vividly than when awake seems to be secondary in importance to the possibility that a hypnotic induction may make a person *believe* that he or she can imagine more vividly.

Behavior therapy stems from the behaviorism-learning branch of psychology, which sees its purpose to be the objective observation of overt behavior and which has formulated laws describing learning. Behavior therapists believe that abnormal behavior is acquired according to the same learning principles as normal behavior and that the very designation of a person as ill reflects a social judgment. More traditionally trained clinicians look for the inner conflict supposedly causing disturbed behavior and tend more than behavior therapists to think in terms of mental illness. Langer and Abelson reasoned that behavior therapists might be less swayed by being told that a person was ill than would traditionally trained clinicians. To test this supposition, they conceived the following experiment. A group of behavior therapists and another of therapists trained in _psychoanalysis_ were shown a videotape of an interview in progress between two men. Before viewing this videotape, half the subjects in each group were told that the interviewee was a job applicant, the other half that he was a patient. The traditional clinicians who

were told that the interviewee was a patient were expected to rate him as more disturbed than those who considered him a job applicant. It was also predicted that the ratings of the two groups of behavior therapists would be unaffected by the labels and thus rather similar.

The videotape shown to all subjects depicted a bearded professor interviewing a young man in his mid-twenties. The interviewee had been recruited through a newspaper advertisement that offered ten dollars to someone who had recently applied for a new job and was willing to be interviewed and videotaped. The fifteen-minute segment chosen from the original interview contained a rambling, autobiographical monologue by the young man in which he described a number of past jobs and dwelt on his conflicts with bureaucrats. His manner was considered by Langer and Abelson to be intense but uncertain; they felt that he could be regarded either as sincere and struggling or as confused and troubled.

A questionnaire measured the clinicians' impressions about the mental health of the interviewee. When the young interviewee was identified as a job applicant, there were no significant differences in the adjustment ratings given by the traditional clinicians and the behavior therapists. But the patient label, as expected, produced sharp differences (Figure 1.2). When the interviewee was identified as a patient, the traditional clinicians rated him relatively disturbed—significantly more so than did the traditional clinicians who viewed the man as a job applicant. In contrast, the behavior therapists rated the ''ill'' interviewee as relatively well adjusted, in fact, no less adjusted than the other behavior therapists rated the man they considered a job applicant.

Qualitative evaluations obtained from the clinicians supported their ratings. Whereas the behavior therapists described the man as ''realistic,'' ''sincere,'' and ''responsible,'' regardless of label, the traditional clinicians who viewed him as a patient used phrases such as ''tight, defensive person,'' ''conflict over homosexuality,'' and ''impulsivity shows through his rigidity.''

Why, in this particular experiment, did the behavior therapists appear to be unbiased? Langer and Abelson explain it this way. The behavioral approach encourages clinicians to concentrate on overt or manifest behavior and to be skeptical about illness that is not readily apparent. Those with such an orientation had the advantage in this particular study because, however the inter-

viewee rambled, his behavior on balance was not overtly disturbed. The traditional therapists, on the other hand, had presumably been trained to look beyond what is most obvious in a client. Therefore, when the traditional therapists heard the negative ramblings about bureaucrats, they probably paid too much attention to them.

Langer and Abelson properly alert readers to the limitations of their experiment, reminding them that a different study—perhaps using an interviewee who is obviously disturbed—might put behavior therapists at a disadvantage. The purpose of the experiment, and this discussion of it, is not to pit one orientation against another but rather to illustrate how a theoretical persuasion can affect perception. Indeed, psychopathology can be in the eye of the beholder.

Thus subjective factors in the guise of theoretical persuasions pervade psychology and very much affect our conception of the nature of abnormal behavior. Scientists, whatever their field, do not resign from the family of man when they formulate hypotheses and conduct investigations and controlled research. Perhaps it is especially appropriate for the psychologist-as-scientist to remain aware of this simple, although frequently overlooked, point.

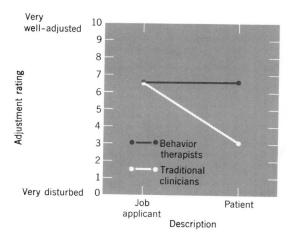

FIGURE **1.2**
The mean adjustment ratings given the interviewee, depending on the investigators' description of him and the diagnosticians' training. Adapted from Langer and Abelson, 1974.

Summary

The study of abnormal behavior is a search for why people behave in unexpected, sometimes bizarre, and typically self-defeating ways. Much less is known than we would like; this book will focus on the ways in which psychopathologists have been trying to learn the causes of abnormal behavior and what they know about alleviating it.

A history of the field was provided, indicating its origins in ancient demonology and crude medical theorizing. Since the beginning of scientific inquiry into abnormal behavior, two major points of view have vied for attention: the somatogenic, which assumes that every mental aberration is caused by a physical malfunction; and the psychogenic, which assumes that the sufferer's body is intact and that difficulties are to be explained in psychological terms.

Scientific inquiry was presented as a special way in which human beings acquire knowledge about their world. In a very important sense people see only what they are prepared to see, and certain phenomena may go undetected because scientists can discover only the things about which they already have some general idea. There is subjectivity in science as there is in everyday perception and problem solving.

Hypnosis was reviewed in some detail, both because it occupies an important position in the historical development of the field and because the controversies about hypnosis provide a good example of how the paradigms of science—the sets of basic assumptions that determine the kinds of scientific questions to be asked and the procedures to be used in collecting data—can vary and thus affect the conclusions drawn.

chapter 2

CURRENT PARADIGMS IN PSYCHOPATHOLOGY AND THERAPY

This chapter is concerned with the principal paradigms or perspectives that have been used to conceptualize abnormal behavior, how it develops, and how best to treat it. Some authors have applied the term model rather than paradigm to these points of view. The term model implies that concepts from one domain, for example, learning theory, are applied to another, such as abnormal psychology, with the expectation that understanding of the second will be increased. Or, as another example, the brain can be thought of as a computer. Adopting a computer model of the brain does not mean that we believe the brain to be a computer, constructed of electronic circuitry, tape decks, and typewriter terminals. Rather, we assume that the *functioning* of the brain might be better understood by likening it to the operation of a computer (Maher, 1966; Price, 1972a).

The term model, however, implies a degree of precision that does not seem to fit the way people have thought about abnormal behavior and its treatment. Instead of formulating models, different investigators have adopted various perspectives, loose sets of general *assumptions* about what should be studied, how to gather data, and how to think about behavior. We shall discuss five major paradigms of contemporary abnormal psychology, the _statistical_ paradigm, the _physiological_, the _psychoanalytic_, the _learning_, and the _humanistic_. The particular postulates of each paradigm cannot be listed item by item. Instead, we shall try to convey the flavor of the five general points of view.

Many people go about the study of abnormal psychology without explicitly considering the nature of the paradigm that they have adopted. But, as this chapter will indicate, the choice of a paradigm has some very important consequences for the way abnormal behavior is defined, investigated, and treated. In fact, our discussion of paradigms will lay the groundwork for the in-depth examination of the major categories of disorder and of intervention that makes up the rest of the book.

The Statistical Paradigm

Those who adopt the statistical approach measure specific characteristics of people, such as personality traits and ways of behaving, and the distribution of these characteristics in the population. One type of population distribution, the _normal curve_ (Figure 2.1), depicts the majority of people as being in the middle as far as any particular characteristic is concerned: that is, very few people fall at either extreme. Within a statistical paradigm an assertion that a person is normal implies that he or she does not deviate from the average in a particular trait or behavior pattern. For example, if we take anxiety as one dimension of abnormality, persons who are "average" in anxiety level will be considered normal. In contrast, people who are extremely anxious and people who suffer little or no anxiety will be considered abnormal. To apply more traditional diagnostic labels (see Chapter 3), we would say that a person with profuse anxiety has an anxiety disorder and that a person with very little is sociopathic. Similarly, a person very low in intelligence will be regarded as abnormal and so will a genius. To make a decision about a person's

normality or abnormality, we merely assess the characteristic in question and determine the person's position on the bell-shaped curve.

As an example, let us consider a system proposed by Eysenck (1960) for linking measurable personality characteristics to diagnosis. He bases his classification on what he believes are the three most pertinent dimensions of personality. The first, neuroticism, refers primarily to emotionality, or the ease with which people can become aroused. The second, introversion-extroversion, refers for the most part to conditionability: extroverts are said to acquire conditioned responses slowly and to lose them rapidly, whereas the reverse is true of introverts. The third, psychoticism, relates to the person's contact with reality. Each of the three dimensions is assumed to be measurable through various techniques, such as personality questionnaires, laboratory tests, and the like. After people's scores on each of the three dimensions have been determined, they are fit into the more traditional diagnostic scheme. Figure 2.2 indicates how this is done for two of the dimensions, neuroticism and introversion-extroversion. Those persons who are deviant, that is, those who are rated either high or low on a particular dimen-

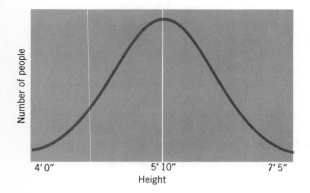

FIGURE **2.1**
The distribution of height among adults, illustrating a normal or bell-shaped curve.

FIGURE **2.2**
Eysenck's statistical paradigm, indicating how various clinical groups can be described according to their positions on the dimensions of neuroticism and introversion-extroversion

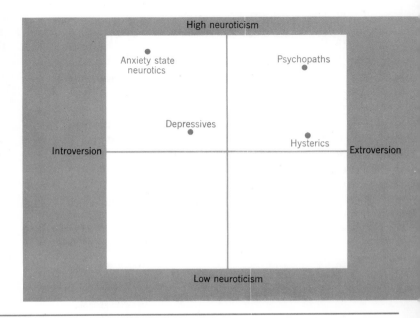

sion, are judged abnormal; for example, someone rated high in both neuroticism and extroversion is regarded by Eysenck as psychopathic.[1]

How useful is the statistical approach to abnormal behavior? The investigator relies on the fact that low and high frequencies of occurrence are defined as deviant. Low and high frequencies of behavior are indeed often regarded as abnormal, but there are also instances in which this relationship breaks down. Low IQs may be a proper subject for study by abnormal psychologists, but can the opposite, high IQs, be considered within their province? And just how low or high does the frequency of occurrence have to be to judge the behavior abnormal? Moreover, the paradigm fails to specify what phenomena we should measure and gives us no hints about what variables may be related to the development of abnormal behavior. Few of us would seriously make decisions about psychological normality or abnormality on the basis of characteristics such as height, weight, and hair color; rather, a person's tendency to be anxious or to hallucinate would generally be viewed as more appropriate criteria. Any decision, then, about *which* variables or dimensions to measure must be made on some other basis. Although the statistical paradigm can provide a partial description and classification of abnormality, it must be considered inadequate. Furthermore, unlike the other paradigms to be examined, this one suggests no particular approach to treatment.

The Physiological Paradigm

What we designate as the physiological paradigm of abnormal behavior is often referred to as the *medical* or *disease model*. We prefer our term for two reasons. First, it has proved difficult to define exactly what is meant by medical model. Second, and more important, arguments about the so-called medical model most often reduce to whether or not behavior is abnormal because of physiological defects.

The Choice of Terms

Let us first examine the prevalent definition of the medical model. As indicated in Chapter 1, the study of abnormal behavior is historically linked to medicine. Many early workers and many contemporaries as well have used the model of physical illness as the basis for defining deviant behavior. Clearly, within the field of abnormal behavior the terminology of medicine is pervasive. As Maher (1966) has noted, "(deviant) behavior is termed *pathological* and is classified on the basis of *symptoms*, classification being called *diagnosis*. Processes designed to change behavior are called *therapies* and are applied to patients in mental *hospitals*. If the deviant behavior ceases, the patient is described as *cured*" (p. 22).

The critical assumption of the medical model is that abnormal behavior may be likened to a disease. To determine how a disease model can be applied to abnormal behavior, we must first examine the concept of disease as it is employed in medicine. During the Dark Ages a disease was thought to consist simply of observable signs and symptoms, such as a rash and high temperature. As medical science, particularly autopsy studies, increased in sophistication, the observable symptoms were attributed to internal malfunctions. Then, when Louis Pasteur discovered the relation between bacteria and disease, and soon thereafter postulated viruses, the *germ theory* of disease provided a new explanation of pathology. External symptoms were assumed to be produced through infection of the body by minute organisms and viruses. For a time this germ theory was the paradigm of medicine. But it

[1] Eysenck's view of psychopaths as having a high level of neuroticism conflicts with most other theoretical accounts, as will be discussed in Chapter 9.

soon became apparent that not all diseases could be explained by the germ theory. Diabetes, for example, a malfunction of the insulin-secreting cells of the pancreas, cannot be attributed to infection. Nor does it even have a single cause. As another example, consider heart disease. A multitude of factors—genetic makeup, stress produced by smoking and obesity, a person's degree of physical fitness—are all related to the frequency of heart disease. Is there a single paradigm here?

We think not. Because medical diseases themselves vary in their causes and symptoms, asserting that abnormal behavior can be considered a disease clarifies little (see Box 2.1). But all diseases *are* disturbances of the body's physiological processes. This is why we have chosen the term physiological paradigm. It is meaningful to say that a behavioral abnormality may be attributed, at least in part, to a disruption in one or more physiological processes.

There is now a considerable literature, both research and theory, dealing with physiological factors relevant to psychopathology. Some, for example, believe that heredity predisposes a person, through physiological malfunction, to develop schizophrenia (see Chapter 14). Depression may result from a failure of the usual processes of neural transmission (Chapter 8). Anxiety disorders have been considered to stem from a defect within the autonomic nervous system that causes a person to be too easily aroused (Chapter 5). Other so-called organic brain syndromes can be traced to impairments in structures of the brain (Chapter 16). In each case a type of psychopathology is viewed as caused by the disturbance of some physiological process. Those working with this paradigm assume that answers to the puzzles of psychopathology will be found by concentrating on somatic, that is, bodily, causes.

Physiological Approaches to Treatment

An important implication of the physiological paradigm is that surgery or a drug able to alter bodily functioning may well be effective in treating or even preventing certain abnormalities. Certainly if a deficiency in a particular biochemical substance is found to underlie or contribute to some problem, it makes sense to attempt to correct the imbalance by providing appropriate doses of the deficient chemical. Here the connection between viewing disorder as physiological defect and attempting to correct the fault through a physiological intervention is demonstrably direct.

As another example, phenylketonuria (PKU) is a form of mental retardation caused by a genetically determined enzyme deficiency that results in an inability to metabolize phenylalanine into tyrosine. The prevention of some of these ravages is a successful example of physiological intervention to correct a physiological anomaly. State laws require routine testing of an infant's blood for excess phenylalanine; if the test is positive, a specific diet low in the amino acid is prescribed. Children otherwise doomed to profound mental deficiency can thereby be brought closer to the normal range of intelligence.

Other physiological interventions in widespread use do not necessarily derive from knowledge of what causes a given disorder in the first place. Again, we are notably short on information about etiology. But the minor tranquilizers, like Valium, can be effective in reducing the tension associated with anxiety disorders and with some forms of depression. The controversial electroconvulsive shock treatment (ECT) seems to be useful in alleviating severe depression. Neither of these somatic therapies is as yet known to be related meaningfully to possible causes of these disorders, but both are to be regarded as physiological treatments.

BOX 2.1 Criticisms of the Medical or Disease Model of Abnormal Behavior

Although we have argued that the term medical model is not very valuable, it is so widely discussed by psychopathologists and clinicians that an overview of some of its problems may be useful. A common criticism of the medical model is that in examining the abnormal behavior of an individual, the clinician has no independent means of verifying the existence of a disease. In medicine both the symptoms and the factors producing them, that is, the disease process, can often be assessed. It is possible, for example, to determine that an individual has a temperature of 104 degrees. Moreover, the particular germ or microorganism that has initiated the processes raising temperature can also be independently determined, say by taking a throat culture and analyzing the foreign organisms present. When a disease model is applied to abnormal behavior, however, it is often not possible to assess independently both the symptoms and the supposed cause of the symptoms. Certain behavior or symptoms are categorized as mental illnesses and given names, but then the name of the illness itself is often cited as an explanation for or cause of these same symptoms. For example, a patient who is withdrawn and hallucinating is diagnosed as schizophrenic; however, when we ask why the patient is withdrawn and hallucinating, we are often told that it is because the patient is schizophrenic. Thus the label schizophrenia is applied to certain behavior and then in addition is specified as a cause of this same behavior, a clear example of circular reasoning.

This criticism of the way mental illnesses are assessed is reasonable, but it is not always entirely applicable. Someone holding a medical or disease model point of view could take a somewhat more sophisticated position. He or she could assert that we may make a diagnosis of schizophrenia on the basis of symptoms without claiming that these symptoms are produced by the presence of schizophrenia. This diagnostician would propose that although we do not now know the cause of the symptoms, such knowledge will eventually be forthcoming. Some deviant chemical may eventually be located within schizophrenics and be identified as the cause of the disorder. In sum, the more sophisticated disease modeler may acknowledge that we currently have little information about causes, but that when such information becomes available, it will, in principle, be possible to assess independently both the symptoms and the _etiology_ as is the case in medicine.

A second common criticism of applying medical models to abnormal behavior involves an alleged difference between the symptoms of physical illness and the symptoms of mental illness. This argument, most often associated with Thomas Szasz (1960), holds that so-called mental symptoms are a patient's communications about himself and others. When we call such statements symptoms, Szasz asserts, we are making a judgment within a particular social and cultural context. For example, a patient's belief that he is Christ might be enough for an observer to make a diagnosis of paranoid schizophrenia. Even in this extreme case, however, the diagnosis depends on the observer's disbelieving the patient's assertion. If the observer gives credence to the patient's assertion, the behavior will clearly not be judged a symptom of mental illness.

Szasz and his followers also say that the symptoms of mental illness are _subjective_, whereas those of physical illness are _objective_. This assertion has some merit, but the distinction is not as clear-cut as Szasz would have it (Ausubel, 1961b). For example, a patient who has entered a physician's office may complain that he is suffering pain. But because tolerance of pain differs widely among individuals, how can the physician determine the actual amount of pain the patient is experiencing? Although the importance of subjective factors as they enter into the definition of so-called mental illness should not be minimized, distinguishing between mental and physical illnesses on this basis alone is a questionable procedure. Subjective factors appear to be implicated in determining the presence of physical diseases as well, although the exact nature of a medical disorder is likely to be assessed further by objective laboratory tests.

Finally, many people have alleged that so-called mental illnesses have neither a specific etiology nor a specific set of symptoms and thus do not qualify as diseases (for example, Milton and Wahler, 1969). Our knowledge of the etiologies of psychopathologies is indeed extremely limited. As we have indicated, however, the fact that these etiologies have not been uncovered as yet does not mean that we should stop looking for them.

Our failure to define specific sets of symptoms for many categories of deviant behavior may be a more damning criticism. Specific syndromes have simply not been discerned for all psychopathologies. Again, however, a person wishing to maintain a medical model for mental illness may counter this criticism with the following line of reasoning. Many medical diseases do *not* have a set of specific symptoms. Paresis is a good example. Before it was discovered to be infectious, there was considerable debate whether the symptoms had a physical cause or whether paresis should be considered a psychological disturbance. Proponents of the psychological view argued that the symptoms were not entirely consistent from one person to another, for some patients suffer depression rather than delusions of grandeur. Therefore they did not consider paresis a medical disease. Although paresis was indeed found to have a *single* causal agent, the manifestations of its *later* stage may *differ markedly from patient to patient*. Thus even an infectious disease may not necessarily have a homogeneous set of symptoms.

The information just presented indicates that the decision whether to view abnormal behavior as a medical disease is partly determined by subjective factors. The medical model is subject to many potential criticisms. For each of these, however, there is a possible rejoinder.

The Psychoanalytic Paradigm

Probably the most widespread paradigm in psychopathology and therapy is the psychodynamic or psychoanalytic, originally developed by Sigmund Freud.

Structure of the Mind

Freud came to divide the mind or the psyche into three principal parts, the _id_, _ego_, and _superego_; each of these are metaphors for specific functions or energies. The id is present at birth and is the part of the personality that accounts for all the energy to run the psyche. Freud, trained as a neurologist, regarded the source of all energy of the id as physiological; it is later converted by some means into psychic energy, all of it unconscious, below the level of awareness.

Within the id Freud postulated two basic instincts, Eros and Thanatos. The more important is Eros, which Freud saw as a life-integrating force, principally sexual. The energy of the instinct Eros is called _libido_. Eros, libido, and sexual energy are sometimes indiscriminately equated, but libido and Eros are also occasionally expanded to include all integrative, life-furthering forces, some of which may not be strictly sexual. Thanatos, the death instinct, plays a relatively small role in Freudian thinking, and indeed its energy never received a name.

The id seeks immediate gratification and operates on what Freud called the _pleasure principle_. When the id is not satisfied, tension is produced, and the id strives to eliminate this tension as quickly as possible. For example, the infant feels hunger, an aversive drive, and is impelled to move about, sucking, in order to reduce the tension arising from the unsatisfied drive. This behavior, called reflex activity, is one means by which the id obtains gratification; it represents the organism's first commerce with the environment. The other means is _primary process_, generating images of what is desired. The infant who wants its mother's milk imagines the mother's breast and thereby obtains some short-term satisfaction of the hunger drive through its wish-fulfilling fantasy. Even in adult life id impulses remain relatively dissociated from the reality-oriented, adaptational processes of the ego. The id, with its need to reduce and eliminate tension, seeks a state of quiescence, which, perhaps ironically, can be achieved only in death.

The second part of the personality, primarily conscious and called the ego, begins to develop out of the id in the second six months of life. The ego is the part of the id that is modified by the direct influence of the environment. It must deal with reality and hence often attempts to delay the immediate gratification desired by the id. The ego frowns upon primary process, for fan-

tasy will not keep the organism alive. Through its planning and decision-making functions, called _secondary process_, the ego realizes that operating on the pleasure principle at all times, as the id would like to do, may not be the most effective way of maintaining life. The ego then operates on the _reality principle_ as it mediates between the demands of reality and those of the id.

The ego, however, derives all its energy from the id and may be likened to a horseback rider who receives energy for riding from the horse. But a real horseback rider directs the horse with his or her own energy, not depending on that of the horse for thinking, planning, and moving. The ego, on the other hand, derives _all_ its ener-

The photograph at top left shows the room in which Freud saw many of the patients written about in his famous psychoanalytic cases. Below left, the ailing Freud sits working at his desk. Above is a portrait of Freud at twenty with his fiancée, Martha Bernays.

gies from the id and yet must direct what it is entirely dependent on for energy.

The superego is the third part of the personality, being essentially the carrier of society's moral standards as interpreted by the child's parents. The superego develops through the resolution of the oedipal conflict, to be discussed shortly, and is generally equivalent to what we call conscience. When the id pressures the ego to satisfy its needs, the ego must cope not only with reality constraints but also with the "right-wrong" moral judgments of the superego. The behavior of the human being, as conceptualized by Freud, is thus a complex interplay of three psychic systems, all vying for the achievement of goals that cannot always be reconciled. This interplay of active forces is referred to as the _psychodynamics_ of the personality.

Freud was drawn into studying the mind by his work with Breuer on hypnosis and hysteria (see page 27). The apparently powerful role played by factors of which patients seemed unaware led Freud to postulate that much of our behavior is determined by forces that are inaccessible to awareness. Both the id instincts and many of the superego's activities are not known to the conscious mind. The ego is primarily conscious, for it is the metaphor for the psychic systems that have to do with thinking and planning. But the ego too has important unconscious aspects, the _defense mechanisms_ which protect it from anxiety; these will also be discussed shortly. Basically, Freud considered most of the important aspects of behavior to be _unconscious_.

Freud saw the human personality as a closed energy system; at any one time there is a fixed amount of energy in the id to run the psychic apparatus. The three parts of the personality therefore battle for a share in a specific amount of energy. Moreover, Freud's theorizing was totally deterministic. Natural scientist that he was, Freud saw every bit of behavior, even seemingly trivial slips of the tongue, as having specific causes, some of them unconscious.

Stages of Psychosexual Development

Freud conceived of the personality apparatus as developing through a series of four separate psychosexual stages. At each stage a different part

The oral and anal stages of psychosexual development.

of the body is the most sensitive to sexual excitation and therefore the most capable of providing libidinal satisfaction to the id. The first is the _oral_ stage, during which the infant derives maximum gratification of id impulses from excitation of the sensory endings around the mouth. Sucking and feeding are the principal pleasures. In the second year of life the child enters the _anal_ stage as enjoyment shifts to the anus and the elimination and retention of feces. In the _phallic_ stage, which extends from age three to age five or six, maximum gratification comes from stimulation of the genitalia. Between ages six to twelve the child is in a _latency_ period, which is not considered a psychosexual stage. During these years the id impulses presumably do not play a direct role in motivating behavior. The child behaves asexually, although according to Freud's theoretical schema all behavior is _basically_ driven by id impulses. The final and adult stage is the _genital_, during which heterosexual interests predominate.

The manner in which the growing person at each stage resolves the conflicts between what the id wants and what the environment will provide determines basic personality traits which will last throughout the person's life. A person who in the anal stage experiences either excessive or deficient amounts of gratification, depending on his or her toilet-training regimen, and thus does not progress beyond this stage, is called an _anal personality_. One type, the anal retentive, is considered stingy and sometimes obsessively clean. These traits, appearing throughout life but receiving the greatest attention in adulthood, when people typically consult psychoanalysts, are traced back to early events and to the manner in which gratification was provided or denied the child. Freud referred to this "freezing" of development at an earlier psychosexual stage as _fixation_.

Perhaps the most important crisis of development occurs during the phallic stage, around age four, for then, Freud asserted, the child is overcome with sexual desire for the parent of the opposite sex. Through the threat of dire punishment from the parent of the same sex, he or she may repress the entire conflict, unconsciously pushing it into the unconscious. This desire and repression is referred to as the _Oedipus complex_ for the male and the _Electra complex_ for the female.

The dilemma is usually resolved through increased identification with the parent of the same sex and through the adoption of society's mores, which forbid the child to desire its parent. Through this learning of moral values the superego is developed.

Anxiety and Defense

Freud proposed two different theories of anxiety. In the first formulation, published in 1895, _neurotic anxiety_ was regarded as stemming from the blockage of unconscious impulses. Such impulses are blocked, for example, under conditions of extreme sexual deprivation. When repressed they become susceptible, according to Freud's first theory of anxiety, to transformation into neurotic anxiety. The first theory did not pay much attention to the circumstances surrounding the repression of an unconscious impulse. In his second theory, proposed in 1926, Freud made more explicit the situations that may cause the individual to repress an unconscious impulse, and he reversed the relationship between neurotic anxiety and repression. According to the first theory, neurotic anxiety develops through repression of impulses. In the second, anxiety about impulses signals the need for their repression. In a sense, according to the first theory we become anxious because we want things that we do not get; according to the second we are anxious because we fear our wants (Wachtel, 1977).

The second theory viewed birth as the prototypic anxiety situation, for the infant is flooded with excitation over which it can exert no control. After the development of the ego in the first year of life, anxiety becomes a signal of impending overstimulation. The person is warned that he or she is in danger of being reduced to an infantile state of helplessness through overstimulation by id impulses and other forces. Anxiety thus plays a functional role, signaling the ego to take action before being overwhelmed.

Three kinds of anxiety were differentiated by Freud, depending on their source. _Objective anxiety_ refers to the ego's reaction to danger in the external world, as for example the anxiety felt when life is in real jeopardy. This kind of anxiety is the same as realistic fear. _Moral anxi-_

ety, experienced by the ego as guilt or shame, is really fear of the punishment that the superego imposes for failure to adhere to standards of moral conduct. *Neurotic anxiety* is the fear of the disastrous consequences that are expected to follow if a previously punished id impulse is allowed expression. Neurotic anxiety has its roots in reality anxiety. As Hall (1954) has noted,

> Neurotic anxiety is based upon reality anxiety in the sense that a person has to associate an instinctual demand with an external danger before he learns to fear his instincts. As long as instinctual discharge does not result in punishment, one has nothing to fear from [the instincts]. . . . However, when impulsive behavior gets the person into trouble, as it usually does, he learns how dangerous the instincts are. Slaps and spankings and other forms of punishment show the child that impulsive instinctual gratification leads to a state of discomfort. The child acquires neurotic anxiety when he is punished for being impulsive (p. 67).

What must be added is that this conflict between desiring something and fearing that desire *has to be repressed,* or driven out of conscious awareness, before we can properly speak of neurotic anxiety. It is this type of anxiety that will concern us throughout the book, whenever we discuss psychoanalytic theories of disorder and treatment.

Perhaps because Freud's earlier views held that repression of id impulses would create neurotic anxiety, we often hear that Freudians preach as much gratification of impulses as possible, lest a person become neurotic. But this is not the case. For Freudians the essence of neurotic anxiety is repression. Being unaware of conflicts lies at the core of neurotic anxiety, rather than simply being reluctant, unwilling, or unable to reduce the demands of the id. A celibate Catholic priest and a nun, for example, are not considered candidates for neurosis provided they consciously acknowledge their sexual or aggressive tendencies. Such individuals do not have to act on these felt needs in order to avoid neurotic anxiety. They must only remain aware

of these needs whenever they vie for expression.

Initially, Freud postulated that traumatic childhood sexual experiences lay behind the neurotic problems of his patients. But by 1897 he came to realize that perverted acts against children would have to be far more prevalent than he was willing or able to assume. He then coupled his patients' reports of such trauma with his own supposition that the unconscious does not distinguish between fact and fantasy. Performing what one commentator has termed a stunning intellectual tour de force (Wachtel, 1977), he proposed that his patients were reporting to him not actual events of their childhood but rather their fantasies. Young children, he assumed, have to deal with intense feelings and longings. Ill-equipped to do so, they are prone to *invent* gratifications. Scientists, wishing to retain certain tenets of their theorizing, can be remarkably creative in adjusting particular aspects of their thinking in order to accommodate newly emerging evidence. By switching from actual events to fantasies, Freud was able to retain early childhood trauma as the central cause of neurotic anxiety.

Forms of neurotic anxiety

Neurotic anxiety can be expressed in several ways: as *free-floating anxiety,* as *phobia,* and as *panic reaction.* The stimuli triggering all these expressions of neurotic anxiety are actually internal, stemming from previously punished id impulses. In free-floating anxiety the person appears to be apprehensive nearly all the time, in the absence of reasonable danger. The theory assumes that the person is actually afraid of his own id—which, of course, is always with him. Phobias are intense irrational fear and avoidance of specific objects and situations, such as kittens, open spaces, closed spaces, and nonpoisonous snakes. The feared objects and situations are hypothesized to be symbolic representations of the object or situation chosen earlier for gratification of the id impulse. That choice and thus the impulse were subsequently punished, and then the whole conflict was repressed. "Behind every neurotic fear there is a primitive wish of the id for the object of which one is afraid" (Hall, 1954, p. 65). Finally, neurotic anxiety may become manifest as a panic reaction, a sudden and inexplicable outburst of severe and prolonged fear.

Defense mechanisms

According to Freud, the discomfort experienced by the anxious ego can be reduced by several maneuvers. Objective anxiety, rooted in reality, can often be handled by removing or avoiding the danger in the external world, or by dealing with it in a rational way. Neurotic anxiety, and sometimes moral anxiety, may be handled through an unconscious distortion of reality by means of one of the defense mechanisms. A defense mechanism is a strategy, unconsciously utilized, which serves to protect the ego from anxiety. Perhaps the most important is _repression_, whereby impulses and thoughts unacceptable to the ego are pushed into the unconscious. Repression not only prevents awareness but also keeps buried desires from growing up (Wachtel, 1977). By remaining repressed, these infantile memories cannot be corrected by adult experience and therefore retain their original intensity. Another defense mechanism, important in paranoid disorders (see Chapter 14), is _projection_, attributing to external agents characteristics or desires that are possessed by an individual and yet are unacceptable to conscious awareness. For example, a hostile woman may unconsciously find it aversive to regard herself as angry at others and may project her angry feelings onto them; thus she sees others as angry with her. Other defense mechanisms are _displacement_, redirecting emotional responses from a perhaps dangerous object to a substitute, for instance, kicking the cat instead of the boss; _reaction formation_, converting one feeling such as hate into its opposite, love; _regression_, retreating to the behavioral patterns of an earlier age; and _rationalization_, inventing a reason for an action or attitude.[2] All these defense mechanisms allow the ego to discharge some id energy while at the same time not facing frankly the true nature of the motivation. Because defense mechanisms are more readily observed than other symptoms of a disordered personality, they very often make

people aware of their troubled natures and persuade them to consult a therapist.

Psychoanalytic Therapy

Since Freud's time the body of psychoanalytic thinking has changed in important ways, but all treatments purporting to be psychoanalytic have some basic tenets in common. Classical psychoanalysis is based on Freud's second theory of neurotic anxiety, that it is the reaction of the ego when a previously punished and repressed id impulse presses for expression (Freud, 1949). The unconscious part of the ego, encountering a situation which reminds it of a repressed conflict from childhood—one usually having to do with sexual or aggressive impulses—is overcome by debilitating tension. Psychoanalytic therapy attempts to remove the earlier repression and to help the patient face the childhood conflict and resolve it in the light of adult reality. The repression, occurring so long ago, has prevented the ego from growing in an adult fashion; the lifting of the repression is supposed to enable this relearning to take place.

The essence of psychoanalysis has been captured by Paul Wachtel (1977) in the metaphor of the _woolly mammoth_. Some of these gigantic creatures, frozen alive eons ago, have been recovered so perfectly preserved that their meat can actually be eaten. Neurotic problems were considered by Freud to be the encapsulated residue of conflicts from long ago. Present adult problems are merely reflections or expressions of these "frozen" intrapsychic conflicts.

The patient's neurosis is seen as deriving most essentially from his continuing and unsuccessful efforts to deal with internalized residues of his past [the "woolly mammoth"] which, by virtue of being isolated from his adaptive and integrated ego, continue to make primitive demands wholly unresponsive to reality. It is therefore maintained that a fully successful treatment must create conditions whereby these anachronistic inclinations can be experienced consciously and integrated into the ego, so that they can be controlled and modified (Wachtel, 1977, p. 36).

[2] A psychoanalytic quip defines a rationalization as a _good_ reason for an action—but not the _real_ reason.

A number of techniques are employed by analysts in their efforts to lift repressions. Perhaps the best known is _free association_. The patient, reclining on a couch, is encouraged to give free rein to his or her thoughts, verbalizing whatever comes to mind, without the censoring ordinarily done in everyday life. It is assumed that the analysand can gradually learn this skill, and that defenses built up over many years can eventually be bypassed. _Dream analysis_ is another classic analytic technique. Psychoanalytic theory holds that, in sleep, ego defenses are relaxed, allowing normally repressed material to enter the sleeper's consciousness. But since this material is extremely threatening, it usually cannot be allowed into consciousness in its actual form. Rather, the repressed material is disguised; dreams take on heavily symbolic content. For example, a woman concerned about aggressive sexual advances from men may dream of being attacked by savages who throw spears at her; the spears are considered phallic symbols, substituting for an explicit sexual advance.

Analysis of defenses, long a focus of psychoanalysis, is emphasized even more by contemporary psychoanalysts, who are sometimes referred to as _ego analysts_. They dispute the relatively weak role that Freud assigned to the ego. Defense mechanisms, as we have seen, are the ego's unconscious tools for warding off a confrontation with anxiety. For instance, a man who appears to have trouble with intimacy may look

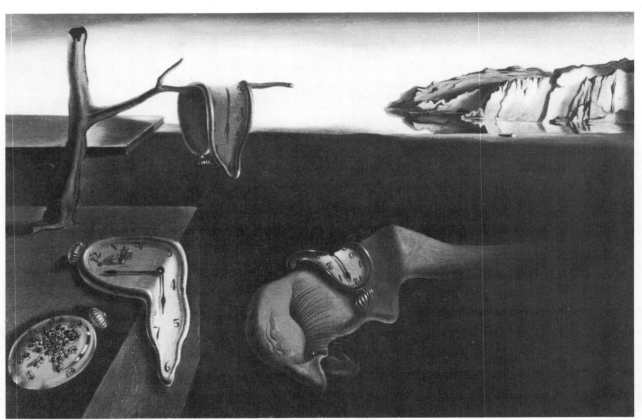

Salvador Dali, _The Persistence of Memory._

In psychoanalytic therapy the symbolic content of dreams provides clues to important unconscious conflicts. Surrealistic art was influenced by psychoanalytic theory and represents an attempt to bypass conscious control and to express unconscious process directly on canvas.

out the window and change the subject whenever anything touches on closeness during the course of a session. The analyst will attempt at some point to offer an _interpretation_ of the patient's behavior, pointing out its defensive nature, in hopes of stimulating the patient to acknowledge that he is, in fact, avoiding the topic.

Psychoanalytic treatment has in the past extended over several years, with as many as five sessions a week. Often a distinction is made between psychoanalysis and psychoanalytic psychotherapy, the more contemporary mode of treatment. Sessions of this therapy are not as frequent, nor does the patient as regularly lie down on the proverbial couch. To our mind, however, these procedural changes do not reflect important theoretical differences. Session frequency and body position do not matter. What does is that the patient, with support from the therapist, slowly examines the true sources of tension and unhappiness by a lifting of repression.

BOX **2.2** Methodological and Conceptual Problems in Freud

Perhaps no investigator of the vagaries of human life has been honored and criticized as much as Freud. During the late nineteenth century, when he was first espousing his views of infantile sexuality, he was personally vilified. At that time sexuality was little discussed among adults. How scandalous, then, to assert that infants and children were also motivated by sexual drives! In the history of science few have shown greater intellectual integrity and personal bravery than Freud.

Because of his very great importance in the field, some current criticisms of his methodology and concepts will be reviewed. Although we attach considerable importance to case reports compiled by clinicians who are "on the front line," clinical reporting by its very nature presents problems that are extremely difficult to avoid. Freud's theorizing, as well as the thinking of the "_Neo-Freudians_," those who have adapted and changed his basic framework, rest primarily on case studies. Like many clinicians, Freud did not take careful notes during his sessions and had to rely almost completely on recollection. The reliability of his perceptions and recollections is impossible to evaluate. Furthermore, the behavior of a listener affects what a speaker has to say. It is possible that Freud's patients were influenced, at least to some degree, to talk about the childhood events that he was most interested in.

The inferential leaps that are made by Freud and other psychoanalysts may be difficult to accept unless one has a prior commitment to the point of view. The distinction between observation and interpretation is sometimes blurred. Consider an example from the analyst Main (1958). "The little boy who babbles tenderly to himself as he soaps himself in his bath does so because he has taken into himself his tender soaping mother." What, in fact, is readily observed by the average onlooker is the child bathing himself. To see his mother incorporated in the soapy bath play is to operate at a very high level of inference. The paradigm problem is once again evident. What we perceive is strongly colored by the paradigm we adopt.

There is considerable disagreement whether Freud's theorizing should be considered scientific, for it is difficult to disprove or prove. Few of the statements are very explicit. If our view of science requires concepts to be measurable, and theories testable, psychoanalytic thinking cannot be regarded as scientific.

Freud's findings do not have general applicability because his sample of patients was very selective and small. Nearly all his patients were from the upper middle class of early twentieth-century Vienna, hardly a representative sampling of human beings. Nonetheless, Freud was prepared to apply his findings to all humankind. In a related vein, after making limited observations, Freud held that a repressed homosexual inclination was the basis for all paranoid disorders. But he never considered, nor for that matter have others who have accepted his point of view, how many paranoids have not had homosexual desires in the past and, indeed, how many people with repressed homosexuality do not develop into paranoids.

Although Freud insisted that he used concepts like id, ego, superego, and the unconscious as metaphors to describe psychic functions, they seem reified, that is, they are made into independent, behavior-determining agents whose own actions must still be explained. For example, Freud spoke of ". . . immediate and unheeding satisfaction of the instincts, such as the id demands. . . . The id knows no solicitude about ensuring survival . . ." (1937, p. 56). Thus the id "demands" immediate satisfaction and "knows" certain things. In spite of occasional reminders in psychoanalytic writings that these concepts are meant as metaphors, or as summary statements of functions, they are typically written about as though they had an existence of their own and had a power to push things around, to think, and to act.

It should be obvious by now that the authors of this book view the validity and usefulness of Freud's work with some skepticism. On the other hand, it would be a serious mistake to minimize his importance in psychopathology or, for that matter, in the intellectual history of Western civilization. Freud was an astute observer of human nature. Moreover, his work has elicited the kind of critical reaction that helps to advance knowledge. He was instrumental in getting people to consider nonphysiological explanations for disordered behavior. It is impossible to acquire a good grasp of the field of abnormal psychology without some familiarity with his writings.

Behaviorism and Learning Paradigms

The Rise of Behaviorism

Before we discuss learning paradigms, it will be helpful to trace briefly the rise of behaviorism within psychology. Early twentieth-century psychology was dominated by structuralism, which held that the proper subject of study was mental functioning and structure. The goal of psychology was to learn more about what goes on in the mind by analyzing the elementary constituents making up its contents. To do this, psychologists used what is called the _introspective method_. Trained subjects were asked to report on their conscious experience and inner sensations in response to controlled stimuli. What, for example, is the experience "red" like? During this same period a controversy raged whether thought did or did not always involve images. Understandably, such a controversy was extremely difficult to resolve and, even with the advances that have been made, is still unsolved today. But because introspection provided no means of settling this question at that time, psychologists became discouraged with it as a method and began to question the definition of psychology as the study of the building blocks of consciousness. This dissatisfaction was brought to a head by John B. Watson, who in 1913 revolutionized psychology with statements such as the following:

Psychology as the behaviorist views it is a purely objective experimental branch of natural science. Its theoretical goal is the prediction and control of behavior. Introspection forms no essential part of its methods, nor is the scientific value of its data dependent upon the readiness with which they lend themselves to interpretation in terms of consciousness (p. 158).

To replace introspection, Watson looked to the experimental procedures of contemporary psychologists who were investigating learning. He also came to feel that the principles uncovered explained much of behavior. In this way learning rather than thinking became the dominant focus of psychology in the post-Watsonian period. Finding out which stimuli would elicit which directly observable responses was now considered the task of psychology. With such objective S–R information it was hoped that human behavior could be both predicted and controlled.

Classical conditioning

With the focus of psychology now on learning, a vast amount of research and theorizing was generated. Two types of learning attracted the research efforts of psychologists. The first type, *classical conditioning*, had originally been discovered quite by accident by the Russian physiologist Ivan Pavlov at the turn of the century. In his studies of the digestive system, a dog was given meat powder to make it salivate, the amount of saliva then being measured with the help of a complicated apparatus in which the dog was restrained. Before long Pavlov's laboratory assistants became aware that the dog began salivating when it saw the person who fed it and then even earlier, when it heard the footsteps of its feeder. Pavlov was intrigued and excited by what his laboratory had happened upon and decided to study the dog's reactions systematically. In the first of many experiments, the dog was positioned facing a window, a bell was rung be-

John B. Watson (1878–1958), American psychologist, who was influential in making psychology the study of observable behavior rather than an investigation of subjective experience.

Ivan P. Pavlov (1849–1936), Russian physiologist and Nobel Laureate, responsible for extensive research and theory in classical conditioning. His influence is still very strong in Soviet psychology.

hind the animal, and then the meat powder was placed in its mouth. After this procedure had been repeated a number of times, the dog began salivating as soon as it heard the bell ring.

When the dog is first given meat powder, it salivates instinctively without prior learning. Since the meat powder automatically elicits sali-

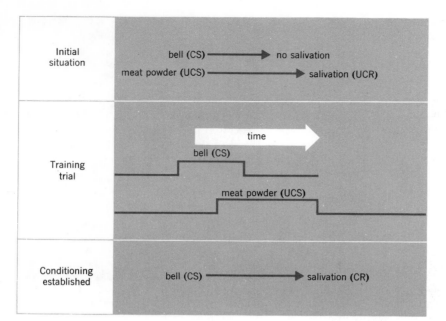

FIGURE **2.3**
The process of classical conditioning: (a) before learning the meat powder (UCS) elicits salivation (UCR), but the bell (CS) does not; (b) a training or learning trial consists of presentations of the CS, followed closely by the UCS; (c) classical conditioning has been accomplished when the previously neutral bell elicits salivation (CR).

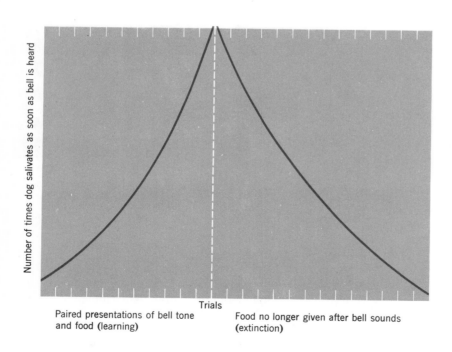

FIGURE **2.4**
Classical conditioning: typical learning curve (a); typical extinction curve (b).

vation, the powder is termed an _unconditioned stimulus_ (UCS) and the response of salivation an _unconditioned response_ (UCR). Then when the offering of meat powder is preceded several times by a neutral stimulus, the ringing of a bell (Figure 2.3), the sound of the bell itself (the _conditioned stimulus_, CS) is able to elicit the salivary response (the _conditioned response_,[3] CR). Figure 2.4a is a typical _learning curve_. As the number of paired presentations of the bell tone and the meat powder increases, the number of salivations elicited by the bell increases. The _extinction curve_ in Figure 2.4b indicates what happens to the established CR when the repeated soundings of the bell tone are later not followed up by the administrations of meat powder. Fewer and fewer salivations are elicited, and the CR is extinguished rather rapidly.

Another famous experiment, one in which John Watson and Rosalie Rayner (1920) made an eleven-month-old boy fear a white rat, indicates the possible relation between classical conditioning and the development of certain emotional disorders, in this instance a phobia. When the infant, Little Albert, was first shown the white rat, he indicated no fear of the animal and appeared to want to play with it. But whenever he reached for the rat, the experimenter made a loud noise (the UCS) by striking a steel bar behind Albert's head, causing him great fright (the UCR). After five such experiences Albert became very disturbed (the CR) by the sight of the white rat, even when the steel bar was not struck. The fear initially associated with the loud noise had come to be elicited by the previously neutral stimulus, the white rat (now the CS).

Operant conditioning

The second principal type of learning drew primarily on the work of Edward Thorndike, begun in the 1890s. Rather than investigating the association between stimuli as Pavlov was to do, Thorndike was interested in the effect that conse-

quences have on behavior. He had observed that alley cats, angered by being caged and making furious efforts to escape, would eventually and accidentally hit the latch that freed them. Recaged again and again, they would soon immediately and purposely touch the latch. Thorndike formulated what was to become an extremely important principle, the _law of effect_: behavior that is followed by consequences satisfying to the organism will be repeated, and behavior that is followed by noxious or unpleasant consequences will be discouraged. Thus the behavior or response that has consequences serves as an instrument, encouraging or discouraging its own repetition. For this reason learning that focuses on consequences was first called instrumental learning.

Over fifty years ago Burrhus Frederick Skinner began applying the law of effect to many different aspects of human behavior. He renamed it the principle of _reinforcement_, the word he prefers to consequences. He argues that freedom of choice is a myth and that all behavior is determined by the positive and negative reinforcers provided by the social environment. The goal of Skinner (1953) and the Skinnerians, like that of Watson, their mentor, is the prediction and control of behavior. These experimenters hope that by analyzing behavior in terms of stimuli, responses, and reinforcement, they will be able to determine when certain responses will occur. The information gathered should then help to indicate how behavior is acquired, maintained, changed, and eliminated. In the Skinnerian approach, often called _operant_ because it studies behavior that operates on the environment, abstract terms and concepts are avoided. For example, references to needs, motivation, and wants are conspicuously absent in Skinnerian writings. To provide an entirely satisfactory account of human behavior, Skinner believes that psychology must restrict its attention to directly observable stimuli and responses and to the effects of reinforcement. Psychologists who hold this view do _not_, as human beings, deny the existence of inner states of mind and emotion. Rather, they urge that investigators not employ such _mediators_ in trying to develop a science of behavior.

In a prototypical _operant conditioning_ experiment a hungry rat might be placed in a box that

---

[3] Some research (for example, Kimble, 1961) has shown that the CR is sometimes different from the UCR. Moreover, a number of writers believe that the terms "unconditional" and "conditional" are preferable to "unconditioned" and "conditioned." Such subtleties, although important for the learning theorist, are relatively unimportant for our purposes and are beyond the scope of this book.

B. F. Skinner, perhaps the most influential living psychologist, responsible for the in-depth study of operant behavior and for the extension of experimental findings to American education and society as a whole.

has a bar located at one end (the well-known "Skinner box"). Initially the rat will explore its new environment and, by chance, will come close to the bar. At this time the experimenter may drop a food pellet into the receptacle located near the bar. After a few such rewards the animal will come to spend more and more time in the area around the bar. But now the experimenter may drop a pellet into the receptacle only when the rat happens to touch the bar. After capitalizing on a few chance touches, the rat begins to touch the bar frequently. With bar touching well established, the experimenter can make the criterion for reward more stringent. The animal must actually press the bar. Thus the desired operant behavior, bar pressing, is gradually _shaped_ by rewarding a series of responses that are _successive approximations_. The number of bar presses increases as soon as they become the criterion for the release of pellets and decreases as soon as the pellet is no longer dropped into the receptacle after a bar press (Figure 2.5).

FIGURE **2.5**
Operant conditioning (a), or instrumental learning, is concerned with the development and maintenance of behavior as a function of its consequences; a typical learning curve (b), showing increases in responding when the operant behavior is reinforced; a typical extinction curve (c), showing decreases in responding when the accustomed reward is withheld.

b   c

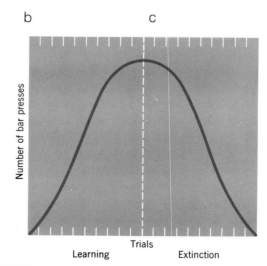

a

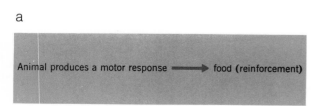

Modeling

In recent years there has been an increased interest in yet a third type of learning, _modeling_. We all realize that we learn by watching and imitating others. Experimental work has proved that witnessing someone perform certain activities can increase or decrease diverse kinds of behavior, such as sharing, aggression, and fear. For example, Bandura and Menlove (1968) used a modeling treatment to reduce fear of dogs in children. After witnessing a fearless model engage in various activities with a dog, initially fearful children showed a decided increase in their willingness to approach and handle a dog.

Mediational learning paradigms

By now it should be apparent that there are a number of learning paradigms. Modeling brings us again to an important issue, namely the role of mediators in learning and behavior. Consider what happens in the kind of modeling experiment just mentioned. A person watches another do something and immediately shows a change in behavior. No overt responding is necessary for the learning to take place, nor for that matter need the observer be reinforced. Something is learned before the person makes any observable response. Outcomes similar to this one had led learning theorists of the 1930s and 1940s to infer mediators of various kinds in order to explain overt behavior.

In the most general terms, a _mediational_ theory of learning holds that an environmental stimulus does not initiate an overt response directly; rather it does so through some intervening process. This process is conceptualized as an internal response, known affectionately as the little r. Without divorcing themselves from behaviorism, mediational learning theorists adopt the paradigmatic position that, under certain conditions, it is both legitimate and important to go beyond observables. Psychologists, who fondly aspire to the status accorded physicists and chemists, will point out that in these natural sciences ample and effective use is made of supposed entities, like the quark, which are not directly observed but whose existence is guessed at or inferred in order to make sense of existing data and to encourage the search for new data.

Perhaps the behavioral analysis of anxiety, as developed by O. Hobart Mowrer and Neal Miller in the late 1930s, will make mediation theory more understandable. In the years since John Watson and Rosalie Rayner had provoked a phobia in Little Albert,[4] American learning theorists, working mostly with rats, had shown little concern with behavior commonly thought to reflect anxiety. The study of anxiety was at the time more actively pursued by clinicians, particularly Freudians, who of course construed it as the threat of or the flooding of the ego by excessive and worrisome stimulation from impulses. Mowrer (1939) is credited with bringing the study of anxiety into the mainstream of experimental psychology. He suggested that anxiety be considered an internal response which can be learned by means of classical conditioning.

In a typical experiment rats were shocked repeatedly in the presence of a neutral stimulus such as the sound of a buzzer. The shock (UCS) produced a UCR of pain, fear, and flight. After several pairings the fear that was naturally produced by the shock came to be produced by the buzzer, fear being assumed the learnable component of the pain-fear response. It was observed that shock could eventually be omitted, and yet the animal would continue to react fearfully to the previously neutral stimulus (CS). In addition, it was shown (for example, Miller, 1948) that the rat could learn new responses to avoid the CS. The question became how to conceptualize the finding that animals would learn to _avoid_ a harmless event. Mowrer (1947) and others suggested that in this, a typical _avoidance learning_ experiment, two bits of learning were taking place (Figure 2.6): (1) the animal, by means of classical conditioning, learned to fear the CS, that is, acquired a fear-drive; and (2) the animal, by means of operant conditioning, learned an overt behavior to remove itself from the CS and thus to reduce the fear-drive.

The essential features of this theorizing are that fear or anxiety can be conceived of both as an internal response, which can be learned as ob-

[4] They had intended to condition away Little Albert's fear, but the child was taken from the hospital where he had been living and where the tests were conducted before their work was completed.

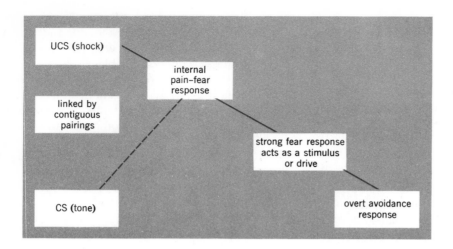

FIGURE **2.6**
Schematic representation of Mowrer's account of avoidance learning. The dotted line indicates that the subject is learning to fear the buzzer tone, the solid line that the subject is learning to avoid the shock.

servable responses are learned, and as a drive, which can mediate avoidance behavior. Anxiety, then, becomes amenable to the same kind of experimental analysis employed in the investigation of observable behavior. Mowrer and Miller speak of "mediating fear-responses" to point up their assumption that such responses, although inferred, are much the same as overt responses. The knowledge gleaned about overt behavior can, it is therefore hoped, be transferred to the study of mental and emotional life (see Box 2.3). For instance, if we know that repetition of an overt response without reinforcement leads to the extinction of the response, we can predict that repeated evocation of a fear-response while withholding the expected pain or punishment will reduce the fear. This is no trivial possibility, and indeed, as will be indicated (see page 56), treatments based on such reasoning have helped people become less fearful of animals and of objects and situations that do not merit such reactions.

Cognition and learning

Cognition is a term that groups together the mental processes of perceiving, recognizing, conceiving, judging, and reasoning. The focus of cognitive psychology is on how people (and animals as well!) *structure* their experiences, how they make sense of them, transforming environmental stimuli into information that is usable. At any given moment we are bombarded by far more stimuli than we can possibly respond to. How do we filter this overwhelming input, put it into words or images, form hypotheses, and arrive at a perception of what is out there? Cognitive psychologists consider the learning process to be much more complex than passively forming new stimulus-response associations. They regard the learner as aware and actively interpreting a situation in the light of what has been acquired in the past, as imposing a perceptual funnel on experience, so to speak. The learner fits new information into a hierarchically organized network of already accumulated knowledge. This new information may fit or, if not, the learner reorganizes the network to the necessary extent.

Contemporary experimental psychology is very much concerned with cognition. The following illustrates how a *cognitive set* may alter the way information is processed and remembered.

The man stood before the mirror and combed his hair. He checked his face carefully for any places he might have missed shaving and then put on the conservative tie he had decided to wear. At breakfast, he studied the newspaper carefully and, over coffee, discussed the possibility of buying a new washing machine with his wife. Then he made several phone calls. As he was leaving the house he thought about the fact that his children would probably want to

BOX 2.3 A Study of the "Thinking-Response"

An early experiment by Miller (1935) was designed to assess the usefulness of construing mental life in mediational stimulus-response terms. Imagine that as a subject in his experiment you have shock electrodes attached to your left hand. The experimenter then asks you to say the letter T and the number 4 when they are presented randomly on a memory drum. You are shocked everytime you say T, never when you say 4. Careful physiological recordings are made of your sweat gland activity when the letter T and the number 4 are pronounced. Results show that you perspire more when saying T than when saying 4. The most interesting part of the experiment then follows. You are instructed to *think* of the letter T, then the number 4 in continuing alternation as you view a series of identical dots one by one. What happens?

Thinking about the letter T, which had previously been paired with shock, elicits more sweat gland activity than thinking about the number 4. This outcome is consistent with the assumption that the image or thought of the letter T functions in the same way as saying the letter. Thought, like fear, is thus construed as a response, which in turn can elicit the sweat gland activity.

go to that private camp again this summer. When the car didn't start, he got out, slammed the door and walked down to the bus stop in a very angry mood. Now he would be late (Bransford and Johnson, 1973, p. 415).

Now read the excerpt again, but add the word "unemployed" before the word "man." Now read it a third time, substituting "stockbroker" for "man." Notice how differently you understand the passage. Ask yourself what parts of the newspaper these men read. If this query had been posed on a questionnaire, you might have answered "the want ads" for the unemployed man, "the financial pages" for the stockbroker. In actual fact, the passage does not specify which part of the paper was read. Your answers would have been erroneous, but in each instance the error would have been a meaningful, predictable one.

Cognitive psychologists study how we acquire, store, and use information. Strict behaviorists, those who follow Skinner in describing behavior in terms of openly observable events, cannot accept cognitive explanations. Cognitive psycholo-gists have until recently paid little systematic attention to how their research findings bear on psychopathology or how they might help generate effective therapies. Now cognitive explanations come up more and more often in the search for the causes of abnormality and for new methods of intervention. A widely held view of depression places the blame on a cognitive set, the individual's overriding sense of helplessness (see page 240). Many who are depressed supposedly believe themselves to have no important effect on their surroundings, regardless of what they do. Their destiny seems to them out of their hands. If depression does develop through a sense of helplessness, this fact would have implications for how clinicians might treat the disorder.

Some clinicians assert that cognitive theorizing is nothing more than a mediational stimulus-response analysis of behavior (for example, Wolpe, 1980), similar to the historically important contributions of Mowrer and Miller. We would disagree. A cognitive explanation of behavior is *fundamentally different* from a "little r" analysis. The mediational researcher asserts that an environmental stimulus automatically evokes an internal mediational response, which is subject to the same reinforcement principles as are overt responses (recall Box 2.3). The cognitive researcher, in contrast, does not conceptualize perception or thinking as a little response. Rather, this worker focuses on how people actively interpret environmental stimuli, and how these transformed stimuli affect behavior. Reinforcement plays a minor role in the theorizing of cognitive psychologists (Davison, 1980).

Applying Learning Points of View to Deviant Behavior

We are now ready to examine, in general, the application of behavioral principles to the study of deviant behavior. The crucial assumption of behavioral and learning approaches is that abnormal behavior is learned in the same manner as most other human behavior. This view minimizes the importance of physiological factors. It focuses instead on elucidating the learning processes that supposedly produced the maladaptive behavior. The gap between normal and abnormal behavior is reduced, since both are viewed within the same general framework; thus a bridge is forged between general experimental psychology and the field of abnormal psychology. Moreover, according to many who have adopted a learning paradigm, abnormality is a *relativistic* concept. Labeling someone or some behavior as abnormal is inextricably linked to a particular social or cultural context. For example, in the United States hallucinating may be one of the grounds for commitment to a mental institution. In some African tribes, however, witch doctors and shamans rely on their trances and visions to help them cure the sick and predict events affecting the welfare of their people.

One very important advantage of applying a learning view in psychopathology is the increased precision of observation. Stimuli must be accurately observed and controlled; the magnitude and rate of responses, and their latency, the rapidity with which they are made, are measured and recorded; and relationships among stimuli, responses, and outcomes are carefully noted. What will be taken to indicate unobservable processes such as fear and thought must be stated explicitly. Although we judge these and

other features of learning approaches to deviant behavior to be extremely advantageous, it is difficult to persuade those not already committed to the paradigm that it is adequate. The learning paradigm of abnormal behavior is in much the same position as the physiological. Just as pertinent physiological malfunctions have not been uncovered, abnormality has not yet been convincingly traced to particular learning experiences, as will be documented in later chapters. Although adopting a learning explanation of abnormal behavior has clearly led to many treatment innovations (see the following section on behavior therapy), the effectiveness of these treatments does not mean that the particular deviant behavior was learned in the first place. The fact that a treatment based on learning principles is effective in changing behavior does *not* show that the behavior was itself learned in a similar way. For example, if the mood of depressed persons is elevated by providing them with rewards for increased activity, this fact cannot be considered evidence that the depression and apathy were initially produced by an absence of rewards (Rimland, 1964).

Behavior Therapy

In recent years a number of therapeutic techniques have been developed that are an outgrowth of the learning paradigms. The terms "behavior therapy" and "behavior modification" are applied to them because they were at least initially asserted to be based on the experimentally tested laws of learning formulated by the behaviorists.

Since in mediation theory anxiety is assumed to be classically conditioned, an effective way to eliminate fear is to associate the conditioned stimulus with a nonfearful response. Referred to as <u>counterconditioning</u>, this principle of behavior change holds that (see Figure 2.7) a response (R_1) to a given stimulus (S) can be eliminated by eliciting a new response (R_2) in the presence of that stimulus. For example, if a child is afraid (R_1) of a harmless animal (S), the therapist might attempt to elicit a playful reaction (R_2) in the presence of the animal. Clinical and experimental evidence suggests that this counterconditioning, or substitution of a response, can eliminate R_1.

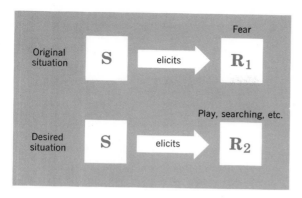

FIGURE **2.7**
Schematic diagram of counterconditioning, whereby an original response (R₁) to a given stimulus (S) is eliminated by evoking a new response (R₂) to the same stimulus.

The counterconditioning principle has played a central role in the innovative thinking of Joseph Wolpe (1958), who devised a set of behavior therapy techniques which he asserts are effective for the reasons just stated. The most widely used technique is _systematic desensitization_. A person who suffers from anxiety works with the therapist to compile a list of feared situations, starting with those that arouse minimal anxiety and progressing onward to those that are the most frightening. He or she is also taught to relax deeply. Then step by step, while relaxed, the person imagines the graded series of anxiety-provoking situations. The relaxation tends to inhibit any anxiety that might otherwise be elicited by the imagined scenes. The fearful person becomes able to tolerate increasingly more difficult imagined situations, as he or she climbs the hierarchy over a number of therapy sessions. Clinical and experimental evidence has confirmed that this technique is useful in reducing a wide variety of fears.

The thirty-five-year-old substitute mail carrier who consulted us had dropped out of college sixteen years ago because of crippling fears of being criticized. Earlier, his disability had taken the form of extreme tension when faced with tests and speaking up in class. When we saw him, he was debilitated by fears of criticism in general and of evaluations of his mail-sorting performance in particular. As a consequence, his everyday activities were severely constricted and, though highly intelligent, he had apparently settled for an occupation that did not promise self-fulfillment.

After agreeing that a reduction in his unrealistic fears would be beneficial, the client was taught over several sessions to relax all the muscles of his body while in a reclining chair. A list of anxiety-provoking scenes was also drawn up in consultation with the client.

You are saying "Good morning" to your boss.
You are standing in front of your sorting bin in the post office, and your supervisor asks why you are so slow.
You are only halfway through your route, and it is already 2:00 p.m.
As you are delivering Mrs. Mackenzie's mail, she opens her screen door and complains about how late you are.
Your wife criticizes you for bringing home the wrong kind of bread.
The officer at the bridge toll gate appears impatient as you fumble in your pocket for the correct change.

These and other scenes were arranged in an _anxiety hierarchy_, from least to most fear-evoking. Desensitization proper began with the client being instructed first to relax deeply as he had been taught. Then he was to imagine the easiest item, remaining as relaxed as possible. When he had learned to confront this image without becoming anxious, he went on to the next scene, and so on. After ten sessions the man was able to imagine the most distressing scene in the hierarchy without feeling anxious, and gradually his tension in real life became markedly less.[5]

Another behavioral technique is _assertion training_, which encourages people to speak up and react openly when with others, expressing both their positive and negative feelings. In _aversive "conditioning"_ an attractive stimulus is paired with an unpleasant event, such as shock to the fingertips, in hopes of endowing it with

[5] Case reports such as this one, which is not referenced, have been drawn from our own clinical files. Identifying features are changed to protect the confidentiality of the individual.

negative properties. Aversive techniques, somewhat controversial as might be imagined, have been employed to reduce the socially inappropriate attraction that objects have for some people, such as the irresistible appeal a woman's boots may have for a fetishist.

Several behavioral procedures derive from operant conditioning. For example, children who misbehave in classrooms can be systematically rewarded by the teacher for their socially acceptable behavior while their undesirable behavior is ignored and thus eventually extinguished. The _token economy_, a program established in many mental hospitals to encourage severely disturbed patients to behave more appropriately, is an operant treatment. Explicit rules are set up for obtaining rewards in the form of tokens or other moneylike scrip. At predetermined intervals patients can trade in their tokens for specific reinforcers, such as a trip to the canteen or a more desirable sleeping arrangement.

Modeling has enjoyed increasing attention as a therapeutic intervention. Bandura, Blanchard, and Ritter (1969) were able to help people reduce their phobias of nonpoisonous snakes by having them view both live and filmed close and successful confrontations between people and snakes. In an analogous fashion, some behavior therapists use _role playing_ in the consulting room. They demonstrate to a patient patterns of behaving that might prove more effective than those he or she usually engages in and then have the patient practice them. Lazarus (1971), in his _behavior rehearsal_ procedures, demonstrates exemplary ways of handling a situation and then encourages the patient to imitate them during the therapy session. For example, a student who does not know how to ask a professor for an extension on a term paper would watch the therapist portray an effective way of making the request. The clinician would then help the student practice the new skill in a similar contrived role-playing situation.

Finally, the cognitive point of view has recently gained widespread attention in behavior therapy. Generally speaking, cognitively oriented behavior therapists attempt to change the thinking processes of their patients in order to influence their behavior. The following is an early example of _cognitive restructuring_ (Davison, 1966).

A man had been diagnosed as paranoid schizophrenic, primarily because of his complaints of "pressure points" on his forehead and other parts of his body. He believed that these pressure points were signals from outside forces helping him to make decisions. These paranoid delusions had been resistant to drug treatment and other psychotherapeutic approaches. The behavior therapist, in examining the man's case history, hypothesized that the patient became very anxious and tense when he had to make a decision, that his anxiety took the form of muscular tension in certain bodily parts, and that the patient misconstrued the tension as "pressure points," signals from helpful spirits. Both patient and therapist agreed to explore the possibility that the pressure points were in fact part of a tension reaction to specific situations. For this purpose the therapist decided to teach the man deep-muscle relaxation, with the hope that relaxation would enable him to control his tensions, including the pressure points.

But it was also important to have the man question his delusional system. So in the first session the therapist asked the patient to extend his right arm, clench his fist, and bend his wrist downward so as to bring the fist toward the inside of the forearm. The intent was to produce a feeling of tension in his forearm; this is precisely what happened, and the man noted that the feeling was quite similar to his pressure points.

Extensive relaxation training enabled the client to begin to control his anxiety in various situations within the hospital and at the same time to reduce the intensity of the pressure points. As he gained control over his feelings, he gradually came to refer to his pressure points as "sensations," and his conversation in general began to lose its earlier paranoid flavor.

The relaxation training apparently allowed the patient to test a nonparanoid hypothesis about his pressure points, to see it confirmed, and thereby to shake off a belief about these sensations that had contributed to a diagnosis of paranoia.

A prominent cognitive therapist, Albert Ellis (1962), holds that maladaptive feelings and activity are caused by _"irrational beliefs."_ Through mistaken assumptions people place excessive demands on themselves. A man who believes that he must always be perfect in everything he does spends too much time on each task—and feels let down whenever he makes a mistake. A woman may think "I should be able to win the love and approval of everyone" and then exhaust herself trying to please others. Ellis and his followers, the so-called "*rational-emotive* therapists," help their patients challenge such assumptions and teach them to substitute ideas like "Although it would be terrific never to make a mistake, that doesn't mean I *have* be without fault."

Behavior therapists ally themselves philosophically with their colleagues from experimental psychology. Thus behavior therapy is best defined not in terms of a set of techniques but rather as an approach to improving behavior that takes a particular epistemological stance, demanding rigorous proof that treatment is indeed effective. Specific techniques will be revised as new research uncovers better ways of altering abnormal behavior. The implications of this emphasis on experimental research will become clearer when behavior therapy is discussed in depth in Chapter 19.

The Humanistic Paradigm

Reacting against the dominance of psychology and psychiatry by psychoanalytic and behavioristic views, Abraham Maslow began exhorting his colleagues of the 1950s to work toward the development of a "third force" in the study of human behavior (Maslow, 1968). Maslow had a much more positive opinion of human nature and potential. He held that the individual is basically sound, whole, healthy, and unique, with an innate drive for growth and *self-actualization*; that humankind is by nature active, resourceful, purposive, and good; that human suffering comes from denial of this basic goodness.

Consider what the paradigm—known variously as humanistic psychology, existential analysis,[6] the human potential movement, and the personal growth movement—says in contrast to the psychoanalytic and behavioral views already examined. The psychodynamic paradigm assumes that human nature, the id, is something in need of restraint, that effective socialization requires the ego to mediate between the environment and the basically antisocial, or at best asocial, impulses stemming from physiological urges. The behavioral point of view, in considering environmental contingencies of activity—reward and punishment—to be the major determinants of effective and normal behavior, stresses the social consequences of beliefs and actions. In contrast, Carl Rogers (1951), a leading figure in humanistic psychology, asserts that the developing personality goes astray when it concerns itself with the evaluations and expectations of others instead of following its own innate drive for self-fulfillment.

The *phenomenological world* of individuals is of utmost importance to the humanists. They regard each of us as having an internal frame of reference which is the product of the totality of earlier perceptions. This subjective universe, made up of the phenomena of personal and private experiences, renders each of us unique and gives each of us our own truth. To contact one

---

[6] Although often grouped together, humanistic and existential approaches are in fact different in some respects. The subtleties are spelled out in Chapter 18 (page 577).

another, each human being must attempt to view the world through the perspective of the other person. As for immediate behavior, it is guided by the experienced stimulus rather than the external stimulus. A person's actions—in fact entire existence—are decided by the way he or she experiences the world at any given moment.

Finally the humanistic view has an abiding belief in free will. Human beings possess freedom of choice; they initiate action instead of being passively influenced by the environment or driven by internal id impulses. The freedom-determinism issue is an exceedingly complex one, running through philosophy, literature, psychology, and politics. We shall have occasion to grapple with it many times in this book.

Existential Neurosis

Although the disorder is not formally recognized in the current diagnostic classification scheme (DSM-III, to be presented in Chapter 3), clinicians have noticed what they call an _existential neurosis_. They attribute it to an inability to exert will and to seek fulfillment. The essence of existential philosophy, as of humanistic psychology, is that people are responsible for their lives and realize their existence the most fully by making choices. Maddi (1967) has described the neurosis.

The cognitive component of the existential neurosis is meaningless or chronic inability to believe in the truth, importance, usefulness, or interest value of any of the things one is engaged in or can imagine doing. The most characteristic [emotional] features . . . are blandness and boredom, punctuated by periods of depression which become less frequent as the disorder is prolonged. As to the realm of action, activity level may be low to moderate, but more important than the amount of activity is the introspective and objectively observable fact that activities are not chosen. There is little selectivity, it being immaterial to the person what if any activities he pursues. If there is any selectivity shown, it is in the

direction of ensuring minimal expenditures of effort and decision making (p. 313).

Maddi suggests that even before the individual suffers from existential neurosis, he or she has developed a _premorbid personality_, a way of behaving that predisposes the individual to the disorder. Such a person satisfies the physiological needs of the body quite adequately—eating, drinking, keeping warm, and avoiding physical danger—and plays social roles, perhaps very well indeed. These talents are important, as Maddi hastens to point out. People whose lives consist _only_ of these acquired skills, however, are candidates for existential neurosis, for they have merely "gone along with" society instead of creating a personal destiny. Such people will feel a great sense of emptiness and lack of fulfillment, _in spite of the fact that they may be extremely effective in satisfying society's demands in every possible way._ Conditions of stress—for example, the imminence of death; a gross disruption in the social order, such as war or an economic depression; or the repeated failure to experience other people and themselves at what Maddi regards as a "deep and comprehensive level"—can easily trigger the onset of the neurosis itself.

Maddi suggests further that children can be taught to become premorbid existential neurotics if they are valued and rewarded only for their ability to satisfy their physiological needs and for their performance of society's social roles. For a healthier development they should be encouraged to make independent decisions based on some system of values, which may be shared by other people, and to have an active internal life, which they can maintain whatever happens in the external world.

Humanistic Therapy

The humanistic paradigm holds that therapists should help people to get in touch with their inner selves, with their true feelings, and to learn to express them without undue concern for what others think. The most prevalent and best-developed form of humanistic therapy is the _client-centered_ approach of Carl Rogers. The person seeking therapy is regarded as client rather than patient and becomes responsible for much of his or her own treatment. Consistent with the view that a mature and well-adjusted person chooses what is innately satisfying and actualizing, therapists do not impose goals on their clients. Rather they create conditions during the therapy hour, conditions which enable clients to discover their own basic natures and make their own judgments about what they need, what they want, and how they might maintain and enhance themselves. True to the humanist's positive view of people, the decisions reached by clients are assumed to be good ones.

Pathology supposedly results from undue sensitivity to the judgments of others and a denial of the individual's own nature. People come to adopt negative, limiting attitudes toward themselves and do not remain open to experiences. The basic tool of the client-centered therapist is therefore _unconditional positive regard_, that is, complete and unqualified acceptance and respect for the client's feeling and actions. Through skillful inquiry and attentive listening, the therapist helps clients uncover, clarify, and express their deepest concerns and conflicts. Gradually clients learn to talk in a more honest and emotional way about themselves and thereby gain access to their basically healthy inner natures.

Rogers and other humanistic therapists believe that people must take responsibility for themselves, even when they are troubled. It is often difficult for a therapist to refrain from giving advice, from taking charge of a client's life, especially when the client appears incapable of making his or her own decisions. But workers like Rogers hold steadfastly to the rule that an individual's innate capacity for growth and self-direction will assert itself provided the therapeutic atmosphere is warm, attentive, and receptive. Indeed, if the therapist steps in, the process of growth and self-actualization will only be thwarted. Whatever short-term relief might come from the therapist's intervening will sacrifice long-term growth. The therapist must not become yet another person whose wishes the client strives to satisfy.

Humanistic therapists tend to de-emphasize techniques, but most of them utilize _empathy_. In

Carl Rogers, the American humanistic psychologist. The aim of his client-centered individual and group psychotherapy is to provide a warm and sympathetic ambience in which the individual recognizes conflicts and goes on to broaden and extend the self.

the following excerpt a Rogerian therapist tries to enter the phenomenological universe of the client and view her complaint from her own frame of reference. He then restates what she has expressed in order to help her clarify her thoughts and feelings—and also to be perceived as someone who understands and cares.

Client: I just can't stand not knowing what Fred's feelings are. Is he really involved with me, or he is just stringing me along?

Therapist: I can see how frustrating it is for you not to know how Fred feels about you, how he views the relationship.

This reflection of feeling is not a simple parroting of the client's words. Rather, the therapist attempts to extract the essence of what she is trying to express—sometimes a feeling only hinted at—and then communicates her concerns back to her, in hopes that she will better understand and acknowledge what is truly at issue. Gradually, encouraged by the empathic acceptance of the therapist, she should gain the self-confidence to listen to feelings from within, which she has shut off as not part of herself.

Consequences of Adopting a Paradigm

The student of abnormal behavior who adopts a particular paradigm necessarily makes a prior decision concerning what kinds of data will be collected and how they will be interpreted. Thus he or she may very well ignore possibilities and overlook other information in advancing what seems to be the most probable explanation. A behaviorist is prone to attribute the prevalence of schizophrenia in lower-class groups to the paucity of social rewards that these people have received, the assumption being that normal development requires a certain amount and patterning of reinforcement. A physiologically oriented theorist will be quick to remind the behaviorist of the many deprived people who do *not* become schizophrenic. The behaviorist will undoubtedly counter with the argument that those who do not become schizophrenic had different reinforcement histories. The physiologically oriented theorist will reply that such *post hoc* or after-the-fact statements can always be made.[7]

Our physiological theorist may suggest that certain biochemical factors that predispose both to schizophrenia and to deficiencies in the intellectual skills necessary to maintain occupational status account for the observed correlation between social class and schizophrenia. The behaviorist will be entirely justified in reminding the physiological theorist that these alleged factors have yet to be found, to which the physiological theorist might rightfully answer, "Yes, but I'm placing my bets that they are there, and if I adopt *your* behavioral paradigm, I may not look for them." To which the learning theorist may with justification reply, "Yes, but *your* assumption regarding biochemical factors makes it less likely that you will look for and uncover the subtle reinforcement factors that in all likelihood account for both the presence and the absence of what you call schizophrenia."

The fact that our two colleagues are in a sense correct and in another sense incorrect is at the same time both exasperating and exciting. They are both correct in asserting that certain data are more likely to be found through work done within a particular paradigm. But they are incorrect to become unduly agitated because each and every social scientist is not assuming that one and the same factor will ultimately be found crucial in the development of all mental disorders. Abnormal behavior is much too diverse to be explained or treated adequately by any of the current paradigms (see Box 2.4). As we subsequently examine various categories of psychopathology, we will find substantial differences in the extent to which physiological and learning paradigms are applicable. As for future discoveries, it is well that psychologists do *not* agree on which paradigm is the *best*. We know far too little to make hard-and-fast decisions on the exclu-

"THERE ARE SEVERAL REASONS FOR YOUR PROBLEM: ENVIRONMENTAL STRESS, EARLY CHILDHOOD EXPERIENCE, CHEMICAL IMBALANCE, AND PRIMARILY, THE FACT THAT BOTH OF YOUR PARENTS ARE AS CUCKOO AS A BAVARIAN CLOCK."

---

[7] The behavioral concept of *reinforcement history* poses an interesting dilemma for those sympathetic to any of the learning paradigms. It is invariably invoked whenever a given individual's development is to be explained or when differences between people raised in apparently the same environment are to be accounted for. For example, if identical twins reared by their natural parents become schizophrenic later in life, the clinician holding a learning view will usually assert that they had similar reinforcement histories. When fraternal twins—they do not develop from the same egg and can be so physically unlike that they are of different genders—are raised at home and only one becomes schizophrenic, the learning "explanation" is that their reinforcement histories were different. Such explanations are as circular and as unsatisfactory as the psychoanalyst's inference of unconscious processes, a practice deplored by behaviorists. And with good reason. Neither hypothesis explains anything, nor does either encourage the search for new data.

BOX 2.4 Eclecticism in Psychotherapy: Practice Makes Imperfect

A word is in order about paradigms and the activities of therapists. The several types of treatment have been presented as though they were practices of separate, nonoverlapping schools of therapy. The impression may have been conveyed that a behavior therapist would never listen to a client's report of a dream, nor would a psychoanalyst be caught dead prescribing assertion training to a patient. Such suppositions could not be farther from the truth. Most therapists describe themselves as _eclectics_, workers who employ ideas and techniques from a variety of schools (Garfield and Kurtz, 1974). Therapists often behave in ways that are not entirely consistent with the theories they might hold. For years practicing behavior therapists have listened empathically to clients, trying to make out their perspectives on events, on the assumption that this understanding would help them plan a better program for changing troublesome behavior. Behavioral theories do not prescribe such a procedure, but on the basis of clinical experience, and perhaps through their own humanity, behavior therapists have realized that empathic listening helps them in establishing rapport, in determining what is really bothering the client, and in planning a sensible therapy program. By the same token, Freud himself is said to have been far more directive and done far more to change immediate behavior than would be concluded from his writings alone. And today especially, psychoanalysts are paying more attention to overt behavior and the relieving of symptoms than analytic theory would lead them to do. Some contemporary writers, like Paul Wacthel (see page 622), even propose that analysts employ behavior therapy techniques, openly acknowledging that behavior therapy has something to offer in the alleviation of behavior pathology.

These are weighty issues; the final section of this textbook will give them the attention they need and deserve. The reader should be aware of this complexity at the beginning, however, and be spared misconceptions about the intricacies and realities of psychotherapy.

sive superiority of any one paradigm, and there is enough important work to go around. And we will often see that a plausible way of looking at the data is to assume multiple causation. A particular disorder may very well develop through an interaction of physiological defects and learning factors, a viewpoint we turn to next.

Diathesis-Stress: A Proposed Paradigm

A general point of view, one which meaningfully links both physiological and learning factors, does in fact guide our own search for answers. Termed the *diathesis-stress* approach, it considers the often subtle interactions between a *predisposition* toward disease—the diathesis—and environmental, or life, events disturbing people—the stress. Diathesis refers most precisely to a constitutional predisposition toward illness, but the term may be extended to any tendency or inclination a person may have to respond in a particular way to an environmental stress. The cognitive set already mentioned, the chronic feeling of helplessness sometimes found in the depressed, may be considered a diathesis for depression.

It is a fact that some people break down in certain ways when exposed to certain stressors, whereas others come through even more terrible trauma apparently unscathed. Certain people have, for example, inherited a physiological predisposition that places them at high risk for schizophrenia (see Chapter 14). Given a certain amount of stress, they are so physiologically constituted that they stand a good chance of becoming schizophrenic. Other people, those at low risk, are not likely to develop schizophrenia, regardless of how difficult their lives are.

Different Perspectives on a Clinical Problem

It will be useful to recall now the case of the policeman with which this book began. The material provided is open to a number of interpretations, depending on the paradigm adopted. For instance, if you hold a physiological point of view, you will be attentive to the similarity between the man's alternately manic and depressed states and the cyclical swings of mood suffered by his father. For you are mindful of the research (to be reviewed in Chapter 8) that suggests a genetic factor in bipolar affective disorder. You do not, however, discount environmental contributions to his problems, but you hypothesize that some inherited, probably biochemical, defect predisposes him to break down under stress. After all, not everyone who experiences a difficult childhood and adolescence develops the kinds of problems Ernest H. has. For treatment you may prescribe lithium carbonate, a drug which many consider helpful in reducing the magnitude of mood swings in manic-depression.

Now suppose that you are committed to a learning perspective, which encourages you to analyze human behavior in terms of reinforcement patterns as well as cognitive variables. You may focus on Ernest's self-consciousness at college, which seems related to the fact that, compared to his fellow students, he had grown up with few advantages. Economic insecurity and hardship may have made him unduly sensitive to criticism and rejection. Moreover, he regards his wife as warm and charming, pointing up his own perceived lack of social skills. Alcohol has been his escape from such tensions. But heavy drinking, coupled with persistent doubt about his own worth as a human being, has interfered with sexual functioning, worsening an already deteriorating marital relationship. As a behavior therapist, you may employ systematic desensitization, having Ernest relax deeply as he imagines a hierarchy of situations in which he is being evaluated by others. Or you may decide on rational-emotive therapy, to convince Ernest that he need not obtain universal approval for every undertaking. Or, given Ernest's deficiency in social skills, you may choose behavior rehearsal in order to teach him how to function effectively in social situations in which he has had little experience. His sexual problems might be breached via a Masters and Johnson therapy program of undemanding but increasingly more intimate sexual encounters with his wife.

A psychoanalytic point of view will cast Ernest H. in yet another light. Believing that events in early childhood are of great importance in later patterns of adjustment, you may hypothesize that Ernest has blamed his father for his mother's early death. Such strong anger at the father has been repressed, but Ernest has not been able to regard him as a competent, worthwhile adult and to identify with him. Fixation at the oedipal stage of psychosexual development may have produced Ernest's anxieties about authority and kept him from functioning as an adult male. For treatment you may choose dream analysis and free association to help Ernest lift his repressions and deal openly and consciously with his hitherto buried anger toward his father.

If you are a humanist, you will say that Ernest H. has consistently chosen not to follow his inner feelings, his basic nature, and that his pattern of seeking security rather than self-expression has caused his current difficulties and frustrations. He did not follow his inclination to attend law school, but rather became a policeman in order to obtain the instant respect accorded a uniform. He thought about having a child as something he *should* do at the age of thirty-two and thus transformed his sexual relationship into one of duty rather than self-expression. These failures to follow his authentic feelings ended in accusations, frustration, and an explosive outburst. In your sessions with Ernest, you will try to help him trust his innermost feelings and take chances in pursuing his own life goals rather than acting only to counter fear and social pressures. Your empathic listening will help Ernest to uncover his own needs and to decide for himself what he wants out of life.

Summary

This chapter has reviewed the major paradigms, or points of view, that are current in the study of psychopathology and therapy. In the *statistical* paradigm a characteristic, such as anxiety, is measured in a group of people, and a distribution of scores is derived. Individuals whose levels of anxiety are at either extreme are designated as abnormal. Which particular behavior or trait is to be measured is decided outside the purview of this paradigm, however. The *physiological* paradigm assumes that psychopathology is caused by an organic defect. Previous discussions of this point of view have taken the form of arguments, pro and con, about a "medical" or "disease" model. But an examination of the meaning of the term medical model reveals that it is actually too vague about etiology to enjoy the status of a formal model of psychopathology. The medical model does have one implication— that psychopathology may be attributed to physiological malfunctions and defects. Therefore we have proposed instead the physiological paradigm. Physiological therapies attempt to rectify the specific organic defects underlying disorders or to alleviate symptoms of other disorders that have not been traced to such defects.

The third paradigm derives from the work of Sigmund Freud. The *psychoanalytic* point of view directs our attention to repressions and other unconscious processes that are traced to early childhood conflicts. Whereas present-day ego analysts who are part of this tradition place greater emphasis on conscious ego functions, the psychoanalytic paradigm has generally searched the unconscious and early life of the patient for the causes of abnormality. Therapeutic interventions based on psychoanalytic theory usually attempt to lift repressions so that the analysand can examine the infantile and unfounded nature of his or her fears.

Behavioral, or *learning,* paradigms suggest that aberrant behavior has developed through classical conditioning, operant conditioning, modeling, or particular cognitive sets. Investigators who believe that abnormal behavior may have been learned share a commitment to examine carefully all situations affecting behavior, as well as to define concepts carefully. Behavior therapists try to apply learning and cognitive principles to the direct alteration of overt behavior, thought, and emotion. Less attention is paid to the historical causes of abnormal behavior than to what maintains it, such as the reward and punishment contingencies encouraging problematic response patterns. Finally, the *humanistic* paradigm assumes that humankind is by nature good and that psychopathology develops from a blockage or denial of this innate worthiness. Therapists encourage clients to discover and trust their inner true selves and to express their needs and impulses.

The *diathesis-stress* paradigm is one that may integrate the best features of several points of view. People are assumed disposed to react differently to particular environment stresses. The diathesis may be constitutional, as appears to be the case in schizophrenia, or it may be extended to the psychological, for example, the chronic sense of helplessness considered a factor contributing to depression.

The most important implication of paradigms is that they determine where and how investigators look for answers. Paradigms necessarily limit their perceptions of the world, for investigators will interpret data differently according to their points of view. In our opinion it is fortunate that workers are not all operating within the same paradigm, for at this point too little is known about psychopathology and its treatment to settle on any one of them.

chapter 3

CLASSIFICATION AND ASSESSMENT

B y the end of the nineteenth century, medicine had progressed far beyond the stage it had been in during the Middle Ages, when a common technique, bloodletting, was at least part of the treatment of virtually all physical problems. It was gradually recognized that different illnesses required different treatments. Diagnostic procedures were improved, diseases classified, and applicable remedies administered. Impressed by the successes that new diagnostic procedures had achieved in the field of medicine, investigators of abnormal behavior also sought to develop classification schemes that grouped disorders according to symptoms. Moreover, advances in other sciences such as botany and chemistry had followed the development of classification systems, reinforcing hope that similar efforts in the field of abnormal behavior might bring progress.

But during the nineteenth century, and indeed into the twentieth as well, there had been great inconsistency in the way abnormal behavior was classified. By the end of the nineteenth century, the diversity of classifications in use was recognized as a serious problem, greatly impeding communication among people in the field. In 1889 in Paris, the Congress of Mental Science adopted a single classification system, but it was never widely used. Earlier, in Britain in 1882,

the Statistical Committee of the Royal Medico-Psychological Association had produced a classification scheme which, even though going through several revisions, was never adopted by the members. In the United States, in 1886, the Association of Medical Superintendents of American Institutions for the Insane, a forerunner of the American Psychiatric Association, adopted a somewhat revised version of the British system. Then in 1913 this group accepted a new classification incorporating some of Kraepelin's ideas. But again, consistency did not emerge. The New York State Commission on Lunacy, for example, insisted on retaining its own system (Kendell, 1975).

More contemporary efforts at achieving uniformity of classification have not been totally successful either. In 1939 the World Health Organization added mental disorders to the *International List of Causes of Death*. In 1948 WHO expanded the previous list, and it became the *International Statistical Classification of Diseases, Injuries, and Causes of Death*, a comprehensive listing of all diseases, including a classification of abnormal behavior. Although this nomenclature was unanimously adopted at a WHO conference, the mental disorders section failed to be widely accepted. In the United States, for example, even though American psychiatrists had a prominent role in the WHO effort, the American Psychiatric Association published its own *Diagnostic and Statistical Manual* (DSM-I) in 1952.

In 1969 the WHO published a new classification system, and it was more widely accepted. A second version of the American Psychiatric Association's DSM (DSM-II, 1968) was similar to it, and in Britain a glossary of definitions was produced to accompany it (General Register Office, 1968). But whether a true consensus had been reached was doubtful. The WHO classifications are simply a listing of diagnostic categories; the actual behavior or symptoms that are the basis for the diagnoses are not specified. DSM-II and the British Glossary provided this crucial information, but the symptoms listed by each were not always similar. Therefore actual diagnostic practices still varied widely. At present, a newer version of the WHO system is in use, and the American Psychiatric Association's DSM-III (1980) is closely linked to it.

In this chapter the major DSM-III categories are given in brief summary. We then examine criticisms of classification in general, of the DSM in particular, and then consider the assessment procedures that provide the data on which diagnostic decisions are based. Finally, we describe assessment techniques different from the traditional DSM approach, ones more closely aligned to behavior therapy.

DSM-III—The Diagnostic System of the American Psychiatric Association

The Axes

A number of major innovations distinguish the third edition of the American Psychiatric Association's *Diagnostic and Statistical Manual*. Perhaps the most sweeping is that classification has become *multiaxial*; each individual is to be rated on five separate dimensions or axes (Table 3.1). The multiaxial system, by requiring judgments to be made on each of the five axes, forces the diagnostician to consider a broad range of information in making a diagnosis. Axis I includes all categories except for the personality and specific developmental disorders, which make up axis II. Thus axes I and II comprise the classification of abnormal behavior and are analogous to the domain of DSM-II. Axes I and II were separated to ensure that the possible presence of long-term disturbances is considered when attention is directed to the current one. For example, a person who is now a heroin addict would be diagnosed on axis I as having a substance use disorder; he might also have a long-standing antisocial personality disorder, which should be listed for axis II.

On axis III the clinician indicates any current physical disorders believed to be relevant to the mental disorder in question. In some individuals a physical disorder, a neurological dysfunction, for example, may be the cause of the abnormal behavior, whereas in others it may be an important factor in their overall condition, for example, diabetes in a child with a conduct disorder. Axis IV codes the level of psychosocial stress that the person has been experiencing and that may be contributing to the disorder. A rating scale of 1 (none) to 7 (catastrophic, for example, multiple family deaths) is to be used. Finally, on axis V, the clinician indicates the person's highest level of adaptive functioning during the past year. Life areas to be considered are social relationships, occupational functioning, and use of leisure time. Axis V ratings, from 1 to 7 (superior to grossly impaired), are included because the better the person has been functioning, regard-

TABLE **3.1**
DSM-III Multiaxial Classification System*

Axis I	Axis II	Axis III
Disorders Usually First Evident in Infancy, Childhood, or Adolescence	Personality Disorders: paranoid, schizoid, schizotypal, histrionic, narcissistic, antisocial, borderline, avoidant, dependent, compulsive, passive-aggressive	Physical Disorders and Conditions
Organic Mental Disorders		
Substance Use Disorders	Specific Developmental Disorders: reading, arithmetic, language, articulation	
Schizophrenic Disorders		
Paranoid Disorders		
Affective Disorders		
Anxiety Disorders		
Somatoform Disorders		
Dissociative Disorders		
Psychosexual Disorders		
Psychological Factors Affecting Physical Condition		

Axis IV

Severity of Psychosocial Stressors

1 none

2 minimal (e.g., small loan)

3 mild (e.g., argument with neighbor)

4 moderate (e.g., pregnancy)

5 severe (e.g., serious illness)

6 extreme (e.g., death of close relative)

7 catastrophic (e.g., natural disaster)

Axis V

Highest Level of Adaptive Functioning Past Year

1 superior: unusually effective in social relations, occupation, and use of leisure time (e.g., single parent in reduced circumstances takes excellent care of children, has warm friendships and a hobby)

2 very good: better than average in job, leisure time, and social functioning (e.g., retired person does volunteer work, sees old friends)

3 good: no more than slight impairment in either occupational or social functioning (e.g., individual with many friends does a difficult job extremely well but finds it a strain)

4 fair: moderate impairment in either social or occupational functioning or some impairment in both (e.g., lawyer has trouble carrying through assignments, has almost no close friends)

5 poor: marked impairment in either social or occupational functioning or moderate impairment in both (e.g., man with one or two friends has trouble holding a job for more than a few weeks)

6 very poor: marked impairment in social and occupational functioning (e.g., woman is unable to do any housework and has violent outbursts)

7 grossly impaired: gross impairment in virtually all areas of functioning (e.g., elderly man needs supervision in maintaining personal hygiene, is usually incoherent)

* This listing is generally selective rather than complete. A comprehensive comparison of DSM-III listings with those of DSM-II is given on the back endpaper of this book.

less of what problems they have for axes I and II, the better the outlook for the future.

The following major *diagnostic categories* are to be considered when determining how the patient should be described for axes I and II.

Disorders Usually First Evident in Infancy, Childhood, or Adolescence   Within this broad-ranging category are the intellectual, emotional, physical, and developmental disorders that usually begin in infancy, childhood, or adolescence. Some of the problems covered are mental retardation; conduct disorders; eating disorders, such as anorexia nervosa, involuntary avoidance of eating; and infantile autism. These disorders are discussed in Chapters 15 and 16.

Organic Mental Disorders   In organic mental disorders the functioning of the brain is known to be impaired, either permanently or transiently. The primary symptoms, which vary with the location and extent of the dysfunction, are delirium—clouding of consciousness, wandering attention, incoherent stream of thought, misperceptions; dementia—deterioration of intellectual capabilities, of memory, abstract thinking, judgment, and control over impulses; persistent and recurrent hallucinations; and disturbed emotions. These disorders are studied in Chapter 17.

Substance Use Disorders   In substance use disorders the ingestion of various substances—alcohol, opiates, cocaine, amphetamines, and so on—has changed behavior enough to impair social or occupational functioning. The individual may become unable to control ingestion of the substance, or to discontinue it, and may develop withdrawal symptoms if he or she stops using it. Substance use disorders are examined in Chapter 10.

Schizophrenic Disorders   The self-care, social relations, and work of patients with schizophrenic disorders have deteriorated from a previous level. Their language and communication are disordered, and they may shift from one subject to another only obliquely related or even completely unrelated. Delusions, such as believing that thoughts not their own have been placed in their heads, are common. Hallucinations, in particular hearing voices that come from outside themselves, plague them. Their emotions are blunted, flattened, or inappropriate, and they have lost contact with the world and with others. These serious mental disorders are discussed in Chapters 13 and 14.

Paranoid Disorders   The most obvious symptoms of people with paranoid disorders are their delusions of being persecuted. The diagnosis can also be applied to extreme and unjustified jealousy, as when a spouse becomes convinced, without reasonable cause, that his or her partner is unfaithful. DSM-III indicates the difficulty in distinguishing paranoid disorders from *schizophrenia, paranoid type,* noting that in schizophrenia, the more serious disorder, delusions tend to be more bizarre and fragmented and the person also has hallucinations. Paranoid disorders are discussed in Chapter 14.

Affective Disorders   Affective disorders are primarily disturbances of mood. In *major depression* the person is deeply sad and discouraged and is also likely to lose weight and energy, to have suicidal thoughts and feelings of self-reproach. The person suffering mania may be described as euphoric, more active than usual, distractable, and possessed of unusually great self-esteem. *Bipolar disorder* is diagnosed if the person experiences episodes of mania or of both mania and depression. The disorders of mood are surveyed in Chapter 8.

Anxiety Disorders   Anxiety disorders are those that have some form of anxiety as the central disturbance. Individuals with a *phobia* fear an object or situation so intensely that they must avoid it, even though they know their fear is unwarranted and unreasonable and disrupts their lives. In *panic disorder,* the first of three so-called anxiety states, the person is subject to sudden but brief attacks of intense apprehension, so upsetting that he or she is likely to tremble and shake, feel dizzy, and have trouble breathing. The anxiety of *generalized anxiety disorder* is pervasive and persistent. Individuals are jumpy and may have a lump in the throat and a pounding heart. They ruminate and feel generally on edge. The person with *obsessive-compulsive disorder* is subject to persistent obsessions or compulsions. Obsessions are recurrent thoughts, ideas, and images which, uncontrollably, dominate a person's consciousness. A compulsion is

In recent years heroin use has increased among members of the middle and upper socioeconomic classes.

Depression frequently reduces the individual to solitary crying.

Alcohol, one of the most dangerous of drugs, is also one of the most common substances of potential abuse.

an urge to perform a stereotyped act with the seeming but usually impossible purpose of warding off an impending feared situation. Attempts to resist a compulsion create so much tension that the individual usually yields.

The anxiety and numbness suffered in the aftermath of a traumatic event outside the usual range of human experience is called *posttraumatic stress disorder*. Individuals have painful, intrusive recollections by day and bad dreams at night. They find it difficult to concentrate and feel detached from others and ongoing affairs. The anxiety disorders are reviewed in Chapter 5.

Somatoform Disorders   The physical symptoms of somatoform disorders have no known physiological cause but seem to serve a psychological purpose. Persons with *somatization disorder,* or Briquet's syndrome, have a long history of multiple physical complaints for which they have taken medicine or consulted doctors. In *conversion disorder* the person reports the loss of motor or sensory function, such as a paralysis, an anesthesia, or blindness. Individuals with *psychogenic pain disorder* suffer from severe and prolonged pain. *Hypochondriasis* is the misinterpretation of minor physical sensations as serious illnesses.

Dissociative Disorders   Psychological dissociation is a sudden alteration in consciousness affecting memory and identity. Persons with *psy-*

chogenic amnesia may forget their whole past or more selectively lose memory for a particular time period. With *psychogenic fugue* the individual suddenly and unexpectedly travels to a new locale, starts a new life, and is amnesic for his or her previous identity. The person with *multiple personality* possesses two or more distinct ones, each complex and dominant one at a time. *Depersonalization disorder* is a severe and disruptive feeling of self-estrangement or unreality. Somatoform and dissociative disorders are examined in Chapter 6.

Psychosexual Disorders   The psychosexual disorders section of DSM-III consists of three principal subcategories. People with *gender identity disorders* have feelings of discomfort and inappropriateness concerning their anatomical sex. Transsexuals, for example, want to alter their genitals and live as someone of the opposite sex. In *paraphilias* the choice of objects for sexual gratification—as in fetishisms, being preoccupied with an inanimate object such as shoes—and of activities—as in sadism and masochism—is unconventional. Finally, persons with *psychosexual dysfunctions* are unable to complete the usual sexual response cycle. Inability to maintain an erection, premature ejaculation, and inhibition of orgasm are examples of their problems. A separate diagnosis, *ego-dystonic homosexuality,* is applied to distressed homosexuals who deeply yearn to be heterosexual. These sexual disorders are studied in Chapters 11 and 12.

Psychological Factors Affecting Physical Condition   If an illness appears to be caused, in part, or exacerbated by a psychological condition, the diagnosis for axis I is *psychological factors affecting physical condition.* Referred to in DSM-II as psychophysiological disorders, these conditions are reviewed in detail in Chapter 7.

Personality Disorders   Personality disorders are defined as "inflexible and maladaptive" patterns of behavior. They are listed on axis II. Eleven distinct personality disorders make up the category. In *schizoid personality disorder,* for example, the person is aloof, has few friends, and is indifferent to praise and criticism. The individual with a *narcissistic personality* has an overblown sense of self-importance, fantasizes about great successes, requires constant attention, and is

likely to exploit others. The *antisocial personality* has surfaced before the age of fifteen, through truancy, running away from home, delinquency, and general belligerency. Now, in adulthood, he or she is indifferent about holding a job, being a responsible mate or parent, planning ahead for the future and even for tomorrow, and staying on the right side of the law. Chapter 9 covers the personality disorders and examines sociopathy in particular.

Specific Developmental Disorders   Specific developmental disorders, which are listed on axis II, cover delays in the development of language, reading skills, articulation, and arithmetic competence. They are studied in Chapter 15.

Classification Changes in DSM-III

Since DSM-III has only recently been published, it will be useful to comment on the most important differences between it and its predecessor, DSM-II. Additional comparisons will be made in later chapters when the various disorders are discussed in depth. A summary comparison of DSM-II and DSM-III is presented on the back endpaper of the book.

1. The old DSM-II section on <u>neuroses</u> has been dropped and replaced with several new and separate major categories: anxiety disorders (phobias, generalized anxiety disorders, obsessive-compulsive disorder), somatoform disorders (somatization disorder, conversion disorder), and dissociative disorders (amnesia, fugue, multiple personality). This is a significant change, for the DSM-II section linked together widely varied complaints that were *assumed* to reflect either conscious or unconscious anxiety. For example, people with the observable anxiety of a phobia were considered together with people with conversion disorders, such as paralysis, because both groups of problems were assumed to be caused by unconscious and unobservable anxiety. The DSM-III listing, then, pays more attention to behavior and less to psychoanalytic theory.

   Because of the long-standing and widespread usage of terms like "neurosis" and "neurotic," however, DSM-III does give "neurotic disorders" as an alternate *descriptive* term for several of the affective, anxiety, somatoform, and dissociative disorders. For example, conversion disorder, one of the somatoform disorders, is referred to parenthetically by its DSM-II label, hysterical neurosis, conversion type.

2. In DSM-II Psychoses Not Attributed to Physical Conditions was a major section and covered schizophrenia, paranoid states, and major affective disorders. This section no longer appears in DSM-III. But it is still recognized that people with certain diagnoses—pervasive developmental disorders, schizophrenic and paranoid disorders, some affective disorders, and some organic mental disorders—are *psychotic*. By the term is meant loss of contact with reality, which becomes evident through the person's delusions, hallucinations, and severely disorganized behavior. The psychotic individual suffers from "gross impairment in reality testing."

3. According to DSM-II a depressed person could be diagnosed as having manic-depressive illness, depressed type; involutional melancholia; psychotic depression; or neurotic depression. It was difficult to choose the proper diagnosis. For example, psychotic and neurotic depressions were supposedly distinguished from manic-depressive illness, depressed type, as being precipitated by a stressful event. But research did not support this distinction. Similarly, involutional melancholia was differentiated from other depressed states primarily by age of onset, during "changes of life," a factor of questionable importance. In DSM-III the category is simply affective disorders, with two principal forms: major depression for those who are deeply sad, and bipolar disorder for those with a history either of mania or of both mania and depression. The difficult distinctions of DSM-II are thus avoided; the DSM-III diagnoses are made on the basis of observed behavior, not assumed etiologies.

4. DSM-II contained a psychophysiological disorders section listing a number of specific illnesses in which emotional factors were thought to be the principal cause. There were two major problems with this assumption. First, most physical diseases are brought on by a multitude of factors, not a single one. Second, emotional factors or stress are now considered to play a significant role in a much broader range of medical diseases than those covered by the DSM-II list. DSM-III uses its multiaxial system to handle the former psychophysiological disorders. If a psychological factor appears to be linked to an illness, the designation for axis I is "psychological factor influencing physical condition." The specific physical condition is listed for axis III.

5. The personality disorders section of DSM-II has been completely revised. Personality disorders have always been problematic for diagnosticians because of the vague way they were described. The DSM-III system hopes to improve this state of affairs by eliminating several poorly defined disorders and making descriptions of retained and additional personality disorders more complete.

6. The DSM-II sexual deviations, alcoholism, and drug dependence categories, which were listed in the section Personality Disorders and Certain Other Nonpsychotic Mental Disorders, are covered in two new and separate sections, Substance Use Disorders and Psychosexual Disorders.

7. The sexual deviation category, now in the new section Psychosexual Disorders, is renamed paraphilias (*para-*, deviation; *philia*, liking for). Thus this category covers sexual interest in unconventional activities and objects. Two other groupings of this section, gender identity disorders and psychosexual dysfunctions, are new. In DSM-II some of the psychosexual dysfunctions were considered to be psychophysiological disorders; DSM-III's listing makes clear their essential sexual nature.

8. The DSM-II section Behavior Disorders of Childhood and Adolescence has been extensively revised and expanded in DSM-III. In addition to retaining, with different names, some of the DSM-II childhood disorders, the

new DSM-III section includes diagnoses that appeared in other places in DSM-II, as well as a few completely new ones. Mental retardation; eating disorders; stereotyped movement disorders, such as tics and Tourette's disorder; enuresis; encopresis; sleepwalking; and childhood onset pervasive developmental disorder, the new term for childhood schizophrenia, are examples of DSM-II diagnoses that have been relocated in the DSM-III section Disorders First Evident in Infancy, Childhood, or Adolescence. New diagnoses include elective mutism, continuous, deliberate refusal to talk; oppositional disorder, made obvious by tantrums, argumentativeness, and noncompliance with rules; identity disorder, a severe subjective distress of adolescence regarding career choice, morals, and friendships; and infantile autism, an almost complete disinterest in others and in learning any means of communicating with them.

Issues in the Classification of Abnormal Behavior

The earlier review of the major categories of abnormal behavior was brief, for they will be examined in more detail throughout this volume. On the basis of this overview, however, let us scrutinize the usefulness of the system as it exists today. Two major lines of criticism can be distinguished. One group of critics argue that classification per se is irrelevant to the field of abnormal behavior. These critics hold that there is a *continuum* ranging from adjustment to maladjustment and consider discrete judgments inappropriate. The second group of critics find specific deficiencies in the way diagnoses have been made.

The Relevance of Classification Per Se

Those opposed to any attempt to classify argue that whenever we do so we lose information and hence overlook some of the uniqueness of the person being studied. The simple example of casting dice will help to explain this argument. Any of the numbers one through six may come up on a given toss of a single die. Let us suppose, however, that we classify each outcome as odd or even. Whenever a one, three, or five comes up on a roll, we call out "odd," and whenever a two, four, or six appears, we say "even." A person listening to our calls will not know whether the call "odd" refers to a one, three, or five, or whether a two, four, or six has turned up when he or she hears "even." In classification some information must inevitably be lost.

What matters, however, is whether the information lost is *relevant,* which in turn depends on the *purposes* of the classification system. Any classification system is designed to group together objects having a common property and to ignore differences in the objects that are not relevant to the purposes at hand. If our intention is merely to count odd and even rolls, it is irrelevant whether a die comes up one, three, or five or two, four, or six. In judging abnormal behavior, however, we cannot so easily decide what is wheat and what is chaff, for the relevant and irrelevant dimensions of abnormal behavior are uncertain. Thus when we do classify, we may indeed be grouping people together on rather trivial bases while ignoring their extremely important differences.

It may also be argued that classification, because it postulates discrete entities, does not allow the continuity between normal and abnormal behavior to be taken into consideration. Those who advance this argument, for example psychopathologists operating within a learning paradigm, hold that abnormal and normal behavior differ only in intensity or degree, not in kind. Therefore discrete diagnostic categories foster a false impression of discontinuity. Rimland (1969) has summarized this position and, in our opinion, effectively criticized it.

> . . . The idea is that if it is difficult to make a distinction between two neighboring points on a hypothetical continuum, no valid distinctions can thereafter be made even at the extremes of the continuum. There are thus persons who would argue that the existence of several variations of gray precludes a distinction between black and white. Hokum. While I will agree that some patients in mental hospitals are saner than nonpatients, and that it is sometimes hard to distinguish between deep unhappiness and psychotic depression, I do not agree that the difficulty sometimes encountered in making the distinction between normal and abnormal necessarily invalidates all such distinctions. (pp. 716–717).

In other words, the fact that some distinctions are difficult to make, such as deciding whether sundown is night or day, does not mean it is impossible to distinguish between noon and midnight.

Another problem of classification lies in its application. Clinicians working within an illness model may tend to see pathology even where it does not exist (see Box 3.1 and also page 32). An incident witnessed in part by one of the authors illustrates how preconceptions can destroy perspective and in this instance even common sense.

A patient hospitalized for anxiety and depression was observed by both the ward psychiatrist and the patient's own therapist. The ward psychiatrist eventually came to feel that the man was hallucinating and reported to the therapist what he considered the significant incident. The previous day, in talking about how depressed he had been feeling, the patient had looked behind him, up toward the ceiling, and declared "It's that little black cloud following me around." On the basis of this single comment, the ward psychiatrist had suggested changing the diagnosis of the patient's condition from a neurosis to a psychosis.

The therapist, however, had observed no signs of psychosis and decided to investigate further. The next time the therapist visited the patient, he queried him: "Can you tell me a little bit about the black cloud that you mentioned to Dr. X the other day?" The patient looked at him quizzically for a long moment and then asked, "You mean that black thing hovering over my left shoulder and my head? Well, what would you like to know about it?" As a more precise description of the cloud was requested, the patient grinned broadly and asked rhetorically, "Haven't you ever heard of a metaphor?"

Classification may also stigmatize a person. We have already seen that diagnostic labels can be "sticky," remaining with a person after discharge. Consider how you might be affected by being told, for example, that you are a schizophrenic. You might become guarded and suspicious lest someone recognize your disorder. Or you might be chronically on edge, fearing the onset of another "attack." Furthermore, the fact that you are a "former mental patient" could have a great impact on your life. Friends and loved ones may now treat you differently, and employment may be difficult to obtain.

There is little doubt that diagnosis can have such negative consequences, but social stigmatization does not appear to be as extensive as once believed. Gove and Fain (1973), for example, followed up a large sample of patients one year after discharge from a hospital. The former patients were interviewed about jobs, social relationships, and outside activities. The patients' descriptions of how they were functioning now and had in the past were not very different. Thus, although we must recognize and be on

BOX **3.1** On Being Sane in Insane Places

Over a period of three years David Rosenhan (1973) arranged for a number of sane people to be admitted to various psychiatric hospitals on the East and West coasts. Care was taken to ensure that none of the participants had had psychiatric problems or was otherwise disordered. Each pseudopatient complained at the admissions desk of hearing voices that said "empty," "hollow," and "thud."

But this one system, chosen by Rosenhan because it is nowhere reported in the clinical literature, was the only one they feigned. Rosenhan wanted to limit the symptoms because a diagnosis of schizophrenia is properly made on the basis of disturbances in thinking and affect, as well as for withdrawn or bizarre behavior, but not solely for having had an hallucination. Furthermore, each pseudopatient accurately reported family history and the circumstances of his present life, except for the psychologists in the research group. Being identified as a fellow mental health professional might have unduly affected the behavior of the staff.

All the pseudopatients were diagnosed as psychotic; on eleven occasions the diagnosis was schizophrenia, and on one occasion manic-depressive psychosis. And all were admitted to the hospital, where they stayed an average of nineteen days. *In no instance did any of the staff detect that the pseudopatient was actually quite sane,* even though, immediately after admission was secured, *the pseudopatient stopped talking about the alleged hallucination and behaved in his usual fashion.* The anxiety of the initial period after admission, which was felt by all the participants, quickly disappeared; if anything, the pseudopatients tended to be somewhat bored. The only instances of detection were those made by their ward companions, the actual hospitalized patients.

Rosenhan found that the circumstances of the patients' past history were sometimes distorted to "explain" the disordered behavior seen on admission. He provides the example of one pseudopatient who had reported accurately a

close relationship with his mother and a remote one with his father. As he grew up, however, the pseudopatient had become closer to his father and somewhat alienated from his mother. The discharge summary concluded that "This white thirty-nine-year-old male . . . manifests a long history of considerable ambivalence in close relationships, which begins in early childhood. . . . Affective stability is absent. His attempts to control emotionality with his wife and children are punctuated by angry outbursts and, in the case of the children, spankings. And while he says that he has several good friends, one senses considerable ambivalence embedded in those relationships also . . ." (1973, p. 253).

Rosenhan comments on the tendency of those who think within an illness model to interpret almost any behavior as a *presumed* illness. But since the behavior of the pseudopatients was completely unremarkable, the only basis for construing their behavior as abnormal was the fact that they were encountered as patients on a psychiatric ward and bore a diagnostic label describing them as psychotic. Thus, Rosenhan argues, the psychiatric diagnosis had little or no relationship to the patients' actual behavior. If this is true, current psychiatric diagnosis is surely a worthless enterprise.

As we might expect, Rosenhan's article describing his study elicited a rash of comments from many mental health professionals. Indeed, some even alleged the study to be so flawed that is was irresponsible of *Science* magazine to have published the article or for textbooks to discuss the study favorably. Let us examine what appear to be the crucial issues.

Each patient was diagnosed twice, on admission and then again on discharge. So we must examine these diagnoses and their relation (or lack of it) to behavior. On admission the patients reported a single symptom, an auditory hallucination. There is no psychiatric diagnosis that can be made on such a basis. But the presence of auditory hallucinations is *consistent with* a diagnosis of psychosis. At this point we can say then that the diagnosis did have some relation to behavior, but that it was based on rather flimsy evidence. In such a case a diagnostician has the option of deferring diagnosis until more information is collected. Yet this tack was not taken by any of the clinicians observed in Rosenhan's study.

From Rosenhan's point of view the discharge diagnoses are even more telling. Upon release from the hospital, nearly all the patients were given a diagnosis of schizophrenia, in remission. Thus psychiatric labels are "sticky," Rosenhan argues, taking on an independent existence of their own. Since the patients behaved normally after admission, how can it be said that they were schizophrenic, even with the qualifier "in remission," on discharge? The discrepancy between the diagnoses and the patients' behavior is obvious. Robert Spitzer (1975), the chairman of the committee which produced DSM-III, however, has challenged Rosenhan's interpretation by carefully analyzing the meaning of the term "in remission." By examining the records of several hospitals, he determined that it is rarely used as a discharge diagnosis for schizophrenics. Instead, schizophrenics are usually discharged with diagnoses of schizophrenia, somewhat improved, or schizophrenia, much improved. Therefore, Spitzer argues, the diagnosticians in Rosenhan's study had indeed recognized that the patients were normal on discharge and chose the "in remission" phrase to make this point.

Spitzer's arguments are not totally acceptable, in our opinion. His data may indicate that discharge diagnoses did have some relation to behavior, but another DSM-II diagnostic category, "no mental disorder," could and should have been used by the diagnosticians.* This diagnostic term "is used when, following psychiatric

examination, none of the previous disorders [the whole range of psychiatric diagnoses] is found. It is not to be used for patients whose disorders are in remission" (APA, 1968, p. 52). If the psychiatrists had been truly attentive to the behavior of the patients, we should have expected the "no mental disorder" diagnosis to be used. But it was not.

Another criticism asks whether the pseudopatients really acted as though they were normal once they were admitted. This is a key point, for Rosenhan's conclusions rest on the assumption that the pseudopatients behaved normally. The pseudopatient did not immediately ask to be released. Would not the normal person wrongfully hospitalized seek to get out? Therefore did not the pseudopatients act abnormally? These questions raise the issue of what behavior is normal in a mental hospital. In our view, the pseudopatients had committed themselves to a project that required them not only to be admitted to a mental hospital but to remain there in order to make the kinds of observations that form part of the published report. Hence they would have been remiss in their responsibilities if they had sought release right after admission. Research protocol demanded that they stay. By way of contrast, many patients who are properly admitted to hospitals do immediately ask to be released. Indeed, such requests are sometimes viewed as an indication of severe disturbances. Therefore the relationship between seeking release and being normal is more complex than one might think.

In sum, Rosenhan has documented the fact that diagnoses are not as closely related to behavior as would be desirable. He has also alerted us to the kinds of errors that even skilled professionals can make. But, as we have tried to show, the diagnoses were not totally *unrelated* to behavior either. Thus we cannot conclude that psychiatric diagnosis is worthless. Indeed, the greater clarity of DSM-III promises to improve the relationship between diagnoses and behavior.

* As publication dates indicate, Rosenhan's study was conducted before the adoption of DSM-III.

guard against the possible social stigma of a diagnosis, the problem may not be as serious as generally believed.

Assuming that various types of abnormal behavior do differ one from one another, however, it is essential to classify them, for these differences may constitute keys to the causes and treatments of the various deviant behaviors. For example, the form of mental retardation already mentioned, phenylketonuria, is attributed to a deficiency in the metabolism of the protein phenylalanine, resulting in the release of incomplete metabolites which injure the brain (see page 498). A diet drastically reduced in phenylalanine prevents some of this injury. As Mendels (1970) has noted, however,

> . . . . had we taken 100, or even 1000, people with mental deficiency and placed them all on the phenylalanine-free diet, the response would have been insignificant and the diet would have been discarded as a treatment. It was first necessary to recognize a subtype of mental deficiency [retardation], phenylketonuria, and then subject the value of a phenylalanine-free diet to investigation in this specific population, for whom it has been shown to have value in preventing the development of mental deficiency (p. 35).

Forming classes may thus further knowledge, for once a class is formed, additional information may be ascertained about it. Even though the class is only an asserted and not a proven entity, it may still be heuristically useful in that it facilitates the acquisition of new information. Only after a diagnostic class has been formed can people who fit its definition be studied in hopes of uncovering factors that were responsible for the development of their problems and of devising treatments that may help them.

Criticisms of Actual Diagnostic Practice

More specific criticisms are commonly made of psychiatric classification, the principal ones being that diagnostic classes are heterogeneous and that they are neither reliable nor valid. These criticisms were frequently leveled at DSM-II and its predecessor. At the close of this section, we see how DSM-III has come to grips with them.

Heterogeneity within diagnostic classes

In a classification scheme each grouping that categorizes a person and his or her particular pattern of behavior must convey specific and discriminating information about that person. If we know that a given patient is classified as an "obsessive-compulsive," the system is useful only when membership in this category reveals something specific about the patient that differentiates him or her from nonmembers of the class. Intrusive thoughts which the patient seems unable to control—for example, worrying continually about the presence of germs—are one of the defining characteristics of an obsessive-compulsive. In order for the relation between this symptom and its category to be truly meaningful, people *not* diagnosed as obsessive-compulsive should *not* display this particular kind of behavior. By the same token, intrusive thoughts should be found in any and all persons considered to be obsessive-compulsive. To state this point another way, whenever a class is formed, the behavior of all its members should be similar along the dimensions distinguishing the classification. Thus, pursuing the example, if we were to examine a group of people who had been diagnosed as obsessive, we would expect all of them to have intrusive thoughts. Others not classified as obsessive should *not* have intrusive thoughts.

Science, alas, is a difficult taskmaster, for research indicates that this important criterion of homogeneity is frequently not met. For example, in a well-known study Zigler and Phillips (1961) found that knowing what diagnostic category a patient falls into does not allow us to predict with great accuracy the actual behavior of the person. Similarly, they found that certain symptoms appeared in a number of diagnostic categories, thus making it difficult to move reliably from a specific symptom to a specific diagnostic category.

Table 3.2 summarizes the principal findings of the study Zigler and Phillips conducted on 793 patients. After reviewing the hospital records, these investigators categorized the patients into four relatively broad diagnostic groups: manic-

TABLE **3.2**

Percentage of Individuals in Each
Diagnostic Category Showing
Particular Symptoms

(from Zigler and Phillips, 1961)

Symptom	All patients (N = 793)	Manic-depressive (N = 75)	Neurotic (N = 152)	Character disorder (N = 279)	Schizo-phrenic (N = 287)
Depressed	38	64	58	31	28
Tense	37	32	46	33	36
Suspiciousness	35	25	16	17	65
Drinking	19	17	14	32	8
Hallucinations	19	11	4	12	35
Suicidal attempt	16	24	19	15	12
Suicidal ideas	15	29	23	15	8
Bodily complaints	15	21	21	5	19
Emotional outburst	14	17	12	18	9
Withdrawn	14	4	12	7	25
Perplexed	14	9	9	8	24
Assaultive	12	5	6	18	5
Self-depreciatory	12	16	16	8	13
Threatens assault	10	4	11	14	7
Sexual preoccupation	10	9	9	6	14
Maniacal outburst	9	11	6	7	12
Bizarre ideas	9	11	1	2	20
Robbery	8	0	3	18	3
Apathetic	8	8	8	4	11
Irresponsible behavior	7	3	7	9	7
Headaches	6	7	10	4	5
Perversions (except homosexuality)	5	0	5	10	2
Euphoria	5	17	2	2	5
Fears own hostile impulses	5	4	9	5	2
Mood swings	5	9	5	4	4
Insomnia	5	11	7	3	5
Psychosomatic disorders	4	7	6	3	5
Does not eat	4	9	4	2	4
Lying	3	0	1	7	0
Homosexuality	3	3	3	8	2
Rape	3	0	3	8	1
Obsessions	3	8	3	1	4
Depersonalization	3	4	1	0	6
Feels perverted	3	0	3	1	5
Phobias	2	4	5	0	2

depressive, neurotic, character disorder (personality disorder), and schizophrenic. Next, they examined the frequency of particular symptoms in each of these groups. As indicated in the second line of the table, for example, each diagnostic category contained a substantial number of patients who were rated as tense: 32 percent of the manic-depressives, 46 percent of the neurotics, 33 percent of those with character disorders, and 36 percent of the schizophrenics. Thus knowing only that a patient was tense tells us very little about the category to which he or she was assigned. Similarly, knowing that a person was schizophrenic allows us to make only a rather poor guess whether or not the individual was regarded as tense, for the table shows that only 36 percent of the schizophrenics were considered to have this symptom. Moreover, all the percentages for tenseness are within fourteen points of one another, although many of the other characteristics do show a wider range from category to category.

Although these data raise an important question about diagnosis, they do not totally negate its usefulness. The symptom tenseness, for instance, may not be useful in differential diagnosis, but others may prove more valuable in this regard. We would suppose the symptom of depression to characterize many manic-depressives and neurotics, and indeed the figures of 64 percent and 58 percent respectively bear out our expectations. Again, since one of the subcategories of schizophrenia is paranoid schizophrenia, characterized by suspiciousness, it is not surprising that 65 percent of the schizophrenics in this study were regarded as suspicious. This figure is substantially and significantly greater than the percentage figures for suspiciousness in the other three categories.

Furthermore, we must keep in mind that the four diagnostic categories used by Zigler and Phillips were indeed *very broad,* and thus their study cannot be considered a definitive test of the point that they were trying to make regarding homogeneity. For example, the general category of schizophrenia is itself made up of several smaller categories; the percentage figures for suspiciousness might be considerably higher for a group of people diagnosed as paranoid schizophrenics.

The Zigler and Phillips study was necessarily limited because it looked only at the presence or absence of specific isolated symptoms. Most psychiatric diagnostic categories, however, are defined by the *joint presence* of a *number* of particular sypmtoms, rather than simply by the presence or absence of a single one. Psychiatrists and psychologists who find diagnosis useful emphasize the importance of syndromes or clusters of symptoms. For example, schizophrenia is generally defined by a number of symptoms such as disordered thought, delusions, hallucinations, and bizarre motor behavior. The problem is that the diagnostic system then in use did not adequately describe these symptoms, nor did it specify how *many* of these various symptoms must be present in order to make a diagnosis, or the degree to which they must be manifest.

Lack of reliability
Whether or not different diagnosticians will agree that a given diagnostic label should be applied to a particular person is the test of its *reliability*. Clearly, for a classification system to be useful, those applying it must be able to agree on what is and what is not an instance of a particular class. Thus reliability becomes the primary requisite for judging any classification system.

Before the evidence is discussed, a problem in assessing the reliability of diagnosis should be addressed. In medicine a diagnosis made by a physician can usually be checked by some sort of laboratory test. That is, an objective measurement is available by which the reliability of a physician's diagnosis can be determined. For diagnosing abnormal behavior no such infallible measurement exists; the only means of assessing reliability is whether or not diagnosticians agree.

The reliability of psychiatric diagnosis has been well researched. One exemplary investigation was reported by Beck and his colleagues (1962). Four highly experienced psychiatrists diagnosed 153 patients within one week of their admission to a psychiatric facility. Each patient was interviewed twice in succession by two different psychiatrists. Before beginning their study, the four psychiatrists had met to discuss the current diagnostic manual so that they could agree on its application. No attempt was made to ensure that the four interviewers would employ the same techniques in gathering the information necessary to make their diagnoses, however.

The overall agreement among the psychiatrists, calculated as the number of diagnoses on which they agreed divided by the total number of diagnoses made, was a disappointingly low 54 percent. The amount of diagnostic agreement within the six most frequently applied categories is presented in Table 3.3. The percentage of agreement varied considerably from one category to another, ranging from a low of 38 percent for personality trait disturbance to a high of 63 percent for neurotic depression. Later, the same data were reanalyzed using only three larger categories, psychosis, neurosis, and character disorder. Diagnostic agreement then reached 70 percent, approaching levels that satisfy most clinical researchers.

The data of the Beck study were later reexamined by Ward and his colleagues (1962), in an attempt to determine why diagnosticians might disagree. Meeting again after they had completed the interviews and made their diagnoses, the psychiatrists found three major reasons why they had not always reached the same determination. First, accounting for 5 percent of the disagreements, were *inconsistencies in the information presented by the patients.*

A young woman was referred for evaluation of a somatic complaint which neither diagnostician could be sure was psychogenic in nature. One of the diagnosticians could therefore make only the diagnosis of "no psychiatric disease." However, to the other examiner, the patient volunteered the history of a previous gastric ulcer . . . information she had previously directly denied to the first examiner. The second physician therefore diagnosed psychophysiological gastrointestinal reaction (p. 200).

The second major group of diagnostic disagreements, 32.5 percent of them, were attributed to *inconsistencies on the part of the diagnostician.* Differences in interview techniques, in judging the importance of particular symptoms and in interpreting the same pathology, constituted most of these inconsistencies.

The third and largest group of disagreements, comprising 62.5 percent of them, were considered to stem from *inadequacies of the diagnostic system.* The diagnosticians found the criteria unclear. Either too fine distinctions were required, or the classification system seemingly forced the diagnostician to choose a major category that was not specific enough.

TABLE 3.3
Percentage of Diagnostic Agreement Within Various Diagnostic Categories

(from Beck et al., 1962)

Category	Number of diagnoses	Agreement, percent
Neurotic depression	92	63
Anxiety reaction	58	55
Sociopath	11	54
Schizophrenic reaction	60	53
Involutional melancholia	10	40
Personality trait disturbance	26	38

. . . A twenty-one-year-old single white female . . . was seen whose chief complaints were nervous tension and self-consciousness since she was three years old. In recent years, she had been unable to hold down a job, although she had some secretarial training. . . . She had received various forms of psychiatric treatment over the past four years and had seen twelve psychiatrists in all, remaining with only one for a period as long as seven months and leaving all of them with open hostility. . . . It was open knowledge in the family that the patient was supposed to have been a boy; and her parents, especially the somewhat alcoholic father, had told her that she was no good because she was a girl and had approved of her only when she was successfully competitive with boys. The patient finished high school with difficulty, having to leave one school because of her marked discomfort in efforts to make speeches before mixed groups, and also because of much daydreaming, which still continued. She now felt frustrated, bitter, and had long felt that life was not worthwhile. She had never had a serious interpersonal involvement of a positive nature, and to the extent that she let herself react with others, the pattern was that of hostile anticipation, poorly modulated aggression, and suspiciousness. She often wished she were dead and had frequent thoughts of turning on the gas or jumping in front of a car, but at the same time she was aware of an excessively strong fear of death. She was compelled to wash her hands after touching certain articles of furniture; she had phobias of eating with other people. She had many physical symptoms of . . . anxiety and autonomic tension. . . . She had a sleep pattern which was a mixture of anxiety and depression, was not rarely awakened by nightmares in which she saw herself dead or bad things happening to her family. She had on several occasions [experienced] . . . visual images upon awakening from these dreams and had remained anxious and unable to sleep long afterwards. However, she definitely had had no auditory or visual hallucinations in the waking state and had had no clear delusions. There was a peculiar quality to her affect which suggested flatness or a manifestation of depression, though it was hard to distinguish between the two, and neither observer felt that she was making any substantial attempt to be melodramatic or impressive.

Both observers were impressed with the borderline nature of her problem. One was reminded of a previous patient who became "overtly psychotic"; the resemblance was less in specific, recognizable details and more in terms of a vague general feeling of the examiner's. He was also impressed with the chronicity, quantity, and multiplicity of her symptoms. The other examiner volunteered that on another day he might well agree, but as the patient struck him now, after an hour's interview, he felt she had a certain integration and inner consistency; he had seen similar patients who consolidated themselves and improved their adjustment without any clearly psychotic episode. In view of the absence of any clear break with reality; because

of the reactive elements in the picture; because the patient was intelligent and did well on routine tests of similarities, differences, and proverb interpretation; because of the potential damage to the patient of being labeled with a psychotic diagnosis; and because of personal antipathy to the poorly conceived phrase "chronic undifferentiated schizophrenic," he gave the patient the benifit of a very sizable doubt as to where schizoid personality left off and schizophrenia began. Diagnostic conflict: chronic undifferentiated schizophrenic reaction vs. chronic anxiety reaction in a severely schizoid personality[1] (pp. 203–204).

Lack of validity

Whether or not accurate statements and predictions can be made about a class once it has been formed is the test of its *validity*. We should state at the outset that validity bears a particular relation to reliability; the less reliable a category is, the more difficult it is to make valid statements about the category. If the reliability of diagnosis is not entirely adequate, we can expect that its validity will not be either.

A psychiatric diagnosis can have three kinds of validity: etiological, concurrent, and predictive. It has *etiological validity* if the same historical antecedents have caused the disorder in the patients diagnosed. In other words, for a diagnosis to be considered etiologically valid, the same factors must be found to have caused the disorder in the people who comprise the diagnostic group. Consider, for example, the supposition that bipolar disorder is, in part, genetically determined. According to this theory, people with episodes of both depression and mania must have a "family tree" that contains other bipolars. As we shall see in Chapter 8, evidence that supports this theory has been collected, giving this diagnostic category some etiological validity.

A psychiatric diagnosis has *concurrent validity* if other symptoms or disordered processes not part of the diagnosis itself are discovered to be characteristic of those diagnosed. Finding that most people with schizophrenia have difficulty

[1] Schizoid personality is a personality disorder characterized by seclusiveness and emotional aloofness.

holding jobs is an example. _Predictive validity_ refers to similar future behavior on the part of the disorder or patient. The disorder may have a particular "natural history," that is, take a certain course. Or members of the diagnostic group may be expected to respond in a similar way to a particular treatment. Bipolar patients, for example, tend to respond well to a relatively new drug, lithium carbonate. The fact that this drug does not work well for people in other diagnostic classes supports the predictive validity of the bipolar diagnosis. Clearly, because we have organized this book around the major diagnostic categories, we believe that they indeed possess some validity. Certain categories have greater validity than others, however; these differences will become apparent as we discuss each diagnostic classification.

DSM-III and Criticisms of Diagnosis

DSM-III was devised to be responsive to some of the criticisms just reviewed. In DSM-III each diagnostic category in axes I and II is described much more extensively than was the case in DSM-II. First there is a description of "essential features," then of "associated features." Given next are statements, drawn from the research literature, about age of onset, course, degree of impairment and complications, predisposing factors, prevalence and sex ratio, familial pattern, and differential diagnosis. Finally, specific _diagnostic criteria_ for the category are spelled out in a precise fashion. These are the symptoms and other factors that must be present to justify the diagnosis. Table 3.4 compares the descriptions of a manic episode given in DSM-II to the diagnostic criteria given in DSM-III. Clearly the bases for making diagnoses are decidedly more detailed and concrete in DSM-III.

The explicitness of the DSM-III criteria can be expected to reduce the descriptive inadequacies found by Ward and his colleagues to be the major source of diagnostic unreliability. Spitzer, Forman, and Nee (1979), in field trials of DSM-III, found diagnostic agreement of 81 percent for schizophrenic disorders and 83 percent for affective disorders, which is particularly encouraging given the importance of these two major axis I categories. Reliability for the personality disor-

ders is lower, 65 percent, consistent with the problems diagnosticians have always had with this category.[2]

Thus far the description of DSM-III has been in positive terms. The classification changes discussed and the attainment of adequate diagnostic reliability are considerable achievements. But problems remain. The reliability of axes III, IV and V, for example, is unknown, and the descriptions of criteria for ratings on these axes is fairly brief. Furthermore, the reliability of axes I and II may not always be as high in everyday usage, for diagnosticians may not adhere as precisely to the criteria as have those whose work was being scrutinized in formal studies. And the improved reliability of DSM-III _may_ lead to more validity but does not guarantee it. The diagnoses made according to it may not reveal anything useful about the patients. Finally, not all DSM-III's classification changes seem as positive as the ones already mentioned. The developmental disorders of childhood—of reading, arithmetic, language, and articulation—and oppositional disorder really cover the waterfront! Should a specific problem like difficulty in learning arithmetic really be considered a "psychiatric disorder"? By expanding its coverage, DSM-III seems to have made too many childhood problems into psychiatric disorders, without good justification for doing so.

In sum, although we regard DSM-III as promising, it is far from perfect. Throughout this book, as we present the literature on various disorders, there will be further opportunites to describe both the strengths and weaknesses of this most recent effort of health professionals to categorize mental disorders.

---

[2] Progress has also been made in dealing with the second largest source of diagnostic unreliability, inconsistency on the part of the diagnostician. The use of standardized, reliably scored interviews, discussed later in this chapter, greatly reduces this problem.

TABLE 3.4
Description of Manic Disorder in DSM-II Versus DSM-III

DSM-II (APA, 1968, p. 36)

Manic-depressive illness, manic type. This disorder consists exclusively of manic episodes. These episodes are characterized by excessive elation, irritability, talkativeness, flight of ideas, and accelerated speech and motor activity. Brief periods of depression sometimes occur, but they are never true depressive episodes.

DSM-III   Diagnostic Criteria for a Manic Episode (APA, 1980, p. 208)

A. One or more distinct periods with a predominantly elevated, expansive, or irritable mood. The elevated or irritable mood must be a prominent part of the illness and relatively persistent, although it may alternate or intermingle with depressive mood.

B. Duration of at least one week (or any duration if hospitalization is necessary), during which, for most of the time, at least three of the following symptoms have persisted (four if the mood is only irritable) and have been present to a significant degree:

   (1) increase in activity (either socially, at work, or sexually) or physical restlessness,
   (2) more talkative than usual or pressure to keep talking,
   (3) flight of ideas or subjective experience that thoughts are racing,
   (4) inflated self-esteem (grandiosity, which may be delusional),
   (5) decreased need for sleep,
   (6) distractability, i.e., attention is too easily drawn to unimportant or irrelevant external stimuli,
   (7) excessive involvement in activities that have a high potential for painful consequences which is not recognized, e.g., buying sprees, sexual indiscretions, foolish business investments, reckless driving.

The Assessment of Abnormal Behavior

The account with which this book began, that of the policeman with drinking and marital problems, allowed no opportunity to find out why he was behaving as he was. We had no possibility of learning more about him by any of the means commonly available to clinicians—interviews, tests, and a variety of other procedures for assessing behavior. These modes of assessment may occasionally be given different, perhaps more impressive-sounding names. An interview may be called "the psychiatric interview," "the diagnostic interview," or "a depth interview"; tests "psychologicals" or "projectives." All _assessment procedures_ are more or less formal ways of finding out what is wrong with a person, what may have caused a problem or problems in the past, and what steps may be taken to improve the individual's condition.

Clinical Interviews

Most of us have probably been interviewed at one time or another, although the conversation may have been so informal that it was not regarded as an interview. To the layperson the word interview connotes a formal, highly structured conversation, but we find it useful to construe the term as any interpersonal encounter, conversational in style, in which one person, the interviewer, uses language as the principal means of finding out about another, the interviewee. Thus a Gallup pollster who asks a college student whom she will vote for in an upcoming presidential election is interviewing with the restricted goal of learning which candidate she prefers. And a clinical psychologist who asks a patient about the circumstances of his most recent hospitalization is similarly conducting an interview.

One way in which a _clinical interview_ is perhaps different from a casual conversation and from a poll is the attention the interviewer pays to _how_ the respondent answers questions—or does not answer them. For example, if a client is recounting her marital conflicts with her husband, the clinician will generally be attentive to any emotion accompanying her comments. If the woman does not seem upset about a difficult situation, her answers will probably be interpreted differently than if she were to cry while relating her story.

The paradigm within which an interviewer operates determines the type of information sought and obtained. A psychoanalytically trained clinician can be expected to inquire about the person's childhood history. He or she is also likely to remain skeptical of the verbal reports because the analytic paradigm holds that the most significant aspects of a disturbed or normal person's developmental history are repressed into the unconscious. By the same token, the behaviorally oriented clinician is likely to focus on current environmental conditions that can be related to changes in the person's behavior, trying to determine, for example, the circumstances under which the person may become anxious. Thus the clinical interview does not follow a prescribed course, varying rather with the paradigm adopted by the interviewer. Clinical interviewers in some measure find only the information they look for.

Great skill is necessary to carry out good interviews, particularly clinical interviews, for they are conducted with people who are often under considerable personal stress. Clinicians, regardless of their theoretical orientations, recognize the importance of establishing _rapport_ with the client. The interviewer must obtain the trust of the person; it is naive to assume that a client will _easily_ reveal information to another, even to an authority figure with the title "Dr." Furthermore, even a client who sincerely, perhaps desperately, wants to recount intensely personal problems to a professional may not be able to do so without assistance. Indeed, psychodynamic and humanistic clinicians assume that people entering therapy usually are not even aware of what is truly bothering them. And behavioral clinicians, although concentrating more on observables, also appreciate the difficulties people have in sorting out the factors responsible for their distress.

Most clinicians employ the kinds of empathy statements discussed in connection with humanistic therapy (see page 60) in order to draw clients out, to encourage them to elaborate on their concerns, and to examine different facets of a problem. A simple summary statement of what

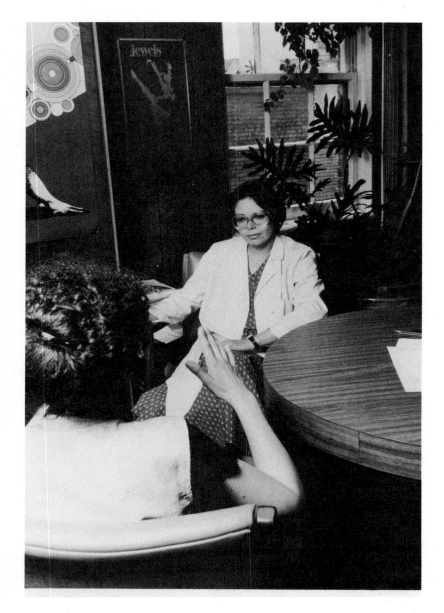

A clinical interview.

the client has been saying can help sustain the momentum of talk about painful and possibly embarrassing events and feelings. And an accepting attitude toward personal disclosures dispels the fear that revealing terrible secrets to another human being will have disastrous consequences.

Vast amounts of information can be obtained by means of the interview; its importance in ab-

normal psychology is unquestioned. Whether the information gleaned can always be depended on is not so clear, however. In the Ward study, as we have seen, patients sometimes gave different interviewers different information in response to the same questions. Often clinicians tend to overlook *situational* factors of the interview that may exert strong influences on what the patient says or does. Consider, for a moment, how a teenager is likely to respond to the question "How often have you used illegal drugs?" when it is asked by a young, long-haired psychologist in jeans and again when it is asked by a sixty-year-old, bald-headed psychologist in a three-piece suit.

Interviews may also vary in the degree to which they are structured. In practice, most clinicians operate from only the vaguest outlines. Exactly *how* such information is collected is left largely up to the particular interviewer. Through years of clinical experience and of both teaching and learning from students and colleagues, each clinician has developed ways of asking questions with which he or she is comfortable and which seem to extract the information that will be of maximum benefit to the client. Thus, to the extent that an interview is unstructured, the interviewer must rely on intuition and general experience, which may be either good or bad, for obvious reasons.

One system of imposing more structure in interviewing is the Schedule for Affective Disorders and Schizophrenia. The SADS is an extensive structured interview with one section covering current problems, the other past history. Many symptoms are rated on a six-point scale of severity, others on a three-point scale indicating absense or presence.

The two sample items given in Table 3.5 indicate the questions that are asked to probe in depth the content of hallucinatory experiences. Training materials which accompany the SADS include case records to be rated and videotapes of actual interviews. A section called Research Diagnostic Criteria gives criteria for most diagnoses and definitions of many key terms. Reliability in using the SADS is impressive (Endicott and Spitzer, 1978). It has proved to be a very useful interview schedule with which to collect information about the patient's current and past mental status.

Psychological Tests

Psychological tests structure still further the process of assessment. The same test is administered to many people at different times, and the responses collected are analyzed to indicate how certain kinds of people tend to respond. Statisti-cal norms for the test can thereby be established as soon as the data collected are extensive enough. This process is called *standardization*. The responses of a particular patient can then be compared to the statistical norms. Psychological tests may be easier to administer and interpret than an interview. Several classes of psychological tests have been developed: projective personality tests, personality inventories, tests of organic damage, and tests of intelligence.

Projective personality tests

The Rorschach inkblot test and the Thematic Apperception Test are perhaps the best-known *projective techniques*. In both of these tests a set of standard stimuli, vague enough to allow variation in responses, is presented to an individual. In an inkblot test the subject is shown ten blots, one at a time, and asked to tell what figures or objects he or she sees in each of them. Similarly, in the Thematic Apperception Test the examinee is shown a series of pictures one by one and asked to tell a story related to each. In both these tests it is assumed that because the stimulus materials are unstructured, the patient's responses will be determined primarily by unconscious processes and will reveal his or her own attitudes, motivations, and modes of behavior. This is referred to as the *projective hypothesis*. For example, reporting eyes on the Rorschach has been said to indicate paranoia. Those of the psychoanalytic bent tend to favor such tests, since they presumably afford an opportunity for the unconscious to express itself. By the same token, those who use these tests tend to think in psychoanalytic terms. This preference for ambiguous stimuli is entirely consistent with the psychoanalytic assumption that people defend against unpleasant thoughts and feelings by repressing them into the unconscious. In order to bypass the defense mechanism of repression (see page 44) and get to the basic causes of distress, the real purposes of a test are best left unclear.[3]

[3] A behaviorist might also make use of projective tests, although for different purposes. The Rorschach and the TAT, being unstructured, may be viewed as making ambiguous demands on the person taking them. Determining the degree of tension evidenced by the respondent when asked to operate in these highly unstructured situations may then be considered a sample of his or her typical reactions to life stresses.

TABLE **3.5**
Sample Items from the SADS Interview
(from Spitzer and Endicott, 1978)

HALLUCINATIONS

Hallucinations are perceptions in the absence of identifiable external stimulation. For the purpose of this assessment, hallucinations are recorded here only if they occurred when the subject was fully awake, and neither febrile nor under the influence of alcohol or some drug. Hallucinations should not be confused with illusions, in which an external stimulus is misperceived, or normal thought processes which are exceptionally vivid. Always get the subject to describe the perception in detail. A rating of "suspected" indicates that the rater suspects, but is not certain, that the subject has experienced the particular kind of hallucination noted, as for example, when it is not clear if the subject is describing an illusion rather than a true hallucination. If the hallucination occurred in the setting of a "religious experience," inquire to determine if this is an expected perception that is idiosyncratic to the subject.*

If there is no evidence from the case record, informants, or from your interview to suggest hallucinations, ask the following questions and any others from the section on hallucinations which you think are appropriate.

Has there been anything unusual about the way things looked, or sounded, or smelled?

Have you heard voices or other things that weren't there or that other people couldn't hear, or seen things that were not there?

☐ If there is still no evidence to suggest hallucinations, check here and skip to Bizarre Behavior.

Experienced auditory hallucinations of voices, noises, music, etc. (Do not include if limited to hearing name being called.)*

0	No information
1	Absent
2	Suspected or likely
3	Definite

The (sounds, voices) that you said you heard, did you hear them outside your head, through your ears, or did they come from inside your head?

Could you hear what the voice was saying?

(Did it talk about you or repeat your thoughts?)

Did you hear anything else? What about noises?

Auditory hallucinations in which a voice keeps up a running commentary on the subject's behaviors or thoughts as they occur.

0	No information
1	Absent
2	Suspected or likely
3	Definite

Did the voice describe or comment upon what you were doing or thinking?

Auditory hallucinations in which 2 or more voices converse with each other.

0	No information
1	Absent
2	Suspected or likely
3	Definite

Did you hear 2 or more voices talking with each other?

Non-affective Verbal Hallucinations Spoken to the Subject. A voice or voices are heard by the subject speaking directly to him, the content of which is unrelated to depressed or elated mood (although he may be depressed or elated at the time). Rate absent if limited to voices saying only 1 or 2 words. Examples: A woman heard voices telling her that she was having a baby and should go to the hospital. A man heard a voice telling him he was being watched by his neighbors for signs of perversion.

0	No information
1	Absent
2	Suspected or likely
3	Definite

*See footnote on next page.

Visual hallucinations.*

Have you had visions, or seen things that are invisible to other people?

0	No information
1	Absent
2	Suspected or likely
3	Definite

Olfactory hallucinations. (Do not include delusion that subject himself smells.*)

Have you noticed strange or unusual smells that other people didn't notice?

0	No information
1	Absent
2	Suspected or likely
3	Definite

Somatic or tactile hallucinations (e.g., electricity, things creeping, snake in his body).*

What about strange feelings in your body?

0	No information
1	Absent
2	Suspected or likely
3	Definite

Hallucinations of any type with a grandiose or persecutory content. Examples: Voices insult him. Voices praise him. Electrical rays torture him.

0	No information
1	Absent
2	Suspected or likely
3	Definite

CHARACTERISTICS OF HALLUCINATIONS OF ANY TYPE

The following items should be rated for the period when the subject had the hallucinations.

Severity of hallucinations of any type. (It may also include hallucinations not listed above.) Consider conviction in reality of hallucination, preoccupation, and effects on his actions.

(Did you ever think.......... was your imagination?)

(What did you do about it?)

0	No information
1	Definitely no hallucinations
2	Suspected or likely
3	Definitely present, but subject is generally aware that it is his imagination and is usually able to ignore it
4	Generally believes in the reality of the hallucination but it has little, if any, influence on his behavior
5	Convinced his hallucination is real and it has a significant effect on his actions, e.g., locks doors to keep pursers, whom he hears, away from him
6	Actions based on hallucinations have major impact on him or others, e.g., converses with voices so much that he is unable to work

Skip to Bizarre Behavior.

(What about during the past week?)

PAST WEEK 0 1 2 3 4 5 6

---

*If the subject reports only unformed visual (spots, flashes, etc.) or auditory (roaring, ringing, rumbling, etc.) hallucinations, or only somatic or tactile hallucinations, the rater should be extremely cautious about scoring the symptom as definitely present. Such phenomena may be a drug reaction or an illusion rather than a hallucination. The item should be rated as "suspected" unless that rater is certain that it is a real hallucination.

Picture from the Thematic Apperception Test, introduced in 1935 by Henry Murray and his associates at the Harvard Psychological Clinic. Like the Rorschach, this projective test is designed to reveal unconscious conflicts and concerns.

son. Generally, the information gathered through a projective technique concerns unconscious conflicts and repressed anxieties. Behavioral psychologists find it difficult to assess the validity of such data, for how can it be known whether the test is in fact measuring unconscious conflicts and repressed anxieties if they are by definition hidden from direct observation?

On the other hand, the inferences drawn from projective test data do sometimes permit attempts at validation. For example, if a patient is asserted to be homosexual on the basis of his Rorschach responses, the validity of this assertion can be determined. But the inferences made about aspects of personality through projective testing do not generally prove accurate. After conducting an extensive survey of the literature, Nunnally (1967) has written that

> *. . . Most projective techniques do a rather poor job of measuring personality traits. . . . In applied settings, the evidence is clear that projective techniques have, at most, only a low level of validity. . . . They do a poor job of differentiating normal people from people who are diagnosed as neurotic and they do a poor job of differentiating various types of mentally ill persons (p. 497).*

Certain responses to projective tests continue to be viewed as diagnostic signs, even though an association between the response and a particular diagnosis does not exist. Many clinicians rely to a considerable extent on such signs in making their diagnoses. Moreover, as noted by Chapman and Chapman (1969), clinicians often show considerable consensus in assigning meanings to various signs, even though there is little evidence to back up their interpretations. Let us examine this issue of consensus.

Chapman and Chapman conducted a study that you may participate in right now. Imagine yourself part of a psychological experiment in which you are asked to rate the amount of association between homosexuality and particular Rorschach responses. Specifically, you are to rate the degree to which each of the responses signifies homosexuality, using the following six-point

As might be imagined, the interpretation of the responses to projective tests poses a severe problem, for the examinee is not merely answering yes or no to a series of questions or indicating which of a series of statements are true and which are false. Rather, the person is providing a complex response to a complex stimulus, which is, by design, open to a fantastic range of interpretations. In many instances the reliability of the scoring of the Rorschach and Thematic Apperception tests is quite low. With extensive training in a particular scoring system, however, examiners can achieve satisfactory levels of agreement (Goldfried, Stricker, and Weiner, 1971). A more serious problem is the often woefully low validities of responses in projective tests. We assume that these responses tell us something important and useful about the per-

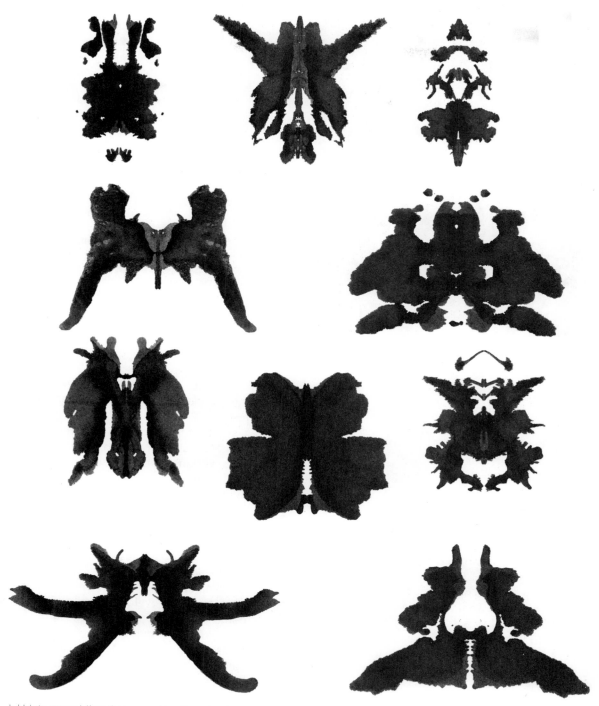

Inkblots resembling those used by Rorschach.

Hermann Rorschach (1884–1922), Swiss psychiatrist who during a ride in the country with his two children noticed that what they saw in clouds reflected their personalities. From this observation came his famous inkblot test.

TABLE **3.6**
Rorschach Responses To Be Rated as Signs of Homosexuality

Response	Rating
Feminine clothing	
Food	
Rectum and buttocks	
Maps	
Figure, part man—part woman	
Sexual organs	
Monsters	
Figure, part animal—part human	

scale; 6, very strong; 5, strong; 4, moderate; 3, slight; 2, very slight; and 1, no tendency at all. The eight Rorschach responses to be rated are presented in Table 3.6.

Now you may compare your ratings to those actually obtained from a sample of undergraduate students. In Table 3.7 the responses are divided into three different classes. The popular invalid signs are those that clinicians tend to *believe* reflect homosexuality, although they have *not* been validated by research evidence. The unpopular but valid signs are infrequently listed by clinicians, but they do have some modest research support as being indicators. The filler items are unrelated to homosexuality and to how clinicians assess it. The students in the Chapmans' study gave much higher ratings to the *popular but invalid signs* than to the other responses.

Professional clinicians may rely on particular signs in making a diagnosis because they *assume* such responses are valid indicators of homosexuality. But as Chapman and Chapman themselves noted, "The popular meanings of many test signs, as reported by clinicians, are *illusory correlations* [italics added] based on verbal associative connection of the test sign to the symptom" (p. 272). No research has established such connections through observation. Chapman and Chapman are saying that, in our culture, we all seem to have developed similar ideas of what homosexuals say, think, or do. In this study of how students rated Rorschach responses, the students *assumed*, as clinicians have, that homosexuals would be inclined to see such things as buttocks in the inkblots, and they accepted such responses as indicators. But these accepted popular signs are *not* valid. There is no evidence to indicate that such responses differentiate between homosexuals and heterosexuals, yet they

TABLE 3.7
Mean Rated Strength of Association Between Particular Rorschach Responses and Homosexuality

(from Chapman and Chapman, 1969)

Response	Rated strength
Popular invalid signs	
Rectum and buttocks	4.38
Figure, part man–part woman	3.53
Feminine clothing	3.12
Sexual organs	4.47
Unpopular valid signs	
Figure, part animal–part human	1.93
Monsters	1.68
Filler items	
Food	1.09
Maps	1.09

continue to be taken as signs and to be applied in diagnoses.[4]

Personality inventories

In *personality inventories* a large number of statements are typically presented to the examinees, who are asked to indicate whether they do or do not apply to them. The investigators who have been involved in the construction of such instruments have usually been well schooled in the general principles of test construction and standardization. It is therefore rare for a personality inventory to lack reliability. Validity, however, still presents a problem, especially if the personality inventory has been designed to reveal unconscious conflicts and the like. Some personality inventories have been constructed

with more specific purposes in mind. Perhaps the best-known of these is the Minnesota Multiphasic Personality Inventory (MMPI), which was developed in the early 1940s as an inexpensive device to simplify the differential diagnosis of mental patients.

In developing the test, the investigators relied on factual information. First, many clinicians provided large numbers of statements that they considered indicative of various mental problems. Second, these items were rated as self-descriptive or not by people already diagnosed as abnormal according to the DSM. Items that served to discriminate among the patients were retained: that is, items were selected if patients in one clinical group responded to them more often in a certain way than did those in other groups. With additional refinements, sets of these items were established as scales for determining whether or not a respondent should be diagnosed in a particular way. If the individual answered a large number of the items in a scale in the same way as had a certain diagnostic group, his or her behavior was expected to resemble that of the particular diagnostic group. The scales of the instrument do, in fact, relate well to psychiatric diagnoses (but see Box 3.2). Thus the MMPI has been widely used to screen large groups of people for whom clinical interviews are not feasible. Items similar to those on the various scales are presented in Table 3.8.[5]

We may well wonder whether answers that would designate the subject as normal might not be easy to fake. A superficial knowledge of contemporary abnormal psychology would alert even a seriously disturbed person to the fact that, if he wants to be regarded as normal, he must not admit to worrying a great deal about germs on doorknobs. In fact, there is evidence that these tests *can* be "psyched out." In many testing circumstances, however, people do not *want*

---

[4] More promising, but still controversial, is analyzing the *formal* properties of a person's responses to the Rorschach cards (Exner, 1978). The examiner pays little attention to the content of the responses and instead analyzes such things as whether the whole card is incorporated in what is seen, whether color affects responses, and whether the figures seen are moving or static. Dr. Rorschach himself suggested this approach in his original manual, *Psychodiagnostics: A Diagnostic Test Based on Perception,* but he died only eight months after publishing his ten inkblots, and his followers devised other methods of administering the test.

[5] The manner in which the MMPI was constructed is referred to as *empirical,* that is, relying on data or experience rather than speculation. It is also worth noting that the MMPI's diagnostic scheme is based on symptoms listed in the DSM. Not surprisingly, clinicians who dislike the DSM are unenthusiastic about the MMPI. Moreover, because the MMPI was devised using older versions of the DSM, it may not predict DSM-III diagnoses well (Winters, Weintraub, and Neale, 1981).

BOX   **3.2** Predictive Validity in Clinical Assessment Procedures

Strictly speaking, our discussion of the validity of the MMPI and other assessment devices has been restricted to concurrent validity, the extent to which one measure correlates with other currently available data. Thus the depression scale of the MMPI has concurrent validity if an individual who has been diagnosed as depressed on the basis of other information receives a high score on this scale.

Predictive validity, or the degree to which a measure can predict a characteristic or behavior that will develop at a later time, is also important. For example, we might wish to predict, on the basis of an MMPI profile, how well a person will do in psychotherapy, or, indeed, how well he or she will do without it. The assessment devices we have reviewed possess little validity for this purpose. Is it because the tests are poor? Perhaps. The authors of this textbook suggest, however, that the tests cannot predict the usefulness of psychotherapy because we know so little about therapy. When we examine theory and research in various forms of therapy (Part Six), it will become painfully clear how little is known about whether psychotherapy works, and if it seems to, under what conditions and why. It is therefore premature to expect an assessment procedure to be able to predict a future outcome that is itself not well understood. To draw an analogy, suppose that a personality test is examined for its validity in predicting how well examinees will get along with Martians. How can we expect good prediction without knowing what is required to get along with such extraterrestrial beings? Personality tests have been expected to predict a great many ill-defined outcomes. For this reason their disappointing predictive validity is not surprising and, indeed, should probably have been anticipated (Mischel, 1968).

TABLE 3.8
Typical Clinical Interpretations of Items
Similar to Those on the MMPI

(adapted from Kleinmuntz, 1967)

Scale	Sample item	Interpretation
Cannot say	This is merely the number of items marked in the "cannot say" category.	A high score indicates evasiveness.
Lie	I have never had a bad night's sleep (false).*	Persons trying to look good (i.e., wholesome, honest) obtain high scores.
Frequency	Everything tastes salty (true).	High scores on this scale suggest disinterest or a wish to appear abnormal.
Correction	I am more satisfied with my life than most of my friends (true).	High scores on this scale suggest a guarded test-taking attitude.
Hypochondriasis	I wake up tired most mornings (true).	High scorers have been described as cynical and dissatisfied.
Depression	I rarely see the bright side of things (true).	High scorers are usually withdrawn, sad, and troubled.
Hysteria	My fingers sometimes feel numb (true).	High scorers have multiple bodily complaints.
Psychopathic deviate	I did not like school (true).	High scorers tend to be adventurous and antisocial.
Masculinity-femininity	I do not like sports (true).	Men with high scores tend to be artistic and sensitive. High-scoring women have been described as rebellious and assertive.
Paranoia	I am envied by many people (true).	High scorers on this scale tend to be suspicious and jealous.
Psychasthenia	I have a great deal of self-confidence (false).	High scorers are described as anxious, self-doubting, and rigid.
Schizophrenia	I sometimes smell strange odors (true).	Adjectives such as seclusive and bizarre describe high scorers.
Hypomania	I never have any difficulty making decisions (true).	High scorers tend to be outgoing and impulsive.
Social introversion–extroversion	I avoid getting together with people (true).	High scorers are modest and shy; low scorers are sociable and exhibitionistic.

* The true or false responses in parentheses indicate the answer expected if the respondent is to accumulate a high score on this scale.

to falsify their responses, for they want to be helped. Moreover, the test designers have included as part of the MMPI several scales designed to detect deliberately faked responses (see Table 3.8). In one of these, the lie scale, a series of statements sets a trap for the person who is trying to "look too good." One such item from the lie scale declares "I read the newspaper editorials every night." The assumption is that few people would be able to endorse such a statement honestly. Thus persons who do endorse a large number of the statements in the lie scale might well be attempting to present themselves in a particularly good light. Their scores on other scales are usually viewed with more than the usual skepticism.

Tests such as the MMPI are subject to certain other difficulties. It has been found that many people tend to answer test questions on bases other than the specific content of the question. For example, suppose the statement is "I attend a party at least once a week." If the individual answers "Yes," or "True," can we conclude without reservation that he or she really attends social gatherings frequently? Research suggests that such answers cannot be accepted as necessarily true, for a certain test-taking or questionnaire "set" may have determined the response.

Several types of _response sets_, as these orientations are called, have been identified. _Response acquiescence_, or "yea saying," is the tendency to agree with statements regardless of their content. _Response deviation_ is the tendency to answer items in an uncommon way regardless of their content. People with a _social desirability_ response set will give what they judge to be the most socially acceptable answer, whether or not the response accurately describes them. For instance, in the example just given, individuals who abhor and avoid parties may say that they attend them at least once a week because they wish to be viewed as typical and believe that such a response is likely to be considered "right" or appropriate.

One obvious means of avoiding this problem is to structure the test-taking situation in such a way that the respondent is motivated to answer honestly. If we are working with an individual in a clinical setting, this is not too difficult to ac-

complish. But what can be done if the test is administered to a group or as part of a research project, where it is difficult to motivate all respondents to answer frankly? The pioneering work of Edwards (1957) illustrates one way of handling the response set of social desirability. He began with an investigation designed to assess the relation between the social desirability of an item and the likelihood that it would be endorsed. First, a large number of undergraduates were asked to judge 140 different self-descriptions on a nine-point scale in terms of ". . . the degree of desirability or undesirability of these traits in people. . . ." Among the items were the following.

1. _To like to punish your enemies._

2. _To like to read psychological novels._

3. _To like to make excuses for friends._

4. _To like to go out with your friends._

In the next phase of the study, Edwards presented the same 140 items to a different sample of undergraduates who were asked to respond yes if the particular item was characteristic of their own behavior and no if it was not. The percentage of subjects responding yes to each of the items was computed and then correlated with the judged social desirability of the response. An impressively high correlation was obtained, leading Edwards to conclude that if we know where a statement lies on the social-desirability–undesirability dimension, ". . . we can then predict, with a high degree of accuracy, the proportion of individuals who will say, in self-description, that the statement does describe them" (p. 3). Moreover, even when respondents are led to believe that they will remain anonymous, they still ascribe to themselves socially desirable attitudes and activities.[6]

---

[6] There is more than one possible interpretation of these data. For example, if behavior that is judged the most desirable in a particular culture is also the most common, the probability of endorsing statements describing such behavior would be high, even when subjects were not misrepresenting themselves. But the evidence does not favor this interpretation.

Several methods have been devised for controlling the social-desirability response set. In one of these methods, the _forced-choice inventory_, items that describe different attitudes and activities, which have been independently determined equal in terms of the social desirability of the behavior, are given in pairs to the respondent. Thus the person is forced to choose between two statements describing equally desirable or undesirable alternatives. Edwards himself used this technique in constructing his Personal Preferences Schedule. The manner in which this method forces respondents to make a content-related response is indicated by the following two examples.

Choose A or B for each of the following items:

Item I
A: _I like to tell amusing stories and jokes at parties._
B: _I would like to write a great novel or play._

Item II
A: _I feel like blaming others when things go wrong for me._
B: _I feel that I am inferior to others in most respects._

Like others who have judged these statements before them, respondents will probably consider the alternatives of each pair equivalent in social desirability. Thus they are more likely to choose the statement that actually describes themselves.

The forced-choice inventory is a widely used technique for reducing the likelihood that questionnaire responses will reflect only the degree to which the respondent wishes to appear conventional or likable. By excluding or at least minimizing the role of social-desirability factors, those who rely on data from personality inventories can with greater confidence regard responses as valid indicators of the personality characteristics the particular test purports to measure.

Tests for organic brain dysfunction

As indicated at the beginning of this chapter, one major section of DSM-III, Organic Mental Disorders, refers to behavioral problems brought on by brain abnormalities. Neurological tests such as checking the patellar reflex, examining the retina for any indication of blood vessel damage, and evaluating motor coordination and perception are useful procedures in diagnosing brain dysfunction. The X-ray can sometimes detect tumors, and the electroencephalograph (EEG) abnormalities in the brain's electrical activity. Computerized axial tomography, the CAT scan, is a recent advance in assessing brain abnormalities; a series of X-rays, taken from different angles, are analyzed by a computer to produce a representation of the brain in cross section. We might reasonably assume that neurologists and physicians, with the help of such procedures and technological devices, can observe the brain and its functions more or less directly and thus assess brain abnormalities. Many brain abnormalities, however, involve alterations in structure so subtle that they have thus far eluded direct physical measurement. Moreover, we still know very little about how the brain works.

Since the way the person functions is the problem—what he or she does, says, thinks, or feels—a number of tests assessing behavioral disturbances that are caused by organic brain dysfunctions have been developed by psychologists. The literature on these tests is extensive and, as with most areas of psychology, so too is disagreement about them. The weight of the evidence, however, does seem to indicate that psychological tests have some validity in the assessment of brain damage. The best psychological test of brain damage is Reitan's modification of a battery or group of tests previously developed by Halstead. The concept of using a battery of tests, each tapping different functions, is critical, for only by studying a person's pattern of performance can an investigator judge accurately whether the person is indeed brain-damaged. But the Halstead-Reitan battery can do even more than this, locating the area of the brain that has been affected. Some of the tests in the battery are the following.

1. **Tactual Performance Test.** While blindfolded, the subject tries to fit variously shaped blocks into spaces in a board, using each hand in turn. After finishing this part of the test, the

subject tries to draw the board from memory, showing the spaces and the blocks filling them in their proper locations.

2. **Trail-Making Test**—see Figure 3.1.

3. **Finger Oscillation Task.** In this procedure the subject depresses a key with the index finger as fast as he or she can for five trials of ten seconds each. The index finger of each hand is tested.

4. **Categories Test.** The subject, seeing an image on a screen that suggests one of the numbers between one and four, presses a button to show which number he or she thinks it is. A bell indicates that the choice is correct, a buzzer that it is wrong. The subject must keep track of these images and signals in order to figure out the rules for making the correct choices.

5. **Aphasia Screening Test.** A number of language abilities are studied by asking the subject to name numbers, to spell, read, write, and pronounce words.

A modified Halstead-Wepman Aphasia Screening Test also asks subjects to identify body parts, to follow directions, and to pantomime simple actions.

Performance on the tests is interpreted by drawing on knowledge of the relation between certain brain structures and behavior. Finger tapping, for example, is thought to be controlled by a brain area just in front of the central sulcus (see Box. A.1, page 714). And control of speech and language tends to be localized in the left cerebral hemisphere. Thus particular deficits suggest that a problem exists in a specific brain area and in one or the other hemisphere. In examining sixty-four brain-damaged patients, Reitan (1964) was able to locate the affected brain area specifically and accurately about 70 percent of the time. That is, his predictions based on test performance were highly related to results of neurological procedures, such as brain scans and surgery.

Intelligence tests

Psychological measures of intelligence enter into diagnoses of mental retardation. Alfred Binet, a French psychologist, originally constructed mental tests to help the Parisian school board predict which children were in need of special schooling. _Intelligence testing_ has since developed into one of the largest psychological industries. The word aptitude is frequently applied to these widely used standardized procedures. The Scholastic Aptitude Test, The Graduate Record Examination, and the individually administered tests, such as the Wechsler Adult Intelligence Scale and the Stanford-Binet, are all based on the assumption that one sample from an individual's current intellectual functioning can predict how well he or she will perform in school.

When such tests are evaluated, it is important to keep in mind two points that are only infrequently made explicit by those who have a heavy professional commitment to intelligence testing. First, strictly speaking, the tests measure only what a psychologist considers intelligence to be. The tasks and items on an IQ test are, after all, invented by psychologists—they did not come down to us inscribed on stone tablets. Second, the tests are widely used because they do indeed accomplish what they were designed for, that is, predict who will succeed in our educational system. If and when there are major changes in our school systems, we can expect

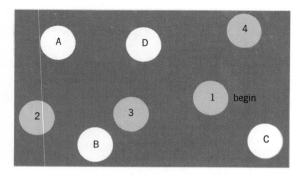

FIGURE **3.1**
Sample item from the Trail-Making Test. The subject is instructed to alternate numbers and letters, for example, by drawing a line from 1 to A, A to 2, 2 to B, and so on.

analogous changes in our definition and assessment of intelligence. Further discussion of IQ tests can be found in Chapter 16.

Behavioral Assessment

Many of the assessment devices in use today are intimately related to the DSM as well as to variations of psychoanalytic theory. As already mentioned, within a psychodynamic framework it makes sense to use a projective test because truly important material is assumed repressed in the unconscious, and ambiguous stimuli rather than direct questions are viewed as the best means to bypass defense mechanisms. Although the MMPI is a more direct, _self-report_ measurement, it too is intimately related to the DSM because the test was developed to make diagnoses according to DSM categories.

In recent years, as part of the continuing development of behavioral approaches to the study of psychopathology and treatment, interest has been growing in assessment procedures that are different from those examined so far. In Chapter 2 behaviorists are described as being interested in _situational determinants_ of behavior, that is, in the environmental conditions that precede and follow certain responses. In addition, with the growing interest in cognitive explanations, we can expect their assessments to include self-reports as well; but, as we shall see, interpretations of self-reports within a behavioral framework differ from those in more traditional assessment.

Traditional assessment concentrates on measuring underlying personality structures and _traits_, such as "anal personality," "obsessive personality," "paranoid personality," coldness, self-importance, self-dramatization, and so on. "A chief aim of the trait approach is to infer the underlying personality structure of individuals and to compare persons and groups on trait dimensions" (Mischel, 1968, pp. 5–6). Behavioral clinicians, on the other hand, focus on specifying conditions under which behavior does or does not occur. Clients typically consult a therapist with vague, generalized complaints such as "I'm all messed up," or "I'm depressed all the time."

It is a considerable challenge to the behavior therapist to obtain from clients information that can prove useful in analyzing the problem in learning terms and, more importantly, in planning various therapy programs.

Behavioral clinicians are concerned with four sets of variables, sometimes referred to by the acronym _SORC_. The S stands for stimuli, the environmental situations that precede the problem. For instance, the clinician will try to ascertain which situations tend to elicit an especially high degree of anxiety. The O stands for organismic, referring to both physiological and psychological factors assumed to be operating "under the skin." Perhaps the client's fatigue is caused in part by excessive use of alcohol, or by a tendency to deprecate the self with such statements as "I never do anything right, so what's the point in trying?" The R refers to overt responses, which probably demand the most attention from behavioral clinicians. They must determine what behavior is problematic, its frequency, intensity, and form. For example, a client might say that she is forgetful and procrastinates. Does she mean that she does not return phone calls, comes late for appointments, or both? Finally, C or consequent variables are events that appear to be reinforcing the behavior in question. When the client avoids a feared situation, does his spouse offer sympathy and excuses, thereby unwittingly discouraging the person from facing up to his fears?

SORC factors are those that a behavioral clinician attempts to specify for a particular client. It might be mentioned in passing that O variables are understandably underplayed by Skinnerians; similarly, C variables receive less attention from cognitively oriented behavior therapists than do O variables.

The information necessary for a _behavioral assessment_ is gathered by several methods. These include direct observation of the behavior in real life as well as in contrived settings, interviews and self-report measures, role playing in the consulting room, and physiological measurement.

Direct observation of behavior

It is not surprising that behavior therapists have paid considerable attention to careful observation of behavior in a variety of settings. But it should not be assumed that they simply go out and *observe*. Like other scientists, they try to fit actual physical events into a framework consistent with their point of view. This excerpt from a case report by Patterson and his colleagues (1969), describing an interaction between a boy named Kevin and his mother, father, and sister Freida, serves as the first part of an example.

> *Kevin goes up to father's chair and stands alongside it. Father puts his arms around Kevin's shoulders. Kevin says to mother as Freida looks at Kevin, "Can I go out and play after supper?" Mother does not reply. Kevin raises his voice and repeats the question. Mother says "You don't have to yell; I can hear you." Father says "How many times have I told you not to yell at your mother?" Kevin scratches a bruise on his arm while mother tells Freida to get started on the dishes, which Freida does. Kevin continues to rub and scratch his arm while mother and daughter are working at the kitchen sink (p. 21).*

This informal description could probably be provided by any observer. But a behavioral observer would divide the uninterrupted sequence of behavior into various parts and apply terms that make sense within a learning framework. "Kevin begins the exchange by asking a routine question in a normal tone of voice. This ordinary behavior, however, is not reinforced by the mother's attention, for she does not reply. Because she does not reply, the normal behavior of Kevin ceases and he yells his question. The mother expresses disapproval—punishing her son—by telling him that he does not have to yell. And this punishment is supported by the father's reminding Kevin that he should not yell at his mother." This behavioral rendition acknowledges the consequences of ignoring a child's question. At some point the behavior therapist will undoubtedly advise the parents to attend to Kevin's requests when expressed in an ordinary tone of voice, lest he begin yelling. This example indicates an important aspect of behavioral assessment, namely its link to *intervention*.

The clinician's way of conceptualizing a situation often implies a way to change it.

It is difficult to observe most behavior as it actually takes place, and little control can be exercised over where and when it may occur. For this reason many therapists contrive artificial situations in their consulting rooms or in a laboratory so that they can observe how a client or a family acts under certain conditions. The sequence just described might well have happened in such a contrived setting.

The foregoing operant interpretation of a family scene employs no inferential concepts; the observations are interpreted in a fairly straightforward way. Behavioral assessment techniques can also be applied within a framework that does make use of mediators. For instance, Gordon Paul (1966) was interested in assessing the "anxiety" of public speakers. He decided that a good way to determine the anxiety of the speaker was to count the frequency of behavior that is deemed indicative of this emotional state. One of his principal measures, the Timed Behavioral Checklist for Performance Anxiety, is shown in Table 3.9. Subjects were asked to deliver a speech in front of a group, some members of which were raters trained to consider each subject's behavior every thirty seconds and to record the presence or absence of twenty specific behaviors. By summing the scores, Paul arrived at a behavioral index of anxiety. This study is one example of how observations of overt behavior have been used to infer an internal state.

In Paul's study people other than the speaker whose behavior was being described made the observations. For several years behavior therapists and researchers have also asked individuals to observe their *own* behavior, to keep track of various categories of response. The general approach is called _self-monitoring_. An early application of self-monitoring was in research to reduce smoking. Subjects were provided with booklets in which they recorded the time each cigarette was lighted at baseline, before treatment had been introduced, during treatment, and after.

Although some research indicates that self-monitoring can provide accurate measurement of such behavior as smoking and the eating of cer-

TABLE 3.9
Timed Behavioral Checklist for
Performance Anxiety

(from Paul, 1966)

Behavior observed	Time period								
	1	2	3	4	5	6	7	8	Σ
1. Paces									
2. Sways									
3. Shuffles feet									
4. Knees tremble									
5. Extraneous arm and hand movement (swings, scratches, toys, etc.)									
6. Arms rigid									
7. Hands restrained (in pockets, behind back, clasped)									
8. Hand tremors									
9. No eye contact									
10. Face muscles tense (drawn, tics, grimaces)									
11. Face "deadpan"									
12. Face pale									
13. Face flushed (blushes)									
14. Moistens lips									
15. Swallows									
16. Clears throat									
17. Breathes heavily									
18. Perspires (face, hands, armpits)									
19. Voice quivers									
20. Speech blocks or stammers									

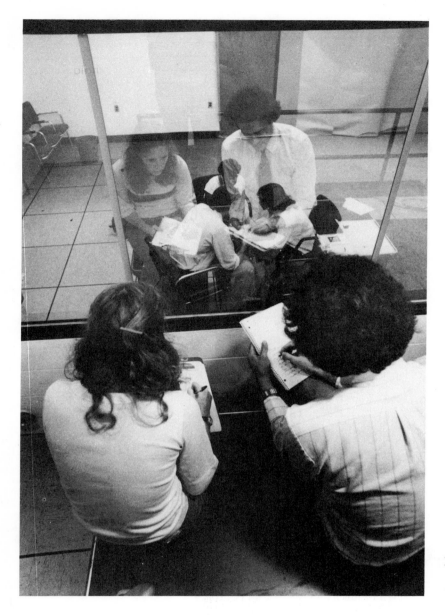

Assessment of behavior by direct observation through a one-way mirror. Those being observed cannot see the experimenters making the observations.

tain foods, many report that the information collected is unreliable (Nelson, 1977). And yet there are ways to improve the accuracy of self-monitoring: by rewarding people for accuracy (Lipinski et al., 1975), by taking care to motivate subjects to be honest and conscientious (Bornstein et al., 1977), by training them in the demands of the particular self-monitoring task (Nelson, Lipinski, and Boykin, 1978), and by

informing people that their self-monitoring is in turn being watched by other observers (Nelson, Lipinski, and Black, 1975). At the same time, however, considerable research indicates that behavior may be altered by the very fact that it is being self-monitored. _Reactivity_ of behavior is the phenomenon of its changing because it is being observed. Generally speaking, desirable behavior, such as engaging in social conversation, often increases in frequency when self-monitored (Nelson, Lipinski, and Black, 1976), whereas behavior the subject wishes to reduce, like cigarette smoking, diminishes (McFall and Hammen, 1971). Such findings suggest that the reactivity which is an outcome of self-monitoring can be taken advantage of in therapeutic interventions.

Self-monitoring of overt behavior should be viewed as a necessary compromise to direct observation by trained people. Researchers have come to realize that much of the behavior they want to observe cannot, in any practical or ethical way, be directly monitored by other people. Recent efforts to collect information on people's thoughts indicate how dependent clinicians are on the ability of people to report on their own behavior. For many years the field of psychology has wrestled with the challenge of gaining knowledge about people's cognitive processes or, to use a perhaps old-fashioned term, consciousness. Today, as we have seen, many behavioral clinicians believe that thoughts affect mental health. If a therapist finds, as does Ellis (see page 58), that what people tell themselves or what they think is a source of psychological distress, it becomes important to know their exact thoughts in a wide variety of circumstances.

Research on the self-monitoring of thinking has only recently begun. Hurlburt (1979) has developed a novel procedure for gathering information on how people think as they go about their normal day-to-day activities. A small boxlike device which he invented is carried in the subject's pocket, with a wire leading from it to a hearing aid earplug. The device emits on a random basis a sound that is audible only through the plug. The subject is trained to note in a booklet whatever is in the mind when the tone sounds and to categorize the thought by its sexual content, whether it is about the present, past, or future, and so on. The fact that the machine sounds its tone on a random basis is important, for such sampling can be assumed to provide a reasonable measure of thought in general. In one study Hurlburt found that among male undergraduates one percent of their total sampled thoughts had sexual content. Considering the stereotype that men of this age are preoccupied with sex, the

low percentage of their thoughts about the subject is surprising. But some subjects may be inhibited about making such reports. The clinical usefulness of Hulburt's technique, thought sampling, is yet to be evaluated.

Interviews and self-report measures

For all their interest in direct observation of behavior, behavioral clinicians still rely very heavily on the interview to assess the needs of their clients. Like other clinicians, they make every effort to establish good rapport, creating an atmosphere of trust and caring which encourages clients to reveal aspects of their lives that they may not have shown any other person—what London (1964) has poetically called "secrets of the heart." Within this trusting relationship the behavior therapist's job is to determine, via skillful questioning and careful observation of the client's emotional reactions during the interview, the SORC factors already mentioned—the situations in which the problematic behavior occurs, the internal conditions mediating the influence of the environment, the particular patterns of behavior causing distress, and the events that may help to maintain the problem. The authors of this textbook, in their behaviorally oriented clinical work, conduct an initial interview with the goal of writing an intake report like the one shown in Table 3.10.

The self-report inventories that behavior therapists develop are a great deal more specific and detailed than those typically used by nonbehavioral clinicians. For example, McFall and Lillesand (1971) employed a Conflict Resolution Inventory, containing thirty-five items which focus on the ability of the respondent to refuse unreasonable requests. Each item describes a specific situation in which a person is asked for something unreasonable. For example, "You are in the thick of studying for exams when a person you know slightly comes into your room and says 'I'm tired of studying, mind if I come in and take a break for a while?'" Subjects are asked to indicate the likelihood that they would refuse such a request and how comfortable they would be in doing so. This and similar inventories have helped behavioral researchers measure the out-

TABLE **3.10**
A Behaviorally Oriented Intake Report

(after Goldfried and Davison, 1976)

Name: BRIAN, James (fictitious name)   Age: 22   Sex: Male

Class: Senior   Date of interview: March 25, 1982
                                       Therapist: John Doe

1. Behavior during interview and physical description:

   James is a clean-shaven, long-haired young man who appeared for the intake
   interview in well-coordinated college garb: jeans, wide belt, open shirt, and
   sandals. He came across as shy and soft-spoken, with occasional minor speech
   blocks. Although uneasy during most of the session, he nonetheless spoke freely
   and candidly.

2. Presenting problem:

   (a) Nature of problem: Anxiety in public-speaking situations and in other
   situations in which he is being evaluated by others.

   (b) Historical setting events: James was born in France and arrived in this
   country seven years ago, at which time he experienced both a social and language
   problem. His social contacts had been minimal until he entered college; there a
   socially aggressive friend helped him to break out of his shell. James describes
   his father as an overly critical perfectionist who would, on occasion, rip up
   his son's homework if it fell short of the mark. His mother he pictures as a
   controlling, overly affectionate person who always shows concern about his
   welfare. His younger brother, who has always been a good student, is continually
   thrown up to James by his parents as being far better than he.

   (c) Current situational determinants: Interaction with his parents, examinations, family gatherings, participation in classes, initial social contacts.

   (d) Relevant organismic variables: The client appears to be approaching a
   number of situations with certain irrational expectations, primarily unrealistic
   strivings for perfection and an overwhelming desire to receive approval from
   others. He is not taking any medication at this time except as indicated under
   10 below.

   (e) Dimensions of problem: The client's anxiety about social relationships and
   evaluations of himself is long standing and occurs in a wide variety of day-to-
   day situations.

   (f) Consequences of problem: His chronic level of anxiety resulted in an ulcer
   operation at the age of 15. In addition, he has developed a skin rash on his
   hands and arms, apparently from excessive perspiration. He reports that his
   nervousness at one time caused him to stutter, but this problem appears to
   have diminished in recent years. His anxiety when taking examinations has
   typically interfered with his ability to perform well.

3. Other problems:

   (a) Assertiveness: Although obviously a shy and timid individual, James says
   that lack of assertiveness is no longer a problem with him. At one time in the
   past, his friends would take advantage of him, but he claims that this is no
   longer the case. His statements should be followed up, for it is unclear what
   he means by assertiveness.

(b) Forgetfulness: The client reports that he frequently misses appointments, misplaces items, locks himself out of his room, and is generally absentminded.

4. Personal assets:

   The client is fairly bright and comes across as a warm, friendly, and sensitive individual.

5. Targets for modification:

   Unrealistic self-statements about how he should fare in social evaluative situations; possible behavioral deficits associated with unassertiveness; and forgetfulness.

6. Recommended treatment:

   It appears that relaxation training would be a good way to begin, especially in light of the client's high level of anxiety. Treatment should then undertake the restructuring of his unrealistic expectations. Behavior rehearsal is a possibility. The best strategy for dealing with forgetfulness is unclear as yet.

7. Motivation for treatment:

   High.

8. Prognosis:

   Good.

9. Priority for treatment:

   High.

10. Expectancies:

    On occasion, especially when going out on a date, James takes half a sleeping pill to calm himself down. He wants to get away from this and feels that he needs to learn to cope with his anxieties by himself. It would appear that he will be receptive to whatever treatment plan we finally decide on, especially if the emphasis is on self-control of anxiety.

11. Other comments:

    Considering the brief time available between now and the end of the semester, between-session homework assignments should be given.

come of clinical interventions and can be used by the practicing clinician as well.[7]

Role playing
Because some clinical problems cannot be observed directly in the real-life situation, many behavior therapists enact little plays, if you will, in the consulting room. The therapist assumes the role of a particular individual in the client's life and creates an opportunity for observing responses. Not frequently clients object that the created scene is "just make-believe, too artficial, could not possibly show anything." But in many instances the client becomes quite involved in the *role playing*, enabling the therapist to obtain useful information about how the client responds in real life.

Physiological measurement
In recent years experimentally minded behavioral clinicians and therapy researchers have availed themselves of sophisticated procedures for measuring physiological aspects of behavior. The discipline of *psychophysiology* is concerned with the bodily changes that accompany psychological events (see Box 3.3). For example, we know that the heart rate of most people will increase markedly under conditions of psychological, as well as physical, stress.

Experimenters have studied such changes, as well as alterations in the conductivity of the skin, tension in the muscles, blood flow in various parts of the body, and even brain waves (see page 285), while subjects are afraid, depressed, asleep, imagining, solving problems, and so on. Special attention has also been paid to the *patterning* of such responses, as when heart rate increases while skin conductivity remains constant.

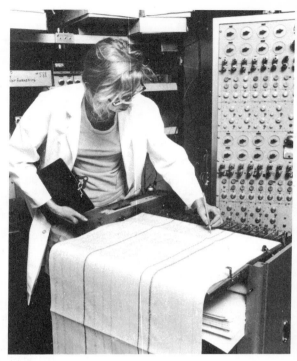

Here a psychologist monitors the output of several channels of a polygraph, a device for measuring a number of physiological responses such as heart rate, blood pressure, respiration, and electrodermal activity.

Behavioral clinicians have come to realize that a more complete picture of the human being is obtained by assessing physiological functioning along with overt behavior and cognitive activity. If experimenters wonder whether showing schizophrenic patients pictures of their mothers is stressful, they can, in addition to asking the patients how they feel about looking at the pictures, measure their heart rate and electrical skin activity. Psychophysiological measuring procedures, which are constantly being improved and added to, are relatively unobtrusive. Once the person has adapted to having electrodes pasted on his or her arm, for example, measurement of heart rate does not interfere with many experimental tasks, such as listening to a story or solving a mathematical problem.

Inasmuch as psychophysiology employs highly sophisticated electronic machinery, and inasmuch as many psychologists aspire to be as scientific as possible, it sometimes happens that

---

[7] Determining behavior through self-report raises issues similar to these posed by Hurlburt's research on thought sampling, for the clinician relies on the ability of individuals to introspect and report on events observable only to themselves, whether the assessment takes place during an interview, as they fill out a questionnaire, or when the beep sounds randomly from Hurlburt's device. A person self-monitoring in his or her everyday surrounding makes an observation at the very moment thoughts occur, however. In contrast, both interviews and self-report inventories require the person to reflect backward in time, to provide a retrospective report of his or her behavior, feelings, and thoughts in certain situations. "When someone criticizes you in class, what thoughts go through your mind?" is a question a client might be asked in an interview or on a paper-and-pencil inventory. The reply in this kind of assessment might well be different from what the client would report were he or she able to do so at the moment of criticism.

3.3 Measurement of Autonomic Nervous System Activity

The mammalian nervous system can be considered to have two relatively separate functional divisions: the _somatic_ or voluntary, and the _autonomic_ or involuntary. Because the autonomic nervous system is especially important in the study of emotional behavior, it will be useful to review its principal characteristics and the ways in which its activity can be monitored.

Skeletal muscles, such as those that move our limbs, are innervated by the voluntary nervous system. Much of our behavior, however, is dependent on a nervous system that operates generally without our awareness and has traditionally been viewed as beyond voluntary control. Hence the term autonomic. The autonomic nervous system (ANS) innervates the endocrine glands, the heart, and the smooth muscles which are found in the walls of the blood vessels, stomach, intestines, kidneys, and other organs. This nervous system is itself divided into two parts, the _sympathetic_ and _parasympathetic_ nervous systems (Figure 3.2), which sometimes work against each other, sometimes in unison. The sympathetic portion of the ANS, when energized, accelerates the heartbeat, dilates the pupils, inhibits intestinal activity, and initiates other smooth muscle and glandular responses that prepare the organism for sudden activity and stress. Indeed, some physiologists view the sympathetic nervous system as primarily excitatory, whereas the other division, the parasympathetic, is viewed as responsible for maintenance functions and more quiescent behavior, such as deceleration of the heartbeat, constriction of the pupils, and speeding up contractions of the intestines. Division of activities is not quite so clear-cut, however, for the parasympathetic system may be active during situations of stress. Animals, and humans to their consternation, may urinate and defecate involuntarily when extremely frightened.

The activities of the ANS are frequently assessed by electronic and chemical measurements and analyses in attempts to understand the nature of emotion. One important measure is heart rate. Each heartbeat generates spreading changes in electric potential, which can be recorded by an electrocardiograph or on a suitably tuned polygraph. Electrodes are usually placed on both arms and lead to a galvanometer, an instrument for measuring electric currents. The deflections of this instrument may be seen as waves on an oscilloscope, or a pen recorder may register the waves on a continuously moving roll of graph paper. Both types of recordings are called electrocardiograms. More recently available is the cardiotachometer, a device that measures the precise elapsed time between two heartbeats and then instantaneously provides heart rate on a beat-to-beat basis. This technological advance is especially important for experimental psychologists, who are typically interested in bodily changes that occur over short periods of time in response to rapidly shifting circumstances. Generally a fast heart rate is taken to indicate increased arousal.

A second measure is _electrodermal responding,_ sometimes referred to as the _galvanic skin response_ (GSR). Anxiety, fear, anger, and other emotions elicit greater sweat gland activity. The electrophysiological processes in the cells of these glands change the electric conductance of the skin as well as producing sweat. There are two methods of measuring the electrodermal response. Skin potential may be measured by recording with surface electrodes the very small differences in electric potential that always exist between any two points on the skin. This voltage shows a pronounced rise after the sweat glands have been stimulated to activity. Or we may determine the current that flows through the skin when a known small voltage derived from an external source is passed between two electrodes pasted to the palm and back of the hand. This current also shows a pronounced increase after activation of the sweat glands. The percentage of change from the normal or baseline reading is for either method the measure of reactivity. High conductance, or alternatively low resistance, is thought to reflect increased autonomic activity. Since the sweat glands are innervated only by the sympathetic nervous system, increased sweat gland activity indicates sympathetic autonomic excitation and is often taken as a measure of anxiety.

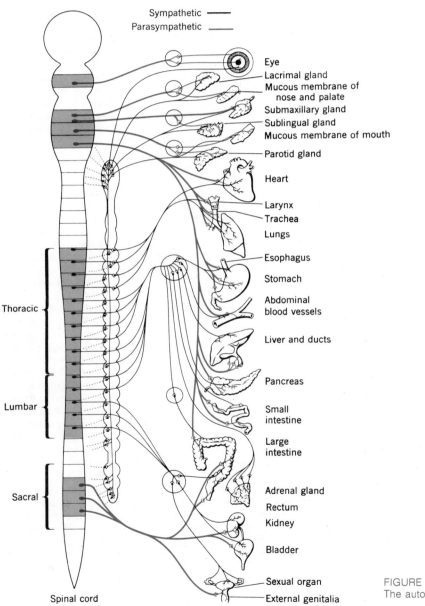

FIGURE **3.2**
The autonomic nervous system.

Many issues in assessment can be appreciated by considering efforts to measure anxiety, one of the most prevalent emotions and one of great concern to psychopathologists and therapists. They have generally relied on three modes of measurement: self-report questionnaires, observations of overt behavior, and physiological measurements.

Allowing people to describe the phenomena of their emotions in their own terms, as is done in clinical interviews, provides useful information about the one individual interviewed; but this strategy alone makes it difficult to compare the experiences of a number of people and, even more important, to quantify what they say. Researchers have therefore devised various self-report questionnaires which attempt to direct the individual's impressions into standardized terms. The following are some sample items from the Taylor Manifest Anxiety Scale (Taylor, 1953), which consists of fifty items drawn from the MMPI.

I work under a great deal of strain.	<u>True</u> False
I am usually calm and not easily upset.	True <u>False</u>
I sweat very easily even on cool days.	<u>True</u> False
I always have enough energy when faced with difficulty.	True <u>False</u>
My sleep is restless and disturbed.	<u>True</u> False

An anxious person would underline the true and false responses as indicated. The test is scored by simply summing the number of "anxious" responses made by the subject. This score is then assumed to represent the person's general level of anxiety.

The second means of assessing anxiety is to observe overt behavior for reactions and movements that are believed to reflect the internal emotional state—trembling, perspiring, nail biting, fleeing from a situation. Observers trained to administer Paul's (1966) Timed Behavioral Checklist for Performance Anxiety time-sampled the overt behavior of subjects in a stressful situation, recording instances of twenty indices of anxiety whenever they were observed.

Physiological measurements of activities of the autonomic nervous system and the output of certain endocrine glands also indicate levels of anxiety. The availability of these measurements has encouraged researchers to define anxiety in physiological terms. The situation in which physiological measurements are taken is very important, however. What would be revealed, for example, if recording electrodes were attached to a woman who is about to have sexual relations? Both before and during sexual activity the heartbeat is very likely to be faster, blood pressure higher, perspiration greater, and breathing more rapid, all physiological responses that are generally regarded as indicators of sexual excitement as well as of anxiety. But why would we not conclude that our female subject is, indeed, anxious as she contemplates sexual intercourse? As we shall see in Chapter 12, many people are debilitated by fear in sexual situations. How can an investigator distinguish rapid breathing that reflects sexual excitement from rapid breathing that reflects anxiety? Part of the answer necessarily lies in other observations being made concurrently. If at the time physiological measures are being taken the female subject convincingly reports that she is looking forward to what is to come, and if she ultimately derives great enjoyment from her sexual partner, we would almost certainly choose to interpret her rapid breathing and other physiological responses as indicating sexual arousal. The situation and her self-report of it must be taken into consideration.

Not only are the physiological indicators of anxiety evident in other emotional states, but the many measures of anxiety have been found time and again *not* to correlate well with one another (see Martin, 1961; Lang, 1969). In a stressful situation such as being threatened with painful electric shock, many people report being very nervous, but their heart rates may be lower rather than elevated. An individual taking an important examination for which he or she is ill-prepared may deny feeling anxious and yet be observed trembling.

The discrepancy in different indices of anxiety was examined in a recent study by Weinberger, Schwartz, and Davidson (1979). They proposed that people who report low levels of anxiety actually divide into two distinct subgroups. One group, people who truly have little anxiety, accurately perceive themselves and truthfully report their anxiety levels. The other group, people who cope by repressing their feelings, do not admit to anxiety on verbal report measures, but examinations of their overt behavior and physiology reveal considerable anxiety. This group is responsible for the lack of correlation between anxiety assessed by psychophysiological observation and that reported verbally.

To test their hypothesis, Weinberger and his colleagues (1979) first selected subjects using measures both of anxiety—the short form of the Taylor Manifest Anxiety Scale; and of the tendency to deny or repress feelings—the Marlowe–Crowne Scale (Crowne and Marlowe, 1964). Three groups of subjects were formed, those with truly little anxiety (they had low scores on both the MAS and the repression scale), anxiety repressors (they made low MAS scores but high repression scores), and people with considerable anxiety (their MAS scores were high, their repression scores low). Subjects were then tested in a procedure in which they had to associate to phrases provided by the experimenter. Some phrases were relatively neutral, others sexual and aggressive in content. The extent to which the task elicited anxiety was assessed by scoring signs of disturbance in the subjects' verbal replies, such as avoiding the actual content of the phrase, and by reaction time. Several psychophysiological measurements were also recorded while the participants performed the task. The data corroborated the hypothesis. Anxiety repressors had more verbal disturbances and took longer to reply, indicating significantly more anxiety than did the minimally anxious subjects. Similarly, the repressors gave more physiological indications of anxiety—for example, higher heart rate, stronger electrodermal responses—than did the truly unanxious subjects.

On a more general level many workers regard the concept of anxiety as a useful one for organizing and interrelating data from numerous sources. Maher (1966) and Lang (1969), for example, consider anxiety to be a hypothetical *construct*, a convenient fiction or inferred state that mediates between a threatening situation and the observed behavior of an organism. They also assume that the construct is multifaceted or multidimensional, and that each facet is not necessarily evoked by a given stressful situation or always expressed to the same degree, another explanation of the low intercorrelations for the measures of anxiety.

As a scientific construct, anxiety must be tied to observables, the conditions that produce it and the effects that follow its induction. For this very reason Skinner (1953), as we indicated earlier (see page 51), argues that mediators are *not* essential in accounting for behavior. Since the construct of anxiety is linked to stimuli and responses, why not dispense with it and talk only of observables? Furthermore, might not the inference of an internal state lead us to believe that an adequate explanation has been found and thereby discourage the continuing search for ways to predict and control behavior?

These are cogent objections, and they have forced workers to exercise great care in their use of the anxiety construct. As will be noted in Chapter 4, investigators who employ mediators such as anxiety do so in hopes of better organizing their data and of generating hypotheses. We seldom find experimental psychologists speaking about anxiety without being able at any time to explain how and why they infer that the emotional state exists.

Finally, certain experiments would not be undertaken or could not be explained without inferring the mediating state. To illustrate, let us consider an experiment reviewed by Rescorla and Solomon (1967). Dogs were taught to avoid a stimulus (CS) by pairing it repeatedly with a painful shock (UCS). Then they were totally paralyzed with injections of curare, a drug which prevents movement of the skeletal muscles. One group of animals, while paralyzed, were repeatedly presented with the CS, but shock did not accompany it. In Pavlovian, classical conditioning terms, these would be considered attempts to extinguish the conditioned response. Did these animals learn, while paralyzed and unable to move, that the CS was in fact no longer followed by shock? Phrased another way, did the previously learned fear of the CS undergo any extinction? The answer was obtained on a subsequent day when the dogs in this group had completely recovered from the curare and were confronted with the CS. The unshocked presentations of the CS a day or two earlier had indeed reduced avoidance behavior, even though no overt response could have occurred during the curare paralysis. The control animals, who had not been confronted with the CS while paralyzed, did not show a reduction in avoidance behavior.

How do we account for such remarkable findings? Rescorla and Solomon deem it necessary, and legitimate, to infer a mediating fear which was lessened when the dogs were presented with the CS while paralyzed with curare. Clearly something was being unlearned during the time that the dogs could not respond by avoiding the CS. By positing a mediating fear, we can make sense of these findings and relate them to a wealth of other theory and research. The experiment just described does indicate that anxiety, or fear, can be useful as an explanatory device. Nonetheless, the anxiety construct poses continual difficulties for those who employ it.

they believe uncritically in these apparently objective assessment devices without appreciating their real limitations and complications. Many of the measurements do not differentiate clearly among emotional states. Heart rate, for example, increases with a variety of emotions, not just with anxiety. Special care must be taken to ensure a proper setting for taking measurements so that the data collected are meaningful. And experimenters can introduce bias by the way they treat their willing subjects.

Behavioral assessment for behavioral change

We have already mentioned that a principal aspect of behavioral assessment is its close ties to procedures for changing behavior. Behavior therapists always search thoroughly for the situational determinants of behavior because they believe it can be altered by manipulating the environment. One behavior therapy procedure, systematic desensitization, seems to be effective in reducing a variety of fears. This technique requires that the therapist know the particular situations that make the patient fearful. Rather than make a general diagnosis, such as phobic reaction, and then begin to search for underlying personality dynamics, behavior therapists believe that quicker and greater progress can be made by ascertaining the specific situations in which people are phobic and then lessening their fears of them. To take another example, an aggressive youngster might be directly observed to see whether teachers and parents reinforce his abrasive behavior with their attention. If this is the case, they can be cautioned to ignore the outbursts as much as possible. These steps contrast with diagnosing the boy as having a conduct disorder and then seeking the reasons for his problem. The range of behavior therapies for different disorders, to be described in later chapters, will reveal again and again this direct link between assessment and intervention.

Reliability of behavioral assessment

We have now surveyed the major approaches to behavioral assessment. The reader has probably become aware of how much more *direct* this type of assessment is than the traditional techniques, such as the Rorschach described earlier in this chapter. If the behavioral researcher wants to determine how anxious a person is, he or she decides what will be taken to indicate anxiety, such as hand tremors or a particular pattern of psychophysiological response recorded on a polygraph, and then measures the person's responses under controlled conditions, as when taking a test.

Are things really so simple? Because a behavioral researcher directly observes a bit of behavior, are better data necessarily being collected? The answer is maybe. Let us examine the problem in terms first of reliability and then of validity.

The reliability of diagnoses depends on whether various diagnosticians agree on how to categorize patients' problems. That of assessment procedures too depends on whether outcomes are similar. Do two raters using a particular coding system make similar observations of the same event, and does a respondent, when taking two versions of a test judged to be roughly equivalent, make similar scores? Behavioral clinicians have been concerned about the reliability of their measures. For example, Paul (1966), in employing the behavioral checklist shown in Table 3.9, trained his research assistants extensively until two of them, while watching the same subject give a speech, could reach similar judgments of the frequency of the several signs of anxiety.

Over the years the reliability of behavioral assessment has been shown to be affected by several factors. The complexity or difficulty of the assessment task can lower reliability. If an investigator is using a time-sampling procedure as Paul did, whereby raters watch for certain indicators at fixed time intervals, reliability can be enhanced if the interval between observations is long enough to allow raters time to make careful judgments—every minute rather than every ten seconds, for instance; and if the behaviors to be watched for are few rather than many—five, for example, rather than twenty.

Another consideration is the way observers are monitored. At the earliest stages of a research project, the people with overall responsibility, the investigators, usually work very closely with the experimenters, those who actually have contact with the subjects. Often experimenters are graduate students. Before actually running a study, the investigators spend many hours with their assistants, ensuring that instructions are being followed and that any behavioral assessments are being done reliably. It has been shown that once the experimenters are left unsupervised—or, more precisely, once they *believe* themselves to be on their own—they tend to become slipshod and hence less reliable as observers (Romanczyk et al., 1973). An effective and ethical way to increase reliability is to inform the experimenters that their work will be checked now and again, without telling them exactly when. This unscheduled observing of the observers seems to keep them on their toes and thus increases reliability (Bernstein and Nietzel, 1980).

Finally, _observer drift_ should be mentioned. When two raters work together for a lengthy period of time, they may begin to agree on ways of recording behavior that are idiosyncratic to *them*. The ratings of the two may achieve high levels of reliability but be different from those of another pair of raters working on the same project. Methods of applying or scoring a particular measure can actually vary markedly from one pair of observers to another. Or, in a similar fashion, a pair of raters in experiment A at University X may use the very same observation procedures differently from a pair of raters in experiment B at University Y. Two raters may be in close agreement and yet as a pair "drift" away from other pairs, thus making it risky to compare results from different experiments. A fairly easy and effective way to deal with this problem is to rotate people from one observer pair to another, so that any given rater works with many different fellow raters.

Validity of behavioral assessment

Behavioral researchers have only recently attended to the validity of their measures. As implied earlier in this chapter, the validity of any measure is the extent to which it reflects what it is supposed to reflect. For example, if an investigator asserts that frequent lateness is an indicator of hostility, he or she is making a statement about the validity of lateness as a measure of hostility. Is this researcher justified in making such an assertion? Or, put differently, are we prepared to agree that hostility can be assessed by taking note of lateness?

Because behavioral assessment is so much more direct and obvious than traditional personality assessment, we can be seduced into assuming validity uncritically and perhaps prematurely. Common sense and the already discussed reactivity of self-monitored behavior, however, suggest that people behave or think differently when they are aware of being watched. For example, Zeigob, Arnold, and Forehand (1975) found that mothers acted more positively toward their children when they knew that they were being observed than when observations were made surreptitiously. Therefore the behavior of the mothers aware of being watched may not provide a valid assessment of their typical level of positive mothering.

Not all behavior, however, is reactive to being measured, and much remains to be learned about this possible source of invalidity. We do know that clients and subjects must become accustomed to being observed before the information being collected can be taken seriously. For example, a recorder might run for half an hour before the taped conversation of a group becomes a source of data on group interaction.

Another problem is the _external_ or _ecological validity_ of an assessment, whether it applies to other situations. Imagine that a therapist has a client role-play in the office to determine whether the young woman asserts herself to her mother, the therapist taking the part of the parent. If she proves to be assertive, can the therapist conclude that she has no assertion problems with her mother? It would be hasty to do so. The most obvious consideration is that the therapist is not the client's mother! Moreover, the particular situation selected for role playing, such as asking the mother not to telephone so often, might not touch on other problems requiring more assertion. The client might be able to ask her mother for a loan but not for some baby-sitting help. Any observation made of behavior is necessarily limited. We can _never_ observe all conceivable situations; assessment, like any other knowledge-gathering enterprise, always touches on less than exists or could exist. Behavioral assessors must be mindful how restricted their observations are and maintain a modest and cautious attitude

about the external validity of their assessments.

Yet another issue are the many distortions that can creep into any observation made by a human being. We have discussed in Chapters 1 and 2 the important roles that paradigms play in science. Any assessor has a point of view and is subject to the effects of this bias. Most importantly, assessors may have expectations and communicate them to subjects. Some years ago Robert Rosenthal (1966) reported on a series of experiments that shocked experimental psychologists and clinicians alike. He demonstrated through review of others' work and by his own ingenious techniques that experimenters, without being dishonest, can often influence the outcome of a study by virtue of having certain expectations about the results. This difficulty of experimenter bias has come to be called the _Rosenthal effect_. But in an interesting demonstration by Kent, O'Leary, and their colleagues (1974), experimenter bias was shown to affect overall conclusions rather than specific behavioral observations. In this study observers used a behavioral coding system as they watched videotapes of children who were being treated for disruptive behavior. One group of observers was told that the treatment would decrease disruptive behavior, the other that no change was expected. As Rosenthal's studies would suggest, observers afterward made the judgment that disruptive behavior had increased if they had been told it was expected to. More importantly, however, their _specific behavior recordings_ did not show bias. These results indicate the usefulness of relatively objective coding schemes in observing behavior.

Finally, the most basic issue in the validity of behavioral assessment are the indicators we choose for measuring what we are interested in. Consider the example mentioned earlier, measuring hostility by counting instances of lateness. Is this the best measure of hostility we can select? People might be late frequently for reasons other than hostility. Any person who has had to fight traffic at rush hour can surely come up with at least one example! We would have to take care, then, that a person whose hostility we wish to assess will not be late for nonemotional reasons.

There are additional ways to evaluate how meaningful our measures are. Weiss, Hops, and

Daniel O'Leary, Stony Brook psychologist, observing and recording the behavior of children in a classroom. He is coding their behavior at regular intervals according to a predetermined set of dimensions.

Patterson (1973), for example, have developed an inventory that each member of a married couple fills out at the end of a day. The items of the inventory tap into such aspects of marriage as the frequency of pleasing behavior on the part of the spouse. In evaluating the validity of this Spouse Observation Checklist, Margolin (1978) determined that fewer "pleases" were reported by couples complaining of a distressed marriage than by couples reporting marital satisfaction. In another study Margolin and Weiss (1978) found that the frequency of displeasing behavior de-

creased markedly during a month in which couples underwent therapy to improve their communication. Such relationships strongly suggest that this instrument is valid as a measure of marital satisfaction.

These, then, are some of the problems in determining the validity of behavioral assessment and some of the strategies employed to handle them. Behavioral assessment has emerged as one of the liveliest and most important areas of work in clinical psychology and psychiatry.

The Consistency and Variability of Behavior

Walter Mischel, in *Personality and Assessment* (1968), has argued that the environment is a more important determinant of behavior than are personality traits. Trait theorists, as stated earlier, believe that human beings can be described as having a certain "amount" of a characteristic, such as "stinginess," or "obsessiveness," and that their behavior in a variety of situations can be predicted by the degree to which they possess this characteristic. This position implies that people will behave consistently in a variety of situations—for example, an aggressive person will be aggressive at home, at work, and at play. Mischel's analysis of the evidence bearing on this question, however, indicates that the behavior of people is often not very consistent from situation to situation.

Not surprisingly, Mischel's attack on trait theory elicited a heated debate in the literature. For example, the psychodynamic theorist Paul Wachtel (1977) argues that social-learning theo-

Walter Mischel, prominent psychologist whose work stimulated the current debate concerning whether traits or situations are the most powerful determinants of behavior.

rists like Mischel ignore current psychoanalytic thinking, which does not entirely overlook the way behavior varies in different situations. Moreover, Wachtel argues, the behavior of individuals whom clinicians tend to encounter may indeed be predictable on the basis of some underlying trait or disposition. Clinical problems may, in fact, be associated with a rigidity or inflexibility to changing conditions.[8]

Wachtel also suggests that people tend to perceive certain kinds of situations in a particular fashion; the perception in effect renders situations that look different to an experimenter equivalent in their own eyes. For example, a person who might be described as paranoid sees threats in seemingly innocuous situations. Insensitivity to circumstances is not his or her problem; rather this person perceives a great many situations as threatening events. In addition, people can *elicit* certain kinds of reactions from their surroundings. The paranoid individual may not only perceive people as threatening but make them so by attacking them first. In effect, he transforms different situations into similar and dangerous ones. As a result his own behavior varies little.

Wachtel goes on to argue that the experiments Mischel attends to are generally done with normal college undergraduates, whose behavior is probably more flexible than that of patients. As just mentioned, one of the hallmarks of mental disorder may be rigidity and inflexibility, which is another way of saying that behavior is consistent in a variety of situations. Therefore, by studying basically normal people, social-learning theorists have concluded that people are more variable than they might had they studied patients.

Thus, contrary to what some behavioral critics contend, contemporary psychodynamic thinkers do not dispute the important role that environmental events play in determining behavior. They argue instead that people perceive situa-

---

[8] It has been suggested that people at the other extreme, those who "shift with the wind," so to speak, may also be subject to emotional disorder. That is, some forms of disorder may be connected to overdependence on the environment as a guide to behavior. To be totally at the mercy of one's surroundings, like a rudderless ship, would seem to pose as many problems as being insensitive to varying environmental demands (Phares, 1979).

tions in certain ways, even transforming them, and then respond in a rather consistent manner.

Mischel, in an important paper published in 1973, replies to some of his critics by suggesting that social-learning theory can indeed incorporate certain personality variables in a more systematic fashion than was made clear in his original pronouncements in 1968. He suggests a set of primarily cognitive "person variables." The expectancy of affecting or not affecting the environment may, for example, be a major factor determining behavior and allowing its prediction. This and other person variables, argues Mischel, should be derived from experimental research and not from speculation, as tends to be the case in psychodynamic theorizing.

In the course of the debate touched off by Mischel's important book, several pieces of evidence have emerged showing that his original position was too extreme. Jack Block has challenged Mischel's conclusions regarding the inconsistency of behavior. In examining the studies Mischel used to support his claim, Block finds that most of them have serious flaws. For example, Mischel cites a single study (Burwen and Campbell, 1957) to support his contention that attitudes toward authority figures are not consistent. In this study, Block notes, reliability is not reported for some of the assessments made, and for others the reliability figures were quite low. Low reliability precludes finding strong relationships in measurements and thus of course any degree of consistency in the attitudes assessed. Block also presents information that does show consistency of behavior and was not considered by Mischel. A notable example is Block's own longitudinal study (1971), which indicated considerable consistency of personality as it was assessed in young people when they were attending junior high school, then senior high school, and later when they were adults.

Bem and Allen (1974) also found evidence of greater behavioral consistency than Mischel's book implied. They administered to a large undergraduate class a questionnaire which presented the students with a number of situations and asked them to indicate whether they would be consistently or variably friendly and conscientious in these circumstances. Bem and Allen then obtained permission from a small number of these men and women to have their behavior observed and rated by people familiar to them, including their parents and roommates. In addition, Bem and Allen arranged for several unobtrusive measures to be taken of these subjects. For example, "spontaneous friendliness" was measured by having each subject observed as he or she waited in a room with a confederate of the experimenter; the observer recorded how long it took the subject to initiate a conversation with the confederate.

Bem and Allen divided their subjects into those with great or little variability in friendliness and conscientiousness, based on the subjects' own ratings of themselves via the questionnaire. They next compared this self-rated consistency or variability with how consistently friendly and conscientious subjects had appeared in the observed real-life situations. The results showed that people can be predicted to behave in a friendly fashion in a number of circumstances if they view themselves as consistently friendly. But the behavior of subjects who believe themselves to vary considerably in friendliness from situation to situation could not be predicted. Basically, Bem and Allen conclude that certain people—those who believe that they are consistent—will generally be so in all situations. In contrast, the behavior of others depends on the specific situation.

Additional evidence of consistency and stability of behavior comes from Epstein (1979), who also criticized the studies used by Mischel to buttress the situationist position. These studies, noted Epstein, looked only at small bits of behavior, a strategy as inappropriate as it would be to measure IQ by looking at a person's score on a single item. More appropriate is an *averaging* of behavior from a range of situations. In the experiments he conducted, Epstein collected data on a number of occasions and was indeed able to demonstrate marked consistency in behavior.

A trait position need not claim that a person is *entirely* controlled by an internal disposition, such as honesty or aggressiveness. All organisms are sensitive to their surroundings, as even Freud asserted—and yet psychoanalytic theory is commonly held up by situationists like Mischel as a prime example of a trait theory. What trait theory does assume is that, over a broad range of different situations, people will exhibit enough consistency within themselves that their behavior can be differentiated from that of others in the same situations. A basically honest person will not cheat under most circumstances, a basically dishonest person will. If, as demonstrated by Epstein, enough situations are sampled so that people have numerous opportunities to indicate the influence of a particular trait on their behavior, enough stability will emerge to justify inferring a generalized disposition or trait (see also Box 3.5).

BOX **3.5** Trait Versus Situation Anxiety: Two Methods of Assessment

A comparison of different self-report anxiety questionnaires provides an opportunity to examine further the consistency and variability of behavior. The aim of the Taylor Manifest Anxiety Scale, mentioned earlier, is to place a person somewhere on a continuum with respect to anxiety. People scoring as highly anxious on the MAS are assumed to carry this personality trait around with them all the time. This ongoing level of tension helps to determine how they will behave as compared, for example, with individuals with a low MAS score.

Contrasting with this scale to measure the trait of anxiety is one developed by Mandler and Sarason (1952). Their Test Anxiety Scale consists of a number of questions concerning heartbeat, perspiration, uneasiness, interfering emotions, and worry before and during intelligence tests and course examinations. Like the MAS, the TAS has contributed to our understanding of the relationship between anxiety and behavior. Individuals with high test anxiety scores typically perform more poorly on exams than do those who have low scores on this scale.

What are the relative contributions of trait and situation to individual differences in anxiousness? One questionnaire directed toward this issue, the S-R Inventory of Anxiousness, asks subjects to indicate how they respond to a number of situations (Endler, Hunt, and Rosenstein, 1962). The questionnaire presents situations such as "You are going to meet a new date," and "You are entering a competitive contest before spectators." Subjects indicate their degree of reaction to each of these situations on variables such as "Heart beats faster," "Perspire," "Enjoy the challenge," and "Experience nausea." A complete sample item appears in Table 3.11.

TABLE 3.11
Sample Item from the S-R Inventory of Anxiousness

"You are just starting off on a long trip."

1. Heart beats faster	1 2 3 4 5
	Not at all　　　　　　　　Much faster
2. Get an uneasy feeling	1 2 3 4 5
	None　　　　　　　　Very strongly
3. Emotions disrupt action	1 2 3 4 5
	Not at all　　　　　　　Very disruptive
4. Feel exhilarated and thrilled	1 2 3 4 5
	Not at all　　　　　　　Very strongly
5. Want to avoid situation	1 2 3 4 5
	Not at all　　　　　　　Very strongly
6. Perspire	1 2 3 4 5
	Not at all　　　　　　　Perspire much
7. Need to urinate frequently	1 2 3 4 5
	No　　　　　　　　Very frequently
8. Enjoy the challenge	1 2 3 4 5
	Not at all　　　　　　　Very much
9. Mouth gets dry	1 2 3 4 5
	Not at all　　　　　　　Very dry
10. Become immobilized	1 2 3 4 5
	Not at all　　　　　　　Very immobilized
11. Stomach feels full	1 2 3 4 5
	Not at all　　　　　　　Very full
12. Seek such experiences	1 2 3 4 5
	Not at all　　　　　　　Very much
13. Have loose bowels	1 2 3 4 5
	Not at all　　　　　　　Very loose
14. Experience nausea	1 2 3 4 5
	Not at all　　　　　　　Very nauseous

This inventory therefore provides separate scores on how anxious people rate themselves in a variety of settings. They may, for example, consider themselves highly anxious about taking a test but not very anxious about situations involving interpersonal relations. The inventory is important because it allows us to examine how much variability in anxiety is attributable to situations and how much to the trait of anxiousness. Research with the questionnaire has indicated that neither situation nor trait alone can best account for anxiety. Instead, both the person's general anxiety level and the situations he or she fears must be determined. Such information allows us to consider the interaction of trait and situation and provides the most telling account of anxiety. Bowers (1973), after a comprehensive review of similar studies, came to a similar conclusion, that both general anxiety level and situations feared must be known, and then their interaction charted.

Summary

The third edition of the Diagnostic and Statistical Manual of Mental Disorders (DSM-III), published in 1980 by the American Psychiatric Association, is the latest in a series of efforts by mental health professionals to categorize the various psychopathologies. A novel feature of DSM-III is its multiaxial organization: every time a diagnosis is made, the clinician must describe the patient's condition according to each of five axes, or dimensions. Axes I and II make up the mental disorders per se; on axis III are listed any physical disorders believed to bear on the mental disorder in question; axis IV is used to indicate the degree of psychosocial stress the person has been experiencing; and axis V rates the person's highest level of adaptive functioning during the preceding year. A multiaxial diagnosis made on the basis of DSM-III is believed to provide a more adequate and useful description of the patient's mental disorder.

Because DSM-II has been in use since 1968, and because much of the research on reliability and validity of psychiatric diagnosis has been done on this version, comparisons were drawn between it and DSM-III. Personality disorders are now to be designated on axis II, which means that a judgment about them has to be made with each diagnosis. Neurosis is for the most part a descriptive term in DSM-III; the manual no longer lists a group of neuroses having a basis in psychoanalytic theory. Diagnoses of depression have been simplified. Sexual problems, such as fetishism and erectile problems, constitute a principal section, rather than being distributed elsewhere with other disorders.

Both general and specific issues in the classification of abnormality were discussed. Because DSM-III is far more concrete and descriptive than its predecessor, diagnoses based on it are expected to be more reliable. Validity, however, remains an open question. It is too soon to know whether more useful knowledge about psychopathology, its prevention, and treatment will be gained through widespread use of DSM-III.

Whether or not DSM-III is employed, clinicians rely on several modes of assessment in trying to find out how best to describe a patient, in their search for the reasons he or she is troubled, and in designing effective treatments. Described in some detail were clinical interviews, projective tests such as the Rorschach, standardized personality inventories such as the MMPI, tests for organic brain dysfunction, and intelligence tests.

In their assessment, behavior therapists gather information on four sets of factors: situational determinants, organismic variables, responses, and the consequences of behavior. While traditional assessment, of which DSM-III is an example, seeks to understand people in terms of general traits or personality structure, behavioral assessment is concerned more with how people act, feel, and think in particular kinds of situations. Specificity is the hallmark of behavioral assessment, the assumption of behavioral clinicians and researchers being that by operating within this framework they will gather more useful information about people. Some of the procedures adopted by behavior therapists, such as direct observation of behavior and behaviorally oriented interviews, were also described. Problems of reliability and validity in behavioral assessment were examined.

No concept is at the same time more important and more difficult to define and to measure than anxiety. A separate study was made of this elusive concept.

Finally, the lively controversy about how stable human behavior is in varying situations was reviewed. The issue has for years been of both theoretical and practical interest to psychologists. Now, with the development of behavioral models of psychopathology and treatment, it has assumed special importance. The answers are far from in, but it appears prudent to say that behavior is probably more variable than was once thought by traditional personality theorists and also more stable in different situations than those working in the learning paradigm believe. ■ ■

chapter 4

From our discussion of different ways of conceptualizing and treating abnormal behavior and of problems in its classification and assessment, it should be clear that there is less than total agreement on how abnormal behavior ought to be studied. Our approach to the field is based on the belief that more progress will be made through scientific research than armchair speculation. Abnormal behavior, as we have already noted, has been the subject of theorizing for centuries. We are studying a field that has a high ratio of speculation to data. Because facts are hard to come by, it is important to discuss in some detail the contemporary research methods that are applied in psychopathology.

Science and Scientific Methods

In Chapter 1 we indicated the important role that subjective factors play in the collection and interpretation of data, indeed, in the very definition of what constitutes an observation. Thus there is actually no one science or scientific method, although we often read in college textbooks of "the scientific method." The phrase "as currently practiced" should really be added.

Let us consider science from the point of view of Baruch Spinoza, a famous Dutch philosopher of the seventeenth century. He believed that the scientist's role was to discover God's law. Today we say that Spinoza did not hold a "constructive" view of science. We do not necessarily imply that Spinoza's views were not useful, rather that they can be differentiated from perspectives that emphasize the active role people play in constructing laws and principles. Contemporary scientists tend to regard the laws and theories in existence as constructions or inventions made by scientists. And the rules to be followed in formulating and evaluating these hypotheses and laws are also constructed by people and might very well be changed at any time. Science, as currently practiced, is the pursuit of systematized knowledge through observation. Thus the term refers to a method, the systematic acquisition and evaluation of information. It also refers to a goal, the development of principles that explain the information. Contemporary science strives for explanations that are an outgrowth of, and can be modified by, publicly observed evidence. Both observations and explanations must meet certain criteria.

Testability and falsifiability

A scientific approach requires first that propositions and ideas be stated in a clear and precise way. Only then can scientific claims be exposed to systematic probes and tests, any one of which could negate the scientist's expectations about what will be found. Statements, theories, and assertions, regardless of how plausible they may seem, must be testable in the public arena and be subject to being disproved. The attitude of science is an extremely doubting one. It is not

The control room of a modern psychophysiology laboratory.

enough to assert that particular traumatic experiences during childhood may produce psychological maladjustment in adulthood, or that various stresses in adult life may create problems. These are no more than possibilities or propositions. According to a scientific point of view, such propositions must be amenable to testing and to being found false.

Reliability

Closely related to testability is the demand that each observation forming a scientific body of knowledge be reliable. Whatever is observed must occur under prescribed circumstances not once but repeatedly. The event cannot be seen or detected only by a single individual or individuals in a given laboratory, community, or country. Instead, it must be reproducible under the circumstances stated, anywhere, anytime. If the event cannot be reproduced, scientists become wary of the legitimacy of the original observation.

The role of theory

A *theory* is a set of propositions meant to explain a class of phenomena. A primary goal of science is to advance theories to illuminate, often by proposing cause-effect relationships, the information with which it deals. The results of empirical research allow the adequacy of theories to be evaluated. Theories themselves can also play an important role in guiding research by suggesting that certain additional data be collected. The generation of a theory is perhaps the most challenging part of the scientific enterprise—and one of the least understood. It is sometimes asserted, for example, that a scientist formulates a theory simply by considering data that have been previously collected and then deciding, in a rather straightforward fashion, that a given way of talking about them is the most economical and useful and suggests still further experimentation for testing its own adequacy.

Although some theory building follows this course, not all does. Aspects too seldom mentioned are the *creativity* of the act and the excitement of finding a novel way to conceptualize things. A theory sometimes seems to leap from the scientist's head in a wonderful moment of insight. New ideas suddenly occur to the scientist, and connections hitherto overlooked are suddenly grasped. What seemed obscure or meaningless just a moment before now makes a new kind of sense within the framework that the new theory provides.

In formulating a theory, scientists must often make use of theoretical concepts, of unobservable states or processes that are inferred from observable data. Although theoretical concepts are inferred from observable data, they go beyond what can actually be seen or measured. Several advantages may thus be gained. First, theoretical concepts often bridge spatiotemporal relations. For example, in early physics it was noted that a magnet placed close to some iron filings would cause some of the filings to move toward it. How does one piece of metal influence another over the spatial distance? The inferred concept of magnetic fields proved to be very useful in accounting for this phenomenon. Similarly, in abnormal psychology we may often want to bridge temporal gaps with theoretical concepts. If a child has had a particularly frightening experience and his or her behavior is changed for a lengthy period of time, we need to explain how the earlier event is able to exert an influence over subsequent behavior. The unobservable and inferred concept of *acquired fear* has been very helpful in this regard.

Theoretical concepts may also be used to account for already observed relationships. Let us take a classic example proposed by a philosopher of science, Carl Hempel (1958). An early observer of nature has been studying what happens to various objects as they are placed in water. He or she formulates some lawlike generalizations, such as "Wood floats in water, iron sinks." In addition to the fact that a large number of such generalizations would be needed to describe exhaustively the behavior of all objects placed in liquids, exceptions to the generalizations are likely. Iron in a particular shape (boatlike) will float on water. A water-logged piece of wood will sink. The solution is to propose a theoretical term, in this case specific gravity, which can both simplify descriptions of what will and will not float and allow errorless statements to be made. Specific gravity is the ratio of the weight of an object to its volume. And with this theoretical term we can now easily and without error specify what will happen to *any* body placed in *any* liquid. If the specific gravity of the object is less than that of the liquid displaced, the object will float.

Let us now examine a similar and familiar instance, closer to the field of abnormal behavior. We may observe that people who are taking an examination, who expect a momentary electric shock, or who are fighting with a companion all have sweaty palms, trembling hands, and a fast heartbeat. If we ask them how they feel, they all report that they are agitated. The relationships can be depicted as shown in Figure 4.1a. Or we could say that all the situations have made these individuals anxious, and that anxiety has in turn

caused the reported agitation, the sweaty palms, the faster heartbeat, and the trembling hands. Figure 4.1b shows anxiety as a theoretical concept explaining what has been observed. The first part of the figure is much more complex than the second, where the term anxiety becomes a mediator of the relationships.

With these advantages in mind, we must consider the criteria to be applied in judging the legitimacy of a theoretical concept. One earlier school of thought, the *operationist,* proposed that each such concept take as its meaning a single observable and measurable operation. In this way each theoretical concept would be nothing more than one particular measurable effect. For example, anxiety might be identified as *nothing more* than scoring 50 on an anxiety question-

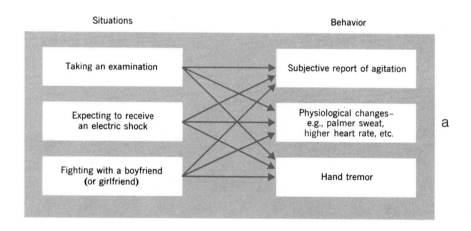

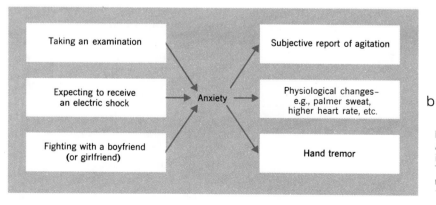

FIGURE **4.1**
An illustration of the advantages of using anxiety as a theoretical concept. The arrows in part b are fewer and more readily understood. After Miller, 1959.

naire. It was soon realized, however, that this approach would take away from theoretical concepts their greatest advantage. If each theoretical concept is *operationalized* in only one way, its generality is lost. If the theoretical concept of learning, for instance, is identified as a *single* operation or effect that can be measured, such as how often a rat presses a bar, other behavior such as a child performing arithmetic problems or a college student studying this book cannot also be called learning, and attempts to relate the different phenomena to one another might be discouraged. The early operationist point of view quickly gave way to the more flexible position that a theoretical concept can be defined by *sets* of operations or effects. In this way the concept may be linked to several different measurements, each of which taps a different facet of the concept (see Figure 4.1b).

The Research Methods of Abnormal Psychology

All empirical research entails the collection of observable data. Sometimes research will stay at a purely descriptive level, but more often researchers will observe more than one event and try to determine how they are associated or related. In the field of abnormal psychology, for example, there is a large literature concerning the typical symptoms of people who have been diagnosed as having particular disorders. The association or relationship is between a particular diagnostic category and a set of characteristic symptoms. But science demands more than describing relationships. We often want to understand the *causes* of the relationships we have observed. For example, we want to know not only that phobics tend actively to avoid a feared situation but also why they do so.

In this section we describe the most commonly used research methods in the study of abnormal behavior: the *case study;* the *correlation;* the *experiment,* both with *groups* and *single subjects;* and the *mixed design*. Each of the methods varies in the degree to which it permits the collection of adequate descriptive data and the extent to which it allows causal relationships to be inferred.

The Case Study

The most familiar method of observing others is to study them one at a time and to record their behavior. In making a case study, the clinician collects historical and biographical information from the individual and other sources. A comprehensive case study would cover family history and background, medical history, educational background, jobs held, marital history, and details concerning development, adjustment, personality, the life course, and the current situation. Clinicians may also carefully describe all efforts to treat the individual. Case reports from practicing clinicians may lack the degree of control and objectivity of research done by other methods, but these descriptive histories have played some important roles in the study of abnormal behavior. Specifically, the case history has been used in each of the following ways: (1) to provide a detailed account of a rare or unusual phenomenon and of important, often novel, methods or procedures of interviewing, diagnosis, and treatment; (2) to disconfirm allegedly universal aspects of a particular theoretical proposition; and (3) to generate hypotheses that can be tested through controlled research.

Descriptive uses

In a famous case history of multiple personality reported in 1954, Thigpen and Cleckley described a patient, "Eve White," who assumed at various times three very distinct personalities. Their description of the case required an entire book, *The Three Faces of Eve*. The following very brief summary emphasizes the moments in which new personalities emerged and what the separate selves knew of one another.

Eve White had been seen in psychotherapy for several months because she was experiencing severe headaches accompanied by blackouts. Her therapist described her as a retiring and gently conventional figure. One day during the course of an interview, however, she changed abruptly and in a surprising way.

As if seized by sudden pain, she put both hands to her head. After a tense moment of silence, both hands dropped. There was a quick, reckless smile, and, in a bright voice that sparkled, she said, "Hi there, Doc!" The demure and constrained posture of Eve White had melted into buoyant repose. . . . This new and apparently carefree girl spoke casually of Eve White and her problems, always using she or her in every reference, always respecting the strict bounds of a separate identity. . . . When asked her name, she immediately replied, "Oh, I'm Eve Black" (p. 137).

After this rather startling revelation, Eve was observed over a period of fourteen months in a series of interviews that ran to almost a hundred hours. A very important part of Eve White's therapy was to help her learn about Eve Black, her other infectiously exuberant self, who added seductive and expensive clothing to her wardrobe and lived unremembered episodes of her life. During this period still a third personality, Jane, emerged while Eve White was recollecting an early incident in which she had been painfully scalded by water from a washpot.

Jane, who from then on knew all that happened to the two Eves, although they did not share in her existence, was "far more mature, more vivid, more boldly capable, and more interesting than Eve White." She also developed a deep and revering affection for the first Eve, who was considered somewhat of a ninny by Eve Black. Jane, however, knew nothing of Eve White's earlier life, except as she learned of it through Eve's memories.

Some eleven months later, in a calamitous session, with all three personalities present at different times, Eve Black emerged and reminisced for a moment about the many good times she had had in the past but then remarked that she did not seem to have real fun anymore. She began to sob, the only time Dr. Thigpen had seen her in tears. She told him that she wanted him to have her red dress to remember her by. All expression left her face and her eyes closed. Eve White opened them. When Jane was summoned a few minutes later, she soon realized that there was no longer any Eve White either and began to experience a terrifying lost event. "No, no. . .! Oh no, Mother. . . .I can't. . . .Don't make me do it," she cried. Jane, who earlier had known nothing of Eve's childhood, was five years old and at her grandmother's funeral. Her mother was holding her high off the floor and above the coffin and saying that she must touch her grandmother's face. As she felt her hand leave the clammy cheek, the young woman screamed so piercingly that Dr. Cleckley came running from his office across the hall.

The two physicians were not certain who confronted them. In the searing intensity of the remembered moment, a new personality had been welded. Their transformed patient did not at first feel herself as apart, and as sharply distinct a person, as had the two Eves and Jane, although she knew a great deal about all of them. When her initial bewilderment lessened, she tended to identify herself with Jane. But the identification was not sure or complete, and she mourned the absence of the two Eves, as though they were lost sisters. This new person decided to call herself Mrs. Evelyn White.

The case of Eve White, Eve Black, Jane, and eventually Evelyn constitutes a valuable classic in the literature because it is one of only a few detailed accounts of a rare phenomenon, multiple personality. Moreover, in addition to illustrating the phenomenon itself, the original report of Thigpen and Cleckley provides valuable details about the interview procedures that they followed; and it sheds light on the way in which the woman's behavior may have developed and how the treatment progressed in this one case of multiple personality.

The case history as evidence

Case histories can provide especially telling instances that negate an assumed universal relationship or law. Freud, for example, initially believed that his female patients' reports of sexual assaults by their fathers or uncles were accurate descriptions of events and, moreover, that these events had a bearing on the problems being treated. Later, on the basis of a chance finding that the supposed sexual assailant of one of his patients could not have been physically present at the time indicated, he came to recognize that some of these sexual assaults were fantasies. This single case provided a negative instance and led Freud to reject his previously held belief that his patients' recollections of early sexual assaults were necessarily true.

But the case history fares less well in providing evidence *in favor of* a particular theory or proposition. In the presentation of a case history, the means for confirming one hypothesis and ruling out alternative hypotheses are usually absent. To illustrate this lack of validity, let us consider another case that received a great deal of public attention in the 1950s, the case of "Bridey Murphy."

When hypnotized, a sedate New England woman "regressed," apparently beyond her early childhood and back into a previous life in which she claimed to be Bridey Murphy, an Irish lass. Under hypnosis the woman was able to report, in a distinct Gaelic brogue, many remarkable details of a town in Ireland which she had never visited. Her case history supposedly demonstrated a true instance of reincarnation. Later, however, it was learned that the woman had been reared, in part, by an Irish maid who had described to her most of the long-ago happenings later reported under hypnosis. The maid had also provided an excellent model for the brogue that the hypnotized subject used so convincingly. In this instance the reincarnation hypothesis presented by the case history was indeed discounted.

Similarly, Chris Sizemore's book *I'm Eve* (Sizemore and Pittillo, 1977) indicates the incompleteness of Thigpen and Cleckley's case study discussed earlier. This woman—the real Eve White—claims that following her period of therapy with them her personality continued to fragment. In all, twenty-one separate and distinct ''strangers'' have come to inhabit her body at one time or another. Contrary to Thigpen and Cleckley's report, Sizemore maintains that nine of them existed before Eve Black ever appeared. One set of personalities—they usually came in threes—would weaken and fade, to be replaced by others. Eventually her personality changes were so constant and numerous that she might become her three persons in rapid switches re-

Chris Sizemore, one of the most famous cases of multiple personality, shown here with her own painting ''Three Faces in One.'' This symbolic representation of herself indicates that the personalities who in the past took over her life came in sets of three.

sembling the flipping of television channels. The debilitating round robin of transformations and the fierce battle for dominance among her selves filled her entire life. After resolving what she hopes is her last trio, by realizing finally that her alternate personalities were true aspects of herself rather than strangers from without, Chris Sizemore decided to reveal her story as a means of minimizing the past.

Generating hypotheses

Finally, the case study plays a unique and important role because it is very often exploratory in nature. Through exposure to the life histories of a great number of patients, clinicians gain experience in understanding and interpreting them. Eventually they may notice similarities of circumstances and outcomes and formulate important hypotheses that could not have been uncovered in a more controlled investigation.

> . . . It is a serious mistake to discount the importance of clinical experience per se. There is nothing mysterious about the fact that repeated exposure to any given set of conditions makes the recipient aware of subtle cues and contingencies which elude the scrutiny of those less familiar with the situation. Clinical experience enables a therapist to recognize problems and identify trends that are usually beyond the perception of novices, regardless of their general expertise. It is at this level that new ideas will come to the practitioner and often constitute breakthroughs that could not be derived from animal analogues or tightly controlled investigations. Different kinds of data and different levels of information are obtained in the laboratory and the clinic. Each is necessary, useful, and desirable (Lazarus and Davison, 1971, p. 197).

In summary, the case study is an excellent way of examining the behavior of a single individual in great detail and in generating hypotheses that can later be evaluated by controlled research. Thus it is useful in clinical settings, where the focus is on just one person. In the fields of clinical and personality psychology some investiga-

tors argue that the essence of psychological studies always lies in the unique characteristics of an individual (for example, Allport, 1961). The case history is an ideal method in an individualistic or *idiographic* context. But in a *nomothetic* context, when only general, universal laws apply, the case study is of limited usefulness. Information collected on a single person may *not* reveal principles that are characteristic of people in general. Furthermore, the case history is unable to provide satisfactory evidence concerning cause-effect relationships.

The Correlational Method

In contrast to the case study, which is a rather informal gathering of information about a single individual, the correlational method requires a more systematic collection of data on particular aspects of a group of research participants. Correlational techniques address questions of the form "Are variable X and variable Y associated in some way so that they vary together (correlate)?" In other words, questions are asked concerning relationships; for example, "Is schizophrenia related to social class?" or "Is anxiety related to scores obtained on college examinations?" Thus the correlational method establishes whether there is a relationship between or among two or more variables. Numerous examples can be drawn from everyday life. Income correlates positively with the number of luxuries purchased: the higher the income, the more luxuries purchased. Height tends to be positively correlated with weight: taller people are usually heavier. This second relationship, that between height and weight, is by no means perfect, for many individuals are "overweight" or too fat for their height and "underweight" or too thin for their height. The relationship, however, is a strong and positive one.

The correlational method involves obtaining pairs of observations, such as height and weight, on each member in a group of subjects (Table 4.1). Once such pairs of observations are obtained, we can determine how strong the relationship is between the two sets of observations. The most prevalent means of measuring such a relationship was devised by Karl Pearson and is referred to as the Pearson product-moment *corre-*

lation coefficient, denoted by the symbol r. This statistic may take any value between −1.00 and +1.00 and measures both the magnitude and the direction of a relationship. The higher the absolute value of r, the larger or stronger the relationship between the two variables. An r of either +1.00 or −1.00 indicates a perfect relationship, whereas an r of .00 indicates that the variables are unrelated. If the sign of r is positive, the two variables are said to be *positively related*. As the values for variable X increase, those for variable Y also tend to increase. Conversely, when the sign of r is negative, variables are said to be *negatively related*; in this instance as values for one variable increase, those for the other tend to decrease. The correlation between height and weight, based on the data in Table 4.1, is +.96, indicating a very strong positive relationship; as height increases so does weight.

Plotting a relationship graphically will often impart a better feel for it. Figure 4.2 presents diagrams of several of the correlations just discussed. In the diagrams each entry point corresponds to two values determined for the given subject, the value of variable X and that for variable Y. In perfect relationships all the points fall on a straight line: if we know the value of only one of the variables for an individual, we can state with certainty the value of the other variable. Similarly, when the correlation is relatively large, there is only a small degree of scatter about the line of perfect correlation. The values tend to scatter increasingly and become dispersed as the correlations become lower. When the correlation reaches .00, knowledge of a person's score on one variable tells us nothing about his or her score on the other.

Thus far we have established that the magnitude of a correlation coefficient tells us the strength of a relationship between two variables. But scientists demand a more rigorous evaluation of the importance of correlations and use the concept of *statistical significance* for this purpose. Essentially, statistical significance has to do with the likelihood that the obtained relationship happened by chance and thus would be very unlikely to occur again were the research conducted a second time. A statistically significant correlation is one that is *not* likely to have occurred by chance. Traditionally, in psychological research, a correlation is considered statistically significant if the likelihood is five or less in one hundred that it is a chance finding. This level of significance is called the .05 level, commonly written as $p < .05$. In general, as the size of the correlation coefficient increases, the result is more and more likely to be statistically significant.[1]

Statistical significance should not be confused with the social or real-life significance of re-

TABLE 4.1
Data for Determining a Correlation*

Individuals	Height	Weight, pounds
John	5'10"	170
Asher	50"	58
Eve	58"	79
Carol	5'8"	130
Gail	5'3"	105
Jerry	5'10"	172
Bob	6'1"	175
Gayla	5'2"	100
Steve	5'8"	145
Margy	5'5"	128
Gert	5'6"	143
Alan	5'7"	150
Sean	48"	54

* For these figures r = +.96

[1] Whether a correlation attains statistical significance also depends on the number of observations that were made. The greater the number of observations, the smaller r needs to be in order to reach statistical significance. Thus a correlation of r = .30 is statistically significant when the number of observations is large, for example, 300, although it would not be significant if only 20 observations have been made.

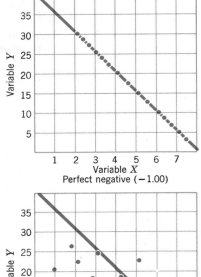

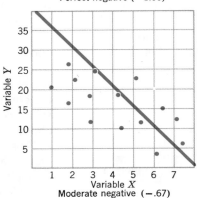

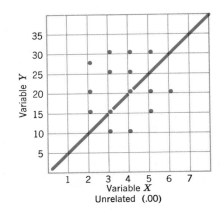

FIGURE **4.2**
Scatter diagrams showing various degrees of correlational relationship.

search results. Research can yield findings that are statistically significant yet devoid of practical importance. Moreover, the level of statistical significance considered acceptable is determined by *social convention,* that is, the rules by which contemporary scientists agree to play the game. Thus if the results of a correlational study have a probability of .10 or less that they occurred by chance rather than a probability of .05 or less, it is nowhere mandated that these are chance events and that the study is therefore totally worthless. Investigators may decide that, given the nature of a particular study, these results are quite encouraging and should not be disregarded. Then they must convince their colleagues that these findings are indeed valid. In a sense, science is a game of *persuasion.*

The correlational method is widely used in the field of abnormal psychology. Whenever we compare people assigned to a diagnostic category with normal people or with those in another diagnostic category, the study is correla-

tional. Many investigators, for example, have compared the performances of schizophrenics and normal people on laboratory tasks such as proverb interpretation or size estimation and on tests of reaction time (for example, Kopfstein and Neale, 1972). Or two diagnostic groups may be compared to see how many members of each experienced a high level of stress before the onset of their disorders. Often such investigations are not recognized as correlational, perhaps because—as is often so in experiments—subjects come to a laboratory for testing, or data are analyzed by comparing the average scores of the groups on each test or measure. But the logic of such studies is correlational: the correlation between two variables—being schizophrenic or nonschizophrenic and the average scores of each group on the laboratory test—is what is being examined. Variables such as being schizophrenic or nonschizophrenic are called *classificatory variables.* Schizophrenics have already been so diagnosed before they perform the laboratory task.

Other examples of classificatory variables are age, sex, social class, and body build. These variables are naturally occurring patterns and are not manipulated by the researcher, an important requirement for the experimental variables to be discussed shortly. Thus classificatory variables fall into the domain of correlational research.

Nor should a classificatory variable such as a psychopathology be manipulated, for both practical and moral reasons. Although inflicting mild pain or discomfort might be (or might not be) ethically acceptable, inducing in an experiment extremely painful but psychologically significant experiences—of the kind people are only too often subjected to in their everyday lives—would be without question highly unethical. Inducing enough distress to cause psychopathology would be indefensible. Thus the correlational technique is the major strategy in studying the vagaries of psychopathology. By this technique the psychopathologist can determine whether the responses and characteristics of a person correlate with his or her abnormality.

Directionality and third-variable problems

The correlational method, although often employed in abnormal psychology, has a serious flaw. It does not allow us to determine cause-effect relationships because of two major problems of interpretation, the _directionality problem_ and the _third-variable problem._ With respect to directionality, a sizable correlation between two variables tells us only that they are related or tend to covary with one another, but we do not really know whether one is caused by the other, or even if they are at all causally related. For example, correlations have been found between the diagnosis of schizophrenia and social class; lower-class people with emotional problems are more frequently diagnosed as schizophrenic than are middle- and upper-class people. One possible explanation is that the stresses of living in the lower social classes produce the behavior that is subsequently labeled schizophrenic. But a second and perhaps equally plausible hypothesis has been advanced. It may be that the disorganized behavior patterns of schizophrenic individuals cause them to lose their jobs and thus to become impoverished. The problem of directionality is present in many correlational research designs; hence the often-cited dictum "Correlation does not imply causation."[2]

As for the third-variable problem, it may be that neither of the two variables studied in the correlation produces the other. Rather, some as yet unspecified variable or process may be responsible for the correlation. Consider the following example, which points out an obvious third variable.

. . . _One regularly finds a high positive correlation between the number of churches in a city and the number of crimes committed in that city. That is, the more churches a city has, the more crimes are committed in it. Does this mean that religion fosters crime or does it mean that crime fosters religion? It means neither. The relationship is due to a particular third variable—population. The higher the population of a particular community the greater . . . the number of churches and . . . the frequency of criminal activity (Neale and Liebert, 1973, p. 86)._

Are there any solutions to the directionality and third-variable problems? In general, the answer is yes, although the solutions are only partially satisfactory and do not permit unambiguous causal inferences to be made from correlational data. To illustrate the problems involved, we shall discuss ex post facto analysis, the technique which is most often used in attempting to control third variables.

Ex post facto analysis

In _ex post facto analysis_ subjects are matched on a third variable in an effort to simulate experimental procedures. For example, the investigator may be comparing the performances of schizophrenics and hospital aides on a test of cognitive ability. Let us assume that the schizophrenics are

---

[2] Although correlation does not imply causation, the determination of whether or not two variables correlate may allow for the _disconfirmation_ of certain causal hypotheses. That is, _causation does imply correlation._ For example, if an investigator has asserted that cigarette smoking causes lung cancer, he or she implies that lung cancer and cigarette smoking will be positively correlated. Studies of the two variables must show this positive correlation, or the theory will be disproved.

People from the lower socioeconomic classes are more likely to develop schizophrenia. This New York City bag lady may well be suffering from the disorder.

found to perform much more poorly than the aides. Clearly, the investigator is interested in attributing the difference between the two groups to the fact that one group is schizophrenic and the other not. Because the variable of interest, schizophrenia, is only classificatory, however, it may not be the factor responsible. The investigator did not directly manipulate it and then observe the effects on cognitive performance. The presence of a third variable may affect the results. By ex post facto analysis the investigator attempts to match subjects beforehand on what seem particularly plausible third variables. In the example we are considering, variables such as social class, intelligence, and years of education are likely candidates for such a matching process; technically this matching is known as *controlling* for the effects of these variables. If their effects can be eliminated, the investigator can with more confidence attribute any differences between the two groups to the presence of schizophrenia in one of them.

The ex post facto technique, however, cannot entirely eliminate the problem of the third variable. First, regardless of the number of variables on which matching occurs, there can be no guarantee that some other unknown variable is not the important controlling factor determining the differences between the two groups. In other words, the term "third variable" is really a misnomer, for *any* number of variables might account for the observed effects in a way that is masked by the correlational research design.[3]

The ex post facto technique is also subject to other difficulties. For example, matching may drastically reduce the generality of any conclusions that may be drawn from a study. Let us assume that schizophrenics generally complete less schooling than do hospital aides. Noticing

[3] This is but one illustration of why scientists seldom make absolute statements. There always seems to be a qualification that must be added in any scientific generalization or conclusion.

this fact, the investigator decides to match subjects on amount of education in order to eliminate the effects of this variable. He or she may then be forced to select for study only the schizophrenics who have educational levels close to those of the hospital aides. Thus the researcher ends up studying an *unrepresentative subpopulation* of schizophrenics. The results of such an investigation cannot be generalized to the entire population of schizophrenics, for the subjects who were studied have, on the average, completed more education than most schizophrenics.

With no viable alternative method available, investigators who study clinical groups must rely on correlational techniques. But they must always keep in mind that certain differences between clinical groups and those they are compared to may make the correlations very difficult to interpret.

The Experiment

The factors causing the associations and relationships revealed by correlational research cannot, as we have seen, be determined with absolute certainty. The experiment is generally considered to be the most powerful tool for determining causal relationships between events. As an introduction to the basic components of experimental research, let us consider a study of how violence seen on television influences the aggressive behavior of children (Liebert and Baron, 1972). A group of 136 children participated in the research. Each child was first taken to a room containing a television monitor and was told he could watch it for a few minutes until the experimenter was ready for him. For all the children the first two minutes of film consisted of two commercials. After that, *half* the children viewed a sequence from "The Untouchables" which contained a chase, two fistfights, two shootings,

Experimental investigations have shown that seeing violence on television increases the likelihood that children will behave aggressively.

and a knifing. The remaining children saw an exciting sports sequence. For all subjects the last minute of the film was another commercial.

Each child was then escorted to a nearby room and seated in front of a large box which had wires leading to another room. On the box was a white light, below which were a green button labeled HELP and a red button labeled HURT. The experimenter explained that the wires were connected to a game a child in the other room was going to play. The game involved turning a handle, and each time the other child did this the white light would come on. The experimenter explained that by pushing the buttons the subject could either help the other child by making the handle easier to turn or hurt him by making the handle hot. Each time the white light came on, the subject was to push one of the buttons, the longer he pushed it, the more he would help or hurt the other child. After making certain that the instructions were understood, the experimenter left the room. Each subject was given twenty trials; that is, the white light came on twenty times.

Table 4.2 shows the average length of time that a subject in each of the two groups—the children who had seen the violent episodes on television and those who had seen the sports sequence—pushed the HURT button. Children who had viewed the violent television sequences were more aggressive than those who had not.

TABLE 4.2
Effect of Television Viewing on the Aggresiveness of Children

(from Liebert and Baron, 1972)

Television program viewed	Average duration of each aggressive response, seconds
Aggressive—"The Untouchables"	9.92
Nonaggressive—sports sequence	7.03

Basic features of experimental design
The foregoing example illustrates many of the basic features of an experiment. The researcher typically begins with an *experimental hypothesis.* Liebert and Baron hypothesized that viewing violence would stimulate aggressive behavior. Second, the investigator chooses an *independent variable* that can be manipulated, that is, some factor that will be under the control of the experimenter. Liebert and Baron exposed some children to an aggressive sequence on television and others to a nonaggressive sequence. Finally, the researcher arranges for the measurement of a *dependent variable,* which is expected to depend on or vary with manipulations of the independent variable. The dependent variable in this study was the duration of the HURT response, an operational definition of aggression. When in such an investigation differences between groups are indeed found to be a function of variations in the independent variable, the researcher is said to have produced an *experimental effect.*

Internal validity
An additional feature of any experimental design is the inclusion of at least one *control group.* A control group is necessary if the effects in any experiment are to be attributed to the manipulation of the independent variable. In the Liebert and Baron study the control group saw the non-violent sports sequence.

To illustrate this point with another example, consider a study of the effectiveness of a particular therapy in modifying some form of abnormal behavior. Let us assume that persons with initially poor self-concepts have asked for treatment and that they undergo therapy designed to remedy their condition. At the end of six months the patients are reassessed, and it is found that their self-concepts have improved compared to what they were at the beginning of the study. Unfortunately, such an investigation would not produce valid data. The improvement in self-concept from the beginning of the treatment to the end could have been brought about by several factors in addition to or instead of the particular treatment employed. For example, it may be that certain environmental events occurred within the six months and produced the improvement. Or it may be that people with a poor self-concept acquire better feelings about themselves with the mere passage of time. Variables such as these are often called _confounds;_ they, like the third variables in correlational studies, confound the results, making them impossible to interpret.[4] Studies in which the effect obtained cannot be attributed with confidence to the independent variable are called _internally invalid_ studies. The design of _internally valid_ research, that is, research in which the effect obtained can be confidently attributed to the manipulation of the independent variable, is a primary goal in the social sciences.

In the example just outlined, _internal validity_ could have been secured by the inclusion of a control group. Such a group might have consisted of individuals with poor self-concepts who did _not_ receive the therapeutic treatment. Changes in the self-concepts of these control subjects would constitute a _baseline_ or standard against which the effects of the independent variable can be assessed. If a change in self-concept is brought about by particular environmental events, quite beyond any therapeutic intervention, the experimental group receiving the treatment and the control group receiving no treatment are equally likely to be affected. On the other hand, if after six months the self-concepts of the treated group have improved more than those of the untreated control group, we can be relatively confident that this difference is, in fact, attributable to the treatment.

The mere inclusion of a control group, however, does not ensure internal validity. To illustrate, let us consider another study of therapy, this time the treatment of two hospital wards of psychiatric patients. An investigator may decide to select one ward to receive an experimental treatment and then select another ward as a control. When the researcher later compares the frequencies of deviant behavior in these two groups, he or she will want to attribute any differences between them to the fact that patients in one ward received treatment and those in the other did not. But the researcher cannot legitimately draw this inference, for a competing hypothesis cannot be disproved—that even before treatment the patients who happened to receive therapy might have had a lower level of deviant behavior than the patients who became the control group. The principle of experimental design disregarded in this defective study is that of _random assignment._

Random assignment is achieved by ensuring that every subject in the research has an equal chance of being assigned to any of the groups. For example, in a two-group experiment a coin can be tossed for each subject. If the coin turns up heads, the subject is assigned to one group; if tails, he or she is assigned to another. This procedure minimizes the likelihood that differences between or among the groups after treatment will reflect pretreatment differences in the samples rather than true experimental effects.

Even with both a control group and random assignment, the results of the research may still be invalid. An additional source of error is the potential biasing influence of the experimenter or observers. This is the "Rosenthal effect" already mentioned in Chapter 3. As Rosenthal (1966) has suggested, the expectancies of an experimenter about the outcome of a study may conspire to produce results favorable to the initial hypothesis. He or she may subtly manipulate the subject to give expected and desired responses. Although the pervasiveness of these effects has been questioned (Barber and Silver, 1968; Kent et al., 1974), experimenters must remain on guard lest their results be tainted by their own expectations. To avoid biases of this type, many studies apply the so-called _double-blind_ procedure. For example, in an investigation comparing the psychological effects of two drugs, the person dispensing the pills is kept ignorant (that is, blind) about their actual content, and the subject is also not informed about the treatment he or she is receiving. With such controls the behavior observed during the course of the treatment is probably not influenced by biasing.

Earlier, we briefly defined the term experimental effect, but we have yet to learn how it can be decided that an effect is important. To evaluate

---

[4] These confounds, and others described in this chapter, are unfortunately widespread in research on the effects of psychotherapy, as will be documented often throughout this book, especially in Part Six.

the importance of experimental results, as with correlations, researchers determine their statistical significance. A significant difference between groups is one that has little probability of occurring by chance alone. Thus this difference can be expected to be found again whenever the same experiment is repeated. And a difference between groups in an experiment, like a correlation, is typically considered statistically significant and therefore admissible as evidence if the likelihood is five or less in one hundred that it is a chance finding.

External validity

The extent to which the results of any particular piece of research can be generalized beyond the immediate experiment is the measure of their external validity. For example, if investigators have demonstrated that a particular treatment helps a group of patients they have tried it on, they will undoubtedly want to determine whether this treatment will be effective in ministering to other patients, at other times, and in other places. Liebert and Baron would hope that the findings of their television experiment apply to violence of many kinds, shown on home television sets to children other than those who served as subjects in the contrived experimental setting.

The external validity of the results of a psychological experiment is extremely difficult to determine. For example, there is the reactivity of observed behavior. Merely knowing that one is a subject in a psychological experiment often alters behavior, and thus results are produced in the laboratory that may not automatically be produced in the natural environment. In many instances results obtained from investigations with laboratory animals such as rats have been generalized to human beings. Such generalizations are hazardous, since there are enormous differences between *Homo sapiens* and *Rattus norvegicus*. Researchers must be continually alert to the extent to which they claim generalization for findings, for there are, in fact, no entirely adequate ways of dealing with the question of external validity. The best that can be done is to perform similar studies in new settings with new participants so that the limitations, or the generality, of a finding can be determined.

Analogue experiments

The experimental method is judged to be the most telling way to determine cause-effect relationships. As you may well have surmised, however, *the method has in fact been little used by those seeking the causes of abnormal behavior.* Suppose that a researcher has hypothesized that a child's emotionally charged, overdependent relationship with his or her mother causes schizophrenia. An experimental test of this hypothesis would require assigning infants randomly to either of two groups of mothers! The mothers in one group will have undergone an extensive training program to ensure that they are able to create a highly emotional atmosphere and foster overdependence in children. The mothers in the second group will have been trained not to create such a relationship with the children they care for. The researcher then waits until the subjects in each group reach adulthood and determines how many of them become schizophrenic. Obviously, such an experimental design already contains insurmountable practical problems. But practical issues are hardly the principal ones that must concern us. Consider also the ethics of such an experiment. Would the potential scientific gain of proving that an overdependent relationship with a person's mother brings on schizophrenia outweigh the suffering that would surely be imposed on some of the participants? In almost any person's view it would not.

Experiments are used, though, in some areas of abnormal psychology. The effectiveness of treatments for psychopathology is usually evaluated by the experimental method, for it has proved a powerful tool for determining whether a therapy reduces suffering. Experimental research on the causes of abnormal behavior, however, has taken the analogue approach. Investigators have attempted to bring a *related* phenomenon, that is, an analogue, into the laboratory for more intensive study. In this way internally valid results may be obtained, although the problem of external validity may be accentuated. In one type of analogue study, behavior is rendered temporarily abnormal through experimental manipulations such as the administration of drugs, hypnotic suggestions, sensory deprivation, or operant shaping. If "pathology" can be experimentally induced by any one of these manipulations, the same variable, existing in the natural environment, might well be a cause of the disorder. Results of such experiments must be interpreted with great caution, but they do provide valuable hypotheses about the origins of psychopathology.

Whether the animal experiments mentioned earlier are regarded as analogues depends not on the experiment itself but rather on the use to which it is put. We can very readily study avoidance behavior in a white rat by running experiments with rats. The data collected from such studies are not analogue data if we limit our discussion to the behavior of rats. They become analogue data only when we draw implications from them and apply them to other domains, such as anxiety in human beings.

Some of the experiments we examine in later chapters are analogue in nature, with their results being generalized to human beings. It will be important to keep in mind that we are arguing by analogy when, for example, we attempt to relate reactions to stress of white rats to anxiety in people. At the same time, however, we do not agree with those who regard such analogue research as totally and intrinsically worthless as far as the study of human behavior is concerned.

Early in their development monkeys need a mother, even if only a cloth surrogate like this one. Monkeys reared in isolation later show signs of both emotional distress and depression. When we generalize these findings about monkeys to human beings, we have used the monkey studies as analogues.

Although human beings and other mammals differ on many important dimensions, it does not follow that principles of behavior derived from animal research are necessarily irrelevant to human behavior.

Single-Subject Experimental Research

Experiments do not always have to be conducted on *groups* of people. In this section we shall consider experimental designs for studying a single subject.

The strategy of relying on a single subject appears to violate many of the principles of research design that we have discussed. As with the case study, no control group can act as a check on a single subject. Moreover, generalizations will be difficult because the findings may relate to a particular or unique aspect of the one individual whose behavior we have explored. Hence the study of a single individual would appear unlikely to yield any findings that could possess the slightest degree of internal or external validity. But, as we shall see, the experimental study of a single subject *can* be an effective research technique for certain purposes.

A method developed by Tate and Baroff (1966) for reducing the self-injurious behavior of a nine-year-old boy, Sam, serves as an example. The child, who had been diagnosed as psychotic, engaged in a wide range of self-injurious behavior, such as banging his head against the floors and walls, slapping his face with his hands, punching his face and head with his fists, hitting his shoulder with his chin, and kicking himself. Despite his self-injurious behavior, Sam was not entirely antisocial. In fact, he obviously enjoyed contact with other people and would cling to them, wrap his arms around them, and sit in their laps. This affectionate behavior gave the investigators the idea for an experimental treatment.[5]

[5] The use of the adjective experimental in this context prompts us to distinguish between two different meanings of the word. As applied to the research methods that have been discussed, the adjective refers to the manipulation of a variable that allows conclusions of a cause-effect relationship to be drawn. But here the word refers to a treatment whose effects are unknown or only poorly understood. Thus an "experimental drug" is one about which we know relatively little; however, such a drug might well be used in a correlational design or reported in a case study.

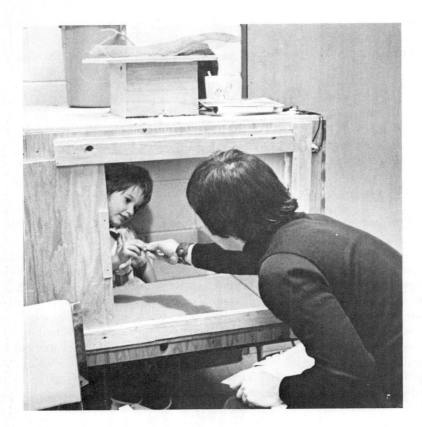

A teaching box used to increase a child's attention span. When the boy is attending and working well, the therapist rewards him with a small piece of food.

The study ran for twenty days. For a period of time on each of the first five days, the frequency of Sam's self-injurious actions was observed and recorded. Then on each of the next five days the two adult experimenters accompanied Sam on a short walk around the campus, during which they talked to him and held his hands continuously. The adults responded to each of Sam's self-injurious actions by immediately jerking their hands away from him and not touching him again until three seconds after such activity had ceased. The frequency of the self-injurious acts was again recorded. As part of the experiment, the schedule was then systematically reversed. For the next five days there were no walks, and Sam's self-afflicting behavior was again merely observed. Then for the last five days the experimenters reinstated their experimental procedure. The dramatic reduction in undesirable behavior induced by the treatment is shown in Figure 4.3. Such designs, usually referred to as *reversal,* (or

ABAB), *designs,* involve the careful measurement of some aspect of the subject's behavior during a given time period, the baseline (A), during a period when a treatment is introduced (B), during a reinstatement of the conditions that prevailed in the baseline period (A), and finally during a reintroduction of the experimental manipulation (B). If behavior in the experimental period is different from that in the baseline period, reverses when the experimentally manipulated conditions are reversed, and ''re-reverses'' when the treatment is again introduced, there is little doubt that the manipulation, rather than chance or uncontrolled factors, has produced the change.

The reversal technique cannot always be employed, however, for the initial state of a subject may not be recoverable, as when treatment produces an irreversible change. Moreover, in studies of therapeutic procedures, reinstating the original condition of the subject or patient would generally be considered an unethical practice.

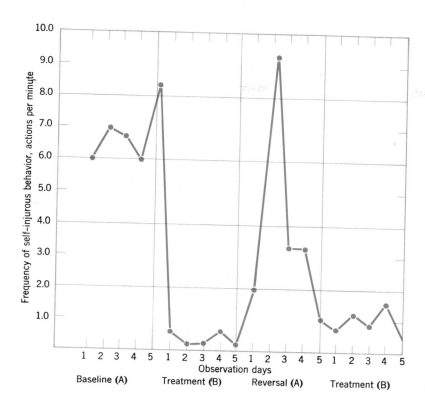

FIGURE **4.3**
Effects of a treatment for injurious behavior in an experiment with an ABAB single-subject design. Adapted from Tate and Baroff, 1966.

Most therapists would be extremely unwilling to act in any way that might bring back the very behavior for which a client has sought help, merely to prove that a particular treatment was indeed the effective agent in changing the behavior.

When the reversal technique does not apply, the _multiple-baseline_ procedure, wherein two or more behaviors are selected for study, is the method of choice. For example, if a child has "learning problems," both mathematical and reading performances might be picked as the two areas for treatment. When observing the child, the experimenter may notice that he or she is inattentive during lessons and proceed to collect baseline data on the degree of attentiveness during _both_ mathematics _and_ reading sessions. Rewards are then given the child for attention paid to the mathematics lessons but not for attention paid during reading sessions. Again, the attentiveness of the child during both kinds

of lessons is measured. Finally, in a third phase of the experiment, the child is rewarded for attention paid during reading as well as mathematics lessons.

A hypothetical pattern of the attentiveness of the child during the course of the experiment is shown in Figure 4.4. If such a pattern were indeed obtained, it would provide convincing evidence that the introduction of reward, and not other factors, was responsible for modifying the child's behavior. Had some uncontrolled environmental influence improved the child's attention, it presumably would have worked equally well during both mathematics and reading classes. Moreover, if reward were not the agent responsible for change, attentiveness during mathematics lessons would not have markedly improved as compared to attentiveness during reading sessions. Thus, by choosing two baselines of behavior to be modified (hence the term multiple baselines), the investigator was able to

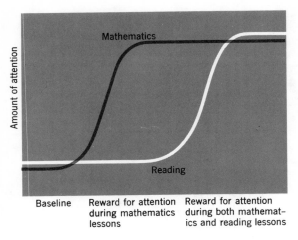

FIGURE **4.4**
Outcome of a multiple-baseline, single-subject experiment
that rewarded attention, initially during lessons in mathematics, ultimately during both mathematics and reading
instruction.

eliminate certain possible sources of invalidity.

As indicated earlier, even though an experiment with a single subject demonstrates an experimental effect, no generalization may be possible. The fact that a particular treatment works
for a single subject does not necessarily imply
that the treatment will be universally effective. If
the search for more widely applicable treatment
is the major focus of an investigation, the single-
subject design has a serious drawback. It may
well help investigators to decide whether large-
scale research with groups is warranted, however.

Mixed Designs

The experimental and correlational research
techniques that we have just discussed can be
combined in what is called a mixed design. In a
mixed design subjects who can be divided into
two or more discrete and typically nonoverlapping populations are assigned as groups to each
experimental condition. The two different types
of populations, for example, schizophrenics and
phobics, constitute classificatory variables. That
is, the variables schizophrenia and phobia were
not manipulated, nor were they created by the

investigator, and they can only be correlated
with the manipulated conditions, which are true
experimental variables.

To illustrate how a mixed design is applied,
we shall consider an investigation of the effectiveness of three types of therapy (the experimental variable) on psychiatric patients who were
able to be divided into two groups on the basis
of the severity of their illnesses (the classificatory
variable). The question was whether the effectiveness of the treatments varied with the severity
of illness. The hypothetical outcome of such a
study is presented in Figure 4.5. The b part of
the figure shows the results obtained when the
patients were divided into two groups on the basis of the severity of their problems. The a part of
the figure illustrates the unfortunate conclusions
that would be drawn were the patients not able
to be divided into those with severe and those
with less severe illnesses. When all patients were
grouped together, treatment 3 produced the
greatest amount of improvement. Therefore,
when no information about differential characteristics of the patients is available, treatment 3
would be preferred. When the severity of the patients' difficulties is considered, however, treatment 3 would no longer be the therapy of
choice for *any* of the patients. Rather, as seen in
Figure 4.5b, for those with less severe illness
treatment 1 would be selected and for patients
with more severe illness treatment 2 would be
preferred. Thus a mixed design can identify
which particular treatment applies best to which
group of subjects.

In interpreting the results of mixed designs, we
must be continually aware of the fact that one of
the variables (severity of illness in our example)
is not manipulated. Therefore the problems we
have previously noted in interpreting correlations
are to be found in interpreting the results of
mixed designs as well.

And yet the inclusion of a manipulated variable, particularly one with multiple levels, does
offer some advantages. Consider a study (Neale,
1971) in which schizophrenic and control subjects were administered an information-process-
ing task of four different levels of complexity.
The subjects were briefly presented with visual
displays containing one, four, eight, or twelve al-

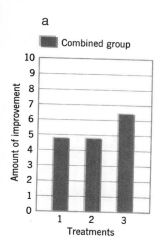

a

Amount of improvement

Combined group

Treatments

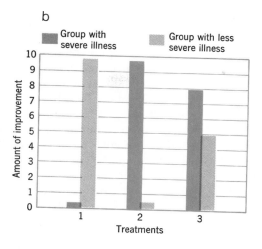

b

Amount of improvement

Group with severe illness   Group with less severe illness

Treatments

FIGURE **4.5**
Effects of three treatments on patients whose symptoms are severe and less severe. The amount of improvement brought about by each treatment varies, depending on how it is administered. When the severity of the illness is not known, the patients are treated together (a). When the severity is known, they are divided into two groups and treated separately (b).

phabetic characters. Their task was to search the display and tell the experimenter whether it contained a *T* or an *F*. The results of this investigation showed that schizophrenics differed from control subjects whenever the two groups saw more than one letter. This pattern is referred to as a _differential deficit._ The schizophrenics' performance was poorer than the control subjects' in one but not all the conditions. A differential deficit is more informative than a simple deficit on a single task. Maher (1974) explains why.

> With the hypothesis that bulls are characterized by a desire to break Royal Worcester China, we stock a shop exclusively with that item, turn the bulls loose, and watch the ensuing destruction. Our hypothesis is duly confirmed—especially if our control group is composed of mice (p. 2).

Maher goes on to point out, "Just as bulls tend to break any kind of china, patient populations tend to do poorly at many tasks." In other words, the demonstration of a simple deficit provides little specific information, because the poor performance could be caused by any number of factors. A differential deficit, however, allows certain plausible rival hypotheses to be ruled out. The equality of performance of schizophrenics and control subjects when only a single letter

was presented makes it unlikely that the schizophrenics' difficulties with larger displays could be attributed to a general failure to comprehend the task. If the schizophrenic subjects had been unable to understand the task or comply with the experimenter's instructions, they would not have done as well as control subjects in determining whether a single letter was a *T* or an *F*.

Summary

Science represents an agreed-upon problem-solving enterprise, with specific procedures for gathering and interpreting data in order to build a systematic body of knowledge. Scientific statements must have the following characteristics: they must be testable in the public arena, they must be subject to falsification, they must derive from reliable observations, and although they may contain references to unobservable processes, the concepts inferred must be linked to observable and measurable events or outcomes.

It is important to consider the various methods that scientists employ to collect data and arrive at conclusions. Clinical case studies serve unique and important functions in psychopathology, such as allowing rare phenomena to be studied intensively in all their complexity. Case studies also encourage the formulation of hypotheses which can be tested later through controlled research.

Correlational methods are the important means of conducting research in abnormal psychology, for diagnoses are classificatory and not experimentally manipulated variables. In correlational studies statistical procedures allow us to determine the extent to which two or more variables correlate or co-vary. Conclusions drawn from nearly all correlational studies cannot legitimately be interpreted in cause-effect terms, however, although there is great temptation to do so.

The experimental method entails the manipulation of independent variables and the careful measurement of their effects on dependent variables. An experiment usually begins with a hypothesis to be tested, that manipulation of one variable will cause another to change in a specific way. Subjects are generally assigned to one of at least two groups: an experimental group, which experiences the manipulation of the independent variable, and a control group, which does not. If differences between the experimental and control groups are observed on the dependent variable, we can conclude that the independent variable did have an effect. Since it is important to ensure that experimental and control subjects do not differ from one another before the introduction of the independent variable, they are usually assigned randomly to groups. Experimenters must guard against bias by keeping themselves unaware of what group a given subject is in, experimental or control. If these conditions are met, the experiment has internal validity. The external validity of the findings, whether they can be generalized to situations and people not studied within the experiment, can be assessed only by performing similar experiments in the external domain with new subjects.

Single-subject experimental designs that expose one subject to different treatments over a period of time can provide internally valid results, although the generality of conclusions may be limited. Mixed designs are combinations of experimental and correlational methods. For example, two different kinds of patients (the classificatory variable) may be exposed to various treatments (the experimental variable).

A science is only as good as its methodology. Thus students of abnormal psychology must appreciate the rules that social scientists currently abide by if they are to be able to evaluate the research and theories that form the subject matter of the remainder of this book.

Joan Miro, "Dutch Interior" (1928). Collection, The Museum of Modern Art, New York. Mrs. Simon Guggenheim Fund.

part two
emotional disorders and reactions to stress

chapter 5

ANXIETY DISORDERS

Phobias
Anxiety States

How would you like to be a tame, somewhat shy and unaggressive little boy of nine, somewhat shorter and thinner than average, and find yourself put three times a week, every Monday, Wednesday, and Friday, as regularly and inexorably as the sun sets and the sky darkens and the globe turns black and dead and spooky with no warm promise that anyone anywhere ever will waken again, into the somber, iron custody of someone named Forgione, older, broader, and much larger than yourself, a dreadful, powerful, broad-shouldered man who is hairy, hard-muscled, and barrel-chested and wears immaculate tight white or navy-blue T-shirts that seem as firm and unpitying as the figure of flesh and bone they encase like a mold, whose ferocious, dark eyes you never had courage enough to meet and whose assistant's name you did not ask or were not able to remember, and who did not seem to like you or approve of you? He could do whatever he wanted to you. He could do whatever he wanted to me (Heller, 1966, p. 236).

This excerpt from Joseph Heller's second novel, *Something Happened*, portrays the terrified helplessness of a nine-year-old boy who has to interact every other school day with a burly gym teacher. As described by his equally fearful father, the youngster has an overwhelming anxiety about his gym class, a situation into which he is forced and from which he cannot escape, a situation which makes demands on him that he feels utterly unable to meet. Once again a gifted novelist captures the phenomenology—the direct experience—of an important human emotion in a way that speaks vividly to each of us.

There is, perhaps, no other single topic in abnormal psychology that is as important and controversial as anxiety. This emotional state can occur in many psychopathologies and is a principal aspect of the disorders to be considered in this chapter. Furthermore, anxiety plays an important role in the study of the psychology of normal people as well, for very few of us go through even a week of our lives without experiencing in at least some measure of what we would all agree is the emotion anxiety or fear. But the briefer periods of anxiety that beset the normal individual are hardly comparable in intensity or duration, nor are they as debilitating, as those suffered by someone with an anxiety disorder.

The specific disorders considered in this and the next chapter were for a considerable period all regarded as varieties of neuroses. The conceptualization of them became extablished through Freud's clinical work with his patients, and thus the diagnostic category of neuroses was inextricably bound up with psychoanalytic theory. DSM-II offered the following definition:

> Anxiety is the chief characteristic of the neuroses. It may be felt and expressed directly, or it may be controlled unconsciously and automatically by conversion, displacement and various other psychological mechanisms. Generally, these mechanisms produce symptoms experienced as subjective distress from which the patient desires relief (p. 39).

The behavior encompassed by the forms of neuroses varied greatly—the fear and avoidance of the phobic, the irresistible urge to perform certain acts over and over again found in compulsives, the paralyses and other "neurological" symptoms of conversion hysterics. How could such diverse problems be grouped into a single category? Although the observed symptoms differ, all neurotic conditions were assumed, according to the psychoanalytic theory of neuroses, to reflect an underlying problem with repressed anxiety. Over the years many psychopathologists questioned this assumption, however, and their doubts are reflected in the manner in which DSM-III progressed through several drafts on the way to its final form. At one point the category of neuroses was dropped entirely. But in the introduction to the final version it is noted that "the omission of the DSM-II diagnostic class of Neuroses has been a matter of great concern to many clinicians," and the category has been restored, at least partially. In DSM-III the old categories of neuroses are distributed in several new diagnostic classes which form new sections: anxiety disorders, the topic of this chapter; and somatoform disorders and dissociative disorders, both of which are covered in Chapter 6. When a DSM-II neurotic category appears in one of the new sections, the new diagnosis, for example, phobic disorder, is followed by the old, for example, phobic neurosis, given in parentheses. Thus DSM-III has tried for a middle-of-the-road approach, which is not likely to please anyone. In our view neurosis is an undersirable diagnostic category because no data support the assumption that all such patients share some common problem or set of symptoms. In all likelihood many people will continue to use the term—indeed it is part of our everyday vocabulary and appears throughout the book—but in this chapter and the next the presentation is organized according to the newer diagnostic categories.

This chapter covers the _anxiety disorders,_ those in which a subjectively experienced feeling of anxiety is clearly present. DSM-III proposes three principal categories: _phobic disorders;_ the _anxiety states,_ which are _panic disorder, generalized anxiety disorder,_ and _obsessive-compulsive disorder;_ and _posttraumatic stress disorder._ We discuss the first two categories in some detail, but little empirical information is available about the third. In posttraumatic stress disorder an extremely traumatic event or catastrophe, such as rape,[1] combat, or a natural disaster, brings in its aftermath anxiety, depression, poor concentration, disturbed sleep, and a tendency to be easily startled. Previously enjoyed activities lose their interest; there is a feeling of estrangement from other people and from "the passing parade"—and a sense of guilt if companions have not survived a shared ordeal. As for the experience itself, the person has great difficulty keeping it out of mind, and recurring nightmares and dreams are common. Posttraumatic stress disorder may be acute, delayed, or chronic and is apparently more severe and longer lasting when the disaster is man-made (see Box 5.1).

---

[1] The aftermath of sexual assault is discussed in a separate section on rape in Chapter 11 (page 355).

BOX   5.1 Posttraumatic Stress Disorder and the Vietnam War

In addition to the many, widely known tragedies of the Vietnam war, serving in it has had long-term negative repercussions for many servicemen. For the most part they went, served their twelve months, and returned home alone. Ironically, because in many men stress reactions were delayed, it was originally thought that the unpopular Vietnam war had produced far fewer "psychiatric casualties" than had World War II. But subsequent research, reviewed by Figley (1978), has convincingly documented among Vietnam veterans, particularly those who were in combat, many overriding problems—high unemployment, low morale, pessimism, and feelings of estrangment from society. Depression, nightmares, a sudden reliving of unbearable events of the war, inability to relax, and difficulty in getting close to other people constitute specific evidence that some suffer from posttraumatic stress disorder. A professor's experience with one veteran poignantly illustrates one aspect of the problem.

He always sat in the back row, as far away as he could get: long skinny body and long face, thin curly hair, dark mustache. Sometimes his bony shoulders were hunched as he peered down at his notebook lying open on that bizarre prehensile arm that grows out of college classroom chairs. Or else he leaned way back, the lopsided chair balanced on two legs and propped against the rear wall, his chest appearing slightly concave beneath his white shirt, and one narrow leg, in jeans, elegantly stretched out to rest on a nearby empty chair.

Casual but tense, rather like a male fashion model. Volatile beneath the calm: someone you would not want to meet on a dark street. His face was severely impassive in a way that suggested arrogance and scorn.

He must have been about twenty-seven years old, an extremely thin young man—ascetic, stripped down to the essentials. His body looked so brittle and so electrically charged that I almost expected crackling noises when he moved, but in fact he slipped in and out silently, in the wink of an eye. His whole lanky, scrutinizing demeanor was intimidating. He would have no patience with anything phony, I imagined; would not suffer fools gladly.

About every fourth or fifth class he was absent, common enough for evening session students, who had jobs, families, grown-up lives and responsibilities. I was a trifle relieved at his absences—I could relax—yet I missed him, too. His presence made a definite and compelling statement, but in an unintelligible language. I couldn't interpret him as readily as I could the books on the reading list.

I was hired in the spring of 1970. It was wartime. Students were enraged. When I went for my interview at Hunter College I had to walk past pickets into a building where black flags hung from the windows. I would use the Socratic method, I earnestly told the interviewer, since I believed in the students' innate intelligence. To myself, I vowed I would win their confidence. After all, I was scarcely older than they were and I shared their mood of protest. I would wear jeans to show I was one of them, and even though I had passed thirty and was married and had two children I would prove that I could be trusted. I was prepared—even eager—for youthful, strident, moral indignation.

Far from strident, he was totally silent, never speaking in class discussions, and I was reluctant to call on him. Since he had a Spanish name, I wondered whether he might have trouble with English. Bureaucratic chaos was the order of the day, with the City University enacting in microcosm the confusion in the nation at large; it was not unusual for barely literate or barely English-speaking students to wind up in an Introduction to Literature class. His silence and his blank arrogant look could simply mean bewilderment. I ought to find out, but I waited.

His first paper was a shocker. I was surprised to receive it at all—I had him pegged as the sullen type who would give up at the first difficult assignment, then complain that college was irrelevant. On the contrary, the paper, formidably intelligent, jarred my view of the fitness of things. It didn't seem possible—no, it didn't seem *right*—that a person so sullen and mute should be so eloquent. Someone must have helped him. The truth would come out in impromptu class papers, and then I would confront him. I bided my time.

After the first exam he tossed his blue book onto my desk, not meeting my eyes, and, wary and feline, glided away, withdrawing into his body as if attempting a disappearing act. The topic he had chosen was the meaning of "the horror" in Joseph Conrad's "Heart of Darkness," the novella we had spent the first few sessions on.

He compared it to Faulkner's "Intruder in the Dust." He wrote at length about racial hatred and war and their connection in the dark, unspeakable places in the soul from which both spring, without sentimentality but with a sort of matter-of-fact, old knowledge. He knew Faulkner better than I did; I had to go back and skim "Intruder in the Dust" to understand his exam. I do know that I had never before sat transfixed in disbelief over a student paper.

The next day I called him over after class and asked if he was aware that he had an extraordinary mind. He said, yes, he was. Close up, there was nothing arrogant about him. A bit awkward and shy, yet gracious, with something antique and courtly in his manner.

Why did he never speak in class, I asked.

He didn't like to speak in front of people. His voice and his eye turned evasive, like an adolescent's as he told me this. Couldn't in fact. Couldn't speak.

What do you mean, I said. You're not a kid. You have a lot to say. You write like this and you sit in class like a statue? What's it all about?

He was in the war, he said, and he finally looked at my face and spoke like the adult that he was. He was lost for a long time in the jungles of Vietnam, he explained patiently, as if I might not know what Vietnam was, or what a jungle was, or what it was to be lost. And after that, he said, he couldn't. He just found it hard to be with people. To speak to people.

But you're so smart. You could do so much.

I know. He shrugged: a flesh and blood version of the rueful, devil-may-care, movie war hero shrug. Can't be helped.

Anything can be helped, I insisted.

No, he insisted back, quietly. Not after that jungle.

Hunter had a counseling service, free. Go, I pleaded.

He had already gone. They keep asking me questions about my childhood, he said, my relationship with my parents, my toilet training. He grinned quickly, turning it on and off. But it doesn't help. It's none of that. It's from when I was lost in that jungle.

You must work, I said. Don't you have to talk to people when you work?

No, he was a meter man.

A what?

He went around checking on cars, to see if they had overstayed their time at the parking meters.

You can't do that forever, I said. With your brains!

Well, at least he didn't have to talk to people, he said sweetly. For now. Maybe later on he would get braver.

And what would he do if I called on him in class? If I made him talk?

Oh no, don't do that, he said, and flashed the wry grin again. If you did that I'd probably run out of the room.

I never called on him because I didn't want to risk seeing him run out of the room. But at least we stopped being afraid of each other. He gave up his blank look, and occasionally I would glance at his face, to see if I was still making sense or drifting off into some seductive, academic cloud of words.

I thought of him a lot this summer after I saw young men lined up at post offices to register for military service. I thought of him also when I heard Ronald Reagan and John Anderson, on television, solemnly pledge themselves to the defense of this country's shores. No candidate has yet pledged himself to the defense of this country's young men, to "taking every measure necessary" to "insure" that their genius does not turn mute and their very lives become the spoils of war (Schwartz, 1980).

*Copyright © 1980, by The New York Times Company. Reprinted with permission

Phobias

Psychopathologists define a phobia as a disrupting fear-mediated avoidance, out of proportion to the danger posed by a particular object or situation. For example, when people are extremely fearful of heights, closed spaces, snakes, or spiders, provided there is no objective danger and their distress is sufficient to disrupt their lives, the label phobia is likely to be applied to their avoidance and fear.

Over the years complex terms have been formulated as names for such unwarranted avoidance patterns. In each instance the suffix -phobia is preceded by a Greek word for the feared object or situation. The suffix is derived from the name of the Greek god Phobos, who frightened his enemies. Some of the more familiar terms are claustrophobia, fear of closed spaces; agoraphobia, fear of open spaces and of leaving the house; and acrophobia, fear of heights. More exotic fears have also been given Greek-derived names, for example, ergasiophobia, fear of writing; pnigophobia, fear of choking; and taphephobia, fear of being buried alive. All too often the impression is conveyed that we understand how a particular problem originated or even how to treat it merely because we have an authoritative-sounding name for it. Nothing could be farther from the truth, however. As with so much else in the field of abnormal psychology, there are more theories and jargon pertaining to phobias than there are firm findings.

In comparison to other diagnostic categories, phobias are relatively common in the general population. For example, Agras, Sylvester, and Oliveau (1969) found a rate of 77 per 1000 in a population study done in New England. This same investigation, however, revealed that most of the phobias recorded were relatively mild, only 2.2 per 1000 being rated as severely disabling. Indeed, many specific fears do not cause enough hardship to compel an individual to seek treatment. If a person with an intense fear or phobia of nonpoisonous snakes lives in a metropolitan area, he or she will probably have little direct contact with the feared object and may therefore not believe that anything is seriously wrong.

Subclassification of Phobias

Up to now we have been discussing phobias as though they are alike in every respect except the object or situation that is fearfully avoided. Behaviorists have been remiss in not considering whether the differences between fearing a small animal and fearing the prospect of leaving the house are important. This neglect of the content of the phobia seems consistent with the fact that behaviorists take a _functional_ stance rather than a topographical one (Wilson and Davison, 1969). _Topography_ here means specification of the actual physical behavior. Thus avoidance of a snake is topographically different from avoidance of heights, for the simple reason that a snake is not a height. According to the functional approach adopted by most behaviorists, however, the two responses may be treated as equivalent because both perform the same function, removing the individual from a fear-eliciting situation. Within a functional framework fear of snakes and fear of heights are viewed as equivalent in the means by which they are acquired, in how they might be changed, and so on.

If behaviorists underplay the content of phobias, analysts go to the other extreme, seeing great significance in the phobic object as a symbol of an important unconscious fear. In a celebrated case reported by Freud, Little Hans was afraid of encountering horses if he went outside (see Box 5.2). Freud paid particular attention to Hans's reference to the "black things around horses' mouths and the things in front of their eyes." The horse was regarded as "standing for the father," who wore eyeglasses and had a moustache. Freud theorized that fear of the father had become transformed into fear of horses, which were then avoided by Hans. Countless other such examples might be cited; the principal point is that psychoanalysts believe that the content of phobias has important symbolic value.

Marks (1969) has an extensive scheme for classifying various phobias. He has noted many potentially important differences, which behaviorists have paid little if any attention to, and which analytically oriented workers have also ignored, but for other reasons. The variables ex-

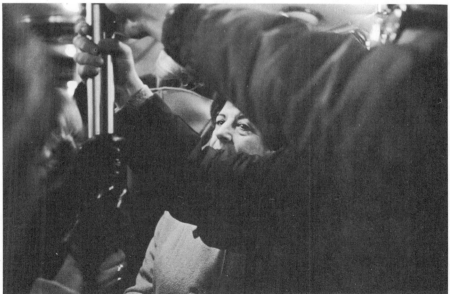

Three common sources of phobias—heights, closed spaces, and crowds.

BOX   **5.2** Little Hans

A classic case of phobia, reported by Freud in 1909, was that of a five-year-old boy, Little Hans, who was afraid of horses and thus would not venture out of his home. The importance of this case is attested to by many psychoanalytic scholars. Ernest Jones, Freud's famous biographer, calls it "the brilliant success of child analysis" (1955, p. 289); and Glover, a respected scholar, terms it "a remarkable achievement . . . [constituting] one of the most valued records in psychoanalytic archives" (1956, p. 76).

"Why can't you be more like Oedipus?"

Drawing by Charles Adams; © 1972 The New Yorker Magazine, Inc.

Freud's analysis of Little Hans was based on information reported in letters written to Freud by the boy's father; Freud actually saw the child only once. Two years before the development of his phobia, when he was three, Hans was reported to have "a quite peculiarly lively interest in the part of his body which he used to describe as his widdler." When he was three and a half his mother caught him with his hand on his penis and threatened to arrange for his penis to be cut off if he continued "doing that." At age four and a half, while on summer vacation, Hans is described as having tried to "seduce" his mother. As his mother was powdering around his penis one day, taking care not to touch it, Hans said, "Why don't you put your finger there?" His mother answered "Because that would be piggish." Hans replied "What's that? Piggish? Why?" Mother: "Because it's not proper." Hans, laughing: "But it's great fun." These events were taken by Freud as proof that Hans had strong sexual urges, that they were directed toward his mother, and that they were repressed for fear of castration. According to the first theory of anxiety (see page 43), this sexual privation would ultimately be transformed into neurotic anxiety.

The first signs of the phobia appeared about six months later while Hans was out for a walk with his nursemaid. After a horse-drawn van had tipped over, he began crying, saying that he wanted to return to "coax" (caress) with his mother. Later he indicated that he was afraid to go out because a horse might bite him, and he soon elaborated on his fears by referring to "black things around horses' mouths and the things in front of their eyes."

Freud considered this series of events to reflect Hans's oedipal desires to have his father out of the way so that he could possess his mother. His sexual excitement for his mother was converted into anxiety because he feared that he would be punished. Hans's father was considered the initial source of his son's fear, but the fear was then transposed to a symbol for his father—horses. The black muzzles and blinders on horses were viewed as symbolic representations of the father's eyeglasses and moustache. Thus, by fearing horses, Hans was said to have succeeded unconsciously in avoiding the fear of castration by his father—even though it was the *mother* who had threatened this punishment—while at the same time arranging to spend more time at home with his principal love-object, his mother.

There are many other details in the case study, which occupies 140 pages in Freud's *Collected Papers*. In our brief account we have attempted to convey the flavor of the theorizing. We agree with Wolpe and Rachman (1960) that Freud made large inferential leaps from the data of the case. First, the evidence for Hans's wanting sexual contact with his mother is minimal, making it debatable that Hans wanted to possess his mother sexually and replace his father. Second, there is little evidence that Hans hated or feared his father, and in the original case report it is stated that Hans directly denied any symbolic connection between horses and his father. This denial was interpreted as evidence *for* the connection, however. Third, there is no evidence, or any reason to believe, that intense sexual excitement was somehow translated into anxiety. Indeed, the fact that Hans became afraid of horses after being frightened by an accident involving a horse may be more parsimoniously explained by the classical conditioning model, although this interpretation has its own problems (see page 156).

amined by Marks are frequency, sex distribution, age of onset, whether or not additional symptoms are present, the course of the problem, and psychophysiological responses.

Agoraphobia

A complicated syndrome, _agoraphobia_ is a cluster of fears centering around open spaces. Fears of other situations such as shopping, encountering crowds, and traveling and even of being alone are often a part of agoraphobia. From a patient's point of view, agoraphobia is surely very distressing. Consider how limiting it must be to be afraid of leaving the house. Perhaps for this reason agoraphobia is the most common phobia seen in the clinic, constituting roughly 60 percent of all phobias examined.[2] The restrictive nature of the syndrome forces the agoraphobic to seek help. Most agoraphobics are women, and the majority develop their problems in adolescence and early adulthood. Numerous other neurotic symptoms are also evident, including panic attacks, tension, dizziness, depression, rumination, and minor checking compulsions— seeing that the screen door is latched, no one is under the bed, the iron is off. Psychophysiological responses confirm the clinical impression that agoraphobics are subject to a rather diffuse, non-specific anxiety. Recordings taken of their autonomic activity typically show high levels of arousal, even when they are supposedly relaxing (Marks, 1969).

Social phobias

A _social phobia_ is a collection of fears generally linked to the presence of other people. The individual feels compelled to avoid situations in which he or she might be scrutinized and reveal signs of anxiousness or behave in an embarrassing way. Eating and speaking in public, or virtually any other activity that might be carried out in the presence of others, can elicit extreme anxiety. Although this phobia is not uncommon, social phobics seek help much less frequently than do agoraphobics. Women are seen in therapy for these difficulties slightly more often than are men. As might be expected, onset is generally

during adolescence, when social awareness and interaction with others are assuming much more importance in the person's life. Few additional symptoms are generally present, although recordings of psychophysiological responses indicate rather high levels of arousal.

Animal and other simple phobias

Although easy to define, phobias of animals are the rarest seen in clinical practice. Only 3 percent of all phobics have them. The majority of _animal phobias_ occur in women, and they begin very often in early childhood (Marks and Gelder, 1966). It is likely that among both boys and girls animal phobias are quite common, but that boys extinguish their phobias because of social pressures to approach and confront what they dread. Thus in adulthood the problems are much more common in women. Recordings of autonomic activity while the subject is at rest indicate that arousal levels are within the normal range. At the sight of the feared animal, however, arousal does increase.

Also included in the catch-all category of simple phobias are those of heights, thunder, darkness, travel, closed spaces, driving, infections, running water, and the like. Few other symptoms are generally present. Further evaluation of this category is not possible because few data have been collected.[3]

A summary of the important differences in various clinical phobias appears in Table 5.1. Some, like agoraphobia and social phobias, are associated with high arousal levels, indicating that the autonomic nervous system may be especially important in their etiology. Therapy procedures aimed at reducing such fears may have to take this high level of autonomic arousal into account. Therefore the topographical features of a phobia may have important implications for both etiology and treatment.

The Psychoanalytic Theory of Phobias

As is true of many of the anxiety disorders (neuroses), Freud was the first to attempt to account systematically for the development of phobic be-

---

[2] A cruel irony about the prevalence of agoraphobia is that it is probably underestimated, for those with the more severe cases are unable to leave their homes to go to a clinic or private office for therapy.

[3] Phobias of childhood will be discussed in Chapter 15, which covers nonpsychotic childhood disorders.

TABLE 5.1
Summary of Classification of Phobias

(adapted from Marks, 1969)

Variables	Agoraphobia	Social phobias	Animal phobias	Simple phobias
Frequency	Common	Not uncommon	Rare	Not uncommon
Sex incidence	75% women	60% women	95% women	50% women
Onset age	After puberty	After puberty	Childhood	Anytime
Associated symptoms	Multiple—general anxiety, depression, panic	Few	Few	Not determined
Psychophysiology	High arousal	High arousal	Normal	Not determined

havior. According to Freud, phobias are a defense against the anxiety that is produced by repressed id impulses. This anxiety is displaced from the id impulse that is feared to an object or situation that has some symbolic connection to it. These objects or situations—for example, elevators or closed spaces—then become the phobic stimuli. By avoiding them, the person is able to avoid dealing with repressed conflicts. As discussed in Chapter 2 (page 44), the phobia is the ego's way of warding off a confrontation with the real problem, a repressed childhood conflict.

More recently, another psychoanalytic theory of phobias has been proposed by Arieti (1979). According to him, repression is of a particular interpersonal problem of childhood rather then of an id impulse. Arieti theorizes that, as children, phobics first lived through a period of innocence during which they trusted the people around them to protect them from danger. But then these children came to fear that adults, usually the parents, were not reliable. This mistrust, or generalized fear of others, was something they could not live with; in order to be able to trust people again, they unconsciously transformed this fear of others into a fear of impersonal objects or situations. The phobia supposedly surfaces when, in adulthood, the person undergoes some sort of stress. As is true of most psychoanalytic theorizing, evidence in support of these views is restricted to conclusions drawn from uncontrolled clinical case reports.

Behavioral Theories of Phobias

As in psychoanalytic theory, the primary assumption of all behavioral accounts of phobias is that such reactions are learned. But the exact learning mechanisms and what is actually learned in the development of a phobia are specified differently in the various behavioral theories.

The classical conditioning model

Historically, Watson and Rayner's (1920) demonstration of the apparent conditioning of a fear or phobia in Little Albert (see page 51) is considered the model of how a phobia may be acquired. Learning theorists have elaborated on the case by asserting that the classically conditioned fear of an objectively harmless stimulus forms the basis of an operant avoidance response. This formulation, based on the two-factor theory originally proposed by Mowrer (1947), holds that phobias develop from two related sets of learning. (1) Via classical conditioning a person can learn to fear a neutral stimulus (the CS) if it is paired with an intrinsically painful or frightening event (the UCS). (2) Then the person can learn to reduce this conditioned fear by escaping from or avoiding the CS. This second kind of learning is assumed to be operant conditioning; the response is maintained by its reinforcing consequences.

Certain clinically reported phobias seem to fit such a model rather well. For example, a phobia of a specific object has sometimes been reported to have developed after a particularly painful experience with that object. Some people become intensely afraid of driving an automobile after a serious accident, or of descending stairs after a bad fall. Other phobias apparently originate in similar fashion.

> A young boy would often pass a grocery store on errands and when passing would steal a handful of peanuts from the stand in front. One day the owner saw him coming and hid behind a barrel. Just as the boy put his hand in the pile of peanuts the owner jumped out and grabbed him from behind. The boy screamed and fell fainting on the sidewalk.
>
> The boy developed a phobia of being grasped from behind. In social gatherings he arranged to have his chair against the wall. It was impossible for him to enter crowded places or to attend the theater. When walking on the street he would have to look back over his shoulder at intervals to see if he was closely followed (Bagby, 1922).

A major problem exists in the application of this model, however. The fact that Little Albert's fear and certain clinically reported phobias were acquired through conditioning can *not* be taken as evidence that *all* fears and phobias are acquired by this means. Rather, the evidence demonstrates only the *possibility* that some fears *may* be acquired in this particular way. Indeed, other clinical reports suggest that phobias may develop *without* prior frightening experience. Many individuals with severe fears of snakes, germs, airplanes, and heights tell clinicians that they have had no particularly unpleasant experiences with any of these objects or situations.[4] In a systematic study Keuthen (1980) found that half of a sample of phobics could recall no upsetting experience in the feared situation. Similarly, many people who have had an unpleasant automobile

accident or a bad fall down stairs do *not* become phobic to automobiles or stairs. Thus the classical conditioning model cannot account for the acquisition of all phobias.

Furthermore, attempts to replicate Watson and Raynor's experiment and demonstrate again the acquisition of fear via classical conditioning have for the most part *not* been successful. For example, English (1929) attempted to condition fear in a fourteen-month-old girl by pairing the presentation of a duck with a loud noise. Despite fifty trials, no conditioned response to the duck was established. In a more extensive investigation Bregman (see Thorndike, 1935) tried to condition fear in fifteen infants of about the same age as Little Albert, using various CSs and a loud bell as the UCS. Again, relatively few fears were acquired by the subjects. (From an ethical point of view, it is fortunate that these workers failed to produce phobias in their young subjects.)

There is actually very little experimental evidence to support the contention that human beings can be classically conditioned to fear neutral stimuli even when such stimuli are paired repeatedly with primary aversive stimuli, such as electric shock (for example, Davison, 1968b). Ethical considerations have of course restrained most researchers from employing highly aversive stimuli with human beings, but considerable evidence indicates that fear is extinguished rather quickly when the CS is presented a few times without the reinforcement of moderate levels of shock (Bridger and Mandel, 1965; Wickens, Allen, and Hill, 1963).

In sum, the data we have reviewed suggest that not all phobias are learned through classical conditioning. Such a process *may* be involved in the etiology of some phobias, but other processes must also be implicated in their development (see Box 5.3).

Modeling

Phobic responses may also be learned through imitating the reactions of others. As we have previously noted (see page 53), a wide range of behavior, including emotional responses, may be learned by witnessing a model. The learning of phobic reactions by observing others is generally referred to as <u>vicarious conditioning.</u> In one study Bandura and Rosenthal (1966) arranged for

---

[4] Such accounts are called *retrospective* reports, that is, reports made by people looking back into their past, sometimes for many, many years. Since memory of long-ago events is often distorted, such reports must be viewed with some skepticism. The fact that many phobics cannot recall traumatic experiences with their now-feared objects may indeed be distortions of memory. Accounts of traumatic episodes may be questioned on the same grounds. Retrospective reports are discussed again on page 281.

BOX **5.3** Classical Conditioning and Preparedness

Perhaps the classical conditioning view of phobias would be more valid if modified slightly to take into account the fact that certain neutral stimuli may be more likely to become conditioned stimuli than others. Pavlov (1928) did not address this question, stating that "... every imaginable phenomenon of the outer world affecting a specific receptive surface of the body may be converted into a CS" (p. 88).

Seligman (1971) has suggested that phobias may well reflect classical conditioning to stimuli that an organism is physiologically predisposed to be sensitive to. Accordingly, classical conditioning experiments that show quick extinction of fear may have employed CSs that the organism was really not "prepared" to learn to associate with UCSs.

An example from the research that has given rise to this _preparedness_ notion may make this hypothesis clearer. Garcia and his associates (Garcia, McGowan, and Green, 1972) found that rats could learn to avoid the _taste_ of a given food if nauseated following its ingestion—even if the nausea did not begin for many hours. In contrast, they could not be negatively conditioned to the _sight_ of food if they were nauseated in its presence but had not actually tasted it. Similarly, rats could readily learn to avoid a light paired with shock (a common experimental finding), but they could not learn to avoid taste paired with shock. Thus, as seen in Figure 5.1 gustatory sensations and illness (taste-nausea) are readily associated, as are visual and tactile modalities (light-shock). But visual stimuli and illness (sight of food-nausea) and gustatory and tactile sensations (taste-shock) are not.

Seligman has provided a personal illustration of the operation of this process.

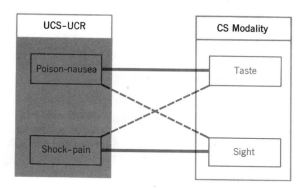

FIGURE 5.1
The organisms may be prepared through innate sensitivity to learn certain associations but not be prepared to learn others. Solid lines indicate easily made associations; dotted lines connect classes of stimuli that are difficult to associate.

Sauce Béarnaise is an egg-thickened, tarragon-flavored con-coction, and it used to be my favorite sauce. It now tastes awful to me. This happened several years ago. . . . After eating filet mignon with Sauce Béarnaise, I became violently ill and spent most of the night vomiting. The next time I had Sauce Béarnaise, I couldn't bear the taste of it. At the time I had no ready way to account for the change, although it seemed to fit a classical conditioning paradigm: CS (sauce) paired with US (illness) and UR (vomiting) yields CR (nau-seating taste). [Although I learned that flu had caused the nausea and others with me did not get sick . . .], I could not later inhibit my aversion (Seligman and Hager, 1972, p. 8).

This and related research prompted Seligman to hypothesize that some associations, and thereby phobias, are easily learned by human beings and thus are not readily extinguished. Marks (1969), in a related observation, points to the fact that human beings tend to be afraid of certain types of objects and events. People may have phobias of dogs, cats, and snakes—but few lamb phobics have been encountered. It is even more remarkable how few people phobically avoid electric outlets, which do present certain dangers under spec-ified circumstances.

Some more direct evidence that certain fears are easily learned comes from a condition-ing study in which different types of stimuli were used as the CS (Öhman, Erixon, and Löfberg, 1975). All subjects viewed three sets of pictures varying in content—snakes, houses, and faces. Half the participants received a shock (UCS) immediately after viewing each slide of snakes. The remainder received shocks after viewing slides either of houses or of faces. The GSR served as the CR and was analyzed for both the conditioning trials and for a subsequent extinction series. During the conditioning part of the study, the GSRs of the groups of participants receiving shocks after viewing slides of any of the three classes of stimuli were about the same. During extinction, however, the CR to the slides of houses or faces quickly diminished, whereas the CR to slides of snakes remained strong. Thus the CR was more durably associated with the sight of snakes, which are a fairly common elicitor of clinical phobias.

In a later study (Hugdahl, Fredrikson, and Öhman, 1977) the subjects' level of physio-logical arousal (see page 107) was also found to be related to the extent to which fears can be conditioned. People with high levels of arousal were more readily made fearful of stimuli easily associated with the emotion than were those with lower levels. These find-ings suggest that people are "prepared" to fear certain stimuli, particularly people with high levels of arousal.

Seligman has also linked his preparedness theory to psychoanalytic concepts. He pro-posed that the kind of symbolism mentioned in psychoanalytic theory may one day be found to have a basis in the sensitivities of people and what they are prepared to associate and to learn. Hans, after all, came to fear horses after he saw one of them fall down in the street in a rather memorable incident. But he did not become afraid of the van which tipped over, and he must have observed other dramatic incidents and been struck by par-ticularly vivid aspects of them during his walks with the nursemaid. Although the symbolic connection with the father is still unclear unless Freud's hypothesis is accepted, it does seem significant that the particular incident mentioned in the case report loomed larger than others, and that in its aftermath Hans came to be afraid of horses. Even though not all investigators are convinced that people are prepared to acquire conditioned responses to certain stimuli (see Bitterman, 1975; Evans, 1976), the preparedness hypothesis neverthe-less appears worth exploring.

subjects to watch another person, the model, in an aversive-conditioning situation. The model was hooked up to an impressive-looking array of electrical apparatus. Upon hearing a buzzer, the model withdrew his hand rapidly from the arm of the chair and feigned pain. The physiological responses of the subjects witnessing this behavior were recorded. After the subjects had watched the model ''suffer'' a number of times, they showed an increased frequency of emotional responses when the buzzer sounded. The subjects began to react emotionally to a harmless stimulus even though they had had no direct contact with a noxious event.

Vicarious learning may also be accomplished through verbal instructions. That is, phobic reactions can be learned through another's description of what might happen as well as by observing another's fear. As an example from everyday life, a mother may repeatedly warn her child not to engage in some activity lest dire consequences ensue. Vicarious examples can apparently be provided through words.

As with classical conditioning, however, vicarious learning experiments fail to provide an adequate model for all phobias. In the first place, the vicarious fear extinguishes quickly. Second, phobics who seek treatment do not often report that they became frightened after witnessing someone else's distress. And third, many people have been exposed to the bad experiences of others but have not themselves developed phobias.

Operant conditioning

Finally, we may consider the possibility that phobic reactions are learned by virtue of the consequences they produce. Avoidance responses may be directly rewarded and thereby learned. For example, a child who wants to stay close to a parent may invent excuses so that she does not have to attend school. If the mother or father gives in to these excuses, the child is directly rewarded by the positive consequence of being allowed to stay home with the adult. In this instance fear is not mentioned as a mediator. The child avoids school simply because it produces favorable results.

Although some phobias may develop because of the payoff provided by the environment, the fact that many phobics suffer because they are compelled to avoid harmless situations strains the general applicability of the theory.

Physiological Factors Predisposing to the Development of Phobias

Both psychoanalytic and learning theories look to the environment for the cause and maintenance of phobias. Indeed, as already indicated, the primary assumption of both theories is that phobias are learned. But why do some people acquire unrealistic fears whereas others do not, given similar opportunities for learning? Perhaps those who are adversely affected by stress have a physiological malfunction (the diathesis) that somehow predisposes them to develop a phobia following a particular stressful event.

Autonomic nervous system

What characteristic may be important in determining the susceptibility of individuals to particular environment experiences? One way people may react differently to certain environmental situations is the ease with which their autonomic nervous systems become aroused. Lacey (1967) has referred to a dimension of autonomic activity which he calls stability-lability. Labile or ''jumpy'' individuals are those whose autonomic systems are readily aroused by a wide range of stimuli. Clearly, because of the extent to which the autonomic nervous system is involved in fear and hence in phobic behavior, a dimension such as _autonomic lability_ would assume considerable importance. Since there is reason to believe that autonomic lability is to some degree genetically determined (Eysenck, 1957; Lacey, 1967), the heredity (see Box 5.4) of individuals may very well have a significant role in the development of phobias.

Genetic studies

Several studies have questioned whether a genetic or innate factor is involved in anxiety disorders, although none has been directly concerned with whether such a factor is implicated in the formation of phobias per se. Brown (1942) investigated the incidence of neuroses in relatives of people who had already been diagnosed as neurotic. Consistent with the view that a predisposi-

BOX 5.4 Behavior Genetics

When the ovum, the female reproductive cell, joins with the male's spermatozoan, a zygote or fertilized egg is produced. It has forty-six chromosomes, the number characteristic of the human being. Each chromosome is made up of thousands of *genes*. The genes are the carriers of the genetic information that is passed on from parents to child. Each cell of the human body will contain a full complement of chromosomes and genes in its nucleus.

Behavior genetics is the study of individual differences in behavior that are attributable in part to differences in genetic makeup. The total genetic makeup of an individual, consisting of the inherited genes, is referred to as the *genotype.* An individual's genotype is the unobservable, physiological genetic constitution, in contrast to the totality of observable characteristics, which is referred to as the *phenotype.* The genotype is fixed at birth, whereas the phenotype changes and is generally viewed as the product of an interaction between the genotype and experience. For example, an individual may be born with the capacity for high intellectual achievement. Whether he or she develops this genetically given potential depends on such environmental factors as rearing and education. Any measure of intelligence (IQ) is therefore best viewed as an index of the phenotype.

On the basis of the distinction made between phenotype and genotype, we realize that various clinical syndromes are disorders of the phenotype. Thus it is not proper to speak of the direct inheritance of schizophrenia or anxiety disorders. At most, only the genotypes for these disorders can be inherited. Whether these genotypes will eventually engender the phenotypic behavioral disorder will depend on environment and experience; a predisposition (diathesis) may be inherited but not the disorder itself.

The two major methods of study in behavior genetics are to compare members of a family and pairs of twins. Members of a family are compared because we can determine, on the average, how many genes are shared by two blood relatives. For example, children receive half their genes from one parent and half from the other. Siblings will, on the average, be identical in 50 percent of their genetic background. In contrast, relatives not as closely related share fewer genes. For example, an uncle shares 25 percent of the genetic makeup of his nephews or nieces. If a predisposition for a mental disorder can be inherited, a study of the family should reveal a correlation between the number of shared genes and the incidence of the disorder in relatives. The starting point in such investigations is to collect a sample of individuals who bear the diagnosis in question; these are referred to as *index cases* or *probands.* Then relatives are studied to determine the frequency with which the same diagnosis might be applied to them.

In the twin method *dizygotic* (DZ) and *monozygotic* (MZ) pairs of twins are compared. MZ twins develop from a single fertilized egg and are genetically identical. DZ pairs develop from separate eggs and on the average are only 50 percent alike genetically, actually no more alike than two siblings. MZ twins are always the same sex, but DZs or fraternal twins can be either the same sex or opposite in sex. Again, such studies begin with diagnosed cases and then search for the presence of the disorder in the other twin. When the pair of twins are similar diagnostically, they are said to be *concordant.* To the extent that a predisposition for a mental disorder can be inherited, concordance for the disorder should be greater in MZ pairs than in DZ pairs.

Although the methodology of the *family* and *twin studies* is clear, the data they yield are not always easy to interpret. Let us assume that neurotic parents have been found to produce more than the average number of neurotic offspring. Does this mean that anxiety disorders are genetically transmitted? Not necessarily. The increased frequency of anxiety disorders could as well reflect child-rearing practices and exposure of the children to neurotic adult models. Consider also a finding of greater concordance for schizophrenia among MZ than among DZ twins. Again, such data do not necessarily implicate heredity, since MZ twins, perhaps because they look so much alike, may be raised in a more similar fashion than are DZs, thus accounting for the greater concordance for schizophrenia among them. There are, however, special but infrequent circumstances that are not subject to the aforementioned problems: children reared completely apart from their abnormal parents and MZ twins reared separately from very early infancy. A high frequency of anxiety disorders in children reared apart from their anxious parents would offer convincing support for the theory that genetic factors figure in these disorders. Similarly, greater concordance among separately reared MZ twins than among DZ twins would offer compelling evidence that a predisposition for a disorder can be inherited.

In family studies the investigator capitalizes on the degree of genetic similarity in family members. Shown here is a marked similarity in physical appearance.

tion for a disorder can be genetically transmitted, he found the incidence of neurosis in first-degree relatives—siblings, mothers, and fathers—to be 16.8 percent. In contrast, for a control group made up of nonneurotic individuals, the incidence of neurosis in first-degree relatives was only 1.1 percent. Similarly, Noyes and his associates (1978) found that 15 percent of the first-degree relatives of individuals diagnosed as having anxiety neurosis[5] also suffered from the disorder. The corresponding figure for the first-degree relatives of the controls, a group of surgical patients, was only 3 percent. Rosenthal (1970) has summarized the available studies of the incidence of neurosis in the co-twins of neurotic probands. Again, consistent with the theory of genetic transmission, among monozygotic or identical pairs of twins there was a 53 percent concordance or similarity in diagnosis. Among dizygotic or fraternal pairs of twins there was only a 40 percent concordance.

These data do not unequivocally implicate innate factors, however. Although close relatives share genes, they also have considerable opportunity to observe one another. The fact that a son and his father are both afraid of heights may indicate not a genetic component but rather direct modeling of the son's behavior after that of his father. In sum, although there is some reason to believe that genetic factors are involved in the etiology of phobias, there has yet been no clear-cut demonstration of the extent to which they may be important.

Therapies for Phobias

Throughout the book, after reviewing theories about the causes of the various disorders, we will briefly describe the principal therapies for them. The theoretical treatment sections of Chapter 2 were meant to furnish the reader with a context for understanding these discussions of therapy. An in-depth study and evaluation of therapy, however, is reserved for the final section of the book.

[5] Anxiety neurosis is a DSM-II diagnosis that covered both panic attacks and generalized anxiety disorder.

Psychoanalytic approaches

Psychoanalytic treatments of phobias generally attempt to uncover the repressed conflicts that are assumed to underlie the extreme fear and avoidance characteristic of these disorders. Because the phobia itself is regarded as *symptomatic* of underlying conflicts, it is not dealt with directly. Indeed, direct attempts to reduce phobic avoidance are contraindicated because the phobia is assumed to protect the person from repressed conflicts that are too painful to confront. The various techniques that have been developed within the psychoanalytic tradition are used in various combinations to help lift the repression. During free association (see page 46) the analyst listens carefully to what the patient mentions in connection with any references to the phobia. The analyst also attempts to discover in the manifest content of dreams clues to the repressed origins of the phobia. Exactly what the therapist believes these repressed origins to be depends, of course, on the particular psychoanalytic theory held. An orthodox analyst will probably look for sexual conflicts, whereas an analyst holding to Arieti's interpersonal theory will encourage patients to examine their generalized fear of other people.

The contemporary ego analysts, however, focus less on historical insights and encourage the patient to confront the phobia, even though they continue to view it as an outgrowth of an earlier problem. Alexander and French in their classic book, *Psychoanalytic Therapy* (1946), spoke of the "corrective emotional experience" in therapy, by which they meant the patient's confrontation of what is so desperately feared. They observed that "Freud himself came to the conclusion that in the treatment of some cases, phobias for example, a time arrives when the analyst must encourage the patient to engage in those activities he avoided in the past" (p. 39). Wachtel (1977) has even more boldly recommended that analysts employ the fear reduction techniques of behavior therapists, such as systematic desensitization.

Behavioral approaches

The principal behavioral treatment for phobias is systematic desensitization (Wolpe, 1958). The

Identical or monozygotic twins are genetically identical. Fraternal or dizygotic twins are no more alike genetically than siblings and can be either the same or opposite in sex.

phobic individual imagines a series of increasingly frightening scenes while in a state of deep relaxation. Both clinical and experimental evidence indicates that this technique is effective in eliminating or at least reducing phobias (Wilson and O'Leary, 1980). Some behavior therapists have, over the years, come to recognize the importance of exposure to real-life phobic situations, sometimes during the period in which a patient is being desensitized in imagination, sometimes instead of the imagery-based procedure. Thus an agoraphobic might be encouraged to venture forth from his or her home a little farther each day, in hopes that the fear will gradually lessen and extinguish.

Fearful clients who are treated through modeling are exposed to either filmed or live demonstrations of other people interacting fearlessly with the phobic object. _Flooding_ therapy forces exposure to the source of the phobia at full intensity. The extreme discomfort that is an inevitable part of this procedure has tended to discourage therapists from employing it, except perhaps as a last resort.

Behavior therapists who favor operant techniques ignore the fear assumed to underlie phobias and attend instead to the overt avoidance of phobic objects and to the approach behavior that must replace it. They treat approach like any other operant and shape it according to the principle of successive approximation. The real-life exposures to the phobic object are graded, and the client is rewarded for even minimal successes in moving closer to it.

Many behavior therapists attend both to fear and to avoidance, using techniques like desensitization to reduce fear and operant shaping to encourage approach. Lazarus, Davison, and Polefka (1965) first proposed this two-pronged strategy for a school-phobic youngster. At the initial stages of treatment, when fear and avoidance are both very great, the therapist concentrates on reducing the fear through relaxation training and graded exposures to the phobic situation. As therapy progresses, however, fear becomes less of an issue and avoidance more. A phobic individual has often over time settled into an existence in which other people cater to his or her incapacities and thus in a way reinforce the person for having a phobia. As the person's anxieties diminish, he or she is able to approach what used to be terrifying; this overt behavior should be positively reinforced by relatives and friends as well as by the therapist.

Cognitive behavior therapists like Albert Ellis employ rational-emotive therapy with phobias, on the assumption that the phobia is maintained by an irrational belief—such as "If something seems dangerous or fearsome, you must be terribly occupied with and upset about it" (Ellis, 1977, p. 10). The client is taught to dispute the irrational belief whenever encountering the phobic object or situation. But even Ellis, with his strong emphasis on cognitions, encourages clients to approach and confront what they actually fear. His intellectual debates with clients about their irrational beliefs help to goad them into real-life exposures.

All these various therapies for phobias have a recurrent theme, namely the need for the phobic to desist from customary avoidance of the phobic object or situation and to begin facing what has been deemed too fearsome, too terrifying. To be sure, analysts consider the fear to reside in the buried past and therefore delay direct confrontation, but eventually they too encourage it. Thus all these therapies reflect a time-honored bit of folk wisdom, one which tells us that we must face up to what we fear. As an ancient Chinese proverb puts it, "Go straight to the heart of danger, for there you will find safety."

Somatic approaches

Psychoactive drugs, principally _tranquilizers_ like Valium and Librium, are a widely used therapy for phobics. Physicians, whether they be general practitioners or psychiatrists, prescribe them in hopes of enabling their patients to deal more calmly with their fears. Physicians, or psychologists working cooperatively with physicians, may also combine drug treatment with a program of graduated exposure. Tranquilizers are relied on to quiet the patient in much the same way that deep relaxation does in systematic desensitization.

The problem with drug treatment of phobias and other anxiety disorders, however, is that it may be difficult to discontinue. All too often people calmed down by tranquilizers find themselves still fearful when weaned from the drugs; consequently, they tend to rely on them in a dependent fashion for long periods of time. In fact, in their efforts to reduce their anxiety, many phobics and other anxious people use tranquilizers and alcohol on their own. The use and abuse of drugs and alcohol are not uncommon among anxiety-ridden people.

Anxiety States

The anxiety states consist of panic disorder, generalized anxiety disorder, and obsessive-compulsive disorders. In *panic disorder* there is a sudden and inexplicable attack of a host of jarring symptoms—labored breathing, heart palpitations, chest pain, feelings of choking and smothering; dizziness, sweating, and trembling; and intense apprehension, terror, and feelings of impending doom. _Depersonalization_ and _derealization,_ feelings of being outside one's body and of the world's not being real; and fears of losing control, of going crazy, or even of dying may beset and overwhelm the patient. Panic attacks occur frequently, usually last minutes, rarely hours, and are sometimes linked to specific situations, such as driving a car. Unfortunately, little information other than the symptoms of the disorder is available. The other two anxiety states are better understood, however.

Generalized Anxiety Disorder

The individual with generalized anxiety disorder is chronically and persistently anxious in many life situations. So pervasive is this distress that it is sometimes referred to as "free-floating anxiety." Moreover, the person is upset in so many different situations and so much of the time that many psychopathologists have regarded as fruitless any systematic search for specific eliciting causes. Somatic complaints—sweating, flushing, heart pounding, upset stomach, diarrhea, frequent urination, cold, clammy hands, a dry mouth, a lump in the throat—are frequent and reflect hyperactivity of the autonomic nervous system. Pulse and respiration rates too may be high. The person may also report disturbances of the skeletal musculature: muscle tension and aches, especially of the neck and shoulders; eyelid and other twitches; trembling, becoming tired easily, and an inability to relax. He or she is easily startled, fidgety, restless, and sighs often. As for the state of mind, the person is generally apprehensive, often imagining and worrying about impending disasters, such as losing control, having a heart attack, or dying. Impatience, irritability, insomnia, and distractibility are also common, for the person is all "on edge." Easily discouraged, extremely sensitive to criticism, indecisive, and often mildly depressed, these individuals are a considerable trial to themselves and sometimes others, but they usually manage to struggle through their days.

> The patient, a twenty-four-year-old mechanic, had been referred for psychotherapy by his physician, whom he had consulted because of dizziness and difficulties in falling asleep. He was quite visibly distressed during the entire initial interview, gulping before he spoke, sweating, and continually fidgeting in his chair. His repeated requests for water to slake a seemingly unquenchable thirst were another indication of this extreme nervousness. Although he first related his physical concerns, a more general picture of pervasive anxiety soon emerged. He reported that he nearly always felt tense. He was apprehensive of possible disasters that could befall him as he worked and interacted with other people. He reported a long history of difficulties in interpersonal relationships, which had led to his being fired from several jobs. As he put it, "I really like people and try to get along with them, but it seems like I fly off the handle too easily. Little things they do upset me too much. I just can't cope unless everything is going exactly right."

Psychoanalytic view

Psychoanalytic theory regards the source of generalized anxiety as an unconscious conflict between the ego and id impulses. The impulses, usually sexual or aggressive in nature, are struggling for expression, but the ego cannot allow this because it unconsciously fears that punishment will follow. Since the source of the anxiety is unconscious, the person experiences apprehension and distress without knowing why. The true source of anxiety, namely previously punished id impulses which are striving for expression, is ever present. In a sense there is no way to evade anxiety; if the person escapes the id, he is no longer alive. Anxiety is felt nearly all the time. The phobic may be seen as more fortunate since, according to psychoanalytic theory, his or her anxiety is displaced onto a specific object or situation, which can then be avoided. The per-

son with generalized anxiety disorder has not developed this type of defense and thus is constantly anxious.

Learning view

Learning theorists (for example, Wolpe, 1958) attempting to account for generalized anxiety would, by the very nature of their paradigm, reject a concept of "free-floating anxiety." Instead, they look with greater persistence for external causes. For example, a person anxious most of his or her waking hours might well be fearful of social contacts. If that individual spends a good deal of time with other people, it may be more useful to regard the anxiety as tied to these circumstances rather than to any internal factors. This behavioral model of generalized anxiety, then, is identical to one of the learning views of phobias. The anxiety is regarded as having been classically conditioned to external stimuli, although the range of conditioned stimuli is considerably broader.

Cognitive-behavioral views

One cognitive-behavioral model of generalized anxiety focuses on control and helplessness. Mandler (1966) suggests that the feeling of not being in control is a central characteristic of all views of anxiety. According to psychoanalytic theory, the ego is anxious because it is threatened with overstimulation that it cannot control. Learning theory sees people as confronted with painful stimuli over which they have no control until they learn to avoid them. This concept of _helplessness_ had earlier been examined by workers in several disciplines.

Richter (1957), in an article entitled "On the Phenomenon of Sudden Death in Animals and Man," quoted the following anthropological observation from an earlier source.

> A Brazilian Indian condemned and sentenced by a so-called medicine man is helpless against his own emotional response to this pronouncement—and dies within hours. In Africa a young Negro knowingly eats the inviolably banned wild hen. On discovery of his "crime" he trembles, is overcome by fear and dies in twenty-four hours. In New Zealand a Maori

woman eats fruit that she only later learns has come from a taboo place. Her chief has been profaned. By noon the next day she is dead. (Basedow, 1925, cited in Richter, 1957, p. 191).

That such seemingly supernatural events actually occur in primitive societies may be difficult for us to believe. Walter Cannon, a well-known American physiologist of the earlier part of this century, studied reports of such "voodoo" deaths and concluded that they do take place and are worthy of serious scientific study (Cannon, 1942). He drew on his own experimental work on the emotions of rage and fear in cats to propose that a person whose autonomic nervous system is maintained in a highly aroused state, with little opportunity for effective action to re-

duce the tension, may indeed die. Under such tension, Cannon suggested, certain vital bodily organs can be irreparably harmed, and death is actually brought about by severe fright.

Bettelheim's (1960) descriptions of the reactions of certain prisoners to conditions in the Nazi concentration camps indicate another instance in which a feeling of having lost control overcame people.

Prisoners who came to believe the repeated statements of the guards—that there was no hope for them, and that they would never leave the camp except as a corpse—who came to feel that their environment was one over which they could exercise no influence whatever [emphasis added], these prisoners were in a literal sense, walking

Prisoners in Nazi concentration camps experienced an extreme sense of helplessness; many gave up all hope.

corpses. . . . *They were people who were so deprived of affect, self esteem, and every form of stimulation, so totally exhausted, physically and emotionally, that they had given the environment total power over them (pp. 151–152).*

These people, typically well educated, reacted in a helpless and self-defeating manner because they believed that they had no control over their lives.

Experimental psychologists have also been interested in related phenomena. Mowrer and Viek (1948) trained rats to obtain food by making a particular operant response. Then they were all shocked at the feeding place. One group was able to terminate the shock by jumping. Each member of the second group was yoked to, that is paired with, a member of the first so that the amount and duration of shock received by the pair were identical. But the members of the second group were unable to jump in a way that would give them control. The group of rats who had control over shock exhibited less fear than did those animals who were yoked helplessly to a partner.

Thus far we have examined anecdotal accounts of human helplessness and a report of rats rendered helpless by experiment. But rats are not people, and uncontrolled variables make it impossible to know what may really cause voodoo deaths and extreme apathy in prisoners. Fortunately, some experimental work has been done with human beings. Haggard (1943) showed that human subjects who administered electric shocks to themselves were less anxious about the situation than those who received the same amount and intensity of shock but who had no control over its administration. Furthermore, Pervin (1963) found that electric shocks that could be controlled were preferred to those that could not be controlled. Another study has indicated that intellectual performance is superior when the subjects believe that they have control over the order in which they take a series of tests (Neale and Katahn, 1968). And in yet another study, in which human beings received aversive stimulation, Staub, Tursky, and Schwartz (1971) indicated that "The ability to predict and control events in the environment is

important for the comfort and safety of organisms. Consequently . . . lack of control . . . may become intrinsically aversive" (p. 157). In all this experimental work with human beings, stressful events that the subjects could exert some control over were less anxiety-provoking than those over which no control could be exercised.

The work done with both animals and human beings led Geer, Davison, and Gatchel (1970) to ask whether a relevant variable might be the subject's *perception* of control in a situation rather than the actual amount of control exercised. In a baseline test to establish the amount of arousal produced by uncontrolled aversive stimulation, subjects were presented with a series of ten painful electric shocks. The subjects were instructed to press a switch as each shock was administered so that the amount of time it took them to react could be determined. Each shock lasted six seconds and was always preceded by a ready signal. The amount of arousal, as measured by the electrodermal response, was recorded for each shock (Figure 5.2). In the next part of the study, half of the subjects, those who were to perceive themselves in control, were told that the duration of each of the next ten shocks would be cut in half if their reaction time achieved a certain speed. Thus these subjects were led to believe that they could exert control over the next ten shocks. The remaining subjects were simply told that the next ten shocks would be of shorter duration. In actuality, the experimenter arranged for *all* subjects to receive three-second shocks in the second part of the experiment rather than six-second shocks, thus holding constant the actual amount of aversive stimulation.

As expected, during the second part of the experiment, the subjects who assumed that they could control the duration of shocks evidenced significantly less arousal, as measured by the GSR. Believing that they could control the amount of shock—even though they really were not able to do so—made the shocks easier to tolerate.

Within the context of this cognitive-behavioral model, the individual who has not learned effective ways of coping with a variety of challenges will feel helpless and pervasively anxious. Even

People who live through natural disasters such as earthquakes are often anxious for a very long time. The realization that they have no control over such events is probably a factor.

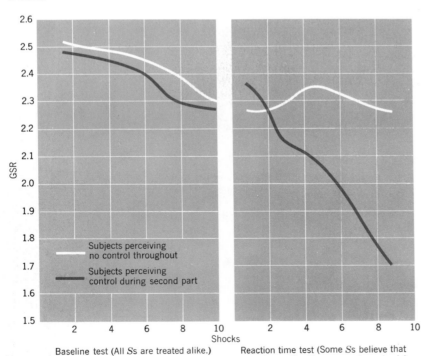

Baseline test (All Ss are treated alike.)

Reaction time test (Some Ss believe that speedy reaction time can reduce shock.)

FIGURE 5.2
Anxiety as a function of whether subjects perceive themselves as capable of shortening the duration of shock. Adapted from Geer, Davison, and Gatchel, 1970.

people who are competent yet *believe* themselves unable to act effectively to control a situation are likely to experience generalized anxiety. The helplessness theory of anxiety also suggests a novel explanation of how anxiety develops. Most theories propose that anxiety is a learned response to certain situations. But perhaps anxiety is instead the inevitable *unlearned* reaction of people to a situation in which they are helpless or believe that they have no control. Later, they may develop a certain amount of control by acquiring behavioral repertoires that allow them to deal with challenging situations. By this process they may *learn* both control and *how not to be anxious*.

Another cognitive theory is worth considering. Albert Ellis has applied his theory concerning irrational beliefs quite specifically to anxious people, proposing that they learn ways of thinking about their world that create anxiety. Consider, for example, two irrational beliefs mentioned earlier. How much anxiety might you create for yourself if you believed that to be a worthwhile person you had to be perfectly competent in everything you do? Or how socially anxious might you be if you considered it essential to be loved or approved of by everyone you meet? Some support for Ellis's theory comes from a study in which a questionnaire, designed to assess a person's degree of endorsement of various irrational beliefs, was administered to neurotics, normal controls, and patients with personality disorders (Newmark et al., 1973). As expected, many more neurotic subjects than others endorsed the irrational beliefs that Ellis has proposed as causing anxiety (Table 5.2).

Humanistic view

A statement on how humanistic workers explain phobias and generalized and other anxiety disorders has not been offered until now because their thinking about all of them is generally the same and not specific. As indicated in Chapter 2, humanists hold human nature to be basically good and beautiful, with psychological problems resulting from a denial of this innate worth. Thus the individual becomes anxious in various ways when his or her basic nature is not expressed. Humanistic psychologists believe that neurotic individuals are particularly preoccupied with two conflicting self-concepts. They have accepted the unfavorable opinion of themselves held by oth-

TABLE **5.2**

Responses to Ellis's Set of Irrational Beliefs by Neurotics, Normal Controls, and Patients with Personality Disorders

(from Newmark et al., 1973)

Irrational belief	Neurotic, percent	Normal, percent	Personality disorder, percent
It is essential that one be loved or approved of by virtually everyone in his community.	65*	2	5
One must be perfectly competent, adequate, and achieving to consider oneself worthwhile.	80	25	30
It is easier to avoid than to face certain life difficulties and responsibilities.	75	29	34
Past experiences and events are the determinants of present behavior; the influence of the past cannot be eradicated.	89	38	45
Some people are bad, wicked, or villainous and therefore should be blamed or punished.	70	40	48

* Entries are percentages of subjects in each group who endorsed the statement. The table shows only the items on which the groups differed substantially.

ers, which interferes with their own more natural, self-enhancing image. Their energy is expended on this conflict rather than on self-actualization.

Genetic studies

Genetic researchers have also examined generalized anxiety disorder. In one study (Slater and Shields, 1969) comparisons were made of seventeen identical pairs of twins and twenty-eight fraternal pairs of twins; one twin of each pair had been diagnosed as having anxiety neurosis. Of the identical co-twins, 49 percent were also diagnosed as having anxiety neurosis. In contrast, only 4 percent of the fraternal co-twins were so diagnosed. Although this pattern of incidence is consistent with genetic transmission, the more crucial adoptee studies, and those of identical twins reared apart, have not been done. Thus we can draw no firm conclusion.

Therapies for generalized anxiety disorder

As might be expected from their view of generalized anxiety disorder, that it stems from repressed conflicts, most psychoanalysts work to help patients confront the true sources of their conflicts. Treatment is much the same as that for phobias.

Behavioral clinicians approach generalized anxiety in various ways. If they can *construe* the anxiety as a set of responses to identifiable situations, the free-floating anxiety can be reformulated into one or more phobias. For example, through situational assessment (see page 99) a behavior therapist may determine that the generally anxious client seems more specifically afraid of criticizing others and of being criticized by them. The anxiety only appears free-floating because the client spends so many hours with other human beings. Systematic desensitization becomes a possible treatment.

If a feeling of helplessness seems to underlie the pervasive anxiety, the therapist will help the client acquire whatever skills might engender a sense of competence, of what Bandura has termed ''self-efficacy'' (1977). The skills may be taught by verbal instructions, modeling, or operant shaping—and very likely some judicious combination of the three (Goldfried and Davison, 1976).

Rational-emotive therapists will bring to their client's attention the self-defeating sentences that

In this group therapy session participants are learning more assertive ways, which they and the therapist hope will allow them to feel less helpless.

they are generating internally, such as "It's a catastrophe that I did not please that person; what a horrible wretch I am"; and their abiding faith in the irrational assumptions behind them, here that they must be loved and approved by everyone. Therapists will help clients identify and dispute their assumptions and encourage them to substitute more realistic statements about the self.

Humanistic treatment of generalized anxiety encourages the person to sense what he or she truly needs and wants at any given time and to develop the trust to express those needs and satisfy those wants. For example, an aim of *Gestalt therapy,* one of the humanistic therapies, is to help the client become aware of moment-to-moment feelings and perceptions. Ingenious exercises are often used to achieve this goal. In the *empty-chair technique* the client is instructed to talk to an important person or to a feeling as though that individual or emotion were sitting in an empty chair nearby. Gestalt therapists believe that by this unusual procedure clients will confront their most basic wants and fears. The increased awareness and insight that follow are assumed to be both necessary and sufficient for the alleviation of a host of psychological problems, including anxiety. Client-centered therapists, following the work of Carl Rogers, provide a warm, nonjudgmental atmosphere in which the client will be better able to come upon his or her innermost feelings.

Tranquilizers, such as those mentioned earlier for the treatment of phobias, are probably the most widespread treatment for generalized anxiety disorder. A psychoactive drug is viewed by medical practitioners as especially appropriate for a disorder defined by its pervasiveness, for the simple reason that, once it takes effect, a drug will continue to work for several hours. Unfortunately, as will be seen in Chapter 20, many tranquilizing drugs have undesirable side effects, ranging from drowsiness and depression to physical addiction and damage to certain bodily organs.

Community psychologists or psychiatrists have yet another approach to generalized anxiety, and to most other psychological disorders. They view human suffering as a normal reaction to abnormal or untenable living conditions. Rather than help the individual cope with or adjust to an environment considered brutalizing, community workers strive for social change. Their work is very different indeed from any discussed so far; much of Chapter 20 is devoted to a close examination of *community psychology.*

Obsessive-Compulsive Disorder

Obsessive-compulsive disorder is one of the rarest behavior disorders. It accounts for less than 5 percent of psychiatric patients and occurs in about 0.05 percent of the general population (Ingram, 1961; Woodruff and Pitts, 1964). The disorder itself usually begins in early adulthood, following some stressful event, although most obsessive-compulsives were highly anxious as children (Kringlen, 1970).

Obsessions are intrusive and recurring thoughts and images which appear irrational and uncontrollable to the individual experiencing them. Whereas many of us may have similar fleeting experiences, the obsessive has them with such force and frequency that they interfere with normal functioning. Cameron (1963) gives an example illustrating the onset of an obsessive thought in a forty-two-year-old mother.

> She was serving the family dinner one evening when she dropped a dish on the table and smashed it. The accident appalled her. While clearing up the fragments she was seized with an unreasonable fear that bits of glass might get into her husband's food and kill him. She would not allow the meal to proceed until she had removed everything and reset the table with fresh linen and clean dishes. After this her fears, instead of subsiding, reached out to include intense anxiety over the possibility that she herself and the children might be killed by bits of glass (p. 384).

A *compulsion* is an irresistible impulse to repeat some ritualistic act over and over again. The activity, however, is not realistically connected with its apparent purpose or is clearly excessive. Lady Macbeth washed her hands continually after the murder of King Duncan. Often an individual who continually repeats some action

The famous "Out damned spot! out, I say!" scene from Macbeth.

fears dire consequences if the act is not performed. The sheer frequency with which an act is repeated may often be staggering. One woman treated by the authors of this book washed her hands over 500 times per day, despite the painful sores that resulted. She reported that she had a very strong fear of contamination by germs and could temporarily alleviate this concern only by washing her hands. Frequently reported compulsions have to do with cleanliness and orderliness, sometimes achieved only by elaborate ceremonies which take hours and even most of the day; with avoiding particular objects, such as staying away from anything brown; with repetitive "magical" protective practices, such as counting, saying particular numbers, touching a talisman or a particular part of the body; and with checking, going back seven or eight times to make certain that already performed acts were actually carried out—lights, gas jets, faucets turned off, windows fastened, doors locked, the silver chest hidden away beneath the guest tablecloths.

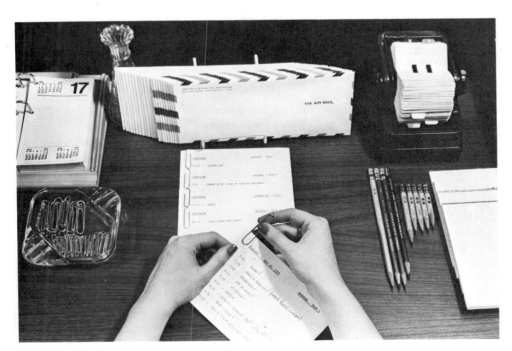

The orderly world of the obsessive-compulsive.

Bernice was forty-six when she entered treatment. This was the fourth time she had been in outpatient therapy, and she had previously been hospitalized twice. Her obsessive-compulsive disorder had begun twelve years ago, shortly after the death of her father. Since then it had waxed and waned and currently was as severe as it had ever been.

Bernice was obsessed with a fear of contamination, a fear she vaguely linked to her father's death from pneumonia. Although she reported that she was afraid of nearly everything, because germs could be anywhere, she was particularly upset by touching wood, "scratchy objects," mail, canned goods, and "silver flecks." By silver flecks Bernice meant silver embossing on a greeting card, eyeglass frames, shiny appliances, and silverware. She was unable to state why these particular objects were special sources of possible contamination.

To try to reduce her discomfort, Bernice engaged in a variety of compulsive rituals which took up almost all her waking hours. In the morning she spent three to four hours in the bathroom, washing and rewashing herself. Between each bath she would have to scrape away the outside layer of her bar of soap so that it would be totally free of germs. Mealtimes also lasted for hours, as Bernice performed her rituals—eating three bites of food at a time, chewing each mouthful three hundred times. These were meant "magically" to decontaminate her food. Even Bernice's husband was sometimes involved in these mealtime ceremonies, and he would shake a teakettle and frozen vegetables over her head to remove the germs. Bernice's rituals and fear of contamination had reduced her life to doing almost nothing else. She would not leave the house, do housework, or even talk on the telephone.

The clinical definition of a compulsion differs somewhat from the way the term is used in common parlance. We hear people described as compulsive gamblers, compulsive eaters, and compulsive drinkers. But even though such individuals may report an irresistible urge to gamble, eat, and drink, such behavior is not clinically regarded as a compulsion because it is often engaged in with pleasure and is not "ego-alien." A true compulsion is viewed by the person as somehow foreign to his or her personality. Stern

and Cobb (1978), for example, found that 78 percent of a sample of compulsives viewed their rituals as either "rather silly" or "absurd."

A frequent consequence of obsessive-compulsive disorder is the negative effect it can have on the individual's relations with other people, especially with members of the family. A person saddled with the irresistible need to wash his hands every ten minutes, or touch every doorknob he passes, or count every tile in a bathroom floor is likely to cause concern and even resentment in a spouse, children, friends, or coworkers. And the antagonistic feelings experienced by these significant others are likely to be tinged with guilt, for at some level they understand that the person cannot really help doing these senseless things. Finally, the undesirable effects on others can, in turn, be expected to have additional consequences, engendering feelings of depression and generalized anxiety in the obsessive-compulsive person and setting the stage for even further deterioration of personal relationships.

The content of obsessions and compulsions has been investigated by Akhter and his colleagues (1975). After interviews with eighty-two obsessive-compulsive patients, five distinguishable forms of obsession and two of compulsion were identified.

Obsessions

1. **Obsessive doubts.** Persistent thoughts that a completed task had not been adequately accomplished were found in 75 percent of the patients. "Each time he left his room a twenty-eight-year-old student began asking himself 'Did I lock the door? Am I sure?' in spite of a clear and accurate remembrance of having done so" (p. 343).

2. **Obsessive thinking.** Seemingly endless chains of thoughts, usually focusing on future events, were reported by 34 percent of those interviewed. A pregnant woman tormented herself with these thoughts: "If my baby is a boy he might aspire to a career that would necessitate his going away from me, but he might want to return to me and what would I do then, because if I . . ." (p. 343).

3. **Obsessive impulses.** Seventeen percent had powerful urges to perform certain actions, ranging from rather trivial whims to grave and assaultive acts. "A forty-one-year-old lawyer was obsessed by what he understood to be the 'nonsensical notion' of drinking from his inkpot but also the serious urge to strangle an apparently beloved only son" (p. 343).

4. **Obsessive fears.** Twenty-six percent were anxious about losing control and doing something that would be socially embarrassing. "A thirty-two-year-old teacher was afraid that in the classroom he would refer to his unsatisfactory sexual relations with his wife, although he had no wish to do so" (p. 344).

5. **Obsessive images.** Persisting images of some recently seen or imagined event plagued 7 percent of the sample. A patient " 'saw' her baby being flushed away in the toilet whenever she entered the bathroom" (p. 344).

Compulsions

1. **Yielding compulsions.** Urges seemingly forced actions on 61 percent of the patients. "A twenty-nine-year-old clerk had an obsessive [notion] that he had an important document in one of his pockets. He knew that this was not true, but found himself impelled to check his pocket, again and again" (p. 344).

2. **Controlling compulsions.** Diverting actions apparently allowed 6 percent of the patients to control an obsessive urge without giving in to it. "A sixteen-year-old boy with incestuous impulses controlled the anxiety these aroused by repeatedly and loudly counting to ten" (p. 344).

Theories of obsessive-compulsive disorder

In **psychoanalytic theory** obsessions and compulsions are viewed as similar, resulting from instinctual forces, primarily aggressive, which are not under control because of overly harsh toilet training. The person is thus fixated at the anal stage. The symptoms observed represent the outcome of the struggle between the id and the defense mechanisms; sometimes the id predominates, sometimes the defense mechanisms. For example, when obsessive thoughts of killing intrude, the forces of the id are dominant. More often, however, the observed symptoms reflect the partially successful operation of one of the defense mechanisms. An individual fixated at the anal stage may by reaction formation resist his urge to soil and become compulsively neat, clean, and orderly. Similarly, in undoing the individual engages in a ritualistic behavior which represents a magical attempt to cancel out the forbidden impulse. Or the ritual may serve as penance, erasing guilt for misdeeds.

Alfred Adler (1931), an early colleague of Freud who broke with the master because he did not agree with Freud's libido theory, viewed obsessive-compulsive disorders within the framework of his theory that pathology results when children are kept from developing a sense of competence by their doting or excessively dominating parents. Saddled with an inferiority complex, people may adopt compulsive rituals in order unconsciously to carve out for themselves a domain in which they exert control and can feel proficient. Adler proposed that the compulsive act allows a person mastery of *something*, even if only the positioning of writing implements on a desk.

Behavioral accounts of obsessions and compulsions (Meyer and Chesser, 1970) consider them learned behavior reinforced by their consequences. One set of consequences is the reduction of fear. For example, compulsive hand washing is viewed as an operant escape-response which reduces an obsessional preoccupation with contamination by dirt or germs. Anxiety as measured by self-report (Hodgson and Rachman, 1972) and psychophysiological responses (Carr, 1971) can indeed be reduced by such compulsive behavior.

Or the consequences may be a more direct but chance reward, as in Skinner's famous demonstration of the acquisition of so-called superstitious behavior in pigeons. The birds were reduced to 75 percent of their normal body weight and then presented with food at regular intervals, whatever their behavior happened to be. In this way and quite by chance, as Skinner described it,

*One bird was conditioned to turn counter-
clockwise about the cage. . . . Another repeatedly thrust its head into one of the upper corners of the cage. A third developed
a "tossing" response, as if placing its head
beneath an invisible bar and lifting it repeatedly (1948, p. 168).*

The implication is that obsessive behavior in human beings is similarly learned through chance
reward.

In a related but more **cognitive view,** Carr
(1974) proposes that obsessive-compulsives,
when in a situation that has a potentially undesirable or harmful outcome, overestimate the
likelihood that the harmful outcome will occur.
In other words, the obsessive-compulsive has an
"If anything can go wrong, it will" view of life.
This cognitive set, according to Carr, necessitates
avoiding the sources of threat and thus increases
the likelihood of obsessive-compulsive behavior.

As plausible as these formulations appear, we
still have much more to learn about the etiology
of obsessive-compulsive disorder.

Therapies for obsessive-compulsive disorder

Psychoanalytic treatment for obsessions and
compulsions resembles that for phobias and generalized anxiety, namely lifting repression and allowing the patient to confront what he or she is
truly afraid of, that a particular impulse will be
gratified. The intrusive thoughts and irresistible
behavior are not appropriate targets for therapeutic change, serving as they do to protect the ego
from the repressed conflict.

In contrast and as before, behavioral treatment
focuses far more directly on the obsessive
thoughts and compulsions themselves. Generally
speaking, behavioral treatment of obsessive
thoughts has concentrated either on reducing the
anxiety assumed to underlie them, in procedures
such as desensitization, or on a technique called
thought stopping. This straightforward procedure
has the client signal to the therapist when an obsessive thought creeps into consciousness, at
which time the therapist shouts "Stop!" Not surprisingly, the client is startled and realizes immediately that this interruption has driven out the
unwanted cognition. The client is then trained to

utter "Stop" subvocally whenever intrusive
thoughts or images invade consciousness. Data
on the efficacy of this technique are meager indeed, however.

Behavior therapy for compulsive rituals usually
entails what is called *response prevention,* dissuading the person from performing the act
whenever the urge arises (Rachman and Hodgson, 1978). Although in the short term such curtailment is very arduous and unpleasant for
clients, the extreme discomfort is believed worth
enduring in order to be rid of these disabling
problems. Clearly, however, conditions must be
such that the client can be persuaded to go
along with the treatment. Sometimes control
over rituals is possible only in a hospital; Victor
Meyer (1966), a renowned behavioral expert in
the treatment of compulsions, has pioneered the
development of a controlled environment at
Middlesex Hospital in London, England. There
staff members have been specially trained to restrict the patient's opportunities for engaging in
ritualistic acts. Generalization of the treatment to
the home requires that family members become
involved. Suffice it to say that preparing them for
this work is no mean task, requiring as it does
skills and care that go beyond whatever specific
behavioral technique is being employed.

The monoamine oxidase inhibitors and the tricyclics, drugs which are more commonly used
in treating depression (see Chapter 8), are sometimes given to obsessive-compulsives. Unfortunately, obsessive-compulsive disorder is overall
one of the most difficult psychological problems
to treat.

Summary

People with anxiety disorders, alternately called anxiety neuroses, feel an overwhelming apprehension that seems unwarranted. DSM-III lists three principal diagnoses: phobic disorders; the anxiety states, which are panic disorder, generalized anxiety disorder, and obsessive-compulsive disorder; and posttraumatic stress disorder. The last diagnosis, about which little is actually known, is applied to the anxiety reactions people experience following catastrophes and traumatic events, such as a natural disaster or a rape.

Phobias are intense, unreasonable fears that disrupt the life of an otherwise normal person. They are relatively common. Agoraphobia is fear of being outside one's home and in open, unfamiliar surroundings; social phobia is fear of social situations in which one may be scrutinized by other people. Other simple phobias are fears of animals, of closed-in spaces, and of heights. The psychoanalytic view of phobias is that they are a defense against repressed conflicts. Behavioral theorists have several ideas of how phobias are acquired—through classical conditioning, the pairing of an innocuous object or situation with an innately painful event; operant conditioning, whereby a person is rewarded for continuing avoidance; and modeling, imitating the fear and avoidance of others. But not all people who have such learning experiences develop a phobia. Perhaps a physiological diathesis, lability of the autonomic nervous system, predisposes certain people to acquire phobias. None of these theories enjoys strong empirical support.

A patient suffering from panic disorder has sudden inexplicable and periodic attacks of intense anxiety. In generalized anxiety disorder, sometimes called ''free-floating anxiety,'' the individual's life is beset with virtually constant tension and apprehension. Psychoanalytic theory regards the source as an unconscious conflict between the ego and id impulses. Behavioral theorists assume that, with adequate assessment, this pervasive anxiety can be pinned down to a finite set of anxiety-provoking circumstances, thereby likening it to a group of phobias. A sense of helplessness or irrational beliefs can also cause people to be anxious in a wide range of situations. Humanistic theorists find that people go into anxiety states when they accept the unfavorable opinions others hold of them and do not express their basic self-worth.

Obsessive-compulsive problems are the final anxiety disorder. People with this diagnosis have intrusive, ego-alien thoughts and feel pressured to engage in stereotyped rituals lest they be overcome by frightening levels of anxiety. This disorder can become quite disabling, interfering not only with the life of the unfortunate who experiences the difficulties but also with the lives of those close to the person. Psychoanalytic theory posits strong id impulses that are under faulty and inadequate ego control. In behavioral accounts obsessions and compulsions are considered learned avoidance responses.

There are many therapies for the anxiety disorders. Psychoanalytic treatment tries to lift repression so that childhood conflicts can be resolved; direct alleviation of the manifest problems is discouraged. In contrast, behavior therapists employ a range of procedures, such as systematic desensitization and modeling, designed to reduce the fear and avoidance. Dissuading compulsives from their rituals is an apparently effective although initially arduous technique. Rational-emotive therapy attempts to substitute more realistic self-statements for irrational beliefs. Humanistic therapies help the person discover his or her denied needs and wants and assume responsibility for satisfying them.

Perhaps the most widely employed treatments are tranquilizing drugs, dispensed by medical practitioners. Drugs, however, are subject to abuse, and their long-term use may have untoward and still inadequately understood side effects. Weaning a person from reliance on a chemical that reduces anxiety is also a problem.

chapter 6

C omplaints of bodily symptoms that suggest a physical defect, some rather dramatic in nature, but for which no physiological basis can be found, are now diagnosed as *somatoform disorders.* In DSM-II these problems were called hysterical conversion neurosis and hypochondriacal neurosis. *Dissociative disorders* are rarer, even more dramatic disruptions of consciousness, memory, and identity. The DSM-II designation for them was hysterical dissociative neurosis. The somatoform and dissociative disorders seem to serve some purpose or need of those who suffer them.

Somatoform Disorders

T he physical symptoms of somatoform disorders, which have no known physiological explanation, are assumed to be linked to sometimes rather discernible psychological factors. Two major forms of somatoform disorders are distinguished, *conversion disorder* and *somatization disorder,* sometimes called *Briquet's syndrome.* DSM-III proposes two other somatoform disorders, about which little information is available. In *psychogenic pain disorder* the person reports severe, long-lasting pain that cannot be accounted for by organic pathology, even after extensive investigation. The pain may have a temporal relation to some conflict or stress, or it may allow the individual to avoid some hated activity and to secure attention and sympathy not otherwise available. In *hypochondriasis,* which was called hypochondriacal neurosis in DSM-II, the person is preoccupied with fears of having a serious disease. He or she overracts to ordinary physical sensations and minor abnormalities—such as irregular heartbeat, sweating, occasional coughing, a sore spot, stomachache—as evidence for this belief and cannot be medically persuaded otherwise. Hypochondriasis is not very well differentiated from somatization disorder.

Conversion Disorder

In conversion disorders the operations of the musculature or sensory functions are impaired, although the bodily organs themselves are sound. We find reports of partial or complete paralyses of arms or legs; anesthesias (Figure 6.1), the loss or impairment of sensations; anal-gesias, insensitivity to pain, all occurring in physiologically normal people. Vision may be seriously disturbed: the person may become partially or completely blind or have "tunnel vision," wherein the visual field is constricted as it would be were the observer peering through a tunnel.

Conversion symptoms by their very nature suggest that they, like psychogenic pain, are linked to psychological factors. They usually appear suddenly in stressful situations, allow patients to avoid some activity or responsibility, or secure them badly wanted attention. The term "conversion" originally derived from Freud, who thought that the energy of a repressed instinct is diverted into sensory-motor channels and blocks functioning. Thus anxiety and psychological conflict were believed to be *converted* into physical symptoms. Some of the people suffering conversion disorders may in fact seem complacent, even serene, and not particularly eager to part with their symptoms. Nor do they connect them with whatever straits they may be in.

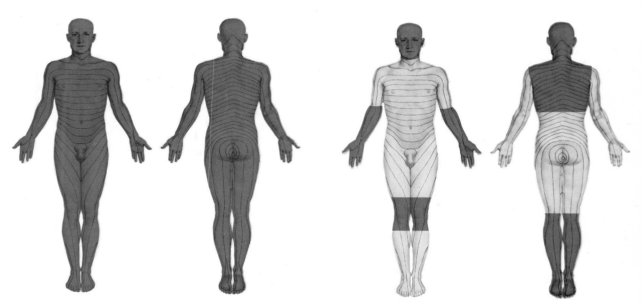

FIGURE 6.1
Hysterical anesthesias can be distinguished from neurological dysfunctions. On the left are shown the patterns of neural innervation of the skin. On the right are superimposed typical areas of anesthesias in hysterical patients. The hysterical anesthesias do not make anatomical sense. (Adapted from an original painting by Frank H. Netter, M.D. From *The CIBA Collection of Medical Illustrations,* copyright by CIBA Pharmaceutical Company, Division of CIBA-GEIGY Corporation.)

Hysteria, the earlier term for such reactions, has of course a long history dating back to the earliest writings on abnormal behavior. Hippocrates considered it an affliction limited solely to women and brought on by the wandering of the uterus through the body. The Greek word *hystera* means womb. Presumably the wandering uterus symbolized the longing of the body for the production of a child. Freud considered the specific nature of the hysterical symptom to relate either to the repressed instinctual urge or to its repressing counterforce, representing them in disguised form. A hysterical convulsion might be the symbolic expression of a forbidden sexual wish, a hysterical paralysis the manifestation of self-punishment for a hidden aggressive urge. The consensus among writers is that conversion disorders are found primarily in females. During both world wars, however, a large number of males also developed conversionlike difficulties in combat (Ziegler, Imboden, and Meyer, 1960).

Diagnostic problems

Diagnostically, it is important to distinguish a conversion paralysis or sensory dysfunction from similar problems that have a true neurological basis. Sometimes this is an easy task, as when the paralysis does not make anatomical sense. But in other cases the diagnostic decision is more difficult and may require special procedures. A case in point was described by Theodor and Mandelcorn (1973). The patient, a sixteen-year-old, had experienced a sudden loss of peripheral vision, reporting that her visual field had become tubular and constricted. Although a number of neurological tests had proved negative, the authors wanted to be even more certain that they were not dealing with a neurological problem. So they arranged a special visual test in which a bright, oval target was presented either in the center or in the periphery of the patient's visual field. On each trial there were two time intervals which were bounded by the sounding of a buzzer. The target was illuminated during one of the intervals, and the young woman's task was to report which one.

When the target was presented in the center of the visual field, the patient always correctly identified the time interval during which it was illuminated. This had been expected since she

had not reported any loss of central vision. What happened when the oval was presented peripherally? The patient could be expected to be correct 50 percent of the time by chance alone; the authors reasoned that this would be the outcome if she were truly "blind" in peripheral vision. For the peripheral showings of the target, however, the young woman was correct only 30 percent of the time. She had performed significantly more poorly than would a person who was indeed blind! The clinicians reasoned that she must have been in some sense aware of the illuminated stimulus, and that she wanted, either consciously or unconsciously, to preserve her "blindness" by performing poorly on the test.

A second diagnostic problem with conversion disorders is differentiating them from *malingering,* which is faking an incapacity in order to avoid a responsibility. In trying to discriminate conversion reactions from malingering, clinicians may attempt to decide whether the symptoms have been consciously or unconsciously adopted.[1] This means of resolving the issue is at best a dubious one, for it is difficult if not impossible to know with any degree of certainty whether behavior is consciously or unconsciously motivated. One aspect of behavior is sometimes revealing, however, *la belle indifférence*—a relative lack of concern, the adoption of a blasé attitude toward the symptoms out of keeping with their severity and supposedly long-term consequences. But these patients also appear willing and eager to talk endlessly and dramatically about them. In contrast, the malingerer is likely to be more guarded and cautious, perhaps because he or she considers interviews a challenge or threat to the success of the lie. But this distinction is not foolproof, for only about one-third of people with conversion disorders show *la belle indifférence* (Stephens and Kamp, 1962).

---

[1] Two DSM-III diagnoses, *malingering* and *factitious disorders,* should also be mentioned. Both are applied to people whose conversionlike symptoms or psychological symptoms are under voluntary control. In malingering the symptoms are obviously linked to a recognizable goal, the altering of the individual's circumstances. An example would be a claim of physical illness to avoid standing trial. In a factitious disorder the motivation for adopting the physical or psychological symptoms is much less clear. Apparently the individual wants to assume the role of "patient," for some unknown reason.

Misdiagnosis of conversion disorder

Since the majority of paralyses, analgesias, and sensory failures do have organic causes, true neurological problems may sometimes be misdiagnosed as conversion disorders. Slater and Glithero (1965) have investigated this disturbing possibility. Their study was a follow-up of patients who nine years earlier had been diagnosed as suffering from conversion symptoms. An alarming number, in fact 60 percent, of these individuals had either died in the meantime or developed symptoms of physical disease! A high proportion had diseases of the central nervous system. Similarly, Whitlock (1967) compared the incidence of organic disorders in patients earlier diagnosed as having conversion disorders and in patients earlier diagnosed as having depressive reactions, anxiety reactions, or both. Organic disorders were found in 62.5 percent of the patients earlier diagnosed as having conversion disorders and in only 5.3 percent of the other groups. The most common organic problem was head injury, generally found to have occurred about six months before the onset of the conversion symptoms. Other common organic problems were stroke, encephalitis, and brain tumor. Finally, Watson and Buranen (1979) found that 25 percent of patients whose symptoms had been considered conversion reactions actually had physical disorders.

From these data we can see that some symptoms labeled as conversion reactions and thought to have psychological causes may, in fact, be physical disorders. We have already learned that the assessment of organic problems is still rather crude. Therefore it is not always possible to distinguish between psychologically and organically produced symptoms. The diagnosis of conversion disorder may be applied too frequently; some individuals diagnosed in this way may have an organic problem that has gone undetected. The damage that such inappropriate diagnoses can do is sobering to contemplate.

Somatization Disorder (Briquet's Syndrome)

In 1859 the French physician Pierre Briquet described a syndrome which has since borne his name and now in DSM-III is referred to as somatization disorder. Recurrent, multiple somatic complaints for which medical attention is sought but which have no apparent physical cause are the basis of this diagnosis. Common complaints include headaches, fatigue, allergies, abdominal, back, and chest pains, genitourinary symptoms, and palpitations. Conversion symptoms may also be present. Visits to physicians, sometimes to a number of them simultaneously, are frequent, as is the use of medication. Hospitalization and even surgery are common (Guze, 1967). Patients are given to histrionics, presenting their complaints in a dramatic, exaggerated fashion or as part of a long and complicated medical history. Many believe that they have been ailing all their lives.

The colloquial term for these problems is hypochondria, but DSM-III draws a distinction be-

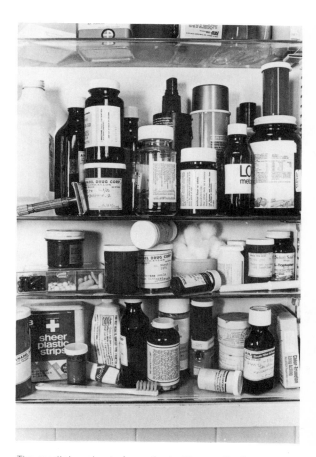

The medicine chest of a patient with somatization disorder.

tween hypochondriasis and somatization disorder. In the first the patient is preoccupied with the fear of having a specific and serious physical disease, whereas in the second the patient's concern is with the many symptoms themselves. As noted at the beginning of this chapter, such a distinction appears to be of dubious value. Table 6.1 gives a picture of the pervasiveness of health problems reported by people with Briquet's syndrome.

Somatization disorder typically begins in late adolescence and is more common in women than in men (Kroll et al., 1979). Anxiety and depression are frequently reported, as are a host of behavioral and interpersonal problems, such as truancy, poor work records, and marital difficulties. Somatization disorders also seem to run in families; they are found in about 20 percent of the first-degree relatives of index cases (Arkonac and Guze, 1963). The following case indictes one woman's complaints.

Alice was referred to the psychological clinic by her physician, Joyce Williams. Dr. Williams had been Alice's physician for about six months and in that time period had seen her twenty-three times. Alice had dwelt on a number of rather vague complaints—general aches and pains, bouts of nausea, tiredness, irregular menstruation, and dizziness. But various tests—complete blood workups, X-rays, spinal tap, and so on—had not revealed any pathology.

Upon meeting her therapist, Alice immediately let him know that she was a somewhat reluctant client: "I'm here only because I trust Dr. Williams and she urged me to come. I'm physically sick and don't see how a psychologist is going to help." But when Alice was asked to describe the history of her physical problems, she quickly warmed to the task. According to Alice, she had always been sick. As a child she had had episodes of high fever, frequent respiratory infections, convulsions, and her first two operations, appendectomy and tonsillectomy. As she continued her somewhat loosely organized chronological account of her medical history, Alice's descriptions of her problems became more and more colorful (and probably exaggerated as well): "Yes, when I was in my early twenties I had some problems with vomiting. For weeks at a time I'd vomit up everything I ate. I'd even vomit up liquids, even water. Just

the sight of food would make me vomit. The smell of food cooking was absolutely unbearable. I must have been vomiting every ten minutes."

During her twenties Alice had gone from one physician to another. She saw several gynecologists for her menstrual irregularity and dyspareunia (pain during intercourse) and had dilatation and curettage (scraping the lining of the uterus). She had been referred to neurologists for her headaches, dizziness, and fainting spells, and they had performed EEGs, spinal taps, and even a CAT scan, a highly sophisticated and very expensive procedure for studying bodily and brain structures. Other physicians had ordered X-rays to look for the possible causes of her abdominal pain and EKGs for her chest pains. Both rectal and gallbladder surgery had also been performed.

When the interview finally shifted away from Alice's medical history, it became apparent that she was a highly anxious person in many situations, particularly those in which she thought she might be evaluated by other people. Indeed, some of her physical complaints could be regarded as consequences of anxiety. Furthermore, her marriage was quite shaky, and she and her husband were considering divorce. Their marital problems seemed to be linked to sexual difficulties stemming from Alice's dyspareunia and her general indifference toward sex.

Theories of Somatoform Disorders[2]

According to classical **psychoanalytic theory,** conversion disorders are rooted in an early, unresolved Electra complex. The young female child becomes incestuously attached to her father, but these early impulses are repressed, producing both a preoccupation with sex and, at the same time, an avoidance of it. At a later period of her life, sexual excitement or some happenstance reawakens these repressed impulses, at which time they are transformed or converted into physical symptoms that represent in distorted

[2] Much of the theorizing in this area has been directed toward hysteria and thus assumes that conversion disorder and somatization disorder are similar etiologically. Although this assumption is unsupported, we have little choice but to present the theories as they exist.

TABLE 6.1
Various Symptoms and Their
Frequency as Reported by a Sample of
Patients with Briquet's Syndrome

(after Perley and Guze, 1962)

Symptom	Percent reporting	Symptom	Percent reporting	Symptom	Percent reporting
Dyspnea (labored breathing)	72	Weight loss	28	Back pain	88
Palpitation	60	Sudden fluctuations in weight	16	Joint pain	84
Chest pain	72	Anorexia	60	Extremity pain	84
Dizziness	84	Nausea	80	Burning pains in rectum, vagina, mouth	28
Headache	80	Vomiting	32		
Anxiety attacks	64	Abdominal pain	80	Other bodily pain	36
Fatigue	84	Abdominal bloating	68	Depressed feelings	64
Blindness	20	Food intolerances	48	Phobias	48
Paralysis	12	Diarrhea	20	Vomiting all nine months of pregnancy	20
Anesthesia	32	Constipation	64		
Aphonia (loss of voice above a whisper)	44	Dysuria (painful urination)	44	Nervous	92
		Urinary retention	8	Had to quit working because felt bad	44
Lump in throat	28	Dysmenorrhea (painful menstruation, premarital only)	4		
Fits or convulsions	20			Trouble doing anything because felt bad	72
Faints	56	Dysmenorrhea (prepregnancy only)	8		
Unconsciousness	16			Cried a lot	60
Amnesia	8	Dysmenorrhea (other)	48	Felt life was hopeless	28
Visual blurring	64	Menstrual irregularity	48	Always sickly (most of life)	40
Visual hallucination	12	Excessive menstrual bleeding	48	Thought of dying	48
Deafness	4	Sexual indifference	44	Wanted to die	36
Olfactory hallucination	16	Frigidity (absence of orgasm)	24	Thought of suicide	28
Weakness	84	Dyspareunia (painful sexual intercourse)	52	Attempted suicide	12

form the repressed libidinal urges or the repressing forces. Modern psychoanalytic theorists, however, do not all agree that conversion disorders stem from the Electra complex. Some (for example, Sperling, 1973) see the problem originating much earlier, during the oral period.

A contemporary psychodynamic interpretation of one form of somatoform disorder, hysterical blindness, has been offered by Sackheim, Nordlie, and Gur (1979). The starting point of their analysis is experimental studies of hysterically blind people whose behavior on visual tests shows that they are being influenced by the stimuli, even though they explicitly deny seeing them. In Theodor and Mendelcorn's case report (1973) the young woman claiming peripheral blindness did more poorly on a visual task than the 50 percent score she could have achieved by chance. Grosz and Zimmerman (1970), on the other hand, observed almost perfect visual performance by a hysterically blind person. Sackheim and his colleagues argue that a two-stage defensive reaction can account for the data. First, perceptual representations of visual stimuli are blocked from awareness, and on this basis people report themselves blind. Second, information is still extracted from the perceptual representations. If subjects feel that they must deny being privy to this information, they do more poorly than they would do by chance on perceptual tasks. If subjects do not need to deny to themselves having such information, they perform the task well but still maintain that they are blind. Whether hysterically blind people unconsciously need to deny receiving perceptual information is viewed as being dependent on personality factors and motivation.

Are the people who claim that they are blind and yet on another level respond to visual stimuli being truthful? Sackheim and his colleagues report that some patients with lesions in the visual cortex say that they are blind and yet perform well on visual tasks. So it is possible for people to claim truthfully that they cannot see and at the same time give evidence that they can. On a more general level, a dissociation between awareness and behavior has been reported in many perceptual and cognitive studies (see Box 6.1). To test their assumption that motivation has bearing, Sackheim and his colleagues hypnotized two susceptible subjects, gave each a suggestion of total blindness, and then tested them on a visual discrimination task. One was given instructions designed to motivate her to maintain her blindness. She was expected to deny her perceptions and perform more poorly than chance on the visual task. The other subject was not so explicitly urged to maintain her blindness and was expected to do better than chance on the task. A third subject was asked to simulate the behavior of someone who had been hypnotized and given a suggestion of total blindness.

The results agreed with the predictions. The subject highly motivated to maintain blindness indeed performed more poorly than chance, and the less motivated subject performed perfectly, even though still reporting that she was blind. The simulator performed, for the most part, at a chance level. In a postexperimental interview she stated that she had deliberately tried to simulate chance performance. As Sackheim and his colleagues have proposed, verbal reports and behavior can apparently be unconsciously separated from one another. Hysterically blind persons will say that they cannot see and yet at the same time be influenced by visual stimuli. And the way in which they show signs of being able to see may depend on how much they need to be considered blind.

Sociocultural theories are based on the supposed decrease in conversion disorders over the last century. Although Charcot and Freud seemed to have had an abundance of female patients with this sort of difficulty, contemporary clinicians rarely see anyone with such problems. A number of hypotheses have been proposed to explain this apparent decrease. For example, those of a psychoanalytic bent point out that in the second half of the nineteenth century, when the incidence of conversion reactions was apparently high in France and Austria, sexual attitudes were quite repressive and may have contributed to the increased incidence of the disorder. The decline of the conversion reaction, then, is attributed to a general relaxing of sexual mores and also to the greater psychological and medical sophistication of twentieth-century culture, which is more tolerant of anxiety than it is of dysfunctions that do not make physiological sense.

A study by Proctor (1958) is often cited as providing evidence for this theory. The incidence of conversion reaction was found to be particularly high among children who were patients at the University of North Carolina Medical School Psychiatric Clinic. In interpreting this very high incidence, 13 percent, the author noted that most of the children came from rural areas where the socioeconomic status of the inhabitants was low and little education was provided for them. Moreover, the religious background of these people was generally strong and fundamentalist. The mid-twentieth-century conditions in this area of North Carolina may have approximated in some respects those prevailing in nineteenth-century France and Austria.

Ironically, *there is in fact little evidence that the incidence of conversion disorders is decreasing.* For example, Stephens and Kamp (1962) compared the outpatient diagnoses of two periods, the first from 1913 to 1919 and the second from 1945 to 1960. In both they found the incidence of conversion reaction to be 2 per-

BOX 6.1 Awareness, the Unconscious, and Behavior

In recent years research in cognition and perception has demonstrated that people's behavior can be influenced by stimuli of which they are unaware. Let us first provide some examples. In studying selective attention, researchers often use a dichotic-listening task in which separate tapes are played to each ear; subjects are asked to attend to only one of them. Subjects usually report that they know very little about the sounds coming into the unattended ear. But these unattended stimuli can affect behavior. For example, Wilson (1975) had people listen to a human voice while tone sequences were played in the unattended ear. Subjects reported having heard no tones. Furthermore, in a memory task in

Subject being given a dichotic-listening task. Different tapes are played simultaneously to the left and right ears; the woman attends only to what is coming in one ear.

which they listened to tone sequences played earlier and others that had not been played, the subjects were unable to distinguish between the two types. Despite this demonstration that the subjects did not recognize tone stimuli played previously, another measure had a startling result. It is known that familiarity affects judgments of tone stimuli similar to those Wilson used. Familiar sequences are liked better than novel ones. When subjects in Wilson's study were asked to rate the degree to which they liked a series of tone sequences, the ones that had been presented earlier to their unattended ears were preferred to novel sequences. Some aspects of the tone sequences played during the dichotic-listening task must have been absorbed, even though subjects said that they did not hear them and demonstrated thay they did not recognize them.

A series of studies reported by Nisbett and Wilson (1977) also indicate that awareness, as measured by verbal report, is not a very accurate indication of the effect stimuli have on behavior. In one of their studies Nisbett and Wilson first had subjects memorize a list of word pairs. For some subjects the pairs of words were specially constructed so that they would be likely to have an effect on subjects' performances in a second part of the study. For example, one of the word pairs these subjects first memorized was "ocean-moon." This pair was expected to make them more likely to respond "Tide" when they were later asked to name a detergent. The results agreed with expectation: subjects who had memorized the special word pairs gave double the number of expected associations as subjects who had not memorized them. Right after the second part of the test, subjects were asked why they had given their particular responses. Even though they could still recall the word pairs, subjects almost never mentioned them as bringing their responses to mind. Instead they gave reasons such as "My mother uses Tide," or "Tide is the most popular detergent."

The studies just reviewed, which are but a small sampling of current research making a similar point, are closely related to the psychoanalytic concept of the unconscious. Contemporary investigators have begun to corroborate Freud's view that much of human behavior is determined by unconscious processes. But the unconscious processes are understood in a different way. Freud postulated the existence of "the" unconscious, a repository of instinctual energy and repressed conflicts and impulses. Contemporary researchers reject the repression and energy reservoir, holding more simply that we are not aware of everything going on around us and of some of our cognitive processes. At the same time, these stimuli and processes of which we are unaware can affect behavior powerfully. This recent research suggests that understanding the causes of human behavior will be a difficult task. It will not be sufficient merely to ask someone "Why did you do that?"

cent. We can also find reasons that explain away the seemingly high incidence of conversion disorders found in the nineteenth century. The large numbers seen by clinicians such as Charcot and Freud may have reflected a selective process. Patients with these particular difficulties may have come to these clinicians because they were known to be successful in treating hysterias. Similarly, the high incidence of conversion reactions reported by Proctor may reflect not a "true" high incidence but rather differences in diagnostic practices. In view of the difficulties in assessing incidence at different periods of time, it would seem ill-advised to use alleged changes in frequency of occurrence as validation for an etiological theory of a disorder.

A **behavioral account** of the development of conversion disorders has been proposed by Ullmann and Krasner (1975). In their opinion the person with a conversion reaction attempts to behave according to his or her own conception of how a person with a disease affecting the motor or sensory abilities would act. This theory raises two questions. Are people capable of such behavior? Under what conditions might such behavior be most likely to occur?

Considerable evidence supports an affirmative answer to the first question, that people can adopt patterns of behavior that match many of the classic conversion symptoms. For example, paralyses and analgesias, and blindness as we have seen, can be induced in people under hypnosis. Similarly, chemically inert drugs called placeboes have reduced the pain of patients who had been considered truly ill. As a partial answer to the second question, Ullmann and Krasner specify two conditions that increase the likelihood that motor and sensory disabilities will be imitated. First, the individual must have some experience with the role to be adopted. He or she may have had similar physical problems or may have observed them in others. Second, Ullman and Krasner note that the enactment of a role must be rewarded. An individual will assume a disability only if it can be expected either to reduce stress or to reap other positive consequences. For Ullmann and Krasner conversion disorders are the same as malingering in that the person adopts the symptom to gain some end.

Ullmann and Krasner describe the case of a veteran originally reported by Brady and Lind (1961). Two of the patient's aunts had been totally blind during their last years. While in the army the patient had developed an infection in one of his eyes, which scarred the cornea and had greatly reduced visual acuity. Thereafter he was given a medical discharge from the army and a small pension. During the twelve years following his discharge, he held a series of semiskilled jobs, remaining at none more than a year. He returned three times to the hospital with recurrences of his eye infection. Each time after returning to the hospital he applied for a larger pension, but he was refused because there had been no additional loss of vision.

Twelve years after his discharge, while shopping with his wife and mother-in-law, he suddenly "became blind" in both eyes. At this time, the authors state, "His wife and mother-in-law were being more demanding than usual, requiring him to work nights and weekends at various chores under their foremanship. One immediate

consequence of his blindness was, then, partial escape from this situation." During the next two years the patient received various treatments and was enrolled in a course of training for the blind. In addition, he was awarded a special pension for his total disability and received financial assistance from the community for his children and some money from his relatives. Ullmann and Krasner's contention that conversion disorders may develop when the role that is to be adopted is known and rewards are to be expected is plausible; yet, except for case studies like this one reported by Brady and Lind, their theory has not been substantiated.

Another behavioral view of somatoform disorders, at least of Briquet's syndrome, holds that the various aches and pains, discomforts and dysfunctions are unrealistic anxiety manifesting itself in particular bodily systems. Perhaps the extreme tension of an individual localizes in his stomach muscles, and he feels nauseous and even vomits. Once normal functioning is disrupted, the maladaptive pattern may strengthen because of the attention it receives or the excuses it provides.

Genetic and physiological factors have been suggested as playing some role in the development of conversion disorders. Slater (1961) investigated concordance rates in twelve identical and twelve fraternal pairs of twins. Probands of each pair had been diagnosed as having the disorder, but none of the co-twins in either of the two groups manifested a conversion reaction. Similarly, Gottesman (1962) found the reactions of identical twins to statements on the hysteria scale of the MMPI to be no more similar than those of fraternal twins. Genetic factors, then, from the studies done so far, seem to be of no importance.

An intriguing case study suggests the neurophysiological mechanisms by which a conversion disorder involving a sensory system might be produced (Hernández-Peón, Chávez-Ibarra, and Aguilar-Figueroa, 1963). A fifteen-year-old patient had an analgesia in her left arm. To determine the basis of her affliction, the investigators recorded electrical activity of the brain while her arms were pricked by a pin. The usual pattern of cortical responses was found for the right arm, but no brain response was detected when the left analgesic arm was pricked. These results, consistent with clinical reports, suggest that sensory input to the left arm was being inhibited. Other research has demonstrated that neural pathways descending from the cortex can exert an inhibitory influence on incoming sensory pathways. That is, certain messages from the brain can block out or inhibit the impulses traveling along incoming sensory nerve fibers. An increase in the activity of these descending inhibitory pathways, then, may be a mechanism by which sensations are altered in conversion disorders. But the possibility that neural pathways are implicated in conversion disorders need not mean that the explanation for them is somatogenic rather than psychogenic, for the increased activity of these descending pathways would still have to be accounted for in some manner.

A hint of a similar neurophysiological explanation of why emotions connected with conversion disorders remain unavailable to conscious awareness comes from studies showing that conversion symptoms are more likely to occur on the left side of the body than on the right (Galin, Diamond, and Braff, 1977; Stern, 1977). In most instances these left-side body functions are controlled by the right hemisphere of the brain. Thus the majority of conversion symptoms may be related to the functioning of the right hemisphere. Research on patients who have had the hemispheres of their brains surgically disconnected to prevent the spread of epileptic seizures has shown that the right hemisphere can separately generate emotions, and indeed it is suspected of generating more of them than does the left hemisphere. Conversion symptoms would in this way be neurophysiologically linked to emotional arousal. Furthermore, this same research indicates that the right hemisphere depends on the neural passageways of the corpus callosum (see page 714) for connection with the left hemisphere's verbal capacity to describe and explain emotions and by these means to gain awareness of them. In conversion disorders it may be that the left hemisphere somehow blocks impulses carrying painful emotional content from the right hemisphere. Thus individuals with a conversion disorder make no connection between it and

their troubling circumstances or their emotional needs. This is an intriguing bit of speculation.

Therapy for Somatoform Disorders

Psychoanalysis of course has a special connection to somatoform disorders, inasmuch as many of Freud's patients were women who suffered from these phenomena. The "talking cure" that psychoanalysis developed into was based on the assumption that a massive repression had forced psychic energy to be transformed or converted into puzzling anesthesias or paralyses. The catharsis of the patient as she faced up to the infantile origins of the repression was assumed to help, and even today free association and other efforts to lift repression are a common approach.

Behavior therapists have applied to somatoform disorders a wide range of techniques intended either to make it worthwhile for the patient to give up the symptoms or to reduce the anxiety assumed to be causing the disorder. A case reported by Liebson (1967) is an example of the first tack. A man had relinquished his job because of pain and weakness in the legs and attacks of giddiness. Liebson helped the patient return to full-time work by persuading his family to refrain from reinforcing him for his idleness and by arranging for the man to receive a pay increase if he succeeded in getting himself to work. A reinforcement approach, then, attempts to provide the patient with greater incentives to get better than to remain incapacitated. An important consideration with any such operant tactic, as noted by Walen, Hauserman, and Lavin (1977), is to make it possible for the patient not to lose face when parting with the disorder; that is, the therapist should appreciate the possibility that the patient will feel humiliated at becoming better through treatment that does not deal with the "medical" problem.

Behavioral clinicians consider the high levels of anxiety that they associate with somatization disorder, or Briquet's syndrome, to be linked to certain situations. Alice, the woman described earlier, revealed herself to be extremely anxious about her shaky marriage and about situations in which other people might judge her. Techniques like systematic desensitization or any of the cognitive therapies could be addressed to her fears. But it is likely that more treatment would be needed, for a person who has been "sick" for a period of time has grown accustomed to weakness and dependency, to avoiding everyday challenges rather than facing them as an adult. Assertion training and _social-skills training_— coaching Alice in effective ways to approach and talk to people, to keep eye contact, give compliments, accept criticism, make requests— could be useful in helping her acquire, or reacquire, means of relating to others and meeting her needs that do not begin with the premise "I am a poor, weak, sick, person." Because somatoform disorders are rarer than other problems people take to mental health professionals, no true research has been done on the relative efficacy of different treatments. Case reports and clinical speculation are, for now, the only sources of information on how to help people with these puzzling disruptions in bodily functioning.

Dissociative Disorders

DSM-III distinguishes among three major dissociative disorders—_psychogenic amnesia_, _psychogenic fugue_, and _multiple personality_—in all of which there is "a sudden, temporary alteration in the normally integrative functions of consciousness, identity, or motor behavior" (p. 253). Important personal events cannot be recalled, or customary identity is temporarily lost. The individual may even wander far from his or her usual surroundings. _Depersonalization disorder_, in which the person's perception or experience of the self is disconcertingly and disruptively altered,[3] is also described as a dissociation disorder. But its inclusion is recognized as controversial because there is no disturbance of memory.

In **psychogenic amnesia** the person suddenly becomes unable to recall important personal information, usually after some stressful episode. Most often the memory loss is for all events during a limited period of time following some traumatic experience, such as witnessing the death of a loved one. More rarely the amnesia is for only selected events during some period of time or is total, covering the person's entire life. During the period of amnesia, the person's behavior is otherwise unremarkable, except that the memory loss may bring some disorientation, perplexity, and purposeless wandering. With total amnesia the patient will not recognize relatives and friends, but he or she will retain the ability to talk, read, and reason and perhaps his or her talents and whatever knowledge of the world and how to function in it had previously been acquired. The amnesic episode may last several hours or as long as several years. Then it usually disappears as suddenly as it came on, with complete recovery and only a small chance of recurrence.

[3] In a depersonalization episode individuals rather suddenly lose the sense of self. Their limbs may seem drastically changed in size, or they may have the impression that they are outside their bodies, viewing themselves from a distance. Sometimes they feel mechanical, that they and others too are robots, or they move as though in a dream, in a world that has lost its reality. Similar, but much more intense, episodes sometimes occur in schizophrenia. The schizophrenic's experience, however, does not have the "as if" quality that the person in depersonalization reports. The schizophrenic's estrangement from the self is real and complete.

Dissociative disorders are usually preceded by a severe stress, such as a death in the family or service in a war.

Memory loss is also common in many organic brain disorders. But psychogenic amnesia and memory loss caused by a brain disease can be fairly easily distinguished. In organic disorders memory fails slowly over time and is not linked to life stress. Furthermore, recovery is rare or incomplete, and other symptoms, such as inattention and emotional upset, are also present.

If a person not only becomes totally amnesic but also moves away from home and work and assumes a new identity, the diagnosis of **psychogenic fugue** is made. Sometimes the assumption of the new identity can be quite elaborate, with the person taking on a new name, new home, new job, and even a new set of personality characteristics. He or she may succeed in establishing a fairly complex social life, all without questioning the inability to remember the past. More often, however, the new life does not crystallize to this extent and the fugue is of briefer duration. Fugues typically occur after the person has experienced some severe stress. Recovery, although varying in the time it takes, is usually complete; the individual does not recollect what took place during the flight from his or her usual haunts.

Multiple personality, the presence of two or more distinct personalities within an individual, is certainly the most dramatic of the dissociative disorders. The famous ''three faces of Eve'' case was discussed in Chapter 4. Each personality, fully intergrated and complex with its own behavior patterns, memories, and relationships, takes its turn at coming forth and being in control for a particular time period. Usually the personalities are quite different, sometimes even opposites of one another.[4] The original personality is seldom aware of the existence of the others, although the subpersonalities may more or less know the primary personality and one another (see Box 6.2) The original and subordinate personalities are all aware of lost periods of time, and the voices of the others may sometimes echo into their consciousness, even though they

do not know to whom these voices belong. Multiple personality is more chronic and serious than other dissociative disorders; recovery may be less complete.

Theories of Dissociative Disorders

According to the **psychoanalytic view** of each of the three dissociative disorders, one part of the mind or consciousness splits off or becomes dissociated from another part. The types of dissociative disorder are tied together etiologically in psychoanalytic theory, being viewed as instances of a massive repression, usually relating back to the unacceptable infantile sexual wishes of the oedipal stage. In adulthood these oedipal yearnings increase in strength until they are finally expressed, often as an impulsive sexual act. The ordinary form of repression is obviously no longer sufficient; the whole event must be obliterated from consciousness. The person succeeds in this by splitting off an entire part of the per-

[4] Cases of multiple personality are frequently mislabeled in the popular press as schizophrenic reactions. This diagnostic category, discussed in greater detail in Chapters 13 and 14, derives part of its name from the Greek root *schizo,* which means ''splitting away from.'' Hence the confusion. A split in the personality, wherein two or more fairly separate and coherent systems of being exist alternately in the same person, is different from the split between cognition and affect that is said to produce the schizophrenic's bizarre behavior.

BOX 6.2 The Three Faces of Evelyn

Consider what it would be like to have a multiple personality. People have told you about things you have done that seem out of character, events that you have no memory of. You yourself have been waking up each morning with the remains of a cup of tea by your bedside—and you do not like to drink tea. How can you explain these happenings? If you were to seek treatment, might you not worry whether the psychiatrist or psychologist will believe you? Perhaps the clinician will think you psychotic.

Each of us has days when we are not "quite ourselves." This is assumed to be quite normal and is not what is meant by multiple personality. According to DSM-III, a proper diagnosis of multiple personality requires that a person have at least two separate "ego states," two different modes of being and feeling and acting that exist independently of each other, coming forth at different times. At least one ego state usually has no contact with the other, that is, the person in ego state A has no memory for what state B is like, or even any knowledge of having an alternate state of being. The existence of different states must furthermore be chronic and severe, not attributable to the ingestion of some drug, for example.

Until recently the case of Eve White, mentioned in Chapter 4, was the most carefully documented report of multiple personality in the clinical literature. But now several other cases have been described. One such account appeared in 1976 in the *Journal of Abnormal Psychology*. "The Three Faces of Evelyn" is a detailed history by Robert F. Jeans, the psychiatrist who treated the woman. The case history is accompanied by exchanges between him and a team of psychologists at a distant university. The investigators had been asked whether they would be interested in describing the patient and advancing some hypotheses about her past history on the basis of her scores on a particular psychological test, taken while she was in each of her different "ego states." Thigpen and Cleckley had adopted a similar procedure in 1954 in their work with Eve White. Osgood, Luria, and Smith's intriguing bit of psychological detective work both sheds light on the fascinating phenomenon of multiple personality and offers

some concurrent validation of a psychological test, the Semantic Differential, which is meant to reveal how a person feels about a number of people, situations, and ideas (Table 6.2).

TABLE 6.2
Sample Item from the Semantic Differential
(from Osgood, Suci, and Tannenbaum, 1957)

	My mother	
valuable	_ _ _ _ _ _ _	worthless
clean	_ _ _ _ _ _ _	dirty
tasty	_ _ _ _ _ _ _	tasteless
large	_ _ _ _ _ _ _	small
strong	_ _ _ _ _ _ _	weak
deep	_ _ _ _ _ _ _	shallow
fast	_ _ _ _ _ _ _	slow
active	_ _ _ _ _ _ _	passive
hot	_ _ _ _ _ _ _	cold
relaxed	_ _ _ _ _ _ _	tense

* Subjects mark any one of the seven lines between each pair of bipolar adjectives, indicating the degree to which they apply.

Jeans provides the following background on his patient. He was consulted in December 1965 by a Gina Rinaldi, referred to him by her friends. Gina, single and thirty-one years old, lived with another single woman and was at the time working successfully as a writer at a large educational publishing firm. She was considered an efficient, businesslike, and productive person, but her friends had observed that she was becoming forgetful and sometimes acted out of character. The youngest of nine siblings, Gina reported that she had been sleepwalking since her early teens; her present roommate had told her that now she would sometimes scream in her sleep.

Gina described her mother, then age seventy-four, as the most domineering woman she had ever known. She reported that as a child she had been quite a fearful and obedient daughter. At age twenty-six Gina got braces for her teeth, and at age twenty-eight she had had an "affair," her first, with a former Jesuit priest, although it was apparently not sexual in nature. Then she became involved with "T.C.," a married man who assured her he would get a divorce and marry her. She indicated that she had been faithful to him since the start of their relationship. Partly on the basis of Jean's analysis of one of Gina's dreams, the psychiatrist concluded that she was quite uncomfortable about being a woman, particularly when a close, sexual relationship with a man might be expected of her. But T.C. did not come through with his promised divorce, stopped seeing Gina regularly, and generally fell out of her favor.

After several sessions with Gina, Jeans began to notice a second personality emerging. "Mary Sunshine," as she came to be referred to by Jeans and Gina, was quite different from Gina. She seemed to be more childlike, more traditionally feminine, ebullient, and seductive. Gina felt that she herself walked like a coal miner, but Mary certainly did not. Some quite concrete incidents indicated Mary's existence. Sometimes Gina found in the sink cups that had had hot chocolate in them—neither Gina nor her roommate liked this beverage. There were large withdrawals from Gina's bank account that she could not remember making. One evening while watching television, Gina realized that she was crying and remarked to herself that it was stupid to feel sad about the particular program she was viewing. She even discovered herself ordering a sewing machine on the telephone, although she disliked sewing; some weeks later she showed up for her therapy session wearing a new dress that Mary had sewn. At work, Gina reported, people were finding her more pleasant to be with, and her colleagues took to consulting her on how to encourage people to work better with one another. All these phenomena were entirely alien to Gina. Jeans and Gina came to realize that sometimes Gina was transformed into Mary.

Then one day T.C. showed up again. Gina was filled with scorn and derision for him, yet she heard herself greeting him warmly with the words "Gee, I missed you so much! It's good to see you!" (Apparently the psychoanalytically oriented therapy was softening the hitherto impermeable boundaries between the separate ego states of Gina and Mary.) Gina was also surprised to hear T.C. reply on this occasion, "All you ever wanted was to please me. You've done nothing but cater to my every whim, nothing but make me happy." Mary must have been active in the earlier relationship that Gina had had with this man.

Now more and more often Jeans witnessed Gina turning into Mary right before his eyes in the consulting room. T.C. accompanied Gina to a session during which her posture and demeanor became more relaxed, her tone of voice warmer. When T.C. explained that he really cared for her, Gina, or rather Mary, said warmly, "Of course, T., I know you do."

At another session Mary was upset and, as Jeans put it, chewed off Gina's fingernails. Then the two of them started having conversations with each other in front of Jeans.

A year after the start of therapy, an apparent synthesis of Gina and Mary began to emerge. At first it seemed that Gina had taken over entirely, but then Jeans noticed that Gina was not as serious as before, particularly about "getting the job done," that is, working extremely hard on the therapy. Jeans, probably believing that Mary wanted to converse with him, encouraged Gina to have a conversation with Mary. The following is what was said by the patient: "I was lying in bed trying to go to sleep. Someone started to cry about T.C. I was sure that it was Mary. I started to talk to her. The person told me that she didn't have a name. Later she said that Mary called her Evelyn. . . . I was suspicious at first that it was Mary pretending to be Evelyn. I changed my mind, however, because the person I talked to had too much sense to be Mary. She said that she realized that T.C. was unreliable but she still loved him and was very lonely. She agreed that it would be best to find a reliable man. She told me that she comes out once a day for a very short time to get used to the world. She promised that she will come out to see you [Jeans] sometime when she is stronger" (Jeans, 1976, pp. 254–255).

Throughout January Evelyn appeared more and more often, and Jeans felt that the patient was improving rapidly. During this stage of therapy he administered the Semantic Differential to each of the three personalities, for now he had access to all three ego states. Within a few months the patient seemed to be Evelyn all the time, and this woman soon married a physician. Now, years later, she still has had no recurrence of the other personalities.

On the basis of the Semantic Differential responses of Gina, Mary, and Evelyn, Osgood, Luria, and Smith (1976) were able to describe the patient in ways that concurred impressively with Jeans's clinical data. Not only do their conclusions have concurrent validity—each personality is described in a manner consistent with Jeans's clinical reports; but their work has etiological validity as well—Osgood and his colleagues were able to suggest accurately various features of the patient's earlier history, for example, that her father was less dominant than her mother. The similarity of their conclusions and Jeans's observations, although not total, is impressive.

sonality from awareness (Buss, 1966) or by acquiring a new identity for the dissociated portion of the self.

Learning theorists have generally construed these rare phenomena as avoidance responses that serve to protect the individual from highly stressful events. Although not employing the concept of repression and not emphasizing the overriding importance of infantile sexual conflicts, the behavioral view of dissociative disorders is not dissimilar to psychoanalytic speculations about them.

If dissociative disorders are regarded as problems in memory, experimental research on memory might be brought to bear in trying to understand them. A recent area of investigation, *state-dependent memory,* offers some promise. In this phenomenon people are better able to recall an event if they are in the same psychic state as when it happened. If they are in a greatly different state when they try to remember, for example, sad now and happy then, memory of the earlier event is poor. Experimental research on state-dependent memory has manipulated mood by hypnosis and confirmed that recall is much better if mood at the time of learning matches mood at the time of recall (Bower, 1981). In applying this concept to dissociative disorders, Bower notes that there are often major mood differences between or among the several ego states of a person with multiple personality. Similarly, in fugue a person escapes from an emotionally charged situation into a calmer existence. The different emotional states may, in part, account for the selective memory loss.

We are unfortunately able to go little beyond these rather vague theories, since there are so few concrete data available on this type of problem. Information is scant, principally because of the rarity of these disorders. Dissociative disorders remain among the most poorly understood clinical syndromes.

Therapies for Dissociative Disorders

Dissociative disorders suggest, perhaps better than any other, the plausibility of Freud's concept of repression. For in all three—amnesia, fu-

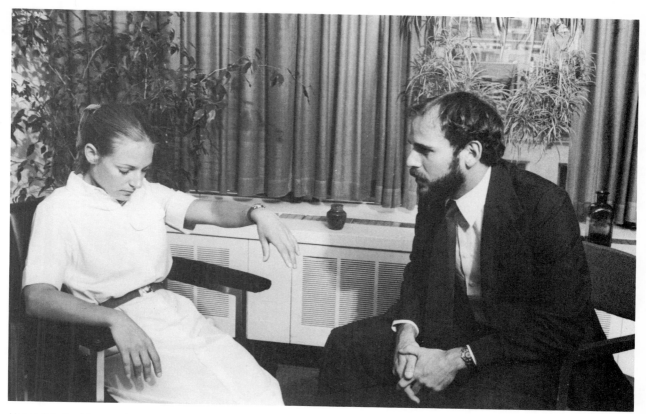

Hypnotist checking on depth of hypnotic trance by suggesting that a gas-filled balloon has been tied to the woman's arm.

gue, and multiple personality—people whose pasts are usually known behave in ways that very assuredly indicate they have forgotten earlier parts of their lives. And since these people may at the same time be unaware even of having forgotten something, the hypothesis that they have repressed massive portions of their lives is a compelling one.

Consequently, for dissociative disorders psychoanalytic treatment is perhaps administered with more élan than for other psychological problems. The goal of lifting repressions is the order of the day, pursued in ways with which we are already familiar.

As discussed in Chapter 1, psychological theorizing about mental disorders began with the work on hypnosis of Mesmer in Vienna and Paris in the late eighteenth century and of Charcot in Paris in the second part of the nineteenth century. They apparently succeeded in removing

various hysterical symptoms[5] by rather direct suggestion. Then Breuer and Freud encouraged patients to talk, while hypnotized, about their problems and especially about the earlier origins of them. Therefore psychoanalysis had its beginnings in hypnosis. But Freud eventually abandoned the practice in favor of techniques like free association, for he came to believe, mistakenly it may be, that enduring cures are not possible by means of hypnosis.

Through the years practitioners have continued to hypnotize patients suffering from dissociative

[5] Hysteria is of course the familiar vernacular diagnosis of several milleniums' standing. Hysterical neurosis was one of the neurotic diagnoses in both DSM-II and DSM-I, covering both conversion disorder and the dissociative disorders. In DSM-III conversion disorder is one of the somatoform disorders, and the dissociative disorders make up a separate major section. Thus contemporary psychiatric thinking regards as fundamentally different two sets of problems formerly considered closely related. But hypnotism was and still is employed in treatment for hysteria, meaning both conversion and the several dissociative disorders.

disorders, supposing that something special about the hypnotic state would permit the person access to hidden portions of the personality—to his or her lost identity or to a set of events precipitating or flowing from a trauma. Implicit in the choice of hypnosis for dissociative disorders are the assumptions that the problem, such as amnesia, is caused by a massive repression which protects the ego from intolerable anxiety, and that hypnosis can help lift the repression.

Some physicians have used sodium Amytal, the "truth serum," to induce a hypnoticlike state, again assuming that painful repressed memories will be brought forth and remove the "need" for the dissociative disorder. A number of dramatic case studies in the clinical literature attest to the efficacy of both hypnosis and sodium Amytal, but little of certainty can be said about their actual effectiveness because nothing even approximating controlled research has been done.[6]

Perhaps because of the rarity of dissociative disorders, the behavioral treatment of them has been little discussed in the published literature. Walton (1961) reported on the successful therapy he devised for a sleepwalker who tried to harm his wife nearly every night for six months during somnambulistic episodes. (Somnambulism was listed as a hysterical dissociative disorder in DSM-II.) Analyzing the case much as a psychoanalyst would, Walton determined that the thirty-five-year-old man, an architectural assistant, was very shy and inhibited, especially in relation to his authoritarian and rigid mother. His wife was at the time trying to force him to do things he objected to and reminded him of his domineering mother. Assertion training helped the man to treat his mother with firmness and to express his negative feelings directly. The sleepwalking incidents were soon eliminated. In general, behavioral clinicians might encourage the person to imagine and discuss aspects of the trauma being avoided in memory and might even desensitize him or her to situations related to the onset of the disorder. Recovering memory of the stressful event of course signals that it is no longer avoided.

[6] To illustrate the problem inherent to case studies, we offer this personal observation. While working in a mental hospital some years ago, one of the authors encountered on the ward a man suffering from partial amnesia. He did not recognize members of his family when they came to visit him but could still recall most other events in his life. Many efforts were made to restore his memory, ranging from hypnotic suggestions to drug therapy. Both sodium Amytal and Methedrine, a powerful stimulant, were administered, Methedrine intravenously. It was hoped that Methedrine would energize his nervous system and "dislodge" the blocks to memory, much as Drano is used to open a clogged drain. In all these attempts the patient was cooperative and even eager for a positive outcome, but none of them worked. The unsuccessful treatment was never written up for publication. There is a strong editorial bias against publishing reports of failed clinical treatments, as indeed there is against publishing inconclusive results of experiments. This, a general problem for psychology and psychiatry, is a special detriment when, as for dissociative disorders, there is little in the way of controlled research.

Summary

In somatoform disorders physical symptoms for which no physiological basis can be found are the problem. The sensory and motor dysfunctions of conversion disorders, one of the two principal types of somatoform disorders, suggest neurological impairments, but ones that do not make anatomical sense; the symptoms do, however, seem to serve some psychological purpose. In somatization disorder, or Briquet's syndrome, multiple physical complaints, which are not adequately explained by physical disorder or injury, eventuate in frequent visits to physicians, hospitalization, and even unnecessary surgery.

Theory concerning the etiology of these disorders is very speculative and focuses primarily on conversion disorders. Psychoanalytic theory proposed that in conversion disorders repressed impulses are converted into physical symptoms. Behavioral theories focus on the more or less conscious and deliberate adoption of the symptoms as a means of obtaining a desired goal. As for therapies, analysts try to help the client face up to the repressed impulses, and behavioral treatments attempt to reduce anxiety and to reinforce behavior that will allow relinquishment of the symptoms.

Dissociative disorders are disruptions of consciousness, memory, and identity. An inability to recall important personal information, usually after some traumatic experience, is diagnosed as psychogenic amnesia. In psychogenic fugue the person moves away, assumes a new identity, and is amnesic for his or her previous life. The person with multiple personality has two or more distinct and fully developed ones, each with unique memories, behavior patterns, and relationships which determine the individual's nature and acts when it comes forth. Psychoanalytic theory regards dissociative disorders as instances of massive repression of some undesirable event or aspect of the self. Behavioral theories similarly consider dissociative reactions to be avoidance responses motivated by high levels of anxiety. Both analytic and behavioral clinicians focus their treatment efforts on the anxiety, since it is viewed as etiologically significant.

chapter 7

In Chapter 5 we discussed voodoo death, a seemingly supernatural phenomenon whereby a curse from a witch doctor dooms his victim to extreme physical suffering and death. To explain such events, Cannon (1942) proposed that vital bodily organs are irreparably harmed if the autonomic nervous system is maintained in a highly aroused state through prolonged psychological stress, during which time there is no opportunity to take effective action. Inasmuch as the arousal of the autonomic nervous system is also regarded as one of the bodily indications of emotion, it is not surprising that psychopathologists have concerned themselves with physical diseases involving this system, in the belief that psychological factors may be implicated. In the expression of emotion, the bodily changes of autonomic arousal are viewed as transient; in psychophysiological disorders the usually reversible autonomic and hormonal responses to stress can cause irreversible tissue damage.

Psychophysiological disorders, such as asthma and ulcers, are characterized by genuine physical symptoms that are caused or can be wors-
ened by emotional factors. The present term, psychophysiological disorders, is now preferred to one that is perhaps better known, psychosomatic disorders. _Psychosomatic_ connotes quite well the principal feature of these disorders, that the psyche or mind is having an untoward effect on the soma or body. The structure of both these terms, in fact, implies that mind and body are separate and independent, although they may, at times, influence each other (see Box 7.1). Dualism is a deeply ingrained paradigm of human thought. And yet the hope was that these terms would foster a monistic rather than dualistic view of the human being, since ''. . . all functioning and all diseases are both mental and physical, because both mental and physiological processes are going on continuously'' (Sternbach, 1966, p. 139). Instead of speaking of the emotions as causing body dysfunctions, we could instead, as Graham (1967) has noted, regard the psyche and soma as one and the same. Psychological and physical explanations of disease are then simply two different ways of describing the same events.

BOX **7.1** Descartes and the Mind-Body Problem

One of the most influential statements about the "mind-body" problem is found in the writings of the brilliant French philosopher of the seventeenth century, René Descartes. Being a deeply religious Catholic, he assumed that human beings differed from other animals by virtue of having a soul and thus being partly divine. But like the other animals, human beings had a body as well. Although the body was said to work on mechanical principles—Descartes was fascinated by the mechanical models of the body's workings that were prevalent at the time—these mechanics were seen to be under the control of the soul, or mind. But how could the body, operating like a machine, be affected by the soul, which is spiritual and nonphysical? How could two such basically different substances, in fact, "touch" each other? If the mind was to affect the body, there must be some point of *contact*. The pineal gland, located in the midbrain, was postulated by Descartes as the locus of this critical interaction, the point at which the mind could direct the mechanics of the body. By dualizing human beings in this way, with this vital connection between the mind and the body, Descartes felt that he could retain his religious view of people as being partly divine and yet an integral part of the rest of the animal world.

René Descartes (1596–1650), the French philosopher who proposed a dualistic view of mind and body.

At the outset, two important points must be firmly established. First, a psychophysiological disorder is a real disease involving damage to the body. The fact that such disorders are viewed as being caused by emotional factors does not make the affliction imaginery. People can just as readily die from "psychologically produced" high blood pressure or ulcers as from similar diseases produced by infection or physical injury. Second, psychophysiological disorders should be distinguished from conversion disorders, which were discussed in Chapter 6. Conversion disorders do not involve actual organic damage to the body, and they are generally considered to affect function of the voluntary musculature. In contrast, in psychophysiological disorders bodily tissues *are* damaged.

The classic psychophysiological disorders are generally grouped together according to the organ system affected. Some of the major ones are given in the following list.

1. Psychophysiological skin disorders. Skin reactions such as neurodermatitis (inflammation), pruritis (itching), and hyperhydrosis (dry skin).

2. Psychophysiological respiratory disorders. Bronchial asthma, hyperventilation (breathing very rapidly), sighing, and hiccups.

3. Psychophysiological cardiovascular disorders. Tachycardia (heart racing), hypertension (high blood pressure), and migraine headache.

4. Psychophysiological gastrointestinal disorders. Peptic ulcers, chronic gastritis, ulcerative or mucous colitis, constipation, hyperacidity, and heartburn.

5. Psychophysiological genitourinary disorders. Disturbances in menstruation and urination, dyspareunia (painful sexual intercourse), and impotence (difficulty obtaining or maintaining an erection, or both).[1]

6. Psychophysiological musculoskeletal disorders. Backache, muscle cramps, and tension headaches.

[1] In DSM-III sexual dysfunctions, including dyspareunia and impotence, are now in their own section, Psychosexual Dysfunctions (see Chapter 12).

Stress and Illness

Psychophysiological symptoms and disorders are quite common in industrialized societies, although they are apparently rare among nonindustrialized groups, such as the Australian aborigines and the American Indians. Schwab, Fennell, and Warheit (1974), for example, interviewed a randomly selected sample of close to 1700 Americans (Table 7.1). Over 40 percent of the respondents reported having had headaches during the previous year, and 50 percent reported a range of gastrointestinal symptoms. Actual disorders such as hypertension, however, were not as common as the less serious symptoms they were questioned about.

Psychophysiological disorders as such do not appear in DSM-III as they did in DSM-II. Because virtually all physical diseases are now viewed as potentially related to psychological stress, a psychophysiological disorders category would become a complete listing of all diseases. Instead of such a cumbersome, overlapping system, DSM-III requires that a diagnostic judgment be made on axis I, to indicate the presence of a psychological factor influencing a physical condition, and also on axis III, to specify that physical condition.

What is the evidence for this view that all illness is, in part, stress-related? For years it had been known that various physical diseases could be produced in laboratory animals who were exposed to severe stress. Usually the diseases studied in this fashion were the classic psychophysiological disorders, such as ulcer and hypertension. More recent evidence has broadened the range of diseases that appear to be stress-related. Sklar and Anisman (1979), for example, first induced tumors in mice with a transplant of cancerous tissue and then studied the impact of stress on growth of the tumors. In animals exposed to electric shock, the tumors grew more rapidly and the animals died earlier.

Research with human beings poses an ethical problem: the experimental method cannot be used. Instead, researchers have sought to measure the amount of life stress a person has experienced and then correlate this with illness. A number of instruments have been developed to measure life stress. One such test, whose items appear in Table 7.2, is the Social Readjustment

TABLE 7.1
Percentages of People* Reporting Psychophysiological Symptoms and Conditions for the Previous Year

Symptoms and conditions	Yes—regularly, percent	Yes—occasionally, percent	No, percent
Symptoms			
Headaches	8.7	38.0	53.4
Indigestion	6.4	27.5	66.1
Constipation	6.9	19.6	73.5
Nervous stomach	5.2	17.5	77.3
Stomachaches	3.7	18.8	77.5
Diarrhea	0.9	14.4	84.8
Conditions			
Hypertension	6.2	8.0	85.8
Asthma	1.9	2.9	95.2
Ulcers	0.9	1.4	97.6
Colitis	0.4	0.9	98.7

* N = 1647.

Rating Scale (SRRS). In using the SRRS, the respondent simply checks off the life events that have been experienced during the time period in question. But merely summing the *number* of events would not work, for different *amounts* of stressfulness are inherent in different events. To solve this problem, Holmes and Rahe (1967) gave a list of life events to a large group of subjects and asked them to rate each item according to its "intensity and [the] length of time necessary to accommodate . . . *regardless of the desirability of the event.*"[2] Marriage was arbitrarily assigned a stress value of 500; all other items were then evaluated using this reference point. For example, an event twice as stressful as marriage would be assigned a value of 1000, and an event one-fifth as stressful as marriage would be assigned a value of 100. The average ratings assigned to the events by the respondents in Holmes and Rahe's study are also shown in Table 7.2.

The ratings that indicate differential stressfulness of events are totaled for all the events actually experienced to produce a Life Change Unit (LCU) score, a weighted sum of events. The LCU score is then related to illness. Rahe and Holmes (unpublished), for example, studied a sample of 200 physicians. Health problems (infectious diseases, allergies, musculoskeletal problems, and psychophysiological disorders) were strongly related to LCU scores. With an LCU score of less than 200, 37 percent of the life crises were associated with deterioration of health. But with an LCU score greater than 300, 79 percent of the life crises were accompanied by health problems. Other studies have shown that LCU scores are related to heart attacks (Rahe and Lind, 1971), fractures (Tollefson, 1972), leukemia onset (Wold, 1968), and colds and fevers (Holmes and Holmes, 1970).

We have, then, some promising information on the relationship between psychological stress and physical illness. But caution is in order before we assert that the relationship is a causal one. Many of the studies have used a retrospective method; participants were asked to recall both the illnesses and the stressful life events that they had experienced over the previous two

[2] Note that Holmes and Rahe's rating procedure makes *change* the crucial variable, not whether an event is pleasant or unpleasant. There is considerable controversy whether change per se is the best index of life stress.

TABLE 7.2
Social Readjustment Rating Scale
(from Holmes and Rahe, 1967)

Rank	Life event	Mean value
1	Death of spouse	100
2	Divorce	73
3	Marital separation	65
4	Jail term	63
5	Death of close family member	63
6	Personal injury or illness	53
7	Marriage	50*
8	Fired at work	47
9	Marital reconciliation	45
10	Retirement	45
11	Change in health of family member	44
12	Pregnancy	40
13	Sex difficulties	39
14	Gain of new family member	39
15	Business readjustment	39
16	Change in financial state	38
17	Death of close friend	37
18	Change to different line of work	36
19	Change in number of arguments with spouse	35
20	Mortgage over $10,000	31
21	Foreclosure of mortgage or loan	30
22	Change in responsibilities at work	29
23	Son or daughter leaving home	29
24	Trouble with in-laws	29
25	Outstanding personal achievement	28
26	Wife begins or stops work	26
27	Begin or end school	26
28	Change in living conditions	25
29	Revision of personal habits	24
30	Trouble with boss	23
31	Change in work hours or conditions	20
32	Change in residence	20
33	Change in schools	20
34	Change in recreation	19
35	Change in church activities	19
36	Change in social activities	18
37	Mortgage or loan less than $10,000	17
38	Change in sleeping habits	16
39	Change in number of family get-togethers	15
40	Change in eating habits	15
41	Vacation	13
42	Christmas	12
43	Minor violations of the law	11

* Marriage was arbitrarily assigned a stress value of 500; no event was found to be any more than twice as stressful. Here the values are reduced proportionally and range up to 100.

years. In this type of study causal inferences are hazardous indeed. Recall is less perfect, and it is difficult to unravel cause and effect. Illness, for example, could cause a high life change score, as when chronic absenteeism brings dismissal from a job. And the reports of stressful events in such studies could also be contaminated by knowledge of subsequently occurring illnesses.

A few studies have used a prospective methodology wherein individuals are followed over time, and life changes and illness are repeatedly assessed (for example, Holmes and Holmes, 1970). Even these investigations, however, are subject to the possible influence of third variables; a factor could cause both the life events preceding the illness and the illness itself. Definite conclusions about the effects of life stresses await further studies that use more sophisticated prospective methodologies and also try to assess the potential role of third variables.

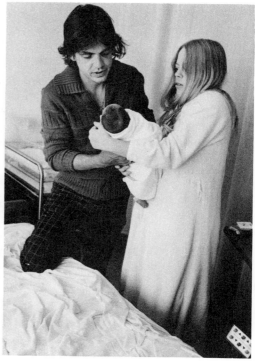

Major life events bring stress which can in turn cause medical and psychological problems.

Theories of Psychophysiological Disorders

In the remainder of the chapter we consider theory and research on the interaction of psychological and physiological factors in causing and alleviating disease. Our primary concerns are how psychological stress affects physiological functioning and causes or exacerbates an illness and, at the end of the chapter, how psychological therapies can prevent or ameliorate physical illnesses.

In considering the etiology of psychophysiological disorders, we are confronted with three questions: (1) Why does stress produce difficulties in only some people who are exposed to it? (2) Why does stress sometimes cause an illness and not a psychological disorder? (3) Given that stress produces a psychophysiological disorder, what determines which one of the many disorders it will be? We have already discussed the concept of stress as it is related to various anxiety disorders, and we shall discuss it further in the chapters on schizophrenia. How is it that this general concept can be used to "account for" such a wide range of disorders?

Answers to these questions have been sought by both physiologically and psychologically oriented theorists. Physiological approaches attribute particular psychophysiological disorders to specific weaknesses or overactivity of an individual's organ systems in responding to stress. Psychological theories account for specificity by positing either particular emotional states or maladaptive attitudes for particular disorders.

Physiological Theories

Somatic-weakness theory

Genetic factors, earlier illnesses, diet, and the like may disrupt a particular organ system, which may then become weak and vulnerable to stress. According to the _somatic-weakness theory,_ the connection between stress and a particular psychophysiological disorder is the weakness in a specific bodily organ. By way of analogy, a tire blows out at its weakest or thinnest portion. And

in the human body a congenitally weak respiratory system might predispose the individual to asthma.

Specific-reaction theory

Some investigators argue that there are differences, probably genetically determined, in the ways individuals respond to stress. People have been found to have their own particular patterns of autonomic response to stress. The heart rate of one individual may increase, whereas another person may react with increased respiration rate but no change in frequency of heartbeats (Lacey, 1967). Thus individuals respond to stress in their own idiosyncratic way, and the body system that is the most responsive may be a likely candidate for the locus of a subsequent psychophysiological disorder. Someone reacting to stress with secretion of stomach acid may be more vulnerable to ulcers, and someone reacting to stress with blood pressure elevation may be more susceptible to essential hypertension. Later in this chapter, when we consider particular psychophysiological disorders, substantial evidence in support of both somatic-weakness and _specific-reaction_ theories will be given.

Evolution theory

A psychophysiological disorder usually affects a single organ system that is controlled by the autonomic nervous system. In a healthy body the actions of the two branches of this system, the sympathetic and the parasympathetic—which work sometimes in unison, sometimes against each other to manage the body's internal affairs—must always be kept in a complex and delicate balance. The two systems act in concert. A burst of sympathetic activity must soon be redressed by increased activity of the parasympathetic. The healthy body can sustain prolonged overactivity of one or the other system on occasion, but for the viscera, blood vessels, and glands to act effectively and to remain unharmed, neither system can overexpend energy for protracted periods of time.

External, physical danger stimulates the sympathetic system to prepare the body for fight or flight. It increases heart rate, blood pressure, and rate of breathing. The liver releases into the bloodstream a large supply of sugar. The blood vessels of the limb muscles and other skeletal muscles dilate to ready them for strenuous activity. At the same time blood vessels of the stomach, intestines, skin, and brain constrict. But actual physical danger is usually transient. After the body has either fled or fought, its muscles relax, heart rate slows down again to normal, blood flow to the brain increases, and digestion resumes, all under the direction of the parasympathetic system.

Imagined and social dangers bring about the same preparations by the sympathetic system. Our brains have evolved to the point that they perceive other than physical threats (Simeons, 1961), and people can continually torment themselves even when real dangers are absent. Anger provoked by an annoying present situation, regrets about the past, and worries about the future all stimulate sympathetic activity. But resentment and regret and worry cannot as readily be fought or escaped from as external threats, nor do they easily pass. They may keep the sympathetic system aroused and the body in a continual state of emergency, sometimes for far longer than it can bear. Under these circumstances, moreover, the necessary balancing of sympathetic and parasympathetic actions is made that much more difficult and can go awry. Thus the bodily changes accompanying the distressed thoughts that evolution has made possible, besides being inappropriate in their nature, both persist longer than they were meant to and contribute to an imbalance between sympathetic and parasympathetic activity.

Psychological Theories

Psychoanalytic theory
Franz Alexander (1950) has perhaps been the most prominent of the psychoanalytic theorists who have concerned themselves with psychophysiological reactions. In his view the various psychophysiological disorders are products of unconscious emotional states specific to each disorder. For example, ". . . it would appear that the crucial factor in the pathogenesis of ulcer is the frustration of the dependent, help-seeking and love-demanding desires. When these desires

cannot find gratification in human relationships, a chronic emotional stimulus is created which has a specific effect on the functions of the stomach'' (p. 103). Alexander assumed that ulcer patients have repressed their longing for parental love in childhood, and that this repressed impulse causes the overactivity of the autonomic nervous system and of the stomach, leading to ulcers. Physiologically, the stomach is continuously preparing to receive food, which the person has symbolically equated with parental love.

Undischarged hostile impulses are viewed as creating the chronic emotional state responsible for essential hypertension.

The damning up of his hostile impulses will continue and will consequently increase in intensity. This will induce the development of stronger defensive measures in order to keep pent-up aggressions in check. . . . Because of the marked degree of their inhibitions, these patients are less effective in their occupational activities and for that reason tend to fail in competition with others, . . . envy is stimulated and . . . hostile feelings toward more successful, less inhibited competitors are further intensified (p. 150).

Alexander formulated his theory on the basis of his observations of patients undergoing psychoanalysis. Although some subsequent research appeared to substantiate the theory—for example, finding that hypertensives score high on measures of anger or hostility—such data were collected *after* the onset of the disease and thus cannot support the assertion that anger or hostility was a cause. Indeed, the results from studies using more sophisticated research designs do not agree with Alexander's theory. Cochrane (1973), for example, studied volunteers in a heart attack prevention clinic, before the onset of any clinical disorder. Participants were given the Maudsley Personality Inventory as a measure of neuroticism and the Direction of Hostility Questionnaire to assess how they customarily handle their angry impulses. After the initial assessment some of the participants did develop hypertension. But, contrary to Alexander's theory, these individuals had not differed from the other subjects on the personality measures. Similarly, Mann (1977) found that although a sample of *diagnosed* hypertensives were more hostile than controls, a group of *undiagnosed* hypertensives, discovered through a large population survey, did not differ from the control group on any personality measures. Thus the personality differences that have been reported in the literature could be a reaction to being diagnosed and undergoing treatment.

A psychodynamically oriented researcher would, however, dismiss the findings just presented. Alexander's theory deals with unconscious personality dynamics, which are not likely to be reflected in responses to paper-and-pencil personality inventories. Although there is no agreed-upon methodology for tapping these unconscious dynamics, some clinicians would argue that projective tests are at least more suitable than paper-and-pencil tests. Thus it is interesting that Harvard psychologist David McClelland (1975), using the Thematic Apperception Test (see page 87), has provided some evidence rather consistent with Alexander's theory.

One of the needs that McClelland assumes can be measured in the stories told to TAT cards is the need for power (n Power), more specifically, the desire to have an impact on others. A person receives a high score on n Power if his or her stories contain many elements reflecting argumentation, attempts to persuade others or to control them, and efforts to help people who have not themselves requested aid.

How might n Power relate to essential hypertension? First, McClelland saw in the hypertension literature that sufferers are frequently described as extremely competitive, aggressive, and impatient. These characteristics suggest chronically high levels of sympathetic nervous system activity. Furthermore, people who score high in n Power on the TAT may be described in a similar way, indicating a possible connection between n Power and essential hypertension. The question then becomes how to test the strength of this relationship.

McClelland has followed several lines of inquiry. Laboratory studies have indicated, for example, that n Power scores can be raised if TAT stories are told after viewing an inspirational film (Steele, 1973). Furthermore, these "power-

David McClelland, Harvard psychologist, who uses the TAT to assess motivation. One of his theories links hypertension and cardiovascular disease to a strong need for power.

aroused" subjects had higher levels of epinephrine in their urine after seeing the film, one which showed President John F. Kennedy giving his inaugural address. Epinephrine is a hormone released through the activities of the sympathetic nervous system. That this elevation in n Power scores and epinephrine level could not be attributed to an overall arousal of needs is suggested by the fact that scores on the need for achievement (n Ach), another need revealed in TAT stories and studied by McClelland, were not similarly increased. Therefore sympathetic nervous system activity may be associated with the desire to exercise power over others.

The next question is whether these short-term analogue findings are supported by data with more clinical relevance. What evidence is there that the power motive might be the kind of chronic, long-term activation that is related to hypertension and cardiovascular disease? McClelland examined longitudinal TAT data collected over many years on college students from a selective Eastern private college. In the fall of 1960, 235 male college freshmen took a TAT test and also had their blood pressure measured as part of their physical examination as incoming students. Those who scored high in n Power on the TAT had significantly higher blood pressure than those who scored low. Moreover, Mc-Clelland obtained access to data on men who had graduated from this college between 1939 and 1944 and who had been followed up regularly since their college years. Available in the files were n Power TAT data as well as blood pressure measurements. McClelland found that blood pressure at about age fifty-one could be predicted from n Power scores obtained when the men were thirty years of age. In addition, there was a clear link between n Power scores and cardiovascular disease: of twenty-five men who had cardiovascular disease in their early fifties, fourteen had scored high in n Power years earlier.

In evaluating this web of evidence, we should be mindful, as McClelland is, of the host of uncontrolled factors in all this research, especially in the longitudinal work. Many things happen to people after they leave college that could bear on the development of hypertension and heart disease as well—financial reverses, marital difficulties, legal entanglements, and the like. In addition, McClelland does not rule out a role for physiological factors in the development of hypertension. Given the additional factors that might be important, the possible relationships revealed between the disorder and n Power by laboratory and historical investigations are all the more remarkable.

Specific-attitudes theories

Graham has proposed another psychological theory to account for the specificity of psychophysiological disorders. According to him, particular attitudes, rather than chronic emotional states, are associated with particular patterns of physiological changes and hence specific psychophysiological disorders (Grace and Graham, 1952). A number of patients having psychophysiological disorders were interviewed to determine their characteristic attitudes. A partial list of psychophysiological disturbances and the attitudes that were found to be related to them follows.

1. Urticaria (hives). Patients see themselves as being mistreated and are preoccupied with what is happening to them, not with retaliation.

2. Raynaud's disease (cold hands). The individual wants to undertake hostile physical action but may not have any idea what the actual activity should be.

3. Asthma. Patients are facing a situation that they would rather avoid or escape. The most important part of their attitude is their desire to have nothing to do with the situation at all and to deal with it by simply ignoring it.

4. Hypertension. Individuals feel that they must be constantly on guard and prepared to ward off the ever-present threat of danger.

5. Duodenal ulcer. Individuals are seeking revenge and wish to injure the person or thing that has injured them.

The seeming remoteness of connection between such attitudes and these psychophysiological disorders makes Graham's findings quite striking. But the connections are, of course, correlational in nature and hence subject to the problems of interpretation discussed in Chapter 4. An experimental analogue study was undertaken to test these suggested correlations. After hypnotizing normal subjects, Graham, Stern, and Winokur (1958) gave them suggestions designed to produce the attitudes specific either to hives, in which the skin swells in intensely itching wheals, or to Raynaud's disease, in which the hand and fingers become cold, moist, and numb. These two disorders were selected for comparison because skin temperature changes with both but in different directions. The skin temperature of someone suffering from hives is higher than normal, that of the person with Raynaud's disease lower than normal. After the particular attitude had been induced in the subject, the temperature of his or her skin was measured. The actual instructions given to the subjects were as follows.

Hives. *Dr. X is now going to burn your hand with a match. When he does so you will feel very much mistreated, but you will*

*be unable to do anything about it. You
can't even think of anything you want to
do about it. You are thinking only of what
happened to you.*

Raynaud's disease. *Dr. X is now going to
burn your hand with a match. You feel mistreated and you want to hit Dr. X. You want
to hit him as hard as you can, you want to
hit him and choke him and strangle him.
That's all you are thinking about, how
much you want to hit him.*

Each subject was tested twice, receiving first
one set of instructions and then the other. The
results showed that the "hives attitude" produced a small rise in skin temperature of a finger
and that the "Raynaud's disease attitude" produced a decrease. In another study the hypertension attitude was induced and blood pressure increased (Graham, Kabler, and Graham, 1962).
These demonstrations support Graham's theory
to some extent, although it must be remembered
that hives, Raynaud's disease, and hypertension
were not actually produced.

Other research, however, has not been very
supportive of Graham's theory. Kogan, Dorpat,
and Holmes (1965), for example, found that the
specific attitudes in Graham's theory could not
be reliably identified. An experimental study (Peters and Stern, 1971) also failed to replicate Graham's work in which he had manipulated attitudes and linked them to the skin temperature
changes of hives and Raynaud's disease. Given
these contradictory findings, Graham's intriguing
theory should be viewed with skepticism.

Conditioning theories

Both classical and operant conditioning have
been suggested as having a role in psychophysiological disorders, although conditioning is
probably best viewed as a factor that can exacerbate an already existing illness rather than cause
it. Consider a person who is allergic to pollen
and thus subject to asthma attacks. It has been
theorized that through classical conditioning
neutral stimuli paired with pollen could also
come to elicit asthma, thus broadening the range
of stimuli that can bring on an attack (Bandura,
1969). The asthmatic attacks might also be
viewed as operant responses producing rewards.

For example, a child could "use" asthma as an
excuse for not participating in unpleasant activities. Dworkin and his colleagues (1979) have
proposed that hypertension too may be reinforcing. Their hypothesis begins with the assumption
that many people live in surroundings that stimulate their aggressive tendencies but also discourage overt aggression. Animal research has shown
that rage reactions can be inhibited by stimulation of the baroreceptors, which are pressure-
sensitive neural cells located, among other
places in the cardiovascular system, within the
walls of the arch of the aorta and of the nearby
carotid sinuses.[3] Perhaps, then, a similar mechanism operates in human beings. High blood
pressure may stimulate the baroreceptors and
thus help inhibit maladaptive aggressive responses.

*None of these accounts excludes the impor-
tance of physiological factors in psychophysiological disorders.* Classical and operant conditioning hypotheses typically assume that the physical
symptoms already exist. Thus any learning
model of a psychophysiological disorder requires
a physiological predisposition, a diathesis of
some kind.

Multifactorial theory

When the germ theory of disease was established
by Louis Pasteur, the hope was that a single
cause would be found for every medical disorder. It is now known, however, that most diseases have multiple causes. Heart disease, for
example, is attributed to a complex intertwining
of genetic factors, diet, cigarette smoking, lack of
exercise, and stress. The multifactorial point of
view has found its way into current theorizing
about both the stress and the emotional and physiological reactions associated with psychophysiological disorders.

Both the somatic-weakness and the specific-reaction hypotheses state that these physiological
predispositions to illness are activated by stress.
But what kind of stress? Are we dealing with
events or situations that are almost universally

---

[3] The carotid sinus is a slight enlargement of the carotid artery at the
point where it bifurcates into an external branch supplying the face,
scalp, tongue, teeth, and other external parts of the head and an internal branch supplying the brain, eye, and other internal structures. The
rich supply of sensory nerve endings in its walls constitutes a major
mechanism regulating heart rate and blood pressure.

stressful, such as loss of job, death of a family member? Probably not, at least not entirely. The evidence seems to indicate that more idiosyncratic stressors, such as spilling a glass of water at a dinner party, can have a powerful impact on illness (for example, Lazarus, 1974). The specific emotional states and maladaptive attitudes pointed out by the psychological theories could be expected to play the important role of "sensitizing" a person to overrespond to unpleasant but not necessarily catastrophic life experiences. Thus a complete diathesis-stress theory of psychophysiological disorders requires an integration of several of the theories already considered.

Our overview of theories concerning the etiology of psychophysiological disorders is complete. We turn now to a detailed review of the disorders that have attracted the most attention from researchers—*ulcer, hypertension, coronary heart disease, asthma, and migraine headache.*

Ulcer

Ulcers are craterlike lesions or holes in the lining of the stomach or duodenum. In the digestive process gastric juice, made up of dilute hydrochloric acid and pepsin, acts on ingested food to break it down into components that the body can use. Ordinarily, the inner walls of the stomach and duodenum are protected from these gastric secretions by a layer of mucus. A reduction in the normal blood supply to the mucosa, excessive gastric secretions, or both may allow gastric juice to erode the mucous lining and then to digest the wall (Weiss, 1977). Autonomic overactivity can reduce blood supply to the mucosa and increase the secretion of stomach acid. Thus a physiological process is linked to possible psychological factors through the relation between autonomic activity and emotions. The following case history illustrates the development of an ulcer.

Background. As a child, Mr. A was quiet and obedient, whereas his brother who was three years older was aggressive and independent. Socially, Mr. A was very close to his brother and his brother's companions and was always under the protection of his brother. Mr. A also spent much time with his parents, who provided him with much attention.

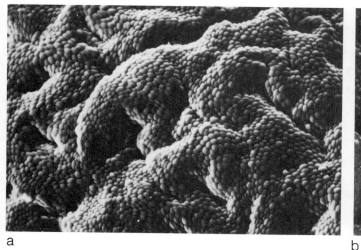
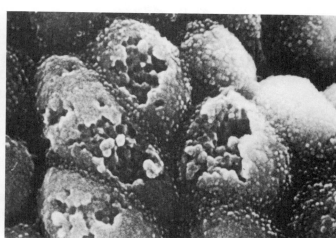

a   b

Scanning electron micrographs of a normal stomach (a) and a stomach with ulcers (b).

Emotion-Arousing Situations. When Mr. A was thirteen his brother died; about two years later his father also died. Both of those events were of major significance in Mr. A's young life. Following the death of his father, his mother became psychologically dependent on him, consulting him about important problems and requiring him generally to substitute for both his older brother and his father, a situation for which Mr. A was completely unprepared intellectually and otherwise. While maintaining a secure outer appearance, Mr. A was aroused emotionally, and his emotional reactions were repeatedly intensified by the excessive expectations of his mother. . . . At age eighteen, Mr. A experienced a short period of stomach discomfort that was followed by the initial hemorrhaging of a duodenal ulcer. When psychotherapy began about five years later, X-ray findings and general symptoms indicated an active ulcer. *Follow-up.* Follow-up study during a three-year period after conclusion of this initial psychotherapy disclosed the following facts. Mr. A had a mild relapse shortly after his marriage when he accepted a very strenuous assignment abroad and had an unsuitable diet; a second mild relapse occurred immediately prior to the birth of his first child, which corresponded in time with his mother's considering remarriage. A few psychotherapeutic consultations at that time involved examination of the existing emotion-provoking problems and apparently resulted in the resumption of more stable functioning. At the end of the three-year period (following conclusion of initial psychotherapy), Mr. A was on a normal diet with minimal daily medication (Lachman, 1972, pp. 1–2).

Stress and Ulcers

Many stressors have been implicated in the formation of ulcers. Among the first identified was *immobilization* (Selye, 1936). Wrapping rats in towels or tying their legs together reliably produced lesions in their stomachs. Approach-avoidance conflicts have also been extensively researched. Sawrey devised several illustrative experiments with rats to investigate whether prolonged approach-avoidance conflicts could produce ulcers. The animals lived in an environment in which shock was administered whenever they approached food or water. Thus they were in conflict over whether to approach the

food or avoid the shock. At the end of approximately two weeks many had developed ulcers, and some had even died from hemorrhages (Sawrey and Weisz, 1956; Conger, Sawrey, and Turrell, 1958).

Several qualities of stressful stimuli have also been found to be related to the production of ulcers. Unpredictable shock, for example, is more likely to cause lesions than shock that is preceded by a signal and is thus predictable (Weiss, 1970). Similarly, the ability to control a stressor reduces the severity of ulcers that are produced in experimental situations (Weiss, 1968).

Various stressors may operate similarly in human beings. Cobb and Rose (1973), for example, found that ulcers were twice as frequent among air traffic controllers as among pilots. The stress pilots are under may be less because they have more control over their planes than do the air traffic controllers. There are alternative explanations, however, that do not involve the concept of control. Today's commercial jet planes are so automated that, except for takeoff and landing, pilots actually have little to do com-

"THE FUNNY THING IS, I GOT MY ULCER AFTER I BECAME A BUM."

Air traffic controllers are at high risk for ulcers, perhaps because their job is chronically stressful.

pared to the constant vigilance that a traffic controller must maintain for hours on end. Moreover, at any given moment the decisions of an air traffic controller can affect the survival of many more human beings than can those of the pilot of a single passenger plane. There would seem to be a marked difference, then, in the extent of personal responsibility shouldered by people in these two emotionally demanding occupations.

Physiological Predisposition

In the studies using various stressors to produce ulcers, only *some* of the animals actually develop a lesion. Thus stress is apparently not the whole story in causing ulcers. Some predisposing factor or factors are also necessary. Rats, for example, have been bred to be ulcer-sensitive. Sines (1963) established a strain of animals, every one of which developed an ulcer when restrained. These rats appeared to be very "emotional." When placed in an open field they defecated more often than other animals.

Another possible candidate for a physiological predisposition is the amount of pepsinogen secreted by the peptic cells of the gastric glands in the stomach. Pepsinogen is converted into pepsin, the stomach enzyme which digests proteins and which in combination with hydrochloric acid is the principal active agent in gastric juice. Pepsinogen levels are therefore implicated in the formation of ulcers. By taking measurements through the umbilical cord, Mirsky (1958) was able to detect marked individual differences in pepsinogen levels in newborns. Furthermore, young infants with high levels of pepsinogen were found to be members of families with a high incidence of excessive pepsinogen levels. That only some people secrete large amounts of pepsinogen, depending on their genetic inheritance, does demonstrate that this variable has a possible causal role in the development of ulcers. Much stronger evidence would come from a prospective study showing that individuals who do not yet have ulcers but do have high levels of pepsinogen secretion are more likely to develop ulcers than another group, also without ulcers but with lower pepsinogen levels.

Such an investigation has in fact been conducted by Weiner and his co-workers (1957). These researchers measured the level of pepsinogen in 2073 newly inducted draftees. From this large number two smaller groups were selected, the 63 with the highest levels of pepsinogen and the 57 with the lowest levels. A complete gastrointestinal examination, given before basic training, showed that none had ulcers at that time. The majority of these men were then reexamined during the eighth and sixteenth weeks of their basic training. Nine cases of ulcers had developed, all of them in the group with high pepsinogen levels. Another study (Mirsky, 1958) of a population of children and civilian adults who had earlier been classified as high and low pepsinogen secreters revealed a similar tendency for ulcers to develop among those with high levels of pepsinogen.

In sum, the data available on ulcers are consistent with a diathesis-stress theory implicating in their development both stress and the physiological predisposition to secrete excessive amounts of pepsinogen. Consistent with the specific-reaction theory, individuals who develop ulcers appear to be predisposed to react to stress with excessive gastric secretions, which then produce lesions.

Cardiovascular Disorders

Essential Hypertension

Without question, one of the most serious psychophysiological disorders is hypertension, commonly called high blood pressure. This disease disposes people to atherosclerosis (clogging of the arteries), heart attacks, and strokes (see Chapter 17). It is estimated that more than half the deaths each year in the United States are caused by these diseases of the heart and brain. Were this statistic not alarming enough, in recent years the incidence of high blood pressure and related illnesses has increased markedly in younger age groups; heart attacks in men in their thirties are no longer as uncommon as they once were (Benson, 1975).

The pressure produced in the arteries as the heart pumps blood through them is referred to as blood pressure. Blood pressure may be elevated by increased cardiac output (the amount of blood leaving the left ventricle of the heart per minute), by increased resistance to the passage of blood through the arteries, that is, by vasoconstriction, and by an increase in fluid volume. *Essential hypertension* is a disorder characterized by chronic high blood pressure that cannot be traced to an evident organic cause; recent estimates are that varying degrees of hypertension are found in 15 to 33 percent of the adult population of the United States, and that no more than 10 percent of these cases are attributable to an identifiable physical cause, which is usually kidney dysfunction (Benson, 1975).

Lyght (1966) has offered the following description of the course of hypertension and the symptoms associated with the disorder.

> . . . Hypertension frequently is present for many years without symptoms or signs other than an elevated blood pressure. In the majority of cases, increased blood pressure first appears during early adult life (mean age of onset, the early thirties). These patients may complain of fatigue, nervousness, dizziness, palpitation, insomnia, weakness and headaches at some time in the course of the disorder. . . . The mean age of death for untreated patients is in the

fifties, and their average life expectancy probably is close to twenty years from the onset, with extremes of from several years to many decades (pp. 218 ff).

Unless people have their blood pressure checked, they may go for years without knowing that they are hypertensive. The disease, then, is known as "the silent killer."

Control over stress and blood pressure increase

Short-Term Effects. Various stressful conditions have been examined to determine their role in the etiology of essential hypertension. Stressful interviews, natural disasters, anger, and anxiety have been found to produce elevations in blood pressure (Innes, Millar, and Valentine, 1959; Ruskin, Board, and Schaffer, 1948; Ax, 1953). Kasl and Cobb (1970) have examined the effects of the loss of employment on blood pressure. They studied a group of workers beginning two months before their jobs were to be terminated and for two years subsequent to loss of employment. A control group, consisting of men in similar occupations who did not lose their jobs, was examined for the same twenty-six-month period. Each participant in the study was visited at home several times by a nurse during six separate periods so that blood pressure could be measured. For the control subjects there were no overall changes in blood pressure. In the men who lost their jobs, however, elevated blood pressure was found with anticipation of job loss, after termination of employment, and during the initial probationary period of a new job. Those who had great difficulty finding stable employment suffered the longest periods of high blood pressure.

In another group of studies (Hokanson and Burgess, 1962; Hokanson, Burgess, and Cohen, 1963, Hokanson, Willers, and Koropsak, 1968; Stone and Hokanson, 1969), based in part on psychoanalytic theory, Jack Hokanson and his colleagues attempted to determine whether blood pressure elevation is associated with the inhibition of aggression. Subjects were given a task but were angered almost immediately by the interruptions of a supposed fellow subject, actually a confederate of the experimenter. Later on, half of the subjects were given the opportunity to retaliate against their harasser.

The results of this series of investigations indicate that harassment of course causes blood pressure to rise but that, for males, aggressing against a source of frustration then helps blood pressure to decrease. With no opportunity to aggress against the frustrator, blood pressure is significantly slower to decrease after frustration. Only aggression directed at a low-status frustrator (college student) proved helpful in decreasing blood pressure, however, not that directed toward a high-status frustrator (visiting professor). These findings did not hold for female subjects.

Hokanson favors the following interpretation of his data: ". . . *Any* social response can be viewed as having arousal-reducing concomitants, if that response has been previously instrumental in terminating or avoiding aggression in others" (Stone and Hokanson, 1969, p. 72).

Hokanson's interpretation explains why aggression directed toward a high-status frustrator was not effective. Presumably, subjects have learned that it does not pay to retaliate against a high-status aggressor. Thus an aggressive response will *not* help to reduce arousal since such responses have not previously been rewarding. Similarly, Hokanson's position accounts for the fact that aggressive responses do not seem to reduce arousal for females. Social and cultural conditions prevailing for them when these studies were conducted dictated that the response to frustration not be aggression. This sex difference may disappear with growing social support for greater assertiveness in women.

The results of these studies seem to indicate that, consistent with our earlier discussion of control and helplessness (see page 166), any response giving *control* to the subject can decrease blood pressure. This possibility was directly examined in a study (Hokanson et al., 1971) in which subjects performed a symbol-matching task, with shocks delivered for poor performance. The task was set up so that subjects would receive, on the average, one shock every forty-five seconds. Participants were to spend twenty minutes working at the task but were allowed to take one-minute rest breaks so that they would not "become overly fatigued." Subjects who had "control" could take as many breaks as they wanted whenever they wanted. "No control" subjects were matched to the "control" subjects in the amount of time spent working and resting, but the number and timing of their rest periods were determined for them. The results (Figure 7.1) indicated clearly that control, not actual amount of rest, produced lower levels of blood pressure. Not having control, then, increases blood pressure and is perhaps an elicitor of essential hypertension.

A study by Harburg and others (1973) extends Hokanson's ideas to the natural environment and to the high incidence of hypertension among black Americans. Harburg and his colleagues chose two areas of Detroit in which to conduct their investigation. In one area, the high-stress location, the crime rate was substantial, population density, mortality rates and frequency of marital breakups were all high, and the socioeconomic status of residents was generally low. Conditions in the low-stress area were more favorable.

In each area groups of married black and white men were selected for study. During a visit to the participants' homes, a nurse took blood pressure readings, the respondents were interviewed, and a specially designed test was administered. The test presented hypothetical situations and asked the participants how they would respond. An example follows.

Now imagine that you were searching to find another place to live in, and finally found one for sale or rent which you liked, but the owner told you he would not sell or rent to you because of your religion, national origin or race. How would you feel about that? The response categories. . . were as follows: (1) "I'd get angry or mad and show it, (2) I'd get annoyed and show it, (3) I'd get annoyed, but would keep it in, (4) I'd get angry or mad but would keep it in, (5) I wouldn't feel angry or annoyed" (p. 280).

Participants were also asked how they would feel if they had become angry and showed it. The dimension assessed here was guilt, and the possible responses ranged from very guilty to no feelings of guilt at all.

Blood pressure was higher among the black males than among the whites; and blacks living in the high-stress area had higher blood pressure than blacks living in the middle-class neighborhoods. Thus previous statistics revealing racial differences in blood pressure were substantiated, but with the important reservation that environmental stress is also a major factor. When responses on the test were related to blood pres-

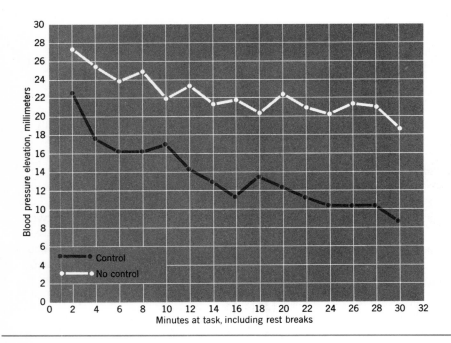

FIGURE **7.1**
Differences in blood pressure of subjects who controlled their rest breaks while performing a task and of subjects who did not, although they rested as much. After Hokanson et al., 1971.

Harburg and his co-workers found that blacks living in high-stress areas were likely to have high blood pressure, particularly if they felt guilty about expressing anger.

sure, the following pattern emerged. For all subjects except blacks in the low-stress area, holding anger in and guilt were related to higher blood pressure levels. The connection to Hokanson's work seems clear: not expressing anger and feeling guilty if anger is expressed would both be correlates of a sense of having no control. So again we see that lack of control may be a crucial variable in determining blood pressure.

Long-Term Effects. Thus far we have discussed stressors that can produce a temporary increase in blood pressure in normal individuals. But can such short-term increases develop into sustained, long-term hypertension? The mechanism inducing long-term hypertension would necessarily involve some structural changes in the organism.

For ethical reasons no experimental work has been done with human beings to determine whether short-term increases in blood pressure will develop into prolonged hypertension, but some research has been done on animals.

In general, true hypertension has proved elusive in the laboratory. In many studies using electric shock as a stressor, blood pressure increased during the period when the animal was stressed but returned to normal when the stress was removed. Somewhat more successful in producing long-term blood pressure elevations are studies that have used more naturalistic stress, such as competing with other animals for food (Peters, 1977). But the overall picture indicates that some predisposing factor or factors are required for stress to bring on hypertension.

Predisposing factors

In research with animals, several powerful diatheses have been identified—rearing in social isolation (Henry, Ely, and Stephens, 1972), level of emotionality (Farris, Yeakel, and Medoff, 1945), and sensitivity to salt (Friedman and Dahl, 1975). In the study having to do with salt, the researchers worked with two strains of rats who had been bred to be either sensitive or insensitive to the impact of salt in their diet. The sensitive rats reliably developed hypertension and died on a high-salt diet. These salt-sensitive rats were also likely to show sustained blood pressure elevations when placed in an experimentally created conflict situation.

Unfortunately, the information on physiological predispositions for hypertension in human beings is not very clear. Several studies have, however, demonstrated that hypertensives show greater blood pressure reactivity, reacting to stress and other novel situations with blood pressure increases that are larger than those of normal people (Engel and Bickford, 1961; Shapiro, 1961). In the Engel and Bickford study twenty female hypertensive patients and twenty control subjects were exposed to various stressors. Fifteen of the twenty hypertensives showed an increase in blood pressure, but only five of the controls did. In a similar vein Hodapp, Weyer, and Becker (1975) studied the blood pressure of hypertensive patients and normal controls while they rested, while they attended to colored slides of landscapes, and while they performed a demanding cognitive task (the stressor). The blood pressure of all subjects increased during the stress task. But in the hypertensives blood pressure was elevated in relation to that recorded during the rest period, even when they were simply viewing the slides.

This research on blood pressure reactivity as a possible physiological predisposition cannot be regarded as conclusive, however, for the individuals being studied were *already* hypertensive. Their reactivity might have been a *result* rather than a *cause* of their hypertension. To be conclusive, studies must begin with individuals who have the predisposition but have not yet developed essential hypertension. In one such longitudinal study (Rose, Jenkins, and Hurst, 1978) air traffic controllers were followed over a three-year period. Consistent with the other research we have discussed, men who initially showed greater blood pressure reactivity to their work were more likely to develop hypertension later on.

Coronary Heart Disease

A characterization of the disease

Coronary heart disease (CHD) takes two principal forms, angina pectoris and myocardial infarction or heart attack. The symptoms of <u>angina pectoris</u> are periodic chest pains, usually located behind the sternum and frequently radiating into the left shoulder and arm. The principal cause of these paroxysms of pain is an insufficient supply of oxygen to the heart, which, in turn, is traced to coronary atherosclerosis, a narrowing or plugging of the coronary arteries by deposits of fatty material. Angina is generally precipitated by physical or emotional exertion and is commonly relieved by rest or medication. Serious physical damage to heart muscle rarely results from an angina attack, for blood flow is reduced but not cut off. <u>Myocardial infarction</u> (MI) is a much more serious disorder and is one of the leading causes of death in the United States today. Like angina pectoris, myocardial infarction is caused by an insufficient oxygen supply to the heart. The oxygen insufficiency, more extreme than in angina pectoris, results either from a general curtailment of the heart's blood supply through ath-

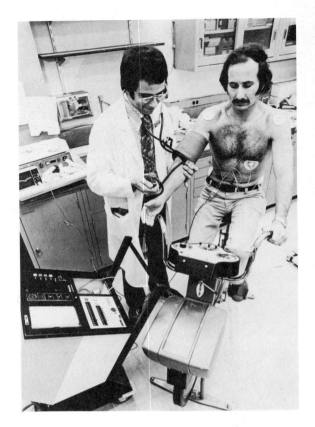

During a heart stress test the individual exercises at an increasing expenditure of energy under controlled conditions. His heartbeat is monitored throughout and during the following rest period, and blood pressure is taken periodically.

erosclerosis or from coronary occulsion, a sudden obstruction of a large coronary artery by deposits or by a blood clot. In both instances parts of the heart muscle die. In addition to this greater severity and possibility of death, myocardial infarction differs from angina in that it is not necessarily precipitated by exertion, and the pain is longer and more severe (Friedberg, 1966).

The American Heart Association lists seven factors related to increased risk for CHD: age, sex (males are at a greater risk), cigarette smoking, elevated blood pressure, elevated serum cholesterol, an increase in the size of the left ventricle of the heart, as revealed by electrocardiogram, and diabetes (Insull, 1973). The risk for heart disease generally increases with the number and severity of these factors. Still, Jenkins (1976) has concluded that these traditional risk factors leave at least half of the etiology of CHD unexplained.

Type A and type B behavior patterns

The search for other causes of CHD has sometimes focused on psychological factors such as stress and personality. Some evidence indicates a relationship between CHD and such stressors as an overload of work, chronic conflict, and the life stressors tapped by the SRRS (Jenkins, 1971, 1976; Rahe and Lind, 1971). The most promising evidence linking CHD to psychological variables, however, comes from investigations pioneered by Friedman and Rosenman (Friedman, 1969; Rosenman et al., 1975). In 1958 they identified a coronary-prone behavior pattern, called _type A._ Glass (1977) describes the type A individual as having an intense and competitive drive for achievement and advancement; an exaggerated sense of the urgency of passing time, of the need to hurry; and considerable aggressiveness and hostility toward others. Type A persons are overcommitted to their work, often attempt to carry on two activities at once, and believe that to get something done well, they must do it themselves. They cannot abide waiting in lines and they play every game to win, even when their opponents are children. Fast-thinking, fast-talking, and abrupt in gesture, they often jiggle their knees, tap their fingers, and blink rapidly. Too busy to notice their surroundings or to be interested in things of beauty, they tabulate success in life in numbers of articles written, projects underway, and material goods acquired. The type B individual, on the other hand, is relaxed and relatively free of such pressures.

Type A and B individuals have been reliably identified by means of a stress interview (Rosenman et al., 1964) in which questions are asked about the intensity of ambitions, competitiveness, the urgency of deadlines, and hostility. A self-report inventory, the Jenkins Activity Survey (Jenkins, Rosenman, and Zyzanski, 1974), covers similar topics. Glass (1977) has documented differences between identified type A and B persons that support the validity of these behavior patterns. In one study, for example, students were asked to walk continuously on a treadmill. Measurements of expired air indicated that the uncompromising type A individuals had worked closer to their physical limits yet reported less fatigue.

Evidence supporting the predictive validity of the type A pattern comes from the Western Collaborative Group Study (WCGS) (Rosenman et al., 1975). In a double-blind prospective investigation, 3524 men aged thirty-nine to fifty-nine were to be followed over a period of eight and a half years. Some 3154 men completed their participation in the study. Individuals who had been identified as type A in a stress interview were more than twice as likely to develop CHD than were type B men. In addition, type A men with CHD were more then five times as likely to have a second myocardial infarction than were other individuals with CHD. Traditional risk factors—parental history of heart attacks; high blood levels of cholesterol, triglycerides, and lipids; diabetes; elevated blood pressure; cigarette smoking; lack of education; and lack of exercise—were also found to be related to CHD, but even when these factors were controlled for, type A individuals were still twice as likely to develop CHD. These findings from the WCGS have provided strong evidence that type A behavior contributes to the development of CHD.

Further research has been spurred by the success of the WCGS. Recent work includes the identification and study of type A women (Waldron, 1978) and attempts to identify subsets of type A behavior that may be related to specific manifestations of coronary disease (Jenkins, Zyzanski, and Rosenman, 1978). Evidence collected by this second investigation suggests that "future angina" individuals may be even more in a hurry, irritable, and competitive than "future MI" individuals.

But how does a set of _psychological_ characteristics mediate a _physiological_ disease of the heart? In response to stress, type As have higher norepinephrine levels in the blood than do type Bs (Simpson et al., 1974).[4] High levels of norepi-

[4] Norepinephrine is a hormone released by the adrenal medulla. It and epinephrine, a somewhat similar hormone released with it, are called into play by and largely back up the sympathetic nervous system. Norepinephrine raises diastolic pressure. And it is a very powerful vasoconstrictor, narrowing even the blood vessels of the skeletal muscles. Norepinephrine is also a neurotransmitter, a substance by which information is passed from one neuron to the next (see page 253). As well as working in some of the nerve tracts of the brain, norepinephrine is the principal neurotransmitter secreted by the sympathetic nerve fiber endings.

nephrine can lead to arterial damage and lesions in the heart. Furthermore, high levels of norepinephrine can increase the extent to which blood platelets aggregate and thus make blockage in the arteries more likely. These are plausible, though speculative, links between the type A pattern and physiological mechanisms that are related to CHD.

Asthma

A Characterization of the Disease

Purcell and Weiss (1970) have described asthma in the following way.

> Asthma is a symptom complex characterized by an increased responsiveness of the trachea, major bronchi, and peripheral bronchioles to various stimuli, and is manifested by extensive narrowing of the airways which causes impairment of air exchange, primarily in expiration, [thus inducing] wheezing. [The airways may be narrowed] because of edema [an accumulation of excess watery fluid in the tissues] of the walls, increased mucus secretion, spasm of the bronchial muscles, or the collapse of the posterior walls of the trachea and bronchi during certain types of forced expiration (p. 597).

The major structures of the respiratory system are shown in Figure 7.2.

Most often, asthmatic attacks begin suddenly. The patient has a sense of tightness in the chest, wheezes, coughs, and expectorates sputum. Subjective reactions include panic-fear, irritability, and fatigue (Kinsman et al., 1974). A severe attack is a very frightening experience. The immense difficulty of getting air into and out of the lungs feels like suffocation, and the raspy, harsh noise of the gasping, wheezing, and coughing compounds the individual's terror. He or she may become exhausted by the exertion and fall asleep as soon as breathing is more normal.

The asthma sufferer takes a longer time than normal to expire air, and whistling sounds can be detected throughout the chest. These sounds are referred to as rales. Symptoms may last an hour or less or may continue for several hours or sometimes even days. Between attacks no abnormal signs may be detected when the individual is breathing normally, but forced, heavy expiration will often allow the rales to be heard through a stethoscope.

One patient, to be described in the following case history, had his first attack at age nine. His condition worsened until he was thirteen, after which he was symptom-free for ten years. From that time on, however, his condition deteriorated

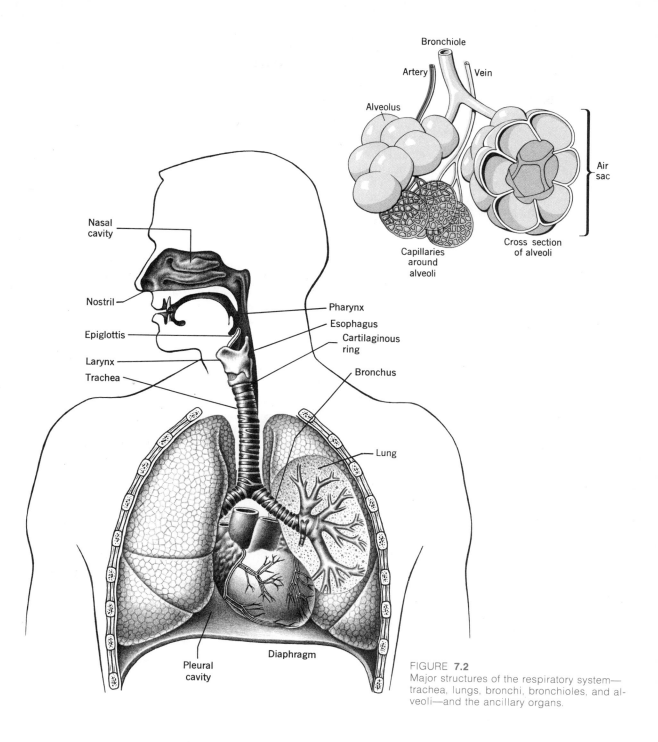

Bronchiole

Artery

Vein

Alveolus

Air
sac

Capillaries
around
alveoli

Cross section
of alveoli

Nasal
cavity

Nostril

Epiglottis

Larynx

Trachea

Pharynx

Esophagus

Cartilaginous
ring

Bronchus

Lung

Pleural
cavity

Diaphragm

FIGURE **7.2**
Major structures of the respiratory system—
trachea, lungs, bronchi, bronchioles, and alveoli—and the ancillary organs.

to an unusual degree, and the patient eventually died of respiratory complications—an outcome which fortunately is rare.

> Abundant data from this patient's life suggest the importance of emotional factors in precipitating exacerbations of his asthma. He gives a graphic description of developing wheezing and shortness of breath upon separation from his mother. Once, while away on a trip with either her or his grandmother (it is not clear which), in a strange hotel, separated from his companion by a wall, he suffered through the night, having the feeling that his wheezes might be loud enough to be heard and bring her in to rescue him.
>
> He described clearly the relationship of his symptoms to odors. His response to the scent of flowers may have had an allergic basis. That seems less likely in the case of the scent of "lovely ladies," which he stated also gave him asthma. So did certain "bad" smells, of asparagus and cigar smoke. . . . He had many conflicts around weeping, frequently described being dissolved in tears, but always with the implication that he never really was exhausting the reservoir of "sobbing." . . .
>
> At the time of his brother's marriage, the patient was jealous; he managed to forget to mail the 150 invitations to the ceremony that had been entrusted to him. In the church he was almost more prominent than the bride, walking down the aisle just before the ceremony, gasping for breath, and wearing a fur coat, although the month was July (Knapp, 1969, p. 135).

Somewhere between 2 and 5 percent of the population is estimated to have asthma. A third of asthma sufferers are children, and about two-thirds of these youngsters are boys (Graham et al., 1967; Purcell and Weiss, 1970). Williams and McNicol (1969) studied 30,000 seven-year-old Australian school children. They found a high correlation between the age of onset of the symptoms and the length of time the disorder lasted. If the age of onset was less than one, 80 percent were found to be still wheezing five years later. With ages of onset from three to four, 40 percent were still wheezing five years later, and with an onset age of five or six, only 20 percent were still wheezing five years later. Thus the earlier the disorder begins, the longer it is likely to last.

The Etiology of Asthma

Much of the debate concerning the importance of psychological factors in the development of asthma relates to whether or not emotionality is always implicated. To investigate the etiology of asthma, Rees (1964) divided the various possible causes into three categories, allergic, infective, and psychological. The cells in the respiratory tract may be especially sensitive to one or more substances or allergens such as pollen, molds, fur, and dust, bringing on asthma. Respiratory infections, most often acute bronchitis, can also make the respiratory system vulnerable to asthma. Anxiety, tension produced by frustration, anger, depression, and anticipated pleasurable excitement are all examples of psychological factors that may, through induced emotionality, disturb the functioning of the respiratory system and thus cause asthma.

The part played by allergic factors was assessed through the case histories that were taken and by making cutaneous and inhalation reaction tests with suspected allergens. Patients were also exposed to suspected allergens and inert substances without their knowing which was which. The importance of infective factors was determined through the case histories and X-rays, by examining sputum, and by searching for pus or other evidence of infection in the nose, sinuses, and chest. The potential importance of psychological factors was assessed through the case histories and by direct behavioral observations. The principal results of Rees's study demonstrate the importance of conceptualizing asthma as a disease with multiple causes. As can be seen from Table 7.3, psychological factors were considered a dominant cause in only 37 percent of the cases. And in 30 percent of the cases psychological variables were regarded as totally unimportant—a conclusion at odds with the popular notion that asthma is always psychosomatic.

Rees's data showed also that the different causes of asthma varied in importance depending on the age of the individual. For those asthmatic individuals less than five years of age, the infective factors predominated. From ages six to sixteen the infective factors still predominated, but psychological variables increased in importance. In the range from ages sixteen to sixty-

TABLE 7.3
Relative Importance of Allergic, Infective, and Psychological Factors in the Etiology of Asthma
(from Rees, 1964)

Factors	Relative importance, percent		
	Dominant	Sub-sidiary	Unim-portant
Allergic	23	13	64
Infective	38	30	32
Psychological	37	33	30

five, psychological factors decreased in importance until about the thirty-fifth year, thereafter becoming more consequential again.

Psychological factors producing asthma
Rees's studies have demonstrated that some, but by no means all, cases of asthma have psychological factors as a primary cause. Yet even when asthma is originally induced by an infection or allergy, psychological stress can precipitate attacks. Eysenck (1965), for example, has related a case study originally described by Katsch, who had

> . . . arrived at the hypothesis that the patient's mother-in-law, with whom he had many conflicts, constituted the source of the emotional trouble producing the asthmatic attacks and that a very large picture of her which hung in the bedroom of the patient was a . . . stimulus for these attacks. . . . [This hypothesis was tested as follows.] Katsch turned the mother-in-law's face to the wall, as it were, and immediately the asthmatic attacks ceased. They could be brought back at will, by turning the picture round again, and they could again be terminated by turning it to the wall once more; in other words, Katsch had achieved complete control over the asthmatic attacks of his patient (p. 207).

In another study exploring somewhat the same ground, Kleeman (1967) interviewed twenty-six patients over an eighteen-month period. According to the reports of these patients, 69 percent of their attacks began with an emotional disturbance.

Dekker and Groen (1956) were able to produce asthma attacks in the laboratory using the following procedure. Before the actual investigation twelve asthmatic patients had described environmental situations that precipitated attacks. When these situations were reproduced in actual or pictorial form in the laboratory, three of the twelve patients developed full-blown asthma attacks, and three others showed less severe respiratory symptoms. The stimuli to which the subjects ascribed their asthma included the national anthem, perfume, the sight of dust, horses, and waterfalls.

Finally, another study indicates the "power of suggestion" in inducing asthma attacks, even among individuals whose allergic reactions are regarded as the primary cause of their disorder (Luparello et al., 1971). Forty asthmatics and a control group of another forty persons were told that they were participating in a study of air pollution. The experimenter explained to each subject that he wanted to determine what concentrations of various substances would induce wheezing. The asthmatics were told that they would inhale five different concentrations of an irritant or allergen that had previously been established as a contributing cause of their asthma attacks. They were led to believe that each successive sample would have a higher concentration of the allergen, but in fact they were given only five nonallergenic saline solutions to inhale. The control subjects were told that they were inhaling pollutants which could irritate the bronchial tubes and make it difficult for them to breathe. Fourteen out of the forty asthmatic patients reacted with significant airway obstruction, and twelve went on to develop full-fledged attacks. None of the controls exhibited pathological respiratory reactions. Later the twelve subjects who had developed asthma attacks were given the same saline solution to inhale but were told that the solution was a bronchodilator. The condition of all twelve improved, confirming the role of suggestion in some asthmatics.

Classical conditioning

The two investigations just described suggest the possibility that asthma may be induced in a variety of situations as a result of conditioning. One conditioning experiment done with human beings as subjects had almost completely negative results, however. Dekker, Pelser, and Groen (1957) paired a known allergen with a neutral solvent. The classical conditioning hypothesis would argue that through repeated pairings of the CS and UCS, the CS should acquire the ability to elicit the asthmatic reaction. In this study, after repeated pairings, only two of a hundred subjects were found to have been successfully conditioned. Moreover, "In a personal communication dated October, 1961, Dekker reported that he was unable to replicate even these results" (Purcell and Weiss, 1970, p. 607). At this time there is no support for a classical conditioning account of asthma.

The role of the family

Several researchers have considered parent-child interactions to be important in the etiology of asthma. The investigators at the Children's Asthma Research Institute and Hospital in Denver routinely categorize their patients into those for whom psychological factors are considered the primary cause and those whose respiratory tracts are more greatly disturbed by other factors. In one investigation Purcell and his colleagues (1969) chose a group of twenty-two children. For thirteen children psychological factors were considered the principal precipitants of their asthma. For the other nine allergic or infective factors were considered more significant. These twenty-two children were studied over a considerable length of time which was subdivided into four periods. The first was an initial baseline period during which the children lived as usual with their families. In the second period the children still lived with their families, but all were informed that all family members except for the asthmatic child would soon be moved out for a two-week period. In the third period the children lived in their own homes but with a substitute mother, and in the fourth they were reunited with their parents. If the psychological factor disturbing one subgroup was the parent-child rela-

tionship, these children should improve when their parents lived apart from them. The children whose asthma was considered induced principally by allergic or infective factors would show no such improvement. The data supported the predictions remarkably well. Daily measurements and observations were made of the following variables: peak expiratory air flow, the force with which the individual can expel air; amount of medication required; wheezing; and frequency of asthma attacks. Seventy percent of the group who were predicted to do well without their parents improved during the separation phase (Figure 7.3). Of the nine children who were not predicted to do well without their parents, only one benefited from being separated.

Another study by Rees (1963) supports the theory that disturbed parent-child relationships may be a cause of asthma. He classified the attitudes of the parents of hospitalized asthmatic children as either satisfactory—the parents promote feelings of security and are affectionate and accepting; or unsatisfactory—parents are rejecting, perfectionistic, and overprotective. Only 44 percent of the parents of asthmatics were rated as having satisfactory attitudes, whereas 82 percent of the parents of control children, (accident cases in the same hospital), were rated in this way.

The research that we have discussed reveals the importance of the home life of asthmatics. It should be noted, however, that we cannot always tell whether various familial variables are causal agents or maintaining agents. Although certain emotional factors in the home may be important in eliciting early asthmatic attacks in some children, in others the illness may originally develop for nonfamilial reasons, and then the children's parents may unwittingly reward various symptoms of the syndrome. For example, the parents may cater to the child and treat him specially because of his asthma. Current recommendations for the treatment of asthmatic children supply indirect support for this thesis. Doctors prescribe no special treatment and no overprotection. Instead, asthmatic children are urged to lead as normal a life as possible, even to the extent of participating in athletic events. An attempt is made, then, to keep the children from considering their sickness as the dominating factors in their lives. This attitude is well illus-

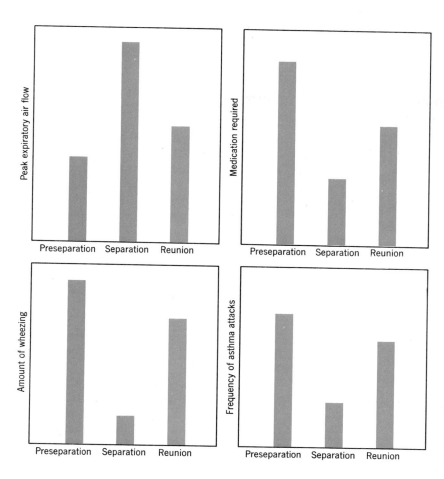

FIGURE **7.3**
Improvement on several measures of asthma among children who were predicted to do well after being separated from their parents. After Purcell et al., 1969.

trated in the following interaction presented by Kluger (1969).

Patient: I can't go to school today because my asthma is worse.

Doctor: I know, but since it's not contagious why can't you be in school?

Patient (irritated): Because I'm having trouble breathing!

Doctor: I can see that, but you'll have trouble breathing whether you go to school or not. Remaining in bed won't help your breathing.

Patient (Disgustedly): Boy, they don't even let you be sick in this hospital! (p. 361).

Personality and asthma
It has often been suggested that particular constellations of personality traits are linked to asthma. Several investigators have found that asthmatic individuals have a great many so-called neurotic symptoms: dependency and maladjustment (Herbert, 1965), meekness, sensitivity, anxiety, meticulousness, perfectionism, and obsessions (Rees, 1964). But most of this work consisted of comparing asthmatics to a normal control population. Neuhaus (1958) compared the personality test scores of asthmatic children to those of both a normal group of children and a group of children with cardiac conditions. As in other studies, the asthmatics were found to be more neurotic than those who were normal. But, and this is the important point, *the cardiac children were also more neurotic than normal children.* Thus the increased neuroticism of asthmatic children may reflect only reactions to a chronic illness; neuroticism scores on personality tests are always higher the longer the patient has been sick (Kelly and Zeller, 1969).

Physiological predisposition

Now that the importance of various stresses in eliciting asthmatic attacks has been documented, we must attempt to account for the fact that not all individuals exposed to such stressors develop asthma. Rees (1964) found that 86 percent of the asthmatics examined had had a respiratory infection before asthma developed. Only 30 percent of his control subjects had been so afflicted. This study can be regarded as evidence that inheriting a weak organ, establishing a reaction pattern, or both may figure in the etiology of asthma. Individuals whose asthma is primarily allergic may have an inherited hypersensitivity of the respiratory mucosa, which then overresponds to usually harmless substances such as dust or pollen. There is evidence that the incidence of asthma has a familial pattern consistent with genetic transmission of a diathesis (Konig and Godfrey, 1973). Finally, there is some indication that asthmatics have a less than normally responsive sympathetic nervous system (Miklich et al., 1973; Mathe and Knapp, 1971). Activation of the sympathetic nervous system is already known to reduce the intensity of an asthmatic attack.

In conclusion, a diathesis-stress explanation once again seems to fit the data on a psychophysiological disorder. Once the respiratory system is predisposed to asthma, any number of psychological stressors can interact with the diathesis to produce the disease.

Therapies for Psychophysiological Disorders

Therapists of the various persuasions agree in the most general terms that reducing anxiety is the best way to alleviate the suffering from psychophysiological disorders. The particular disorder, whether it be ulcer, essential hypertension, coronary heart disease, or an asthma attack, is considered a consequence of anxiety or to be linked with it in some way. Psychoanalytically oriented workers employ techniques such as free association and dream analysis, as they do with other anxiety sufferers, in their efforts to help the egos of their patients confront the supposed infantile origins of their fears. Ego analysts, however, like Franz Alexander, consider specific emotional states to underlie the several disorders and try to strengthen present functioning. Thus they would encourage someone with essential hypertension, viewed as laboring under a burden of undischarged hostility, to assert himself and thereby siphon it off.

Client-centered therapists similarly regard people beset with psychophysiological disorders as needing to reduce anxiety, but they place special blame on the individual's conflict with society. Ulcers, hypertension, and coronary heart disease are considered the physiological evidence of the stress felt by those who comply with an establishment whose values go against their own best interests. The goal of the attentive listening and empathic reflection of client-centered therapists is to help clients see the physiological price paid for social conformity and make responsible decisions about changing their mode of living.

Behavior therapists employ their usual range of procedures for reducing anxiety—systematic desensitization, rational-emotive therapy, and assertion training—depending on the source of tension. If the person does not know how to act in a particular situation, behavior rehearsal and shaping may help him or her acquire necessary skills.

Behavioral medicine, a new area of specialization in behavior therapy, focuses on psychological factors that are linked to physical problems. Obviously psychophysiological disorders are of special interest to these mental health workers. Several forms of relaxation training are given as a part of medical treatment for a number of these disorders. One important area of research is to help people stop smoking cigarettes, which has been linked to a host of medical problems. These therapists also work on methods to help people lose weight (Marston and Marston, 1980). Carrying around extra pounds, especially as people grow older, can contribute to coronary heart disease and to hypertension.

In recent years behavioral researchers have been exploring the clinical uses of _biofeedback_ as a means of improving somatic functioning. Biofeedback provides people with prompt and exact informaton, otherwise unavailable, on heart rate, blood pressure, brain waves, skin temperature, and other autonomic bodily functions. The particular internal physiological process is detected and amplified by a sensitive electronic recording device. The person knows instantaneously, through an auditory or visual signal, the rate of the process, whether it is too high or too low or just right. Numerous studies have shown that most people, if given the task, for example, of raising their heart rates or lowering their blood pressure, can do so with the help of biofeedback (Elmore and Tursky, 1980; Shapiro, Tursky, and Schwartz, 1970). What is not yet clear is whether through biofeedback they can achieve results that are of clinical significance. Several studies have demonstrated improvement in essential hypertension (Blanchard and Miller, 1977) and in tension headache (Budzynski et al., 1973), but perhaps other factors, such as relaxation training, have been responsible for the favorable results obtained. Biofeedback will be evaluated in greater depth in Chapter 19. Box 7.2 presents a recent example of promising clinical research.

Researchers in behavioral medicine also address the challenge of altering the driven, overcompetitive patterns of the type A individual, who has been shown to be at high risk for heart disease. A five-year study, funded by the National Heart, Lung and Blood Institute, is investigating the possibility of reducing the impatience and overcommitment to work, the anger and the hostility of 600 type A heart attack victims, with the hope of lowering the risk of their having second heart attacks. These people meet regularly in small groups with a professional leader to discuss their life strategies and problems and to role-play troublesome situations. They are also given exercises to practice, such as standing in line, and advice on how to reduce the irritation they usually feel. Members of the control group, another 300 type A people who have had at

Biofeedback procedures are being applied in the treatment of a number of psychophysiological disorders. Shown here is a demonstration of techniques sometimes used to relieve headaches.

BOX 7.2 Migraine Headache and Biofeedback

When I am in a migraine aura (for some people the aura lasts fifteen minutes, for others several hours), I will drive through red lights, lose the house keys, spill whatever I am holding, lose the ability to focus my eyes or frame coherent sentences, and generally give the appearance of being on drugs, or drunk. The actual headache, when it comes, brings with it chills, sweating, nausea, a debility that seems to stretch the very limits of endurance. That no one dies of migraine seems, to someone deep into an attack, an ambiguous blessing. (From Joan Didion, The White Album, *pp. 170–171. Copyright © 1979, by Joan Didion. Reprinted by permission of Simon and Schuster, a Division of Gulf and Western Corporation.)*

Migraine headaches are estimated to afflict up to 10 percent of the general population. Some people have these attacks as often as every few days, others only a few times in their lives. The headache pain itself is usually on one side, almost as though the head were divided in two by an impermeable wall. It has been said that only those actually afflicted with this most common of psychophysiological disorders can know how extreme is the suffering associated with migraine.

A distinction is usually made between classic migraine and common migraine. In classic migraine the person has prodromal symptoms, symptoms experienced before the onset of the headache itself. They take the form of tension, wakefulness, declining energy and drive, and sometimes visual disturbances which are seen first as a shimmering haze, then as zigzag lines. In both types of migraine it is known that the headache itself is caused by sustained dilation, or increase in size, of the extracranial vasculature, principally of the temporal artery which trifurcates to supply the side of the head. Almost universally, the headache is initially a pulsing pain on one side of the head, coinciding with each heartbeat as the blood is pumped through the expanded extracranial arteries. The pain is caused by these dilated arteries triggering pain-sensitive nerve fibers in the scalp. As the headache progresses, the pain becomes steadier. The arteries thicken and rigidify, making stimulation

of the extracranial nerve fibers constant rather than pulsing (Elmore, 1979). Recent evidence indicates that the scalp arteries of migraine victims are more sensitive to autonomic nervous stimulation than those of normal people. Other evidence points to a general instability in vasomotor control, which appears to be the inherited diathesis that predisposes these unfortunates to reacting to stress with this debilitating disorder.

For many years there has been a controversy about the causes of the extracranial vascular dilation. In classic migraine, it will be recalled, visual disturbances are among the prodromal symptoms. These precursors to the headache itself, according to some researchers, are caused by intense constriction, or narrowing, of the internal carotid artery and its branches, the cranial arteries supplying blood to the brain and to the visual system. Somehow, the theorizing goes, this initial constriction of the internal cranial arteries produces the subsequent dilation of the external carotid artery and its branches, in particular of the temporal arteries, that is the immediate cause of the migraine headache itself.

Consequently, there are two competing schools of thought regarding the best kind of treatment for migraine: one concentrates on the intracranial vasoconstriction during the prodromal stage, the other on the extracranial vasodilation of the headache phase. The first tries to dilate internal arteries by reducing sympathetic activity, the second to constrict external arteries by increasing sympathetic activity. Sympathetic activity can be reduced through such psychological techniques as deep-muscle relaxation training (Jacobson, 1929); autogenic training, a method promoting relaxation through suggestions of heaviness and warmth* (Luthe and Schultz, 1969); and a Westernized version of transcendental meditation (Benson, 1975). Of particular importance for our present discussion are studies that employ biofeedback to increase finger temperature as a means of promoting vasodilation in the body generally. Clinical reports of research conducted originally at the famous

* A series of six exercises train patients to regulate their breathing and heart rates and to make their extremeties feel heavy and warm, the stomach warm, the forehead cool. Autogenic training is considered a combination of relaxation training and self-hypnosis.

Menninger Clinic in Topeka, Kansas (Sargent, Green, and Walters, 1972, 1973), claimed marked improvement in a number of migraine patients who were taught to warm their hands through biofeedback training and then to initiate hand warming on their own at the slightest warning that a headache was coming on. Unfortunately, these studies were flawed by serious methodological problems. Nothing indicated that patients actually learned to warm their hands, and the judgments of improvement were unsystematic and impressionistic (Elmore, 1979). The Menninger reports, however, did stimulate a series of more rigorous clinical studies.

The second treatment for migraine focuses on increasing sympathetic activity in order to halt extracranial artery dilation. Through biofeedback the individual is trained to reduce the amplitude of pulsations in the superficial temporal arteries, in other words to constrict the arteries at the site of the actual migraine headache.

Graham and Wolff (1938) had earlier given migraine sufferers ergotamine tartrate, a powerful vasoconstrictive drug, and found significant lowering of pulse in the superficial temporal arteries and in the occipital, the extracranial arteries at the side and rear of the head; patients also reported less headache pain. As with many drugs, however, the very vasoconstriction that appeared to alleviate the migraine had some serious side effects, such as nausea and numbness and even gangrene in the extremities. These side effects encouraged work on psychological methods of contricting just the extracranial arteries. A number of researchers have demonstrated that patients find relief from migraine by learning to lower extracranial artery pulse via biofeedback (for example, Friar and Beatty, 1976).

From an examination of the migraine treatment literature, Elmore (1979) concluded that a study was needed to compare the two competing approaches to treatment. He also wanted to demonstrate by careful physiological measurement that whatever response was asserted to have been acquired via biofeedback was in fact acquired; and to determine whether therapy gains were maintained by following up patients for a period of time after their training.

Elmore divided a sample of twenty-three adults suffering from migraine into two groups: one received eight sessions of biofeedback training to raise hand temperature, the other eight sessions of biofeedback training to lower temporal pulse. Both groups had a ninth session without feedback to test whether members could perform the learned response on their own. To achieve the respective goals of their groups, raising hand temperature or lowering temporal pulse, subjects were to generate images of warmth or coolness, or to adopt any technique, other than tensing the muscles, that seemed to work for them. They were also encouraged to practice these strategies every day for about fifteen minutes and at the slightest warning that a headache was about to begin. For a month before and following treatment all subjects recorded the occurrence and intensity of headache in a specially designed pain and discomfort diary. If the people lowering temporal pulse did better than the hand-warming people, it could be concluded that migraine should be treated by *increasing* sympathetic nervous system activity. To relieve migraine headaches people need merely constrict the extracranial arteries. Superiority of hand warming, in contrast, would indicate that earlier on vasodilation is necessary in order to prevent the intracranial vasoconstriction believed by the Menninger group to trigger the later extracranial vasodilation.

Physiological measurements taken during the biofeedback training showed that members of each group did in fact learn the skill they were being taught. Moreover, the subjects lowering temporal pulse showed a pattern of general sympathetic nervous system activation, the hand-warming group deactivation of this system, demonstrating that the respective training procedures had the intended effects on the autonomic nervous system. Finally, the all-important treatment results: the people lowering temporal pulse achieved significantly more improvement during the one-month posttreatment evaluation than did the hand-warming subjects. Specifically, they reported fewer than half the headaches suffered before treatment, ingested significantly less headache medication, and tended to rate as less painful whatever headaches they had. In contrast, members of the hand-warming group rated their posttreatment headaches as significantly more painful and somewhat longer lasting than those suffered before treatment. The results, then, pose a serious challenge to the view that migraine is caused by sympathetic overarousal and that, generally speaking, people with this disorder should try to reduce their sympathetic nervous activity through relaxation training or tension-reducing drugs. Rather, treatment should be aimed more directly at constriction of the extracranial arteries.

least one heart attack, meet periodically with a cardiologist to discuss heart disease. It is expected that what is learned through this long-term study will help many who survive their first heart attack avoid a second one.

Since psychophysiological disorders are true physical dysfunctions, sound psychotherapeutic practice calls for close consultation with a physician. Whether the high blood pressure is organically caused or, as in essential hypertension, linked to psychological stress, the diuretic chlorthalidone will increase excretion by the kidneys of sodium chloride and thus reduce its presence in arterial walls and in turn their constriction. Reserpine has a sedative effect and also reduces arterial pressure. Antacids relieve the discomfort of ulcers, and anticholinergic drugs, which act like the sympathetic nervous system, decrease the secretion of gastric juice. Asthma attacks can be alleviated by oral inhalation or injection of agents that dilate the bronchial tubes, one of the most effective being epinephrine. The help that drugs provide in ameliorating the damage and the discomfort in the particular body systems cannot be underestimated. Mental health and medical professionals recognize, however, that most drug interventions are only symptomatic; they do not deal with the fact that the person is reacting emotionally to psychological stress. Although the evidence suggests that the predisposition for a particular organ breakdown is inherited or at least somatically based, nonetheless, the manner in which a person responds psychologically probably is not, and it is to this realm that psychotherapeutic interventions are directed.

Summary

Psychophysiological disorders are physical diseases produced by psychological factors, primarily stress. Such disorders usually affect organs innervated by the autonomic nervous system, such as those of the respiratory, cardiovascular, gastrointestinal, and endocrine systems. Research has focused on the question of how psychological stress produces a particular psychophysiological disorder. Some workers have proposed that the answer lies in the specifics of the stressor. One piece of evidence singles out great personal responsibilities as creating enough pressure to give an individual an ulcer. Theories and some evidence link the need for power and inhibition of aggression to hypertension, the type A personality to heart attacks. Other theories propose that stress must interact with a physiological diathesis; for ulcers the diathesis may be a tendency of the stomach to secrete too much acid, for hypertension a labile circulatory system, for heart attacks a sympathetic nervous system that releases too much norepinephrine, and for asthma a respiratory system that overresponds to an allergen or one that has been weakened by prior infection. Although we have spoken of psychological stress affecting the body, it must be remembered that the *mind* and the *body* are best viewed as two different ways of talking about the same organism.

The general aim of therapies for psychophysiological disorders is to reduce anxiety and regulate autonomic arousal. Behavioral medicine, a new field of specialization in behavior therapy, tries to find psychological interventions that can alleviate these disorders. It has developed ways of helping people to relax, smoke less, eat fewer fatty foods, and, via biofeedback, gain control over various autonomic functions, such as heart rate and blood pressure. One study is developing methods by which type A victims of heart attacks can abandon their angry, driving ways. But since psychophysiological disorders represent true physical dysfunctions, medications are usually called for as well.

chapter 8

AFFECTIVE DISORDERS

Melancholia, a term derived from the Greek words *melan* meaning black and *choler* meaning bile, and mania, derived from the Greek word *mainesthai*, to be mad, were two of the three types of mental disorder recognized by Hippocrates in the fourth century B.C. By the second century A.D. the physician Aretaeus of Cappadocia had suggested a relationship between melancholia and the apparently opposite emotional state of mania. In the late nineteenth century, as we have seen, the famous German psychiatrist Emil Kraepelin listed two major types of psychoses. One, schizophrenia, will be discussed in Chapters 13 and 14. The other, *manic-depressive illness,* which was considered to be the disturbance of all patients showing "affective excess," is the subject of this chapter.

General Characteristics of Depression and Mania

Depression

"Depression is the common cold of psychopathology, at once familiar and mysterious" (Seligman, 1973). It has been estimated that at least 12 percent of the adult population have at least one episode of *depression* serious enough that individuals should seek professional help (Schuyler and Katz, 1973). Just as most people experience at least moments of anxiety every week of their existence, so will each of us probably have more than an ample amount of sadness during the course of our lives, although perhaps not to the degree or with the frequency that the diagnosis depression is warranted. Often depression is associated with other psychological problems and with medical conditions. The man who has trouble maintaining his erection during intercourse is usually depressed about his sex life. The woman who has had a hysterectomy often suffers depression over what she incorrectly believes to be a loss of her femininity. Agoraphobics may become despondent because of their inability to venture out of their homes. In these and many other instances depression is best viewed as secondary to another condition. Our discussion of depression in this chapter will focus on people for whom this affective disorder is the primary problem.

The following eloquent account is from a person who would be regarded as suffering from profound depression. Clearly, anxiety also plays a part in deepening the despair.

> *I was seized with an unspeakable physical weariness. There was a tired feeling in the muscles unlike anything I had ever experienced. A peculiar sensation appeared to travel up my spine to my brain. I had an indescribable nervous feeling. My nerves seemed like live wires charged with electricity. My nights were sleepless. I lay with dry, staring eyes gazing into space. I had a fear that some terrible calamity was about to happen. I grew afraid to be left alone. The most trivial duty became a formidable task. Finally mental and physical exercises became impossible; the tired muscles refused to respond, my "thinking apparatus" refused to work, ambition was gone. My general feeling might be summed up in the familiar saying "What's the use." I had tried so hard to make something of myself, but the struggle seemed useless. Life seemed utterly futile (Reid, 1910, pp. 612–613).*

Depression has been studied from several perspectives in addition to such phenomenological reports. Psychoanalytic views emphasize the unconscious conflicts associated with grief and loss; cognitive theories focus on the depressed person's self-defeating thought processes; learning theorists contend with the curtailment of activity associated with depression; and physiologi-

cal theorists concentrate on what the central nervous system is doing at the neurochemical level.

There is general agreement on the most common signs and symptoms of depression (Robins and Guze, 1970; DSM-III, 1980).

1. Sad, depressed mood.

2. Poor appetite and weight loss or increased appetite and weight gain.

3. Difficulties in sleeping (insomnia): not falling asleep initially, not returning to sleep after awakening in the middle of the night, and early morning awakenings; or in some depressed patients a desire to sleep a great deal of the time.

4. Shift in activity level, becoming either lethargic (psychomotor retardation) or agitated.

5. Loss of interest and pleasure in usual activities.

6. Loss of energy, great fatigue.

7. Negative self-concept; self-reproach and self-blame, feelings of worthlessness and guilt.

8. Complaints or evidence of difficulty in concentrating, such as slowed thinking and indecisiveness.

9. Recurrent thoughts of death or suicide.

Paying attention is an exhausting effort for the depressed. They cannot take in what they read and what other people say to them. Conversation is also a chore, for many prefer to sit alone and to remain silent. They speak slowly, after long pauses, using few words and a low, monotonous voice. Others are too agitated and cannot sit still. They pace, wring their hands, sighing and moaning all the while or complaining. When depressed individuals are confronted with a problem, no ideas for its solution occur to them. Every moment has a great heaviness, and their heads fill and reverberate with self-recriminations. Depressed people may also neglect personal hygiene and appearance and make numerous hypochondriacal complaints of aches and pains that apparently have no physical basis. Utterly dejected and completely without hope and

Depression was Marilyn Monroe's frequent adversary and a disrupter of her personal and professional life. She fought many bouts of it throughout her career and earlier and then lost a final one.

initiative, they may be apprehensive, anxious, and despondent much of the time.

A single individual seldom shows all the aspects of depression; the diagnosis is typically made if at least a few signs are evident, particularly a *mood* of profound sadness that is out of proportion to the person's life situation. Fortunately, most depression, although recurrent, tends to dissipate with time. But an average untreated episode may stretch on for six to eight months or even longer. When depression becomes chronic, the patient does not always snap back to an earlier level of functioning between bouts. The following case description conveys the course of depression.

Mr. J. was a fifty-one-year-old industrial engineer who, since the death of his wife five years earlier, had been suffering from continuing episodes of depression marked by extreme social withdrawal and occasional thoughts of suicide. His wife had died in an automobile accident during a shopping trip which he himself was to

have made but had canceled because of professional responsibilities. His self-blame for her death, which became evident immediately after the funeral and was regarded by his friends and relatives as transitory, deepened as the months, and then years, passed by. He began to drink, sometimes heavily, and when thoroughly intoxicated would plead to his deceased wife for forgiveness. He lost all capacity for joy—his friends could not recall when they had last seen him smile. His gait was typically slow and labored, his voice usually tearful, his posture stooped. Once a gourmet, he had lost all interest in food and good wine, and on those increasingly rare occasions when friends invited him for dinner, this previously witty, urbane man could barely manage to engage in small talk. As might be expected, his work record deteriorated markedly, along with his psychological condition. Appointments were missed and projects haphazardly started and then left unfinished. He was referred by his physician for psychotherapy after he had spent a week closeted in his home. Not long afterward, he seemed to emerge from his despair and began to feel his old self again.

Mania

Some people who suffer from episodic periods of depression also at times suddenly abound with joyful elation and become very active, confident, and full of plans. Although there are clinical reports of individuals who experience _mania_ but not depression, such a condition is apparently quite rare. Mania has the following signs and symptoms.

1. Elevated, expansive, or irritable mood.

2. Increase in activity level—at work, socially, or sexually.

3. Unusual talkativeness, rapid speech, and the subjective impression that thoughts are racing.

4. Less than the usual amount of sleep needed.

5. Inflated self-esteem; belief that one has special talents, powers, and abilities.

6. Distractibility; attention easily diverted.

7. Involvement in activities that are likely to have undesirable consequences, such as reckless spending.

The manic stream of remarks is loud and incessant, full of puns, jokes, plays on words, rhyming, and interjections about nearby objects that have diverted the speaker's attention. This speech is very difficult to interrupt. It also reveals the manic's so-called _flight of ideas._ Although small bits of talk are coherent, the individual shifts from topic to topic with great rapidity. The manic need for activity may cause the individual to be annoyingly sociable and intrusive, constantly and sometimes purposelessly busy, and unfortunately oblivious to the obvious pitfalls of his or her endeavors. Any attempt to curb all this momentum can bring quick anger and even rage. Mania usually comes on suddenly, over the period of a day or two. Untreated episodes may last from a few days to several months.

The following description of a case of mania comes from our files. The irritability that is often part of this state was not found in this patient.

Mr. M., a thirty-two-year-old postal worker, had been married for eight years. He and his wife lived comfortably and happily in a middle-class neighborhood with their two children. In retrospect there appeared to be no warning for what was to happen. On February the twelfth Mr. M. let his wife know that he was bursting with energy and ideas, that his job as a mail carrier was unfulfilling, and that he was just wasting his talent. That night he slept little, spending most of the time at a desk, writing furiously. The next morning he left for work at the usual time but returned home at eleven a.m., his car filled to overflowing with aquaria and other equipment for tropical fish. He had quit his job and then withdrawn all the money from the family's savings account. The money had been spent on tropical fish equipment. Mr. M. reported that the previous night he had worked out a way to modify existing equipment so that fish ". . . won't die anymore. We'll be millionaires." After unloading the paraphernalia, Mr. J. set off to canvass the neighborhood for possible buyers, going door to door and talking to anyone who would listen.

The following bit of conversation from the period after Mr. M. entered treatment indicates his incorrigible optimism and provocativeness.

Therapist: Well, you seem pretty happy today.

Client: Happy! Happy! You certainly are a master of understatement, you rogue! (Shouting, literally jumping out of seat.) Why I'm ecstatic. I'm leaving for the West coast today, on my daughter's bicycle. Only 3100 miles. That's nothing, you know. I could probably walk, but I want to get there by next week. And along the way I plan to contact a lot of people about investing in my fishing equipment. I'll get to know more people that way— you know, Doc, "know" in the biblical sense (leering at therapist seductively). Oh, God, how good it feels. It's almost like a nonstop orgasm.

Formal Diagnostic Listings

Two major *affective disorders* are listed in DSM-III, *major depression* and *bipolar disorder.* The symptoms of major depression, sometimes also referred to as *unipolar depression,* are the profoundly sad mood and disturbances of appetite, weight, sleep, and activity level just described. Major depression is one of the most widespread of the disorders considered in this book. Approximately 5 to 10 percent of men and 10 to 20 percent of women will be clinically depressed at least once in their lives (Weissman and Myers, 1978; Woodruff, Goodwin, and Guze, 1974). The critical symptoms of bipolar disorder are the elated or irritable mood, talkativeness, and hyperactivity of mania, as well as episodes of depression. In addition, people who suffer only manic episodes are diagnosed as having bipolar disorder. The incidence of bipolar disorder is much lower than that of major depression—about one percent of the population (for example, Weissman and Myers, 1978).

The bases for distinguishing major (unipolar) depression and bipolar disorder

There is abundant evidence that the bipolar-unipolar distinction is an important one. Those suffering the two disorders differ in ways other than whether they have manic episodes. For example, when bipolars are depressed, they typically sleep more than usual and are lethargic, whereas unipolars have insomnia and are agitated. Unipolar depression usually has a later age of onset than does bipolar disorder, the average ages being thirty-six and twenty-eight, respectively. Moreover, more relatives of individuals with bipolar disorder have affective disorders than do the relatives of those with unipolar depression. Lithium carbonate is more therapeutic for bipolars who are currently depressed than it is for unipolars. All these differences add to the validity of the bipolar-unipolar distinction (Depue and Monroe, 1978).

Unipolar depressions

A problem remaining in the classification of affective disorders, however, is the great heterogeneity of unipolar depressives. In the previous edition of the DSM, various attempts were made to deal with this diversity. The factors distinguishing among various types of unipolar depression were age of onset, the presence or absence of stress, and whether or not the patient was psychotic. Involutional melancholia, one of the DSM-II categories, was thought to occur at the "change of life," when both men and women go through physiological changes that make it less likely that they will be able to reproduce. Stress was not viewed as an important etiological factor; rather physiological (hormonal) changes were believed to cause this kind of depression. But no evidence substantiates this belief. We know that, in addition to somatic changes, individuals in their forties and fifties face considerable other difficulties: doubts about sexual attractiveness, realization that certain life goals may never be achieved, and loss of contact with children. All are likely contributors to depression in people of this age. In two other DSM-II diagnoses, neurotic and psychotic depression, a life event was assumed to have brought on the reactions. But deciding whether depression was indeed caused by environmental stress proved troublesome.

DSM-III retains the option of diagnosing a depressed patient as psychotic but drops the notion of neurotic depression. Depressed patients are diagnosed as psychotic if they are subject to delusions and hallucinations. Among such depressives delusions and hallucinations are usually *mood-congruent.* Psychotically depressed patients may believe that they are being punished for past sins. Or their feelings of inadequacy may be elaborated into delusions of past inabilities and failures. Sometimes they think that the world is coming to an end. Nelson and Bowers (1978) have reported data that validate the psychotic-nonpsychotic distinction. Psychotically depressed patients do not usually respond well to the usual drug therapies for depression. But they do respond favorably to these drugs when they are combined with the drugs commonly used to treat other psychotic disorders such as schizophrenia.

Finally, according to DSM-III, some unipolar depressives may also have melancholic symptoms. They find no pleasure in any activity and are unable to feel better even temporarily when something good happens. Their depressed mood is distinctly different from "normal" grief and is worse in the morning. They awaken about two hours too early, lose appetite and weight, have strong feelings of guilt, and are either lethargic or extremely agitated. The validity of the distinction between depressions with or without melancholia is at present unknown. Depression with melancholia, however, is similar to an older concept, endogenous depression, which did seem to be useful (for example, Mendels and Cochrane, 1968).

Psychological Theories of Depression

As is true of theorizing about other abnormal syndromes, that concerning depression points to both psychological and physiological factors. It will be seen that each theoretical position emphasizes one or another aspect of depression at the expense of others. In this section we discuss several theories that are couched in psychological terms.

Psychoanalytic Theory

It is not always easy to distinguish between sadness, which is normal, and depression, which is not. The contrast between normal grief and abnormal depression is the focal point of Abraham's (1911) original attempt to interpret depression through psychoanalytic theorizing and of Freud's (1917) celebrated paper, "Mourning and Melancholia." Abraham was Freud's student. They both saw self-centeredness as differentiating depression from normal grief. Freud's work was an elaboration of Abraham's theorizing.

Predictably, Freud saw the potential for depression being created early in childhood. He theorized that during the oral period the child's needs may be insufficiently or oversufficiently gratified. The person therefore remains "stuck" in this stage and dependent on the instinctual gratifications particular to it. With this arrest in psychosexual maturation, this fixation at the oral stage, he or she may develop a tendency to be excessively dependent on other people for the maintenance of self-esteem.

From this happenstance of childhood, how can the adult come to suffer from depression? The reasoning is complex, assuming as it does that several unconscious processes are a part of mourning. Freud hypothesized that after the loss of a loved one the mourner first _introjects_ or incorporates the lost person: he or she identifies with the lost one, perhaps in a fruitless attempt to undo the loss. Because, as Freud asserted, we unconsciously harbor negative feelings against those we love, the mourner now becomes the object of his or her own hate and anger. In addition, the mourner also resents being deserted and feels guilt for real or imagined sins against the lost person. The period of introjection is followed by the period of _mourning work,_ during which the mourner recalls memories of the lost one and thereby separates himself from the person who has died and loosens the bonds that introjection has imposed.

The grief work can go astray in overly dependent individuals and develop into an ongoing process of self-abuse, self-blame, and depression. Such individuals do not loosen their emotional bonds with the person who has died, continuing to castigate themselves for the faults and shortcomings perceived in the loved one who has been introjected. The mourner's anger toward the lost one continues to be directed inward. This theorizing is the basis for the widespread psychodynamic view of depression as anger turned against oneself.

One further point must be made. Since many people can become depressed and remain so _without_ having recently suffered the loss of a loved one, it became necessary to invoke the concept of _"symbolic loss"_ in order to keep the theoretical formulation intact. For example, a person may unconsciously interpret a rejection as a total withdrawal of love.

We see numerous problems in this formulation. First, since the person presumably both hates and loves the individual he or she has lost, why is it that only the hate and anger are turned inward and not the love that is also there? Since the depressed person is said to have introjected the loved one, thus directing inwardly the feelings previously directed to the loved one, why do anger and resentment predominate? If the mourner directed positive feelings about the lost one inwardly, he or she would be a happy person rather than a depressed one. Psychoanalytic theorists have tried to resolve this inconsistency by postulating that the loss of a loved one is viewed as a rejection or withdrawal of affection. Interpreted in this way, a negative emotional state is more likely to predominate. The crucial point, though, is the absence of direct evidence that depressives do interpret death as rejection by the deceased.

A second difficulty is common to all Freud's hypotheses that involve the concept of fixation at an earlier psychosexual stage of development. Freud states that fixation at the oral stage can come about _through either too little or too much gratification._ How much, it could be asked, is _enough_ to prevent fixation? Freud's theory, being nonquantitative, does not deal adequately with this question.

The concept of "symbolic loss" presents a third problem. From our critical perspective, this concept is introduced only after the fact to account for depression when no actual object loss can be specified. The concept would not be invoked for people who are not depressed. If it is inferred only _after_ a diagnosis of depression and only _after_ no actual object loss can be discerned, the diagnostician is engaging in the kind of confused reasoning referred to as _post hoc, ergo propter hoc,_ after this, therefore because of this.

Little research has been generated by psychoanalytic points of view, neither Freud's nor those of others that are not discussed here. The little information available does not support the theory. Dreams and projective tests should theoretically be means of expressing unconscious needs and fears. Beck and Ward (1961) analyzed the dreams of depressed people and found themes of loss and failure, not of anger and hostility. An examination of responses to projective tests established that depressives identify with the victim, not the aggressor. Other data also contradict the views of Abraham and Freud. If depression comes from anger turned inward, we would expect depressed people to express little hostility toward others. This was not found to be the case; depressed individuals often express intense anger and hostility toward people close to them (Weissman, Klerman, and Paykel, 1971).

At the same time, however, psychoanalytic ideas have found their way into more recent theorizing. For instance, irrational self-statements such as "It is a dire necessity that I be universally loved and approved of," to which Ellis attributes much human suffering, might plague Freud's "oral personality" in the deepening depression following the loss of a loved one. Although Freud cloaked his clinical impressions in theoretical terms that have been rejected by many contemporary writers, we must appreciate that some of his basic suppositions have a continuing influence.

Cognitive Theories

Discussions of the feeling of helplessness in Chapter 5 and of Ellis's concept of irrational beliefs in Chapter 2 and elsewhere indicate that cognitive processes play a decisive role in emotional behavior. In some theories of depression as in some concerning anxiety, thoughts and beliefs are regarded as causing the emotional state. In a way Freud is a cognitive theorist too, for he viewed depression as resulting from a person's *belief* that loss is a withdrawal of affection.

Perhaps the most important contemporary theory of depression to regard thought processes as causative factors is Aaron Beck's (1967). His central thesis is that depressed individuals feel as they do because they commit characteristic logical errors. From an examination of his therapy notes, he found that his depressed patients tended to distort whatever happened to them in the direction of self-blame, catastrophes, and the like. Thus an event interpreted by a normal person as irritating and inconvenient, for example, the malfunctioning of an automobile, would be interpreted by the depressed patient as yet an-

other example of the utter hopelessness of life. Beck's position is not that depressives think poorly or illogically in general. Rather, depressives draw illogical conclusions in evaluations of themselves, their immediate world, and their future.

Beck calls these errors in thinking "schemata" or characteristic sets which color how the person actually perceives the world. The depressed person is seen as operating within a schema of *self-deprecation* and *self-blame*. This set and those for the outer world and current experiences and for the future dispose the individual to interpret or label events in a way that justifies saying "What a jerk I am," "How empty and meaningless that is," and "How can anything ever get better?" (1970).

Beck describes several logical errors committed by depressed people in interpreting reality. Here the most damaging of the schemata, negative self-evaluation, is at work.

Aaron T. Beck, psychiatrist at the University of Pennsylvania. His cognitive theory of depression suggests that it is caused by excessive self-blame.

1. **Arbitrary inference.** A conclusion drawn in the absence of sufficient evidence or of any evidence at all. For example, a man concludes that he is worthless because it is raining the day that he is hosting an outdoor cocktail party.

2. **Selective abstraction.** A conclusion drawn on the basis of but one of many elements in a situation. A worker blames herself entirely for the failure of a product to function, even though she is only one of many people who have produced it.

3. **Overgeneralization.** An overall sweeping conclusion drawn on the basis of a single, perhaps trivial, event. A student regards his poor performance in a single class on one particular day as final proof of his worthlessness and stupidity.

4. **Magnification and minimization.** Gross errors in evaluating performance. A woman believes that she has completely ruined her car (magnification) when she sees that there is a slight scratch on the rear fender; or a man still believes himself worthless (minimization) in spite of a succession of praiseworthy achievements.

It is important to appreciate the thrust of Beck's position. Whereas many theorists have seen people as victims of their passions, creatures whose intellectual capacities can exert little if any control over feelings—this is Freud's basic position—in the theory just outlined the cause-effect relationship operates in the opposite direction. Our emotional reactions are considered to be a function of how we construe our world, and indeed the interpretations of depressives are found not to mesh very well with the way most people view the world. Beck sees depressives as the victims of their own *illogical self-judgments*.

At least two points need to be demonstrated when evaluating Beck's theory. First, depressed patients, in contrast to nondepressed individuals, must actually judge themselves in the illogical ways that Beck has enumerated. This first point was initially confirmed by Beck's clinical observations, which suggest that depressed patients do, in fact, manifest at least some of the errors in logic listed by him (Beck, 1967). More recently, further studies have lent additional support to Beck's general theory (for example, Beck et al., 1974; Nelson, 1977).

Second, it should be demonstrated that this cognitive distortion is not a function of a primary emotional disturbance, that it does in fact *cause* the depressed mood. Many studies in experimental psychology have in a general way shown that a person's feelings can be influenced by how he or she construes events. The Geer, Davison, and Gatchel study (1970), for example, indicated that people are less aroused when they believe that they have control over painful stimulation, even when that belief is false. No study that we know of, however, directly demonstrates that the various noncognitive aspects of depression are truly secondary to or a function of the distorted cognitive schemata that Beck believes operate in this disorder. Beck has found that depression and cognitive distortions are *correlated*, but a specific causal relationship cannot be determined from such data; depression could cause illogical thoughts or illogical thoughts could cause depression. Or the relationship could reflect some third variable, such as a biochemical disturbance.

In spite of these difficulties, an important advantage of Beck's theory is that it is testable and

has encouraged considerable research on depression. Even more important, as discussed later in this chapter (see page 256), it has encouraged therapists to work directly on depressed patients' thinking in order to change and alleviate their feelings (Beck, 1976).

Learning Theories

Depression through reduction in reinforcement One current learning conceptualization of depression bears some resemblance to Freud's theory, although, of course, the metaphors differ. Freud proposed as a causative factor the loss of a loved one by people whose oral dependencies retained from childhood make them particularly vulnerable to a lessening of external supports. It seems but a short step to connect depression to the reduction in activity that occurs when accustomed reinforcement is withdrawn. When a loved one dies, an important source of positive reinforcement is certainly lost.

For some learning theorists the concept of *reduction in reinforcement and activity* is central (Eastman, 1976); unconscious mourning processes and introjection of the lost loved one play no part in their explanation of depression. Once people stop behaving as they used to do before the loss, when reinforcement was plentiful (Ferster, 1965; Lazarus, 1968b), the new lower level of activity and social participation may itself be reinforced (Ullmann and Krasner, 1975). For example, depressed people may receive sympathy or special dispensations from others, who expect less of them than they did before the loss of the loved one. The outlook for improvement is all the more bleak for those who lack social skills for acquiring in new or different ways the rewards that used to be available. In fact, this learning theory explains more directly than did Freud the depression that is not preceded by the loss of a loved one; accustomed reinforcements may be cut off for a number of reasons, for example, changes in occupational status or of locale.

The learning conceptualization attributing depression to a reduction in activity when reinforcement is lacking has been elaborated on and researched by Lewinsohn and his colleagues (for example, Lewinsohn, 1974). Figure 8.1 is a schematic representation of Lewinsohn's model of depression. The following assumptions are made.

1. The feeling of depression and other symptoms of the clinical syndrome, such as fatigue, are elicited when behavior receives little reinforcement.

2. This "thin" schedule of positive reinforcement, in turn, tends to reduce activity even more, and then reinforcements are even fewer.

3. The amount of positive reinforcement likely to be available is a function of three sets of variables: (a) the individual's personal characteristics, such as age, sex, and attractiveness to others; (b) the environment that the person is in, such as being at home rather than in prison; and (c) the person's repertoire of behavior that can gain reinforcement, for example, vocational and social skills.

As Figure 8.1 indicates, a low rate of positive reinforcement reduces still further the activities and expression of qualities that might be rewarded. Both social participation and rewards decrease in a vicious cycle.

Research evaluating Lewinsohn's theory has generally assessed the relation between self-reports of mood and the number of pleasant events subjects indicate they have participated in. The items people check off each day on the Pleasant Events Schedule (MacPhillamy and Lewinsohn, 1973), a list of 320 events generally regarded as pleasurable—such as talking about sports, playing in a musical group—affirm the frequency of reinforcement. These studies show that the more depressed people are, the fewer pleasant events they report taking part in (Lewinsohn and Libet, 1972); the data indicate as well that depressed people declare having fewer pleasant experiences than do nondepressed people (MacPhillamy and Lewinsohn, 1974).

This information, however, constitutes only weak support for the theory. First, there is the problem of ascertaining the direction of these correlational relationships. Depressed mood could precede rather than follow a reduction in the number of pleasant experiences; a depressed person might report few pleasant events because his gloomy mood alters the way he feels about participating in them. Second, pleasant events are not necessarily reinforcers. A reinforcer is defined as having the capacity to make behavior more frequent. Some pleasant events will have this reinforcing property for particular individuals, but it cannot be assumed that each event on the Pleasant Events Schedule is each time a reinforcer. Finally, the accuracy of the self-reports being collected can be questioned. There is rea-

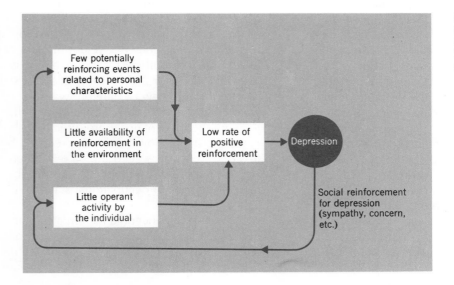

FIGURE **8.1**
Schematic of Lewinsohn's model of depression, which takes into account the inactivity and dejection of the depressive. After Lewinsohn, 1974.

son to doubt the reliability of depressed people's recollections of pleasant occasions, as indicated by the following experiment (Nelson and Craighead, 1977).

Subjects were depressed and nondepressed college students, so defined on the basis of the Beck Depression Inventory (Table 8.1). They were told that they would be shown a series of out-of-focus slides of nonsense syllables, each one presented for half a second. After viewing each nonsense syllable, they were to select from a set the one that had been shown. They would be informed whether they had made a correct or an incorrect choice.

TABLE 8.1
Sample Items from the Beck
Depression Inventory
(after Beck, 1978)

Attitudes		Depression inventory
Sadness*	0	I do not feel sad.
	1	I feel sad.
	2	I am sad all the time and I can't snap out of it.
	3	I am so sad or unhappy that I can't stand it.
Pessimism	0	I am not particularly discouraged about the future.
	1	I feel discouraged about the future.
	2	I feel I have nothing to look forward to.
	3	I feel that the future is hopeless and that things cannot improve.
Guilt	0	I don't feel particularly guilty.
	1	I feel guilty a good part of the time.
	2	I feel quite guilty most of the time.
	3	I feel guilty all of the time.
Self-dislike	0	I don't feel disappointed in myself.
	1	I am disappointed in myself.
	2	I am disgusted with myself.
	3	I hate myself.
Self-accusations	0	I don't feel I am any worse than anybody else.
	1	I am critical of myself for my weaknesses or mistakes.
	2	I blame myself all the time for my faults.
	3	I blame myself for everything bad that happens.
Suicidal ideas	0	I don't have any thoughts of killing myself.
	1	I have thoughts of killing myself, but I would not carry them out.
	2	I would like to kill myself.
	3	I would kill myself if I had the chance.

* The words to the left do not appear in the actual inventory but are given here to indicate what attitudes each group of items is meant to measure.

Actually, the syllables were presented in such poor focus that they could not be accurately detected. This allowed the experimenter to manipulate the rate at which subjects were either rewarded or punished. Subjects in the reward groups were told that at the end of the study they would receive 5¢ for each "correct" response; through manipulation by the experimenter, half were to receive rewards for 70 percent and half for 30 percent of their responses. These two reward groups included depressed and nondepressed students in equal numbers. Subjects in the punishment groups were told that they would lose 5¢ for every "incorrect" response; through manipulation half were to be punished for 70 percent of the responses and half for 30 percent. Again, these two punishment groups included depressed and nondepressed students in equal numbers. At the end of forty trials, the subjects in the reward and punishment groups were asked to recall the number of their correct and incorrect answers, respectively.

The results are given in Table 8.2. Notice first the row for the subjects who were to be rewarded 70 percent of the time. If they were depressed, these subjects inaccurately recalled significantly fewer correct answers than if they were not—22.5 versus 29.5. Now look at the row for those to be punished for 30 percent of responses. Here the depressed students accurately recalled more incorrect answers than did the nondepressed students—13.0 versus 7.62. Thus

depressed people seem to underestimate the frequency of rewards. In contrast, normal people underestimate the frequency of punishments but depressives recall them accurately. If depressed people behaved similarly in one of Lewinsohn's studies, depressed mood would correlate with participation in few pleasant events. But the correlation would actually reflect biased recall and not the effect of pleasant events on mood.

Thus existing data do not give strong support to Lewinsohn's theory. More sophisticated research with more objective measurements of mood and reinforcement will be needed for a better evaluation of their relationship.

Depression through learned helplessness

Martin Seligman (1974) has proposed that depression comes about through *learned helplessness.* He suggests that although anxiety is the initial response to a stressful situation, it is replaced by depression if the person comes to believe that control is unattainable. In some ways this model is similar to the ego-analytical view of Bibring (1953), who proposed that depression follows ". . . the ego's shocking awareness of its helplessness in regard to its aspirations" (p. 39).

Both Lewinsohn's low-reinforcement–reduced-activity view of depression and Seligman's learned-helplessness model are learning-based theories of depression. There are, however, important differences between them. The first view is a noncognitive one, assuming that inactivity

TABLE 8.2
Recall of Rewards and Punishments by Depressed and Nondepressed Students

(from Nelson and Craighead, 1977)

Outcome	Frequency of rewards and punishments, percent	Number of responses to be rewarded or punished	Recalled number of correct and incorrect responses	
			Depressed	Nondepressed
Reward	30	12	7.5	9.3
	70	28	22.5	29.5
Punishment	30	12	13.0	7.62
	70	28	30.33	29.13

and depressed mood are a direct function of environmental consequences. If a person's reinforcement becomes "thin," activity will be reduced in frequency, positive reinforcement will become even scarcer, and the person will feel depressed. Seligman's formulation has come to emphasize the way the individual learns to *construe* the relationship between activity and outcome, which is that he or she is helpless and all efforts will be in vain.

To examine Seligman's theory, we first describe a typical learned-helplessness experiment with animals. Dogs receive painful electric shock in two different situations. In the first part of the experiment some dogs are put in a box with electric grids in the flooring and subjected to numerous painful electric shocks from which they cannot escape. In the second part these animals, as well as dogs who did not have this prior experience with inescapable shock, are placed in a similar apparatus. Now painful shock can be avoided if the dogs learn to leap over a partition to another compartment of the so-called shuttle box as soon as they hear a warning buzzer or see a light come on. The behavior of the dogs is markedly affected by whether they were earlier exposed to inescapable shock. Animals who have not had the earlier experience become quite upset when they receive the first few electric shocks but fairly soon thereafter learn to leap over the partition when they hear or see the conditioned stimulus and thereby avoid further painful shock. The animals who have had the earlier experience with inescapable shock behave quite differently. Soon after receiving the first shocks, they stop running around in a distressed manner; instead they seem to give up and passively accept the painful stimulation. Not surprisingly, they do not acquire the avoidance response as efficiently and effectively as the control animals do. Most of them in fact lie down in a corner and whine. Such experiments imply that animals can acquire what might be called a "sense of helplessness" when confronted with uncontrollable aversive stimulation. This helplessness later tends seriously and deleteriously to affect their performance in stressful situations that *can* be controlled. They appear to lose the ability and motivation to learn to respond in an effective way to painful stimulation.

On the basis of this and other work on the effects of uncontrollable stress, Seligman felt that learned helplessness in animals can provide a model for at least certain forms of human depression. He noted similarities between the manifestations of helplessness observed in animal laboratory studies and at least some of the symptoms of depression. Like many depressed people, the animals appear passive in the face of stress, failing to initiate action that might allow them to cope. They develop anorexia, having difficulty in eating or retaining what is eaten, and lose weight. On the physiological level, one of the neurotransmitter chemicals, norepinephrine, was found to be depleted in Seligman's animals (see Box 8.4, page 253). Drugs that increase levels of norepinephrine have been shown to alleviate depression in human beings. Although effectiveness of treatment does not, as we have often indicated, prove etiology, the fact that depression is reduced by a drug that increases the level of norepinephrine is consistent with the finding that learned helplessness in animals is associated with lower levels of the chemical.

Building on these behavioral and physiological parallels, Seligman then examined possible commonalities in the causes of helplessness and depression. What makes the dog behave in a helpless, apparently depressed manner is known, for the carefully controlled experiments *create* the condition. The causes of human depression are much less clear, for the information available consists primarily of clinical observations. It is noteworthy, however, how often clinicians of diverse theoretical persuasions mention events over which the depressed person has had little or no control, such as the loss of loved ones, physical disease, aging, and failure.

Experiments with human beings have yielded results similar to those of experiments done with animals. People who have been subjected to inescapable noise or inescapable shock or who have been confronted with unsolvable problems fail later to escape noise and shock and solve simple problems (for example, Hiroto and Seligman, 1975; Roth and Kubal, 1975). Moreover, the performance of tasks by college students who rate as depressed on the Beck Depression Inventory (Beck, 1967) is similar to that of nonde-

pressed students who have earlier been subjected to these same helplessness-inducing
experiences (Miller, Seligman, and Kurlander,
1975; Klein and Seligman, 1976). This is very
important, for it suggests that we can, in a laboratory setting, elicit from nondepressed subjects
behavior similar to that observed in depressed
individuals (Figure 8.2).

In 1978 a revised version of the learned-helplessness model was proposed by Abramson, Seligman, and Teasdale.[1] It is basically a cognitive
theory of depression. Two inadequacies of the
original theory stimulated the reformulation.
First, the initial view did not distinguish between
situations of *universal helplessness,* in which no
one is able to control outcomes, and those of
personal helplessness, in which a particular person is unable to make the responses necessary to
control outcomes. The original helplessness theory had been criticized because data indicated
that some helpless individuals blamed themselves for their failures (for example, Abramson
and Sackheim, 1977; Blaney, 1977). How can
people who believe that they are helpless hold
themselves responsible for their failures? The answer lies in whether the helplessness is universal
or personal. When helplessness is personal, people will believe that they are responsible for the
failure. In contrast, in situations of universal
helplessness people attribute failure to external
circumstances. The universal-personal distinction
is related to another important aspect of depression not adequately handled by the original theory, *low self-esteem.* Although both forms of
helplessness are expected to cause depression,
only personal helplessness is predicted to produce feelings of low self-worth or low self-esteem.

The second problem with the original theory
lay in its vagueness in predicting both the range
of situations in which helplessness might be felt
and the duration of the state. The revised theory
deals with this issue by postulating that generality and chronicity will depend on how people
construe their failure. If, for example, the cause
of the failure is perceived to be a stable personal
characteristic, such as stupidity, the effects of

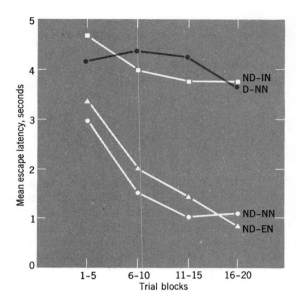

FIGURE **8.2**
Subjects who were depressed and those who were not de-
pressed but had experienced inescapable noise acted
more slowly to escape noise than did those in the
other groups. After Klein and Seligman, 1976.
   D–NN: *S*s rated as depressed on Beck Depression In-
        ventory; were not previously subjected to noise.
 ND–NN: *S*s rated as nondepressed; were not previously
        subjected to noise.
 ND–IN: *S*s rated as nondepressed; were previously sub-
        jected to inescapable noise (the "helpless"
        group).
 ND–EN: *S*s rated as nondepressed; were previously sub-
        jected to escapable noise.

helplessness are likely to be very general and enduring.

The essence of the revised theory lies in the
concept of *attribution* (Weiner et al., 1971).
Given a situation in which a person has experienced failure, the individual will try to attribute
the failure to some cause. In Table 8.3 the
Abramson, Seligman, and Teasdale formulation
is applied to indicate the ways in which a college student might attribute his failure on the
mathematics portion of the Graduate Record Examination. Three questions are asked. Are the
reasons for failure believed to be internal (personal) or environmentally caused (universal)? Is
the problem believed to be stable or short-term?
How global or specific is the inability to succeed
perceived to be?

---

[1] Miller and Norman (1979) have independently published a theory
very similar to this reformulation.

TABLE 8.3
Attributional Schema of Depression:
Why I Failed My GRE Math Exam

Degree	Internal (personal)		External (universal)	
	Stable	Unstable	Stable	Unstable
Global	I lack intelligence.	I am exhausted.	These tests are all unfair.	It's an unlucky day, Friday the thirteenth.
Specific	I lack mathematical ability.	I am fed up with math.	The math tests are unfair.	My math test was numbered "13."

The attributional revision of helplessness theory postulates that the way the person attributes failure will determine its subsequent effects. Global attributions should increase the generality of the effects of failure. Attributions to stable factors will make them long-term. Finally, attributing the failure to internal characteristics is more likely to diminish self-esteem, particularly if the personal fault is also global and persistent.

People then become depressed when they believe either that desired outcomes are unattainable or that negative outcomes are unavoidable. Whether self-esteem collapses too depends on whether they blame the bad outcome on their own inadequacies, and the generality and chronicity of their depression and loss of self-esteem depend on the globality and persistence of the characteristic blamed. In fact, the depression-prone individual is thought to show a "depressive attributional style," a tendency to attribute bad outcomes to personal, global, stable faults of character. When persons with this style have unhappy, adverse experiences, they become depressed and self-esteem shatters (see Box 8.1).

Some research gives direct support to the reformulated theory. Seligman and his colleagues (1979) have devised an attributional-style questionnaire (Table 8.4) and, as predicted by the theory, found that depressed college students did indeed more often attribute failure to personal, global, persistent inadequacies than did nondepressed students.

Metalsky and his colleagues (in press) have recently linked attributional style to depressed mood. A study was conducted with college students taking a course in abnormal psychology. Early in the semester the students completed the attributional-style questionnaire, an adjective checklist assessment of current mood, and a questionnaire concerning their grade aspirations. Eleven days later they again completed the adjective checklist assessing mood. Finally, five days later, after the midterm exam grade was returned, the students reported on their mood for a third time.

According to the reformulated helplessness theory, a tendency to attribute negative events to personal, global, and persistent inadequacies, as determined by the attributional-style questionnaire, should predict a more depressed mood in those students who received a poor grade. Students were divided into two groups, one consisting of those receiving good grades, another of those receiving poor grades. "Good" and "poor" depended on how their actual grades compared to their aspirations. A poor grade was defined as one equal to or less than the grade the student had earlier indicated he or she would be *un*happy with. A good grade was one equal to or greater than that the student had said he or she would be pleased with. For each group correlations were then computed between measures from the attributional-style questionnaire and change in depressed mood from before to after the midterm exam. Consistent with the theory, correlations within the good-grade group were not significant, for an increase in depressed mood requires *both* a particular attributional

BOX **8.1** Depression in Women: A Consequence of Learned Helplessness?

Depression appears to occur more often in women than in men. Why? A large-scale survey carried out by the National Institute of Mental Health Center for Epidemiologic Studies (Radloff, 1975) suggests some reasons.

   More than 2500 men and women of all ages and from a broad range of educational and socioeconomic backgrounds were interviewed in two American cities. Among the questions asked were twenty that comprised a self-report measure of depression, such as how often had the person slept restlessly during the previous week, and how often had he or she felt sad.

Several of the numerous findings are important for our present purposes.

1. Consistent with work done previously, married men were found to be significantly less depressed than married women.

2. Contrary to earlier thinking (for example, Gove and Tudor, 1973; Bernard, 1973), however, it was concluded that the role of housewife per se does not account for the higher levels of depression in married women, for working wives were also more depressed than married men. Having a job outside the home, then, does not appear to insulate married women from depression. Indeed, working wives were no less depressed than those who did not have outside employment.

3. Contrary to the findings of previous studies, the working wives were not more depressed than working men because they felt overworked by having two jobs, one as homemaker and one outside the house. Although the working wives did more housework than working husbands, this was not associated with their higher levels of depression.

Radloff speculates that the higher levels of depression among women are best explained as a consequence of learned helplessness. The feminist literature would agree (for example, Bernard, 1973; Chesler, 1972), for it blames the greater incidence of mental problems among women on their lack of personal and political power. Feminists take the position that more women than men become depressed because their social roles do not encourage them to feel competent. What women do does not seem to count compared to the greater power that men have in society. In fact, it may be that little girls are *trained* to be helpless (Broverman, Broverman, and Clarkson, 1970). And the more helpless woman, unable to tolerate the single life (Bernard, 1973), is probably more likely to marry.

These are interesting hypotheses, even plausible ones. But we need to know, for example, whether a woman's depression is preceded by a series of events that force her to recognize a feeling of helplessness already instilled in her. This and other questions have to be dealt with before lending too much credence to a helplessness explanation of depression in women. Learned helplessness may, however, prove a fruitful framework within which to conduct research on the depression of women.

TABLE 8.4
Instructions and Sample Item from the
Attributional-Style Questionnaire
(from Seligman et al., 1979)

Please try to vividly imagine yourself in the situations that follow. If such a situation happened to you, what would you feel would have caused it? While events may have many causes, we want you to pick only one—the *major* cause if this event happened to *you*. Please write this cause in the blank provided after each event. Next we want you to answer some questions about the *cause* and a final question about the *situation*. To summarize, we want you to:

1. Read each situation and vividly imagine it happening to you.
2. Decide what you feel would be the *major* cause of the situation if it happened to you.
3. Write one cause in the blank provided.
4. Answer three questions about the *cause*.
5. Answer one question about the *situation*.
6. Go on to the next situation.

YOU HAVE BEEN LOOKING FOR A JOB UNSUCCESSFULLY FOR SOME TIME.

1. Write down *one* major cause _____.

2. Is the cause of your unsuccessful job search due to something about you or something about other people or circumstances? (Circle one number)

Totally due to   Totally due
other people   to me
or circumstances
             1   2   3   4   5   6   7

3. In the future when looking for a job, will this cause again be present? (Circle one number)

Will never again   Will always
be present   be present
             1   2   3   4   5   6   7

4. Is the cause something that just influences looking for a job, or does it also influence other areas of your life? (Circle one number)

Influences just this   Influences all
particular situation   situations in my life
             1   2   3   4   5   6   7

5. How important would this situation be if it happened to you? (Circle one number)

Not at all   Extremely
important   important
             1   2   3   4   5   6   7

style *and* a negative event. For the poor-grade group two of three dimensions—internality and stability of faults—from the attributional-style questionnaire did predict an increase in depression. Students who were prone to attribute negative events to personal and persistent inadequacies became more depressed after a negative event, a poor grade, as predicted by the theory.

Over the past few years the original learned-helplessness theory and its attributional reformulation have clearly been at the forefront of psychological research on depression. In fact, in 1978 an entire issue of a major professional publication, the *Journal of Abnormal Psychology*, was devoted to theoretical and experimental studies on depression and learned helplessness. Although the theory is promising, some problems do need to be addressed in future work (see also Box 8.2).

1. **Which type of depression is being modeled?** In his original paper Seligman attempted to document the similarity between learned helplessness and "reactive depression," depression indicated in DSM-II to be brought on by stressful life events. But Depue and Monroe (1978) have demonstrated that learned helplessness resembles the symptoms of a bipolar patient in a depressive episode more than it does those of any form of unipolar depression. Clearly, neither Seligman's dogs nor human beings in helplessness studies have exhibited both mania and depression. Seligman's (1978) solution to this problem is to bypass the traditional classification schemes and regard learned helplessness as a model for "helplessness depressions." In so doing, he proposes a new diagnosis based on presumed etiology. Only future research will tell whether his solution is more than a circular statement.

2. **Can college student populations provide good analogues?** Although some research on learned helplessness has been done with clinical populations (for example, Abramson et al., 1978), by far the majority of studies have examined college students who are selected on the basis of scores on the Beck Depression Inventory. The Beck inventory was not, how-

ever, designed to *diagnose* depression, only to allow an assessment of severity in a clinically diagnosed group. Thus whether high scores on the BDI separate out subjects who can serve as good analogues for clinical depressives is unclear.

3. **Are the findings specific to depression?** This issue is raised by the results of a recent learned-helplessness study that Lavelle, Metalsky, and Coyne (1979) conducted with subjects classified as having high or low test anxiety. The subjects with high test anxiety performed as depressed subjects have in previous research. Thus the learned-helplessness phenomenon may not be specific to depression.

4. **Are attributions relevant?** At issue here is the underlying assumption that people actively attempt to explain their own behavior to themselves and that the attributions they make have subsequent effects on behavior. Some research indicates that making attributions is not a universal process. For example, Hanusa and Schulz (1977) allowed subjects in a helplessness experiment to make open-ended attributions about why they had succeeded or failed. Subjects did not spontaneously report them, and even after probing, the attributions given did not fall into specific categories. Furthermore, relating attributions to behavior has been difficult (Nisbett and Wilson, 1977). Indeed, in a series of experiments Nisbett and Wilson have shown that people are frequently unaware of the causes of their behavior.[2]

---

[2] The attribution literature makes the basic assumption that people *care* what the causes of their behavior are. This central idea is the brainchild of psychologists whose business it is to explain behavior. It may be that psychologists have projected their own need to explain behavior onto other people! Laypeople may simply not reflect on why they act and feel as they do to the same extent that psychologists do.

BOX 8.2 Sadder But Wiser

The learned-helplessness theory of depression suggests that depressives believe themselves to have little control and their behavior to have little effect on the outcome of events. Alloy and Abramson (1979) have evaluated this hypothesis in a series of investigations which, although not strongly supporting helplessness theory, offer an interesting perspective on the cognitive processes of depressives.

The basic task in the studies was a series of trials in which subjects could either press or not press a button. Each trial had one of two outcomes. A green light was or was not turned on. The subjects were to try to turn on the green light by pressing the button. The actual degree of control a subject had could then be manipulated by the experimenter. For example, the experimenter could arrange for the green light to go on 75 percent of the time a subject pressed the button and 25 percent of the time that the button was not pressed. In this situation the subject would be said to have 50 percent control (75% − 25%). After a series of trials, subjects would be asked to judge how much control they had had over the outcome.

In one of their studies, Alloy and Abramson exposed depressed and nondepressed students to one of two situations. In both subjects had no actual control, but in one the frequency with which the green light turned on was 75 percent and in the other it was 25 percent. When the light turned on relatively infrequently—in only 25 percent of the trials—the depressed and nondepressed students did not differ in their judgments of the degree of control they had had. Both groups were relatively accurate and indicated that they had had little real control. But when the green light turned on frequently, the nondepressed students markedly *overestimated* the degree of control they had had; depressed students did not.

In another study the investigators manipulated the consequences of turning on or not turning on the green light. Depressed and nondepressed students were put in one of two experimental situations. Subjects in one, the "lose" situation, were told that they were starting with $5 and would lose 25¢ each time the light did not come on after they had pressed the button; in the other, the "win" situation, subjects started with no money but were told that they would win 25¢ each time the light came on after they had pressed the button. The money was to be given to the subjects at the conclusion of the study. In both situations the light turned on following a button press 50 percent of the time and following a nonpress 50 percent of the time. Thus subjects actually had no control. Both depressed and nondepressed students in the "lose" situation judged that they had had little control. But nondepressed students in the "win" situation greatly overestimated their degree of control. In a subsequent study, this time giving all subjects 50 percent control, nondepressed students in a "lose" situation *underestimated* the degree of control they had had. The depressed students, in contrast, were quite accurate in their judgments.

What are the implications of these findings? First, the deductions from helplessness theory were not supported. Depressed students did not underestimate the degree of control their responses exerted over outcomes. Indeed, the depressed subjects were very accurate in these judgments. Instead it was the nondepressed students who revealed inaccuracies, believing themselves to have greater control or less control than was actually the case in different situations. Alloy and Abramson summarized their findings as follows.

. . . depressed people are "sadder but wiser" than nondepressed people. Nondepressed people succumb to cognitive illusions that enable them to see both themselves and their environment with a rosy glow (pp. 479–480).

Why do nondepressed people engage in these distortions? One answer is that they do so to maintain or enhance their self-esteem. Taking credit for good outcomes and disowning responsibility for bad ones, the pattern observed in Alloy and Abramson's experiments, would indeed seem to be a good strategy for preserving self-esteem. What, then, of depressed people? Perhaps they are not motivated to maintain self-esteem, and as Bibring has argued, their ability for self-deception has broken down. It is ironic to contemplate that people may remain cheerful because they deceive themselves into believing that the world is better than it actually is. A modicum of illusion, given our troubled times, may be a good thing.

Physiological Theories of Affective Disorders

Since physiological processes are known to have considerable effects on moods, it is not surprising that investigators have sought physiological causes for depression and mania. Moreover, disturbed physiological processes must of course be part of the causal chain if a predisposition for an affective disorder can be genetically transmitted. Evidence indicating that an affective disorder is, in part, inherited would, then, provide some support for the theory that the disorder has a physiological basis.

The Genetic Data

Research on genetic factors in unipolar depression and bipolar disorder has used both the family and twin methods. Estimates of the frequency of affective disorders in first-degree relatives of bipolars range from about 10 to 20 percent (Slater, 1938; Perris, 1969; Brodie and Leff, 1971; Hays, 1976). These figures are higher than those for the general population. Notably, among the first-degree relatives of bipolar index cases, there are more cases of unipolar depression than bipolar disorder. For example, James and Chapman (1975), in a thorough study conducted in New Zealand, found the morbidity risk estimates for the first-degree relatives of bipolars to be 6.4 percent for bipolar disorder and 13.2 percent for unipolar depression. Allen (1976) has reviewed concordance data for bipolar disorder in twins. Overall, the concordance rate for bipolar disorder in identical twins was 72 percent, in fraternal twins only 14 percent. The evidence clearly supports the notion that bipolar disorder has a heritable component (see Box 8.3).

Less research has been done on unipolar depression, but the information available indicates that genetic factors, although important, do not figure to the same extent that they do in bipolar disorder. Perris (1969), for example, found that 7.4 percent of the first-degree relatives of unipolar index cases had also experienced a depressive episode. The relatives of unipolar cases do not appear to be at risk for bipolar disorder. Studies of unipolar depression in twins typically

BOX 8.3 A Theory of the Genetic Transmission of Bipolar Disorder

Throughout this book we have often been faced with theories couched in sufficiently vague terms to be untestable. A notable exception is the proposal of Winokur and his colleagues at the University of Iowa, that bipolar disorder is caused by a dominant gene on the X chromosome, one of two which together determine the sex of the fetus. The theory is easily tested. According to Mendelian genetics, the forty-six chromosomes in the body cells of human beings, and the genes they carry, act together in pairs. A dominant gene is one that will find expression, regardless of the other gene it is paired with. Women have a pair of similar sex chromosomes, XX, men a dissimilar pair, XY. The fetus gets one of its pair from the ovum of the mother and one from the spermatozoan of the father; each of these sex cells contains only twenty-three chromosomes, for the pairs have earlier divided. The mother, then, always contributes an X chromosome. If the father also contributes an X chromosome, the child will be female. If the father contributes a Y chromosome, the child will be male.

Winokur's theorizing grew out of an early study of the family histories of patients with affective disorders (Winokur and Clayton, 1967). The patients were separated into two groups, those whose families had incidences of affective disorders and those whose families did not. In the first group 96 percent of 112 probands were bipolars. In the second only 3 percent of 129 probands were bipolars. The relatives of bipolar probands were obviously at high risk. To investigate bipolar patients further, Winokur, Clayton, and Reich (1969) collected a new sample of 89 index cases. The data from this investigation are shown in Table 8.5. The A part of the table indicates that female relatives were at much

TABLE 8.5

A Study of the First-Degree Relatives of Bipolar Probands

(from Winokur, Clayton, and Reich, 1969)

A.	Morbidity risk of relative of a proband	
	Relationship to proband	*Risk, percent*
	mother	55
	father	17
	sister	52
	brother	29

B.	Relationships of depressive pairs	Number of pairs
	father–son	0
	father–daughter	13
	mother–son	17
	mother–daughter	17

higher risk than males, which would bear out the prediction that bipolar disorder is controlled by a dominant gene on the X chromosome. Part B of the table shows no instances of father-son pairs of bipolars. Again, this is precisely what Winokur's theory predicts. The reasoning is as follows. The gene causing bipolar disorder in a father is on his X chromosome. Since the father gives only his Y chromosome to a male child, his son cannot be affected.

Winokur's data supported his theory, but before long disconfirmations appeared. Goetzl and his colleagues (1974), Hays (1976), and James and Chapman (1975) have all reported father-son pairs of bipolars. Therefore Winokur's theory cannot account completely for the genetics of bipolar disorder. It may be, however, that bipolar disorder is etiologically heterogeneous, in which case Winokur's theory might apply to a subset of bipolar patients.

---

report MZ concordances of about 40 percent and DZ concordances of about 11 percent (Allen, 1976).

Earlier we mentioned the great heterogeneity among unipolar depressives. Some of the genetic data collected over the past decade bear on this issue. Winokur (1979) has noted differences in the disorders found in the first-degree relatives of unipolars. Both male and female first-degree relatives of men whose depression occurs for the first time rather late in life, after age forty, are at about equal risk for depression. But for male and female first-degree relatives of women whose first episode of depression begins earlier, the pattern is different. The female relatives are at greater risk for depression than male relatives, who are at greater risk for alcoholism and sociopathy. Although these data are not yet fully understood, they do suggest that the diagnosis unipolar depression may actually cover several disorders with different etiologies.

Taken together, the family and twin studies suggest that both *bipolar disorder and unipolar depression have heritable components*. And this conclusion is further supported by recent studies that have used the adoption method. Mendlewicz and Rainer (1977) found more affective disorders in the biological parents than in the adoptive parents of bipolar adoptees. Similarly, Cadoret (1978) found more affective disorders in adopted children whose biological parents had an affective disorder.

Biochemistry and Affective Disorders

Two major theories have been proposed relating depression to *neurotransmitters* (see Box 8.4). One theory suggests that depression results from low levels of *norepinephrine;* the other points to low levels of *serotonin.* The norepinephrine theory also postulates that an excess of this neurotransmitter causes mania (Schildkraut, 1965).

The actions of drugs provided the clues on which both theories are based. In the 1950s two particular groups of drugs, the *tricyclics* and the *monoamine oxidase inhibitors* (see page 664), were found to be effective in relieving depression. Studies revealed that they also increase the levels of both serotonin and norepinephrine in the brains of animals. This information only suggested that depression is caused by low levels of these substances, but it encouraged further explorations. Another piece of evidence favoring both theories was provided by reserpine, a drug now used primarily in the treatment of hypertension. Early in the same decade reserpine had been isolated by a research team working in Switzerland. It is an alkaloid of the root of *Rauwolfia serpentina,* a shrub which grows in India. Hindu physicians have for centuries administered powdered rauwolfia as a treatment for mental illness. Reserpine became one of the compounds to initiate the modern era of psychopharmacology and to revolutionize the care and treatment of mental patients. This drug and chlorpromazine (see page 439) were given to schizophrenics

BOX **8.4** Communication in the Nervous System

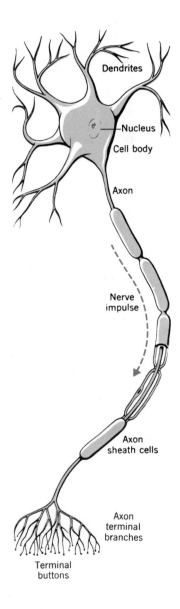

FIGURE **8.3**
The neuron, the basic unit of the nervous system.

The nervous system is composed of billions of neurons. Although differing in some respects, each neuron has four major parts (Figure 8.3): (1) the cell body; (2) several dendrites, its short and thick extensions; (3) one or more axons, but usually only one, long and thin, extending a considerable distance from the cell body; and (4) terminal buttons on the many end branches of the axon. When a neuron is appropriately stimulated at its cell body or through its dendrites, a nerve impulse, which is a change in the electric potential of the cell, travels down the axon to the terminal endings. Between the terminal endings of an axon and other neurons there is a small gap, the synapse (Figure 8.4). For a nerve impulse to pass from one neuron to another, it must have a way of bridging the synaptic space.

The terminal buttons of each axon contain synaptic vesicles, small structures which are filled with chemicals called neurotransmitters. Each neuron synthesizes and stores only one particular neurotransmitter. The nerve impulse causes the synaptic vesicles to release their transmitter substance, which floods the synapse and can then stimulate an adjacent neuron. The molecules of the transmitter fit into receptor sites in the postsynaptic neuron and thereby transmit the impulse.

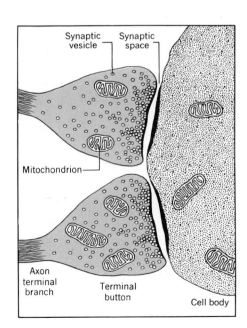

FIGURE **8.4**
A synapse showing the terminal buttons of two axon branches in close contact with a very small portion of the cell body of another neuron.

Several neurotransmitters have been identified; those belonging to two major compound groups, the catecholamines and the indoleamines, have been implicated in mood and emotion and therefore in psychopathology. Substances in both groups are monoamines, which means that their molecules contain a single amino group (NH_2). The catecholamines, each with a catechol portion ($C_6H_6O_2$), are norepinephrine, epinephrine, and dopamine. The two indoleamines, each with an indole portion (C_8H_7N), are serotonin and tryptamine. Serotonin and tryptamine are found in greater quantities in other bodily tissues than in the central nervous system. Serotonin, for example, occurs in large amounts in cells of the mucous membranes of the intestines. Its release from these cells helps to regulate peristalsis. Norepinephrine is a neurotransmitter of the peripheral sympathetic nervous system. Of these monoamines, norepinephrine, dopamine, and serotonin appear for certain to be neurotransmitters of the central nervous system. At least some of the particular pathways in the brain served by these transmitters have been identified.

To understand the theory and research relating neurotransmitters to psychopathology, we need to know how these substances are synthesized within the neuron from the amino acids tryosine and tryptophan. Table 8.6 presents this information. Finally, we need to consider the mechanisms by which the neurotransmitters are inactivated following their release. The catecholamines norepinephrine and dopamine are for the most part pumped back into the presynaptic neuron. The remainder of these substances is deactivated in the synapse by the enzyme catechol-O-methyltransferase (COMT). Catecholamines within the presynaptic neuron can be deactivated by the enzyme monoamine oxidase (MAO), which is present in the mitochondria, the powerhouses supplying the energy for the activities of all cells. Serotonin is also taken up again into the presynaptic neuron. It is deactivated within the presynaptic neuron and in the synapse by MAO.

TABLE 8.6
Biosynthesis of the Catecholamines and Indoleamines

Catecholamines	Indoleamines
Tyrosine	Tryptophan
↓ tyrosine hydroxylase*	↓ tryptophan hydroxylase tryptophan decarboxylase
Dopa	5-Hydroxytryptophan →Tryptamine
↓ dopa decarboxylase	↓ dopa decarboxylase
Dopamine	Serotonin
↓ dopamine-β-hydroxylase	
Norepinephrine	
↓ norepinephrine-N-methyltransferase	
Epinephrine	

* The substances on the arrows are the enzymes that catalyze the reactions.

to calm their agitation. Reserpine did indeed relax and sedate them but was soon contraindicated, for a serious side effect in about 15 percent of the patients taking it was depression (for example, Lemieux, Davignon, and Genest, 1956). Reserpine was discovered to reduce levels of both serotonin and norepinephrine and of all the brain amines. It impairs the process by which these substances are stored within the synaptic vesicles and allows them instead to become degraded by monoamine oxidase.

So far we have examined *indirect* evidence for each theory. It would be ideal if the levels of norepinephrine, serotonin, or both could be measured within the brains of depressed people. This is not possible with existing technology, so we must take another tack. Two approaches have been used. The first measures metabolites of these neurotransmitters, the by-products of the breakdown of serotonin and norepinephrine, as they are found in urine, blood serum, and the cerebrospinal fluid. The problem with such measurements is that they are not direct reflections of *brain* levels of either serotonin or norepinephrine, since serotonin is involved in other bodily processes and norepinephrine acts in the peripheral nervous system. 3-Methoxy-4-hydroxyphenylethylene glycol (MHPG), for example, is considered to be a major metabolite of norepinephrine. Although several studies have found low levels of MHPG in the urine of depressives (for example, Greenspan et al., 1970), the inactivity of individuals can also decrease MHPG levels (Post et al., 1973). Since depressives are typically less active than is normal, their urine may contain lesser amounts of MHPG after the onset of depression rather than before.

A second strategy would be to choose drugs other than the antidepressants and reserpine that are known either to increase or to decrease the brain levels of serotonin and norepinephrine. A drug raising the level of a neurotransmitter should alleviate depression; one reducing it should deepen depression or induce it in normal subjects. This strategy also has its problems, however. Most drugs have multiple effects, making it difficult to choose one that accomplishes a specific purpose without complicating side effects. The drug L-dopa, for example, *should* enter the brain and allow a greater amount of catecholamines, including norepinephrine, to be produced. If the norepinephrine theory were true, L-dopa should be therapeutically effective in depression. But it is not (Mendels et al., 1975). This evidence, though, is not regarded as a conclusive refutation of the norepinephrine hypothesis. L-dopa may not really increase levels of norepinephrine in the brain, and it has other potential effects, including a reduction in serotonin levels.

Significant evidence has been collected by these strategies, however.

1. **Low levels of serotonin.** 5-Hydroxyindoleacetic acid (5-HIAA), the major metabolite of serotonin that is present in cerebrospinal fluid, can be measured to determine the level of the transmitter in the brain and spinal cord. A fairly consistent body of data indicates that 5-HIAA levels are low in the cerebrospinal fluid of depressives (Ashcroft, Crawford, and Eccleston, 1966; Mendels et al., 1972; Van Praag, Korf, and Schut, 1973). Studies also show that ingestion of L-tryptophan, which acts as a serotonin precursor, relieves depression, especially when used in combination with other drugs (Coppen et al., 1972; Mendels et al., 1975). Furthermore, *p*-chlorophenylalanine (PCPA), which suppresses serotonin synthesis by blocking tryptophan hydroxylase, reduces the therapeutic effect of drugs that usually lessen depression (Shopsin, Friedman, and Gershon, 1976).

2. **Catecholamines as determiners of mania or depression.** We have already noted that low levels of MHPG, the principal metabolite of norepinephrine, have been found in several studies of depressives. Furthermore, studies have revealed that drugs that increase norepinephrine levels can precipitate an episode of mania in a bipolar patient (Bunney et al., 1970). Additional evidence comes from a series of studies on bipolar patients performed by Bunney and Murphy and their colleagues at the National Institute of Mental Health. The norepinephrine levels of a group of bipolar patients were watched over a period of

time as patients cycled through stages of depression, mania, and normalcy. Urinary levels of norepinephrine decreased when patients became depressed (Bunney et al., 1970) and increased as patients became manic (Bunney, Goodwin, and Murphy, 1972). This study was able to relate the low and high levels of norepinephrine more closely to the onset, rather than the aftermath, of depression and mania.

A synthesis of the two theories has been proposed by Prange and his associates (1974): a low level of serotonin may be a predisposing factor for affective disorders in general; and an imbalance of norepinephrine determines the direction of bipolar disorder, a low amount producing depression and a high level producing mania. Another way of interpreting the seemingly conflicting data is again to raise the possibility that the disorders being considered are etiologically heterogeneous. Some depressions may be linked to low levels of norepinephrine and others to low serotonin levels. Cobbin and his co-workers (1979), for example, found that depressed patients with low levels of MHPG, and thus, presumably, also of norepinephrine, responded favorably to the tricyclic drug imipramine, whose primary effect is to prevent reuptake of norepinephrine from the synapse, thus keeping more available for transmission of impulses. Depressed patients with normal or elevated levels of MHPG, in contrast, responded favorably to the tricyclic amitriptyline, whose major effect is thought to be in blocking reuptake of serotonin, making more available for neural transmission. Although tentative, these data carry a major implication: important findings may be masked by lumping all depressed patients together into a single group and looking statistically only at the group's average. If etiology is heterogeneous, a more individual, case by case investigation will be required.

These biochemical data lend some support to theories that affective disorders have physiological causes. Does this mean that psychological theories are irrelevant or useless? Not in the least. To assert that behavioral disorders have a basis in somatic processes is to state the obvious. No psychogenic theorist would deny that behavior is mediated by some kinds of bodily changes. The question rather is how psychological and physiological factors interact. We have already grappled with this philosophical issue in Chapter 7. It may well be, for example, that depletion of norepinephrine does cause certain kinds of depression, but that an earlier link in the causal chain is "the sense of helplessness" or "paralysis of will" that psychological theorists have proposed as the disabler.

Therapy for Affective Disorders

Psychological Therapies

Because depression is considered derived from anger unconsciously turned inward, psychoanalytic treatment tries to help the patient achieve insight into the repressed conflict and often encourages outward release of the hostility supposedly working inward. In the most general terms, the goal of analytic therapy is to uncover latent motivations for the patient's depression. A man may, for example, blame himself for the death of a loved one, as did the engineer described earlier, but repress this belief because of the pain it causes. The patient must first be made to confront the fact that he holds this belief, after which the therapist can help him realize that his guilt is unfounded. The recovery of memories of stressful circumstances of the patient's childhood, when feelings of inadequacy and loss may have developed, should also bring relief.

Research on the effectiveness of dynamic psychotherapy in alleviating depression is sparse. The few investigations carried out have not found such treatment making a significant impact on the problem (Hollon and Beck, 1979). For example, psychoanalytic therapy combined with tricyclic drugs, which have proved useful, does not lift mood any more than do the drugs by themselves (Daneman, 1961; Covi et al., 1974).

In keeping with their cognitive theory of depression, that the profound sadness and shattered self-esteem of depressed individuals are caused by errors in their thinking, Aaron Beck and his associates have worked for several years to devise a cognitive therapy aimed at altering aberrant thought patterns. The therapist tries to persuade the depressed person to change his or her opinions of events and of the self. When a client states that she is worthless because "Nothing goes right. Everything I try to do ends in a disaster," the therapist offers examples contrary to this overgeneralization, such as competences that the client is either overlooking or discounting. The therapist also instructs the patient to monitor her "private monologues" with herself and to identify all patterns of thought that contribute to depression. She is then taught to think through her negative prevailing beliefs, to understand how they prevent her from making more realistic and positive assumptions and from more accurately interpreting adversity.

Although developed independently of Ellis's rational-emotive method, Beck's analyses are similar to it in some ways. For example, he suggests that depressed people are likely to consider themselves totally inept and incompetent if they make a mistake. This can be considered an extension of one of Ellis's irrational beliefs, that the individual must be competent in all things in order to be a worthwhile person.

Beck also includes more strictly behavioral components in his treatment of depression. Especially when patients are severely depressed, Beck encourages them to *do* things, such as getting out of bed in the morning, and discourages them from doing other things, such as attempting suicide. Beck gives his patients activity assignments that will provide them with successful experiences and allow them to think well of themselves. But the overall emphasis is on cognitive restructuring, on persuading the person to think differently. If a change in overt behavior will help in achieving that goal, fine. Behavioral change by itself, however, without altering the logical errors that Beck asserts depressed people commit, cannot be expected to alleviate depression in any significant way.

A widely cited comparative therapy study by Rush and his colleagues (1977), discussed in Chapter 19 (page 612), has indicated that Beck's cognitive therapy is more successful in alleviating depression than the common regimen of administering an antidepressant drug, the tricyclic imipramine (Tofranil). This superiority was maintained at a six-month follow-up and has encouraged many other researchers to adopt the therapy and to develop it further. Previous research had shown imipramine to be superior to insight-oriented psychotherapy in treating depression, which renders all the more impressive the finding that Beck's cognitive therapy was better than a standard course of pharmacotherapy.

Because Lewinsohn considers depression to be brought on by the reduction of activity and social participation when important sources of reinforcement are withdrawn, therapy based on his view focuses on behavioral deficits. Depressed people are asked to engage in more activities, such as shopping, participating in hobbies, and talking to other people. They are also trained to behave in ways that are likely to be regarded more positively by others. Assertion training, role playing, and modeling are all important methods of helping them develop the necessary social skills. In contrast to Beck's therapy, what people are thinking as they make changes in their overt behavior is not explicitly considered.

A study by Shaw (1977) compared four groups of depressed people. One group received training in social skills, based on Lewinsohn's theory; the second, Beck's cognitive-restructuring therapy. Members of the third, called an attention-placebo group, had nondirective discussions with a therapist about their feelings and the possible reasons for them. This group was included in order to evaluate what gains depressed people might make through the _placebo effect_ (see page 560), through hoping and expecting to be helped by an interested and sympathetic professional. The fourth group was not treated. After sixteen hours of therapy, members of the cognitive-treatment group were less depressed than all the others, and those in the social-skills group were no better off than the attention-placebo subjects. Methodological problems have been mentioned for this study (Wilson and O'Leary, 1980), but

nonetheless it did indicate that training people in social skills is not an especially effective treatment for lifting depression.

Although Seligman's learned-helplessness theory is a widely held conception of depression, as yet no specific program of therapy based on this view has been developed. Seligman did undertake to cure his helpless dogs, but it proved difficult. Removing the partition in the shuttle box did not encourage the animals to move, nor did supplying food on the side with the safe floor. When the buzzer or light came on, signaling that a painful shock was forthcoming, they still cowered in the corner on the unsafe side and then passively absorbed shock. Finally, the dogs were leashed and dragged to the other side when the buzzer or light came on. Some dogs started moving on their own after twenty-five draggings, others only after two hundred. They had to be forced to experience success in avoiding shock before they were able to move on their own. The growing research literature on learned helplessness has sensitized therapists in a general way to the need that many depressed people have to achieve a sense of competence and of control over events in their lives, and indeed to the need that all human beings have to believe that they command their own destinies (see Box 8.5).

Assertiveness training can be used in treating depression. In this workshop, sponsored by the National Organization of Women, participants are engaging in an exercise in which they say positive things about themselves to the person next to them.

BOX 8.5 An Existential Theory of Depression and Its Treatment

In 1959 a remarkable book, *From Death Camp to Existentialism,* was published by Viktor Frankl, an Austrian psychiatrist who during World War II had spent three horrible years in Nazi concentration camps. His wife, brother, and parents, imprisoned with him, all lost their lives. Revised since its initial appearance and retitled *Man's Search for Meaning* (1963), Frankl's book vividly describes the humiliation, suffering, and terror experienced by camp prisoners. Frankl goes on to tell how he and others managed to survive psychologically in the brutalizing conditions of the death camps.

Frankl concluded that he was sustained emotionally by having succeeded somehow in finding meaning in his suffering and relating it to his spiritual life. The spirit gives the individual freedom to transcend circumstances, and freedom makes him responsible for his life. Maddi's concept of existential neurosis would suggest (see page 60) that each human being has the responsibility to find purpose and meaning in life, even when the external

Viktor Frankl's best-known technique is called paradoxical intention. Patients are told to indulge their symptoms intentionally. If a depressed man has been unable to leave his bed until noon, he should stay there until evening. Exaggeration will bring his symptom under conscious control.

world provides little evidence of them. Frankl believes that psychopathology, particularly depression, ensues when a person has no purpose in living. He developed out of his concentration camp experiences a psychotherapeutic approach called _logotherapy,_ after the Greek word _logos,_ translatable as meaning.

The task of logotherapy is to restore meaning to the client's life. This is accomplished first by accepting in an empathic way the subjective experience of the client's suffering, rather than conveying the message that suffering is sick and wrong and should therefore not be accepted as normal. The logotherapist then helps the client make some sense out of his or her suffering by placing it within a larger context, a philosophy of life in which the individual assumes responsibility for his or her existence and for pursuing the values inherent in life. Nietzsche has said, ''He who has a why to live for can bear with almost any how.''

It may be useful to relate Frankl's views on depression and its treatment to learned helplessness. Certainly the concentration camp induced helplessness and hopelessness, an utter disbelief that an individual could exert any control over his or her life. Profound depression was commonplace. Logotherapy might be an effective way to reverse the helplessness depressed people experience in contemporary society, under less horrific and brutal conditions. By accepting responsibility for their lives and by seeking some meaning even in trying circumstances, they may achieve a sense of control and competence indispensable to forging an acceptable existence.

Somatic Therapies

There are a variety of somatic therapies for depression and mania. Perhaps the most dramatic, and controversial, treatment for depression is _electroconvulsive therapy_ (ECT). Carried out usually in a hospital, ECT is the deliberate induction of a seizure and unconsciousness by passing a current of between 70 and 130 volts through the patient's brain by means of electrodes placed at each side of the forehead; recently unilateral ECT has been used as well. In the past electric shock has often created frightening contortions, sometimes even causing bone fractures. Now the administration of tranquilizers and strong muscle relaxants prior to an ECT treatment has eliminated these negative aspects.

Why should anyone in his right but depressed mind agree to undergo such radical therapy, or how could a parent or a spouse consent to such treatment if the patient is judged legally incapable of giving consent? The answer is simple: ECT may be the optimal treatment for severe depression (Klerman, 1972). Most professionals, though, acknowledge the risks involved—memory loss which can be prolonged, confusion,

perhaps even some brain damage when administered repeatedly—and resort to ECT only after less drastic treatments have been tried and found wanting. In considering _any_ treatment that has negative side effects, the person making the decision must be aware of the consequences of not providing any treatment at all. Given that suicide is a real possibility among depressed people, and given a moral stance that values the preservation of life, the use of ECT, at least after other treatments have failed, is regarded by many as defensible and responsible.

Antidepressant drugs are available and easy to take. Even if a chemical agent manages to alleviate a bout of depression only temporarily, that benefit in itself should not be underestimated, given the suicide potential in depression and given the extreme anguish and suffering borne by the individual, and usually by the family as well. Moreover, the judicious use of a drug may make unnecessary an avenue of intervention and control that many regard as very much a last resort, namely being placed in a psychiatric hospital.

The two major categories of antidepressant

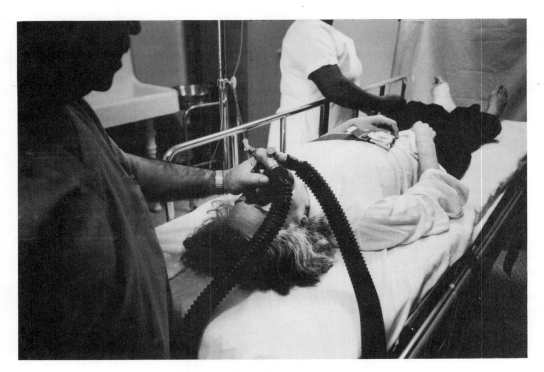

This woman has just undergone shock treatment. Oxygen is being administered because the muscle relaxant given earlier interferes with breathing.

drugs are the tricyclics, such as imipramine (Tofranil) and amitriptyline (Elavil), and the monoamine oxidase (MAO) inhibitors, such as Parnate. Since the MAO inhibitors have by far the more serious side effects, the tricyclics are more widely used. These medications, discussed more fully in Chapter 20 (page 664) have been established as effective in a number of double-blind studies (Morris and Beck, 1974). Patients and their families must be forewarned, however, that one to several weeks may elapse before any therapeutic effect is observed. This delay can make for a difficult waiting period and points up once again the need to intervene psychologically as well as somatically. Practitioners do not rely exclusively on drugs like Tofranil for another reason. Once the patient has withdrawn from the drug, relapse is more often the rule than the exception (Klerman et al., 1974). "Symptomatic relief" is, as already stated, of no small importance in problems like depression, but the patient should be able to stop taking the drug during periods when symptoms have lessened. The simple truth is that, at least so far, no chemical has been found that can "cure" depression.

People with the mood swings of bipolar disorder are often helped by carefully monitored dosages of _lithium_, an element, taken in a salt form, _lithium carbonate._ The fact that lithium carbonate cannot be patented like other drugs discouraged pharmaceutical companies for years from marketing it; only minimal profits are to be made. Lithium is now taken regularly and prophylactically, that is every day in the absence of problems in order to prevent radical shifts in mood (Davis, 1976). One of the consequences of the medication, however, is that it prevents bipolars from feeling extremely good on occasion (Honigfeld and Howarth, 1978), and it is not always easy for them to forgo occasional euphoria. Because of possibly serious, even fatal side effects, lithium has to be prescribed and used very carefully.

Suicide

In some religions _suicide_ is considered a mortal sin. As late as 1823 a citizen of London who took his own life was buried with a stake pounded through his heart (Shneidman, 1973). Moreover, until 1961, suicide in England was a criminal offense. Sanctions, then, have been quite strong in many societies. And yet it is fair to say that the idea of killing oneself comes to many people at one time or another. Indeed, many acts of self-annihilation are praised by some societies, as when Japanese Kamikaze pilots crashed their planes into enemy ships during World War II to wreak destruction on their foes for the glory of their Emperor; or when a soldier saves his comrades by falling on an exploding grenade.

Suicide is discussed in the present chapter because many depressives have suicidal thoughts and sometimes make genuine attempts to take their own lives; moreover, it is generally believed that more than half of those who try to kill themselves are depressed and despondent at the time of the act. A significant number of people who are not depressed, however, make suicidal attempts and commit the act. An adequate understanding of suicide cannot come by concentrating only on the tendency of many depressed people to think about suicide.

Facts about Suicide

No single theory is likely to take into account all the available information about suicide. The diversity of known facts may help us appreciate how complex and multifaceted self-intentioned death is (Resnik, 1968; Gibbs, 1968; Douglas, 1967; Shneidman, 1973; Seiden, 1974).

1. Every thirty minutes someone in the United States kills himself, and this rate is probably a gross underestimate.

2. As many as 200,000 in this country attempt suicide each year—and one in ten succeeds.

3. About half of those who commit suicide have made at least one previous attempt.

4. Three times as many men kill themselves as women.

5. Three times as many women as men attempt to kill themselves but do not die.

6. Suicide is found in both the very old and the very young—even in those older than ninety years and younger than ten years.

7. Suicide is found at all social and economic levels but is especially frequent among psychiatrists, physicians, lawyers, and psychologists.

8. No other kind of death leaves in friends and relatives such long-lasting feelings of distress, shame, guilt, puzzlement, and general disturbance.

9. Guns are the most common means of suicide in the United States. Men usually choose to shoot or hang themselves. Women are more likely to use sleeping pills. Elsewhere in the world methods vary by country. For example, coal gas is often chosen in England; gas and hanging are common means in Austria, pills and poisons in the Scandinavian countries.

10. Suicide ranks tenth as a leading cause of death among adults and second, after accidents, among college students.

11. Most of the people who kill themselves in the United States are native-born Caucasian males between forty-five and sixty years of age.

12. Many more college students commit suicide than do their peers who do not attend; it is estimated that each year upwards of 10,000 college men and women attempt to kill themselves.

13. The rates for suicide among whites and native American youths are more than twice those for blacks.

14. The rates of suicide for adolescents and children in the United States are increasing.

15. Hungary is the country with the highest rate of suicide in the world. Czechoslovakia, Finland, Sweden, and Austria also have high incidences.

The suicide rate is especially high among young people. This young woman threatened to throw herself to the pavement, fifty feet below, but was talked out of it by police officers.

16. Suicide rates go up during depression years, remain stable during years of prosperity, and decrease during war years.

Theories of Suicide

Mintz (1968) has summarized the numerous motivations for suicide mentioned in the literature: aggression turned inward; retaliation by inducing guilt in others; efforts to force love from others; efforts to make amends for "perceived" past wrongs; efforts to rid oneself of unacceptable feelings, such as sexual attraction to members of one's own sex; the desire for reincarnation; the desire to rejoin a dead loved one; and the desire or need to escape from stress, deformity, pain, or emotional vacuum. Two traditional theoretical positions, the psychoanalytic and Durkheim's sociological theory, have influenced suicidologists.

Psychoanalytic theories of suicide

Freud proposed two major hypotheses to account for suicide. One is an extension of his theory of depression. When a person loses someone whom he or she has ambivalently loved and hated, and introjects that person, aggression is directed inward. If these feelings are strong and murderous enough, the person will commit suicide. The second theory postulates that the death instinct, Thanatos, can turn inward and make the person take his or her life.

Freud's views on suicide are subject to many of the problems raised earlier in this text about psychoanalytic theorizing. Moreover, a careful analysis of suicide notes by Tuckman, Kleiner, and Lavell (1959) provides information that is in marked disagreement with the psychoanalytic position. They found that only a very small minority of the notes expressed hostility. In fact,

BOX 8.6 Some Myths about Suicide

There are many prevalent misconceptions about suicide (Pokorny, 1968; Shneidman, 1973).

1. *People who discuss suicide will not commit the act.* The fact is that up to three-quarters of those who take their lives have communicated the intent beforehand, perhaps as a cry for help, perhaps to taunt. On the other hand, the vast majority of people who contemplate suicide do not actually attempt to kill themselves.

2. *Suicide may be committed without warning.* The falseness of this belief is readily indicated by the preceding statement. There seem to be many warnings, such as the person's saying that the world would be better off without him, or making unexpected and inexplicable gifts to others, often of his most valued possessions.

3. *Only people of a certain class commit suicide.* Suicide is actually neither the curse of the poor nor the disease of the rich. People in all classes commit suicide.

4. *Membership in a particular religious group is a good predictor that a person will not consider suicide.* It is mistakenly thought that the strong Catholic prohibition against suicide makes the risk that Catholics will take their lives much lower. This is not supported by the evidence, perhaps because an individual's formal religious identification is not always an accurate index of true beliefs.

5. *The motives for suicide are easily established.* The truth is that we have only the poorest understanding of why people commit suicide. For example, the fact that a severe reverse in finances precedes a suicide does not mean that the reversal adequately explains the suicide.

6. *All who commit suicide are depressed.* This fallacy may account for the tragic fact that signs of impending suicide are overlooked because the person is not depressed. Although reliable data are difficult to collect, some experts believe that many of the people who take their lives are *not* depressed. In fact, some people appear calm and at peace with themselves after having decided to kill themselves.

7. *A person with a terminal physical illness is unlikely to commit suicide.* A person's awareness of impending death does not preclude suicide. Perhaps the wish to end their own suffering or that of their loved ones impels many to choose the time of their death.

8. *To commit suicide is insane.* Although most suicidal persons are very unhappy, most do appear to be completely rational and in touch with reality.

9. *A tendency to commit suicide is inherited.* Since suicides often run in families, the assumption is made that the tendency to think in terms of self-annihilation is inherited. There is no evidence for this.

10. *Suicide is influenced by seasons, latitude, weather fronts, barometric pressure, humidity, precipitation, cloudiness, wind speed, temperature, and days of the week.* There are no good data to substantiate any of these myths.

11. *Suicide is influenced by cosmic factors such as sunspots and phases of the moon.* No evidence confirms this.

12. *Improvement in emotional state means lessened risk of suicide.* The fact is that people often commit the act after their spirits begin to rise; this appears to be especially true of depressed patients.

13. *Suicide is a lonely event.* Although the debate whether to commit suicide is waged within the individual's head, deep immersion in a frustrating, hurtful relationship with another person—a spouse, a child, a lover, a colleague—may be a principal cause.

14. *Suicidal people clearly want to die.* Most people who commit suicide appear to be ambivalent about their own deaths.

about half expressed gratitude and affection for others. A possible rebuttal—which we find unsatisfactory—might be that a suicide note, written at the conscious level, could not be expected to reflect repressed hostility.

Durkheim's sociological theory of suicide
Durkheim (1897), after analyzing the records of suicide for various countries and during different historical periods, viewed self-annihilation as a sociological phenomenon and distinguished three different kinds. *Egoistic suicide* is committed, according to Durkheim, when a person has too few ties to the society and community. These people feel alienated from others, cut off from the social supports that are important to keep them functioning adaptively as social beings. *Altruistic suicides,* in contrast, are viewed by Durkheim as responses to societal demands. Some people who commit suicide feel very much a part of a group and sacrifice themselves for what they take to be the good of society. The self-immolations of Buddhist monks and nuns to protest the fighting during the Vietnam war would fit into this category. Some altruistic suicides, such as the hara-kiri of the Japanese, are literally required as the only honorable recourse in the circumstances. Finally, *anomic suicide* may be triggered by a sudden change in a person's relations to society. A successful businesswoman who suffers severe financial reverses may experience *anomie,* a sense of disorientation, because what she believed to be her normal way of living is no longer possible for her. Anomie can pervade a society in disequilibrium, making suicide more likely.

As with all sociological theorizing, Durkheim's hypotheses have trouble accounting for the different reactions of individuals in a given society to the same demands and conditions. Not all those who unexpectedly lose their money commit suicide. It appears that Durkheim was aware of this problem, for he suggested that individual temperament would interact with any of the social pressures that he found causative. Perhaps at the most general level a person's suicide may be regarded as what he or she considered the best means for withdrawing from a particular and apparently unsolvable problem in living. Even this

Jo Roman, in her early sixties and suffering from breast cancer that was not yet critical, methodically planned her death for fifteen months. She was determined to spare herself and her dear ones the pain and great emotional strain of a terminal illness. While she could still "function to my satisfaction," she bid her husband, daughter, and a close friend goodnight and farewell, swallowed thirty-five sleeping pills and a glass of champagne, and went quietly to bed.

suggestion, however, is inadequate, for it does not explain why person A chooses suicide whereas person B withdraws from stress by "going crazy." All explanations remain strictly *post hoc* until and unless a theory better predicts why individuals differ in their reactions to the same set of social conditions.

Prediction of Suicide from Psychological Tests

Psychologists have attempted to predict suicide on the basis of scores on psychological tests. It would of course be of immense theoretical and practical advantage to be able to predict from the results of tests who might consider the act. Theoretically, knowing what characteristics a potential suicide has would help us understand what makes people contemplate killing themselves. On practical, social-action grounds, being able to detect who is likely to make an attempt would obviously help those who wish to intervene and save lives.

Many investigators have studied the personality characteristics of those who have attempted suicide. An unavoidable difficulty with this kind of research stems from the fact that personality tests can seldom be given to numbers of people who may *later* kill themselves. Furthermore, in addition to this problem of obtaining data before a suicide attempt has been made, it is impossible to obtain information, other than biographical accounts from relatives and a few other sources, after the deed has been done. The literature, then, consists mostly of reports of psychological tests given to people *after* they have made an aborted attempt at suicide. Clearly, the information obtained from such tests will reflect the fact that those tested have recently tried and failed to kill themselves. Their state of mind is likely to be quite different from what it had been before the attempt. For example, many who have tried unsuccessfully to take their lives feel extremely guilty and embarrassed. It is impossible to know with any exactness how test scores and interview behavior are affected by such postattempt factors.

Although these problems might have affected the results, several studies have found significant correlations between suicide intent and hopelessness. For example, Beck, Kovacs, and Weissman (1975) found that hopelessness, as measured by the Hopelessness Scale, was more highly correlated with suicide intent than was depression. The expectation that, at some point in the future, things may look no better than they do right now seems to be more instrumental than depression per se in propelling a person to take his or her life.

On the other hand, an investigation by Leonard (1974) suggested different factors. Leonard gave the MMPI and the Self-Rating Depression Scale (Zung, 1965) to ninety patients voluntarily admitted to a psychiatric hospital. About one-third of them were rated as seriously suicidal by these tests. The most surprising finding was that suicidal inclination did not correlate strongly with depression, rather with a feeling of being out of control and a sense of physical disequilibrium. Perhaps the person felt extremely restless or believed that his or her heart beat faster than usual, that it was not as easy to do things as it once had been. Problems in channeling energy emerged rather than hopelessness and despondency.

Another avenue of research has focused on several cognitive characteristics of people who attempt suicide. It has been suggested that suicidal individuals may be more rigid in their approach to problems (for example, Neuringer, 1964), less flexible in their thinking (Levenson, 1972). Constricted thinking could account for their apparent inability to seek solutions to life problems other than taking their own lives. Others have suggested that such people may also be impulsive, the assumption being that they would not attempt to kill themselves were they to reflect carefully on their behavior. A recent study by Patsiokas, Clum, and Luscomb (1979) addressed some of these questions. They administered several tests to a group of psychiatric patients who had been admitted to a hospital for having attempted suicide, as well as to a control group made up of psychiatric patients with no history of having tried to take their own lives. Flexibility of thinking was measured by the Alternative Uses Test (Wilson et al., 1975), in which the person has to list as many different uses for a series of common objects as possible. Also given was the Matching Familiar Figures Test (Kagan, 1965), in which the person chooses correct matching figures from several alternatives. The impulsive person supposedly responds too quickly and makes many errors, rather than taking the time to reflect and choose carefully.

In general, the results confirmed the hypothesis that people who attempt suicide are more rigid than control subjects, lending support to the clinical observation that they seem almost myopically incapable of thinking of alternative solutions to problems and might therefore tend to settle on suicide as the only way out. Little evidence linked impulsiveness to attempted suicide, however. The researchers speculate that the measure used may not be a valid index of impulsiveness as it relates to suicide. Another interpretation, more plausible to us, is that taking one's own life is not an impulsive act at all but is generally done after considerable reflection and doubt.

Prediction of Suicide from Demographic Variables

Instead of employing psychological tests devised for other purposes, many workers advocate the development of assessment procedures specifically designed to predict suicide. Attention is paid to demographic factors such as age, sex, marital status, and living arrangements, which turn out to be very useful predictors—more helpful than the personality and cognitive variables just considered.

Suicide prevention centers rely on demographic factors (Shneidman, Farberow, and Litman, 1970). Workers receiving phone calls from people in suicidal crises have before them a checklist to guide their questioning of each caller, for they must immediately assess how great the risk of suicide may be. For example, a caller would be regarded as a lethal risk if he were male, middle-aged, divorced, and living alone and had a history of previous suicide attempts. And usually the more detailed and concrete the suicide plan, the higher the risk. More details on suicide prevention centers are provided in Chapter 20 (page 647). Box 8.7 discusses some general clinical issues and gives guidelines for handling suicidal patients.

Another procedure is the "*psychological autopsy*," pioneered at the Los Angeles Suicide Prevention Center (Shneidman, Faberow, and Litman, 1970). In effect, these workers analyze information obtained from crisis phone calls, from interviews with relatives and friends of those who are thinking about suicide or have committed the act, and from notes left behind by those who have ultimately killed themselves. This type of clinical case study has yielded a wealth of provocative and often useful information.

Of particular interest is a study (Shneidman and Farberow, 1970) of notes left by people who subsequently committed suicide. In the Los Angeles area, at the time this work was done, about 15 percent of suicides left notes, and the contents of these notes were analyzed by judges trained to rate them on the presence or absence of instructions and specific themes, such as self-blame, discomfort, death as relief, and the like. Having determined that such ratings could indeed be made reliably by independent judges, Shneidman and Farberow compared these actual suicide notes with simulated notes prepared for them by individuals who were *not* oriented toward killing themselves but who were matched to those who had on such demographic variables as age, sex, and social class. These control subjects had been instructed to write *as if* they were about to commit suicide. The genuine notes contained a greater number of instructions, such as suggestions about raising the children and explicit orders about how to dispose of the body; there was also evidence of significantly more anguish.

As is the case in nearly all areas of abnormal psychology, not as much is known about suicide as we would like. In this instance the lack of information is all the more worrisome, since the very existence of many people is at stake. Fortunately, those who have devoted their professional lives to preventing suicide are not waiting for all the data to come in before attempting to intervene. The absence of a good theory does not preclude action. Working principles can be derived from available statistical studies, which already identify at least some of the individuals who are likely to make lethal attempts.

A LIVING WILL

Prepared by

CONCERN FOR DYING

an educational council

IMPORTANT

Declarants may wish to add specific statements to the Living Will to be inserted in the space provided for that purpose above the signature. Possible additional provisions are suggested below:

1. a) I appoint _____ to make binding decisions concerning my medical treatment.

   OR

   b) I have discussed my views as to life sustaining measures with the following who understand my wishes

   _____,
   _____,
   _____

2. Measures of artificial life support in the face of impending death that are especially abhorrent to me are:

   a) Electrical or mechanical resuscitation of my heart when it has stopped beating.

   b) Nasogastric tube feedings when I am paralyzed and no longer able to swallow.

   c) Mechanical respiration by machine when my brain can no longer sustain my own breathing.

   d) _____

3. If it does not jeopardize the chance of my recovery to a meaningful and sentient life or impose an undue burden on my family, I would like to live out my last days at home rather than in a hospital.

4. If any of my tissues are sound and would be of value as transplants to help other people, I freely give my permission for such donation.

A Living Will, to be completed by a person who does not want his or her life prolonged by extreme artificial means. Should this will be considered an expression of suicide intent? At what point can society be denied efforts to prolong life?

BOX **8.7** Dealing with Suicide

Although it is not true, as stated at the beginning of this section, that people are invariably depressed when they commit suicide or attempt to do so, suicide must always be considered a danger when working with those who are profoundly depressed. The despair and utter hopelessness of their existence may make them see suicide as the only solution, the only exit. In fact, sometimes the sole reason a depressed individual does *not* attempt suicide is that he or she cannot summon the energy to formulate and implement a suicide plan. In working with a seriously depressed individual, the clinician must be especially careful as the patient *emerges from* the low point of depression, for the sadness and hopelessness may still be strong enough to make self-annihilation appear the only option *and* now the person begins to have enough energy to do something about it. Because so many who commit suicide are depressed, treatment of this condition is at the same time an intervention that clinicians hope will reduce the risk of suicide.

Clinicians have to work out for themselves an ethic regarding a person's right to end his or her life. What steps is the professional willing to take to prevent a suicide? Confinement in a straitjacket on the back ward of a hospital? Or, as is more common in these modern times, sedation administered against the patient's wishes and strong enough that the person is virtually incapable of taking any action at all? And for how long will extraordinary measures be taken? The clinician realizes, of course, that many, perhaps even most, suicidal crises pass; the suicidal person is likely to be grateful afterward that he or she was prevented from destroying the self when it seemed the only course. But to what extremes is the professional prepared to go in order to prevent a suicide attempt?

The therapist should not hesitate to inquire directly whether the client has thought of suicide. Experienced clinicians and suicidologists do not believe that the idea can be put into another person's head, that the risk of suicide can be increased merely by asking about it. On the contrary, opening up the topic for discussion can be the first step of a therapeutic intervention (Beck et al., 1979). It is important to adopt a phenomenological stance, to view the suicidal person's situation as he sees it, rather than convey in any way that he is a fool or is crazy to have settled on suicide as a solution to his woes. This Rogerian empathy for suicidal people is sometimes referred to as "tuning in" by those who work in suicide prevention centers. In addition, the clinician treating a suicidal person must be prepared to devote more energy and time than he or she usually does even to psychotic patients. Late-night phone calls and visits to the patient's home may be frequent. Finally, the therapist should realize that he or she is likely to become a singularly important figure in the suicidal person's life—and be prepared both for the extreme dependency of the patient and for the hostility and resentment that sometimes greets efforts to help.

Summary

DSM-III lists two principal affective disorders. In major or unipolar depression the person experiences profound sadness as well as a number of related problems, such as sleep and appetite disturbances, loss of energy and self-esteem. In bipolar disorder the person has episodes either of mania alone or of both mania and depression. With mania the person's mood is elevated or irritable, and he or she becomes extremely active, talkative, and distractible.

Psychological theories of depression have been couched in psychoanalytic, cognitive, and learning terms. Psychoanalytic formulations stress unconscious identification with a loved one whose desertion of the individual has made him or her turn anger inward. Beck's cognitive theory ascribes causal significance to illogical self-judgment. Operant learning theorists attribute depression to an unrewarding, inactive existence. And according to Seligman's cognitive-learning appraisal, early experiences in inescapable, hurtful situations instill a sense of helplessness which can evolve into depression. Physiological theories suggest an inherited predisposition for bipolar disorder in particular and relate the phenomena of depression and mania to abnormally depleted and copious amounts of the neurotransmitters that pass on neural impulses in particular nerve tracts of the brain.

There are a number of psychological and somatic therapies for affective disorders and especially for depression. Psychoanalytic treatment tries to give the patient insight into childhood loss and inadequacy and into later self-blame. The aim of the cognitive therapy of Aaron Beck is to uncover illogical patterns of thinking and teach more realistic ways of viewing events, the self, and adversity. Behavioral therapists encourage greater levels of activity in the belief that more frequent reinforcement will lighten the sad mood and encourage more social participation by depressed individuals. The learned-helplessness view of depression, although not as yet identified with a particular set of therapy procedures, does make therapists aware of the apparent need of people to believe that they exercise control over their lives. Finally, the existential logotherapy encourages depressed people to make spiritual sense of their suffering, to feel free and responsible for their lives, and to find meaning and purpose in existence.

A range of somatic treatments are also available; often used in conjunction with a psychological treatment, they can be very effective. Electroconvulsive shock and several antidepressant drugs have proved their worth in lifting depression. In recent years it has been possible for patients to avoid the excesses of manic and depressive periods through careful administration of lithium carbonate.

Finally, the topic of suicide was explored, although self-annihilative tendencies are not restricted to those who are depressed. A review of the facts and myths about suicide suggests that any single theory is unlikely to account for its great diversity, but that the information already gathered can be applied to prevent it.

Most large communities have suicide prevention centers, and most therapists at one time or another have to deal with patients in suicidal crisis. Clinical evidence suggests that suicidal persons need to have their fears and concerns understood but not judged, and that workers must gradually and patiently point out to them that alternatives to self-destruction are there to be explored.

Jacob Lawrence, "The Migration Gained in Momentum" (1940–1941). Collection, The Museum of Modern Art, New York. Gift of Mrs. David M. Levy.

part three
social problems

chapter 9

Personality disorders are a group of diagnoses based on a trait approach to personality (see page 115). DSM-III puts it this way.

> . . . When personality traits *are inflexible and maladaptive and cause either significant impairment in social and occupational functioning or subjective distress . . . they constitute* Personality Disorders. *The manifestations of Personality Disorders are generally recognized by adolescence or earlier and continue throughout most of adult life, though they often become less obvious in middle or old age.*
>
> *Many of the features characteristic of various Personality Disorders . . . may be seen during an episode of another mental disorder, such as Major Depression. The diagnosis . . . should be made only when the characteristic features are typical of the individual's long-term functioning and are not limited to discrete periods of illness (p. 305).*

According to DSM-III *personality disorders* are to be indicated on axis II, which means that their presence or absence is to be considered when-ever a diagnosis is made. The names given to the specific personality disorders differ considerably from those in DSM-II. But name changing does not solve the many problems of this category. Personality disorders have been shown to possess little diagnostic reliability as they were defined in previous editions of the DSM (for example, Beck et al., 1962). Although DSM-III attempts to improve the clarity of the definitions, in the field trials of DSM-III the reliability of diagnoses of personality disorders was lower than that of most other categories. Critics could also point to the problems involved in basing a diagnostic category on a trait conception of personality. As indicated in Chapter 3, saying that someone has a particular trait is not always a powerful predictor of behavior. Perhaps, though, personality disorders reflect the phenomenon discovered by Bem and Allen (1974): some people, and those with personality disorders may be among them, behave consistently enough in a wide range of situations to be described as having traits. A final problem is that there is simply very little information available on many of the personality disorders, not enough to indicate whether they are valid diagnoses.

Specific Personality Disorders

Personality disorders are grouped into three clusters in DSM-III. Individuals with the first three in the following list seem odd or eccentric, those with the next three dramatic, emotional, or erratic, and those with any of the last cluster of four disorders anxious or fearful.

Paranoid Personality Disorder   The *paranoid personality* is suspicious of people. He or she expects to be mistreated by others and thus becomes secretive and is continually on the lookout for possible signs of trickery and abuse. Such individuals are extremely jealous and tend to blame others even when they themselves are at fault. Paranoid personalities are also overly sensitive, quick to take offense, argumentative, and tense. Their emotional responses are shallow, and they appear cold and humorless to others.

Schizoid Personality Disorder   The *schizoid personality* has difficulties in forming social relationships and usually has few close friends. He or she appears dull and aloof and without warm, tender feelings for other people. Indifferent to praise, criticism, and the sentiments of others, individuals with this disorder are "loners" and pursue solitary interests. They may daydream a great deal and sometimes seem "not with it," but they, unlike the schizophrenic, are basically in good contact with reality.

Schizotypal Personality Disorder   The *schizotypal personality* usually has the interpersonal difficulties of the schizoid personality. But along with these are a number of other symptoms which, although eccentric, are not severe enough to

A schizoid personality has few friends and disengages himself from others.

warrant a diagnosis of schizophrenia (see Chapter 13). Schizotypal personalities may have *"magical thinking"*—superstitiousness, beliefs that they are clairvoyant and telepathic—and perceptual disturbances such as depersonalization, derealization, and *illusions*—they sense the presence of something that is not actually there. Speech may also contain words used in unusual and unclear fashion. Under stress such persons can appear psychotic. This diagnosis is acknowledged in DSM-III to overlap often with borderline personality disorder.

Borderline Personality Disorder   The *borderline personality* indicates instability in relationships, mood, and self-image. For example, attitudes and feelings toward other people may vary considerably and inexplicably over short periods of time. Emotions are also erratic and can shift abruptly, particularly to anger. Unpredictable and impulsive behavior, such as gambling, spending, sex, and eating sprees, is potentially self-damaging. Borderline personalities lack a clear sense of self and are uncertain about their values, loyalties, and choice of career. They cannot bear to be alone. Like the schizotypal personality, these persons can appear psychotic under emotional stress.[1]

Histrionic Personality Disorder   The diagnosis *histrionic personality,* formerly called hysterical personality, is applied to people who are overly dramatic and always drawing attention to themselves. These individuals, emotionally expressive to an unusual degree, are also given to angry overreactions to minor annoyances and to quick boredom with normal routines. Interpersonal problems are frequent and include manipulativeness, seductiveness, dependence, and constant demands on others. The histrionic personality is sometimes regarded as superficially charming by other people, but also as vain, shallow, ungenuine, and inconsiderate.

Narcissistic Personality Disorder   *Narcissistic personalities* have a grandiose view of their own uniqueness and abilities. They are preoccupied with fantasies of great successes and crave the

Narcissistic personalities have an inflated sense of their self-importance and are likely to overestimate their physical attractions.

admiration and attention of others. To say that they are self-centered is almost an understatement. Their interpersonal relationships are disturbed by their lack of empathy; by exploitiveness, taking advantage of others; and by feelings of entitlement, expecting others to do special, not-to-be-reciprocated favors for them.

Avoidant Personality Disorder   *Avoidant personalities* are keenly sensitive to the possibility of social rejection and humiliation and are therefore reluctant to enter into relationships, even though they yearn for closeness and for the affection and acceptance of others. They suffer from low self-esteem, being dismayed by their

[1] Patients with both borderline and schizotypal personality disorders would probably have been diagnosed as schizophrenic using DSM-II criteria. Designating the behavior of these people as the criteria for these two personality disorders is one way that DSM-III has narrowed the schizophrenic diagnosis (see Chapter 13).

own personal shortcomings and devaluing all their achievements.

Dependent Personality Disorder *Dependent personalities* lack self-confidence and self-reliance, passively allowing other people to assume responsibility for deciding where they should live, what jobs they should hold, with whom they should be friendly. They are unable to make demands on others, and they subordinate their own needs to ensure that they do not break up the protective relationships they have established. Their belittlement of themselves brings to mind the colloquialism "inferiority complex."

Compulsive Personality Disorder *Compulsive personalities* are perfectionists, preoccupied with details, rules, schedules, and the like. They are work- rather than pleasure-oriented and have inordinate difficulty making decisions and allocating time. Their interpersonal relationships are often poor because they demand that everything be done their way. They are generally serious and formal and are unlikely to express warmth and friendliness.[2]

Passive-Agressive Personality Disorder *Passive-aggressive personalities* *indirectly* resist the demands of others, either socially or at work. The resistance, which is thought to be aggression in disguise, takes the form of thoroughgoing stubbornness and ineffectuality. They are habitually late for appointments, do not return phone calls, procrastinate, and "forget." This persistent behavior pattern usually provokes further problems, such as marital discord and not being offered promotions. The dawdling of passive-aggressive personalities can be considered a hostile way of controlling others without assuming responsibility for their own anger.

The personality disorders make up what many workers regard as an unreliable, cluttered grab bag of a category. Ironically, the descriptions of them may seem to fit some of the members of our families and some of our own acquain-

tances! Each of us develops over the years some apparently persistent means of dealing with life's challenges, a certain "style" of relating to other people. One person is overly dependent, another challenging and aggressive; yet another is very shy and avoids social contact, and another is more concerned with appearances and bolstering his or her precious ego than with relating honestly and on a deep level with others. To be sure, DSM-III would not have these personalities diagnosed unless the patterns of behavior are long standing and pervasive, but the essential disturbances listed for the various personality disorders no doubt bring to mind the shortcomings of friends, colleagues—and oneself.

The reader may also have noticed that descriptions of some of the personality disorders are similar to those of diagnostic categories discussed elsewhere. Generally speaking, a person judged to have, for example, a paranoid personality disorder is less disturbed than a person with paranoid schizophrenia or a paranoid disorder (see pages 416-417). People given all three diagnoses, however, do have in common a tendency to be overly suspicious, guarded, and thin-skinned. But it can be very difficult to distinguish personality disorders from others that bear a resemblance (Nathan et al., 1968), underlining once again their problematic status as a separate group of psychological disturbances.

Although data are few on the disorders just described, one personality disorder omitted from the foregoing list is more reliably diagnosed and has attracted the attention of workers for many years. In short, *antisocial personality disorder* may be a useful diagnosis. The rest of this chapter will be devoted to what is known about the disruptive and essentially self-destructive individuals whose deep-seated ethical and moral maladjustments frequently bring them into serious conflict with their associates and with society.

[2] It may occur to the reader that these traits can be very adaptive in certain situations. It is a standing joke, for example, that success in graduate school goes to those who are compulsive. The issues are more serious, however, for they go to the heart not only of the appropriateness of considering such people to have a mental disorder, but also of the demands placed on people working for advanced degrees. Consider as well the kinds of people selected for graduate study, and the kinds of professionals these students are likely to become.

Antisocial Personality Disorder (Sociopathy)

In current usage the terms *sociopath* and *psychopath* appear interchangeably with antisocial personality. The concept has an interesting history. At the very beginning of the nineteenth century, Philippe Pinel conceived of *manie sans délire*. Pinel chose this term to indicate that the patient he described was violently insane (*manie*) but did not show other symptoms (*sans délire*) common among the insane. In 1835 James Prichard, an English psychiatrist, described the disorder "moral insanity" in an attempt to account for behavior so far outside the usual ethical and legal codes that it seemed a form of lunacy. The man whose nature prompted Pinel's term was an easily angered aristocrat who had whipped a horse, kicked a dog to death, and thrown a peasant women into a well. Since the early concept was used to explain a wide range of strange behavior, it is not surprising that it came to function somewhat as a wastebasket diagnosis, encompassing those inclined not only to violence but to unconventional practices as well.

Before considering current views of these problems, we shall examine excerpts from two case histories that illustrate the scope of sociopathic reactions. The first case illustrates many of the classic characteristics of the sociopath but is unusual in that the person described was neither a criminal nor in psychiatric treatment at the time that the data for the case study were collected. This is an important point, for the majority of sociopaths who are the subjects of research studies have broken the law and been caught for doing so. Only rarely do we have the opportunity to examine in detail the behavior of an individual who fits the diagnostic definition but yet has managed not to break the law. The second case history presents the more usual picture of the criminal sociopath.

The Case of Dan

This case history was compiled by a psychologist, Elton McNeil (1967), who happened to be a personal friend of Dan's.

Dan was a wealthy actor and disc jockey who lived in an expensive house in an exclusive suburb and generally played his role as a "personality" to the hilt. One evening, when he and McNeil were out for dinner, Dan made a great fuss over the condition of the *Shrimp de Johnge* that he had ordered. McNeil thought that the whole scene had been deliberately contrived by Dan for the effect it might produce, and he said to his companion,

"I have a sneaking suspicion this whole scene came about just because you weren't really hungry." Dan laughed loudly in agreement and said, "What the hell, they'll be on their toes next time." "Was that the only reason for this display?" . . . "No," he replied, "I wanted to show you how gutless the rest of the world is. If you shove a little they all jump. Next time I come in, they'll be all over me to make sure everything is exactly as I want it. That's the only way they can tell the difference between class and plain ordinary. When I travel I go first class."
"Yes, . . . but how do you feel about you as a person—as a fellow human being?"
"Who cares?" he laughed. "If they were on top they would do the same to me. The more you walk on them, the more they like it. It's like royalty in the old days. It makes them nervous if everyone is equal to everyone else. Watch. When we leave I'll put my arm around that waitress, ask her if she still loves me, pat her on the fanny, and she'll be ready to roll over any time I wiggle my little finger" (p. 85).

Another incident occurred when a friend of Dan's committed suicide. Most of the other friends whom Dan and McNeil had in common were concerend and called the psychologist to see whether he could provide any information about why the man had taken his life. Dan did not. Later, when McNeil mentioned the suicide to Dan, all he could say was "That's the way the ball bounces." In his public behavior, however, Dan's attitude toward the incident appeared quite different. He was the one who collected money and presented it personally to the new widow. In keeping with his character, however, Dan remarked that the widow had a sexy body that really interested him.

These two incidents convey the flavor of Dan's behavior. McNeil had witnessed a long succession of similar events which led him to conclude that

> [The incidents] painted a grisly picture of life-long abuse of people for Dan's amusement and profit. He was adept at office politics and told me casually of an unbelievable set of deceptive ways to deal with the opposition. Character assassination, rumor mongering, modest blackmail, seduction, and barefaced lying were the least of his talents. He was a jackal in the entertainment jungle, a jackal who feasted on the bodies of those he had slaughtered professionally (p. 91).

In his conversations with Dan, McNeil was also able to inquire into Dan's life history. One early and potentially important event was related by Dan.

> I can remember the first time in my life when I began to suspect I was a little different from most people. When I was in high school my best friend got leukemia and died and I went to his funeral. Everybody else was crying and feeling sorry for themselves and as they were praying to get him into heaven I suddenly realized that I wasn't feeling anything at all. He was a nice guy but what the hell. That night I thought about it some more and found that I wouldn't miss my mother and father if they died and that I wasn't too nuts about my brothers and sisters for that matter. I figured there wasn't anybody I really cared for but, then, I didn't need any of them anyway so I rolled over and went to sleep (p. 87).

The moral depravity described long ago by Pinel and Prichard clearly marks Dan's behavior. A person may be otherwise quite rational and show no loss of contact with reality and yet behave in a habitually and exceedingly unethical manner. The final excerpt illustrates Dan's complete lack of feeling for others, a characteristic that will later be seen to have considerable relevance in explaining the behavior of the sociopath.

The Case of Jim

Jim, the fourth child in a family of five, grew up in the lower social class of a small Midwestern town. During his childhood the member of his family who made the greatest impression on him was his older brother, whom he described as follows.

> He was always a bully, promiscuous, and adventurous. He was always involved with some local girl, before I was even old enough to realize what was going on. He started drinking early, and had several scrapes with the law. He had rough companions, whom I later inherited, who helped me on my way.
>
> He married a tramp, ended up in a stolen car, and was given the choice of jail or the army, as this was the Korean war time. I cannot directly link him to my life of crime, although he introduced me to those who later helped me along. Also, he condoned some of my early petty thievery (Bintz and Wilson, as reprinted in Milton and Wahler, 1969, p. 92).

During early adolescence Jim engaged in many petty antisocial acts. For example, on one occasion he stole some change from his mother's pocketbook. His father reacted by whipping both brothers until Jim confessed. Once Jim had admitted taking the money, however, the punishment ended. This became standard practice for the family, with Jim being able to avoid punishment by confessing as soon as he was accused of misbehavior, regardless of whether or not he was guilty. Moreover, the petty thievery that Jim committed in the community was generally successful, and even when he was caught consequences were minimal.

Jim's first serious trouble with the law occurred when he was charged with raping a young woman whom he had picked up at the local skating rink. He was sentenced to five years at a reform school but received an immediate parole on the condition that his sentence would be activated if he violated it. After several parole violations such as petty theft, and being detained for speeding, he was sentenced to one year at the reform school. By the time he returned to his hometown a year later, he had become a young hoodlum. Jim himself stated that the principal consequence of the year in reform school had been the opportunity afforded him to fraternize with more experienced thieves. Shortly thereafter Jim and a friend committed their first major theft, stealing $1700 from a tavern safe. Then the same pair attempted to burglarize a lumberyard but were unable to open the safe. The next day they were arrested, and the burglary tools were found in Jim's car. He served a ninety-day sentence for attempted burglary. Three months after being released, Jim was incarcerated again, this time for statutory rape. As soon as he was free again, he and a friend planned another robbery. They reasoned that a bootlegger would be a good target for a holdup for, being outside the law himself, he would be reluctant to report the incident to the police. They bungled the job badly, however, and both were sentenced to five-year terms. Jim served three of the five years and upon his release met the woman he was soon to marry. He described her as follows.

Diane was a tramp, I could tell from the start. She forced the introduction and the first date. I had sexual relations with her on the first date, she was my third sexual partner on that particular day. She was neat, but not really attractive. The next four and a half months we were intimate almost every night. She wanted to marry, I did not. I could not see myself married to this plain-looking tramp. In fact, toward the last, I was trying to think of a scheme to get rid of her . . . (p. 100).

During this period Jim held a job, but he soon began to get deeper and deeper into debt. Eventually, an opportunity for another theft presented itself. Again the job was spectacularly unsuccessful and Jim was sentenced to ten years in the state penitentiary. While in the county jail, before the trial, he was visited often by Diane and finally married her just before going to prison. As a substitute for a wedding ring, Jim had the words "Love me, Diane" tattooed on his penis.

Cleckley's Concept of Sociopathy

Both of these case histories illustrate many of the symptoms of the sociopathic syndrome as it has been defined by Hervey Cleckley (1976). On the basis of his vast clinical experience, he formulated a set of criteria by which to recognize the disorder. Cleckley's work continues to be accepted as providing the classic description of _sociopathy._

1. Considerable superficial charm and average or above average intelligence.

2. Absence of delusions or other signs of irrational thinking.

3. Absence of anxiety or other "neurotic" symptoms; considerable poise, calmness, and verbal facility.

4. Unreliability, disregard for obligations; no sense of responsibility, in matters of little and great import.

5. Untruthfulness and insincerity.

6. Lack of remorse, no sense of shame.

7. Antisocial behavior which is inadequately motivated and poorly planned, seeming to stem from an inexplicable impulsiveness.

8. Poor judgment and failure to learn from experience.

9. Pathological egocentricity, total self-centeredness; incapacity for real love and attachment.

10. General poverty of deep and lasting emotions.

11. Lack of any true insight, inability to see oneself as others do.

12. Ingratitude for any special considerations, kindness, and trust.

13. Fantastic and objectionable behavior, after drinking and sometimes even when not drinking—vulgarity, rudeness, quick mood shifts, pranks.

14. No history of genuine suicide attempts.

15. An impersonal, trivial, and poorly integrated sex life.

16. Failure to have a life plan and to live in any ordered way, unless it be one promoting self-defeat.

Cleckley's indicators of sociopathy are somewhat different from DSM-III's criteria for the diagnosis of antisocial personality disorder. The DSM-III criteria refer to more specific aspects of behavior, such as inability to hold a job and be a responsible parent and failure to honor financial obligations. But DSM-III also omits some of the characteristics that Cleckley would regard as being of central importance, such as superficial charm, blitheness, and shamelessness. Indeed, the DSM-III indicators bring the concept of antisocial personality dangerously close to criminal behavior in general. Earlier, for example, Hare (1978) found that 76 percent of a sample of prison inmates met the proposed DSM-III criteria for antisocial personality disorder. In contrast, Cleckley's description fit only 33 percent of these prisoners.

For the concept of sociopathy to be useful, it must be easily differentiated from criminal behavior. A definition that focuses on the reactions of the individual to his or her own antisocial behavior accomplishes this purpose. Thus Cleckley's criteria *no sense of responsibility* and *no sense of shame* are particularly important. The sociopath is viewed as not responding emotionally after committing an act that generally elicits shame and guilt in most people. Moreover, the lack of these affective reactions is presumably linked to the sociopath's inability to learn from experience, particularly to avoid punishment. The sociopath continues to engage in the same antisocial activities, even though they prove unsuccessful, and even though his or her intelligence is perhaps above average. Learning to avoid actions that continually fail may be mediated by emotional arousal; because sociopaths do not become emotionally aroused, they may be less likely to suffer from and to change their unproductive and antisocial ways.

Three percent of adult American men and one percent of women are estimated to have antisocial personalities. Business executives, politicians, and physicians, plumbers, salespeople, carpenters, and bartenders—they are to be found in all walks of life. Prostitutes, pimps, confidence men, murderers, and drug dealers are by no means the only sociopaths.

Before examining the existing research on the sociopathic syndrome, we should emphasize again that most of it has been conducted on sociopaths who have already been convicted as criminals. Individuals such as Dan have rarely been studied in research settings. We must therefore keep in mind that the available literature may not allow us to generalize about the behavior of sociopaths who elude arrest and the subsequent label of criminal.[3] A method that may make these noncriminal sociopaths available for study is presented in Box 9.1.

---

[3] Nor indeed are all criminals sociopaths. In fact, the majority of criminals cannot be described as sociopathic. We consider it important to draw a distinction between sociopathy and criminal behavior. *Criminality* refers to law breaking as defined by a given society at a given point in time. Crime in general is much too extensive a subject to be covered in a textbook on abnormal psychology. Whenever possible, we restrict our discussion to sociopathy, taking special note when investigators have studied criminality rather than sociopathy.

BOX 9.1 A Methodology for Studying Noninstitutionalized Sociopaths

Until recently the problem of collecting for study a sample of "successful" sociopaths who have avoided incarceration seemed unsolvable. Now a method that may allow them to be contacted in sufficient numbers has been proposed by Widom (1977).

In order to recruit subjects, Widom placed an advertisement in a "counterculture" newspaper in the Boston area. The ad attempted to attract the attention of sociopaths by referring to key aspects of their behavior in a nondemeaning way.

Wanted charming, aggressive, carefree people who are impulsively irresponsible but good at handling people and at looking after number one. Send name, address, phone, and short biography proving how interesting you are . . . .

The ad ran for eight months, and in this period of time forty-five males and twenty-three females responded. Its message was apparently deciphered by one respondent, who wrote "Are you looking for hookers or are you trying to make a listing of all the sociopaths in Boston?" On the basis of the biographies, and in some instances telephone conversations, twenty-three males and five females were selected as likely sociopaths (a ratio consistent with the far greater prevalence of sociopathy in men). These subjects were then contacted, and appointments were arranged for rather extensive testing.

The critical question that these tests were meant to answer was whether these subjects, upon closer examination, would actually prove to have the rather clear-cut characteristics of sociopaths. Seventy-eight percent of the sample fit Robins's (1966) description of sociopathy: they had poor work and marital histories, used drugs excessively, drank heavily, and were physically aggressive and sexually promiscuous. True to the MMPI sociopathic profile, they peaked on the mania and psychopathic deviate scales of this questionnaire. Other results, for example, low scores on empathy and socialization tests, corroborated the conclusion that the members of this sample were truly sociopathic. Thus it now seems possible to collect subjects who can be studied to determine the etiology of sociopathy in noncriminal populations.

Theory and Research on the Etiology of Sociopathy

The Role of the Family

Since much sociopathic behavior violates social norms, it is not surprising that many investigators have focused on the primary agent of socialization, the family, in their search for the explanation of such behavior. McCord and McCord (1964) concluded, on the basis of a classic review of the literature, that lack of affection and severe parental rejection were the primary causes of sociopathic behavior. Several other studies have related sociopathic behavior to the parents' inconsistencies in disciplining their children and in teaching them their responsibilities to others (Bennet, 1960). Furthermore, the fathers of sociopaths are likely to be antisocial in their behavior.

But such data on early rearing must be interpreted with extreme caution. They were gathered by means of _retrospective reports._ Information about early family experiences and about how the child was taught to behave socially was obtained either from an adult sociopath or from parents, relatives, and friends at a time very much later than when the events actually occurred. Studies of the reliability of the information obtained in this way indicate that such data may be of little use. As Garmezy has noted,

> Studies of normal families have revealed the unreliability of the case history, with its exclusive reliance on retrospective reconstruction of an earlier time period. . . . Investigations conducted with normal mothers of primary school age (and younger) children provide evidence that not only do mothers suffer deficits in recalling events in the early years of their children's lives but that the deficiency is particularly acute [in remembering] emotions and affectively-tinged attitudes . . . (1971, p. 105).

When people are asked to recollect the early events in the life of someone who is now known to be a sociopath, their knowledge of adult status may have some effect on what they remember or report about childhood events. Potentially deviant incidents are more likely to be recalled, whereas those that do not dovetail with the person's current behavior may be overlooked.

One way of avoiding the problems of retrospective data is to follow up in adulthood a large group of individuals who as children were seen at a child guidance clinic. In one such study very detailed records had been kept on the children, including the type of problem that had brought them to the clinic and considerable information relating to the family (Robins, 1966). Ninety percent of an initial sample of 584 cases were located thirty years after their referral to the clinic.[4] In addition to the clinic cases, 100 control subjects who had lived in the same geographic area served by the clinic but who had _not_ been referred to it were also followed up in adulthood.

By interviewing the now-adult individuals chosen for both the experimental and control samples, the investigators were able to diagnose and describe any maladjustments of these individuals. Then adult problems were related back to the characteristics that these people had had as children to find out which of them predicted sociopathic behavior in adulthood. Robins summarized these as follows.

> If one wishes to choose the most likely candidate for a later diagnosis of sociopathic personality from among children appearing in a child guidance clinic, the best choice appears to be a boy referred for theft or aggression who has shown a diversity of antisocial behavior in many episodes, at least one of which could be grounds for Juvenile Court appearance, and whose antisocial behavior involves him with strangers and organizations as well as with teachers and parents . . . more than half of the boys appearing at the clinic [with these characteristics were later] diagnosed sociopathic personality. Such boys had a history of truancy, theft, staying out late, and refusing to obey parents. They

---

[4] It should be appreciated that being able to track down this large a percentage of individuals thirty years after their contact with the clinic is an incredible feat.

lied gratuitously, and showed little guilt over their behavior. They were generally irresponsible about being where they were supposed to be or taking care of money. They were interested in sexual activities and had experimented with homosexual relationships . . . (p. 157).

In addition to these characteristics, aspects of family life mentioned earlier were again found to be important. Both inconsistent discipline and no discipline at all predicted sociopathic behavior in adulthood, as did antisocial behavior of the father.

In sum, the research we have reviewed emphasizes the importance of child-rearing practices. The fathers of sociopaths appear to provide a model for antisocial behavior. We must caution, however, that poor training in socialization has been implicated in the etiology of a *number* of clinical syndromes, including delinquent, neurotic, and even psychotic behavior (Wiggins, 1968), and that many individuals who come from what appear to be similarly disturbed social backgrounds do *not* become sociopaths or develop any other behavior disorders. This point is important: adults may have no problems whatsoever in spite of the inconsistent and otherwise undesirable manner of their rearing. Thus, although family experience is probably important in the development of sociopathic behavior, it can *not* be the whole story.

Genetic Correlates of Sociopathic Behavior

Twin and adoptee studies

Most of the studies concerned with the possible genetic basis for sociopathic behavior have focused on criminality or antisocial behavior rather than on sociopathy per se. The data collected are therefore difficult to interpret since, as already emphasized, not all sociopaths are criminals nor are all criminals sociopaths. Lange's research (1929) comparing concordance rates for criminality in identical and fraternal twins showed them to be a great deal higher for identical twins, supporting the theory that genetic factors may be involved. Kranz (1936), in a study

that used better sampling procedures, found the following patterns of concordance: identical twins, 66 percent; fraternal twins of the same sex, 54 percent; fraternal twins of the opposite sex, 14 percent. Although at first glance these data also seem to support the notion that genetic factors are important, they in fact give only slight support to this hypothesis. The critical piece of information is the marked *difference* in concordance rates of fraternal twins of the same sex and those of fraternal twins of the opposite sex. Both of these pairs of twins are equally alike genetically, but we can expect the parental rearing practices to which they are exposed to be markedly different. Fraternal twins of the same sex are probably treated more alike than are fraternal twins of the opposite sex. This evidence, in point of fact, implicates environmental factors.

But more recent adoptee studies suggest that heredity may indeed play a role in both criminality and sociopathy. With the help of the extensive social records kept in Denmark, Hutchings and Mednick (1974) examined rates of criminality in the adoptive and biological relatives of adoptees who had acquired criminal records, and Schulsinger (1972) performed a similar study with sociopathy as the variable of interest. Hutchings and Mednick found a higher rate of criminality in the biological relatives of criminals than in the general population, and Schulsinger found more sociopathy in the biological relatives of sociopaths. Studies done in the United States of adopted children whose biological parents were antisocial personalities also point to a genetic predisposition (Crowe, 1974; Cadoret, 1978).

XYY

One genetic aberration that has received considerable publicity is the presence of an extra male sex chromosome in men who have committed particularly violent crimes.[5] As indicated in Box 8.3 (page 250), the normal male cells have one X and one Y chromosome, the normal female cells two X chromosomes. The cells of some men have been reported to have one Y chromosome too many, XYY, and thus they may be con-

[5] Again we must caution that such data may be of only limited relevance to sociopathy.

Richard Speck, accused slayer of eight nurses who had lived together in a Chicago apartment, listens in 1966 as his lawyer demands a sanity hearing. Speck has the XYY syndrome.

sidered "supermales." But Rosenthal (1970) noted that of the large number of criminals and delinquents tested to date, only about 1.5 percent had shown this pattern. And these studies, because only criminals had been tested, could not provide definitive information on the relation between the XYY syndrome and violence in noncriminal populations.

A more adequate study was performed in Denmark by Witkin and a large group of investigators (1976). All men born in Copenhagen between 1944 and 1947 ($N = 31,436$) formed the population, and from this group the investigators culled for study those who were over six feet tall

($N = 4591$). Height was used as a selection criterion to ensure that an adequate number of XYY males would be found; previous research had shown that XYY males tend to be taller than average. Over 90 percent of the selected group participated in the research, which involved taking blood and a buccal smear—one from the mucous membranes of the cheek—so that the sex chromosomes could be studied. Existing records of criminal offenses were the measure of aggression-criminality; school reports and army screening tests provided estimates of intelligence.

Twelve XYY men were found, a prevalence rate of 2.9 per thousand. Five of these (41.7 percent) had been convicted of one or more criminal offenses; the nature of their crimes is indicated in Table 9.1. Of the 4579 normal XY men, 9.3 percent had been convicted of a crime. Thus with superior methodology it has now been shown that XYY men are more likely to be convicted of crimes. But do the convictions reflect a greater tendency of these men to be aggressive and violent? Inspection of Table 9.1 reveals that only one man committed an act of aggression against another person. Thus the XYY male, at least in his criminal offenses, does not appear to be highly violent. Why, then, are XYY men more likely to be convicted of crimes? Their lower intelligence is a possible explanation. The XYY men scored significantly lower than the XYs on both measures of intelligence. And the data revealed that low intelligence was related to higher rates of criminality. It may be, then, that low intelligence is causally related to criminality. It is equally possible, though, that people of low intelligence are less able to escape detection once they have committed a criminal act. The XYY men may have a higher rate of being *apprehended* for crimes, rather than a higher rate of committing them.

Central Nervous System Activity and Sociopathy

Many studies have examined patterns of brain wave activity (see Box 9.2) in sociopaths and various groups of control subjects. Ellingson (1954) reviewed these studies and reported that in thirteen out of fourteen of them, investigating a total of about 1500 sociopaths, between 31

TABLE 9.1
Nature of Offenses of XYYs Convicted
on One or More Criminal Charges
(adapted from Witkin et al., 1976).

Case 2. This man is a chronic criminal who, since early adolescence, has spent 9 of 15 years in youth prisons and regular prisons. By far his most frequent criminal offense, especially in his youth, has been theft or attempted theft of a motor vehicle. Other charges included burglary, embezzlement, and procuring for prostitution. On a single occasion he committed a mild act of violence against an unoffending person; for this together with one case of burglary he received a sentence of about three-quarters of a year. This aggressive act was an isolated incident in a long period of chronic criminality. Except for this act, and the charge of procuring, all his nearly 50 offenses were against property, predominantly larceny and burglary. His single most severe penalty was somewhat less than a year in prison. Most of his crimes were committed in the company of other persons.

Case 3. This man committed two thefts, one in late adolescence, the second when he was in his early twenties. The penalties for both were mild—a small fine for the first and less than 3 months in prison for the second. His last offense was committed 7 years ago.

Case 5. Ten years ago as a young adult this man committed two petty offenses, the second within a short time of the first. One was the theft of a motorcycle, the other a petty civil offense; the penalties were detentions of approximately 2 weeks and less than 2 weeks, respectively.

Case 7. Five years ago when in his twenties this man committed his only criminal offenses within a short period of time: falsely reporting a traffic accident to the police and starting a small fire. On both occasions he was intoxicated. The penalty was probation.

Case 12. This man was under welfare care as a child and has spent only 3 to 4 of the last 20 years outside of institutions for the retarded. He is an episodic criminal. When very young he committed arson. Later his crimes included theft of motor vehicles, burglary, larceny, and embezzlement. His more than 90 registered offenses were all against property, mostly theft and burglary. For crimes committed while he was free, the penalty imposed was placement in an institution for the mentally retarded. For crimes committed while he was in such an insitution—once theft of a bicycle, another time theft of a quantity of beverage—the penalty was continued institutionalization.

and 58 percent of the sociopaths showed some form of electroencephalogram (EEG) abnormality. The most frequent form of abnormality was *slow-wave activity*, which is typical of the infant and young child but not of the normal adult. The slow waves came generally from throughout the brain. There is, however, some evidence that among extremely impulsive and aggressive sociopathic individuals the EEG abnormalities are localized in the temporal lobes of the cerebral hemispheres (Hill, 1952). Finally, some individuals who respond with impulsive, aggressive, and destructive acts to seemingly trivial stimuli show what are referred to as *positive spikes*. These occur in the temporal area of the brain and consist of bursts of activity with frequencies of 6 to 8 cycles per second (cps) and 14 to 16 cps.

More recent findings reviewed by Syndulko (1978) generally agree with the earlier ones. Most studies report rather high frequencies of EEG abnormalities in sociopaths and the presence of slow waves and positive spikes in particular. Not all sociopaths show EEG abnormalities, however, and it is unclear whether those who do

BOX 9.2 The Electroencephalogram

The *electroencephalogram* or EEG is a graphic recording of the electrical activity of the brain. The brain is known to be continuously active, chemically and electrically, through-out life, even in sleep. Individual neurons of the central nervous system fire spontaneously at regular or irregular intervals, creating differences in electric potentials, that is, fluctua-tions in voltage. The fluctuations in voltage in the cortex, the portion of the brain immedi-ately below the skull, can be picked up by two or more sensitive electrodes pasted to the scalp. The recording machine, the *electroencephalograph,* amplifies the pulsations one to two million times and connects them to a pen record (or recorders) which registers them on a continuously moving role of graph paper as a pattern of oscillations. The spontaneous activity of the brain, known as its *waves,* varies in different cortical areas and in the other, less accessible portions of the brain. Perhaps most importantly, the dominant brain waves reflect the degree to which the brain has been aroused.

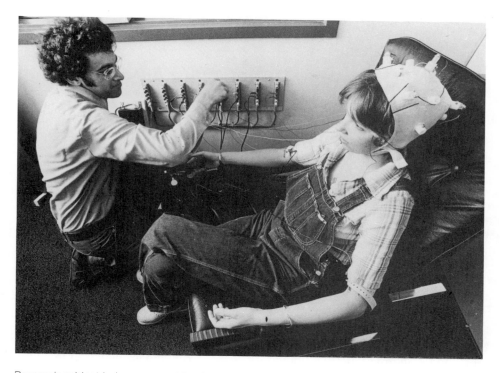

Research subject being prepared for the recording of her brain waves by an electroencephalograph. The cap en-sures that the recording electrodes will contact the proper locations on her skull.

In a normal adult subject, awake but resting quietly with eyes closed, the dominant rhythm has a frequency of between 8 and 13 pulsations or cycles per second (cps) and an amplitude of from 40 to 50 microvolts. This low-frequency, high-voltage wave is called the _alpha_ rhythm. When a stimulus is presented, the alpha rhythm is replaced by a high-frequency (14 to 25 cps), low-voltage rhythm, the _beta_ rhythm. If very low-frequency waves are found dominant in the awake adult, they are considered abnormal. These slow waves, which are sometimes found in sociopaths while they are awake, are referred to as the _theta_ (4 to 7 cps) and the _delta_ (less than 4 cps) rhythms. Delta rhythms occur during deep sleep; theta waves are commonly recorded from subcortical parts of the brain. Examples of these various rhythms as well as the positive spikes referred to in the text may be seen in Figure 9.1.

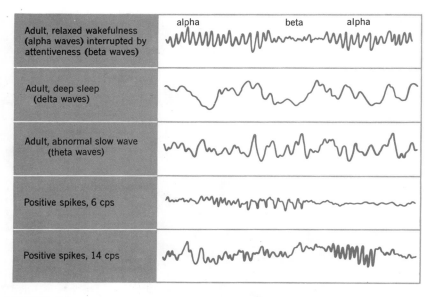

FIGURE **9.1**
Patterns of electrical activity in the brain recorded by the electroencephalograph. After Hare, 1970.

differ in any other way from those who do not. It should also be borne in mind that the EEG is a very gross measure of brain function, reflecting the mass action of hundreds of thousands of neurons. Specific interpretations of the sociopath's EEG abnormalities remain highly speculative at this time. Hare (1970), for example, interprets the high frequency of slow-wave activity to indicate a dysfunction in inhibitory mechanisms which, in turn, lessens the impact of punishment on sociopaths. Although this interpretation is consistent with studies of the effects of punishment on sociopaths, it certainly is not the only one possible. But the _inability_ of sociopaths _to learn to avoid_ or escape from _punishment_ has been an important subject of research.

Avoidance Learning, Punishment, and Sociopathy

As we have previously noted, in defining the so-ciopathic syndrome Cleckley pointed out the inability of these persons to learn from experience. In particular, they seemingly feel no need to avoid the negative consequences of social misbehavior. Cleckley also remarked that they were not neurotic and seldom anxious. Lykken (1957) deduced that sociopaths may have few inhibitions about committing antisocial acts because they experience so little anxiety. He performed several tests to determine whether sociopaths do indeed have low levels of anxiety. One of these tests involved avoidance learning.

A group of male sociopaths, judged to be so on the basis of Cleckley's criteria for recognizing the syndrome, were selected from a penitentiary population. Their performance on an avoidance learning task was compared to that of nonsocio-pathic penitentiary inmates[6] and of college students. It was of course critical that only avoidance learning and not learning mediated by other possible rewards be tested. If a subject perceives that his task is to learn to avoid pain, he may be motivated not only by the desire to avoid the pain but also by a desire to demonstrate his cleverness to the investigator. To ensure that no other motives would become manifest, Lykken made the avoidance learning task *incidental*. He used the following apparatus. On a panel in front of the subject there were four red lights in a horizontal array, four green lights below each of the red ones, and a lever below each column, as illustrated in Figure 9.2. The subject's task was to learn a sequence of twenty correct lever presses, but for each he first had to determine by trial and error which of the four alternatives was correct. The correct lever turned on a green light. Two of the remaining three incorrect levers turned on red lights, indicating an error. The third incorrect lever delivered an electric shock to the subject. The location of the correct lever was of course not always the same. The subject was told simply to figure out and to learn the series of twenty correct lever presses.

[6] In the literature such people are sometimes referred to as neurotic sociopaths. We have avoided using this confusing term since, by definition, a sociopath is not neurotic.

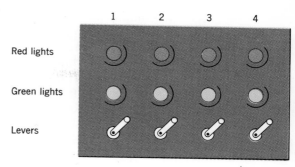

FIGURE **9.2**
The apparatus devised by Lykken (1957) for his study of avoidance learning in sociopaths.

For the first lever press assume that lever 3 is correct, that is, that pressing it lights the green bulb; that levers 1 and 4 are incorrect, lighting red bulbs; and that pressing lever 2 lights a red bulb and gives the subject a shock. For the second lever press the meaning of the levers may change entirely; for example, lever 2 may be correct, levers 3 and 4 incorrect, and lever 1 may give the shock. The subjects had to learn a sequence of twenty correct lever presses.

He was not informed that avoiding shock was desirable or possible, only that shock was randomly administered as a stimulant to make him do well. Thus the task yielded two measures of learning: the total number of errors made before the subject learned the correct sequence of twenty presses and the number of errors made that produced shock. Avoidance is measured by this second index.

In terms of the overall number of errors made, there were no significant differences among any of the groups in Lykken's study. The college students, however, were apparently best able to remember the sequence of presses that produced shock and thus sharply decreased their proportion of shocked errors. The sociopaths made the most shocked errors, but the differences between their shocked errors and those of the other penitentiary inmates only approached statistical significance. The results of Lykken's investigation therefore tentatively support the hypothesis that sociopaths operate under lower levels of anxiety than do normal individuals.

Lykken also tried to verify his reduced-anxiety hypothesis by giving his subjects standard psychological tests for measuring anxiety, such as the Taylor Manifest Anxiety Scale. On these tests the sociopaths did indeed show lower levels of anxiety. In addition, Lykken devised his own instrument, the Activity Preference Questionnaire, which presents subjects with a series of items, each forcing a choice between two unpleasant events. One is unpleasant in a social way, such as having an accident in a borrowed car or spilling a glass of water in a restaurant. The other is merely distasteful or tedious, such as cleaning up a bottle of syrup or draining and cleaning a cesspool. It was thought that, by virtue of their minimal anxiety in social situations, sociopaths would choose relatively more of the socially unpleasant incidents. Control subjects, on the other hand, were expected to choose more of those that were unpleasant but not socially so. Lykken's hypothesis again received clear support: sociopaths chose more of the socially unpleasant incidents than did the controls, indicating less sensitivity to social mores.

Lykken's pioneering work was subsequently followed up by Schachter and Latané (1964). These investigators reasoned that if sociopaths fail to learn to avoid unpleasant stimuli because they have little anxiety, a procedure that in-

creases their anxiety should help them learn to shun punishment. Inasmuch as anxiety is viewed as being related to activity of the sympathetic nervous system, they injected Adrenalin, an agent whose effects mimic sympathetic activity, in order to increase anxiety.

Sociopathic and nonsociopathic prisoners from a penitentiary were studied with the same task and apparatus that had been devised by Lykken. This time each subject was tested twice. The subjects were led to believe that the effects of a hormone on learning were being investigated. Half received a placebo injection on the first day of testing and half an injection of Adrenalin. On the second day of testing the injections received by the subjects were reversed.

The results of Schachter and Latané's experiment were important in several ways. First, the overall number of errors provided confirmation for Lykken's results: no difference was found between the sociopathic and nonsociopathic prisoners in the total number of errors committed in learning the sequence, whether they had been injected with Adrenalin or the placebo. Second, the nonsociopathic prisoners injected with the placebo markedly reduced their proportion of shocked errors after a number of runs, but the sociopaths injected with the placebo showed no such improvement. In this part of the study the difference between the performances of the two groups of prisoners was greater than that revealed in Lykken's experiment and considerably larger than the amount necessary for statistical significance. Third, and most important, when injected with Adrenalin, the sociopaths showed a great reduction in the number of shocked errors, but the prisoners who were not sociopaths were adversely affected by the Adrenalin and did not learn to avoid the shock in their state of high arousal (Figure 9.3). Thus the hypothesis of the anxiety-free and *underaroused* sociopath received considerable support from the work of Schachter and Latané.[7]

Chesno and Kilmann (1975) have provided further confirmation of Schachter and Latané's work. Sociopaths, as well as several other groups

Stanley Schachter, social psychologist at Columbia University, known for his theory that emotion has both cognitive and physiological aspects. He has investigated the relation between arousal in the autonomic nervous system, emotion, and sociopathy.

[7] The finding that the Adrenalin injection apparently worsened the avoidance learning performance of the nonsociopathic prisoners is difficult to interpret. A follow-up test by Schachter and Latané did not reproduce this effect.

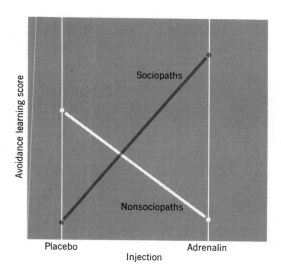

FIGURE **9.3**
Results of Schachter and Latané's study (1964) of the effects of adrenalin on avoidance learning in sociopathic and nonsociopathic prisoners. Higher scores reflect better avoidance learning; arousal through adrenalin helped the sociopaths to learn to avoid shock by activating their otherwise underaroused autonomic nervous systems.

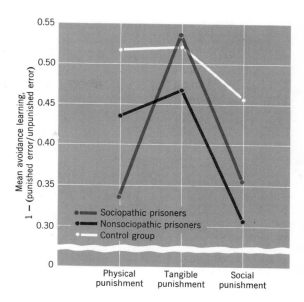

FIGURE **9.4**
Mean avoidance learning scores plotted for three subject groups confronted by three different punishments, physical, tangible, and social. The sociopaths readily learned to avoid punishment when it cost them money. After Schmauk, 1970.

of subjects, participated in a shock avoidance learning test. While they performed the task the subjects were exposed to bursts of noise which varied in intensity. One-third of the subjects in each group were exposed to noise of 35 decibels, one-third to 65 decibels, and the remainder to 95. The varying levels of noise were expected to produce different levels of arousal, as had the Adrenalin injections in Schachter and Latané's work. And the sociopaths were expected to learn to avoid shock more readily as noise became more intense, which is exactly what happened.

An avoidance learning study by Schmauk (1970) qualifies the findings of Lykken as well as those of the other studies we have discussed. He showed that a particular kind of punishment, losing money, *can* have an effect on sociopaths. His study involved three groups, sociopathic prisoners, nonsociopathic prisoners, and a control group consisting of farmworkers and hospital attendants. As in the previous studies, an avoidance learning task was devised, but this time three different aversive stimuli could be avoided:

a physical punishment—electric shock; a tangible punishment—losing a quarter from an initial pile of forty; and a social punishment—the experimenter's saying "wrong" to the subject. There were again no differences among the groups in the total number of errors made before the task was mastered. The major finding of this study (Figure 9.4) indicated that the sociopath's avoidance performance varies with the nature of punishment. When the punishments confronting them were physical and social, the members of the control group were vastly superior to the sociopaths in learning to avoid punishment. But the sociopaths outdid them in learning to avoid the tangible punishment of losing a quarter. The nonsociopathic prisoners did better than the sociopaths in learning to avoid physical punishment but less well in avoiding social punishment.

It appears then that sociopaths *can* learn to avoid punishment. The differences found between sociopaths and nonsociopaths in previous investigations may reflect *not* a general deficit in avoidance learning ability but rather the fact that some punishments have no meaning for the sociopath. Evidently, sociopaths will learn to avoid punishment that is relevant to their system of values, and money may very well be particularly important to them.

In the avoidance learning studies discussed thus far, punishment was inevitable if a particular incorrect response was made. But many crimes remain unsolved, so in real life the sociopath is actually in a situation in which punishment is uncertain. According to some clinicians, the sociopath almost magically believes that his antisocial behavior will not be punished. Therefore it may be that sociopaths are particularly insensitive to *uncertain punishment*. Siegel (1978) examined this notion by testing sociopaths, nonsociopathic prisoners, and college students in a card game in which different probabilities of losing poker chips, which could be redeemed for money, were the punishment. As expected, punishment had the least impact on sociopaths when its probability was in the middle range, from 40 to 70 percent. And the sociopaths also underestimated the likelihood of subsequently losing poker chips after a session in which the probability of loss was in the midrange. In these circumstances the nonsociopathic prisoners and the college students were not so cavalier about chancing the loss of chips. As in previous studies, then, sociopaths were affected less by punishment; more importantly, they behaved as though they believe punishment to be unlikely when it does not certainly follow a misstep.

Underarousal and Sociopathic Behavior
Sociopaths have often been described as not responding emotionally when confronted by both familiar and new situations that most people would fine either stressful or unpleasant. Cleckley (1976) has written about this aspect of their behavior.

Regularly, we find in [the sociopath] extraordinary poise rather than jitteriness or worry, a smooth sense of physical well-being instead of uneasy preoccupations with bodily functions. Even under concrete circumstances that would for the ordinary person cause embarrassment, confusion, acute insecurity, or visible agitation, his relative serenity is likely to be noteworthy (p. 340).

This description is remarkably consistent with the Schachter and Latané finding that sociopaths do not ordinarily avoid electric shock but that they do so when their autonomic arousal is increased by injections of Adrenalin. Because of the assumed central role of the autonomic nervous system in states of emotion, several investigators have examined sociopaths both for their resting levels of autonomic activity and for their patterns of autonomic reactivity to various classes of stimuli.

Most studies indicate that in resting situations sociopaths have lower than normal levels of skin conductance. Furthermore, their skin conductance is less reactive when they are confronted with intense or aversive stimuli. A different picture emerges, however, when heart rate is examined. The heart rate of sociopaths is like that of normal people under resting conditions, and their heart rate reactivity to stimuli is also unremarkable. But in situations in which sociopaths anticipate a stressful stimulus, their hearts beat faster than those of normal people anticipating stress.

These physiological reactions indicate that the sociopath cannot be regarded as simply underaroused, for measurements of skin conductance and heart rate are inconsistent. Basing his theorizing in part on Lacey's work (1967), Hare (1978) focuses on the *pattern* of psychophysiological responses of sociopaths. Faster heartbeats are viewed as a concomitant of gating out or reducing sensory input and thus lowering cortical arousal. Thus the increased heart rate of sociopaths who are anticipating an aversive stimulus would indicate that they are "tuning it out." Their skin conductance is then less reactive to an aversive stimulus because they have already construed it to be less negative than it appears to normal people. That is, with skin conductance considered an index of anxiety, that of sociopaths does not increase to any extent after expected aversive stimulation because they have already dealt with it by screening it out.[8] This interpretation of the physiological reactions of sociopaths is plausible and consistent with the studies reviewed earlier on avoidance learning.

The fact that sociopaths are underaroused or are better able to control their arousal has additional implications. Quay (1965) has suggested that the impulsiveness, thirst for excitement, and inability to tolerate routine and boredom of sociopaths are fostered by their lesser emotional reactivity and by their ability to block out arousing sensory input and thus stem cortical arousal. Quay's reasoning is based on the hypothesis that there is an optimal level of arousal for human beings. When arousal is too high an individual will take steps to reduce it, and when it is too low the individual will take steps to increase it. Much of the sociopath's "thrill seeking" behavior could then be viewed as an attempt to increase his or her arousal enough to approach this optimal state.

If it is true that sociopaths seek excitement to raise their arousal levels, we might expect their performance on a tedious and monotonous task to be especially poor. Orris (1967) tested prisoners on such a task. The findings bore out the prediction. Sociopathic prisoners performed less well than did the others. We might also predict that given a choice, sociopaths will prefer novel and complex stimuli. Such stimuli are generally viewed as having high-arousal properties, and thus the sociopath might be expected to show a preference for them. Skrzypek (1969) tested this hypothesis on a sample of sociopathic and other prisoners and found that sociopaths indeed showed a somewhat greater preference for novelty and complexity than did the other prisoners.

The case histories, studies, and theories that we have reviewed show the sociopath to be an individual who does not experience the same emotions that most of us do. Thus anxiety can have no deterrent effect. Moreover, because the sociopath is in greater control of his or her emotional reactions, arousal is actually sought. These are possible reasons for the sociopath's misconduct without regret and for his thrill seeking without regard for society's rules.

[8] Recent psychophysiological studies of sociopathy have focused on what is called *recovery time*, the period it takes for the level of skin conductance to return to baseline after the body has responded to a stimulus. Slow recovery time is associated with criminal behavior and is even found in children of aggressive fathers (Mednick and Hutchings, 1978). The recovery time of sociopaths is more complicated. Hare (1978) found them to have slow recovery only when conductance from their left hands was checked and only when the stimuli had been unexpected or aversive. Slow recovery could also indicate the greater ability of sociopaths to ignore or "tune out" aversive stimuli like punishment.

Therapies for Personality Disorders

There is as little information on treating personality disorders as there is on how they develop. Few such people probably even go to therapists because they regard their behavior as "natural" and in no need of professional attention. It has even been asserted that their disorders, if such they be, cause them little if any discomfort (Nathan and Harris, 1980). Because disordered personalities do not believe that they need help and relate no better to the therapist than they do to others, they take no responsibility and make no effort in their own treatment. In fact, they may terminate it in short order.

Behavior Therapy for Disturbed Personalities

Behavior therapists, in keeping with their attention to situations rather than to traits, have no specific treatments as such for histrionic personality, borderline personality, or any of the other personality disorders designated by DSM-III. Rather they analyze the problems that, taken together, might be considered by an enthusiast of DSM-III to reflect a personality disorder. For example, the man diagnosed as having a paranoid personality will be very sensitive to criticism. This sensitivity may be treated by systematic desensitization or rational-emotive therapy. His argumentativeness and hostility when he disagrees with other people will push them away from him and provoke counterattacks from them. The behavior therapist may practice with the man more adaptive ways of disagreeing with other people.

One aspect of a personality disorder commands the attention of any skilled behavior therapist, as well as that of any other professional helper, namely, the alleged deeply ingrained, long-standing, and pervasive nature of the problem. A man will bear the diagnosis of paranoid personality only if his tendency to be suspicious and guarded is chronic and permeates his overall psychological functioning. Any therapist working with him must therefore consider the broad implications of his problem. Before a highly suspicious person can express emotion openly and appropriately, he must make major and difficult changes in his assumptions about people and in general mode of functioning. In other words, therapy must take into consideration the pervasive, wide-ranging nature of a person's particular personality disorder and, in addition, the person's general intractableness.

Therapy for Sociopathy

As for the treatment of antisocial personality disorder, there is unusual—and unfortunate—agreement among therapists of varying theoretical persuasions: sociopathy is virtually impossible to treat (Cleckley, 1976; McCord and McCord, 1964).

It may be that people with the classic symptoms listed by Cleckley are, by their very natures, incapable of benefiting from any form of psychotherapy. The most likely reason is that they are unable to form any sort of trusting, honest relationship with a therapist. A person who lies almost without knowing it, who cares little for the feelings of others and understands his own even less, who appears not to realize that what he is doing is morally wrong, who lacks any motivation to obey society's laws and mores, and who, living only for the present, has no concern for the future is all in all an extremely poor candidate for therapy. In fact, one clinician, experienced in working with sociopaths, has suggested three general principles.

First, the therapist must be continually vigilant with regard to manipulation on the part of the patient. Second, he must assume, until proven otherwise, that information given him by the patient contains distortions and fabrications. Third, he must recognize that a working alliance develops, if ever, exceedingly late in any therapeutic relationship with a psychopath (Lion, 1978, p. 286).

To be sure, many valiant attempts have been made to establish tenable connections with sociopaths, but both the published literature and informal communications among mental health professionals support the conclusion that true sociopathy cannot be reached through clinical efforts. Similar negative conclusions are to be drawn as well about somatic methods—electroconvulsive shock, drugs such as Dilantin, stimulants, and sedatives, and psychosurgery.

Since many sociopaths spend time in prison for crimes that they have been convicted of, the discouraging results of imprisonment as rehabilitation are traced at least in part to the inability to modify sociopathic behavior. As criminologists have stated repeatedly (for example, Wilkins, 1969), our prison system seems to operate more as a school for crime than it does as a place where criminals, and sociopaths, can be rehabilitated. Ramsey Clark, former Attorney General, put it this way: "Prisons in the United States today are more often than not manufacturers of crime. . . . [They] are usually little more than places to keep people—warehouses of human degradation" (1970, p. 213). For a time in the 1970s there was interest in developing new therapy programs for prisoners, such as operant conditioning regimens, usually token economies, for especially violent prisoners and different kinds of group therapy aimed at encouraging the more tractable prisoners to assume some responsibility for their behavior. For a variety of reasons, including the claims of civil liberties groups that therapy in a prison setting is unconstitutional, fewer therapeutic efforts are now made on behalf of prisoners. Indeed, the trend seems to be to regard imprisonment as simply punishment for transgressions against society. Little attention is paid to trying to help those convicted so that they will "go straight" upon release.

An interesting argument in favor of incarceration is that psychopaths often "settle down" in middle age and thereafter. Whether through physiological changes, eventual insight into their self-defeating natures, or simply becoming worn out and unable to continue in their finagling ways, many sociopaths grow less disruptive as they approach forty. Prison, therefore, protects society from the antisocial behavior of "active" sociopaths, with release considered more plausible when the prisoner enters a stage of life in which the excesses of his sociopathy are less in evidence (see Box 9.3).

BOX 9.3 Aggression Alone Does Not a Sociopath Make

The social-learning literature on both the acquisition and elimination of aggressive behavior is extensive. Some writers (for example, Mahoney, 1980) refer to this theory and research in an effort to understand both the etiology and possible treatment of sociopathy. In our view, however, the kind of aggressive behavior studied by social-learning theorists is very different from that of an antisocial personality. Social-learning theorists (for example, Bandura, 1973) conduct experiments showing that basically normal children and adults can acquire sometimes complex and novel patterns of aggressive behavior by watching models perform such actions. The tendency to imitate has been shown to be related to how the model is rewarded for being aggressive, the status of the model, and how the observer is reinforced for aggression. Such research is informative about aggression in normal people under normal circumstances, but it does not address the issue of sociopathy. For example, none of the social-learning experiments on aggression has assessed whether subjects who imitate an aggressive model feel guilt or shame. Nor do these studies really touch on the *persistent* and *pervasive* monstrous cruelty that is a true hallmark of sociopathy and is clearly something apart from ordinary aggression. As for treatment, prosocial behavior may indeed be fostered in delinquent adolescents by systematically rewarding them for it in a homelike environment (see page 654). But the natures and inclinations of the young people living in residential treatment settings must be scrutinized. Although they have clearly run afoul of the law and stand every chance of spending many of their adult years in prison, very few, if any, of these youngsters can be described as sociopaths.

Summary

The category of personality disorders is an extremely broad and heterogeneous one. There is little information on most of them. The notable exception is sociopathy, the dominant pattern of which is repeated antisocial behavior without regret or shame. In addition, sociopaths are thought to be unable to learn from experience, to have no sense of responsibility, and to establish no genuine emotional relationships with other people. Research on their families indicates that sociopaths had fathers who themselves were antisocial and that discipline was either absent or inconsistent. Genetic studies, particularly those using the adoptee method, suggest that a predisposition to sociopathy is inherited. The core problem of the sociopath may be that impending punishment creates no inhibitions about committing antisocial acts. A good deal of overlapping evidence supports this view: (1) sociopaths have abnormal amounts of slow-wave EEG activity, which may reflect a failure of the usual inhibitory processes; (2) sociopaths are slow at learning to avoid shock, a deficit which can be reduced by heightening the sociopath's level of physiological arousal; and (3) sociopaths, according to their electrodermal responses, show little anxiety but, as indicated by their faster heart rates, seem better able than normal people to tune out aversive stimuli.

Little is known about effective therapy for the various personality disorders, for several reasons. The poor reliability of the diagnoses and the tendency to use the category as a grab bag make it difficult to evaluate reports of therapy. Therapy for the sociopath in particular holds little promise for a successful outcome. In addition to the pervasiveness and apparent intractability of the uncaring and manipulative life style, the antisocial personality is by nature a poor candidate for therapy. People who habitually lie and lack insight into their own or others' feelings—and have no inclination to examine emotions—will not readily establish a trusting and open working relationship with a therapist.

chapter 10

SUBSTANCE USE DISORDERS

From prehistoric times humankind has used various substances in the hope of reducing physical pain or altering states of consciousness. Almost all peoples have discovered some intoxicant that affects the central nervous system, relieving physical and mental anguish or producing euphoria. Whatever the aftermath of taking such substances into the body, their effects are usually pleasing, at least initially.

Alcoholic beverages from the fermentation of many fruits and grains, of milk, honey, and molasses, and even of tree sap; opium, the dried milky juice obtained from the immature fruit of the opium poppy; hashish and marijuana from *Cannabis,* the hemp plant; and cocaine, an alkaloid extracted from coca leaves—these are the major natural drugs that have a long history of both use and abuse, and that continue today to present problems for society. In the United States and other Western countries, morphine, an alkaloid extracted from opium, and heroin, derived from morphine, are more prevalent than the raw opium, and dried marijuana is used more often than hashish. Also available are a number of newer synthetic and synthesized drugs, most importantly the barbiturates, the amphetamines, and LSD. Of all the potentially dangerous drugs, the one craved by the greatest number of people is nicotine, the principal alkaloid of tobacco.

In DSM-II drug problems appeared in the Personality Disorders and Certain Other Nonpsychotic Mental Conditions section. DSM-III, however, has created an entirely separate section for these problems, Substance Use Disorders.

The pathological use of substances that affect the central nervous system falls into two categories, *substance abuse* and *substance dependence.* A person is considered to abuse a substance when he or she is, for example, often intoxicated from it throughout the day and, despite all efforts, unable to cut consumption in any consistent way. The state of intoxication reached will be deep enough that the person fails in important obligations to friends and family and at work. And he or she may also get into legal difficulties by causing harm when intoxicated or by behaving criminally in order to secure money to purchase the substance. The abuse must be of at least a month's duration to be considered a disturbance. A yearly New

Year's Eve binge on the part of a person who during the rest of the year drinks in only moderate amounts is clearly not substance abuse.

Substance dependence is a more severe form of disorder in which there is evidence of physiological dependence on the drug, in addition to the abuser's other problems. Dependence in this sense, or _addiction_ as we prefer to call it, is the physiological process by which the body responds to certain drugs. When addicting drugs are ingested for prolonged periods of time, greater and greater amounts of them are _tolerated_. The bodily systems habituate to the particular chemical so that larger and larger doses are necessary to maintain similar intoxicating effects. Then when the frequency of ingestion or the amount of the drug is suddenly decreased, the person suffers _withdrawal reactions._ The prolonged use of the drug has so altered the physiological conditions of the body that it is disturbed when the drug is not administered. For example, an addict who suddenly ceases to take morphine usually suffers from hypertension and cramps, is restless, and sweats profusely.

The physiological mechanisms responsible for _tolerance_ and withdrawal reactions are as yet unknown. In the case of alcohol, it is evident that tolerance can _not_ be attributed to the drug's entering the bloodstream at a slower rate and being more rapidly metabolized by the liver. Most current hypotheses focus on alterations in the process of neural transmission, but none has unequivocal support.

But not all drugs, even if they are taken regularly, bring on either tolerance or the later withdrawal reactions when their use is terminated. For this reason the term _psychological dependency_[1] is often applied to reliance on drugs that are not addicting. A drug may be taken because its effects make stressful or anxiety-provoking situations more bearable. But the dosage of the drug does not have to be continually increased to produce these effects, nor is there a withdrawal reaction if the drug is not taken. This is not to say that the individual with a psychological dependence on a drug feels no unpleasant effects when the drug is not available. If people are deprived of _anything_ that they have come to rely on, they are likely to react negatively to its absence by becoming restless, nervous, or otherwise upset. These reactions sometimes resemble the withdrawal symptoms obtained with addictive drugs, but they should not be regarded as such _unless_ there is also evidence of tolerance.

The DSM-III section Substance Use Disorders considers only the _behavior_ associated with the regular use of substances that interfere with everyday life. If a person who is addicted to a drug is denied it and therefore thrown into withdrawal, a diagnosis in addition to substance dependence would also be applicable. In the section Organic Mental Disorders are listed _substance-induced organic mental disorders,_ an example of which is _alcohol withdrawal delirium,_ commonly known as the DTs (see page 302). In this chapter, then, which covers all psychological and physical problems created by drugs, we necessarily deal with facets of drug abuse that DSM-III puts into more than one major section.

---

[1] The term psychological dependency must not be confused with DSM-III's use of the word dependence, which is, as noted, synonymous with addiction. But, generally speaking, drugs that are not known to be addictive, such as cocaine and LSD, nonetheless interfere with people's lives, for their use creates the problems described for substance abuse. Therefore finding a person to be psychologically dependent on a substance is equivalent to the substance abuse diagnosis of DSM-III.

Aloholism

Written reports of the use of wines, beers, and other alcoholic beverages date back to 3000 B.C., but not until about 800 B.C. was the distillation process applied to fermented beverages, making possible the preparation of the highly potent liquors that are available today. It has been estimated that in the United States about 100 million people consume alcohol and about 12 million are judged alcoholic according to some definitions. There are about 200,000 new cases of _alcoholism_ each year, and in this last decade teenage alcoholism has greatly increased. In older studies male alcoholics outnumbered females by about four to one. But this gap is diminishing and, particularly among younger age groups, women's consumption of alcohol is on the upswing (Becker and Kronus, 1977). Although most of the people who have a drinking problem do not seek professional help, alcoholics do constitute a large proportion of new admissions to mental and general hospitals. The suicide rate of alcoholics, especially of women alcoholics, is much higher than that of the general population. A third of all suicides have alcohol as a contributing cause. Moreover, some estimate that alcohol is implicated in at least 25,000 highway deaths each year, about half the total number. Alcohol also presents law enforcement problems, for about one-third of all arrests in the United States are for public drunkenness. Homicide is an alcohol-related crime—over half of all murders are believed committed under its influence—and so too are parental child abuse and sexual offenses (Brecher, 1972; Special Report of the National Insitute on Alcohol Abuse and Alcoholism, 1978).

As in the more general diagnoses of substance abuse and dependence, DSM-III distinguishes between _alcohol abuse_ and _alcohol dependence_. The second is applied when there are classic signs of addiction—either tolerance or withdrawal reactions, such as morning "shakes" and malaise which can be only relieved by taking a drink. Persons who begin drinking early in life develop their first withdrawal symptoms in their thirties or forties. For both diagnoses the pattern of drinking must indicate that it is out of control. Individuals will need to drink daily, being unable to stop or cut down despite repeated efforts to

Teenage drinking has been increasing steadily in recent years.

abstain completely or to restrict drinking to certain periods of the day. They may go on occasional binges, remaining intoxicated all through two, three, or more days. Sometimes they consume a fifth of spirits at a time. They suffer "blackouts" of the events that took place during a bout of intoxication; their craving may be sufficient to make them drink alcohol in a nonbeverage form, such as hair tonic. Such drinking of course causes social and occupational difficulties, and signs of them are necessary for both diagnoses: quarrels with family or friends, violence when intoxicated, frequent absences from work or loss of job, and arrest for intoxication or for traffic accidents.

Short-Term Effects of Alcohol

Physiological effects

After being swallowed, alcohol does not undergo any of the processes of digestion. A small part of the alcohol ingested passes immediately into the bloodstream through the stomach walls, but most of it goes into the small intestines and from there is absorbed into the blood. It must then be metabolized by a process referred to as oxidation. In this process alcohol fuses with oxygen and is broken down so that its basic elements leave the body as carbon dioxide and water.[2] The primary site of oxidation is the liver, which can break down about one ounce of 100 proof (that is, 50 percent alcohol) whiskey per hour. Quantities in excess of this amount remain in the bloodstream. Whereas absorption of alcohol can be very rapid, removal is always slow. Many of the effects of alcohol vary directly with the level of concentration of the drug in the bloodstream, which in turn depends on the amount ingested in a particular period of time, the presence or absence in the stomach of food to retain the alcohol and reduce its absorption rate, the size of the individual's body, and the efficiency of the liver.

Because the drinking of alcoholic beverages is accepted in most societies, alcohol is rarely regarded as a drug, especially by those who drink. But it is indeed a drug, affecting the central nervous system. Alcohol, acting as a depressant, first numbs the higher brain centers, those that are primarily inhibiting. Thus the initial effect of alcohol is stimulating. Tensions and inhibitions are reduced, and the individual may experience an expansive feeling of sociability and well-being. Some people, though, become suspicious and even violent. Larger amounts interfere with complex thought processes; then motor coordination, balance, speech, and vision are impaired. At this stage of intoxication, some individuals become depressed and withdrawn. Alcohol is capable of blunting pain and in larger doses of inducing sedation and sleep. Before modern techniques of anesthesia were discovered, liquors were often administered to a patient about to undergo surgery.

Cognitive effects

Studies have determined that short-term effects of alcohol on social drinkers are complex. Jones and Parsons (1975) have reviewed a number of experiments that suggest, among other things, that effects vary depending on whether the person is becoming drunk or sobering up. In one such experiment Jones and Parsons (1971) assessed the abstract problem-solving ability of drinkers. Those on the downward part of the curve, that is, drinkers becoming sober, performed significantly better with a particular level of alcohol in their blood than did those who were getting high and had the same level. A person apparently thinks better, at a given stage of intoxication, if he or she is becoming less drunk than if becoming more so. The short-term memories of those becoming sober appear to be similarly good and those becoming intoxicated to be similarly poor (Jones, 1973).

Other studies have addressed a problem experienced by many social drinkers, namely remembering clearly what happened while they were drinking. It seems indeed that the state of consciousness entered through intoxication is somewhat separate from the normal, sober state. Overton (1966) demonstrated what is termed *state-dependent learning* in a series of experiments with rats. A rat taught something while drugged later remembers it better when tested in a drugged state than when tested in an undrugged state. The same phenomenon has been demonstrated with alcohol intoxication and the learning and retention of human beings (Goodwin et al., 1969).

It now appears that some of the short-term effects of ingesting small amounts of alcohol are more strongly related to beliefs about the effects of the drug than to its chemical action on the body. For example, alcohol is commonly thought to stimulate aggression, reduce anxiety, and increase sexual responsiveness. Recent research has shown, however, that these reactions may not be caused by alcohol itself but by beliefs about alcohol's effects. Subjects are told that they will be consuming a quantity of alcohol but, in fact, are given an alcohol-free beverage with its taste disguised so that they will not see through the ruse. They subsequently become more aggressive (Lang et al., 1975), more sex-

[2] Various types of alcohol differ in the rate at which they can be oxidized. Ethyl alcohol, the type found in alcoholic beverages, oxidizes the most rapidly, whereas methyl or wood alcohol oxidizes much more slowly. Because of slow oxidation, large amounts of methyl alcohol may accumulate in the blood, causing death or blindness. Another type of alcohol, denatured alcohol, is a deadly poison because of the toxic substances added to it.

ually aroused (Wilson and Lawson, 1976), and less anxious (Wilson and Abrams, 1977). Indeed, subjects who merely believe that they have drunk alcohol, but have not, usually act in the same way as subjects who have actually consumed the drug. Once again, cognitions have a demonstrably powerful effect on behavior.

Sexual effects

On the other hand, greater quantities of alcohol confirm Shakespeare's observation that "Lechery, sir, it provokes, and it unprovokes: it provokes the desire but it takes away the performance" (*Macbeth*, Act II, Scene 3). In the first experiment published on the effects of alcohol on the physiology of sexual responding, a plethysmograph was used to determine genital blood flow (see Box 11.2, page 348). Farkas and Rosen (1976) showed male subjects an erotic film after they had drunk one of four concentrations of alcohol ranging from 0 percent (pure orange juice) to 0.075 percent, which corresponds to about five drinks of straight whiskey. In each case the amount of alcohol could not be detected by the taste of the drink. The more alcohol the men ingested, the less the penile erection. Thus, in a laboratory setting, the more alcohol drunk, the more it took away from "performance."

Do women respond in the same way? Wilson and Lawson (1976) confirmed that their physiological sexual arousal was also reduced by drinking a large amount of alcohol. But when the women *believed* that they had drunk alcohol, they reported feeling sexually aroused even though, if the amount was large, their vaginal blood flow indicated little arousal. As psychologists have learned more then once, the Bard of Avon had the greatest insight into the workings of humankind.

Long-Term Effects of Prolonged Alcohol Use

The possible long-term effects of prolonged drinking are vividly illustrated in the following case history.

> At the time of his first admission to a state hospital at the age of twenty-four, the patient, an unmarried and unemployed laborer, already had a long history of antisocial behavior, promiscuity

and addiction to alcohol and other drugs. . . . There had been eight brief admissions to private sanatoria for alcoholics, a number of arrests for public intoxication and drunken driving, and two jail terms for assault.

> The patient had been born into a wealthy and respected family in a small town. The patient's father, a successful and popular businessman, drank excessively and his death at the age of fifty-seven was partly due to alcoholism. The mother also drank to excess. The parents exercised little control over the patient as a child, and he was cared for by nursemaids. His father taught him to pour drinks for guests of the family when he was very young and he reported that he began to drain the glasses at parties in his home before he was six; by the time he was twelve he drank almost a pint of liquor every weekend and by seventeen was drinking up to three bottles every day. His father provided him with money to buy liquor and shielded him from punishment for drunken driving and other consequences of his drinking.

> The patient was expelled from high school in his freshman year for striking a teacher. He then attended a private school until the eleventh grade, when he changed the data on his birth certificate and joined the Army paratroops. After discharge, he was unemployed for six months; he drank heavily and needed repeated care at a sanatorium. When a job was obtained for him he quit within a month. On his third arrest for drunken driving he was jailed. His father bailed him out with the warning that no more money would be forthcoming. The patient left town and worked as an unskilled laborer—he had never acquired any useful skills—but returned home when his father died. During the next few years he was jailed for intoxication, for blackening his mother's eyes when he found a male friend visiting her, and for violating probation by getting drunk. He assaulted and badly hurt a prison guard in an escape attempt and was sentenced to two additional years in prison. When released, he began to use a variety of stimulant, sedative and narcotic drugs as well as alcohol (Rosen, Fox, and Gregory, 1972, p. 312).

Behavioral effects

The life histories of male alcoholics are considered to share a common progression. On the basis of an extensive survey of 2000 such men, Jellinek (1952) described the male alcoholic as passing through four stages on the way to his addiction. The first *prealcoholic* phase lasts from several months up to two years. In this stage the individual drinks socially and also on occasion rather heavily to relieve tension and to forget about his problems. At first the heavy drinking is infrequent, but in time the crises and the occasions for seeking the bolstering effects of alcohol recur with greater regularity. In the second *prodromal stage* drinking may become furtive and may also be marked by blackouts. The drinker remains conscious, talks coherently, and carries on other activities, without even appearing to be greatly intoxicated, but later he has no recall of the occasion. Alcohol begins to be used more as a drug and less as a beverage; the individual may gulp down his first drink or two. He becomes preoccupied with drinking, feeling guilty about it but at the same time worrying where and when he will have his next drink.

Jellinek terms the third phase *crucial,* choosing this adjective because he sees the alcoholic in this stage as being in severe danger of losing everything that he values. He has already lost control of his drinking. Once he takes a single

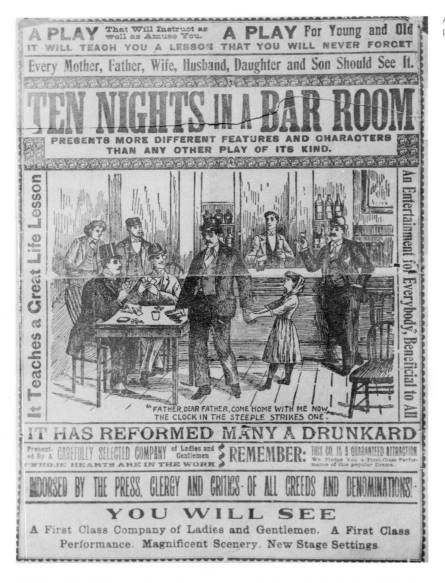

Advertisement for a nineteenth-century play which portrayed the evils of alcohol.

drink, he continues to consume alcohol until he is too sick or in too much of a stupor to drink anymore. The individual's social adjustment also begins to deteriorate. He starts to drink during the day, and this becomes evident to his employer, family, and friends. He may at this point begin to avoid friends and to quit or lose jobs. The alcoholic neglects his diet, has his first bender, a several-day period of excessive drinking, and may experience hallucinations and delirium when he stops drinking. At this stage the individual still has the ability to abstain. He can give up alcohol for several weeks or even months at a time, but if he has just one drink the whole pattern will begin again. The alcoholic even comes to feel that he needs a drink to steady himself for the day, and he starts to drink in the morning.

In the final *chronic stage* drinking is continual, and benders are frequent. The individual lives only to drink. His bodily systems have become so accustomed to alcohol that they must be supplied with it or he suffers withdrawal reactions. If liquor is not available to him, he will consume any liquid he can find that contains alcohol—shaving lotion, hair tonic, various medicinal preparations, whatever. He suffers from malnutrition and other physiological changes. He ne-

glects his personal appearance and, having lost his self-esteem, feels little remorse about any aspect of his behavior. Finally, he ceases to care at all about family and home, about friends, occupation, and social status.

Jellinek's description has been widely cited, but the available evidence is not always corroborative. One study found that blackouts do *not* occur in conjunction with modest drinking and that many alcoholics have never experienced a blackout (Goodwin, Crane, and Guze, 1969). Data now available also question the commonly accepted notion that a single drink stimulates an irresistible impulse to continue drinking (Marlatt, Demming, and Reid, 1973). Alcoholics "primed" with an initial drink, one they believed to be nonalcoholic, later consumed no more alcohol than did social drinkers. Finally, there is much less consistency in the progression from problem drinking to alcoholism than Jellinek implied. In a four-year follow-up of problem drinkers, Clark and Cahalan (1976) found much variability in outcome.

A growing body of evidence indicates that Jellinek's account does not apply to alcoholic women. Alcoholism usually begins at a later age in women than in men and very often after an inordinately stressful experience, such as the

Alcoholism cuts across age groups and all strata of society.

death of a husband or a serious family crisis. For women the time interval between the onset of problem drinking and alcoholism is briefer. Alcoholic women tend more than men to be steady drinkers and to drink alone; they are also less likely to engage in binge drinking (Hill, 1980; Wolin, 1980).

Physiological effects

In addition to the psychological deterioration brought on by alcoholism, severe physiological damage is a serious consequence of chronic drinking. Almost every tissue and organ of the body is affected by the prolonged consumption of alcohol. The malnutrition suffered may be severe. Because alcohol provides calories—a pint of 80 proof spirits supplies about half a day's caloric requirements—alcoholics often reduce their intake of food. But the calories provided by alcohol are "empty"; they do not supply the nutrients essential for health. Alcohol also contributes directly to malnutrition by impairing the digestion of food. In the older chronic alcoholic a deficiency of B-complex vitamins is believed to cause severe memory loss (Korsakoff's psychosis, page 716). A drastic reduction in the intake of protein contributes to the development of cirrhosis of the liver, a disease in which an excessive amount of fibrous connective tissue forms, replacing active liver cells and thus impeding blood circulation. Cirrhosis ranks seventh among causes of death, and in urban areas it ranks third for people aged twenty-five to sixty-five (Lieber, 1976). The disease is more common in women alcoholics than in male. Alcohol per se also disturbs liver functions and damages liver cells. Other common physiological changes include damage to the endocrine glands, heart failure, hypertension, and capillary hemorrhages, which are responsible for the swelling and redness in the face, and especially of the nose, of chronic alcoholics. Prolonged use of alcohol also appears to damage brain cells, especially those in the frontal lobes, causing cortical atrophy and other changes in structure (Parsons, 1975).

Heavy alcohol consumption during pregnancy can retard the growth of the fetus and infant and can cause cranial, facial, and limb anomalies as well as mental retardation. The condition is known as _fetal alcohol syndrome._ Even moderate drinking can produce less severe but undesirable effects on the fetus, leading the National Institute on Alcohol Abuse and Alcoholism to counsel total abstention during pregnancy as the safest course (_Alcohol, Drug Abuse and Mental Health Administration News,_ May 2, 1980).

The effects of the abrupt withdrawal of alcohol from an alcoholic may be rather dramatic, for the body has become profoundly accustomed to the drug. Subjectively, the patient is often frightened, depressed, weak, restless, and unable to sleep. Tremors of the muscles, especially of the small musculatures of the fingers, face, eyelids, lips, and tongue, may be marked, and there is an elevation of pulse, blood pressure, and temperature. The patient sweats profusely, and the pupils of his eyes react slowly to changes in light. An alcoholic who has been drinking for a number of years may also suffer from _delirium tremens_ (DTs) when the level of alcohol in the blood drops suddenly. He becomes delirious as well as tremulous. His hallucinations are primarily visual but they may be tactile as well. Unpleasant and very active creatures—snakes, cockroaches, spiders, and the like—may appear to be crawling up the wall or all over the alcoholic's body, or they may fill the room. Feverish, disoriented, and terrified, the alcoholic may claw frantically at his skin to rid himself of the vermin, or he may cower in the corner to escape an advancing army of fantastic animals.

If body heat continues to rise, a significant percentage of brain cells may be destroyed. Indeed, the nervous system may be so disturbed that physiological functioning becomes erratic. Breathing may stop and the body may be thrown into convulsions. Death is imminently possible if the alcoholic in withdrawal from the drug is not hospitalized and given immediate medical care.

The delirium and physiological paroxysms caused by withdrawal of alcohol indicate that the drug is addictive. Increased tolerance is also evident. Mello and Mendelson (1970) found that alcoholics could drink a quart of bourbon a day without showing signs of drunkenness. Moreover, levels of alcohol in the blood were unexpectedly low after what would usually be viewed as excessive drinking.

In short, _the psychological, physiological, and social effects of prolonged consumption of alco-_

hol are extremely serious. Because the alcoholic's own functioning is so severely disrupted, the people he interacts with are also deeply affected and hurt by his conduct. Society too suffers, for the alcoholic is unlikely to be able to hold a job. The accumulated costs—the money spent on liquor, the time lost in work efficiency, the damage of traffic accidents, the expense of physicians and psychologists—run to tens of billions of dollars each year. The human tragedy, much more devastating, is virtually incalculable.

Theories of Alcoholism

In trying to understand alcoholism, we must draw a distinction between conditions that induce a person to *start* drinking and those that play the central role in *maintaining* the behavior. Chronic drinking can become an addiction; an alcoholic eventually continues drinking because his or her body demands alcohol. But the later physical need does not explain why an individual initially develops a drinking habit. Those who attempt to explain the origins of habitual drinking refer to either psychological or physiological factors. Within each of these two broad categories there are several theories.

Psychological theories

Psychoanalytic Views   Most analytic accounts of alcoholism point to *fixation at the oral stage* of development as the precipitating cause. Early mother-child interactions supposedly either frustrate dependency needs during this stage of maturation or satisfy them to too great an extent. The various psychoanalytic theories therefore differ in the function attributed to excessive drinking. For example, Knight (1937) proposed that the male alcoholic's experience with an overprotective mother has developed a strong need to remain dependent. When this need is frustrated, he becomes angry and aggressive and feels guilty about his impulses. He drinks heavily to reduce these impulses and also to punish those who withhold affection from him. Fenichel (1945), in contrast, stated that being neglected by the mother turns the young male child toward his father, which in turn produces unconscious homosexual impulses. These repressed impulses

compel him to drink in bars with other men, an activity that supposedly allows the alcoholic to obtain some of the emotional satisfaction he has not received from women. (It is not clear what the psychodynamic significance of solitary drinking would be.) Bergler (1946), emphasizing the self-destructive nature of alcoholism, hypothesized that alcohol addiction is a means of attempting to destroy a bad mother with whom the individual has identified. Little evidence is available to support these notions.

Other analytic accounts of alcoholism describe excessive drinking as a defense mechanism adopted to reduce emotional conflicts or eliminate guilt (see Box 10.1). A common analytic quip defines the superego as the part of the personality that is soluble in alcohol.

Learning Views   The notion that the consumption of alcohol can *reduce distress* is also advanced in learning-based accounts of alcoholism. An early experiment by Conger (1951) demonstrated that alcohol can relieve fear. First, animals were trained in a classic approach-avoidance situation: after having been trained to feed in a particular place, the animals were subjected to shock when they approached their food. Half of the animals were then injected with alcohol. These animals were found to approach the food more readily than did the controls. The fear that had become associated with the goal was apparently decreased by the alcohol in the bloodstream of the animals. Some recent investigations have replicated this work and also shown that conflict increases alcohol consumption (Freed, 1971; Von Wright, Pekanmaki, and Malin, 1971).

Generalizing from these studies, we might argue that drinking alcohol is a learned response that is acquired and maintained because it reduces distress. Alcohol, however, has other effects besides the immediate allaying of tension, as our review of the long-term deleterious effects of continual drinking has revealed. Should not these extremely serious long-term negative effects outweigh the transient relief from stress felt when alcohol is first consumed? Dollard and Miller (1950) offered as a solution to this seeming paradox the concept of a *delay of reward gradient.* According to this formulation, the effectiveness of both rewards and punishments, in

BOX   **10.1** Alcoholism and the Need for Power

David McClelland has advanced a rather novel psychodynamic theory of the origins of both social and excessive drinking, linking them to a personality trait, the _need for power_ (McClelland et al., 1972). He proposes that men drink to increase their sense of power. Ingesting alcohol in small doses supposedly brings to mind a greater number of thoughts about social power—being able to affect others for their own good—and larger doses increase thoughts of personal power, and in particular of sexual and aggressive conquests.

In one experiment lending support to the theory, men were recruited to participate in a study of the effects of social atmosphere on imaginativeness. On arriving at the laboratory, each member of the group responded to a series of four TAT-like pictures. Twenty-five minutes of social interaction followed, during which the experimental manipulation took place. Half the men were allowed to drink alcohol, but the others consumed only soft drinks. Then the subjects responded to four more TAT cards. In support of the theory, only those who drank alcohol told in the second testing a greater number of power-related TAT stories—stories that involved prestige, dramatic settings, and positive feelings aroused in others—than they had related in the first testing.

According to McClelland's theory, the need for personal power that makes the alcoholic drink heavily is intense and excessive. Moreover, instead of fostering operant behavior that might indeed earn increased power, this excessive need impels the alcoholic to choose drinking as an alternate path to his goal. Two studies did indeed show that the experimental induction of concerns about power led to increased drinking. What remains unclear is how an excessive need for power develops, why some individuals with this need attempt to fulfill it by drink rather than action, and whether the findings apply to women.

terms of their impact on any particular behavior, tends to decrease as they become farther and farther removed in time from the response. Thus a small but immediate reward can often exert a more powerful effect than can a larger one that does not immediately follow the response. Similarly, an immediate punishment is a much more effective agent of change than a pushishment imposed several days, weeks, or even months later. In this sense the short-term reduction of distress offered by alcohol is seen as a rather large and immediately reinforcing benefit. Conversely, the longer-term effects of alcohol are relatively ineffective in discouraging its consumption because they are suffered so long after the actual drinking.

The theory that the alcoholic drinks because alcohol reduces tension must be viewed as an incomplete explanation, however. First, studies of the effect of alcohol on other behavior related to tension, such as avoidance, have not always provided data supporting the theory (Cappell, 1975). Furthermore, the theory may explain why many people _begin_ drinking, but it does not appear to account for the continuation of drinking over long periods of time. For example, Nathan and his colleagues (1970) have reported a study in which alcoholics residing in a specially designed hospital ward were carefully observed. The patients were allowed to work to obtain points which could later be exchanged for alcohol. Although the patients themselves reported that they drank to relieve anxiety and depression, an assessment of their moods by means of a self-report adjective checklist indicated that they were actually _more_ anxious and depressed after drinking. Similar results were reported by Mendelson (1964).

We might well ask why it has so long been assumed that drinking is initially maintained because it reduces anxiety. Perhaps the theorists have failed to distinguish between chronic consumption of alcohol and social drinking. Those who have theorized about alcoholism are, after all, unlikely to be chronic or addicted alcoholics. They are more likely to be social drinkers who enjoy an occasional cocktail in the company of others, especially after a trying day. It may be, then, that closeness to the subject matter has prevented until recently a critical examination of the view that prolonged drinking reduces tension.

Personality and Alcoholism   Many investigations have attempted to measure the personalities of alcoholics. Two points must be made about this research. First, no profile of a single "alcoholic personality" has been obtained. More typically a number of personality patterns are found among alcoholics (for example, Skinner, Jackson, and Hoffman, 1974). Second, the research design of such studies suffers from the problems of interpretation that are inherent in correlational work. For example, if a given personality pattern is highly correlated with alcoholism, did the former cause the latter, or vice versa? Some studies, though, have employed the more appropriate longitudinal design.

In the 1930s a long-term research project was begun in Oakland, California. Called the Oakland Growth Study, it examined a large sample of children in great detail and followed them up at periodic intervals. In the mid-1960s many of these middle-aged individuals were contacted again and interviewed concerning their current alcohol consumption patterns, their reasons for drinking, their attitudes toward drinking, and the like (Jones, 1968, 1971). On the basis of their answers to these questions, the individuals were classified into five categories: (1) problem drinkers, (2) heavy drinkers (two or three drinks every day), (3) moderate drinkers, (4) light drinkers, and (5) nondrinkers and abstainers. The information that had been collected on the members of the population sample during their junior and senior high school years was extensive. Parents

had contributed details about background and homelife, teachers had reported on classroom behavior, classroom peers had rated one another, and the individuals in the sample had rated themselves on personality tests and in interviews. All these data collected during their adolescence were correlated with the subjects' adult drinking patterns.

Jones found that the adult male problem drinkers still had some of the same traits that had characterized them in adolescence: impulsiveness which was never controlled, extroverted behavior, and a tendency to overemphasize their masculinity. Moreover, as compared to high school contemporaries who did not later become excessive drinkers, adult male problem drinkers had been described in adolescence as less aware of impressions made on others, less productive, less calm, more sensitive to criticism, and less socially perceptive. The traits of the future problem drinker had apparently caused him social difficulties even in high school. Later these difficulties may have served as the source of stress that induced him to begin drinking.

Among the women, the picture was much less clear, for Jones found in adolescence marked similarities between those who later became problem drinkers and those who abstained altogether from alcohol in adulthood. Both groups had been characterized in high school as vulnerable, withdrawn, dependent, irritable, and sensitive to criticism. The pattern of apparently *poor social adaptation*—which correlated with heavy drinking in men—was in women associated with *either* problem drinking *or* total abstinence.

The Sociocultural View   It has been argued that ethnic groups such as the Jews, Italians, and Chinese, who specify appropriate ceremonial, nutritional, or festive uses of alcohol, have lower rates of alcoholism. Although these people condone the drinking of alcohol under specified circumstances, they frown on overindulgence. For other national groups, such as the Irish and the English, the circumstances in which the consumption of alcohol is deemed appropriate are less clear.

A study carried out by McCord, McCord, and Gudeman (1959, 1960) reveals the importance of *ethnic and cultural backgrounds* in the etiology of alcoholism of males in the United States. Young men who had been intensively studied several years earlier as adolescents were followed up. In examining the earlier histories of those who had become alcoholics, the investigators found no support for theories relating the habit to oral fixation, parental pampering, or self-destructive tendencies, but they did find the relation of alcoholism and ethnic background to be significant. More young men with American Indian, western and eastern European, and Irish backgrounds were alcoholic than were those of Italian and other Latin extractions. The investigators also found a relation between alcoholism and social class: more of the alcoholics were from the middle class than from the lower class.

Although social and cultural factors are clearly important, they obviously cannot be the only ones. The relationship between ethnic background and alcoholism is not one to one; some Jews are alcoholics, and not every Irishman is addicted to the beverage. Furthermore, comparisons of various countries reveal a pattern of alcoholism not entirely consistent with this view. The rate of alcoholism in Ireland, for example, is actually quite low, and Italians have the second highest rate.

Epidemiologists pursue their own methods when studying alcoholism and examine the broad social contexts in which people live. Fillmore and Caetano (1980) found unusually high levels of alcoholism among sailors, railroad workers, and people in the "drink trade"—resturant owners, bartenders, waiters, and liquor dealers. In all these occupations heavy drinking is normative, that is, almost expected as part of the job, and alcohol is readily available to these men. A survey of occupational drinking by Mannello and Seaman (1979) showed that 14 percent of railroad workers drank on the job, 5 percent came to work drunk or got drunk on duty, and 20 percent reported to work with hangovers. These are alarming statistics, considering the fact that railroad personnel are responsible for the physical safety of hundreds of thousands of people each day. Improvements in working conditions might help, such as more generous allowances for sick leave and modifying the requirement that railroad workers be on call for eight hours following every work shift.

Physiological theories

Inasmuch as chronic alcoholism becomes a physiological addiction, theorists point to physiological factors in attempting to explain why some people begin a drinking pattern that eventuates in addiction. Among animals a preference for alcohol or indifference to it varies with the species. By selective mating within a species showing a preference, animals that greatly prefer alcohol to other beverages can be bred (Segovia-Riquelme, Varela, and Mardones, 1971). And there is evidence that alcoholism in human beings runs in families. A number of studies indicate that relatives and children of alcoholics have higher than expected rates of alcoholism. Although these findings are consistent with the genetic transmission of a predisposition, these individuals might also have become alcoholics through exposure to drinking.

One study, however, examined alcoholism in the adopted offspring of alcoholics, thus allowing the role of heredity to be more precisely specified (Goodwin et al., 1973). One hundred seventy-four subjects were chosen from an initial pool of 5483 male babies who were adopted in Copenhagen between 1924 and 1947. Subjects were divided into the three following experimental and control groups.

1. $N = 67$: One and sometimes both biological parents of each subject (proband) in the experimental group had been hospitalized for alcoholism. The probands had been adopted within six weeks of birth by nonrelatives and had had no subsequent contact with biological relatives.

2. $N = 70$: Each subject in this control group was matched for age and time of adoption with a subject in group 1. None of the biological parents of these control subjects had a record of psychiatric hospitalization.

3. $N = 37$: The subjects in this control group were matched for age and time of adoption with subjects in group 1. At least one biological parent of each of these control subjects had been hospitalized for a psychiatric condition other than alcoholism or schizophrenia.

When this original sample was followed up, 133 subjects were located and interviewed. (Those who could not be located or who refused to be questioned were proportionately distributed across groups.) The subjects, who had a mean age of thirty at the time of the follow-up, were interviewed by a psychiatrist blind to their group assignment. Questions covered their drinking practices, psychopathology, and demographic variables. Since the subjects in the two control groups did not differ on any of the classificatory variables except having or not having a parent with a record of psychiatric hospitalization, they were combined into one comparison group for purposes of analysis. Problems that significantly discriminated between the experimental group and the comparison group are given in Table 10.1

As can be seen, the two groups are easily distinguished one from the other on the basis of alcohol-related measures. Thus the results suggest that in men a predisposition toward alcoholism can be inherited.

TABLE **10.1**
The Alcohol-Related Problems of Offspring of Alcoholics, Adopted and Raised by Others, Compared with Those of Controls

(from Goodwin et al., 1973)

Problems	Probands, percent ($N = 55$)	Controls, percent ($N = 78$)
Ever divorced	27	9
Any psychiatric treatment	40	24
Psychiatric hospitalization	15	3
Drinking problems Hallucinations (as withdrawal symptoms)	6	0
Loss of control	35	17
Repeated morning drinking	29	11
Treated for drinking	9	1
Alcoholic diagnosis	18	5

This picture is different for women, however. Goodwin and his colleagues (1977) conducted a study of daughters of alcoholic parents who had been adopted and raised by others. The rate of alcoholism in both the adopted daughters of alcoholics and the control adopted daughters of nonalcoholic parents was about the same and higher than the rate in the general population.

In speculating on what might be inherited as a diathesis for alcoholism, Goodwin (1979) proposes the ability to tolerate alcohol. To become an alcoholic, a person first has to be able to drink a lot, in other words, be able to tolerate large quantities of alcohol. Some ethnic groups, notably Orientals, may have a low rate of alcoholism because of their physiological intolerance. Indeed, about three-quarters of Orientals experience unpleasant effects from small quantities of alcohol. Noxious effects of the drug may then protect a person from alcoholism.

Therapy for Alcoholism
The havoc created by alcoholism, both for the drinkers themselves and for their families, friends, employers, and communities, makes this problem the most serious public health issue in this country. As already mentioned, no dollar figure can be put on the human tragedy that is a direct result of this most prevalent form of drug abuse. For these reasons industry spends large sums of money in support of various alcohol rehabilitation programs for employees, in the knowledge that for every dollar spent in this way, many more dollars will be returned in improved functioning of workers. Television and radio carry public service messages about the dangers of alcoholism, in attempts to discourage people from beginning to drink to excess and to encourage those already addicted to own up to their problem and seek help. Calling excessive drinking a disease is believed preferable to holding persons responsible for their drinking; presumably this lessens guilt and allows them to mobilize their resources to seek help and combat their alcoholism.

Traditional hospital treatment
Both public and private hospitals around the world have for many years provided retreats for

alcoholics, sanctums where individuals can "dry out" and avail themselves of a variety of individual and group therapies, which they will need. The withdrawal from alcohol—*detoxification*—can be very painful, both physically and psychologically, and even fatal if not done under medical supervision. Tranquilizers are sometimes given to ease the anxiety and general discomfort of withdrawal. Because many alcoholics misuse tranquilizers, some clinics try gradual tapering off without tranquilizers rather than sudden cutoff of alcohol. The alcoholic will need carbohydrate solutions and B vitamins either way and perhaps an anticonvulsant. Disulfiram, or Antabuse, can discourage the patient from drinking; this drug, if taken reliably each morning, causes violent vomiting should the person drink alcohol. Many alcoholics are naturally reluctant even to take the drug, but if they can be motivated to do so, Antabuse is an effective therapy (Bourne, Alford, and Bowcock, 1966).

Alcoholics Anonymous

The largest and most widely known self-help group in the world is Alcoholics Anonymous (AA), founded in 1935 by two recovered drinkers. It currently has 30,000 chapters and a membership numbering more than a million people in the United States and ninety-one other countries throughout the world. An AA chapter runs regular and frequent meetings at which newcomers rise to announce that they are alcoholics, and older sober members give testimonials, relating the stories of their alcoholism and indicating how their lives are better now. The group provides emotional support, understanding, and close counseling for the alcoholic and a social life to relieve isolation. Members are urged to call upon one another around the clock when they need companionship and encouragement not to relapse into drink.

The belief is instilled in each AA member that alcoholism is a disease one is never cured of, that continuing vigilance is necessary to resist taking even a single drink lest uncontrollable drinking begin all over again. The important religious and spiritual aspect of AA is evident in the twelve steps of AA shown in Table 10.2. Two related self-help groups are of more recent origin. The relatives of alcoholics meet in Al-Anon

Family Groups for mutual support in dealing with their alcoholic family members. Ala-Teen is for the offspring of alcoholics, who also require support and understanding.

Unfortunately, the claims made by AA about the effectiveness of its treatment have rarely been subjected to scientific scrutiny. Available findings indicate that they should be viewed with some caution. For example, as many as 80 percent of people who join AA drop out (Edwards et al., 1967). Furthermore, without follow-up it is impossible to know how enduring are the short-term changes that AA may effect. Since return to excessive drinking is the norm rather than the exception for alcoholics, the absence of such information prevents an adequate evaluation of what many regard as the best treatment for alcoholism.

Aversion therapy

Behavioral researchers have been studying the treatment of alcoholism for many years. In fact, one of the earliest articles on behavior therapy concerned aversive "conditioning" of alcoholism (Kantorovich, 1930). With these procedures a problem drinker is shocked or made nauseous while looking at, reaching for, or beginning to drink alcohol. The aversive stimulus may also be presented in imagination in a procedure called *covert sensitization* (Cautela, 1966). The following excerpt describes a situation recommended as an imagined noxious stimulus. A client in this form of treatment would imagine this scene both in sessions with the therapist and at home.

You are walking into a bar. You decide to have a glass of beer. You are now walking toward the bar. As you are approaching the bar you have a funny feeling in the pit of your stomach. Your stomach feels all queasy and nauseous. Some liquid comes up your throat and it is very sour. You try to swallow it back down, but as you do this, food particles start coming up your throat to your mouth. You are now reaching the bar and you order a beer. As the bartender is pouring the beer, puke comes up into your mouth. You try to keep your mouth closed and swallow it down. You reach for the glass of beer to wash it down. As soon

TABLE 10.2
Twelve Suggested Steps of Alcoholics Anonymous

1. We admitted we were powerless over alcohol—that our lives had become unmanageable.
2. Came to believe that a power greater than ourselves could restore us to sanity.
3. Made a decision to turn our will and our lives over to the care of God *as we understood Him*.
4. Made a searching and fearless moral inventory of ourselves.
5. Admitted to God, to ourselves, and to another human being the exact nature of our wrongs.
6. Were entirely ready to have God remove all these defects of character.
7. Humbly asked Him to remove our shortcomings.
8. Made a list of all persons we had harmed, and became willing to make amends to them all.
9. Made direct amends to such people wherever possible, except when to do so would injure them or others.
10. Continued to take personal inventory and, when we were wrong, promptly admitted it.
11. Sought through prayer and meditation to improve our conscious contact with God *as we understand Him*, praying only for knowledge of His will for us and the power to carry that out.
12. Having had a spiritual awakening as the result of these steps, we tried to carry this message to alcoholics and to practice these principles in all our affairs.

Source: *The Twelve Steps and Twelve Traditions*. Reprinted with permission of A. A. World Services, Inc. © 1952.

as your hand touches the glass, you can't hold it down any longer. You have to open your mouth and you puke. It goes all over your hand, all over the glass and the beer. You can see it floating around in the beer. Snots and mucus come out of your nose. Your shirt and pants are full of vomit. The bartender has some on his shirt. You notice people looking at you. You get sick again and you vomit more and more. You turn away from the beer and immediately you start to feel better. As you run out of the bar room, you start to feel better and better. When you get out into clean fresh air you feel wonderful. You go home and clean yourself up (1966, p. 37).

Ethical considerations inhibit investigators in their selection of aversive procedures, for they entail, by their very nature, an assault on the person being treated. Although some drinkers who have undergone aversion therapy of one sort or another drink less or not at all at the end of treatment, it is doubtful that they do so because of conditioning (Kazdin and Wilson, 1978). Aversion therapy for alcoholism probably works because of the nonspecific, placebo effects of the treatment.

Behavioral contracting
Making a contract with the alcoholic is somewhat more promising. An alcoholic in an institution agrees to refrain from excessive drinking in exchange for particular rewards, such as weekend passes or better living conditions on the ward. Provided a given patient can be persuaded to enter into the necessary contract, there is some evidence that control over drinking can be achieved (Nathan and Goldman, 1979).

Controlled drinking
Until recently it was generally agreed that alcoholics had to abstain completely if they were to

be cured, for they were said to have no control over their imbibing once they had taken that first drink. Although this continues to be the abiding belief of Alcoholics Anonymous, the research mentioned earlier calls the supposed constitutional weakness into question. Drinkers' *beliefs* about themselves and alcohol may be as important as the physiological addiction to the drug itself. Indeed, considering the difficulty in our society of avoiding alcohol altogether, it may even be *preferable* to teach the problem drinker to imbibe with moderation. A drinker's self-esteem will certainly benefit from being able to control a problem and from feeling in charge of his or her life.

In treatment sessions an outpatient is allowed to drink to a moderate level of intoxication and blood alcohol. He or she is then informed if the level of blood alcohol rises above a certain percent (Lovibond and Caddy, 1970). Thereafter when the person does drink, he or she is supposedly able to keep blood level of alcohol low. Recent information indicates that problem drinkers have more difficulty than others in determining the alcohol content of the blood, however (Huber, Karlin, and Nathan, 1976).

Preliminary findings of one treatment program suggest that at least some alcoholics can learn to control their drinking and improve other aspects of their lives as well (Sobell and Sobell, 1976). Alcoholics who are attempting to control their drinking are shocked when they choose straight liquor rather than mixed drinks, gulp their drinks down too fast, or take large swallows rather than sips. They are also given problem-solving and assertiveness training, watch videotapes of their inebriated selves, and identify the situations precipitating their drinking so that they can settle on a less self-destructive course of action. Their improvement is greater than that of alcoholics who try for total abstinence and are shocked for any drinking at all. Nonetheless, some workers in the field of alcoholism continue to question the wisdom of controlled drinking for alcoholics, being concerned that for many the belief that they can imbibe with moderation will prove an illusory goal, a cruel hoax, as it were. They may be left unable to manage the drug that often threatens their very lives and with no motivation for complete abstinence.

Clinical considerations

A general problem with attempts to control or eliminate alcoholism has been the therapist's often unstated assumption that all people who drink to excess do so for the same reasons. Thus an analyst may assume that problem drinkers are trying to escape from intolerable feelings of dependency. A humanistic theorist may hold that the excessive drinker escapes into the haze of alcohol because he or she lacks courage to face problems and deal with them in an open, direct fashion. A behavior therapist favoring aversive treatment believes that reducing the attraction alcohol or its taste has for drinkers will help them abstain. As is true of people with other human problems, however, those who drink are not likely to be this simple (Lazarus, 1965). A more sophisticated and comprehensive clinical assessment considers the place that drinking occupies in the person's life. A woman in a desperately unhappy marriage, with meaningless time on her hands at home, especially as children need her constant attention less than they did before entering school, may seek the numbing effects of alcohol just to help the time pass and to avoid facing her life dilemmas. Making the taste of alcohol unpleasant for this woman by pairing it with shock or an emetic seems neither sensible nor adequate. The therapist should concentrate on the marital and family problems and try to reduce the psychological pain that permeates her existence. Since she is probably a true addict, she will also need help in tolerating the withdrawal symptoms that come with reduced consumption. And without alcohol as a reliable anesthetic, she will need to mobilize other resources to confront her hitherto avoided problems. Social-skills training may help her to do so.

Sedatives and Stimulants

Until 1914 addiction to drugs was disapproved in the United States, but it was tolerated. The 1914 Harrison Narcotics Act changed this, making the unauthorized use of various drugs illegal and those addicted to them criminals. The drugs to be discussed, not all of which are illegal, may be divided into two general categories. The major _sedatives,_ called "downers," slow the activities of the body and reduce its responsiveness. In this group of drugs are the organic narcotics—opium and its derivatives morphine, heroin, and codeine—and the synthetic barbiturates. The second group, the _stimulants_ or "uppers," act on the brain and the sympathetic nervous system to increase alertness and motor activity. The amphetamines are synthetic stimulants; cocaine is a natural stimulant extracted from the coca leaf.

Sedatives

Narcotics

Opium, the principal drug of illegal international traffic, was known to the people of the Sumerian civilization dating back to 7000 B.C. They gave the poppy that supplied this narcotic the name by which it is still known and which means "the plant of joy." Opium is a mixture of about eighteen alkaloids, but until 1806 people had no knowledge of these substances to which so many natural drugs owe their potency. In that year the alkaloid _morphine,_ a bitter-tasting powder, was separated out from raw opium. It proved to be a powerful sedative and pain reliever. Before its addictive properties were noted, it was commonly used in patent medicines. In the middle of the century, when the hypodermic needle was introduced in the United States, morphine began to be injected directly into the veins to relieve pain. Many soldiers wounded in battle and suffering from dysentery during the Civil War were treated with morphine and returned home addicted to the drug. Concerned about administering a drug that could disturb the later lives of patients, scientists began studying morphine. They thought that part of its molecule might be responsible for relieving pain and another part for its addictiveness. In 1874 they found that

morphine could be converted into another powerful pain relieving drug which they named _heroin._ It was used initially as a cure for the withdrawal symptoms of morphine and was substituted for morphine in cough syrups and other patent medicines. So many maladies were treated with heroin that it came to be known as G.O.M. or "God's own medicine" (Brecher, 1972). Heroin proved to be even more potent than morphine, however, acting more quickly and with greater intensity, and it is more addictive. Heroin in fact is converted to morphine by the brain, but it has first passed the blood-brain barrier faster and possibly in greater concentration than morphine does. By 1909 President Theodore Roosevelt was calling for an international investigation of opium and the opiates.

Opium and its derivatives morphine and heroin produce euphoria, drowsiness, reverie, and sometimes a lack of coordination. Heroin has an additional initial effect, the "rush," a feeling of warm, suffusing ecstasy immediately following an injection. The addict sheds worries and fears and has great self-confidence for four to six hours. Then letdown, bordering on stupor. Because these drugs are central nervous system depressants, they relieve pain. All three are clearly addicting in the physiological sense, for users show both increased tolerance of the drugs and withdrawal reactions when they are unable to obtain another dose.

A recent breakthrough may greatly increase our understanding of the process of addiction to opiates. In the early 1970s several laboratories reported the presence in vertebrate brains of what appeared to be specific opiate receptors, that is, cell components to which opiates bind to produce euphoria and analgesia. Because it seemed unlikely that such receptors had been developed to interact with opiate alkaloids in the environment, a search began for internally produced (endogenous) opiates. By 1975 such compounds, called _endorphins,_ had been discovered in several species, including human beings (Goldstein, 1976). Apparently we all can produce our own opiates. Endorphins are thought to be the body's own pain relievers and may play a crucial role in addiction. Ingesting an exogenous opiate, such as heroin, may halt the normal production of endorphins. If later the exogenous

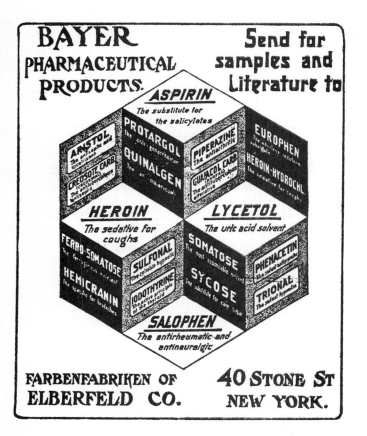

Early advertisement from the Bayer Company illustrating the legal sale of heroin as a medicant for coughing.

substance is no longer supplied, an individual could be left with no opiates in the body, either exogenous or endogenous, precipitating withdrawal reactions.

The National Institute on Drug Abuse (NIDA) noted a decline in the number of heroin addicts in the United States, from about 550,000 in 1975 to about 380,000 in 1978, and a decline in heroin-related deaths, from 2600 in 1976 to 800 in 1978 (*ADAMHA News,* March 21, 1980).

The actual cause of deaths, often attributed to overdoses, remains in doubt. Among the possible effects of prolonged narcotic addiction are loss of sexual interest, respiratory and circulatory difficulties, and malnutrition. Because narcotics greatly reduce hunger and thirst, addicts eat very poorly and may lose considerable weight. In addition, there is an ever-present danger of abscesses and of contracting bloodstream infec-

tions, tetanus, and hepatitis from the use of unsterile needles.

Reactions to not having a dose of heroin may begin within eight hours of the last injection, at least after high tolerance has built up. During the next few hours the individual will typically have muscle pain, will sneeze, sweat, become tearful, and yawn a great deal; the symptoms resemble influenza. Within thirty-six hours the withdrawal symptoms have become more severe. There may be uncontrollable muscle twitching, cramps, chills alternating with excessive flushing and sweating, and a rise in heart rate and blood pressure. The addict is unable to sleep, vomits, and has diarrhea. These symptoms typically persist for about seventy-two hours and then diminish gradually over a five- to ten-day period.

A new kind of heroin has recently been described by the staff of the Haight-Ashbury Clinic in San Francisco (as reported by Leibtag, 1980). Imported from Iran, ''Persian'' is considerably more potent than other forms of street heroin— 92 percent pure as compared with the usual 2 to 4 percent. Persian is usually smoked or ''snorted'' rather than injected. This kind of ingestion of the drug presents new hazards of pulmonary complications as well as of rapid addiction. Withdrawal from Persian, as might be expected, is markedly more severe than that from weaker preparations of the drug. Dealers have been trying to meet this new competition by mixing their weaker heroin with instant coffee, to give it the brown powdery appearance of Persian. More ominously, they have been selling cleaner heroin, up to 50 percent pure.

Even more serious than the physical effects are the social consequences of narcotic addiction. The drug and obtaining it become the center of existence, structuring all activities and social relationships. Since narcotics are illegal, addicts must deal with the underworld in order to maintain their habits. The high cost of the drugs—addicts must often spend $100 and more per day for their narcotics—means that they must either have great wealth or acquire money through illegal activites.[3] Thus the correlation between addiction and criminal activities is rather high,

[3] Recent indications are that heroin use is increasing in the upper socioeconomic classes.

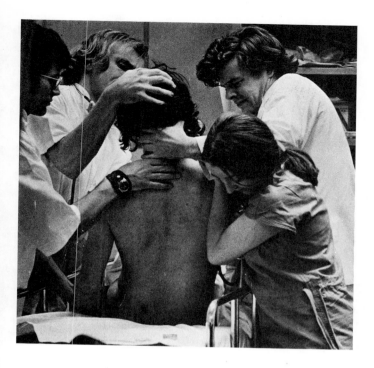

Medical team trying to revive a heroin OD case.

drug abusers choose a barbiturate or other sedative as one of them.

Barbiturates are depressants,[4] relaxing the muscles and in small doses producing a mildly euphoric state. With excessive doses, however, speech becomes slurred and gait unsteady. Impairment of judgment, concentration, and ability to work may be extreme. The user loses emotional control and may become irritable and combative before falling into a deep sleep. Very large doses can be fatal because the diaphragm muscles relax to such an extent that the individual suffocates. As we have indicated in Chapter 8, barbiturates are frequently chosen as a means of suicide. But many users accidentally kill themselves by drinking alcohol, which potentiates, or magnifies, the depressant effects of barbiturates. With prolonged excessive use the brain can become damaged and personality deteriorates.

Barbiturates—the street for the most part offers pentobarbital, secobarital, and amobarbital—are the second most common class of drug to which people become addicted. Increased tolerance follows prolonged use, and the withdrawal reactions after abrupt termination are particularly severe and long lasting and can even cause sudden death. The delirium, convulsions, and other symptoms resemble those following abrupt withdrawal of alcohol. The following is a description of one stage of the withdrawal reaction of a middle-aged woman who had been taking barbiturates for many years.

undoubtedly contributing to the popular notion that drug addiction per se causes violence.

Barbiturates

Barbiturates were synthesized as aids for sleeping and relaxation. The first was produced in 1903 and since then hundreds of derivatives of barbituric acid have been made. Two types are usually distinguished—long-acting barbiturates for prolonged sedation and short-acting barbiturates for prompt sedation and sleep. The short-acting drugs are usually viewed as addicting. Initially, the drugs were considered highly desirable and were prescribed very frequently. In the 1940s, however, a campaign was mounted against them because they were discovered to be addicting, and physicians prescribed barbiturates less frequently. Today in the United States they are manufactured in vast quantities, enough, it is estimated, to supply each man, woman, and child with fifty pills per year. Many are shipped legally to Mexico and then brought back into the country and trafficked illegally. The majority of poly-

> She has a marked tremor and was unsteady on her feet. She had hallucinated, thought she heard the voice of her husband telling her that he was coming to get her in a taxi and she cried out to him. Soon she began seeing people climbing trees and looking through the window at her. She became violent and abusive to the staff. Even after receiving sedative medication she remained restless, muttering to herself incoherently. Her tremor increased, her face became flushed and she began to perspire exces-

[4] Methaqualone, a sedative sold under the trade names Quaalude and Sopor, is similar in effect to barbiturates and has become a popular ''street'' drug. Besides being addictive, it has other dangers—internal bleeding, coma, and even death from overdose.

BOX 10.2 Polydrug Abuse

Many of those who abuse drugs use more than one drug at any given time. _Polydrug abuse_ poses a serious health problem because the effects of some drugs when taken together are _synergistic,_ that is, the effects of each interact to produce an especially strong reaction. Mixing barbiturates with alcohol is a common means of suicide, be it intentional or accidental. Alcohol is believed to have contributed to deaths from heroin as well, for evidence indicates that alcohol can dramatically reduce the amount of narcotic that need be taken for it to be a lethal dose. Many early studies found that heroin addicts disliked alcohol, using it only as a substitute during withdrawal. In recent years, however, addicts seem to alternate between alcohol and heroin because the price of heroin is so high. Thus deaths such as the following may be caused by an interaction between alcohol and heroin.

The quart bottle of Southern Comfort that she held aloft on-stage was at once a symbol of her load and a way of lightening it. . . . Last week, Janis Joplin died on the lowest and saddest of notes. Returning to her Hollywood motel room after a late-night recording session and some hard drinking [emphasis added] with friends at a nearby bar, she apparently filled a hypodermic needle with heroin and shot it into her left arm (Time, October 19, 1970).

sively. At times she twitched convulsively. A little later she began picking up imaginary objects and muttering "thank you" as if someone were handing them to her. Later she was observed reaching for an imaginary glass and drinking from it. She ate imaginary food and picked imaginary cigarettes out of the air; she heard nonexistent doorbells and an ambulance siren (Rosen, Fox, and Gregory, 1972, pp. 317–318).

Stimulants

Amphetamines

In seeking a treatment for asthma, the Chinese-American pharmacologist Chen studied ancient Chinese descriptions of drugs. He found a desert shrub mahuang commended again and again as an effective remedy. After systematic effort Chen was able to isolate an alkaloid from this plant, which belongs to the genus _Ephedra;_ ephedrine

did indeed prove highly successful in treating asthma. But relying on the shrub for the drug was not viewed as efficient, and so a search began for a synthetic substitute. The _amphetamines_ were the result of this search (Snyder, 1974).

The first amphetamine, Benzedrine, was synthesized in 1927. Almost as soon as it became commercially available in the early 1930s as an inhalant to relieve stuffy noses, the public discovered its stimulating effects. Physicians thereafter prescribed it and the other amphetamines soon synthesized to control mild depression and appetite. During World War II soldiers on both sides were supplied with the drugs to ward off fatigue; today amphetamines are used to treat hyperactive children (see page 663).

Amphetamines such as Benzedrine, Dexedrine, and Methedrine produce effects similar to those of norepinephrine in the sympathetic nervous system. They are taken orally or intravenously and can be addicting. Wakefulness is heightened, intestinal functions are inhibited, and appetite is reduced—hence their use in dieting. The heart rate is increased, and blood vessels in the skin and mucous membranes constrict. The individual becomes alert, euphoric, and more outgoing and is possessed with seemingly boundless energy. Larger doses can make the person nervous, agitated, and confused, subjecting him or her to palpitations, headaches, dizziness, and sleeplessness. There are some reports that large doses taken over a period of time induce a state quite similar to paranoid schizophrenia, which can persist beyond the time that the drug is present in the body.

Tolerance develops rapidly so that mouthfuls of pills are required to produce the stimulating effect. As tolerance increases, the user may stop taking pills and inject Methedrine, the strongest of the amphetamines, directly into the veins. The so-called speed freaks give themselves repeated injections of the drug and maintain intense and euphoric activity for a few days, without eating or sleeping, after which they are exhausted and depressed and sleep or "crash" for several days. Then the cycle starts again. After several repetitions of this pattern, the physical and social functioning of the individual will have deteriorated considerably. Behavior will be quite erratic and hostile, and the speed freak may become a danger to himself and to others.

Cocaine

The Spanish conquistadors introduced *coca* leaves to Europe. The Indians of the Andean uplands, to which the coca shrubs are native, chew the leaves, but the Europeans chose to brew them instead in beverages. The alkaloid *cocaine* was extracted from the leaves of the coca plant in 1844 and has been used since then as a local anesthetic. In 1884, while still a young neurologist in Vienna, Sigmund Freud began using cocaine to combat his depression. Convinced of its wondrous effects, he prescribed it to a friend with a painful disease and published one of the first papers on the drug, "Song of Praise," which was an enthusiastic endorsement of the exhilarating effects he had experienced.[5] One of the early

[5] Freud subsequently lost his enthusiasm for cocaine after nursing a physician friend, to whom he had recommended the drug, through a night-long psychotic state brought on by it.

products using coca leaves in its manufacture was Coca-Cola, the recipe for which was concocted by an Atlanta druggist in 1886. For the next twenty years Coke was the real thing, but in 1906 the Pure Food and Drugs Act was passed and the manufacturer switched to coca leaves from which the cocaine had been removed.

Cocaine itself is very costly, and the rituals of taking it are elaborate; the paraphernalia people use can add to the overall expense (see Box 10.3). Cocaine can be sniffed ("snorted"), smoked in pipes or cigarettes, swallowed, or even injected into the veins like heroin; some heroin addicts in fact mix the two drugs in a combination known as "speedball," which is taken orally.

In addition to its pain-reducing effects, cocaine acts on the cortex of the brain, heightening sensory awareness and inducing a state of euphoria. Sexual desire is accentuated, and feelings of self-confidence, well-being, and indefatigability suffuse the user's consciousness. An overdose may bring on chills, nausea, and insomnia, as well as a paranoid breakdown and terrifying hallucinations of insects crawling beneath the skin. Although people can become psychologically dependent on cocaine, it does not appear to be addicting.

The use of cocaine increased significantly in the 1970s. According to the National Institute on Drug Abuse (Kelly, 1980), cocaine is second only to marijuana in its increasing popularity. In 1977 an estimated 19 percent of young adults had tried the drug; by 1979 the number had risen to 28 percent. Of this group of young people, one-third have used it between eleven and ninety-nine times. Overall, NIDA estimates that 6.5 million Americans tried cocaine at least once in 1978, up from 4 million in 1976.

Theories of the Origins of Drug Addiction

Physiological theories

Many have regarded the physiological changes in the body effected by drugs as the most important factor in drug addiction. Because the physiology of the body has been changed by the drug, it reacts when the substance to which it

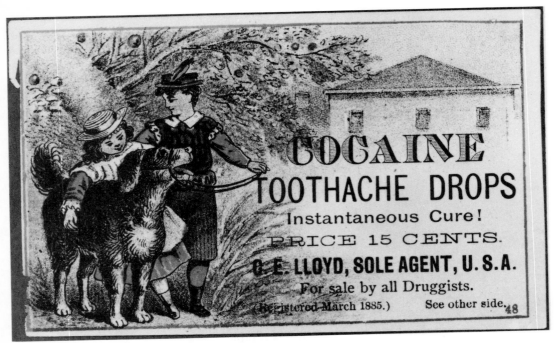

At one time cocaine was sold legally as a local anesthetic for toothache.

Cocaine, which is expensive and provides a notable euphoria, has become a fashionable drug of the rich.

has become accustomed is no longer administered. To avoid withdrawal reactions, the addict continues taking the drug. Physiological alterations are, in turn, viewed as having been established through accident or curiosity. A person may take the drug by chance or because he or she wants to experience its effects. With enough repetition—how much is not known—the person is ensnared by changes in bodily chemistry and the concomitant severity of withdrawal reactions. The addict is regarded as an unwitting victim of physiological reactions, continuing to use the drug to ward off the distress of withdrawal.

Ausubel (1961a) has challenged this interpretation by alleging that the effects of withdrawal from heroin, for example, are in reality no more severe than a bad case of influenza. Anecdotal evidence exists to support Ausubel's claim that the effects of withdrawal are not as severe as is often imagined. Synanon (Yablonsky, 1967), a self-governing corporation which offers a community-living treatment for drug addiction, does not "allow" a severe withdrawal reaction among the participants in its program. Rather, the heroin addict is told that the effects of withdrawal will not be severe and that he or she will be able to

BOX 10.3 Free Enterprise: Meeting Demands of the Marketplace

A person window-shopping in many cities and towns will come upon displays of paraphernalia designed to enhance the use of illicit drugs, particularly of cocaine and marijuana. Although the sale of these drugs remains illegal virtually everywhere, it is not (yet) against the law to sell tiny spoons, gram scales, roach clips with which to hold a marijuana cigarette so that virtually all of it can be smoked, hash pipes, and any of the various tools employed by people who seek the maximum effects of narcotics, stimulants, and marijuana. For many of the more affluent drug users, the style and elegance of one's pipe or spoon are as much a part of the drug-taking ritual as the purity of the drug being ingested.

"Head shops," stores in which drug paraphernalia are sold, have become more and more prevalent in recent years.

In the first report of its kind, the National Institute on Drug Abuse has surveyed one of this country's newest growth industries (Weisman, 1980). More than 20,000 retail outlets cater to the demands of drug users. These include not only "head shops" but more conventional businesses such as record stores, food markets, and clothing stores. The lure of selling such items appears irresistible. Many of the "straight" outlets report that sales of such items, which have a high profit margin, account for up to 20 percent of their total profits. Total retail sales in the United States are estimated to be anywhere between $50 million to $3 billion a year. Sales of cocaine paraphernalia have increased the most, up 50 percent between 1977 and 1978. Considering the increasing use of this fashionable drug, sales figures would appear likely to continue their upward movement.

Only the state of Georgia now prohibits the sales of drug paraphernalia to minors. Community groups are becoming more and more concerned about the proliferation of shops selling these items, however, and are agitating for restriction, if not elimination, of the sale of such materials.

continue ordinary daily life. In fact, strong social pressures are applied to make the addict meet responsibilities during withdrawal. Apparently the method has some success, and severe withdrawal reactions are not often reported among people who live at the various Synanon centers. As noted earlier, however, the apparent increase in availability of purer forms of heroin is likely to exacerbate the withdrawal problems of addicts.

Psychological theories

Psychological theories of the origin of drug addiction usually emphasize reduction of distress and the pleasant feeling and euphoric state that the drugs produce. These theories also attempt to explain why particular kinds of people seem to "need" these effects. An association has often been noted between criminality, drug abuse, and antisocial personality disorder. In this context drug abuse may be considered as part of the thrill-seeking behavior of the sociopath discussed in Chapter 9. We might also expect narcotics to be used by anxious individuals in order to reduce the distress that they often experience. Drug addicts have also been found to be deviant on various personality questionnaire measures. But we must question whether these personality characteristics antedated the addiction and caused it. For example, we might find that drug addicts tend to be more suspicious than non-

users. To conclude that suspiciousness contributes to the use of drugs would not be justified, for it might well be the addict's *reaction to* his illegal status as a drug user. Longitudinal data on personality variables such as those that were collected by Jones on alcoholism (page 305) are not available on narcotics addiction.

Some similarities in family background have been identified in the life histories of drug addicts (Chein et al., 1964). In many cases the father is absent from the home of the future addict. If the father is present, he tends to be a shadowy figure or to be overtly hostile and distant. If present he may also serve as a model for criminal behavior, and the relations between the mother and father are likely to be stormy. Chein and his colleagues therefore proposed that the personality defects of the drug addict, whatever they are, were developed through family background. Initial experiences with addicting drugs were also shown to be nonaccidental. Most addicts were found to have been introduced knowingly to the drugs, not by an adult but rather by a member of their peer group, suggesting the importance of peer pressure and curiosity. Boredom and aggravation are probably contributing factors. In ghettoes where narcotics are readily available, and the culture of the streets prevails, the incidence of drug use is especially high.

An intriguing explanation of ghetto drug use

and drug dealing has been proposed by Preble and Casey (1969). In their eyes addiction and all that goes with it become a challenge and a full-time occupation. In order to maintain his or her habit, the addict must be actively and resource-fully engaged in a variety of money-making enterprises, such as theft, fencing stolen property, selling drugs, and prostitution. The addiction, then, becomes the organizing principle of life, providing a focus for how the person, now a fully committed hustler, spends his or her days and nights.

In sum, there is little evidence available concerning the origins of drug addiction. Personality characteristics, peer pressure, family background, the ease with which the drug can be acquired, and the frequency with which it is used in a particular culture are all possible factors, but as yet the role of any of them has been only vaguely specified.

Therapy for Drug Use

Central to the treatment of hard drug use is detoxification, withdrawing the person from the drug itself. Heroin withdrawal reactions range from relatively mild bouts of anxiety, nausea, and restlessness for several days, to more severe and frightening bouts of delirium and apparent madness, depending primarily on the purity of the heroin that the individual has been using. Someone high on amphetamines can be brought down by appropriate dosages of one of the phenothiazines, a class of drugs more commonly used to treat schizophrenics (see page 439), although it must be kept in mind that the speed freak may also have been using other drugs in conjunction with amphetamines. As for barbiturates, withdrawal reactions from these drugs, as already noted, are especially severe, even life-threatening; they begin about twenty-four hours after the last dose and reach their maximum two to three days later. They have usually abated by the end of the first week, but they may last a month if doses have been large. Withdrawal from these drugs is best done gradually, not "cold turkey," and should take place under close medical supervision (Honigfeld and Howard, 1978).

Withdrawal is but the first way in which therapists try to help the addict or drug abuser, and perhaps ironically it is the easiest part of the rehabilitation process. Finding a way to enable the drug user to function on his or her own, without drugs, is an arduous task, which promises more disappointment and sadness than success for both helper and client. Nonetheless, a great number of efforts are made, many of them financed heavily by federal and state governments.

Two widely used drug therapy programs for heroin addiction are the administration of _heroin substitutes_ and of _heroin antagonists_. In the first category are _methadone_ and methadyl acetate, both synthetic narcotics. Originally developed by Dole and Nyswander (1966), these agents are designed to take the place of heroin. Since they are themselves narcotics, successful treatment merely converts the heroin addict into a methadone addict. The addict must come to a clinic several times a week and swallow the drug in the presence of a staff member, thereby improving his or her lot by no longer having to resort to needles or to criminal activity to satisfy a physical need. Although early reports were encouraging, problems have been noted as well. For one thing, since methadone does not give the addict a euphoric high, many will return to heroin if it becomes available to them. In addition, when methadone is injected, rather than taken orally as it is supposed to be, its effects on some addicts are similar to those of heroin (Honigfeld and Howard, 1978). Not surprisingly, an illegal market in methadone has developed, which would seem to be defeating the purpose of its use. Finally, a great number of people drop out from methadone programs (Luria, 1970).

Cyclazocine and naloxone are heroin antagonists. After being gradually withdrawn from heroin, addicts receive increasing dosages of either of these drugs, which prevents them from experiencing any high should they later take heroin. The drugs have great affinity for the cells that heroin usually binds to. Their molecules occupy the cells, without stimulating them, and heroin molecules have no place to go. The antagonist, then, changes the whole nature of heroin; it simply will not produce the euphoric effect that the addict seeks. As with methadone, however, addicts must make frequent and regular visits to the clinic, which requires motivation and responsibility on their part. In addition, addicts do not for some time lose the actual craving for heroin.

Drug abuse, though, cannot be dealt with solely by some form of chemotherapy. People turn to drugs for many reasons, and even though in most instances their current drug taking is controlled primarily by a physical addiction, the entire pattern of their existence is bound to be influenced by the drug and must therefore command the attention of whoever would hope to remove the drug from their lives.

Drug abuse is treated in the consulting rooms of psychiatrists, psychologists, and other mental health workers. The several kinds of psychotherapy are applied to drug use disorders as they are to the other human maladjustments. Little can be said, however, about the relative efficacy of psychoanalytic, behavioral, and humanistic therapies in helping people to break their dependence on drugs.

The most widespread psychological approach to heroin addiction and other drug abuse are the self-help residential homes or communes with which most readers are familiar. Modeled after Synanon,[6] a therapeutic community of former drug addicts founded by Charles Dederich in Santa Monica, California, in 1958, these residences are designed to restructure radically the addict's outlook on life so that illicit drugs no longer have a place. Daytop Village, Phoenix House, Odyssey House, and other drug rehabilitation homes share the following features.

1. A total environment in which drugs are not available and continuing support is offered to ease the transition from regular drug use to a drug-free existence.

2. The presence of often charismatic role models, former addicts who appear to be meeting life's challenges without drugs.

3. Direct, often brutal confrontation in group therapy, in which the addict is goaded into accepting responsibility for his problems, and for his drug habit, and urged to take charge of his life.

4. A setting in which the addict is respected as a human being rather than stigmatized as a failure or a criminal.

5. Separation of the addict from previous social contacts, on the assumption that these relationships have been instrumental in fostering the addictive life style.

There are several obstacles to evaluating the efficacy of residential drug treatment programs. First, since entrance is voluntary and the dropout rate high, those who remain cannot be regarded as representative of the population of people addicted to opiates or to other hard drugs. Their motivation to go straight is probably much higher than average; therefore any improvement they might make will in part reflect their uncommon desire to rid themselves of their habit, rather than the specific qualities of the treatment program. Second, the role of mental health professionals is either nonexistent—because of an explicit antagonism toward "shrinks" and social workers—or very marginal; adequately designed research on the outcomes of these programs has not yet been undertaken.

[6] Like its founder, Charles Dederich, who was charged in 1979 for criminal offenses and found unfit to stand trial because of alcoholism and related psychiatric problems, Synanon has fallen on hard times. Emulated by others, Synanon itself eventually lost its mission. It has grown large and wealthy through its business enterprises, and it has been brought to court for acts of violence and for holding residents against their will.

Nicotine and Cigarette Smoking

The history of tobacco smoking bears much similarity to the use of other addictive drugs (Brecher, 1972). Its popularity spread through the world from Columbus's commerce with the native American Indians. It did not take long for sailors and merchants to imitate the Indians' smoking of rolled leaves of tobacco—and to experience, as the Indians did, the increasing craving for the stuff. When not smoked, tobacco was chewed or else ground into small pieces and inhaled as snuff.

Some idea of the addictive qualities of tobacco can be appreciated by considering how much people would sacrifice to maintain their supplies. In sixteenth-century England, for example, tobacco was exchanged for silver ounce for ounce. Poor people squandered their meager resources for their several daily pipefuls. Even the public tortures and executions engineered as punishment by the Sultan Murad IV of Turkey during the seventeenth century could not dissuade those of his subjects who were addicted to the weed.

Prevalence and Consequences of Smoking

The threat to health that smoking poses has been documented convincingly by the United States Surgeon General in a series of reports since 1964. Among the medical problems associated with, and almost certainly caused or exacerbated by, long-term cigarette smoking are lung cancer, emphysema, cancer of the larynx and of the esophagus, and a number of circulatory diseases. These ill tidings appear, after many years, to be having some limited influence on smokers and their consumption of tobacco. Since the first report there has been a welcome decrease in smoking among adults (Warner, 1977). And yet about 54 million American adults still smoke about 620 billion cigarettes a year. What is even more alarming, smoking among teenage boys did not at once change and that among teenage girls actually *increased*. Perhaps of even greater concern is that children have been taking up the habit at earlier ages. In 1968 it was estimated that about 12 percent of young people between twelve and eighteen years of age were regular smokers; in 1974 the numbers smoking regularly had risen to 16 percent (National Institutes of Health, 1976). And of youngsters between the ages of twelve and fourteen, 12 percent were smokers in 1974 as compared to 6 percent in 1968. The attraction of smoking for young people has caused concern, particularly since it is very difficult to give up once the habit and the addiction have been established.

Recently gathered statistics suggest that daily smoking among young people is finally reversing its upward trend. According to a 1980 survey of high school seniors conducted by University of Michigan researchers on behalf of the National Institute on Drug Abuse, 21 percent smoked cigarettes daily as compared to 29 percent in 1977, a drop of more than 25 percent. And even though the young women in the survey still smoked more than the young men, their rate of decline since 1977 was found to be especially steep. The researchers surmise that the widely publicized health dangers of smoking may be making an impact. Peer pressures against smoking also appear to be growing stronger: in 1975 over half the seniors, 55 percent, believed that their friends would disapprove of their smoking, but in 1980 a full 74 percent thought so (*ADAMHA News*, February 9, 1981). If these trends are maintained, there is reason to anticipate still further declines in smoking among young adults.

Since most cigarette smokers take up the habit in their teens, researchers have investigated the reasons why young people begin smoking. Evidence currently available suggests that pressure from peers and having parents who smoke are important factors (Evans and Henderson, 1979). It is common knowledge that teenagers are strongly influenced by standards set by their age-cohorts; conformity is not a trivial characteristic of young people, as any visit to a junior high or high school confirms. Especially strong is the influence of a "best friend." Levitt and Edwards (1970) found a significant correlation between smoking in young people from the fifth through twelfth grades and having friends who smoked.[7]

---

[7] Since the studies mentioned are all correlational, cause-effect conclusions can be drawn only tentatively.

Whether parents and siblings smoke has also been determined to be a major factor. In fact, if both parents and an older sibling smoke, a youngster is four times as likely to smoke than if none of the other family members does.

Cigarette smoking is an enormous health hazard in this country and around the world. It was estimated that in 1978 the health costs associated with cigarettes in the United States were $27 billion (Pinney, 1979) and that 325,000 died prematurely as a result of smoking (United States Department of Health, Education and Welfare, 1979). Most people who smoke acknowledge that it is hazardous to their health and yet they continue to engage in what might be viewed as suicidal behavior. Perhaps one of the most tortured addicts was Sigmund Freud, who continued smoking up to twenty cigars a day in the full knowledge that they were seriously taxing his heart and causing cancerous growths in his mouth. With his jaw later almost entirely removed and replaced by an awkward artificial one, Freud suffered great difficulty swallowing and endured excruciating pain. But he was still unable to bear the anguish of abstaining. Although many heavy smokers do succeed in stopping, Freud's tragic case was certainly not the exception.

The health hazards are not restricted to those who smoke. The smoke coming from the burning end of a cigarette, the so-called sidestream smoke, contains higher concentrations of ammonia, carbon monoxide, nicotine, and tar than does the smoke actually inhaled by the smoker. Nonsmokers can suffer lung damage, possibly permanent, from extended exposure to cigarette smoke (Bennet, 1980). Moreover, when mothers-to-be smoke, their infants are more likely to be born prematurely and to have lower birth weights and birth defects.

In recent years various local governments have passed, or tried to pass, ordinances regulating where cigarettes may or may not be smoked in public places. In New York City, for example, it is against the law to smoke in supermarkets and on elevators; similar laws exist on a statewide basis in Minnesota and Utah. Many nonsmokers express enthusiastic approval of such measures, but pressure from smokers and from the tobacco industry sometimes defeats efforts to enact them.

The objections of smokers to what they view as undue infringement on their rights often find virulent expression. Otherwise amiable, law-abiding people become defensive and even combative when threatened with such restrictions on their freedom, which appears consistent with the view that heavy cigarette smoking is an addiction.

Is Smoking an Addiction?

In the literature on smoking, however, there has been controversy whether _nicotine_ is an addictive drug. It would be a serious mistake to overlook the social and psychological factors that encourage people to _begin_ smoking. For some, smoking is a necessary and pleasurable accompaniment of their relaxing activities. One authority speculates that cigarette smoking is part and parcel of coping with social situations and of establishing identity in our achievement-oriented society; therefore its benefits may outweigh the accepted physical dangers (Mausner, 1973).

Part of the addiction controversy may stem from a failure to distinguish among different kinds of smokers. These smoking more than two packs a day may well be addicted to nicotine, whereas those who limit smoking, for example, to social situations, and consume less than a pack a day do indeed smoke from habit, but they may not be addicted.

Although upwards of four million American smokers are estimated to quit on their own each year, over three-quarters of them return to smoking within twelve months. Krasnegor (1979), a research psychologist at the National Institute on Drug Abuse, hypothesizes that the pain of withdrawal from nicotine is the culprit. Regular smokers trying to escape from the weed report problems such as disruption of sleep, nausea, headaches, constipation, excessive eating, increased anxiety, difficulty in concentrating, irritability—in short, all the signs and symptoms we are accustomed to seeing portrayed humorously by screen characters or displayed by friends and loved ones in the throes of "nicotine fits." And these withdrawal symptoms can persist for many weeks, even months. As with other addictions, the most readily available relief is a bit more of the same—another cigarette and the nicotine it

Most cigarette smokers report that their habit is relaxing (Ikard, Green, and Horn, 1968), yet smoking a cigarette typically increases the heart rate from fifteen to twenty-five beats per minute, as well as elevating blood pressure (United States Department of Health, Education and Welfare, 1964). An experiment was designed to investigate these two paradoxical effects.

Nesbitt (1973) arranged for both smokers and nonsmokers to undergo a series of increasingly uncomfortable electric shocks under three conditions: when not smoking, when smoking a high-nicotine cigarette, and when smoking a low-nicotine cigarette. He reasoned that if smoking is at the same time physiologically arousing yet psychologically relaxing to *regular smokers,* they would endure greater levels of painful shock when smoking and would also endure even more shock when smoking a high-nicotine cigarette than

FIGURE **10.1**

Average numbers of shocks endured by smokers compared to those endured by nonsmokers taking in the same amounts of nicotine. After Nesbitt, 1973.

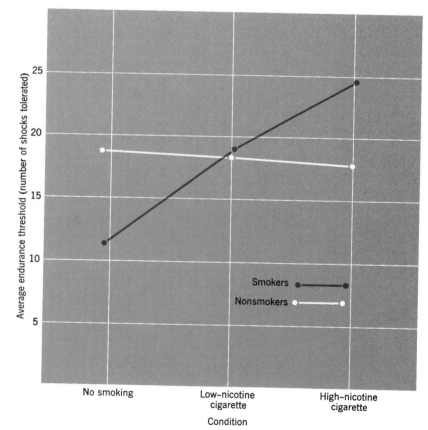

when smoking one low in nicotine. Inasmuch as nonsmokers were not expected to experience a cigarette as relaxing, he did not believe that he would find this improvement in ability to endure shock among the subjects of the nonsmoker control group.

First, by monitoring the heartbeats of his subjects with the electrocardiograph, he was able to demonstrate that smoking a cigarette does indeed increase heart rate, especially when the cigarette contains a high concentration of nicotine. More interesting was the ability of a regular smoker to endure increasingly higher-voltage electric shock as a function of whether he was smoking. As Figure 10.1 indicates, regular smokers took more shock when smoking, especially when smoking a high-nicotine cigarette. Smoking did not alter the shock-taking behavior of the nonsmokers.

Assuming that increased endurance of shock is a valid measure of reducing anxiety, Nesbitt concluded that smoking relaxes those who are accustomed to smoking, even while physiological arousal is increasing. Nonsmokers, unfamiliar with the effects of smoking—indeed, feeling even somewhat queasy—do not relax psychologically while physiologically aroused by cigarettes. Nesbitt proposed then that there does seem to be a paradox in smoking: although cigarettes arouse any smoker physiologically, they relax regular smokers psychologically.

These results can be interpreted in another way, however. Perhaps rather than actually helping smokers feel better, absorbing the drug nicotine before the shock tolerance test merely kept them from feeling *worse* because it prevented withdrawal. The increased shock tolerance of regular smokers, particularly after they had smoked a high-nicotine cigarette, might mean merely that they did not feel especially bad rather than that the cigarette had done something positive for them (Silverstein, 1976).

provides to a body grown dependent on it (see Box 10.4). Nonsmokers tend to berate the nicotine addict with allegations of no will power and lack of concern for self and others. From all we know, however, these people are waging an extremely difficult battle with a true addiction (Jarvik, 1979). In fact, it has been estimated that one out of five people who has refrained from smoking for as long as nine years continues at least occasionally to crave a cigarette (Fletcher and Doll, 1969).

Evidence collected in Stanley Schachter's laboratory of Columbia University more clearly supports the notion that smoking is an addiction. He has shown that smokers adjust their habit to maintain a relatively constant level of nicotine in their systems (Schachter, 1977) and has suggested further that their rate of smoking is controlled by the pH (a measure of acidity-alkalinity) of the urine. Said another way, "The smoker's mind is in his bladder" (Schachter, Silverstein, and Perlik, 1977). Urinary pH is related to smoking in the following way. When urine is acidic,

nicotine is excreted at a greater rate than when urine is nonacidic. Therefore when urine is acidic, there should be more smoking to replace the nicotine being excreted. This prediction was confirmed in a study in which smokers ingested vitamin C; their urine was acidified and their rate of smoking increased (Schachter, Kozlowski, and Silverstein, 1977). Furthermore, if Schachter's thesis is correct, smoking should also increase in other circumstances that acidify the urine. Stress appears to operate in this fashion, increasing both the acidity of the urine and smoking (Silverstein, Kozlowski, and Schachter, 1977; Schachter et al., 1977). The usual effects of stress can even be short-circuited via a manipulation that prevents urine from becoming too acidic. After drinking sodium bicarbonate, which makes urine more alkaline, subjects under stress did not increase their smoking (Schachter, Silverstein, and Perlik, 1977).

The rather general agreement that nicotine is addictive, and that at least heavy smokers are addicted, has raised concern about the proliferation of low-nicotine cigarettes. Smokers who switch to such cigarettes in the numbers they are accustomed to smoke each day will experience acute withdrawal symptoms, as happens to smokers who stop "cold turkey" in an effort to abstain from cigarettes altogether (Schachter, 1977). Regular smokers will therefore smoke more of these "improved" cigarettes or take greater numbers of puffs and inhale more deeply than they did when smoking those containing higher levels of nicotine. Thus Schachter (1978) questions current social policy that encourages the development and marketing of low-nicotine cigarettes. Since the products of incomplete combustion of tar during the smoking process itself, rather than nicotine, are the principal agents causing cancer and other harm, it might be preferable to develop low-tar—*high*-nicotine cigarettes; these would provide the nicotine addict with the drug he or she craves but at the same time reduce the risks associated with tar. Nicotine may, however, through stimulation, bring on cardiovascular disease. All things considered, it is better not to begin smoking at all, or, if the habit is established, to concentrate personal and professional efforts on reducing or eliminating it.

Treatment and Prevention of Cigarette Smoking

Of the twenty-nine million smokers who have quit since 1964, it is believed that 95 percent did so without professional help (National Cancer Institute, 1977).[8] Some smokers attend smoking clinics or consult with professionals for specialized smoking reduction programs. The American Cancer Society and the Church of the Seventh Day Adventists have been especially active in offering programs to help people stop smoking. There is also considerable social support nowadays for smokers to stop. Indeed, as mentioned earlier, more and more nonsmokers object to people smoking in restaurants, trains, airplanes, and public buildings. The social con-

text, then, provides many more incentives to stop smoking than existed nearly twenty years ago, when the Surgeon General first warned of the serious health hazards associated with cigarette smoking. Even so it is estimated that not more than half of those who go through smoking cessation programs succeed in abstaining by the time the program is over; and only about one-third of those who have succeeded in the short term actually remain away from cigarettes after a year (Hunt and Bespalec, 1974).

The most encouraging results come from behavioral programs, especially those employing so-called *rapid-smoking treatment* (Lando, 1977; Lichtenstein and Danaher, 1977). The procedure calls for a smoker to sit in a poorly ventilated room and puff much faster than normal, perhaps as often as every six seconds. After a number of such daily sessions, many smokers report less desire to smoke; in fact, as might be expected, the rapid-smoking sessions make most of the participants ill. In aversive-conditioning terms rapid smoking uses the natural consequences of the act, smoke, as an aversive UCS to discourage puffing on a cigarette. What appears to be a promising behavior therapy procedure may, however, also be dangerous to the health of some smokers, especially those with cardiopulmonary disease—ironically those who most need to stop smoking (Horan, Linberg, and Hackett, 1977).

Unfortunately, research on smoking cessation is marred by numerous methodological errors and procedural oversights; in particular, most studies fail to include a placebo group, in order to assess the contributions of faith and expectancy (Pechacek, 1979). When placebo effects are not evaluated, even meager achievements cannot be attributed to the program or method being examined.

Behavioral treatments have thus far focused on the overt act of smoking. Given the addictive nature of the smoking habit, the disappointing results are not surprising. Until more is known of how to eliminate the addiction or at least of how ex-smokers might learn to tolerate withdrawal symptoms for long periods of time, it is unrealistic to expect great advances in treatment.

And yet, as important as addiction is in heavy smoking, smoker A may also have trouble quit-

---

[8] It is interesting, perhaps disconcerting, that virtually no investigations have been conducted on these large numbers of people who quit without being in a formal program. What enables a particular individual to stop? How does this person survive the withdrawal from nicotine, a hellish period of time that can last for months, some say even years? What homegrown techniques do these people use? What commonalities exist among these do-it-yourselfers?

ting for psychological reasons, and they may be quite different from those plaguing smoker B. When two such smokers are exposed to the same treatment package, the outcomes are likely to be different. This seems sensible enough; unfortunately, in their zeal to make an impact on the smoking problem, workers have for many years put smokers in standardized programs. There are probably a number of reasons why people have trouble quitting, which means that there will have to be diverse methods to help them stop.

In light of the difficulties in desisting from smoking once the habit and addiction are established, *prevention* of smoking, developing ways of discouraging young people even from experimenting with tobacco, has become a top priority among health researchers, with encouragement from the Surgeon General. What measures hold promise for persuading young people to resist smoking? Although many young people now apparently do fear disastrous consequences later in life and resist cigarettes, smokers, young and old alike, seem able to discount the possibility that they are at higher risk of coronary heart disease or lung cancer—the "It won't happen to me" syndrome. Indeed, although heavy smokers are eleven times as likely as nonsmokers to develop lung cancer, large numbers of heavy smokers live longer and healthier lives than do nonsmokers. Our scientific understanding of how environmental dangers interact with individual differences in body chemistry is limited; responsible scientists are not able to "guarantee" a twelve-year-old that his or her own particular body will deteriorate more quickly from smoking than if the habit were never established. Moreover, young people have a limited time perspective. Teenagers would seem to be occupied more with next Saturday evening's festivities or next Friday's math exam than with their life situation at age sixty.

The fact that more and more adults are quitting may influence young people. Whether an admired teacher or health professional smokes can be expected to affect a young person's decision to begin or continue. An interesting disparity between the actual and believed rate of smoking among teachers suggests an intervention. In one survey close to 70 percent of teen-agers thought it likely that their teachers smoked (Jarvik et al., 1977). Another survey, however, found that only about 20 percent of teachers do in fact smoke (American Cancer Society, 1976). Perhaps conveying more accurate information to students would allow them to regard teachers as nonsmokers.

Recent programs in the public schools may prove effective. Aware of the effects of peer pressure, Evans has developed films that portray teenagers resisting appeals from friends to try smoking. The hope is that youngsters will acquire assertive ways and refuse invitations to partake. McAlister, another researcher, has focused on enhancing the self-esteem of young people, on the assumption that, feeling good about themselves, they will be better equipped to stand up to social pressure and perhaps even ridicule. Preliminary findings are promising (*ADAMHA News*, November 2, 1979).

Millions of Americans, most of them reasonable and intelligent, smoke cigarettes from packages bearing the ominous label "Warning—The Surgeon General Has Determined That Cigarette Smoking Is Dangerous to Your Health." Few challenges to behavioral and medical scientists are more important and difficult than to understand better why people begin smoking, why they continue, and why it is so very difficult for most of them to give up the habit.

Marijuana

Marijuana consists of the dried and crushed leaves and flowering tops of the hemp plant, *Cannabis sativa*. It is most often smoked, but it may be chewed, prepared as a tea, or eaten in baked goods. *Hashish,* much stronger than marijuana, is produced by removing and drying the resin exude of the tops of high-quality cannabis plants. Both marijuana and hashish have been known for thousands of years, and their poor reputation among the general public dates back many centuries. For example, the English word assassin comes from the Arabic word *hashshāshīn,* which means those addicted to hashish, and which was the name given an order of Muslims who took hashish and murdered Christians at the time of the Crusades. In early American history the plant was extensively cultivated, not for smoking but for its fibers, which were used in the manufacture of cloth and rope. By the nineteenth century the medicinal properties of *Cannabis* resin were noted, and it was a recommended treatment for rheumatism, gout, depression, cholera, and neuralgia, as well as being smoked for pleasure. Until 1920 marijuana was little seen in the United States, but with the passage of the Eighteenth Amendment, which prohibited the sale of alcohol, marijuana began to be brought across the border from Mexico and smoked for intoxication by members of the lower classes. Unfavorable reports in the press attributing crimes to marijuana use led to the enactment of a federal law against the sale of the drug in 1937.

Patterns of Marijuana Use

According to periodic surveys conducted by the National Institute on Drug Abuse, marijuana use has been increasing significantly in recent years, especially among young people. Some of the data can be summarized as follows (Marijuana Research Findings, 1980; National Survey on Drug Abuse, 1979).

1. In 1979, 8 percent of twelve- and thirteen-year-olds had tried marijuana at least once. For ages fourteen and fifteen the percentage was up to 32, and by ages sixteen and seven-teen 51 percent of youths had used the drug. Overall, for the twelve-to-seventeen age group, those who had used marijuana at least once increased from 14 percent in 1972 to 31 percent in 1979.

2. Daily use of marijuana by high school seniors increased markedly between 1975 and 1979: whereas in 1975 only 5.8 percent of this group reported daily use, 10.3 percent did so in 1979.[9]

3. Marijuana use appears to be beginning at earlier ages, as evidenced by annual surveys of high school seniors. Thus 16.9 percent of the class of 1975 had used the drug before the tenth grade. This percentage rose steadily with the classes of 1976, 22.3 percent; 1977, 25.2 percent; 1978, 28.2 percent, and 1979, which reported 30.4 percent. From 1975 to 1979, then, the percentage of high school seniors who had been introduced to marijuana in the ninth grade or earlier nearly doubled.

4. From 1971 to 1974 the percentage of adults ages eighteen to twenty-five who had tried marijuana at least once jumped from 39 to 53 percent. By 1979 the percentage was up to 68. And in this group current use, defined as having used the drug some time during the month preceding the particular survey, is also up, from 27 percent in 1977 to 35 percent in 1979.

5. Among eighteen-to-twenty-five-year-olds, 40 percent reported in 1979 having used marijuana more than 100 times in their lives. Of those using it on a regular basis, two-thirds do so five or more days a month.

6. For people over twenty-six years of age, use

---

[9] As noted earlier for cigarette smoking, recent surveys of high school seniors indicate a drop in marijuana use from 1979 to 1980; daily use of the drug was down by 12 percent in just one year (Reinhold, 1981). This decrease and similar decreases in the use of inhalants and hallucinogens like PCP (angel dust) may reflect a growing recognition and acceptance by young people of the documented dangers of many of the illicit drugs. Nonetheless, the 12 percent decline in daily marijuana use among high school seniors still finds more than 9 percent using the drug on a daily basis and millions more Americans smoking or eating it with some frequency. Although the latest statistics are encouraging, at least to those who believe marijuana is dangerous, it is too soon to know whether this one-year dip will be maintained in coming years.

Early recreational use of hashish in a fashionable apartment in New York City. An 1876 issue of the *Illustrated Police News* carried this picture with the title "Secret Dissipation of New York Belles: Interior of a Hasheesh Hell on Fifth Avenue."

was much lower as of 1979 than in the younger age groups just reviewed. Even so, usage among these individuals had also increased over preceding years. Thus, whereas 7.4 percent had used marijuana at least once in 1972, nearly 20 percent had in 1979.

7. Although men have consistently been heavier users of marijuana than women, women are using the drug more often now; the sex difference can be expected to vanish before too long.

8. Marijuana use was, in the early 1970s, far more prevalent among adults who had attended college than among those who had not. This difference was virtually gone by 1979.

9. During 1978 it is estimated that more than twenty-six million Americans used marijuana at least once, nearly 20 percent more than in 1976.

In sum, although there are regional differences, use being greater in the West and the Northeast than in other parts of the United States, millions of Americans, ranging considerably in age but from the high school and even junior high ranks in particular, are smoking marijuana.

Reasons for Use

For a number of years it has been fairly obvious why marijuana is popular, and recent surveys confirm earlier impressions. People report enjoying good feelings of being "high" and relaxed, usually without the hangover common with alcohol. They generally find that space seems larger, time is drawn out, and perceptions are enhanced; a feeling of serene detachment and composure is created. Many consider marijuana an easy escape from their everyday lives; and many value the sociality of sharing joints and the accompanying camaraderie—sitting quietly with friends and acquaintances, touching, conversing, listening to music, and so forth. Devotees of rock concerts and science fiction movies assert that more interesting and intense experiences are available to them if they get high before or during performances. Now that penalties for use of marijuana have been reduced and people in all walks of life are among its champions, the sweet scent of marijuana smoke in parks and even some theaters has become almost commonplace in some parts of the country.

In the middle and late 1960s, when social activism among young people was prevalent, use of marijuana appeared to have political and generational significance. Along with psilocybin and LSD, marijuana was declared to be the drug of the young, and its illegality may have enhanced its appeal among those who were in their then magical years below the age of thirty. By the same token, the harsh penalties meted out to those unlucky enough to be caught may have reflected the antipathy felt by the "establishment" toward the long-haired, raucous, and politically radical youth counterculture, which appeared to pose a threat to standards and institutions. Thus marijuana may have been viewed as abetting the destruction of the prevalent social order. There are few perceived threats a society reacts more strongly against than that of its own destruction.

According to current information, marijuana is no longer the drug of the young or a chemical used for making sociopolitical statements. But do its markedly increased availability and usage reflect commensurately more positive attitudes toward marijuana? Not necessarily, according to recent surveys. For example, nearly three-quarters of youth, people between the ages of twelve and seventeen, and 79 percent of people older than twenty-six believe either that marijuana should be illegal or that laws against use should be even stricter than at present. Of the eighteen-to-twenty-five-year-olds, whose usage is greatest, a full 40 percent advocate these restrictive positions. And in 1979, when more than a third of high school seniors were using the drug at least occasionally, two-thirds disapproved of regular use, as they did of regular use of alcohol and conventional cigarettes. In addition, almost half of those between the ages of twelve and twenty-five believe that marijuana is addictive, compared to over 80 percent who regard alcohol and heroin as such (National Survey of Drug Abuse, 1979). Thus resistance to legalizing the drug is considerable, and a significant proportion

of people disapprove of regular use.[10] Perhaps attitudes will become even more adamant as new findings emerge on both the short-term and long-term psychological and physical consequences of smoking marijuana.

Effects of Marijuana

A great deal of research has been conducted on marijuana in recent years. Because any discussion of the drug has inevitable social and political overtones, the evidence needs to be considered as soberly as possible. Marijuana, like most other drugs, is apparently not without its risks. Science has generally found that the more we learn about a drug, the less benign it turns out to be, and marijuana is no exception.

Psychological effects of marijuana

The intoxicating effects of marijuana, as of most drugs, depend in part on potency and size of the dose. We have already stated that smokers of marijuana find it makes them feel relaxed and sociable. Large doses have been reported to bring rapid shifts in emotion, to dull attention, fragment thought, and impair memory. Extremely heavy doses have sometimes been found to induce hallucinations and other effects similar to those of LSD.

The major active chemical in marijuana has been isolated and named delta-9-tetrahydrocannabinol (THC). Since 1974 the marijuana available in this country has come from Jamaica, Mexico, and Colombia and has been very potent, as much as ten times stronger than that sold earlier.[11] Thus in the early 1970s the most widely available domestic *Cannabis* contained about a fifth of a percent of THC; samples studied in 1979, in contrast, averaged more than 2 percent. Hash oil, a concentrated liquid marijuana extract only recently available on the street, has been found to be as much as 28 per-

---

[10] Those who use marijuana may not be the same people who express negative attitudes toward it. Nonetheless, the widespread objection to the drug as well as its frequent use should be appreciated.

[11] The potency of the leaves is thought to vary with the region in which the hemp plant is cultivated. The leaves of plants grown in hot, relatively dry climates contain larger amounts of THC.

cent THC. The picture is complicated, however, by the fact that *Cannabis* contains more than 400 compounds, in addition to THC. Many of these compounds are believed to exert psychological effects either by themselves or in conjunction with one another and with THC.

Let us examine more closely the psychological effects of marijuana. An abundance of scientific evidence indicates that marijuana interferes with a wide range of cognitive functions. And since *Cannabis* available in recent years is stronger, actual short-term effects on people's minds are probably greater than they were found to be in the laboratory studies, which were conducted for the most part in the late 1960s. A number of tests—digit-symbol substitution (substituting symbols for numbers), reaction time tests, repeating series of digits forward and backward, arithmetic calculations, reading comprehension and speech tests—all revealed intellectual impairment (Marijuana Research Findings, 1980). Of special significance are loss of short-term memory and state-dependent learning, the inability, when sober, to recall material learned when high. Given both the numbers of high school students who use marijuana regularly and the strength of *Cannabis* today, it would seem that significant numbers of students may be seriously hindering their learning.

Several studies have demonstrated that being high on marijuana diminishes complex psychomotor skills necessary for driving. And highway fatality and driver arrest figures indicate that marijuana plays a role in a significant proportion of accidents and arrests; a recent study in California, for example, found that of 1800 blood samples taken from people arrested for driving while intoxicated, 24 percent had detectable levels of marijuana (Reeve, 1979, cited in Marijuana Research Findings, 1980). Marijuana has similarly been found to impair manipulation of flight simulators. Some performance decrements can persist even after a person believes he or she is no longer high, creating the very real danger that people will attempt to drive or to fly when they are not functioning adequately.

Does long-term use of marijuana affect intellectual functioning in any sort of consistent way? Studies requiring memory and problem solving conducted in Egypt and in India in the late 1970s indicated some deterioration in users compared to nonusers (Soueif, 1976; Wig and Varma, 1977). It is impossible to know, however, whether these differences existed before heavy drug use and whether they might have been associated with poor diet. American college students do not show these deficits, so it would be premature to conclude that chronic use of the drug brings intellectual deterioration.

People who have had psychological problems before using any psychoactive drug are generally believed to be at highest risk for having negative reactions to it. Until recently, anxiety, general distress, and paranoia from marijuana intoxication were infrequently reported. But the more people who try marijuana, especially the stronger type now available, the more likely, on a strictly statistical basis, is it to be used by those who might become frightened by the altered sensations and the feeling of lost control. The federally sponsored Drug Abuse Warning Network is a nationwide system that provides information on how often drug use is implicated when people seek help in such places as hospital emergency rooms; between May 1976 and April 1977 marijuana ranked thirteenth among drugs that were mentioned, but during 1978 it rose to sixth place.

Somatic effects of marijuana

Some preliminary, tentative evidence indicates that marijuana may be harmful to reproduction. Two studies of male chronic users found lower sperm counts and less motility of the spermatozoa, suggesting that fertility might be decreased, especially in men who are already marginally fertile (Hembree, Nahas, and Huang, 1979; Issidorides, 1979). It is conceivable, notes the 1980 Public Health Service Marijuana Report, that negative effects on sperm may be greatest in young smokers. The junior high and high school male students of today may be tampering with their present and future fertility.

As for female reproduction, a study with female "street users" yielded consistent findings, namely frequent failure to ovulate normally and shortened fertility periods. Moreover, researchers have discovered that marijuana constituents can cross the placental barrier[12] in rats and thus may affect the development of a fetus (Vardaris et al., 1976). Experiments with female rhesus monkeys, using THC levels comparable to fairly heavy use by human beings, found abnormally frequent loss of the fetus in those who became pregnant (Sassenrath, Chapman and Goo, 1979). Marijuana also shows up in the milk of squirrel monkeys to whom the drug is administered, thus raising the possibility that nursing mothers may pass on its effects to their babies (Chao et al., 1976). All these studies have their share of methodological problems, but the outcomes for animals and human beings do raise the possibility that moderate and heavy use of marijuana interferes with reproduction. People interested in bearing children need to exercise caution and prudence.

In the short term marijuana makes the eyes bloodshot and itchy, dries the mouth and throat, increases appetite, and may raise blood pressure somewhat. There is no evidence that smoking marijuana has untoward effects on the normal heart. The drug apparently poses a danger to people with already abnormal heart function, however, for it does elevate heart rate, sometimes dramatically. As a NIDA report suggests, this fact may become of particular concern as present smokers grow older. The relatively healthy thirty-year-old marijuana users of today are the fifty-year-olds of tomorrow with a statistically greater chance of having a cardiovascular system impaired for other reasons, such as heart disease. It they are still using the drug then, their hearts will be more vulnerable to its effects. In addition, it is possible that long-term use of marijuana, like the chronic use of tobacco, may be harmful in ways that cannot be predicted from the short-term effects studied so far (Jones, 1980).

Indications are that long-term use of marijuana may seriously impair lung structure and function. Even though marijuana users smoke far fewer cigarettes than do persons using tobacco, most inhale marijuana smoke more deeply and retain it in their lungs for much longer periods of time.

Any harmful elements present in marijuana smoke may exert effects far greater than would be expected were only the absolute number of cigarettes or pipefuls considered. What are these unfavorable pulmonary effects? First, a research team at the University of California at Los Angeles found that the amount of air a person can expel following a deep breath, called vital capacity, is reduced as much from smoking one marijuana cigarette a day as from smoking sixteen conventional cigarettes a day (Tashkin et al., 1978, cited in Marijuana Research Findings, 1980). Second, since marijuana cigarettes are generally ''homemade,'' they are not filtered as are most tobacco cigarettes nowadays; the smoke contains significantly higher levels of tar which, like the tar from conventional cigarettes, has been found to cause cancer when applied to the skin of laboratory animals. Moreover, because marijuana smoke also contains 70 percent more benzopyrene, another known cancer-causing agent, than do regular cigarettes, the risk of lung cancer from regular, prolonged use of marijuana cannot be overlooked. Although not yet clearly demonstrated in human beings, another potential hazard is increased susceptibility to infection, specifically a serious form of pneumonia; marijuana smoke reduces the antibacterial defense systems of the lungs.

Some well-known and highly publicized studies of chronic ganja[13] users in Jamaica, Greece, and Costa Rica (Coggins, 1976; Rubin and Comitas, 1976; Stefanis, Bonlougouris, and Liakos, 1976), however, did not uncover lung pathology associated with regular use of the drug. But, as the 1980 report from the United States Public Health Service suggests, users in these countries do not inhale the smoke as deeply or retain it in their lungs as long as Americans seem to. It may not be prudent, therefore, to rely on findings from other countries.

Whether marijuana is addictive has been a matter of some interest. Recent information suggests that indeed marijuana may be, contrary to widespread earlier belief that it is not. It began to be suspected that tolerance could develop when American servicemen returned from Viet-

---

[12] The placenta is the porous membrane forming the sac in which a fetus develops. In studying whether a chemical in the pregnant woman's body might affect the fetus, scientists try to determine whether it can permeate the placenta or whether this membrane filters it out. If the agent can get through this barrier, there is presumptive—suggestive but not definite—evidence that the fetus is affected.

[13] Ganga is the *Cannabis* smoked especially in India and in some other countries as well.

nam accustomed to concentrations of THC that would be toxic to domestic users. Controlled observations have confirmed that habitual use of marijuana does produce tolerance (Nowlan and Cohen, 1977). Whether long-term users suffer physical withdrawal when accustomed amounts of marijuana are not available is less clear. After a period of heavier-than-normal smoking in the laboratory, appetite is lost and other withdrawal symptoms such as irritability, nausea, and diarrhea do develop when it is stopped (Jones, 1977; Jones and Benowitz, 1976). Withdrawal was also found in a study in which users selected their own number of joints, smoked in their usual manner, and then stopped (Mendelson, Rossi, and Meyer, 1974). Future studies may confirm these initial indications that long-term, heavy use of marijuana can be addicting.

Ours is known to be a drug-taking culture. At any one time many individuals have circulating in their bloodstreams one or more chemicals that have been swallowed, injected, sniffed, or smoked. How drugs *interact* with one another, the combination of marijuana and alcohol in particular, is of no little concern. People often take these two drugs together or close enough in time for them to be mixing in the body.

Evidence from studies of both animals and human beings indicate that simultaneous use of alcohol and marijuana more seriously impairs perception, cognition, and motor activity than does either drug alone. The synergistic effect also extends to physiological processes; for example, heart rate is faster and eyes become more bloodshot. Marijuana can enhance the effects of other drugs such as barbiturates and amphetamines. Although this interactive force of THC is complex and inadequately understood, people should be aware of it and govern themselves accordingly (Siemens, 1980).

Therapeutic effects of marijuana

In a seeming irony, therapeutic uses of marijuana have come to light during the same period that negative effects of regular and heavy usage of the drug have been indicated. In the 1970s a number of double-blind studies (for example, Sallan, Zinberg, and Frei, 1975) showed that THC and related drugs can reduce for some cancer patients the nausea and loss of appetite that

accompany chemotherapy. Marijuana often appears to reduce nausea when other antinausea agents fail. It is also a treatment of glaucoma, a disease in which outflow of fluid from the eyeball is obstructed. Abnormally high pressure builds up and vision gradually fails. A 1971 study by Hepler and Frank had shown that smoking marijuana reduced intraocular pressure in normal subjects. This discovery led to clinical trials. Oral ingestion of delta-9-THC, especially when combined with conventional treatment of the eye disease, reduces intraocular pressure in glaucoma sufferers (Hepler, Frank, and Petrus, 1976).

Research continues on these and other therapeutic uses of marijuana, but as yet none is regarded as standard medical practice (Cohen, 1980). Moreover, since such medical treatments tend to be attempted with older people, the potential benefits have to be measured against physical risks. It will be unfortunate if the illegality of marijuana in many states hinders scienfitic study of its positive uses, especially for serious medical conditions inadequately dealt with by existing conventional interventions.[14]

[14] And yet new disclosures reveal risks that may have to be considered even for very ill cancer patients. Dr. Steven Kagen (as reported by *The New York Times*, February 19, 1981) has found that marijuana contains a fungus particularly dangerous to people whose immune systems are impaired, and those of cancer patients undergoing chemotherapy are. In the lungs of a healthy person the immune system fights off the fungus, and the individual suffers mild cough or fever. Patients with immune systems weakened by the drugs fighting their cancer may develop a more serious version of the infection, which can cause death.

LSD and Other Psychedelics

In 1943 a Swiss chemist, Albert Hofmann, recorded a description of an illness he had seemingly contracted.

> Last Friday . . . I had to interrupt my laboratory work . . . I was seized with a feeling of great restlessness and mild dizziness. At home, I lay down and sank into a not unpleasant delirium, which was characterized by extremely exciting fantasies. In a semiconscious state with my eyes closed . . . fantastic visions of extraordinary realness and with an intense kaleidoscopic play of colors assaulted me (cited by Cashman, 1966, p. 31).

Earlier in the day Dr. Hofmann had manufactured a few milligrams of *d*-lysergic acid diethylamide, a drug which he had first synthesized in 1938. Reasoning that he might have unknowingly ingested some and that this was the cause of his unusual experience, he deliberately took a dose and confirmed his hypothesis.

After Hofmann's experiences with *LSD* in 1943, the drug was referred to as psychotomimetic because it was thought to produce effects similar to the symptoms of a psychosis. Then the term *psychedelic,* from the Greek words for soul and to make manifest, was applied to emphasize the subjectively experienced expansion of consciousness reported by users of LSD and two other drugs, *mescaline* and *psilocybin.* In 1896 mescaline, an alkaloid and the active ingredient of peyote, was isolated. Peyote is obtained from small, disklike growths of the top of the peyote cactus, most of which extends below ground. The drug has been used for centuries in the religious rites of Indian peoples living in the Southwest and northern Mexico. Psilocybin is a crystalline powder which Hofmann isolated from the mushroom *Psilocybe mexicana* in 1958. The early Aztec and Mexican cultures called the sacred mushrooms "god's flesh," and the Indians of Mexico still use them in their worship today.

During the 1950s these drugs were given in research settings to study what were thought to be psychotic experiences. In 1960 Timothy Leary and Richard Alpert of Harvard University began an investigation of the effects of psilocybin on institutionalized prisoners. The early results, although subject to several confounds, were encouraging: released prisoners who had had a psilocybin trip proved less likely to be rearrested. At the same time the investigators started taking trips themselves and soon had gathered around them a group of people interested in experimenting with psychedelic drugs. By 1962 their activities had attracted the attention of law enforcement agencies. As the investigation continued, it became a scandal, culminating in Leary and Alpert's departure from Harvard. The scandal seemed to give tremendous impetus to the use of the *hallucinogens,* particularly since the manufacture of LSD and the extraction of mescaline and psilocybin were found to be relatively easy and inexpensive.

After leaving Harvard, Leary and Alpert founded the International Foundation for Internal Freedom, an organization which emphatically espoused the desirability of psychedelic trips. It can probably be said that the proselytizing efforts of Leary and Alpert shifted attention from the supposedly psychotic experiences induced by the drugs to their mind-expanding effects.[15] The user's state of consciousness and intensification of sensory perceptions were considered extremely positive and beautiful. Among the mind expansions often cited and sought after are a marked slowing of time; the feeling that the body and limbs have lost their boundaries with space; a dreamy light-headedness and detachment from reality; gratifying and illuminating images seen in great richness and profusion of colors; occasional synesthesias, the merging of one sense modality with another so that, for example, colors are heard and sounds seen; enlightenments; ecstasy; and a sense of being in empathic connection with all of humankind.

---

[15] Like many of the "old timers" in the psychedelic drug revolution, Alpert now espouses an Eastern meditation philosophy that urges people to forsake drugs and work instead on creating their own meaningful "trips" without the aid of chemical agents. Known as Baba Ram Dass, he has lectured and written eloquently about the possibility of cultivating expanded states of consciousness; those who would devote the necessary time and energy to meditation techniques will be open to such experiences, according to Ram Dass.

BOX   **10.5** PCP—Not an Upper or a Downer But an
Inside-Outer

In 1956 Park, Davis and Company, a large pharmaceutical firm, synthesized a new anesthetic. Although effective in large doses, it was found to cause agitation and disorientation as the patient regained consciousness. When administered in smaller doses, it induced a psychoticlike state. In 1965 this new drug, _phencyclidine,_ was taken off the market, and by 1978 its legal manufacture was discontinued in the United States.

Phencyclidine (PCP) was first seen in illegal use in Los Angeles in 1965. It soon turned up in the Haight-Ashbury district of San Francisco under the name "PeaCe Pill" and was sold as a mild psychedelic, but it quickly gained a bad reputation because many users had negative reactions. In the late 1960s and early 1970s the drug spread to other parts of the country until, by 1979, it had turned up in most states.

As sold on the street, PCP is known by dozens of names—among which are angel dust, cadillac, cozmos, Detroit Pink, embalming fluid, Killerweed, horse crystal, PeaCe Pill, wac, and zombie—and has been marketed falsely as LSD, psilocybin, cocaine, and other drugs. It is available in many forms and degrees of purity and in most colors. In granular

This PCP user became so violent that several policemen
had to use a net to restrain him.

form it is often sold as angel dust and contains between 50 and 100 percent phencyclidine. Angel dust is usually available as mint or parsley that has been sprinkled with PCP powder or liquid and sealed in zip-lock plastic bags. The most popular ways to take PCP are in mint or parsley joints and in commercial cigarettes that have been dipped in liquid PCP or had a string dipped in liquid PCP passed through them. But the drug can also be injected intravenously, swallowed, put in the eyes as drops, "snorted" like cocaine, and smoked in a pipe.

The effects of PCP depend largely on the dosage. The user generally has jerky eye movements (nystagmus) alternating with a blank stare, is unable to walk heel-to-toe in a straight line (gait ataxia), and has great rigidity of the muscles. Hallucinations and delusions are also experienced by some. Individuals become agitated and combative. Some people under the influence are so violent that it takes several others to restrain them. Their incoherence and lack of communicativeness do not allow them to be "talked down" from their high. With very high dosages—actually, as little as a single gram—there are usually a deep and prolonged coma, seizures, apnea or periods of no breathing, sustained high blood pressure, and sometimes even death. No medication to reverse the effects of PCP has yet been found.

Phencyclidine is not an upper or a downer, nor is it a psychedelic. Some workers refer to it as an "inside-outer," a term which to some extent conveys the bizarre and extreme nature of its effects.

How long do the effects of PCP last? The way it is ingested and the dosage seem to play a role. Onset is usually between one and five minutes after smoking a treated cigarette; effects peak after about half an hour and then do not dissipate for up to two days. Since PCP remains in the body for several days, it can accumulate if ingested repeatedly. Chronic users who have taken the drug several times a week for six months experience cognitive distortions and disorientation for several months afterward, even for as long as two years after use has ceased. In addition, the personality often changes, there can be memory loss, and the person may experience severe anxiety, depression, and aggressive urges.

Organ damage has not yet been linked to chronic use of this drug. More than 100 deaths were reported in Los Angeles County in 1978 alone, however. These fatalities were caused in a number of ways. One man who was swimming drowned because he lost his spatial orientation; others have expired because of severe respiratory depression or uncontrollable increase in body temperature. Information about the drug is too limited at this time to know more about its long-term effects. Its addictiveness and other consequences are likely to be difficult to determine because most PCP users take other drugs as well.

In light of how terrifying and dangerous the drug is, why, according to the NIDA survey of 1979, has use increased significantly since 1976 among young people, ages twelve to seventeen, and older adults, twenty-six and over? A number of reasons have been proposed, but given the relative recency of PCP abuse, they are very tentative indeed. The drug is inexpensive and both readily available and easily synthesized in a home laboratory, making it a quick and easy escape from unpleasant realities. Peer pressure may be great among the young to show that one is "tough" enough to stay in control. The sheer intensity of the experience is enticing. And the fact that scare tactics have been applied with other illicit drugs throughout the years reduces the credibility of warnings about PCP.*

* The foregoing is based on *Phencyclidine Abuse Manual*, published 1980 by the University of California Extension, Los Angeles, pursuant to a contract from the State of California Department of Alcohol and Drug Abuse.

Research on the Effects of Psychedelics

The typical dose of LSD is extremely small, from about 100 to 350 micrograms, administered as a liquid absorbed in sugar cubes or as capsules or tablets; for psilocybin the usual dose is about 30,000 micrograms; and for mescaline the usual dose is between 350,000 and 500,000 micrograms. The effects of LSD and mescaline usually last about twelve hours, those of psilocybin about six.

The effects of varying doses of LSD were studied by Klee and his associates (1961). Neither the subjects nor the observers knew the amounts of drug that had been administered. Nonetheless, experienced observers could readily judge the dose levels ingested by a particular subject from his reports of visual effects and from his somatic or bodily reactions, particularly of the sympathetic nervous system; intellectual impairment and also confusion increased with higher doses. There is no indication that LSD or the other psychedelics are addicting.

The effects of the psychedelics, like those of other kinds of drugs, depend on a number of psychological variables in addition to the dose itself. A subject's set, that is, attitudes, expectancies, and motivations about taking drugs, are widely held to be important determinants of reactions to psychedelics.

Some of the individual studies on psychological variables have been relatively simple, others complex. Expectancies were examined by Metzner, Litwin, and Weil (1965). Before receiving 25,000 to 30,000 micrograms of psilocybin, subjects were asked, "How apprehensive are you about taking the drug?" and "How good do you feel about taking the drug today?" Reports of greater apprehension about taking the drug correlated significantly with increased anxiety, headache, and nausea during the drug experience itself. Similarly, Linton and Langs (1964) administered a battery of personality tests before giving the subjects a dose of 100 micrograms of LSD. Those who were judged to be guarded and overdependent on the basis of the personality tests had the greatest number of bodily reactions, particularly of the sympathetic nervous system, and experienced the greatest anxiety during the

LSD session. Persons who had shown themselves to be mistrustful, complaining, and fearful had paranoiac reactions from taking LSD (Klee and Weintraub, 1959; Von Felsinger, Lasagna, and Beecher, 1956).

Pahnke (1963) performed a considerably more remarkable and original piece of research. He attempted to maximize all the situational variables that might contribute to a religious or mystical experience. Subjects in his investigation were theological students who first attended a meeting at which they were told of the possibilities of having religious experiences after taking psilocybin. Twenty students were given psilocybin and twenty an active placebo by a double-blind procedure. Nicotinic acid was given as the placebo because it does produce some effects, such as a tingling sensation in the skin. After receiving the drug or the placebo, each subject participated in a two-and-a-half-hour-long religious service which included meditation, prayers, and the like. To heighten the significance of the occasion, Pahnke had chosen to conduct the experiment on Good Friday. After the service each subject wrote a description of his experience and answered an extensive questionnaire. The mystical and transcendental experiences of the group who took psilocybin were found to be significantly greater than those of the group who took the placebo.

The Problem of Flashbacks

One of the principal concerns about ingesting LSD is the possibility of _flashbacks_—"the transient recurrence of psychedelic drug symptoms after the pharmacologic effects of such drugs have worn off and [there has been] a period of relative normalcy" (Heaton and Victor, 1976, p. 83). Little is known about these flashback "trips" except that they cannot be predicted or controlled. The available evidence does not support the hypothesis that they are caused by drug-produced physical changes in the nervous system. For one thing, only 15 to 30 percent of users of psychedelic drugs are estimated ever to have flashbacks (for example, Stanton and Bardoni, 1972). Moreover, there is no independent evidence of measurable neurological changes in these drug users. The flashback, which seems to have a force of its own and may come to haunt people weeks and months after they have taken the drug, is a very upsetting phenomenon for those it besets.

Heaton and Victor (1976) determined to explore a possible psychological explanation of flashbacks. Heaton had been mindful of previous evidence indicating that extreme relaxation and sensory deprivation can produce in some people sensations and experiences closely similar to those reported during flashbacks. In an earlier study (1975) he had demonstrated that *expectancy* of a flashback increased the chances that former LSD users, after swallowing a placebo capsule and then undergoing mild sensory deprivation, would report such experiences, whether or not they had previously had flashbacks. The belief that they had taken a drug that would produce a flashback proved more important than a past history of such phenomena.

Heaton and Victor therefore speculated that some drug users, believing that flashbacks are likely, may *attend selectively* to naturally occurring altered states of consciousness and then *label* them flashbacks of a previous drug trip. But why would they allow their thinking to take such a course? Employing various scales from the MMPI, the two researchers developed measures of thinking in a logical, reality-oriented fashion and in a looser, inner-fantasizing mode. They then recruited thirty male volunteer drug users from clinics and counseling agencies serving young people, including "street people," in a Western metropolitan area. Half claimed no previous history of flashbacks; the others reported such experiences. The two groups, satisfactorily matched on classificatory variables such as age and numbers of previous psychedelic experiences, were tested on the selected MMPI scales. Then all subjects swallowed a capsule, which they were told would probably produce a flashback in experienced drug users like themselves, and underwent brief sensory deprivation. On a second occasion all subjects were given a different capsule, this time with the expectation that it would *not* produce a flashback. Both capsules were placeboes.

The group of LSD users reporting earlier flashbacks did show significantly more loose fantasizing, as measured by the MMPI scales. They were also found to have poorer social and sexual adjustment, an uneven school and work history, and often a history of bizarre thinking. And the subjects who scored especially high in loose thinking did indeed report many flashback experiences during the sensory deprivation, even when they had been told that the capsule ingested would *not* produce such effects.

Although it is impossible to know whether the personality described predated the tendency to have flashbacks, the results are useful. They suggest that

> Under environmental conditions which pull for altered states of consciousness anyway, [loose-thinking] subjects have less ability (and possibly less desire) to maintain reality-oriented mental activity. . . . [Furthermore,] if the subject labels his initial sensations as the beginning of a flashback, expectations . . . are self-fulfilling to the extent that they selectively direct attention to psychedelic sensations (Heaton and Victor, 1976, p. 89).

A contrasting psychological explanation comes from a study by Matefy (1980), who hypothesized that psychedelic-drug users who have flashbacks may be highly disposed to role taking.

> For example, an individual who frequently "tripped" during a rock music festival might experience flashbacks in [a] similar social crowd. . . . Under appropriate conditions, such as [being given] cues associated with actual drug highs, one may willingly or unwillingly enact the role of a drugged person. Accordingly, subjects experiencing flashbacks should exhibit a greater propensity for deep engrossment in role-playing. . ., resulting in altered feelings and perceptions congruent with the role (p. 551).

To test this hypothesis, Matefy recruited one group of psychedelic-drug users who were experiencing flashbacks and another group who were not. People using no drugs served as controls. Matefy gave all subjects a battery of paper-and-pencil and behavioral tests designed to measure their ability to assume different roles, their willingness to lose themselves in these roles, and their capacity to imagine vividly. Those who experienced flashbacks scored significantly higher than the other two groups on every measure. In essence, they manifested greater ability to submerge themselves in various roles and situations, "reflecting a . . . willingness to relinquish personal control for the sake of a peak experience, and altering of consciousness" (p. 552).

Summary

Using substances to alter mood and behavior is virtually a human characteristic, and so also is the tendency to abuse them. DSM-III follows contemporary practice in distinguishing between substance abuse and substance dependence. Abuse is usage that interferes with a person's customary functioning. Substance dependence, or addiction, is a physiological dependence on a drug in which tolerance builds up—ever-increasing amounts are required to achieve a particular effect—and there are withdrawal reactions should the person desist from taking the drug.

Alcohol has a variety of short-term and long-term effects on human beings, and many are tragic in nature, ranging from poor judgment and motor coordination, and their dire consequences for the alcoholic and society, to addiction, which makes an ordinary productive life impossible and is extremely difficult to overcome. As with other addicting drugs, people come to rely on alcohol less for how good it makes them feel than for an escape from feeling bad.

Less prevalent but more notorious, perhaps because of their illegality, are the so-called hard drugs, the narcotic heroin and the barbiturates such as Seconal, which are sedatives, and the amphetamines and cocaine, which are stimulants. Of these, only cocaine appears at present not to be addicting. Heroin has been of special concern in recent years because stronger varieties have become available. Barbiturates have for some time been implicated in both intentional and accidental suicides; they are especially lethal when alcohol is taken at the same time. Cocaine use has risen dramatically in the past few years; its high cost and elaborate paraphernalia have made it a rather "trendy" drug in some circles.

Nicotine, especially when taken into the body via the inhaled smoke from a cigarette, has worked its addictive power on humankind for centuries and, in spite of somberly phrased warnings from public health officials, continues in widespread use. Of special concern is the smoking of school-aged youngsters and teenagers. Each year the government and private individuals spend millions of dollars to dissuade people from beginning the habit or to help those already addicted to desist from smoking; and each year millions of dollars are spent by the government and private individuals promoting the cultivation and sale of tobacco products. Neither the psychological-medical nor economic-political issues have easy solutions.

But of all the drugs around which controversy swirls, none generates more furor than marijuana. Its use by Americans has veritably skyrocketed in recent years, and it is being tried at earlier ages. About one-third of Americans between the ages of eighteen and twenty-five smoke marijuana with some frequency. Arguments for deregulation of marijuana have stressed its supposed safety, in comparison to the known harm caused by the habitual use of alcohol, which is a legal and integral part of our culture. But currently available evidence indicates that marijuana when used with regularity is not benign. Significantly stronger varieties of marijuana are now available than were in the early 1970s. Furthermore, there is evidence that marijuana constituents may adversely affect fertility, fetal development, heart function in people who already have coronary problems, and pulmonary function. The debate continues whether marijuana is addicting; although withdrawal has not been conclusively demonstrated, it does appear that tolerance develops over time. Ironically, at the same time that the possible dangers of this drug began to be uncovered, marijuana was found to ease the nausea of cancer patients undergoing chemotherapy and to reduce the excessive intraocular pressure of glaucoma sufferers.

Phencyclidine, known as PCP or angel dust, is a newcomer on the drug abuse scene. Concern about it dwarfs that surrounding other illicit drugs, for people on PCP are unpredictable and often violent and have such seriously impaired judgment that they can inadvertently kill themselves.

The so-called psychedelics, LSD, mescaline, and psilocybin, are taken by many to alter or expand consciousness. Their continuing popularity attests to humankind's desires not only to escape from unpleasant realities but probably to explore inner space as well.

Therapies to discourage usage of many of these drugs are often confrontational in nature. Residential and outpatient programs confront alcoholics and other drug addicts with the immorality or stupidity of their behavior and encourage in them a resolve to alter the mode of their lives, leaving no room for chemical crutches. Behavioral clinicians, until fairly recently, employed primarily aversive techniques with abusers of alcohol and tobacco, but they now include in their repertoire procedures designed to reduce anxiety and enhance social skills. Anxiety and the lack of such skills may be underlying reasons why people turn to drugs as a means of coping with life.

■ ■

chapter 11

PSYCHOSEXUAL DISORDERS: GENDER IDENTITY DISORDERS AND THE PARAPHILIAS

Gender Identity Disorders
The Paraphilias
Ego-Dystonic Homosexuality

William V. is a twenty-eight-year-old computer programmer who currently lives alone. He grew up in a rural area within a conservative family with strong religious values. He has two younger brothers and an older sister. William began to masturbate at age fifteen; his first masturbatory experience took place while he watched his sister urinate in an outdoor toilet. Despite considerable feelings of guilt, he continued to masturbate two or three times a week while having voyeuristic fantasies. At the age of twenty he left home to spend two years in the navy.

On a summer evening at about 11:30 p.m., William was arrested for climbing a ladder and peeping into the bedroom of a suburban home. Just before this incident he had been drinking heavily at a cocktail lounge featuring a topless dancer. When he had left the lounge at 11:15 p.m. he had intended to return to his home. Feeling lonely and depressed, however, he had begun to drive slowly through a nearby suburban neighborhood, where he noticed a

lighted upstairs window. With little premeditation, he had parked his car, erected a ladder he found lying near the house, and climbed up to peep. The householders, who were alerted by the sounds, called the police, and William was arrested. Although this was his first arrest, William had committed similar acts on two previous occasions.

The police referred William's case for immediate and mandatory psychological counseling. William described a lonely and insecure life . . . to his therapist—six months before the arrest, he had been rejected in a long-term relationship, and he had not recovered from this emotional rejection. As an unassertive and timid individual, he had responded by withdrawing from social relationships and increasing his use of alcohol. His voyeuristic fantasies, which were present to begin with, became progressively more urgent as William's self-esteem deteriorated. His arrest had come as a great personal shock, although he recognized that his behavior was both irrational and self-destructive (Rosen and Rosen, 1981, pp. 452–453).

Of all the aspects of human suffering that command the attention of psychopathologists and clinicians, few touch the lives of more people than problems involving sex. Oftentimes the human suffering is exacerbated by bad counsel and misinformation—such as the belief held not so long ago that masturbation should be avoided at all costs because it was immoral and might even weaken the mind. This chapter and the next consider the full range of human sexual thoughts, feelings, and actions that are generally regarded as abnormal and dysfunctional and are listed in DSM-III as *psychosexual disorders* (Table 11.1). In the present chapter our study is of the *gender identity disorders,* the *paraphilias,* and *ego-dystonic homosexuality,* all of them sexual problems that are viewed as particularly serious and aberrant and that are found in only a small minority of people. The next chapter focuses on *psychosexual dysfunctions,* disruptions in normal sexual functioning to be found among many people who are in otherwise reasonably sound psychological health.

In the earlier nosology, DSM-II, what are now termed the paraphilias were grouped with personality disorders, as were alcoholism and drug dependence, in a large, heterogeneous section, Personality Disorders and Certain Other Nonpsychotic Mental Disorders. A few of the psychosexual dysfunctions were considered as psycho-

TABLE **11.1**
Psychosexual Disorders
(from DSM-III)

A. Gender Identity Disorders
   1. Transsexualism.
   2. Gender identity disorder of childhood.
   3. Atypical gender identity disorder.

B. Paraphilias
   1. Fetishism.
   2. Transvestism.
   3. Zoophilia.
   4. Pedophilia.
   5. Exhibitionism.
   6. Voyeurism.
   7. Sexual masochism.
   8. Sexual sadism.
   9. Atypical paraphilia (for example, coprophilia, frotteurism, necrophilia).

C. Psychosexual Dysfunctions
   1. Inhibited sexual desire.
   2. Inhibited sexual excitement.
   3. Inhibited female orgasm.
   4. Inhibited male orgasm.
   5. Premature ejaculation.
   6. Functional dyspareunia.
   7. Functional vaginismus.
   8. Atypical psychosexual dysfunction.

D. Other Psychosexual Disorders
   1. Ego-dystonic homosexuality.
   2. Psychosexual disorder not elsewhere classified.

physiological disorders in DSM-II. The fact that in DSM-III all the disorders that concern human sexuality are now brought together into a single section called Psychosexual Disorders indicates that the psychiatric profession considers the *sexual* component of these problems to be a defining characteristic, one setting them apart from other psychological problems. This represents a major shift in thinking about these disorders.

When workers speculate on how people become *dis*ordered in their sexual lives, the impression is conveyed that we rather fully understand how people develop *normally* as sexual beings. Actually, we know little of how or why a physically mature male has both the desire and ability to interact with a physically mature woman, so that, at some point, he will insert his penis into her vagina and one or both of them will have an orgasm after a period of thrusting. The most widely held belief is that people are "doin' what comes naturally." This may be true in some limited degree, but left out of such an explanation are the complex rules we all learn about how to initiate a sexual encounter, what makes it sexually stimulating, how it is paced. These aspects of our sexual lives are what Gagnon and Simon (1973) call our *sexual scripts,* the rules we carry in our heads to guide our actions to a maximum of positive sexual consequences and a minimum of negative ones.

Gender Identity Disorders

"**A**re you a boy or a girl?" "Are you a man or a woman?" For virtually all people—even those with serious mental disorders such as schizophrenia—the answer to such questions is immediate and obvious. Also unequivocal is the fact that others will agree with the answer given. Our sense of ourselves as male or female, or what is called *gender identity,* is so deeply ingrained from earliest childhood that, no matter the stress suffered at one time or another, the vast majority of people are certain beyond a doubt of their gender.

Some people, however, and more often they are men, feel deep within themselves from early childhood that they are of the opposite sex. The evidence of their anatomy—normal genitals and the usual secondary sex characteristics, such as beard growth for men and developed breasts for women—does not persuade them that they are what others see them to be. A male transsexual, then, can look at himself in a mirror, see an ordinary man, and yet announce to himself, and more often nowadays to the world as well, that he is a woman. Furthermore, he will often try to convince the medical profession to bring his body in line with his gender identity; many transsexuals undergo radical surgery and hormone treatment to make their bodies assume as much as possible the anatomy of the opposite sex.

Transsexualism

DSM-III defines a *transsexual* as an adult who has a persistent, deep sense of discomfort in his, less often her, anatomic sex, often wishes to be rid of his genitals and live as a woman, and has felt this way for more than two years. This last stipulation excludes people who may, under specific stress, temporarily reject their anatomic gender. Excluded also are schizophrenics who on very rare occasions claim to be of the other sex, as well as people who are biologically intersexed, that is, possess both male and female sex organs, as in hermaphroditism.

Transsexuals generally suffer from anxiety and depression, not surprising in light of their psychological predicament. Occasionally the transsexual's sexual orientation is homosexual, although a male transsexual's interest in men will be interpreted by him as a conventional heterosexual preference, given that he is "really" a woman. Predictably, transsexuals often arouse the disapproval of others when they choose to cross-dress in clothing of the other sex.

The question is often raised whether a transsexual should be considered psychotic, for is it not delusional for a person with a penis to believe that he is a woman. DSM-III asserts that "The insistence by an individual with Transsexualism that he or she is of the other sex is, strictly speaking, not a delusion since what is invariably meant is that the individual *feels like* a member of the other sex rather than truly believing he or she *is* a member of the other sex" (p. 263). Case studies of many transsexuals reveal, however, that such people express the conviction that they are, in fact, members of the opposite sex. Their statements imply more than the "as if" feelings that DSM-III claims are prevalent. Research concerning whether transsexuals are psychotic has provided conflicting findings (for example, Langevin, Paitich, and Steiner, 1977). But perhaps it matters little whether transsexuals are psychotic or not; their condition remains what it is.

The long-standing and apparently unchangeable nature of the transsexual's incongruous gender identity has led researchers to speculate that transsexuals are hormonally different from those with normal gender identity. Perhaps a woman who believes that she is a man has an excess of androgens such as testosterone and androsterone, hormones known to promote the development of and maintain male secondary sex characteristics. In a review of several such investigations, Meyer-Bahlburg (1979) finds the results to be equivocal: some female transsexuals have elevated levels of male hormones, but most of them do not. Differences, when they are found, are difficult to interpret, however. Many transsexuals use sex hormones in an effort to alter their bodies in the direction of the sex to which they believe they belong. Even though a researcher studies only transsexuals who have not taken such exogenous hormones for a few months, relatively little is known at present about the long-

term effects of earlier hormonal treatment. In any event, the available data do not support an explanation of transsexualism in terms of hormones. Even less conclusive is the research on possible chromosomal abnormalities.

Gender Identity Disorder of Childhood

Virtually all transsexuals who have been studied by sex researchers report retrospectively that they engaged in cross-gender behavior as young children. An examination of *gender identity disorder of childhood* should provide clues to the etiology of transsexualism. The children given this diagnosis are profoundly feminine boys and profoundly masculine girls, youngsters whose behavior, likes, and dislikes do not fit at all our culture's rules for what is appropriate for the two sexes. Thus a boy may not like rough-and-tumble play, prefer the company of little girls, don women's clothing, and insist that he will grow up to be a girl. He may even claim that his penis and testes are disgusting. The onset of the disorder is before the age of six or earlier.

The very categorization of boys and girls as having their own masculine and feminine ways is so heavily laden with value judgments and stereotyping that considering opposite behavioral patterns abnormal may seem unjustified. But clear lines of evidence indicate that the disturbance is real. Human and other primate offspring of mothers who have taken sex hormones during pregnancy may frequently behave like the opposite sex *and* have anatomical abnormalities. For example, girls whose mothers took synthetic progestins during pregnancy, to prevent uterine bleeding, were found to be "tomboyish" during their preschool years (Ehrhardt and Money, 1967). Progestins are considered precursors of androgens, the male sex hormones. Similar findings come from other studies as well (see Green, 1976). These young tomboys also had genitalia with male characteristics, which suggests a link between the progestins taken by their mothers and male physical features. Young boys whose mothers ingested female hormones when they were pregnant were found to be less athletic as young children and to engage less in rough-and-tumble play than their male peers (Yalom, Green, and Fisk, 1973). Although such children were not necessarily abnormal in their gender identity, the prenatal sex hormones did give them higher than usual levels of cross-gender interests and behavior.

The role of the parents and relatives is apparently quite strong in reinforcing the cross-gender behavior that many, perhaps most, little children engage in now and then. Interviews with the parents of children who have become atypical frequently reveal that they did not discourage, and in many instances clearly encouraged, cross-dressing and other cross-gender behavior. This is especially true for feminine boys. Many mothers, aunts, and grandmothers found it "cute" that the little fellow enjoyed putting on mommy's old dresses and high-heeled shoes, and very often they instructed the youngster on how to apply lipstick, eyeshadow, and rouge. Family albums often contain photographs of the young boys fetchingly attired in woman's clothing. Such reactions on the part of the family of an atypical child have probably contributed in a major way to the conflict between his or her anatomical sex and the acquired gender identity (Green, 1974).

Research with infants and very young children whose genitals have both male and female characteristics and who often undergo surgery to correct the problem indicates that by the age of three a child has achieved a sense of gender identity that is virtually impossible to change later on (Money, Hampson, and Hampson, 1955). Indeed, the gender assigned several of these children was later found to conflict with at least one anatomic sex criterion, such as the indication of sex by their chromosomes. Such children already over the age of three kept the gender to which they had been assigned (see Box 11.1). The web of evidence, then, points to the criticalness of how a very young child, under three years of age, is treated by the adults around him. Dressing a child as a boy, giving him (or her!) a male name, and encouraging him to engage in traditional masculine activities are major influences on the development of gender identity. In contradiction to widespread belief, anatomy is not always destiny.

These findings, however, should *not* be interpreted to mean that encouraging gentleness in a little boy or assertiveness, even aggressiveness, in a little girl will probably lead to a gender

BOX **11.1** An Accidental Change of Gender Identity

Sometimes we can learn something very important from a rare, and in this case shocking, accident. Money and Ehrhardt (1972) describe what happened to one member of a pair of identical male twins. As they were being circumcised at seven months of age, the penis of one of them was irreparably destroyed through a surgical accident. After almost a year of torment and indecision, the parents decided to go along with a suggestion by a physician that this twin be reared as a female. Surgery transformed the boy's genitals into a vagina. His birth certificate was changed, and the parents began to treat the child in every way as a little girl. Within a few years this twin had developed a female gender identity and looked and acted in feminine ways, quite unlike her male brother. When she reaches puberty, she will be given female sex hormones to stimulate breast growth and other secondary female characteristics. Although she will never menstruate and never be able to have children, her physical appearance will be very much that of a normal woman. This remarkable case study underlines how critical our social environment is in determining our sense of ourselves as a man or a woman.

identity disorder. Investigators working in this field are very much aware of the culture-relative aspects of masculinity and femininity, and of the difference between enjoying activities more typical of the opposite sex and actually believing that one *is* of the opposite sex. Even though an anatomically male child can indeed acquire a female identity after being treated like a little girl, little is known about the family dynamics and the exact reinforcement histories that account for such atypical developments. We do not know either whether some somatic diathesis must be present at the outset for environmental forces to interact with. Moreover, we do know that the vast majority of little boys engage in varying amounts of "feminine" play and little girls in varying amounts of "masculine" play with no identity conflicts whatsoever (Green, 1976). Gender identity disorder of childhood and the adult disorder of transsexualism—one of its end points, the others being transvestism and homosexuality—are rare, far less prevalent than could be expected from the numbers of little boys who play with dolls and of little girls who engage in vigorous, physical-contact sports.

Therapies for Gender Identity Disorders

Sex-change surgery

Innovations in surgical procedures, coupled with advances in hormonal treatments and a sociocultural atmosphere that would permit their implementation, have allowed many transsexuals to pursue their wish to become in most respects a member of the opposite sex. In _sex-change surgery_ for men the genitalia are almost entirely removed, with some of the tissue retained to form an artificial vagina. Appropriate female hormones are given at least a year before the operation to produce bodily changes such as development of the breasts and softening of the skin (Green and Money, 1969). At the same time the transsexual begins to live as a member of the other gender in order to experience as fully as possible what it is like. Conventional heterosexual intercourse is possible for male-to-female transsexuals, although pregnancy is out of the question since only the external genitalia are altered. For female-to-male transsexuals the pro-

Young Judy Patton and Jude Patton as he is today.

cess is more arduous and the outcome more problematic. The penis that can be constructed is small and not capable of normal erection; artificial supports are therefore needed for conventional sexual intercourse.

The first sex-change operation took place in Europe in 1930, but the surgery that attracted worldwide attention was performed on an ex-soldier, Christine (originally George) Jorgensen, in Copenhagen in 1952. More recently, Jan (originally James) Morris, a well-known journalist, published *Conundrum* (1974), a sensitive and highly personal account of her life as a man and her subsequent alteration to a female. For many years the Gender Identity Clinic at Johns Hopkins University School of Medicine was a leading American facility for these operations, but now their sex-change program has been terminated, apparently because transsexuals whom surgeons had operated on failed to show better life adjustment than those who did not have surgery (Meyer and Reter, 1979). But sex-change programs continue elsewhere, such as at Stanford University and the University of Minnesota; it is estimated that upwards of 1000 transsexuals are surgically altered each year in the United States.

The long-term effectiveness, or even wisdom, of sex transformation surgery is difficult to evaluate (Lothstein, 1980). Given that people who go to great lengths to have this surgery performed claim that their future happiness depends on the change, should this surgery be evaluated in terms of how happy such people are afterward? If so, it can be safely said that some transsexuals who have crossed over anatomically are better off, others are not. But as people make their way through life, many events bring them a greater or lesser amount of fulfillment or even just ease. If a surgically altered transsexual becomes terribly unhappy, is the venture to be indicted as antitherapeutic? Transsexuals who undertake these procedures often cut their ties to former friends and family members and to aspects of their previous lives—"Was it *I* who played tailback on the football team?" Considerable stress is the fate

BEFORE   **AFTER**   **TODAY**

Christine Jorgensen, shown before her surgery in 1943, after it in 1952, and again in 1972, was the first transsexual whose operation was widely publicized.

of anyone who chooses to divorce himself from the past, for the past contributes to our sense of ourselves as people, as much as do the present and the future. A transsexual who has surgery, then, confronts challenges most people do not even conceive of; adjustment to the new life should perhaps be evaluated more leniently.

All experienced therapists, whatever their theoretical persuasion, are wary of a client who says "If only. . . ." The variations are legion: "If only I were not so fat. . . ." "If only I were not so nervous. . . ." "If only I had not left school before graduation. . . ." Following each "if only" clause is some statement indicating that life would be far better, even wonderful . . . if only. Most of the time the hopes expressed are an illusion; things are seldom so simple. The transsexual, understandably focusing on the discrepancy between gender identity and biological makeup, blames his or her present dissatisfactions on the horrible trick nature has played. But he or she usually finds that sex change falls short of solving life's problems. It may handle this one set of them, but it usually leaves untouched other difficulties that all human beings are subject to.

Alterations of gender identity

But are sex-change operations the only option? Until recently they have been considered the only viable treatment, for psychological attempts to shift gender identity had consistently failed. Gender identity was assumed too deep-seated to alter. Two apparently successful procedures for altering gender identity through behavior therapy have now been reported, however. One treatment (Rekers and Lovass, 1974) was of a five-year-old boy who, since age two, had been cross-dressing and showing the other familiar signs of gender identity disorder. Concurring with the therapist's judgment that conforming to societal standards of masculinity would benefit the boy in both the short and long run, the child's parents began, as instructed, to compliment and otherwise support him whenever he played with traditionally male toys, rather than those commonly preferred by girls, and whenever he engaged in other little-boy activities. Feminine mannerisms were to be discouraged. After only six months of intensive treatment, the boy was

typically masculine, and he was still so at a two-year follow-up. Although it might be objected that encouraging play with guns while discouraging play with dolls only reinforces cultural stereotypes (Winkler, 1977), this child was probably spared considerable psychological hardship by bringing his gender identity into conformity with his biological makeup.

An even more dramatic reversal of gender identity was reported by Barlow, Reynolds, and Agras (1973). In their behavioral treatment of a seventeen-year-old male transsexual, gender role was broken down into concrete components, such as mannerisms, interpersonal behavior, and fantasies, and the client was given training to change each component. He was initially made aware of the effeminate manner in which he stood, sat, walked, and talked, and through modeling, rehearsal, and video feedback, and through voice retraining, he was taught the ways of doing them judged masculine by the culture. Almost immediately the staring and ridicule of his peers lessened, and he returned to high school part time. The young man's social skills improved as he was taught to make eye contact and conversation and to express his positive feelings through appropriate smiles and other means.

He still felt himself to be a female, however, and had fantasies and urges to have intercourse with men. Therapy then focused on his fantasy life. During training sessions a female therapist encouraged him to imagine himself in sexual situations with attractive females; she also embellished his fantasies by describing foreplay in explicit detail. He was instructed to generate such fantasies when encountering women as he went about his daily activities. After thirty-four training sessions over a period of two months, the client's desires to change sex dropped dramatically, and fantasies about men decreased in number as those about women increased. He was now beginning to think of himself as a man, and the attraction he still occasionally felt toward men was taking place without gender role reversal, that is, the attraction was that felt by one man toward another.

Measures of sexual arousal with the penile plethysmograph (see Box 11.2) more definitely revealed that he was still attracted to men and

BOX 11.2 Psychophysiological Assessment of Sexual Arousal

Let us examine closely some important innovations in physiological measurement. In 1966 Masters and Johnson startled researchers and lay people alike by their direct physiological assessments of men and women during states of great sexual arousal. The measures they used primarily were muscle tension and blood volume in various parts of the cardiovascular system. In addition, they employed ingenious photographic devices to record changes in the color of various tissues of the vagina during the sexual arousal of women. More recently behavioral researchers have been using two genital devices for measuring sexual arousal in men and in women, and each of them enjoys considerable validation in giving rather specific measurements of sexual excitement. Both are sensitive indicators of vasocongestion of the genitalia, that is, the flooding of their veins with blood, a key physiological process in sexual arousal.

The penile plethysmograph (Freund, 1963; Bancroft, Jones, and Pullan, 1966) has been used successfully to measure the sexual arousal of men in a variety of experiments. A plethysmograph is a device that measures blood flow. The most widely used penile plethysmograph is a strain gauge, consisting of a very thin rubber tube filled with mercury or a circular piece of light surgical steel, either of which can be placed around the penis (Barlow, et al., 1970) with ease and in privacy. As the penis fills with blood during sexual excitement, the tube or steel stretches, changing the electrical resistance of the mercury or steel; through appropriate wiring the increase in resistance is transformed into tracings on a complex apparatus called the polygraph. Increase in the length of the penis correlates highly with increase in circumference, and both of them are a function of engorgement of the penis with blood during sexual excitement. The strain gauge, then, provides a very useful measure of sexual responding in men.

Similarly direct and specific measurement of female sexual arousal was not at first possible. Only indirect measures such as those used by Masters and Johnson were available, and these are unsatisfactory for both aesthetic and practical reasons. Fortunately, a vaginal plethysmograph was eventually invented by Sintchak and Geer (1975). This device is shaped like a small menstrual tampon and has a light at the tip. The light reflected from the vaginal walls is recorded and provides a measure of the amount of blood they contain. Like the penile strain gauge, the vaginal probe is a reliable instrument and is easily put in place by subjects in total privacy. An important validational study of this device was reported by Geer, Morokoff, and Greenwood (1974). They showed female undergraduates erotic and nonerotic films and measured engorgement of their vaginal walls during the viewings. In the erotic film a young man and a young woman have an explicit sexual encounter, including foreplay, oral-genital sex, and intercourse. The nonerotic film, entitled *The Crusades,* depicts battle scenes and court life during the time of the Crusades. Since each film was readily identified as erotic or nonerotic, any differences between the measurements of the two groups of subjects obtained with the vaginal probes could be taken as evidence that the instruments do provide a valid measure of sexual excitement. The women watching the sexual film showed much greater blood flow than did the subjects watching the control film. It is of interest that heart rate measurements taken concurrently did not differentiate the two groups of subjects, confirming the desirability of specific genital measures.

Subjects soon become relatively unaware of the presence of genital plethysmographs on their bodies and of the wiring to the polygraph. This degree of unobtrusiveness, desirable in any assessment procedure, is particularly important in studying sexual behavior, about which many people are self-conscious. The technical innovations and availability of these devices have spurred a remarkable volume of research on human sexual behavior. Of course, it would be naive to assert that these genital devices have no effect on how subjects respond in a laboratory. And as valuable as these new devices appear to be in assessing sexual arousal, it would be unwise to view them as able to gauge all sexual interest. The sexual significance of a particular image or idea may not always translate directly into an increase in penile size or vaginal blood flow. Not all sexuality can be measured in terms of genital responding.

The data being collected by sex researchers around the world do indicate that, at least with those volunteering for such experiments, meaningful and important studies can be done. The accumulating literature is beginning to shed light on an area of human conduct previously shrouded in mystery, embarrassment, and an often harmful mythology.

not women, so therapeutic effort was now devoted to increasing the arousal felt toward women and decreasing that felt toward men. This was achieved by pairing slides of women with slides of men, the idea being to classically condition sexual arousal to slides of women by associating them with the arousal felt toward slides of males. This procedure, when followed by aversion therapy sessions to reduce the attractiveness of slides of males, promoted the desired change to a heterosexual pattern of arousal. Interestingly, during this period the young man's manner of standing, sitting, and walking became even more traditionally masculine. He also felt much better about himself and had returned to high school on a full-time basis. Five months after the end of treatment, the young man reported for the first time masturbating to orgasm while imagining himself with a woman. A one-year follow-up found him going steady with a young woman and engaging in "light petting." He no longer thought of himself as a woman. Five years later the man's gender identity continued to be masculine, his sexual orientation heterosexual (Barlow, Abel, and Blanchard, 1979).

The work of Barlow and his colleagues represents the first successful change of gender identity in an adult transsexual and as such raises the possibility that cross-sex identity is amenable to change. The clinicians themselves acknowledge that this particular client might have been different from other transsexuals because he did consent at the outset to participate in a therapy program aimed at changing his gender identity. Most transsexuals refuse such treatment as inappropriate; for them sex reassignment surgery is the only legitimate goal.[1]

[1] In their follow-up report on the seventeen-year-old transsexual, Barlow, Abel, and Blanchard (1979) described two additional cases treated in the same way. These two men, in their mid-twenties, were on the route to sex-change surgery but then had second thoughts. The behavioral retraining succeeded again in altering gender identity but not their attraction to men.

The Paraphilias

The term paraphilias replaces DSM-II's sexual deviation. It denotes that there is a deviation (*para-*) in what the person is attracted to (*-philia*). In those suffering the disorders,

> . . . unusual or bizarre imagery or acts are necessary for sexual excitement. Such imagery or acts tend to be insistently and involuntarily repetitive and generally involve either: (1) preference for use of a nonhuman object for sexual arousal, (2) repetitive sexual activity with humans involving real or simulated suffering or humiliation, or (3) repetitive sexual activity with nonconsenting partners. . . . [The paraphilias] in varying degrees may interfere with the capacity for reciprocal affectionate sexual activity (DSM-III, pp. 266, 261).

This definition of paraphilias indicates that a person need not actually engage in overt acts to be given the diagnosis; the deviant sexual activity may be solely imaginal, as when certain fantasies or pictorial materials are relied on for sexual arousal during masturbation. Another aspect of a paraphilia is that the deviant components are *necessary* for sexual excitement, not merely a variation that a person may on occasion choose to lend variety to his or her sex life. Paraphilias may, according to DSM-III, be multiple rather than single and also be an aspect of other mental disorders, such as schizophrenia or one of the personality disorders. Finally, the fact that in some of these patterns of existence nonconsenting partners are specifically sought indicates that they will have legal consequences.

Fetishism

A fetishist, almost always a male, is sexually enthralled by some inanimate object or some specific nongenital part of a person. His disorder of *fetishism* takes the form of using

> nonliving objects (fetishes) as a repeatedly preferred or exclusive method of achieving sexual excitment. The diagnosis is not made when the fetishes are limited to articles of female clothing used in cross-dressing, as in Transvestism, or when the object is sexually stimulating because it has been designed for that purpose, e.g., a vibrator (DSM-III, p. 268).

Beautiful shoes, sheer stockings, gloves, toilet articles, fur garments, and especially underpants are common sources of arousal for fetishists. Some carry on their fetishism by themselves in secret by fondling, kissing, smelling, or merely gazing at the adored object as they masturbate. Others need their partner to don the fetish as a stimulant for intercourse. Fetishists sometimes become primarily interested in making a collection of the desired objects, and they will burgle week after week to add to their hoard.

Other individuals make fetishes of parts of the female body. Locks of hair, feet, ankles, hands, fingernails, delicately shaped ears, and large bosoms may be the narrowed focus of all passion. To secure contact with them, the fetishist may engage in rather extraordinary maneuvering—such as working as a shoe salesman, even though he could qualify for a better-paying position—and may even commit assault.

Subjectively, the attraction felt by the fetishist toward the object or part of the body is involuntary and irresistible. Because it has such a strong, compulsive quality, the fetishism may be a dominant force in the man's life. The degree of the erotic focalization distinguishes fetishisms from the ordinary attraction that high heels and net stockings may hold for heterosexual men and from their normal appreciation of beautiful hair, bosoms, and ankles.

Psychoanalytic theorists generally consider fetishisms and the other paraphilias to serve some sort of defensive function, warding off anxiety about normal sexual contacts. Learning theorists usually invoke some kind of classical conditioning in the person's social-sexual history. For example, a young man may, early in his sexual experiences, masturbate to pictures of women dressed in black leather. Indeed, one experiment (Rachman, 1966) lends some mild support to learning propositions. Male subjects were repeatedly shown slides of nude and alluring females interspersed with slides of women's boots. The subjects were eventually aroused by the boots alone. The "fetishistic attraction" induced, however, was weak and transient.

Box 5.3 (page 157) discussed the possibility that people are "prepared" to learn to become phobic to certain objects. It is also possible that human beings are prepared to learn to be sexually stimulated by certain classes of stimuli. If mere association with sexual stimulation were all there is to acquiring a fetishism through classical conditioning, would not objects such as ceilings and pillows be found high on the list of fetishes (Baron and Byrne, 1977)? At this point it would be premature to conclude that fetishisms are established through classical conditioning.

Transvestism

When a man is sexually aroused by dressing in the clothing of the opposite sex while still regarding himself as a member of his own sex, the term _transvestism_ is applied to his behavior. A transvestite may also enjoy appearing socially as a woman; some female impersonators become performers in nightclubs, catering to the delight that many sexually conventional people take in skilled cross-dressing. When arousal is the primary motivation of transvestites, they often masturbate when cross-dressed. Transvestism should not be confused with homosexuality; transvestites are heterosexual, and only a few homosexuals ever on occasion "go in drag." In many jurisdictions it is illegal to appear cross-dressed in public.

Transvestites, who are always males according to DSM-III, by and large cross-dress episodically rather than on a regular basis. They tend to be otherwise masculine in appearance, demeanor, and sexual preference. Most are married. The cross-dressing usually takes place in private and in secret and is known to few members of the family. The compulsion to cross-dress may become more frequent but only rarely develops over time to a change in gender identity, that is, to the man's believing that he is actually a member of the female sex.

Case histories of transvestites often refer to childhood incidents in which the little boy was praised and fussed over for looking "cute" when wearing female attire. Learning accounts assume the disorder results from the conditioning effects of repeatedly masturbating when cross-dressing,

A transvestite imitating Marilyn Monroe in a Parisian nightclub act.

similar to the supposed classical conditioning connection between arousal and the object adopted as a fetish. Some clinicians believe transvestism represents for a bealeaguered male a refuge from the responsibilities he sees himself bearing solely by virtue of being male in our society. Female clothing, then, is believed to have _meaning_ for transvestites that is more complex and encompassing than sheer sexual arousal; trying to explain transvestism solely in sexual terms may therefore be an oversimplification.

Incest

The taboo against _incest_ seems virtually universal in human societies (Ford and Beach, 1951). A notable exception were the marriages of Egyptian pharoahs to their sisters or other females of their immediate families. In Egypt it was believed that the royal blood should not be contaminated by that of outsiders. Some anthropologists consider the prohibition against incest to have served the important function of forcing larger and wider social ties than would have been likely had family members chosen their mates only from among their own.

Incest, which includes all varieties of sexual relations that culminate in at least one orgasm, seems most common between brother and sister. The next most common form, which is considered more pathological, is between father and daughter. Gebhard and his associates (1965) found, in their well-known study on sex offenders, that most fathers who had relations with physically mature daughters tended to be very devout, moralistic, and fundamentalistic in their religious beliefs. More recent evidence, however, indicates that incestuous relationships can be found in familes of all religious and socioeconomic backgrounds (Rosen and Rosen, 1981). Very few instances of mother-son incest have been reported.

Statistics on the incidence of incest are notoriously difficult to collect; since this behavior occurs within the family, other members are very reluctant to report the offenders to the authorities. Explanations of incest run the gamut from sexual deprivation to the Freudian notion that human beings have basic human desires for such relationships. Gagnon (1977) speculates that an incestous relationship between father and daughter begins when the father is under considerable stress outside the home and receives insufficient emotional and sexual support from his wife. He turns to an available, sometimes prepubescent daughter, who takes on the role of substitute wife. Whether the incest continues depends in large measure on the response of the man's wife, who may choose to ignore what is going on in the interest of keeping the family together. The reactions of the daughter are, of course, highly variable and can be expected to change over time. Perhaps initially flattered that she can take

good care of daddy, the growing young woman may later feel trapped by the whole affair and run away from home. Or she may become pregnant, thus _forcing_ other family members to deal with the father's behavior. There is little firm evidence bearing on the long-term effects of incest on either children or parents.

Pedophilia

Pedophiles are adults, usually men at least as far as police records indicate, who derive sexual gratification through physical and often sexual contact with prepubertal children. Older adolescents may also be pedophiles, although the disorder most frequently begins in middle age. Violence is seldom a part of the molestation, but society's reaction to pedophiles is far more punitive than it is toward rapists, who employ physical force. Often the pedophile, or child molester, is content to stroke the child's hair, but he may also manipulate the child's genitalia, encourage the child to manipulate his, and less often, attempt intromission. The molestations may be repeated over a period of weeks, months, or years if they are not discovered by other adults or protested by the child. There are both heterosexual and homosexual pedophiles, but it is of interest that most homosexuals restrict their sexual attentions to other adults and regard with disdain those who do not.

Pedophiles tend to be rigidly religious and moralistic. As with most of the aberrant sexual behavior that has been described, there is a strong subjective feeling of compulsion in the attraction that draws the pedophile to the child. According to Gebhard and his colleagues (1965), pedophiles typically know the children they molest, being a next-door neighbor, friend of the family, or relative. It has been estimated that up to 30 percent are related to their victims. Most older heterosexual pedophiles are or have been married at some time in their lives.

A group of pedophiles were investigated by Mohr, Turner, and Jerry (1964). The pedophiles in their sample were found to cluster into three age groups, adolescent, mid-to-late thirties, and mid-to-late fifties, with the mid-thirties group the largest. Adolescent pedophiles were found to be sexually inexperienced with people of their own age. Those in their mid-thirties had developed serious mental and social maladjustments, including alcoholism, which was frequently associated with the act. The older pedophiles were better adjusted but usually suffered from loneliness and isolation. These differences indicate that etiological factors vary with the age of the offender.

It has been suggested that the drive to approach a child sexually can reflect a sense of having failed in the adult world, socially and professionally as well as sexually. Occasionally, though, an adult prediposed toward pedophilia may be aroused by a child's innocent, uninhibited show of affection. Unbeknown to the child, the pedophile perceives sexual overtones in demonstrativeness. In defining pedophilia, state laws prescribe an upper age limit for those who are to be considered children, making it a crime to approach sexually any younger person. The age varies in different states.

When a child tells a parent that an adult has fondled him or her, the parents face the dilemma of how to react. Many experts feel that the child tends not to interpret the interaction in the same sexual terms that adults do (Gagnon, 1977). Even if the molester has an orgasm, it is not always clear to the child what was happened, and to react with adult alarm can lend needless negative meaning to an unfortunate incident. But at the same time the young child must be protected from a prolonged and harmful sexual relationship with an adult.

Voyeurism ("Peeping")

Now and then a man may by chance happen to observe a nude woman without her knowing he is watching her. If his sex life is primarily conventional, his act is voyeuristic, but he would not generally be considered a voyeur. *Voyeurism* is

repetitive looking at unsuspecting people, usually strangers, who are either naked, in the act of disrobing, or engaging in sexual activity, as the repeatedly preferred or exclusive method of achieving sexual excitement. The act of looking ("peeping") is for the purpose of achieving sexual excitement,

and no sexual activity with the person is sought. Orgasm, usually produced by masturbation, may occur during the voyeuristic activity, or later in response to the memory of what the individual has witnessed. Often these individuals enjoy thinking about the observed individuals' being helpless and feeling humiliated if they knew they were being seen (DSM-III, pp. 272–273).

A true voyeur, who is almost always a man, will not find if particularly exciting to watch a woman who is undressing for his special benefit. The element of risk seems important, for he is excited by his anticipation of how the woman would react if she knew he was watching.[2] Some voyeurs derive special pleasure from secretly observing couples having sexual relations. As with all categories of behavior that are against the law, frequencies of occurrence are difficult to assess, since the majority of *all* illegal activities go unnoticed by the police.

From what we know, voyeurs tend to be young, single, submissive, and fearful of more direct sexual encounters with others (Katchadourian and Lunde, 1972; McCary, 1973). Their peeping serves as substitute gratification and possibly gives them a sense of power over those watched. They do not seem to be otherwise disturbed, however. After all restrictions against the sale of pornographic materials to adults had been lifted in Denmark, one of the few observed effects of this liberalization was a significant reduction in peeping, at least as reported to the police (Kutchinsky, 1970). It may be that the increased availability of completely frank pictorial and written material, which is typically used in masturbation, satisfies the needs that had earlier made some men without other outlets voyeurs.

[2] That voyeurs have an impoverished social life and engage in surreptitious peeping instead of making conventional sexual and social contacts with women suggests another way to understand their preference for spying on unaware women. If the women were to be aware of the man's actions and continue nonetheless to allow herself to be watched, the man might well conclude that she has some personal interest in him. This possibility would be very threatening to the voyeur and, because of his fear, less sexually arousing. Perhaps then it is not the risk of being discovered that arouses the voyeur. Rather, protection from a possible relationship with a woman renders undiscovered peeping the least frightening way for the heterosexual voyeur to have visual contacts with women.

The surreptitious voyeur, unable to manage closer sexual encounters, invades the privacy of a disrobing stranger from afar.

Exhibitionism

Voyeurism and exhibitionism together account for close to a majority of all sexual offenses that come to the attention of police. Again, the frequency of _exhibitionism_ is much greater among men. A quip holds that a man surreptitiously looking at a nude woman is a voyeur, but that a woman looking at a naked man is watching an exhibitionist. Like many statements about human sexuality, this one implies that women are less sexual than men. The exhibitionist repeatedly exposes

> the genitals to an unsuspecting stranger for the purpose of sexual excitement, with no attempt at further sexual activity with the stranger. The wish to surprise or shock the observer is often consciously perceived or [is] close to conscious awareness, but these individuals are usually not physically dangerous to the victim. Sometimes the individual masturbates while exposing himself (DSM-III, p. 272).

The urge to expose seems overwhelming and virtually uncontrollable to the exhibitionist or "flasher" and is apparently triggered by anxiety and restlessness as well as by sexual arousal. Be-

cause of the compulsive nature of the urge, the exposures may be repeated rather frequently and even in the same place and at the same time of day. Apparently exhibitionists are so strongly driven that, at the time of the act, they are oblivious to the social and legal consequences of what they are doing (Stevenson and Jones, 1972). In the desperation and tension of the moment, they may suffer headache and palpitations and have a sense of unreality. Afterward they flee in trembling and remorse (Bond and Hutchison, 1960). Generally, the exhibitionist is immature in his approaches to the opposite sex and has difficulty in interpersonal relationships. Over half of all exhibitionists are married, but their sexual relationships with their wives are not satisfactory (Mohr, Turner, and Jerry, 1964).

Younger exhibitionists may not manifest other kinds of psychopathology, but some of those who expose themselves come from the ranks of the mentally retarded and the senile. Some who exhibit do so while having a temporal lobe epileptic seizure (see page 717). Because the behavior of these men may be without deliberation and intent and sometimes even awareness, it is problematic whether they should be considered exhibitionists. When the label of exhibitionism is applied, not only overt behavior but also intent should be established, which may be difficult.

The fact that the exhibited penis is sometimes flaccid (Langevin et al., 1979) raises interesting questions about the *sexual* aspects of the act. How sexually arousing can it be for a man to expose himself if his penis is not erect when doing so? The exhibitionist, deficient as he seems to be in more conventional social skills, may regard his act of exposure as the best social interaction that he can manage. The fact that a nonchalant reaction on the part of the observer is not satisfying to the exhibitionist confirms that he is seeking to startle those to whom he exposes himself. These are only a few of the aspects of exhibitionism about which we have no certain knowledge at present.

The search to determine how exhibitionism develops has turned up very little. One of many psychodynamic theories views the problem as stemming from a repressed fear of castration and the exhibitionist's need to reassure himself that he is still a man. Such speculations are unsupported by any data, nor have they contributed to the development of effective therapies. An intriguing learning hypothesis emphasizes the reinforcing aspects of masturbation. McGuire, Carlisle, and Young (1965) reported on the development of exhibitionism in two young men who were surprised during urination by an attractive woman. When the embarrassment had passed and they were in private, the thought of being discovered in this way aroused them and they masturbated while fantasizing the earlier experience. After repeated masturbating to such fantasies, they began to exhibit. The report suggests that repeated association of sexual arousal with images of being seen by a woman classically conditioned the men to become aroused through exhibiting. No experimental evidence, however, clearly supports a learning explanation of exhibitionism.

Rape

The crime

Few other antisocial acts are viewed with more disgust and anger than the obtaining of sexual gratification from an unwilling partner through *forcible rape.* A second category, *statutory rape,* refers to sexual intercourse between a male and any female who is a minor. The typical age of consent, as decided by state statutes, is eighteen years. It is assumed that a younger person should not be held responsible for her sexual activity, but it has been suggested in recent years that the age be lowered. A charge of statutory rape can be made even if it is proved that the girl entered into the situation knowingly and willingly. Thus statutory rape need not involve force, being simply a consummated intercourse with a female minor that was reported to the police. The focus here is on rape other than statutory.

In the past rape was considered an offense not against the victim but against the property rights of the woman's husband, father, or brothers. Even now in most states a forcible sexual assault by a husband on his wife is not legally recognized as rape. Moreover, certain women have "bad" reputations with the police of their communities. Under these circumstances a truly forceful and even violent rape may not be categorized as such in the station house, especially when the status in the community of the man involved is higher than that of the victim. Thus a biased incidence of rape, as well as of other unconventional sexual behavior, may be obtained if attention is restricted to police records. Overriding these considerations, however, is the unfortunate fact that the woman may feel great shame is attached to her involuntary role in rape. More than three times as many rapes are estimated to occur than are reported to the police; but even though underreported, the incidence of rape is increasing faster than incidences of murder, assault, and robbery. Rape is the fastest-growing violent crime in the United States.[3]

The attack

A prevalent belief is that the victims of rape are always young and attractive. This is a myth. Although many victims do indeed fit this description, many others do not. Age and physical appearance are no barriers to some rapists; they may choose children as young as one year old and women in their eighties. Rapists usually in-

[3] In many jurisdictions the definition of rape includes not only vaginal penetration but oral and anal entry as well (Geis, 1977).

flict at least a degree of bodily injury in forcing themselves sexually upon their victims. And if a woman struggles against her attacker, ligaments in the pelvic area can be torn. Some rapists may, after the sex act, murder and mutilate the women they have attacked.

Rape victims are often traumatized by the experience, both physically and mentally. In the minutes or seconds preceding rape, the woman begins to recognize her dangerous situation but can scarcely believe what is about to happen to her. During the moments of the attack, she is first and foremost in great fear for her life. The physical violation of her body and the ripping away of her freedom of choice are enraging. But the victim also feels her vulnerability in not being able to fight off her stronger attacker and usually finds her capacity for resistance seriously compromised by her terror. For weeks following the rape, many victims are extremely tense and deeply humiliated; they feel guilt that they were unable to fight harder and have angry thoughts of revenge. Many have nightmares about rape. In a study of women admitted to a large city hospital for emergency treatment immediately following rape, Burgess and Holmstrom (1974) found that half of the women ultimately changed their place of residence or at least their telephone number. A large number had trouble in their sexual relationships with husbands or lovers. Masters and Johnson (1970) too found among their dysfunctional couples a number of women who had developed negative attitudes toward sex with their husbands following rape. Some victims of rape develop phobias about being outdoors or indoors, or in the dark, depending on where the rape took place. They may also for a time fear being alone or in crowds or having anyone behind them.

The rapist

The vast majority of rapes are almost surely planned—it is inaccurate to say that rape is the spontaneous act of a man whose sexual impulses have gone out of control (Harrington and Sutton-Simon, 1977). The rapist may have a sadistic streak, but unlike the sadist he often does not know the victim beforehand and attacks someone who is unwilling. Moreover, the sadist usually has an established, ongoing relationship

with a masochist. In many cases a pattern of repeated rape is part of a sociopathic life style (see page 277).

The incidence of sexual dysfunction during rape may be unusually high. Interviews with 170 men convicted of sexual assault revealed that maintaining an erection and premature and retarded ejaculation had been considerable problems for a third of these men in their criminal act, although almost none reported having them in his consenting sexual relations. Only one-fourth of the men gave no evidence of sexual dysfunction during rape (Groth and Burgess, 1977). One interpretation of such reactions is that rape is not invariably sexual. In fact, because rape is a mixture of both sex and aggression, the motivation is difficult to determine.

Sexism and the subjugation of women through rape have been explored in depth by Susan Brownmiller (1975) in her best-selling book *Against Our Will*. Her thesis holds rape to be "nothing more or less than a conscious process of intimidation by which all men keep all women in a state of fear" (p. 5). She garners evidence from history, both ancient and modern. In the Babylonian civilization (3000 B.C.), for example, a married woman was the property of her husband. If she was raped, both she and the rapist were bound and tossed into a river. The husband could choose to save her, or he could let her drown, just punishment for "her adultery." The views of the ancient Hebrews were no more enlightened: a married woman who had been raped was commonly stoned to death along with her attacker. When an unbetrothed virgin was raped within the walls of the city, she was similarly stoned, for it was assumed that she could have prevented the attack simply by crying out.

These penalties that different societies have imposed on raped women, together with the fact that men with their generally superior strength can usually overpower women, buttress Brownmiller's argument that rape has served in the past and still serves to intimidate women. The Crusaders raped their way across Europe in the eleventh through thirteenth centuries on their holy pilgrimages to free Jerusalem from the Muslims, the Germans in World War I raped as they rampaged through Belgium, and American forces raped in Vietnam as they "searched and destroyed." Brownmiller contends that rape is actually *expected* in war. In her view membership in the most exclusive males-only clubs in the world—the fighting forces of most nations—encourages a perverse sense of masculine superiority and creates a climate in which rape is acceptable.

Who is the rapist? Is he primarily the psychopath who seeks the thrill of dominating and humiliating a woman through intimidation and often brutal assault? Is he an ordinarily unassertive man with a fragile ego who, feeling inadequate after disappointment and rejection in work or love, takes out his frustrations on an unwilling stranger? Or is he the teenager, provoked by a seductive and apparently available young woman who, it turns out, was not as interested as he in sexual intimacy? Is he a man whose inhibitions against expressing anger have been dissolved by alcohol? The best answer is that the rapist is all these men, probably in a combination of several of these circumstances.

If we rely for information on crime reports, men arrested for rape tend to be young—usually between fifteen and twenty-five years of age—poor, unskilled, and not well educated. They come from the lower classes, in which, sociologists assert, violence is more the norm than in the middle class. About half of them are married and living with their wives at the time of the crime. A fourth to a third of all rapes are carried out by two or more men. Given the knowledge that rape is seriously underreported, however, it would be a mistake to generalize about rapists from information gleaned from police files.

Some theoreticians believe that rape is part and parcel of the cultural stereotypes of masculinity and femininity, whereby the male's role in sexual relationships is to be aggressive, the female's passive yet seductive. The woman is expected to resist the man's advances; the man is expected to overcome her resistance. It may be that some acts of rape are committed through faulty communication between the man and the woman. The woman's "Maybe" is interpreted as a "Yes" by the man, who proceeds on the assumption that the woman "really" wants to be intimate, only to be sorely disappointed and unable to accept her ultimate refusal (Gagnon, 1977). This view of rape would of course apply only to instances in which the two people know each other—in more than a third of reported rapes they do—not to the large number of assaults that occur on streets and through forced entry into the woman's home. Nor does this view account for the extreme brutality that is often part of the assault.

Emerging from the study of rape, and of other patterns of unconventional sexual behavior, is the fact that sexuality can serve many purposes. Indeed, an act we label as sexual because it involves the genitalia may sometimes be better understood in nonsexual terms. The classic study of sex offenders (Gebhard et al., 1965) concluded that up to 33 percent of rapists carried out the act to express aggression rather than for sexual satisfaction. Rapists, in the opinion of many (for example, Brownmiller, 1975; Gagnon, 1977), aggress against others for reasons having only remotely to do with sex per se (see Box 11.3). Many feminist groups object to the classification of rape as a *sexual* crime at all, for it can mask the basically assaultive and typically brutal nature of the act, and it creates an atmosphere in which the sexual motives of the *victim* are questioned. Although a person who is beaten and robbed (without being sexually abused) is hardly suspected of secretly wanting to be attacked, by cruel irony the victims of rape must often prove their moral "purity" to husbands, friends, police—and even to themselves. What, after all, did *they* do that might have contributed to the incident, especially if the rapist was not a complete stranger? But there are indications that the stigma of rape is being removed by more enlightened views, coming in large measure from women's liberation groups and from books such as Brownmiller's.

Sexual Sadism and Sexual Masochism

The majority of <u>sadists,</u> as indicated earlier, establish relationships with masochists to derive mutual sexual gratification. Sadomasochism is found in both heterosexual and homosexual relationships. The sadist may derive full orgastic pleasure by inflicting pain on his or her partner, and the masochist may be completely gratified by being subjected to pain. For other partners the sadistic and masochistic practices are a prel-

BOX   11.3 A Psychophysiological Analysis of Rape

Discussions of rape are based almost entirely on the work of historians, sociologists, political analysts, and journalists. Recently, experimental psychologists have been trying to bring something of the phenomenon into the laboratory. The work of Abel and his colleagues (1977) is a good example of this kind of research.

In their initial study these workers developed a methodology that relied on the penile plethysmograph to help them distinguish between rapists and nonrapists. Most of the rapists had long histories of forcible sexual assaults on women, and some on men as well. Control subjects had histories of other types of unconventional sexual behavior, such as exhibitionism, pedophilia, and homosexuality.

The independent variable in the experiment consisted of two kinds of erotic audiotapes. The story recorded on one tape was of mutually enjoyable intercourse with a suitable partner; the other audiotape was of a rape of that same partner. The enjoyable scene of intercourse portrayed the partner as willing, loving, and utterly involved with the subject. In the rape scene the victim resisted and was in physical as well as emotional pain. According to the plethysmograph, rapists were significantly more aroused by the rape tape than were the nonrapist subjects, the expected pattern. But interestingly, the rapists were highly aroused by the mutually enjoyable intercourse tape as well! In fact, this tape aroused them no less than the rape scene. And the nonrapists, although much more aroused by the lovemaking than by the rape, nonetheless showed some mild arousal when listening to the rape story.

The finding that the rapists were responsive to the enjoyable sex scene as well as to the rape scene does not support the usual image of the rapist as a man who is *incapable* of finding stimulation in conventional, loving intercourse. It is possible, however, that had Abel and his colleagues queried the subjects afterward, they would have found that the rapists were adding imagined violence and hurtful elements to the loving encounter in an attempt to enjoy it more.

Abel then went on to use the same method to investigate the rapist's response to aggression. Are rapists aroused by aggression if the incident does not conclude with sexual assault? How does arousal from aggression relate to arousal from rape? Some of the rapists already studied listened to three additional tapes. One of them depicted a rapist slapping, hitting, and holding a woman down against her will, but without ensuing intercourse. On the second the man had forcible intercourse with the same victim. The rapists also listened to a tape of nonviolent sexual intercourse with a willing partner. Results revealed that the aggression scene generated some sexual arousal, but only 40 percent of that generated by the rape scene and an even smaller percentage of that generated by the tape of mutually satisfying nonaggressive intercourse.

Abel and his colleagues went on to compare the plethysmograph records of individual rapists with their case histories. Some case histories indicated a preference for conventional intercourse, with rape resorted to if the victim was unwilling. These men had relatively small erections to the aggression story, greater response to the rape, and the greatest response to the conventional intercourse. For other rapists, whose histories showed repeated, often sadistic assaults on women, erections to mutually enjoyable intercourse were minimal, but arousal was markedly augmented when aggression was added to sex to equal rape. Moreover, high levels of arousal were elicited by the aggression tape. Hence the picture is not a simple one. Some men apparently resort to rape only when loving intercourse is unavailable, whereas others seem to *require* violence-with-sex forced on an unwilling and frightened victim.

How does this sort of research relate to the discussions in the text? Consider, for example, Brownmiller's thesis that rape is man's way of intimidating, even denigrating, women. Her historical-political analysis might at first appear a world apart from the laboratory research of Abel. But this is not really the case, even though investigators like Brownmiller and experimentalists seldom converse. Abel and his colleagues have shown that some rapists do, indeed, become sexually aroused by scenes depicting aggression, and that this arousal can be greater than that they experience when scenes of conventional intercourse are presented. The question this kind of laboratory research does not address—and can probably *never* address—is *why*. Why are certain men sexually stimulated when pain is inflicted on an unwilling victim? What is there about the one-down relationship between a rapist and his victim that excites him? Brownmiller and others find the causes in the broad sweep of history and more particularly in the power relationships between men and women. Their independent variables, if you will, are male machismo, the deliberate degradation of women, and the desire to intimidate by aggression. Abel and others in their laboratory work examine men at the end of a long behavior-shaping process. The rapists they have studied are products of their social-learning history. To figure out *why* they aggress is the larger, more important question. The search should take investigators into the domain of sociologists, political scientists, and historians.

ude to sexual intercourse. A married couple seen for behavior therapy had practiced the following ritual.

> As a prelude to sexual intercourse, the young man would draw blood by cutting a small incision on the palm of his wife's right hand. She would then stimulate his penis, using the blood of her right palm as a lubricant. Normal intercourse would then ensue, and the moment the wife felt her husband ejaculating, she was required to dig her nails deep into the small of his back or buttocks (Lazarus and Davison, 1971, pp. 202–203).

Masochists seem to outnumber sadists, however. For this reason "bondage and discipline" services may constitute a considerable portion of the business of a house of prostitution. The manifestations of sexual masochism are also varied. Some of course are self-inflicted.

Some sadists murder and mutilate. Fortunately, however, most of the time sadism and masochism are restricted to fantasies and are not then regarded as disorders, according to DSM-III. The increasing number of "sex shops" in large cities do a lucrative business in providing pictorial and written materials to those who need at least the vicarious experience of pain in order to satisfy themselves sexually.

How can it happen that a person, often quite normal in other respects, must inflict or experience suffering, directly or vicariously, in order to become sexually aroused? If it is assumed, as some psychoanalysts do, that pain provides sexual pleasure, the answer is readily available; unfortunately, this "explanation" really explains nothing. Another psychoanalytic theory, restricted to men, holds that the sadist has a castration complex and inflicts pain to assure himself of his power and masculinity. It may also be that in childhood or adolescence sadomasochistic elements were present while orgasms were experienced. Although it is plausible to suggest that classical conditioning may have occurred, there are as yet no data to support this theory. A related hypothesis suggests that the physiological arousal from inflicting and experiencing pain is not, in fact, dissimilar to sexual excitement. In the early stages of being sexualized, discriminations may be more difficult to make, especially if the pain-inducing act also includes sexual elements. In this way the individual may learn to label pain-produced arousal as sexual. Interesting as it may be, this hypothesis is also purely speculative at this point.

Atypical Paraphilias

The final category of paraphilias are called atypical; they are a miscellaneous group of unconventional activities, all of them having impressive and mysterious names, none of them being well understood. In each instance the act is necessary for sexual excitement, not merely a variation of conventional behavior. Among them are the following.

Coprophilia. Obtaining sexual gratification from handling feces.

Frotteurism. Obtaining sexual gratification by rubbing against another person, without engaging in sexual intercourse.

Klismaphilia. Achieving sexual excitement by means of an enema administered by another person.

Necrophilia. Being sexually intimate with a corpse.

Telephone scatologia. Making obscene phone calls for sexual gratification.

Sexual oralism. Exclusive reliance on oral-genital sex.

Sexual analism. Exclusive reliance on anal sex.

Gerontosexuality. Marked preference for older people as sexual partners.[4]

Therapies for the Paraphilias

Neither the psychoanalytic school nor the humanistic has made notable contributions to therapy for paraphilias, although interesting case studies abound in their clinical literatures.

In the earliest stages of behavior therapy, paraphilias were narrowly viewed as attractions to in-

---

[4] This paraphilia highlights the subjectivity or cultural relativism that permeates psychiatric diagnosis. How much older must a person's sex partner be for the relationship to be considered abnormal? Widespread ignorance of how sexually active people can be well into their eighties (see page 546) may be the reason why a diagnosis pertaining to this preference was ever suggested.

appropriate objects and activities. Looking to experimental psychology for ways to reduce these attractions, workers fixed on aversion therapy. Thus a boot fetishist would be given mild shock or an emetic when looking at a boot, a transvestite when cross-dressing, a pedophile when gazing at a photograph of a nude child, and so on. Sometimes these negative treatments were supplemented by training in social skills and assertion, for many of these individuals only poorly relate to others in ordinary social situations and even more poorly if at all through conventional sexual intercourse. There is some reason to believe that aversion therapy can alter pedophilia, transvestism, exhibitionism, and fetishism (Marks and Gelder, 1967; Marks, Gelder, and Bancroft, 1970), although to what extent the improvements are achieved through the placebo effect is unclear.

More recently the aversive stimulus has been presented in imagination, via covert sensitization (Cautela, 1966; see page 308). Instead of being shocked or made nauseous with a drug while confronting the objects or situations to which he is inappropriately attracted, the paraphiliac, with assistance and encouragement from the therapist, pairs in imagination the pleasurable but unwanted arousal and an aversive stimulus. In a variation called covert punishment, the fantasized aversive stimulus may concern the aftermath of his act. The pedophile may imagine that his wife and daughter catch him fondling a little girl, that the police arrest him in the street, that his crime is reported in the newspapers, that he loses his job, and so on to jail.

Paraphiliacs have also been behaviorally treated by _orgasmic reorientation,_ which attempts to help them respond sexually to stimuli or situations that for them do not have the accustomed appeal. Individuals are confronted with a conventionally arousing stimulus while they are responding sexually for other, undesirable reasons. In an early clinical demonstration of this technique, Davison (1968a) instructed a young man troubled by sadistic fantasies to masturbate at home in the following manner.

When assured of privacy in his dormitory room. . . he was first to obtain an erection by whatever means possible—undoubtedly *with a sadistic fantasy, as he indicated. He was then to begin to masturbate while looking at a picture of a sexy, nude woman (the "target" sexual stimulus). . . . If he began losing his erection, he was to switch back to his sadistic fantasy until he could begin masturbating effectively again. Concentrating again on the . . . picture, he was to continue masturbating, using the fantasy only to regain erection. As orgasm was approaching, he was at all costs to focus on the . . . picture . . . (p. 84).*

The client was able to follow these instructions and over a period of weeks began to find conventional pictures, ideas, and images sexually arousing. The therapist, however, had to complement the orgasmic procedure with some covert sensitization for the sadistic imaginings. The follow-up after a year and half found the client capable of conventional arousal, although he apparently reverted to his sadistic fantasies every now and again. This dubious outcome has been reported for other instances of orgasmic reorientation, but behavior therapists continue to explore its possibilities.

A sensible program of treatment must always consider the multifaceted nature of a particular disorder. Individual A may cross-dress for one reason, individual B for another. An exhibitionist, for example, may experience a great deal of tension in connection with his urge to expose himself; it would therefore make sense to desensitize him to women of the type who appeal to him. After imagining them in a succession of street and other public scenes, until they no longer make him anxious, he may be more relaxed when he encounters appealing women in public places and so may not feel the urge to expose (Bond and Hutchison, 1960). Other paraphiliacs might be questioned about social situations and aspects of relating to women that cause them undue discomfort. They could be desensitized to these, in hopes of making them generally less anxious.

The paraphilias have been the focus of considerable behavior therapy research. The evidence for the effectiveness of aversion therapy, assertion training, social-skills training, covert sensitization, desensitization, and other behavior therapy procedures in effecting enduring and significant changes in the paraphilias is meager when the usual standards of scientific evidence are applied (see Chapter 4). In our zeal to be rigorous, however, we should not dismiss the fact that behavior therapy has, for whatever constellation of reasons, proved far more effective than either psychoanalysis or humanistic-existential therapies in treating these very difficult and resistant human problems. Although the role of insight per se appears important in treating anxiety and depression, clinical and experimental reports reveal that for the paraphilias a focused, action-oriented, directive program, especially one that includes the teaching of specific social skills, may be the most appropriate.

Therapy for Rape

Unlike most of the disorders dealt with in this book, rape has the dubious distinction of presenting two different challenges to the mental health professional: treating the man who has committed the act and treating the woman who has been the victim.

A number of therapy programs have been developed to reduce the tendency of men to rape. In some prisons group therapy of a confrontational nature has been employed in efforts to encourage convicted rapists to take responsibility for their violence toward women and to explore more decent ways of handling their anger and relating to the opposite sex. But the effectiveness of these programs has for the most part not been studied. Most rapists perpetrate their assaults many times in their lives, and prison terms have little demonstrable effect on reducing the future incidence of rape. Therapists who try to help men who rape have to consider a wide range of causes that might underlie the problem—loneliness, deficient social skills, fear of dealing with women in conventional ways, actual hatred for women, inability or unwillingness to delay gratification, perhaps especially after excessive drinking, and exaggerated conceptions of masculinity that relegate women to an inferior position.

Considerable effort has recently been expended in helping the victims of sexual assaults (for example Peters, 1977; Sutherland and

BOX 11.4 Sex Offenders: A Problem for Society

Sex offenders, those who are convicted of rape, child molesting, voyeurism, and exhibitionism, are usually imprisoned. Sometimes, but not always, specially designed treatment programs are available to help the prisoner with his problem, but the success rates are not encouraging.

To begin with, virtually all therapies require the active cooperation of the patient. They generally have little chance of succeeding when forced on a person. Moreover, when therapy takes place in a prison, other conditions, the routines of the place, are too restrictive for the prisoner to become truly involved in his treatment. Finally, above and beyond the inherently coercive surroundings, professional knowledge of how to treat unconventional patterns of sexuality is quite limited. Until recently, therapeutic efforts were very punitive in nature, consisting for the most part of aversion therapy and even of surgical castration of the testes. Many workers believe that such radical treatments reflected society's wish to punish the offender for his heinous acts rather than any desire to help him.

Then the 1970s saw a curtailment of treatment. Lawsuits were brought on behalf of prisoners who objected to certain therapeutic interventions on the grounds that their civil rights were being violated. And indeed, some sex offenders were being subjected to extremely painful and unethical practices in the name of behavior modification. Actions by the courts have brought much-needed protection to many prisoners, but at the same time it may have a price. Clinicians have been discouraged from developing treatments that could conceivably have controlled behavior threatening to society as well as to the offender himself. Finally, the descriptions of sex offenders indicate the complexity of their behavior. A man who feels compelled to exhibit himself to unwilling observers would seem to suffer from a host of underlying psychological problems. If he is a lonely person, unable to initiate even casual, let alone intimate, relationships with women, chances are that many areas of his life require careful attention. Such work requires much skill, patience, and time—which our society does not have in abundance when it comes to treating the imprisoned sex offender.

Scheri, 1977). A number of rape crisis centers and telephone hotlines have been established across the country, some of them associated with existing hospitals and clinics, others operating on their own. Staffed both by professionals and by female volunteers, who may themselves have been rape victims in the past, these centers offer support and advice. Women from the center accompany the rape victim to the hospital and to the police station, where they help them with the legal procedures and with recounting the events of the attack. They may later arrange for examinations for pregnancy and venereal disease and for psychological counseling. These empathic companions help the victim get started in expressing her feelings about her ordeal, and they urge her to continue her venting with her own relatives and friends. If the attacker or at-tackers have been apprehended, the women from the center urge the victim to go through with the prosecution. They attend both her meetings with the district attorney and the trial itself.

As already indicated, rape victims, far more than the victims of other violent crimes, tend to examine their own role in provoking or allowing the attack; counseling, therefore, has to concentrate on alleviating the woman's feelings of responsibility and guilt. When long-term counseling is available, attention is often paid to the woman's ongoing relationships, which may be disrupted or otherwise negatively affected by the rape. Husbands and lovers often acquire the culture's suspicion of the victim and must be kept from viewing their loved one as guilty or tainted by the experience.

Rape-counseling centers are now offering assistance to rape victims, helping them through their ordeal and urging them to prosecute rapists.

Ego-Dystonic Homosexuality

From the time DSM-II was published in 1968 until 1973, it listed _homosexuality_ as one of the "sexual deviations." During 1973 the Nomenclature Committee of the American Psychiatric Association, under pressure from many professionals, and particularly from gay activist groups, recommended to the general membership the elimination of the category homosexuality and the substitution of _sexual orientation disturbance._ This new diagnosis was to be applied to gay men and women who are "disturbed by, in conflict with, or wish to change their sexual orientation." The

members of the psychiatric association voted on the issue, in itself a comment on the conduct of science in the twentieth century. The change was approved, but not without vehement protests from a number of renowned psychiatrists who had for some time been identified with the traditional view that homosexuality reflects a fixation at an early stage of psychosexual development and is inherently abnormal.

The controversy continued among mental health professionals, but as DSM-III was being developed during the late 1970s, it became increasingly clear that the new nomenclature would maintain the tolerant stance toward homosexuality that had become evident in 1973. The current category, _ego-dystonic homosexuality,_ refers to a person who is homosexually aroused, finds this arousal to be a persistent source of distress, and wishes to become heterosexual.

The new category

As for acceptance of homosexuality, the statements in DSM-III about ego-dystonic homosexuality bring to mind the ironic comment, "There is less here than meets the eye." This new category of psychosexual disorder is restricted to homosexuals; by definition it does not apply to heterosexuals who find their sex lives with members of the opposite sex a source of persistent concern and wish them to be different. Diagnosticians examine individuals dissatisfied with heterosexuality with a view toward improving their functioning as heterosexuals. For example, a woman might be unhappy with a heterosexual relationship because she has been pressured continually to engage in sex when she does not feel like doing so. A likely diagnosis would be "inhibited sexual desire," the assumption being that the normal desire for heterosexual sex is being blocked, or inhibited, by something that should be discovered and removed. Or a woman might find sexual intercourse aversive, distasteful, or simply uninteresting because she does not become aroused or, if she does, does not have orgasms. Her diagnosis would likely be "inhibited sexual excitement" if the first is true and "inhibited female orgasm" if the second is. (These sexual dysfunctions are discussed in Chapter 12.) Again, the unspoken assumption is

BOX   11.5
Homophobia
and Exclusive
Homosexuality

Those who argue that heterosexuality is normal and homosexuality abnormal often make the statement that exclusive homosexuality is unknown in the animal kingdom when members of the opposite sex are available. It is also proposed that heterosexual contacts are maximized in all species so that adequate reproduction can take place. Moreover, it is apparently the case that in no human culture has exclusive homosexuality been encouraged for sizable numbers of people.

These arguments are cogent, but they overlook one essential characteristic of human sexuality, namely that *bisexuality is more prevalent than exclusive homosexuality* (Kinsey, Pomeroy, and Martin, 1948). Churchill (1967) has made the provocative suggestion that exclusive homosexuality may well be encouraged by antihomosexual societies such as our own. Because sexual contacts between members of the same sex are so severely condemned, some bisexuals may be forced into making a choice and *thereby* become committed to contacts with members of their own sex rather than continuing to find sexual relationships with members of both sexes meaningful. What some call *homophobia* (Weinberg, 1972) may actually help create exclusive homosexuality.

that difficulties with sex involving an opposite-sexed partner are disruptions or inhibitions of the norm, namely, heterosexuality. A greater *value* is placed on achieving satisfactory heterosexual functioning. The fact that "ego-dystonic *heterosexuality*" is not a diagnosis reflects a continuing implicit belief that homosexuality is abnormal. The difference between DSM-III and earlier nosologies is that the negative view of homosexuality is more subtle.

As for all categories of disorder, DSM-III contains for ego-dystonic homosexuality a discussion of predisposing factors.

> *Since homosexuality itself is not considered a mental disorder, the factors that predispose to homosexuality are not included in this section [or anywhere in DSM-III]. The factors that predispose to Ego-dystonic Homosexuality are those negative societal attitudes toward homosexuality that have been internalized. In addition, features associated with heterosexuality, such as having children and [a] socially sanctioned family life, may be viewed as desirable and incompatible with a homosexual arousal pattern (p. 282).*

What do these statements mean? Consider the plight of the homosexual growing up in contemporary society.

> *To suggest that a person comes voluntarily to change his sexual orientation is to ignore the powerful environmental stress, oppression if you will, that has been telling him for years that he should change. To grow up in a family where the word "homosexual" was whispered, to play in a playground and hear the words "faggot" and "queer," to go to church and hear of "sin" and then to college and hear of "illness," and finally to the counseling center that promises to "cure," is hardly [to live in] an environment of freedom and voluntary choice. The homosexual is expected to want to be changed and his application for treatment is implicitly praised as the first step toward "normal" behavior (Silverstein, 1972, p. 4).*

BOX **11.6** Sexual Preference and Our Understanding of Human Behavior

The Kinsey reports (Kinsey, Pomeroy, and Martin, 1948; Kinsey, Pomeroy, Martin, and Gebhard, 1953) documented for the first time that a great many men and women have homosexual feelings at various times in their lives. So it became less and less defensible to divide people up into two mutually exclusive categories based on the gender of their sexual partners. A continuum seemed more appropriate. But, as Gagnon has pointed out, the very fact that homosexuality and heterosexuality appear at opposite ends of Kinsey's continuum reveals an *assumption* that human behavior will be better understood if individuals are placed somewhere on a continuum of sexual preference. An infinite array of characteristics might have anchored Kinsey's scale:

In United States culture the gender of one's sexual partner is crucial, and therefore leads to a key label; however, let us think of a society where gender does not matter, but where it is very important what emotions one feels during sex. People would then divide up by the kind of feeler that they are . . . love-feelers of lust-feelers (the former would obviously be "better" people). In our studies we would find that there are many love-feelers in the society and only just a few lust-feelers; in the middle we would find bi-feelers. Soon we would have theories about why people felt lust (and not love); their childhoods would be studied; the fact that they were not able to feel correctly would tell us that they were immature, neurotic, perhaps even criminal. (From Human Sexualities, p. 236. Copyright © 1977, by Scott, Foresman and Company. Reprinted by permission.)

Is Western society's long-held concern with sexual orientation a useful one? Is our understanding of Michelangelo's genius furthered by our knowing that he had strong homosexual interests? Many have remarked that his sensitive sculpture "David" is a manifestation of his homosexuality, that his brilliant representastion of a young man came from his sexual love for men and for the person who was the model for the sculpture. Are we then to "explain' the beauty of the Sistine Chapel in a similiar fashion?

DSM-III takes the position then that a homosexual is abnormal if he or she has been persuaded by this prejudiced society-at-large that his or her sexual orientation is inherently deviant, something which DSM-III itself asserts is not the case! Ego-dystonic homosexuality could also develop when a homosexual is frustrated or hurt by societal prejudices against his or her desire to establish a home with another person of the same sex. If DSM-III's explicit support of homosexuality is able to help win for the life style greater acceptance than it has today, eventually there will be fewer social and legal sanctions against homosexual partners' setting up households and raising children, whether they be adopted or the offspring of earlier heterosexual mariages of one or both of them. The homosexual will then be able to enjoy more of what is now the heterosexual "package." The DSM will have influenced itself out of this new category, ego-dystonic homosexuality.

A comment on past theory and research

For many years theories have been proposed, and data collected, on the origins of homosexuality. Psychoanalysts, learning theorists, and physiologically oriented workers have compared homosexuals with heterosexuals for differences in their psychological or physical makeup. Perhaps the most widely cited study is that carried out by Bieber and several of his colleagues (1962). Case records of 106 homosexual patients and 100 heterosexual patients who were being seen by 77 New York psychoanalysts were compared. Among the differences found was that the homosexual male analysands more often had "close-binding intimate mothers" and emotionally detached, hostile fathers. Overlooking for present purposes a number of methodological flaws in the study—the most important being that all the 107 homosexuals were being analyzed and were not representative of homosexuals en masse, most of whom are not in therapy—we ask whether these differences demonstrate that homosexuality per se is pathological and that having such parents is pathogenic, that is, causes illness.

Bieber and his colleagues clearly believe so.

[The close-binding intimate mother] exerted an unhealthy influence on her son through preferential treatment and seductiveness on the one hand and inhibiting, over-controlling attitudes on the other. In many instances, the son was the most significant individual in her life and the husband was usually replaced by the son as her love object. . . .[5] We are led to believe that . . . maternal close-binding intimacy and paternal detachment-hostility is the "classic" pattern and most conducive to promoting homosexuality . . . in the son (pp. 47, 144).

The implication of this study and of many others is that any differences found between homosexuals and heterosexuals constitute evidence that homosexuality is abnormal and that the difference itself is pathogenic. Is there anything wrong with this line of reasoning?

Let us take an analogous situation. Suppose we found that women who are now good golfers had as children attended public schools more often than did women who are poor golfers. Suppose also that the difference in their golfing ability is the only consistent one between the two groups. Under what circumstances would we conclude that childhood experiences in private schools are pathogenic, causing pathology or illness? The answer is simple: going to a private school is pathogenic if its outcome, being a poor golfer, has already been judged pathological. If we do not make this a priori judgment, we cannot talk of a difference between two groups as indicative of pathology in one of the groups, and we cannot regard the presumed cause a pathogenic one. The most we can say is that the two groups are *different* from each other.

This logic can be applied to Bieber's study.

One cannot attach a pathogenic label to a pattern of child rearing unless one a priori labels the adult behavior pattern as pathological. . . . What is wrong with [a "close-binding intimate mother"] unless you hap-

---

[5] The presumed replacement of the father by his son as a "love object" did not refer to explicit sexual activities.

BOX 11.7 Gender Identity and Homosexual Preference

Psychoanalytic theory and to a degree behavioral theories as well hold male homosexuality to be a problem in gender identity: a man can become homosexual because he has not adopted his society's definition of manhood. Making love to a man rather than to a woman is assumed to be possible only for men who do not share a given society's conception of masculinity.

Other theorists and writers dispute whether homosexuals have an inappropriate gender identity. Churchill (1967), for example, refers to the comradeship and homosexual love that existed among many Greek warriors; Plato commented on the military advantages of homosexual relationships, for they seemed to foster great ferocity in battle on the part of men driven to protect their lovers. Is it reasonable to regard a brave soldier as lacking a masculine gender identity?

Moreover, in the Bieber study (1962) only 2 percent of the homosexuals were rated by their analysts as "effeminate"; this finding of masculinity among male homosexuals was borne out in a study by Evans (1969), in which 95 percent of the homosexuals rated themselves as "moderately or strongly masculine." Indeed, in his renowned "Three Contributions to the Theory of Sex" (1905), Freud asserted, "In men, the most perfect psychic manliness may be united with . . . homosexuality."

Many male homosexuals have a firm identification of themselves as men (Silverstein, 1972); the same holds true for lesbians, who usually identify themselves as women (Martin and Lyon, 1972). To be sure, the stereotype of the limp-wristed, lisping "fag" probably contributes to the misconception, or at least overgeneralization, of male homosexuality as feminine behavior. And the stereotype of the "butch" or "dyke" who wears her hair clipped and dresses in tailored clothing similarly fosters the misconception that the lesbian is somehow less of a woman, more of a man. But we must bear in mind that homosexuals grow up in the same cultures as everyone else! They learn that preferring a same-sexed partner implies being less of a man or less of a women and they may consciously adopt traits of the opposite gender. To explain homosexuality itself as simply an error in gender identity is probably wrong. "Gender roles are not a mold in which we pour our sexuality" (Gagnon, 1977 p. 242).

pen to find her in the background of people whose current behavior you judge beforehand to be pathological? (Davison, 1976, p. 159).

Future research

If the mental health professions take seriously the DSM-III position that homosexualty itself is not pathological unless a person internalizes society's views that it is, research into ego-dystonic homosexuality should not concern itself with finding reasons why attraction to same-sexed partners develops. Rather, the search should be for the reasons why some homosex-

uals cannot resist pressures from others to believe that homosexuality is abnormal. And, as discussed in Box 21.7 (page 707), mental health workers might well spend less time trying to make homosexuals into heterosexuals and more time trying to eliminate the prejudices of society against homosexuality. If such efforts succeed, we can expect laws discriminating against homosexuals to be eliminated, and social prejudices may mollify as well. In short, the very societal conditions that bring on ego-dystonic homosexuality may disappear and with them, as indicated earlier, the last vestige of homosexuality from the list of mental disorders.

Summary

In this chapter we examined three categories of psychosexual disorders. The gender identity disorders—transsexualism and gender identity disorder of childhood—are deep and persistent convictions of individuals that their anatomic sexual makeup and the psychological sense of self as a man or a woman and as a boy or a girl are discrepant. Thus a man who is a transsexual is masculine in his physical endowment but considers himself a woman and would like to live as such. Early child-rearing practices may have encouraged the young child to believe that he or she was of the opposite sex. These problems are of significant theoretical interest, for they illustrate the plasticity of our beliefs about ourselves as men and women. Until recently, the only kind of help available to such individuals was sex-change surgery, to bring their bodies into line in some degree with gender identity. In the past few years, however, behavior therapy has successfully altered specific aspects of the transsexual's behavior—mannerisms, tone of voice, sexual fantasies—and brought gender identity into line with anatomy.

In the paraphilias unusual imagery and acts are necessary for sexual excitement or gratification; fetishism, transvestism, and sexual sadism are examples of such problems. Rape, although it is not described in DSM-III, is a pattern of behavior of considerable social and psychological trauma for the victim. The very inclusion of rape in a discussion of human sexuality is a matter of some controversy, for many workers regard rape as an act of aggression and violence rather than of sex. The most promising treatments for the paraphilias are behavior therapies, such as aversion therapy to reduce unwanted attraction and training in social skills to help the person have ordinary relations with members of the opposite sex.

DSM-III's new diagnosis ego-dystonic homosexuality is given to people whose homosexuality is a source of persistent distress and who clearly wish to be heterosexual. The inclusion of this category in the new nomenclature and descriptive statements about it are not completely logical, but they may eventually help eliminate prejudice against homosexuality.

chapter 12

PSYCHOSEXUAL DYSFUNCTIONS

In the preceding chapter the unconventional patterns of sexual behavior of a small minority of the population were described. But many "ordinary" people are likely to have problems that interfere with conventional sexual enjoyment at least to some extent during the course of their lives. Our concern in this chapter is with a range of sexual problems that are considered to represent inhibitions in the normal sexual response cycle.

A psychological problem has consequences not only for the individual but also for those with whom he or she is involved. Individuals unable to interact socially with others are inevitably cut off from many opportunities in life and, furthermore, often have low opinions of themselves. They can be a source of frustration and guilt for a spouse, a child, or a friend. This aspect of human emotional problems is especially important

in our consideration of _psychosexual dysfunctions,_ for they almost always are evident in interpersonal, intimate relationships. A marriage is bound to suffer if one or both of the partners fear the sexual situation. And most of us, for better or for worse, base part of our self-concept on our sexuality. Do we please the people we love, do we gratify ourselves, or, more simply, are we able to enjoy the fulfillment and relaxation that can come from a pleasurable sexual experience? Sexual difficulties can be of such severity that tenderness itself is lost, let alone the more intense satisfaction of sexual activity. It will be helpful to keep these points in mind in this review of the various sexual dysfunctions and, at the end of the chapter, of some of the therapies for them.

The Sexual Response Cycle

We begin by describing the _sexual response cycle._ It has been conceptualized in several ways. Havelock Ellis (1906), one of the earliest sexologists, spoke of _tumescence_ and _detumescence_—the flow of blood into the pelvic area during arousal and orgasm and its flow out of these areas afterward. A three-stage model—desire, excitement, and orgasm—has been proposed by Helen Singer Kaplan (1974), a noted sex therapist. What is significant about her model is the inclusion of "desire" as the initial stage.

William H. Masters and Virginia Johnson (1966), in their highly publicized research, overlooked the importance in everyday life of an inclination or decision by the individual to begin sexual activity in the first place. The four-stage cycle of sexual arousal delineated by them (Figure 12.1) was based on direct observations of normal volunteers who consented to be observed and to have their physiological responses to sexual stimulation recorded in a laboratory.[1] The reponses of men and women were found to be unexpectedly similar.

Havelock Ellis (1859–1939), a British writer on the psychology of sex and a humane and discerning man, understood at the turn of the century the sexual capacities of women and children and old people.

> The excitement phase is initiated by whatever is sexually stimulating to a particular individual. If stimulation is strong enough, excitement builds quickly, but if it is interrupted or if it becomes objectionable, this phase becomes extended or the cycle may by stopped. If effective sexual stimulation is continued, it produces increased levels of sexual tension. . . . This increased tension is called the plateau phase. If the individual's drive for sexual release in this phase is not strong enough, or if stimulation ceases to be effective or is withdrawn, the man or woman will not experience orgasm, but will enter a long period of gradually decreased sexual tension. The climactic or orgasmic phase, a totally involuntary response, consists of those few seconds when the body changes resulting from stimulation reach their maximum intensity. During the resolution phase, after orgasm, there is a lessening of sexual tensions as the person returns to the unstimulated state. Women are capable of having another orgasm if there is effective stimulation during this phase. The resolution period in the male includes a time, which varies among individuals, when restimulation is impossible. This is called the refractory period. In both sexes, the basic responses of the body to sexual stimulation are myotonia (increased muscle tension) and vasocongestion (filling of the blood vessels with fluid), especially in the genital organs, causing swelling. Of course these basic physiologic responses take on a different appearance in a man

[1] Although it is generally assumed that the data collected by Alfred Kinsey in the 1940s and 1950s were based almost entirely on interviews, John Gagnon, formerly associated with Kinsey's Institute for Sex Research in Bloomington, Indiana, has called attention to the extent to which Masters and Johnson built on work done earlier at the Institute. Many findings of the Kinsey group, published later in the Kinsey reports, were obtained through the direct observation and filming of sexual activity. The social climate of the day, however, discouraged Kinsey from acknowledging that his group had, in fact, gathered information on human sexuality through direct observation (Gagnon, 1977).

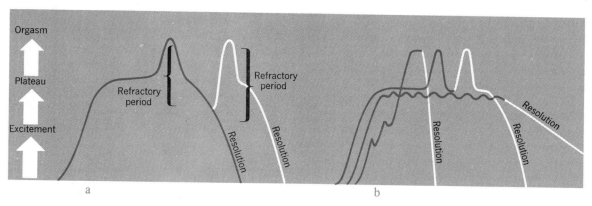

FIGURE **12.1**
Graphs of male (a) and female (b) sexual response cycles. The blue lines indicate the most common patterns of response, the white lines variations. The female cycle does not always climb to orgasm, but when it does there is not the inevitable refractory period found in the male cycle. Many women are able to have multiple orgasms in fairly rapid succession. After Masters and Johnson, 1966, p. 5.

The noted sex researchers and therapists, William H. Masters and Virginia Johnson. Their pioneering work helped launch a more candid and scientific appraisal of human sexuality.

than they do in a woman. Interestingly enough, the basic physiologic sexual responses remain the same regardless of the stimulation—coital, manipulative, mechanical, or fantasy. (Belliveau and Richter, 1970, pp. 33–34).

It is important to note that the various sexual response phases pointed out by Masters and Johnson do not represent actual quantitative changes in any particular physiological or psychological dimension. Heart rate, or vaginal lubrication, or engorgement of the penis does not steadily increase during excitement, remain constant during plateau, shift markedly upward during orgasm, and slowly diminish during resolution. Nor did Masters and Johnson claim to have shown the sexual interest of their subjects to wax and wane in this manner. What they and Ellis and Kaplan have proposed are schemes for talking about human sexuality. The scheme is an *invention* of the scientist, a device for organizing and discussing a body of information (Gagnon, 1977). It is also worth mentioning that sex researchers speak in terms of group averages; an average is after all by definition a convenient way to summarize a *range* of scores or experiences. So a given individual's responses can differ noticeably from a group average without being considered deviant or abnormal.

The impact of Masters and Johnson's work was considerable, contributing to our knowledge of the physiology of human sexuality. Perhaps more important, it helped make the scientific study of sex legitimate and acceptable. Even before their book was published, the information obtained through research was put to use in the treatment phase of their work (Masters and Johnson, 1970). By knowing how the body functions to achieve maximum sexual response, Masters and Johnson were able to elaborate methods of treating sexual dysfunction. These and other treatments are discussed later in this chapter.

The artificial circumstances in which Masters and Johnson gathered their findings limit their generality somewhat, however. And we should be mindful how little physiological research can tell us about the *psychological* components of human sexuality. Masters and Johnson were nonetheless able to provide firm data on certain controversial points and to dispel a few myths.

1. Although the _clitoris_ (Figure 12.2) is very important in transmitting sexual stimulation in the female, it has been a mistake to advise men to try to stimulate it continually during intercourse. During the plateau phase the cli-

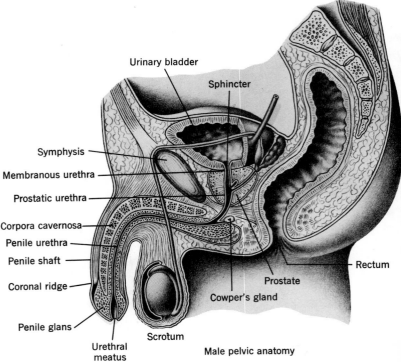

FIGURE **12.2**
Exterior view of female genitalia, cross section of male. (From Alvin Nason and Robert DeHaan, *The Biological World*, New York: Wiley, 1973.)

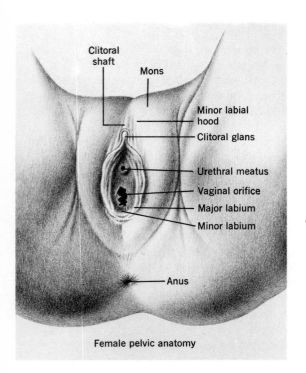

Female pelvic anatomy

Clitoral shaft
Mons
Minor labial hood
Clitoral glans
Urethral meatus
Vaginal orifice
Major labium
Minor labium
Anus

Male pelvic anatomy

Urinary bladder
Sphincter
Symphysis
Membranous urethra
Prostatic urethra
Corpora cavernosa
Penile urethra
Penile shaft
Coronal ridge
Penile glans
Urethral meatus
Scrotum
Cowper's gland
Prostate
Rectum

toris retracts, making access to it extremely difficult and even painful for some women. In point of fact, it is very difficult to have intercourse without stimulating the clitoris *indirectly,* which is the type of stimulation that some women seem to prefer.

2. Masters and Johnson were able to document that orgasms in women obtained from stimulation of the clitoris, without entrance into the vagina, are as intense as and indeed physiologically indistinguishable from orgasms obtained by having an erect penis in the vagina.

Probably few pieces of misinformation have caused more consternation than Freud's insistence that the vaginal orgasm is superior to the clitoral orgasm. He asserted, and practitioners have parroted to hundreds of thousands of people for years since, that a woman who can have an orgasm only by stimulation of her clitoris is settling for second best; further, that failure to have an orgasm via stimulation of the vagina by the man's penis is a sign of psychosexual fixation and immaturity. The Freudian theory has been explained rather precisely by John Gagnon.

Everyone goes through certain psychosexual stages, one of which involves masturbation as the important overt sexual activity. This stage occurs early in life as part of the parade of changes toward heterosexual genital maturity, that is, intercourse with a person of the opposite sex. Masturbation is infantile; intercourse is mature; being mature is better than being infantile. When women masturbate, they touch the clitoris; when women have intercourse, they have a penis in the vagina. Since masturbation is infantile, pleasures achieved by touching the clitoris are infantile. Sexual maturity [therefore] requires that women move from having orgasms produced by touching the clitoris to having orgasms produced by the penis in the vagina. The site of sensation [is] supposed to move from clitoris to vagina (From Human Sexualities, *p. 138. Copy-*

right © 1977, by Scott, Foresman and Company. Reprinted by permission.)

Even before the work of Masters and Johnson, some sexologists had been trying to disabuse people of this notion (for example, A. Ellis, 1961), pointing out that the walls of the vaginal barrel are poorly supplied with sensory nerve endings, whereas the clitoris, like the glans of the penis, is amply supplied. The fact that orgasms achieved by masturbation and manual manipulation by the partner, both of which typically concentrate on the clitoris and surrounding areas, were found to create at least as much excitation as intercourse pretty much puts to rest the bugaboo about clitoral orgasms.

Many authorities now believe that all female orgasms are evoked by stimulation of the clitoris, whether the friction is applied directly or through coitus. The orgasm itself, however, is expressed by rhythmic contractions of vaginal muscles. This dichotomy may be the source of the myth of clitoral and vaginal orgasms (Kaplan, 1974). Of course these findings in no way imply that the insertion of the penis and the movements of coitus are not extremely enjoyable to women.

3. Having simultaneous orgasms, a goal held up in numerous marriage manuals as indicating true love and compatibility, was not shown to be a mark of superior sexual achievement. In fact, it can often distract each of the partners from his or her own sexual pleasure.

4. It was also found that not only do most women *not* object to intercourse during menstruation, but they even tend to enjoy it more, particularly during the second half of the period.

5. During the second three months of pregnancy, women seem to desire intercourse at least as much as when not pregnant. Although there is some danger of spontaneous abortion in the early stages, particularly for women who have a history of spontaneous miscarriage, most women continue to desire sexual stimulation, sometimes until they go into labor. At any rate, little harm seems to

come to the woman and to the fetus in the uterus through intercourse, at least during the first six months of the pregnancy.

6. Various facts about the male's penis were also confirmed. The size of a man's erect penis was not found to be a factor in the enjoyment he can derive himself and impart to his sexual partner. The vagina is a potential not an actual space; that is, it distends just enough to accommodate the penis. Hence a very large penis will not create more friction for the man or the woman than a smaller one. Furthermore, penises that are small when flaccid may double in size when erect, whereas penises that are large in the limp state increase less proportionately. In other words, there does not seem to be as much variation in the size of the *erect* penis as had been assumed. The idea that the size of a man's penis is an index of his virility was completely dispelled.[2]

[2] Some women have voiced disagreement with Masters and Johnson's conclusion about the merits of a large penis. No doubt psychological variables, as well as the purely physiological ones that Masters and Johnson have dealt with, play a part in determining how an individual woman reacts.

The Sexual Dysfunctions: Descriptions and Causes

There have been several attempts to classify *sexual dysfunctions* (see LoPiccolo and Hogan, 1979, for a comprehensive review). Although no scheme is universally accepted, that of DSM-III is as reasonable as any others that have been proposed.

In general, the categories listed represent disturbances in one or more of the phases of the response cycle, as viewed by DSM-III: the appetitive phase, the equivalent of Kaplan's stage of desire; the excitement stage; the orgasm; and the resolution. DSM-III omits the plateau stage described by Masters and Johnson, and it indicates that inhibition of the resolution phase is rarely of clinical significance. A particular disorder may be lifelong, or it may have been acquired after a period of normal functioning; it may be generalized, or it may occur only in particular situations or with certain partners; and it may be total or partial. Each of the disorders may show up either during sexual activity with another person or during masturbation. DSM-III does not state whether the sexual partner is of the opposite or same sex, a sign of the growing liberalization of the attitude of the mental health professions toward homosexuality. The prevalence of these disturbances is believed to be very great, so great in fact that people should not assume that they need treatment only because they sometimes experience one or more of these problems. In the diagnostic criteria for each sexual dysfunction, DSM-III uses the phrase "recurrent and persistent" to underscore the fact that a problem must be serious indeed before a diagnosis is made.

In our discussions of the DSM-III categories of sexual dysfunctions, we describe what is believed to cause these human problems. It is important to bear in mind, however, that most of these generalizations about etiology are based on clinical reports of investigators like Masters and Johnson (1970), Kaplan (1974), and other sex therapists. As with all clinical reports, information provided by clients and interpreted by therapists is subject to distortion and selective attention. Moreover, no studies compare groups of dysfunctional patients with appropriate control groups for the presence or absence of causative factors (LoPiccolo and Hogan, 1979). For example, an unpleasant experience with a prostitute at age seventeen may seem to be a major cause of a thirty-year-old man's erectile problem, but countless other men have had a similar negative experience *without* developing a sexual problem.

Any points made about etiology are therefore necessarily tentative. Although this caveat can be issued for any section of this book, it is particularly appropriate to bear in mind here, considering the likelihood that the lives of many readers will be touched in some way by what is being discussed.

Inhibited sexual desire

The psychosexual dysfunction *inhibited sexual desire* did not appear in DSM-II. Its presence in DSM-III reflects a formal recognition that some people are troubled by what they, and especially their partners, perceive to be abnormally little interest in initiating or having sexual intimacies. The colloquialism is ''low sex drive.''

Of all the sexual dysfunctions covered by DSM-III, this one seems to be the most problematic. How frequently ''should'' a person be interested in sex? How often ''should'' a person actually have intercourse or masturbate? The diagnosis inhibited sexual desire may owe its very existence to the greater openness about sex in contemporary society—and perhaps to the higher expectations people are acquiring about being sexual.

Sexual drive may appear diminished to a partner because the other person wishes to be sexually intimate much less often than he or she does. There is no absolute frequency to point to as a criterion. During intercourse a woman may show some of the physical signs of sexual excitement, such as lubrication of the vaginal walls, yet claim she feels nothing and manifest little interest in repeating the experience. A man may readily have erections when in bed with someone he cares for and yet assert that he can take sex or leave it. In extreme cases a person may have an actual aversion to sex altogether. Sexual disinterest was formerly thought to be rare and

found only in women. Contemporary sex researchers and therapists recognize the phenomenon in men as well, and among those who seek help at some sex therapy centers inhibited sexual desire is more and more often the diagnosis.

We know little about the causes of this disorder, if indeed it is legitimate to call it a disorder. Probably the most definite evidence is that certain drugs, especially sedatives and narcotics, can dull a person's sexual desires. Sexual dysfunctions of the partner may also be implicated. A woman who is constantly frustrated by her partner's erectile problems or inept lovemaking may decide that sex is just not worth the aggravation and disappointment. Interpersonal problems of the partners can also be expected to affect their interest in sex with each other. In general, the role that sex plays in someone's life can vary tremendously. For whatever reasons—and the truth of the matter is that we can only speculate—some people are far less interested in sex than others. Unlike hunger and thirst, an ''appetite'' for sex need not be satisfied or even exist in order for the individual to survive and, it seems, to live happily.

Inhibited sexual excitement

DSM-II referred to ''impotence'' in the male. Its equivalent in women would be ''frigidity.'' The problem of inhibition during the excitement stage of the response cycle is, according to DSM-III, evidenced

> In males, [by] partial or complete failure to attain or maintain erection until completion of the sexual act, or
>
> In females, [by] partial or complete failure to attain or maintain the lubrication-swelling response of sexual excitement until completion of the sexual act (p. 279).

The diagnosis *inhibited sexual excitement* is appropriate only if ''the individual engages in sexual activity that is adequate in focus, intensity, and duration'' (p. 279). Should a woman, for example, be unresponsive to the overtures and technique of a man whom she does not particularly like, the diagnosis is not made.

Helen Singer Kaplan (1974) has outlined a

wide range of erectile problems for men. Some get an erection easily but lose it as they enter the woman's vagina. Others are flaccid when intercourse is imminent but maintain an erection easily during fellatio. Some men are erect when the partner dominates the situation, others when they themselves are in control. Some suffer complete erectile failure, being unable to maintain an erection under any circumstances. Others have problems only with people they care for deeply. Moreover, an obvious aspect of the problem is that it is, in fact, obvious. A woman can at least go through the motions of lovemaking, but sexual intercourse is usually stalemated if the man is not erect. A great deal is at stake if the penis becomes flaccid when it "should" be erect.[3] For this reason, perhaps, an "impotent" male is sometimes and unfortunately regarded as less than a man.

The causes of erectile problems are many. Possible organic factors include certain medications, such as Mellaril, one of the phenothiazines used in treating psychoses; some drugs for hypertension, angina, and heart disease; alcohol in large amounts; obesity; and generally any disease or hormonal imbalance that can affect the nerve pathways or blood supply to the penis. If one of these is believed to be the sole cause, a diagnosis of a psychosexual dysfunction is not made, according to DSM-III. And yet it is important to realize that physical causes sometimes play a major role when a man loses or does not have any erection at all. The majority of erectile difficulties, however, are believed to be psychological in nature (Rosen and Rosen, 1981), brought

on by performance fears and other preoccupations that distract men from "egoless" involvement in and enjoyment of sexual relations. The inhibition of sexual excitement in women is discussed in the following section on inhibited female orgasm.

Inhibited female orgasm

Sometimes called orgasmic dysfunction or anorgasmia, the persistent inability of a woman to have orgasms following sexual stimulation judged adequate for a climax is to be diagnosed as *inhibited female orgasm,* according to DSM-III. Oftentimes a woman also has difficulty during the excitement phase and would therefore receive the diagnosis of inhibited sexual excitement as well.

Until recently a distinction was not generally made between problems a woman may have in becoming sexually aroused and those she may have in reaching an orgasm. Although as many as 20 percent of all adult women rarely if ever experience an orgasm (Kinsey et al., 1953), far fewer are believed to remain unaroused during lovemaking. Kaplan (1974) argues that this distinction, recently made in DSM-III, is an important one, for "As a general rule, women who suffer from orgasmic dysfunction are responsive sexually. They may fall in love, experience erotic feelings, lubricate copiously, and also show genital swelling" (p. 343). In fact, she argues that failure to have orgasms should not be regarded as a disorder at all, rather as a normal variation of female sexuality.

Numerous reasons have been put forward to explain anorgasmia. Perhaps many women, unlike men, have to *learn* to become orgasmic. That is, the capacity to have an orgasm may not be innate in females as it is in males. In men ejaculation, which almost always is accompanied by orgasm, is necessary for reproduction. A woman may to some extent learn to have coital orgasms through earlier masturbation; survey findings indicate that women who masturbated little or not at all before they began to have intercourse were much more likely to be inorgasmic than women who had (Kinsey et al., 1953; Hite, 1976). These are, of course, correlational data; some third factor may be responsible both for infrequent masturbation and for dimin-

[3] Male erectile problems are complicated and important. Although an extended discussion is beyond the scope of this book, a few additional observations would seem in order. The fact that the state of a man's penis is evident both to him and to his partner is generally regarded as placing a unique set of pressures on him that are not the fate of a woman who suffers from inhibited sexual excitement. True enough, but the woman's situation is not easy either. The very fact that she can have sexual relations without being aroused has no doubt contributed to neglect of the woman's needs and desires. Moreover, the man's self-esteem is not the only one threatened if he becomes flaccid; the partner too, whether it be a woman or another man, often has doubts about sexual adequacy—is she not sexy enough, not lovable enough, not creative or "liberal" enough? Finally, replacement of impotence and frigidity by the phrase inhibited sexual excitement can be considered an advance. Impotence implies that the man is not potent, or in control, or truly masculine, and negatively backs up the macho conception of masculinity that many people are challenging (see page 652). Frigidity implies that the woman is emotionally cold, distant, unsympathetic, unfeeling. Both terms are derogatory and encourage as well a search for causes *within* the person, rather than focusing attention on the relationship, the domain contemporary investigators explore for answers and solutions.

ished ability to have orgasms during lovemaking. Lack of sexual knowledge also appears to play a role according to clinical data; many inorgasmic women, as well as those who experience little excitement during sexual stimulation, are unaware of their own genital anatomy and therefore have trouble communicating their needs to a partner or to themselves.

Women have different "thresholds" for orgasm. Although some have orgasms quickly and without much clitoral stimulation, others seem to need intense and prolonged stimulation, whether during foreplay or intercourse. A high threshold may contribute to anorgasmia if the woman does not appreciate that she simply requires relatively more stimulation than average, or if she is reluctant to communicate to her partner what she knows she needs. Her partner's reaction if she does can contribute to the problem; a man may conclude that he and his penis are inadequate if the female asks for manual stimulation of her clitoris during intercourse.

Another factor may be fear of losing control. The French have an expression for orgasm, *le petit mord,* the little death. Some women fear that they will begin screaming uncontrollably, make fools of themselves, or faint. A related source of inhibition is a belief, perhaps poorly articulated, that to let go and allow the body to take over from the conscious, controlling mind is somehow unseemly. The state of a relationship is also not to be overlooked: although some women can enjoy making love to a person they are angry with, or even despise, most hold back under such circumstances.

Inhibited male orgasm

Masters and Johnson (1970) used the somewhat pejorative term ejaculatory incompetence for the inability of the man to ejaculate within the vagina. The DSM-III diagnosis *inhibited male orgasm* would be applied to problems of ejaculating during intercourse, masturbation, manual or oral manipulation by a partner, and anal intercourse.

Difficulty in ejaculating is relatively rare, although some have suggested it is becoming more prevalent as men deem it desirable to delay their orgasms for long periods of time (Rosen and Rosen, 1981); indeed, sex without orgasm has even

been proposed in recent years as an ultrasophisticated form of male sexuality. It may be that some men are learning the skill too well! More prosaic causes have also been put forth: fear of impregnating a female partner, withholding love, expressing hostility, and, as with female anorgasmia, fear of letting go. In rare instances the problem may be traced to a physical source, such as taking certain tranquilizers. As with most of the other sexual dysfunctions, practically no experimental data exist, only speculation based on clinical case reports (Munjack and Kanno, 1979).

Premature ejaculation

Masters and Johnson (1970) define ejaculation as being premature when a man is unable to inhibit his orgasm long enough for his female partner to climax in 50 percent of their sexual encounters. Many people have been concerned about stipulating the male problem of *premature ejaculation* in terms of a *partner's* responsiveness. In DSM-III this difficulty is handled as follows: "Ejaculation occurs before the individual wishes it, because of recurrent and persistent absence of reasonable voluntary control of ejaculation and orgasm . . ." (p. 280). The focus is now on the preference of the man himself.[4] As with many other of the sexual dysfunctions, considerable judgment is required by clinicians who employ the DSM, for they must take into account such factors as the man's age, whether the sexual partner is new, and how often the man customarily has intercourse.

Premature ejaculation is probably the most prevalent sexual dysfunction among males, occurring also on an occasional basis, in which case the diagnosis is not appropriate. In general, the problem is associated with considerable anxiety. Sometimes the man ejaculates even before he penetrates the vagina but more usually within a few seconds of intromission. Although the human being is more than a relatively hairless ape, evolutionary theory informs us that rapid ejaculation has survival value, for any animal is particularly vulnerable to surprise attack when copulating. Hence the more quickly copulation can

---

[4] It would be naive, however, to overlook the extent to which a partner may influence the man's judgment that ejaculation is occurring before he wishes it.

occur, the better. Kinsey, himself a biologist, suggested that ejaculating quickly should not be considered a problem in human beings. Such a view, however, considers only the reproductive function of intercourse, ignoring its recreational and interpersonal functions (Rosen and Rosen, 1981). Indeed, concern about ejaculating "too soon" may be regarded as part and parcel of the undue emphasis placed on coitus as the ultimate in sexual behavior. The problem for a couple who prizes conventional sexual intercourse above all other sexual activities is that erection is slowly lost after an ejaculation, with many men finding continued stimulation unpleasant and sometimes painful. If lovemaking stops when the penis is no longer hard, ejaculation may indeed sometimes be premature. But if, as sex therapists advise, couples expand their repertoire of activities to include techniques not requiring an engorged penis, gratification of the partner is eminently possible *after* the man has climaxed. Indeed, when the focus is removed from penile-vaginal intercourse, the couple's anxieties about sex usually diminish sufficiently to permit greater ejaculatory control in the male and sexual intercourse of longer duration. As mentioned earlier, less and less emphasis is being placed nowadays on simultaneous orgasms during conventional sexual intercourse. It will be interesting to observe whether shifts in sexual norms and practices alter the concept of premature ejaculation.

The possible causes of premature ejaculation were examined in a doctoral dissertation by Spiess (1977). In his study men who complained of premature ejaculation when they sought assistance at a university sex therapy clinic were compared with controls recruited from the nearby community. The two groups were shown erotic slides and listened to an erotic audiotape while penile circumference was monitored by a plethysmograph (see Box 11.2, page 348). One prevalent theory holds that ejaculation occurs quickly because the man is unusually sensitive to erotic stimulation. Spiess's physiological measurements indicated otherwise.

Another hypothesis supposes that premature ejaculators climax at lower levels of sexual excitement than do other men. Spiess asked both premature ejaculators and normal controls whether they felt fully aroused when they ejaculated during intercourse. The premature ejaculators tended significantly more often to answer "Sometimes," the normal controls "Always." Spiess examined yet another hypothesis, namely that premature ejaculation may be caused by too little sex (Hastings, 1966). He asked both premature ejaculators and control subjects how often they had had intercourse and ejaculated during the two weeks preceding the study. The average number of ejaculations for these two weeks were 3.8 times for the premature ejaculators, 8.6 for the controls. This correlational information tends to back up the theory. The premature ejaculators could, however, have been avoiding the experience of climaxing quickly rather than responding early through infrequency of orgasm. A final hypothesis tested was Kaplan's (1974) suggestion that premature ejaculators are out of touch with their arousal levels, in essence less informed than controls of how close they are to ejaculating. To evaluate this hypothesis, Spiess had subjects rate their arousal several times while watching erotic slides and correlated their replies with penile circumference. The figures for both groups of subjects varied considerably, with no differences emerging. Overall, Spiess's research lends a certain amount of support to the view that some men tend to ejaculate at levels of sexual excitement that are lower than normal.

Functional vaginismus

During sexual excitement, especially when intercourse or other sexual intimacy is imminent, some women have involuntary spasms of the musculature of the outer third of the vagina. Coitus or even the insertion of a finger becomes impossible. This condition, _functional vaginismus,_ is not strictly sexual in nature, for the woman usually cannot undergo a routine pelvic examination, which entails insertion of a speculum.

Since the spastic contractions of the muscles prevent intercourse, it is not surprising one theory supposes that the woman wishes, perhaps unconsciously, to deny herself, her partner, or both the pleasures of sexual intimacy. As plausible as this idea may seem, no evidence supports it. Indeed, women with this problem can often have sexually satisfying lives through clitoral stimulation, if the partner is so inclined. Clinical reports also suggest fear of pregnancy and negative attitudes about sex in general. Masters and Johnson found that for a number of couples the man's inability to maintain an erection preceded the development of vaginismus in his wife; for some women, then, the sexual problems of their partners are so anxiety-provoking that a condition like vaginismus may develop.

Functional dyspareunia

Sometimes a man or a woman finds it painful to have intercourse. If this problem is not caused exclusively by a physical disorder, or if, in a woman, there are no vaginal spasms or lack of lubrication—which would indicate functional vaginismus or inhibited sexual excitement—DSM-III says _functional dyspareunia_ is to be diagnosed. Masters and Johnson, as well as other authorities on sexual dysfunctions, however, have found dyspareunia to be caused almost always by physical problems, such as infections of the vagina, cervix, and uterus and of the glans of the penis; pulled ligaments in the pelvic region; and scar tissue in the vaginal opening from incisions made during childbirth.

Theories of Psychosexual Dysfunctions: General Considerations

Earlier Sexology

Psychoanalytic views have assumed that sexual dysfunctions are symptoms of underlying repressed conflicts. The analyst considers the symbolic meaning of the "symptom" both to understand its etiology and to guide treatment. Since sexual dysfunctions bring discomfort and psychological pain to both the individual and to his or her partner, and since unimpaired sexuality is inherently pleasurable, the theme of repressed anger and aggression competing with the gratification of sexual needs pervades psychoanalytic writings. Thus a man who ejaculates so quickly that he frustrates his female partner may be expressing repressed hostility to women who remind him unconsciously of his mother. A woman with vaginismus may be expressing her repressed penis envy by threatening to castrate a man who would hope to enter her vagina. There is little evidence for the validity or even the usefulness of psychoanalytic theories of psychosexual dysfunctions. In fact, many contemporary psychoanalysts now confess the inability of their therapy to help people with sexual dysfunction and supplement it with the more direct techniques of behavior therapy (LoPiccolo, 1977).

Humanists view psychosexual dysfunctions in the same way that they do other disorders. A sexual dysfunction is considered to reflect the crippling anxiety and inhibition of a person who is failing to fulfill his or her own potential (see Box. 12.1).

Most contemporary sexologists, however, operate within a social-learning framework, although it is not always labeled as such. The most comprehensive account of the etiology of human sexual dysfunction was offered by Masters and Johnson in their widely acclaimed book _Human Sexual Inadequacy_ (1970). Let us first examine their suggestions and then consider modifications and extensions of their ideas that have been proposed more recently.

12.1 Psychosexual Dysfunction: A Bioenergetic Approach

Wilhelm Reich (1942), an Austrian psychoanalyst, agreed with Freud in placing human sexuality at the center of psychology but, unlike Freud, he studied sexual functioning directly. He concluded that the basis for all anxiety was the inability to achieve full and repeated sexual satisfaction. Thus the goal of therapy was to teach people to achieve sexual satisfaction by releasing muscular tension and allowing the free flow of sexual energy. Although one of Reich's extreme notions—that a vital energy "orgone" pervades nature and can be accumulated for bodily use by sitting in a specially designed box— discredited his other theories in the early fifties, they reemerged in the work of Alexander Lowen (1958). The _bioenergetic movement_ is a force in American psychology and psychiatry, especially on the West coast.

Bioenergetic therapy considers sexual dysfunctions to be caused by chronic anxiety and tension. Here Alexander Lowen performs deep-muscle massage to remove tension.

According to the bioenergetic view, sexual dysfunctions such as premature ejaculation and inhibited orgasm are caused by chronic tension and anxiety as they affect the muscles of the body. These chronic tensions are said to develop when powerful emotions like fear, anger, and sexual excitation are "blocked." The "blocking" is described as being not only cognitive but physical. Bioenergetic analysts speak of such phenomena as "the dead pelvis" in describing the body posture of those individuals who do not experience orgasm as the full and rhythmic involuntary pelvic movements indicative of sexual satisfaction. The task of bioenergetic therapy is to teach people to relax the body's musculature and establish freedom of movement during sex.

Bioenergetic therapy generally proceeds at both the cognitive and physical levels. At the cognitive level the therapist employs traditional psychodynamic procedures to help the patient achieve insight into the thoughts and feelings maintaining a rigid and sexually dysfunctional body posture. At the physical level the patient is instructed in a series of exercises designed to remove body tensions and breathing irregularities and to promote freedom of pelvic movement. Some bioenergetic therapists loosen tense areas of the body through deep-muscle massage. While the patient is being massaged, he or she is encouraged to recall and express any emotions that are experienced in order to ensure that emotional blocks and muscle tensions are not reinstated.

Bioenergetics, following Reich, places sexual dysfunction at the heart of all emotional and behavioral problems and has the same therapy goal for all clients, the restoration of sexual functioning. This goal may be appealing to some, but others have criticized it as contributing to a cultural obsession with sexual gratification and kindling unrealistic expectations of sexual fulfillment (Keen, 1979).

Because bioenergetic therapy has not been properly evaluated in controlled studies, its effectiveness is difficult to judge. Bioenergetics does, however, offer a unique view of human sexual inadequacy.

The Findings of Masters and Johnson

Current factors

Masters and Johnson discovered in the backgrounds of their patients a number of untoward attitudes and events that they consider responsible for sexual problems. The two researchers distinguish *historically* relevant factors and two *currently* relevant variables that they believe underlie the *maintenance* of all human sexual inadequacies. Sexual disorders are maintained, they suggest, because during intercourse one or both of the participants either adopt a *spectator role* or have crippling *fears about performance.* These two attitudes focus undue attention on performance rather than allowing a relatively passive and uncritical acceptance of sexual stimulation, which if unimpeded leads naturally to sexual enjoyment, including orgasm. As Masters and Johnson have stated, "fear of inadequacy is the greatest known deterrent to effective sexual functioning, simply because it so completely distracts the fearful individual from his or her natural responsivity by blocking reception of sexual stimuli . . ." (1970, pp. 12–13).

Historical factors

How do people come to adopt the spectator role and harbor performance fears? Masters and Johnson proposed that unfortunate attitudes instilled by upbringing and difficult experiences of earlier years feed into the current causes of sexual problems (Figure 12.3).

Religious Orthodoxy   One or both partners may have negative attitudes toward sex because they have been brought up with strict religious beliefs that denigrate sexual enjoyment. For example, a woman with vaginismus who was interviewed by Masters and Johnson had been

. . . taught that almost any form of physical expression might be suspect of objectiona-

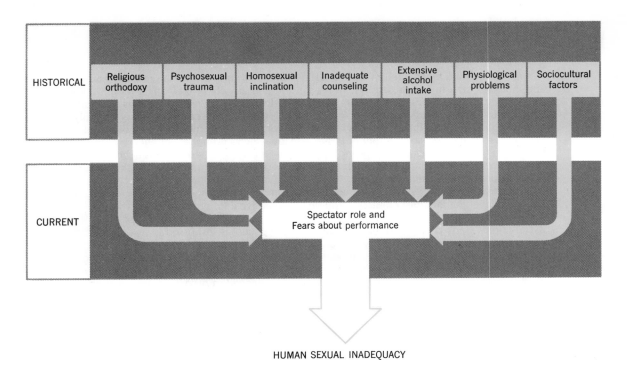

FIGURE **12.3**
Historical and current causes of human sexual inadequacies, according to Masters and Johnson.

ble sexual connotations. . . . She was prohibited when bathing from looking at her own breasts either directly or from reflection in the mirror for fear that unhealthy sexual thoughts might be stimulated by visual examination of her own body. Discussion with a sibling of such subjects as menstruation, conception, contraception, or sexual functioning were taboo. . . . Mrs. A. entered marriage without a single word of advice, warning, or even good cheer from her family relative to marital sexual expression. The only direction offered by her religious advisor relative to sexual behavior was that coital connection was only to be endured if conception was desired (p. 254).

Psychosexual Trauma   Some patients trace their fears of sexual contact to paricularly frightening or degrading experiences during initial sexual exposures. One young man had been assured by a

prostitute that ''He would never be able to get the job done for any woman—if he couldn't get it done here and now with a pro.'' One woman could date her vaginismus to a gang rape from which she suffered severe physical and psychological damage.

Homosexual Inclinations   Men with erectile problems and inorgasmic women may be unable to enjoy heterosexual relations because they have homosexual inclinations.[5]

---

[5] When Masters and Johnson published their clinical report on the nature and treatment of ''human sexual inadequacy'' in 1970, the sociopolitical climate was not as accepting of homosexuality as it is today. Their treatment program was exclusively heterosexual in its focus; hence the presence in one of the partners of a homosexual preference was seen as an etiological factor. The alternative view that the problem lay with a decision of the homosexual partner to try to maintain a heterosexual marriage was not explicitly considered. Similarly, until recently professionals have not attended systematically to sexual dysfunctions in homosexual relationships; contributions like Silverstein's A Family Matter: A Parent's Guide to Homosexuality (1977) are likely to redress the imbalance and help focus attention on homosexual interests, practices, and concerns.

Inadequate Counseling Bad advice from professional workers may create or exacerbate sexual inadequacies. Some men were told by physicians that erectile problems are incurable, others that they are a natural part of the aging process. A few had been warned by clergymen that their problem was God's punishment for sins.

Excessive Intake of Alcohol An erectile problem sometimes begins with undue concern about a normal reduction in sexual responsiveness brought on by excessive drinking (see page 299). In the typical pattern suggested by Masters and Johnson, a man who works very hard may develop a habit of drinking a good deal. Large amounts of alcohol are known to interfere with erections, while at the same time, ironically, lowering inhibitions. Having drunk too much, the man may find later in bed that no erection develops. Instead of attributing his lack of sexual arousal to his drinking, however, he begins to ruminate. Fear accumulates, and after a number of failures he may become unable to have an erection. The wife often attempts to be understanding and supportive of the husband. He, for any number of reasons, interprets this solicitude as further questioning of his masculinity. Or the wife, concerned that she may no longer be sexually attractive to her husband, pushes for sexual encounters, and aggravates the situation. Soon she may refrain from any physical contact whatsoever, even affectionate hugs and kisses, for fear that the husband will interpret this as a demand for intercourse. The communication of the couple worsens, intensifying the man's anxiety and setting a pattern difficult to reverse without professional assistance.

Vaginismus As yet another example of the intimate relation between the sexual reactions of the two partners, Masters and Johnson found that some men develop erectile problems because of the partner's vaginismus.

Physiological Causes Some of the disorders are attributable to physical damage. As indicated earlier, clitoral or vaginal infections, torn ligaments in the pelvic region, scar tissue at the vaginal opening from incisions made during childbirth (episiotomies), and—especially in older, postmenopausal women—insufficient lubrication of the vagina may make intercourse painful for women. Infection of the glans of the penis, which can develop when it is not kept clean, may cause dyspareunia in men. A minority of men with erectile problems are found to suffer from metabolic disturbances through diabetes, and in some sexual arousal is dulled by the use of certain tranquilizers.[6]

Sociocultural Factors Especially in female dysfunctions, cultural biases play a role. "Sociocultural influence more often than not places the woman in a position in which she must adapt, sublimate, inhibit, or even distort her natural capacity to function sexually in order to fulfill her genetically assigned role. Herein lies a major source of woman's sexual dysfunction" (p. 218). The man has the blessing of society to develop sexual expressiveness, but the woman, at least until recently, has not had this freedom, and her needs have often been ignored. And of course compounding her difficulties is the fact that she does not require sexual arousal in order to function adequately as a partner during sexual intercourse.

According to laboratory studies reported in *Human Sexual Response*, women seem capable both of multiple orgasms and of more sustained, more frequent, and more physiologically intense sexual arousal then men, which makes the neglect of their sexuality particularly ironic.

Other Contemporary Views

Figure 12.3 illustrates graphically the distinction Masters and Johnson made between the several historically relevant factors in the development of sexual problems and the two variables believed to operate in the here and now, spectator role and fear of performance. One question that suggests itself is whether causes alleged to be of only historical importance might not be of more immediate concern to some people. Might not a woman's *current* religious beliefs inhibit her involvement in and enjoyment of sexual relations?

---

[6] Spinal cord lesions, depending on how complete they are and where they are located, may cause paralysis and loss of sensation either in the legs (paraplegia) or in both arms and legs (quadraplegia). A person who cannot move his or her arms and legs is sometimes considered incapable of sexual excitement. This is not so. A recent review by Higgins (1978) documents erections and ejaculations in a number of paralyzed men.

Or consider the woman who was traumatized as a teenager by a gang rape. Might not the memory of that incident intrude itself upon her consciousness whenever she finds herself in an intimate situation? Masters and Johnson would reply that a religious belief or memory acts on the present by making the person a spectator rather than an uncritical participant, thus preserving the integrity of their theoretical model. Be that as it may, religious beliefs and sexual traumas might conceivably hinder a person's sexual behavior in a very direct and immediate way.

Masters and Johnson considered sexual dysfunctions as problems in and of themselves and not inevitably caused by deeper-seated intrapsychic or interpersonal difficulties. The couples whose treatment formed the basis of their second book, *Human Sexual Inadequacy* (1970), had marriages which, in spite of the sexual problems, were marked by caring and closeness. But as the Masters and Johnson general orientation became widespread and their therapy techniques were applied by others, sex therapists saw people whose relationships were seriously impaired. It is not difficult to imagine why a marriage or other relationship might deteriorate when the couple has not had intercourse for years. By the time a therapist is consulted, he or she is faced with the chicken-and-egg conundrum. It is impossible to know whether the hostility between the two people caused the sexual problem or vice versa. The working assumption of most therapists is that couples have both sexual and interpersonal problems. Clearly, it is unrealistic to expect a satisfying sexual encounter when, for example, the man is angry with the woman for spending more and more time outside the home or when the woman resents the man's insensitive dealings with their children. Such negative thoughts and emotions can intrude themselves into the sexual situation and thereby inhibit whatever arousal and pleasure might otherwise be found.

As with other disorders, Albert Ellis (1971) emphasizes the role of irrational thinking in the development and maintenance of sexual dysfunctions. Thus a woman who cannot have orgasms during intercourse is assumed to be *demanding* of herself that she have one. Indeed, the often-used phrase "achieve an orgasm" may reflect our society's maladaptive view of sexual satisfaction as something to be pursued and won, much as people chase after approval and recognition. Many sexologists, including Masters and Johnson, appreciate that self-defeating thoughts can preclude sexual enjoyment.

"Why doesn't he touch me more there, rather than here?" "Why does she stop stroking just as I'm getting excited?" As mentioned earlier, people may lack knowledge of sexual anatomy and functioning and more specifically be unaware of the likes and dislikes of a partner. Unfortunately, just caring for the partner may not be enough in establishing a mutually satisfying sexual relationship. People who have sexual problems are often found to lack knowledge and skill (LoPiccolo and Hogan, 1979). A woman may be left "hanging" short of orgasm by a lover who does not appreciate the importance of clitoral stimulation; the husbands of inorgasmic women are often reported to be awkward lovers (Kaplan, 1974; LoPiccolo, 1977).

A related problem is poor communication between partners. For any number of reasons—embarrassment, distrust, dislike, resentment, depression, to name but a few—one lover may not inform the other of his or her preferences, likes, and dislikes. Then he or she often misinterprets the failure of the partner to anticipate or mind-read as not really caring. Although sexual communication is frequently inadequate in distressed marriages and is therefore tended to in marital therapy (see page 635), it can also be poor in people who are otherwise compatible. Open discussions of sex by partners, among friends, in the media, and even in professional training programs are after all relatively recent phenomena.

Finally, as with many of the other psychological problems dealt with in this book, it is not known why some people have in their backgrounds or in their present lives one or more of the factors believed to be of etiological significance and yet do not have a sexual dysfunction. Why a person develops one sexual dysfunction rather than another is also a puzzle.

Behavior Therapy for Psychosexual Dysfunctions

P erhaps in no area of psychotherapy has behavior therapy been more successful than in treating psychosexual dysfunctions. Therapists, some of whom specialize as sex therapists, work directly with the sexual problems in question, paying relatively little attention to the intrapsychic and personality problems focused on by psychodynamic and humanistic therapists. Although to date few adequately controlled outcome studies have been done (Heiman and LoPiccolo, 1981), the overwhelming weight of clinical evidence clearly indicates the effectiveness of a general learning approach in treating sexual dysfunctions.

LoPiccolo and Hogan (1979) offer a useful scheme for describing the treatment of sexual dysfunctions. Sex education, techniques for reducing anxiety, skills and communication training, procedures to change attitudes and thoughts, shifts in routines, marital therapy, psychodynamic techniques, and medical and physical procedures are all considered as means. A therapist may choose only one technique to treat a given case, but the multifaceted nature of sexual problems usually demands several.

Sex Education   Because many dysfunctional people are ignorant of basic facts about human sexuality, most therapists devote time and effort to educating their clients in sexual anatomy and the physiological processes of intercourse. An unintentional but important effect of such instruction is to make legitimate the explicit discussion of sex, taking it out of the realm of unspoken taboo and mystery and dismissing some of the anxiety and embarrassment surrounding this previously avoided topic.

Anxiety Reduction Techniques   Well before the publication of the Masters-Johnson therapy program (see Box 12.2), behavior therapists appreciated that their frightened clients needed gradual and systematic exposure to anxiety-provoking aspects of the sexual situation. Wolpe's systematic desensitization and *in vivo desensitization,* that is, by real-life encounters, have been employed with apparently high degrees of success (Hogan, 1978), especially when they are combined with skills training. (People highly anxious about sex have often failed to learn to do a number of necessary and preliminary things.) In vivo desensitization would appear to be the principal technique of the Masters-Johnson program, although additional components probably contribute to its overall effectiveness.

Skills and Communication Training   To improve sexual skills and communication, therapists assign written materials, show clients videotapes and films that demonstrate explicit sexual techniques, discuss techniques with them, and encourage them to express their likes and dislikes to their partners. All these training procedures expose the client to anxiety-laden material; this desensitizing aspect appears to contribute to their effectiveness.

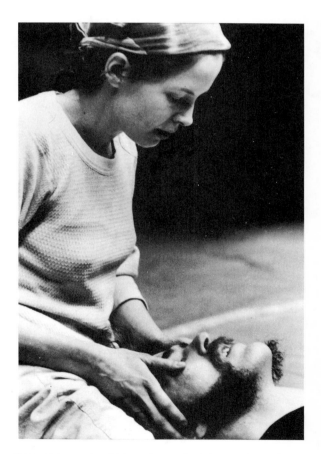

Sensate focus, in which partners give pleasure to each other through touching, is one of the techniques used in early phases of therapy for sexual dysfunction.

BOX **12.2** Therapy for Psychosexual Dysfunctions by Masters and Johnson

In 1970 the publication of Masters and Johnson's *Human Sexual Inadequacy* generated an excitement in the mental health community that is seldom encountered. This book reported on a therapy program carried out with close to 800 sexually dysfunctional people. Each couple had traveled to St. Louis and spent two weeks attending the Reproductive Biology Research Foundation for intensive therapy by day and doing sexual homework in a motel at night. Away from home, they were free of domestic distractions and able to make their stay a sort of second honeymoon. Many of the Masters and Johnson techniques had been used by therapists for some time, and some serious methodological problems have been uncovered by workers who have examined their report closely (Zilbergeld and Evans, 1980). Even so, the work of Masters and Johnson virtually created the sex therapy movement and therefore deserves a detailed description.

The therapy attempts to reduce or eliminate fears of performance and to take the participants out of their maladaptive roles as spectators. Then, it is hoped, the couple will be able to enjoy sex freely and spontaneously.

Each day the couple meets with a dual-sex therapy team, the assumption being that men best understand men and women best understand women. For the first several days the experiences of all couples are the same, regardless of their specific problem. An important stipulation is that for the time being any sexual activity between the two partners is expressly forbidden. A complete social and sexual history is obtained during the first two days, and physical examinations are conducted so that any organic factors can either be excluded or be found and dealt with.

In the assessment interviews considerable attention is paid to the so-called *sexual value system,* the ideas of each partner about what is acceptable and needed in a sexual relationship. Sometimes this sexual value system must be changed for one or both partners before sexual functioning can improve. For example, if one partner regards sexuality as ugly and unacceptable, it is doubtful whether even the most powerful therapy can help that person and the partner enjoy sex.

On the third day the therapists begin to offer interpretations about why problems have arisen and why they are continuing. In all cases the emphasis is on problems in the relationship, not on particular difficulties of either partner. A basic premise of the Masters and Johnson therapy is that ". . . there is no such thing as an uninvolved partner in any marriage in which there is some form of sexual inadequacy" (1970, p. 2). Whatever the problem, the couple is encouraged to see it as their mutual responsibility. At this time the clients are introduced to the idea of the spectator role. They are told, for example, that a male with erectile problems usually worries about how well or poorly he is doing rather than participating freely. It is pointed out to the couple that this pattern of observing himself, although totally understandable in context, is blocking his natural responses and greatly interfering with sexual enjoyment.

At the end of the third day an all-important assignment is given to the couple, namely to engage in _sensate focus._ The couple is instructed to choose a time when they feel "a natural sense of warmth, unit compatibility . . . or even a shared sense of gamesmanship" (Masters and Johnson, 1970, p. 71). They are to undress and give each other pleasure by touching each other's bodies. The co-therapists appoint one marital partner to do the first "pleasuring" or "giving"; the partner who is "getting" is simply to enjoy being touched. The one being touched, however, is *not* required to feel a sexual response and, moreover, takes responsibility for immediately telling the partner if something becomes distracting or uncomfortable. Then the roles are switched. Attempts at intercourse are still forbidden. To Masters and Johnson this approach is a way of breaking up the frantic groping common among these couples. The sensate-focus assignment may promote contact where none has existed for years; if it does, it is a first step toward gradually reestablishing sexual intimacy.*

Sensate focusing may uncover deep animosities that have hitherto remained hidden. Most of

---

* Details of other direct therapies, some of them going beyond what Masters and Johnson describe, are available in LoPiccolo and LoPiccolo, 1978; Rosen and Rosen, 1981; Gagnon, 1977; Kaplan, 1974.

the time, however, partners begin to realize that encounters in bed can be intimate without necessarily being a prelude to sexual intercourse. On the second evening the partner being pleasured is instructed to give specific encouragement and direction by placing his or her hand on the hand of the giving partner in order to regulate pressure and rate of stroking. The touching of genitals and breasts is also now allowed. Still, however, there is no mention of an orgasm, and the prohibition on intercourse remains in effect. Diagrams are presented if the partners are ignorant of basic female and male anatomy, as they often are. After this second day of sensate focusing, treatment branches out according to the specific problem or problems of the couple. As an illustration, we will outline the therapy for orgasmic dysfunction in the female.

After the sensate-focus exercises have made the couple more comfortable with each other in bed, the wife's attention is directed to maximizing her own sexual stimulation without trying to have an orgasm. As a result her own sexual excitement generally builds. The therapists give explicit instructions about generally effective means of manually manipulating the female genital area, although ultimate decisions are made by the female partner, who is encouraged to make her wishes clear to the man, moment by moment. In the treatment of other dysfunctions, as in the treatment for this one, it is emphasized that at this stage having orgasms is not the focus of interaction between partners.

After the woman has begun to enjoy being pleasured in this way, the next step is to move the source of sensate pleasure from the man's hand on her body to his penis inside her vagina. She is told to place herself on top of the man and gently insert the penis; she is encouraged simply to tune in to her feelings. When she feels inclined, she can begin slowly to move her pelvis. She is encouraged to regard the penis as something for her to play with, something that will provide her with pleasure. The male can also begin slowly to thrust. At all times, however, the wife must be able to decide when and what should happen next.

When the couple is able to maintain this containment for minutes at a time, without the man's thrusting forcefully toward orgasm, a major change has usually taken place in their sexual interactions: for perhaps the first time the woman has been allowed to feel and think sexually, and indeed selfishly, about her own pleasure. In their subsequent encounters most couples begin to have mutually satisfying intercourse.

Clinicians must be extremely sensitive in presenting these various treatment procedures to a couple whose problems may stretch back many years. Sometimes the couple discuss sex for the very first time at the Masters and Johnson clinic. The calm and open manner of the therapists puts the couple at ease, encouraging in them both a commitment to follow certain instructions, and a more open attitude toward sex and the activities that people may engage in together when making love. Although behavioral prescriptions are specific, the therapists can never lose sight of the atmosphere that must be maintained in the consulting room and, it is hoped, transferred over to the privacy of the bedroom, where much of the *actual* therapy takes place. As in other forms of behavior therapy, there is a strong emphasis on technique, but interpersonal factors set the stage for behavior to change.

In recent years sex clinics have sprung up everywhere, based in general on the Masters and Johnson model, and many mental health professionals have incorporated direct sex therapy techniques into their practices. Researchers are investigating various aspects of the treatment package. One question being asked is whether a dual-sex therapy team is really necessary for all couples (Fordney-Settlage, 1975); this does not seem to be the case. Another question concerns the effectiveness of daily, intensive therapy as compared to the more usual outpatient practice of once-weekly sessions; data indicate no advantage to the intensive Masters-Johnson regimen (Heiman and LoPiccolo, 1981). Some clinicians now rely on electrically powered vibrators when treating female orgasmic dysfunction; with proper instructions many inorgasmic women first learn to enjoy orgasms through self-stimulation with these little machines (Barbach, 1975; Dodson, 1974). The pursuit and enhancement of sexual pleasure for its own sake is being legitimized. Although some are concerned about this trend and dub it "sexual athletics," on the whole the relaxation of strictures regarding sexuality promises greater satisfaction for most people (Gagnon and Davison, 1974).

Procedures To Change Attitudes and Thoughts

In what are called *sensory-awareness proce-dures,* the client is encouraged to tune in to the pleasant sensations that accompany even incipient sexual arousal. The sensate-focus exercises described in Box 12.2, for example, are a way of opening the individual to truly sensual and sexual feelings. Rational-emotive therapy tries to substitute less self-demanding thoughts for "musturbation," the "I must" thoughts often making a catastrophe of things for sexually dysfunctional people.

Shifts in Routines   Therapists may encourage a couple to make "dates" with each other, to take the phone off the hook, hang a "Do Not Disturb" sign on the bedroom door, or agree not to have intercourse for a given period of time. The assumption is that any such specific shifts from habitual behavior will have positive reinforcing consequences and be beneficial to the sexual relationship.

Marital Therapy   As noted earlier, sexual dysfunctions are often embedded in a distressed marital or other relationship. Troubled couples usually need special training in communication skills. Marital therapy is discussed in more detail in Chapter 20 (page 635).

Psychodynamic Techniques   A man may not at first admit that he cannot have an erection, in which case the therapist must listen between the lines of what he says. A woman may be thought reluctant to take the initiative in sexual encounters because, although she may not verbalize it to the therapist, she considers such assertiveness unseemly and inappropriate to her traditional female role. In such instances the general analytic view of clients as often unable to express clearly to their therapists what truly bothers them can help in proper assessment and planning for behavioral treatment. Kaplan (1974) articulates well the blend of psychodynamic therapy with direct behavioral treatment. No doubt elements of non-behavioral therapy are to be found in the actual practices of sex therapists, even if they are not made explicit by these workers when they discuss their work in journals or with colleagues. Readers may wish to hearken back to the earlier discussion of eclecticism in therapy (Box 2.4, page 63) to remind themselves of the complexity of the therapeutic enterprise.

Medical and Physical Procedures   Although our study of sexual dysfunctions has referred to relatively few underlying somatic problems, therapists must not ignore their possibility, especially if dyspareunia and complete erectile dysfunction are the disorders. When depression is part of the clinical picture and has severely diminished sex drive, antidepressant drugs can be helpful (Winokur, 1963). Tranquilizers are also used as an adjunct to anxiety reduction techniques, although the depressant effects of these drugs may be detrimental to sexual functioning. Most therapists use drugs only when psychological procedures are found wanting.

The self-help trend is quite evident among sexually dysfunctional people as well as among those who strive to enhance already satisfying sex lives. For greater arousal and ecstatic enjoyment of sex, some people rely on chemicals. Amyl nitrate is a peripheral vasodilator, but unfortunately it sometimes has the potentially fatal side effect of heart failure. Alcohol disinhibits in small amounts; marijuana, hashish, cocaine, LSD, and other psychedelics have effects that are variable and often dramatic. Other chemicals are touted for their presumed aphrodisiac, or sexually stimulating, properties; for example, cantharides or Spanish fly creates itching in the genitals, sensations experienced by some people as sexually arousing. The most that can be said about any of these drugs is that their efficacy is yet to be established, although their benefits to some people under some circumstances, as well as their dangers to others, are attested to by enthusiastic testimonials and by dire warnings.

Implanting a rigid plastic rod or a system of hydraulic tubes in a chronically flaccid penis and removal of the clitorial hood, in hopes of enhancing clitoral stimulation, are surgical procedures. These are radical steps to take, but implantations in the penis will allow the physically disabled man to have an erection. Alteration of the female genitalia is seemingly unnecessary, since the clitoris can be gently rubbed either during or separately from intercourse. Finally, simple physical exercise may have some favorable impact on sexual difficulties, although the effects may be general and placebo in nature; people who jog or otherwise maintain their bodies in good physical condition probably feel generally better about themselves and may thereby improve their sex lives. One set of exercises does appear to have some specific benefit for inorgasmic women, namely the Kegel (1952) exercises for regularly contracting and thereby strengthening the pubococcygeal masculature surrounding the vagina.

Summary

Few emotional problems are of greater interest to people nowadays than the psychosexual dysfunctions, disruptions in the normal sexual response cycle which seem to be caused by inhibitions and which rob many people of sexual enjoyment. DSM-III categorizes these disturbances as occurring in one or more of four phases of the response cycle: the appetitive phase (whether the person wishes to have sex), the excitement phase (whether the individual can respond with arousal to stimulation he or she deems acceptable), orgasm, and resolution. Disorders can vary in severity, in chronicity, and in their pervasiveness, occurring generally or only with certain partners and in particular situations. In no instance should a person believe himself or herself to have a psychosexual dysfunction unless the difficulty is persistent and recurrent; all of us quite normally experience sexual problems on an intermittent basis throughout our lives.

Descriptions and presumed causes of the range of sexual dysfunctions were given in detail. Although organic factors must be considered, especially for instances of dyspareunia and complete erectile failure, the etiology of the disorders usually lies in a combination of unfavorable attitudes, difficult earlier experiences, fears of performance, assumption of a spectator role, and lack of specific knowledge and skills. Sex role stereotypes may play a role in some dysfunctions: a man who has trouble maintaining his erection is often called impotent, the implication being that he is not much of a man; and a woman who does not have orgasms with regularity is often termed frigid, the implication being that she is generally cold and unresponsive. The problems of females in particular appear to be linked to cultural prejudices against their sexuality, ironic in light of laboratory data indicating that women are capable of greater and more frequent sexual enjoyment than men.

Information on the causes of psychosexual dysfunction derives almost entirely from uncontrolled case studies and must therefore be viewed with caution. The absence of solid data on etiology has not deterred therapists from devising seemingly effective interventions. Direct sex therapy, behavioral in nature and aimed at reversing old habits and teaching new skills, was propelled into public consciousness by the appearance of the Masters and Johnson book *Human Sexual Inadequacy* in 1970. Their method, anticipated by several behavior therapists years earlier, hinges on gradual, unthreatening exposure to increasingly intimate sexual encounters and the sanctioning of sexuality by credible and sensitive therapists. Education in sexual anatomy and physiology; anxiety reduction techniques; skills and communication training; procedures to change attitudes and thoughts; shifts in routines; marital therapy, when the sexual problem is embedded, as it often is, in a snarled relationship; psychodynamic techniques; and a variety of medical and other physical procedures are other means applied by sex therapists. Controlled data are only just beginning to appear, but there is good reason to be optimistic about the ultimate ability of the mental health professions to help most people achieve at least some relief from crippling sexual inhibitions.

Yves Tanguy, "The Rapidity of Sleep" (1945). The Joseph Winter-
bothen Collection. Courtesy The Art Institute of Chicago.

part four
the
schizophrenias

chapter 13

SCHIZOPHRENIA: DESCRIPTION

History of the Concept
Clinical Symptoms of Schizophrenia
Subcategories of Schizophrenia
Laboratory Research with Adult Schizophrenics

Schizophrenia is one of the most serious of the mental disorders. About 50 percent of hospitalized mental patients are diagnosed schizophrenic. And even though the typical length of the period of hospitalization for these patients has shortened markedly over the past decades, rehospitalization is frequent. Within two years following initial discharge, about 50 percent of schizophrenics have reentered mental hospitals (Gunderson et al., 1974). Thus, because it is one of the most serious and the commonest form of psychotic behavior, schizophrenia has understandably been one of the most thoroughly investigated disorders in the field of abnormal psychology. The sometimes massive and extreme disruptions of thought, perception, and behavior

that are schizophrenia are what people generally refer to as madness. Those in close contact with it are themselves very much shaken by the breakdown, for they witness the surfacing of an inner, discordant realm, out of control and beyond their comprehension.

In this chapter and the following we review the literature on schizophrenia. In this first chapter we examine the history of the diagnosis, the symptoms of the disorder, its various forms, and some research on the more exact nature of a few symptoms. In Chapter 14 we consider the different theories of the etiology of schizophrenia, the etiological research, and the treatment of schizophrenia.

History of the Concept

Kraepelin's and Bleuler's Early Descriptions

The concept of _schizophrenia_ was initially formulated by two European psychiatrists, Emil Kraepelin and Eugen Bleuler. Differences in their approaches to schizophrenia and their definitions of the disorder have continued to have a major impact and have produced a good deal of controversy. Kraepelin first presented his concept of _dementia praecox,_ the early term for schizophrenia, in a paper titled "The Diagnosis and Prognosis of Dementia Praecox," which he delivered to the Twenty-ninth Congress of Southwestern

German Psychiatry in Heidelberg in 1898. Two major groups of endogenous, or internally caused, psychoses were differentiated, manic-depressive illness and dementia praecox. Dementia praecox included several diagnostic concepts— dementia paranoides, catatonia, and hebephrenia—already singled out and regarded as distinct entities by nineteenth-century clinicians in the few previous decades. The term dementia praecox is itself descriptive of two major aspects of the disorder: an early onset (praecox) and a progressive intellectual deterioration (dementia). They had been observed in a fourteen-year-old boy and named _démence précoce_ by the Belgian psychiatrist Morel in 1860. Among the major symptoms that Kraepelin saw in such patients

Emil Kraepelin (1856-1926), the German psychiatrist whose descriptions of dementia praecox have proved remarkably durable in the light of contemporary research.

Eugen Bleuler (1857-1939), the Swiss psychiatrist who contributed importantly to our conceptions of schizophrenia and coined the term.

were hallucinations, delusions, negativism, attentional difficulties, stereotyped behavior, and emotional dysfunctions. Thus Kraepelin focused on both course and symptoms in defining the disorder, although he often emphasized the former over the latter.

Kraepelin did not move much beyond a descriptive level. In the eighth edition of his textbook, for example, he grouped the symptoms of dementia praecox into thirty-six major categories, assigning hundreds of them to each. He made little effort to interrelate these great numbers of separate symptoms and stated only that they all reflected dementia and a loss of the usual unity in thinking, feeling, and acting. In contrast to Kraepelin's descriptive approach, the view of the next major figure, Eugen Bleuler, represented both a specific attempt to define the "core" of the disorder and a move away from Kraepelin's emphasis on prognosis in defining the disorder.

From 1885 to 1897, Bleuler was the director of a mental hospital in Rheinau, Switzerland. In 1898 he was appointed professor of psychiatry at the University of Zurich and head of the Burghölzli Clinic. In describing schizophrenia, Bleuler broke with Kraepelin on two major points, for he believed that the disorder in question did not necessarily have an early onset and that it did not inevitably progress toward dementia. Thus Bleuler was much less attentive to the *course* of the disorder than was Kraepelin, and the label dementia praecox was no longer considered appropriate. In 1908 Bleuler proposed his own term, schizophrenia, to capture what he viewed as the essential nature of the disorder.

Psychoanalytic theory had a major influence on Bleuler's view of schizophrenia. First, he thought that Freudian concepts could account for the specific content of symptoms such as delusions and hallucinations.[1] They were viewed as attempts to replace the existing world from which the schizophrenic had retreated. Second, and even more importantly, Bleuler was led to

attempt for schizophrenia what Freud had tried to accomplish for the neuroses—to specify underlying psychological processes that might be at the root of the various disturbances of schizophrenic patients.

Bleuler, like Kraepelin, had noted the great range of distress and dysfunction evident in schizophrenic patients. But Bleuler went much further than Kraepelin in trying to specify a common denominator or essential property that would link the various disturbances together. The metaphorical concept that he adopted for this purpose was the "breaking of associative threads." For Bleuler associative threads joined not only words but thoughts. Thus goal-directed, efficient thinking and communication were possible only when these hypothetical structures were intact. The notion that associative threads are disrupted in schizophrenics was then used to "account" for other problems. The attentional difficulties of schizophrenics, for example, were viewed by Bleuler as resulting from a loss of purposeful direction in thought, which in turn caused passive responding to objects and people in the immediate surroundings. In a similar vein, blocking, a seeming total loss of a train of thought, was considered a complete disruption of the associative threads for the subject under discussion.

Kraepelin's writings then fostered a narrow definition of schizophrenia and an emphasis on description. Although he recognized that a small percentage of patients who originally manifested symptoms of dementia praecox did not deteriorate, he preferred to limit this diagnostic category to patients who had a poor prognosis. Bleuler's work, in contrast, led to a broader concept of schizophrenia and a more pronounced theoretical emphasis. He placed patients with a good prognosis in his group of schizophrenias and even proposed the existence of "latent" schizophrenia, a term to be applied to patients who "have the disorder" but do not manifest overt schizophrenic symptoms. In addition, he included as schizophrenic "many atypical melancholias, and manias of other schools, especially hysterical melancholias and manias, most hallucinatory confusions, some 'nervous' people and compulsive and impulsive patients, and many prison psychoses" (1923, p. 436).

---

[1] Also relevant here is Bleuler's association with C. G. Jung, who too was at the Burghölzli Clinic and whose 1907 paper was a classic attempt to apply Freudian theory to dementia praecox. Jung maintained that in the disorder the unconscious is unusually strong so that a great many atavistic tendencies are not brought into adjustment with modern life.

The Broadened American Concept

Bleuler has had a great influence on the American conception of schizophrenia. Over the first part of the twentieth century its breadth was extended considerably. At the New York State Psychiatric Institute, for example, about 20 percent of patients were diagnosed schizophrenic in the 1930s. The numbers increased through the 1940s and in 1952 peaked at a remarkable 80 percent. In contrast, the European concept of schizophrenia has remained narrower. The percentage of patients diagnosed schizophrenic at the Maudsley Hospital in London remained relatively constant, at 20 percent for a forty-year period (Kuriansky, Deming, and Gurland, 1974).

The reasons for the increase in the frequency of American diagnoses of schizophrenia are not difficult to find; several prominent figures in the history of American psychiatry, following Bleuler's lead, have expanded the concept of schizophrenia to an even greater extent and also diverted attention from diagnosis itself.

Adolf Meyer (1866–1950), considered by many to have been the dean of American psychiatry (for example, Zilboorg and Henry, 1941), argued that diagnostic categories were often arbitrary and artificial (for example, Meyer, 1917, 1926). Although Meyer visited Kraepelin in Heidelberg in 1896 and was influential in introducing American psychiatrists to the concept of dementia praecox, he was not enthusiastic about the diagnostic process and placed greater emphasis on the *individual* characteristics of each patient and on his or her whole personality. His approach to schizophrenia was flexible and did not rely on either specific symptoms or progressive deterioration for a definition of the disorder. He viewed it as an accumulation of faulty habits which had been building for a very long period of time. What he called substitutive reactions had replaced the ones appropriate to daily living and become established as the person settled into a rut of least resistance.

The American conception of schizophrenia was also broadened by investigators who suggested additional schizophrenic subtypes.[2] For example, in 1933 Kasanin described nine patients who had all been assigned diagnoses of dementia praecox. The onset of the disorder had been sudden for all of them and their recovery relatively rapid. Noting that theirs could be said to be a combination of both schizophrenic and affective symptoms, Kasanin suggested the term "schizoaffective psychosis" to describe the disturbances of these patients. This diagnosis subsequently became part of the American concept of schizophrenia, being listed in DSM-I (1952) and the revisions thereafter.

The schizophrenia category was further expanded by Hoch and his colleagues, who argued that schizophrenia often "masquerades" as other disorders. They suggested the terms "pseudoneurotic schizophrenia" (Hoch and Polatin, 1949) and "pseudopsychopathic schizophrenia" (Hoch and Dunaif, 1955) to describe anxious, withdrawn persons with serious interpersonal problems who also have neurotic or psychopathic symptoms. Hoch argued that even though these patients often lacked the more classic symptoms of schizophrenia, they would reveal, on closer examination, the cognitive and emotional disorganization he considered the hallmark of the disorder. As a result of such opinions, many patients who would otherwise have been diagnosed as suffering from neuroses, affective disorders, and personality disturbances came in this country to be considered schizophrenic.

In the 1960s and 1970s the *process-reactive* dimension was another key means of maintaining the broad concept of schizophrenia in the United States. As soon as Bleuler had observed that the onset of schizophrenia was not always at a young age and that deterioration was not a certain course, clinicians began to observe other differences between those whose onset was later and who sometimes recovered and those whose onset was earlier and who usually deteriorated further. Some schizophrenics had been relatively deviant, apathetic individuals for many of their young years, suffering gradual but insidious depletion of thought, emotion, interests, and activity. Others, usually later in life, had a rather rapid onset of more severe symptoms. The term *process*, indicating some sort of basic physiological malfunction in the brain, was chosen for insidiously developing schizophrenia and *reactive*

---

[2] Both Kraepelin and Bleuler had suggested that schizophrenia could be divided into specific types (see page 403), but the subtypes discussed here went considerably beyond their proposals.

for what appeared suddenly after stress. For the last thirty years in the United States the process-reactive dimension has been extensively studied. Earlier social and sexual adjustment, as measured, for example, by the Phillips Scale (1953), became a means of distinguishing schizophrenics and determining their chances for recovery. Those with a *good premorbid* adjustment were more likely to have only an episodic problem and to have a good prognosis. Process schizophrenia, then, which has followed an earlier poor adjustment of patients at school, work, and in their sexual and social lives, may be equated with Kraepelin's original description of dementia praecox. The inclusion of reactive patients in the definition helped extend the American concept.

A prevailing interest in treatment also played a role in broadening the American conception of schizophrenia. Both Bleuler and Meyer had rejected the notion that deterioration was inevitable, thus allowing the possibility of intervention and the restitution of reason. Harry Stack Sullivan (1892–1949) shared this optimistic view and became the first major theorist to develop a systematic psychological treatment for schizophrenia. He emphasized the *underlying* emotional and cognitive factors motivating what he considered to be the schizophrenic's withdrawal from interpersonal relationships. Other behavior did not play an important role in Sullivan's definition of the disorder. Because he believed that personality could be observed only in interpersonal relations, he, in fact, maintained that there were *no* fundamental criteria for the disorder (1929).

Empirical Data on Differences in Diagnoses

The differences in the American and European diagnoses of schizophrenia have been empirically studied in the United States–United Kingdom Cross-National Project (Cooper et al., 1972). In one part of the overall investigation, a number of patients admitted consecutively to several hospitals in London and New York were interviewed by members of the project staff, who later reached diagnoses. These diagnoses were then compared with those made on the same patients by the staffs of the respective institutions.

The numbers of patients diagnosed schizophrenic by the special project staff were about the same, in New York hospitals 59, in London hospitals 61. The numbers of schizophrenic diagnoses made by the staffs of each institution, in New York 118 and in London 59, were not the same. The difference between New York staff and project staff diagnoses can be pinpointed by examining how the project staff diagnosed the patients considered schizophrenic by the New York staff but not by them. Table 13.1 indicates that a substantial proportion of New York-diagnosed schizophrenics were considered to have an affective illness by the project staff. In fact, many patients considered by the project staff to fit in all categories other than schizophrenia were regarded as schizophrenic by New York diagnosticians. "Sixty-three percent of those with a project diagnosis of depressive psychosis, 91 percent of those with a project diagnosis of mania, 69 percent of those with a project diagnosis of neurosis, and 63 percent of those with a project diagnosis of personality disorder all have hospital diagnoses of schizophrenia" (Cooper et al., 1972, p. 104). Thus the American concept of schizophrenia (or at least the New York concept) was shown to be considerably broader than that used either by project staff or by hospital staff in London (Figure 13.1).

Having established that there are clear differences between American and British diagnostic

TABLE **13.1**
Project Diagnosis of Patients Considered Schizophrenic by New York Staff

Project diagnosis	Of New York schizophrenics
Schizophrenic	50
Affective illness	42
Neurosis	3
Personality disorder	5
Other	18

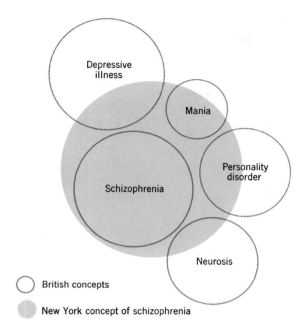

○ British concepts

● New York concept of schizophrenia

FIGURE **13.1**

A Venn diagram indicating the difference between the New York and British concepts of schizophrenia before the development of DSM-III. The British concept is narrower than the New York one and does not overlap with other diagnostic categories. After Cooper et al., 1972.

practices, we must now ask whether one system is in some ways better than the other. Since there is no absolute criterion by which to judge, we can only examine the reliability and validity of each approach. A narrower diagnostic concept seems superior on both counts. Using British diagnosis, Wing and his associates (1967), for example, found an interjudge reliability of 92 percent for schizophrenia. Contrast this with the 53 percent figure found in America by the Beck (1962) study discussed in Chapter 3! Validity can be assessed by relating diagnosis to other measures such as performance on laboratory tasks and evidence of predisposition in the family. Although few studies have compared the validity of different diagnostic systems, those that have suggest that a narrower definition of schizophrenia is preferable. We discuss two such studies, one

later in this chapter (Oltmanns, O'Hayon, and Neale, 1978) and one in the next (Gottesman and Shields, 1972).

The DSM-III Diagnosis

With the publication of DSM-III, the American conception of schizophrenia has moved considerably from the excessively broad definition we have been discussing. The new definition narrows the range of patients diagnosed schizophrenic in three ways. First, the diagnostic criteria are presented in explicit and considerable detail. Second, patients with symptoms of an affective disorder are excluded. In the U.S.–U.K. study, you will remember, many with a DSM-II diagnosis of schizophrenia were considered to have an affective disorder by British clinicians. Schizophrenia, schizoaffective type, is now listed as *schizoaffective disorder*[3] in a new separate section, Psychotic Disorders Not Elsewhere Classified. Third, DSM-III requires that the person have continuous signs of schizophrenia for at least six months. Thus are eliminated the patients who have a brief psychotic episode, often stress-related, and then recover quickly. DSM-II's acute schizophrenic episode is now diagnosed as either *schizophreniform disorder* or *brief reactive psychosis,* which are also listed in the new section. Schizophreniform disorder must not persist for more than six months or for fewer than two weeks. A brief reactive psychosis must not last longer than two weeks and is brought on by stress.

The foregoing has served as background for a more detailed description of the behavior of schizophrenics. The diagnostic symptoms to be presented rely heavily on the DSM-III criteria as well as on information collected in a large-scale investigation of schizophrenia, the International Pilot Study of Schizophrenia (IPSS), conducted by the World Health Organization (Sartorius, Shapiro, and Jablonsky, 1974).

[3] Schizoaffective disorder is to be diagnosed only when the clinician cannot decide between affective disorder and schizophrenia or schizophreniform disorder. Onset and usually resolution are rapid, as indicated earlier.

Clinical Symptoms of Schizophrenia

The symptoms of schizophrenic patients can be organized into disturbances in several major areas—thought, perception and attention, motor behavior, affect or emotion, and life functioning. The range of problems of people diagnosed as schizophrenic is very extensive, although patients who are so diagnosed will typically have only *some* of them. DSM-III determines for the diagnostician how many problems must be present, and in what degree, to justify the diagnosis. The heterogeneity of schizophrenia suggests that it would be appropriate to try to subdivide schizophrenics into types who manifest particular constellations of problems. After reviewing the major symptoms, we shall examine the types of schizophrenia.

Disorders of thought

The term *thought disorder* refers to problems both in the *form* of thought—the organization of ideas, speaking so that a listener can understand; and in its *content*—the actual ideas that are expressed. We examine first the form of thought in schizophrenia.

Disorders of Thought Form   In response to an initial, seemingly simple question to a schizophrenic patient, this conversation ensued.

> "How old are you?"
> "Why I am centuries old, sir."
> "How long have you been here?"
> "I've been now on this property on and off for a long time. I cannot say the exact time because we are absorbed by the air at night, and they bring back people. They kill up everything; they can make you lie; they can talk through your throat."
> "Who is this?"
> "Why, the air."
> "What is the name of this place?"
> "This place is called a star."
> "Who is the doctor in charge of your ward?"
> "A body just like yours, sir. They can make you black and white. I say good morning, but he just comes through there. At first it was a colony. They said it was

heaven. These buildings were not solid at the time, and I am positive that this is the same place. They have others just like it. People die, and all the microbes talk over there, and prestigitis you know is sending you from here to another world. . . . I was sent by the government to the United States to Washington to some star, and they had a pretty nice country there. Now you have a body like a young man who says he is of the prestigitis."
> "Who was this prestigitis?"
> "Why, you are yourself. You can be prestigitis. They make you say bad things; they can read you; they bring back Negroes from the dead" (White, 1932, p. 228).

This excerpt illustrates the *incoherence* sometimes found in the conversation of schizophrenics. Although the patient may make repeated references to central ideas or a theme, the images and fragments of thought are not connected. It is difficult to understand exactly what the patient is trying to tell the interviewer. In addition, the patient used the word "prestigitis" several times, a *neologism* or new word which he has made up himself and which is probably meaningless to the listener.

Thought may also be disordered by *loose associations,* in which case the patient may be more successful in communicating with a listener but has difficulty sticking to one topic. He or she seems to drift off on a train of associations evoked by an idea from the past. Schizophrenic patients have themselves provided descriptions of this state.

> My thoughts get all jumbled up. I start thinking or talking about something but I never get there. Instead, I wander off in the wrong direction and get caught up with all sorts of different things that may be connected with things I want to say but in a way I can't explain. People listening to me get more lost than I do. . . .
> My trouble is that I've got too many thoughts. You might think about something, let's say that ashtray and just think, oh! yes, that's for putting my cigarette in, but I would think of it and then I would think of

a dozen different things connected with it at the same time (McGhie and Chapman, 1961, p. 108).

Another aspect of the schizophrenic's associative problems is termed _clang associations._ The patient's speech contains many rhyming words, for example, "How are you today by the bay as a gay, Doctor?" The words follow one another because they rhyme, not because they make grammatical or logical sense. Other disturbances in thought form are _poverty of speech_—either the amount of discourse is reduced or it conveys little information; _perserveration_—words and ideas are persistently repeated; and _blocking_—a train of speech is interrupted by silence before an idea is completed and then the thought being conveyed cannot be recalled.

Disturbances in the form of thought were regarded by Bleuler as the principal clinical symptom of schizophrenia and remain one of the DSM-III criteria for the diagnosis. But recent evidence indicates that it is a relatively rare one. In the IPSS, for example, only about 10 percent of schizophrenic patients showed disorder of thought form (Sartorius, Shapiro, and Jablonsky, 1974). Furthermore, the presence of thought disorder does not discriminate well between schizophrenics and other psychotic patients, such as some of those with affective disorders (Andreasen, 1979).

Disorders of Thought Content   Deviance in _content_ of thought seems more central to schizophrenia than confusion in form of thought. The thoughts of 97 percent of schizophrenics in the IPSS were found disordered in a very fundamental way, through _"lack of insight."_ When asked what they thought was wrong or why they had been hospitalized, schizophrenics seemed to have no appreciation of their condition and little realization that their behavior was unusual. In addition, many schizophrenics are subject to _delusions,_ holding beliefs that the rest of society would generally disagree with or view as misinterpretations of reality.

No doubt each of us is, at one time or another, rather concerned because we believe that others think badly of us. Perhaps much of the time this belief is well justified. Who, after all, can be universally loved? Fortunately, we either learn to live with this belief, or, if it is false, are readily able to dispel it. Consider for a moment, however, what life would be like if you were firmly convinced that numbers of people did not like you, indeed that they disliked you so much that they were plotting against you. Some of these persecutors have sophisticated listening devices which allow them to tune in on your most private conversations and gather evidence in a plot to discredit you. None of those around you, including your loved ones, is able to reassure you that these people are not spying on you. In fact, even your closest friends and confidants are gradually joining your tormentors and becoming members of the persecuting community. You are naturally quite anxious or angry about your situation, and you begin your own counteractions against the imagined persecutors. Any new room you enter must be carefully checked for listening devices. When you meet a person for the first time, you question him or her at great length to determine whether he or she is part of the plot against you.

Simple _persecutory_ delusions were found in 65 percent of the IPSS sample. Schizophrenics' delusions may also take several other forms. Some of the most important of these have been described by the German psychiatrist Kurt Schneider (1959). The following catalogue of these delusions is drawn from Mellor (1970).

1. **Delusional percept.** A normal perception, for some reason, takes on a special significance for the patient and an often elaborate delusional system quickly develops. To give an example of such a transformed percept,

   A young Irishman was at breakfast with two fellow-lodgers. He felt a sense of unease, that something frightening was going to happen. One of the lodgers pushed the salt cellar towards him (he appreciated at the time that this was an ordinary salt cellar and his friend's intention was innocent). Almost before the salt cellar reached him he knew that he must return home, "to greet the Pope, who is visiting Ireland to see his family and to reward them. . . because Our Lord is going to be born again to one of the women. . . . And because of this

Kurt Schneider, a German psychiatrist, proposed that particular forms of hallucinations and delusions, which he calls first-rank symptoms, are central to defining schizophrenia.

A twenty-nine-year-old housewife said "I look out of the window and I think the garden looks nice and the grass looks cool, but the thoughts of Eamonn Andrews come into my mind. There are no other thoughts there, only his. . . . He treats my mind like a screen and flashes his thoughts on to it like you flash a picture" (p. 17).

4. **Thought broadcast.** The patient's thoughts are transmitted so that others know them.

A twenty-one-year-old student [found that] "As I think, my thoughts leave my head on a type of mental ticker-tape. Everyone around has only to pass the tape through their mind and they know my thoughts" (p. 17).

5. **Thought withdrawal.** The patient's thoughts are "stolen" from his or her mind by an external force—suddenly, unexpectedly, and without arousing anxiety.

A twenty-two-year-old woman [described such an experience]. "I am thinking about my mother, and suddenly my thoughts are sucked out of my mind by a phrenological vacuum extractor, and there is nothing in my mind, it is empty . . ." (p. 16–17).

The next three delusions pertain to the experiencing of feelings and the carrying out of actions and impulses that have been imposed on the patient by some external agent.

6. **"Made" feelings.** A twenty-three-year-old female patient reported, "I cry, tears roll down my cheeks and I look unhappy, but inside I have a cold anger because they are using me in this way, and it is not me who is unhappy, but they are projecting unhappiness onto my brain. They project upon me laughter, for no reason, and you have no idea how terrible it is to laugh and look happy and know it is not you, but their emotions" (p. 17).

7. **"Made" volitional acts.** A twenty-nine-year-old shorthand typist described her [simplest] actions as follows: "When I reach my hand for the comb it is my hand and arm which

they [all the women] are all born different with their private parts back to front" (p. 18).

2. **Somatic passivity.** The patient is a passive, unwilling recipient of bodily sensations imposed by an external agency.

A twenty-nine-year-old teacher described "X-rays entering the back of my neck, where the skin tingles and feels warm, they pass down the back in a hot tingling strip about six inches wide to the waist. There they disappear into the pelvis which feels numb and cold and solid like a block of ice. They stop me from getting an erection" (p. 16).

3. **Thought insertion.** Thoughts, which are not the patient's own, have been placed in his or her mind by an external source.

move, and my fingers pick up the pen, but I don't control them. . . . I sit there watching them move, and they are quite independent, what they do is nothing to do with me. . . . I am just a puppet who is manipulated by cosmic strings. When the strings are pulled my body moves and I cannot prevent it'' (p. 17).

8. **"Made" impulses.** A twenty-nine-year-old engineer [who had] emptied the contents of a urine bottle over the ward dinner trolley [tried to explain the incident]. "The sudden impulse came over me that I must do it. It was not my feeling, it came into me from the X-ray department, that was why I was sent there for implants yesterday. It was nothing to do with me, they wanted it done. So I picked up the bottle and poured it in. It seemed all I could do'' (p. 18).

Disorders of perception and attention

Schizophrenic patients frequently report that the world seems somehow different or even unreal (derealizations) to them. Some mention changes in the way their bodies feel. Parts of their bodies may seem too large or too small, objects around them too close or too far away. Or there may be numbness or tingling and electrical or burning sensations. Patients may feel as though snakes are crawling inside the abdomen. Or the body may become so depersonalized that it feels as though it is a machine. Some patients become hypersensitive to sounds, sights, and smells. Others remark that their surroundings are not as they used to be, that everything appears flat and colorless. Some schizophrenics report difficulties in attending to what is happening around them.

I can't concentrate on television because I can't watch the screen and listen to what is being said at the same time. I can't seem to take in two things like this at the same time especially when one of them means watching and the other means listening. On the other hand I seem to be always taking in too much at the one time, and then I can't handle it and can't make sense of it. . . . [Or, as another patient stated] When people are talking, I just get scraps of it. If it is just

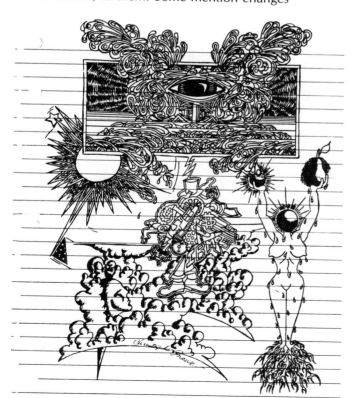

Drawing done by a hospitalized patient during art therapy sessions. He described the picture as a depiction of "my way of being safe at the time of judgment." In the center is a representation of the material world, the profile at bottom left is his own, the woman at the right represents a marijuana plant, and the eye at the top is God.

one person who is speaking, that's not so bad, but if others join in then I can't pick it up at all. I just can't get in tune with the conversation. It makes me feel all open—as if things are closing in on me and I have lost control (McGhie and Chapman, 1961, p. 106).

The most dramatic distortions of perception are called _hallucinations_, sensory experiences in the _absence_ of any stimulation from the environment. They occur most often in the auditory modality and less often in the visual. Seventy-four percent of the IPSS sample reported having auditory hallucinations.

As with delusions, some hallucinations are thought to be particularly important diagnostically because they occur more often in schizophrenics than in other psychotic patients. Schneider (1959) has described these, and we again rely on Mellor (1970) for examples.

1. **Audible thoughts.** _A thirty-two-year-old housewife complained of a man's voice speaking in an intense whisper from a point about two feet above her head. The voice would repeat almost all the patient's goal-directed thinking—even the most banal thoughts. The patient would think "I must put the kettle on" and after a pause of not more than one second the voice would say "I must put the kettle on." It would often say the opposite "Don't put the kettle on"_ (p. 16).

2. **Voices arguing.** _A twenty-four-year-old male patient reported hearing voices coming from the nurse's office. One voice, deep in pitch and roughly spoken, repeatedly said "G.T. is a bloody paradox," and another higher in pitch said "He is that, he should be locked up." A female voice occasionally interrupted, saying "He is not, he is a lovely man"_ (p. 16).

3. **Voices commenting.** _A forty-one-year-old housewife heard a voice coming from a house across the road. The voice went on incessantly in a flat monotone describing everything she was doing with an admixture of critical comments. "She is peeling potatoes, got hold of the peeler, she does not want that_ potato, she is putting it back, because she thinks it has a knobble like a penis, she has a dirty mind, she is peeling potatoes, now she is washing them. . . ."_ (p. 16).

Motor symptoms

Disturbances in motor activity are obvious and bizarre. The schizophrenic may grimace or adopt strange facial expressions. He or she may gesture repeatedly, using peculiar and sometimes complex sequences of finger, hand, and arm movements—which often seem to be purposeful, odd as they may be. Some schizophrenics manifest an unusual increase in the overall level of activity. There may be much excitement, wild flailing of the limbs, and great expenditure of energy similar to that seen in mania. At the other end of the spectrum is _catatonic immobility:_ unusual postures are adopted and maintained for very long periods of time. A patient may stand on one leg, with the other tucked up toward the buttocks, and remain in this position virtually all day. The limbs of catatonic patients may have what is referred to as _waxy flexibility._ Another person can move them about and put them into strange positions that will then be maintained.

Affective symptoms

Two affective abnormalities are found in a number of schizophrenic patients. In some affect is said to be _flat;_ virtually no stimulus can elicit an emotional response. This shallowness or complete blunting of emotions renders the schizophrenic apathetic. The patient may stare vacantly, the muscles of his face flaccid, his eyes lifeless. When spoken to he answers in a flat and toneless voice. Flat affect was found in 66 percent of the IPSS schizophrenics. Other patients have _inappropriate affect._ The emotional responses of these individuals are out of context—the patient may laugh on hearing that her mother has just died or become enraged when asked a simple question about how a new garment fits. These schizophrenics are likely to shift rapidly from one emotional state to another for no discernible reason. Although this symptom is quite rare, when it does appear it is of considerable diagnostic importance.

Impairments in life functioning

Besides the specific symptoms that have been described, schizophrenics have many impairments of what should be the daily routines of their lives. In adolescence the preschizophrenic usually has few social skills, few friends, and no intimates. Dating is infrequent and academic difficulties are common. After leaving high school most schizophrenics are relatively unsuccessful in obtaining and holding a job. And they become ever more seclusive and actively avoid the company of other people. They even keep a definite physical distance and may have difficulty looking people in the eye. Personal hygiene and grooming may become quite cursory. Later, after they have experienced full-blown episodes of schizophrenia, they continue to have many similar problems even between episodes.

Subcategories of Schizophrenia

Three of the types of schizophrenic disorders that are now included in DSM-III—*hebephrenic, catatonic,* and *paranoid*—were initially proposed by Kraepelin many years ago. The present descriptions of Kraepelin's original types provide further information on what schizophrenia is like and on the great diversity of behavior that relates to the diagnosis.[3]

Disorganized schizophrenia

Kraepelin's hebephrenic form of schizophrenia is called *disorganized* schizophrenia by DSM-III and is characterized by a variety of rather diffuse and regressive symptoms. Hallucinations and de-

A man diagnosed as a disorganized schizophrenic, largely because of his inappropriate mirth.

[3] Several other of the old DSM-II types of schizophrenia are no longer part of the DSM-III category. Schizophrenia, simple and latent types, would now be diagnosed as schizotypal and borderline personality disorders. Schizophrenia, childhood type, is now diagnosed as either infantile autism or childhood onset pervasive developmental disorder (see Chapter 16).

lusions—sexual, hypochondriacal, religious, and persecutory—are profuse and less organized than those of the paranoid schizophrenic. The patient may be subject to bizarre ideas, often involving deterioration of the body. He is constantly changeable, breaking into inexplicable fits of laughter and crying. Much of the patient's behavior is marked by a pattern of silliness and absurdity. He may grimace or have a meaningless smile on his face. He giggles childishly and speaks incoherently, stringing together similar-sounding words and inventing neologisms. All in all, his life seems a tangled skein of delusions, mannerisms, and busy, inconsequential rituals. He may tie a ribbon around his big toe or move incessantly, pointing at objects for no apparent reason. He frequently deteriorates to the point that he becomes incontinent, voiding anywhere and at any time. And he completely neglects his appearance, never bathing, brushing his teeth, or combing his hair.

The patient was a twenty-four-year-old single woman. After graduation from college she worked for two years with an advertising agency. Both during her college days and later she was very seclusive and had few friends. She had never had any sexual experience, either homosexual or heterosexual. In the few weeks before hospitalization she had stopped going to work, remaining in her apartment and becoming inattentive to personal hygiene and grooming.

When she was admitted to the hospital, she was unkempt, disheveled, and dirty. Meaningful conversation with her seemed impossible. She maintained a silly grin and occasionally would burst into spontaneous and wild fits of laughter, even though she might be describing how her bones were melting. Her verbal behavior was nonsensical. Asked whether she wanted to go on a ward outing, she replied, "Outing, inning, being out is in and in is out" (*laughter*).

Catatonic schizophrenia

The most obvious symptoms of the *catatonic* type of schizophrenia are the motor disturbances discussed earlier. Such individuals typically alternate between catatonic immobility and wild excitement, but one or the other type of motor symptoms may predominate. The onset of cata-

tonic reactions may be more sudden than other forms of schizophrenia, although the person has probably already shown some apathy and withdrawal from reality. The limbs of the immobile catatonic may become stiff and swollen; in spite of apparent obliviousness, he or she may later relate all that has happened during the stupor. In the excited state the catatonic may shout and talk continuously and incoherently, all the while pacing with great agitation. This form of schizophrenia is seldom seen today, perhaps because drug therapy works effectively on these bizarre motor processes (Arieti, 1955). The following description is taken from our files.

Bob, a twenty-two-year-old, was admitted to the hospital after a brief period of withdrawal and then peculiar motor agitation at home. His parents reported that for several days he had stayed in his room, coming out only for meals. Then, at dinner one evening, he suddenly "became rigid." Alarmed, the parents called the family physician, but by the time he arrived Bob had entered a period of intense activity. He ran through the house, rolled on the floor, and strenuously resisted efforts to restrain him. Finally, he was sedated and taken to the hospital.

In the hospital Bob continued to alternate between periods of catatonic immobility and wild excitement. He refused to speak or eat and often did the exact opposite of what was requested of him, remaining in bed when asked to get up and remaining up when asked to go to bed.

Initially, Bob was placed on a drug therapy regimen which lasted for several months. He showed little improvement. Then a course of electroconvulsive therapy was begun, but again there was little improvement. The periods of excitement abated, but Bob remained mute and withdrawn and frequently adopted catatonic postures.

Paranoid schizophrenia

A more common diagnosis is paranoid schizophrenia. The key to this diagnosis is the presence of prominent delusions. Usually they are of persecution, but sometimes they may be _grandiose_ delusions. Individuals may have an exaggerated sense of their own importance, power, knowledge, or identity. Or they may be plagued by _delusional jealousy,_ believing the sexual partner to

This patient, diagnosed as a catatonic schizophrenic, spends nearly all his waking hours in a crouching position.

be unfaithful. Vivid auditory and visual hallucinations may also accompany the delusions. These patients often develop what are referred to as *ideas of reference:* they incorporate unimportant events within a delusional framework, reading personal significance into the seemingly trivial activities of others. They think that phrases of overheard conversations apply to them, and the continual appearance of a person on a street where they customarily walk means that they are being watched. What they see on television or read in magazines also somehow refers to them. Paranoid schizophrenics are agitated, argumentative, angry, and sometimes violent. But they remain emotionally responsive, although they may be somewhat stilted, formal, and intense with others. And they are more alert and verbal than

other schizophrenics; their thought processes, although deluded, have not fragmented. Another case from our records illustrates these symptoms.

Roger was initially seen as an outpatient. He had come for treatment because he had been rejected by the army for psychiatric reasons and ''wanted to do whatever was necessary to get into the army and go to Vietnam.'' He thought that he was a ''born soldier'' and related several incidents to support this assertion. In one of them he had been registering at a hotel desk, and the clerk had asked him how long his ''leave'' was going to be. Roger was unable to see that his short hair, marching gait, and the fact that he wore an army jacket were the likely cues the clerk was responding to.

Over the course of several weeks of outpatient therapy little happened. Roger remained very guarded and maintained that there really wasn't anything wrong. He showed almost no affective responses and claimed that his ideal was Mr. Spock, the intellectual, unemotional Vulcan of "Star Trek." One week, as he was leaving, he announced that he had "figured out what was going on and knew what to do."

Three days later he was hospitalized. He had threatened to blow up an army recruiting post, claiming that aliens from another planet had taken over. He now believed that he was one of the last "true" earthmen. The aliens had already infiltrated the bodies of most human beings, beginning first with those of army men and then moving into the bodies of the rest of the human race as well.

study (page 77) indicated, psychiatric labels are "sticky!" Clearly, schizophrenia is a disorder with a wide range of possible symptoms. Indeed, Bleuler wrote of the "group of schizophrenias," implying that it is not one but a set of disorders, each perhaps with a different etiology.

Evaluation

The Kraepelinian types still form the basis of current diagnostic systems, yet many have questioned their usefulness. Diagnosing types of schizophrenia is extremely difficult, which often means that diagnostic reliability is dramatically reduced. Furthermore, the types have little predictive validity: knowing that a patient has been diagnosed as having one or another form of schizophrenia does not give us information that will be helpful in treatment or in predicting the course of the problems. Finally, there is considerable overlap among types. For example, patients with all forms of schizophrenia may have delusions. Thus the Kraepelinian system of subtyping has not proved to be an optimal way of trying to deal with the variability in schizophrenic behavior.

Supplemental types that have been added by the DSM are also flawed, as definitions of the *undifferentiated* and *residual* types will indicate. The undifferentiated type is for patients who either have psychotic symptoms that do not fit into any other type or have symptoms of more than one of them. The diagnosis residual schizophrenia "should be used when there has been at least one episode of Schizophrenia but the [current] clinical picture . . . is without prominent psychotic symptoms, though signs of the illness persist" (DSM-III, p. 192). As Rosenhan's (1973)

Laboratory Research with Adult Schizophrenics

In their quest for a better understanding of schizophrenia, researchers have examined a number of psychological processes, among them motivation, learning, perception, and cognition. The primary goal of this research has been to obtain a detailed and precise knowledge of processes that may become deviant and are thus relevant to certain important types of schizophrenic behavior. Researchers attempt to answer questions such as "Why do schizophrenics make deviant associations?" "How is schizophrenic attention deviant?" "What produces hallucinations?"

We have already noted, for example, that historically disorders of thought and language were viewed as crucial signs of schizophrenia. But what exactly is disordered in thought disorder? Chapman and Chapman (1973) report the following answer that a schizophrenic patient gave to the question "Why do you think people believe in God?"

> Uh, late, I don't know why, let's see balloon travel. He holds it up for you, the balloon. He don't let you fall out, your little legs sticking out down through the clouds. He's down to the smoke stack, looking through the smoke trying to get the balloon gassed up you know. Way they're flying on top that way, legs sticking out, I don't know, looking down on the ground, heck, that'd make you go dizzy you just stay and sleep you know, hold down and sleep there. The balloon's His home you know up there. I used to sleep outdoors, you know, sleep outdoors instead of going home. He's had a home but His not tell where it's at you know (p. 3).

The patient's response is clearly disordered, but can we specify the nature of the disorder more precisely? It would seem that the patient wanders off the topic, bringing in details, such as sleeping outdoors, that seem irrelevant to the question asked. Chapman and Chapman note that different observers might account for irrelevancy in varying ways.

1. The patient is unable to organize his thoughts coherently. A disordered associative process leads the patient from thinking of God's home, which he believes to be in the sky, to thinking of balloons because they are also in the sky.

2. The patient can deal with only one idea at a time.

3. The question was too abstract for the patient.

4. The patient's own personal feelings of being weak and alone intrude into his answer. He mentions the possibility of "falling out," "little legs," and so on.

These several descriptions of a single bit of schizophrenic dialogue illustrate how clinical data can be explained in a variety of ways. Laboratory research tries to determine which account is best by arranging special tests that pit the competing explanations against one another and allow incorrect ones to be discarded.

In any research on pertinent psychological processes, the performance of a group of adult schizophrenics is compared to that of a nonschizophrenic *contrast group*. Generally, schizophrenics are found to do more poorly than the contrast group, and the poor performance of the patients is termed a _psychological deficit_. The type of contrast group to which schizophrenics are compared is important. It is relatively easy to find that schizophrenics differ from college sophomores, but it has been much more difficult to show that schizophrenics differ from other psychotic patients (Neale and Oltmanns, 1980). But such a demonstration is crucial in determining whether any observed deficit is *specific* to schizophrenia.

The major difficulty of this research, discussed previously in Chapter 4, is that it is correlational in nature. The variable of primary interest is schizophrenic-nonschizophrenic, which is classificatory and has *not* been manipulated by an experimenter. Thus differences between schizophrenic and contrast groups in addition to the diagnosis may be regarded as plausible rival hypothesis to account for the varying perform-ances. And there are many such differences and rival hypotheses. The schizophrenic and contrast groups are likely to vary in intelligence and so-cial class, as indicated earlier; moreover, the schizophrenics are likely to be taking a tranquil-izing medication. We must keep in mind that be-cause this research is correlational, the conclu-sions drawn can be only tentatively accepted.

Before reviewing some of the research con-ducted on psychological deficits, we should mention that a good deal of this work has been directed toward disorder in form of thought. Fol-lowing Bleuler's belief that thought disorder is the key symptom of schizophrenia, researchers have oriented their efforts toward it and com-pared schizophrenics and contrast groups on var-ious cognitive tasks with the hope of discovering the mechanism responsible. Such research is problematic because only some of the schizo-phrenics in these samples are actually likely to have this problem. A more profitable method is to study cognitive processes only in schizophren-ics who have thought disorder. We shall examine one study (Rochester, Martin, and Thurston, 1977) that illustrates this research tactic of select-ing only schizophrenics with thought disorder.

Cognitive Research

Referential communication

In a study by Cohen, Nachmani, and Rosenberg (1974), colors were presented on disks in dis-plays that varied in two ways, the number of disks in each display and the "hue steps" be-tween the colors of the disks. Twenty-four first-admission schizophrenics and twenty-four medi-cal center employees were tested individually in the speaker role. Each participant was shown a series of disk displays; for each display he was asked to describe the color of the disk desig-nated by the experimenter "so that another per-son with the same colors in front of him will know which color you are talking about." The subject's descriptions were tape-recorded and his reaction times—the number of seconds between presentation of the display and the beginning of his response—were noted. Later, to measure the

associative accuracy of these tape-recorded de-scriptions, experimenters played them for a panel of people who were asked to pick out the colored disk that had been described. Finally, a week after the subjects were initially tested in the speaker role, they were tested as listeners to their own descriptions.

As expected, schizophrenics were significantly poorer at devising useful descriptions than were the controls. When depending on their descrip-tions of the colors, the listener panel made sub-stantially more errors in choosing the correct disk, except when the disks in the display were not very similar in color. For example, for a two-disk display with quite dissimilar colors, a pur-ple-blue and a red, and with the purple-blue as the referent, the following descriptions were given.

Normal S1: "Purple."

Normal S3: "This is purple-blue."

Schizophrenic S1: "Blue."

Schizophrenic S3: "The bluer."

But with similar colors, a red and a slightly more yellowish red, and with the red as the referent, the following descriptions were typical.

Normal S1: "Both are salmon-colored. This one, however, has more pink."

Normal S3: "My God this is hard. They are both the same except that this one might be a little redder."

Schizophrenic S2: "This is the stupid color of a shit ass bowl of salmon. Mix it with mayon-naise. Then it gets tasty. Leave it alone and puke all over the fuckin' place. Puke fish."

Schizophrenic S3: "Make-up. Pancake make-up. You put it on your face and they think guys run after you. Wait a second! I don't put it on my face and guys don't run after me. Girls put it on them."

Schizophrenics were also less accurate than the controls when choosing disks on the basis of their own recorded descriptions. Finally, the reaction times of the schizophrenics were usually longer than those of the controls. When the displays contained more disks or disks of similar color, the reaction times of members of both groups were longer than when disks were few and dissimilar, reflecting the greater difficulty of the task. But the reaction times of the schizophrenics were more than proportionately longer.

In discussing their results, Cohen, Nachmani, and Rosenberg evaluated several models that might explain the schizophrenics' associative inadequacy. In all the models they evaluated, the associative process was conceptualized as consisting of two stages, sampling and comparison. In the sampling stage the person thinks of a number of ways of describing the referent. In the comparison stage he or she determines the degree of association between each of the tentative descriptive phrases and the referent, decides whether they distinguish it from the nonreferent colors, and then picks the best phrase.

One model, called the *Tower of Babel*, asserts that schizophrenics sample from a repertoire of idiosyncratic phrases. Thus they would be poor describers but, and this is the important point, they should be able to respond accurately to their own descriptions. Since the outcome belied this second prediction, the model was abandoned. The *impulsive-speaker* model asserts that schizophrenics sample normally from a nondeviant repertoire of phrases but then fail to go through the comparison stage, that is, they fail to self-edit. Failure to self-edit should lessen the effectiveness of the schizophrenic's description for both the listener panel and self. These two predictions of the impulsive-speaker model were supported by the data. If schizophrenics spend no time comparing phrases, however, their reaction time should *not* change when the number of disks in a display is increased or when their colors are more similar. The findings indicated otherwise.

Finally, the authors considered and tentatively accepted a *perseveration-chaining* model. This position asserts that schizophrenics are unable to ignore a phrase that occurs to them, even though they recognize it to be a poor description. Most phrases would rather inadequately distinguish among many and similar colors. But the schizo-

phrenic perseverates or samples and resamples the same first inappropriate phrase until it is emitted as a response. He cannot let go of it and search for a more appropriate one. Then the schizophrenic begins the chaining process, uttering a new response evoked by the one already given, and then another and another one to each immediately preceding response, without concern for their relevance to the color at hand. This model predicts the inadequacy of the descriptions, both for the listener panel and self, and also the observed increases in reaction time. Finally, this model implies that the utterances of schizophrenics should be longer than normal, which they are.

Increased distractibility

Another interpretation of thought disorder blames unusual _distractibility._ Because the attention of schizophrenics is supposedly too easily diverted either by irrelevant stimuli in the surroundings or by their own thoughts, bodily processes, and the like, their train of thought and speech become disorganized. Some research has indeed found that schizophrenics are particularly distractible. Rappaport (1967) investigated the performance of schizophrenics and normal subjects on a competing-message task. Several auditory messages were presented simultaneously. The subjects were required to attend to only one of them and then repeat it back. The number of simultaneously presented messages varied from one to seven. The performance of the schizophrenics was always deficient whenever more than one message was offered. But not all research has found that schizophrenics are especially distractible (for example, Taylor and Hirt, 1975). Perhaps the conflicting results can be attributed in part to differences in the way the schizophrenic populations of the various studies had been diagnosed. This question, as well as several others, was studied by Oltmanns, O'Hayon, and Neale (1978).

Testing distractibility in relation to diagnosis required a complicated procedure. It was necessary to diagnose patients according to two different systems. First, patients who had been diagnosed schizophrenic by hospital personnel were chosen as subjects. Distractibility was tested by a digit span task. In the no-distraction version of the task selected, subjects heard a voice presenting a sequence of numbers at a rate of one every two seconds. After listening to the string, the participant tried to recall as many digits as possible. In the distraction version another voice presented several *irrelevant* digits after each relevant digit, before the next one was heard. The difference in performance of these two tasks was the measure of distractibility. Hospital-diagnosed schizophrenics were no more distractible than controls, at least to no statistically significant degree. But then the schizophrenic subjects were rediagnosed using more stringent, Europeanlike diagnostic rules developed by Spitzer, Endicott, and Robins (1975). The schizophrenics separated out by the second diagnosis were found to be quite distractible, significantly more so than both the normal controls and the remaining patients who had now been judged not schizophrenic.

Additional evidence collected by Oltmanns and his colleagues also attests to the potential importance of distractibility in schizophrenia. The symptoms of each patient as recorded in their case histories were graded for severity and then related to distractibility. Since distractibility is hypothesized to be a determinant of thought disorder, the correlation between these two variables was expected to be high. This is exactly what was found. Finally, a new sampling of patients, some still receiving medication, others not, were tested. Since certain drugs are known to improve schizophrenic behavior (see page 439), they should affect distractibility, if indeed it is an important component of schizophrenia. The schizophrenics who had been withdrawn from medication were found more distractible than those still taking it.

Oltmanns's research, in contrast to many psychological-deficit studies, had as one of its purposes determining whether distractibility is related to thought disorder. This is clearly an improvement over simply *assuming* that the measure is related to disordered thought. Another line of recent research, conducted by Rochester and her colleagues, had a similar desirable purpose.

Analysis of schizophrenic speech

Rochester was interested in specifying empirically the characteristics of schizophrenics' speech that lead clinicians to infer that their thoughts are disordered. To do so she collected speech samples from thought-disordered schizophrenics, schizophrenics without thought disorder, and normal subjects. Thought disorder was determined on the basis of clinical ratings. Rochester was concerned with variables that allow a listener to follow someone's ideas as he or she speaks. The ties a speaker makes between sentences or clauses provide their cohesion, which takes several forms. For example, two sentences with temporal cohesion are linked by information about the temporal order of events: She opened the door. *Then* she came over here. Examples of the types of cohesion considered by Rochester, Martin, and Thurston (1977) are listed in Table 13.2. The speech samples of all three groups of speakers were rated by two independent coders to determine the extent and form of cohesion utilized. The schizophrenic patients without thought disorder produced the same proportions of each type of cohesion as the normal subjects, but thought-disordered patients deviated from both of these groups. Thought-disordered speakers used fewer conjunctive ties and relatively more lexical ties (Table 13.3).

Noun phrases often require additional information in order to be understood. For example, pronouns can often be understood only by referring back to nouns that have appeared previously. Rochester, Martin, and Thurston (1977) formed several categories of sentences with reference cohesion that differed in the amount of information provided to the listener. Some sentences provided clear information to a listener, for example, "The man opened the book. *He* began turning the pages." But other constructions posed problems for a listener, for example, "Bill and Pete are walking down the street and *he* looks tired." Rochester and her colleagues had two raters code all the noun phrases produced by each speaker according to the adequacy of their referents. Thought-disordered speakers produced more noun phrases that either were ambiguous or required additional, unavailable information.

TABLE 13.2
Three Categories of Cohesion
(from Rochester, Martin, and Thurston, 1977)

Category	Subcategory	Examples
Reference	(1) Pronominal (2) Demonstrative (3) Comparative	We met "Joy Adamson" and had dinner with *her* in Nairobi.* We went to "a hostel" and oh *that* was a dreadful place. "Six guys" approached me. The *last* guy pulled a knife on me in the park.
Conjunction	(1) Additive (2) Adversative (3) Causal (4) Temporal (5) Continuative	I read a book in the past few days *and* I like it. They started out for England *but* got captured on the way. It was a beautiful tree *so* I left it alone. My mother was in Ireland. *Then* she came over here. What kind of degree? *Well,* in one of the professions.
Lexical	(1) Same root (2) Synonym (3) Superordinate (4) General item	Mother needed "Independence." She was always *dependent* on my father. I "got angry" at M. but I don't often *get mad.* I love catching "fish." I caught a *bass* last time. The "plane" hit some air pockets and the bloody *thing* went up and down.

* Cohesive elements are in italics; tied-in information is indicated by quotation marks.

TABLE 13.3
Distribution of Cohesive Ties
(from Rochester, Martin, and Thurston, 1977)

Group	Proportion of ties per category*		
	Reference	Conjunction	Lexical
Thought-disordered schizophrenics	.34	.23	.41
Schizophrenics without thought disorder	.33	.30	.34
Normal subjects	.30	.36	.33

* Proportions sum to less than 1.0 because two minor categories are not reported.

In summary, then, Rochester and her co-workers succeeded in demonstrating differences in the speech samples of thought-disordered speakers and speakers without thought disorder. They found that thought-disordered schizophrenics make poor cohesive ties. They less frequently provided conjunctive ties between sentences, and, although they gave as many reference ties as other subjects, they used ambiguous noun phrases and failed to provide the listener with clear pronoun referents. Rochester's research is a useful confirmation and extension of Cohen's studies. Taken together, these two lines of investigation demonstrate that the communication difficulties of some schizophrenics may stem from a failure to encode or consider what information will be required by the listener.

Hallucinations

Another schizophrenic disturbance that has been researched, this a perceptual one, is the hallucination. Mintz and Alpert (1972) hypothesized that having a predisposition for *vivid imagining* and an *impaired perception of reality* may explain why schizophrenics hallucinate. They administered two tests to three groups of hospitalized mental patients—hallucinating schizophrenics, nonhallucinating schizophrenics, and nonschizophrenic patients. In the first test the subject was asked to close his eyes and imagine hearing a phonograph record playing "White Christmas" with both words and music. After thirty seconds the subject rated the vividness of the image he was able to produce on a scale ranging from "I heard a phonograph record of 'White Christmas' clearly and believed that the record was actually playing" to "I did not hear the record." For a second test earphones were placed on the subject through which he was to hear a set of twenty-four sentences, each with an intelligibility level of about 50 percent. Each time a sentence was presented, the subject tried to repeat exactly what he had heard and rated his confidence in the accuracy of his rendition on a scale ranging from "positive correct" to "positive incorrect."

On the imagination task 85 percent of the hallucinating schizophrenics reported either that they heard "White Christmas" and believed that the record was actually playing or that they had heard the song clearly but knew that a record was not really playing. One of the hallucinating schizophrenics who had not heard "White Christmas" said that his voices were talking too loudly for him to listen to the record. In contrast, only 5 percent of the nonhallucinating schizophrenics reported having heard the record with any vividness. The accuracy scores on the sentence detection task and the ratings by which the subject had indicated his confidence in his own renditions were compared. The correlation was +.54 for the hallucinating schizophrenics and +.84 for the nonhallucinating schizophrenics. Hallucinating schizophrenics were poorer at judging the accuracy of their performance.

What do these results reveal about hallucinations? How well the subject imagined hearing "White Christmas" was assumed to reflect his vividness of imagery. His capacity to perceive reality was supposedly measured by the correlation between the actual accuracy of his sentence renditions and his confidence in their accuracy—for anyone in contact with reality is assumed able to assess accurately his performance of a task. Hallucinating schizophrenics showed *both* vivid imagery *and* a defective capacity for perceiving reality. Hallucinations may therefore reflect a failure to discriminate between self-produced images and stimulation in the external world. A greater capacity for vivid imagery and loss of contact with reality should increase the likelihood of hallucinations.

In a corroborative study McGuigan (1966) instructed patients to press a key whenever they experienced an auditory hallucination. At the same time recordings were made of electrical activity in the subject's larynx. In this fashion McGuigan could compare the outputs of the larynx when the patient was experiencing auditory hallucinations and when he was not. The patient's report that he was hallucinating correlated remarkably with an increase in electrical activity in the larynx. Patients reporting auditory hallucinations may merely be talking to themselves by interpreting the internal speech as coming from the external world.

Summary

The pioneering efforts of Kraepelin and Bleuler led to two views of schizophrenia. Kraepelin's work fostered a descriptive approach and a narrow definition, whereas Bleuler's theoretical emphasis led to a very broad diagnostic category. Bleuler had a great influence on the American conception of schizophrenia. His influence, together with the American interest in treatment and the addition of several poorly defined types of schizophrenia, served to make the American concept excessively inclusive. By mid-twentieth century the differences in the way schizophrenia was diagnosed in America and Europe were vast. These differences were studied in depth by the U.S.–U.K. project. With the advent of DSM-III, the American concept of schizophrenia has become narrower and more similar to a European view. The basic symptoms are disturbances in thought—incoherence, loose associations, lack of insight, and delusions; in perception and attention—derealization, distractibility, and hallucinations; in motor behavior—grimacing, gesturing, and flailing of limbs or catatonia and waxy flexibility; and in affect—flat or inappropriate. Schizophrenics also have little social competence and considerable difficulty holding jobs. A review of the schizophrenic types proposed by Kraepelin and in DSM-III indicates the great variability in the behavior of schizophrenic patients.

The performance of schizophrenics on laboratory tasks has indeed furthered our understanding of some schizophrenic behavior. Cognitive research has tried to pinpoint crucial processes that may explain thought disorder. Cohen's study has shown that schizophrenics' association problems may result from perseveration and chaining. In selecting descriptive words, schizophrenics are unable to ignore what first occurs to them and then are off on a chain of associations to that phrase. Oltmanns determined that distractibility is related to thought disorder. Rochester and her colleagues have observed poor cohesive ties in the sentences of schizophrenics. Research on hallucinations indicates that these experiences may reflect schizophrenics' vivid imaginings and their failure to distinguish their own images from environmental stimuli. Any theory of the etiology of schizophrenia will have to account for the descriptive and laboratory data presented in this chapter.

chapter 14

SCHIZOPHRENIA: THEORY AND RESEARCH ON ETIOLOGY AND THERAPY

Major Theoretical Positions
Research on the Etiology of Schizophrenia
Therapies for Schizophrenia

A t the end of the preceding chapter we reviewed some research undertaken to determine *how* schizophrenics differ from normal people in the ways they think, speak, perceive, and imagine. We are now ready to ask *what* can explain the scattering and disconnections of their thoughts, their wanting or inappropriate emotions, their delusions and bewildering hallucinations. To borrow from the words of a poet, we might ask "What could frame their fearful dissymmetries?" In contrast to other disorders considered in this book, broad theoretical perspectives like psychoanalysis and learning theory have not had much of an impact on research in schizophrenia. Therefore we provide only a brief overview of major theoretical positions and then turn to a more detailed examination of specific areas of etiological research.

Major Theoretical Positions

Psychoanalytic Theory

Because Freud himself dealt primarily with neuroses, he had relatively little to say about schizophrenia. He did occasionally speculate on its origins, though, using some of the psychoanalytic concepts that he applied to all disordered personalities. His basic notion was that schizophrenics have regressed to a state of "primary narcissism," a phase early in the oral stage before the ego has differentiated from the id. There is thus no separate ego to engage in reality testing—a crucial function whereby the ego takes actions that test the nature of its social and physical environment. By regressing to narcissism, schizophrenics have effectively lost contact with the world; they have withdrawn the libido from attachment to any objects external to themselves. Freud thought that the cause of the regression was an increase, during adulthood, in the intensity of id impulses, especially sexual ones. Contemporary psychoanalytic theorists give primacy to aggressive impulses. Whether the threats of the intense id impulses provoke schizophrenia or a neurosis depends on the strength of the ego. Neurotics, having developed a more stable ego, will not regress to the first psychosexual stage, as schizophrenics do, and consequently will not lose contact with reality.

Some of the major symptoms of schizophrenia—lack of interpersonal relationships and passivity—are considered reflections of this regression. Other symptoms such as hallucinations and bizarre speech are regarded as the outcomes of attempts to deal with the id impulses and with reality—attempts to cope with the flood of id impulses demanding discharge and at the same time to reestablish contact with something other than the self. The patient, having withdrawn from reality, creates an inner world of hallucinations.

Few data bear on the psychoanalytic position. The theory has generated intriguing and speculative analysis of case history material (see Box 14.1) but little research. The material on cognitive deficits presented in Chapter 13 as well as similar data collected by analytically oriented researchers (for example, Bellak, Hurvich, and Gediman, 1973) could be said to demonstrate that the egos of schizophrenics have been impaired. But even so, ego impairment need not be precipitated by an increase in id impulses, nor need it end in a regression to a childhood state. Finally, no one has presented evidence that ego impairments cause schizophrenia.

Labeling Theory

In a radical departure from the traditional conceptualization of schizophrenia, Scheff (1966) has suggested that the disorder is a *learned social role*. This position, also known as *labeling theory,* is essentially unconcerned with etiology. Rather, Scheff argues that the crucial factor in schizophrenia is the act of assigning a diagnostic label to the individual. Presumably this label then influences the manner in which the person will continue to behave, based on the stereo-

typic notions of mental illness, and at the same time determines the reactions of other people to the individual's behavior. The social role, therefore, *is* the disorder, and it is determined by the labeling process. Without the diagnosis, Scheff argues, deviant behavior—or to use his term, residual rule breaking—would not become stabilized. It would presumably be both transient and relatively inconsequential.

By *residual rules* Scheff means the rules that are left over after all the formal and obvious ones, about stealing and violence and fairness, have been laid down. They concern ways of behaving that are so taken for granted that they are rarely if ever stated and come to mind only when they are breached. "Do not stand still staring vacantly in the middle of a busy sidewalk." "Do not talk to the neon beer sign in the delicatessen window." "Do not sing glad songs at your mother's graveside." "Do not spit in the piano." The examples are endless. Scheff believes that one-time violations of residual rules are fairly common. Normal people may think that they know when they can safely violate such rules, but through bad luck or poor judgment they are caught in their acts and the diagnoses assigned them take over. Then they are very likely to accept the social role of being mentally ill. Once judged so, they find it very difficult to rejoin the sane, for employment will be denied them and other people will know about their pasts. In the hospital they will receive attention and sympathy and be free of all responsibilities. So once there they actually perceive themselves as mentally ill and settle into acting crazy as is expected of them.

Scheff's theory has some intuitive appeal. Most people who have worked for any amount of time at a psychiatric facility have witnessed abuses of the diagnostic process. Patients are sometimes assigned labels that are poorly justified (recall the Rosenhan study, page 76). Many factors other than symptomatology can influence both the diagnostic and hospitalization processes, such as number of beds available. Furthermore, a few studies have indicated that schizophrenic patients are able, in some situations, voluntarily to manipulate the diagnostic impression they give to others. In one such study (Braginsky, Grosse, and Ring, 1966) acute and chronic pa-

BOX 14.1 Paranoid Delusions and Repressed Homosexuality

According to DSM-III, paranoid delusions are the most obvious symptom of both paranoid schizophrenia and the _paranoid disorders._ A person with a paranoid disorder is troubled by persistent persecutory delusions or by delusional jealousy, the unfounded conviction that the spouse or lover is unfaithful. But unlike the paranoid schizophrenic, he or she has no thought disorder, no hallucinations, and no bizarre delusions, such as the belief that thoughts are being broadcast. The person speaks and reasons coherently and carries out daily responsibilities. A circumscribed delusional system is the one and fundamental loss of contact with reality. People with this order of paranoia rarely seek treatment through their own volition, but when they become contentious and initiate series of litigations, others may bring them for care.

Freud's theory, commonly accepted even today, is that paranoid delusions result from repressed homosexual impulses which are striving for expression. The anxiety stemming from their threatened expression is handled primarily by the defense mechanism of projection, attributing to others feelings that are unacceptable to one's own ego (Freud, 1915). The basic unconscious thought is "I, a man, love him" or "I, a woman, love her." Freud considered the common paranoid delusions of persecution and grandiosity to derive from distortions, and then projection, of this basic homosexual urge.

In _delusions of persecution_ the homosexual thought "I, a man, love him," being unacceptable to the ego, is converted into the less threatening statement "I, a man, hate him." Since the emotion expressed by this premise is also less than satisfactory, it is further transformed by projection into "He hates me, so I am justified in hating him." The final formulation may be "I hate him because he persecutes me." Freud asserted that the persecutor is always a person of the same sex who is unconsciously a love object for the individual.

Delusions of grandiosity (megalomania) begin with a contradiction of the homosexual impulse. The sentence "I, a man, love him" is changed

into "I do not love anyone." But since libido must be invested in or attached to something or someone, the psychic reality becomes "I love only myself."

One of Freud's lesser-known cases of a patient with paranoid delusions is of special interest, for it seems initially to challenge Freud's basic tenet that the persecutor must be a person of the same sex. The kinds of inferences that constitute the argument of this case study are typical of those made by Freud in his attempts to understand his clinical data and to test his hypotheses.

Freud was consulted by a lawyer in Vienna who had been hired by a woman to sue a male business associate for making indecent allegations about her. She stated that the man had had photographs taken of them while they were making love and was now threatening to bring disgrace upon her. Because of the unusual nature of her allegation, the lawyer had persuaded her to see Freud so that he could offer an opinion.

The woman, about thirty years of age, was an attractive single person who lived quietly with her mother, whom she supported. A handsome man in her firm had recently begun to court her. After much coaxing he had persuaded her to come to his apartment for an afternoon together. They became intimate, at which point she was frightened by a clicking noise coming from the direction of a desk in front of the window. The lover told her that it was probably from a small clock on the desk. As she left the house that afternoon, she encountered two men, one of them carrying a small package. They appeared to whisper something to each other secretively as she passed. By the time she reached home that evening, she had put together the following story. The box was a camera, the men were photographers, and her lover was an untrustworthy person who had arranged for photographs to be taken of them while they were undressed. The following day she began to berate the lover for his untrustworthiness, and he tried equally hard to rid her mind of her unfounded suspicions. Freud read one of the letters that the man had written to the woman. It struck him that the lover was indeed sincere and honest in denying involvement in such a plot.

At this point Freud faced a dilemma common in scientific inquiry. What should the investigator do when confronted by an instance that negates his hypothesis? The persecutor of the young woman appeared to be a member of the opposite sex. Freud could, of course, have completely abandoned his theory that paranoid delusions originate in homosexual impulses. Instead, he looked more closely into the case to see whether there were subtle factors that would allow him, in the end, to preserve the integrity of his theory.

During the second meeting with Freud, the woman changed the story somewhat. She admitted that she had visited the man twice in his apartment, not once, and that only on the second occasion had she heard the suspicious noise. After the first and uneventful visit—as far as her paranoia was concerned—she had been disturbed by an incident that she had witnessed at the office. The next day she had seen her new lover speaking in low tones to an older woman who was in charge of the firm. The older person liked the younger woman a great deal, and the younger woman in turn found that her employer reminded her of her own mother. She was therefore very concerned about their conversation and became convinced that her suitor was telling the woman about their lovemaking the previous afternoon.

Then it occurred to her that her lover and her employer had been having a love affair for some time. At the first opportunity she berated her lover for telling their employer of their lovemaking. He naturally protested and after a while succeeded in undoing her suspicions. Then she made her second visit to his apartment and heard the reputed clicking.

Let us examine Freud's comments on this portion of the case history.

These new details remove first of all any doubts

as to the pathological nature of her suspicion. It is easy to see that the white haired elderly manageress is a mother-substitute, that in spite of his youth the lover had been put in the place of the father, and that the strength of the mother-complex has driven the patient to suspect a love-relationship between these ill-matched partners, however unlikely such a relation might be. Moreover, this fresh information resolves the apparent contradiction with the view maintained by psychoanalysis, that the development of a delusion of persecution is conditioned by an overpowerful homosexual bond. The original persecutor—the agency whose influence the patient wishes to escape—is here again not a man but a woman. The manageress knows about the girl's love-affairs, disapproves of them, and shows her disapproval by mysterious allusions. The woman's attachment to her own sex hinders her attempts to adopt a person of the other sex as a love object (1915, p.155).

To protect herself from her own homosexual impulses, the young woman is presumed to have developed a paranoid delusion about the man and her employer. A crucial aspect of the case, according to Freud, was the click that the woman had heard and interpreted as the sound of a camera shutter. Freud assumed that this click was actually a sensation or beat in her clitoris. Her sexual arousal, then, provided the basis for her paranoid delusion of being photographed.

Freud allowed himself a remarkable amount of unverified inference in this particular case. Because he wanted to hold to a homosexuality-based theory of paranoia, he inferred that the woman regarded her female superior as a substitute for her mother, that she had an undue homosexual attachment to her own mother and by generalization to this older woman, and that the click that she had heard and construed in paranoid fashion to be the sound of a camera shutter was really sexual excitement.

tients completed a short form of the MMPI. Some patients were told that the more items answered true, the more severely ill they were, and the more likely they were to remain in the hospital for a long time. Others were told that the more items answered true, the more they knew about themselves, the less severely ill they were, and the more likely they were to remain in the hospital for only a short period.

It was hypothesized that the chronic patients, who had been in the hospital for a long period of time, actually wished to remain there since they had adjusted to the hospital milieu. In contrast, acute patients, those for whom the onset of the disorder had been rapid and who were in a great panic because they did not understand what was happening to them, were thought to be eager to leave. Assuming that patients can indeed manage the impression that they create on others, the following outcomes were expected. Acute patients would give more true responses when they thought these answers reflected self-insight, fewer when they believed them to reflect mental illness. Chronic patients would give more true responses when they believed them to prove mental illness, fewer when they considered them to prove self-insight. The results (Table 14.1) clearly supported the hypotheses. It indeed appeared that patients would try to manipulate the impression that they created on others in order to enhance their chances of either staying in the hospital or leaving it.

A number of serious problems with Scheff's theory indicate, however, that it is, at most, of secondary importance to our understanding of schizophrenia. First of all, Scheff refers to deviance as residual rule breaking, and as described it is indeed merely that. Violating cultural norms governing the nature of interpersonal interaction is, however, very different from the phenomena included in most definitions of schizophrenia and certainly from Schneider's descriptions of delusions and hallucinations. Calling schizophrenia residual rule breaking trivializes a very serious disorder. Second, very little evidence indicates that unlabeled norm violations are indeed transient, as Scheff implies. Third, information regarding the detrimental effects of the social stigma associated with mental illness is inconclusive at best (Gove, 1970). And finally, the ability of schizophrenic patients voluntarily to manage other people's impressions appears to be extremely limited, according to the results of studies somewhat similar to Braginsky's research (Price, 1972b; Ryan and Neale, 1973). Thus holding that schizophrenia may most usefully be thought of as simply a label arbitrarily assigned to hapless rule breakers is not a satisfactory position.

An Experiential Theory

Ronald Laing, a Scottish existential psychiatrist, has offered a view of schizophrenia that is similar in some respects to labeling theory. For him schizophrenia is not an illness but a label for another kind of problematic experience and behavior.

> . . . The experience and behavior that gets labelled schizophrenic is a special sort of strategy that a person invents in order to live in an unlivable situation . . . the person has come to be placed in an untenable position. He cannot make a move or make no move without being beset by contradictory pressures both internally, from himself, and externally, from those around him. He is, as it were, in a position of checkmate (1964, p. 186).

Under such stress he will no longer masquerade as the false outer self society expects of him. Rather he retreats from reality backward into his

TABLE **14.1**

Average Number of "True" Responses Made by Chronic and Acute Patients

(from Braginsky et al., 1966)

Groups	True means mental illness	True means self-insight
Chronic patients	18.80	9.70
Acute patients	13.00	18.80

Ronald D. Laing, the Scottish existential psychiatrist who believes that schizophrenia is a behavioral strategy adopted as a means of escaping the reality of an unlivable world.

inner world. There he passes through regressive changes, but it is a voyage of discovery on which he may meet and make peace with his true inner self. Then he may emerge again into reality with a whole and authentic identity. Laing considers the family to be the primary culprit producing the behavior that is labeled schizophrenia. In what Laing calls *mystification*, the parent has systematically stripped the child's feelings and perceptions about himself and the world of all validity, so that he has come to doubt his hold on reality.

Rather than trying to remove the patient's symptoms, Laing argues that we should accept his or her experience as valid, understandable, and potentially meaningful and beneficial. The schizophrenic is on a psychedelic trip, necessitated by untenable environmental demands, and is in need of guidance—not control—if the destination of that trip is to be a state of enlightenment.

Laing's ideas are popular among those who object to what they consider to be hypocrisies of society and of the mental health establishment. Those who experience the suffering associated with schizophrenia may also take comfort in the belief that they are going through a positive growth process. At this point, however, there is little evidence that experiencing schizophrenia can make a "better person" of the patient. When released from the hospital, most schizophrenics who had a poor premorbid adjustment live a marginal existence, isolated from social relationships. Nor, as we shall see later in this chapter, is there much evidence to support Laing's assertion that schizophrenia is caused by familial experiences.

In sum, none of the major theoretical positions discussed has much support. Freud's views on regression to the oral stage, labeling theory, which emphasizes role taking reinforced by the attitudes of diagnosticians and mental hospital staff, and Laing's hypothesis that schizophrenia is a trip to improved functioning—all are without substantiating evidence.

Rather than construct elaborate theories, it may prove more fruitful to determine the etiological significance of particular discrete variables. A review of these variables will indicate how very complicated a theory will have to be to account for the problems called schizophrenia.

Research on the Etiology of Schizophrenia

Social Class and Schizophrenia

Numerous studies have shown a relation between social class and the diagnosis of schizophrenia. The highest rates of schizophrenia are found in central city areas inhabited by the lowest socioeconomic classes (for example, Hollingshead and Redlich, 1958; Srole et al., 1962). The relationship between social class and schizophrenia does not show a continuous progression of higher rates of schizophrenia as the social class becomes lower. Rather, there is a sharp *discontinuity* between the number of schizophrenics in the lowest social class and those in others. In the ten-year Hollingshead and Redlich study of social class and mental illness in New Haven, Connecticut, the rate of schizophrenia was found to be twice as high in the lowest social class as in the next to the lowest (see Box 14.2). The findings of Hollingshead and Redlich have been confirmed cross-culturally by similar community studies carried out in countries such as Denmark, Norway, and England (Kohn, 1968).[1]

The correlations between social class and schizophrenia are consistent, but they are still difficult to interpret in causal terms. Some people believe that being in a low social class may in itself cause schizophrenia. This is called the *sociogenic hypothesis.* The degrading treatment a person receives from others, the low level of education, and the unavailability of rewards and opportunity, taken together, may make membership in the lowest social class such a stressful experience that the individual develops schizophrenia.

But another explanation of the correlation between schizophrenia and low social class has also been suggested, the *social-drift theory.* During the course of their developing psychosis, schizophrenics may "drift" into the poverty-ridden areas of the city. The growing cognitive and motivational problems besetting these individuals may so impair their earning abilities that they cannot afford to live elsewhere. Or they may by choice move to areas where little social pressure will be brought to bear on them and where they can escape intense social relationships.

One way of resolving the conflict is to study the social mobility of schizophrenics. Three studies (Schwartz, 1946; Lystad, 1957; Turner and Wagonfeld, 1967) have found that schizophrenics are downwardly mobile in occupational status. But an equal number of studies have shown schizophrenics *not* to be downwardly mobile (Hollingshead and Redlich, 1958; Clausen and Kohn, 1959; Dunham, 1965). Kohn (1968) has suggested another way of examining this question. Are the fathers of schizophrenics also from the lowest social class? If they are, this could be considered evidence in favor of the hypothesis that lower-class status is conducive to schizophrenia, for class would be shown to *precede* schizophrenia. If the fathers are from a higher social class, the drift hypothesis would be the better explanation.

Goldberg and Morrison (1963) conducted such a study in England and Wales. The occupations of male schizophrenic patients were found to be less remunerative and prestigious than those of their fathers. Turner and Wagonfeld (1967) conducted a similar study in the United States and found evidence for both the sociogenic and drift hypothesis. Fathers of schizophrenics were more frequently from the lowest social class, supporting the sociogenic hypothesis. But at the same time many schizophrenics were lower in occupational prestige than their fathers, supporting the drift hypothesis. Thus it appears that both theories are partially correct. Some, but not all, of the relationship between social class and schizophrenia can be accounted for by the drift hypothesis. Social class appears to play a causal role, but the exact way in which the stresses associated with it exert their effect remains unknown.

The Role of the Family

Many theorists have regarded family relationships, especially those between a mother and

---

[1] There is perhaps one exception to this finding: the relationship may disappear in nonurban areas (Clausen and Kohn, 1959).

BOX 14.2 The Adequacy of Indices of Schizophrenia

Perhaps the most important decision facing a researcher interested in the relationship between social class and schizophrenia is determining how schizophrenia will be indexed. Many studies use hospital admission rates, especially those of state hospitals. But lower-class individuals are more likely to come to a public hospital than to a private one. Furthermore, many studies have shown that some people who suffer serious mental disorders never enter a mental hospital at all.

Researchers have attempted to make their sampling more complete by picking individuals from all treatment facilities in a given area. But the same kind of problem holds. For example, there are social class differences between people who have been treated for mental illness and severely impaired people who have never had any kind of treatment (Srole et al., 1962). Thus using treatment as an index of schizophrenia is suspect.

An alternative approach is to go into the community and examine everyone, or a representative sample of everyone. The problem of relying exclusively on treatment is solved, but other difficulties are raised. Operating in the community makes diagnostic reliability and even the definition of abnormal behavior a difficult proposition. The raters employed in the community studies have usually received much less training than those who conduct studies in psychiatric facilities. In addition, community studies settle for what is termed _prevalence_ rather than _incidence_ data. Incidence refers to the number of new cases found in various population groups during a particular period of time and thus is theoretically the most relevant measure in an investigation of this sort. In community studies, however, a simple count of the number of abnormal people is made. This prevalence measure is somewhat inappropriate, for it reflects both incidence and duration of illness. Since there is a correlation between duration of illness and social class (Hollingshead and Redlich, 1958), we cannot determine from prevalence data whether a correlation between social class and schizophrenia reflects incidence or duration of the disorder.

All in all, however, workers have continued to find a relation between social class and schizophrenia, whatever the methodologies employed, indicating that their data can be accepted.

her son, as crucial in the development of schizophrenia. The view has been so prevalent that the term _"schizophrenogenic mother"_ has been coined for the supposedly cold and dominant, conflict-inducing parent who is said to produce schizophrenia in her offspring (Fromm-Reichmann, 1948). These mothers have also been characterized as rejecting, overprotective, self-sacrificing, impervious to the feelings of others, rigid and moralistic about sex, and fearful of intimacy.[2]

[2] It is noteworthy that most theories implicating family processes in the etiology of abnormal behavior focus almost exclusively on the mother. Sexism?

Methods of study

Three methods have been employed to assess the potential role of the family. First, when patients are in treatment, their families can be studied by the *clinical observational method*. Although such studies may provide hypotheses, the data collected cannot serve as scientific proof (see Chapter 4), for the observations are not made under controlled conditions. Second, in *retrospective studies of child rearing*, parents and other relatives and friends of the patient being treated are questioned about historical events related to family life. The information collected by this method is also subject to a severe problem, the fallibility of recall over time. Third, in the *family interaction method* structured situations are devised to reveal how family members interact with one another. One of these procedures is the *revealed-differences technique*. Members of a family are given several questions to respond to, such as "What is the appropriate time for teenagers to begin dating?" Then they are asked to resolve any differences in the answers given by the individual members of the family. As they attempt to resolve their differences, their interaction is video-recorded so that the information can be reliably coded. The family interaction method has a clear advantage over the other two in the quality of the evidence that it can provide. It also has limitations, however. One of them is reactivity (see page 102). Knowledge that the family conversation is being studied may alter communication patterns. Moreover, since one member of the family is already psychotic, the validity of the information collected rests on the assumption that the currently observed family interaction patterns are the same as those existing *before* one member of the family became schizophrenic. The parents, however, may be *reacting* to the fact that an offspring is schizophrenic rather than acting as they did earlier when they may have been instrumental in causing the development of the disorder. If problems are noticeable in the family of a schizophrenic, the directionality of the correlation is therefore difficult to ascertain. The family problems may have caused schizophrenia in one of its members, or the schizophrenia may be causing family problems that did not exist earlier.

Fontana (1966) has found that the great majority of family studies are inadequate in various ways and has recommended some basic rules about methodology that should be followed in setting up these studies. Only families of schizophrenics should constitute the experimental group, the families of male and female patients should be analyzed separately, and all the diagnoses of schizophrenia should be reliable. Moreover, families of patients hospitalized for a physical illness must constitute the control group, for *all* families with a member hospitalized for any reason have been found to have problems.

Of the hundreds of family studies of schizophrenia, Fontana was able to find only five that met these criteria. And on the basis of these five he was able to draw only two conclusions.

1. There is more conflict between the parents of schizophrenics than between the parents of control patients.

2. Communication between the parents of schizophrenics is less adequate than that between control parents.

When the most stringent controls are applied, conflict and poor communication between parents assume more significance than any qualities of the supposed schizophrenogenic mother. But whether the difficulties between the parents antedate the development of schizophrenia in an offspring remains to be settled. Two noteworthy attempts to resolve this issue are described in Box 14.3.

The double bind

Thus far we have examined the role of the family in a rather general way and found the amount of conflict and accuracy of communication to be problems. More specific hypotheses have also been advanced, the most prominent being the *double bind* proposed by Bateson and his colleagues (1956). These writers believe that an important factor in the development of schizophrenic thought disorder is the constant subjection of an individual to a so-called double-bind situation. A double bind has the following aspects.

1. The individual has an intense relationship to another, so intense that it is especially impor-

In a detailed and careful study, Mishler and Waxler (1968) attempted to determine what family interaction patterns correlated with schizophrenia. They used the revealed-differences technique with two sessions for each family. In one session the parents participated with their schizophrenic child, and in the other with a nonpsychotic offspring of the same sex and approximately the same age as the patient. The design included in the experimental group both male and female patients and patients with good and poor premorbid adjustment. The control families had pairs of normal siblings of the same sex and nearly the same age. An attempt was made to balance the two groups so that family incomes, father's occupation, parents' education and religion, and parents' and grandparents' birthplaces were not too different.

By having two revealed-differences sessions, the researchers hoped to determine whether the patient's presence or absence affected the parents' behavior. If, for example, the parents expressed less emotion and were uncommunicative only in the session with the patient, their behavior might be interpreted as a *response* to the disturbed child. But if the parents of a schizophrenic child were unexpressive and uncommunicative toward both the disturbed child *and* the normal sibling, their behavior was less likely to be a specific reaction to a schizophrenic child.

Strategies of control were one of the variables studied in the two sessions. In normal families there was a coalition between mother and father and a clear status hierarchy. In contrast, in families with a schizophrenic son the father was excluded and a coalition between the mother and son was evident. In families with a schizophrenic daughter, she was the excluded one. These patterns were observed only when the patient was present, not during the session that the parents had with their normal offspring, suggesting that control strategies were a reaction to the schizophrenic child's behavior.

Speech disruptions—fragments of thought, repetitions, and incomplete sentences—were also observed. Contrary to expectation, the greatest frequency of speech disruptions occurred in the sessions with families of normal children. They were less noticeable in the conversations of families whose schizophrenic child was a poor premorbid and even less frequent in the conversations of familes whose schizophrenic child had had a good premorbid adjustment. Thus disrupted verbal communications could not be implicated as causative factors.

Overall, Mishler and Waxler were unable to establish a definite causal relationship between any aspect of parental behavior and the development of schizophrenia in an offspring, but their study did go well beyond a simple and general comparison of the behavior of normal families and that of families with a schizophrenic child.

In another study, one which focused on communication, Liem (1974) had a number of families with a schizophrenic son and control families with a normal son participate in an object identification task. The "communicator" was given the task of describing common objects, such as lamp or match, and concepts, such as teacher or child, so that a listener could identify them. During a session five "communications" about each of three objects or concepts were tape-recorded. Each schizophrenic son and each normal son had a turn in the role of communicator. Each set of parents took the role together as a communicating pair. Later parents and sons responded to different tapes, giving an answer after each description. The parents responded to tapes made by their own son, by an unknown non-schizophrenic son, and by an unknown schizophrenic son. The sons responded to tapes made by their own parents, unknown parents of a normal son, and unknown parents of a schizophrenic son.

How does this study relate to the possible role of the family in the etiology of schizophrenia? If unclear communication by the parents of a schizophrenic is assigned a *causal* role, we might expect their descriptions to be indeed inadequate and confusing to anyone who listens to them. In contrast, if the parents of a schizophrenic are *reacting* to their child's disorder, we would not expect their descriptions to be inadequate, but we would expect *all* parents to have difficulty interpreting the tape-recorded communications of a schizophrenic son. This second pattern is the one borne out by Liem's study.

On several measures of adequacy of communication, there were no important differences between the parents of normal and schizophrenic sons. The schizophrenic sons were inferior to normal sons, however, as would be expected from Cohen's work described in Chapter 13. *All* parents were confused by the descriptions formulated by schizophrenic sons, making more misidentifications when they listened to their own schizophrenic son's tape or that of an unknown schizophrenic son. In the author's own words,

The communication disorder of schizophrenic sons had an immediate, observable, negative effect not only on the parents of schizophrenic sons but on all parents who heard and attempted to respond to them. Disorder was not observed in the communications of parents of schizophrenic sons nor were their communications found to adversely affect sons who heard and responded to them (p. 445).

tant to be able to understand communications from the other person accurately so that the individual can respond appropriately.

2. The other person expresses two messages when making a statement, one of which denies the other.

3. The individual cannot comment on the mutually contradictory messages and cannot withdraw from the situation or ignore the messages.

The parent rarely communicates with the child in a simple an direct way. What a mother says to her son may be contradicted by how she says it, by what she does, or by emotion conveyed in

other ways. And the child cannot complain that he does not understand, nor can he ask for clarification. It becomes impossible for him to order his thinking; his responses may eventually become even more confused than the communications he receives. In their original paper Bateson and his colleagues gave the following example.

A young man who had fairly well recovered from an acute schizophrenic episode was visited in the hospital by his mother. He was glad to see her and impulsively put his arm around her shoulders whereupon she stiffened. He withdrew his arm and she asked, "Don't you love me anymore?" He then blushed and she said

"Dear, you must not be so easily embarassed and afraid of your feelings." The patient was able to stay with her only a few minutes more and following her departure he assaulted an aide. . . .

Obviously, this result could have been avoided if the young man had been able to say, "Mother, it is obvious that you become uncomfortable when I put my arm around you, and you have difficulty accepting a gesture of affection from me." However, the schizophrenic patient doesn't have this possibility open to him. An intense dependency in training prevents him from commenting upon his mother's communicative behavior, though she comments on his and forces him to accept and to attempt to deal with the complicated sequence. . . .

The impossible dilemma thus becomes: "If I am to keep my tie to my mother, I must not show her that I love her, but if I do not show her that I love her then I will lose her" (pp. 258–259).

Although the double bind has been a popular and widely known explanation of how schizophrenia develops, it is not supported as a factor of great etiological significance by any available data. Most of the literature on the double-bind hypothesis is uncontrolled and descriptive, consisting of case histories and transcripts of therapy sessions. In one controlled study Ringuette and Kennedy (1966) had different groups of judges try to identify double binds communicated in letters.[3] Two sets of letters were used, those written by parents to their hospitalized schizophrenic and nonschizophrenic offspring, and letters that had been written by volunteers instructed to compose them as though they were writing to hospitalized offspring. The groups of judges included three of the people closely involved in originally formulating the double-bind hypothesis, psychiatric residents who had been taught earlier how to recognize a double-bind communication, and experienced clinicians who also knew the double-bind interpretation.

[3] Although the use of letters in this study may seem strange, many of those who have studied the double bind have paid particular attention to the contents of letters written by parents of schizophrenics. They believe that written communications are likely to resemble spoken ones.

The judges did not agree on which letters did and did not contain a double-bind communication. *The correlation among the judgments of the experts was only +.19.* Furthermore, the experienced judges were unable to discriminate between the letters written by the parents of a schizophrenic and those written by the other parents and by volunteers. This investigation, then, provided little support indeed for the viability of the double-bind hypothesis.

At this point we can clearly put to rest the two theories proposing the schizophrenogenic mother and the double bind as causes of schizophrenia. Although both theories have been around for over twenty years, no evidence lending them any definite support has been collected. Information on hand does indicate that communication is often unclear, however, and that there is much conflict in families with a schizophrenic son or daughter. But whether these family processes should be viewed as playing a causal role in the development of schizophrenia is questionable. It is equally plausible that the conflict and unclear communication are a response to having a young schizophrenic in the family. Indeed, some evidence favors this interpretation (for example, Liem, 1974).

Although the etiological significance of family interaction remains unclear, a series of studies conducted in London indicate that the family can have an important impact on the adjustment of patients *after* they leave the hospital. Brown and his colleagues (1966) conducted a nine-month follow-up study of a sample of schizophrenics who returned to live with their families after being discharged from the hospital. Interviews were conducted with the parents or spouses before discharge and rated for the number of critical comments made about the patient and for expressions of hostility toward or emotional overinvolvement with him or her. On the basis of this variable, called *expressed emotion* (EE), families were divided into those revealing a great deal, high-EE families, and those revealing little, low-EE families. At the end of the follow-up period, 10 percent of the patients returning to low-EE homes had relapsed. In marked contrast, 58 percent of the patients returning to a high-EE home had gone back to the hospital in the same period! This research, which has since been replicated (Vaughn and Leff, 1976; Leff, 1976), indicates that the environment to which patients are discharged has great bearing on whether or not they are rehospitalized.

The Genetic Data

Suppose that you wish to select an individual who will one day be diagnosed as schizophrenic and that no behavior patterns or other symptoms can be considered. This problem, suggested by Paul Meehl (1962), has one solution with at least an even chance of picking a potential schizophrenic. *Find an individual who has a schizophrenic identical twin.* There now exists a convincing body of literature indicating that a predisposition for schizophrenia is transmitted genetically. The major methods employed in this research, as in other behavior genetics research projects, are the family and twin studies. The findings obtained from them will be discussed first and thereafter studies of adopted children.

Family studies

Table 14.2 presents a summary, compiled by Zerbin-Rüdin (1972), of the risk for schizophrenia in various relatives of schizophrenic index cases. In evaluating the figures of this table, bear in mind that the general risk for schizophrenia is about one percent. Quite clearly, relatives of schizophrenics are at increased risk, and the risk increases as the genetic relationship between index case and relative becomes closer. Therefore the data gathered by the family method support the notion that a predisposition for schizophrenia can be transmitted genetically. And yet relatives of a schizophrenic proband share not only genes but also common experiences. A schizophrenic parent's behavior could be very disturbing to a developing child. The influence of the environment cannot be discounted as a rival explanation for the higher morbidity risks.

Twin studies

A summary of the available twin studies appears in Table 14.3. The concordance rates reported in the several studies of identical twins range with great variability from 0 to 86 percent. The rates of concordance for the fraternal twins range from 2 to 34 percent. Concordance for the identical twins is generally greater than that for the fraternal, but it is always less than 100 percent. This is important, for if genetic transmission were the whole story of schizophrenia and one twin was schizophrenic, the other twin would be guaranteed a similar fate because MZ twins are genetically identical.

Gottesman and Shields (1972) studied all twins treated at the Maudsley and Bethlem hospitals in London, England, between the years 1948 and

TABLE 14.2

Morbidity Risk for Schizophrenia Compiled from the Most Important Investigations of Various Authors

(from Zerbin-Rüdin, 1972)

Relationship to a schizophrenic	Morbidity risk, percent
Parents	5–10
Children	9–16
Siblings	8–14
Children of two affected parents	40–68
Half-siblings	1– 7
Stepsiblings	1– 8
Grandchildren	2– 8
Cousins	2– 6
Nieces and nephews	1– 4
Uncles and aunts	2– 7
Grandparents	1– 2

David Rosenthal, a psychologist who has made a major contribution to understanding the genetics of schizophrenia and of other mental disorders.

TABLE 14.3
Concordance Rates in the Major Twin Studies of Schizophrenia

(after Rosenthal, 1970)

Study	Country	Monozygotic twins		Dizygotic twins	
		Number of pairs'	Concordance, percent	Number of pairs	Concordance, percent
Luxenburger, 1928, 1934	Germany	17–27	33–76.5*	48	2.1
Rosanoff et al., 1934–1935	United States and Canada	41	61.0	101	10.0
Essen-Möller, 1941	Sweden	7–11	14–71	24	8.3–17
Kallmann, 1946	New York	174	69–86.2	517	10–14.5
Slater, 1953	England	37	65–74.7	115	11.3–14.4
Inouye, 1961	Japan	55	36–60	17	6–12
Tienari, 1963, 1968	Finland	16	6–36	21	4–10
Gottesman and Shields, 1972	England	24	42	33	9
Kringlen, 1967	Norway	55	25–38	172	4–10
Fischer, 1973	Denmark	16	24–58	34	10–34
Hoffer and Pollin, 1970	United States	80	13.8	145	4.1

* The ranges in the concordance figures reflect different definitions of what would constitute a concordant pair.

1964. One of the problems of any twin study of schizophrenia is how to judge concordance. Recognizing the potential problems and biases involved in making psychiatric diagnoses, often of people who were not hospitalized, Gottesman and Shields devised a three-grade system of concordance. All probands were, of course, hospitalized schizophrenics. The co-twins with the first grade of concordance were also hospitalized and diagnosed schizophrenic. Co-twins with the second grade of concordance were hospitalized but not diagnosed as schizophrenic; those with the third grade were abnormal but not hospitalized. Concordance rates for the MZ and DZ twins in the sample, figured cumulatively for the three grades, are shown in Table 14.4. As the definition of concordance is broadened, its rate increases in both MZ and DZ pairs, but concordance of the MZs is always significantly higher than that of the DZs.

The data in Table 14.4 are of cases in which British hospital diagnoses were the basis for deciding concordance and discordance of pairs. But Gottesman and Shields went beyond this, having each case rediagnosed from case history material by a group of eminent psychopathologists from several countries. Concordance rates obtained by pooling their diagnoses were for

MZs 50 percent and for DZs 9 percent. More interesting, though, are the differences the judgments of individual diagnosticians bring to concordance rates. These data were alluded to in Chapter 13 as evidence of the low validity of the broad American concept of schizophrenia. The

TABLE 14.4
Concordance in MZ and DZ Twins as Defined in Three Ways

(from Gottesman and Shields, 1972)

Definition of concordance	Concordance, percent	
	MZ	DZ
1. Hospitalized and diagnosed schizophrenic	42	9
2. Hospitalized but not schizophrenic, plus those with first-grade concordance	54	18
3. Not hospitalized but abnormal, plus those with first-grade and second-grade concordance	79	45

greatest number of schizophrenia diagnoses were made by an American psychopathologist; when his diagnoses were used, the concordance rates for MZ and DZ pairs were 54 and 21 percent respectively. When those of some conservative diagnosticians who found fewer cases of schizophrenia were applied, the concordance rate for MZs was four times as large as for DZs.

Gottesman and Shields have also examined the relationship between severity of schizophrenia in the proband and the rate of concordance. Severity was defined in terms of the total length of hospitalization and the outcome, that is, whether the patient recovered enough to leave the hospital and then engage in gainful employment. When one of a MZ pair was judged severely ill, concordance rates went up dramatically. For example, pairs of MZ twins were divided into two groups; in one group the probands had had less than two years of hospitalization, in the other more than two years of hospitalization. The concordance rate for the first group was 27 percent, for the second 77 percent.

Questions have been raised about the interpretation of data collected on twins. Some have argued that the experience of being an identical twin may itself predispose toward schizophrenia. If schizophrenia is considered an "identity problem," it might be argued that being a member of an identical pair of twins could be particularly stressful. But schizophrenia occurs about as frequently in single births as in twin births. If the hypothesis were correct, simply being twins would have to increase the likelihood of becoming schizophrenic—which it does not (Rosenthal, 1970).

But the most critical problem of interpretation remains. Since the twins have been reared together, a common deviant environment rather than common genetic factors could account for the concordance rates. A few pairs of identical twins, at least one of whom developed schizophrenia, have been reared apart from very early childhood, enabling the relative contributions of heredity and environment to be separately determined. Of the sixteen cases in the literature, ten were concordant and six discordant (Rosenthal, 1970). The concordance rate of this limited sample was therefore 62.5 percent, a finding that certainly supports the view that a predisposition for schizophrenia is genetically transmitted. Because of the small sample size and the unsystematic way in which the sample was collected, however, the data cannot be regarded as conclusive.

A clever analysis, supporting a genetic interpretation of the high concordance rates found for identical twins, was performed by Fischer (1971). She reasoned that if these rates indeed reflected a genetic effect, the children of even the discordant, or nonschizophrenic, identical co-twins of schizophrenics should be at high-risk for schizophrenia. These nonschizophrenic twins would presumably have the genotype for schizophrenia, even though it was not expressed behaviorally, and thus might pass along an increased risk for the disorder to their children. In agreement with this line of reasoning, the rate of schizophrenia and schizophreniclike psychoses in the children of nonschizophrenic co-twins of schizophrenic probands was 9.4 percent. The rate among the children of the schizophrenic probands themselves was only slightly and nonsignificantly higher, 12.3 percent. Both rates are substantially higher than those found in an unselected population.

Adoptee studies

A study of children of schizophrenic mothers reared from early infancy by adoptive parents has provided more conclusive information on the role of genes in schizophrenia. This study too eliminated the possible effects of a deviant environment. Heston (1966) was able to follow up forty-seven people who had been born to schizophrenic mothers while they were in a state mental hospital. The infants were taken away from the mothers shortly after birth and given either to relatives or foundling homes, which arranged for their adoptions. Fifty control subjects were selected from among those adopted through the same foundling homes that the children of schizophrenic mothers had been sent to. The followup assessment consisted of an interview, MMPI, IQ test, social class ratings, and the like. A dossier on each of these subjects was then rated independently by two psychiatrists, and a third

TABLE 14.5
Subjects Separated from Their
Schizophrenic Mothers in Early Infancy

(from Heston, 1966)

Assessment	Offspring of schizophrenic mother	Control offspring, mothers not schizophrenic
Number of subjects	47	50
Mean age at follow-up	35.8	36.3
Overall ratings of disability (low score indicates more pathology)	65.2	80.1
Number diagnosed schizophrenic	5	0
Number diagnosed mentally defective	4	0
Number diagnosed sociopathic	9	2
Number diagnosed neurotic	13	7

evaluation was made by Heston. Ratings were made on a 0 to 100 scale of overall disability and, whenever possible, psychiatric diagnoses were offered. Ratings of disability proved to be quite reliable, and when the number of diagnostic categories was reduced to four—schizophrenia, mental deficiency, sociopathy, and neurosis—diagnostic agreement was also acceptable.

The control subjects were rated as less disabled than were the children of schizophrenic mothers. Similarly, thirty-one of the forty-seven children of schizophrenic mothers (66 percent) were given a psychiatric diagnosis, but only nine out of fifty control subjects (18 percent) were. None of the control subjects was diagnosed schizophrenic, but 16.6 percent of the offspring of schizophrenic mothers were so diagnosed.[4] In addition to this greater likelihood of being diagnosed schizophrenic, the children of schizo-

phrenic mothers were more likely to be diagnosed mentally defective, sociopathic, and neurotic (Table 14.5). They had spent more time in penal institutions, had been involved more frequently in criminal activity, and had more often been discharged from the armed services for psychiatric reasons. Heston's study clearly supports the importance of genetic factors in the development of schizophrenia. Children reared without contact with their so-called "pathogenic mothers" were still more likely to become schizophrenic than were the controls.

A study similar in intent to Heston's has been carried out in Denmark under Kety's direction (Kety et al., 1968, 1976). In Denmark a lifelong and up-to-date listing of the address of every resident is kept, and a National Psychiatric Register maintains records on every psychiatric hospitalization in the country. The starting point for the investigation was a culling of the records of all children who had been adopted at an early age between the years 1924 and 1947. All adoptees who had later been admitted to a psychiatric facility and diagnosed schizophrenic were selected as the index cases. From the remaining cases the investigators chose a control group who had no

[4] The 16.6 percent figure was age-corrected. By this process raw data are corrected to take into account the age of the subjects involved. If a subject in Heston's sample was only twenty-four at the time of the assessment, he might still have become schizophrenic at some later point in his life. The age correction procedure attempts to account for this possibility.

psychiatric history and who were matched to the index group on variables such as sex and age. Both the adoptive and the biological parents and the siblings and half-siblings of the two groups were then identified, and a search was made to determine who of them had a psychiatric history. As might be expected if genetic factors figure in schizophrenia, the biological relatives of the index cases were diagnosed schizophrenic more often than were members of the general population. The adoptive relatives were not.

Evaluation

All the data collected so far indicate that genetic factors play an important role in the development of schizophrenia. Earlier twin and family studies deserved the criticism of environmentalists, who found that investigators had not acknowledged upbringing as a possible contributing factor. But later studies of children of schizophrenic mothers and fathers, who were reared in foster and adoptive homes, plus the follow-up of relatives of adopted schizophrenics, indicate the importance of genetic transmission, for the potential biasing influence of the environment had been virtually removed. As Seymour Kety, the highly regarded schizophrenia researcher, has quipped, "If schizophrenia is a myth, it is a myth with a heavy genetic component" (1974).

We cannot conclude, however, that schizophrenia is a disorder completely determined by genetic transmission. The less than 100 percent concordance rate of identical twins would argue against this, and we must always keep in mind the distinction made between phenotype and genotype (see page 160). The diathesis-stress model, introduced in Chapter 2, seems appropriate for guiding theory and research into the etiology of schizophrenia. Genetic factors can only be predisposers for a disorder. Stress is required to render this predisposition an observable pathology. And yet, the exact sources of stress are rather vague at this point. Low social class and certain patterns of family interaction are two areas we have already discussed. There is also some evidence that, in the weeks preceding hospitalization, schizophrenics experience an increased number of stressful life events (Brown and Birley, 1968). But, on the whole, additional

Seymour Kety, a prominent figure in research into both the genetics and the biochemistry of schizophrenia.

research is needed on how particular environmental stressors trigger schizophrenia in an already predisposed person.

Biochemical Factors

Speculation concerning possible biochemical[5] causes of schizophrenia began almost as soon as the syndrome was identified. Kraepelin thought in terms of a chemical imbalance, as already indicated, for he believed that poisons secreted from the sex glands affected the brain to produce the symptoms. Carl Jung suggested the presence of "toxin X," which he thought would eventually be identified. The demonstrated role of genetic factors in schizophrenia also suggests that bio-

[5] This section is necessarily technical, and it may be unusually difficult to follow for readers who have not studied biochemistry. We want to provide the details, however, for those who have this background. For those who lack it, we hope at least to convey the logic and general trends in the research on biochemical factors.

chemicals should be investigated, for it is through the body chemistry that heredity may have an effect.

The extensive and continuing search for possible biochemical causes has a principal difficulty to overcome. If an aberrant biochemical is found in schizophrenics and not in control subjects, the difference in biochemical functioning may have been produced by a third variable rather than by the disorder. Most schizophrenic patients, for example, take tranquilizing medication. Although the effects of such drugs on behavior diminish quite rapidly once they are discontinued, traces of them may remain in the bloodstream for very long periods of time, making it difficult to attribute a biochemical difference between schizophrenic and control subjects to schizophrenia per se. Institutionalized patients may also smoke more, drink more coffee, and have a less nutritionally adequate diet than various control groups. They may also be relatively inactive. All these variables can conspire to produce biochemical differences in schizophrenic and control patients that confound attempts to seek deviant biochemicals in the schizophrenics. Nonetheless, the search for biochemical causes of schizophrenia proceeds at a rapid rate. Tremendous advances now allow a much greater understanding of the relation between biochemistry and behavior. At present no biochemical theory has unequivocal support. But because of the great amount of effort that continues to be spent in the search for biochemical causes of schizophrenia, we shall review several of the best-researched factors.

Early theories

Over the past two decades two major classes of biochemical theories of schizophrenia have been advanced. One type has proposed deviant blood proteins as a factor. Heath, for example, theorizes that schizophrenics produce a gamma globulin, a deviant antibody called taraxein, which interferes with neural functioning (Heath and Krupp, 1967). Frohman has proposed that an alpha globulin (a lipoprotein), one with an abnormal molecular structure, may disrupt normal neural transmission (Frohman et al., 1971). The other type of theory has suggested that the bodily systems of schizophrenics add methyl (CH_3) por-

tions to the neurotransmitters dopamine, serotonin, and tryptamine, making the molecules of these substances structurally more similar to those of hallucinogens such as mescaline and psilocybin (for example, Friedhoff and Van Winkle, 1962). The methylated transmitters are supposedly capable of bringing on the psychosis. Although early research findings supported these theories, more contemporary work has been negative and these hypotheses have largely been abandoned.

Excess dopamine activity

Another theory, that schizophrenia is brought on by excess activity of the neurotransmitter dopamine, appears more promising at this time. It is based principally on information concerning the mode of action of drugs that are effective in treating schizophrenia. If the biochemical activity of a therapeutically effective drug is understood, or a least hypothesized, the process responsible for the disorder may be guessed at too.[6] The _phenothiazines_ (see page 660), in addition to alleviating schizophrenia, produce side effects resembling Parkinson's disease. Parkinsonism is known to be caused, in part, by low levels of dopamine in a particular nerve tract of the brain (see page 722). It is therefore supposed that phenothiazines interfere with dopamine activity. Phenothiazine molecules are assumed, because of the structural similarities to the dopamine molecule (Figure 14.1), to fit into and thereby block postsynaptic receptors in dopamine tracts. From this speculation about the action of the drugs that help schizophrenics, it is but a short inductive leap to view schizophrenia as resulting from excess activity in dopamine nerve tracts, although the specific dopaminergic tracts malfunctioning in schizophrenia have not been identified.

Further indirect support for the theory of _excess dopamine activity_ comes from the literature on amphetamine psychosis. There is general agreement that amphetamines can produce a state that closely resembles paranoid schizophre-

---

[6] Although the therapeutic effects of a drug may provide a _clue_ to the causes of the disorder it helps to alleviate, we must be mindful once again that treatment effects cannot logically prove the case for etiology or even for the current causes of the problem in question.

nia and that they can exacerbate the symptomatology of a schizophrenic (Angrist, Lee, and Gershon, 1974). The amphetamines are thought to
act either by directly releasing catecholamines
into the synaptic cleft or by preventing their inactivation (Snyder et al., 1974). We can be relatively confident that the psychosis-inducing effects of amphetamines come from their impact
on dopamine, rather than norepinephrine, for
phenothiazines are antidotes to amphetamine
psychosis.

Work has been done on monoamine oxidase,
for a deficiency on this enzyme, which can inac-
tivate dopamine within the presynaptic neuron,
might explain excess dopamine activity. Murphy
and Wyatt (1972) studied blood platelet MAO in
thirty-three chronic schizophrenics and twenty-
two normal controls matched for age and sex.
The blood platelets of schizophrenics were much
lower in MAO than those of the controls; a subsequent investigation with drug-free patients confirmed this result. But acute schizophrenics,
those who had suddenly been beset with florid
and obvious symptoms, were not found to differ
from controls in platelet MAO levels (Carpenter,
Murphy, and Wyatt, 1975). Moreover, Friedman

and his colleagues (1974) studied platelet MAO
of schizophrenics, depressives, and normal controls and found no significant differences. Postmortem studies of levels of MAO in the brains of
eight schizophrenics and nine controls by
Schwartz and his colleagues (1974) found no differences, nor did similar work done by Domino,
Krause, and Bowers (1973).

The major metabolite of dopamine, homovanillic acid, has also been examined, with the expectation that it would be present in greater
amounts in schizophrenics. Homovanillic acid
can be measured in cerebrospinal fluid by treating patients with probenecid, a drug which prevents the transfer of homovanillic acid from cerebrospinal fluid to blood. But Bowers (1974)
found that before drug treatment schizophrenics
had lower levels of homovanillic acid than patients with affective illness, and that levels of
homovanillic acid in schizophrenics increased
when they were reassessed during treatment.
Post and his colleagues (1975) found no differences in levels of homovanillic acid in schizophrenics and several control groups.

Meltzer, Sachar, and Frantz (1974) have also
indirectly evaluated the excess-dopamine-activity

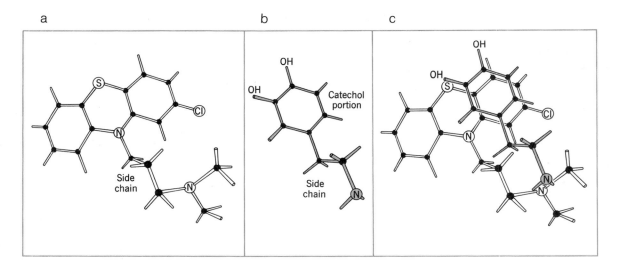

FIGURE **14.1**
Conformations of chlorpromazine (a), a phenothiazine, and
dopamine (b) and their superimposition (c), determined by
X-ray crystallographic analysis. Chlorpromazine blocks im-
pulse transition by dopamine by ftting into its receptor sites.
Adapted from Horn and Snyder, 1971.

hypothesis, by examining levels of the hormone prolactin. The dopaminergic system controls to some extent the release of prolactin inhibiting factor and thus prolactin levels in blood serum. If schizophrenics have excessive dopamine transmission, more inhibiting factor should be released and blood serum should contain less prolactin. Serum prolactin of thirty newly admitted drug-free patients was compared to that of a sample of normal controls, and no differences were found.

The theory of excess dopamine transmission is not strongly refuted by the evidence collected in the studies of MAO, homovanillic acid, and prolactin. Dopaminergic overactivity has not, perhaps, been specified precisely enough. The predictions of depleted MAO and increased levels of homovanillic acid assume that the dopamine-releasing neurons are overactive. But it may be that in schizophrenia dopamine *receptors* are overactive or oversensitive. In fact, the work on the phenothiazines' mode of action would suggest that the dopaminergic receptors are a more likely locus of disorder. Indeed, some postmortem studies of schizophrenics' brains have revealed that dopamine receptors may have either increased in number or been hyperactive (Lee and Seeman, 1977). If increased activity of the dopaminergic receptors is the key to schizophrenia, the data concerning levels of MAO and homovanillic acid are not crucially relevant. As for serum prolactin, its levels are affected by a host of variables, including stress, and thus it is hazardous to conclude that they provide an accurate reflection of the activity of dopaminergic neurons.

In sum, the dopamine theory has two powerful, but indirect, pieces of evidence in its favor: the effectiveness of phenothiazines in treating schizophrenia, through the supposed blocking of dopamine receptors; and the inducement of a paranoidlike psychosis by amphetamines, through the release of dopamine into the synaptic cleft or a forestalling of its inactivation. But the theory has not been supported by all investigations, and it has difficulty handling some other effects. For example, antipsychotic drugs gradually improve schizophrenic symptoms over a period of several weeks. But the drugs rapidly block dopamine receptors, and after several

weeks tolerance should have developed (Davis, 1978). This disjunction between the clinical and pharmacological effects of phenothiazines is difficult to understand within the context of the theory. It is also puzzling that phenothiazines have to reduce dopamine levels to *below normal,* producing Parkinsonian side effects, if they are to be therapeutically effective. According to the theory, reducing dopamine levels or receptor activity to normal should be sufficient for a therapeutic effect. But apparently it is not. Thus, although the dopamine explanation remains the most actively researched biochemical position, it is not likely to be a complete theory of the biochemistry of schizophrenia.

Evaluation

The history of research on whether biochemicals figure in schizophrenia has been one of discovery followed by failures to replicate. Many methodological problems plague this research, and many confounds, unrelated to whether or not a subject is schizophrenic, can produce biochemical differences. Thus we must maintain a cautious attitude toward the excess-dopamine-activity theory. Furthermore, studies on biochemicals can indicate only that a particular substance and its physiological processes are associated with schizophrenia. Dopamine activity might become excessive *after* rather than *before* the onset of the disorder.

High-Risk Studies of Schizophrenia

How does schizophrenia develop? An earlier method of answering this question was to construct developmental histories by examining the childhood records of those who had later become schizophrenics. This research did indeed show that those who were to become schizophrenics were different from their contemporaries even before any serious problems were noted in their behavior. Albee and Lane and their colleagues repeatedly found preschizophrenics to have a lower IQ than members of various control groups, which usually consisted of siblings and neighborhood peers (Albee, Lane, and Reuter, 1964; Lane and Albee, 1965). Investigations of the social behavior of preschizophrenics yielded some interesting findings; for example, teachers have described male schizophrenics as being disagreeable in childhood, female schizophrenics as being passive (Watt et al., 1970; Watt, 1974). Both have been described as delinquent and withdrawn (Berry, 1967).

But these findings are gross and nonspecific; certainly the traits mentioned would also be found in children and adolescents who are not destined to become schizophrenic. The major limitation of this type of developmental research is that the data on which it relies were not originally collected with the intention of describing preschizophrenics or of predicting the development of schizophrenia from childhood behavior. More specific information is required if developmental histories are to be a source of new hypotheses.

Perhaps the most desirable way of collecting information about the development of schizophrenia would be to select a large sample of individuals and follow them for the twenty to forty-five years that are the period of risk for the onset of schizophrenia. But such a method would be prohibitively expensive, for only about one individual in a hundred eventually becomes schizophrenic. The yield of data from such a simple longitudinal study would be small indeed. The _high-risk method_ overcomes this problem; only

individuals whose risk of becoming schizophrenic in adulthood is greater than the average are selected for study. In most of the current research projects using this methodology, individuals who have a schizophrenic parent are selected as subjects for, as we saw earlier, having a schizophrenic parent increases a person's risk for developing schizophrenia.

This method has three other major advantages.

1. Variables that have direct relevance to the development of schizophrenia can be chosen for study.

2. The data are collected before the individual becomes schizophrenic. Therefore, unlike studies of hospitalized adult schizophrenics, these investigations will not be confounded by variables such as drugs, diet, and inactivity.

3. Finding variables that predict the occurrence of schizophrenia in adulthood may allow early intervention and the prevention of this serious disturbance.

In the early 1960s one of the first and most extensive high-risk studies was begun in Denmark by Sarnoff Mednick and Fini Schulsinger.

Sarnoff Mednick and Fini Schulsinger, pioneers in applying the high-risk longitudinal method of studying schizophrenia.

The Danish registries make it much easier to follow up individuals. Mednick and Schulsinger selected as their high-risk subjects 207 young people whose mothers were chronic schizophrenics and had had poor premorbid adjustment. It was decided that the mother should be the parent suffering the disorder because paternity is not always easy to determine and because schizophrenic women have more children than do schizophrenic men. Then 104 low-risk subjects, individuals whose mothers were not schizophrenics, were matched to the high-risk subjects on variables such as sex, age, father's occupation, rural-urban residence, years of education, and institutional upbringing versus rearing by the family. A summary of the design and expected results may be seen in Figure 14.2.

Now a number of other high-risk projects are in progress, and descriptions of the characteristics of high-risk children based on several studies are available.

Characteristics of high-risk children

School Adjustment   Since the social problems of the adult schizophrenic are so obvious, we might expect to find some early indications of them in the school-aged child. Several studies have indeed found this to be so (Beisser, Glasser, and Grant, 1967; Rolf, 1972). In one conducted by Weintraub, Liebert, and Neale (1975) teachers rated the classroom behavior of three groups of children. Members of one group had schizophrenic mothers, those of the second depressed mothers, and those of the third normal mothers. The two groups whose mothers were patients disturbed the classroom with their impatience, disrespect, defiance, inattentiveness, and withdrawal. The teachers also rated both groups as low in comprehension and creative initiative and remote in their relationships to their teachers. Although the social and academic difficulties experienced by the children of schizophrenics seemed severe, these young people could *not* be differentiated from the offspring of depressive mothers. Thus the disruptive behavior described is unlikely to be a specific predictor of schizophrenia.

Psychophysiology   Many hypotheses link schizophrenia to alterations in levels of arousal and responsiveness. Perhaps the psychophysiological patterns in the high-risk children will resemble those seen in adult schizophrenics.

FIGURE **14.2**
Design and expected results of Mednick and Schulsinger's study (1968) of young people with a high risk of developing schizophrenia.

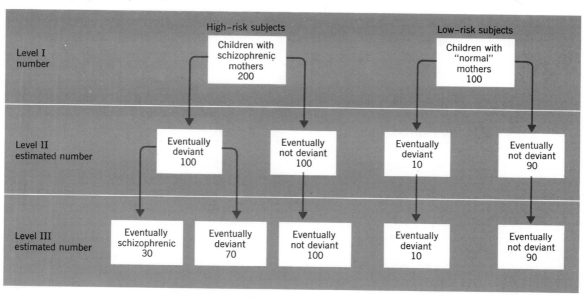

Itil (1972) has analyzed the EEG tracings from the cortexes of children with schizophrenic mothers, children with a parent who has another psychological problem, and children with normal parents. The offspring of schizophrenics had more delta and beta brain waves and fewer alpha than the controls. Furthermore, the tracings of the brain waves of high-risk children showed smaller amplitudes and less variability of amplitude. These are important findings, for the pattern reported for adult schizophrenics (for example, Goldstein et al., 1965) is quite similar.

The principal study of autonomic nervous system psychophysiology is Mednick and Schulsinger's (1966). Heart rate, muscle potential, and GSR were measured during a conditioning situation in which a neutral buzzer (CS) was paired with an irritating 96-decibel noise (UCS). After the children had been conditioned to react to the neutral buzzer, others similar in tone but of slightly different frequencies were sounded. The responses to them indicated the extent to which the conditioning of the children became generalized and carried over to similar stimuli.

The high-risk children differed from their controls on several measures, showing stronger GSR to the UCS as well as stronger conditioning. They also showed less of what is called habituation. If persons become habituated to stress, their GSRs occur only after lengthening periods of time following the onset of the stressful event. In contrast to the controls, the high-risk children showed no habituation. In fact, their GSRs occurred with increasing speed, suggesting greater responsiveness. Finally, the time it takes for the skin to return to baseline conductance after the presentation of a stimulus, which is called recovery time or GSR recovery, was determined. This measure discriminated between the groups better than any other, with the high-risk children showing particularly rapid recovery. Overall, then, the high-risk children showed a pattern of autonomic overreactivity.[7]

[7] Although failures to replicate this research have been reported (for example, Erlenmeyer-Kimling, 1975), Mednick (1978) has indicated that they may reflect differences in the samples being studied. One such difference is family intactness. Only about 25 percent of Mednick and Schulsinger's subjects were from intact families—perhaps because they studied only children of schizophrenic mothers who were chronically ill—whereas Erlenmeyer-Kimling required that all families in her sample be intact. In a reanalysis of his original data, Mednick (1978) showed that deviant psychophysiological responses were present only in the high-risk children from nonintact homes.

Measurements of Cognitive Processes and Attention Several teams have found in high-risk children deficits in thought processes and attention that closely resemble those of adult schizophrenics. Mednick and Schulsinger (1966), for example, found that on a continuous-association task high-risk children tended to drift away from the stimulus word. Instead of continuing to give associations to a single stimulus, as they had been instructed to do, the children gave them to words that they themselves were using as responses. Oltmanns, Weintraub, and Neale (1976) found that the conceptual patterns of high-risk children were quite similar to those of schizophrenics. Asarnow and his co-workers (1977) compared high-risk children, adopted away from their schizophrenic mothers, to other adoptees and nonadopted controls, using an entire battery of attention-measuring tasks. Among the best discriminators in this battery was a task assessing their ability to pick up briefly presented information. The adopted high-risk children, like adult schizophrenics (Neale, 1971), were notably deficient in apprehending within brief spans of time. Finally, high-risk children are also more distractible than other children (Harvey et al., 1981), showing exactly the same pattern of response on a digit span test that Oltmanns, O'Hayon, and Neale (1978) had found in adult schizophrenics diagnosed by stringent European-like rules.

To sum up, the data on the characteristics of high-risk children appear significant. The high-risk children, although not in treatment or viewed as highly disturbed, differ from controls on a variety of measures. But will these differences predict what happens in adulthood? Only one high-risk study has been underway long enough to have collected data on this question, Mednick and Schulsinger's.

Longitudinal data from Mednick and Schulsinger's project

During the initial phase of Mednick and Schulsinger's study, an alarm network was set up in Denmark to ensure that children who began to show psychiatric difficulties would be detected. In a 1968 report the histories of twenty of the initial high-risk group who had by then required psychiatric care were reviewed. For comparison purposes each of these disturbed high-risk young people was matched with one high-risk subject who had not broken down and with one low-risk subject. The matching variables were age, sex, and social class. In addition, the disturbed high-risk subjects were matched with the well high-risk subjects in their 1962 level of adjustment rating, which had been determined by a psychiatrist's interview. The major findings of these comparisons were as follows.

1. Young people in the disturbed high-risk group tended to lose their mothers to a mental hospital early and permanently. Their mothers were also rated as being more severely ill. These facts can be interpreted in two ways. Losing one's mother is stressful; or the severity of the mother's illness may mean that a stronger genetic predisposition is passed on. In a later report B. Mednick (1973) presented illuminating information about the fathers of the disturbed and nondisturbed high-risk subjects. Eighteen fathers of the young people in the disturbed group could be traced. Seven of them had themselves had psychiatric treatment for disorders "that ranged from chronic paranoid schizophrenia to chronic alcoholism." None of the fathers of children in the nondisturbed high-risk group had a psychiatric history. The impressive finding raises into prominence the role of the father, either genetic or rearing, in potentiating schizophrenia in a predisposed person.

2. Teachers had reported that more members of the disturbed high-risk group, once they had become upset or excited, remained that way for a longer period of time than did members of the other two groups. More members of the disturbed high-risk group had also been rated by the teachers as being aggressive, domineering, and disturbing to the class.

3. During the continuous-association test, members of the disturbed high-risk group had tended to drift away from the original stimulus word, to an even greater extent than had the high-risk young people who were still well.

4. The disturbed high-risk group had shown to an even greater degree than the well high-

risks the pattern of psychophysiological responding already described for high-risk children in general—greater responsiveness to the UCS, greater generalization of the conditioning, less habituation, and faster GSR recovery.

In interpreting the information collected, Mednick focused on the psychophysiological responses. In an earlier paper (Mednick, 1958) he had postulated that schizophrenia is a learned thought disorder produced by autonomic hyperactivity. The tangential thinking of schizophrenics was suggested to be a set of operantly conditioned avoidance responses that help the individual control his or her autonomic responsiveness, in other words, his or her intense and excessive emotional arousal. These avoidance responses—the irrelevant thoughts—are learned on those occasions when the preschizophrenic escapes from arousal by switching to a thought that interrupts the arousal stimulus. Because the irrelevant associations enable the individual to avoid a stressful stimulus, they are reinforced by less arousal and the probability is great that the preschizophrenic will engage in similar behavior in the future.[8] The preschizophrenic learns to escape from a very great anxiety by thinking just about any thought that can be summoned. Mednick supposed that many such thoughts would be irrelevant and tangential.

In a later report (Mednick, 1970) additional significant information was presented. Earlier Mednick and Schulsinger had examined the frequency of individual birth complications in the various groups in their study. The many complications that might have been reported by the midwife—prematurity, anoxia or oxygen deprivation, prolonged labor, placental difficulty, umbilical cord complications, illness of mother during pregnancy, multiple births, and breech presentations (baby emerging feet first instead of head first)—were analyzed separately, but no conclu-

---

[8] One of the key aspects of the theory is the finding of faster GSR recovery in the subjects who experienced breakdown. According to Mednick and Schulsinger (1968), the fast recovery means that avoidance behavior is more quickly and thoroughly reinforced. But this interpretation is controversial, and research with adult schizophrenics has not always found them to have fast recovery (for example, Maricq and Edelberg, 1975).

sions could be drawn. One of Mednick's students, after grouping all the pregnancy and birth complications into a single category, made a startling finding. Seventy percent of of the mothers of disturbed high-risk children had suffered one or more pregnancy or birth complication (PBC) while carrying or delivering the child, as compared to 15 percent of the mothers of the nondisturbed but high-risk group and 33 percent of the mothers of the controls. Then in reexamining the psychophysiological differences previously discussed, Mednick determined that psychophysiological responses were deviant only in the subjects whose mothers had had one or more PBCs. Thus complications in the birth process may upset bodily control of responses to stress and thereby potentiate schizophrenia in a predisposed individual.[9]

In 1972 and 1973 the entire sample was reevaluated to establish diagnoses. Seventeen of the high-risk subjects and one of those at low risk had developed schizophrenia (Schulsinger, 1976). Interestingly, the majority of the schizophrenics were *not* from among those who had earlier been designated as disturbed. Therefore a new set of analyses, currently underway, will have to be conducted to locate the variables that predict schizophrenia specifically rather than just general psychiatric breakdown (for example, Griffith et al., 1980).

The high-risk method holds great promise of furthering our understanding of schizophrenia. By using specially selected samples, the investigator is able to study the actual unfolding of the disorder. In the next few years the high-risk investigations that are already in progress may yield important information on the development of schizophrenia, pinpointing the environmental factors that potentiate a genetically transmitted diathesis.

[9] The mechanism by which PBCs may produce their effect is the subject of debate. Mednick (1970) proposed that they produce brain damage through anoxia, and that the hippocampal area is particularly vulnerable, but a good deal of other evidence (reviewed by Kessler and Neale, 1974) does not favor this view.

Therapies for Schizophrenia

The puzzling, often frightening array of phenomena found in schizophrenics makes one wonder how they can possibly be helped. The history of psychopathology, reviewed in Chapter 1, is in many respects a history of humankind's efforts, often brutal and unenlightened, to deal with schizophrenia. Although some of the insane people condemned centuries ago as witches or confined in foul asylums may have suffered from problems as prosaic as food poisoning or syphilis (see pages 16 and 23), there seems little doubt that many, were they to be examined now, would carry a diagnosis of schizophrenia. Box 14.4 contains a general discussion of the mental hospital; somatic and psychological therapies for schizophrenia are for the most part administered within a hospital.

Somatic Treatments

The general warehousing of severely disturbed patients in mental hospitals earlier in this century, coupled with the shortage of professional staff, created a climate that allowed, perhaps even subtly encouraged, experimentation with radical somatic interventions. In the early 1930s the induction of a coma via large dosages of insulin was introduced by Sakel (1938), who claimed that up to three-quarters of the schizophrenics he treated showed significant improvement. But later findings by others were far less encouraging, and *insulin coma therapy,* which presented serious risks to health, was gradually abandoned.

In 1935 Moniz, a Portuguese psychiatrist, introduced the *prefrontal lobotomy,* a surgical procedure which destroys the tracts connecting the frontal lobes to lower centers of the patient's brain. His initial reports, like those of Sakel for insulin coma therapy, claimed high rates of success (Moniz, 1936), and for twenty years thereafter hundreds of mental patients underwent variations of psychosurgery, especially if their behavior was violent. Many of them did indeed quiet down and could even be discharged from hospitals. But during the 1950s this intervention too fell into disrepute, for several reasons. Many patients suffered serious losses in their cognitive capacities—which is not surprising, given the destruction of parts of their brain believed responsible for thought—became dull and listless, or even died. The principal reason for its abandonment, however, was the introduction of drugs that seemed to reduce the behavioral and emotional excesses of many patients.

Electroconvulsive therapy (ECT) has been in use since its development in 1938 by Cerletti and Bini. Electrodes are placed on both temples, more recently on only one temple, and a current of between 70 and 130 volts is applied for a fraction of a second. A seizure is thereby induced, followed by a period of unconsciousness. In the treatment of schizophrenia, ECT has, like psychosurgery, given way to the several psychotropic medications, although it remains an apparently effective treatment for profoundly depressed patients (see page 259).

Without question the most important development in the treatment of the schizophrenic disorders was the advent in the 1950s of several drugs collectively referred to as antipsychotic medications. They are also called _neuroleptics_ because, in addition to their beneficial effects,

they have side effects similar to the behavioral manifestations of neurological diseases. The phenothiazines, especially _chlorpromazine_ (Thorazine), not only control the emotional and behavioral excesses of most mental hospital patients but also, in a manner still inadequately understood, improve the disordered thinking of many schizophrenics, often to the point that they can be released from confinement. And these beneficial consequences are over and above the ubiquitous placebo effect (Klein and Davis, 1969). Problems and unanswered questions still abound, however, in the use of these antipsychotic drugs. Additional details about them and the other somatic treatments just discussed are provided in Chapter 20.

Psychological Treatments

Efforts to treat schizophrenia have by no means all been somatic. Freud himself worked little, either in his clinical practice or through his writings, on adapting psychoanalysis to the treatment of schizophrenics; he believed them to be incapable of establishing the close interpersonal rela-

With the advent of neuroleptic medication, the drug table has become a major feature of mental hospitals.

BOX 14.4 The Mental Hospital

Each year about two and a half million Americans are hospitalized for mental disorders. It has been estimated that one in ten people in this country will enter a mental hospital at least once (Atthowe, 1976). Treatment in public mental institutions is primarily custodial in nature, the existence of patients monotonous and sedentary for the most part. After Pinel's revolutionary work in La Bicêtre (see page 21), the hospitals established in Europe and in this country were for a time relatively small and privately supported. Patients had close contact with attendants, who talked and read to them and encouraged them to purposeful activity. Residents were to lead as normal lives as possible and in general take responsibility for themselves within the constraints of their disorders. This moral treatment, which is estimated to have achieved enviable discharge rates, had to be abandoned in the second half of the nineteenth century,

however. The staffs of the larger, public mental hospitals being built to take in the many patients for whom the private ones had no room could not provide such individual attention (Bockoven, 1963). Moreover, these hospitals came to be administered by physicians, who were more interested in the physiological aspects of illness and in the physical well-being of mental patients. The money that had paid the personal attendants went into equipment and laboratories.

Mental hospitals in this country today are usually funded either by the federal government or by the various states. In fact, the term "state hospital" is taken to mean a *mental* hospital run by the state. They are often old, grim, and somewhat removed from major metropolitan centers. Their costs to society in economic terms are utterly staggering. Some Veterans Administration Hospitals and general medical hospitals also contain psychiatric wards.

The dramatic contrast between private and state mental hospitals. On the left is a living room of the Sheppard and Enoch Pratt Hospital. The enormous quarters on the right are in a state institution.

In addition, there are private mental hospitals. Sheppard and Enoch Pratt near Baltimore, Maryland, and McLean Hospital, in Belmont, Massachusetts, are two of the most famous. The physical facilities of private hospitals tend to be superior to those of state hospitals for one simple reason: the private hospitals have more money. The daily costs to patients in these private institutions ran, in 1980, close to $200 per day and might not include individual therapy sessions with a member of the professional staff! Although some patients may have medical insurance, usually with a ninety-day limit, such hospitals are clearly beyond the means of most citizens.

A somewhat specialized mental hospital is reserved for people who have been arrested and have been judged unable to stand trial or have been acquitted of a crime by reason of insanity (see Chapter 21, page 671). They have not been sent to prison, but armed guards and tight security regiment their lives. Treatment of some kind is supposed to take place during their internment.

Many fine books and articles have been written about mental hospitals (Stanton and Schwartz, 1954; Goffman, 1961; Rosenhan, 1973; Moos, 1974). They agree with our own clinical experiences that, even in the best of hospitals, patients usually have precious little contact with psychiatrists or clinical psychologists. Most of a patient's days and evenings are spent either alone or in the company of other patients and of aides, individuals who often have little more than an elementary school education. The Rosenhan study of pseudopatients, described in Box 3.1 (page 76), provides some valuable insights on the attention patients receive, and Kesey's remarkable work of fiction, *One Flew over the Cuckoo's Nest*, although ex-

aggerated, portrays vividly what life can be like inside one of these institutions. As with imprisonment, the overwhelming feeling is of helplessness and depersonalization. Patients sit endless hours in hallways waiting for dining halls to open, for medication to be given out, and for consultations with psychologists, social workers, and vocational counselors to begin.

Except for the most severely disturbed, patients have access to the various facilities of a hospital, ranging from woodworking shops to swimming pools, from gymnasia to proverbial basketweaving shops. Most hospitals require patients to attend group therapy—here a general term indicating only that at least two patients are supposed to relate to each other and to a group leader in a room for a specified period of time. And for some patients there are the few sessions alone with a professional therapist.

By and large, in our opinion, the hospital serves primarily to isolate from the general community disturbed persons who are unable to adapt to social norms and whose life styles are not tolerated by society at large. The reasons for their maladaptions are the varied ones already discussed. Some writers (for example, Scheff, 1966) hold the view that people are placed in hospitals only because they are *labeled* sick or insane. But there is more to mental disorder than a diagnostic statement from a policeman, a judge, a teacher, or a psychiatrist. The majority of patients would be very much at a loss outside the haven and confines of a mental hospital.

One nagging problem is that institutionalization is difficult to reverse once people have resided in mental hospitals for more than a year. The mental hospital has certainly not proved its worth by preparing patients for their return to the community. We recall asking a patient who had improved markedly over the previous several months why he was reluctant to be discharged. "Doc," he said earnestly, "it's a jungle out there." Although we cannot entirely disagree with his view, there nonetheless appear to be at least a few advantages to living on the outside. But this man—a veteran and chronic patient with a clinical folder more than two feet thick— had become so accustomed to the restrictions and care of various Veterans Administration hos-

pitals that the prospect of leaving was as frightening to him as the prospect of entering a mental hospital is to those who have never lived in one. Recent deinstitutionalization sweeps have reduced the number of patients in mental hospitals, but the problems of the chronic patient have yet to be handled adequately.

One treatment now widely applied is *milieu therapy,* in which the entire hospital becomes a "therapeutic community" (for example, Jones, 1953). All its ongoing activities and all its personnel become part of the treatment program. Milieu therapy appears to be a return to the moral practices of the nineteenth century. Social interaction and group activities are encouraged so that through group pressure the patients are directed toward normal functioning. Patients are treated as responsible human beings rather than custodial cases (Paul, 1969). They are expected to participate in their own readjustment, as well as that of their fellow patients. Open wards allow them considerable freedom. Evidence of the efficacy of milieu therapy, however, is scant.

In a milestone project at a unit in a new Illinois state mental health center, Paul and Lentz (1977) demonstrated encouraging improvement in twenty-eight chronic "hard-core" patients through *social-learning therapy.* A token economy, which reached into many details of the patients' lives, was combined with other behavior therapy interventions tailored to the particular needs of each resident. A host of measures were taken on the behavior of both staff and patients over four and a half years of treatment, with a later eighteen-month follow-up on patients who had since been discharged. The social-learning program was markedly more successful than both milieu therapy, carried out for a matched group at another unit of the mental health center, and routine hospital management of a second matched group in an older Illinois state hospital. Since mental hospitals will be needed for the foreseeable future, especially by people who demonstrate time and again that they have difficulty functioning on the outside, Paul's work is of special importance. It suggests specific ways the chronic patient can be helped to cope better not only within the hospital but during periods of discharge as well.

tionship that is essential for analysis. It was Harry Stack Sullivan, the American psychiatrist, who pioneered in doing psychotherapy with hospital patients. Sullivan established a ward at the Sheppard and Enoch Pratt Hospital in Towson, Maryland, in 1923 and developed a psychoanalytic treatment reported to be markedly successful. He held that schizophrenia reflected a return to early childhood forms of communication. The fragile ego of the schizophrenic, unable to handle the extreme stress of interpersonal challenges, had regressed. Therapy therefore requires the patient to learn adult forms of communication and achieve insight into the role that the past has played in current problems.[10] Sullivan advised the very gradual, nonthreatening development of a trusting relationship. For example, he recommended that the therapist sit somewhat to the side of the patient in order not to force eye contact, which is deemed too frightening in the early stages of treatment. After many sessions, and with the establishment of greater trust and support, the analyst begins to encourage the patient to examine his or her interpersonal relationships.

A similar ego-analytic approach was proposed by Frieda Fromm-Reichmann (1889–1957), a German psychiatrist who emigrated to the United States and worked for a period of time with Sullivan at Chestnut Lodge, a private mental hospital in Rockville, Maryland. Fromm-Reichmann was sensitive to the symbolic and unconscious meaning of behavior, attributing the aloofness of schizophrenics to a wish to avoid the rebuffs suffered in childhood and thereafter judged inevitable. She treated them with great patience and optimism, making it clear that they need not take her into their world or give up their "sickness" until they were completely ready to do so. Along with Sullivan, Fromm-Reichmann (1952) helped establish psychoanalysis as a major treatment for schizophrenia.

Paradoxes are inherent to psychoanalytic thought. Whereas Sullivan and Fromm-Reichmann trod gingerly and gently into the defensive structure of their patients, John Rosen (1946) in his _direct analysis_ drives a Mack truck. He

agrees with his analytic colleagues that therapy must establish communication and foster insight, but he parts company with them about the fragility of the schizophrenic's ego. Rosen believes it strong enough to handle direct, often brutal confrontation, although always in a supportive relationship.[11] The following excerpt describes part of a therapy session with a young male catatonic schizophrenic.

> For the first hour, his productions were repetitious and revealed that he was actively hallucinating. He made reference to numerous sexual adventures. He spoke as follows: "This is a wonderful airplane. It's over the Atlantic Ocean. I can see her down there. My mother. She's floating. Here I go. A dive bomb. I have her centered. Here I go. Here I go."
>
> Following this symbolic incestuous experience, the patient screamed in terror and appeared to plead for mercy with his father. "Don't cut off my balls. Please don't cut them off. Please, papa, please." Since the plea was directed toward "papa," the physician said he was "papa," that he had seen what happened and that everything would be all right. The patient received permission to have these thoughts about his mother and was promised that there would be no punishment (1946, p. 193).

Rosen becomes the omnipotent, nurturant protector of his patients. In some instances he actually feeds and caresses them to lend reality to their regression and enable them to reexperience problems from early childhood that are assumed to underlie their psychosis. Patients spend virtually all their waking hours in the company of the therapist and his assistants, being harangued through threats and coaxed through promises to interpret and relinquish their psychotic behavior. Rosen is, understandably, a controversial figure, and his claims for a 100 percent cure rate do little to reduce the controversy.

Existential and humanistic therapies have made little if any impact on schizophrenic disor-

---

[10] Sullivan's work is discussed more generally in Chapter 18 .

[11] Those who have worked with Rosen attest to his unusual ability to establish a supportive relationship with many patients so that they are not frightened or otherwise disturbed by his unorthodox techniques.

ders. As writers in this tradition have themselves suggested (for example, Corey, 1977), to make responsible choices and thus become truly human, to face the existential realization that the individual is ultimately alone in the world are high-level demands and very probably beyond the capacities of the people described in this and in the preceding chapter. A schizophrenic's response to the expounding of existential-humanistic goals might well be "They should be my worst problems." When people must struggle even to reason logically, to avoid violating social norms, and to attend to the world as most people see it, rather than to their own of frightening demons and persecutors, they do not have the luxury of contemplating ultimate aloneness and the awesome responsibility of making choices, of creating existence anew every day. But empathic listening and efforts to reassure patients that they will not be hurt are certainly beneficial. Clinical lore, for example, tells us not to challenge the paranoid's delusions, lest we become part of them. The person who believes that the C.I.A. is broadcasting messages into his or her mind and keeping tabs on daily thoughts and activities needs an empathic ear.

The overall evaluation of insight-oriented psychotherapy with schizophrenics, although truly in its infancy, thus far justifies little enthusiam for applying it with these severely disturbed people (Feinsilver and Gunderson, 1972). Earlier, great claims of success were made for the analyses done by Sullivan and Fromm-Reichmann, but a close consideration of the patients they saw indicates that many tended to be only mildly disturbed and might not even have been diagnosed schizophrenic by the strict DSM-III criteria for the disorder. What little research has been done on Rosen's direct analysis is methodologically flawed; in any event, it does not find value in this approach. A widely cited study by Carl Rogers and his associates (1967) examining client-centered therapy with schizophrenics indicated that empathic listening by an exceptionally genuine therapist can help establish a good therapeutic relationship, but no inroads on the actual clinical problems of schizophrenics were made (May, 1974). Finally, a study by May (1968; May et al., 1976) failed to show that psychoanalysis

added anything to a phenothiazine regimen. Although experienced clinicians often believe that they themselves, or other highly gifted therapists, can make a positive impact on certain schizophrenics, and this may indeed happen when some therapists work with some patients, evidence obtained through controlled scientific research does not indicate that insight into themselves and the past is of much help to schizophrenics.

Family therapy was conceived in the 1950s in response to theories of schizophrenia that proposed abnormal family relationships as causes. Even though suppositions about double-bind communication and the schizophrenogenic mother (the term originated with Frieda Fromm-Reichmann) lack empirical support, it is possible, once the problem exists, that the schizophrenic patient's symptoms may be relieved by correcting relationships within the home. If a parent sends conflicting messages to a schizophrenic son, the parent could be helped to clarify his or her statements, and the son could be taught that people do not always say to others what they really mean. The literature contains reports of improvement brought about by family therapy, but fundamental changes are rarely achieved. The research on family therapy suffers from methodological problems that preclude drawing firm conclusions (Massie and Beels, 1972). A more promising family therapy project, described in Chapter 20 (page 637), was designed to reduce stress in patients returning home after hospitalization.

In recent years behavior therapy has been developed for schizophrenia, particularly operant conditioning techniques. As discussed in greater detail in Chapter 19, hundreds of hospitalized patients, most of them carrying a diagnosis of schizophrenia, have lived in a token economy instituted to eliminate specific behavior, such as hoarding towels, to teach more socially appropriate responses, such as combing hair and arriving on time at dining halls, and to encourage activity, such as doing chores on the ward. The study by Paul and Lentz (1977) demonstrated the potential of a carefully designed and meticulously implemented therapy program based on social-learning principles. Seriously ill schizophrenics were released to shelter care and three even to independent living.[12] At the present time it is generally acknowledged among mental health professionals that therapy programs with a learning framework are the most effective psychological procedures for helping schizophrenics function better. But behavior therapy is seldom claimed to make such thoroughgoing changes that we can speak of curing people with this group of mental illnesses. These interventions do, however, reverse somewhat the effects of institutionalization, fostering social skills such as assertiveness in people whom attendants have reinforced for passiveness and compliance.

The justified enthusiasm for drugs that stop hallucinations and delusions and even improve clarity of thought should not blind us to the always-existing need of patients to learn or relearn ways of interacting with their world, of dealing with the troubling emotional challenges all people face as they negotiate life. Schizophrenia is almost assuredly an illness that certain people are predisposed to develop when under stress. A wonder drug that alleviates symptoms still leaves untouched the basic tendency of the individual to react abnormally on later occasions. Perhaps schizophrenics can be taught effective coping skills so that, in the future, they will be able to keep their emotional reactions under better control. Well before all the answers are in on this puzzling and serious group of mental disorders, logic dictates that comprehensive treatment of schizophrenia be both somatic and psychological.

Summary

Labeling theory and broad theoretical views such as those of Freud and Laing have not had great impact on research undertaken to determine the etiology of schizophrenia. Each of the theories places undue and unsupported emphasis on particular causal factors. Freud thought that schizophrenia resulted from regression to the first psychosexual stage in which the ego is not differentiated from the id. In labeling theory schizophrenia is regarded as a social role maintained in large part by mental health professionals who reinforce "sick" behavior. For Laing schizophrenia is a label for the experience and behavior that constitute a person's attempts to cope with an impossible situation. Although popular and plausible, these theories lack empirical support. New information appears pertinent and suggests other explanations.

Most research has tried to determine the etiological role of more specific variables such as social class, the family, and genetic and biochemical factors. The diagnosis of schizophrenia is more frequently applied to members of the lowest social class. Available information indicates this is so in part because the stresses of lower-class existence are great enough to bring on schizophrenia and in part because the disorder keeps schizophrenics from achieving higher social status. Vague communications and conflicts are evident in the family life of schizophrenics, but it is unclear whether such factors contribute to schizophrenia or whether the presence of a schizophrenic family member disrupts the home.

The data on genetic transmission are impressive. The adoptee studies, which are relatively free from most criticisms that can be leveled at family or twin studies, show a strong relation between having a schizophrenic parent and the likelihood of developing the disorder. Perhaps the genetic predisposition has biochemical correlates, although reseach in this area permits only tentative conclusions. At this time the excess-dopamine-activity theory appears the most promising. Much of the data we have reviewed are consistent with a diathesis-stress view of schizophrenia. Recently, investigators have turned to the high-risk method, studying children who are

[12] The criterion of being discharged from a mental hospital is more complicated than may appear on the surface. A treatment may help a person leave a hospital, yet that person may still be able to live only a marginal existence. Keith and his colleagues (1976) concluded that only half of schizophrenics who are released from mental hospitals are able to assume full occupational and social responsibilities.

particularly vulnerable to schizophrenia by virtue
of having a schizophrenic parent. They have
found that these children are indeed different
from controls in a variety of measurable ways—
for example, in psychophysiology, thought processes, and attention—that have also been studied
in adult schizophrenics. Mednick and Schulsinger have found that two characteristics of high-
risk offspring—complications during the baby's
term and birth and GSR responsiveness—predicted maladjustment in adulthood.

There are both somatic and psychological
therapies for schizophrenia. Insulin and electroshock treatments and even brain surgery were in
vogue earlier in the century, but none is employed to any extent nowadays, primarily because antipsychotic drugs, in particular the phenothiazines, are now available. In numerous
studies these medications have been found to
have a major and beneficial impact on the disordered lives of schizophrenic patients. They have
also been very much a factor in the deinstitutionalization of hospital patients. But drugs alone are
unlikely to be the answer, for schizophrenics
need to be taught or retaught ways of dealing
with the challenges of everyday life, and perhaps
as well to resolve the intrapsychic problems believed by some therapists to underlie their symptoms. Psychoanalytic theory assumes that schizophrenia represents a retreat from the pain of
childhood rejection and mistreatment; the relationship gradually and patiently established by
the analyst offers the patient a safe haven in
which to explore repressed traumas. Direct analysis agrees that childhood conflicts lie at the
core of schizophrenia but regards the patient's
ego as not too fragile for an assaultive analysis of
defenses. Good evidence for the efficacy of these
treatments is not plentiful, although case studies
of dramatic cures are many in both the professional and popular literature. More recently behavioral treatments have helped patients discharged from mental hospitals to meet the
inevitable stresses of family and community living, and, when discharge is not possible, to lead
more ordered and constructive lives within an
institution.

Marisol, "The Family" (1962). Collection, The Museum of Modern
Art, New York. Advisory Committee Fund.

part five
developmental disorders

chapter 15

NONPSYCHOTIC CHILDHOOD DISORDERS

"**N**othing is more precious than a young child" (O'Leary and Wilson, 1975, p. 39). And few events in an adult's life are more emotionally draining than being close to a child who is hurt, physically or psychologically. Until now in this book the psychological problems discussed have been those that beset a significant proportion of the adult population. As upsetting as it may be to have a friend or relative who suffers from depression, or from unpredictable bouts of anxiety, or from the myriad of thought and emotional disruptions of schizophrenia, it is much more disturbing to see these problems in a child. Children are judged to have few emotional resources with which to cope with problems. The extreme dependency of troubled children on their parents and guardians adds to the sense of responsibility these people feel, and to their guilt, whether it be justified or not.

Most psychodynamic, behavioral, and even biological theories find childhood experience and development to be critically important to adult mental health. In addition, most theories regard children as more malleable than adults and thus more amenable to treatment. We would therefore expect the disorders of children to have been the focus of voluminous research into etiology, prevention, and treatment. Until recently, however, they have been given considerably less attention than adult problems.

Disorders associated with the course of adult development and aging have received even less attention than those of childhood. The disorders of these two periods, childhood and aging, can be treated together as a new research endeavor, the study of the problems of life-span development. In this chapter we discuss the major _nonpsychotic childhood disorders._ Chapter 16 covers first mental retardation and then the psychotic disorders of the childhood years. In Chapter 17 the problems linked with aging are reviewed.

Classification

The classification of childhood disorders has changed radically over the last thirty years. Consistent with the scant research efforts then being expended on the problems of childhood, DSM-I and DSM-II treated them primarily as downward extensions of adult disorders. Children were often given diagnoses that had originally been created for adults. The major adult categories of psychoses, neuroses, and personality disorders of DSM-II, for example, were all applied to children as well. The only unique section for disorders of children was Behavior Disorders of Childhood and Adolescence. The ineffectiveness of this system is indicated by the fact that most children seen by mental health professionals received a diagnosis of adjustment reaction, a very broad one indeed, or no diagnosis at all (Achenbach, 1974).

Recognizing a need for change in the classification system, the Group for Advancement of Psychiatry (GAP), an organization of psychiatrists devoted to a careful scrutiny of their field, proposed a very different diagnostic scheme for children (GAP, 1966). Although the work was still linked to psychodynamic theory, the GAP committee began creating a developmentally oriented diagnostic system tailored specifically for childhood disorders. These efforts were incorporated and extended in DSM-III. Whereas DSM-II contained one section with seven specific diagnoses to be applied uniquely to children, DSM-III contains a section with forty specific diagnoses gathered in nine general groups. The expansion of childhood diagnoses in the three DSMs is traced in Table 15.1, which summarizes the schemes employed by each version.[1]

Although the validity of the broader and more detailed system employed by DSM-III has not yet been established, its reliability can be addressed at this time. Initial studies with childhood diagnoses of DSM-III indicate that reliability is not particularly high—the agreement of diagnosticians averages 54 percent—but it is higher than the reliability of the GAP system (Beitchman et al., 1978). Indeed, the fact that reliability studies are being done at all is a positive sign for the new system, for no reliability studies were ever conducted on the section for childhood disorders of either DSM-I or DSM-II (Cantwell et al., 1979).

Factor analysis has also had a major influence on the classification of childhood disorders. Ratings of the behavior of disordered children are collected and analyzed, allowing clusters of symptoms that are related to one another to be separated out. These symptom clusters are called factors. A review of the major factor-analytic studies of disordered children found consistent evidence for at least two broad clusters of childhood symptoms. Children with symptoms from one cluster are called either undercontrolled or externalizers and are said to show behavior excesses. Children who have symptoms from the other cluster are said to be overcontrolled, to be internalizers, or to have behavior deficits[2] (Achenbach and Edelbrock, 1978). Although the names picked for the two broad clusters depend on theoretical orientation—we have chosen _undercontrolled_ and _overcontrolled_—the key to the distinction between them lies in whether the child's ways of reacting, such as disobedience, creates more of a problem for others or, such as anxiety, affects the self.

In this survey of the major nonpsychotic childhood disorders, we draw from both DSM-III listings and the undercontrolled-overcontrolled dimension for chapter organization. Developmental deviations will be reviewed first. This category, which DSM-III calls specific developmental disorders, covers extreme deviations from the average in a specific area of development, such as learning arithmetic and how to read. Following the section on developmental deviations are a section each on undercontrolled and overcontrolled behavior and a final one on two disorders of special interest, anorexia nervosa and Gilles de la Tourette's syndrome.

---

[1] DSM-III still applies adult diagnoses to children if their symptoms meet the criteria.

[2] Narrower clusters have been found, but they can be covered by the broader terms of undercontrolled and overcontrolled.

TABLE **15.1**
Diagnoses Applied Exclusively to
Children in Three Versions of the DSM

Listings	DSM-I	DSM-II	DSM-III
Overall Major Category N of subcategories	None Six	One Ten	Nine Forty
Psychoses Major category N of subcategories Example	None One Schizophrenic reaction, childhood type	None One Schizophrenic reaction, childhood type	Pervasive Developmental Disorders Three Infantile autism
Developmental Deviations Major category N of subcategories Example	None None –	None None –	Specific Developmental Disorders Six Developmental reading disorder
Problems of Undercontrol Major category N of subcategories Example	None One Adjustment reaction, conduct disturbance	Behavior Disorders of Childhood and Adolescence Five Hyperkinetic reaction	Attention Deficit Disorder Three Hyperactivity Conduct Disorders Five Undersocialized aggressive
Problems of Overcontrol Major category N of subcategories Example	None Two Adjustment reaction, neurotic traits	Behavior Disorders of Childhood and Adolescence Two Withdrawing reaction	Anxiety Disorders Three Separation anxiety Other Disorders Five Elective mutism
Other Major category N of subcategories Example	None Three Adjustment reaction of infancy	None Three Adjustment reaction of infancy	Eating Disorders Five Bulimia Stereotyped Movement Disorders Five Tourette's disorder Other Disorders with Physical Manifestations Five Stuttering

BOX 15.1 Problem Environment or Problem Child?

Childhood disorders differ from adult disorders in a very important way; whereas many adults identify *themselves* as having a problem, most children are so identified *by others*. The difference between "I have a problem" and "You have a problem" is great.

The Rosenhan study discussed in Chapter 3 illustrated how surroundings can influence people's perception of behavior. And our discussion of ego-dystonic homosexuality in Chapter 11 (see page 363) raised a similar issue. When people refer themselves for treatment, we can be reasonably sure that they have problems for which they desire help. When a child is referred for treatment, on the other hand, all we really know is that someone perceives this child as disordered. Why does the person see this child as needing treatment? Child mental health workers must continually ask themselves questions that are not readily answered. Is this boy really unmanageable or does he just remind his mother of her divorced husband? Is this girl really distractible or is she merely bored by school? The evidence indicates that although the child's actual behavior is at least partly the basis for how adults perceive him or her, many other factors also enter into the perception (Ross, 1981).

Griest, Wells, and Forehand (1979) investigated this issue by studying a group of young children referred to a clinic for noncompliance with their parents. Mothers gave their perceptions of their child's maladjustment and also completed a paper-and-pencil inventory indicating their own depression. In addition, the children were visited in their homes so that instances of noncompliance and deviant behavior could be observed and recorded. These three pieces of data were then correlated. Surprisingly, mothers' perceptions of maladjustment in their children related significantly to their own depression ratings but *not* to observed child behavior! Children perceived as deviant actually behaved no worse than other children according to the outside observers. The depression of mothers may have more to do with their perception of deviance in their sons and daughters than do any acts of their children.

The study by Griest, Wells, and Forehand, although provocative, can be criticized on several grounds. For one, its design is correlational and therefore causality cannot be inferred. But despite its flaws the study indicates that what is considered a child's problem may well be a problem of the environment. For this reason many therapists see only entire families rather than individual children (Framo, 1975), and others have called for changes in schools rather than in school children (Winett and Winkler, 1972). We recognize the importance of the issue of labeling by the adult society and will raise it again in the course of the chapter. We also believe, however, that many identified problems are "real" childhood disorders. It is to them that this chapter is primarily devoted.

Specific Developmental Deviations

In Chapter 2 the statistical paradigm was introduced as one way of defining abnormal behavior. According to this model, large deviations from the average are to be regarded as abnormal. Developmental deviations are an explicit application of the statistical paradigm. These diagnoses are applied to children who differ from age-appropriate norms in a specific area of development, such as acquiring language. Two exclusions are made by DSM-III, however. If the specific deviation is an integral part of another disorder, such as language deficit in an autistic child, or if it is but one of many general delays in development, as in mental retardation, the diagnosis of _specific developmental disorder_ is inappropriate.

DSM-III lists four specific developmental deviations: _developmental reading disorder, developmental arithmetical disorder, developmental language disorder,_ and _developmental articulation disorder._ Because these problems are so frequent in children with other behavioral disorders, for example, hyperactivity, DSM-III codes the specific developmental disorders on axis II. We have chosen to include two additional developmental deviations, _enuresis_ or wetting and _encopresis_ or soiling, in this section. As noted in Chapter 2, the statistical model tells us nothing about _which_ deviations are to be considered abnormal. Where then does the DSM-III list come from? This is a good question, one asked by those who object to the childhood diagnoses in DSM-III (_APA Monitor_, January, 1980). Is a child who is doing very poorly in math really suffering a psychiatric disorder?

We prefer to collapse the DSM-III scheme. The two of the four DSM-III specific developmental disorders to be discussed have to do with behavior that is for the most part measured and promoted in schools, institutions operating within a statistical paradigm. These specific problems, in learning reading and arithmetic, are frequently called _learning disabilities_ and will be discussed as such later in this section. The two disorders _enuresis_ and _encopresis_ are usually considered earlier problems for both children and parents.

Enuresis

Infants have no bladder or bowel control and must continually be diapered. As the child becomes older, toilet training begins. Some children learn toileting at eighteen months, others at thirty months, and so on. When is it no longer "normal" to be unable to control the bladder? The answer is fairly arbitrary, as determined by cultural norms and the statistical paradigm.

DSM-III and other classification systems distinguish between those who wet during sleep, which is nocturnal enuresis, and those who wet themselves while awake with or without bed-wetting, which is called diurnal enuresis. Daytime continence is established earlier. When a child falls behind in bladder control, it is usually for the nighttime hours. Using census data and incidence rates at different ages, Baller (1975) projects what he calls a conservative estimate of close to four million bed wetters in the United States today! The majority of bed wetters are male; there are approximately two male enuretics for every female (DeJonge, 1973). Calculation of prevalence rates is not a straightforward task, however.

Figure 15.1 shows Lovibund's (1964) calculations of the incidence of bed wetting in England as a function of age. Certainly the cutoff on this graph, after which bed-wetting is designated a problem, cannot be set at two years, when the rate is over 40 percent. In the United States the most commonly accepted cutoff is between three

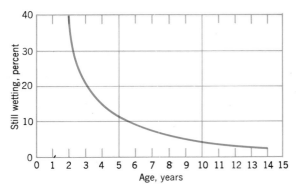

FIGURE **15.1**
Incidence of bed-wetting in England. After Lovibond, 1964.

and four years of age, at which time the estimated incidence of bed-wetting is 10 to 15 percent of the age group (Baller, 1975). In contrast, Bettelheim (1969) reported that on an Israeli kibbutz 40 percent of the nine-year-olds wet their beds, but the caretakers do not consider this a problem. Apparently there is more bed-wetting but less enuresis in Israel!

Clearly, age is not the only factor that enters into a diagnosis of enuresis. Baller (1975) offers a four-part definition of nocturnal enuretics as

persons who (1) involuntarily wet the bed; (2) show no evidence of urinary, organic pathology; (3) are three and one half years of age or more; and (4) have simply continued the nighttime wetting habits of infancy ("primary enuresis") or have . . . fallen into a pattern of bed-wetting ("secondary enuresis") that averages more than twice a week (p. 15).

This fourth criterion is a commonly made distinction, one found also in DSM-III. Primary enuretics, who represent two-thirds of all enuretics (Starfield, 1972), have wet the bed from infancy, whereas secondary enuretics were once able to remain dry at night but have apparently lost the capacity.

One consistent finding about enuresis is that the likelihood of an enuretic having a first-degree relative who also wets is very high, approximately 75 percent (Bakwin, 1973), evidence for either physiological or psychological theories of etiology. Bed-wetting is usually done during the first third of the night, when the child is not dreaming. If it does take place during a period of dreaming, the child may later recall a dream having to do with urination. Hospitalization between the ages of two and four, the birth of a sibling, and entering school are predisposing stresses.

Theories of enuresis

As many as 10 percent of all cases of enuresis are caused by purely medical conditions. The most common of the known physical causes is urinary tract infection. Approximately one in twenty female and one in fifty male enuretics have such an infection. Treatment of the infec-tion oftentimes does not stop the enuresis, however. Other infrequent but known physical causes are chronic renal or kidney disease, tumors, diabetes, and seizures (Kolvin, Mackeith, and Meadow, 1973). Because of the substantial incidence of physical causes of enuresis, most professionals refer enuretics to physicians before beginning psychological treatment.

Starfield (1972) has offered an interesting physiological theory on the etiology of enuresis. She supposes that enuretics void more frequently, that they have smaller functional bladder capacities, that is, they can hold only a small volume of urine before voiding, and that they tend to wet during the predream period of sleep, a time when they are moving from very deep sleep to a state of greater arousal. According to Starfield, enuresis is an abnormal response during a period of sleep when arousal is increasing. She also holds that sleepwalking and night terrors happen during this same period. Starfield suggests a procedure designed to increase functional bladder capacity as the best treatment for enuresis (see page 456). Unfortunately, this treatment has not met with much success, indicating that the small functional bladder capacity is not the principal cause of their wetting (Doleys, 1977). Furthermore, EEG tracings determine that enuresis, as well as sleepwalking and night terrors, is more likely to occur earlier in the deep-sleep cycle, sometimes just after delta waves have acquired especially great amplitude.

Some psychoanalytic theorists have suggested that enuresis serves as a symbol for other conflicts. Enuresis has been hypothesized to be both symbolic masturbation and a disguised means of demonstrating spite toward parents (Mowrer, 1950). A related notion considers enuresis a symptom of a more general psychological disorder. Many investigators disagree, however, finding other personal problems to be a reaction to the embarassment and guilt of wetting, rather than being causes of enuresis. Children will of course lose self-esteem if their peers ostracize them and their parents become angry and rejecting. When bladder control is gained, most of the correlated emotional problems are also likely to disappear (Starfield, 1972; Baller, 1975).

Learning theorists propose that children wet when toilet training begins at too early an age,

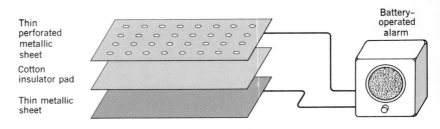

Thin
perforated
metallic
sheet

Cotton
insulator pad

Thin metallic
sheet

Battery-
operated
alarm

FIGURE **15.2**
The bell and pad apparatus for halting bed-wetting, devised by Orval Hobart and Willie Mae Mowrer.

when training is lax and insufficient reinforcement is given for proper toileting, and more specifically when children do not learn to awaken as a conditioned response to a full bladder or to inhibit sufficiently relaxation of the sphincter muscle controlling urination (Mowrer and Mowrer, 1938; Young, 1965; Baller, 1975). Bladder control, the inhibition of a natural reflex until voluntary voiding can take place, is after all a skill of considerable complexity. Although no single learning theory has received much empirical support, treatments based on learning models have proved quite successful (Doleys, 1977).

Treatment of enuresis
In the late 1930s Mowrer and Mowrer (1938) introduced the *bell and pad,* a treatment for nocturnal enuresis based on learning principles. Over the years the procedure has proved markedly successful in reducing or eliminating bed-wetting. Although relapses can be common, it is estimated that 75 percent of enuretic children will learn to stay dry through the night with the help of this remarkably simple device (Doleys, 1977).

The bell and a battery are wired to the pad, which is composed of two metallic foil sheets, the top one perforated, separated by a layer of absorbent cloth (Figure 15.2). The pad is inserted into a pillowcase and placed beneath the child at bedtime. When the first drops of urine, which acts as an electrolyte, reach the absorbent cloth, the electric circuit is completed between the two foil sheets. The completed circuit sets off the bell, which awakens the child immediately or

soon after he begins to wet. He is then able to stop urination, turn off the device, and go to the bathroom.

Mowrer and Mowrer (1938) viewed the bell and pad as a classical conditioning procedure wherein an unconditioned stimulus, the bell, wakens the child, the unconditioned response. The bell is paired with the sensations of a full bladder so that they eventually become a conditioned stimulus which produces the conditioned response of awakening, before the bell sounds. Others have questioned the classical conditioning theory, suggesting instead that the bell, by awakening the child, serves as a punisher and thus reduces the undesirable behavior of wetting.[3] Other methods that use an operant conditioning rationale instead of or in addition to the bell and pad procedure have also proved quite successful (Doleys, 1977).

A rather different learning treatment for enuresis is based on the theory already mentioned, that enuretics have an abnormally small functional bladder capacity. Children perform exercises to increase gradually the volume of urine that they can retain before voiding (Starfield, 1972). For instance, a child may be asked to drink a large glass of water and not to urinate for thirty minutes. The next day the time might be stretched to thirty-five minutes, and so on; rewards are provided for the steps along the way. In this manner the child's capacity to hold urine

[3] In actual practice the bell usually wakens the child's parents too; their reactions may serve as an additional incentive for the child to remain dry.

without voiding is gradually increased, the hope being that the enlarged capacity will reduce wetting. Although often useful, retention control training has not proved as effective as the bell and pad (Doleys, 1977).

Encopresis

In comparison to enuresis, encopresis, involuntary defecating, is a less common and much less well understood problem. Approximately 1.5 percent of children ages seven and eight are encopretic. By the age of sixteen the incidence figures drop to nearly zero (Schaefer, 1979). Encopresis too is both primary and secondary and much more common in boys than girls. About one in twenty cases of encopresis is attributable to physical causes; the remainder are believed to be psychogenic in origin. Many encopretic children also suffer from constipation and enuresis. Encopresis is regarded as more serious than enuresis.

In contrast to enuresis, which is usually a nighttime problem, soiling happens mostly during the day, very often in the late afternoon after school. It creates serious social problems for the child. Schoolmates will avoid the malodorous child, teachers will object to his presence in the classroom, parents may become very angry and upset, and the youngster himself suffers greatly from shame and embarrassment. He often devises clever ways of concealing incidents from parents by hiding dirty underwear (Ross, 1981).

The behavior therapist gives rewards for appropriate toiletings and mild punishment for failure to maintain bowel control, such as letting the child be responsible for the natural consequences of soiling. But the therapist is well advised to attend to the family situation in general. If, for example, the mother subtly rewards the child for soiling because it infuriates the father, whom she wishes to anger, the therapist must also deal with the troubled marital relationship.

Learning Disabilities

Ross (1974) considers learning dysfunctions, as he calls these disabilities, severe impairments in learning efficiency that are not attributable to (1) mental subnormality; (2) impairment of visual or auditory functions; (3) psychological disorders; or (4) cultural disadvantage. As Ross acknowledges, this is a definition by exclusion. The definition does not tell us what a learning disability is, only what it is not. His failure to define learning disability adequately is just one instance of the definitional confusion in the field. Parents, teachers, and child specialists continually see children who fail to perform up to their apparent capabilities in a given subject area, but persuasive explanations for their various performance deficits are not forthcoming. Nor for this diagnosis does DSM-III provide any improvement on a definition by exclusion. It states that the "subclass is for disorders of specific areas of [cognitive] development not due to another disorder" (DSM-III, p. 92).

Determining when a child is not fulfilling a "capacity" to learn is an additional problem in diagnosing a learning disability. Because academic performance is usually evaluated within a statistical model, there will *always* be some children at the lower end of the achievement curve. The learning-disabled child is found at the low end of this curve but presumably has the ability to perform at a higher level. But how do we measure this untapped ability? DSM-III suggests that individually administered IQ tests and academic achievement tests serve as indicators of the capacity for learning reading and arithmetic. Measures such as IQ tests, however, assess both native ability and academic achievement.

Because of the definitional confusion, the prevalence of learning disabilities is difficult to estimate. Prevalence rates as low as one percent and as high as 20 percent of the school-age population have been proposed (Cruickshank, 1977). One consistent finding is that more boys than girls have learning disabilities (Ross, 1974), but the reported sex ratio varies. There is no indication that all these children will "catch up" with time. Many continue to have signs of these disturbances as adolescents and as adults.

Etiology of learning disabilities

Two major theoretical positions have dominated the explanations put forth for learning disabilities, *perceptual-deficit theory* and *academic-instruction theory* (Wong, 1979). Perceptual-deficit theory asserts that learning disabilities are caused by a dysfunction in one or more levels of perceptual processing. According to this theory, children fail to learn because they make errors in perceiving sensory stimuli. For example, one popular early hypothesis suggested that children with developmental reading disorder, or *dyslexia,* perceive printed letters in reverse order or mirror image, mistake one letter for another, for example, a *d* for a *b,* or are unable to recall the sound connected with the letter. The learning-disabled child was believed actually to *see* the alphabet and words differently from other children. In fact, in the writing of these children letters are frequently reversed and words written backward. Although there has been a general failure to pinpoint perceptual deficits in many learning-disabled children (Wong, 1979), some researchers still continue the search (Cruickshank, 1977).

Academic-instruction theory proposes that a learning disability reflects a problem of teaching rather than a problem of learning (Englemann, 1969). The child is not incapable of learning; rather the teacher has failed to instruct properly. As might be expected, those who blame academic instruction are more concerned with identifying new methods of teaching than with describing learning-disabled children. Although it is doubtful that failures to teach properly explain all instances of learning disability, the assumption that at least many of these children have not learned certain skills has led to some encouraging treatments.

Intervention for reading problems

Special programs for teaching reading illustrate the general treatment of learning disabilities. Early on Staats and Butterfield (1965) established the operant approach as a useful means of helping youngsters overcome reading difficulties. The client was a fourteen-year-old boy from a large Mexican-American family who was reading at only the second-grade level. His academic and occupational prospects were rather grim, and he had already been in trouble with the police. Staats and Butterfield broke down the task of learning to read into several small steps. The young man's first task was to master a number of words written on file cards. All the words were from a story that his therapists hoped to have him read as the next step. Using tokens that the boy could "cash in" later for things he wanted, they systematically reinforced him for correctly pronouncing each new word. Whenever the boy failed, the trainer said the word correctly and then returned to it somewhat later. When all the new words for the story had been learned, reinforcement was made contingent on reading entire paragraphs of the story correctly. The tokens

A learning-disabled child receiving individualized instruction in recognizing words.

given at this stage were worth more than those the young man had obtained earlier for reading single words. Ultimately the boy had to read stories silently and answer comprehension questions correctly in order to earn tokens. After forty hours of such individualized instruction over a period of four and a half months, the boy had advanced more than two grade levels in reading ability.

Building on the pioneering work of Staats, Schwartz (1977) carried out a more ambitious and comprehensive study of behavioral tutoring of reading-disabled youngsters. His population consisted of 1265 seventh graders reading between 1.5 and 4.5 years below grade level. He assigned pupils to an experimental group or to one of four control groups. Students in the first control group were informed that they had been chosen for special attention, that they had the ability to improve their reading, and that their classroom teacher would monitor their progress and give them special help. Teachers were left to their own devices in providing this assistance. Members of the second control group were given the experimental program to be described, but it became part of the regular school curriculum and was conducted by the classroom teacher. Nothing changed for the students in the third control group. The fourth was an attention-placebo group; college student tutors met with these pupils an hour a week for the ten weeks of the program and helped them with their homework, but they did not use any of the special skill-training procedures.

What were these special training procedures? Children in the experimental group were tutored an hour a week for ten weeks by undergraduates who had been trained by Schwartz in principles of reinforcement and in applying these principles to reading problems. The tutor first assessed the particular needs of each pupil and then systematically reinforced the pupil for gradual progress in reading words, sentences, and paragraphs.

The children also practiced at home between the weekly sessions. A contract was established between tutor and pupil whereby the pupil could earn points for reading books at home and then correctly answering comprehension questions about their contents during the weekly tutoring sessions. Points could also be earned by making a good effort and by coming to sessions on time. These points were to be considered in establishing report card grades, presumably a powerful reinforcer.

The experimental program had other elements designed to improve reading habits and abilities. Tutors praised each of their pupils whenever they made positive statements about reading, in an effort to reverse negative attitudes. And to sustain whatever gains were achieved during the ten weeks of special training, each pupil made a contract with his or her tutor for summer reading. The children's goal was to earn as many points as they had during the tutoring program. It was assumed, however, that the most powerful reinforcement would come from their enhanced sense of competence in acquiring an important academic skill and from their appreciation of the pleasures of reading.

The five groups of youngsters were compared immediately following the termination of the program and again at a six-month follow-up. The results strongly favored the individualized experimental instruction. The growth in reading skills of experimental subjects, as measured by standardized tests, far surpassed that of children in all four control groups. Furthermore, this superiority was maintained and even consolidated at the follow-up. For example, the increase in grade level of reading expected for average students in the period from just before the program began until the six-month follow-up was 1.0 grade; experimental subjects showed an increase of 2.6 grades, the control subjects 1.6 grades. The appreciable jump of the experimental group was especially gratifying, considering that these students were below average. Their previous growth rate had been only 0.7 of a grade per year.

Other measures were consistent with these results. Pupils in the experimental group were reading many more books and enjoying them far more. Some reported that they could sit for two and three hours at a stretch reading a book; earlier their attention span had been less than an hour. Librarians reported seeing more of these youngsters, and teachers and parents commented on their greater self-confidence about schoolwork in general. Since the ability and willingness to read is central to academic as well as social development of children and adolescents, the need to deal effectively with reading problems cannot be underestimated. This program and others like it around the country have worked by assuming that most children have the capacity to learn, and that special professional attention can help them develop their abilities.

Disorders of Undercontrolled Behavior

The undercontrolled child lacks or has insufficient control over behavior that is expected in a given setting and is appropriate to the child's age. Because of such failings the undercontrolled child is frequently an annoyance to both adults and peers. Two general categories of _undercontrolled behavior_ are frequently differentiated, hyperactivity and conduct problems.

Problems of undercontrol are not as clearly derived from applying the statistical model of abnormal behavior as are the developmental deviations. These disorders are defined by the type and form of the behavior, its _topography_. The high frequency of much "problem" behavior in the general population of children, such as fidgeting in class, makes it questionable, however, whether isolated incidences should be considered abnormal. Other behavior, such as assaulting a teacher, is by topography alone considered abnormal by most people.

Hyperactivity

Jerry was a four-year-old child whose mother stated that she had never noticed anything unusual about him until he was almost two years old. At that point he had a severe case of mumps and this illness seemed to be the turning point from a calm infancy to a disruptive preschool period. The abruptness of the change suggests that his mumps _may_ have been a mumps encephalitis with subsequent brain damage, but there was no mention of this possibility in his pediatric history. His activity [coupled] high speed . . . with an erratic quality. He rarely stood still: when he was not running, jumping, or climbing he jiggled up and down in place much as a boxer does while waiting for his opponent's next move. He lacked fine motor skill and some of his gross motor behavior was characterized by clumsiness and awkwardness. [At preschool he] spent a major part of each morning running, climbing, and swinging. If an adult offered to push him or help him with any project he sometimes accepted the help, but at other times he burst into screams of rage and often pounded the adult with his fists. When he went to the toy corner he would throw all the toys off the shelves until he found the one he wanted. If another child had the toy he wanted, he took it by force; then, when an adult intervened, he had a tantrum. He had a short attention span and was unable to sit in a group and listen to a short story.

His speech was somewhat delayed. Although his IQ on the Stanford-Binet was 120, he never seemed to learn from experience; he repeatedly tried to stand on the seat of his tricycle even though he had many nasty falls. He rarely cried on falling but he often sobbed disconsolately over minor frustrations and hurts. At times he seemed almost desperate for attention and would engage in what could best be described as daredevil and reckless behavior to get it. On one occasion he climbed a tall tree in the preschool yard and attracted a fascinated audience by his promises to "go down the chimney like Santa Claus." To reach the roof he had to make a difficult jump from the tree, which he did without any hesitation or overt evidence of fear, and was prevented from going down the chimney only because it was too small for him to enter. When he was brought down from the roof he exhibited only pleasure at his feat and at "having all the kids watch me like that." On another occasion he picked up some bottles of prescription pills that had been carelessly discarded in a trash can and set himself up as doctor outside the preschool, dispensing pills to children as they entered (many came by themselves from a nearby housing development). When he was severely reprimanded his only comment was that he liked having "every kid do what I tell them." His behavior in any one session had a Jekyll and Hyde quality, with periods of calm interspersed with frequent . . . intense upset. The other children generally feared him, so even his serene periods were never reinforced by positive peer attention. Although he appeared to enjoy the preschool he often tried to climb the fence and was successful on several occasions (Ross, 1961, as reprinted in Ross and Ross, 1976, pp. 34–35).

Hyperactivity or hyperkinesis in children is defined as a behavioral pattern of persistent restlessness and inattentiveness that begins in early childhood. Such children are not simply more active than their peers; rather they seem to have particular difficulty in controlling their activity in situations that call for sitting still, such as at school or at mealtime (Pope, 1970). When required to be quiet, they appear completely unable to stop moving or talking. The problem usually comes to the attention of the family doctor when parents complain that Johnny is "driving them crazy," or when teachers repeatedly send the child to the school principal for disciplinary action.

This poor control in structured situations may be a result of a key symptom of hyperactivity, poor attention. The hyperactive child's inability to sustain attention is believed by some to be the root cause of the child's overactivity. Rather than attending to the task at hand, hyperactive children are distracted by a variety of things or events that cause them then to engage in activity inappropriate to the current situation. So important is this aspect of hyperactivity that DSM-III calls it _attention deficit disorder with hyperactivity_. It is noteworthy that this DSM-III term indicates a particular hypothesis about the etiology of hyperactivity. The category name, attention deficit disorder, is therefore not descriptive, as category names like enuresis are; rather it makes a statement about a presumed cause.

Minimally brain-damaged is another term applied by some writers to hyperactive children. This label also designates a _presumed_ etiology for the behavior pattern of restlessness and inattentiveness. Hyperactive children, however, do not give clear evidence of specific brain damage, although they often have what are termed "soft" neurological signs, such as clumsiness, confusion of right and left, poor balance, coordination, and speech, as well as problems in perceiving. On the basis of these signs, it has been inferred that these children have "minimal" brain damage. We prefer the term hyperactivity to either of the other two because it does not carry with it a presumption concerning etiology. Indeed, as we shall see later, hyperactivity may have multiple causes.

In addition to their core problems, hyperactive children have a number of difficulties. As evidenced by poor academic and test performance (Weiss et al., 1971), between 40 and 50 percent have learning problems. Oftentimes, then, hyperactivity and learning disabilities are found in the same child and a diagnostic decision becomes difficult (Lahey et al., 1978). Which problem is the primary one?

Misconduct at school is found in about 80 percent of hyperactive children (Satterfield et al., 1972). And they are commonly described by adults as immature. They may choose to play with children younger then themselves and with toys inappropriate to their age; they also persist in baby talk (Weiss et al., 1971).

The problems of hyperactive children begin in early infancy: they are more likely than their peers to develop colic (Stewart et al., 1966), and they fail to reach developmental milestones, such as walking, at the expected ages (Denhoff, 1973). Furthermore, even during infancy there are deviations in activity level; some are overactive but others, interestingly enough, are too passive (Werry, Weiss, and Douglas, 1964). By the preschool years their overactivity and inattentiveness are evident. They do not follow through when given small chores by their parents, and they knock over their baby sister's pile of blocks when asked to play with her. At this stage in their lives, they are often considered temperamental and emotional children (Schain and Reynard, 1975). Their problems attract real notice when they enter school, probably because of the greater degree of structure evident in most elementary school settings. One study (Stewart et al., 1966) compared teacher ratings of the behavior of hyperactive and control children (Table 15.2). The actions and attitudes rated make a good catalogue of hyperactivity.

It is estimated that 8 to 9 percent of elementary school boys and 2 to 3 percent of girls are hyperactive (Miller, Palkes, and Stewart, 1973). At one time it was thought that hyperactivity simply went away by adolescence. Problems

TABLE **15.2**
Classroom Behavior of Hyperactive and Control Children
(from Stewart et al., 1966)

Behavior	Control, Percent ($N = 33$)	Hyperactive, percent ($N = 37$)
Overactive	33	100
Can't sit still	8	81
Fidgets	30	84
Leaves class without permission	0	35
Can't accept correction	0	35
Temper tantrums	0	51
Fights	3	59
Defiant	0	49
Doesn't complete project	0	84
Doesn't stay with games	3	78
Doesn't listen to whole story	0	49
Moves from one activity to another in class	6	46
Doesn't follow directions	3	62
Hard to get to bed	3	49
Unpopular with peers	0	46
Talks too much	20	68
Wears out toys, furniture, etc.	8	68
Gets into things	11	54
Unpredictable	3	59
Destructive	0	41
Unresponsive to discipline	0	57
Lies	3	43

with activity level do diminish somewhat, but many adolescent youngsters diagnosed as hyperactive in childhood still have difficulty maintaining attention (Weiss et al., 1971; Hoy et al., 1978). Deficits in learning and perception may persist (Mendelson, Johnson, and Stewart, 1971), and social relationships at home and with peers may remain problematic (Huessy, Metoyer, and Townsend, 1974). In young adulthood the formerly hyperactive child may continue to have some problems, but they are usually less serious. Hyperactives change residences more often and have more car accidents than controls, which is evidence of their continuing impulsiveness. A minority show signs of antisocial behavior. On the brighter side, hyperactives attain job status and satisfaction equal to those of controls and are only slightly lower in educational achievements (Weiss et al., 1979). Clearly some of the problems of hyperactive children lessen with age. A summary of their difficulties and reactions, as linked to specific ages, appears in Table 15.3.

TABLE 15.3
Behaviorial Characteristics of Hyperactives
(after Ross and Ross, 1976)

Age	Description of individual
Infancy	Difficult and unpredictable
	Apoplectic to calm
	Querulous, irritable
	Rarely smiles
	Erratic sleep
Preschool	Sharp temper
	Strong-willed
	Excessively demanding
	Light sleeper
	Short attention span
Middle childhood	Extremely active
	Difficulty sitting still
	Unable to remain seated during meal
	Distractible
	Light sleeper
	Often sad or depressed
	Poor school performance
Adolescence	Poor self-image
	Poor school performance
	Lack of social skills
	Rejection by parents and siblings
	Decrease in activity level
	Aggressiveness
Adulthood	Personality disorders
	Explosive personality
	Alcoholism

Physiological theories of hyperactivity
A predisposition toward hyperactivity does appear to be inherited. Morrison and Stewart (1971), for example, found that 20 percent of hyperactive children had a parent who had been hyperactive. The corresponding figure for control children was 5 percent. Similar results have been reported by Gross and Wilson (1974), and the findings have held up in more methodologically sophisticated adoption studies (Morrison and Stewart, 1973; Cantwell, 1975).

A biochemical theory of hyperactivity, proposed by Feingold (1973), has enjoyed much attention in the popular press. He had been treating a woman for allergies while she was concurrently being seen by a psychiatrist for uncontrollable, frenetic behavior. Feingold thought that the patient might be allergic to aspirin and other salicylate compounds, so he prescribed a diet free of them. Both her allergic symptoms and her overactivity rapidly and dramatically diminished. Feingold soon noted the prevalence of salicylates and other similar chemicals in food additives and embarked on a study in which hyperactive children were kept on a diet free of food additives. Many responded favorably, and his work was subsequently replicated (Hawley and Buckley, 1974). Thus it is possible that the central nervous systems of some hyperactive children, perhaps through a genetically transmitted predisposition, are upset in some way by food additives. It is unlikely, though, that all cases of hyperactivity are caused by sensitivity to food additives. Well-controlled studies of the Feingold diet have found that very few such children respond positively (Goyette and Conners, 1977).

Hyperactive children show some signs of possible brain damage. Their mothers have often had difficult pregnancies (Pasamanick, Rogers, and Lilienfeld, 1956), and in infancy hyperactive children are more likely to have had seizures, encephalitis, cerebral palsy, and head injury (Conners et al., 1972). Furthermore, hyperactivity can be brought on by lead poisoning (Wiener, 1970). And many hyperactive children show abnormal EEGs (Gross and Wilson, 1974) in addition to the soft neurological signs already mentioned. All this evidence points to some brain malfunction, but what parts of the brain might be impaired? Or is the problem biochemical, in the neurotransmitters, rather than structural? Unfortunately, no data currrently available allow greater and more meaningful specification of the vague term brain damage (Sroufe, 1975).

The success of psychostimulant medication in treating hyperactive children was once considered to be additional evidence in support of a physiological theory of hyperactivity. Amphetamines, as discussed in Chapter 10, heighten the adult's sense of energy. Yet they have the effect of increasing attention and decreasing activity level in hyperactive children. This apparently paradoxical effect was taken as evidence for abnormal physiological processes in hyperactive children. Such an interpretation is no longer viable, for recent evidence demonstrates that normal children also respond to amphetamines with increased attention and decreased activity (Rapoport et al., 1978). The once presumed "paradoxical effect" has proved to be the normal response of children to psychostimulants.

Psychological theories of hyperactivity

Bettelheim (1973) proposed a diathesis-stress theory, suggesting that hyperactivity develops when a predisposition to the disorder is coupled with unfortunate rearing by parents. A child with a disposition toward overactivity and moodiness is stressed further by a mother who easily becomes impatient and resentful. The child is unable to cope with the mother's demands for obedience, the mother becomes more and more negative and disapproving, and the mother-child relationship ends up a battleground. With a disruptive and disobedient pattern already established, the demands of school cannot be handled, and the behavior of the child is usually and often in conflict with the rules of the classroom.

The Fels Research Institute's longitudinal study of child development supplies some evidence that is consistent with Bettelheim's position (Battle and Lacey, 1972). Mothers of hyperactive children were found to be critical of them and relatively unaffectionate, even during the children's infancy. These mothers continued to be disapproving of their children and dispensed severe penalties for disobedience. The parent-child relationship, however, is bidirectional, the behavior of each being determined by the reactions of the other. The influence of hyperactive children's behavior on the actions of their mothers has recently been demonstrated (Barkley and Cunningham, 1979). It is plausible, though, that a critical and unaffectionate mother might exacerbate the problems of a hyperactive child (Cunningham and Barkley, 1979).

Finally, although no comprehensive theory has been proposed, two ways in which learning might figure in hyperactivity should be mentioned. First, hyperactivity could be reinforced by the attention it elicits, even negative attention, as Jerry's was. Second, as Ross and Ross (1976) suggest, hyperactivity may be modeled on the behavior of parents and siblings.

Treatment of hyperactivity

As already indicated, two somatic treatments for hyperactivity are widespread. Stimulant drugs, especially methylphenidate or Ritalin, have become increasingly popular medication for this disorder since the early 1960s (Sprague and Gadow, 1976). One estimate is that during the school year as many as 700,000 American children are given Ritalin or one of the amphetamines in efforts to control their hyperactivity. Drug companies advertise heavily in psychiatric journals to encourage prescription of these medications. The other somatic intervention is the so-called Feingold diet, promulgated by Feingold's 1975 book, *Why Your Child Is Hyperactive*, and by numerous parent associations throughout the country. These associations publish complete diets made up of foods that do not contain such things as artificial flavors and colorings, preservatives, and natural salicylates. Reports on the efficacy of these two interventions are mixed. A number of controlled studies comparing stimulants with placeboes in double-blind designs indicate short-term lessening of fidgeting and greater obedience in school (Cantwell and Carlson, 1978; O'Leary, 1980). Little research indicates that over the long haul such drugs favorably influence academic achievement, however (Weiss et al., 1975); in fact, they may sometimes *interfere with* academic performance when administered in doses strong enough to reduce hyperactive behavior (Sprague and Sleator, 1977). Very little evidence supports the efficacy of the Feingold diet (Harley, in press).

Despite the absence of a comprehensive theory, treatments of hyperactive children based on learning principles have demonstrated at least short-term success in improving both social and academic behavior. In these treatments the behavior of the children is monitored both at home and in school, and they are reinforced for doing the appropriate thing, such as remaining in their seats and working on assignments. Point systems and star charts, akin to the token economies used on hospital wards, are frequently a part of these programs; the youngsters earn points and the younger children stars for behaving in certain ways. They can then of course ''spend'' their earnings for back-up rewards. It is of special interest that the focus of these operant programs is on improving academic work rather than on reducing signs of hyperactivity, such as running around and jiggling (O'Leary et al., 1976). The therapists devising them treat hyperactivity as a deficit in certain skills rather than as an excess of disruptive behavior. Although hyperactive children have proved very responsive to these programs, the optimal treatment for hyperactivity, discussed in more detail in Chapter 20, seems to require the use of both stimulants and behavior therapy.

Conduct Disorders and Delinquency

The term *conduct disorders* encompasses a wide variety of undercontrolled behavior. There is no single definition. Rather, any undercontrolled behavior that is deemed noxious or unacceptable by others may be viewed as a conduct problem. Aggression, defiance, and disobedience, verbal hostility, lying, destructiveness, vandalism, theft, promiscuity, and early drug and alcohol use are attitudes and actions usually covered by the general, and rather vague, category of conduct disorders. The patterns and severity of the acts go beyond the mischief and pranks common among children and adolescents. A lack of concern for the feelings, wishes, and well-being of others is another serious shortcoming of those with conduct problems.

Two diagnostic types of conduct disorders are commonly identified (Jenkins and Glickman, 1947; Quay, 1964). The diagnosis *socialized conduct disorder* applies to children who perpetrate frequent antisocial or delinquent acts—truancy, running away, serious lying, stealing—in the company of peers. *Undersocialized conduct disorder* is the diagnosis when the antisocial acts more closely resemble those of the adult antisocial personality—vandalism, rape, breaking and entry, fire setting, mugging, assault, extortion, purse snatching, armed robbery—and the children committing them have no stable bonds and apparently no concern for how their actions affect others. In fact, the disorder may be a precursor of antisocial personality, for many of these children will have conflicts with the law as adults (Robins, 1966).

Perhaps more than any other childhood disorder, conduct problems are defined by the impact of the child's behavior on people and surroundings. Schools, parents, and peers usually decide what undercontrolled behavior is unacceptable conduct. Preadolescents and adolescents are often identified as conduct problems by legal authorities. Because the diagnosis of conduct disor-

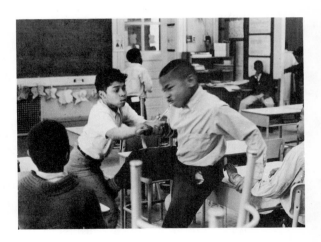

Conduct-disordered children are frequently aggressive and disruptive in the classroom.

TABLE 15.4
Frequency of Illegal Activities in
Nondelinquent Male Populations

(from Short and Nye, 1958)

Delinquent act	Admit committing act, percent			Admit committing act more than once or twice, percent		
	Midwestern students	Western students	Training school boys	Midwestern students	Western students	Training school boys
Driving a car without a license	81.1	75.3	91.1	61.2	49.0	73.4
Skipping school	54.4	53.0	95.3	24.4	23.8	85.9
Fist fighting	86.7	80.7	95.3	32.6	31.9	75.0
Running away	12.9	13.0	68.1	2.8	2.4	37.7
School probation or expulsion	15.3	11.3	67.8	2.1	2.9	31.3
Defying parents' authority	22.2	33.1	52.4	1.4	6.3	23.6
Stealing items worth less than $2	62.7	60.6	91.8	18.5	12.9	65.1
Stealing items worth from $2 to $50	17.1	15.8	91.0	3.8	3.8	61.4
Stealing items worth more than $50	3.5	5.0	90.8	1.1	2.1	47.7
Gang fighting	24.3	22.5	67.4	6.7	5.2	47.4
Drinking beer, wine, or liquor	67.7	57.2	89.7	35.8	29.5	79.4
Using narcotics	1.4	2.2	23.1	0.7	1.6	12.6
Having sex relations	38.8	40.4	87.5	20.3	19.9	73.4

der is so closely linked to the reaction it elicits from other people, we must be particularly aware of the potential labeling biases discussed at the beginning of this chapter. Moreover, since much of the behavior considered a conduct problem has a high base rate in the general population, a certain level of aggression or disobedience must be "normal." Even delinquency is difficult to define. As indicated in Table 15.4, a wide variety of illegal acts are committed by a significant proportion of "nondelinquent" populations.

An excerpt from the case history of Tom serves to illustrate the difficulty of defining conduct disorders in terms of behavior alone.

He entered the church, now, with a swarm of clean and noisy boys and girls, proceeded to his seat and started a quarrel with the first boy who came handy. The teacher, a grave, elderly man, interfered; then turned his back a moment and Tom pulled a boy's hair in the next bench, and was absorbed in his book when the boy turned around; stuck a pin in another boy, presently, in order to hear him say "Ouch!" and got a new reprimand from his teacher (p. 454).

Based on this sample of Tom's behavior, are we to conclude that he has a conduct disorder? Certainly he is aggressive and disobedient, two of the more frequent indications. And the impact of Tom's behavior on his companions and the Sunday school session is a disruptive one, as we can be sure both Tom's Sunday school teacher and his classmates would report. The excerpt, however, was taken from *The Adventures of Tom Sawyer,* by Mark Twain (1876). Tom Sawyer a conduct problem? No! For one hundred years Tom has been considered the prototypical all-American boy. Something about Tom, perhaps his cleverness and his affection for Becky, keeps us from thinking of him as a boy with conduct problems. Although he was devilish, even Aunt Polly acknowledged that Tom was not *really* a ruffian.

> *"But as I was saying," said Aunt Polly, "he warn't bad, so to say—only mischeevous. Only, just giddy, and harum-scarum, you know. He warn't any more responsible than a colt. He never meant any harm, and he was the best-hearted boy that ever was"* (p. 503).

The factors that make the actions of one child be considered a conduct problem and the same actions of another be accepted as "normal" are intriguing. Unfortunately, they are largely unspecified in the psychological literature. Fertile ground for speculation is provided by the contrast between Tom Sawyer and Huck Finn, who would likely be diagnosed as having a conduct disorder. "Huckleberry was cordially hated and dreaded by all the mothers of the town, because he was idle, and lawless, and vulgar and bad" (p. 464). The fact that Huck had no "proper" family may have been one factor swaying the opinions of the townspeople.

We do not wish to overstate the labeling bias of society, however. Many qualities of the child's behavior itself must be considered in the diagnosis of conduct disorders. Perhaps the two most important criteria for deciding whether a given act is aggressive or problematic are the frequency with which it occurs and the intensity of the behavior (Herbert, 1978). Thus one fight in a year is not a problem, but one fight per week is. (The percentage of young people committing a delinquent act the second time is sometimes dramatically less than those who do it once, as indicated in Table 15.4.) Similarly, stealing a candy bar is a minor incident; stealing a car is a felony. These criteria of frequency and intensity do not fully solve the problem of defining conduct disorders, but they are initial considerations.

Because of the definitional difficulties, the prevalence of conduct disorders is impossible to estimate accurately. With little doubt, however, they are quite common. Approximately one-third of all referrals made to child guidance clinics are for conduct problems (Wiltz and Patterson, 1974). Furthermore, since it is estimated that most children with conduct problems do not receive treatment (Bahm et al., 1961), clinic referrals would not reflect the true prevalence of these problems. If both of these suppositions are accurate, conduct disorders must be the most frequent psychological problem of childhood.

Conduct problems are from three to ten times more frequent in males than in females, although their incidence in females may be increasing (Herbert, 1978). Generally, the more serious the delinquent act, the greater the ratio of males to females committing it. Juvenile crime is a major problem. In 1975 it was estimated that 44 percent of the seven most serious types of felonies—for example, murder, rape, and robbery—were committed by juveniles (Federal Bureau of Investigation, 1976).

The prognosis for children diagnosed as having conduct disorders is poor. Robins (1966, 1972), in her thirty-year follow-up study of adults who had as children been seen in a child guidance clinic (see page 281), found that fully 50 percent of them had in their younger years been incarcerated in correctional institutions, and that the majority of the people in this clinic sample continued to be antisocial in their behavior during adulthood. As is the case with hyperactivity, it is clear that conduct problems are not simply outgrown.

Etiology of conduct disorders

Numerous theories have been offered as explanations of the etiology of conduct disorders. Physiological explanations are suggested by the fact that a higher incidence of antisocial behavior is found in the relatives of delinquent children than in the general population (Cloninger, Reich, and Guze, 1975). Furthermore, twin studies show consistently higher concordance rates

BOX **15.2** The Role of Marital Discord in Conduct Disorders

The role that separation and divorce play in fostering conduct problems and delinquency has been an issue of debate. The incidence of delinquency has frequently been found greater in one-parent families than in two-parent families (for example, Glueck and Glueck, 1959). Some have argued that separation from a parent by itself causes delinquency (Bowlby, 1973). If this assumption is correct, parents would be wise to stay together "for the child's sake."

But research evidence contradicts this conclusion. McCord, McCord, and Thurber (1962) compared the rates of gang delinquency in the sons from three groups of homes. The three types consisted of happy single-parent homes, happy homes inhabited by both parents, and unhappy single-parent homes. The researchers found that the rates of delinquency of sons from the two types of happy homes were very similar, but the unhappy single-parent homes produced a greater percentage of delinquents. On the basis of this finding, they concluded that discord, not separation, was the more likely cause of delinquency. The confounding of two factors, separation and marital conflict, would explain the misinterpretations of the results of other studies. More recent evidence, including comparisons of homes broken by death with homes broken by divorce, supports the conclusion that discord is the important factor (Rutter, 1979). Although separation per se does have disruptive effects, family conflict is apparently the key contributor to delinquency and conduct problems.

for antisocial behavior in MZ pairs than in DZ pairs (Eysenck, 1975). The effects of rearing are indicated by findings that discipline of conduct-disordered children has been inconsistent, yet harsh (Glueck and Glueck, 1959), that families of these children frequently lack cohesiveness (Craig and Glick, 1963), and that they have experienced the stresses of marital discord and divorce (Rutter, 1971; Emery and O'Leary, 1979; see Box 15.2).

Several psychological theories have unique merits. Learning theories that look to both modeling and operant conditioning have received considerable attention as explanations of the development and maintenance of conduct problems. Bandura and Walters (1963) were among the first to point out the obvious, that children can learn aggressiveness from parents who behave in this way. Children may also imitate aggressive acts that are seen elsewhere, such as on television (Liebert, Neale, and Davidson, 1973). Since aggression is an effective, albeit unpleas-

ant, means of achieving a goal, it is likely to be reinforced. Thus, once imitated, aggressive acts will probably be maintained.

Bandura and Walters (1959) found that the families of antisocial adolescents use physical punishment more often than control families and are more likely to reward aggressive acts. Their study, although limited by a cross-sectional design,[4] supports their theory, that *modeling and reinforcement* are part of the etiology of at least *some* conduct problems.

Patterson and Reid (1970) have offered a more specific explanation of how conduct problems are rewarded in families. Their coercion hypothesis is best demonstrated by an example from our clinical files.

---

[4] The findings are only correlational. In such cross-sectional studies it is possible that the aggressiveness of the children elicits physical punishment from their parents. A longitudinal study would permit a cause-effect conclusion. Say, for example, a child is not aggressive at age five but lives in a home in which he is punished physically. By age ten he may have become an aggressive youngster.

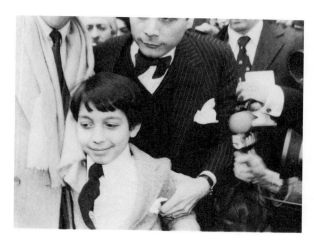

New York City's nine-year-old bank robber. His plea of innocence was based on the claim that he was just acting out what he had seen on television.

Chris was an eight-year-old boy brought to the clinic by his mother, who described him as unmanageable. Whenever his mother refused to comply with Chris's requests, he became upset. At these times Chris would be stubborn, uncooperative, and verbally abusive. Occasionally he would throw a temper tantrum and lie down on the floor, kicking his feet and screaming. His mother usually ignored Chris's behavior for a few minutes, but she gave in to his demands when his tantrums became too difficult for her to bear. This sequence of agitation and giving in had become habitual, particularly when the mother was busy. When she felt rushed and perturbed, she gave in to Chris almost immediately.

The coercion hypothesis postulates that both Chris and his mother are rewarded in this sequence of events. Chris is rewarded by getting his own way, his mother by the cessation of Chris's obnoxious behavior. Through this mutual rewarding both Chris's conduct problems and his mother's acquiescence are likely to be maintained. Therapy based on the coercion hypothesis would direct the mother never to give in to Chris while he is misbehaving and thereby extinguish his conduct problems. The coercion hypothesis seems a likely model, but it explains only how obstreperous behavior is *maintained,* not how it first *develops.*

Some psychodynamic theorists have explained conduct problems and delinquency as a ". . . disorder(s) in the functioning of the superego" (Kessler, 1966, p. 303). In psychoanalytic theory the superego is the part of the psyche that governs behavior according to societal and parental rules; thus conduct problems are traced to a failure of conscience and moral development.

In any discussion of conduct disorders and delinquency, the work of sociologists must be recognized. Social class and urban living in particular are related to the incidence of delinquency. High unemployment, poor educational facilities, disrupted family life, and a subculture which deems delinquency acceptable have all been found to be contributing factors (Gibbons, 1975). The correlation coefficients given in Table 15.5 indicate the relation of demographic indices to delinquency in three cities. Any comprehensive

TABLE **15.5**
Relation of Several Demographic Indices to Delinquency in Three Cities
(from Chilton, 1964)

Demographic index	Delinquency, correlation coefficient		
	Baltimore	Detroit	Indianapolis
Education	−.51	−.47	−.64
Rented dwellings	−.54	−.35	−.57
Owner-occupied dwellings	−.80	−.61	−.64
Foreign-born	−.16	−.44	−.11
Nonwhite	.70	.52	.41
Overcrowding	.73	.65	.85
Substandard housing	.69	.62	.81

theory of delinquency and conduct disorders would need to include these consistent sociological findings.

Conduct disorders versus hyperactivity

The similarities between conduct disorders and hyperactivity are obvious; moreover, the two problems often occur together. In fact, most empirical work has been unable to distinguish between the two disorders. For instance, on the most frequently used measure of hyperactivity, the Conners Teacher Rating Scale (Conners, 1969), the two scales designed to measure these two different disorders actually correlate .77 (Werry, Sprague, and Cohen, 1975).

Recently factor analysis has proved better able to distinguish the two disorders. Three key symptoms were found for each. Lack of control, negative affect, and interpersonal aggression are the key symptoms of conduct problems, poor judgment, agitation, and inattention the key symptoms of hyperactivity (Loney, Langborne and Paternite, 1978). Although these two sets of symptoms can occur together, factor analysis suggests that they do not *always* occur together.

Treatment of conduct disorders

The management of conduct disorders poses a formidable challenge to contemporary society. Sociologists and politicians, working on the assumption that poor economic conditions create most of the problem, argue for a fairer distribution of income, for job programs and other large-scale efforts to alleviate the material deprivation of the lower classes, among whom, as previously noted, delinquency is often found.

As meritorious as such proposals might be on moral and political grounds, the broad sociological view gives too little consideration to two simple facts: only a minority of lower-class youngsters are "hoods," and conduct problems are to be found in sizable numbers among children and adolescents of middle- and upper-class families.[5]

[5] One view of the juvenile delinquency of young people from affluent backgrounds holds that, with time on their hands, they sometimes make the conscious choice to engage in antisocial acts, not out of any felt economic need but as a way to fill their leisure hours. They supposedly engage in a bit of deliberation, weighing the positive consequences against the negative. This view of antisocial behavior is inconsistent with considering it to have an underlying pathology (Richards, Berk, and Forster, 1979).

Mischief and crime of well-to-do young people are of course underrepresented in police statistics because the status and social influence of their families often keep these children from being booked and incarcerated, as poorer youngsters are. Although sociological considerations may play some role in planning treatments, we emphasize here psychological methods aimed more at the particular individuals themselves.

Some of the young people with undersocialized conduct disorder are the sociopaths of tomorrow. Just as precious little in the way of effective psychological treatment has been found for sociopathy, so are there few ways to reach young people who commit violent and antisocial acts with little remorse or emotional involvement. These callous young individuals, most of them male, "graduate from" training schools and youth farms to lives of crime and dissoluteness, interrupted by extended periods of incarceration in prisons. Recidivism is the rule. One of society's most enduring problems is how to deal with people whose social consciences appear grossly underdeveloped.

Some behavior therapists find in people whose behavior violates societal norms

> a failure to have learned . . . to postpone immediate and often unlawful gratification and . . . a lack of socially endorsed skills for finding alternate, legal forms of gratification. . . . It follows that intervention must be aimed at teaching needed controls and missing skills. [Furthermore,] the norm-violator may not have acquired the ability to discriminate between acceptable and unacceptable behavior, [hence] the logical treatment is the teaching of this discrimination (Ross, 1981, p. 148).

These therapists advocate positive reinforcement of new prosocial responses rather than the punishment of existing antisocial behavior. Two kinds of efforts can be distinguished. First, therapists may try merely to change the behavior of residents while they are in an institution. Or they may try to create changes during institutionalization that generalize to life on the outside, so that discharged people will do better in school, hold jobs longer, and avoid legal hassles with the police.

Several studies have demonstrated that systematically reinforcing prosocial acts can improve the overt behavior of young men with conduct disorders while they are in an institution (for example, Barkley et al., 1976). The second method is of greater importance. An architect, Harold Cohen, and his associates developed a one-year special program at the National Training School for Boys in Washington, D.C., a federally run residential center for male teenagers who have been convicted of crimes such as robbery, auto theft, and even murder (Cohen and Filipczak, 1971). This project, referred to as CASE II, was a comprehensive educational program consisting of sixteen courses. The American Revolution, electronics, and remedial mathematics and reading are a sampling of those offered. The young men were able to earn money by demonstrating their competence; making grades 90 percent or better earned them extra points. They used their money to pay for better living arrangements, to order clothing, and to gain admittance to a recreational lounge. The young men acquired better study skills than they possessed before entering the program and, following release, used these skills to good advantage in the public school system. Moreover, for two years they had less trouble with the law; their recidivism rate the first year was only one-third of the average.

Delinquent youngsters who live at Achievement Place, a small, familylike home supervised by live-in surrogate parents, attend regular schools in the community. They earn points for completing homework, for reading books and newspapers, for keeping neat and clean, and for helping with household tasks (Table 15.6). Even-

TABLE **15.6**
Behavior That Earns and Loses Points at Achievement Place
(from Phillips, 1968)

Behavior that earns points	Points
1. Watching news on TV or reading the newspaper	300 per day
2. Cleaning and maintaining neatness in one's room	500 per day
3. Keeping one's person neat and clean	500 per day
4. Reading books	5 to 10 per page
5. Aiding houseparents in various household tasks	20 to 1000 per task
6. Doing dishes	500 to 1000 per meal
7. Being well dressed for an evening meal	100 to 500 per meal
8. Performing homework	500 per day
9. Obtaining desirable grades on school report cards	500 to 1000 per grade
10. Turning out lights when not in use	25 per light
Behavior that loses points	**Points**
1. Failing grades on the report card	500 to 1000 per grade
2. Speaking aggressively	20 to 50 per response
3. Forgetting to wash hands before meals	100 to 300 per meal
4. Arguing	300 per response
5. Disobeying	100 to 1000 per response
6. Being late	10 per minute
7. Displaying poor manners	50 to 100 per response
8. Engaging in poor posture	50 to 100 per response
9. Using poor grammar	20 to 50 per response
10. Stealing, lying, or cheating	10,000 per response

tually they earn their release through good behavior, and for two years their recidivism rates too are generally low. Repairing the academic and social deficits of youngsters seems a promising way to begin the attack on the serious social and psychological problem of delinquency.

Success in teaching specific skills suggests that taking preventive measures during earlier child rearing might prove useful in reducing the incidence of antisocial behavior. An exemplary program of clinical research on the families of aggressive boys has been conducted for a number of years by Gerald Patterson and his colleagues at the Oregon Research Institute (Patterson, Cobb, and Ray, 1973). Parents of young boys who could be considered "predelinquent" were trained to monitor their interactions with their aggressive sons; to desist from reinforcing their misbehavior with attention, a pattern often found in the families of aggressive youngsters; and to reward prosocial behavior more consistently. A follow-up study of a number of families with aggressive and coercive sons a year after treatment suggested that such interventions had been helpful for at least some of the youngsters (Patterson, 1974b). Behavioral treatments may help prevent the development of full-blown conduct disorders in children and adolescents.

Disorders of Overcontrolled Behavior

O *vercontrolled behavior,* as indicated earlier, usually creates more problems for the individual child than for others.[6] Withdrawn children receive only the amount of attention from teachers that normal children do, but children with conduct problems receive a greater amount of their vigilance (Scarlett, 1980). And unlike undercontrolled children whose behavior is judged by others, children with problems of overcontrol themselves frequently complain of bothersome fears and tenseness; of feelings of shyness, of being unhappy and unloved; and of being inferior to other children. Symptoms of overcontrolled behavior are similar to those of the adult problems of anxiety and depression. The three specific problems of overcontrol to be discussed are childhood fears, social withdrawal, and depression. The first two problems are roughly equivalent to the DSM-III listings *separation anxiety disorder* and *avoidant disorder.* Childhood depression is not a specific diagnostic category in DSM-III; as will be seen, the evidence for depression in children is controversial.

Childhood Fears

Most children have many fears that are apparently "outgrown" in the normal course of development. For example, Jersild, Markey, and Jersild (1933) interviewed 398 children of ages five to twelve. Fears of the following were expressed by substantial numbers: supernatural events, for example, ghosts and witches, 19.2 percent; being alone, in the dark, or in a strange place, being lost, 14.6 percent; attack or danger of attack by animals, 13.7 percent; bodily injury, falling, illness, operations, hurt and pains, 12.8 percent. The results of a similar study of generally younger children appear in Figure 15.3. Certain types of fears diminish as children become older. Experience with various everyday objects apparently takes away their fearsomeness. But imaginary fears magnify and are acquired by more

[6] We must not, however, underestimate the toll taken on parents, family members in general, and teachers by the problems described in this section.

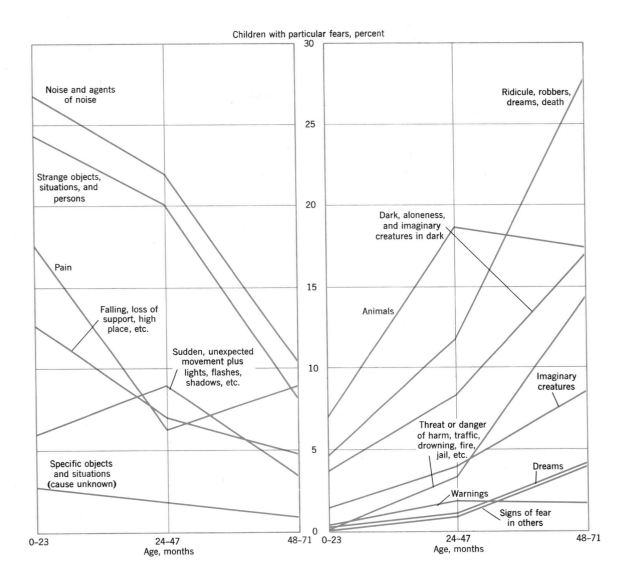

Children with particular fears, percent

FIGURE **15.3**
Relative frequency of fears of various kinds shown by children of different ages who were observed by parents and teachers in the Jersild and Holmes (1935) study. After Gray, 1971.

and more children as they gain in months and years. Later on, by the time children are in the sixth grade, fears of imaginery creatures have been abandoned, but fear of bodily injury and physical danger have increased (Bauer, 1976).

The suffering experienced by a fearful child should not be underestimated. As recounted in DSM-III, children's fears often affect them physically; they have headaches, stomachaches, and nausea, and they vomit. Children may have a near-obsessive concern that parents will be hurt during an absence, or that they will never see their parents again. They may be subject to nightmares and insomnia, indeed, to an overwhelming sense of dread and apprehension that permeates their young lives and robs them of the simple pleasures that childhood can bring. Perhaps the sense of helplessness spoken of earlier aggravates a situation already grim in the eyes of the child.

The first day of school for an obviously frightened child.

School phobia

One childhood fear has attracted much attention, for not only is it disabling to the child and disruptive to the household, but it also appears to be a true phobia, an extreme avoidance that does not usually just go away with the passage of time. _School phobia,_ furthermore, has serious academic and social consequences for the youngster. Waldfogel (1959) offers the following definition.

> School phobia refers to a reluctance to go to school because of acute fear associated with it. Usually this dread is accompanied by somatic symptoms with the gastrointestinal tract the most commonly affected. . . .The somatic complaints come to be used as an auxiliary device to justify staying at home and often disappear when the child is reassured that he will not have to attend school. The characteristic picture is of a child nauseated or complaining of abdominal pain at breakfast and desperately resisting all attempts at reassurance, reasoning, or coercion to get him to school. In its milder forms, school phobia may be only a transient symptom; but when it becomes established, it can be one of the most disabling disorders of childhod, lasting even for years (pp. 35–36).

The frequency of school phobias has been estimated at 17 per 1000 children per year (Kennedy, 1965), and unlike most childhood disorders, they are more common in girls than in boys. School phobia is commonly thought to be rooted both in actual fear of being in school and in separation anxiety, but primarily in separation anxiety. Since the beginning of school is often the first circumstance that requires lengthy and frequent separations of children and their parents, separation anxiety is frequently a principal cause of school phobia.

If separation anxiety largely accounts for school phobias that commence with enrollment in school, how are the serious ones that develop later to be explained? Johnson and his colleagues (1941) have offered one interpretation.

First some environmental event, which may be related to the school setting itself, elicits increased anxiety in the child. At the same time the mother becomes increasingly anxious about some problem of her own. A dependent relationship between mother and child may then conspire to increase further the anxiety that occurs naturally when mother and child are separated by the child's going to school. Thus the child starts to avoid school, and the mother does not protest too strongly. She may even unwittingly reward the child's nonattendance for her own purposes. Given that the dependent relationship works both ways, the child being dependent on the mother and the mother being dependent on the child, the mother may not wish to lose her child to the school each day. Several factors may therefore conspire to keep the child from school. Initial, perhaps realistic, fears may make the young child withdraw from school to seek the comforting figure of her mother. This dependency on her mother is consoling and reinforces both mother and daughter for avoiding the feared situation. Finally, since the object of fear is not confronted, actual fears are not reduced and may, in fact, be worsened.

Treatment of childhood fears

How are childhood fears overcome? As Figure 15.3 indicates, many simply dissipate with time and maturation. Perhaps the most widespread means of helping children overcome fears, employed by millions of parents, is to expose them gradually to the feared object, often while acting simultaneously to inhibit their anxiety. If a little girl fears strangers, a parent takes her by the hand and walks her slowly toward the new person. Mary Cover Jones (see page 587) was the first psychologist to explain this bit of folk wisdom as a counterconditioning procedure.

Indeed, contemporary therapists have by and large built on folk wisdom in helping children overcome fears. *Exposure* is generally agreed to be the most effective way of eliminating fear and avoidance of something that does not merit caution and diffidence. Modeling has also proved effective, both in laboratory studies (for example, Bandura, Grusec, and Menlove, 1967) and in countless clinical treatments; another child, one the fearful child is likely to imitate, demonstrates fearless behavior. Offering rewards for moving closer to a feared object or situation can also en-

courage a child to venture forth. When the fear and avoidance of a school phobic child are very great and of long duration, they may require desensitization through direct graduated exposure plus operant shaping. The therapist started with walks to school with nine-year-old Paul. Next the boy, one step at a time on successive days, entered the schoolyard, then an empty classroom after school, attended the opening morning exercises and then left, sat at a desk, spent time in school, all with the therapist beside him, then with the therapist out of sight but still nearby. In the last steps, when anxiety seemed to have lessened, promises to play the guitar with Paul at night, comic books, and tokens that would eventually earn the boy a baseball glove were the enticements for attending school (Lazarus, Davison, and Polefka, 1965).

Finally, some new situations may be threatening, not only for children but for adults as well, because the person lacks the knowledge and skills to deal with them. Thus a child's fear of the water may very well be based on a reasonable judgment that danger lurks there because he or she cannot swim. Parents and therapists must see to it that children have the opportunity to acquire knowledge and relevant skills.

Social Withdrawal

Most classrooms have in attendance at least one or two children who are quiet and shy. Oftentimes these same children will play only with family members or familiar peers, avoiding strangers both young and old. Their shyness may prevent them from acquiring skills and participating in a variety of activities that most of their age-mates enjoy, for they avoid playgrounds and games played by neighborhood children. Although some youngsters who are shy may simply be "slow to warm up," withdrawn children never do, even after prolonged exposure to new people. Extremely shy children may refuse to speak at all in unfamiliar social circumstances; this is called _elective mutism_. In crowded rooms they cling and whisper to their parents, hide behind the furniture, and cower in corners. At home they ask their parents endless questions about situations that worry them.

Withdrawn children usually have warm and

Shy children keep to themselves at playgrounds.

satisfying relationships with family members and family friends, and they do show an eagerness for affection and acceptance. Because the point at which shyness or withdrawal becomes a problem varies, no statistics on the frequency of _social-withdrawal disorder_ have been compiled. The problem is assumed to be common, however, for it is readily observed in many social settings. Theories of the etiology of social withdrawal are not well worked out. It is often suggested that anxiety interferes with social interaction and thus causes the child to avoid social situations. Or withdrawn children may simply not have the social know-how that facilitates interaction with their age-mates. The finding that isolated children make fewer attempts to structure peer relations and are less imaginative in their play may indicate a deficiency in certain social skills. Finally, isolated children may have become so because they have in the past spent most of their time with adults; they do interact more freely with adults than with other children (Scarlett, 1980).

Treatment for withdrawal or social avoidance disorders is similar to the treatment of childhood fears. In one innovative study youngsters were shown films in which other isolated children gradually engage in and come to enjoy play with their peers (O'Connor, 1969). Shy children may

be given attention by day-care personnel and teachers as reinforcement for socializing with peers but none when they remain alone (Hart et al., 1968). They may also be taught skills needed for using play equipment, thus increasing the likelihood of social contact (Buell et al., 1968).

Affective Disorders in Childhood

Clinical reports in the literature describe what appear to be instances of both major depression and bipolar disorder in children. According to DSM-III, the symptoms of affective disorders of children are the same as those of adults. At the same time, however, there is controversy whether many children have affective disorders and how they should be defined (Lefkowitz and Burton, 1978).

Rutter, Tizard, and Whitmore (1970), using conservative criteria, conducted an extensive survey of children on the Isle of Wight; they found that fewer than one percent were depressed. In marked contrast, some other studies (for example, Weinberg et al., 1973) have reported much higher figures. The discrepancy hinges on two points. First, some of the behavior defining adult depression is common in childhood. For example, 37 percent of girls and 29 percent of boys

BOX 15.3 Play Therapy and Family Therapy—Two General Methods of Treating Childhood Problems

Many of the childhood disorders discussed in the present chapter, and even the more serious problems to be reviewed in the next, are treated by two general methods, _play therapy_ and _family therapy._

Children are usually less verbal than adults, at least in the sense that is needed for psychoanalytic and client-centered therapy. Moreover, children are often more reluctant than older clients to voice their concerns and complaints directly and openly. Through the pioneering work of Melanie Klein (1932) and Anna Freud (1946), play became a vehicle for delving into a child's unconscious, taking the place of the free association and recounting of dreams that means so much in analytic treatment of adults. It is assumed that in play therapy a child will express his or her feelings about problems, parents, teachers, and peers. A play therapy room is equipped with puppets, blocks, games, puzzles, drawing materials, paints, water, sand, clay, toy guns and soldiers, and a large inflated rubber clown, Bobo, to punch. These toys will, it is hoped, help draw out inner tensions and concerns. A dollhouse inhabited by parental and child dolls is a common fixture. The therapist may encourage a young male client to place the figures in "any room you wish," or to position the dolls in a way "that makes you feel good." The child may assemble members of the little family in the living room, except for the father, who is placed in his study. "What is Daddy doing?" the therapist will ask. "He's working. If he weren't such a meanie, he'd come out and play with the kids." The therapist will then, as he or she would for an adult, interpret for the boy the wish he seems reluctant to express openly. Little in the way of controlled research has been done to evaluate the claims made for play therapy by its adherents. What evidence is available, however, does not find it to be notably effective (Barrett, Hampe, and Miller, 1978; Levitt, 1971).

Whatever ultimate purposes may be served by play therapy, at the very least, it is likely to help the adult therapist establish rapport with a youngster. An adult client might respond favorably to a therapist who is empathic, kindly, and replete with professional degrees, but a little girl is likely to be suspicious and regard "Dr. X" as an ally of her parents or teacher with no real interest in her. Therapists of varying persuasions, including behavior therapists who would eschew the symbolic significance an analytic worker might see in the child's play, commonly use a play room to establish a relationship with a young client and perhaps also to determine from what the child says and does with toys the youngster's perspective of the problem.

Because children usually live with their parents and siblings, and because their lives are so inextricably bound up with them, many therapists examine and attempt to alter patterns of interactions in families rather than seeing the troubled child or young adolescent alone. Family therapy (page 635) too is practiced by therapists of all persuasions. Practitioners hold that the child's problem has been caused or is maintained by disturbed relationships within the family. For example, the father may have defaulted on his own responsibilities, forcing a male child to take a more adult role than he feels ready to assume. As we have pointed out many times, however, treatments that help alleviate a problem may in no way indicate its etiology. The fact that clarifying and altering disturbed family relationships relieves the disorders of children does not mean that the disturbed relationships themselves caused their problems in the first place. Many clinical reports and the intrinsic plausibility of family therapy suggest that future studies will back up claims of success made by enthusiasts.

have poor appetites at age six (MacFarlane, Allen, and Honzik, 1954). Should this relatively frequent behavior of eating little be given clinical significance? Studies that do will find more childhood depression. Second, some researchers have chosen a very broad range of behavior to indicate the presence of childhood depression. To this range they couple the notion of "masked depression." Behavior not considered indicative of depression in adults—such as hyperactivity, psychophysiological reactions, school problems, aggression—is nonetheless thought to reflect an "underlying" depression in children. Clearly, such an expansive definition, which is unsupported by data, means that a large number of diagnoses will probably be invalid.

In sum, affective disorders probably do occur in children, although they are likely to be rare. A good set of diagnostic criteria have yet to be established, and many important questions, such as whether childhood depression predicts depression in adulthood, have not yet been answered. Until the controversy over just what constitutes childhood depression is settled, such issues cannot be addressed.

Two Special Disorders of Childhood and Adolescence

A variety of other problems with psychological components occur either principally or exclusively during childhood and adolescence. Two of the most important and intriguing are _anorexia nervosa_ and _Gilles de la Tourette's syndrome._

Anorexia Nervosa

Anorexia nervosa[7] is a life-threatening disorder unaccounted for by any known physical disease. Serious weight loss, an intense fear of becoming obese, and a refusal to eat sufficiently to gain or maintain body weight are three principal symptoms of this mysterious disorder. The self-starvation imposed by anorexics brings about physiological changes sometimes difficult to reverse; estimates vary, but approximately 5 percent die. Another 25 percent of anorexics continue in the unremitting course of their disorder at two-year follow-up, and the remainder gain weight back as a result of treatment and over the course of time (Hsu, 1980).

Anorexia is far more common in girls than boys. Ratios as high as twenty female anorexics for every male have been reported; approximately one of every 200 school-aged girls is anorexic (Crisp, Palmer, and Klucy, 1976). Onset of the weight loss most commonly begins during adolescence, shortly after the beginning of menstruation. Amenorrhea, failure to menstruate regularly, is reported in almost all anorexic young women, often before weight loss has become noticeable. They begin losing weight because, being a little plump or sometimes obese, they decide to diet; but the dieting continues far beyond reasonable bounds. Anorexics may take laxatives and exercise extensively and frantically to lose weight. The manic energy expended in

---

[7] Anorexia nervosa is one of several _eating disorders_ described in DSM-III. The others are bulimia, which is episodic binge eating; pica, the eating of nonnutritive substances such as paint, plaster, hair, cloth, sand, bugs, leaves and pebbles; and rumination disorder of infancy, a potentially fatal problem in which the child regurgitates food, then ejects it or chews and reswallows it. A dramatic behavioral treatment of this disorder is described on page 708.

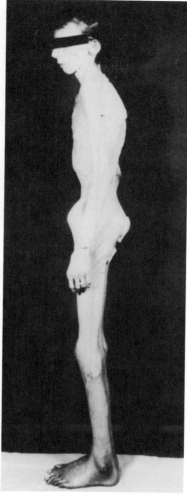

The eighteen-year-old woman dressed for dancing weighed 120 pounds, within the normal range for her five-foot, six-inch frame. She was married that year and immediately began to lose weight. Her menstrual periods also ceased. Nineteen years and a divorce later, she weighed only forty-seven pounds (right) and was in serious danger of dying when she was admitted to the University of Virginia Hospital, in December 1960. She was allowed mail, television, shampoos, and social contacts only when she ate and then only when she gained weight. She managed to add seventeen pounds in a little over three months in the hospital and then ten pounds in another eleven months as an outpatient. Readmitted because of her slow progress, she gained fourteen pounds in five weeks (far right) and was discharged. For four months she maintained this weight and even reached a high point of ninety pounds. Anorexia nervosa is often chronic, however. Sixteen years later this woman weighed fifty-five pounds (Bachrach, Erwin, and Mohr, 1965; Erwin, 1977).

excessive physical activity is amazing, considering their emaciation.

Anorexics are preoccupied with food, even when they are struggling not to ingest it. They become interested in its preparation, collecting cookbooks, trying new recipes, and planning and cooking elaborate meals of many courses and special dishes for others. Many anorexics do not admit to feeling any hunger, but others say they do feel hungry but force themselves not to eat. Admission to feeling hungry is associated with an eating pattern found in almost half of all anorexics, binge eating or bulimia. After ingesting enormous quantities of food, they self-induce vomiting, and therefore receive little or no nourishment. Anorexics who are bulimic are more

impulsive, depressed, and anxious than others and may be particularly difficult to treat (Casper et al., 1980; Garfinkel, Moldofsky, and Garner, 1980). Indeed, anorexics in general deny having a problem that needs treatment.

A commonly reported phenomenon of anorexia is a distorted body image. Despite their protruding ribs and hipbones, their skull-like faces, their broomstick limbs, anorexics do not view themselves as being too thin. Rather, in frequent scrutinizings of their figures in mirrors, they either continue to see themselves as too fat or feel that they have finally arrived at an attractive weight. Anorexics are often described as ''good'' girls. They are well-behaved, conscientious, quiet, and often perfectionistic. They frequently obtain better grades and score higher on IQ tests than controls (Bemis, 1978).

The etiology of anorexia nervosa

Theories accounting for anorexia are varied and largely unsubstantiated. Some psychological explanations of the disorder have been based on Freud's notion that eating can be a substitute for sexual expression. Thus the anorexic's refusal to eat is thought to indicate fear of increasing sexual desires or perhaps of oral impregnation (Ross, 1977). Learning theorists have suggested that anorexia may be a weight phobia (Crisp, 1967) or a striving to effect the image of the beautifully slim woman so extensively modeled and emulated by our society (Bemis, 1978). Others view anorexia as a reflection of conflict, between wanting to attain independence and selfhood within the family and a fear of growing up. Finally, a variety of organic explanations have been offered. Abnormal functioning of the part of the hypothalamus known to control how much we eat, sexual activity, and menstruation is perhaps the leading physiological theory, but specific abnormalities have not been found (Bemis, 1978).

Therapy for anorexia nervosa

The treatment of anorexia is really a two-tiered process. The immediate goal is to help the young woman gain weight in order to avoid medical complications and the possibility of death. An anorexic may have to be hospitalized if any food is to be gotten into her at all. And she has often become so weak and her physiological functioning so disturbed that she badly needs hospital treatment. Intravenous feeding will provide necessary nourishment in life-threatening situations. Behavior therapy programs in which the hospitalized anorexic is isolated as much as possible and given mealtime company, then periods of access to a television set, radio, or phonograph, walks with a student nurse, mail, and visitors as rewards for eating and weight gain have been successful in producing immediate increases in body weight. The second goal of treatment, long-term maintenance of gains in body weight, is not reliably achieved by medical, behavioral, or traditional psychodynamic interventions (Bemis, 1978).

One mode of treatment that may be able to produce long-term gains for anorexics is family therapy. Like most other treatments, family therapy has been insufficiently studied for its long-term effects. One report, however, suggests that as many as 86 percent of fifty anorectic daughters treated with their families were still functioning well when assessed at times ranging between three months to four years after treatment (Rosman, Minuchin, and Liebman, 1976). Salvador Minuchin and his colleagues, who represent but one of several "schools" of family therapy, have done considerable work on anorexia nervosa. The treatment they have developed is called _the family lunch session._

Before the specific treatment is described, a basic assumption in Minuchin's family treatment has to be made clear. He believes that "sick" family members, especially children, serve to deflect attention away from underlying conflict in family relationships. The illness is the family psychopathology become manifest, so to speak. In these families members are both rigid and deeply enmeshed in one another's lives, overprotect the children, and do not acknowledge conflicts. Thus the sickness acts to reduce friction surrounding these basic family disturbances. By providing an alternative focus of attention, the illness lessens the tension between family members. Minuchin believes that troubled families therefore act in a way that keeps the "sick" family member in the patient role (Minuchin et al., 1975). To treat the disorder, Minuchin attempts to redefine it as interpersonal rather than individual and to bring the family conflicts to the fore. Thus, it is theorized, the symptomatic family member is freed from having to maintain his or her problem for it not longer deflects attention from the dysfunctional family.

Families of anorexics are seen by the therapist during mealtime, since the conflicts related to anorexia are believed to be most evident then. There are three major goals for these lunch sessions: (1) changing the patient role of the anorexic; (2) redefining the eating problem as an interpersonal one; and (3) preventing the parents from using their child's anorexia as a means of avoiding conflict. One strategy is to instruct each parent to try individually to force the child to eat. The other parent may leave the room. The individual efforts are expected to fail. But through this failure and the frustration of each, the mother and father may now work *together* to persuade the child to eat. Thus, rather than being a focus of conflict, the child's eating will produce cooperation and increase parental effectiveness in dealing with the child (Rosman, Minuchin, and Liebman, 1975). Given the only moderate successes of other treatments devised for anorexics, family therapy appears promising.

Gilles de la Tourette's Syndrome

At age ten [Matthew] developed a hiccuping tic which was high pitched and whooping. Over the next three years sudden squatting and extension and retraction of the arms appeared. In the next year he developed a grabbing motion directed at his mother's breasts, accompanied by the vocal expletives "tits" and "titties." The last tics to appear were coprolalic[8] utterances of "shit," "God dammit," and "flutchy nay." (The patient explained that this was French for fornication.) The patient had been in psychotherapy for four years, but the condition had become progressively worse, and he was admitted to our hospital for evaluation and treatment in 1963 at age thirteen. On our ward he was observed to have approximately 106 tics per day with a verbal to motor ratio of ten to one. Neurological examination was normal and the WISC placed him in the normal range of intelligence.

The patient was placed on haloperidol [an antipsychotic drug]. His motor tics disappeared when dosage reached 6 milligrams daily and vocal tics vanished in the next few days. On discharge from the hospital in September 1963, the parents felt that his medication had not been "stabilized" because he was quite sleepy and drooled. . . .Two years later, his parents were well pleased with the control of his symptoms and stated that only under stress were there two or three disguised and very mild tics per day (Jenkins and Fine, 1976, pp. 50–51).

In 1885 Gilles de la Tourette, a French physician, described eight patients who had a history of making bizarre and often profane involuntary vocalizations and who also had a variety of mo-

tor tics. The unusual nature of the symptoms of those afflicted with what has since been called Tourette's syndrome has frequently attracted clinical attention, although the disorder is exceedingly rare. An international registry reports only 485 cases known to exist worldwide (Abuzzahab and Anderson, 1976). But other estimates of frequency are higher, for example one case per 10,000 people. Bizarre verbalizations and motor tics occur together in almost all cases of the disorder. "Barking" sounds, clicks, grunts, yelps, sniffs, coughs, profanity, and palilalia, repeating one's own last words and phrases, are some of the involuntary spewings. Motor tics, which are repetitive and rapid and are most frequently seen in the face and upper extremities, include eye blinking, facial grimacing, and jerking of the arms. The tics and swearing can be voluntarily suppressed for short periods of time. Onset of the disorder occurs before twelve years of age in 75 percent of the cases and before twenty years in 96 percent of them. The disorder is about twice as common in males as in females (Anderson and Abuzzahab, 1976). Despite the unusual nature of the symptoms, the disorder is so rare that it is often misdiagnosed. Golden (1977), for example, found that of seventeen cases only one was initially diagnosed correctly. The others were called "habit disorders" or simple tics, or the patients were diagnosed as having organic problems.

A variety of psychogenic and somatogenic hypotheses have been offered as explanations of Tourette's syndrome, but no one hypothesis has received convincing support (Anderson and Abuzzahab, 1976). Most professionals today suspect some form of organic involvement because similar symptoms are found in patients in a number of Western and Eastern countries and because the antipsychotic medication haloperidol is able to reduce symptoms. Although research evidence is not strong, it is possible that the disorder is an infection of the central nervous system. Furthermore, genetic factors are implicated. Occasionally families are found in which several members have Tourette's syndrome (Anderson and Abuzzahab, 1976), and relatives of those with the syndrome often have tics, perhaps a milder form of the disorder (Kidd, Prusoff, and Cohen, 1980).

[8] Coprolalia is the irresistible urge to use obscene language.

Most psychogenic explanations of Tourette's syndrome have been abandoned. Still, the frequently obscene nature of the involuntary speech and a notable increase of symptomatology during times of stress (Anderson and Abuzzahab, 1976) suggest at least some psychogenic component of the disorder. Psychological treatment may benefit those with Tourette's syndrome in one way, helping them adjust to living a lifetime with a bizarre, embarrassing, and at present incurable disorder.

Summary

DSM-III has greatly expanded the range of diagnosis applicable to children. Specific developmental deviations are diagnoses given children whose behavior differs from age-appropriate norms in a specific area of development. Enuresis, for example, is diagnosed when children older than three and a half continue to wet the bed or themselves while awake. Although no theory of enuresis has strong support, a treatment based on learning principles and using a bell and pad is quite successful. Children with learning disabilities, which are also specific developmental disorders, do poorly in reading or mathematics, even though they are believed to have the capacity to achieve greater mastery. Theories of learning disabilities blame either perceptual deficits, for example, seeing letters reversed, or faulty instructional techniques. Special instruction coupled with dispensing rewards has been successful.

Hyperactivity and conduct problems are disorders of undercontrolled behavior. The hyperactive child is too active in situations that call for sitting still and has problems in maintaining attention. The attentional problems of hyperactives are often viewed as primary; in fact, DSM-III's diagnosis is attention deficit disorder with hyperactivity. Genetic studies, evidence of neurological problems, and the fact that hyperactivity can be induced by head injuries, brain diseases, and lead poisoning point to a physiological cause. The role of parents, either as causing or exacerbating the disorder, is also supported by some data. Stimulant drugs and rewards for sitting still and doing homework help to calm hyperactive children. Conduct disorders cover aggression, lying, theft, vandalism, and other acts and attitudes deemed unacceptable by others. A genetic predisposition, marital discord of parents, modeling and direct reinforcement of deviant behavior, and living in city slums are considered etiological factors. Reinforcement of prosocial behavior and teaching specific academic skills have proved promising interventions.

School phobia, social withdrawal, and depression are disorders of overcontrolled behavior. School phobia, a fear of and refusal to go to school, is usually treated by gradual exposure to the feared situation, sometimes coupled with rewards for attending school. Children who withdraw socially are assumed to do so because of anxiety and poor social skills; treatments then are directed either at the anxiety or at reinforcing social interaction and building social skills. The frequency of depression in children is not known for certain. Nor do we know whether depressed children have symptoms different from those of depressed adults. Play therapy and family therapy are often applied to disorders of overcontrolled behavior.

The final two disorders discussed are enigmas. In anorexia nervosa the individual does not eat enough to maintain a healthy weight and, if not stopped, starves herself to death. It is much more common in girls and begins in adolescence. None of the several theories of anorexia—fear of becoming sexually mature, weight phobia, striving for the slim image so esteemed by our society, conflict between wanting selfhood within the family and a fear of growing up, and physiological dysfuncitons—has much support. Treatment of the disorder is difficult, although family therapy appears promising. In Gilles de la Tourette's syndrome, a rare condition, the person has motor tics and makes bizarre, often profane, vocalizations. The disorder is likely to have a physiological basis and responds favorably to drug therapy.

■ ■

chapter 16

MENTAL RETARDATION AND INFANTILE AUTISM

Mental Retardation
Pervasive Disorders of Childhood
Infantile Autism

Mental retardation and infantile autism are two very serious and tragic disorders of childhood. Not only can both of these disorders be extremely severe, in which case they are lifelong and affect all of it, but they are similar in a number of respects. The majority of autistic children score in the retarded range on intelligence tests. And many retarded children make ritualistic hand movements, body-rock, and are injurious to themselves, actions which are just about *sine qua nons* for autism. Both autism and the moderate, severe, and profound forms of mental retardation become evident in infancy or in very early childhood.

Mental Retardation

"What is retardation? It's hard to say. I guess it's having problems thinking." More technical descriptions of mental retardation will be presented, along with theories of some of the causes of this disorder, but we have not encountered a more straightforward definition than this one. It is particularly meaningful and poignant because it comes from a twenty-six-year-old man who, at the age of fifteen, was placed in a state institution for the retarded. An account of his life, in his own words, indicates his sensitivity, warmth, and thoughtfulness.

When I was born the doctors didn't give me six months to live. My mother told them she could keep me alive, but they didn't believe it. It took a hell of a lot of work, but she showed with love and determination that she could be the mother to a handicapped child. I don't know for a fact what I had, but they thought it was severe retardation and cerebral palsy. They thought I would never walk. I still have seizures. . . .

When I was at school, concentrating was almost impossible. . . . That was my major problem all through school that I daydreamed. I think all people do that. It wasn't related to retardation. I think a lot of kids do that and are diagnosed as retarded, but it has nothing to do with retardation at all. It really has to do with how people deal with the people around them and their situations. . . . I kind of stood in the background—I kind of knew that I was different—I knew that I had a problem, but when you're young you don't think of it as a problem. . . . The problem is getting labeled as being something. After that you're not really as a person [sic]. . . . In the fifth grade—in the fifth grade my classmates thought I was different, and my teacher knew I was different. One day she looked at me and she was on the phone to the office. Her conversation was like this, "When are you going to transfer him?". . . . She looked at me and knew I was knowledgeable about what she was saying.

My mother protected me. . . . I can remember trying to be like the other kids and having my mother right there pulling me away. . . . Sometimes I think the pain of being handicapped is that people give you so much love that it becomes a weight on you and a weight on them.

[When he was fifteen, the young man's parents died, and after brief stays with family friends and at an orphanage, he and his sister were sent to a state school.] Right before they sent me and my sister to the State School, they had six psychologists examine us to determine how intelligent we were. I think that was a waste of time. They asked me things like, "What comes to mind when I say 'Dawn'?"—so you say, "Light." Things like that. What was tough was putting the puzzles together and the mechanical stuff. They start out very simple and then they build it up and it gets harder and harder. . . . Another guy I talked to was a psychiatrist. That was rough. For one thing I was mentally off guard. . . . You don't figure what they're saying and how your're answering it and what it all means—not until the end. When the end came, I was a ward of the State. . . . When the psychiatrist interviewed me he had my records in front of him—so he already knew I was mentally retarded. It's the same with everyone. If you are considered mentally retarded there is no way you can win. . . .

I don't like the word vegetable, but in my own case I could see that if I had been placed on the low grade ward I might have slipped to that. I began feeling myself slip. . . . If I would have let that place get to me and de-

press me I would still have been there today. . . . They had me scheduled to go to P-8—a back ward. . . . There was this supervisor, a woman. She came on to the ward and looked right at me and said: "I have him scheduled for P-8." An older attendant was there. He looked over at me and said, "He's too bright for that ward. I think we'll keep him." . . . She made a remark under her breath that I looked pretty retarded to her. . . .

Of course I didn't know what P-8 was then, but I found out. I visited up there a few times on work detail. That man saved my life. . . . At that point I'm pretty positive that if I went there I would have fitted in and I would still be there. . . .

It's funny. You hear so many people talking about IQ. The first time I ever heard the expression was when I was at Empire State School. I didn't know what it was or anything, but some people were talking and they brought the subject up. It was on the ward, and I went and asked one of the staff what mine was. They told me forty-nine. Forty-nine isn't fifty, but I was pretty happy about it. I mean I figured that I wasn't a low grade. I really didn't know what it meant, but it sounded pretty high. Hell, I was born in 1948 and forty-nine didn't seem too bad. Forty-nine didn't sound hopeless. I didn't know anything about the highs or the lows, but I knew I was better than most of them. . . .

[Eight years later the young man was discharged. He has been working as a janitor and living in a boardinghouse with other former residents of state institutions. His thoughts go to a young woman named Joan, whom he had met at the institution.] Is there still any magnetism between that woman and me? I haven't seen her in three months, but there is still something, I can tell. . . . We got pretty close psychologically and physically—not that I did anything. They don't have programs at the Association for Retarded Children that say to adults you are an adult and you can make it. . . . The first time I noticed her was in the eating area; I was having lunch. I looked around and she was the only one there that attracted me. There was just something about her. . . .

Being at the State School and all you never have the chances romantically like you might living on the outside. I guess I was always shy with the opposite sex even at Empire. We did have dances and I felt that I was good looking, but I was bashful and mostly sat. I was bashful with Joan at the movie. In my mind I felt funny, awkward. I didn't know how to approach her. Should I hug her? You can't hug the hell out of her because you don't know how she would take it. You have all the feeling there, but you don't know what direction to go in. If you put your arm around her she might scream and you're finished. If she doesn't scream you're still finished. . . .

As I got older I slowly began to find myself becoming mentally awake. I found myself concentrating. Like on the television. A lot of people wonder why I have good grammar. It was because of the television. I was like a tape recorder—what I heard I memorized. Even when I was ten to twelve I would listen to Huntley and Brinkley. They were my favorites. As the years went by I understood what they were talking about. People were amazed at what I knew. People would ask me what I thought about this and that. Like my aunt would always ask me about the news— what my opinions were. I began to know that I was a little brighter than they thought I was. . . .

I don't know. Maybe I used to be retarded. That's what they said anyway. I wish they could see me now. I wonder what they'd say if they could see me holding down a regular job and doing all kinds of things. I bet they wouldn't believe it (Bogdan and Taylor, 1976, pp. 47–52).

The foregoing comes from edited transcripts of conversations between this man and two psychologists who came to know him. Bogdan and Taylor hold the view that retardation is nothing more than a social construct, a label rather arbitrarily applied to other human beings. They object to the unfortunately widespread tendency to draw sharp distinctions between the "normal" and the "retarded," and their apparent purpose in publishing the article containing the transcripts was to argue how faulty and damaging such generalizations are.

It is important to consider seriously this line of argument, for as the research and theorizing on retardation are reviewed, we must resist the tendency to dehumanize the people so labeled. A person may have "problems thinking," but he is still able to have his feelings hurt, to know justifiable anger, to love, to marry and have children, and to reflect on his life and where it seems to be going. In other words, his commonalities with those of us who score well on the standard tests and who adapt relatively easily are to be appreciated as well as his differences.

But, as will become clear in this chapter, we ourselves cannot accept the thesis that mental retardation is nothing more than a social label. Although there is an important gray area between the intellectually normal and those of subnormal IQ, and yes, although to be labeled mentally retarded can be demeaning, consistent differences *do* exist between retardates and normal individuals, and careful consideration of these differences by behavioral scientists will bring greater understanding, help, and tolerance.

According to DSM-III, the diagnostic criteria for mental retardation are significantly subaverage general intellectual functioning, deficits or impairments in adaptive behavior, and an onset of these difficulties before the age of eighteen. A low IQ score does not by itself designate an individual as a mental retardate; he or she must also experience difficulties adapting to the natural and social demands of everyday living in the home and community. Moreover, the problems of retardates manifest themselves early in life, at least by the eighteenth year and usually much before, distinguishing them from those whose intelligence is impaired later in life, through a severe brain injury, for example. Thus three variables must be considered in deciding whether a person is mentally retarded: measured IQ, degree of social adaptation, and whether the difficulties were early in onset. A diagnosis of mental retardation, DSM-III states, may be made whether or not another disorder is also judged to be present. Indeed, in addition to their mental difficulties, severely and profoundly retarded people almost always have neurological problems—neuromuscular, vision, and hearing abnormalities and sometimes seizures, all of which are coded on axis III. And, especially in these more serious cases, self-injurious and self-stimulatory behavior are often found as well.

Classification and Diagnosis of Mental Retardation

Levels of retardation
Four levels of mental deficiency are now recognized by the DSM, each of them a specific subaverage range on the far left of the normal distribution curve of measured intelligence (see page 36). The significant problems in social ad-

aptation that people who score in these ranges must also have to be considered retarded are discussed later in this section. In the United States those considered retarded by these two measures number close to seven million. The following is a summary of how individuals at each level of mental retardation are described by Robinson and Robinson (1976).

Mild Mental Retardation (50 to 70 IQ)   The mildly retarded comprise about 80 percent of all those who have IQs less than 70. They are not always distinguishable from normal youngsters until the age when they enter school. As children they are eligible for special classes for the educable mentally retarded. By their late teens they can usually learn academic skills at about a sixth-grade level. As adults they are likely to be able to maintain themselves in unskilled jobs or in sheltered workshops, although they may need help with social and financial problems. Only about one percent are ever institutionalized, usually in adolescence for behavior problems. Most of the mildly retarded show no signs of brain pathology and are members of families whose intelligence and socioeconomic levels are low.

Moderate Mental Retardation (35 to 49 IQ)   About 12 percent of those with IQs of less than 70 are moderately retarded. Brain damage and other pathologies are frequent. The moderately retarded may have physical defects and neurological dysfunctions that hinder fine motor skills, such as grasping and coloring within lines, and gross motor skills, such as running and climbing. During childhood these individuals are eligible for special classes for trainable retardates in which the development of self-care skills rather than academic achievement is emphasized. The moderately retarded are unlikely to progress beyond the second-grade level in academic subjects and can manage this learning only in later childhood or as adults. They may, however, learn to travel alone in a familiar locality. Many are institutionalized. Although most can do useful work, few hold jobs except in sheltered workshops or in family businesses. Most live dependently within the family. Few have friends of their own, but they may be left alone without supervision for several hours at a time. Their retardation is likely to be identified in infancy or early childhood, for their sensorimotor coordina-

tion remains poor, and they are slow to develop verbal and social skills. In contrast to mildly retarded children, moderate retardates and those more seriously retarded are found in all socioeconomic groups.

Severe Mental Retardation (20 to 34 IQ)   About 7 percent of those with IQs of less than 70 are severely retarded. They commonly have congenital physical abnormalities and limited sensorimotor control. Most are institutionalized and require constant aid and supervision. For children in this group to be able to speak and take care of their own basic needs requires prolonged training; the self-care training that is provided in the special classes within the school system is usually inadequate except for the upper portion of this group. As adults the severely retarded may be friendly but can usually communicate only briefly on a very concrete level. They engage in very little independent activity and are often lethargic, for their severe brain damage leaves them relatively passive and the circumstances of their lives allow them little stimulation. They may be able to perform very simple work under close supervision. Genetic disorders and environmental insults, such as severe oxygen deprivation at birth, account for most of this degree of retardation.

Profound Mental Retardation (below 20 IQ)   Less than one percent of the retarded are profoundly so, requiring total supervision and often nursing care all their lives. Very little training is usually given them because it is assumed that they can learn little except possibly to walk, utter a few phrases, feed themselves, and use the toilet. Many have severe physical deformities as well as neurological damage and cannot get around on their own. There is a very high mortality rate during childhood.

These categories are difficult to apply, partly because of the assessment devices that are used to measure intelligence and adaptive behavior, and partly because human beings seldom lend themselves to precise categorization. Moreover, the social implications of labeling a child as mildly or moderately retarded must be considered. Ross (1974) points out that social agencies, such as schools, make inferences about the future development of children with low IQ scores, and that these expectations affect markedly the kind of educational settings in which such children are placed. A child labeled as moderately retarded is generally judged to be "trainable." Those who are categorized as mildly retarded are considered "educable." Educable children are expected eventually to reach a sixth-grade level of academic achievement, but trainables are generally considered able to learn very little of the subject matter usually taught in schools. So-called trainable children tend not to be given adequate opportunity to surpass the levels that are expected of them, which means, as Ross points out, that the prophecy of low achievement is self-fulfilling.

Over the past two hundred years attitudes have swung like a pendulum from optimism and interest in educating the "feeble-minded" to bleak pessimism. Édouard Seguin, a French physician and educator of the nineteenth century, was convinced that education was a universal right and that "idiots" were among the neediest. Considering mental retardation a weakness in the nervous system, he devised teaching methods to correct specific disabilities. After leaving Paris in 1848, he settled in Ohio and was instrumental in setting up special schools throughout the northeastern United States, one of them the Pennsylvania Training School for Idiots.[1] But disillusionment set in later in the century when the goals that had been confidently worked toward earlier were not attained. The children did not become normal, and the institutions grew and grew. Perhaps the retarded were just "born that way" and little could be done for them, except to maintain them and protect them from the intellectual demands of society. In the past few decades of this century, there have been more serious and systematic attempts to educate the retarded to as full an extent as possible. These efforts were spurred on, no doubt, by the infusion of federal moneys initiated by President Kennedy, himself the brother of a retarded woman (Crissey, 1975). Some retarded children have acquired skills that they were formerly thought incapable of learning. If such successes continue, the descriptions

of each level of retardation may have to be revised.

Intelligence test scores as a criterion

Because the principal means of diagnosing mental retardation are the IQ tests that are currently available, we should examine the nature of these tests (see page 98). An intelligence quotient[2] is actually nothing more than what an IQ test measures, even though the concept of intelligence has seemingly been reified by these tests, made into "a thing" that exists "out there."

When people take an IQ test, they demonstrate how many problems of those that are being presented to them—whether they be to generate definitions of words or to manipulate small colored blocks to form a design—they can solve at that particular time and place. Scores on IQ tests do allow useful predicitons to be made; Binet, for example, succeeded in predicting school performance on the basis of his test. Current IQ tests are similarly good at predicting academic performance. And people can be categorized by IQ scores so that other aspects of their behavior are anticipated. But the predictive validity of the intelligence test should not blind us to the fact that intelligence itself is a construct, an entity which is inferred as actually existing and supposedly generating measurable phenomena, but which is not at present, and perhaps never will be, fully observable.

Traditional IQ tests pose special problems when they are used to diagnose mental retardation.

1. Most IQ tests have not been standardized on nonwhite populations or institutionalized populations, groups that are heavily represented in the prevalence figures for mental retardation. Items that sample intelligent behavior of a white noninstutionalized population may be very different from those that ought to be used to measure the intelligent behavior of

---

[1] The reader will note how the connotative meanings of terms change. Nowadays health professionals would never use the word idiot, let alone include it in the name of an institution.

[2] Since the late 1930s the intelligence quotient has represented what is technically called a "deviation IQ." Although the mathematics need not concern us here [see Anastasi (1968), for example, for particulars], a person's raw score—the number of test items he or she passes—is transformed into a deviation IQ, which indicates how far the raw score falls away from the average raw score obtained by the age group on which a given test was standardized.

a nonwhite institutionalized population of retardates.

2. Few of the intelligence tests have been validated for IQ scores of less than 70. Individuals of low intellectual functioning were not adequately represented in the groups taking the tests when the scales were being compiled and standardized.

3. Many diagnoses of retardation are made when the child is quite young, less than five years of age. Measurements of the intelligence of very young children do not necessarily correlate highly with those obtained when the child is older, although extremely low scores do predict subnormal intellectual functioning later in childhood.

4. The most reliable and frequently used tests for measuring the intelligence of children, the Stanford-Binet Intelligence Scale and the Wechsler Intelligence Scale for Children (WISC), were not devised to take into account other problems of the mentally retarded that may contribute to their poor performance on an IQ test. The intelligence of blind, deaf, and nonverbal individuals is extremely difficult to assess by either of these instruments, for children who are handicapped in these ways are physically unable to complete all parts of the tests. Those with poor motor coordination may work out an intellectual solution to a problem but have trouble translating it into the verbal or motor behavior required by the test. For these reasons special IQ tests have been developed for the blind, the Hayes-Binet; for the deaf, the Hiskey Nebraska; and for the nonverbal, for whom the second half of the WISC, the performance section of the test, is typically used.

5. Before the IQ test is given, the tester must establish a degree of rapport with the child in order to obtain maximum performance. A poor black child may not readily be put at ease by a white middle-class psychologist. But it is also unclear whether a black psychologist will necessarily "pull" maximum performance from a black child, or a white psychologist maximum performance from a

white child. The important point, however, is that establishing a relaxed atmosphere is especially necessary, for testing may present special problems for the retarded child.

6. Zigler, Butterfield, and Capobianco (1970) have shown that an institution can be a very socially depriving place for a child. When being tested the retarded child's atypical need for social reinforcement may make him attend too much to the adult and look to him for solutions to the test problems. The "outer-directedness" of the retarded child can keep him from concentrating on the tasks, resulting in a spuriously low IQ score.

The problems in testing the IQs of the retarded suggest that the scores obtained cannot be regarded as unerringly valid indicators of their intelligence. At the same time, however, such tests have proved useful in providing information about retardates and in predicting their later intellectual and social achievements.

Adaptive behavior as a criterion
In addition to intelligence, adaptive behavior must be assessed in determining whether a person is mentally retarded. Adaptive behavior is described as the degree to which "an individual meets the standards of personal independence and social responsibility expected of his or her age and cultural group" (DSM-III, p. 37). Unfortunately, there are few objective measures of adaptive behavior. The Vineland Social Maturity Scale (Doll, 1953) is perhaps the best measure currently available, although its norms are not as firmly established as those of the IQ tests. This scale is composed of 117 activities grouped into 8 categories of behavior. An interviewer asks a person well acquainted with the child, often a parent, to evaluate how well the child performs a variety of socially adaptive behaviors. Several sample items are shown in Table 16.1.

The adaptive skills a child is expected to learn are caring for the self; acquiring concepts of time and money; being able to use tools, to shop, and to travel by public transportation; and becoming socially responsive and self-directive. The adolescent is expected to be able to apply academic skills, reasoning, and judgment to daily living and to participate in group activities.

TABLE 16.1
Sample Items from Vineland Social Maturity Scale with Age at Which Performance Is Expected
(from Doll, 1953)

Age	Item
0–1	pulls self upright does not drool
1–2	pulls off socks eats with spoon
2–3	asks to go to toilet dries own hands
3–4	plays cooperatively at kindergarten level buttons coat or dress
4–5	uses pencil or crayon for drawing washes face unassisted
5–6	prints simple words is trusted with money
6–7	uses table knife for spreading goes to bed unassisted
7–8	tells time to quarter hour combs or brushes hair
8–9	uses tools or untensils reads on own initiative
9–10	makes minor purchases goes about town freely

The adult, of course, is expected to be self-supporting and to assume social responsibilities.

Experimental Study of Specific Cognitive Processes

Intellectual functioning is for the most part judged on the basis of IQ scores, but a particular score provides only limited information on *how* a person thinks. The WISC may reveal that a child does very poorly on block design tasks (Figure 16.1), but why? What is there about the problem solving of this task that is particularly difficult and that psychologists might study? In the picture completion subtest of the WISC a series of pictures are presented to the child one at a time. He or she must identify the important part that is missing from each picture. This and other subtests have proved effective in picking out retardates. But what are the deficiencies in thinking that they reveal?

Laboratory testing of the retardate

Experimental psychologists have for years divided intelligence into particular functions such as perception, motor skills, short-term memory, long-term memory, speech, discrimination learning, and other phenomena and have studied them in laboratories. But they have usually tested these functions in individuals whose IQ scores and social behavior are well within the normal range, if not above average. Since the early 1960s, many workers have been studying experimentally, in laboratory settings, the intellectual behavior or mental retardates, giving careful consideration to the specific intellectual functions that are poorly developed in them. Approaching mental retardation in this fashion would seem to have some advantages. Experimentalists may one day be able to isolate variables that underlie subnormal functioning. Through comparison studies they may find out how the learning of retardates differs from that of normal children, and through special studies of retardates they may determine what factors might help them to achieve better patterns and levels of performance.

The developmental versus defect controversy

Much of the experimental research in mental retardation has been devoted to determining whether the retarded person is *quantitatively* or *qualitatively* different from the normal person in thinking and learning processes. The essential question is whether the retardate's cognitive development is the same as that of a normal person but proceeding at a slower rate—the developmental position; or whether he or she suffers from some cognitive deficit that makes intellectual functioning different from that of normal persons—the defect position.

The major developmental theorist is Zigler (1969). He is concerned with the *cultural-familial retarded,* those who have no demonstrated brain pathology, are mildly retarded, and have at least one parent or sibling who is also retarded. He believes that the cultural-familial retardate "is characterized by a slower progression through the same sequence of cognitive stages . . . and a more limited upper stage of cognition . . . than is characteristic of the individual of average intellect" (p. 537).

Milgram (1973) is one of the major defect or difference theorists. His research attempts to isolate specific deficiencies of the retarded to which their low IQs can be attributed, with the hope that eventually deficiencies can be modified or retarded learning can at least be better understood.

The specific qualitative deficiency Milgram is concerned with is the failure of retardates to think of mediators to help them associate words. In a _paired-associates learning_ task, for example, an individual is given several pairs of words to learn, cat–tree, spoon–table, knife–wall. Later he or she is given only the first item of each pair—cat, spoon, knife—and is required to recall the second item—tree, table, wall. Normal children commonly form verbal mediators to link the items of a pair—for example, the phrase "the CAT ran up the TREE." Milgram has argued that because retarded children do not usually form such mediators, they do poorly on this type of task. In support of his argument, he administered a paired-associates test to retarded and normal children under two conditions. First the children were given only the paired words, but in the second round the children were provided a mediator for each pair. The retarded children performed more poorly than the nonretarded _only when mediators were not provided,_ confirming the hypothesis that retarded children have trouble producing verbal mediators.

The short-term memory, selective attention, distractibility, and physiological arousal of the mentally retarded have also been studied in the attempt to discover particular deficiencies. They predictably have poor short-term memory and a brief attention span; they are also distractible and anxious. But in comparing normal children and retardates on laboratory cognitive tasks, investigators have great difficulty controlling the motivational, environmental, and educational variables other than intelligence that might con-

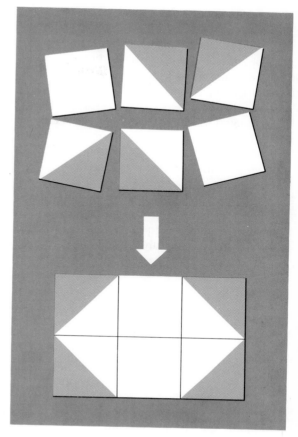

FIGURE **16.1**
In the WISC block design test, blocks and a series of printed designs are presented to the examinee. He or she has to construct the design using the varicolored blocks. Each block has a white side, a colored side, and a side that is half and half, as well as sides with irrelevant colors.

tribute to poor cognitive performance. It is still unclear how best to account for the consistently poor performance of retarded children on these tasks. The developmental versus defect controversy remains a lively one.

The contributions of Piaget
A further attempt to study the mental processes that may underlie mental retardation comes from the tradition of work that originated with the famous Swiss researcher Jean Piaget (for example, 1952; Ginsburg and Opper, 1969), and more particularly with his associate Bärbel Inhelder.

Piaget began studying the growth of intelligence and problem solving in normal children in the 1920s. His efforts to understand the development of adaptive behavior were probably more ambitious and more creative than the work of any other single theorist in this field. It is not surprising that in recent years investigators have attempted to understand mental retardation in Piagetian terms. Before we review some of these efforts, it will be useful to outline briefly Piaget's view of the growth of intelligence.[3]

Piaget was a cognitive theorist, for he believed that human behavior must be understood in terms of how people construe their world, how they attempt to alter it to meet their needs, and how they change their own way of thinking and behaving in order to work within the constraints of their surroundings. Although identified professionally as a psychologist, Piaget was in fact trained as a zoologist. Perhaps this accounts for the notion central to his theory, that cognitive abilities develop in stages. At each stage the individual acquires not a simple quantitative advance in "brainpower" but a *qualitatively different* way of grappling with experience. Piaget's stages of intellectual growth are similar in concept to Freud's psychosexual stages of development. Neither theorist ignored the *interaction* between organism and environment, but both Piaget and Freud postulated a predetermined set of developmental stages through which every human being is thought to progress—unless, of course, there is some sort of aberration in development.

Birth to Two Years: The Period of Sensorimotor Intelligence   At the beginning of the first period, the innate reflexes of infancy, such as sucking, have already been acquired. By the end the ability to manipulate objects and even to anticipate the consequences of behavior has been developed. The very young child gradually learns to perceive, to recognize aspects of the environment, and to realize that he or she can have a predictable effect on it. The child knows that a rattle will move and make noise if grasped and shaken. Sensorimotor intelligence is essentially knowing by doing; presumably the young child does not have an internal, symbolic representa-

tion of the world. According to Piaget, the child is not interested in or capable of understanding *why* behavior affects things, only in the fact that it does. The child's thoughts are very much bound by concrete objects that are immediately in view, although the child eventually realizes that they continue to exist even when not seen. More reflective intelligence is assumed to develop in the next stage.

Two to Seven Years: The Period of Preoperational Thought   The hallmark of this stage of development is the emergence of internal representations of the external world, in other words, images and thoughts about what may not be immediately present. Of course the acquisition of language is the most obvious and remarkable feature of these five years, and much of the child's language is conceptual—it reflects an increasing ability to transcend time and space, to think of the past, present, and future.

These are impressive gains, but preoperational intelligence is still limited. Piaget finds children in this period of development to be egocentric, unable to adopt differing points of view about problems. They tend not to reflect on their own thought processes, on how logical or illogical they are. Perhaps the best-known limitation of this stage of thinking is the difficulty children have in conserving volume. In one way of demonstrating this phenomenon, a child is first presented with identical tall, thin beakers containing equal amounts of water. After the child has agreed that both beakers contain exactly the same amount of liquid, the contents of one of the beakers are poured into a shorter but wider container. The child is then asked whether these two containers have the same amounts of water in them. A preoperational child usually answers no and states that the tall, thin beaker contains more. The child has focused on one salient characteristic of the beakers, namely their height, and has assumed that "taller" means "bigger in volume," which in this instance is not so. The child has not conserved volume when shape was changed.

Seven to Eleven Years: The Period of Concrete Operations   The principal advance at this stage is the acquisition of well-organized cognitive systems, such as notions of time, space, and number and the ability to add and subtract, to esti-

[3] Much of the following discussion of Piaget is based on Robinson and Robinson (1976).

mate and approximate. Piaget's theorizing becomes unusually intricate at this point, so suffice it to say that the child now thinks more and more like an adult—logically and in a complex fashion.

Eleven Years Onward: The Period of Formal Operations This final, highest stage of intellectual development frees the child and adult from the close dependence on concrete, external objects that characterizes the three preceding stages of thought. During the period of formal operations the person can deal with the hypothetical, the possible. Readers can demonstrate this kind of thinking to themselves by formulating an experiment, such as one to test the effects of toilet training on adult attitudes toward parents. In designing such a study, they will be fully immersed in abstract, logical thinking.

Piaget's concepts and his research with normal children offer a way of *describing* the cognitive deficits of retarded children that takes the psychologist much farther than the mere reporting of an IQ score. In fact, Bärbel Inhelder (1968), one of Piaget's closest associates, has described different levels of retardation in terms of cognitive patterns à la Piaget, and her observations have been confirmed by others. She has found, for example, that severely and profoundly retarded adults (IQ from below 20 to 34) have not progressed beyond the sensorimotor stage; moderately retarded adults (IQ 35 to 49) are limited to preoperational thought; and mildly retarded people (IQ 50 to 70) are unable to pass beyond the concrete operations stage. And yet, as we have come to expect, people do not fit this neatly into categories. In general, although the overall findings in Piagetian research lend some support to Inhelder's observations, many retarded children and adults shift back and forth, showing at different times lesser or greater ability to solve problems that are believed to require one or another kind of thinking. As enthusiastic as they are about Piaget's theory, Robinson and Robinson (1976), in their classic text on mental retardation, caution against falling into the trap of expecting all retarded children of a given IQ to function alike in Piagetian terms.

Robinson and Robinson (1976) have discussed other ways in which Piaget's theorizing has contributed to our understanding of mental retarda-

tion, and in particular how it has affected our general attitudes. As we have seen, the theory emphasizes *qualitative* changes in thinking as a person matures and, as such, is consistent with Milgram's position. According to Piaget, knowledge does not simply get added on through experience, rather, individuals deal with their surroundings *differently* as they pass from stage to stage. Piaget's theory encourages (or should encourage) workers to appreciate the unique capabilities of retarded persons rather than emphasizing their obvious limitations.

Piaget was not concerned with the possibility that children might be taught more effectively by developing their cognitive competencies to the fullest as they become evident. But his theory promises to guide other workers in planning curricula suited for children at particular levels of intellectual development (Ginsburg and Opper, 1969). And his work offers clues to what the *content* of remedial programs should be if they are to challenge the retarded child just enough to maintain interest and curiosity, yet not be so difficult that they contribute to feelings of helplessness and incompetence.

Organic Causes of Mental Retardation

The several forms of mental retardation are likely to be caused by any number of factors or combinations thereof. Through the years the issue of whether mental retardation should be attributed primarily to organic factors or to the environment has aroused great controversy. But this debate has really focused on only one level of the disorder, the first, mild retardation. Zigler (1968), Robinson and Robinson (1976), and others following their lead make a distinction between mild retardation on the one hand and moderate, severe, and profound on the other. Cultural-familial or environmental factors are considered likely to be formative in mild retardation; and a single pathological organic factor, such as a defective gene or a brain trauma, is considered determinative in the more severe forms of retardation.

Heber (1970) estimates that damage to the developing brain accounts for no more than 10 to 20 percent of the total population of the mentally retarded. These individuals generally have

IQs of less than 50, their retardation being moderate, severe, and profound. They are fairly evenly distributed throughout all socioeconomic, ethnic, and racial groups. Unlike the so-called cultural-familial retardates, these children may have parents with IQs anywhere in the entire range.

In Table 16.2 are listed a few of the many currently known diseases that are associated with mental retardation. They are grouped in two different ways, by when the problem develops, before or after birth, and by the nature of the disease, genetic, infectious, or traumatic. In some instances a problem will not show itself until some time after birth, but is still categorized as prenatal if the physiological source of the difficulty was established while the child was still in its mother's uterus. Our knowledge is still so limited, however, that the distinctions made in the table should be viewed only as general guidelines. To take but one example, a chromosomal abnormality, which is categorized as a prenatal genetic disease, may itself be attributed to the mother's exposure to radiation (considered a traumatic disease) before the egg was even fertilized.

Genetic conditions causing mental retardation

In genetic conditions the individual's abnormality is almost always determined at the moment of conception. Robinson and Robinson (1976) distinguish two important types, those caused by chromosomal aberrations and those attributable to the unfortunate pairing of two defective recessive genes. Mental retardation attributable to a dominant gene is very rare because the persons affected are generally not able to reproduce. Variations from the normal complement of forty-six chromosomes usually, but not always, cause very noticeable physical abnormalities in the developing child. When defective recessive genes are paired, production of an enzyme necessary for an important metabolic process is usually disturbed.

Chromosomal Aberrations *Down's syndrome* or *mongolism,* first described by Langdon Down in 1866, is the most prevalent single-factor cause of mental retardation, accounting for at least 10 percent of moderately to severely retarded children. It has been estimated that one child in every 600 births is afflicted with this disorder (Robinson and Robinson, 1976). Mongoloid chil-

TABLE **16.2**
Illustrative Organic Diseases
Associated with Mental Retardation

When disease develops	Types of disease		
	Genetic	Infectious	Traumatic
In utero (before birth)*	Down's syndrome Klinefelter's syndrome Phenylketonuria Tay-Sachs disease Niemann-Pick disease Maple Syrup Urine disease Hurler's syndrome Lesch-Nyhan syndrome	Rubella Syphilis Toxoplasmosis Encephalitis	Rh factor Cretinism Malnutrition Poisoning (lead, carbon monoxide, X-ray) Drugs (especially alcohol)
At or following birth		Encephalitis Meningitis	All the above (except Rh factor) *plus* Anoxia Premature birth Head injury

* Conditions in which the head size is grossly distorted are not listed because various factors may have impaired development. Examples are microcephaly or small head in which the development of the brain has been arrested; macrocephaly, large head with abnormal growth of supportive tissues; and hydrocephaly, large head with excessive cerebrospinal fluid.

dren seldom have an IQ over 50. They have many rather distinctive physical signs: eyes slanted upward and outward, a vestigial third eyelid in the inner corner of the eye, flat face and nose, an overly large, protruding, and deeply fissured tongue, misshapen teeth, a small skull, somewhat flattened at the back, sparse fine, straight hair, stubby fingers, fingerprints with ℓ-shaped loops rather than whorls, arms and legs that are smaller than normal, protruding belly, underdeveloped genitalia, and poor muscle tone.

Many children with Down's syndrome, perhaps 40 percent, have heart problems; a small minority may have blockages of the upper intestinal tract; and about 25 percent do not survive the first few years. As adults, mongoloids seldom exceed five feet in height. Menstruation in women tends to follow a normal course, but men are apparently sterile. Mortality after age forty is abnormally high; brain tissue generally shows signs of deterioration similar to that found in Alzheimer's disease (see page 720).

Down's syndrome is caused by a chromosomal abnormality. The vast majority of mongoloid children have forty-seven chromosomes instead of forty-six. During the earliest stage of an egg's development, the two chromosomes of pair 21 fail to separate, perhaps because they are so small. When the sperm and egg unite, chromosome pair 21 will thus have three chromosomes instead of the usual two. This is referred to as a trisomy of chromosome 21.

The risk of having a mongoloid child increases dramatically with the age of the mother. There is a one in 1500 chance of a mother in her twenties having such a child, and a one in 65 risk for a mother over forty-five. Fortunately, the amniotic fluid in which the fetus is immersed within the uterus can now be tested and will reveal whether the child is mongoloid; this procedure, called amniocentesis, raises for the future parent the difficult decision whether to terminate the pregnancy when mongolism is found. In a much rarer and inherited form of mongolism, the extra chromosome 21 becomes attached to another chromosome. The risk of bearing a child with this type of mongolism does not increase with maternal age.

Down's syndrome children have a reputation for being good-natured nd affectionate and rather easily managed. Perhaps because they grow up in widely diverse situations, the rates at which they become toilet-trained and master walking vary more than might be expected from the description of the disorder. The interaction between diathesis, in this case the chromosomal anomaly, and stress, here the environment in which a person with a faulty brain is reared, is complex. The children do much better in a loving home than in an institution. A special program for Down's syndrome children has been developed at the University of Washington. Mother and infant begin weekly visits to a clinic when the child is five weeks old. Until the infant's eighteenth month they do exercises together in visual, auditory, and motor stimulation. From the eighteenth month until the child is three the work is on gross motor skills, language,

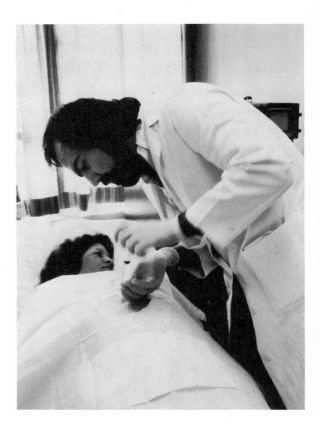

Amniocentesis. Fluid from within the amnion, the sac surrounding the fetus, is being withdrawn for later testing to determine whether there is a chromosomal abnormality.

The development of a child with Down's syndrome, sensitively photographed by his father.

and concept learning. In the last two preschool years the child learns cognitive skills and how to get along with others. The IQs of children in this program have been brought to an astonishing mean of 83, high enough that some of them should be able to attend public schools (Hayden and Haring, 1977). Although it is unrealistic to expect even extensive remedial efforts to eradicate completely the adjustment problems of Down's syndrome children, their potentials for intellectual and social growth have probably not been realized.

In *Klinefelter's syndrome* an extra X chromosome is usually at fault. This syndrome occurs only in males and accounts for about one percent of institutionalized male retardates. Only about 25 percent of males with this syndrome are retarded, and their retardation is likely to be mild or moderate rather than severe. The symptoms are usually noticed at puberty when the testes remain small and the boy develops feminine secondary sex characteristics such as enlarged hips.

Recessive Genes   When a pair of defective recessive genes misdirect the formation of an enzyme, metabolic processes are disturbed. The problem may affect development of the embryo in the uterus or may not become important until much later in life.

In *phenylketonuria* (PKU) the infant, born normal, soon suffers from a deficiency of liver enzyme, phenylalanine hydroxylase, which is needed to convert phenylalanine, an amino acid of protein foods, to tyrosine. Phenylalanine and its derivative phenylpyruvic acid build up in the body fluids, ultimately wreaking irreversible brain damage. The unmetabolized amino acid interferes with the process of myelination, the sheathing of neuron axons. This sheathing is essential for the rapid transmittal of impulses and thus information in the nervous system. The neurons of the frontal lobes are particularly affected. Inasmuch as these areas of the cortex are known to be crucial for normal thinking—although *how* is not known—it is not surprising that mental retardation is profound.

At about six months parents usually begin to notice a retardation in motor development and in general responsiveness. There may also be seizures and an unusual body odor from the presence of phenylpyruvic acid in the urine. Over 60 percent of the children with PKU never learn to talk, about one-third cannot walk, and more than half have IQs of less than 20. In addition to their profound mental impairment, those with PKU have been described as jerky, restless, unfriendly, fearful, and occasionally destructive.

Although a rare disorder, with an incidence of about one in 20,000 births, it is estimated that one person in seventy is a carrier of the recessive gene. Fortunately, prevention of extensive brain damage is facilitated by laboratory tests of an infant's blood for excessive phenylalanine. State laws require that this test be given four or five days after birth. If the test is positive, the parents are urged to provide the infant with a diet low in phenylalanine. When the diet is restricted as early as the third month and until the age of six, when brain differentiation is relatively complete, cognitive development improves, sometimes to within the normal range (*Collaborative Study of Children Treated for Phenylketonuria*, 1975).

Several hundred other recessive-gene disorders have been isolated, many of them causing mental retardation. Only a very minor percentage of the cases of mental retardation are acccounted for by any single disorder, however. *Tay-Sachs disease,* a disorder of lipid metabolism transmitted by the pairing of single recessive genes, is found for the most part among Jewish families of northeastern Europe ancestry. In many metropolitan areas of the United States, large-scale screening programs provide Jewish couples with the blood tests that detect carriers. In Tay-Sachs disease an enzyme is missing in nerve cells, and fats accumulate in the central nervous system. Amniocentesis will detect the absence of the enzyme. The child born with Tay-Sachs disease suffers increasing muscular weakness, visual deterioration, and convulsions. He or she seldom lives beyond the third year (Kolb, 1968).

Niemann-Pick disease, also a fatal inherited dysfunction in lipid metabolism, causes gastrointestinal disturbances, malnutrition, and progressive paralysis. *Maple Syrup Urine disease* is an inherited defect in amino acid metabolism and receives its name from the odor of the infant's urine. Deterioration of the muscles accompanies cerebral deterioration, and the child seldom survives its first year. An infant afflicted with

BOX 16.1 Idiot Savant

One particularly interesting phenomenon, usually regarded as a special form of mental retardation, is the _idiot savant,_ a retardate with superior functioning in one narrow area of intellectual activity. Perhaps the best-documented case history was kept by Scheerer, Rothman, and Goldstein (1945), who studied their subject intensively from his eleventh year through his sixteenth. During this period they gave the boy numerous problem-solving tasks and intelligence tests. L. was described as follows.

1. He had been failing at school, showing little interest in classroom activities and interacting minimally with classmates.

2. L. had developed the unusual talent of being able to provide, with little apparent thought, the day of the week for any date between 1880 and 1950. A favorite pastime was to ask people their birth dates and then immediately tell them on which day of the week they had been born and when their birthday would fall in any other given year, past or future. L. had been performing this feat since the age of seven. Scheerer and his colleagues point out, however, that he had no grasp of which of two people was the older, designating always the person whose birthday fell in an earlier part of the year. For example, he would regard anyone born on June 10 as being older than someone born on September 13, quite overlooking the year of birth or the physical appearance of the two people.

3. L. could quickly spell forward or backward practically any word pronounced to him, _but_ without knowing its meaning or caring to.

4. The boy had a very well-developed but unusual musical ability. He could play many melodies on the piano by ear, that of Beethoven's "Moonlight Sonata," for example, but he seemed to have no grasp of what he was doing and took no enjoyment in it. He ignored any instructions or comments on his playing. Moreover, "He sings the accompaniment or the Italian words [to several operas] as they sound to him. Without knowing the language he reproduces it phonetically" (p. 2).

5. L.'s arithmetic ability was also unusual. He could, for example, add ten to twelve two-digit numbers as fast as they were recited to him, but he was unable to learn to add larger numbers. He could also count by 16 very rapidly—1, 17, 33, 49, and so on—but without any understanding of what the numbers meant; for instance, he could not state that 20 is larger than 8.

6. He easily learned the Gettysburg Address at age fourteen by rote memory, but without understanding its meaning.

Scheerer and his colleagues found L. to test at an IQ of 50 on the Binet scale. In their attempt to explain L.'s behavior, they rejected the idea that an idiot savant has a supernormal _ability_ in one area. Rather they suggested that this kind of individual lacks the crucial ability to reason abstractly and that, given this serious handicap, he copes with the world by channeling his energy into rote memory feats. He develops rote skills to an unusually high degree because he can in essence do little else with his cortex. L.'s IQ rating was low because he could not perform tasks that children must handle in order to score in the normal range when they are eleven or older—namely tasks requiring abstract reasoning. For instance, shown an absurd picture of a man in the rain holding an umbrella upside down, the boy at age fifteen said "Yes, the man is holding an umbrella upside down. I don't know why, there is a lot of rain there" (p. 10). The overall problem was summarized by these workers as ". . . a general impairment of abstract capacity . . . , L. [even] succeeded in his own performance-specialties without having a genuine understanding of their meaning . . ." (p. 59).

Hurler's syndrome, or gargoylism, accumulates a mucopolysaccharide in body and brain cells and soon develops an enlarged head with protruding forehead, bushy eyebrows, thick lips, and deformed limbs. Many of these children survive into their teens. Another metabolic disorder, the _Lesch-Nyhan syndrome,_ is inherited through sex-linked recessive genes and seriously impairs the kidneys. It causes not only severe mental retardation but unusually aggressive and self-mutilating behavior. Although appearing normal at birth, these children, all of whom are boys, begin to manifest a delay in motor development at three or four months of age and then lose considerable motor control. Not surprisingly, institutionalization is the rule. These boys seem to be happiest when physically restrained. They appear terrified and are subject to loud, destructive outbursts when free to move about (Nyhan, 1973).

Infectious diseases causing mental retardation
Even though the developing fetus has had a normal genetic beginning to its journey to life, it faces physical dangers that can bring on mental retardation. The speed and complexity of the development of the fetus's nervous system are unparalleled, especially during the first three months, or trimester. Later, by the time a baby is about six months old, cell division within the central nervous system ceases altogether and forever; the most serious consequence of this fact is that central nervous system cells can never be replaced if they are injured or destroyed. It sometimes appears miraculous that most human infants arrive on the scene unhurt and properly equipped and enter the first years of life unscathed by any degree of damage to the intricate brain. Fortunately, the overwhelming majority of births and subsequent early development are apparently quite normal and routine.

Both before birth—through contagion of the mother—and after birth, an inherently healthy fetus and infant can be subjected to an infection that causes mental retardation. If the mother is infected by _rubella_ or German measles in the last six months of pregnancy, the fetus is usually not adversely affected. If, however, she contracts the disease during the first month of pregnancy, there is a 50 percent chance that her live-born child will suffer both mental abnormality and congenital physical defects, very often cataracts and other eye problems, deafness, and heart anomalies. When the disease is contracted in the second month, the risk is reduced to 15 percent, in the third month to 10 percent (Kolb, 1968). Therapeutic abortions have been available for a number of years for pregnant mothers who have had German measles early in pregnancy; more importantly, vaccination to prevent rubella is now widely available, the happy result being a marked reduction in the _rubella syndrome_ form of mental retardation.

Syphilis too no longer causes as much mental retardation as it used to because pregnant women who are seen in prenatal clinics must have their blood tested. Many of the fetuses afflicted with congenital syphlis die before they are born. Others die during the first weeks of life. Congenital syphilis usually affects the child immediately if he or she lives, frequently causing mental retardation, blindness, and deafness. A rarer form is juvenile paresis. This disease begins to affect the central nervous system only after a number of symptom-free years, but thereafter intellectual deterioration is progressive (Robinson and Robinson, 1976). Other very rare infectious diseases of the mother can affect the unborn child, among them _toxoplasmosis_ (infection from a protozoanlike organism, _Toxoplasma_) and _encephalitis._

After birth, infectious diseases can also affect a child's developing brain. Encephalitis and meningococcal meningitis may cause irreversible brain damage and even death if contracted in infancy or early childhood. These infections in adulthood are usually far less serious, probably because the brain is largely developed by about the age of six. There are several forms of childhood meningitis, a disease in which the protective membranes of the brain are acutely inflamed and fever is very high. Even if the child survives and is not severely retarded, he or she is likely to be moderately or mildly so. Other disabling aftereffects are deafness, paralysis, and epilepsy.

Traumas causing mental retardation
Trauma of many kinds can cause mental retardation and other physical problems, either indi-

rectly to the fetus through the mother or directly to the infant after birth. The specific forms and severity of disorders vary with the trauma; lead poisoning, Rh-factor incompatibility, carbon monoxide poisoning, too frequent exposure to X-rays, poor diet, birth injury, head injury, and certain drugs, including excessive alcohol intake by the mother (see page 302), all have serious aftermaths.

Rh factors are substances that are present in the red blood cells of a large majority of human beings and other higher animals. When they are introduced into the blood of a person whose own does not contain them, they act as antigens or foreign substances and stimulate the production of antibodies. If the blood of a fetus contains Rh factors, through inheritance from the father, but that of the mother is Rh negative, lacking in Rh factors, these substances will be introduced into the mother's blood for the first time by the fetus. The mother produces antibodies which, when they in turn enter the bloodstream of the fetus, destroy red blood cells, and cause oxygen deprivation. Since it takes time for the mother to produce the antibodies, firstborn children are less likely to be affected by _Rh incompatibility_ than are subsequent children. The brain damage from oxygen deprivation in Rh incompatibility can be extensive if not treated. In an earlier treatment newborn infants at risk were given a complete blood transfusion. Although most children recovered, Heber's (1970) summary of various studies indicates that the IQs of children who had suffered from Rh incompatibility and been treated were lower that those of control group children, even though they were still within the average range. Now the Rh-negative mother, immediately after giving birth to her first Rh-incompatible infant, receives antibodies to destroy the fetal Rh factors in her blood. She therefore never builds up her own antibodies, which would be harmful in her next pregnancy.

Cretinism is caused by a severe deficiency in the output of the thyroid gland and is characterized by profound intellectual deficit as well as physical defects. The untreated child who has suffered this deficiency since birth has a large head, coarse features, heavy eyelids, abundant wiry hair, cool, dry skin, a short, dwarflike body, a grossly swollen abdomen, and short, stubby limbs. Although several factors may diminish the activity of the thyroid, historically the major cause has been lack of iodine in the diet of the pregnant mother, iodine being the major ingredient needed for the production of the hormone thyroxin. The infant is born with defective thyroid glands which remain underdeveloped or atrophy. The symptoms of cretinism become apparent during the early months, for development is very slow, and the baby is not responsive or alert. The incidence of cretinism is now very low because of the widespread use of iodized salt. An infant born with a thyroid deficiency can be given thyroid extracts, making a relatively normal development possible in many instances.

It has been estimated that throughout the world 300 million preschool children suffer mild to moderate malnutrition (Behar, 1968). A poor diet, one deficient in proteins in particular, is believed to be especially harmful during the period of the brain's fastest growth. The consequences of moderate and chronic malnutrition are not as well known. The effects of malnutrition have been studied in several ways, by manipulating the diets of animals, by observing those of human beings, and by examining the brains of children who have died of malnutrition. Animal research has convincingly demonstrated the ill effects of poor diet on brain development (Davison and Dobbing, 1966). The total number of brain cells is permanently reduced if the animal suffers from malnutrition during periods when they are dividing. But we cannot easily generalize from species to species, and it would be unethical to try to replicate these studies with human infants. Some research, however, does reveal similar effects in human beings. In one study autopsies were performed on children who had died from malnutrition; all had a subnormal number of brain cells (Winick, Rosso, and Waterlow, 1970). In another study lower-class women in Virginia were given supplements of thiamine, riboflavin, niacin, and iron during pregnancy. They gave birth to children who, at age three, had higher IQs than those whose mothers had not had the special supplements (Harrell, Woodyard, and Gates, 1955). Thus there is some evidence that the pregnant woman's diet can influence the future IQ of the infant.

Eating chips of lead-based paint can cause mental retardation.

Recent years have seen heightened interest in and welcome action against the high levels of lead and mercury that have been allowed to poison the environment, causing brain damage and consequent mental retardation. Screening of children in some of our largest cities, both those who live in slums and those who do not, has often revealed toxic levels of lead in their blood. Slum children sometimes ingest lead by eating chips of paint. The paint applied indoors used to be lead-based. Now laws prohibit indoor household paint from containing lead, and landlords are instructed to remove old coatings that contain this poison. City children living in more fortunate circumstances may also have dangerously high blood levels of lead, apparently because they, as well as slum children, breathe in automobile emissions. For this reason, among others, newer cars are built to run on unleaded gasoline. Adults are not immune to the ravages of lead poisoning, but children, not surprisingly, are more susceptible to its effects (Robinson and Robinson, 1976).

The neurological damage that accompanies mercury poisoning retardation can bring on problems in kidney function and walking and can even cause cerebral palsy. Certain industrial wastes containing mercury, dumped carelessly into rivers and lakes, have led to tragic illnesses in Japan and in this country. Vigorous action has been brought against offending industries. Too often, however, economic considerations bring evasive maneuvers that delay control of both mercury and lead, and they continue to wreak irreversible brain damage.

If the cells of the brain are completely deprived of oxygen for even a few short seconds during any period of the life cycle, they will die. *Anoxia,* which is usually only partial but still causes irreparable damage because the rate of metabolism in the brain is lowered, can occur before, during, or after birth. Research with animals has shown the harmful effects of oxygen deprivation, but generalization to human beings may be unwarranted. Summarizing the results of research with human beings, Heber (1970) concludes that children who suffered oxygen deprivation at birth do not differ greatly in intelligence from controls. He believes that studies stressing the role of neonatal anoxia as an important cause of retardation are usually based on retrospective analysis of the histories of retarded persons and have failed to include appropriate non-retarded control groups.

When *prematurity* of birth is separated from the other variables that commonly accompany it—poor socioeconomic status, maternal age, health, medical care—there seems to be little relationship between it and neurological deficit or mental retardation. Robinson and Robinson (1976) conclude that prematurity per se is not usually dangerous to mental development, although the risk of retardation in children who are very small at birth, whether or not they are premature, is quite high.[4]

Cultural-Familial Causes of Mental Retardation

The vast majority of people considered retarded are only mildly so and do not have any identifiable physiological damage. The diagnosis of cultural-familial retardation is made on the basis of three criteria: mild retardation, no indication of brain pathology that can at present be detected, and evidence of retardation in at least one of the parents or in one or more of the siblings. The mildly retarded have IQs above 50, and the great majority of them are born and raised in deprived environments. Although the genes considered responsible for inheritance of intelligence have been implicated in their retardation, the effects of sociocultural impoverishment are now considered very important as well. Very often mild retardation does not become evident until the child enters school and begins to have difficulty with the intellectual requirements of our educational system. After schooling has been

---

[4] Of course, premature babies tend to be below average in size at birth. Thus an infant premature enough to be very small has a higher risk of being mentally retarded.

completed, the individual may no longer be considered retarded.

The mildly retarded are thus considered backward only within a cultural context that emphasizes the importance of the "three Rs"—reading, writing, and arithmetic. Only in modern societies such as our own have psychologists developed IQ tests to measure the intellectual functioning of children. Given the nature of our educational system and the society for which it is supposed to prepare people, IQ tests are very good at predicting how children will do in school. But it is only because of these tests that we have been able to talk about high IQs versus low and thereby designate children as bright or below normal. Nonindustrilized societies, which are without our kind of intelligence testing, would not conceive of cultural-familial retardation.

Familial backgrounds of the cultural-familial retarded

Robinson and Robinson (1976) report that a sizable proportion of the cultural-familial retarded come from stable lower-class families. There is steady employment, and the child's physical needs are met fairly adequately. But the intellectual and educational level in the home is low; few of the parents have IQs that exceed the borderline range from 71 to 83 (Heber, 1970).

Children classified as cultural-familial retarded may also come from unstable, poverty-stricken families. In such homes shelter, food, clothing, and medical care are inadequate. The intelligence and intellectual achievement of the parents is very low. The family is often disrupted and disintegrating, providing no social, emotional, or motivational support for the child.

Many research findings document the accuracy of these dismal characterizations of the homelife of the child with cultural-familial retardation. Benda and his colleagues (1963) studied the families of 205 institutionalized mentally retarded children. The children had no obvious neurological symptoms, were four to fifteen years old, and had IQs above 50. Only 13 of the 205 children came from homes in which there was no apparent mental retardation in the immediate family. Only one-fourth of the families were both intact and able to provide even minimum food, shelter, clothing, and protection from danger. In most of the families certain members had violated societal norms severely enough to have had legal action taken against them. This study was somewhat biased, however, for a mildly retarded child is usually institutionalized only when the family unit cannot provide for his or her needs. The backgrounds of these children were probably worse than those of mildly retarded children in general.

Not all children who are reared in deprived environments are retarded, however. Heber (1970) correlated the IQ scores of eighty-eight mothers in a Milwaukee slum with their children's test scores and found that a minority of the mothers had given birth to a majority of the children whose IQs were in the mildly retarded range. For example, 17 percent of mothers with IQs of less than 68 had reared 54.5 percent of the children in that range and 32.9 percent of children with IQs of 68 to 83.

Offspring of mothers whose IQs were less than 80, approximately half the sample, showed a decrement in measured intelligence with increasing age; the older children of these mothers had lower IQ scores than their younger siblings. Only 20 percent of the children less than six years of age had IQs lower than 80, but 50 percent of the children between seven and twelve years of age tested below 80, as did over 90 percent of those thirteen years of age. This tendency for scores to decrease as children grow older in

Many children reared in extreme poverty are subject to cultural-familial retardation.

deprived socioeconomic environments is often interpreted as evidence of the serious effects of such environments on intellectual development. The children of mothers who scored closer to the normal range, however, showed no decrease in intelligence as they grew older. Fewer than 20 percent of these children, regardless of their age, had IQs of less than 80. The deleterious effects of living in an impoverished environment are less if the mother's IQ is near average.

Problems of interpretation

The effects of deprivation are very complex. Lower-class mothers tend to have poor diets, which can retard normal development of the fetus. As a growing child the ghetto youngster may eat chips of lead-based paint. The schools may not be as good, and the parents may never read books or even newspapers or intellectually stimulate their children. They may never even talk to them much. The family members may seldom venture from the few blocks of their neighborhood. But even knowing that a child is brought up in physical, cultural, and intellectual poverty does not always mean that environment is totally responsible for retardation. As Zigler (1968) has stated, "It is one thing to assert that the environment plays a role in determining the range of individual differences, and quite another to say that environmental events can cause the individual born with a normal intellect to be retarded or that they can prevent retardation" (p. 528).

Some, however, believe that the relationship between poverty and mental retardation should no longer be regarded as correlational. Hurley (1969) feels that the evidence is sufficient to demonstrate that *poverty causes mental retardation.* The child reared in poverty is affected by innumerable intellectually stunting factors—both organic and environmental—ranging from the poor nutrition and the lack of prenatal care of his mother to his own malnutrition, his emotionally and intellectually deprived home and neighborhood, and the failure of his school system. These factors, either singly or in combination, may cause the kind of retardation that has been termed cultural-familial. The conclusion drawn by Hurley is that by eradicating poverty the majority of cases of mental retardation would be eliminated.

Therapy for Retarded People

Seriously retarded people, who almost always have physical disabilities along with their intellectual deficits, often need care and attention that few families are able to provide. They, like the mentally ill, have been warehoused in large state-supported institutions, grim and often frightening to the outsider as well as to the hapless residents. There is no way to explain the dismal and sometimes brutalizing conditions of many of the hospitals society maintains for its less intelligent citizens.

Exposés of the 1960s and early 1970s (Rivera, 1972) plus the efforts of parents forced public awareness of these conditions and a shift in legal opinion. In 1975 Congress enacted the Developmentally Disabled Assistance and Bill of Rights Act asserting that the retarded have a right to appropriate treatment in the least restrictive residential setting. Deinstitutionalization is now favored for many retarded patients, in a manner similar to the deinstitutionalization of mental patients. Supervised community living arrangements are becoming more common, especially for the moderately retarded, many of whom hold regular jobs in sheltered workshops and other workplaces that look to the potential of these people rather than focusing on what they cannot easily do.

Some of the retarded live at home or in foster homes which are provided with psychological and educational assistance and with money to pay for special medication and sitters. The foster parents have been trained in behavior, speech, and other therapies. Other retarded people live in small-group residences of six to ten adults, supervised by several live-in paraprofessionals. Some are able to live together in semi-independent apartments of three or four retarded adults who are chosen for their complementary skills so that they can help and learn from one another. The aid of a counselor is available to them several hours a day. The retarded do clerical, maintenance, and laundry work; packaging; electronic and other light assembly; cutting metals, drilling, and other machine work; farming, gardening, and carpentry. They are also in the domestic and food services and in other service fields. Some are taught to participate in the care and training of those more retarded than themselves and benefit greatly from the experience. Many of the retarded are very persistent, accurate, and punctual employees.

Therapies based on the writings of Freud and Rogers, which rely so heavily on verbal ability, indeed verbal facility, have had limited applicability in treating many retarded people. But verbal exchanges with the retarded are of course

Many retarded adults can be taught useful skills which enable them to lead more independent lives.

BOX 16.2 Avoidable Mental Retardation

We were reminded earlier that despite the numerous dangers to the developing fetus in utero and to the growing child, the overwheming majority of births yield intact babies. But it is also clear that parents must bear considerable responsibility to make certain that their babies are born healthy. Sensible care during pregnancy is not too difficult, given a minimum economic level. Moreover, through public assistance the indigent have access to the benefits of modern medicine. A woman who even suspects that she is pregnant should immediately make certain that her diet is adequate, avoid unnecessary use of drugs, and decline medical X-rays, such as those that dentists take to detect cavities.

Preventive measures can lessen the incidence or severity of organic disorders causing moderate to severe retardation. Screening at birth identifies infants with phenylketonuria, and a special diet reduces its effects on their still developing brains. Amniocentesis determines whether the fetus has a trisomy of chromosome 21, and Down's syndrome, or whether certain of its enzymes are missing or defective, the so-called inborn errors of metabolism, some of which cause mental retardation. Genetic counseling and tests can determine whether parents are carriers of some of the recessive genes causing inborn errors of metabolism. Public health educational programs inform future parents of the dangers of heavy smoking and drinking by the pregnant woman, the importance of good diet, the threat to the fetus should the mother contract rubella in the first trimester of pregnancy, and the importance of vaccinating all schoolchildren for rubella.

Preventive programs have also been directed at mild retardation. The Milwaukee Project, a very ambitious one to rehabilitate the family and provide the child with better surroundings, stimulation, and motivation, was carried out by Rick Heber (and Garber, 1975) in the Milwaukee slum where he had studied the mothers with IQs of less than 80 and their offspring.

Forty families with mothers whose IQs were less than 75 were chosen. Their infants were three to six months old. Half the families were assigned randomly to the experimental program, half to the control group. The mothers were given a one-month course in adult education to prepare them for six months of vocational training. After they had found jobs, they were trained in home and child care and in ways to stimulate their children.

For the first year a trained adult met one to one with each child for several hours and engaged him or her in lively perceptual-motor activities. Thereafter the children received intensive preschool educational attention at the project's training center, seven hours a day, five days a week, twelve months a year. The program continued until the children were six. They met in small groups for half-hour periods of learning, activity, and play. They were taught language, reading readiness, and how to classify, associate, and generalize. The training of the children has been criticized as geared to intelligence testing (Page, 1975), but at nine years of age, after three years of public school, the mean IQs of these children were, on the several tests used, above average and twenty points or more higher than the mean IQs of the control group children.

possible and necessary. Moderately retarded children can use advice from a counselor or other adult; they all need to be reassured about the competencies that they have, and they can obtain encouragement and support from what kind and trustworthy people tell them (Robinson and Robinson, 1976). Play therapy has been adapted for treatment of retarded children, water and finger paints in unstructured sessions for the severely retarded, for example, coloring books and puzzles in more structured meetings with those less so (Leland and Smith, 1965).

Psychotherapists have in the past, however, for a reason we cannot be proud of, played a minor role in working with the emotional and intellectual problems of retarded people. Given the great numbers of malfunctioning human beings, middle- and upper-middle-class professionals have concentrated on the plight of those who are not disfigured, whose verbal abilities are largely intact, who, despite their psychological problems, seem more like us than the children with Down's syndrome or with a brain ravaged by phenylketonuria. Nonetheless, for the past few decades efforts have been made to educate and to socialize our retarded citizens. Behavior therapy has ushered in what some feel is a revolution in helping retarded people. Therapists have entered institutions and effected positive changes in even the most severely retarded children and adults through operant shaping and modeling techniques.

The specific behavior to be learned is broken down into very small steps; the therapist plans the teaching to provide immediate feedback and frequent reinforcement and to minimize failures. Foxx and Azrin (1973) managed to toilet-train severely retarded children by rewarding successive approximations to voiding in a toilet. Toilet-trained people are more comfortable, are better liked by the staff, and can leave the ward for other rooms and leave the building for recreation on the grounds. Self-injurious behavior has also been brought under control by behavioral procedures (for example, Solnick, Rincover, and Peterson, 1977), freeing the children from physical and chemical restraints, from the straitjackets and drugs that formerly ordered their waking hours.

The children are also taught self-help skills, such as how to make their own beds and how to dress themselves. In instructing a youngster how to remove a sweater, Watson (1973) starts with the last step first. The therapist guides the young boy in pulling the sweater up and over his head and down his left arm, but then allows him to remove it from his wrist and reinforces him as he does so. Gradually the child is manually guided in removing the sweater only so far as the lower arm, the elbow, the upper arm and so on. Eventually the child manages the over-the-head and the pulling-up movements on his own too. A great advantage of behavior therapies is that parents can be taught to work with their own children, who can be kept at home.

The significance of learning self-care and social skills must not be underestimated. Most retardates face discrimination from other people, whose negative attitudes are based in part on the sometimes gross violations of norms committed by them. Being able to act more normally will increase their chances of interacting meaningfully with others. Moreover, the self-esteem that comes from learning to take better care of oneself, to ride a bus, to greet and talk to others, and to read a book—accomplishments well within reach of most retarded children and adults, given the proper learning conditions—is extremely bolstering. The challenge for health professionals today is to develop techniques whereby the seriously retarded may learn the self-care and social skills that will allow them to remain in the community, whether it be in their families' homes or, as they grow up, in community residences under supervision.

What was discovered about the thinking of the retarded in the experimental studies discussed earlier indicates what special efforts should be made in teaching them. For example, the greater distractibility of retarded children and their apparent problems with short-term memory mean that irrelevant stimuli must be kept to a minimum—therapists are advised against bright colors and jewelry—and that the pace of learning must be slow and modest, building from simple tasks to the more complex. Piaget's theory of developmental stages indicates that concrete materials rather than abstract concepts should be chosen (Iscoe and Semler, 1964). As Chinn, Drew, and Logan (1979) put it, in teaching a retarded youngster what a fireman is, it is better to leave the schoolroom and go to a fire station than to show the child pictures in a book.

Ross and Ross (1973) implemented an exemplary program based on Milgram's finding that retardates do not use mediators to make associations as effectively as normal children do. They gave one group of children whose IQs ranged from 40 to 80 special game sessions in which they watched nonretarded children using sentences to link words together. Control retarded children continued in the usual curriculum of the school at which the study was being carried out. During the school year the special group of children showed marked increases in their measured IQ, and eleven of the thirty of them were actually transferred from the special classes to regular ones; the control children did not show such improvement.

The families of moderately retarded children face a problem that, in some ironic ways, may be more difficult than the dilemmas facing those with more seriously retarded youngsters, namely how to provide the best possible education so that the child and young adult can take full advantage of his or her limited intellectual abilities and develop in as normal a fashion as possible as a social being. In 1950 parents founded the National Association for Retarded Children and by the mid-1960s had spread their advocacy for better education for their children to all fifty states. Many local units ran their own day-school programs, but these efforts could not meet the needs of all retarded children. Class action suits were filed in twenty-three states and the District of Columbia to give all persons access to education. In 1975 the United States Congress passed Public Law 94-142, the Education for All Handicapped Children Act. Implemented in 1977, this law provides to the states federal funds for devising free public education for all children in the least restrictive situation possible. The law indicates that children should, whenever practicable, be _mainstreamed,_ that is placed in educational settings that nonretarded children enjoy as a matter of course. Neighborhood public schools now teach retarded and physically handicapped children who would earlier have been out of view, segregated in special schools. Depending on a given child's abilities and achievements, he or she may be able to participate in certain regular gym and home economics classes and mix with other children at recess. They spend their arithmetic and reading time in a special class with other retarded children, under the direction of a teacher with training in what is called "special education." By not being segregated from society-at-large, retarded youngsters are expected to learn more about socializing with others than they would were their schoolmates always other retarded children.

It is too soon to know how beneficial mainstreaming is for retarded children. There is always the chance that a child who knows within himself that he thinks less clearly, less quickly, less accurately than an age-mate will feel worse in a situation forcing constant comparisons. Furthermore, having retarded children sit in the same classroom with normal children does not ensure meaningful social and intellectual interactions. At the same time, and this is the implicit hope, the regular classroom may provide stimulation otherwise available in very limited amounts, and the retarded child may learn more, both academically and socially. There are some indications that this does happen (Budoff and Gottlieb, 1976). The majority of children, the lucky normal ones, stand to gain too. They will know from early in life that there is tremendous diversity among human beings, that a child may be different in some very important ways _and yet_ be worthy of respect and friendship. With support from parents and teachers, normal children may reach adulthood without the burden of prejudice of earlier generations. Such an eventuality would benefit both the normal child and his or her age-mate not blessed with as quick and receptive a mind.[5]

[5] We have expressed a hope, but as yet it is only that. Some evidence indicates that contact with retarded children actually increases prejudice against them (Gottlieb, Cohen, and Goldstein, 1974). Special measures such as discussion groups and films of appealing retarded youngsters may help normal children accept them as different, rather than reject them as deviant.

Pervasive Disorders of Childhood

There has been a good deal of confusion in the classification of serious disorders that begin in childhood. DSM-II used the diagnosis _childhood schizophrenia_ for these conditions, implying that they were simply an early onset form of adult schizophrenia. But the available evidence did not support this supposition and instead demonstrated many differences between childhood and adult schizophrenia. For example, delusions and hallucinations did not seem to be prevalent among the children formerly considered schizophrenic. Although the sex ratio is about equal among adult schizophrenics, the so-designated schizophrenia of childhood was more common among males. Lotter (1966) indicated the ratio as 2.5 to 1, but Rutter (1967) placed it at 4.3 to 1. Moreover, unlike adult schizophrenia, the supposed childhood schizophrenia was not preponderant among the lower classes. Finally, in a well-executed ten-year follow-up study of psychotic children, many of whom could be regarded as childhood schizophrenics, Lockyer and Rutter (1969) did not find that they had become adult schizophrenics. We must therefore conclude that the evidence does not favor viewing adult schizophrenia and the so-called childhood schizophrenia as two closely related disorders.

As a partial replacement for the earlier childhood schizophrenia diagnosis, DSM-III proposes _childhood onset pervasive developmental disorder._ The diagnosis is given children with profound disturbances in social relations and "oddities of behavior" that begin after thirty months but before twelve years of age. The children are not emotionally responsive, have little interest in their peers or in social relationships, and cling to their parents more than is appropriate for their age. They may have sudden episodes of intense anxiety and peculiar motor behavior, such as moving their hands and fingers in a stereotyped manner. Overresponsiveness or underresponsiveness to light, sound, and pain, self-mutilation, speech abnormalities, and an obsessive insistence on maintaining the same routines are other symptoms.

This new diagnosis is clearly applicable to some children who were formerly considered childhood schizophrenics. But children are not to be given the new diagnosis if they have delusions, hallucinations, or signs of thought disorder. According to DSM-III, children with such disturbances are to be diagnosed schizophrenic, for they meet the criteria that are applied to adults. Children with clearly psychotic symptoms may in addition be diagnosed as having major depression or bipolar disorder. Thus a number of fairly distinct psychoses can apparently occur in childhood. Because of the diagnostic problems, we will not consider research findings on childhood schizophrenia but instead describe another pervasive developmental disorder, one which has intrigued and befuddled researchers and clinicians for several decades, infantile autism.

Infantile Autism

In 1943 Leo Kanner, a noted American psychiatrist, described a group of eleven children who had not developed normal relationships with other people, who were severely limited in language, and who had a great obsessive desire that everything about them remain exactly the same. Kanner proposed the term *infantile autism* to describe this disorder. Autism did not appear in DSM-I (1952) or II (1968), but it has finally been included in DSM-III. It is distinguishable from other psychotic disorders of childhood by this constellation of specific symptoms and by the fact that it begins before the age of thirty months. The following case history indicates the distress of one such youngster.

Robbie was four years of age when his parents first sought behavior therapy for him. At that time he was virtually uncontrollable. He would do little that either of his parents told him to and, in fact, would often do the oposite of what they suggested. Although he "looked intelligent," he had never spoken. He seemed to be particularly fond of only one activity, unscrewing nuts and bolts. Whenever left to himself, Robbie would begin, working with just his fingers, to try to undo any nuts he could find. Often he puttered for hours with a single one until it would begin to move. After unscrewing the nut and bolt, he would typically swallow them. He also showed great upset over any change in daily routine, or indeed over any change at all in his surroundings. On one occasion, after his parents had bought new living room furniture, Robbie went into a rage that lasted until he fell asleep from exhaustion.

In interviews Robbie's parents described him as having been a "good baby," not crying very much and not placing very many demands on them. In thinking back to the time when they first noticed that something might be wrong, both parents agreed on one early phenomenon, which they had not considered particularly significant at the time. Robbie had actually seemed *not* to enjoy being held and cuddled by either of his parents. Often, when they tried to hold him and to look into his eyes, he would avoid their gaze and stiffen, seemingly becoming anxious and upset. As Robbie grew older, of course, the parents became worried about their lack of control over his behavior, his negativism, and his failure to talk. And as their concern deepened, they began to seek professional assistance. At various times Robbie had been diagnosed as retarded, as a childhood schizophrenic, as a symbiotic psychotic, as an anaclitic depressive,[6] and as autistic.

In the initial treatment sessions with Robbie, several other aspects of his behavior were clearly exhibited. He apparently had the capacity to understand at least some speech, even though he often appeared not to listen and did the opposite of what was requested. Four players, one of them being Robbie, gathered in a circle for a game of ball. Robbie was asked each time to throw the ball to a different person. In thirty trials not once did he throw the ball to the person whom he had been requested to throw it to. He always threw the ball to someone else. Even if he did not understand the requests, he would be expected to throw the ball to the correct person about one-third of the time simply by chance. The fact that he *never* made the correct response is evidence that he understood and chose deliberately not to comply with the request.

Robbie often gave the appearance of being tired, bored, and passive. When things became difficult during a language training session, for example, he might seem placid and calm and yawn a great deal. His outward appearance, however, was not an accurate reflection of Robbie's internal state. In one instance Robbie, barefoot, got up and walked across the room and left glistening footprints on the tile floor. His feet were literally dripping with sweat.

Descriptive Characteristics

Kanner (1943), Rimland (1964), and Rutter (1974) have expended considerable effort in studying and describing the baffling and tragic symptoms of infantile autism, singling out the three already mentioned as the most important.

---

[6] Symbiotic psychosis is a rare childhood disorder described by Margaret Mahler (1952). Occurring at about four years of age, it is marked by an extreme reluctance to be separated from the mother and by agitated panic attacks. Anaclitic depression is a term applied to the infant's profound sadness when separated from his mother for a prolonged period. Because there has been little systematic investigation of these syndromes, we mention them only in passing.

When together autistic children do not pay much attention to one another, preferring inanimate objects to the company of their peers.

Extreme autistic aloneness

An inability to relate to people or to any situation other than being alone in a crib is found in many autistic children from the very beginning of life. Autistic infants are often reported to be "good babies," apparently because they do not place many demands on their parents. They do not coo or fret or demand attention, nor do they reach out or smile or look at their mothers when being fed. When they are picked up or cuddled, they arch their bodies away from their caretakers rather than molding themselves against the adult as normal babies do. Autistic infants are content to sit quietly in their playpens for hours, completely self-absorbed, never noticing the comings, goings, and doings of other people. Their unusual physical attractiveness has often been

noted. After infancy they do not form attachments with people but instead may become extremely dependent on mechanical objects, such as refrigerators or vacuum cleaners. Because they avoid all social interaction, they fall rapidly behind their peers in development.

The autistic child's failure to relate to people has been studied in laboratory settings. Hutt and Ounsted (1966) observed autistic and control children in a room that had five masks mounted on stands. There were two human faces, one happy and one sad, a blank oval mask, and two animal masks, a monkey and a dog. The children were allowed ten minutes to explore the room. They were observed through one-way mirrors, and the time spent viewing each face was recorded. Corroborating clinical impressions, the autistic children spent the least time looking at the happy face, longer periods viewing the animal faces, and by far the most time looking at fixtures in the room, such as light switches and faucets. In a similar manner, Black, Freeman, and Montgomery (1975) examined the behavior of autistic children as they played in several different environments. Again consistent with clinical lore, the autistic children related more often to objects than to peers and frequently engaged in solitary, repetitive behavior.

Communication problems

Even before the period when language is usually acquired, autistic children show deficits in communication. Babbling, a term used to describe the utterances of children before they actually begin to use words, is less frequent in autistic children and conveys less information then does that of other children. Ricks (1972), for example, played tape recordings of the babbling of both autistic and mentally retarded children to their own mothers and to other mothers. Although all mothers understood best the meaning of the noises of their own children, the babbling of the autistic children was less meaningful to other mothers than was the babbling of the mentally retarded children. Even on a nonvocal level, autistic children manifest a communication deficit. They do not, for example, use gesture as a substitute for speech, and it has proved difficult to train them to do so (Bartak, Rutter, and Cox, 1975).

The difficulties that older autistic children have with language are even more pronounced. _Mutism,_ complete absence of speech, is prevalent; about 50 percent of all autistic children never learn to speak (Rutter, 1966). Even when they do, many peculiarities are found, among them _echolalia._ The child does not use speech for communication but echoes, usually with remarkable fidelity and in a high-pitched monotone, what he or she has heard another person say. In "delayed" echolalia the child may not repeat the sentence or phrase until hours or weeks after hearing it. In one of our own cases, for example, speech was limited to the repetition of television commercials. In fact, the child's memory for these commercials seemed limitless. Mute children who later do obtain some functional speech through training must usually first pass through a stage of echolalia before they can learn to respond meaningfully to questions or to use labels.

Another abnormality common in the speech of autistic children is _pronoun reversal._ The children refer to themselves as "he," or "you," or by their own proper names; the pronouns "I" or "me" are seldom used and then only when referring to others. Pronoun reversal is closely linked to echolalia. Since autistic children often use echolalic speech, they will refer to themselves as they have heard others speak of them; pronouns are of course misapplied. For example,

Parent: "What are you doing, Johnny?"

Child: "He's here."

Parent: "Are you having a good time?"

Child: "He knows it."

As normal speech is built up, this pronoun reversal might be expected to disappear. It has been reported, however, to be highly resistant to change (Tramontana and Stimbert, 1970); some children have required very extensive training even after they have stopped parroting the phrases of other people.

Communication deficiencies are clearly one of the most serious problems of autistic children. The fact that about 70 percent of autistic children score in the mentally retarded range on IQ tests, with 40 percent having IQs below 50, is undoubtedly a reflection of these deficiencies. They may also leave a lasting mark of social retardation on the child. The link between social skills and language is made evident by the often spontaneous appearance of affectionate and dependent behavior in these children after they have been trained to speak (Churchill, 1969; Hewett, 1965).

An autistic child's ability or inability to speak is often an effective means of predicting later adjustment, an additional indication of the central role of language. Rutter (1967) found that of thirty-two autistic children without useful speech at five years of age, only seven had acquired speech when followed up about nine years later. Eisenberg and Kanner (1956) had earlier followed up a sample of eighty autistic children classified according to whether or not they had learned to speak by age five. Fifty percent of the children who had been able to speak at this age were later rated as showing fair or good adjustment, but only 3 percent of the nonspeaking children were so rated. Subsequent studies have also shown a close link between the acquisition of language and later adjustment (Lotter, 1974; Treffert, McAndrew, and Dreifuerst, 1973).

Preservation of sameness

Autistic children become extremely upset over changes in daily routine and their surroundings. An offer of milk in a different drinking cup or a rearrangement of furniture may make them cry or bring on a temper tantrum. Even common greetings must not vary.

> . . . _A beautiful girl of five, with autism, finally made contact with her teacher. Each morning she had to be greeted with the set phrase, "Good morning, Lily, I am very, very glad to see you." If even one of the very's was omitted or another added she would start to scream wildly (Diamond, Baldwin, and Diamond, 1963, p. 304)._

An "obsessional" quality, similar to the preservation of sameness, pervades the behavior of autistic children in other ways. In their play they may continually line up toys or construct intricate patterns out of household objects. They may become preoccupied with train schedules, subway routes, and number sequences. By adolescence full-blown obsessions sometimes appear. This obsessional quality may be related to "overselectivity," an attentional problem studied by Lovaas and his colleagues (1971). Three cues, one visual, one auditory, and one tactile, were presented simultaneously to normal, autistic, and retarded children. They were taught to press a bar in response and were then rewarded with candy. Later only one cue was given at a time. The normal children had considered the situation in its entirety and were thus able to respond to each of the three separate cues. Retarded children pressed the bar for two of the cues, autistic children for only one. They had not attended to the entire pattern of stimulation, rather only one part of it.

Other signs

In addition to the three major signs just described, autistic children have problems in eating, often refusing food or eating only one or a few kinds of food. They are also given to peculiar ritualistic hand movements and to other rhythmic movements, such as endless body rocking and head rolling. They twiddle their fingers in front of their eyes, and they stare at fans and spinning things. They may also become preoccupied with manipulating a mechanical object and be very upset when interrupted. Often the children have sensory problems. Some autistic children are first diagnosed as being deaf because they never respond to any noise; some appear to be insensitive to noise or light or pain or are overly sensitive to them. They seem to prefer touch, smell, and taste to vision and hearing. Bowel training is frequently delayed, and head banging, hair pulling, biting parts of the body, and other self-injurious behavior are common (Rutter, 1974). Finally, autistic children have been shown to be negativistic, looking through or past people, or turning their backs on others and actively resisting whatever is expected of them (Cowan, Hoddinott, and Wright, 1965).

As indicated earlier, most autistic children are also mentally retarded. The fact that autistic children perform very poorly on intelligence tests, however, is not sufficient grounds to regard them as *merely* mentally retarded. Between one-quarter and one-third of autistic children have a nor-

mal IQ. Furthermore, performance may vary widely depending on the ability being tested. Children diagnosed as autistic perform more poorly on verbal tests and relatively better in matching designs in block design tests and in putting together disassembled objects (DeMyer, 1975; Rutter and Lockyer, 1967). Furthermore, prognosis is worse for autistic children than for retardates, and most retardates are not autistic. Thus autism cannot be viewed simply as a form of mental retardation.

Some controversy, though, surrounds the interpretation of the low IQ scores of autistic children. Kanner (1943) observed that autistic children "looked intelligent"; and like the idiot savant they may have isolated areas of great talent, such as multiplying two four-digit numbers rapidly in their heads, and exceptional long-term memory, such as recalling the exact words of songs heard years earlier. A variety of factors, other than poor cognitive ability, may account for poor performance on an IQ test. In one study, for example, autistic children were asked to choose red or square objects from a stimulus array; each correct response was rewarded. Over 80 percent of the children tested made *fewer* correct responses than would be expected on the basis of chance alone. In other words, they actively avoided making correct responses (Cowan, Hoddinott, and Wright, 1965). Such a negativistic response set would, of course, make it difficult to obtain an accurate estimate of intelligence. But other evidence suggests that negativism is not the whole story of the low IQs of autistic children. If it were, the IQs of autistic children would be less reliable and valid than those obtained from testing other groups. But they are not. The IQs of autistic children prove to be stable on test-retest reliability (Lockyer and Rutter, 1969) and predict later adjustment and educational attainment as well as do those of normal children (Rutter, 1974).

Prognosis in infantile autism

What happens to such severely disturbed children when they reach adulthood? Kanner (1973) has reported on the adult status of nine of the eleven children whom he had described in his original paper on autism. Two developed epileptic seizures; by 1966 one of them had died, and the other was in a state mental hospital. Four others had spent most of their lives in institutions.

> Originally fighting for their aloneness and basking in the content that it gave them, originally alert to unwelcome changes and, in their own way, struggling for the status quo, originally astounding the observer with their phenomenal feats of memory, they yielded readily to the uninterrupted self-isolation and soon settled down to a life not too remote from a nirvanalike existence (p. 185).

Of the remaining three, one had remained mute but was working on a farm and as an orderly in a nursing home. The last two have made at least somewhat satisfactory recoveries. Although both still live with their parents and have little social life, they are gainfully employed and have some recreational interests. Other follow-up studies corroborate the generally gloomy picture of adult autistics (for example, Rutter, 1967; Treffert, McAndrew, and Dreifuerst, 1973; Lotter, 1974). From his review of all published studies, Lotter (1978) concluded that only 5 to 17 percent of autistic children had made a relatively good adjustment in adulthood, leading independent lives but with some residual problems, such as social awkwardness. Most of the others had limited lives, and about half were institutionalized.

Etiology of Infantile Autism

Physiological bases of autism

What could underlie the development of such a set of problems, beginning so early in life and affecting the person across the entire life span? Several theories referring to physiological processes have been proposed. Rimland (1964), for example, speculated that autistic children suffer damage to the reticular formation, an area of netlike nerve tissue in the brainstem which plays an important role in modulating arousal levels. As a result of this damage, the autistic child's level of arousal is abnormally low, and this hypoarousal is in turn responsible for a cognitive

defect, an inability to attend to stimuli long enough to relate one relevant one to another or to relate new stimuli to remembered experience. Because of the child's difficulty in integrating sensations, perceptions, and memory into a meaningful whole, new lively things are threatening and inanimate objects are much easier on his or her system.

Several considerations do make organic accounts of autism plausible. First, the age of onset is very early; autism is detectable in the first two years of life. Were a psychological stress to precipitate such disorders, it would indeed have to be a particularly dire event. Yet the available evidence does not indicate that these children are reared in especially unpleasant environments or that they suffered some severe trauma. There is general reason then to believe that autism is not caused by the experiences of the affected child during the first year or two of life. Second, a syndrome quite similar to the symptoms of autism may develop in the aftermath of brain diseases such as encephalitis, congenital rubella, and congenital syphilis. Third, mental subnormality is often associated with some kind of brain dysfunction and, as already noted, the majority of autistic children have low levels of intelligence.

As for what the faulty physiological processes might be, EEG, neurological, and genetic studies have proved illuminating. There has also been some interest in levels of brain amines, especially serotonin, but thus far no conclusions can be drawn (Campbell et al., 1974; Yuwiler et al., 1975; Ritvo et al., 1978).

Neurological Findings   If autism is related to abnormal brain functioning, this should be detectable in the children's EEGs or through a neurological examination, although such correlational evidence would not be sufficient to prove causation. The majority of studies of the electrical activity in the brains of autistic children have indeed found abnormal brain rhythms. Hutt and his colleagues (1964) reported low-amplitude, high-frequency waves and used them as evidence in proposing an overaroused cortex as the cause of autism. Others have failed to find this specific pattern, however, detecting instead slow-wave activity (Hermelin and O'Connor, 1968). Lotter (1974) reports that one-third of autistic children appear to have either seizures or an abnormal EEG. Similarly, Rutter and Lockyer (1967) reported that 14 to 20 percent of autistic children later develop seizures.

Neurological examinations have also revealed signs of damage in a large percentage of autistic children (Bosch, 1970; DeMyer et al., 1973; Gubbay, Lobascher, and Kingerlee, 1970). Thus a large proportion of autistic children appear to have a neurological dysfunction, as assessed by EEG and other neurological tests. The evidence however, does not necessarily support Rimland's specific theory of abnormally low arousal.

Genetic Factors   Genetic studies of autism are difficult to conduct because the disorder is so rare, somewhere between two to four cases per 10,000 children. Indeed, the family method presents special problems because autistic persons almost never marry. But autistics do often have siblings, so that the rate of autism in their brothers and sisters can be assessed. It turns out to be about 2 percent (Rutter, 1967). Although this as a small percentage in and of itself, it represents a fiftyfold increase in risk as compared to the morbidity risk in the general population.

Early twin studies of autism were seriously flawed, principally because of sampling bias. But evidence of the importance of genetic factors in autism is provided by a methodologically sound study conducted by Folstein and Rutter (1978). In ten pairs of fraternal twins, one of whom had autism, there was no concordance of the co-twins. But in the eleven pairs of identical twins, one of whom had autism, the concordance rate was 36 percent. Four of the co-twins had autism. In addition to examining concordance for autism, Folstein and Rutter also looked for cognitive disabilities, such as delayed speech, problems in saying words properly, and low IQ, in the co-twins. Concordance for cognitive impairment was 82 percent for the MZ pairs and 10 percent for the DZ. Thus the identical twin of an autistic is very likely to have difficulties of speech and intellect, but the fraternal twin of an autistic is not. Autism is apparently linked genetically to a broader deficit in cognitive ability. Taken together, the evidence from family and twin studies supports a genetic basis for infantile autism.

Psychological theories of autism

One of the best-known of the psychological theories was formulated by Bruno Bettelheim (1967). The basic supposition of Bettelheim's theory is that autism closely resembles the apathy and hopelessness found among inmates of German concentration camps during World War II (see page 167). Bettelheim hypothesizes that the young infant has rejecting parents and is able to perceive their negative feelings. He finds that his own actions have little impact on their unresponsiveness. The child comes to believe "that [his] own efforts have no power to influence the world, because of the earlier conviction that the world is insensitive to [his] reactions" (p. 46).

This experience of helplessness, which appears similar to the learned helplessness discussed earlier (see page 168), is viewed as extremely frustrating for the child. But he is unwilling to communicate his frustration because he feels that nothing good can come from it. He never really enters the world but builds the "empty fortress" of autism against pain and disappointment. His only activities—his ritualistic hand movements and echolalic speech—are more a means of shutting out the world than of truly meeting it. An elaborate fantasy life is created, and insistence on sameness is the rule that brings permanence and order. Autistic children remain safe only if everything about them stays put. Since the essential purpose of activity is to bring about change, autistic children avoid any sort of action; their universe centers on a static environment, beyond which they will not move.

Social-learning theorists, like those who are psychoanalytically oriented, have postulated that certain childhood learning experiences cause psychotic childhood disorders. Ferster (1961), in an extremely influential article, suggested that the inattention of the parents, especially of the mother, prevents establishment of the associations that make human beings reinforcers. And because the parents have not become reinforcers, they cannot control the child's behavior, the end result being infantile autism. Ferster's reasoning is as follows.

1. Behavior is controlled primarily by its consequences.

2. Initially, the young child responds only to primary reinforcers, such as food and milk.

3. As children grow older, their behavior comes more under the control of secondary and generalized reinforcers, such as praise and love. These social rewards have acquired their reinforcing properties through contiguous association with primary rewards.

4. The behavior of severely disturbed children is a consequence of not having adequate secondary and generalized reinforcers.

5. The parents of disturbed children, especially those of autistic children, neglect the child, for example, by being excessively involved in professional and other non-family-oriented activities.

6. Thus the child learns to function alone or autistically and never becomes responsive to human contact, having been deprived of it during the earlier stages of life.

Characteristics of the parents of autistic children

Both Bettelheim and Ferster, and others, have implied that parents play the crucial role in the etiology of autism. Many investigators have studied the characteristics of these parents; for a psychogenic theory of a childhood disorder to have any plausibility at all, something very unusual and damaging about the parents' treatment of their children would have to be demonstrated.

In his early papers Kanner described the parents of autistic children as cold, insensitive, meticulous, introverted, distant, and highly intellectual (Kanner and Eisenberg, 1955). He summed up his theory of how such traits affect the children by saying that they are reared in "emotional refrigeration." Others (for example, Singer and Wynne, 1963; Rimland, 1964) have also noted the detachment of parents of autistic children, although Rimland has used less pejorative adjectives. Singer and Wynne have described several means by which these parents "disaffiliate" themselves from their children. Some are cynical about all interpersonal relations and are emotionally cold; others are passive and apathetic; and still others maintain an obsessive, intellectual distance from people. But systematic

investigations have failed to confirm these earlier clinical impressions. For example, Cox and his colleagues (1975) compared the parents of autistic children to those of children with receptive aphasia (a disorder in understanding speech); the two groups did *not* differ in warmth, emotional demonstrativeness, responsiveness, and sociability. Similarly, DeMyer and her co-workers (1972) did not find the parents of autistic children to be rejecting, nor did McAdoo and DeMyer (1978) find psychiatric disorders in parents, using standard measures like the MMPI. The weight of the evidence is overwhelming. There is nothing remarkable about the parents of autistic children.

Even if we were to ignore these recent findings, the direction of a possible correlation between parental characteristics and autism is not easily determined. Any deviant parental behavior could be a reaction to the child's abnormality rather than the other way around (see Box 16.3). And if parental behavior causes autism, why is the incidence of similar difficulties so low in siblings? Moreover, although autism is a severe disorder, the parental behavior that has been discussed does not appear likely to be more than mildly damaging. It would seem that only very gross mistreatment, such as keeping the child in a locked closet, could precipitate severe problems so early in life. There have been few reports of exceedingly harsh treatment of autistic children.

It is commonly accepted in contemporary science that the failure to prove an effect does not mean it does not exist. Although investigations have not uncovered harmful parental influences on children of a sort that could reasonably cause infantile autism, this does not mean that such influences do not exist. In a purely logical sense, they may be operating, and so far we have simply failed to discover them. But in the meantime the early onset of autism and neurological and genetic evidence do imply a physiological basis for this puzzling disorder.

Treatment of Infantile Autism

Even though infantile autism is almost assuredly a disorder caused by some physiological aberration, interventions have often been psychological. Certainly until the true causes are discov-

BOX 16.3 The Pernicious Nature of Psychogenic Theories

Readers of this book have no doubt noticed that the authors are very critical of various psychogenic theories, both psychoanalytic and learning. In addition to our aspirations to provide as scientifically accurate a textbook as possible, we are concerned about the impact that theories may have on people. Consider, for a moment, what your feelings might be if a psychiatrist or psychologist were to tell you that your unconscious hostility has caused your child to be mute at the age of six. Or how would you feel if you were told that your commitment to professional activities has brought about the autistic behavior patterns of your child? The fact is, of course, that the truth of these allegations has yet to be demonstrated, and considerable information even contradicts these views. But in the meantime a tremendous emotional burden is placed on parents who have, over the years, been told that they are at fault.

As Rimland (1964) has suggested, considering autism psychogenic in origin may be not only an inadequate hypothesis but also a pernicious one.

ered, preventive efforts, such as those successful in reducing the incidence and severity of several forms of organically caused mental retardation, cannot be made.

Mental health professionals agree that autistic children have been helped through modeling and operant conditioning. On the positive side, behavior therapists have helped autistic children talk (Hewett, 1965), modified their echolalic speech (Carr, Schreibman, and Lovaas, 1975), encouraged them to play with other children (Romanczyk et al., 1975), and helped them become more generally responsive to adults (Davison, 1964).

Wolf, Risley, and Mees (1964) have supplied a case report of their treatment of an autistic child who had tantrums. On the assumption that this behavior was being maintained by adult attention, they isolated the boy in a room for short periods of time whenever he threw a temper tantrum. The acting out was soon eliminated. This

time-out procedure, whereby a person is temporarily excluded from situations in which positive reinforcement might be obtained, has proved effective with a number of behavioral problems and with children other than those diagnosed as autistic. For extreme and dangerous behavior, such as self-mutilation, brief but strong punishment may be necessary. Autistic children may bang their heads so hard against the wall that they have concussions, and they might bite their flesh to the bone. Ivar Lovaas, a leading clinical researcher in therapy for autistic children at the University of California at Los Angeles, has, together with his co-workers, demonstrated the effectiveness of spankings and brief electric shock in halting their self-destructive acts (Lovaas et al., 1965). Some therapists object to procedures that punish psychotic children, but the investigators and the vast majority of other professionals feel that they are justified. Electric shock rapidly eliminates sometimes life-threatening behavior

This autistic child is being taught sign language as a means of encouraging him to communicate with words.

and enables therapists to proceed with more positive instruction and remediation (Lovaas, 1977). The Lovaas group has also found that therapeutic improvement can be sustained if the parents are trained to maintain the same reinforcement contingencies at home; when children treated by the group entered institutions, where reinforcement contingencies were not sustained, the children lost whatever gains they had made (Lovaas et al., 1973).

A very different treatment of autism has been developed over many years by Bruno Bettelheim (1967, 1974) at the Orthogenic School of the University of Chicago. Bettelheim argues that a warm, loving atmosphere must be created to encourage the child to enter the world. Patience and what Rogerians would call unconditional positive regard are believed necessary for the child to begin to trust others and to take chances in establishing relationships. Bettelheim and his colleagues report many instances of success, but the uncontrolled nature of their observations makes it difficult to know what the active ingre-

dients might be. Bettelheim's treatment may contain more direct instruction, systematic reinforcement, and extinction than comes through in the published reports. By the same token, of course, reports of behavior therapists usually underplay the rapport building that undoubtedly provides the context for their programs.

As helpful as behavior therapies for autistic children have proved to be, most of them still remain autistic. Fewer than a fourth of children treated have an even marginal adjustment in later life. Greater knowledge of the true causes of the disorder may bring more thoroughgoing improvements in their lot. Lovaas and his group have a new tack which may be one answer. They now start working intensively with autistic children when they are very young, no older than two and a half years. The children are visited in their homes for four to six hours a day by six to eight undergraduates who work in shifts. The young therapists concentrate on developing the children's language and social skills and help them to eliminate their stereotyped and self-stim-

Bruno Bettelheim, prominent psychoanalytic theorist who founded the Orthogenic School as a treatment residence for autistic children.

ulating movements. After six months the children also attend preschool with normal peers. The children are considered to have responded well to all this help if they no longer make self-stimu-lating movements, play normally with their peers, and complete the first grade. The results have not yet been published, but preliminary in-dications are that 50 to 60 percent of the chil-dren are successful and another 30 percent im-prove appreciably. Such an outcome, if it holds through further research, will be very gratifying indeed.

Summary

The diagnostic criteria for mental retardation are subaverage intellectual functioning and deficits in adaptive behavior, with onset before the age of eighteen. Four levels of retardation are desig-nated, ranging from the profound when IQ is less than 20, to mild when IQ is 50 to 70. Many studies have been conducted on the specific in-tellectual deficits of retarded people. Some re-searchers believe that retardates have defects that separate their thinking qualitatively from that of normal people, such as an inability to think of mediators. Others, however, believe that retarda-tion is simply a quantitative variation from the norm, a slower rate of intellectual development with a more limited upper range. More severe forms of mental retardation usually have a physi-ological basis. These include the chromosomal trisomy that causes Down's syndrome; the reces-sive genes responsible for conditions such as phenylketonuria and Tay-Sachs and Neiman-Pick diseases; infectious diseases suffered by the preg-nant mother, such as rubella and syphilis, or af-fecting the child directly, for example, encephali-tis; and traumas such as Rh incompatibility, thyroid deficiencies, and malnutrition. For the mild range of retardation, which is by far the most prevalent, no identifiable brain damage is evident. These mild cases are often referred to as instances of cultural-familial retardation, reflect-ing the view that environmental factors are the principal causes. Among the specific findings are that the cultural-familial retarded come from lower-class homes in which deprivation is great. Preventive treatment for some forms of mental retardation, such as phenylketonuria, is now available. Using operant conditioning, shaping, and modeling, behavior therapists have been able to treat successfully many of the behavioral problems of retarded individuals as well as im-prove their intellectual functioning.

Infantile autism, one of the pervasive develop-mental disorders, begins before the age of thirty months. The major symptoms are extreme autis-tic aloneness, a complete failure to relate to other people; communication problems, either a failure to develop language or speech irregulari-ties such as echolalia and pronoun reversal; and preservation of sameness, an obsessive desire that daily routines and surroundings be kept exactly the same. Although no certain physiological basis of autism has been found, a number of points make such a cause plausible. Its onset is very early, syndromes similar to autism can develop as a result of encephalitis, and many autistic children have the low intelligence associated with brain dysfunctions. Furthermore, the EEGs of some autistic children are abnormal, and neurological tests also reveal abnormalities. Finally, both family and twin studies give evidence of a genetic predisposition. On the basis of early clinical reports, some theorists concluded that the coldness and aloofness of parents and their rejection of their children bring on autism. But recent research gives no credence to such notions. The most promising treatments of autism have often been by procedures that rely on modeling and operant conditioning. Although specific aspects of behavior can be improved, most autistic children remain intellectually and socially handicapped.

■ ■

chapter 17

AGING AND PSYCHOLOGICAL DISORDERS

The more fortunate readers of this book will grow old one day. When and as you do, physiological changes are inevitable, and there may be many emotional and mental changes as well. The physiological processes are inexorable, although sensible health regimens have been shown to delay many of the ravages of aging. We are concerned here less with physical changes than with the psychological aspects of growing old. Is it reasonable to expect a satisfying sex life in old age? Is the ability to remember and to think rationally subject to unavoidable deterioration? Does society treat the elderly in ways that may set them on a downward slide to senescence and even death? Are earlier emotional problems of anxiety and depression likely to become worse in old age? Do these emotional problems develop in people who did not have them when younger? Finally, are some therapies especially appropriate to our elders, and does society devote suitable monetary and intellectual resources to the development of effective ways of helping our older citizens? As life expectancy extends further and further into the seventies and perhaps even beyond, what is the professional community doing *now* to acquire knowledge and techniques that can make old age more meaningful than it has been for past generations, in the United States and in many other countries?

The elderly in this country are treated badly. The process of growing old, although inevitable for us all, is abhorred, even resented. Perhaps the lack of regard for senior citizens stems from our own deep-seated fear of growing old. The old person, especially one with serious infirmities, is an unwelcome reminder that we too will one day walk with a less steady gait, see less clearly, taste food less sharply, enjoy sex less frequently and with apparently less intensity, and fall victim to some of the many diseases and maladies that are the lot of most old people before they depart this world.

Growing old may be especially disagreeable for women. Even with all the consciousness raising carried out by the feminist movement in the past decade, women still have trouble accepting the wrinkles and sagging which become more and more prominent with advancing years. The cosmetics industry and plastic surgery make billions of dollars a year by exploiting the fear women have been taught to have about looking their age. Although gray hair at the temples and even a bald head are often considered distinguished and attractive in a man, a great many women who have the financial means to buy a few more years of youthful appearance do so. And so the psychological problems of older people may be especially severe for women.

Mental health professionals have almost phobically ignored the behavioral and emotional problems of the elderly. Misinformation is rampant, such as the belief that depression among old people is untreatable, that sex is a lost cause, that intellectual deterioration is widespread and inevitable. Butler and Lewis (1977) have shown that such "ageism" abounds in the writings of academicians and in the treatment regimens of clinicians, often exacerbating the plight of many older adults.

The relative inattention to mental health problems of the aging is both a cause and an effect of the inattention to professional training. As of 1981 only 2 of the 103 doctoral programs in clinical psychology accredited by the American Psychological Association had coherent and high-quality course work, research, and clinical training in aging, those at the University of Southern California and at Northwestern Medical School. Little training in geriatrics is given in medical schools, nursing schools, and schools of social work. Fortunately, several of the health professions have now evidenced considerable interest in aging. In June 1981, for example, the American Psychological Association sponsored a conference on geriatric clinical training. Its purpose was to bring together experts from around the country to formulate guidelines for proper training of clinicians for the aging, as well as to encourage the development of such programs.

Some Basic Facts[1]

Before we consider some of the basic facts of aging, two terms should be introduced. In any discussion of differences between the elderly, usually defined by gerontologists as those over the age of sixty-five, and those not yet old, a distinction is made between the contributions of what are called _age effects_ and _cohort effects._ Cohorts are people who have something in common; in studies of aging, they are people who were born in the same year. When several groups of cohorts are compared, age per se may not have caused the differences observed. For example, suppose we find in 1982 that people seventy years of age like to see romantic movies, people fifty-five Westerns, and those forty science fiction films. Can we conclude that something inherent in being seventy years of age makes people prefer _Gone with the Wind_ to _Star Wars_? No! The fact is that the people in each of the three age groups grew up in different periods, in years with enough cultural variation to affect taste in movies. A study with a cross-sectional design, one comparing different age groups at the same moment in time, masks cohort effects. Specialists in aging are sensitive to them, however, and have devised sophisticated research methods to separate cohort effects from the effects of growing older per se (Schaie, 1977).

Numbers of Older People   The proportion of older people in the population has increased greatly over the past three-quarters of a century. In 1900 only 4 percent of the United States population was over age sixty-five. In 1970 this percentage was 10 percent, or approximately 22 million persons. Since 1960 the number of people sixty-five or older has increased 21 percent, that of people under sixty-five only 13 percent (Brotman, 1973). By the year 2010, when the post-World War II baby boom people begin to reach sixty-five, upwards of 15 percent will be this age or older. These increases are attributed to many factors, but to decreased infant mortality and the widespread use of antibiotics in particular. More people than ever are surviving to age sixty-five and beyond.

[1] We acknowledge Zarit (1980) as a source of much of the content of this chapter.

Prevalence of Psychological Disorders Numerous surveys have been conducted to ascertain whether more old people than young have mental disorders. The question, then, is whether age itself is a contributing factor to mental and emotional malfunction. Estimates range from a low of 2 percent of the elderly to as many as 26 percent suffering from some kind of psychological impairment (Kramer, Taube, and Redick, 1973; Kay, Beamish, and Roth, 1964). As we shall see shortly, some disorders, particularly depression, seem to be more prevalent in old age. Whether psychological disorders are generally more prevalent in older adults is not clear. But it is evident that older people, like those younger, have psychological problems of an order requiring professional attention.

Physical Decline Many physical functions unquestionably decline with age. Both structural and functional losses are observed. For example, upwards of 85 percent of people over sixty-five have one or more chronic health problems, such as heart disease, hypertension, arthritis, and diabetes (Wilder, 1971). A decline in sensory acuity and a slowing of psychomotor responses are two certain hallmarks of advanced age. The lens of the eye yellows and becomes less accommodative, creating visual difficulties (Fozard et al., 1977). About 10 percent of people over sixty-five are blind or have greatly diminished vision. Lenses may help, but vision can seldom be restored to what it was when people were younger. Hearing is also impaired in most older people, and their senses of taste and smell diminish. Energy level is lower. Speed of responding, or reaction time, slows down with age, probably because transmission of neural impulses in the central nervous system is slower (Birren, 1974). Older people are wise to be more conservative when doing such things as driving a car. And younger people should be more tolerant when their elders negotiate highways and streets with less vigor and resolve than traffic conditions might allow.

Yet, in the face of these apparently inevitable losses in bodily performance, it has been estimated that at least 80 percent of the persons sixty-five or over are able to carry out major daily activities and otherwise function with a high degree of independence. Only about 10 percent must live in hospitals or nursing homes or be restricted to their homes because of serious physical disabilities.

IQ Changes Does measured IQ decline with age? Methodological problems abound in research attempting to answer this question, but some tendencies have been observed (Botwinick, 1977). Older people score differently on the verbal and performance sections of IQ tests. Scores on items measuring performance, such as the block design test (see Figure 16.1, page 491) become lower with age (Blum, Jarvik, and Clark, 1970). Because these tests require speed in responding, the declines in sensory functions and reaction time already mentioned would seem to account for the lower scores. In cross-sectional testing of people of different age groups, older people generally make higher verbal scores than performance scores (Doppelt and Wallace, 1955). Longitudinal studies of the same individuals at intervals over a period of years do not show declines in tests of vocabulary and logical reasoning. Indeed, people who have considerable ability when young tend to retain it as they grow old.

There are two general problems, however, in evaluating all this information, and they are relevant as well to memory difficulties. First, the high incidence of depression in older people argues for caution in interpreting IQ test scores, for this affective disorder interferes with a variety of functions, including the intellectual. Second, there is a "terminal drop" in all physical and psychological functions for a period of time before an individual dies; the older the person being tested, the more likely is performance compromised by this terminal slowing down.

Memory Changes The individual's ability to remember is obviously important in IQ testing. If we exclude the small minority of older people who suffer from senile dementia, a chronic brain disorder discussed later in this chapter, it is unclear whether or how memory worsens with age. There is evidence that older people do less well than younger on memory tasks that demand considerable organization of the material to be memorized. They also perform less effectively tasks that require divided attention. The underlying deficit is believed to be attentional; that is,

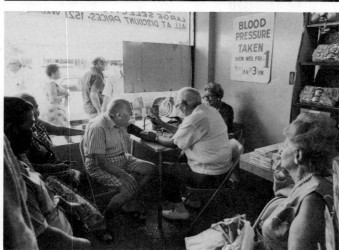

Elderly people are too often considered to be on a steadily declining path. In reality, many continue to work, play, love, and participate in commmunity activities.

older people have problems in concentrating on more than just a few things at a time (Craik, 1977). If we consider long-term memory—the ability to store material and then retrieve it after more than just a few minutes—older people are not as adept as younger ones in what is called free recall; they cannot as well retrieve an item from memory without being given hints or cues (Perlmutter, 1978). "Who was the thirty-fifth president of the United States?" is an example of a free-recall question. A cued-recall question, the kind that older people answer about as well as younger people, would be "Who was the president assassinated in Dallas in November 1963?"

On a practical level, we might ask whether the decrements in memory of older people, as measured in careful laboratory settings, reflect true functional deficits in their everyday lives. The kinds of memory tasks used in experiments may uncover deficits that are readily compensated for, such as by having a note pad nearby to jot things down on rather than relying on long-term memory.

Memory problems point up a general issue of attribution in thinking about aging. Old people are "known" to be forgetful, and when they are, their failing memory is attributed to the inevitable processes of aging. Impairments may be exaggerated, however, both by older people themselves, especially if they are depressed, and by society at large. For example, although half of a sample of people over sixty complained of memory problems, these complaints were not reflected on objective tests of memory (Lowenthal et al., 1967). It may be that elderly people, accepting the cultural stereotype of forgetful old folks, attach special significance to occasions when they have forgotten something (Kahn et al., 1975). This can create worry and anxiety which, in turn, can interfere with memory and other intellectual performance. Readers of this book under the age of sixty-five can confirm for themselves how often they forget another's name, or how often they cannot remember why they have gotten up from studying and gone into another room. Younger people seemingly forget more easily that they have been forgetful, an interesting irony indeed!

Finally, experimental psychologists know little about what we call wisdom and judgment, the complex capacity to use the experiences and knowledge of a lifetime sensibly and wisely. These abilities of old age are never tested.

Personality Changes   Do people undergo predictable personality changes in old age? It is widely assumed that old people are more rigid than young people. A variety of experiments, however, have failed to confirm this assumption (see Zarit, 1980). But there is some evidence that old people are more cautious than younger individuals. In one study (Rees and Botwinick, 1971) young and old people were asked to guess whether a particular sound had been played by the experimenter. When the sound was faint, yet within the hearing capacity of all subjects, the older people tended to say, more often than the younger, that no sound had been played. Other studies present a similar picture: in uncertain situations older subjects refrain more often from hazarding a guess. Of course caution in physical activities is easily observed in the elderly and is probably very adaptive, considering the losses in sensorimotor function common to old age. Living within one's capabilities and being more cautious than one was earlier in life seems evidence of growing sagacity rather than a sign of maladaptive timidity.

Social and Reality Problems Facing the Elderly

Medical care

Medical expenses constitute the greatest financial headache of the elderly. The Medicare program, passed in 1965 as part of the Social Security law, was intended to provide adequate medical care which was within the means of even the poor, but this has not happened. It has been estimated that in 1967 Medicare covered about 46 percent of medical expenses for the elderly; in 1976 this percentage had dropped to 38, indicating a worsening situation. The reasons for this failure are many and so complex that they are beyond the scope of this book. Suffice it to say that regulations keep changing so that old people and even the professionals who try to help them are often confused about what is covered. Some treatments, such as physical rehabilitation after a stroke or fracture, are not consistently covered; certain outpatient services of a preventive nature, such as dental and visual care, are inadequately covered or not covered at all; the increases in medical costs have outdistanced the benefits provided by federal and state governments; and limitations on length of hospital care as well as the premiums to be deducted from Social Security payments deny many old people proper medical attention.

Assuming the elderly can obtain and pay for medical care, how good is it? The answer seems to be, not very. The chronic health problems of old people are not appealing to physicians because they seldom diminish. In fact, many maladies of old people—such as hearing loss, visual impairments, loss of mobility, aches and pains, especially in the feet (Pearson and Gatz, in press), and a steadily declining cardiovascular system—are unlikely to get better and must somehow be adjusted to. The elderly come to rely heavily on their relationships with health care providers, but these providers may become impatient with them because they complain continually about not getting well or they become depressed.[2] Older people do not always take

[2] The situation may be even worse. As Zarit (1980) suggests, the illnesses of older people violate a "law" that the medical profession lives by, for these maladies are often incurable. Some of the impatience may therefore stem from the fact that older patients do not get well.

medication as instructed. Their relationships with family members who must look after them are likely to suffer. The ailing elderly are sometimes torn both by feelings of guilt for needing so much from others, and by anger against these younger people whom they have spent so many of their "good years" looking after and sacrificing for. The sons and daughters have similar feelings of guilt and anger.

At a time when custodial treatment of mental patients in hospitals is being replaced whenever possible by outpatient care, a very small percentage of the mentally ill over sixty-five are treated as outpatients (Kramer, Taube, and Redick, 1973). Indeed, older adults are overrepresented in state hospitals and especially in nursing homes. Many of the older chronic state hospital patients who are discharged "to the community" end up in nursing homes, the numbers of which have doubled over the past twenty years. It has been estimated that 80 percent of nursing home residents have mental health problems (Pfeiffer, 1977). This is an alarming statistic, given the fact that personnel trained to deal with emotional problems are the exception rather than the rule in such residences. Thus few elderly receive therapy in outpatient centers or, when hospitalization is required, rehabilitation to equip them to return to community settings. The bleak assumption seems to be that the mental health problems of old people are either impossible to alleviate or, worse still, not worth the time and effort since they do not have much longer to live anyway.

Poverty

In many respects the greatest challenge of old people is to cope with reality, the gradual loss of loved ones and friends, the deterioration of physical and psychological capacities, the low regard in which they are held by the culture at large. But of all the pressures borne by senior citizens, perhaps none is as cruel as poverty.

Although the Social Security system, begun in 1935 and denounced at the time by opponents of the Roosevelt Administration as socialistic, even communistic, and the Supplementary Security Income program, begun in 1974, have improved the situation for the elderly in the last half century, it is nonetheless the case that be-

Poverty is common among the aged, especially black women. Living in substandard housing is one of their usual deprivations.

tween 15 and 35 percent of old people must make do on incomes that are below the poverty level (Schulz, 1976). This range compares with about 10 percent of the general population who live in poverty. The situation is particularly acute for older women—for those separated from their husbands, for women who have never married, and for black women. According to one estimate, 96 percent of black women live below federally designated poverty levels (Atchley, 1977). Women in the current generation of old people are generally in a bad situation because the jobs they worked at seldom paid well or were covered by pension or Social Security plans. Those who were married receive lower benefits when their husbands die, and women tend to outlive men by an average of seven years.

The difficulty of living on fixed incomes, even though there are adjustments for inflation, has reduced some old people to subsisting on an inadequate diet and living in inadequate quarters. Their final years are a far cry from "the golden years" envisioned when they were younger. The reduction in their standard of living is one of their psychological predicaments.

Housing

Housing conditions may well affect the mental and emotional well-being of older people as indeed they may affect the attitudes all people have about their lives. Financial exigencies impinge here as they do on health care. Only about 5 percent of old people live in nursing homes or other institutions; most live in homes they have owned and occupied for many years or with their sons and daughters. A common problem of the elderly living in their own homes is that neighborhoods have frequently declined. Because they prefer familiar surroundings, and because they cannot afford to move or to make necessary repairs, a great many senior citizens live in deteriorating houses. It is not clear whether age-integrated housing is better than age-segregated, although we often hear "experts" proclaim that old people would rather live among other old people. This is surely true for some of the elderly, but it is very certainly untrue for many others. Retirement communities, with secure fences and guardhouses, social and recreational facilities, and even medical care immediately at hand, may be attractive to some, but, true to the complexity of the human species, others do not choose them, especially those for whom familiar neighborhoods and people have overriding importance.

Crime

Fear of crime is the most frequently reported worry mentioned in surveys of the elderly, and with good reason (Bild and Havighurst, 1976). Although statistics show that people over the age of sixty-five are less likely to be attacked than other age groups, they are more likely to be injured if assaulted. They are special targets for predatory crimes, for purse snatching and mugging in or near their homes. Indeed, most old people are easy marks for unplanned attacks by

A retirement community is now favored by many old people as the place to spend their last years.

inexperienced young thugs, who take advantage of their inability to fight back or to evade assaults. It is not uncommon for senior citizens to avoid being outside by themselves after sundown and sometimes even during the day as well. Their modest, often dilapidated houses and apartments become as much their self-imposed prisons as shelter from the elements. Fears of going about weigh heavily on the old, especially those living in large cities, and reduce the occasions of pleasure they might partake of in the society at large.

Retirement

Much has been made of the dread of retirement, but available information indicates that for most people it is a welcome and generally satisfying stage of life, especially for those who have not been happy with their jobs in the first place (Atchley, 1977)! The belief that retirement is a horror may derive from the fact that half of those retiring do so involuntarily. They have been forced to because of health problems or because their jobs have been eliminated, conditions hardly creating a sanguine context for this step. In general, no large-scale changes in mental or physical health have been found to accompany retirement (Sheppard, 1976). For people whose jobs or profession defined their lives, however, retirement can be stressful, especially when they fail to find activities that lend meaning and enjoyment to their leisure time. For others retirement means serious financial strain, casting a pall over the pleasures available in later years. The quality of retirement depends as well on the marital situation.

Widowhood

Nothing in life faces each person with greater certainty than death, both his or her own and, for many, the death of a loved one. We often feel inadequate and unable to cope with the demands of life, and we are disrupted even further by the death of a person on whom we have depended for support and companionship. For older people, especially women, the likelihood is considerable that their spouse will die before they themselves do. What effects does widowhood have on people?

Surprisingly little research has been done on the subject, perhaps a reflection of our own uneasiness about death and its aftermath. We do know, as common sense informs us, that to lose a spouse is very stressful. Studies have indicated that recently widowed people have many serious mental and physical problems, and widowed men have higher rates of dying themselves (Young, Benjamin, and Wallis, 1963). Negative sequelae—insomnia, difficulty eating, multiple somatic complaints, even hallucinations in previously normal individuals—can continue for many months after the loss of a spouse. Feelings of guilt are common. Perhaps I should have done more to get Joe to ease up. Why did I let him shovel the snow from the driveway? Anger at others is felt as well, especially at the physician who "let her die."

Is it easier to be widowed when old or when young? Answers are tentative and complex. A critical factor in satisfactory adjustment to widowhood may be whether the event was expected. Substantial evidence suggests that tragic events may occasion less trauma if their occurrence is anticipated and advance preparations have been made (Neugarten, 1977). An older married woman is virtually *expected* to become a widow. With about half the women over sixty-five widowed (Butler and Lewis, 1977), the older widow has considerable company. She may also choose to join a self-help widows' group. In contrast, the young widow, a statistical oddity in our culture, has few such supports and usually has a heavier burden of responsibility, such as raising young children. But at least the young widow is more likely to have new intimate relationships and even to remarry. The picture for the older widow is considerably less rosy. She has much less opportunity to socialize with men her own age, for only about 15 percent of men over sixty-five are widowed. Men are widowed less often because they tend to have wives younger than they, and because women outlive men by an average of seven years. As for older women being romanced by younger men, feminism has unfortunately made little impact on the prejudices against such pairings. Men, however, are virtually expected to choose younger women.

The adjustment problems of widowed men—and this may change in coming generations—are exacerbated by their inexperience in managing household affairs, such as cooking, mending

The death of a spouse is one of the most devastating losses facing old people.

clothes, and the like. Men who have depended on their wives for arranging social occasions with other couples will find that they have also lost their "social secretary."

A poignant source of stress for a widow or widower is the decision whether and when to remarry. When a man whose wife has died is fortunate enough to fall in love again, how will his children view his new "girlfriend?" Will they feel that Daddy never really loved Mom, for how could he take up with another woman so soon (how soon?) after her death? Does Dad feel he must get his children's approval? What burden of guilt does he bear? Does loving again make him doubt his feelings for his deceased wife? When two older people marry, they usually bring with them a family of *younger* people, a dramatic reversal of familiar roles. Now the children look over the new lover or fiancé and perhaps pass judgment. A new love interest also brings up for the children, now adults, of course, the issue of their parent's sexuality. The sons and daughters may be ambivalent about this, exacerbating the older people's concerns and puzzlement about how sexual a man and woman over sixty-five "should" or can be.[3]

Loss of friends

An older person loses people other than a spouse. The older we become, the older our long-time friends and confidants become, and the more likely these sources of support and intimacy are to die or become incapacitated. When people are raising children and working, they have built-in reference groups—the local Parent-Teachers Association, colleagues at the office or factory, neighbors—but when the household empties and when occupational ties are severed through retirement, it is more difficult to maintain relationships and to create new ones. So there can be for many older adults an impoverishment in personal relationships that may not be obvious to an outside observer. Then too there is the unfortunate fact that older people are frequently ignored when in public places, treated

[3] Sexuality and aging are discussed later in a separate section of this chapter (see page 546).

virtually as nonpersons. The isolation can be profound and, for some, devastating.

Having a confidant, a person in whom the older individual can confide and with whom he or she can discuss personal problems, acts as a buffer against diminished status and the lessening of other social ties and activities. Older people who enjoy a stable intimacy with another person are less likely to be depressed and are even better able to weather significant losses, such as retirement from a well-liked job and widowhood. Older women are somewhat more likely than older men to have a confidant, married people more likely to have one than widows, and widows more likely to have a confidant than single persons. The confidant is equally likely to be a spouse, a child, or a friend. A confidant does not seem to be able to keep up the individual's morale in the face of physical illness, however, and loss of a confidant plunges morale more than does any other social diminishment (Lowenthal and Haven, 1968).

Brain Disorders of Old Age

Although the vast majority of older people, approximately 95 percent, do not have organic brain diseases, a significant portion of those in hospitals and nursing homes do. Two principal types of brain disorders are distinguished: _delirium,_ often referred to as acute brain syndrome; and _senile dementia,_ a chronic brain syndrome that begins late in life.

Delirium (Acute Brain Syndrome)

Delirium is described by DSM-III as a "clouded state of consciousness." The principal manifestation in older persons is a sudden onset of cognitive difficulties; they have great trouble concentrating and focusing attention, and they cannot maintain a coherent and directed stream of thought. They may be impossible to engage in conversation because of their wandering attention. In severe delirium speech is sparse or pressured and incoherent. Delirious people have illusions and hallucinations, very often visual ones. They think that the bedclothes have become animated objects, or they may see a group of people hovering over the bed when no one is there. They may also become disoriented for time, place, and sometimes for person. When asked where she is, a delirious woman may insist that she is in a hotel, even though the name of the hospital is clearly printed on her bedsheets. But very often delirious people are so inattentive that they cannot be questioned for orientation. They are sometimes mistakenly diagnosed as schizophrenic because their misrepresentations of reality are so florid.

Perhaps as dramatic as their disordered thoughts and perceptions are the accompanying swings in behavior and mood. Delirious people can be erratic, ripping their clothes one moment, sitting lethargically the next. They are in great emotional turmoil and shift rapidly from one emotion to another—depression, anxiety, and fright, anger, euphoria, and apathy. Although the state of delirium varies with the person, symptoms come on rapidly and then fluctuate. They are usually worse during sleepless nights and in the dark. In the course of a twenty-four-hour period, and commonly in the morning hours, the individual has lucid intervals and becomes attentive and coherent. These fluctuations help to distinguish delirium from other brain syndromes.

Profuse sweating, a flushed face, dilated pupils, elevated blood pressure, and rapid pulse are also common. The cycle of sleep and wakefulness is invariably disturbed. Most importantly, symptoms may disappear entirely after a brief period of time, lasting usually no longer than a week if the causes themselves are either self-limiting or are adequately treated. If untreated, some people with delirium can die.

The episodic and reversible nature of delirium can be traced directly to the many organic causes. In general, in acute brain syndrome there is malfunctioning, but not destruction, of a significant number of brain cells. This neural dysfunction is thought to be caused by a range of physical diseases and traumas that interfere with removal of cell wastes and with the metabolic processes that support brain cells, such as supplying oxygen and proteins. Perhaps the most important of the various physical causes in older adults are drug intoxication, from the interactions of multiple medications, from overdoses, and from the side effects of proper and adequate doses; infections and high fever; malnutrition and vitamin deficiencies, especially of thiamine; dehydration; endocrine diseases, especially diabetes, hypothyroidism, and hypoglycemia; head trauma; and cerebrovascular problems, in particular congestive heart failure. Psychological factors may underlie the physical causes, as when an isolated old person becomes undernourished over a long period of time because of her depression; the brain receives an insufficient supply of nutrients, which eventuates in delirium.

People of any age are subject to delirium, but it is especially common in children and after age sixty. Older people are susceptible because of their less robust and efficient metabolism and the many medications prescribed for them. A physician may, for example, prescribe too high a dose of a tranquilizer for an agitated old person in a nursing home. If the resulting delirium then goes unrecognized as drug-induced, still higher doses of the drug will be prescribed, with still further delirium. Eventually, the patient will be considered senile, and indeed her acute problem, developed under the very eyes of professional staff, may have led to the destruction of brain cells (Zarit, 1980). Moreover, since many people with senile dementia suffer occasional bouts of delirium, careful and informed attention is called for. Sometimes a relatively minor adjustment, such as change in medication or allowing the person to go home, can reverse the sudden alteration in functioning that is characteristic of delirium.

Senile Dementia (Chronic Brain Syndrome)

Senile dementia is what laypeople call senility; it is a steady and gradual deterioration of intellectual abilities over several years, to the extent that it interferes with social and occupational functioning. Difficulty in remembering things is the most prominent symptom of dementia. People may leave tasks unfinished because they forget to return to them after an interruption. A person who had started to fill a teapot at the sink will leave the water running. Parents become unable to recall the name of a son or daughter and later do not even remember that they have children. In early stages the individual may deny the problem and attempt to hide the impairment. Zarit (1980) tells of a woman who used to like going out with her husband but began to make excuses not to, apparently concerned that others would notice her gaps in memory. Denial can also take the form of rationalization, such as saying that one dislikes the current president and for that reason cannot remember his name.

Abstract thinking suffers as well; people are confused by any new, rather complex task, especially when they are pressed for time. This loss can be tested by asking the person the meaning of proverbs; he or she will give literal and concrete interpretations. Those with dementia are also unable to find similarities and differences in related words. Judgment becomes faulty, hygiene poor, appearance slovenly. People lose their standards and control of their impulses; they may use coarse language, tell inappropriate jokes, shoplift, and make sexual advances to strangers. Individuals with dementia may also have paranoia, or they may become depressed. Eventually many are withdrawn and apathetic. In the terminal phase of the illness the personality has lost its sparkle and integrity. Relatives and

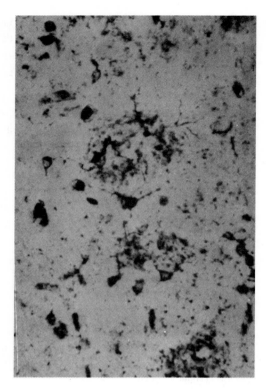

This micrograph of a cross section of degenerating brain tissue shows the small, round areas of granular material and filaments that constitute senile plaques.

friends will say that the person is just not himself any more. Social involvement with others has kept on narrowing. The person is eventually oblivious of his surroundings.[4]

There are numerous organic causes of chronic brain syndrome (CBS) in older adults, all of which lead to the destruction of brain cells and most of which are poorly understood at this time. Not long ago, cerebrovascular diseases, often called "hardening of the arteries," were incorrectly regarded as the primary cause of senile dementia. More recent research (for example, Terry and Wisniewski, 1977) has indicated that fewer than 25 per cent of cases of dementia in the elderly are clearly traceable to heart and circulatory problems. Indeed, over half of them are caused by "Alzheimer-type" brain diseases, in which primary neuronal degeneration occurs. The degeneration consists of diffuse atrophy or

wasting away of cortical cells, to the extent that sulci widen and the ventricles become larger (see Box A.1, page 714); senile plaques, small areas of deterioration in the brain tissue; and neurofibrillary tangles, threadlike structures displacing normal neurons. The Appendix contains a discussion of a wide range of brain disorders, including Alzheimer's disease, a dementia occurring in people as young as forty. Because of the similarity of brain deterioration and intellectual deficits in this disease of younger people and in senile dementia, many dementias in older people are referred to as "Alzheimer-type" brain diseases. Taken together, then, vascular and Alzheimer-type syndromes constitute the vast majority of senile dementias. It is not uncommon, however, to find mixed cases. Alzheimer-type atrophy may coexist with infarctions, or areas of dead cells caused by obstructions in blood supply to the brain, as in a stroke (see Box 17.1). If vascular dementia is the result of the gradual accumulation of small lesions throughout the cortex, brought about by a series of small strokes or extended periods of diffuse circulatory

---

[4] As used here, dementia refers to irreversible psychological deterioration brought on by progressive destruction of nerve cells. But the term is applied as well to any intellectual loss, without giving a particular cause. As noted in the Appendix, some dementias are reversible if the underlying cause is modified.

insufficiency, often referred to as multi-infarct dementia, the manifestations may be difficult to distinguish from Alzheimer-type syndromes. In general, the onset of Alzheimer-type dementias is insidious, with progressive deterioration leading to death within ten to fourteen years. The course of multi-infarct syndromes is less predictable; there is likely to be greater fluctuation in both cognitive and emotional states as the condition worsens.

But the brain is a complex, little understood organ, and the diagnosis of dementia is an imprecise and rather global one. People also vary considerably in how they react psychologically to apparently similar deterioration of the brain. Some persons with extensive brain damage have less behavioral and intellectual deterioration than might be expected, whereas others with minimal damage have considerable psychological loss (Tomlinson and Henderson, 1976). Workers in the field of gerontology acknowledge that factors such as prior education, energy level, and whether the person lives at home play an important role. Nonetheless, psychological deficits are strongly related to extent of brain damage.

Because of the differing ways in which older people manifest similar types of cortical damage, and in which a single individual manifests deterioration and tries to compensate for it throughout the course of an organic brain disorder, a diagnosis of dementia is difficult to make. There are two additional complications; delirium may overlie dementia, and several types of senile dementia with different prognoses may coexist. Moreover, the symptoms of many depressed elderly—memory complaints, difficulties in concentration, and psychomotor changes—mimic those of organic brain syndromes. Such depressive disorders are called "pseudodementia" (Post, 1975). Considerable research on how to determine whether the causes of psychological deficit in the elderly are affective or organic is currently in progress. One way to distinguish between depression and dementia is to motivate the person to improve performance; many depressed people can function better temporarily if exhorted to do so, but the person with dementia cannot.

Several methods of assessing organic brain syndromes are available to clinicians, although some are still in rudimentary stages of development (Eisdorfer and Cohen, 1978).

1. Clinical interviews with the patient, family members, and significant others.
2. Carefully compiled health histories.
3. Formal psychological testing, usually of cognitive performance.
4. Medical and neurological examinations.
5. EEG and radiological techniques, including CAT scans.
6. Medical laboratory tests to assess the metabolism

These diverse methods call for multidisciplinary skills—of physicians, social workers, laboratory technicians, and a relatively new group of professionals, those holding a master's degree in gerontology. Nonetheless, even with systematic use of these assessment techniques, only through the passage of time and by decreasing doses or eliminating drugs one at a time, changing diet, treating infections, and giving psychotherapy can the accuracy of diagnoses be verified.

In light of these diagnostic problems, it is best to be conservative in diagnosing senile dementia (DSM-III, 1980; Zarit, 1980), and instead to explore temporary and reversible causes of the symptoms. Both acute brain syndrome and psychogenic depression are reversible and should be treated. But senile dementia is not, for brain cells do not regenerate, and no known interventions prevent or retard the continuing destruction of cells. Therefore it would seem better to fail to diagnose senile dementia when it is present than to diagnose it when it is not.

Treatment of Delirium

Delirium is usually reversible. An elderly woman was found in a filthy apartment with no food. Initially believed by a poorly informed physician to be senile, she was simply given routine custodial care in a nursing home. Fortunately, a professional knowledgeable about delirium learned that she had become depressed over the loss of a loved one and in her despondency had neglected her diet. Appropriate counseling in tak-

BOX   **17.1** Cerebrovascular Diseases—Stroke and Its Aftermath

The blood vessels supplying the brain are subject to several types of malfunction. In *atherosclerosis* deposits of fatty material narrow the lumen, or inner passageway, of the arteries of the body. When those in the brain are affected, some areas may not receive enough blood and hence insufficient oxygen and glucose. If the shortage is prolonged, the brain tissue, which is particularly dependent on receiving adequate supplies, softens, degenerates, and is even destroyed. The effects of cerebral atherosclerosis vary widely, depending on what area of the brain has clogged arteries and whether it is also supplied by nonaffected blood vessels. About three million Americans are incapacitated in some way by cerebral atherosclerosis (Terry and Wisniewski, 1974).

In *cerebral thrombosis* a blood clot forms at a site narrowed by atherosclerosis and blocks circulation. Carbon dioxide builds up and damages the neural tissues. The loss of consciousness and control is referred to as apoplexy or *stroke.* The patient may die, suffer paralysis or decreased sensation from one side of the body or of an arm or leg, or lose other motor and sensory functions. The impairments of the patients who survive may disappear spontaneously, or they may be lessened through therapy and determined effort. Usually there is some residual damage. When only a small vessel is suddenly blocked, the patient suffers transient confusion and unsteadiness. A succession of these small strokes will bring cumulative damage, however.

A frequent impairment is *aphasia,* a disturbance of the ability to use words. The cause of this damage may be a clot in the middle cerebral artery supplying the parietotemporal region, usually of the dominant cerebral hemisphere. A right-handed person depends on the parietotemporal region in the left hemisphere for language skills; a left-handed person may depend on this region in the right hemisphere or in the left. Interestingly, damage to the right hemisphere in a right-handed person and to the left in a left-handed person disturb's the ability to use language to a lesser extent.

Aphasia is generally divided into two types, receptive or sensory and executive or motor. In sensory aphasias individuals have difficulty in understanding the meaning of words. They may have auditory aphasia and not understand the words spoken to them or visual aphasia and not understand the printed word. They will, however, be able to speak properly; and they may, for example, be able to read but not understand spoken speech, or they may understand spoken speech but not be able to read. With motor aphasia a person suffers no deficit in comprehension but has problems in speaking words and sentences. He or she may transpose syllables, utter words of a sentence out of order, or be unable to recall names of common objects.

In *cerebral hemorrhage* a blood vessel ruptures because of a weakness in its wall, damaging the brain tissue on which the blood spills. Cerebral hemorrhages are frequently associated with hypertension. The psychological disturbance produced depends on the size of the vessel that has ruptured and on the extent and the location of the damage. Often the person suffering a cerebral hemorrhage is overtaken suddenly and rapidly loses consciousness. When a large vessel ruptures, the person suffers a major stroke. All functions of the brain are generally disturbed—speech, memory, reasoning, orientation, and balance. The person usually lapses into a coma, sometimes with convulsions, and may die within two to fourteen days. If the person survives, he or she will probably have some paralysis and difficulties with speech and memory, although in some cases appropriate rehabilitation restores nearly normal functioning. Cerebral thromboses and hemorrhages together kill about 200,000 Americans each year (Terry and Wisniewski, 1974).

The following case illustrates the human impact of a stroke and efforts that can be made to restore some semblance of normalcy.

At age sixty-eight, Mr. H., a retired small businessman, was active in community affairs and with his hobby of woodworking. He had high blood pressure that was well controlled on medication and had had diabetes for several years, which was controlled with insulin. Mr. H. was accustomed to being independent and in charge of things, and this was acceptable to his wife of forty-five years. Mr. H. believed that any reduction of his independent status would be a sign of weakness. He was generally even tempered but would become angry when he was hindered from completing a task he had set out to do. . . .

Mrs. H. was active with her church group and had frequent visitors. She was in good health but had only moderate physical strength. She prepared well-balanced meals for both of them, including the special diet required for Mr. H. because of his diabetes and high blood pressure. They had two children, both of whom were married and living out of state, but who visited at holiday times.

One morning Mrs. H. entered her husband's workshop and found him sitting on a chair and unable to speak. The right side of his face drooped and he was unable to move his right arm or leg. He did not seem to see her when she approached him from his right but could see her when she moved to his left side. He made a few attempts to speak but was unsuccessful. Mrs. H. called their physician, who arranged for ambulance transportation to the hospital. Detailed examination and testing revealed that Mr. H. had sustained a stroke due to the occlusion of an artery supplying the left side of his brain. After receiving acute care including that necessary to prevent complications and reaching a stabilized condition, Mr. H. was transferred to a comprehensive medical rehabilitation center.

Mr. H.'s medical records were reviewed by the rehabilitation physician, he was examined, and his wife was informed of the results. She was also interviewed by a social worker who obtained further background information and answered questions about the facility. Mrs. H. found that she would be part of the rehabilitation process, that the staff would work closely with her, and she would receive training necessary to help in her husband's care when he returned home. She would also receive counseling to aid her in coping skills and help her adapt to this change in their life situation. Mr. H. had a urinary catheter and had become constipated because of his illness and inactivity. These problems were attended to by the rehabilitation nursing staff, which also kept close watch on skin condition, both because of his impaired mobility and his diabetes. They monitored his blood pressure and regularly checked his urine for sugar. As Mr. H. progressed in the program, they taught him how to inject his insulin with his left hand and taught his wife how to draw up the proper amount in the syringe.

Mr. H. began to regain some communication ability, and his function was carefully evaluated by the speech pathologist, who aided him in improving general communication abilities. She informed Mrs. H. and the rehabilitation team members about how best to communicate with Mr. H. Speech therapy was also used to improve the volume and clarity of his speech.

As communication abilities improved, a psychologist evaluated Mr. H.'s mental status and cognitive skills and helped him to adapt to the frustrations of his disability and his feelings of [not] being in control. The psychologist also helped Mr. H. direct his anger in a more productive manner rather than diffusely taking out frustrations on the staff or on his wife. . . .

The physical therapist gradually helped Mr. H. improve his bed mobility and transfers, and eventually he progressed to the point where he was ambulating, first with a broad-based four-pointed cane and maximum assistance, and ultimately with a straight cane with his wife standing by. The occupational therapist worked on teaching Mr. H. to use his non-dominant hand while he was also working to improve function in the weak right hand. He was taught to feed himself, to dress himself, and to perform the basic activities of daily living. He was also given exercises and training that would [allow him to pursue] his woodworking hobby, at least to a limited degree.

The recreational therapist helped Mr. H. to reach some self-fulfillment during his leisure time. His leisure activities were geared to those he had previously enjoyed, adapted to his disability. Transportation and financial status were discussed with Mrs. H. and also with her husband and appropriate community agency referrals were made. An occupational therapist went out to the house to evaluate the existence of architectural barriers and to make recommendations for safety.

During this course of events, the rehabilitation team met weekly to discuss the problems that Mr. H. was experiencing, to compare ideas on solving these problems, and to plan the treatment approach for the forthcoming week. After about a month of this treatment Mr. H. was able to return home with his wife at a semi-independent level, with plans to return for out-patient treatment in order further to increase his strength, mobility, self-care, and communication skills (Zarit, 1980, pp. 179-180).

ing better care of herself was therefore provided, along with special attention to her diet. Her condition improved gratifyingly, enough to allow her eventual discharge to her own home (Zarit, 1980).

This case is not atypical. Old people are often assumed to be senile and therefore beyond help. A decision for long-term, that is terminal, institutional care is all too often viewed as the only sound one, in spite of the fact that many disoriented, despondent, and withdrawn older people may be only delirious and can be helped by proper assessment and therapy. They must be examined for all the possible causes, drug intoxication, infections, fever, malnutrition, dehydration, endocrine diseases, head trauma, and congestive heart failure and treated accordingly.

Families with a senile parent must also be counseled on the realities of acute brain syndrome. A father with senile dementia, for example, may run a high fever from influenza and begin to hallucinate and otherwise act bizarrely. These new symptoms, superimposed on the intellectual deterioration to which members of the family have already become accustomed, may alarm them into concluding that he is losing ground fast and irreversibly. They may be hastened into a premature decision to institutionalize him. Proper diagnosis and treatment can often eliminate the delirium and return the patient to pretty much the same demented condition which, although problematic, was nonetheless being coped with by those taking care of him in the home.

Treatment of Dementia

Zarit (1980) has succinctly summarized the interventions that make sense in senile dementia.

The treatment of persons with senile dementia is basically supportive both of affected individuals and of their social networks. At present there are no methods that effectively restore intellectual function or prevent further deterioration in cases of senile brain disease. Treatment involves minimizing the disruption caused by the disorder. Goals for treatment include: maintaining the person in a community setting;

allowing affected persons the opportunity of discussing their illness and its consequences; giving information to family members and other concerned persons about the nature of this disorder; supporting family members so that they can continue to provide assistance to the affected person; and using behavioral and problem-solving methods to deal with specific issues that arise as the result of the brain disorder (p. 356).

Most people with senile dementia are in hospitals and nursing homes. But today mental health professionals recommend maintaining all but the most seriously ill patients in their homes when adequate support systems are available. For one thing, people with dementia frequently have inordinate difficulty adapting to new places, for their cerebral damage interferes with new learning. For another, staff in some hospitals and nursing homes tend to overmedicate, which can of course bring on delirium and exacerbate the person's emotional and intellectual deterioration.

Of overriding importance is the support provided to the caregivers, to the family members and friends who are faced with taxing demands on their time, energies, and emotions as they look after patients who may be incontinent, irrational, and bedridden. They need accurate information on the nature of the patient's problems. For example, people with dementia have far less difficulty with short-term memory than with long. This means that they can engage in a reasonable conversation but will forget minutes later what had been discussed. A caregiver may become impatient and even abusive unless he or she understands that this impairment is to be expected because of the underlying brain damage. Making increased demands on the patient, perhaps in the belief that he or she is expressing hostility in a passive-aggressive manner, is likely to be aggravating for the person making them and for other family members, and it will not improve the elderly person's recollections. Homespun memory drills are also ill-advised; there are no known techniques for improving the memories of people with dementia.

Caregivers should also be informed that dementia patients often do not appreciate their limitations and may attempt to engage in activities beyond their abilities, sometimes in a dangerous manner. Although it is not advisable to coddle patients, it is important to set limits in light of their obliviousness to their own problems and impairments.

Sometimes the caregiver's reactions to the patient's problems require attention. The daughter-in-law of a senile woman was offended by the woman's color combinations in clothing and wished to take over responsibility for coordinating her wardrobe, even though the woman was capable of dressing herself in an adequate, although not spiffy, fashion. The caregiver was urged not to impose her own standards and taste on the old woman and to understand that her ability to dress herself and take responsibility for her clothes was more important than adherence to conventional standards of appearance.

There are several other ways in which counselors and therapists can help those responsible for looking after people with senile dementia at home. Many caregivers are afraid to leave the infirm person alone, and as a consequence they exhaust themselves paying constant attention to the sick person. They deny themselves simple diversions and pleasures because they view any absence as neglect of the spouse or parent. In many instances their overattention is inappropriate to the situation, and they should be told this. If the infirm person's needs are really critical, outside help from a nurse or other professional should be sought.

The counselor must bear in mind that some of the tensions between caregiver and sick person may well have their roots in aspects of the relationship that predate the onset of dementia. There is a tendency to consider the most obvious facet of a situation, here the impairments of the sick person, as the cause of all difficulties. Counseling directed to long-standing problems may be called for.

The paranoid delusions often found in senile dementia can be very disruptive. As with paranoia generally, the beliefs should not be challenged directly. It is better to try to work around them, concentrating on aspects of the person's behavior that are more intact. The delusions in senile dementia diminish in time, as memory worsens with the progressive cerebral deterioration; the prognosis for this aspect of the illness is, in a sad sort of way, good.

Counseling the organically impaired person is difficult and, with the more severely deteriorated, of apparently little benefit because of their cognitive losses. But some dementia patients seem to enjoy occasional conversations with professionals and others not directly and constantly involved in their lives. It would appear important not to discount entirely their ability to participate in their caregivers' discussions of ways to cope with their infirmities. Their inherent cognitive limitations must be appreciated, however; Zarit (1980) even suggests that no efforts be made to get them to admit to their problems, for their denial of them may be the most effective coping mechanism available to them.

Moreover, the cognitive limitations of senile persons should always be treated with gentleness. Others should not consider them non-beings, talking about their debilities in their presence, making fun of their occasional antics and forgetfulness, discounting their paranoid suspicions about others. Old people, even those with no organic disorder, are often infantilized or ignored by their juniors, a sign of disrespect that demeans not only the elderly person but the person showing the discourtesy.

Perhaps the most heart-rending decision is whether and when to institutionalize the old person. At some point the nursing needs may become so onerous and the mental state of the person so deteriorated that placement in a nursing home is the only realistic option, not so much for the benifit of the impaired person as for his or her family. The conflicts encountered in making this decision are not to be underestimated. The counselor can be a source of information about nearby facilities as well as a source of support for making and implementing the decision.

Psychological Disorders in the Elderly

In an earlier discussion the point was made that transsexuals tend to attribute whatever personal unhappiness they experience to the discrepancy between their anatomy and their gender identity. A similar process operates with old people, at least as they are viewed by others. The most obvious characteristic of a seventy-five-year-old man is that he is old. If he is cranky, it is because he is old. If he is depressed, it is because he is old. Even if he is happy, it is assumed to be because of his age. Moreover, the "old-age explanation" is generally a physical one, even if this is not made explicit. Some ill-defined physical deterioration is assumed to underlie not only the physical problems of old people but all their psychological problems as well.

This physical explanation of psychological disorder locates the cause of old people's problems within them and often blinds us to other factors that may have much to do with whatever mental or emotional distress they are suffering. Although normal aging processes may make people forgetful and diminish sexual capacity, the fact is that most of the psychopathology to be found in the aged has not been directly linked to the physiological processes of aging.[5] Stress from having to live in poverty and from being less mobile and inability to come to terms wtih loneliness after death of a spouse and friends are possible causes. Whether the person brings maladaptive personality traits and inadequate coping skills into old age figures as well.

Depression

In view of the losses inherent to old age—the loss of status, of power, and of control through diminishing physical capacities—it is not surprising that depression is the most prevalent psychological disorder among older people, occurring more often in them than in younger people. The discussion of depression in Chapter 8 should help us understand the severe despondency and hopelessness found in many people over the age of sixty-five, and it may provide some clues about treatment. But it is important to consider as well dissimilarities in the depressions of younger and older people.

Extent of depression among older people
Trouble in sleeping, headaches, and poor appetite are recognized symptoms of depression. Such somatic complaints of older people do not necessarily mean that they are depressed, however; they are commonly beset by physical woes as their bodies naturally run down. But in spite of this and other diagnostic problems, it is generally agreed that the prevalence of depression is particularly high among the aged, upwards of 25 percent, as compared to about 10 percent in people under sixty-five. The majority of major depressive episodes in older adults are recurrences of the disorder (Gurland, 1976). Other people have episodes of depression for the first time in late life. Depression is the most frequent diagnosis for people admitted to mental hospitals after the age of sixty-five. And surveys of non-hospitalized elderly confirm the prevalence of depression, it being the most common complaint of otherwise healthy elderly people residing in the community (Busse, 1970). The complaint is even more common in people with chronic health problems, including senile dementia.

Theories of depression among the elderly
Senile Brain Disorders It used to be thought that the depression found in an old person was caused by the brain damage associated with senile dementia. Recent evidence contradicts this straightforward organic view. Postmortem analyses of the brains of people diagnosed as "functionally" depressed and of those of people diagnosed as having senile dementia revealed much more extensive damage in brains of the dementia group; in fact, the extent of the brain damage in the functionally depressed was within normal limits (Blessed, Tomlinson, and Roth, 1968). Other studies found that old people admitted to a hospital with a diagnosis of depression tended to be released much sooner and to live much

---

[5] This statement needs qualification. The older the old person is, the more important physical deterioration becomes in understanding psychological deficits. The "old, old," people eighty years of age and beyond, are clearly subject to many physical problems, which can affect their mental and emotional functioning.

longer than those admitted with a diagnosis of dementia. And up to six years later no more of them had developed brain disease than is expected in the aged population at large (Post, 1962). Such findings argue against interpreting depression in old people as caused either exclusively or predominantly by brain disease. At the same time, however, people with senile dementia *do* suffer from depression, but only in the earliest stages of the progressive disease; as their intellectual impairment worsens, they have a diminished awareness of their situation.

Biochemical Theories   Can the especially high incidence of depression in the elderly be reconciled with the theories that consider depression to have biochemical bases? Levels of monoamine oxidase are higher in old people than in younger. We know that MAO destroys norepinephrine and serotonin, neurotransmitters found to be lower in depressed people (see page 255). This may be one link between depression and biochemical changes in old age. Another may be the diminishing output of the thyroid gland. Continued research may reveal other possible biochemical bases of depression in older people, but at the present time it would be a mistake to focus attention on them to the neglect of psychological factors.

Psychological Factors   The sense of having no control over stressful events, discussed in connection with generalized anxiety disorder, psychophysiological disorders, and depression, and the reduction in reinforcing events, discussed as another cause of depression, are useful concepts in understanding the prevalence of depression in older people. Having serious and often chronic physical illness; being forced to retire, without finding rewarding postretirement activities; a reduction in social status; and deaths of friends and spouse are all common to the lives of older people and can be expected to create the sense of helplessness and hopelessness that appears to underlie depression in all people. Studies have found that older people often become depressed after the loss of persons important to them (Paykel, 1974). Medical illness has also been found an especially critical factor (Post, 1962); it requires no sophisticated psychological theory to realize that a person who learns of terminal illness, or of a health problem that will seriously limit pleasurable activities and cause constant pain, is likely to become depressed.

Many more old people face adversity than become depressed, however. What might account for this? People may have a premorbid "cognitive style" by which they come to believe, after a single calamity, that nothing is good and that things will never improve. Or they may attribute misfortunes to their own shortcomings, as when a woman blames herself for the death of her ailing husband. Although our focus is on old age, we must continually bear in mind that older people are individuals, each of whom brings to the senior years a developmental history that lends uniqueness to his or her reactions to common problems. The kind of personality individuals bring to old age is a crucial factor in how effectively they respond to the experience of being elderly (Butler and Lewis, 1977).

Treatment

Many depressed older adults can be helped by psychological interventions. Two treatments discussed in Chapter 8 are of special interest. Lewinsohn indicates the importance of motivating depressed people to undertake activities providing positive reinforcement. Social-skills training can help the old person engage in new activities and find opportunities for pleasure and companionship. For example, the depressed widower who has seldom prepared a meal can be urged to take a cooking class at the local junior college as a first step toward more independent living. Beck tries to help depressed people eliminate negative thought patterns and self-talk. Although there is little solid experimental evidence indicating that these therapies help older depressed people, numerous case reports suggest that they can substantially reduce their despondency. In more general terms, Pfeiffer (1977) has indicated that older people have to adapt to losses, many of them inevitable, either by finding substitutions, such as making new friends, or when no replacements are possible, by realizing that they must make do with less. The older person should also be encouraged to remain as physically and mentally active as possible.

Paranoid Disorders

Mrs. Warner was an eighty-year-old widow, in good physical health, alert, and well informed about events around her. She was not disoriented, and there was no other evidence of organic brain disease. However, from time to time she became very concerned and upset over the "fact" her neighbors were putting lint into her washer and dryer. On several occasions she went to the police station to lodge a complaint. She had no good explanation why the neighbors were doing this. Reasoning with her was to no avail. For instance, her daughter tried to prove that this could not be happening because there was nowhere the neighbors could obtain lint to dump into her machine. Apart from this she got along well, but on washdays her complaints and accusations returned.

Mrs. B., age seventy-four, had a happy marriage of fifty-three years until her husband died. After [she had spent] the winter alone in her big house, her son suggested that perhaps she would enjoy going to the spring meeting of the Golden Age Society. This would give her an opportunity to meet new people, see old friends, and have an outing with people her own age. She thought this was an excellent idea, and she looked forward to going.

In the afternoon paper a few days later she saw an article about the meeting to be held the next morning. She noticed that the topic for the meeting was "Correct Way to Prepare Your Will." The article went on to state that questions could be asked, and anyone wishing to make a will could do so that morning. On reading this she "realized" why her son had told her about the meeting and insisted that she go. She became angry, refused to go, and was sure that her son was "in cahoots" with the man making out the wills, and this was his way of seeing to it that she left all her worldly possessions and savings to him (Pfeiffer and Busse, 1973, pp. 127-128).

The delusions and their implications

Although paranoia is not as widespread in older people as depression, it has a more disturbing and immediate impact on others, often bringing angry reactions and contributing to decisions to institutionalize them (Berger and Zarit, 1978). Older people may have delusions that people are eavesdropping on them, opening their mail, plotting to steal their money, or poisoning their food. Some of the old people will have had a marginal adjustment for many of their adult years; it must not be forgotten that the mental and emotional ills of earlier years may extend into old age. But for most old people paranoid ideation is a new thing; and it is not accompanied by the hallucinations, agitation, and argumentativeness of paranoid schizophrenia.

There is an interesting and striking difference between the paranoid delusions of older people and those of younger individuals. The suspicions of older adults are more down to earth, concerned with persons in their immediate surroundings—such as neighbors, sons and daughters, people in stores, and the like. In contrast, the persecutors of younger paranoids are often located far away, in the C.I.A. or the F.B.I. or even outer space. Younger paranoids are given to more grandiosity than older ones.

Older people are especially vulnerable to all kinds of abuse from others, however. They may be talked about behind their backs, or even to their faces, as though they were not present; taken advantage of by others, in many small and larger ways; and deprived of control of their financial assets by greedy and impatient relatives. There is danger that a complaint of persecution from an old person will be blithely dismissed as "just" a sign of late-life paranoid disorder. A client of one of the authors complained bitterly about being followed by private detectives hired by her "evil" husband. Inquiry revealed that the husband was worried that she was having an affair and had indeed hired someone to follow her! It should always be determined whether suspicions have any bases in reality before they are attributed to paranoia.

Causes

Perhaps there is something specific about being old that heightens suspiciousness and eventually precipitates delusions. Brain disorders have been implicated as one possible cause. People with delirium and senile dementia have more than their share of paranoid experiences. Levels of medication that are too high for impaired central nervous systems are a possible chemical cause (Pfeiffer and Busse, 1973). Paranoia may serve a function for the senile dementia sufferer, filling in the gaps in memory caused by the progressive cerebral atrophy. Instead of admitting "I can't remember where I left my keys," he or she thinks, "Someone must have come in here and taken my keys" (Zarit, 1980). As indicated earlier, such instances of paranoia recede over time as brain damage becomes more extensive.

Paranoia is also related to losses in sensory functions, in particular of hearing. More paranoid older people have poor hearing than do older people without paranoid thoughts (Cooper et al., 1974). Not hearing easily, some old people may think that others are saying bad things about them (see Box 17.2). Social isolation must also be a factor, for people living alone or with only limited contacts with others are particularly subject to paranoia. Isolation limits a person's opportunities to check his or her suspicions and ideas about the world, making it easier for delusions to take hold. By the same token, paranoid individuals often avoid others or are excluded by them from normal social intercourse; paranoia may therefore contribute to isolation, as much as isolation contributes to paranoia.

Paranoia may be maintained at least in part, as are other kinds of abnormality, by reinforcement from others. A lonely woman gets action from police and relatives if she complains of intruders. Sadly enough, sometimes such attention is the best that old people can manage to obtain. But it should not be supposed that the adoption of a paranoid belief is deliberate, nor does it seem plausible that reinforcement patterns can explain why a person begins having delusions in the first place.

Treatment

The treatment of paranoia in old people is much the same as for younger individuals. Directly challenging the paranoid delusion is seldom effective; by the time the patient sees a health professional, friends, relatives, and police have no doubt already tried this approach, to no avail. Especially with a forgetful older person, it can be helpful to consider a paranoid delusion to be his or her most available plug for a gap in memory or in knowledge about the surroundings. Toxicity from medications must always be considered as well, given the particular sensitivity of many older people to drugs. Judicious use of phenothi-

azines is sometimes effective, although paranoid individuals are generally suspicious of the motives of those who give them drugs. They may view the pill or capsule as just another clever means of gaining control over their minds, a belief which, in an interesting sort of way, has considerable validity. Clinical lore suggests that a patient, supportive approach is best; the therapist should provide empathic understanding of the person's concerns.

If the person has a hearing or visual problem, a hearing aid or corrective lenses may alleviate the suspiciousness and feelings of persecution. When the individual is socially isolated, efforts can be made to increase his or her activities and contacts. Such direct action is believed by gerontologists to hold more promise for reversing paranoia in older people than any kind of formal psychotherapy. Even if these straightforward measures do not relieve paranoia, they may be beneficial to other areas of the person's life. Institutionalization, best considered a last resort, will seldom do anything positive for the person. In practice, the decision depends more on how tolerant the person's social environment is than on how severe and disruptive are the paranoid beliefs.

Schizophrenia

Does schizophrenia ever appear for the first time in old age? Debate on this question has raged for years; as might be expected, the answer depends on the definition of schizophrenia. According to DSM-III's narrower definition, first-time onset of schizophrenia after the age of sixty-five is very rare indeed.

The next question of interest is what happens to schizophrenic symptomatology as people become older. Answers depend on what generation of schizophrenics we are talking about. Because the advent of the neuroleptics, such as Thorazine, ushered in a veritable revolution in the treatment of schizophrenia, as did political decisions to reduce the numbers of patients in mental hospitals, many more schizophrenics now live at home or in other community settings than was the case twenty or thirty years ago. They are unlikely ever to have been institutionalized for long periods of time and have not suffered from

BOX **17.2** Partial Deafness, Growing Old, and Paranoia

A relation between hearing problems in old age and the development of paranoid thinking was noted many years ago by Emil Kraepelin and has been verified since by careful laboratory studies (Cooper et al., 1974). The connection appears to be specific to paranoia, for the relation between difficulties in hearing and depression in older individuals is not as great. Since hearing losses appear to predate the onset of paranoid delusions, this may be a cause-effect relationship of some importance.

Stanford psychologist Philip Zimbardo and his associates have recently done an experiment to study the relation of poor hearing to paranoia. They reasoned that loss of hearing acuity might set the stage for the development of paranoia if the person does not acknowledge, or is unaware of, the hearing problem (Zimbardo, Andersen, and Kabat, in press). If I have trouble hearing people around me, which makes them seem to be whispering, I may conclude that they are whispering *about me* and that what they say is unfavorable. I will think this way, however, only if I am unaware of my hearing problem. If I know that I am partially deaf, I will appreciate that I do not hear them well because of my deafness and will not think that they are whispering. A hard-of-hearing grandfather may eventually challenge the light-voiced, gesturing grandchildren he believes are whispering about him; and they will deny that they are. A tense cycle of allegations, denials, and further accusations will isolate the increasingly hostile and suspicious grandfather from the company of his grandchildren.

The experiment done by Zimbardo and his group examined the initial stage of this hypothesized development of paranoia. College students previously determined to be easily hypnotized and capable of responding to a posthypnotic suggestion of partial deafness participated in what they believed to be a study of the effects of various hypnotic procedures on creative prob-lem solving. Each of the subjects sat in a room with two other subjects who were actually confederates of the experimenter. The trio were provided a task to perform either cooperatively or by themselves; they were to make up a story concerning a TAT picture. The picture was shown on the screen, and projected first was the word "FOCUS." The confederates, as planned, began to joke with each other as they made decisions about the story, inviting the subject to join them in the cooperative venture. After the story was completed, the subject was left alone to fill out the questionnaires, among them MMPI measures of paranoia and an adjective checklist to assess mood.

As described so far, there is nothing particularly interesting about the experiment. The actual manipulations took place earlier, *before* the TAT picture was presented. Each subject had been hypnotized and then given one of the three following hypnotic suggestions.

1. *Induced partial deafness without awareness.* Each member of the first group was told that when he saw the word "FOCUS" projected on a screen in the next room, he would have trouble hearing noises and whatever other people might be saying, that they would seem to be whispering, and that he would be concerned about not being able to hear. He was also instructed to forget this suggestion until an experimenter removed the amnesia by touching his shoulder.

2. *Induced partial deafness with awareness.* Subjects in the second group, the control group, were given the same partial-deafness suggestion, but they were instructed to remember that their hearing difficulty was by posthypnotic suggestion.

3. *Posthypnotic-suggestion control.* Subjects in the third group, controls for the effectiveness of posthypnotic suggestion, were instructed to react to the word "FOCUS" by experiencing an

itchiness in the left earlobe, with amnesia for this suggestion until touched on the left shoulder by the experimenter.

After being given their posthypnotic suggestions, all subjects were awakened from the hypnotic state and ushered into the next room, where the experiment proceeded as already described. It can now be appreciated that participants who had deafness without awareness might perceive the joking of the confederates as directed toward them, for they would have trouble hearing what was being said and would be unlikely to attribute this difficulty to any hearing problem of their own. Subjects who had deafness with awareness would have the same problem hearing the joking, but they would know that they had temporary decrement in hearing through hypnotic suggestion. The other control subjects would have no hearing problems, just itchy earlobes. At the completion of the study, all subjects were carefully informed about the purposes of the study, and steps were taken to ensure that the posthypnotic suggestions of partial deafness and itchy earlobes had been lifted.

The results are fascinating. The experience of being partially deaf without awareness showed up significantly on cognitive, emotional, and behavioral measures. As compared to members of the two control groups, these subjects scored more paranoid on the MMPI scales and described themselves as more irritated, agitated, and hostile. The two confederates who were in the same room with these subjects rated them as more hostile than the controls. The confederates were of course not aware of which group a given subject was in. When the confederates invited each subject to work with them in concocting the TAT story, only one of six experimental subjects accepted the overture, although most of the control subjects agreed. At the end of the study, just before the debriefing, all subjects were asked whether they would like to participate in a future experiment with the same partners; none of the deafness-without-awareness subjects said that he would, but most of the controls did.

The overall reaction of subjects who had trouble hearing and had no ready explanation for it, other than that others were whispering, was suspicion, hostility, agitation, and unwillingness to affiliate with these people. This pattern is similar to what Zimbardo hypothesizes to be the earliest stage of the development of some paranoid delusions. The creation of this "analogue incipient paranoia" in the laboratory by inducing deafness without awareness of the deafness is consistent with the view that when people's hearing becomes poor in old age, they are susceptible to paranoia *if*, for whatever reasons, they do not acknowledge their deafness.

the withdrawal, compliance, and apathy and the settling in of symptoms that were the secondary problems of institutionalization.

Given that many schizophrenics beyond the age of sixty-five are not in hospitals, and given that their symptoms are controlled somewhat by drugs, what can be said about the symptoms themselves? If these people were not on drugs, would the distortion of their thinking have become less as they entered old age? Would their behavior have become more appropriate? Some researchers claim that schizophrenia sometimes "burns out" (Bridge, Cannon, and Wyatt, 1978; Lawton, 1972), that symptoms become somewhat muted. Hallucinations and delusions decrease in intensity and frequency, mood swings diminish and the capacity for social interactions improves. *But,* as Lawton (1972) cautions, these findings are based primarily on *hospitalized* schizophrenics who *are taking drugs.* At this point then, the course of schizophrenia is old age has not been satisfactorily studied.

Insomnia

Problems in sleeping are common in adulthood, but they are especially common in old age. Estimates are that as many as half the people over the age of sixty-five suffer from insomnia (Feinberg and Carlson, 1968).

Sleep patterns appear to change with age. For example, spontaneous interruptions of sleep increase as people become older. Thus old people generally sleep less but spend more time in bed in an effort to compensate. They spend less sleep time in a phase known as rapid-eye-movement (REM) sleep, and stage 4 sleep, the deepest, is virtually absent. Old people are often not aware that these changes are normal and hence may consider some of them insomnia.

Since sleep disturbance is a common aspect of depression, anyone treating insomnia should recognize that it may be secondary to an affective disorder. We also know that insomniacs underestimate the amount of sleep they actually get (Monroe, 1968); sometimes reassurance on this matter can help ease the person's mind. Whatever the cause of a particular individual's insomnia, it is worsened by ruminating over it, by counting the number of hours slept and those spent waiting to fall asleep, and by other similar self-defeating actions.

The most widely used treatment for insomnia is drugs, especially barbiturates. The little bottle of sleeping pills is a familiar companion to the many medications that sit on the night table of the older person. Aside from the problems older people have with drugs—their special sensitivity to them, the possibly dangerous interactions of medications being taken, the increased risk of suicide from availability of a lethal means—most sleeping medications interfere with REM sleep, and most drugs lose their effectiveness after a while and can even become addicting.

Behavioral treatments such as relaxation training (Borkovec, 1977) hold some promise for helping people sleep. If the problem is severe and truly debilitating, however, attention to other aspects of the person's life may be warranted and necessary.

Suicide

Several factors put people in general at especially high risk for suicide: serious physical illness, feelings of hopelessness, social isolation, loss of loved ones, dire financial circumstances, and depression. Because these problems are widespread among the elderly, we should not be surprised to learn that suicide rates for people over sixty-five are unusually high, perhaps three times greater than the rate for younger individuals (Pfeiffer, 1977). The rate is especially high for white males; they keep on committing suicide at a steadily increasing rate even into their eighties (United States Public Health Service, 1974).[6] Butler and Lewis (1977) speculate that the severe loss of status in old age affects white males in particular, because they have held the greatest power and influence in society. A recent study (Marshall, 1978) has noted a decline between 1948 and 1972 in the rate of suicide of white males, although it is still much higher than that for white women and still climbs with years of age. This study related the decline to better income of the aged. The white men over sixty who

[6] Interestingly, the suicide rate for white women increases through the age of sixty but decreases thereafter. Rates for nonwhite men and women in the United States fluctuate throughout the life-span, with no clear patterns emerging as they enter old age.

committed suicide in Arizona between 1970 and 1975 were likely to have been widowed, to have lost or never had a confidant, and to have recently seen a physician, who apparently had not been able to help them (Miller, 1978).

Higher too are the number of successful suicides compared to unsuccessful attempts; the ratio of attempted to successful suicides is seven to one for people below the age of sixty-five but two to one for those older than sixty-five. These grim statistics are probably underestimates; old people have many opportunities to "give up" on themselves by neglecting their diet or medications, thus killing themselves in a more passive fashion. Indeed, Butler and Lewis (1977) have argued that suicide of older adults may more often be a rational or philosophical decision than that of younger people. Consider, for example, the elderly man who faces the intractable pain of a terminal illness and knows that with each passing day his medical care is using up more and more of the money he might otherwise leave to his widow and his family.

Intervention to prevent the suicide of an older person is similar to that discussed earlier (see page 268). In general, the therapist tries to persuade the person to consider alternatives to the situation seen in such desperate terms. Mental health professionals, who are usually younger and healthier, may unwittingly try less hard to prevent an older person's suicide. But even the older person, once the suicidal crisis has passed, is usually grateful that he or she has another chance at living. Statistics inform us, however, that a previous suicide attempt is a strong predictor of yet another one; and even in institutions most people can take their own lives if they really wnat to.

Hypochrondriasis

Old people are subject to a multitude of physical ills. Complaints of sore feet, aching backs, poor digestion, constipation, labored breathing, and cold extremeties are to be taken seriously by responsible health professionals. But some of the elderly only believe themselves to be ill, as do younger people, and complain unendingly about aches and pains for which there are no plausible physical causes. Often such complaints are part of a more general depressive syndrome. Hypochondriacal problems occupy much of the time of physicians who care for old people, as they do the time and energy of families and friends of a significant proportion of people over the age of sixty-five.

Little is known about the causes of hypochondriasis. It has been suggested that for old people of this and previous generations, emotional concerns and distress are more difficult to talk about than physical ailments. The language they use, then, is somatic. It is not that my feelings are hurt because my son never visits me. Rather I can't keep my food down and my arms keep aching. Studies have indicated that somaticizing is more frequent among lower-middle-class or semiskilled workers (Pilowsky, 1970) than among better-educated people, who presumably have greater psychological sophistication and nonmedical explanations for their unhappiness. Perhaps, then, hypochondriacal complaints in older adults reflect in part a cohort effect. The next generation of old people have, like ourselves, lived in a social climate in which psychological problems are openly discussed and in which seeing a "shrink" and taking a tranquilizer are accepted, as they were not by present and past generations of elderly. These old people of the next decade may express their unhappiness in psychological terms rather than somatic.

In addition, among many older hypochondriacs there exists almost a camaraderie. Not to make light of this, it is possible that going to a doctor or clinic affords some older people a rare chance to socialize, to be attended to and cared for, and otherwise to enjoy a respite from a tedious and isolated existence. And if Dr. A has tired of their complaints and will not take them seriously, there is always Dr. B.

No controlled studies of the treatment of hypochondriasis have been done. Clinicians generally agree, though, that reassuring the person that he or she is really healthy is rather useless, for these people are not swayed by negative laboratory tests or authoritative pronouncements from people in white coats. Some tentative evidence suggests that ignoring the somatic complaints and concentrating instead on more positive aspects of existence can be helpful (Goldstein and Birnbom, 1976). I know that you're feeling bad and that your feet really hurt, but let's take a walk in Palisades Park anyway, and then we'll go out to dinner. Diverting activities may allow hypochondriacs at least to function in the face of their perceived medical ills and perhaps obtain some positive satisfactions from life.

Sexuality and Aging

Biases against the expression of sexuality in old age and disbelief in older people's capacity for sex have abounded in our culture. Men and women alike have been expected to suddenly lose interest in and capacity for sex once they reach their senior years. Some believe that old people are unable to enjoy anything more passionate than an affectionate hug and a kiss on the cheek. An older man who shows sexual interest in much younger women is called a "dirty old man." And, after the strong sexual value placed on them when younger, older women are not considered especially sexual. Their capacity for sexual arousal is confused with their inability to procreate.

The facts are that older people have considerable sexual interest and capacity. As we review them, it will be important to bear in mind that sexual interest and activity vary greatly in younger adults; disinterest or infrequent sex in an older person, then, should not be blithely taken as evidence that older people are inherently asexual. The sixty-eight-year-old man who has no sex life may well have had little if any interest at age twenty-eight.

The frequencies of sexual activity and interest in sex have been determined in several large-scale surveys, among them the famous Kinsey reports (Kinsey, Pomeroy, and Martin, 1948; Kinsey et al., 1953) and the Duke Longitudinal Studies (Pfeiffer, Verwoerdt, and Wang, 1968, 1969; George and Weiler, in press). The picture that emerges from these surveys is as follows.

1. Earlier studies—the Kinsey reports and the first Duke Longitudinal Study (Pfeiffer, Verwoerdt, and Want, 1968, 1969)—revealed a decline in heterosexual intercourse, masturbation, and homosexual intercourse beginning around age thirty, with average activity quite restricted beyond the age of sixty-five.

The second Duke study (George and Weiler, in press) covered the years 1968 through 1974 and indicated *no* decline in the sexual activity of people between ages forty-six and seventy-one. The belief then that sex necessarily becomes less important to people in their middle years and in old age is not substantiated by the most recent research.

2. At the same time there is a considerable variation in the sexual activity of older people, suggesting that biological age per se can be a limiting factor. Physical illness can interfere, as it can in younger people; it is of greater importance in older people for the simple reason that more of them are sick than are younger people. And yet, the actual physical limitations are usually less than what people believe them to be.

3. Erectile problems gradually increase with age.

4. A heterosexual woman's sexual activity centers on having a husband, whether or not he is well and whether or not he initiates sex. Women's sexuality in old age is lower overall than men's, perhaps because they tend both to be married to men older than they and to outlive their husbands.

5. The major factors affecting a man's sexual activity are past frequency, health, and general attitudes toward sex.

These facts can be interpreted in several ways. Clearly older people can be sexually active; even the earlier surveys indicated that. But it is noteworthy that the second Duke Longitudinal Study does not reveal the decline that the first Duke study and the Kinsey studies found. The older people surveyed between 1968 and 1974 may have shown the influence of less negative stereotyping. That is, they may have been the beneficiaries of modern attitudes that sanction sexuality well beyond the childbearing years. They may also have been more willing to discuss their sexual interests and activities with researchers, again because the cultural atmosphere has become more supportive.

Physiological changes with aging in men
Among the volunteer subjects studied by Masters

and Johnson (1966) were a sizable number of people over the age of sixty-five. Physiological measurements showed the following differences in older men as compared to younger men.

1. **Excitement phase.** Older men take longer to have an erection even when they are being stimulated in a way they like.

2. **Plateau phase.** The plateau phase as well lasts longer in older men, and they do not have the urge to ejaculate on every occasion. It is not known whether physiological changes or control learned over the years explains this diminished urge.

3. **Ejaculation-orgasm phase.** Contractions are less intense and fewer in number, and the fluid expelled during ejaculation is less in volume and under less pressure.

4. **Refractory period.** Erection is lost more quickly in older men, and it takes significantly longer for them to be aroused again.

Even allowing for the fact that the men who agreed to be subjects were hardly a random sample of the population, it is clear that older men are capable of the same pattern of sexual activity as younger men, the major difference being that things take longer to happen and, when they do, there is less urgency. But the incidence of erectile failure does increase in older men. Age-related physiological changes in physically healthy men would seem to play a very minor role, but the way in which men and their partners view them may. If a man or his partner react with alarm to a slow build-up of sexual arousal, the stage is set for the performance fears that have been proclaimed a principal reason for psychosexual dysfunction.

Physiology is not irrelevant, however. Conditions known to affect sexual responsiveness and behavior adversely—peripheral nerve damage from diabetes, side effects of tranquilizers and antihypertensive medication, a history of cigarette smoking, abuse of alcohol—are prevalent in older men. Fears of resuming sexual activities after a heart attack have also inhibited older men and their lovers, but for most of them the fears are exaggerated (Friedman, 1978). Unfortunately, physicians often fail to provide accurate information to the postcoronary patient; for example, heart rate is frequently higher during activities such as climbing stairs than it is during intercourse.[7]

Physiological changes with aging in women
A number of age-related differences in older women have also been found, but again none of them justifies the conclusion that they are incapable of a satisfactory sex life.

1. Like men, older women need more time to become sexually aroused. Vaginal lubrication is less, because of lower estrogen levels, and vaginal contractions during orgasm are fewer in number, four or five compared to eight to twelve in younger women. Also like older men, women return more quickly to a less aroused state.

2. Spastic contractions of the vagina and uterus, rather than the rhythmic ones that occur during orgasm in younger women, can cause discomfort and even pain in the lower abdomen and legs. Direct stimulation of the clitoris, often pleasurable to some younger women, is more likely to be painful to the older woman.

3. There is some evidence that these physical changes are not as extensive in women who have had regular intercourse once or twice a week throughout their sexual lives.

Sexual responding, then, is different in older women but still very much in evidence and of a quality that can provide pleasure well into old age. The adage "use it or lose it" seems particularly applicable to women's potential for lessening the negative impact of age-related changes in sexual physiology.

Treatment
Perhaps the best remedy for sexual frustrations experienced by many older people is giving

---

[7] The situation is different for patients with congestive heart failure, however. This condition, in which the heart is unable to maintain an adequate circulation of blood in the tissues of the body or to pump out venous blood returned by the venous circulation, does create a serious risk for a patient wishing to have intercourse. But less strenuous sexual activity is not a problem.

them and the professionals who look after their medical needs the facts of sexuality in the later years. Physicians have been particularly guilty of telling older patients to forget about sex or of not raising the issue when discussing their patients' adjustment, perhaps because of their own discomfort, lack of knowledge, or ageism. Nursing homes are often intolerant of sexuality among the residents; and a married couple residing in the same home may not be allowed to share a room. The authors have witnessed nurses in geriatric wards caution residents against stimulating themselves in public while at the same time not allowing for adequate privacy.

Sexual relations of older people can be fulfilling, especially if the partners understand age-related changes in physiological responding and do not view them as abnormal or in decline. Postmenopausal women are sometimes troubled by decreases in vaginal lubrication and by thinning of the lining of the vagina, which can make intercourse painful. Estrogen replacement therapy or topical application of estrogen creams may alleviate such barriers to enjoyable sex, but the association of these treatments with some forms of endometrial cancer has made physicians cautious about prescribing them. As for the older male, the slowing of sexual responsiveness and the extension of his plateau phase may cancel earlier concerns about ejaculatory control and enhance his own and his partner's enjoyment.

Making information concerning sexuality in old age available to the general public is likely to affect many older people favorably. For those whose problems remain untouched, indications are that older people are good candidates for the type of sex therapy given by Masters and Johnson (Berman and Lief, 1976). Greater attention must be paid to physical condition than is usual with younger clients, however.

General Issues in Treatment and Care

Nursing Homes

In recent years inexcusable brutality in some nursing homes has come to light through hearings held by the Senate Special Committee on the Aging, starting in 1974, and by the New York State Moreland Act Commission in 1975, newspaper exposés, and lawsuits. Violations of building codes, neglect, overmedication, intimidation, excessive billing, and other unethical and illegal practices have made people wary about the honesty of nursing home operators and have occasioned considerable anxiety among families and old people themselves about the nursing home as the best place to spend final months or years.

But these flagrant abuses are probably less a problem than the more subtle disadvantages of nursing homes, which are found even in those with the best-intentioned staffs. A dramatic study by Blenkner (1967) highlights the problem. Elderly people who came to a family service center were *randomly* assigned to one of three treatments, intensive, intermediate, and minimal. Intensive treatment involved the services of a nurse and a social worker, intermediate somewhat less professional attention. Minimal treatment consisted of information and referral to community-based services. We might expect intensive treatment to be the most effective, but quite the opposite was the case. After half a year the death rate of members of the intensive-care group was four times that of people in the minimal-care group! The intermediate-care group was less worse off than the intensive-care group; the death rate of its members was "only" twice that of the minimal-care group. What happened? It turned out that the major culprit was being placed in an institution such as a nursing home. A person was much more likely to be institutionalized if a nurse and social worker were intensively involved in planning his or her care, and the excessive death rates were found among the people so taken care of. Since people had been assigned randomly to the three treatments, it is unlikely that the death rates were related to differences existing before treatment began.

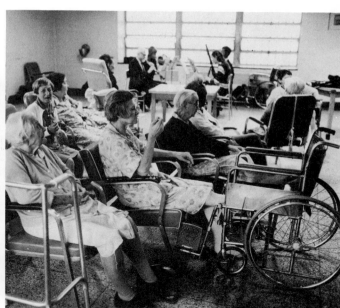

Nursing homes vary in the quality of living that they provide. The woman on the left sits in comfort in her own private room. The elderly on the right are in a large living area in a more crowded home, but musicians have come to play for them.

What is there about nursing homes that contributes to such decline? First, relocation to a new setting is in itself stressful and is believed to play a role in increased mortality (Aldrich and Mendkoff, 1963; Schulz and Brenner, 1977). Once in the nursing home, the extent and nature of care discourage rehabilitation and even maintainance of whatever self-care skills and autonomous activities the resident may be capable of. For example, a resident able to feed herself but only slowly and with occasional spills will be assisted at mealtime and even fed like a child to shorten the time devoted to serving meals as well as to decrease the chances of messes on the floor and stains on the woman's clothing. The resident no longer thinks of herself as someone able to eat without help, which is likely to lead to still more loss of function and lowered morale. Muscles themselves weaken and deteriorate through disuse (DeVries, 1975). Relatives of the resident, anxious to know that they have made the right decision and that Mom is being well cared for, are pleased by the tidiness and orderliness that are the result of excessive staff involvement in all details of living.

Nursing homes are concerned as well with legal liability. If a resident can walk with a cane, but unsteadily, is it not better to have him pushed in a wheelchair than risk his falling? Falls are a common hazard to old people, and their bones heal slowly and imperfectly.

Custodial care may be excessive, but treatments to improve a patient's mental condition do not have priority. We know that depression is the most prevalent psychological disorder of older people, especially of those in nursing homes. The type of psychoactive drug prescribed, however, is more likely to be a tranquilizer than an antidepressant; a less agitated, relatively inactive patient is easier to handle. Psychological interventions are virtually unheard of, for the staff either is untrained in their implementation or operates under the widely held assumption that such therapy is inappropriate for an old person.

In sum, all the problems of institutionalization are in bold and exaggerated relief in nursing homes. Independence is actively discouraged, and both physical and mental deterioration is expected and unfortunately obtained (see Box 17.3). But what are the alternatives? In recent years community-based treatment and care have been proposed.

Principles of Community-Based Treatment

It has been estimated that as many as 80 percent of nursing home residents do not need the level of custodial care provided them (Kistin and Morris, 1972). Zarit (1980) proposes principles that can foster the development of effective noninstitutional services to the elderly.

Comprehensive community-based services
The community should provide individual and family psychotherapy; telephone reassurance, daily phone calls to old persons living alone, to

check that they are all right; home services, such as Meals on Wheels, which brings a hot meal a day to the old person's door, visits from homemakers who cook meals and see to the household, shopping help from young people, and regular social visits from community neighbors; a community day center for older people, which may also serve a hot lunch and provide help with state and federal forms; sheltered housing, apartments in which several old people may live together semi-independently; and home visits by health professionals and social workers who can assess the actual needs of old people and treat them.

Working with members of families caring for old people is especially important. They can overprotect and foster needless dependency and even deterioration every bit as "effectively" as can nursing home staff. They also need support

---

BOX **17.3** Nursing Homes, Loss of Control, and Mindlessness

Ellen Langer, a social psychologist at Harvard, and her associates, have advanced an interesting argument relating lack of control over life circumstances to the deterioration in both physical and mental health often found in some of the elderly. The reasoning behind her research program is this. Since we know that a perceived or actual lack of control leads to deterioration in adaptive behavior, at least some of what we regard as senility—the inactivity of elderly people and their poor adjustment to changing circumstances—may be caused by loss of control rather than progressive brain disease (Langer, 1981).

Langer points out that our society actually *teaches* the elderly—and sometimes the nonelderly as well!—that older adults are incompetent, or at least far less competent than they were before they became old. In our eagerness to help them, we seem to protect old people from having to make decisions that they might, in fact, be able to make. In our concern to protect them from physical harm, we arrange environments that require little effort to control. And, of course, we set ages for compulsory retirement, overlooking the large individual differences of old people. These practices, especially in a society that values competence and activity, do much to destroy an elderly person's belief that he or she is still effective, that indeed life is worthwhile.

In one study Langer and Rodin (1976) posed the question whether the psychological and physical well-being of old people living in a nursing home could be enhanced by giving them responsibility that they would not otherwise have. One group of residents of a nursing home were told that they would be given a variety of decisions to make, instead of the staff's making decisions for them; they were also given plants to take care of. A control group was told how eager the staff was to take care of them; the plants they were given would be looked after by the staff. Although initially matched on variables such as health,

and encouragement, opportunities to vent their feelings of guilt, resentment, and the like. They need permission and support to take time off, or to feel that they will be able to should the pressures become too great. A program in England arranges for the elderly person to be hospitalized briefly so that caregivers can take a vacation (Glasscote, Gudeman, and Miles, 1977). The knowledge that relief is available and *sanctioned* by authority figures lessens the burden of looking after loved ones at home.

Coordination of services

Mere availability of services is not enough, however. They must be coordinated, as regrettably they are not in most localities. All too often an old person and his or her family are shuffled from one agency to another, getting lost in a morass of bureaucratic niceties, frustrated by rules

that often interfere with the very goals for which programs were instituted. In California, for example, Medicare does not always pay for rehabilitation services, such as physical therapy after a broken hip has healed. As a consequence many old people without means do not regain function that they might have and may suffer additional physical and emotional deterioration.

Minimum intervention

Sometimes less is better. Older people should be encouraged to remain as independent as possible. The decreased ability to do many of the things that were part of the normal routine earlier in life may be perceived by the old person as good reason to become more dependent on others. Often lost is the difference between necessary dependency and accepting help that is merely comforting or easier to accede to than re-

---

these two groups of elderly residents differed three weeks later on several measures of alertness, happiness, and general well-being. Members of the group given enhanced responsibility—and presumably a sense of greater control—tested superior on these measures. Even more impressive was the finding eighteen months later that only half as many of the experimental group, seven out of forty-seven, had died as had members of the control group, thirteen out of forty-four. Moreover, the group given responsibilities continued to show better psychological and physical health (Rodin and Langer, 1977).

Not only may our treatment of old people engender in them a sense of lost control, but their repetitious, unchallenging environments—especially the surroundings of those who are hospital patients or live in nursing homes—may encourage a mode of cognitive functioning Langer terms "mindlessness." Mindlessness is a kind of automatic information processing studied by cognitive psychologists, a mode of thinking that is adaptive when people are in situations that recur frequently, for example, remembering a familiar sequence such as tying one's shoes. In fact, attending to such overlearned activities—making the information processing conscious, not mindless—can actually *interfere* with performance!

Research indicates that people respond mindlessly when confronted by familiar situations. It is as though we operate with as little cognitive effort as we can get away with. When a situation is novel and requires our attention, however, we tend to operate *mindfully*.

What are the clinical implications of too much mindlessness, this mode of mental functioning that entails little cognitive effort? The nonelderly have ample opportunities to engage in thoughtful behavior, and it is reasonable to assume that we all need some minimum of thought and planning to feel good about ourselves and to maintain an alert state of mind. The elderly, in contrast, may be afforded too few opportunities to be thoughtful. Because of the restricted mobility of nursing home residents and hospital patients and because little is demanded of them, their experiences in particular tend to be repetitious and boring. The Langer and Rodin nursing home study may well demonstrate that conscious *thinking* per se as well as perceived control is essential in maintaining emotional and physical well-being. Lack of control and mindlessness are probably related, for what is there really to think about when people believe that they have lost control over the events in their lives? In addition to the undeniable losses that come with age, many elderly people develop a pronounced sense of incompetence and worthlessness because so little thinking and so few autonomous decisions are required of them.

ject. Younger and healthier caregivers are victims of a matching tunnel vision. If an old person is in need, the tendency is to meet that need and then some, choosing treatments that are unnecessarily intrusive and restrictive.

There is risk in any therapeutic intervention (see page 633), and some people are worse off for having consulted a mental health professional. Considerable judgment is needed, lest really serious problems be overlooked, but the principle of minimum intervention remains a sound one, especially with the elderly.

Issues Specific to Therapy with Older Adults

As has been mentioned throughout this chapter, discussing a group of people who share only chronological age runs the risk of overlooking important differences in their backgrounds, personalities, and developmental histories. Although adults over sixty-five do have in common physical and psychological characteristics that differentiate them to some degree from younger adults, they are nonetheless *individuals,* each of whom has lived a long time and has experienced unique joys and sorrows. In spite of this uniqueness, there are a few general issues important to consider in the conduct of therapy with older people. They can be divided into issues of content and issues of process.

Content issues

The emotional pain of the elderly is very often caused by major life stresses. More so than younger people, older adults are likely to be distressed by losses, for what they lose is difficult if not impossible to replace. An older woman who has been widowed is less likely, as previously noted, to find a new love relationship than is a younger woman. Medical problems may create irreversible difficulties in walking, seeing, and hearing. Finances are often a particular problem as well, for most older people are retired or have few prospects of improving their earnings through a change of jobs or a promotion. It is therefore essential that the clinician bear in mind that emotional suffering may reflect to a large degree reactions to realistic problems in living. To suggest that it is simply a manifestation of

psychopathology may be unfair and inaccurate.

Another realistic source of distress is the older person's sense of vulnerability, his or her worries about robbery and personal injury, about the losses just mentioned, and, perhaps most importantly, about impending death. Much psychological distress about dying can be averted or reduced by encouraging the client to attend to such concrete details as ensuring that estate and will are in order and that funeral or cremation plans are explicit and satisfactory. If clients deplore and dread the artificial life-support treatments sometimes applied in terminal illnesses, the therapist should suggest that they consider a Living Will (see page 267) to provide to those they choose to be responsible for them. Family members are wisely included in discussions, for their own concerns about death often influence their dealings with the old person.

Older clients may also be counseled to examine their lives from a philosophical or a religious perspective. Leo Tolstoy was but one of many people who become increasingly religious as they grow old. Philosophical and religious perspectives can help the client to transcend the limitations aging imposes on human existence. When the person is finally dying, discussions of the meaning of the individual's life can facilitate self-disclosure and enhance his or her sense of well-being and personal growth. The loved ones, who will experience the inevitable loss, will also benefit from such discussions.

Process issues

Many clinicians who specialize in aging hold that therapists need to be active and directive with older clients, providing information, taking the initiative in seeking out social agencies for necessary services, and helping the client and members of the family to find their way through the maze of federal and local laws and offices that are in place to help the aged.

People working with today's generation of older clients must also be mindful that they have had few encounters with, and have some suspicion of, mental health workers. Older clients may think that only crazy, incompetent persons talk to a therapist. Their concern is often manifested in inquiries about the competence and training of the therapist, an implicit question being "Can you possibly understand me?" Indeed, most clinical gerontologists working today are student trainees or professionals many years under sixty-five.

Although the age difference is not an insurmountable barrier, it has been suggested that older adults should be trained as paraprofessionals to work under supervision with other older adults. Such helpers are seen as a community resource for the elderly; their enthusiasm, dedication, and life experiences have proved of value in enhancing the lives of the peers they serve (Gatz, Smyer, and Lawton, 1981).

Given the many reality-based problems, even disasters of aging, it is a wonder that the prevalence of emotional disorders in the elderly is not greater than it is. Aging implies two achievements. First, over the years, older adults accumulate wisdom and perspective that allow them to cope with challenges that might disable a younger person emotionally. Second, their expectations and aspirations are brought into line with what is possible for them. There would seem to be valuable lessons for all of us to learn from our elders.

Summary

Until recently the psychological problems of older people have been neglected by mental health professionals. As the proportion of people who live beyond sixty-five continues to grow, it will become ever more important to learn about the disorders suffered by some older people and the most effective means of preventing or ameliorating them. Although physical deterioration is an obvious aspect of growing old, it appears that most of the emotional distress to which old people are prone is psychologically produced.

The elderly endure a number of stresses: their deteriorating faculties, the high cost and increased need of medical care, economic exigencies, vulnerability to crime, the loss of spouse and friends. Whether they learn to cope with these challenges has much to do with their psychological well-being.

Serious brain disorders affect only a tiny minority of older people, approximately 5 percent, but their causes and treatment should be considered. Two principal brain disorders have been distinguished, delirium, or acute brain syndrome, and senile dementia, or chronic brain syndrome. In delirium there is sudden clouding of consciousness and other problems in thinking, feeling, and behaving—fragmented and undirected thought, incoherent speech, inability to sustain attention, hallucinations, illusions, disorientation, lethargy or hyperactivity, and mood swings. The condition is reversible, provided the underlying cause is self-limiting or adequately treated. Brain cells malfunction but are not destroyed. Causes include overmedication, infection of brain tissue, high fevers, malnutrition, dehydration, endocrine disorders, head trauma, and cerebrovascular problems. In contrast, senile dementia is a brain disease in which there is steady and gradual deterioration of brain cells and eventually death. The person's intellectual functioning goes downhill; memory, abstract thinking, and judgment deteriorate to the extent that the individual seems another person altogether. He or she is in the end oblivious of surroundings. A variety of diseases can cause this deterioration, the most important of which is an Alzheimer-type disease, in which cortical cells waste away.

The treatments of these two disorders are quite different one from the other. If delirium is suspected, there should be a search for the cause so that the pathogenic situation can be rectified. Senile dementia, on the other hand, cannot be treated, but the person and the family affected by the disease can be counseled on how to make the remaining time reasonable and even rewarding. If adequate support is given to caregivers, many dementia patients can be looked after at home. There usually comes a time, however, when the burden of care impels most families to place the person in a nursing home or hospital.

Older people suffer from the entire spectrum of psychological disorders, in many instances brought with them into their senior years. But some difficulties are felt particularly in old age, none more so than depression, which is far more prevalent in people over sixty-five. Considering the losses suffered as people become older, including their loss of control over important aspects of their lives, it is not surprising that as many as one-quarter of older people are depressed much of the time. The condition can be treated, however. The newer cognitive behavioral therapies are being applied to depression of the elderly, and results so far are encouraging.

Although not as widespread as depression, paranoia is a problem for older people and for those who have a relationship with them. In contrast to the persecutors of young paranoids, distant agencies such as the F.B.I. and aliens from outer space, those of older individuals live closer to home—the neighbor who opens her mail, the ungrateful son who is conniving to steal his mother's money, the physician who prescribes drugs that pollute the mind. Paranoia is sometimes brought on by the brain damage in dementia, but more often it is caused by psychological factors. Paranoia may be a reaction to hearing difficulties; if I cannot hear what they are saying—especially if I do not acknowledge my hearing problem—perhaps it is because they are whispering nasty things about me. Isolation as well can be a factor; when a person has little social intercourse, and indeed many old people have too little, it is difficult to verify impressions and suspicions, setting the stage for delusions to develop.

White males, as they enter old age, are at increasing risk of suicide. More of the suicide attempts of all old people result in death than do those of younger people. Mental health professionals, most of them younger than sixty-five, may assume that, indeed, the old and debilitated have nothing to live for. This attitude may reflect their own fear of growing old.

Considerable mythology has surrounded sexuality and aging, the principal assumption being that at the age of sixty-five sex becomes improper, unsatisfying, and even impossible. Evidence indicates otherwise. Barring serious physical disability, older people, even those well into their eighties, are capable of deriving enjoyment from sexual intercourse and other kinds of lovemaking. There are differences as people age; it takes longer to become aroused and the orgasm is less intense. Dissemination of accurate information about sexual capacity in old age would probably prevent much unnecessary sexual dysfunction and disinterest.

Nursing homes and other extended-care facilities do little to encourage residents to maintain or enhance whatever skills and capacities they still have. Both physical and mental deterioration are the rule, and nowadays care is shifted to the community whenever possible. Three elements are believed essential in effective community-based treatment. There should be comprehensive services in the community, such as Meals on Wheels, regular home visits by health professionals, and support for caregivers. Such services should be coordinated so that people do not have to confront a bureaucratic maze. And intervention should be minimal so that old people remain as independent as their circumstances permit.

Many older people can benefit from psychotherapy, but several issues specific to treating the older adult should be borne in mind. The emotional distress of the elderly is usually realistic in content. They have often suffered irreplaceable losses and face real medical and financial problems; it is unwise to attribute their complaints to a psychopathological condition. Death is a more immediate issue as well. As for the process of therapy, clinicians should be active and directive, providing information and seeking out the agencies that give the social services needed by their clients. The difference in age between an older client and a mental health professional may be an issue. For this reason more and more peer paraprofessionals are being trained in the mental health care of the elderly.

■ ■

Evfa Model, "Open Door" (1962). Collection, The Museum of Modern
Art, New York. Purchase.

part six
treatment

chapter 18

INSIGHT THERAPY

Throughout our account of the various psycho-pathologies, we have considered the ways in which therapists of varying persuasions attempt to prevent, lessen, and even eliminate mental and emotional suffering. The Chapter 2 descriptions of the several paradigms of treatment, physiological, psychoanalytic, learning, and humanistic, laid the groundwork. Some forms of intervention are more appropriate than others for particular problems. Through our understanding of physiological processes, new parents now have means of halting or at least reducing certain forms of genetically transmitted mental retardation. And through better understanding of the process of learning, retarded children are now acquiring more cognitive, social, and self-care skills than was earlier thought possible. Psychoanalytic theory helps therapists in treating dissociative disorders, for it alerts them to the possibility that an amnesic patient, for example, cannot remember because the pain of certain past events forced them to be massively repressed. Humanistic treatment helps clients explore the depth and causes of their psychological pain and encourages them to take action, make choices, and assume responsibility for bettering their lives.

Now it is time to take a closer, more intensive look at therapy to consider issues of general importance, to explore controversies, and to make comparisons. What we have studied so far of psychopathology and treatment should enable us to do so with some sophistication and perspective.

Shorn of its theoretical complexities, any psychotherapy is a set of procedures by which a mental health specialist uses language to help a person in psychological difficulty. The underlying assumption is that particular kinds of verbal exchanges in a trusting relationship can achieve specific goals, such as reducing anxiety and eliminating self-defeating or dangerous behavior.

Simple as this definition may seem, there is little general agreement about what *really* constitutes psychotherapy. A person's next-door neighbor might utter the same words of comfort as would a clinical psychologist, but should we regard this as psychotherapy? In what way is psychotherapy different from such nonprofessional reassurance? Is the distinction made on the straightforward basis of whether the dispenser of reassurance has an academic degree or license? Does it relate to whether the giver of information has a theory that dictates or at least guides what he or she says? Does it depend on how sound the basic assumptions of the theory are? These are difficult questions, and, as in other areas of abnormal psychology, professionals give different answers.

The people who seek or are sent for *professional* help are usually those who have tried the nonprofessional avenues to feeling better and have failed to obtain relief. Before an individual goes to a therapist, he or she has probably confided in friends or in a spouse, perhaps spoken to the family doctor, has often consulted with a member of the clergy, and may have tried several of the vast number of self-help books and programs that are so popular nowadays. For most people in psychological distress, one or more of these options provide enough relief, and they seek no further (Bergin, 1971). But for others these attempts fall short, and individuals are left feeling helpless, often hopeless, and in need of professional help. These people are the ones who go to mental health clinics, university counseling centers, and the private offices of independent practitioners. Whatever the nature and efficacy of any form of psychotherapy, it is appropriate to bear in mind that professionals generally have as clients the especially troubled people who have not been helped by other means.

Therapeutic activities and theories are very great in number. There are scores, perhaps hundreds, of schools of therapy, each with its band of enthusiastic adherents (both therapists and patients) proposing procedures ranging from screaming and writhing nude on the floor to forced inactivity and sleep for several weeks. One could almost say "You name it, someone thinks it's therapeutic." Because it would be impossible and unenlightening to examine every school, we have opted for a focused review of the field, presenting sufficient detail about the major approaches to allow a grasp of the basic

issues and an overall perspective on the enterprise of changing behavior in a therapeutic context.

London (1964) categorizes psychotherapies into *insight* and *action* (behavioral) therapies. Behavior therapy is the subject of Chapter 19. Insight therapy, which is discussed in this chapter, assumes that behavior becomes disordered because people do not adequately understand what motivates their actions, especially when different needs and drives conflict. Insight therapy tries to help them discover the true reasons they behave as they do. The assumption is that greater awareness of motivations will yield greater control over behavior and subsequent improvement in it. The emphasis is less on changing behavior directly than on uncovering its causes—both historical and current. To facilitate such insights, therapists of different theoretical persuasions have employed a variety of techniques, ranging from the free association of psychoanalysis to the reflection of feelings practiced in client-centered therapy.

Our principal concern in this chapter and the next is individual therapy, that is, therapy conducted by a clinician with one patient or client. But is should be noted that nearly everything said in these two chapters is relevant also for therapy in groups, a subject dealt with more completely as one of three principal topics in Chapter 20.

The Placebo Effect

For reasons that will become clear, it is appropriate to begin our discussion of psychotherapy with what has become known as the *placebo effect*. The term refers to improvement in physical or psychological condition that is attributable to a patient's expectations of help rather than to any specific active ingredient in a treatment. Although the word placebo generally refers to a pill or capsule that has no pharmacologically active substance—the familiar "sugar pill"—the term placebo effect need not be restricted to therapy with an inert pill. It can also apply to therapeutic results, both psychological and physiological, brought about by any method that has no demonstrable specific action on the disorder being treated.

Shapiro (1960) concludes that until recently the history of medication has been largely a history of placebo effects, that drugs have benefited people only to the extent they were believed in. Frank (1973) relates placebo effects to faith healing in prescientific or nonscientific societies. For centuries, suffering human beings have derived benefit from making pilgrimages to sanctified places such as Lourdes and from ingesting sometimes foul-smelling concoctions.

Many people tend to dismiss placebo reactions as "not real" or second-best. After all, if a person has a tension headache, what possible benefit can he or she hope to get from a pill that is totally devoid of chemical action or direct physiological effect? The fact is, however, that such benefits can be significant and even long lasting. For example, Lasagna and his colleagues (1965) reported impressive relief from pain in surgical patients receiving saline injections. And Frank (1973) furnishes extensive evidence attesting to improvement in a variety of physical and mental problems after ingestion of pills and from exposure to other ministrations that, in themselves, could not possibly account for this relief. An appreciation of the placebo effect, however, is by no means an endorsement of quackery. A placebo, whether it be an inert pill or an impressive but worthless psychological intervention, will not deal directly with many potentially serious problems of humankind.

A psychotherapist who places great stock in a particular theory may not like to think that his or her professional activities derive much or even all their effectiveness from mobilizing a person's expectancies for help. But research on psychotherapy offers scant reassurance to the contrary.

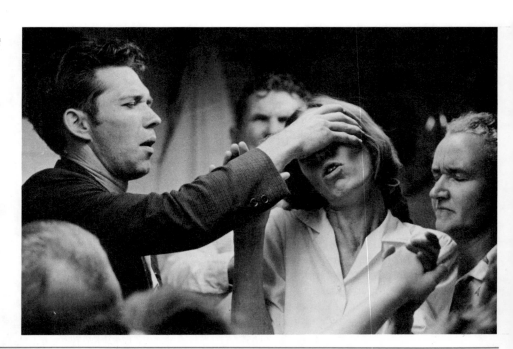

Faith healing would be considered by many an example of the power of the placebo effect.

Many researchers agree that in psychotherapy, as in much of medicine, *the most reliable effect is the placebo effect.*

The phenomenon of the placebo effect has far-reaching implications concerning the controls that must be designed into experiments. If every therapy procedure—however rationalized by its proponents—has placebo elements, it is essential to include a placebo control group in any experiment examining the efficacy of a technique. A good example of this practice is Paul's (1966) experiment on systematic desensitization, discussed in the next chapter. In insight therapy research, however, placebo controls have virtually not been used at all.

Psychoanalytic Therapy

Despite the numerous critical attacks made on psychoanalytic theory and the denials that psychoanalytic therapy is effective, psychoanalysis and its many offshoots remain the dominant force in American psychiatry and clinical psychology. In this section we attempt to summarize the important elements both of classical—that is, traditional—psychoanalysis and of ego analysis.

Basic Techniques of Psychoanalysis

The overall purpose of psychoanalysis derives from the Freudian assumption that psychopathology develops when people remain unaware of their true motivations and fears. They can be restored to healthy functioning only by becoming conscious of what has been repressed. When people can understand *what* is motivating their actions, they have a greater number of choices. Where id is, let there ego be, to paraphrase a maxim of psychoanalysis. The ego, being the conscious, deliberating, choosing portion of the personality, can better guide the individual in rational, realistic directions if repressions are at a minimum.

The steady procession of people to the shrine at Lourdes.

A moment in a psychoanalytic session.

Wachtel's (1977) woolly mammoth (see page 45) is an apt metaphor for the unresolved buried conflicts from which psychoanalytic theory assumes neurotic problems arise. The proper focus of therapy then is not on the presenting problem, such as fears of being rejected, but on unconscious conflicts existing in the psyche from childhood. Only by lifting the repression can the person confront the underlying problem and reevaluate it in the light of present-day reality.

A number of techniques are used by psychoanalysts to facilitate the recovery of conflicts that have been repressed. Perhaps the best known and most important is free association: the patient, reclining on a couch, is encouraged to give free rein to thoughts and feelings, and to verbalize whatever comes to mind. The assumption is that with enough practice free association will facilitate the uncovering of unconscious material. The analysand must follow the fundamental rule of reporting thoughts and feelings as accurately as possible, without screening out the elements he feels are unimportant or shameful. Freud assumed that thoughts and memories occurred in associative chains and that recent ones reported first would ultimately trace back to earlier crucial ones. In order to get to these earlier

events, however, the therapist has to be very careful not to guide or direct the patient's thinking, and the patient must not monitor his thoughts. Ford and Urban (1963) have paraphrased the analyst's directions for free association.

In ordinary conversation, you usually try to keep a connecting thread running through your remarks, excluding any intrusive ideas or side issues so as not to wander too far from the point, and rightly so. But in this case you must talk differently. As you talk various thoughts will occur to you which you like to ignore because of certain criticisms and objections. You will be tempted to think, "That is irrelevant or unimportant or nonsensical," and to avoid saying it. Do not give in to such criticism. Report such thoughts in spite of your wish not to do so. Later, the reason for this injunction, the only one you have to follow, will become clear. Report whatever goes through your mind. Pretend that you are a traveler, describing to someone beside you the changing views which you see outside the train window (p. 168).

But blocks do arise, virtually thrusting themselves across the thoughts supposedly given free rein. Patients may suddenly change the subject or be unable to remember how a long-ago event ended. They will try any tactic to interrupt the session, remaining silent, getting up from the couch, looking out the window, making jokes and personal remarks to the analyst. Patients may even come late or "forget" sessions altogether. Such obstacles to free association—_resistances_—were noted by Freud and contributed to the development of the concept of repression. He asserted that interference with free association can be traced to unconscious control over sensitive areas; it is precisely these areas that psychoanalytic therapists must thoroughly probe.

Akin to free association is dream analysis. Freud assumed that during sleep the ego defenses are lowered, allowing repressed material to come forth, usually in disguised form. Concerns of the patient are often expressed in symbols to help protect the conscious ego from the true significance of dream material. The manifest content of dreams—what is immediately apparent—may be regarded as a sort of compromise between repression of true meaning and a full expression of unconscious material. The latent content of dreams, then, is distorted by unconscious defensive structures which, never completely abandoned, even in sleep, continue their fight to protect the ego from repressed impulses.

As presumably unconscious material begins to appear, another technique comes into play, interpretation. According to Freud, this stage helps the person face the hitherto repressed and emotionally loaded conflict. At the "right time" the analyst begins to point out to the patient his defenses and the underlying meaning of his dreams. Great skill is required lest an interpretation be offered too early, for the patient may so totally reject it that he leaves treatment. To be effective, interpretations should reflect insights that the patient is on the verge of making himself; they can then be claimed by the patient as his own, rather than coming from the analyst. Presumably an interpretation that a patient attributes to himself will be more readily accepted and thereby have stronger therapeutic effect.

Interpretation then is the analyst's principal weapon against the continued use of defense mechanisms. He points out how certain verbalizations of the patient relate to repressed unconscious material, and he suggests what the manifest content of dreams _truly_ means. If the interpretation is timed correctly, the patient can start to examine the repressed impulse in the light of present-day reality. In other words, he begins to realize that he no longer has to fear the expression of the impulse.

Feeling safe under the undemanding conditions arranged by the analyst, the patient presumably uncovers more and more repressed material. Interpretations are held to be particularly helpful in establishing the meaning of the resistances that disturb the patient's free association. The therapist may, for example, point out how the patient manages to avoid a topic, and it is common for the analysand to deny the interpretation. Interestingly, this denial is sometimes interpreted as a sign that the therapist's interpretation is correct rather than incorrect. In the slow process of "working through" the disturbing conflicts, of confronting them again and again, the patient gradually faces up to the validity of the analyst's interpretations, often with great emotion.

The core of psychoanalytic therapy is the _transference neurosis._ Being a good observer, Freud noted that some of his patients acted toward him in an emotion-charged and unrealistic way. For example, a patient much older than Freud would behave in a childish manner during a therapy session. Although these reactions were often positive and loving, many times they were quite negative and hostile. Since these feelings seemed out of character with the ongoing therapy relationship, Freud assumed that they were relics of attitudes, _transferred_ to him from those held in the past toward important people in the patient's history, primarily parents. That is, he felt that patients responded to him as though he were one of the important people in their past. Freud utilized this transference of attitudes, which he came to consider an inevitable aspect of psychoanalysis, as a means of explaining to patients the childhood origin of many of their concerns and fears. This revelation and explanation tended also to help lift repressions and allow the confrontation of hitherto buried impulses. In psychoanalysis transference is regarded as essential to a complete cure. Indeed, it is precisely when analysts notice transference developing that they take hope the important neurotic conflict from childhood is being approached. Analysts encourage the development of transference by intentionally remaining shadowy figures, generally sitting behind the patient while the patient free-associates and serving as relatively blank screens on which the important persons in the neurotic conflicts can be projected. Analysts are also caring persons, which may remind the patient of attributes, real or hoped for, in his or her parents. Because the therapy setting is so different from the childhood situation, analysts can readily point out to patients the irrational nature of their fears and concerns (see Box 18.1).

Related to transference is _countertransference,_ the feelings of the analyst toward the patient. The analyst must take care lest he lay his own emotional vulnerabilities on the analysand. His own needs and fears must be recognized for what they are; he should have enough under-

---

BOX **18.1** Excerpt from a Psychoanalytic Session, an Illustration of Transference

Patient (a fifty-year-old male business executive): I really don't feel like talking today.

Analyst: (Remains silent for several minutes, then) Perhaps you'd like to talk about why you don't feel like talking.

Patient: There you go again, making demands on me, insisting I do what I just don't feel up to doing. (Pause) Do I always have to talk here, when I don't feel like it? (Voice becomes angry and petulant) Can't you just get off my back? You don't really give a damn how I feel, do you?

Analyst: I wonder why you feel I don't care.

Patient: Because you're always pressuring me to do what I feel I can't do.

Comments. This excerpt must be viewed in context. The patient had been in therapy for about a year, complaining of depression and anxiety. Although extremely successful in the eyes of his family and associates, he himself felt weak and incompetent. Through many sessions of free association and dream analysis, the analyst had begun to suspect that the patient's feelings of failure stemmed from his childhood experiences with an extremely punitive and critical father, a man even more successful than the client, and a person who seemed never to be satisfied with his son's efforts. The exchange quoted was later interpreted by the analyst as an expression of resentment by the patient of his *father's* pressures on him and had little to do with the analyst himself. The patient's tone of voice (petulant), as well as his overreaction to the analyst's gentle suggestion that he talk about his feelings of not wanting to talk, indicated that the patient was angry not at his analyst but at his father. The expression of such feelings to the analyst, that is, transferring them from the father to the analyst, was regarded as significant by the therapist and was used in subsequent sessions in helping the patient to reevaluate his childhood fears of expressing aggression toward his father.

standing of his own motivations to be able to see the client clearly, without distortion. For example, when an analyst feels himself becoming angry with a client, he must make certain that the client is doing something to make him feel this way, that he does not feel anger through his own unresolved problems or his own personal sensitivities. Then he will be able to help the client examine his or her personality for what is creating hostility in the analyst.

For this reason a "training analysis," or *Lehranalyse*, is a formal part of the education of an analyst. Although many therapists of different theoretical persuasions consider it useful to have been in therapy themselves, a personal therapy is *required* in analytic training institutes. It is essential that analysts reduce to a minimum the incidence or intensity of countertransference toward their clients.

The analyst, moreover, must *not* become actively involved in helping the analysand deal with everyday problems. He assiduously avoids any intervention, such as direct suggestion how to behave in a troublesome situation. Short-term relief might deflect the patient's efforts to uncover the repressed conflicts. Freud was emphatic on this point, writing in 1918 that the analyst must take care not to make the patient's life so comfortable that he or she is no longer motivated to delve into the unconscious. He put it this way in his criticism of nonanalytic helpers.

> Their one aim is to make everything as pleasant as possible for the patient, so that he may feel well there and be glad to take refuge there again from the trials of life. In so doing, they make no attempt to give him more strength for facing life and more capacity for carrying out his actual tasks in it. In analytic treatment, all such spoiling must be avoided. As far as his relations with the physician are concerned, the patient must be left with unfulfilled wishes in abundance. It is expedient to deny him precisely those satisfactions which he desires most intensely and expresses most importunately (Freud, 1955, p. 164).

The detachment of the analyst has often been satirized or misinterpreted, which does an injustice both to analytic theory and to the people who apply it. When a person is in pain and need, the initial impulse is, figuratively, to take the sufferer into one's arms and comfort him or her, providing reassurance that all will be well, that the client will be taken care of. But the truth is that others have probably already tried to provide solace; if sympathy and support were going to help, they probably would already have done so. The analyst must work hard to *resist* showing concern through expressions of support and with concrete advice. Moreover, acting in a directive fashion will interfere with transference, for the therapist necessarily becomes less of a blank screen if he expresses opinions, voices objections, and gives advice and direction. The distance kept by the analyst from the analysand is intended for his or her betterment. This stratagem is consistent with analytic theory and is rather rigidly applied by the more orthodox of psychoanalysts and by those who see utility in the theory.

Psychoanalysis is directly opposite in thrust to behavior therapy, for behavior therapists, unconcerned with factors that are presumed by analysts to be buried in the unconscious, concentrate precisely on what they ignore, namely helping patients change their attitudes, feelings, and overt behavior in concrete, current life situations. What the analyst, and to a large degree the ego analyst, terms "supportive therapy," the behavior therapist regards as the essence of therapy. By the same token, what the behavior therapist sees as unnecessary and even detrimental to the client—digging into the repressed past and withholding advice on how to make specific changes in the here and now—is judged by the analyst to be essential to complete psychotherapeutic treatment.

Ego Analysis

The most important modifications in psychoanalytic theory come from a group generally referred to as ego analysts. Their views are often seen as constituting contemporary Freudian psychoanalysis. The major figures in this loosely formed movement include Karen Horney (1942), Anna Freud (1946), Erik Erikson (1950), David Rapaport (1951), and Heinz Hartmann (1958). Basically, these writers regard Freud's model of humankind as too dependent on instinctual drives. Although Freud by no means ignored the interactions of the organism with the environment, his view was essentially a "push model," one in which people are driven by intrapsychic urges. The ego analysts place greater emphasis on a person's ability to control the environment and to select the time and the means for satisfying certain instinctual drives. Their basic contention is that the individual is as much ego as id. The concept of control, first introduced in Chapter 5, is quite important to ego analysts. They also focus on current living conditions to a greater extent than Freud did, although they still advocate delving deeply into the historical causes of an individual's behavior.

> The ego analysts do not view man as an automaton pushed hither and yon by imperative innate energies on the one hand and by situational events on the other, constantly seeking some compromise among these conflicting influences. When behavior develops in a healthy fashion, man controls both it and the influence of situational events, selectively responding to consequences he has thoughtfully selected. . . . Man is not at the mercy of either [innate energies or situational events]. He can impose delay and thought between innate energies and action, thus postponing the reduction of such energies indefinitely. Learned responses, primarily thought, make this possible, and although originally they may be learned as a consequence of their energy-reducing function, later they may become relatively independent of such influences (drives) and control them (Ford and Urban, 1963, pp. 187–188).

We have, then, a set of important ego functions which are primarily conscious, capable of controlling both id instincts and the external environment, and which, more significantly, do not depend on the id for their energy. Ego analysts assume that these functions and capabilities are present at birth and then develop through experience. Underemphasized by Freud, ego functions have energies and gratifications of their own,

usually separate from the reduction of id impulses. And whereas society was, for Freud, essentially a negative inhibition against the unfettered gratification of libidinal impulses, the ego analysts hold that an individual's social interactions can provide their own special kind of gratification.

In spite of these changes, however, we cannot conclude that most ego analysts have entirely renounced Freud's repression theory. Consider this from Karen Horney.

> The . . . task awaiting the patient is to change those factors within himself which interfere with his best development. This does not mean only a gross modification in action or behavior, such as gaining or regaining the capacity for public performance, for creative work . . . or losing phobias or tendencies toward depression. These changes will automatically take place in a successful analysis. They are not primary changes, however, but result from less visible changes within the personality . . . (1942, pp. 117–118).

The Interpersonal Views of Harry Stack Sullivan

The views on the development of normal and abnormal behavior held by the American psychiatrist Harry Stack Sullivan (1953) are generally considered to be a variation of ego psychology, although some writers label him "interpersonal,"[1] others Neo-Freudian. His primary contributions derive from his emphasis on the interpersonal nature of emotional problems. The basic difficulty of patients, according to Sullivan, is so-called *parataxic distortions,* which are misperceptions of reality stemming from some disorganization in the interpersonal relations of childhood, primarily those between child and parents. The disturbed attitudes toward parents, siblings, and other people who were significant in the person's past are from that time forward projected unconsciously into all interpersonal re-

---

[1] The interpersonal school holds that mental disorder stems from fear and inadequacy in one or more kinds of interpersonal situations.

BOX 18.2 What Does the Therapist See of the Client in Transference?

Sullivan suggested that the therapist can never be just a blank screen, that he becomes an important participant in the process of therapy. In a searching critique of transference, Wachtel (1977) goes even further. Opposing the orthodox psychoanalytic view that a shadowy therapist enables transference to develop, Wachtel hypothesizes that such unvarying behavior on the part of the therapist frustrates the client, who may be seeking some indication of how the therapist feels about what he or she is doing and saying. The sometimes childish reactions assumed to be part of the transference neurosis Wachtel regards as the normal reactions of an adult who is thwarted! The troubled client sees the analyst as a professional person who remains distant and noncommittal in the face of his or her increasing expression of emotion. Thus, rather than an unfolding of the client's personality, "transference" may actually be his or her extreme frustration with minimal feedback. Moreover, because the analyst restricts his own behavior so severely in the consulting room, and intentionally limits the setting to which the client is exposed, he can sample only a limited range of the client's behavior, attitudes, and feelings. In contrast, behavior therapists and others who believe more than analysts do that behavior is in large part situationally determined often role-play someone in the person's life to see how the client reacts.

lationships, including that between patient and therapist (Wolberg, 1954). The individual has never learned to behave properly in social situations and is therefore too anxious to bear the buffeting to the self of a close association. The principal goal of therapy is to bring these distortions in thinking to the patient's consciousness so that he or she can evaluate present reality and separate it from past conditioning and learning.

So far Sullivan appears traditionally Freudian, with his strong emphasis on the childhood sources of adult problems and the need to help the analysand achieve insight into the infantile origins of current difficulties. But he was also very directive and present-oriented, recommending that the therapist inform the patient of fairly predictable consequences of contemplated actions (Wachtel, 1977). Moreover, Sullivan is perhaps most noted for his conception of the analyst as a "participant observer" in the therapy process. In contrast to the classical or even ego-analytical view of the therapist as a blank screen for the transference neurosis, Sullivan argued that the therapist, like the scientist, is inevitably a part of the process he or she is studying. An analyst does not "see" patients without at the same time affecting them. What patients do and say— or do not do and say—is determined not only by what they bring to the therapy session but by how they interact with the therapist. Even a silent or "invisible" analyst will elicit a reaction from the patient (Box 18.2).

Sullivan was relatively vague, however, about the means by which patients were actually to be helped. For example, it is not clear whether Sullivan assumed that realization on the part of the patient of the role a given interpersonal relationship has played in his or her discomfort will automatically reduce anxiety. Like the other ego analysts, Sullivan provided relatively sparse descriptions of specific therapeutic techniques (Ford and Urban, 1963). He did, however, alert Freudians to the importance of using the interpersonal setting of therapy to help patients understand their maladaptive ways of dealing with the world.

Evaluation of Analytic Therapy

In clinical circles there are few issues more controversial than the question whether psychoanalysis and related therapies work. Some clinicians are uneasy with the psychoanalytic concepts themselves, especially those that seem wedded to a notion of *an* unconscious. As Levy puts it, ". . . nothing can be said by the canons of modern philosophy of science, of the existence of the unconscious as a substantive entity: the assertion of its existence is in principle untestable and hence meaningless" (1963, p. 22).

This harsh judgment points up one of the major themes of this textbook, namely the role of paradigms. Those who think in psychoanalytic terms might themselves take issue with "the canons of modern philosophy of science" on the grounds that a monolithic view of science is not tenable. That is, science itself, no less than psychopathology, is subject to different points of view. These paradigmatic differences bear on any evaluation of the effectiveness of psychoanalysis, in all its various forms. It is very difficult to evaluate scientifically. What, for example, are the criteria for improvement? A principal one is the lifting of repressions, making the unconscious conscious. But how is that to be demonstrated? How do we determine whether a repression has been lifted? In practice, attempts to assess outcome have relied very heavily on projective tests like the Rorschach, which, in turn, rely heavily on the concept of the unconscious. Clearly, if this very concept is rejected a priori, there is little common ground for discussion.

The central concept of insight is also questioned. Rather than accept insight as the recognition by the client of some important, externally valid historical connection or relationship, several writers (for example, Bandura, 1969; London, 1964) propose that the development of insight is better understood as a *social conversion process,* whereby the patient comes to accept the belief system or his or her therapist. Marmor (1962) has suggested that insight means different things depending on the school of therapy; a patient treated by a proponent of any one of the various schools develops insights along the lines of its particular theoretical predilections. Freudians tend to elicit insights regarding oedipal dilemmas, Sullivanians insights regarding interpersonal relationships. Indeed, Levy (1963) goes so far as to say that the concept of the unconscious is actually nothing more than a disagreement between what a psychoanalytically oriented therapist and the analysand believe to be the explanation of the client's predicament.

The insight therapists argue that the worth or validity of a particular insight is to be gauged by its efficacy in producing a desired and beneficial therapeutic change. But there are no generally agreed upon criteria for assessing therapeutic change and few well-controlled studies of whether there has been any.

With all these cautions in mind, let us consider what efforts people have made to evaluate the power of psychoanalytic and ego-analytic therapy to effect desirable changes in people. Like all therapy research, psychoanalytic research can be divided into studies concentrating on *outcome* and on *process.* Outcome studies ask whether therapy works, and whether it works better under one set of conditions than another. Process studies focus on what happens *during* therapy that can be related to the outcome. For example, does transference have to occur for beneficial change to take place?

Outcome research

The following generalizations about Freudian psychoanalysis were made by Luborksy and Spence (1978), who relied on outcome research conducted with some measure of controlled observation.

1. Patients with severe psychopathology (for example, schizophrenia) do not do as well as those with anxiety disorders. This is understandable in view of Freud's admitted emphasis on neurosis rather than psychosis and in view of the heavy reliance psychoanalysis places on rationality and verbal abilities.

2. The more education a patient has, the better

he or she does in analysis, probably because of the heavy emphasis on verbal interactions.

3. The evidence is conflicting whether the outcome of psychoanalysis is any better than what would be achieved through the mere passage of time or by engaging other professional help, such as a family doctor (Bergin, 1971; Eysenck, 1952). This is *not* to say that psychoanalysis does no good, only that clear evidence is as yet lacking. Given the great diversity in the characteristics of both patients and therapists, and in the severity of patients' problems, the question being asked is probably too complex to yield a single, scientifically acceptable answer.

No study with adequate controls has as yet demonstrated a superiority of psychoanalysis or psychoanalytically oriented therapy over a placebo treatment or alternative forms of therapy (Prochaska, 1979). Although numerous studies suggest improvements in patients after analytic therapy, the research designs employed do not allow us to assess whether such patients might have improved as much by raising their hopes for help or by providing other modes of treatment.

A widely cited study of Sloane and his colleagues (1975) is considered by some psychotherapy researchers (for example, Bergin and Lambert, 1978) the best comparative study of therapy yet carried out. At the Temple University Outpatient Clinic three behavior therapists and three analysts—all of them highly experienced and recognized leaders in their respective fields—treated a total of ninety adult patients for a period of four months. In order to judge the effects of having taken steps to enter therapy, there was also a wait-list control group, people who had been promised therapy after a comprehensive assessment but were asked to wait while others were in treatment. Most of the participants in this study can best be described as neurotic; they were the individuals typically seen in outpatient clinics or in private consulting rooms. For the most part they were troubled by anxiety and disturbed relationships. After being matched on age and sex, as well as severity of problems, they were assigned to behavior therapy, to short-

term analytic therapy (meaning ego analysis, presumably), or to the wait-list control group.

Outcome measures, taken immediately after treatment and at an eight-month follow-up, included personality tests such as the MMPI, ratings of how much symptoms had improved, structured interviews to determine how well the clients were doing in their work and social adjustment, and a global rating of improvement. In addition to the psychiatrist or psychologist who had conducted the therapy, the client, a clinician who had not been involved in treatment and did not know which each participant had received, and a close friend or relative joined in the judgments. Depending on how we look at the data, and there are many ways, given the complexity of the study and the several measures taken, the findings favor behavior therapy, analytic therapy, or no treatment at all! Immediately after termination of therapy it was determined that the problems of the clients in the two treatment groups had been relieved about equally and that their functioning was similarly improved. The independent clinicians rated 80 percent of the clients in each treatment group improved or cured and 48 percent of the wait-list control group improved or recovered. *But* at the eight-month follow-up the superiority of the two treated groups over the wait-list control group had vanished, for the subjects in the control group had improved markedly. The people waiting for treatment had received a fair amount of attention, for in addition to the initial and later assessments they were called regularly and given encouragement and support.

This ambitious study is subject to several criticisms that are of general importance to the study of therapy. First, did the use of multiple judges—the client, the therapist, an independent clinician, and a close friend or relative—make the information gathered about improvement especially valid? Unlikely. The ratings made by independent clinicians were based entirely on interviews with the clients. It is not surprising that their ratings correlated significantly with those of the clients. Yet these two ratings correlated much less strongly with those of the therapists, friends, and relatives. Which sets of ratings are valid?

Much of the information collected was obtained through interviews. Improvement was rated by what the client said and how he or she said it during treatment or evaluation interviews—except for the judgments of friends and relatives, who presumably observed the daily living of the client. No other observation of the client in everyday surroundings or in contrived settings, such as the speech anxiety test employed by Paul (1966; see page 100), was attempted, however. By not arranging for such observations, Sloane and his colleagues made the assumption that we can know how a client is doing by sampling his or her behavior in the consulting room.

Clearly the limitations of the outcome measures argue for caution in interpreting the results. But what of the independent variables, the treatments themselves? Did each analytic therapist *do* only analytic work with each client, and did each behavior therapist *do* only behavior therapy? The answer is maybe. Sloane and his colleagues drew up for their therapists a list of defining characteristics of the analytic and behavior therapy that they intended to compare (Table 18.1) and instructed the therapists to adhere to these definitions as closely as possible. Audiotape recordings of the fifth session of each treatment were analyzed to determine whether these rules were being followed. The judgment was made that they were. The fact remains, however, that at least for behavior therapy a broad range of techniques are available, and each one is believed especially appropriate for a particular kind of problem, which must be determined through careful assessment. For example, systematic desensitization will not help a client who is anxious because he lacks social skills. Although the behavior therapists in the Sloane study enjoy sterling reputations among their peers—two of them were Wolpe and Lazarus—researchers prefer to rely less on personal reputation and more on careful specification of procedures.

Process research

It is difficult to draw general conclusions from process studies of analytic therapy, primarily because the variables are so complex and, as already stated, inextricably bound up with concepts referring to the unconscious. A number of projects, entailing intensive study of tape recordings and of analysts' notes for individual cases,

have been underway for years. One of the variables studied is "associative freedom," or the extent to which the analysand can free-associate. If free association helps the analyst get to hitherto repressed material, great facility in free-associating should predict a good outcome. Unfortunately, the relationship is much more complex, for the patient's free association interacts with the analyst's interpretations, and the effectiveness of these, in turn, depends on their timing—not to mention their accuracy. Because of these difficulties, plus the problems of defining outcome criteria and of designing reliable measures, it is not surprising that process research in psychoanalysis and related therapies has thus far shed little light on how they work.

Perhaps the most sobering and thought-provoking statement about research in analytic therapy was made by Luborsky and Spence (1978), two leading psychotherapy researchers. Examined closely, it reveals the minor role that controlled research is expected to play in evaluating psychoanalytic therapy.

> *Quantitative research on psychoanalytic therapy presents itself, so far, as an unreliable support to clinical practice. Far more is known now through clinical wisdom than is known through quantitative, objective studies.* Much of what is contributed by the quantitative literature represents a cumbersome, roundabout way of showing the clinician what he or she already "knows". . . (p. 358).

TABLE 18.1

Characteristics of Behavior Therapy and
Psychoanalytically Oriented Psychotherapy
in the Temple University Study

(from Sloane et al., 1975)

1. Specific advice
   b) Given frequently.*
   p) Given infrequently.
2. Transference interpretation
   b) Avoided.
   p) May be given.
3. Interpretation of resistance
   b) Not used.
   p) Used.
4. Dreams
   b) Polite lack of interest; not used in treatment.
   p) Interest in reported dreams which may be used in treatment.
5. Level of anxiety
   b) Diminished when possible except in implosive therapy.
   p) Maintain some anxiety as long as it does not disrupt behavior.
6. Training in relaxation
   b) Directly undertaken.
   p) Only an indirect consequence of sitting, and perhaps the example of the therapist.
7. Desensitization
   b) Directly undertaken.
   p) Only an indirect consequence of talking in comfortable circumstances with uncritical therapist.
8. Practical retraining
   b) Directly undertaken.
   p) Not emphasized.
9. Training in appropriately assertive action
   b) Directly undertaken and encouraged in everyday life.
   p) Only indirectly encouraged in everyday life. Assertive or aggressive speech which would be
      inappropriate in everyday life permitted in therapeutic session.
10. Symptoms
    b) Interest in the report of symptoms, may explain biologically.
    p) Report of symptoms discouraged, may interpret symbolically.
11. Childhood memories
    b) Usually history taking only.
    p) Usually further memories looked for.
12. Aversion, e.g., electric shock
    b) May be used.
    p) Not used.
13. Observers of treatment session
    b) May be permitted.
    p) Not usually permitted.
14. Deliberate attempts to stop behavior, such as thoughts, which makes the patient anxious
    b) May be used.
    p) Rarely directly attempted.
15. Role training
    b) May be used.
    p) Not used.
16. Repetition of motor habits
    b) May be used.
    p) Not used.

* The items preceded by b apply to behavior therapy, by p psychoanalysis.

Humanistic and Existential Therapies

Humanistic and existential therapies, like psychoanalytic therapies, are insight-oriented, being based on the assumption that disordered behavior can best be changed by increasing the individual's awareness of motivations and needs. But there is a useful contrast between psychoanalysis and its offshoots on the one hand and humanistic-existential approaches on the other: humanistic-existential therapies place greater emphasis on the person's freedom of choice. Free will is regarded as the human being's most important characteristic. Free will is, however, a double-edged sword, for it not only offers fulfillment and pleasure but also threatens acute pain and suffering. It is an innately provided gift that *must* be used and that requires special courage to use. Not all of us can meet this challenge; those who cannot are regarded as candidates for client-centered, existential, and Gestalt therapies.

Carl Rogers's Client-Centered Therapy

Carl Rogers is an American psychologist whose theorizing about psychotherapy grew slowly out of years of intensive clinical experience. After teaching at the university level in the 1940s and 1950s, he helped organize the Center for Studies of the Person in La Jolla, California. Rogers makes several basic assumptions about human nature and the means by which we can try to understand it (Ford and Urban, 1963; Rogers, 1951, 1961).

1. We must adopt a phenomenological point of view (see page 5). People can be understood only from the vantage point of their own perceptions and feelings. It is the way people construe events rather than the events themselves that the investigator must attend to, for a person's phenomenological world is the major determinant of behavior and makes him or her unique.

2. Healthy people are aware of their behavior. In this sense Rogers's system is similar to psychoanalysis and ego analysis, for it emphasizes the desirability of awareness of motives.

3. People are innately good and effective; they become ineffective and disturbed only when faulty learning intervenes.

4. Behavior is purposive and goal-directed; people do not respond passively to the influence of their environment or to their inner drives. They are self-directive. In this assumption Rogers is closer to ego analysts than to orthodox Freudian psychoanalysts.

5. Therapists should not attempt to manipulate events for the individual; rather they should create conditions that will facilitate independent decision making by the client.

Personality development

Rogers postulates an innate tendency to actualize, that is, to realize potentialities. This idea, drawn from Otto Rank (1936), a Viennese psychoanalyst and a member of Freud's inner circle, is basic to Rogers's conception of human beings and therefore crucial to understanding his approach to therapy. In common with Freud and most learning theorists, Rogers holds that people try to reduce the physiological tensions of hunger, thirst, and pain. But Rogers proposes that people by nature seek also to learn new things and otherwise enhance their lives. In other words, people *seek out* pleasurable tension in addition to attempting to reduce the unpleasurable tension. All behavior, for Rogers, originates in some way from this innate self-actualizing tendency. Furthermore, people evaluate behavior for its contribution to personal growth and tend to repeat activity that helps them approach this goal.

Rogers assumes that the most effective learning takes place when a person does not have to struggle for and concern himself with approval from others. The most important evaluations are to come from the person himself, for the self has its innate self-actualizing tendency. When a person receives *unconditional positive regard* from others, he is not distracted and is better able to evaluate how his own behavior is contributing to enhancement of self.

The natural sequence of healthy development can be interfered with by faulty learning. A person may accept evaluations by others instead of paying heed to the internal evaluations provided by his own psyche and body. For example, he may apply the denigrating evaluations of others to his own instrinsically good behavior and actually begin to accept their judgment, as when a student regards himself as a worthless human being after being criticized by a teacher. By accepting the judgments of others, individuals may develop too limited a self-concept, one that, for example, denies the potential for anger and assertiveness and, on the other hand, for gentleness and giving. Individuals with a rigid self-concept based on narrow introjected values must reject or distort large portions of experience. Self-actualization is impeded, and the self-concept is in ever-greater incongruence with experiences.

This incongruence, or conflict, creates anxiety. At some point the conflict begins to operate outside of the person's awareness. By the time he consults a therapist, an individual may not even know why he is unhappy.

Therapeutic intervention

Because a mature and well-adjusted person makes his own judgments based on what is intrinsically satisfying and actualizing, Rogers avoids imposing goals on the client during therapy. The client is to take the lead and direct the course of the conversation and of the session. The therapist's job is to create conditions so that during their hour together the client can return once again to his basic nature and judge for himself which course of life is intrinsically gratifying to him. Again, because of Rogers's very positive view of people, he assumes that their decisions will not only make them happy with themselves but also turn them into good civilized people.

Rogers's thinking has evolved from a clear specification of techniques (Rogers, 1942) to an emphasis on the attitude and emotional style of the therapist and a de-emphasis of specific procedures (Rogers, 1951). The therapist should have three core qualities. Genuineness, sometimes called congruence, encompasses spontaneity, openness, and authenticity. The therapist has no phoniness and no professional facade, self-disclosing himself, his feelings, and his thoughts informally and candidly to the client. In a sense the therapist through honest self-disclosure pro-

vides a model for what the client can become. He is in touch with his feelings and is able to express them and to accept responsibility for doing so. He has the courage to present himself to others as he really is. The second attribute of the successful therapist, according to Rogers, is being able to extend unconditional positive regard. Other people set what Rogers calls "conditions of worth"—I will love you if. . . . The client-centered therapist prizes clients as they are, and conveys unpossessive warmth for them, even if he does not approve of their behavior. People have value merely for being people, and the therapist must care deeply for and respect a client, for the simple reason that he or she is another human being, engaged in the struggle of growing and being alive. The third quality, accurate empathic understanding, is the ability to see the world through the eyes of clients from moment to moment, to understand the feelings of clients both from their own phenomenological vantage point, which is known to them, and from perspectives that they may be only dimly aware of.

Empathy

Empathizing—the acceptance, recognition, and clarification of feelings—is one of the few techniques of Rogerian therapy. It is applied within the context of a warm therapeutic relationship. The therapist encourages the client to talk about his most deeply felt concerns and attempts to restate the emotional aspects, not just the content, of what the client says. This reflection of feelings to the client is meant to remove gradually the emotional conflicts that are blocking self-actualization. Because feelings are mirrored back without judgment of disapproval, the client can look at them, clarify them, and acknowledge and accept them. Feared thoughts and emotions that were previously too threatening to enter awareness can become part of the self-concept. The self-concept enlarges and becomes more complex but also better integrated. The therapist, it should be noted, is not being truly nondirective, a term often applied to Rogers, for he selectively attends to evaluative statements and feelings expressed by the client. He believes that these are the matters the client should be helped to examine.

If therapeutic conditions allowing self-acceptance are established, the client begins to talk in a more honest and emotional way about himself. Rogers assumes that such talk in itself is primarily responsible for changing behavior.

Rogers's application of empathy is sometimes mistakenly assumed to be an easy, straightforward matter, but it is not. In fact, it requires much subtlety and constitutes strong "medicine" indeed. The therapist does not always restrict himself to merely finding words for the emotional aspects of what the client says but, in what one writer calls "advanced accurate empathy" (Egan, 1975), he goes beyond to what he believes *lies behind* the client's observable behavior (see Box 18.3). The therapist makes an inference about what is troubling the client. He interprets what the client has told him in a way that seems different from the client's actual statements. In a sense, advanced empathy represents theory building on the part of the therapist: after considering over a number of sessions what the client has been saying and how he or she has been saying it, the therapist generates a hypothesis about what may be the true source of distress and yet remains hidden from the client.[2] The following is an example.

Client: I don't know what's going on. I study hard, but I just don't get good marks. I think I study as hard as anyone else, but all of my efforts seem to go down the drain. I don't know what else I can do.

Counselor A: You feel frustrated because even when you try hard you fail [primary empathy].

Counselor B: It's depressing to put in as much effort as those who pass and still fail. It gets you down and maybe even makes you feel a little sorry for yourself [advanced empathy] (Egan, 1975, p. 135).

In primary empathy the therapist tries to restate to clients their thoughts, feelings, and experiences *from their own point of view*. The work here is at the phenomenological level; the therapist views the client's world from the client's perspective and then communicates to the client that this frame of reference is understood and appreciated. In advanced empathy the therapist generates a view that takes the client's world into account but conceptualizes things differently and, it is hoped, in a more constructive way. The therapist presents to the client a way of considering himself that may be quite different from the client's accustomed perspective.

To understand this important distinction, we must bear in mind that therapists operating within the client-centered framework assume that the client views things in an unproductive way, as evidenced by the psychological distress that has brought the client into therapy. At the primary empathic level the therapist accepts this view, understands it, and communicates to the client that it is appreciated. But at the advanced or interpretive level the therapist offers something new, a perspective he hopes is better and more productive and implies new modes of action. Advanced empathizing builds on the information made available over a number of sessions in which the therapist has concentrated on making primary-level empathic statements. In actual practice therapists move back and forth between the two kinds of empathy, being careful to put forth any advanced empathic statements in a cautious, tentative way, lest they become untoward pressure on the client to perceive things in a particular way.

Evaluation

Largely because of Rogers's own insistence that the outcome and process of therapy be carefully scrutinized and empirically validated, numerous studies have attempted to evaluate client-centered therapy. Indeed, Rogers can be credited with originating the whole field of psychotherapy research. He and his students deserve the credit for removing the mystique and excessive privacy of the consulting room; for example, they pioneered the tape recording of therapy sessions for subsequent analysis by researchers.

Research on Rogerian therapy has focused principally on relating outcome to the personal qualities of therapists and has yielded inconsis-

---

[2] Whether an advanced empathy statement by the therapist should even be regarded as *accurate* is an interesting question. These interpretations by client-centered therapists can never be known for sure to be true. Rather, like theories in science, they may be more or less *useful.*

BOX 18.3 Excerpt from a Client-Centered Therapy Session

Client (an eighteen-year-old female college student): My parents really bug me. First it was Arthur they didn't like, now it's Peter. I'm just fed up with all their meddling.

Therapist: You really are angry at your folks.

Client: Well, how do you expect me to feel? Here I am with a 3.5 GPA, and providing all sorts of other goodies, and they claim the right to pass on how appropriate my boyfriend is. (Begins to sob.)

Therapist: It strikes me that you're not just angry with them. (Pause) Maybe you're worried about disappointing them.

Client: (Crying even more) I've tried all my life to please them. Sure their approval is important to me. They're really pleased when I get A's, but why do they have to pass judgment on my social life as well?

Comments. Although the emotion expressed initially was one of anger, the therapist felt that the client was really fearful of criticism from her parents. She therefore made an advanced empathic statement in an effort to explore with the client what was only implied but not expressed. Previous sessions had suggested that the client worked hard academically primarily to please her parents and to avoid their censure. She had always been able to win their approval by getting good grades, but more recently the critical eyes of her mother and father were directed at the young men she was dating. The client was beginning to realize that she had to arrange her social life to please her parents. Her neurotic fear of disapproval from her parents became the focus in therapy after the therapist had helped her see beyond her anger.

---

tent results, casting doubt on the widely held assumption that positive outcome is strongly related to the therapist's empathy, genuineness, and warmth (Parloff, Waskow, and Wolfe, 1978). It is probably useful to continue emphasizing such qualities in the training of young clinicians, however, for they would seem to help create for the client an atmosphere of trust and safety within which to reveal the deep inner workings of the self. But it is not justifiable, from a research perspective, to assert that these qualities, by themselves, are sufficient to help clients change.

In keeping with Rogers's phenomenological approach, self-reports by clients are the usual measures of the effectiveness of therapy. Research on Rogerian therapy pays practically no attention to how patients actually *behave* following therapy. Rogers's basic datum is the individual's own phenomenological evaluation and reaction to himself and events in his world; the overt behavior, it is held, follows from these perceptions and is not the proper object of study by the client-centered therapy researcher.

The paradigmatic neglect of behavior outside the therapy session can conceivably create problems for clients. Even though feelings of inferiority are overcome during sessions, the client may very well be at a loss how to behave differently after leaving the consulting room. He may, for example, never have acquired an adequate repertoire of social skills. If he is truly to change his concept of himself, it would seem necessary to do more than help the client understand himself better. He may very well need training in interpersonal skills.

Rogers's emphasis on subjective experience also raises epistemological problems, for the therapist must be able to make accurate and incisive inferences about what the client is feeling or thinking. Although the method seems to rely entirely on what the client says, Rogers asserts that clients can be unaware of their true feelings; indeed, it is this lack of awareness that brings most of them into therapy in the first place. As with psychoanalysis, we must ask how a therapist is to make an inference about internal processes of which a client is seemingly unaware, and then by what procedures is the usefulness or validity of that inference to be evaluated.

Rogers may also be criticized for assuming that self-actualization is the principal human motivation. Postulating any innately given drive or motive raises difficulties. Rogers infers the self-actualization motive from his observation that people seek out situations offering fulfillment. But then the self-actualization tendency is given in *explanation* of the search for these situations. Circular reasoning again!

Then, of course, there is the question of the therapist's own influence on what happens in the therapy session. Rogers no longer refers to his therapy as nondirective, evidently an admission that the therapeutic situation is inherently directive.

Another point to consider is how faulty ideas are learned from the evaluation of others. Why does the master motive not always dominate the individual's learning? If the person is indeed always self-actualizing, under what circumstances does faulty learning take place, and what motives and needs are satisfied by such faulty learning?

Finally, Rogers assumes both that the psychologically healthy person makes choices to satisfy self-actualizing tendencies and that people are by their very natures good. But other social philosophers have taken a less optimistic view of human nature. Thomas Hobbes, for example, stated that life is "nasty, brutish, and short."

How do we explain a person who behaves in a brutish fashion and yet asserts that this behavior is intrinsically gratifying and, indeed, self-actualizing?

It may be that the problem of extreme unreasonableness has not been adequately addressed by Rogers because he and his colleagues have concentrated on people who are only mildly disturbed. As a way to help unhappy but not severely disordered people understand themselves better (and *perhaps* even to help them behave differently), client-centered therapy may very well be appropriate and effective. This humanistic approach remains popular in the encounter group movement (see page 626). Rogerian therapy may not, however, be appropriate for a severe psychological disorder, as Rogers himself has warned.

Existential Therapy

Those most commonly associated with existentialism are the Danish philosopher Kierkegaard and the German philosophers Husserl and Heidegger, with existential therapy the Swiss psychiatrists Binswanger and Boss and the Austrian psychiatrist Viktor Frankl, whose logotherapy and views on depression were discussed earlier (see page 258). In this country the principal proponents of existential therapy, or existential analysis as it is sometimes called, have been Rollo May and the late Abraham Maslow.

Basic concepts of existentialism

The following is a distillation of the existential position.

> Man has the capacity for being aware of himself, of what he is doing, and what is happening to him. As a consequence, he is capable of making decisions about these things and of taking responsibility for himself. He can also become aware of a possibility of becoming completely isolated and alone, that is, nothing, symbolized by the ultimate nothingness of death. This is innately feared. He is not a static entity but in a constant state of transition. He does not exist; he is not a being; rather he is coming into being, emerging, becoming,

Rollo May, the founder of existential therapy in the United States. According to him, the self is centeredness, which we all strive to preserve. But we need too to go forth from it and participate in other beings.

evolving toward something. His ways of behaving toward himself and other events are changing constantly. His significance lies not in what he has been in the past, but in what he is now and the direction of his development, which is toward the fulfillment of his innate potentiality (Ford and Urban, 1963, p. 448).

The existential point of view, like humanism, emphasizes personal growth. There are, though, some important distinctions. Humanism, as exemplified by Rogers's views, stresses the goodness of human nature. If unfettered by groundless fears and societal restrictions, human beings will develop normally, even exceptionally, much as a flower will sprout from a seed if only given enough light, air, and water. Existentialism is gloomier, having a strain of darkness within it. Although it embraces free will and responsibility, existentialism stresses the anxiety that is inevitable in making important choices, the existential

choices on which existence depends, such as staying or not staying with a spouse, with a job, or even with this world. Hamlet's famous soliloquy beginning "To be, or not to be—that is the question" is a classic existential statement. To be truly alive is to confront the anxiety that comes with existential choices. To avoid such choices, to pretend that they do not have to be made, may protect the individual from anxiety, but it also deprives him of living a life with meaning. Thus whereas the humanistic message is upbeat, almost ecstatic, the existential is tinged with sadness and anxiety, but not despair, unless the exercise of free will and the assumption of responsibility that accompanies it are avoided.

The goals of therapy

A person is the sum of the choices he makes. Difficulties in making choices can only be understood by exploring experience. The existential therapist, by offering support and empathy through adoption of the individual's phenomenological frame of reference, helps him explore his behavior, feelings, relationships, and what his life means to him. But the therapist also encourages the client to confront and clarify past and present choices. Present choices are the most important.

Abraham Maslow (1908–1970), the humanistic therapist who made Carl Jung's term self-actualization central to his psychology.

In addition, existential therapy helps people to relate *authentically* to others. People are assumed to define their identity and existence in terms of their interpersonal relationships; a person is threatened with nonbeing—or alienation—if isolated from others. Even though he may be effective in dealing with people and his world (see page 60), he can become anxious if deprived of open and frank relationships. Hence, although the existential view is a highly subjective one, it strongly emphasizes *relating to others* in an open, honest, and loving fashion.[3] The encounter group movement owes much to this existential tenet.

The therapeutic relationship should be an authentic encounter between two human beings so that the patient has some practice in relating to another individual in a straightforward fashion.[4] The therapist, through his own honesty and self-disclosure, helps the client learn authenticity. An incident with a married couple in therapy together (Prochaska, 1979) serves as an example. The husband had been complaining bitterly that his wife did not want to have sex with him. The way he criticized her and refused to take any responsibility whatsoever for the problem impelled the therapist to exclaim, "You make me want to vomit." The husband initally considered this remark unprofessional conduct on the part of the therapist, but he soon came to recognize the therapist's outburst as an authentic expression of feeling which might reflect his wife's own phenomenological state.

The principal goal of existential therapy is to make the patient more aware of his own potential for choice and growth. In the existential view people create their existence anew at each moment. The potential for disorder as well as growth is ever present. The person must be encouraged to accept the responsibility for his own existence and to realize that, within certain limits, he can redefine himself at any moment and behave and feel differently within his own social environment. But this freedom to choose and the responsibility that comes with it are not easy for humankind to accept and work with. Many people are afraid of this freedom, and as they begin to make choices, they realize that fulfillment is a *process*, that they must constantly choose and accept responsibility if they are to be truly human and fulfill their potential. Their prospects then are not cheery; with greater awareness of their freedom to choose comes more existential anxiety. One of the goals of therapy is to bolster their resolve and ability to cope with this inescapable anxiety and to continue growing.

The existential writers, however, are very vague about what therapeutic techniques will help the client grow. Indeed a reliance on technique may be seen as an objectifying process, that is, a process in which the therapist acts upon the client as though he or she were a thing to be manipulated (Prochaska, 1979). The existential approach is a general *attitude* taken by certain therapists toward human nature, rather than a set of therapeutic techniques.

Evaluation

Although existential therapists have published numerous case reports relating striking successes with a variety of clinical problems, no available evidence has scientific rigor. Existential therapy, like the other insight therapies, is difficult to evaluate scientifically. In fact, contemporary science is seen as dehumanizing by existentialists, hence to be *avoided*. They believe that applying science to individuals denies the unique humanness of people. Several of the criticisms of client-centered therapy apply too to existential treatment. Since by definition a person's subjective experience is unique to himself, how can the therapist know that he is truly understanding a patient's world as it appears to him? Yet attention to subjective impressions is not necessarily unproductive. Paying heed to our freedom to choose and ability to change at any time may be an important means of changing behavior. Indeed, the message implicit in existentialism, that

---

[3] At the same time each of us is ultimately and basically *alone*. Although existentialism asserts that we must relate authentically to others, the paradox of life is that we are inherently separate from others, that we came into this world alone and must create our own existence in the world alone.

[4] It is interesting to note that this approach, which places so much emphasis on a person's perceptions, understanding, feelings, and other internal processes, is in a way very behavioristic in the overt sense of the word. The person must at some point during therapy begin to behave differently, both toward the therapist and toward the outside world, in order for his own existential condition to be changed.

our existence is constantly being reaffirmed and that we are not prisoners of our past mistakes and misfortunes, might well be incorporated into *any* therapy.

Gestalt Therapy

Another humanistic therapy that has developed over the past thirty years is Gestalt therapy; its most important proponent was the late Frederick S. Perls (see Box 18.4). After receiving a medical degree in Germany in 1921, Perls became a psychoanalyst. But he was rejected by European analysts because he challenged some of the basic precepts of psychoanalytic theory, particularly the important place accorded to the libido and its various transformations in the development of neurosis (Perls, 1947). He emigrated to Holland in 1933, shortly after Hitler came to power, because he was opposed to totalitarianism, and to South Africa in 1934, as the country's first teaching analyst. There he developed the basics of Gestalt therapy. He took up residence in the United States in 1946 and eventually settled at Esalen, a center for humanistic therapy on the West coast. Here his ideas and techniques of therapy have undergone impressive growth, especially as applied in groups (Perls, Hefferline, and Goodman, 1951; Perls, 1970).

Basic concepts of Gestalt therapy

Like Rogers, Perls holds that people have an innate goodness and that this basic nature should be allowed to express itself. Psychological problems originate in frustrations and denials of this innate goodness. Like other humanistic approaches, Gestalt therapy tends to emphasize the creative and expressive aspects of people, rather than the negative and distorted features on which psychoanalysis seems to concentrate.

A basic assumption of Gestalt therapy is that all of us bring our needs and wants to any situation. We do not merely precieve situations "as they are"; instead we engage our social environment by projecting our needs, or fears, or desires onto what is "out there." Thus if I am talking to a stranger, I do not merely react to the person as that person exists; I react to the stranger in the context of my needs. Gestalt therapists working with groups sometimes have people pair off,

close their eyes, and imagine the face of an individual to whom they have a strong emotional attachment. They are encouraged to concentrate on the feelings they have about that person. Then all open their eyes and look at their partner. After a few moments they are instructed to close their eyes again and think now of something neutral, such as an arithmetic problem. They then open their eyes again and look a second time at their partner. Finally, they are asked whether there was an important difference in the ways they felt about their partner in the two situations. This exercise is designed to exaggerate what is assumed to be inevitable in all our social interactions, namely the intrusion of our feelings into whatever is happening at any particular moment.

Perls and his followers concentrate on the here and now and on the individual as an actor, as a being who is responsible for his or her own behavior and who is capable of playing a central role in bringing about beneficial changes.

The patient who comes for help, seeking to relate more adequately with other people and to be able to express his feelings more directly, is instructed to express what he is feeling at that moment to another person. The ways in which he stops, blocks, and

A Gestalt therapy exercise being performed at the famous Esalen Institute at Big Sur, California.

BOX **18.4** A Glimpse of Fritz Perls

Frederick (Fritz) Perls (1893–1970), colorful founder of Gestalt therapy.

As Joe got on the elevator, he hardly noticed the short, gray-bearded man standing against the wall. Then recognition hit him. "Uh, Dr. Perls, I'm, uh, honored to meet you. I've read your work, and it's such—such an honor to meet—to be in your presence. . . ." Joe's stammering speech trailed away with no effect. The old man did not move.

The elevator slowed and Joe, realizing that an opportunity was slipping away, heard himself say, hopelessly, "I'm really nervous." Perls turned and smiled at him. As the doors opened, he took Joe's arm and said, "Now let us talk" (Gaines, 1974).

frustrates himself quickly become apparent, and he can then be assisted in exploring and experiencing the blockings and encouraged to attempt other ways of expressing himself and of relating.

Thus, the general approach of Gestalt theory and therapy requires the patient to specify the changes in himself that he desires, assists him in increasing his awareness of how he defeats himself, and aids him in experimenting and changing. Blocks in awareness and behavior emerge [during the session] in the same way that they manifest themselves in a person's life; his increased awareness of his avoidances and his relief as he becomes able to expand his experience and behavior are felt immedi- *ately in increases in capacity for living (Fagan and Shepherd, 1970, p. 2).*

The foregoing description of the theorizing behind Gestalt therapy does not distinguish it very well from what Rogers prescribes. But Gestalt therapy is supposedly related to Gestalt psychology, a branch of psychology concerned primarily with perception. Their closest similarity may be in their attention to *wholes*. Perls wanted to make individuals *whole* by increasing their awareness of unacknowledged feelings and having them reclaim the parts of the personality that have been denied or disowned.

The Gestalt therapist focuses on what a client is doing in the consulting room here and now, without delving into the past, for the most important event in the client's life is what is happening at that moment. In Gestalt therapy all that exists is the Now. If the past is bothersome, it is brought into the present. ''Why'' questions are discouraged, for searching after causes in the past is considered an attempt to escape responsibility for making choices in the present, a familiar existential theme. Clients are exhorted, cajoled, sometimes even coerced into awareness of what is happening now. Awareness is an immediate and direct thinking and sensing. Individuals must know what is going on about them, what they think and fantasize, want and feel, what they are doing at the moment, and they must also sense posture, facial expressions, muscular tensions, and gestures, the words they use, the sound of their voice. Perls believed that awareness could be curative. People have only to be moved away from their ideas about themselves to an awareness of what they are feeling and doing at this exact moment.

Gestalt therapy techniques

Gestalt therapy is noted for its emphasis on techniques, in contrast to their paucity in the humanistic therapies discussed so far.[5] The techniques described here are but a small sample of current Gestalt practices.

The Gestalt therapist insists that the client talk in the present tense. This is one way of directing his attention to current feelings and activities. To help him bear continuing responsibility for what he is and what he is to become, the therapist instructs him to change ''it'' language into ''I'' language.

---

[5] Although Gestalt therapy over the years has tended to become identified with a set of techniques, many contemporary workers assert that it is not a set of defined procedures, or for that matter a particular theory of behavior and experience. Rather, Gestalt therapy entails a particular *attitude* toward the nature of humankind and toward treatment. A Gestalt therapist is constantly creative, is open to new experiences, and talks openly to the client on a person-to-person basis, the I-thou which is a tenet of existential philosophy. The core of therapy is to help the client be creative and open too. The Gestalt therapist is trained to ''fine-tune'' the person so that he or she can encounter the world on an immediate, nonjudgmental, nonreflective basis. We agree that equating Gestalt therapy with techniques does not tell the whole story. Gestalt therapy does indeed encourage both therapists and clients to be spontaneous and open to new experience in a general way. At the same time, though, Gestalt therapists employ a body of procedures on a rather consistent basis. Many of them have been adopted by therapists of other persuasions.

Therapist: What do you hear in your voice?

Patient: My voice sounds like it is crying.

Therapist: Can you take responsibility for that by saying, I am crying? (Levitsky and Perls, 1970), p. 142).

This simple change in language, besides allowing the patient to assume responsibility for feelings and behavior, reduces his sense of being alienated from aspects of his very being. It helps the patient see himself as active rather than passive, as an open and searching person rather than as someone whose behavior is determined entirely by external events.

In one procedure of Gestalt therapy, the empty-chair technique, a client projects and then talks to his projection of a feeling, or of a person, object, or situation. Thus, seeing that a patient is crying, the Gestalt therapist might ask him to regard the tears as being in an empty chair opposite him and to speak *to* the tears. This tactic often seems to help people confront their feelings. Indeed, to ask a person to talk *about* his tears is assumed to encourage him to establish still greater distance between himself and his feelings—something Gestalt therapists assert interferes with psychological well-being.

Another technique is to have the person behave opposite to the way he feels. Someone who is excessively timid might be asked during the therapy session to behave like an outgoing person. Perls assumes that the opposite side of the coin actually lies within the being of the person and that acting out feelings not usually expressed allows the person to become aware of a part of himself that has thus far been submerged.

All therapists pay attention to nonverbal and paralinguistic cues given by the client. Nonverbal cues are body movements, facial expressions, gestures, and the like, paralinguistic the tone of voice, the rapidity with which words are spoken, and other audible components of speech beyond its content. People can negate with their hands or their eyes what they are saying with the larynx. Perls placed special emphasis on these nonlinguistic signals, closely observing them in order to determine what clients might really be feeling. ''What we say is mostly lies or bullshit. But the voice is there, the gesture, the posture, the facial expression, the psychosomatic language'' (Perls, 1969, p. 54). At a Gestalt workshop we witnessed a man in his twenties who was bragging about his father's professional accomplishments. As he spoke, his right leg began to shake slightly. The therapist interrupted the story and asked the client to observe his leg. As he did so, he seemed about to cry. Sensing that the client was holding back his tears, the therapist asked him to shake his leg more. Soon the leg was jumping up and down in a violent fashion, and the man began to weep. The resentment toward his father, bottled up since childhood, was now expressed. The session continued, but its focus became the "unfinished business" the client had with his father. Perls believed that unresolved traumas of the past affect new relationships. They should be acted out in the present. By finishing this business, the individual becomes better able to confront the present, for it will not be contaminated by residues from a troubling past.

During the therapy session Gestalt therapists often create unusual scenarios to externalize, to make more vivid and understandable, a problem they believe a client is having. In one session that we observed, a husband and wife sat together on a sofa, bickering about the woman's mother. The husband seemed very angry with his mother-in-law, and the therapist surmised that she was getting in the way of his relationship with his wife. The therapist wanted to demonstrate to the couple how frustrating this must be for both of them, and he also wished to goad both of them to do something about it. Without warning, he rose from his chair and wedged himself between the couple. Not a word was said. The husband looked puzzled, then hurt, and gradually became angry at the therapist. He asked him to move so that he could sit next to his wife again. The therapist shook his head. When the husband repeated his request, the therapist removed his jacket and placed it over the wife's head so that the husband could not even see her. A long silence followed, during which the husband grew more and more agitated. The wife meanwhile was sitting quietly, covered by the therapist's coat. Suddenly the husband stood up, walked past the therapist, and angrily removed the coat; then he pushed the

therapist off the sofa. The therapist exploded in good-natured laughter. "I wondered how long it would take you to do something!" he roared.

The little game drove several points home in a way that mere words might not have. The husband—having been trained already by the therapist to get in better touch with his feelings and to express them without fear or embarassment—reported tearfully that he had felt cut off from his wife by the therapist, in much the same way that he felt alienated from her by her mother. The mother was intruding, and he was not doing anything about it. He did not trust himself to assert his needs and to take action to satisfy them. The fact that he was able to remove the coat and the therapist as well made him wonder whether he might not behave similarly toward his mother-in-law. As he spoke, his wife began to sob; she confided to her husband that all along she had been wanting him to take charge of the problem with her mother. So far so good. But then the therapist turned to the woman and asked her why she had not removed the coat herself! The husband grinned as the therapist gently chided the wife for being unduly passive about her marital problems. By the end of the session, the clients, although emotionally drained, felt in better contact with each other and expressed resolve to work together actively to alter their relationship with her mother.

The interpretation of dreams is another important part of Gestalt therapy. Gestalt analysis of them is quite different from the psychoanalytic. The dream is not considered a rich source of symbolism relating to unconscious processes; rather

> Every image in the dream, whether human, animal, vegetable, or mineral, is taken to represent an alienated portion of the self. By reexperiencing and retelling the dream over and over again in the present tense, from the standpoint of each image, the patient can begin to reclaim these alienated fragments, and accept them, live with them and express them more appropriately (Enright, 1970, p. 121).

For example, a woman in Gestalt therapy dreamt of walking down a crooked path among tall, straight trees. The therapist asked her to *become* one of the trees, and this made her feel serene and more deeply rooted. She then expressed her desire for such security. When she was asked to become the crooked path, tears welled as she confronted the deviousness of the way in which she lived. Once again the Gestalt therapist helped the client to externalize feelings customarily avoided, so that she could become aware of them, acknowledge them as her own, and then perhaps decide to change them.

Consistent with their phenomenological approach, Gestalt therapists encourage clients to recount, with emotion, the meaning that the dream has for them at that very moment. Even though the therapist may have a hypothesis about what a particular dream means to the client, care is taken not to impose that meaning on the dreamer, for it is the dreamer's dream. The only significance it has for the dreamer is the meaning it holds as it is discussed in the session. In this sense Gestalt therapy does not have a theory of dreams; rather it concerns itself with dream *work*, the analysis of dreams by the client, with support from the therapist. Since only the phenomenal world has importance for each client, his or her immediate experience is the one thing worth focusing on.

The Gestalt therapy philosophy of life

As Naranjo (1970) has pointed out, an important aspect of Gestalt therapy is the philosophy of life that the therapist (perhaps unwittingly) conveys to the patient. Although Perls repeatedly emphasized that the therapist should not "lay his own trip" on the patient, nonetheless a patient in Gestalt therapy seems to be provided with what the therapist regards as a desirable mode of living. This mode for living has the following prescription.

1. Be concerned much more with the present rather than with your past or with the future.

2. Deal more with what is here than with what is absent.

3. Experience things rather than imagine them.

4. Feel rather than think.

5. Express feelings rather than justify or explain them or judge those of others.

6. Open your awareness to pain as well as to pleasure.

7. Do not use the word should.

8. Take responsibility for your actions, feelings, and thoughts.

9. Surrender to being the kind of person you are.

This prescription, according to Naranjo, can be subsumed under the rubric of "living in the moment," or as Perls puts it, *living in the now*.

Those who knew or met Fritz Perls are aware that he seemed to personify the ideals of his therapy. He was a very present-oriented, earthy, spontaneous individual, who placed great emphasis on satisfying his needs. This philosophy is well summed up in the following poetic statement by Perls.

> *I do my thing and you do your thing. I am not in this world to live up to your expectations. And you are not in this world to live up to mine. You are you and I am I. And if by chance we find each other, it's beautiful. If not, then not.*

Evaluation

As with nearly every school of therapy, our initial criticism concerns the lack of evidence supporting the efficacy of Gestalt therapy. We do not imply that people who go through such therapy are necessarily wasting their time. On the contrary, many people are undoubtedly helped by therapists who follow Perls's thinking and use his therapeutic techniques. At least a part of the therapeutic improvement may be attributable to the placebo effect, however, or to any number of other factors.

The Gestalt therapy literature suggests that these therapists spend much or most of their time urging clients to be more expressive, spontaneous, and responsive to their own needs. Perls describes this activity as making the person more attentive to emerging gestalts. Therapy also attempts to make the person whole by encouraging a reclamation of parts of the personality hitherto denied. The psychotherapy is therefore aligned with the experimental findings of Gestalt psychology. It is open to question, however, whether Perls's description is the most accurate or parsimonious way of talking about the techniques, and, more importantly, whether such concepts assist in the effective training of good therapists.

Gestalt therapy does forcefully convey the existential message that a person is not a prisoner of his past, that he can at any time make the existential choice to be different, and that the therapist will not tolerate stagnation. No doubt this optimistic view helps many people change. If the person does not know how to behave differently, however, considerable damage can be done to an already miserable individual.

Perls's emphasis on responsibility is not to be confused with commitment or obligation to others. Even as a therapist Perls did not present himself as a person who assumes responsibility for others, and he did not urge this on his patients either. The individual has the responsibility to take care of himself, to meet his *own* needs as they arise. This apparent egocentrism may be troubling for people with a social conscience and for those who have in the past made commitments to others. Indeed, Perls believed that commitments to others should never be made in the first place (Prochaska, 1979).

The same complaint voiced about Rogers's client-centered therapy applies to Gestalt therapy. Indeed, it may be common to all humanistic therapies. According to humanists, people are, by their very nature, good, purposive, and resourceful. If they are, it would be reasonable to trust this intrinsic good nature and to encourage direct expression of needs. But are people always good? Sometimes clients—especially those who are psychologically troubled—feel they must do something that, in the judgment of the professional, is not in their own best interests. Suppose that a client feels the need to murder someone or to engage in other behavior that, to outside observers, is surely undesirable. What is the therapist's responsibility? At what point does the therapist intervene and impose his or her judgment? We believe that Gestalt therapists do *not* abdicate all decisions to their clients and that they *do* exert considerable influence on them, if only by virtue of the models they themselves provide. We have already indicated that Perls was a very charismatic figure. It is likely that most people adopt the values of their therapists (Rosenthal, 1955; Pentoney, 1966), and it seems preferable to us to admit this social influence so that is can be dealt with, rather than to deny that such influence exists and perhaps allow for even greater "tyranny" of therapists over patients. This issue is discussed at length in Chapter 21.

All therapies are subject to abuse; Gestalt is no exception. Indeed, it may present special problems. It is not difficult, even for trainees with a minimum of experience, to induce clients to express their feelings. Some Gestalt techniques may in themselves be so powerful in opening people up that clients can be harmed unintentionally. The forcefulness of Perls's personality and his confrontational style have led some therapists to mimic him without the thoughtfulness, skill, and caring he appeared to possess in unusual abundance. The responsible Gestalt therapist is a professional who keeps the client's interests at the forefront, and who understands that the expression of strong emotion for its own sake is seldom enough to ease an individual's suffering. The nature of Gestalt therapy and the fact that a cult has grown up around the memory of Fritz Perls are reasons why practicing Gestalt therapists should strive for an extra measure of caution and humility.

Summary

Insight therapies share the basic assumption that a person's behavior is disordered because he is not aware of what motivates his actions. Psychoanalysis and ego analysis tend to emphasize factors from the past, whereas most humanistic and existential approaches, such as those of Rogers and Perls, emphasize the current determinants of behavior.

Consistent with Freud's second theory of neurosis, psychoanalysis tries to uncover childhood repressions so that infantile fears of libidinal expression can be examined by the adult ego in the light of present-day realities. Ego analysis puts more emphasis on the need and ability of the patient to achieve greater control over the environment and over instinctual gratifications.

Rogers trusts the basic goodness of the drive to self-actualize, and he proposes the creation of nonjudgmental conditions in therapy. Through empathy and unconditional positive regard for their clients, the therapists help them to view themselves more accurately and to trust their own instincts for self-actualization. Existential therapists, influenced primarily by European existential philosophy, similarly regard people as having the innate ability to realize their potential; they also have the freedom to decide at any given moment to become different. Both Rogers and the existentialists assume that the only reality is the one perceived by the individual; thus the therapist must try to view the world from the client's phenomenological frame of reference, rather than from his own.

The Gestalt therapy of Perls is usually regarded as humanistic, yet it is different in important ways from the therapies of Rogers and the existentialists. Perls stresses living in the now, and the many techniques he and his followers have introduced are designed to help clients experience their current needs and feel comfortable about satisfying them as they emerge. The emphasis is on changing behavior, and yet considerable attention is directed toward increasing the individual's awareness of what he or she is doing at the present moment and accepting responsibility for it.

In addition to the specific criticisms we have made of each of these insight therapies, all have a common problem which impedes progress and refinement. Carefully controlled studies to support the claims of efficacy and the assertions that changes do occur for the reasons expounded by the various theorists are scarce. Some theorists—especially the existentialists—dismiss a priori and paradigmatically the need for and even the possibility of the kind of controlled research that most social scientists deem important. The ultimate question, an important one in view of the large fees people pay to their therapists, is whether people are helped by the therapists. But even when patients do derive benefit, their improvement may be attributable at least in part to the ubiquitous placebo effect.

chapter 19

The insight-oriented therapies described in the preceding chapter all share the assumption that psychopathology can be treated by enabling sufferers to know the reasons for their behavior. And yet behavior has sometimes been ignored during treatment, which would seem to open them to criticism. The manner in which insight therapies developed and their lack of justifying principles also render them vulnerable. The theorists described in Chapter 18 have generally operated outside the mainstream of academic-experimental psychology. Freud did his early work before experimental psychology had become well established. Other insight therapists were primarily practitioners, concerned with helping the individuals who turned to them for assistance, and were seldom well grounded, or interested, in the methodology and principles of experimental psychology. Moreover, the humanistic and existential therapists, except for Carl Rogers, have not had a philosophical commitment to scientific evaluation of their clinical work.

Throughout this book we have taken the view that the study of human behavior in general and abnormal behavior in particular should be scientific. Over the past three decades a method of treating abnormal behavior within a scientific framework has been developed. Called *behavior therapy,* it was initially restricted to procedures based on classical and operant conditioning. Today it has a broader base, all of experimental psychology (see Bandura, 1969; Kanfer and Phillips, 1970). Behavior therapy, as now conceived, is characterized more by its epistemological stance—its search for rigorous standards of proof—than by allegiance to any particular set of concepts (see Davison and Goldfried, 1973; Yates, 1970). In brief, behavior therapy is an attempt to study and change abnormal behavior by drawing on the discoveries made by experimental psychologists in their study of normal behavior.

That the most effective clinical procedures will be developed through science is an *assumption.* There is nothing inherent in the scientific method that guarantees victories for those studying human behavior by its principles. Because we have reached the moon and beyond by playing the science game does not mean that the same set of rules should be applied to human behavior. The existentialists, who emphasize free will, assume that the nature of man cannot be meaningfully probed by following the rules favored by the authors of this textbook. Although we are placing our bets on the scientific work described in this chapter, it nonetheless remains an article of faith that behavior therapy will prove the best means of treating disordered behavior.

Sometimes the term "behavior modification" has been used interchangeably with behavior therapy; therapists using operant conditioning as a means of treatment have often preferred this term. But we have argued elsewhere (Davison and Stuart, 1975) that the term behavior therapy should be employed in order to differentiate this approach from others. After all, every therapy—whether it be psychoanalysis or psychosurgery—has as its ultimate goal the modification of behavior. In the recent past the work done by clinicians of other bents, who do not adhere to the standards of evidence and procedure that are the essence of behavior therapy, has been confused with the efforts of behavior therapists.

Just when behavior therapy first began to be developed is difficult to date. It is, in any event, not the case that some social scientist woke up one morning and proclaimed that from this day on people with psychological problems should be treated with techniques suggested by experimental findings. Rather, over many years people in the clinical field began to formulate a new set of assumptions about the best means of dealing with the problems that they encountered. We have found it helpful to examine four discernibly separate theoretical approaches applied in behavior therapy—counterconditioning, operant conditioning, modeling, and cognitive restructuring.

Counter-conditioning

In counterconditioning, illustrated in Figure 2.7 (page 57), a response (R_1) to a given stimulus (S) is eliminated by eliciting different behavior (R_2) in the presence of that stimulus. For example, if a man is afraid (R_1) of enclosed spaces (S), the therapist attempts to help the man have a calm reaction (R_2) when he is in such situations. Experimental evidence suggests that unrealistic fears can be eliminated in this way. An early and now famous clinical demonstration of counterconditioning was a case by Mary Cover Jones (1924). She successfully eliminated a little boy's fear of rabbits by feeding him in the presence of a rabbit. The animal was at first kept several feet away and then gradually moved closer on successive occasions. In this fashion the fear (R_1) produced by the rabbit (S) was "crowded out" by the stronger positive feelings associated with eating (R_2).

Systematic Desensitization

Three decades later Joseph Wolpe (1958) employed similar techniques with fearful patients. He found that many of his clients, like the child treated by Jones, could be encouraged to expose themselves gradually to the situation or object they feared if they were at the same time engaging in behavior that inhibited anxiety. Rather than have his patients eat, however, Wolpe taught them deep muscle relaxation. His training procedures were adapted from earlier work by Edmund Jacobson (1929), who had shown that strong emotional states like anxiety could be markedly inhibited if a person is in a state of deep relaxation. In Jacobson's many experiments various autonomic indices as well as self-reports indicated that the anxiety of subjects was reduced after they had learned to let go of their muscles through a progressive program of contracting and relaxing muscle groups of the body.

Many of the fears felt by Wolpe's patients were so abstract—for example, fear of criticism and fear of failure—that it was impractical to confront them with *real-life* situations that would evoke these fears. Following earlier proposals by Salter (1949), Wolpe reasoned that he might

Joseph Wolpe, one of the pioneers in behavior therapy. He is known particularly for systematic desensitization, a widely applied behavioral technique.

have fearful patients *imagine* what they feared. Thus he formulated a new technique which he called *systematic desensitization,* a term originally applied to the medical procedure of administering increasing doses of allergens to hay fever and asthma sufferers. In systematic desensitization a deeply relaxed person is asked to imagine a graded series of anxiety-provoking situations; the relaxation tends to inhibit any anxiety that might otherwise be elicited by the imagined scenes. If relaxation does give way to anxiety, the client signals to the therapist by raising an index finger, stops imagining the situation in mind, rests, reestablishes relaxation, and then reimagines the situation. If anxiety drives out relaxation again, the client goes back to an earlier situation and tries later to handle the more difficult one. Over successive sessions a client is usually able to tolerate increasingly more difficult scenes as he or she climbs the hierarchy in imagination. As has been documented by Wolpe

as well as by many other clinicians (for example, Goldfried and Davison, 1976), the ability to tolerate stressful imagery is generally followed by a reduction of anxiety in related real-life situations. The case study on page 57 illustrates the application of this technique.

Between therapy sessions clients are usually instructed to place themselves in progressively frightening real-life situations. These homework assignments help to move their adjustment from imagination to actuality (for example, Davison, 1968b; Sherman, 1972). Clients are also taught to use relaxation skills as a way of *coping with* anxieties as they arise in day-to-day living (for example, Goldfried and Trier, 1974).

In clinical practice systematic desensitization has proved effective with a great variety of anxiety-related problems. The technique appears deceptively simple. But as with any therapy for people in emotional distress, its proper application is a complicated affair. First, the clinician must determine, by means of a comprehensive behavioral assessment, that the situations the client is reacting anxiously to do not warrant it. If a person is anxious because she lacks the skills to deal with a given set of circumstances, desensitization would not be appropriate; to be anxious, for example, about flying an airplane is logical when the individual does not know how to operate the aircraft! Desensitization, then, is an appropriate treatment if a client seems to be inhibited by anxiety from behaving in customary and known ways.

Sometimes the technique can be used when the client does not appear openly anxious. For example, a middle-aged construction worker complaining of depression sought help (Goldfried and Davison, 1976). He was having trouble getting out of bed in the morning and viewed his job and life in general with dread and foreboding. Careful assessment by the clinician revealed that the man was inordinately concerned whether the men working under him liked and approved of him. His depression had set in after he had been promoted to foreman, a position that required him to issue orders and monitor and criticize the activities of other workers. His men would occasionally object to his instructions and comments, and the client found their baleful stares and sullen silences very upsetting.

A small group of dog phobics being treated by systematic desensitization. While remaining deeply relaxed, they are shown a series of pictures of dogs.

He agreed with the therapist that a hierarchy of situations in which he was criticized and rejected by others would be appropriate. The reduction in job-related anxiety that followed treatment by desensitization succeeded in lifting his depression.

As with all the techniques described in this chapter, very rarely is only one procedure used exclusively. A person fearful of social interactions might well be given training in conversational and other social skills in addition to desensitization. In the most general sense, the treatments chosen and their applicability depend largely on the therapist's ingenuity in discovering the source of the anxiety underlying a client's problems.

Researchers became interested in studying desensitization because clinical reports indicated that the technique is effective. Initial steps in the experimental investigation of the procedure were taken by Lazovik and Lang (1960; Lang and Lazovik, 1963). They were concerned primarily with assessing the procedure under relatively controlled laboratory conditions. In the earlier clinical reports improvement had been judged by the clinicians who had given the treatment, and other therapeutic procedures were usually employed along with desensitization. Lang and Lazovik decided that for greater control in evaluating desensitization of the simple phobia chosen, fear of snakes, testers who were *not* treating the subjects should measure their pretreatment and posttreatment ability to approach snakes. They also restricted treatment to desensitization. Their experiments showed that, indeed, desensitization can measurably and significantly reduce avoidance of a phobic object.

One of the most widely known and highly regarded experiments in systematic desensitization, and in psychotherapy research as a whole, was conducted by Gordon Paul (1966). His purpose was to compare systematic desensitization, a placebo, and insight therapy for their effectiveness in reducing unrealistic fear. He recruited students who were taking a required public-speaking course and were all fearful of speaking in front of groups. Prior to treatment all students had to deliver a speech before an audience, and numerous measures of their anxiety were taken—self-reports, behavioral observations, and two physiological measures, of pulse rate and sweat (see page 100).

Students were then assigned to one of three different treatments. The first was systematic desensitization. The second was an attention-placebo treatment. Subjects in this group met with a sympathetic therapist who led them to believe that a pill would reduce their overall sensitivity to stress. To convince them, Paul had them listen to a tape which the therapist told them had been used in training astronauts to function under stress. They listened to this "stress tape" for several sessions after ingesting the "tranquilizer." In reality, the pill was a placebo, and the tape contained various nonverbal sounds that had been shown in other research to be quite boring. In this way Paul raised subjects' expectations that their social anxieties could be lessened by taking a pill. The third treatment was insight therapy. Subjects met with skilled insight-oriented therapists to talk over their anxieties; the therapists were free to structure the sessions in any way they saw fit. All treatments were limited to five sessions, a number settled on by the insight therapists when they were asked how many sessions they would need to make a measurable impact on this kind of problem. An important feature of Paul's experimental design was training insight therapists to do systematic desensitization. In fact, insight therapists gave all three treatments. In this way Paul anticipated the criticism that any superiority of systematic desensitization could be attributed to greater enthusiasm shown by desensitization therapists. A fourth group of students did not receive any treatment; the anxiety of these students was measured as they gave two speeches along with the others, one before and one after the treatment sessions.

The results of this important study revealed that subjects who had received systematic desensitization improved much more than did the no-treatment group and more than did the attention-placebo and insight therapy subjects, who reacted about the same to their forms of therapy. Students receiving these two treatments did, however, show significant improvement. The results, then, indicated that systematic desensitization is superior to both insight therapy and to attention plus a placebo in lessening anxiety about making speeches. These results persisted in a two-year follow-up study (Paul, 1967). Subsequent research has attested to the effectiveness of desensitization in reducing a wide range of anxieties; it is doubtful that these gains are attributable to the placebo effect (Rachman and Wilson, 1980).

Behavioral researchers are interested not only in whether a given techinque works—the out-

come question—but also in *why*—the process question. Wolpe suggests that counterconditioning underlies the efficacy of desensitization; a state or response antagonistic to anxiety is substituted for anxiety as the person is exposed gradually to stronger and stronger doses of what he or she is afraid of. Many experiments (for example, Davison, 1968b) suggest that there may be a specific learning process underlying the technique and that, indeed, it may be counterconditioning. But a number of other explanations are possible. Some workers attach importance to exposure to what the person fears per se; relaxation is then considered merely a useful way to encourage a frightened individual to confront what he or she fears (Wilson and Davison, 1971). At this time many workers believe that the reasons the technique works are still not known (for example, Borkovec and O'Brien, 1976). Our knowledge of how people change is rudimentary; moreover, behavior therapy maintains a healthy skepticism about all aspects of treatment, which may be a particular strength of this approach.

Aversion Therapy

Aversion therapy attempts to attach negative feelings to stimuli that are considered inappropriately attractive. The literature on classical aversive conditioning of animals (that is, pairing a neutral or positive stimulus with an unpleasant unconditioned stimulus such as shock) led therapists to believe that negative reactions can be conditioned in human beings, and they formulated treatment programs along these lines. For example, a boot fetishist (see page 350) may wish to be less attracted to the sight or feel of boots. To reduce the attraction, a therapist gives the client repeated electric shocks when pictures of boots are presented. Instead of creating discomfort and shock, some therapists use emetics, drugs which make the client nauseous. The method is similar to desensitization, but the goal is different, since the new response is anxiety or an aversion reaction which is to be substituted for a positive response. In covert sensitization (see page 308) the attractive stimuli and negative states are imagined by the client. Among the problems treated with aversion therapy are ex-

19.1 Fighting Fear with Fear: Flooding and Implosion Therapies

In systematic desensitization fearful clients expose themselves to fear in a gradual fashion by imagining a series of episodes, each more frightening than the preceding one. The therapist may also force the client to confront a very fearful episode immediately at full intensity in one of two related procedures, flooding and implosion. The principal difference between the two is the inclusion in implosion of cues that are psychodynamic in nature. Thomas Stampfl, the originator of implosion therapy, asserts that the kinds of fears people bring for treatment have been classically conditioned to what psychoanalytic theory holds are problem areas for people, primarily events relating to aggressive and sexual id impulses (Stampfl and Levis, 1967). Flooding procedures are not based on this kind of speculation. Confronting in imagination or in real life the situations bringing the greatest amount of fear is assumed the best way of reducing it. Whereas in desensitization a person first imagines the least fear-provoking episodes and is instructed to drop the image if it is the least bit bothersome, in both flooding and implosion the therapist urges the client to keep on imagining the most stressful situation for long periods of time, as long as an hour at a time! Clinical evidence suggests that by not allowing themselves the relief of escape, individuals are eventually able to decrease or extinguish their fears.

Unlike desensitization, which is a fairly benign procedure, both flooding and implosion are very difficult for clients. Stampfl's implosion therapy is particularly strenuous, and controversial, for the psychodynamic themes are introduced by constructing stories and scenes of sometimes unbelievable horror and degradation. Implosion therapy is of course applied only in imagination! For example, whereas in flooding a snake phobic may have to imagine at the very outset that she is holding a harmless snake as it crawls in her lap, in implosion she may be asked to envision the snake as a gigantic serpent which devours her eyes, crawls into her eye sockets, and systematically chews on her internal organs.

Important to both flooding and implosion is maintaining exposure until fear passes a peak and has substantially subsided, which accounts for the very long exposure times. Rather than escaping from or avoiding altogether an aversive situation, the client confronts his or her worst fears until the fear extinguishes.

Not surprisingly, Stampfl's technique has been attacked by many therapists as inhumane, vulgar, and needlessly cruel. But it has also become clear over the years that many fearful people can overcome their anxieties by implosion (for example, Barrett, 1969). The efficacy of flooding is supported by research with animals. Their fear of a stimulus that has previously been paired with shock can sometimes be rapidly extinguished if they are prevented from escaping it (Baum, 1970; Wilson and Davison, 1971; Stampfl and Levis, 1967).

Controlled laboratory research that measures physiological signs of fear during implosion treatment sessions and compares them to the reduction of fear suggests that improvement is related to the amount of fear experienced. The greater amount of fear aroused and then extinguished, the greater improvement. This finding is consistent with Stampfl's basic view that his treatment works by extinguishing fear of truly aversive situations (Orenstein and Carr, 1975). Careful analyses of various studies (for example Morganstern, 1973; Marshall, Gauthier, and Gordon, 1979) reveal some serious methodological errors, however; it is too early to accept Stampfl's reasons for why implosion therapy works. Research on flooding has similar methodological problems, but many reports of clinical treatments are encouraging, especially treatments of obsessive-compulsive disorders (for example, Meyer, Robertson, and Tatlow, 1975). Those who fear contamination are made to handle dirt; those who must keep checking whether they have locked the door are allowed to check only once.

Although investigators cannot agree whether flooding and implosion are as effective as other fear reduction methods, they do believe that a therapy fighting fear with fear exacts a high cost from the client. *Even if* such a treatment were *as* effective as a more benign method, they would seriously question whether it should be used except when all else fails.

cessive drinking, smoking, transvestism, exhibitionism, and overeating. Although some people have benefited from these procedures, the evidence does not indicate conclusively that these techniques are truly effective (Wilson and O'Leary, 1980).

Aversion therapy is controversial for both ethical and scientific reasons. A great outcry has been raised about inflicting pain and discomfort on people, even when they ask for it. Perhaps the greatest ethical concern and anger have been voiced by the several gay liberation organizations; they hold that homosexuals who request painful treatment are actually seeking to punish themselves for behavior that a prejudiced society has convinced them is dirty. They accuse behavior therapists of impeding the acceptance of homosexuality as a legitimate life style when they accede to such requests (Silverstein, 1972).

The issue is a difficult one to resolve and has led several behavior therapists to question whether therapists should ever agree to help homosexuals change their sexual orientation (see Box 21.7, page 707).

The scientific issue is whether the aversive reactions acquired by human beings through shock and nausea are stable. It is doubtful that a person will continue to react anxiously to an intrinsically harmless stimulus once he sees that he will no longer be shocked. Several experimental investigations of a wide range of aversion treatments (for example, Diament and Wilson, 1975) have failed to demonstrate their superiority over placebo control treatments. Many behaviorists therefore assert that any beneficial outcomes of this treatment cannot be attributed to conditioning.

Behavior therapists who choose aversive pro-

"TODAY WE'LL TRY AVERSION-THERAPY. EVERY TIME YOU SAY SOMETHING STUPID, I'LL SPILL A BUCKET OF WATER ON YOUR HEAD."

BOX   **19.2** Out of the Consulting Room and into the Real World

Whatever their differences, systematic desensitization, flooding in imagination, and implosion do have one feature in common: they all rely on imagery. As mentioned earlier, Wolpe had reasoned that the imaginations of his patients could deal with abstract problems and avoidances that they could not feasibly confront in real life. The use of the imagination was always an acknowledged bowing to practicality.

Early research on desensitization made it obvious that the ability of a client to imagine something fearsome without becoming fearful did not mean that he or she would always encounter it without agitation in real life (Davison, 1968b). Being able to entertain an image of oneself climbing a fire escape and looking down ten stories is not the same as actually being able to do so. And yet it was, and still is, significant that lessening emotional reactions to an imagined fearful situation does diminish fear in the actual situation.

Behavior therapists have compared imagined with in vivo exposures in a number of experimental studies, and almost without exception in vivo exposure is superior to imagined exposure (Wilson and O'Leary, 1980; Bandura, 1969).* Nowadays they are likely, whenever possible, to help fearful clients confront in real life what they would otherwise avoid. More and more therapists are leaving the confines of their consulting rooms and clinics to accompany their clients into the world as it is.

"LEAVE US ALONE! I AM A BEHAVIOR THERAPIST! I AM HELPING MY PATIENT OVERCOME A FEAR OF HEIGHTS."

* As noted in Box 19.1, implosion therapy is restricted to imagery because the client is supposed to expose himself to situations that are grotesquely frightening. Flooding can be conducted in vivo as well as in the imagination.

cedures, however, seldom use them alone. Instead, more positive techniques are instituted to teach new behavior to replace that eliminated. For example, a boot fetishist may also be given training in social skills to allow him more easily to initiate social contacts with women. The effects of aversion therapy may indeed be ephemeral, or short-lived, or the treatment may have only a placebo effect. The temporary reduction in undesirable behavior, however, creates some "space" which can be taken up by responses judged by the person or the culture to be more appropriate. When aversion therapy is the only treatment given, it is generally chosen as a last resort.

Operant Conditioning

In the 1950s a number of investigators, most of whom lived in the United States, suggested that therapists should try to shape overt behavior through rewards and punishments (Skinner, 1953). In the belief that they could through operant conditioning exercise some control over the complex, puzzling, often frenetic behavior of hospitalized patients, many experimentally minded psychologists determined to try to bring practical order into the chaos of institutions for the severely disturbed. Generally speaking, operant treatments work best with clients whose intellectual capacities are limited and in situations in which considerable control can be exercised by the therapist (Wilson and O'Leary, 1980).

The Token Economy

Perhaps the most extensive and best-known work within the operant tradition is the token economy of Ayllon and Azrin (1968). On the basis of earlier work that Staats and Staats (1963) had done with children, they set aside an entire ward of a mental hospital for a series of experiments in which rewards were provided for activities such as making beds and combing hair, and reinforcers were denied for withdrawn, bizarre, and other symptomatic behavior. The forty-five female patients, who averaged sixteen years of hospitalization, were systematically rewarded for their ward work and self-care by giving them plastic tokens that could later be exchanged for special privileges, such as listening to records and going to the movies, renting a private room, and extra visits to the canteen. The entire life of each patient was as far as possible controlled by this regime.

The rules of the token economy—the medium of exchange; the chores and self-care to be rewarded, and by what number of tokens; the items and privileges that can be purchased, and for how many tokens—are carefully established and usually posted. These regimes have demonstrated how even markedly regressed adult hospital patients can be significantly affected by systematically manipulating reinforcement contingencies, that is, rewarding some behavior to increase its frequency, or ignoring other be-

A patient cashing in his tokens for the purchases he wishes to make at the hospital store.

toms, and length of hospitalization and then assigned to one of three wards, social learning, milieu therapy, and routine hospital management. Each ward had twenty-eight residents. The two treatment wards shared extensive objectives: to teach self-care, housekeeping, communication, and vocational skills; to reduce symptomatic behavior; and to release patients to the community.

1. **Social-learning ward.** Located in a new mental health center in Illinois, the social-learning ward was operated on a token economy embracing all aspects of the residents' lives. Their appearance had to pass muster each morning, in eleven specific ways, in order to earn a token. Well-made beds, good behavior at mealtime, classroom participation, and socializing during free periods were other means of earning tokens. Residents learned to do as they should through modeling, shaping,

havior to reduce its frequency. In order to show that a stimulus following behavior actually reinforces it, an experiment has to demonstrate not only that behavior increases when followed by a positive event, but also that behavior declines when nothing positive happens as a consequence. In Chapter 4 the ABAB design was employed to study the effect of contingencies. Ayllon and his associates demonstrated how contingencies affected the behavior of their ward patients. Figure 19.1 indicates that conduct such as brushing teeth and making beds markedly decreased when rewards were withdrawn, but became more frequent again when rewards were reinstated.

Since the publication of Ayllon's early studies of the token economy, many similar programs have been instituted throughout the country. The most impressive was reported by Gordon Paul and Robert Lentz (1977) and has already been mentioned in Box 14.4 (page 442). The long-term, regressed, and chronic schizophrenic patients in their program are the most severely debilitated institutionalized adults ever studied systematically. Some of these patients screamed for long periods, some were mute; many were incontinent, a few assaultive. Most of them no longer used silverware, and some buried their faces in their food. The patients were matched for age, sex, socioeconomic background, symp-

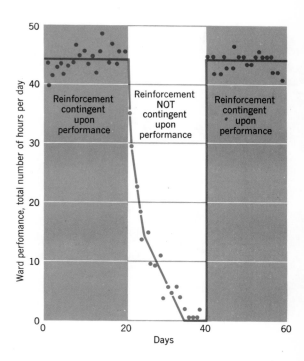

FIGURE **19.1**
When receiving tokens was the contingency, patients on a ward spent more time grooming themselves and doing chores than when they were given no reward. Adapted from Ayllon and Azrin, 1965.

prompting, and instructions. They were also trained to communicate better with one another and participated in problem-solving groups. Tokens were a necessity, for they purchased meals as well as small luxuries. In addition to living on the token economy, each individual received behavioral treatments tailored to his needs. Residents were kept busy 85 percent of their waking hours learning to behave better.

2. **Milieu therapy ward.** Another ward of the center operated on the principles of Jones's (1953) "therapeutic community." These residents too were kept busy 85 percent of their waking hours. They, both individually and as a group, were expected to act responsibly and to participate in decisions about how the ward was to function. In general, they were treated more as normal individuals than as incompetent mental patients. Staff members impressed on the residents their positive expectations of them and praised them for doing well. When they behaved symptomatically, staff members stayed with them, making clear their expectations that they would soon behave more appropriately.

3. **Routine hospital management.** The patients continued their accustomed hospital existence in an older state institution, receiving custodial care and heavy antipsychotic medication. Except for the 5 percent of their waking hours occupied by occasional activity, recreational, occupational, and individual and group therapies, these individuals were on their own.

Before the program began, the staffs of the two treatment wards were carefully trained to adhere to detailed instructions in therapy manuals; regular observations confirmed that they were implementing the principles of a social-learning or a milieu therapy program. Residents were carefully evaluated at regular six-month intervals by meticulous, direct, behavioral observations and structured interviews over the four and a half years of hospitalization and the one and a half years of follow-up.

The results? Both the social-learning and the milieu therapy reduced symptomatic behavior. The residents acquired self-care, housekeeping, social, and vocational skills. The behavior of members of these two groups within the institution was superior to that of the residents of the hospital ward. By the end of treatment, more of them had been discharged. In fact, over 10 percent of the social-learning patients left the center for independent existences; 7 percent of the milieu patients achieved this goal, and none of the hospital treatment patients did. Many more patients from all three groups were discharged to community placements such as boarding homes and halfway houses, where there was supervision, to be sure, but considerably less restraint than patients had been experiencing for an average of seventeen years. Members of the social-learning group were significantly better in remaining in these community residences than were patients in the other two groups.

Considering how poorly these patients had

Gordon Paul, prominent behavior therapist who has demonstrated the beneficial impact that social-learning therapy has on hospitalized chronic patients.

been functioning before this treatment project, these results are remarkable. And the fact that the social-learning program was superior to the milieu program is also significant, for milieu treatment is instituted in many mental hospitals. As implemented by Paul's team of clinicians, it provided more attention to patients than was given those on the social-learning ward. This greater amount of attention of the other treatment would appear to control well for the placebo effect of the social-learning therapy.

These results, though, should not be accepted as confirming the usefulness of token economies per se, for the social-learning therapy contained elements that went beyond operant conditioning of overt motor behavior. Staff provided information to residents and attempted verbally to clarify misconceptions. Indeed, Paul (personal communication, 1981) relegates the token economy to a secondary, although not trivial, role. He sees it as a useful device for getting the attention of severely regressed patients in the initial stages of treatment. The token economy created the opportunity for his patients to acquire new information, or, in Paul's informal phrase, to "get good things into their heads."

Paul and Lentz have never claimed that any of these patients was "cured." Although they were able to live outside the hospital, they continued to manifest many signs of mental disorder, and few of them had gainful employment or participated in the social activities most people take for granted. The outcome, though, is not to be underestimated; chronic mental patients, those typically shut away on back wards and forgotten by society, can be resocialized and taught self-care. They can learn to behave normally enough to be discharged from mental institutions. The marked superiority of the social-learning program argues strongly for reorganizing mental hospital care for severely disturbed patients along these lines.[1]

Operant Work with Children

Some of the best operant conditioning behavior therapy has been done with children, perhaps because much of their behavior is subject to the control of others. Children, after all, tend more than adults to be under continual supervision. At school their behavior is scrutinized by teachers, and when they come home parents frequently oversee their play and other social activities. In most instances the behavior therapist works with the parents and teachers in an effort to change the ways in which they reward and punish the children for whom they have responsibility. It is assumed that altering the reinforcement practices of the adults in a child's life will ultimately change the child's behavior.

The range of childhood problems dealt with through operant conditioning is very broad indeed, including bed-wetting, thumb-sucking, aggression, tantrums, hyperactivity, self-mutilation, disruptive classroom behavior, poor school performance, extreme social withdrawal, and asthmatic attacks. Even gender identity appears susceptible to operant procedures (see page 347). In general, rates of improvement are superior to those reported for traditional forms of therapy (O'Leary, Turkewitz, and Taffel, 1973; Ross, 1981). Operant behavior therapists must of course determine that the behavior being shaped or extinguished is in fact controllable through reward. A child who is crying because of physical pain should be attended to.

Encouraging results have been achieved by applying operant techniques to the training of retarded children. As indicated in Chapter 16, many operant conditioners have challenged assumptions about the limited trainability of the retarded, much to the benefit of some retarded children and their families. Among other problems, they have been able to improve table manners (Plummer, Boer, and LeBlanc, 1977), social skills (Williams et al., 1975), and hyperactive behavior (Doubros, 1966).

Perhaps the most significant and heartening advances have been in intellectual development. One example among many is a study by Ayllon and Kelly (1972). First they showed that measured IQ could be significantly raised in "trainable" retarded children—these had an IQ below 55—simply by giving tokens as rewards for acceptable performances in the various subtests; the average gain was approximately 10 percent of the total possible score. Even more impressive

[1] The aftercare aspects of the Paul and Lentz project are discussed in detail in Chapter 20 (page 656).

BOX **19.3** Token Economies, Asylums, and the Metrics of Human Existence

Paul and Lentz's landmark study promises to establish the token economy as an important component of the institutional treatment of long-term mental patients. Nonetheless, questions will continue to be raised about token economies in institutional settings. Some of these concern certain legal problems, and these are reviewed in detail in Chapter 21. Others have to do with the basic assumptions of these behavior control regimens (Gagnon and Davison, 1976).

David Rothman (1971), a historian, has traced the development of mental hospitals in this country during the nineteenth century. He shows that asylums of the time were instituted as they were because much of the madness of the day was assumed caused by the hurly-burly of a vigorous democratic and industrial society, which offered endless opportunities—and therefore possibilities for failure. Asylums were to be havens for those who could not keep up with the rapid economic and social expansion that had followed the industrial revolution.

Consider how different is this view of the mental hospital from the way token economies are organized. The disease, if you will, now becomes the doctor. The token economy is the nineteenth-century asylum on its head, for this innovation introduces into the hospital the very conditions that were assumed in the previous century to have caused mental disorders. Instead of protecting patients from the strains of an achievement-oriented, money-dominated society, the token economy introduces commercial relationships into the asylum.

Can we on these historical grounds claim that token economies are necessarily bad? Can we really say that commercialism is likely to aggravate mental illness? After all, have we not made some progress in understanding mental disorder since the early nineteenth century? The reader may judge for himself by reflecting on the material presented in the preceding chapters of this book. It would seem that for the more serious disorders—schizophrenia, in particular—genetic factors and the biochemistry of the brain have provided and will provide the major clues to etiology. Economic failure is probably at most a stress activating a predisposition.

Other issues can be raised that are not tied to history. Token economies are effective in ward *management*. They do seem to introduce order where there has been only chaos; helping a regressed schizophrenic dress herself and arrive on time to a hospital dining hall is a significant accomplishment. And if the remarkable success of Paul and Lentz in returning chronic schizophrenics to the community, to live in sheltered residences, can be duplicated by other clinicians, the token economy will have proved of value in helping resocialize mental patients.

But what, in fact, do patients really learn on a token economy? Gagnon and Davison (1976) take an unusual position on this.

One thing that is learned is that producing certain kinds of behavior produces a stable response from the token-emitting behavioral engineer. . . . The value of any act is metrically stable, and its value can be compared to [that of] other acts [in] number of tokens. . . . [Is this a good thing for mental patients to learn if they are to be prepared for life outside the confines of the institution?] The exchanges that characterize most conventional social life [suggest] that things do

*not come out even. . . . Life is largely the capacity to toler-
ate interactions which have low predictability of outcome.
. . . [And] staying out of asylums is a capacity to survive the
fact that life is unjust: sometimes you get what you pay for,
sometimes you get more than you pay for, sometimes you
get less than you pay for (pp. 532–534, emphasis added).*

Finally, a token regimen may encourage people to view themselves and others in ways
that are undesirable. Human relationships and human feelings run the risk of being cheap-
ened when reduced to a monetary metric. If a patient, for example, has to have twenty
tokens to see a clergyman, will this adversely affect how he feels about religion? If thirty
tokens are required for a weekend pass, how will a patient feel about the people she sees
while she is on leave?

We are unaware of attempts by behavior therapists to answer such questions. The failure
to address these issues does *not* represent callousness to the human condition; such an
allegation would be unfair and incorrect. Rather, apparently because of their professional
training, psychologists and psychiatrists are not inclined to view their work in historical
and sociological contexts. Perhaps the kind of critical analysis summarized here will goad
token economy workers into such considerations. Whatever the outcome, the beneficiaries
will be those whom we are all trying to help.

---

were the results of a six-week program at a
school for retarded children. Two groups were
carefully matched on IQ. One group was assigned to an experimental program while the
control subjects continued in the ongoing academic program of the school. In the innovative
program, which used specially designed materials to teach arithmetic, spelling, copying, and
reading, children were reinforced with tokens
depending on their achievements. The children
were able to exchange their tokens for a variety
of desirable things—soft drinks, candy, and extra
privileges such as playing records and watching
television.

Testing at the end of the six-week program
showed that the IQs of the experimental subjects
had increased by an average of almost four
points, whereas those of the control children had
actually decreased by nearly three points. Since
the two groups had been carefully matched before the operant training program began, we can
conclude that the program, whether the teaching
materials, the token economy, or both, was responsible for the improvement.

Although programs such as these may offer
hope to those responsible for the well-being of
retarded children, their effectiveness must not be
overestimated. The improvements in IQ shown
in the Ayllon and Kelly study were statistically
significant, but the children still remained retarded, that is, their posttreatment scores were
still very far below average. Furthermore, the
amount of time and effort required in any training of the retarded is staggering. Even so, such
programs, and scores of others tested throughout
the country, do carry an important message,
namely that one should not despair of making a
beneficial impact on problems simply because
procedures currently available have been unsuccessful.

Biofeedback

A visit to the commercial exhibit area of any
psychological or psychiatric convention will reveal a plentiful display of complex biofeedback
apparatus, touted as an efficient, even miraculous, means for helping people control one or

another bodily-mental state. Basically, biofeedback gives a person prompt and exact information, otherwise unavailable, on muscle activity, brain waves, skin temperature, heart rate, blood pressure, and other bodily functions. It is assumed that a person can achieve greater voluntary control over these phenomena—most of which were once considered to be under involuntary control and completely unresponsive to will—if he or she knows immediately, through an auditory or visual signal, whether a bodily activity is increasing or decreasing. Because anxiety has generally been viewed as a state involving the autonomic ("involuntary") nervous system, and because psychophysiological disorders (Chapter 7) afflict organs innervated by this system, it is obvious why researchers and clinicians have become intrigued with biofeedback.

In a series of studies at Harvard Medical School, Shapiro, Tursky, and Schwartz (1970; Schwartz, 1973) demonstrated that human volunteers could achieve significant short-term changes in blood pressure and in heart rate. They found that some subjects could even be trained to increase their heart rate while decreasing blood pressure. Achievement of this fine-grained control lent impetus to biofeedback work with human beings and awakened hope that certain clinical disorders might be alleviated in this new way.

In the move from analogue studies to the more challenging world of the clinic, at least three vital questions must be asked. First, can persons whose systems are *mal*functioning achieve the same biofeedback control over bodily events that normal subjects can acquire? Second, if actual patients can achieve some degree of control, will it be enough to make a significant difference in their problems? And third, can the control achieved by patients hooked up to and receiving immediate feedback from a remarkable apparatus be carried over to real-life situations in which they will have no special devices to inform them of the state of the bodily functions that they have learned to control?

Research with patients suffering from essential hypertension has been somewhat encouraging, but results have not been certain enough to establish biofeedback as a standard treatment for the problem (Shapiro and Surwit, 1979). More-

over, some (Blanchard et al., 1979) believe that relaxation training, which is often given along with biofeedback, does more to reduce blood pressure than the biofeedback itself. Training takes place in a quiet laboratory, where the patient receives feedback from the apparatus. Being able to control blood pressure in normal living conditions, with no apparatus and in the presence of stress and other competing stimuli, is another matter. Perhaps making laboratory conditions approximate those awaiting the person in real life would help (Surwit, Shapiro, and Good, 1978). Once the person has acquired the skill of reducing blood pressure, the therapist might introduce distractions and emotional stressors in a gradual fashion.

Normal subjects more readily increase heart rate through biofeedback than decrease it (Bell and Schwartz, 1975), perhaps because of the "floor effect." Normal subjects already have a low resting heart rate and can therefore not reduce it as much as they can raise it. As for patients suffering from abnormal heart function, Engel and his associates (Engel and Bleecker; Weiss and Engel, 1975) have taught several whose hearts sometimes beat irregularly to reduce the frequency of their arrhythmias via biofeedback. If further research confirms these initial findings, biofeedback may be applied to some serious coronary conditions.

The highly touted training of the brain to produce increases in alpha waves appears to accomplish less than was originally anticipated. The alpha state has been considered desirable for the feelings of calmness and well-being supposedly associated with it (Kamiya, 1968; Nowlis and Kamiya, 1970). Carefully controlled research, however, has usually failed to confirm earlier findings that the state can be reliably induced. Or it has demonstrated that subjects' expectations of alpha training are responsible for whatever effects are produced (Glaros, 1975). There is no evidence that this treatment has helped patients, or that it allows people to relax any better than if they just sit quietly with their eyes closed (Paskewitz and Orne, 1973).

The control of various forms of epilepsy has been attempted with some success. Several patients have reduced the frequency of seizures through intensive biofeedback training to increase brain activity in the sensorimotor cortex, but this improvement did not invariably persist when training sessions were discontinued (Sterman, 1973). Recent evidence, though, is encouraging, with generalization to periods of time when the biofeedback training has been suspended (Kuhlman and Kaplan, 1979).

A combination of at-home relaxation training and the reduction of tension in the frontalis muscles above the eyes through biofeedback can be effective in controlling tension, or muscle contraction, headaches. An exemplary study by Budzynski and his associates (1973) demonstrated marked reductions both in frontalis contractions and in tension headaches in a group of adult patients who had suffered severely for several years. This improvement was not found in a control group of patients whose auditory feedback did not inform them of the true activity of the frontalis muscles. Indeed, their bogus feedback was programmed to show consistently reduced contractions during training sessions, a manipulation to control for expectancy and placebo effects; the impressive clinical procedure—biofeedback machinery, white coats, and all—is quite persuasive. The clinical improvement of patients who had received true feedback persisted over an eighteen-month follow-up, suggesting that such training, when combined with home practice in relaxation, can have beneficial, long-term effects, even though people are no longer informed of their muscular contractions. Yet the fact that the treatment also included relaxation training makes it impossible to attribute the gains to biofeedback alone. Indeed, other studies applying biofeedback to tension headaches have clearly failed to produce any significant clinical relief (Elmore and Tursky, 1978). Recent reports indicate that straightforward training in muscle relaxation is as effective in controlling tension headache as elaborate biofeedback programs (Rimm and Masters, 1979).

Biofeedback treatment of migraine headache was reviewed earlier in Box 7.2 (page 226). Elmore succeeded in markedly reducing the severity of migraine by teaching sufferers through biofeedback to constrict the extracranial arteries. This constriction requires sympathetic arousal and is the diametric opposite of the relaxation deemed best for tension headaches and of the hand-warming biofeedback treatment of migraine, which is given at the Menninger Clinic and which requires sympathetic deactivation.

Reports on the use of biofeedback for neuromuscular disorders—cerebral palsy, jaw clenching and teeth grinding, paralysis in the aftermath of stroke and other diseases such as poliomyelitis—have been especially heartening. The initial research was done by Basmajian (1977) in the early 1960s. Paralyzed patients proved able to activate single motor cells if informed of their firing by biofeedback. The Biofeedback Society of America is so enthusiastic about the effectiveness of biofeedback for hemiplegia, a paralysis on one side of the body usually caused by stroke, that it is regarded as the treatment of choice (Fernando and Basmajian, 1978). The fact that patients participating in these studies had not earlier been helped by conventional physical therapy lends credibility to the specific effectiveness of biofeedback in allowing them to make minute muscle movements. A 1980 report by the National Institute of Mental Health reasons that biofeedback should be especially useful for neuromuscular disorders because functions that have gone awry are normally under the voluntary control of the central nervous system. If the dysfunction is caused in part by the faintness of the signs of muscle movement in damaged tissue, amplifying these proprioceptive signals by feedback will make the patient aware of them and possibily allow control (Runck, 1980).

Even though biofeedback techniques bring about meaningful improvements in patients, clinicians must remain mindful of the complexities of human problems. A person who has tension headaches, for example, probably also has a host of difficulties that contribute to them, such as marital problems. These will require attention. Similarly, a man with high blood pressure might have to alter a tense, driven life style before he can significantly reduce blood pressure through biofeedback. It is unwise, and a sign of naive clinical practice, to assume that one technique focused on a specific malfunction or problem will invariably cure the patient.[2]

---

[2] Of course, medical consultation is always a part of responsible treatment of psychophysiological disorders such as hypertension.

Finally, two observations on a theoretical level. Biofeedback has been discussed here because most investigators have assumed it to be a special case of operant conditioning. A measurable physiological change, like a reduction in heart rate, is followed by a signal denoting the change. This signal is assumed to function as a secondary reinforcer to increase the strength of the response. But biofeedback, when it works, may do so for other reasons. Several investigators (for example, Lang, 1974; Shapiro and Surwit, 1976, 1979) suggest that biofeedback may be effective because it allows better processing of information rather than because it rewards. The feedback signal may be important because it provides information rather than because it functions as a reward for a particular response. Such questions are of more than theoretical interest, although their importance can readily be justified on this account alone. A better understanding of how something happens may suggest still more effective techniques.

A continuing problem with operant theory is its seeming capacity to include practically *anything* within its purview. If someone acquires a new skill, we look first for environmental reinforcers of a concrete sort, like money, food, or sex. If these are not found, a search is begun for more abstract events, such as receiving praise. If this hunt is similarly fruitless, people "find" reinforcers such as a feeling of well-being. Now awareness of internal events as they are monitored by highly sensitive bioelectric instruments—knowledge that the heart is slowing, blood pressure dropping, or contraction of the frontalis muscle diminishing—is similarly labeled a "reinforcer." We invite the reader to consider the following questions. Does regarding biofeedback as operant conditioning increase our understanding of biofeedback? Does it tell us what *kind* of feedback is best, auditory or visual, for example? Might some physiological systems be more responsive to one kind of feedback signal than to another (Elmore and Tursky, 1978)? More generally, are there behavioral phenomena that are *not* amenable to an operant "explanation"? If there are not—and we sometimes believe this to be the case—can this view of human behavior be accused, as behaviorists have

accused psychoanalytic theory, of explaining everything and therefore explaining nothing?

Generalization of Treatment Effects

As we have indicated, generalizing to real life whatever gains have been achieved in therapy is a problem common to all treatments. Insight therapists assume that therapeutic effects are made more general through restructuring of the personality. As environmentalists, behavior therapists wonder how changes brought about by their manipulations can be made to persist once clients return to their everyday situations, which are often assumed to have produced their problems in the first place!

Intermittent reinforcement

Behavior therapists have tried to meet this challenge in several ways. Because laboratory findings indicate that intermittent reinforcement—rewarding behavior only a small portion of the times it appears—makes new behavior more enduring, many operant programs take care to move away from continuous schedules of reinforcement once desired behavior is occurring with satisfactory regularity. For example, if a teacher has succeeded in helping a disruptive boy spend more time in his seat by praising him generously for each arithmetic problem that he finishes there, he or she will gradually reward him for every other problem, and ultimately only infrequently. The hope is that the satisfactions of being a good pupil will make the child less dependent on the teacher's approval. Another strategy is to move from artificial reinforcers to those that occur naturally in the social environment. A token program might be maintained only long enough to encourage certain desired behavior, after which the person is weaned to natural reinforcers such as praise from peers.

Environmental modification

Another strategy for bringing about generalization takes the therapist into the province of community psychology, which will be discussed in the next chapter. Behavior therapists manipulate surroundings, or attempt to do so, to support changes brought about in treatment. As one small example, Lovaas and his colleagues (1973) found that the gains painstakingly achieved in therapy for autistic children were sustained only when their parents continued to reinforce their good behavior.

Self-reinforcement

Generalization can also be effected by assigning the client a more active role. Work done by Drabman, Spitalnik, and O'Leary (1973) is an example. In a three-month after-school program for disruptive young boys, the teacher rewarded nondisruptive classroom behavior and appropriate reading behavior. Then later the boys were allowed to self-rate their behavior according to the teacher's criteria and reward their own good conduct. That is, the pupils were taught that they could earn special privileges not only by behaving well when the teacher dispensed rewards but through honest evaluation of their own good behavior. The findings for the first part of the study were similar to those of many other studies. Disruptive behavior decreased and academic behavior improved when the teacher judged them and dispensed the tokens. This improvement then generalized to periods of each class during which the child *himself judged* how well he was doing and *reinforced himself* accordingly; in other words, improved performance was extended to periods of time when the pupils were not under direct external control (see Box 19.4).

The implications are clear. At least for disruptive children, self-evaluating and self-rewarding their own good behavior may be one effective way in which they can maintain it when the original controlling agent is absent.

Eliminating secondary gain

When a client learns, for example, to reduce his blood pressure by biofeedback, the therapist then needs to motivate him to practice this newly acquired skill at home and in situations believed to provoke a rise in blood pressure. This is a difficult matter. Relatively little is known how best to accomplish this. Many patients are so resistant to doing on their own what they consciously and rationally agree is in their own best interests that therapists often invoke as an explanation the psychoanalytic concept of secondary

gain, that the patient derives benefit from being disabled. For complex and poorly understood reasons people act as though they unconsciously wish to keep their symptoms. Therapists, whatever their persuasion, may have to examine the client's interpersonal relationships for clues to why a person suffering directly from a problem seemingly prefers to hold on to it.

Attribution to self

Attribution, a subject usually studied by social psychologists, may offer insight on how to maintain treatment gains once therapy is over. How a person explains to himself why he is behaving or has behaved in a particular way presumably helps to determine his subsequent behavior. Might not a person who has been in therapy and attributes improvement in his behavior to an external cause, such as a reinforcer from the environment, lose ground once what he considers the external justification for change is gone? In an analogue study on attribution and the ingestion of a ''drug'' (Davison and Valins, 1969), two groups of college undergraduates were given shock to determine how much they could bear. Then they took a prescribed ''fast-acting vitamin compound'' and were told that they would now be able to endure greater amounts of shock. And indeed they were, at least in their own minds. The experimenters surreptitiously altered the voltage levels to ensure this belief. Members of one group were then told that the capsule ingested was only a placebo, those of the other group that its effects would soon wear off. Those who believed that they had taken a placebo attributed to themselves the greater ability to withstand discomfort and endured higher levels of shock on a third test. Those who believed that the external agent was no longer effective were in the third round able to endure only lesser amounts of shock.

In an experiment with a similar design, conducted with people who were having trouble falling asleep, Davison, Tsujimoto, and Glaros (1973) obtained similar results, indicating that ''real'' problems may be treated by helping patients to attribute improvement to themselves. A clinical report by Levendusky and Pankratz (1975) confirms the benefits to patients of feeling

BOX **19.4** Self-Control—Outside a Behavioral Paradigm?

One of the most exciting areas of speculation in behavior therapy concerns the exercise of self-control (Goldfried and Merbaum, 1973; Mahoney, 1972). Much of the research and theory reviewed in this chapter seems to assume that the human being is a relatively passive recipient of stimulation from the environment. Given this apparent dependence on the external world, how can we account for behavior that appears to be autonomous, willed, and often contrary to what might be expected in a particular situation? How, for example, do we account for the fact that a person on a diet refrains from eating a luscious piece of chocolate cake even when hungry?

Psychoanalytic writers, including the ego analysts, handle the issue by positing within the person some kind of internal agent. Thus many ego analysts assert that the ego can operate on its own power, making deliberate decisions for the entire psychic system—including decisions that go against the wishes of the id. Behaviorists, especially Skinner (1953), have objected to this "explanation," regarding it as simply a relabeling of the phenomena.

Perhaps the most widely accepted behavioral view of self-control is Skinner's: an individual engages in self-control when he or she arranges the environment so that only certain controlling stimuli are present. A person wishing to lose weight rids his or her home of fattening foods and avoids passing restaurants when hungry. Behavior remains a function of the surroundings, but they are controlled by the individual.

A related behavioral conception of self-control is reflected in Bandura's (1969) explanation of aversive conditioning: rather than being passively conditioned to feel distaste for stimuli that have been paired with shock, a person learns a skill of aversive self-stimulation which he or she deliberately applies in real life. According to this view, a person resists a temptation by *deliberately* recalling the earlier aversive experience of being shocked or nauseated during therapy. Here, then, the individual is said to create symbolic stimuli which, in turn, control behavior.

A familiar means of exercising self-control, which is also discussed in the behavior therapy literature, is setting standards for oneself and denying oneself reinforcement unless they are met (Bandura and Perloff, 1967). One example is a tactic often employed by the authors of this book: I will not leave this desk for a snack until I have finished writing this page. When a person sets goals, and makes a contract with himself about achieving them before enjoying a reward, and then keeps to the contract without obvious external constraints, he can said be to have excercised self-control.

Self-control can be applied with *any* therapy technique. The only stipulation is that the client implement the procedure on his own, after receiving instructions from the therapist. For example, a client who was being desensitized decided on his own to imagine some of the hierarchy scenes while relaxing in a warm tub. A highly sophisticated and intelligent man, he felt that he understood the rationale of desensitization well enough and had enough control over the processes of his imagination to meet the procedural requirements of the technique. Consequently, after achieving what he felt to be a state of deep relaxation in his bathtub, he closed his eyes and carried out the scene presentation and scene termination as he had learned to do from the behavior therapist. Later, when he was with the therapist, they were able to skip the items to which he had desensitized himself in the tub and then proceeded more rapidly through the anxiety hierarchy.

Implicit in all conceptions of self-control are three criteria: (1) there are *no external controls* that could explain the behavior; (2) control of self is difficult enough that the person has to *put forth some effort;* and (3) the behavior in question is engaged in with *conscious deliberation and choice.* The individual actively decides to exercise self-control either by performing some action or by keeping himself from doing something, such as overeating. He does not do it automatically, nor is he forced to by someone else.

Let us take the example of a male jogger. If an army sergeant is goading this man along, the first criterion is not met and his running would not be an instance of self-control, even though considerable effort is probably required to maintain the running. Physiological factors inside the body may also be regarded as "external" control, as paradoxical as this may seem. Behavior that is impelled, or driven forward, by some inner physical urgency—such as a man running through a crowded restaurant toward the men's room because he feels himself about to vomit—is not an instance of self-control.

If the jogger finds it pleasurable to run, so enjoyable that he would rather do so than engage in other activities, the running cannot be considered an instance of self-control. In the earliest stages of jogging, the man may indeed be exerting great effort. He groans as he dons his Nikes, looks at his watch after only a few minutes of running to see how long this torture has been going on, and collapses in relief after half a mile, glad that the ordeal is over. But with practice and conditioning—the physical, not the Pavlovian variety!—the man's attitude changes. Jogging becomes a virtual necessity; running through city streets each morning at 6:00 a.m. is an activity sought after and treasured to the ex-clusion of other competing activities.

The third criterion, acting with conscious deliberation and choice, distinguishes self-control from actions people take in a mindless way. It is probably a good thing that much of our everyday action is mindless, for imagine how fatiguing (and boring!) it would be to mull over and make specific decisions to do such things as look out a window, tie our shoelaces, eat our breakfast, and so on. But these very acts would be categorized as instances of self-control if, on a given occasion, we have to decide whether to engage in them. Eating would require self-control if we were on a strict diet and had agreed, with our spouse, or doctor, or ourselves, to reduce caloric intake.

In our opinion, the concept of self-control places a strain on the behavioristic paradigm, for people are described as acting independently, putting forth effort, deliberating and choosing. Each of these verbs supposes the person to be an *initiator* of action, as the place where control *begins.* Ardent behaviorists, though, will counter by asserting with Skinner that our view of the person as an initiator only indicates our ignorance of the external forces that ultimately control behavior. Thus the person who denies himself an extra dessert is not really controlling himself; rather his self-denial is controlled by some subtle reward unappreciated by the observer, or by a distant reinforcer, such as being able later on to wear clothes of a smaller size. The flaw in this line of reasoning is that it is purely *post hoc* and irrefutable. We can *always* assert that, down the road, there will arrive the reinforcer that sustains the behavior. Such an "explanation" should be as unsatisfactory to the behaviorist as the psychoanalyst's invocation of an unconscious defense mechanism to account for an action.

that they have improved through their own efforts.

What are the implications of attribution research? Since in behavior therapy most improvement seems to be controlled by environmental forces, especially therapy relying on operant manipulation, it might be wise for behavior therapists to help their clients to feel more responsible. By encouraging an "I did it" attitude, perhaps by motivating them to practice new skills and to expose themselves to challenging situations, therapists may help their clients to be less dependent on therapy and therapist and to maintain better their treatment gains. Insight therapies have always emphasized the desirability of patients' assuming primary responsibility for their improvement. Behavior therapists have only recently come to grips with the issue (Bandura, 1977; Mischel, 1977). And on a more general level, the question of attributing improvement underscores the importance of cognitive processes in behavior therapy, to be discussed later in this chapter.

Modeling

Modeling is the third theoretical approach employed by behavior therapists. As we noted in Chapter 2, social learning generally encompasses not only classical and operant conditioning but also modeling. The importance of modeling and imitation in behavior is self-evident, for children as well as adults are able to acquire complex responses and eliminate emotional inhibitions merely by watching how others handle themselves.

Problems Treated by Modeling

The effectiveness of modeling in clinical work was shown in a study by Bandura, Blanchard, and Ritter (1969). They were attempting to help people overcome their snake phobias. The researchers had fearful adults view both live and filmed confrontations of people and snakes. In these confrontations the models gradually moved closer to the animals. The fears of the patients were decidedly reduced. Sex therapy researchers have found that inhibited adults can become more comfortable with their sexuality if shown tastefully designed explicit films of people touching themselves, masturbating, and having intercourse (Nemetz, Craig, and Reith, 1978; McMullen and Rosen, 1979). Other films have significantly reduced children's fears of dogs (Hill, Liebert, and Mott, 1968), of surgery (Melamed and Siegel, 1975), and of dental work (Melamed et al., 1975). In the Melamed films initially fearful children gradually cope with their anxieties about preparing for and undergoing medical and dental procedures. So helpful do such films appear to be and so easily are they shown to young patients in clinics and hospitals that it has been suggested they become a routine part of medical and dental practice (Wilson and O'Leary, 1980). These modeling films for reducing the fear of medical interventions are considered one of the new behavioral medicine or "health psychology" procedures.

Some of the clinical work of Arnold Lazarus, one of the leading behavior therapists, is also regarded as modeling treatment. As indicated in Chapter 2 (page 58), in *behavior rehearsal,* Lazarus (1971) demonstrates for a client how to handle a difficult interpersonal problem in a better

Albert Bandura, pioneer in the study of modeling and the alleviation of neurotic fears through imitation.

way. The client observes the therapist's exemplary performance and then attempts to imitate it during the therapy session. By continual practice and observation, the client can frequently acquire entire repertoires of more effective and more satisfying behavior. Often videotape equipment can be creatively used to facilitate such modeling and imitation.

In an attempt to expand the kinds of problems handled, some therapists and researchers have tried covert modeling (Cautela, 1971). The client imagines that he is watching a model, sometimes the client himself, coping with an object he fears or handling a situation requiring assertion. Research suggests that covert modeling reduces fears and promotes more assertive behavior (Rimm and Masters, 1979; Kazdin, 1975). The exact reasons why are not known. Covert procedures, in which the patient does nothing overt and has no real-life contact with what is feared or upsetting, are of course adopted when direct experience is not possible. Imagined substitutes are not expected to be as effective as actual exposure to threat and actual practice in confronting it (Bandura, 1977).

Behavior therapy programs for psychotic patients also make use of modeling. Bellack, Hersen, and Turner (1976) contrived social situations for three chronic schizophrenic patients and then observed whether they behaved appropriately to the situation. For instance, a given patient would be told to pretend that he had just returned home from a weekend trip to find his lawn had been mowed. As he gets out of the car, his next-door neighbor approaches him and says that he has cut the patient's grass because he was already cutting his own. The patient must then respond to the situation. As expected, patients were initially not very good at making a socially appropriate response, which in this instance would have been some sort of thank-you. Training followed; the therapist encouraged the patient to respond, commenting helpfully on his efforts. If necessary, the therapist also modeled appropriate behavior so that the patient could observe and then try to imitate it. This combination of role playing, modeling, and positive reinforcement effected significant improvement in all three patients. There was even generalization to social situations that had not been worked on during the training. This study, and others like it, indicate that many severely disturbed patients can be taught new social behavior which may help them function better both inside *and outside* the hospital.

The Role of Cognition

It is still unclear, however, *how* the observation of a model is translated into changes in overt behavior. In their original writings on modeling, Bandura and Walters (1963) asserted that an observer could, somehow, learn new behavior by watching others. Given the emphasis that much of experimental psychology places on learning through doing, this attention to learning without doing was important. But it left out the processes that could be operating. A moment's reflection on the typical modeling experiment suggests the direction theory and research have taken in recent years. The observer, a child, sits in a chair and watches a film of another child making a number of movements, such as hitting a Bobo doll in a highly stereotyped manner, and he hears the child uttering peculiar sounds. An hour later the youngster is given the opportunity to imitate what he saw and heard earlier. He is able to do so, as common sense and folk wisdom would predict. How shall we understand what happened? Since the observer did not *do* anything of interest in any motoric way while watching the film, except perhaps fidget in his chair, it would not be fruitful to look at overt behavior for a clue. Obviously, the child's cognitive processes were engaged, including his ability to remember later on what had happened.

Behavioral researchers are currently investigating what cognitive processes might account for the effects of modeling. For example, experimental cognitive research informs us that having a code by which to summarize information helps a person retain it better. Bandura, Jeffrey, and Bachicha (1974) found that the use of such a code helped observers pattern their actions on what they had seen modeled. Other theories about memory storage and retrieval may shed light on how people acquire new and complex patterns of behavior "simply" by watching others. The word "simply" is placed in quotation marks because, in fact, the process is not simple at all. The literature on modeling, which at first offered straightforward, commonsensical social-learning explanations, now regards modeling as a cognitive behavior therapy.

Cognitive Restructuring

In the therapies discussed thus far, the emphasis has been on the direct manipulation of overt behavior and occasionally of covert behavior. Relatively little attention has been paid to direct alteration of the thinking and reasoning processes of the client. Perhaps as a reaction to insight therapy, behavior therapists initially discounted the importance of cognition, regarding any appeal to thinking and believing as a return to the "mentalism" that Watson vigorously objected to in the early part of the twentieth century (see page 49).

If behavior therapy is to be taken seriously as applied experimental psychology, however, it should incorporate theory and research on cognitive processes. Indeed, in recent years behavior therapists have paid attention to "private events"—to thoughts, perceptions, judgments, and self-statements—and they have studied and manipulated these processes in their attempts to understand and modify overt and covert disturbed behavior (Mahoney, 1974). The cognitive-restructuring treatment of the man with "pressure points" described in Chapter 2 (page 58) is one example. Cognitive restructuring is a general term for changing a pattern of thought that is presumed to be causing a disturbed emotion or behavior. It is carried out in several ways by behavior therapists.

Rational-Emotive Therapy

For many years the work of a New York clinical psychologist, Albert Ellis, existed outside the mainstream of behavior therapy, but recently it has engaged the interest of behavior therapists. The principal thesis of Ellis's rational-emotive therapy is that sustained emotional reactions are caused by internal sentences that people repeat to themselves. As indicated earlier, anxious persons may create their own problems by adopting unrealistic expectations, such as "I must win the love of everyone." Or a depressed woman may say to herself, several times a day, "What a worthless person I am." Ellis proposes that people interpret what is happening around them, that sometimes these interpretations can cause emotional turmoil, and that a therapist's attention should be focused on these internal sentences, rather than on historical causes or, indeed, overt behavior (Ellis, 1962).

Ellis lists a number of assumptions people can make that may lead to distress (see page 170). One very common notion is that people must be thoroughly competent in everything they do. Ellis suggests that many people actually believe this untenable assumption, and that they evaluate every event within this context. Thus, if a person makes an error, it becomes a catastrophe since it violates his deeply held conviction that he must be perfect. It sometimes comes as a shock to clients to realize that they actually believe such strictures and are as a result running their lives so that it becomes virtually impossible to live comfortably or productively.

After becoming familiar with the client's problems, the therapist presents the basic theory of rational-emotive therapy so that the client can understand and accept it.[3] The following transcript is from a session with a young man who had inordinate fears about speaking in front of groups. The therapist guides the client to view his "inferiority complex" in terms of the unreasonable things he may be telling himself. The therapist's thoughts during the interview are indicated in italics.

Client: My primary difficulty is that I become very uptight when I have to speak in front of a group of people. I guess it's just my own inferiority complex.

Therapist: [I don't want to get sidetracked at this point by talking about that conceptualization of his problem. I'll just try to finesse it and make a smooth transition to something else.] I don't know if I would call it an inferiority complex but I do believe that people can, in a sense, bring on their own upset and anxiety in certain kinds of situations. When you're in a particular situation, your anxiety is often not the result of the situation itself, but rather the

way in which you *interpret* the situation— what you tell yourself about the situation. For example, look at this pen. Does this pen make you nervous?

Client: No.

Therapist: Why not?

Client: It's just an object. It's just a pen.

Therapist: It can't hurt you?

Client: No. . . .

Therapist: It's really not the object that creates emotional upset in people, but rather what you *think* about the object. [*Hopefully, this Socratic-like dialogue will eventually bring him to the conclusion that self-statements can mediate emotional arousal.*] Now this holds true for . . . situations where emotional upset is caused by what a person tells himself about the situation. Take, for example, two people

Albert Ellis's rational-emotive therapy is designed to help patients recognize the impossible "musts" they impose on themselves and become more realistic in their expectations.

---

[3] The usefulness of a theory does not depend on whether it is true. Ellis's views may be only partially correct, or even entirely wrong, and yet it may be helpful for a client to act as though they are true.

who are about to attend the same social gathering. Both of them may know exactly the same number of people at the party, but one person can be optimistic and relaxed about the situation, whereas the other one can be worried about how he will appear, and consequently be very anxious. [*I'll try to get him to verbalize the basic assumption that attitude or perception is most important here.*] So, when these two people walk into the place where the party is given, are their emotional reactions at all associated with the physical arrangements at the party?

Client: No, obviously not.

Therapist: What determines their reactions, then?

Client: They obviously have different attitudes toward the party.

Therapist: Exactly, and their attitudes—the ways in which they approach the situation—greatly influence their emotional reactions (Goldfried and Davison, 1976, pp. 163-165).

Having persuaded the client to construe his problems in rational-emotive terms, the therapist proceeds to teach the person to substitute for irrational self-statements an internal dialogue meant to ease his emotional turmoil. At the present time therapists who implement Ellis's ideas differ greatly on how they persuade clients to change their self-talk. Some rational-emotive therapists, like Ellis himself, argue with clients, cajoling and teasing them, sometimes in very blunt language, to change their minds. Others, believing that social influence should be more subtle and that individuals should participate in changing themselves, encourage clients to discuss their own irrational thinking and then gently lead them to discover more rational ways of regarding the world.

One variation of rational-emotive therapy, *systematic rational restructuring* (Goldfried, Decenteceo, and Weinberg, 1964), is modeled after systematic desensitization. The therapist and client draw up a hierarchy of anxiety-provoking situations, but instead of having the client relax while imagining each, the therapist teaches the client to talk to himself differently about the situation. Anxiety, it is hoped, will be reduced dur-

ing the visualization itself. The following transcript is from a later session with the young man who was afraid of speaking in front of groups. Notice how the therapist shares the perspective of the client in an effort to direct his thinking in a more realistic direction. Once again, the therapist's own thoughts are shown in italics.

Therapist: I'm going to ask you to imagine yourself in a given situation, and to tell me how nervous you may feel. I'd then like you to think aloud about what you might be telling yourself that is creating this anxiety, and then [try] to put your expectations into a more realistic perspective. From time to time, I will make certain comments, and I'd like you to treat these comments as if they were your own thoughts, OK?

Client: All right.

Therapist: I'd like you to close your eyes now and imagine yourself in the following situation: You are sitting on stage in the auditorium, together with the other school board members. It's a few minutes before you have to get up and give your report to the people in the audience. Between 0 and 100 percent tension, tell me how nervous you feel?

Client: About 50.

Therapist: [*Now to get into his head.*] So I'm feeling fairly tense. Let me think. What might I be telling myself that's making me upset?

Client: I'm nervous about reading my report in front of all these people.

Therapist: But why does that bother me?

Client: Well, I don't know if I'm going to come across all right. . . .

Therapist: [*He seems to be having trouble. More prompting on my part may be needed than I originally anticipated.*] But why should that upset me? That upsets me because . . .

Client: . . . because I want to make a good impression.

Therapist: And if I don't . . .

Client: . . . well, I don't know. I don't want people to think that I'm incompetent. I guess I'm afraid that I'll lose the respect of the people who thought I knew what I was doing.

Therapist: [*He seems to be getting closer.*] But why should that make me so upset?

Client: I don't know. I guess it shouldn't. Maybe I'm being *overly* concerned about other people's reactions to me.

Therapist: How might I be overly concerned?

Client: I think this may be one of those situations where I have to please everybody, and there are an awful lot of people in the audience. Chances are I'm not going to get everybody's approval, and maybe that's upsetting me. I want everyone to think I'm doing a good job.

Therapist: Now let me think for a moment to see how rational that is.

Client: To begin with, I don't think it really is likely that I'm going to completely blow it. After all, I have prepared in advance, and have thought through what I want to say fairly clearly. I think I may be reacting as if I already have failed, even though it's very unlikely that I will.

Therapist: And even if I did mess up, how bad would that be?

Client: Well, I guess that really wouldn't be so terrible after all.

Therapist: [*I don't believe him for one moment. There is a definite hollow ring to his voice. He arrived at that conclusion much too quickly and presents it without much conviction.*] I say I don't think it'll upset me, but I don't really believe that.

Client: That's true. I would be upset if I failed. But actually, I really shouldn't be looking at this situation as [indicating] failure.

Therapist: What would be a better way for me to look at the situation?

Client: Well, it's certainly not a do-or-die kind of thing. It's only a ridiculous committee report. A lot of the people in the audience know who I am and what I'm capable of doing. And even if I don't give a sterling performance, I don't

think they're going to change their opinion of me on the basis of a five-minute presentation.

Therapist: But what if some of them do?

Client: Even if some of them do think differently of me, that doesn't mean that I *would* be different. I would still be me no matter what they thought. It's ridiculous of me to base my self-worth on what other people think.

Therapist: [*I think he's come around as much as he can. We can terminate this scene now.*] With this new attitude toward the situation, how do you feel in percentage of anxiety?

Client: Oh, about 25 percent.

Therapist: OK, let's talk a little about some of the thoughts you had during that situation before trying it again (Goldfried and Davison, 1976, pp. 172-174).

Other techniques are used in rational-emotive therapy; the client is not left submerged in thought. Once a client verbalizes a different belief or self-statement during a therapy session, it must be made part of everyday thinking. In recent years Ellis and his followers have paid particular attention to homework assignments designed to provide opportunities for the client to experiment with the new self-talk and to experience the positive consequences of viewing life in less catastrophic ways.

It can be argued that Ellis is preaching an ethical system, for he suggests that a great deal of emotional suffering is engendered by goals that *he* asserts are wrong. He proposes that these goals are subject to modification, and that by altering them a person can reduce subjective discomfort. Indeed, the reduction of stress can often improve performance so that, ironically, it more closely approximates the goal previously viewed as a "must" or a "should." Rational-emotive work appears at present to be one of the most promising and interesting areas in behavior therapy. Several well-controlled clinical studies (for example, Kanter and Goldfried, 1979) confirm that rational-emotive therapy reduces a number of interpersonal anxieties, but much remains to be done to evaluate the long-term efficacy of the therapy and to determine whether it is superior to other treatments.

Other Cognitive Behavior Therapies

Two other cognitive therapies have attracted a great deal of attention, that of Aaron T. Beck (Beck et al., 1979) and the *self-instructional training* of Donald Meichenbaum (1977).

Beck's cognitive therapy

The reader will recall Beck's theory of depression (see page 236). He holds that numerous disorders, particularly depression, are caused by the negative patterns in which individuals think about themselves, the world, and the future. They arbitrarily infer, exaggerate, overgeneralize, and magnify or minimize. Beck questions clients so that they discover for themselves the distortions in their thinking and can make changes that, at least in Beck's view, are more consonant with reality. Thus a depressed patient who bemoans his worthlessness because he burned the roast is encouraged to view the failure as regrettable but not to overgeneralize and conclude that he can do no good on future occasions. The client is encouraged to formulate an alternative, nondepressive hypothesis and then to test it, in a spirit of "collaborative empiricism" (Hollon and Beck, 1979). In this respect Beck's cognitive therapy has explicit behavioral components. Therapy is aimed not just at examining cognitive distortions but at considering implications of viewing the world in other ways. Clients are encouraged to gather information about themselves and to perform experiments that will allow them to disconfirm their false beliefs. For example, if a client is convinced that she is depressed all the time, this belief itself may be causing her to feel all the more depressed and hopeless. Beck will have this client record her moods at regular intervals during the day, by self-monitoring (see page 100). If it turns out that her reports of mood show some *variability,* as indeed sometimes happens even with very depressed people, this information will serve to challenge the client's general belief that life is *always* miserable for her.

Beck also gives his clients graded task assignments. Depressed clients often do very little because tasks seem insurmountable, and they believe that they can accomplish nothing. To test this hypothesis of insurmountableness, the therapist breaks down a particular task into small steps and encourages the client to focus on just one step at a time. If this tactic is skillfully handled, and a good therapeutic relationship is obviously important, the client finds that she can, in fact, accomplish *something.* Her accomplishments are then discussed with the therapist as inconsistent with her general view that she is not up to making an effort. As the client begins to change her view of herself, tasks of greater difficulty appear less forbidding, and success can build upon success, with still further beneficial changes in the client's beliefs about herself and her world.

Although Ellis and Beck share the assumption that thinking influences emotion and behavior, there is an important difference in their views. Ellis has a list of what he considers common or core irrational assumptions; thus he concentrates on the *specific content* of his client's thinking—Is the client making this assumption or that one? Beck, in contrast, has no particular ideas about the content of thought; rather, he focuses on the *form* of his clients' ideation.

The effectiveness of Beck's approach is under intensive study. A noteworthy effort was reported by Rush, Beck, and their colleagues (1977); they compared Beck's treatment with the administration of imipramine or Tofranil, a psychoactive drug widely used for depression, in two groups of severely depressed men and women. After a period of treatment, those in the cognitive therapy group were less depressed. People who terminate therapy prematurely are usually doing poorly. There were fewer dropouts from the cognitive therapy group, an early indication that these people were receiving more help than those who took the drug. Patients who had received cognitive therapy remained less depressed at a six-month follow-up. In light of the demonstrated efficacy of imipramine in treating depression, these findings are praise indeed for Beck's treatment. Other research as well indicates that this cognitive-restructuring therapy is effective in relieving depression (Shaw, 1977).

Meichenbaum's self-instructional training

Meichenbaum's cognitive therapy is designed to help clients cope with stressful conditions by providing them with more adaptive self-talk. These new inner dialogues urge strategies such as "Slow down," "Let's see, first add this column of digits, then move to the left." They help the person to inhibit anxiety and to stick to a task or to handle a situation better.

Meichenbaum helps clients become aware of the private monologues that they have with themselves when they are in distress. He then analyzes the demands of a particular situation in which clients are responding poorly and devises a dialogue they can have with themselves that will better control their behavior. Meichenbaum and Goodman (1971) together worked out a way to help hyperactive children restrain their impulsiveness and to size up and accomplish a task through self-talk. First the teacher performs the task, speaking instructions aloud to herself while the child watches and listens.

> *Okay, what is it I have to do? You want me to copy the picture with different lines. I have to go slow and be careful. Okay, draw the line down, down, good; then to the right, that's it; now down some more and to the left. Good, I'm doing fine so far. Remember go slow. Now back up again. No, I was supposed to go down. That's okay. Just erase the line carefully. . . . Good, even if I make an error I can go on slowly and carefully. Okay, I have to go down now. Finished. I did it (p. 117).*

Then the child listens and draws the lines while the teacher speaks instructions to him. The child repeats the task twice again, first giving himself instructions aloud, then whispering them. Finally he is ready to perform the task while uttering self-talk instructions silently to himself. Meichenbaum and his colleagues have also demonstrated that self-talk reduces test anxiety (Meichenbaum, 1972) and speech anxiety (Meichenbaum, Gilmore, and Fedoravicius, 1971).

Some Reflections on Cognitive Behavior Therapy

Experimental psychologists have for many years been doing research into cognition—into the mental processes of perceiving, recognizing, conceiving, judging, and reasoning, of problem solving, imagining, and other symbolizing maneuvers. Indeed, psychology first became estab-

lished as a science in the late nineteenth century through the work of Wilhelm Wundt in Leipzig and Edward Titchener in Ithaca, New York (Boring, 1953); their laboratories made inquiries into the contents of the mind and the elements of consciousness.

As we have indicated, behavior therapy aligned itself initially with stimulus-response psychology—with the study of classical and operant conditioning—the assumption being that principles and procedures derived from conditioning experiments could be applied to lessen psychological suffering. The S–R orientation came from behaviorists like Watson and Skinner, who had become dissatisfied with Wundt and Titchener's use of introspection to study consciousness. What has now developed and is called "cognitive behavior therapy" may appear to be a radical and novel departure, given the earlier focus of behavior therapists on classical and operant conditioning. But in a historical sense it actually represents a return to the cognitive foci of the earliest period of experimental psychology.

The work of Ellis, Beck, and Meichenbaum exemplifies a formal consideration of cognitive processes within behavior therapy. From the beginning, however, behavior therapists have relied heavily on the human being's capacity to symbolize, to process information, to represent the world in words and images. Wolpe's technique of systematic desensitization is a very clear example. This technique, believed by Wolpe to rest on conditioning principles, is inherently a cognitive procedure, for the client *imagines* what is fearful. Indeed, the most exciting overt behavioral event during a regimen of desensitization is the client's occasional signaling of anxiety by raising an index finger! If anything important is happening, it is surely going on "under the skin," and some of this activity is surely cognitive in nature.

As behavior therapy "goes cognitive," however, it is important to bear in mind that contemporary researchers continue to believe that behavioral *procedures* are more powerful than strictly verbal ones in affecting cognitive *processes* (Bandura, 1977). That is, they favor behavioral techniques while maintaining that it is important to alter a person's beliefs in order to effect an enduring change in behavior. Bandura

BOX **19.5** Assertion Training

"Children should be seen and not heard." "Keep a stiff upper lip." "He's the strong silent type." Our society does not generally value the open expression of beliefs and feelings. And yet people seem to pay an emotional price for concealing their thoughts and suppressing their feelings. Peoples' wants and needs may not be met if they shy away from stating them clearly. As we have seen, poor communication between sexual partners is one of the major factors contributing to an unsatisfying sexual relationship. Therapists of all persuasions spend a good deal of time encouraging clients to discover what their desires and needs are and then to take responsibility for meeting them. If they have trouble expressing their feelings and wishes to others, assertion training may be able to help them.

Andrew Salter, in his book *Conditioned Reflex Therapy* (1949), was the first behavior therapist to set assertiveness as a positive goal for clients. Using Pavlovian, classical conditioning terms,

Salter said that much human psychological suffering is caused by an excess of cortical inhibition; therefore greater excitation is called for. He encouraged socially inhibited people to express their feelings to others in an open, spontaneous way. They are to do so verbally, telling people when they are happy or sad, angry or resolute; and nonverbally with smiles and frowns, what Salter called facial talk. They are also to contradict people they disagree with, and with appropriate feeling; use the pronoun I as often as possible; express agreement with those who praise them; and improvise, that is, respond intuitively in the moment without ruminating. Although Salter's classical conditioning formulation of assertion has not been verified, assertiveness remains a goal for people in therapy, and his impact on therapeutic practice has been great and enduring.

How are we to define assertion? Is it not inconsiderate to put ourselves forward and express

Andrew Salter, the originator of assertion training, which very often employs role playing to help the patient overcome passivity.

our beliefs and feelings to others? What if we hurt someone else's feelings in doing so? Much effort has gone into articulating the differences between assertive behavior and aggressive behavior. A useful distinction has been drawn by Lange and Jakubowski (1976); they consider assertion as

expressing thoughts, feelings, and beliefs in direct, honest, and appropriate ways which respect the rights of other people. In contrast, aggression involves self-expression which is characterized by violating others' rights and demeaning others in an attempt to achieve one's own objectives (pp. 38-39).

Arnold Lazarus regards the expression of positive and negative emotions as important for psychological well-being. He argues (1971) that "emotional freedom" in the most general sense of the term is important for many kinds of clients; they need to express affection and approval as well as dislikes and criticisms. In helping clients to assert themselves, behavior therapists, whether they acknowledge it or not, are doing therapeutic work with goals similar to those of humanistic therapists, who also regard expression of positive and negative feelings as a necessary component of effective living.

People may be unassertive for any number of reasons. The specific therapy procedures chosen will depend on the reasons believed to be causing the individual's unassertiveness. Assertion training, then, is actually a set of different techniques, having in common the goal of enhancing assertiveness. Goldfried and Davison (1976) have suggested several factors that can underlie unassertiveness, one or more of which may be found in an unassertive individual.

1. The client may not know what to say. Some unassertive people lack information on what to say in situations that call for expressiveness. The therapist should supply this information.

2. Clients may not know how to behave assertively. They may not assume the tone and loudness of voice, the fluency of speech, the facial expression and eye contact, and the body posture necessary for assertiveness. Modeling

"Do you have any idea when the meek shall inherit the earth?"

Drawing by Dana Fradon; © 1972 The New Yorker Magazine, Inc.

and role playing will help these people acquire the signals of firmness and directness.

3. Clients may fear that something terrible will happen if they assert themselves. Systematic desensitization may reduce this anticipatory anxiety. In others assertiveness seems to be blocked by negative self-statements, such as "If I assert myself and am rejected, that would be a catastrophe" (Schwartz and Gottman, 1976). They will profit from rational-emotive therapy.

4. The client may not feel that it is "proper" or "right" to be assertive. The value systems of some people preclude or discourage assertiveness. For example, some of the problems of a Catholic nun undergoing therapy seemed to relate to her unassertiveness, but through discussion it became clear that she would violate some of her vows were she more expressive and outspoken. By mutual agreement assertion training was not undertaken; instead, therapy focused on helping her work within her chosen profession in ways that were more personally satisfying and yet not more assertive.

Assertion training may begin with conversations in which the therapist tries to get the client to distinguish between assertiveness and aggression. For people who are submissive, even making a reasonable request or refusing a presumptuous one may make them feel that they are being hostile. Then therapists usually give clients sample situations which will leave them feeling put upon if they are unable to handle them. The situations usually require that they stand up for their rights, their time, and their energies.

You have been studying very hard for weeks, taking no time off at all for relaxation. But now a new film, which will play for only a few days, interests you and you have decided to take a few hours and go late this evening to see it. On the way to an afternoon class your very good friend tells you she has free tickets to a tap dancing exhibition this evening and asks you to go with her. How do you say no?

Behavior rehearsal is a useful technique in assertion training. The therapist discusses and models appropriate assertiveness and then has the client role-play situations. Graded homework assignments, such as asking the garageman to explain the latest bill for repairs, then telling an uncle that his constant criticisms are resented, are given as soon as the client has acquired some degree of assertiveness through session work.

Assertion training raises several ethical issues. To encourage assertiveness in people who, like the nun mentioned earlier, believe that self-denial is a greater good than self-expression would violate the client's value system and could generate an unfavorable "ripple effect" in other areas of the person's life. Drawing a distinction between assertion and aggression is also an ethical issue. Behavior considered assertive by one person may be seen by another as aggressive. If we adopt the distinction made by Lange and Jakubowski, that assertion respects the rights of others whereas aggression does not, we still have to make a judgment about what the rights of others are. Thus assertion training touches on moral aspects of social living, namely the definition of other people's rights and the proper means of standing up for one's own rights.

suggests, in fact, that all therapeutic procedures, to the extent that they are effective, work their improvement by giving the person a sense of mastery, of "self-efficacy." At the same time he finds that the most effective way to gain a sense of self-efficacy, if one is lacking, is by changing behavior. Whether or not we believe self-efficacy to be as important as Bandura does, a distinction can be made between processes that underlie improvement and *procedures* that set these *processes* in motion. Cognitive behavior therapists continue to be behavioral in their use of performance-based procedures and in their commitment to behavioral change, but they are cognitive in the sense that they believe cognitive change to be an important mechanism that accounts for the effectiveness of behavioral procedures.

All cognitive behavior therapists heed the mental processes of their clients in another way. They pay attention to the world as it is perceived by the client. It is not what impinges on us from the outside that controls our behavior, the assumption that has guided stimulus-response psychology for decades. Rather our feelings and behavior are determined by how we view the world. The Greek philosopher Epictetus stated it in the first century, "Men are not disturbed by things, but by the views they take of them." Thus behavior therapy is being brought closer to the humanistic therapies reviewed in Chapter 18. A central thesis of therapists like Rogers and Perls is that the client must be understood from the client's own frame of reference, from his or her phenomenological world, for it is this perception of the world that controls life and behavior.

From the philosophical point of view, such assumptions on the part of those who would understand people and try to help them are profoundly important. Experimentally minded clinicians and researchers are intrigued by how much the new field of cognitive behavior therapy has in common with the humanists and their attention to the phenomenological world of their clients. To be sure, the *techniques* used by the cognitive behavior therapists are usually quite different from those of the followers of Rogers and of Perls. But as students of psychotherapy and of human nature, these surface differences should not blind us to the links between the two approaches.

Some Basic Issues in Behavior Therapy

Behavior therapy is expanding each year; with such a proliferation of activity, everyone concerned should remain aware of the problems and issues that transcend particular experimental findings. The following considerations, many of which have been alluded to earlier, need to be kept clearly in mind.

The behavioral focus on current maintaining variables

An important defining characteristic of behavior therapy is its focus on current maintaining variables rather than on etiology. For example, a married woman is unhappy because she is unable to be assertive with her husband. Her problem might be traced to her inability as a child to deal effectively with her domineering father. A behavior therapist will, however, concentrate on helping her become more open with her husband rather than working on her past relationship with her father. Behavior therapists tend to concentrate their attention on maintaining variables such as unassertiveness, regardless of what factors brought them into being.

Internal behavior and cognition

In Chapter 4 we demonstrated that the inference of intervening processes and other explanatory fictions is useful in interpreting data and generating fruitful hypotheses. Behavior therapists are often thought to hold the radical behavioristic positions of Watson and Skinner, that it is not useful or legitimate to make inferences about internal processes of the organism. Our intent is to present a broader point of view as persuasively as we can, although not all contemporary behavior therapists (for example, Ullmann and Krasner, 1975; Bijou and Baer, 1961) agree on this issue.

The position we share with others (see Bandura, 1969; Kanfer and Phillips, 1970; Mahoney, 1974; MacCorquodale and Meehl, 1948; Meyer and Chesser, 1970; Mischel, 1968; O'Leary and Wilson, 1975) is that behavior therapy, as applied experimental psychology, is legitimately concerned with internal as well as external

BOX 19.6 Multimodal Therapy and the BASIC ID

Arnold Lazarus, a leading behavior therapist.

For many years Arnold Lazarus of Rutgers University has been among the most inventive of behavioral clinicians. He has been particularly concerned that behavior therapists remain *flexible,* not committing themselves to particular points of view regarding techniques or even to particular theories. This position has been formulated in great detail and given the name *multimodal therapy.* It is an approach that aims to tailor therapy interventions to the full range of difficulties presented by clients. Lazarus (1973) proposes the acronym BASIC ID to help the clinician remember the seven modalities in which a given client may be having problems: behavior, affect, sensation, imagery, cognition, interpersonal relations, and drugs. Except for prescribed drugs, which are really an intervention rather than an aspect of the person's functioning, each represents a potential trouble spot for the clinician to attend to. Most clients, Lazarus suggests, have problems in several areas; in focusing on one or just a few of them, a therapist may overlook significant difficulties in others. A client who is depressed, for example, may also be disturbed by some of his or her interpersonal relationships.

But Lazarus develops multimodal therapy even further. He argues that the therapist must apply to the gamut of a patient's problems *any* techniques that promise to work; treatment should not be limited to behavior therapy procedures. Lazarus himself is not reluctant to employ techniques from other theoretical orientations. Psychoanalytic procedures, he argues, may be especially well suited to alleviate problems of affect or cognition, whereas various behavior therapy techniques may be better suited to problems in overt behavior or in interpersonal relations. Table 19.1 is a ''modality profile'' adapted from one that was drawn up by Lazarus for a client.

As might be expected, Lazarus's proposals have not met with universal acceptance among behavior therapists. Some are worried that a ''Do what you think will work'' attitude will pollute the theoretical purity of behavior therapy and divert the attention of behavioral clinicians from their commitment to scientific formulations and evaluation. Further, the apparent antitheoretical flavor of his proposals disturbs those who believe that advances in therapy are made not only through clinical innovations of the sort people like Lazarus are so skillful in producing but by working methodically within a particular theoretical framework. In any event, Lazarus's suggestions serve to caution behavior therapists against being needlessly rigid in their clinical work. Given the incomplete state of our knowledge of how best to help people, this warning is timely and valuable.

TABLE **19.1**

Modality Profile for a Patient in
Multimodal Therapy
(adapted from Lazarus, 1973).

Modality	Problem	Proposed treatment
Behavior	Frequent crying Negative self-statements	Nonreinforcement Positive self-talk assignments
Affect	Unable to express overt anger Absence of enthusiasm and spontaneous joy Emptiness and aloneness	Role playing Positive imagery procedures General relationship building
Sensation	Out of touch with most sensual pleasures Frequent lower back pains	Sensate-focus method Orthopedic exercise
Imagery	Distressing scenes of sister's funeral	Desensitization
Cognition	Irrational self-talk: "I am evil." "I must suffer." "I am inferior."	Deliberative rational disputation and corrective self-talk
Interpersonal relationships	Childlike dependence Easily exploited and submissive	Specific self-sufficiency assignments Assertion training

events, provided the internal mediators are securely anchored to observable stimuli or responses. Behaviorists do not have to ignore the internal life of human beings; but they do differ from psychologists with other views in the rigor of their inferences and in the care they take to ensure the inferences are parsimonious as well as productive of good explanations and testable hypotheses.

Underlying causes

A related misconception is that behavior therapy deals with symptoms whereas other therapies, particularly psychoanalytically oriented ones, are concerned with "root" or "underlying" causes. To many people a determinant of behavior that is assumed to lie in the unconscious or in the past is somehow more "underlying" or "basic" than a determinant that is anchored in the current environment. This conception fails to consider the fact that science searches for the most significant causes of behavior. If "underlying" is defined as "not immediately obvious," behavior therapists indeed search for underlying causes. If such causes are taken to be the most significant ones, that is, the controlling variables, the task of behavior therapists is the same as for all other therapists—to find the most significant causes (Bandura, 1969).

A clinical example will illustrate this point. A twenty-five-year-old man who had been discharged from a mental hospital was treated for problems that included occasional paranoid delusions. A careful behavioral assessment suggested to both client and therapist that these thoughts of persecution were triggered by considerable anxiety. Rather than working directly on the delusional episodes, then, the therapist desensitized the client to a variety of social situations in which he might feel inadequate and be criticized by others. Such occasions seemed often to precede his paranoid "trips." As the client came gradually to be less upset about possible criticism, his paranoid thoughts dropped to near zero. Although there is of course no way of knowing whether desensitization to disturbing social situations was truly responsible for this outcome, the behavior therapist did search for an underlying cause as the strongest controlling variable.

Broad-spectrum treatment

Our review of behavior therapy has necessarily been fragmented because we have dealt with separate techniques one at a time. In clinical practice, however, behavior therapists employ several procedures at once or sequentially in an attempt to deal with all the important controlling variables; this approach is generally referred to as *broad-spectrum behavior therapy* (Lazarus, 1971). For example, a woman fearful of leaving her home might well undergo desensitization by imagining herself walking out of her door and gradually engaging in activities that take her farther and farther from her safe haven. Over the years, however, she may also have built up a dependent relationship with her husband. As she becomes bolder in venturing forth, this change in her behavior may disrupt the equilibrium of the relationship that she and her husband have worked out over the years. To attend only to her fear of leaving home would be incomplete behavior therapy (Lazarus, 1965) and might even lead to replacement of the agoraphobia with another difficulty that would serve to keep the woman at home—a problem frequently called "symptom substitution."

In a related vein, it is often said that behavior therapists invariably focus only on the patient's complaint as it was stated during the first interview. The facts are otherwise. A clinical graduate student was desensitizing an undergraduate for test anxiety. The client made good progress up the hierarchy of imagined situations but was not improving at all in the real world of test taking. The supervisor of the graduate student suggested that the therapist find out whether the client was studying for his tests. It turned out that he was not; worry about the health of his mother was markedly interfering with his attempts to study. Thus the goal of making the client nonchalant about taking tests was inappropriate, for he was approaching the tests themselves without adequate preparation. On the basis of additional assessment, the therapy shifted away from desensitization to a discussion of how the client could deal with his realistic fears about his mother's possible death.

Relationship factors

Because of the scientific language typically employed in the literature on behavior therapy, behavior therapists are considered little if at all concerned with the therapist-client relationship—whether, for example, the client trusts the therapist, believes that he or she can be of assistance, and the like. Although behaviorists have, indeed, tried to emphasize the learning mechanisms that are brought into play by the various techniques, they have never discounted the importance of the client's feelings about the therapist (Goldfried and Davison, 1976). Research in behavior therapy has, in fact, already documented the importance of sometimes vaguely defined relationship factors. In the Paul (1966) study of anxious public speakers, for example, considerable and long-lasting improvement was observed in subjects who were given the attention-placebo treatment. Thus, although desensitization subjects improved more than did the others, the significant improvement in the attention-placebo group demonstrates the substantial contribution of the warm, trusting relationship with a therapist.

A good therapeutic relationship is important for many reasons. As discussed in Chapter 3 (page 85), it seems doubtful that clients will reveal deeply personal information if they do not trust or respect their therapists. Furthermore, since behavior therapy cannot be imposed on an unwilling client, a therapist must obtain the cooperation of the client if there is to be any possibility that techniques will have their desired effect. In desensitization, for example, a client could readily sabotage the best efforts of the therapist by not imagining a particular scene, by not signaling anxiety appropriately, and by not practing relaxation. And in virtually all other behavior therapy procedures clients are able to, and sometimes will, work against the therapist if relationship factors are neglected (Davison, 1973).

Flesh on the theoretical skeleton

Determining the most important controlling variables is related to another overlooked aspect of behavior therapy—indeed, of any therapy—namely moving from a general principle to a concrete clinical intervention.

To illustrate, let us consider a study in which

undergraduates were trained to analyze the behavior of severely disturbed children in operant conditioning terms (Davison, 1964). The students were encouraged to *assume* that the important determinants of these children's behavior were the consequences of that behavior. Armed with M & M candies as reinforcers, these student-therapists attempted to bring the behavior of the severely disturbed children under their control. Eventually, one child appeared to be losing interest in earning the candies. Working within a framework that required an effective reinforcer, the therapist looked around for another incentive. Luckily, he noticed that each time the child passed a window, she would pause for a moment to look at her reflection. The therapist obtained a mirror and was subsequently able to make "peeking into the mirror" the reinforcer for desired behavior; the peeks into the mirror were used in the same *functional* way as the M & M candies. Thus, *although guided by a general principle, the therapist had to rely on improvisation and inventiveness as demanded by the clinical situation.*

An outsider can get the impression that devising therapy along behavioral lines is easy and straightforward, that the application of a general principle to a particular case is a simple matter. Those who have worked as behavioral clinicians, however, know otherwise. Although a given theoretical framework helps to guide the clinician's thinking, it is by no means sufficient.

> . . . *The clinician in fact approaches his work with a given set, a framework for ordering the complex data that are his domain. But frameworks are insufficient. The clinician, like any other applied scientist, must fill out the theoretical skeleton. Individual cases present problems that always call for knowledge beyond basic psychological principles* (Lazarus and Davison, 1971, p. 203).

The preceding quotation from two behavior therapists is very similar to the following one from an article written by two experimental social psychologists.

> *In any experiment, the investigator chooses*

a procedure which he intuitively feels is an empirical realization of his conceptual variable. All experimental procedures are "contrived" in the sense that they are invented. Indeed, it can be said that the art of experimentation rests primarily on the skill of the investigator to judge the procedure which is the most accurate realization of his conceptual variable and has the greatest impact and the most credibility for the subject (Aronson and Carlsmith, 1968, p. 25).

Thus behavior therapists are faced with the same kinds of decision-making challenges that their experimental colleagues face. There are no easy solutions in dealing with human problems.

Psychoanalysis and behavior therapy— a rapprochement?

Is contemporary psychoanalysis compatible with behavior therapy? This question has been discussed for many years, and few professionals are optimistic about a meaningful rapprochement, arguing that these two points of view are incompatible paradigms. But Paul Wachtel, in his book on just such an integration (1977), has offered a scheme that, in our view, holds considerable promise at least for establishing a dialogue between psychoanalytically oriented therapists and behavior therapists.

As indicated in Chapter 18, ego analysts place much more emphasis on current ego functioning than did Freud. Sullivan, for example, alerted his psychoanalytic colleagues to his belief that patients will feel better about themselves and function more effectively if they focus on problems in their current interpersonal behavior. But even Sullivan appears to have been ambivalent about the wisdom of working directly on how people act and feel in the present if this might mean they would not recover memories of repressed infantile conflicts. Wachtel, however, suggests that the therapist *should* help the client change his current behavior, not only so that he can feel better in the here and now but indeed so that he can *change* his childlike fears from the past. For example, if a client takes heart from being able to control present behavior, he may then uncover and alter his "woolly mammoth." By pointing out that a direct alteration of behavior

may help clients attain a more realistic understanding of their past repressed conflicts, traditionally the goal of psychoanalysis, Wachtel hopes to interest his analytic colleagues in the techniques employed by behavior therapists.

Similarly, Wachtel holds that behavior therapists can learn much from their analytic colleagues, especially concerning the *kinds* of problems people tend to develop. For example, psychoanalytic theory tells us that children have strong and usually ambivalent feelings about their parents, and that, presumably, some of these are so unpleasant that they are repressed, or at least are difficult to focus on and talk about openly. Suppose then that a behavior therapist is working with a male client who describes himself as fearful of heterosexual relationships. In most instances the therapist will work to help the client reduce his unrealistic anxieties and perhaps also offer training in social skills. But if the focus is exclusively on heterosexual anxiety, the therapist will not explore the possibility that the client is also *angry* at women. How might the therapists come to consider this possibility? Wachtel suggests that the behavior therapist sensitive to the childhood conflicts that analysts focus on will question the client about his relationship with his mother. The client's reply or manner may give a hint of resentment. Assuming this happens, the therapist will then *see* the client differently. He will hypothesize that the client is not just fearful of women but angry at them as well, because he associates them with a mother who has been the object of both hate and love from early childhood. This additional information will presumably suggest a different behavioral intervention, for the anger must be dealt with.

Wachtel argues further that psychoanalysts are more likely than behavior therapists to consider the nonnormative, or unusual concerns, wishes, and fears of their patients. Guided by the view that emotional problems derive from the repression of id conflicts, they consider them to reflect infantile wishes and fears, dark mysteries of primary process thinking. Behavior therapists tend to have a more straightforward, more prosaic, if you will, view of their patients' problems.

Wachtel would also have the behavior therapist appreciate that reinforcers can be *subtle* and that, furthermore, a client may deny that he or she really wants something. And the client may well be unaware of this denial. In other words, therapists should attune themselves to unconscious motivation, to the possibility that a person may be motivated or reinforced by a set of events that he or she, for psychodynamic reasons, is not conscious of.

Contemporary psychoanalytic thought may also help the behavior therapist become aware of the *meaning* that a particular intervention has for a client. Consider the case of a young woman with whom a behavior therapist decided to do assertion training. As role-playing procedures were described, the client stiffened in her chair and then began to sob. To proceed with the training without dealing with her reaction to the description of it would of course be insensitive and poor clinical practice. An awareness of psychoanalytic theories had sensitized the therapist to the possibility that assertion *symbolized* something to the client. The therapist gently encouraged the woman to talk freely, to free-associate, to the idea of assertion training. She recalled a series of incidents from childhood in which her parents had criticized the way she acted with her friends, without providing support and constructive suggestions about other ways to behave. Without initially being aware of it herself, the client was reminded of this pain from the past when the therapist suggested that she learn more assertive ways of dealing with others. The psychologist was able to distinguish the current enterprise, assertion training, from the unhelpful and negative criticisms made in the past and thereby persuaded the young woman to try role playing. The incident also pointed up the client's unresolved problems with her parents and with authority figures in general.

Summary

In this chapter we have reviewed theory and research in behavior therapy, a branch of clinical psychology which attempts to apply the methodologies and principles of experimental psychology to the therapeutic modification of human behavior. Several areas of this burgeoning field were surveyed. Via counterconditioning a substitute response is elicited in the presence of a stimulus that has evoked an undesired response. Systematic desensitization is believed by some to be effective because of counterconditioning. In operant conditioning desired responses are taught and undesired ones discouraged by applying the contingencies of reward and punishment. The token economy is a prime example of the clinical application of operant conditioning. Modeling—helping the client to acquire new responses and unlearn old ones by observing models—is useful in eliminating fears and efficient in teaching new patterns of behavior. Cognitive-restructuring techniques, such as rational-emotive therapy, alter the thoughts that are believed to underlie emotional disorders. Self-control was examined and found to present some interesting challenges to the behavioral paradigm; an active and conscious human being by autonomous and deliberate choice acts independently of environmental influences. Finally, several important issues in behavior therapy—such as the role of underlying causes, relationship factors, and the possibilities of integrating some parts of psychoanalytic theorizing into behavior therapy—were discussed in the hope of providing the reader with a better and more sophisticated grasp of a field that is both promising and controversial.

chapter 20

GROUP AND MARITAL THERAPY, COMMUNITY PSYCHOLOGY, AND SOMATIC TREATMENT

Group and Marital Therapy
Community Psychology
Somatic Treatment

In this chapter we review three means of therapeutic intervention. Although different from one another in many important ways, they are similar in making far more efficient use of professional time than the one-to-one therapies reviewed in the preceding two chapters. In group and marital therapy a professional treats a number of patients simultaneously; community psychology is oriented toward prevention and treats the problems of patients without removing them from their customary surroundings; and somatic treatments—drugs, surgery, and electroconvulsive therapy—do not require much time to administer. All three, then, are more economical than individual therapy. As we shall soon see, however, economy is not the primary reason that any of the three is chosen. Rather, each treatment has developed from a particular rationale for providing effective help.

Group and Marital Therapy

A single therapist can obviously treat more people by seeing them in groups, and charge lower fees, than would be possible were he or she seeing them individually. But it would be a mistake to estimate the value of group therapy only in economic terms. Most group therapists regard their form of treatment as *uniquely* appropriate for accomplishing certain goals. For example, group members can learn vicariously (see page 53) when attention is focused on another participant. Social pressures, too, can be surprisingly strong in groups. If a therapist tells an individual client that his or her behavior seems hostile even when hostility is not intended, the message may be rejected; however, if three or four other people agree with the interpretation, the person may find it much more difficult to dismiss the observation. In addition, many people derive comfort and support solely from the knowledge that others have problems similar to their own.

As we saw in the two preceding chapters, the literature on individual psychotherapy is confusing and extensive; so too is the information available on group therapy. Virtually every technique or theory employed in individual therapy has been, or can be, used for treating people in groups. Thus there are psychoanalytic groups (Slavson, 1950; Wolf, 1949), Gestalt groups (Perls, 1969), client-centered groups (Rogers, 1970), behavior therapy groups (Lazarus, 1968a; Paul and Shannon, 1966; Upper and Ross, 1980), and countless other kinds, including special-purpose groups such as Alcoholics Anonymous (see page 308). We shall examine closely a few group psychotherapies, in hopes of imparting some idea of the range of prevailing theories and procedures, and then review the evidence bearing on their effectiveness.

Insight-Oriented Group Therapy

Moreno's psychodrama

Jacob L. Moreno, a Viennese psychiatrist, is said to have coined the term "group psychotherapy" in 1931. He was unquestionably one of the most influential and colorful figures in the field. The essence of the form of group therapy he introduced—_psychodrama_—is to have participants take parts and act out their feelings as though they were in a play, with the therapist assuming the role of director of the psychic drama. A male patient might be asked to converse with another group member playing the role of his father. By this spontaneous, unrehearsed playacting the patient is apparently helped to express his feelings and perceptions about his father more effectively than were he to try to verbalize them. "We must stimulate the patients to be concrete, and bring forth their feelings and thoughts in a structured form" (Moreno and Kipper, 1968, p. 56). Like other forms of group therapy, psychodrama makes unique use of the group as a vehicle for changing people. Group members provide a company of potential actors with whom to stage the dramatic presentations.

To facilitate role taking and to give the proceedings the aspect of a true drama, Moreno advised using an actual stage. The presence of an audience also contributes to the theatrical atmosphere. Moreno suggested many kinds of role taking to promote the expression and confrontation of true feelings. For example, the _mirroring_ technique is designed for patients who have difficulty expressing themselves in action or in words: another person, an "auxiliary ego," portrays the patient as best he can, thereby furnishing him concrete information on how others view him. In _role reversal_ actors exchange roles; in _magic shop_ the protagonist may "buy" a desired personal quality by temporarily giving up one already possessed. At all times the aim of

A psychodrama session. The director-therapist (above) is guiding the patients in their roles.

A group of business people at a sensitivity training session. The T-group was originally devised to increase the efficiency of managers by making them more aware of their feelings and more sensitive to other people.

the players is to express in dramatic form true feelings about certain situations. The therapist sometimes actively directs the "play" to ensure that therapeutic gain will be the maximum.

Should psychodrama be classified as insight or action-oriented therapy? Clearly, the therapist assumes responsibility for what happens during the session; furthermore, he or she goads the patients into specific behavior during treatment. On the other hand, the ultimate goal of the treatment was seen by Moreno as insight into motivation. Thus psychodrama appears to be an insight therapy that goes beyond reliance on the verbal interpretive methods of psychoanalysis but still tries to help patients achieve an understanding of their true motivations and needs.

Unfortunately, there is no body of controlled research on psychodrama, so it is not possible to assess the efficacy of Moreno's ideas.

Sensitivity training and encounter groups

Without question, one of the most exciting developments in clinical psychology and psychiatry is the _sensitivity training group,_ or T-group, movement. Aronson (1972) differentiates the T-group from the more radical "encounter group," which grew in popularity primarily on the West coast at such places as the Esalen Institute. T-groups, he contends, tend to rely more on verbal procedures and to avoid the physical contact, touching exercises, and unrestrained expressions of emotion employed by many encounter groups. Aronson's distinction is not accepted by all workers, however. Rogers (1970) traces the development of encounter groups to his training of counselors at the University of Chicago in

1946, in which he emphasized personal growth and improved interpersonal communication. We would agree with his judgment that T-groups and encounter groups are usually impossible to distinguish one from the other nowadays.

The T-group was originally conceived in 1947, and the National Training Laboratory was established through conferences on small-group dynamics held in Bethel, Maine. The impetus came from colleagues of Kurt Lewin, who was a famous social psychologist at MIT. The original groups were made up of people in industry, and the goal was to increase efficiency in business practices at the highest levels of management by making executives more aware of their impact on other people and of their own feelings about others. Over the past thirty years millions of people have participated in such groups, including no doubt some readers of this book. Attention has shifted in these years from group dynamics to individual growth.

The T-group is best viewed as educational; it was not designed for those who are seriously disturbed. The T-group promotes personal growth and better understanding in people who are functioning reasonably well. Generally speaking, members are encouraged to focus on their "here and now" relationships with one another. Individuals are often drawn to T-groups because, even though their lives are not full of problems, they feel that they are missing something, that their days are lived through without intensity and intimacy. Aronson lists some general goals of T-groups.

1. To develop a willingness to examine one's

behavior and to experiment with new ways of behaving.

2. To learn more about people in general.

3. To become more authentic and honest in interpersonal relations.

4. To work cooperatively with people rather than assuming an authoritarian or submissive manner.

5. To develop the ability to resolve conflicts through logical and rational thinking rather than through coercion and manipulation of others.

In the most general terms T-groups and encounter groups provide a setting wherein people are encouraged to behave in an unguarded fashion. They are then helped to receive and give feedback, to see how they come across to and affect others and to examine how they feel about their behavior and that of others. They are expected to become more aware and accepting of themselves and of other group members. Aronson (1972) provides the following descriptions of a group session getting started.

. . . He [the leader] . . . falls into silence.

Minutes pass. They seem like hours. The group members may look at each other or out the window. Typically, participants may look at the trainer for guidance or direction. None is forthcoming. After several minutes, someone might express his discomfort. This may or may not be responded to. Eventually, in a typical group, someone will express annoyance at the leader: "I'm getting sick of this. This is a waste of time. How come you're not doing your job? What the hell are we paying you for? Why don't you tell us what we're supposed to do?" There may be a ripple of applause in the background. But someone else might jump in and ask the first person why he is so bothered by a lack of direction—does he need someone to tell him what to do? And the T-group is off and running (p. 241).

Levels of Communication Figure 20.1 is Aronson's schematic representation of a dyadic or two-person interaction. In our everyday lives we usually operate at level P_3, namely behaving in some verbal or nonverbal way toward another person. Usually the recipient of our P_3 behavior eventually responds at level R_4, evaluating us.

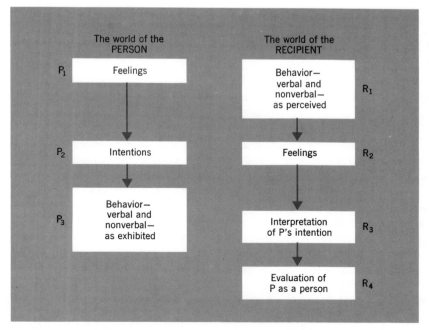

FIGURE **20.1**
Schematic representation of a two-person interaction. The diagram illustrates the different levels of communication possible. After Aronson, 1972.

There are obviously many points at which misjudgments can occur. For example, at level R_3 the recipient may misinterpret P's intention. Even though the person, a man, may feel warmly (P_1) toward his friend the recipient, he may have difficulty expressing warmth and therefore display sarcasm at P_3. The recipient will then interpret P's intention as a wish to hurt him (R_3), rather than as a desire to express warm feelings toward him. Without the open discussion of feelings that is encouraged in a T-group, the recipient can reject (R_4) the person as a nasty individual and never come to understand that the person really feels warmly (P_1) but has not learned to express his feelings (P_3) appropriately. Or the following might occur. A person may be expressing warm feelings in a totally open way, at P_3, but the recipient, for reasons of his own, may be so suspicious of any expression of warmth that he misinterprets (R_3) the person's intentions and rejects him instead of acknowledging and enjoying the expression of warmth. A properly run T-group encourages the participants to break down their interpersonal communications and reactions into all the various components so that they can examine their true feelings toward other persons and their perceptions of what they are receiving from them.

Within the T-group people talk frankly and listen to one another. Usually the group works on the ongoing interactions, rather than examining past histories, as would be the case in a psychoanalytically oriented group. The emphasis on openness is not necessarily a violation of a person's right to privacy, although there is little question that in some groups people feel pressured to reveal more about themselves than they might wish. Experienced and competent group leaders watch for undue coercion and direct the stream of conversation away from an individual when they sense excessive probing into the person's private feelings.

Immediate and open feedback from fellow group members, including the leader, is one of the principal tools for achieving the kind of learning desired in a T-group. Thus A may be continually interrupting B and yet be unaware of her dislike for B. Other group members, or the leader, might interject a comment to A that she is apparently having difficulty expressing certain feelings to B and perhaps would like to do so more directly than by interrupting him. Furthermore, A might be made aware of the negative impact that her constant interruptions have on B, perhaps even more negative than an honest expression of dislike would have. T-group members learn to give constructive feedback tactfully and to receive it without defensiveness.

Role of T-group Leader   Aronson has summarized the role and function of the group leader in a T-group.

1. The leader or trainer is a full member of the group. His or her own feelings, reactions, and effects on others are as legitimate a subject of discourse as are those of any other group member. Unlike some group therapists, T-group leaders do not hold themselves aloof from their clients.

2. Being professionals, however, leaders are busy performing other functions as well. They may occasionally comment on what is going on in the group, or they may step in to help people with difficult encounters and to make certain that participants discuss their feelings about others rather than judging them.

3. On the assumption that discoveries made by one's self are more meaningful and longer lasting than insights and observations doled out by experts, the group leader tries whenever possible not to intervene. At times, for example, he or she finds it best to remain silent.

4. Competent trainers will make every effort not to impose their will and ideas on the other participants, but they are of course aware of the very powerful position that they occupy in the group. It seems likely that some of the unfortunate abuses of encounter groups and T-groups can be attributed to the all-too-human tendency of some trainers to wield this power unwisely.

Variations   Sensitivity or encounter groups vary in a number of ways. Rogers's (1970) groups tend to operate according to his individual client-centered therapy as outlined in Chapter 18; the leader tries to clarify the feelings of

An encounter group exercise designed to foster trust.

group members, on the assumption that growth can occur as people confront their emotions with honesty. The group leader—or "facilitator"—tends to be less active than in the T-groups Aronson describes. Some groups may meet for hours at a time, perhaps over a weekend, with little if any sleep allowed. Such *marathons* (Bach, 1966; Mintz, 1967; Stoller, 1968) rely on fatigue and extended exposure to a particular set of social conditions to weaken "defenses" and help the participants become more open and presumably more authentic. Many encounter group enthusiasts use exercises to break the ice (Schutz, 1967). For example, a man may be instructed to close his eyes and allow himself to be carried around by other group members, which is supposed to help him trust them. In another exericse two people stare into each other's eyes without speaking. Such maneuvers are meant to loosen people up, making clear to them that in this social setting feelings are to be expressed openly without censorship or fear of punishment. Bindrim (1968) introduced nudity as an aid to lowering defenses. Drug addict "Synanon" groups tend even to be brutal in the directness of their confrontations (Yablonsky, 1962).

Behavior Therapy Groups

Individualized behavior therapy in groups
Arnold Lazarus (1968a), a pioneer in group behavior therapy, has pointed out that a behavior therapist may, primarily for reasons of efficiency, choose to treat several people suffering from the same kind of problem by seeing them in a group rather than individually. The emphasis, as in one-to-one therapy, remains on interactions between the therapist and each individual patient or client.[1]

Group desensitization (Lazarus, 1961) is a good example of this individualized approach. A single therapist can teach deep muscle relaxation and present a hierarchy to each member of the group simultaneously, thus saving therapist time. Fears handled in this manner include test anxiety (Nawas, Fishman, and Pucel, 1970), snake phobias (Ritter, 1968), and anxiety about public speaking (Paul and Shannon, 1966).

[1] Gestalt therapy groups generally operate in this fashion as well. The therapist works with one group member at a time; often this individual will sit in a particular chair, or on a particular pillow, referred to as "the hot seat."

Another example of individualized behavior therapy given to members of a group was Lazarus's (1968a) treatment of several impotent men in one group and of several frigid women in another. Treatment for each group consisted of didactic discussion of sexual functioning, including instructions on ways of providing noncoital sexual pleasure to a partner, as well as group desensitization of related sexual fears. Therapeutic messages and instructions emanated from a single therapist to each of a number of people at the same time (Figure 20.2a).

Therapies given to groups to help members lose weight (Wollersheim, 1970) and stop smoking (Koenig and Masters, 1965) have also been successful. Again, a particular technique was used on each member of the group. Whether this should be considered group therapy is open to question. The members of these special-purpose groups do seem to provide valuable encouragement and social support for one another, however.

Social-skills training groups

Social skills are taught to groups of people who have similar deficits in relating to others. The members of these groups rehearse together the skills that they are learning and thus provide one another unique and appropriate help in changing behavior. Because members interact, the lines of communication are among all participants, not just between therapist and participant (Figure 20.2b). Groups of depressed people, for example, have learned social skills that are likely to

bring them more reinforcement from others (Lewinsohn, Weinstein, and Alper, 1970).

Assertion training groups

Assertiveness is a social skill. Lazarus conducts assertion training groups composed of about ten people of the same sex. At the first meeting he describes the general goals of the therapy group, commenting particularly on the problems that unassertiveness can create for individuals in our society. He also suggests that the therapy group can provide a good setting for cooperative problem solving. Like Rogers, he calls for honesty and acceptance within the group and prescribes constructive criticism and the diligent practice of new skills. Then members introduce themselves briefly, and the others are encouraged to comment on the manner in which they presented themselves, especially if it was apologetic.

Members of the group are then given a situation that calls for an assertive response (see page 614). The therapist turns the situation into a skit and demonstrates being assertive. Then group members, in pairs or larger groupings, take turns playing out the skit. The therapist and other members tell the persons practicing assertiveness what they are doing right and doing wrong. Assertiveness is rehearsed again and again in each situation until members feel natural acting in this fashion. Of particular importance are assignments carried out by the members between sessions. People are encouraged to describe both successful and unsuccessful attempts at assertive behavior in their everyday activities, and they

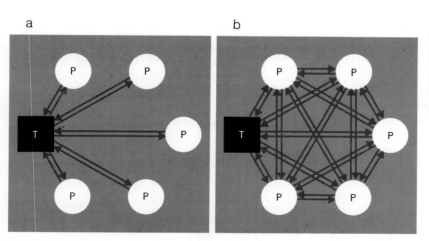

a   b

FIGURE **20.2**
Distinction between individualized group therapy (a) and group therapy in which interactions among all the members are regarded as important (b). Arrows indicate lines of communication and influences; T stands for therapist, P for patient.

often role-play within the group to help them improve on past or anticipated performances. The emphasis is at all times on the benefits to be derived from appropriate and effective expression of both positive and negative feelings. If the therapist is sensitive and skillful, he or she is able to create an atmosphere in which group members begin to trust themselves to express criticism without fearing that they are hurting other people's feelings. Assertion groups may even be effective in reducing the compliant, withdrawn behavior of chronic schizophrenics (Bloomfield, 1973).

There are some similarities between Lazarus's assertion training groups and the sensitivity training groups described earlier, but an important difference is the attention Lazarus pays to between-session activities; people are trained within the group to make specific changes later, outside the group therapy setting. Although T-groups are similarly concerned with helping people change their everyday lives, as yet much less systematic attention has been paid to what clients do between group sessions.

Evaluation of Group Therapy

Like other therapies, the T-group and encounter movement has its share of glowing testimonials.

> *I have known individuals for whom the encounter experience has meant almost miraculous change in the depth of their communication with spouse and children. Sometimes for the first time real feelings are shared. . . . I have seen teachers who have transformed their classroom . . . into a personal, caring, trusting, learning group, where students participate fully and openly in forming the curriculum and all the other aspects of their education. Tough business executives who described a particular business relationship as hopeless have gone home and changed it into a constructive one (Rogers, 1970, p. 71).*

Such observations, especially by a highly skilled and innovative clinician, contribute to the growing faith many people have in encounter groups.

Comments of this nature do not, however, satisfy most scientists of human behavior.

Some critics have suggested that those who participate in T-groups learn only how to participate in T-groups. They are not able to transfer to real-life situations the insights and skills that have been acquired in a group (Houts and Serber, 1972). Transfer of learning is a difficult problem for, whether we like it or not, the real world is not set up to encourage openness and frankness. Those who are not operating by the rules of a T-group may be offended by the open and honest expression of feelings. Indeed, as Aronson reminds us, if someone insists that others be totally open when they do not want to be, he or she is being insensitive to their feelings and so really has *not* learned some of the essentials from what might have seemed a good T-group experience. This is not to say that T-group experiences can never transfer to the real world. Knowledge of how a person feels about others and comes across to them may be extremely useful in everyday activities, even though the overt behavior encouraged in a T-group is not continued.

Because the independent variables are so complex and difficult to control, it is extraordinarily difficult to do good research with groups. As with all psychotherapy research, there is little agreement on what are the best means of measuring success. There is wide disparity in how often groups meet and for how long, and the people assembled are quite diverse. Few studies have employed credible controls for the placebo effect. Most importantly, little attention is paid to what actually *happens* in the group. Mindful of these methodological shortcomings, Smith (1975) has offered the following tentative conclusions about T-groups that met for at least twenty hours and were compared to no-treatment controls.

1. T-group participants tend to view themselves more favorably after a group experience, and this effect often persists for months afterward.

2. Some studies suggest that group members come to view themselves as more in control of their behavior, more responsible for themselves.

3. There is little if any good evidence that T-

groups help participants become more open-minded and less prejudiced.

4. Some documentation suggests that participants are more willing to disclose personal information about themselves.

5. Since the purpose of a sensitivity training group is to foster understanding of others and their needs, it is surprising how little evidence shows participants becoming more empathic.

6. Some evidence suggests that participants improve more than controls in communication skills.

7. Some data indicate that associates of former group participants see them as functioning better in their everyday activities. For example, they seem more relaxed, more communicative. But in most instances the observers knew that their friends and colleagues had been in a group program, thus weakening the import of this observation.

Additional generalizations about other kinds of groups come from a careful review of studies that met certain methodological criteria, such as random assignment of subjects to different treatments; but "... these constraints have excluded the bulk of the potential literature" (Bednar and Kaul, 1978, p. 772), a sad commentary on the state of research in the complicated area of group therapy.

1. Dependent people appear to do better in a highly structured group, whereas independent, better-functioning individuals improve to a greater extent in groups that have less structure and offer more opportunity for self-expression.

2. Virtually no research has been directed at the factors generally assumed to be centrally curative in groups, such as learning by imitation, realizing that others have the same problems, and acquiring feelings of belongingness (Yalom, 1975).

3. Marathon groups may have no particular advantage over similarly constituted groups that meet for shorter periods of time; in fact, concentrating group hours in a few marathon sessions may accomplish less than spreading them over more sessions.

4. Beneficial long-term changes do occur for a variety of group therapies, but seldom have there been appropriate attention-placebo controls for nonspecific factors. (This complaint should by now be familiar to the reader.)

5. Casualties of therapy, people who become worse in the course of treatment, are very few, with most studies finding rates of less than 3 percent. Members who do become worse are usually particularly disturbed. Those responsible for selecting group members try to screen out people who might need more individual attention or for whom the stress of confrontation and open sharing of feelings with others might be too great. Particular *styles* of leadership, such as a challenging, authoritative attitude which pushes group members to deal with more feeling, especially anger, than they are ready for, may be harmful (Lieberman, Yalom, and Miles, 1973; see Box 20.1).

6. No body of evidence supports the superiority of one kind of group therapy over another. Although one theoretical approach may be more suitable than another for treating a particular problem, research has not yet addressed such questions.

7. Cohesive groups apparently produce better results for their members than do less cohesive groups, and self-disclosure provides material for discussion (see Box 20.2).

8. It has long been assumed that progress in group therapy is facilitated by feedback, by candid comments made by one person to another about the feelings he or she arouses, the impressions made, "how you're comin' across." Evidence is beginning to emerge that feedback is indeed useful, especially when negative feedback, "You sound imperious when you ask things of people," is followed by positive feedback, "I like the way you said that" (Jacobs et al., 1973).

BOX 20.1 Therapy, for Better or for Worse

In 1966 Allen Bergin applied the term *deterioration effect* to the harm that can come to someone from therapy. Several reviews of the literature since his initial report (Bergin, 1971; Bergin and Lambert, 1978; Lambert, Bergin, and Collins, 1977; Strupp, Hadley, and Gomes-Schwartz, 1977) indicate an unpleasant fact of life: although individual psychotherapy benefits many people, some are hurt by the experience. Group therapy (Yalom and Lieberman, 1971) and marital and family treatment (Gurman and Kniskern, 1978) also have casualties. Risk of being harmed is of course not peculiar to psychological intervention. Patients have been made worse by a wide range of medical procedures as well, including electroconvulsive therapy (Elmore and Sugarman, 1975) and the prescription of psychoactive drugs (Shader and DiMascio, 1970), both of which aim at psychological change.

Some people who do *not* seek treatment also deteriorate. Avoiding contact with a mental health professional is no guarantee against getting worse!*

What are the factors that might be responsible for the deterioration effect? Highly disturbed people and those with great expectations and a need to improve are among those often harmed. Moreover, therapies of all orientations are subject to the deterioration effect. Reports from the Menninger Foundation, a renowned center for research and training in psychoanalysis, suggest that Freudian therapy may be too stressful for people with little "ego strength," poor interpersonal relationships, and little ability to tolerate anxiety and frustration (Kernberg, 1973; Horwitz, 1974).

The therapist will bear ultimate responsibility for harm to the client. Lieberman, Yalom, and Miles (1973) found casualties in encounter groups that were led by an "aggressive stimulator," by a challenging, authoritative person who insisted on self-disclosure and catharsis of group participants even when they were not ready or willing for it. Any therapy can be abused by a practitioner who follows it foolishly, without tailoring it to the needs of the client. Some clients, desperate for support, reassurance, and advice and lacking in interpersonal skills, may become worse if a client-centered therapist unflinchingly declines to provide some guidance. Other clients, already overly dependent on others, may not be able to make choices and grow if the behavior therapist does not recognize this as a need and, instead, takes total charge of their lives. Any therapist or community worker can err when assessing the patient's problem, thereby embarking on treatment that cannot possibly help him or her. In addition, therapists, it must be remembered, are only human beings! Their training and experience do not qualify them as Superpeople in Mental Health. Their own needs and personal problems, even though they know they should not allow them to intrude, can blind them to the needs of the client and can otherwise reduce their ability and willingness to work on the client's behalf. Sadly, some therapists are unethical as well. A few go so far as to claim that clients, always the more attractive ones, can profit from a sexual encounter with the therapist; these workers sometimes initiate or permit sexual intimacies. Licensing laws and codes of ethics do not themselves ensure that therapists will always act wisely and humanely. Most do, and the vast majority of clients are *not* hurt by them. But the deterioration effect has been observed too often to be disregarded or underestimated.

* Several noted behavior therapists have recently examined the studies on which Bergin and others base their claim of a deterioration effect. They (Mays and Franks,1980; Rachman and Wilson, 1980) suggest that the evidence is far weaker than assumed earlier. It is proving as difficult to show that therapy can sometimes harm as it has been to show that it can help. One problem is insufficient information on "spontaneous deterioration," that is, on the rate at which people who receive no therapy at all become worse. We know that some disturbed and untreated people do get worse. "If spontaneous deterioration did not take place, mental health workers would join the ranks of the unemployed . . ." (Rachman and Wilson, 1980, p. 99). But therapy outcome studies have thus far failed to assess this deterioration adequately. Thus certain people who deteriorate while in therapy may do so not because of the therapy itself, but because of factors outside the consulting room, beyond the control of the therapist. Even so, some patients clearly worsen during therapy, which raises serious empirical and ethical questions.

BOX 20.2 Cohesion and Self-Disclosure in Groups—Some Recent Ways To Pose the Questions

Throughout the literature on group therapy, it is asserted that cohesion and self-disclosure contribute to the success of a group. Members of a cohesive group become accepting and supportive of one another; they are open to influence from the group and feel safe discussing their problems and exploring possible solutions. A cohesive group also allows members to express anger and hostility, without the fear, common to their everyday lives, that relationships will then worsen irreparably (Yalom, 1975). Each of the following factors (Flowers, 1979) reflects group cohesion and, if manipulated, increases group cohesion.

1. Eye contact with whoever is speaking.
2. More interactions among clients than between the group leader and a client.
3. Not allowing one particular group member to become the focus of criticism or other negative messages.
4. Self-disclosure.
5. Trust in other group members.

Clients apparently improve more in groups that have a cohesive atmosphere (Flowers, Booraem, and Hartman, 1977). This is an important finding, for it suggests specific ways of structuring group therapy to enhance its overall effectiveness. For example, a group leader might deliberately make as much eye contact as possible with group members as they speak and encourage members to relate to one another instead of to himself. Yet to be determined are the processes underlying effectiveness of cohesive groups, but it will probably turn out that social influence in the most general sense is stronger when groups are cohesive. The group per se, as indicated earlier, provides unique help, encouragement, and support to people in their efforts to change.

Self-disclosure is also regarded as desirable in all kinds of group therapy, for if members do not bring up problems they wish to work on, the group will have little material to discuss. How can a group leader encourage members to raise problems for examination? A trusting atmosphere must first be created and maintained by the therapist, and oftentimes group members must agree that what is discussed during sessions should remain in the group, that is, it should not be mentioned to people outside the group without first asking permission. "Problem cards" (Goodman, 1969) help members to disclose their troubles. Before a group session each member is asked to write down on a small file card one or two current problems, one judged by the client to be relatively difficult and immediate, the other less difficult and immediate. Then, during the session, the therapist asks each group member whether he or she would like to disclose a problem for the group to work on. The client is free to disclose a problem not previously written on the card; the client may also demur and not divulge anything. Research indicates that systematic use of the cards increases the amount of self-disclosure, perhaps because they prompt clients to mention a problem (Flowers, 1979). In fact, when two problems are written on a card rather than one, self-disclosure is even more frequent.

The ratio of opinion to data is disturbingly high in the literature on group therapy. The kind of focused research just discussed may help provide better-quality information on the processes that lead to beneficial change in group settings.

Family and Marital Therapy

The terms family therapy and marital therapy do not denote a set procedure. Although the focus is on at least two members of a family, how the therapist views the problem, what techniques are chosen to alleviate them, how often family members are seen, and whether children and even grandparents are included are all variables of treatment.

It was noticed that many people who improved through individual therapy, usually in an institution, had a relapse when they returned home. Theories blaming family relationships for schizophrenia were based on such observations. Sometimes forces worked the other way around. The improvement of the "identified patient" was destructive to the family. Apparently the family unit and the relationships within it are sometimes distorted and need restructuring. As an overall approach, family therapy seems to have begun with the work of John Bell (1975), a psychologist working in the 1940s at the Mental Research Institute in Palo Alto, California. In the past forty years an increasing number of mental health professionals have devoted their professional lives to this kind of work. During the 1960s the efforts of Virginia Satir (1967), a psychiatric social worker, and of Donald Jackson (and Weakland, 1961), a psychiatrist, also at MRI, provided the field with fresh impetus.

It is difficult to categorize the theoretical approach of the MRI people, but it is fair to say that their work has been much more behavioral in nature than insight-oriented. Faulty communication patterns are identified, and so too are uneasy relationships and inflexibility. Members of the family come to realize how their behavior affects their relations with others. They then devote their energies to making specific changes. Few family therapists are concerned with past history, and none believes that working with only one member of the family can be fruitful. Whatever the clinical problem, the family therapist views it as that of a *system*, the family, and therefore treated to the best advantage within this group context.

There is almost universal agreement among marital therapists and researchers, regardless of theoretical orientation, that conflict is *inevitable* in a marriage or in any other long-term relationship. The aura of the honeymoon passes when the couple makes unromantic decisions about where to live, where to seek employment, how to budget money, what kind of meals to prepare and who is to prepare them, when to visit in-laws, when to have children if they plan to have a family, and whether to experiment with novel techniques to keep alive the spark of physical attraction. Now, in addition, they have the changing nature of gender roles to negotiate. For example, if both spouses work, shall their place of residence be determined by the husband's employment or by the wife's? This list, some readers might term it litany, of sources of conflict must be handled by any two people living together, whether they are married or not, whether they are of the opposite sex or not.[2] Authorities agree that it is the way couples deal with such inherent conflicts that determines the quality and duration of their cohabitation relationship (for example, Schwartz and Schwartz, 1980).

A strategy some couples adopt, deliberately or unconsciously, is to avoid acknowledging disagreements and conflicts. Because they believe in the reality of the fairy tale ending, "And they lived happily ever after," any sign that their own marriage is not going smoothly is so threatening that it must be ignored. Unfortunately, dissatisfactions and resentments usually develop and begin to take their toll as time goes by. Because the partners do not quarrel, they may appear "a perfect couple" to outside observers. But without discussing things openly, they drift apart emotionally.

Most marital therapy is conjoint; the partners see one therapist or a pair of therapists together. Distressed couples do not react very positively toward each other, which is not surprising! Jacobson and Margolin (1979), two behavioral marital therapists, recommend attending to this problem as an initial step in helping a couple improve their marriage. One strategy is the "caring days" idea of Richard Stuart (1976). The wife agrees to devote herself to doing nice things for her husband on a given day, without expecting anything in return. The husband will do the

---

[2] Most of what is discussed under the rubric of marital therapy is relevant as well to unconventional relationships, such as those of gay people. For this reason the term couples therapy is becoming more common among mental health professionals.

same for her on another day. If successful, this strategy accomplishes at least two important things: first, it breaks the cycle of distance and suspicion and of aversive control of each other in the distressed marriage; and second, it shows the giving partner that he or she is able to affect the spouse in a positive way. This enhanced sense of positive control is achieved simply by pleasing the partner. The giving can be more reciprocal; each partner may agree to please the other in certain specific ways, in anticipation of the partner's reciprocating immediately. For example, a husband may agree to prepare dinner on Tuesdays, and on that day the wife contracts to stop at the supermarket on her way home from work and do the weekly shopping. The improved atmosphere that develops as a consequence of each partner's doing nice things for the other and having nice things done for him or her in return helps each become motivated to please the other person on future occasions.

Behavioral marital therapists generally adopt Thibaut and Kelley's (1959) exchange theory of interaction. According to this view of human relationships, people value others if they receive a high ratio of benefits to costs, that is, if they see themselves getting at least as much from the other person as they have to expend. Furthermore, people are assumed to be more disposed to continue a given relationship if other alternatives are less attractive to them, promising fewer benefits and costing more. Therapists therefore try to encourage a mutual dispensing of rewards by spouse A and spouse B. The number of positive events shared by the couple increases. We might ask what this reciprocity view does to qualities of the relationship, however. Might not a truly satisfactory relationship be one in which partners do things for each other *without* expecting anything in return? Both behavioral marital therapy and other kinds have deterioration effects about 6 percent of the time (Gurman and Kniskern, 1978), which should caution workers that much remains to be studied and explained.

All forms of marital therapy try to improve communication. Each partner is trained to listen empathically to the other and to state clearly to the partner what he or she understands is being said and what the feelings behind the remarks are. One way to improve marital communication

is to distinguish between the intent of a remark and its impact.[3] Partner A, for example, may wish to be helpful by asking partner B whether he can get her something from the store, but this question may have a negative impact if she would prefer him to stay home and help her with a project. The husband's intent, then, would be positive, but his question would affect his wife negatively. Research has shown that the communications of distressed and undistressed couples may not differ so much in intent as in impact. In one study Gottman and his colleagues (1976) found that both types of couples made the same number of positive statements to partners, but distressed spouses reported having heard fewer positive statements than undistressed spouses. Gottman and his colleagues have proposed one specific technique for clarifying intent when two partners are in a heated argument going nowhere. The husband calls "Stop action" and asks his wife to tell him what she believes he is trying to say. Or the wife asks the same of her husband. The feedback indicates immediately whether remarks are having the intended impact.

The therapist must often decide whether to treat the husband and wife as a couple or to concentrate on other problems that are often part of a distressed marriage. A marriage can seemingly be disrupted by a serious behavior problem of a child. Although some marital therapists (for example, Framo, 1975) insist that child problems are caused by marital problems, cause-effect relationships in families are poorly understood. As we have already indicated (see page 425), a child's schizophrenia can upset the stability of the family.

Many operant behavior therapists follow Gerald Patterson's (1974a) practice of working with the parents to alter reinforcement of the child whose behavior is a problem. The child is involved little if at all in treatment. An improvement in the child's behavior often clears up much distress between husband and wife. But sometimes a child's aberrant behavior can be traced to the marital distress; although the child may be the "identified patient," his or her "problems" may better be regarded as reflecting

[3] The reader will find the following similar to Aronson's analysis of a two-person exchange.

BOX 20.3 Behavioral Family Therapy for Schizophrenia

There has been great interest in recent years in family therapy to help acute schizophrenics discharged from a hospital maintain a life outside. Falloon and Liberman are conducting a collaborative project at the University of Southern California and at the University of California at Los Angeles (Falloon, Boyd, and McGill, 1980). As indicated earlier (see page 425), when schizophrenics return home, the "expressed emotion," the level of criticism and hostility directed toward them by family members, bears on how long they manage to remain at home.

Family members, including the patients, participate in sessions in their own homes in which the importance of regular medication is stressed. They are instructed in ways to express both positive and negative feelings in a constructive empathic manner. Information on how to cope with symptoms of the patient and on how to structure the home situation to reduce emotional turmoil is dispensed. It is made clear to patient and family alike that schizophrenia is primarily a biochemical illness, but that proper medication and the kind of psychosocial treatment they are receiving can reduce stress on the patient and prevent relapses and deterioration. Treatment extends over two years, with more frequent sessions during the first nine months when the danger of relapse is especially high.

This behavioral family treatment is being compared to an individual therapy in which the patient is seen alone at a clinic, with supportive discussions centering on problems in daily living and developing a social network. Family members of patients in this control group are seldom seen, and when they are, it is not in conjoint home sessions with the patients.

Ongoing assessments are made of the patient's symptomatology, with special attention given to signs of relapse, such as delusions of control and hallucinations. Family members are also evaluated for their problem-solving skills and for the emotions they express toward the patient. All patients, including the controls, are maintained on antipsychotic medication, primarily Thorazine, which is monitored and adjusted throughout the project by an independent psychiatrist unaware of which patients are receiving family therapy and which individual.

The preliminary findings are encouraging. At the time of the initial report, seven patients were in their third month of family therapy and eight in their third month of individual therapy. None of the family therapy patients had relapsed, but three of the individual therapy control patients had, one of them twice. Most importantly, the families receiving the behavioral family therapy in their homes had improved their emotional communication and their problem-solving skills, whereas the control families had not. The intensive at-home training of families in empathic listening and problem solving is reducing their criticism and hostility. The working hypothesis of the study is, of course, that discharged schizophrenics are more likely to relapse if families are critical and hostile and cannot cope with having in their midst a previously ill patient who may begin to have problems once again. Teaching both patient and family in an explicit manner what is known about schizophrenia, explaining to them the importance of minimizing emotional tension, and providing training in empathic communication and management of family crises may turn out to foster better social adjustment of schizophrenics.*

* Falloon (personal communication, 1981) reports that after a year none of the seven former patients receiving family therapy has relapsed.

marital conflict. In such instances family-marital therapists usually decide to intervene in the marital relationship, hoping that the child's difficulties will diminish if the parents learn to get along better. Unfortunately, there is little decisive information on where it is best to intervene. Some research done by a Stony Brook group suggests that altering the child's problematic behavior can improve the marital relationship (Oltmanns, Broderick, and O'Leary, 1976), but other research done by the same group indicates that successful marital treatment impacts favorably on children's problems (Turkewitz and O'Leary, 1977).

If a husband is depressed because of self-doubts about his job, there is little reason to alter the marital relationship. Such a strategy might lift his depression somewhat, but it will hardly address the source of the problem. Even so, married partners are usually the most significant people in each other's lives and thereby control many of the most powerful reinforcers that can be brought to bear on their partners. If the depressed man will benefit from being assertive at his job, his wife could encourage this by working with him on becoming more assertive in the marriage as well (Jacobson and Margolin, 1979).

Divorce counseling is a new facet of marital therapy. Until recently marital-family therapists have regarded divorce as an evil to be avoided at all costs, but the advocacy of women's rights, the increasing acceptability of single-parent families, and the greater expectations people have of marriage have prompted mental health workers to explore ways of helping people leave a marriage that appears beyond repair. Therapists of this new specialty help the divorced or separated partner deal with the loss of the spouse, regain self-esteem—a person is likely to blame himself or herself for the "failure" of the marriage—and foster independence (Gurman and Kniskern, 1978). Sometimes divorce counseling or therapy begins while the couple are still living together; the participants might regard as successful a resolution of their ambivalence and fear about separating. Divorce counseling is still too new to have generated much in the way of research, but studies will probably be forthcoming in the near future.

Perhaps because the outcomes and processes of family and marital therapies are so complex and vague, controlled research on whether they work, with what kinds of problems, and how has only begun (Gottman et al., 1976; Weiss, Hops, and Patterson, 1973; Jacobson and Margolin, 1979; O'Leary and Turkewitz, 1978; Stuart, 1980; Gurman and Kniskern, 1978). One important finding from the outcome literature is that conjoint therapy for marital problems appears to be much more successful than individual therapy with one spouse. Indeed, the state of about 10 percent of clients seen individually for marital problems worsens (Gurman and Kniskern, 1978). Conjoint therapy is apparently better for problems that are conjoint in nature.

A great virtue of most family therapists is their willingness to make their work public. It is commonplace to have therapy sessions videotaped, and several professional journals, such as *Family Process* and *Family Therapy,* publish detailed accounts of clinical work. Some professionals view family therapy as a revolution in the treatment of human psychological suffering. Whether it will indeed prove this dramatically effective remains to be seen.

Community Psychology

Prevention and Seeking

Community psychology's focus on prevention sets it apart from what we have studied so far. Gerald Caplan (1964), whose writings have had considerable impact, distinguishes three levels of prevention. *Tertiary prevention* is in many respects equivalent to the treatment of disorders already discussed, but it also seeks to reduce the long-term consequences of having a disorder. Mental health workers help those who have recovered from mental illness to participate fully in the occupational and social life of the community. Providing ex-patients with vocational advice and training and planning special outings for them are examples. *Secondary prevention* consists of efforts to detect problems early, before they become serious, and to prevent their development into chronic disabilities. Quick and accurate assessment by community people—physicians, teachers, clergymen, police officers, court officials, social workers—will allow remedial procedures to begin early. Crisis-intervention work and twenty-four-hour emergency services are other means of secondary prevention.

Primary prevention tries to reduce the incidence of new cases of social and emotional problems in a population. Altering stressful and depriving conditions in the environment and strengthening individuals so that they can resist stress and cope with adversity are two primary prevention means. Attention to overcrowding, poor housing, job discrimination, neighborhood recreation, and school curriculums and neighborhood group work with children from broken homes are examples. Genetic counseling, prenatal care for ghetto mothers, school lunches, and Meals on Wheels are also primary prevention measures. Community psychologists concentrate their efforts on primary and secondary prevention.

Nearly all the therapies reviewed thus far are administered by professional persons with advanced degrees who make themselves available by appointment in offices, clinics, and hospitals. They provide assistance to individuals who initiate the contact themselves or are referred by the courts. Such delivery of services has been referred to as in the *waiting mode* (Rappaport and Chinsky, 1974). In contrast, community psychology operates in the *seeking mode,* that is, those who are troubled or are likely one day to be so are sought out by community workers, some of whom are paraprofessionals supervised by psychologists, psychiatrists, or social workers. Mental health services are often provided outside of offices and clinics, in the schools, businesses, and factories, and on the streetcorners of the person's own community.

Are the techniques employed by community psychologists different from those used in private practice so that a seeking mode makes especially good sense? The answer is complex.

Rappaport and Chinsky (1974) have proposed a scheme to clarify a too often confused area. They suggest that every type of mental health care has two components, the delivery and the conceptual. The delivery component relates to the difference between seeking and waiting, to an *attitude* about making services available. As noted, community psychology has a seeking orientation. The conceptual component, on the other hand, consists of the theoretical and data-based underpinnings of the services. Two examples are psychoanalytic and learning approaches. Table 20.1 illustrates how these two conceptual modes combine with either style of delivery. For example, a twenty-four-hour-a-day "hotline" in a suicide prevention center would be in the community psychology seeking mode. But what specifically the people answering the phones say and do when a call comes in depends on the conceptual mode. One worker might be psychoanalytic in approach; another might construe suicide threats in learning terms. Clearly, these two workers would answer the calls differently— but both would be delivering community psychology. The conceptual components section of Table 20.1 could, of course, be expanded almost indefinitely. Whether a particular conceptual orientation is more suited to one of the two delivery modes than to the other is a separate, and crucial, question, one which creates ongoing controversy among community psychologists and psychiatrists.

TABLE 20.1
Some Possible Models for Mental Health Service
(adapted from Rappaport and Chinsky, 1974)

Conceptual component*	Delivery component	
	Waiting mode	Seeking mode
Psychoanalytic conception	Psychodynamic explanations of abnormal behavior. Therapist waits for patient to initiate contact and then uses insight therapy.	Psychodynamic explanations of abnormal behavior. Professional attempts to prevent illness through public education and extends traditional treatments into community settings.
Behavioral conception	Learning theory interpretation of emotional dysfunction. Therapist waits for client to initiate contact and then uses techniques such as systematic desensitization.	Learning theory interpretation of emotional dysfunction. Professional extends services into the community through public education; trains various nonprofessionals in behavior therapy techniques and social-learning principles.

* Listed here as examples are only two of a large number of possible conceptual components.

Values and the Question of Where To Intervene

In a recent effort to explain the essence of community psychology, Rappaport (1977) proposes that we view society as composed of four levels: the individual, the small group, the organization, and the institution. Therapists will intervene at a given level, depending on their values and goals for people. For example, if the therapist assumes that society itself is benign, human problems will be seen as failures to *adjust to* this benign system. Treatment will therefore attempt to change the *individual* so that he or she will fit into society. This tertiary prevention is pursued in a number of ways—from behavior therapy to psychoanalysis to chemotherapy—but in all these modes of intervention society is considered good and people in need of adjustment to it. In contrast, human problems may be assumed to derive from interpersonal difficulties such as conflicts within families, at work, and in other *small groups.* The therapist will apply family and encounter therapy to help members of the group communicate better. The therapist will *not* try to change just the individual because the problem is assumed to lie in group processes.

If the third level, that of *organizations,* is considered at fault, therapists have another view of human disorders. They "blame" the way units such as schools and prisons operate. To help a child who is failing in her academic work, for example, therapists examine the school curriculum and how it is implemented by principals and teachers; they do *not* provide remedial tutoring for the pupil. Community psychology operates at this level and at the *institutional* level, which is closely related to it but is more abstract and all-inclusive. Institutions refer not to physical entities such as school buildings and prisons but to the basic values and ideologies that characterize a society, its religion, and its politics. For example, the community psychologist may assert that people are unhappy because of a lopsided distribution of wealth and power. Professional efforts would then rightly be directed at political parties, the courts, legislatures, and the like, *not* to encourage them to function more efficiently but rather to change entirely their goals and basic assumptions so that they work toward a more equitable social distribution of wealth and power.

Rappaport's analysis makes it clear why some community workers tend to be impatient with individual and group therapy. They do not believe the problems lie with the individual or the group, and they even assert that by concentrating on these levels the therapist will "blame the victim" (Ryan, 1971) and overlook the real problems of organizations and institutions. For these reasons community psychologists work in the seeking mode and make no pretense, as some individual and group therapists unfortunately do, at being politically and ethically neutral.

Why has there been a shift to community activism in the treatment of mental disorders? For many years it had been obvious how few people could avail themselves of psychotherapeutic services, which were typically very expensive, in short supply, and apparently geared to so-called YAVIS clients—individuals who are young, attractive, verbal, intelligent, and successful (Schofield, 1964). Eysenck (1952) had also questioned the effectiveness of most kinds of psychotherapy, finding treated patients' rates of improvement no better than the spontaneous remission rate. Al-though Eysenck's criticisms were compellingly rebutted by a number of scholars (for example, Bergin, 1971), the idea had taken hold among mental health professionals that individual psychotherapy aimed at changing people might not be the best way to alleviate the psychological problems of the majority of people. Focus began to shift from repressions, conflicts, and neurotic fears to large-scale social problems such as poverty, overcrowding, poor education, segregation, the alienation felt in large cities, and the impersonalism of many aspects of present-day living.

The shift from intrapsychic factors to social factors probably reflected the *Zeitgeist* or tenor of the times. The 1960s were a period of tremendous social upheaval and activism. Social institutions of all kinds were being challenged. Cities and college campuses were erupting in riots, and a range of minority groups, from blacks in urban ghettoes to gays in the larger cities, charged racism and political repression. This social upheaval, which at times seemed to border on revolution, further encouraged a search for causes of individual suffering in social institutions. At the same time the Kennedy and Johnson administrations lent the monetary clout of the federal government to a progressive liberalism. Ken-

Recognition that poverty and other social problems such as overcrowding and segregation are related to psychopathology was an important stimulus for the community psychology movement.

nedy's New Frontier and Johnson's Great Society programs poured tens of millions of dollars into attempts at bettering the human condition.

Community Mental Health Centers

The greatest single impetus to the community psychology movement was a practical one. In 1955 Congress authorized the Joint Commission on Mental Illness and Health to examine the state mental hospitals. On the basis of its survey, which went on for six years, the commission concluded that the care offered was largely custodial and that steps must be taken to ensure that treatment is given. In its 1961 report it recommended that no additional large hospitals be built and that community mental health clinics be established. In 1963 President John F. Kennedy sent a message to Congress calling for a "bold new approach" and proposing the Community Mental Health Centers Act to provide comprehensive services in the community and to implement programs for the prevention of mental disturbances. The act was passed. For every 100,000 people a mental health center was to provide outpatient therapy, short-term inpatient care, day hospitalization for those able to go home at night, twenty-four-hour emergency services, and consultation and education to other agencies in the community.

The services provided

The principal objective of a community mental health center is to provide outpatient mental health care in a person's own community and at a cost that is not beyond the means of most people. The increased availability of clinical services presumably means that fewer individuals need be committed to institutions. They can go across town and receive therapy several times a week without leaving their families, friends, and work. The community health center also provides short-term inpatient care, usually on a psychiatric ward of a community general hospital, again where relatives and friends of patients may conveniently visit them. Partial hospitalization, during the day or sometimes for the night, is usually also on a psychiatric ward. A twenty-four-hour walk-in crisis service offers emergency consultation around the clock and "rap sessions" for

members of the community. In Chapter 11 (page 362) we discussed rape crisis work, a service often run by community mental health centers.

The centers are staffed by psychiatrists, psychologists, social workers, and nurses, and by paraprofessionals who live in the community and can help bridge the gap between the middle- and upper-middle-class professionals and community members to whom psychotherapy is sometimes an alien concept. Paraprofessionals and volunteers also of course provide needed numbers for staffing the centers within their limited budgets.

The first program involving paraprofessionals was probably that at Harvard University (Umbarger et al., 1962), in which students spent several hours per week as companions to patients in mental hospitals (see Guerney, 1969, for numerous examples of other programs). Community acceptance of these workers would seem to be a vital factor in community-based programs. They usually bring a fresh commitment to their work and sincere and warm interest in the patients. Yet a nonprofessional may not have all the qualities and talents necessary to make effective therapeutic interventions. Surely much depends on *what* the paraprofessional is supposed to do.

A wide range of services is included under the rubrics of "consultation" and "education." A principal one is to educate other community workers, the teachers, clergymen, and police, in the principles of preventive mental health and in how to extend help themselves (see Box 20.4). Consider the crisis-intervention effort made by the Westside Community Mental Health Center in 1971. The staff tried to help children adjust to enforced school busing in San Francisco.

We designed a program in which we placed a professional staff person on a school bus to ride to and from school with grade school children; in addition this staff person had streetcorner meetings with the parents about their busing concerns, and acted also as their advocate to the schools. Knowing the children would be experiencing separation anxiety in this [situation], we had our Hospital Art Department design coloring books with maps of the territory they would cover on the bus route; we at-

BOX **20.4** Community Psychology and Community Mental Health—Related But Different

Although related, the community mental health movement and community psychology should be distinguished from each other. Community psychology is concerned with changing social systems at a broad, institutional level, community mental health with providing care for the needy troubled people who have traditionally been underserved by the mental health professions. Because community mental health delivers mental health services for needy individuals, its orientation is often as individualistic as traditional consulting room therapy of the kind discussed in Chapters 18 and 19. On the staffs of mental health centers are psychiatrists, clinical psychologists, and social workers who conduct therapy in offices at the center. Community psychology, on the other hand, shows its concern for individuals by trying to alter social systems and by creating different and, it is hoped, better environments for people to live in, both to reduce the forces that are thought to bring maladaptations and to promote opportunities for individuals to realize their potential. Community psychology requires intervention with the courts, police, schools, and city services and planning agencies. Political more than clinical skills are required for such work; in fact, relatively little time is spent dealing directly with the individuals affected by the larger social forces. The two movements are sometimes equated; the inclusion of community mental health in this discussion of community psychology reflects the relationship between these two forces in psychology today. Nonetheless, their differences are as important to appreciate as are their similarities.

---

tempted to introduce play materials and games that would be helpful to the children, would encourage the children to carry "transitional objects" from home . . . such as dolls, teddy bears, special favorite toys. Our staff member met with the children before they boarded the bus, talked to them on the bus, again in their new schoolyard and on the way back home again (Heiman, 1973, p. 60).

Staff members at a mental health center might conceivably call a rent strike, should they decide that better housing would alleviate emotional suffering. Or suggestions might be made by a center's staff to change physical arrangements in a local factory in order to reduce the boredom or tension of performing particular kinds of work.

Moreover, organized interventions such as these need not emanate solely from community mental health centers. Workers can operate from university departments, social welfare agencies, and even private offices and still understate activities that would be best characterized as community psychology.

A behaviorally oriented CMHC

In Oxnard, California, Liberman and his colleagues (1974) established the Behavior Analysis and Modification (BAM) Project. Staff employed a variety of behavior therapy techniques, including systematic desensitization, covert sensitization, assertion training, and token economies. Data were carefully collected on all patients before, during, and after treatment. For example, each week a staff person completed a Behavioral

A rent strike organized in an attempt to coerce landlords into making their properties more secure and safe exemplifies the activism of community psychology.

Progress Record on each patient, indicating whether behavioral goals had been accomplished. The operant treatment of one of the patients in the day section of the Oxnard center is a good example of the carefully planned procedures.

William was a . . . twenty-seven-year-old, single and unemployed man, diagnosed as schizophrenic. [Extremely withdrawn, he] had always lived with his parents, except for one brief hospitalization. William was not only socially withdrawn, but he actively removed himself from the presence of others. At his parents' home, most of his time was spent isolated in his room with the doors closed. He reported no friends, no social contacts, and he only left the house in the company of his parents.

When he first came to the clinic, William spent a large amount of his time outside of the area of the clinic in which most of the activities took place. Not only did he stand in the hall, but William kept his eyes closed, and his fingers stuck in his ears.

The first targeted [change in] behavior for William was [to be present] in the day room of the treatment center. A time sampling recording procedure was used whereby William's therapist observed him ten times during the day and recorded whether William was in the targeted area or not. A reversal design was planned to demonstrate experimental control over this behavior. Figure 20.3 depicts the contingencies used and the results. . . .

. . . The procedures were as follows: For condition A, the therapist was simply to observe William on the predetermined schedule. This condition was the designated baseline phase. In condition B, William was paid coupons for being in the targeted area. The coupons were part of a regular, ongoing token economy at the center. The back-up reinforcers for the coupons were lunch, coffee, snacks, and excursions. In condition C, William was paid coupons but allowed to buy time off from the clinic . . . at the rate of one coupon for five minutes away. He could earn two coupons per observation or a maximum possible of twenty per day.

[The rules for condition D imposed a price on social withdrawal.] For each of the times William was observed outside of the targeted area, he was to relinquish two coupons. The reinforcement contingency was continued with William receiving two coupons with which he could buy time off from the clinic if he was in the day room. With the introduction of condition D, . . . observations of William outside the targeted area decreased to zero and remained there for eight days. At this point, the . . . cost procedure was removed; that is, condition C was reinstated. The effect was to increase the [number of times William was observed] away from people. With the reinstatement of . . . condition D, there was a gradual decrease and elimination of social isolation.

The results of the experiment are informative on several points. First, . . . experimental control was demonstrated over a targeted problem behavior of a patient in a day treatment center. Secondly, the results demonstrate the [importance of evaluating] a treatment program. The first two interventions that were used, conditions B and C, produced no change in William's behavior. It was only with the introduction of the third contingency that a desirable change was produced. In treatment settings many contingencies have to be tried before [an effective] one is found. Thirdly, the results demonstrated improvement in one target behavior, but did not show any changes in other behaviors, such as the amount of time William had his eyes open

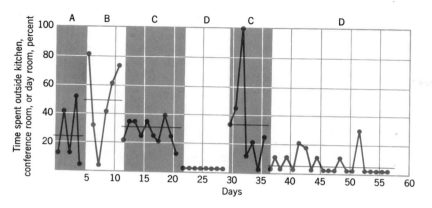

FIGURE **20.3**
Reducing the social isolation of a young male psychotic through contingency management. Condition A is the baseline situation. In condition B coupons are earned by being near others; in C, time away from the clinic can be bought with the coupons; in D, time away from the clinic can still be bought with coupons, but social withdrawal costs the young man some of his earned coupons. After Liberman et al., 1974.

and the amount of time [he] spent in social conversation. [The various aspects of his antisocial behavior might have to be treated separately] (Liberman et al., 1974, pp. 112–114).

Treatment at the Oxnard Center, when compared with that at nearby centers not run according to behavioral principles, was found more effective in increasing the social participation and in decreasing the isolation of chronic mental patients, who are typically withdrawn and apathetic. The underlying purpose of the BAM project, to analyze patients' problems and to evaluate treatments systematically, appears eminently feasible in a community mental health center. With continued experience it should be possible to refine treatments so that they are of maximum assistance to the greatest numbers of people—and this surely is the mandate of the original congressional act that set community mental health in motion in this country.

Environmental Psychology
Do you recall the last time you entered an air-conditioned building after suffering the heat and humidity of a mercilessly steamy summer day? What was your mood after being inside the cool haven for half an hour, compared to how you felt while walking outside? Have you ever visited some of the Gothic cathedrals in France and Germany? As you gazed upward to the soaring heights of the vaults, did you feel uplifted, exhilarated?

Since its beginning American psychology has had a love affair with environmentalism. Over the past fifteen years the study of how elements of the physical environment affect thoughts, feelings, and behavior has involved psychologists in the domain of designers, architects, and urban planners. Their attempts to control behavior through control of environmental stimuli is now called environmental design or environmental management (see Sommer, 1969; Proshansky, Ittelson, and Rivlin, 1972). Given the community psychologists' appreciation of the importance of large social issues in behavior disorder, it is not surprising that they too want psychology applied in the planning of cities and mass transit systems, in the design of apartment and office buildings.

A fascinating example of research work in this field is a study done by Baum and Valins (1973). It investigated a proposal by Calhoun (1970) that within a given physical space there is a limit to the amount of social interaction that animals can tolerate before stress is created. Baum and Valins term as ''unwanted social interaction'' any degree of social contact among people that exceeds some optimal level; any environment that provides unwanted social interaction is regarded as crowded.

In an initial field study they found that students living in older dormitories on a university campus complained of more overcrowding than those living in newer ones. Furthermore, when confronted with miniature bedroom and lounge areas and asked to place miniature figures in them until "you would feel crowded if you were there," the residents of the older dormitories placed far fewer figures than did those from the newer dormitories, indicating that they would feel crowded with fewer people than would those in the newer dormitories. The subjects in this research study were freshmen who had been *assigned* to their dormitories, thus controlling for self-selection factors that might render the analysis of the data more ambiguous.

In a subsequent study a subject coming either from the older dorms or from the newer residences was told to wait in a room in the laboratory with another subject. In reality the other student was the experimenter's "stooge." The students from the older accomodations, being more sensitive to crowding, were expected to sit farther away from the stooge than those coming from newer dorms. This prediction was confirmed. Moreover, hidden observers counted the number of seconds within a five-minute period that each subject glanced in the direction of the stooge. Again significant differences emerged: "older-dorm" students looked at the stooge significantly less often than did "newer-dorm" students, and, moreover, reported being more uncomfortable after the enforced waiting period.

Valins and Baum examined why students would feel more crowded in the older dormitories. The first obvious question was whether, in fact, older dormitories were more crowded in absolute terms than the newer dormitories. This seemed not to be the case, for the numbers of people per square foot of living area were about the same. What differentiated the two sets of dormitories was the *configuration* of the space. The older dormitories were constructed along traditional lines; a typical floor contained a number of bedrooms, with two students to a bedroom, each of which opened out directly onto the hall. All three dozen students on a given floor shared one large bathroom and lounge. By contrast, the newer dormitories, with a comparable number of students per floor, were arranged in individual suites with separate living areas and

bathrooms to accommodate small groups of four to six students, again two to a bedroom. The residents of the older dormitories apparently had to interact with more people than did the residents of newer ones. Privacy was simply more difficult to obtain, and Baum and Valins assumed that such forced interaction with larger numbers of students brought unwanted social contacts. It did not seem surprising that the students in the older dorms felt more crowded.

Thus, although provided with comparable amounts of physical space, students living in older dormitories were subjected to a far greater incidence of unwanted social interaction and were far more sensitive to crowding. The implications of such research are important. Among other things, it suggests that when architects design living quarters, they should take care to minimize unwanted social interaction by providing a certain degree of privacy. Investigations of this nature may cast light on the alarmingly high incidence of violence, emotional turmoil, and other problems that have come to characterize urban living.

Glass and Singer (1972), for example, document some of the deleterious effects of noise pollution. Their study (Cohen, Glass, and Singer, 1973) showed that the reading difficulties of elementary school children were associated with living in noisy apartments in New York City. Controlling for social class, they found that children who lived on the upper stories of a thirty-two story apartment house had higher reading scores than those living on the lower and noisier floors. Since research has shown that verbal skills are related to the ability to make auditory discriminations, they reasoned that noise was causing the reading problems. Indeed, children who had lived in the building fewer than four years were better readers than those who had lived there longer. Such research plus subjective impressions that excessive noise is distracting and unpleasant might encourage urban planners to build better insulation into homes and apartments, which would also make them cheaper to heat and to air-condition.

Suicide Prevention Centers and Telephone Crisis Services

Another community agency is the suicide prevention center, modeled after the Los Angeles Suicide Prevention Center, founded in 1958 by Farberow and Shneidman. Staffed largely by nonprofessionals under the supervision of psychologists or psychiatrists, these centers attempt to provide twenty-four-hour consultation to people in suicidal crises. Usually the initial contact is made by telephone. The center's phone number is well publicized in the community. There are at present more than 200 such centers in the United States. The worker tries to assess the likelihood that the caller will actually make a serious suicide attempt and, most importantly, tries to establish personal contact and dissuade the caller from suicide. The accompanying summary sheets used by telephone workers at the Suicide Prevention Center in Buffalo, New York, speed the recording of crucial bits of information.

Specialists hold that phone attendants in these centers should work toward the following goals (Speer, 1972).

1. "Tuning in," communicating empathy to the caller.

2. Conveying understanding of the problem.

3. Providing information regarding sources of help, for example, mental health clinics, psychologists, psychiatrists.

4. Obtaining an agreement from the caller to take some specific steps away from suicide, for example, making an appointment to come to the center itself.

5. Providing some degree of hope to the caller that the crisis will end and that life will not always appear so hopeless.

The potential value of such community facilities rests in the fact that most suicides give warnings—"cries for help"—before taking their lives (see page 263). Usually their pleas are directed first to relatives and friends, but many potential suicides are isolated from these sources of emotional support; a hotline service may save the lives of such individuals.

It is exceedingly difficult to do controlled research on suicide. Evaluating the effectiveness of suicide prevention centers is similarly problematic, for a large proportion of those who call are not heard from again. For example, Speer (1971) found that more than 95 percent of callers did not use the service repeatedly. Does this mean that the phone contact helped so much that no further consultation was needed? Perhaps so, but it is also possible that many callers killed themselves after the phone call. One study (Weiner, 1969) found no differences in the suicide rates of cities with hotline services and of those without. Although numerous factors might have masked real differences, we cannot conclude from these data that the centers *have* demonstrated their effectiveness.

Speer (1972) attempted to evaluate one crisis phone service. His study sheds light on the kind of research people in the field are doing and on the difficulties such research poses. The subjects were thirty-four callers to a suicide prevention center who subsequently appeared for individual counseling. Some were asked to rate their feelings after the phone call that had led them to the center; others were asked how they had felt after the preceding plea for help, the last one made to a personal acquaintance, friend, or relative before they called the center. In this way Speer hoped to learn whether potential suicides derive

Suicide hotlines, staffed twenty-four hours a day, are a service often provided by a community health center.

SPCS, INC., BUFFALO, NEW YORK

INITIAL CONTACT SHEET (Telephone)

I. Identifying Information: (1-6) ☐☐☐☐☐☐   Case No._____

          1 2 3
(7)   Line: S T P   (8-9) ☐☐ Counselor_____

         Mo. Date Yr.
(10-14) Date: ☐☐☐ (15) ☐ Day:____ (16-19) Call Began ☐☐ A/P ☐

                                 min.
                       (20-22) Call Duration ☐☐☐

          1
(24) ☐ Caller: (for self   other)   Other: Subject of Call_____
         Name:_____   2
                               Name:_____

         Address:_____   Address:_____

         Phone:_____   Phone:_____

(25) ☐ Catchment Area: Relationship to Caller_____

(72-73) ☐☐☐☐ Census Tract

         Caller (or Subject of Call)
                 1 2   1 2 3 4 5
(26-27) Age: ☐☐ (28) ☐ Sex: M F (29) ☐ Marital Status: U M S D W
(30) ☐ Occupation:_____ (32) ☐ Living Situation:___Alone
                                         With:_____
(31) ☐ Education:_____
Affect and Behavior During Call: (33) ☐ Crying____ (34) ☐ Agitated_____
     (35) ☐ Hostile____ (36) ☐ Difficulty talking/unresponsive___
     (37) ☐ Normal_____ (38) ☐ Depressed____ (39) ☐ Intoxicated____
     (40) ☐ Tripping____ (41) ☐ Other____

II. Identification of Problem (Check all Appropriate; double check primary problem):
   (42-43) ☐☐

1 Alcoholism _____	13 Legal _____	Sexual:
2 Anxiety _____	14 Lonely _____	24 Heterosexual_____
3 Confusion _____	15 Medical	25 Homosexual _____
4 Depression _____	Problems_____	26 Other _____
5 Drugs:	16 Pregnancy_____	27 Social Withdrawal____
Type _____	17 Reality	28 Suicidal _____
Amount _____	Distortion _____	29 Other _____
6 Employment _____	Relationship:	
7 Financial _____	18 Marital _____	
8 Homeless/Stranded_____	19 Parental_____	
9 Homicidal _____	20 Dating _____	
Illegal Activities:	21 Family _____	
10 Theft _____	22 Other _____	
11 Assault _____	23 School _____	
12 Other _____		

III. Assessment of Lethality:
   A. Suicidal Behavior:
   (44) ☐ Current Ideation: 0 1 2 3 4 5   None_____
   (45) ☐ Current Suicidal Attempt (describe):_____ None_____
   (46) ☐ Other Suicidal Behavior (describe):_____ None_____
   (47) ☐ History of Attempts: Date_____ Method_____
                     Outcome_____

B. Suicidal Plan:
(48) ☐ Specificity: 1.Vague_____ 2.Explicit_____
(49) ☐ Method: 1.Hi-Lethal_____ 2.Lo-Lethal_____ What:_____
(50) ☐ Availability of Means: 1.Yes____ 2.No_____ 3.Obtainable_____

C. Resources:
(51) ☐ Internal (e.g. coping ability)_____
(52) ☐ External (e.g. significant other)_____

D. (53) ☐ Communication: 1.Significant Other ____ 2.SPCS ____
                          3.Therapist elsewhere ____ 4.Other____

E. (54) ☐ Age: 1.Below 40_____ 2.Above 40_____
F. (55) ☐ Sex: 1.M___ 2.F
G. (56) ☐ Marital Status: 1.U 2.M 3.S 4.D 5.W
H. (57) ☐ Physical Illness: 1.Yes___ 2.No___ What?_____
I. (58) ☐ Drinking: 1.Yes___ 2.No___
J. (59) ☐ Recent Loss or Threat of Loss: 1.Yes____ 2.No___ What?_____
K. (60) ☐ Unexplained Change in Behavior: 1.Yes___ 2.No___
L. (61) ☐ Isolation: 1.Yes___ 2.No___
M. (62) ☐ Depression:
           1.Trouble Sleeping____4.Hopelessness: Severe_____ Moderate_____
           2.Loss of Appetite___ 5.Crying: Frequent_____
           3.Loss of Weight_____ 6.Crying: Uncontrollable_____
   (63) ☐ Estimated Suicidal Risk: 1.Low___ 2.Mod.___ 3.High___ 4.Undet.___

IV. Disposition:
Resources Mobilized (check where appropriate)
(64) ☐ Traced____ (65) ☐ Rescue Squad____ (66) ☐ Police____ (67) ☐ Home Visit____
(68) ☐ Significant Other____ Who?_____
(69) ☐ Appointment Made____ When?_____
(70) ☐ Other:_____

NARRATIVE SUMMARY (including Outcome and Recommendations):

(71) ☐ Follow-Up Requested: 1.Yes___ 2.No___

     Outcome of Follow-Up: (3/1/72)

more comfort and benefit from a service or from a friend or relative, who is presumably not trained in handling a suicide threat.

The results are sobering: of the seven measures used, only one showed that calls to the center were significantly more helpful than calls to a friend. Speer concluded that, in this instance, the hotline service gave no evidence of superiority in achieving the goals specified for it.

Can anything else be said about this study? One possible confound in the design was not considered by Speer. When a person calls a crisis service, he or she may be decidedly more desperate than when phoning a friend or relative. Those who rated phone calls to the service may therefore have been reporting reactions felt in a far more unhappy and more suicidal mood than were the individuals remembering their feelings after calls to friends. If so, there might very well be a significant difference in the efficacy of the two kinds of calls, a difference that would provide much-needed justification for the continuation or even the expansion of such centers.

Once again, we are left with little if any convincing evidence. Human lives are precious, however, and since many people who contact prevention centers weather a suicidal crisis successfully, there is at present no reason to discontinue these efforts.

The Use of Media To Change Harmful Life Styles

Cardiovascular diseases, such as high blood pressure and coronary heart disease, are responsible for more deaths in the United States than any other single group of illnesses. As reported earlier (see page 217), a number of physical and psychological factors are known to increase a person's chances of developing heart disease—a diet producing high blood levels of cholesterol, smoking cigarettes, and not exercising enough. In many respects the life style of an affluent, industrialized society increases risk of premature cardiovascular diseases. Projects underway promise to furnish better information on the relative importance of the many risk factors, but it is not too early to consider how to disseminate information on these risks to the greatest number

of people in the most effective and efficient manner.

A group of researchers at Stanford University, led by Nathan Maccoby, a psychologist noted for his work in communications, have for several years been studying ways to educate large numbers of people about the desirability of altering their life styles, in order to reduce their risk of cardiovascular diseases. The Three Communities Project was designed to evaluate whether mass media and direct, intensive instructional programs can reduce known risk factors and risk-producing behavior. (Maccoby et al., 1977; Maccoby and Alexander, 1980).

Three towns in northern California were studied; Watsonville and Gilroy were the two experimental towns, Tracy was the control town. For two years both experimental towns were bombarded by a mass media program on cardiovascular diseases, consisting of television and radio spots, weekly newspaper columns, and newspaper advertisements and stories. Posters in busses and in stores conveyed briefly and graphically such vital information as the desirability of eating fewer eggs in order to prevent heart attacks. An interesting feature of the design of the study was the participation of a sample of Watsonville residents at "high risk" for heart disease. They received intensive instruction, consisting of group sessions and individual home counseling over a ten-week period; the researchers wanted to examine whether information and exhortations to alter life style delivered face-to-face might add to whatever positive benefits derived from the mass media program.

The control town, Tracy, had media services that were quite different from those of the two experimental towns. Tracy is separated from Watsonville and Gilroy by a range of low mountains and therefore has entirely separate local television stations. The inhabitants of Tracy were of course not imprisoned in their hometown for the duration of the two-year study, but for the most part they did not receive through their media the messages conveyed to the citizens of the two experimental towns. Because all three towns had sizable numbers of Mexican and Chicano people, all media messages were in both Spanish and English.

The findings reveal that through the mass media campaign citizens off Watsonville and Gilroy did significantly increase their knowledge of cardiovascular risk factors; people in the control town did not gain in such knowledge. Egg consumption was reduced more in Watsonville and Gilroy than in Tracy, and clinically significant blood pressure decreases were observed in the two experimental towns, as contrasted with small increases in the control town. The high-risk people of Watsonville who participated in the special intensive instruction program reaped even greater benefits in lowered egg consumption and blood pressure. Finally, the researchers considered the overall measure of risk, a weighted average of the several physical and psychological factors mentioned earlier. Not surprisingly they found highly significant drops in risk in the experimental townspeople, an important result since we know from previous research, the famous Framingham, Massachusetts, longitudinal study of risk factors in cardiovascular diseases (Truett, Cornfield, and Kannel, 1967), that elevated risk scores predict reasonably well the incidence of heart disease over a twelve-year period.

This work of Maccoby and his colleagues is important as a community psychology effort, for it demonstrates that laypeople can learn from the mass media what is known about cardiovascular diseases, and that they will also act in many ways on this knowledge to reduce their overall risk for such diseases. The two-year span of the study is a considerable length of time as far as experiments in psychology are concerned! But in terms of the serious health problems that develop through long-standing detrimental patterns of behavior, this is not a very long time at all. So far the researchers do not know whether cardiovascular diseases will, in fact, be reduced in the experimental towns as compared to the control town. Even so, they have determined that properly designed mass media efforts can significantly alter people's behavior and attitudes in ways that reduce their statistical risk for cardiovascular diseases. The mass media are far less expensive and far more encompassing than individual or group therapy. This demonstrated effectiveness of using the media is a definite plus for community psychology's mission of bringing the greatest good to the greatest number.

Residential Programs

Youth residences

Residential centers for disadvantaged youth have concentrated on teaching vocational and educational skills, even to those who have been diagnosed as having an antisocial personality or perhaps even schizophrenia. Some residential units have been located within a community itself (for example, Goldenberg, 1969) in the belief that training is most effective in a familiar urban setting. Other apparently effective work has been done in state schools located quite a distance from the homes of the attending youths. In view of the deleteriousness of reform schools and prisons—which are often little more than training grounds where inmates learn how, when freed, to commit bigger and better crimes—it is heartening that noninstitutional programs are becoming more and more prevalent.

Most projects tend to be nonspecific in the actual techniques used. In contrast, as discussed in Chapter 15 (page 471), the basic assumption and hope of the one-year CASE II project, conducted at the National Training School for Boys in Washington, D.C. (Cohen and Filipczak, 1971), was that the antisocial behavior of young men, ranging from fourteen to eighteen years of age, would be reduced if they could acquire academic and vocational skills usable in the public schools and neighborhoods to which they would return after discharge. The residents on the educational round-the-clock token economy were called Student Educational Researchers and could earn money by making course grades of 90 percent, by participating in seminars, by studying, and by doing well on achievement tests. By means of their learning young men earned material goods and privileges—special meals, private rooms, room furnishings, and clothing—that made a significant difference in their lives. Those who did not participate or did not earn enough money had to go "on relief" and sleep in bunk beds in an open area, wear issue clothing, and eat issue meals on metal trays. No young man voluntarily spent more than four weeks in this state during the course of the project.

Practical constraints prevented the use of any control groups, but because of the ambitious na-

BOX **20.5** People's Liberation—An Aspect of Community Psychology

Life is change—this is one of the few things we can be certain of. Different demands, different joys, different sorrows, different challenges await us as we go through the life cycle. Much depends on where we grow up, how much money our families have, how sharp a mind we are born with, how well we apply ourselves in school and on our jobs—and luck. This book presents human problems that are fortunately remote from most of our personal lives, though there are surely readers who will find special significance in some of the material in these chapters. But we all experience unhappiness, groundless as well as reasonable fears, depression, perhaps even a touch of irrationality.

Let us spend some time, then, on ourselves, specifically on a set of life problems that confront all of us, those of sex roles and recent shifts in them. Are sex roles a source of stress to little boys and little girls and to men and women? Could such stress underlie some of the unhappiness and occasional psychopathology that we encounter? Generalizations are especially risky when discussing social roles, for society is large and complex. But as a starting point, consider the following broad and contrasting codes for men and women that have applied and still do in much of contemporary Western culture.

Men

1. A man's worth is very much a function of how much money he earns, how much influence he has on his job and in society. A man who earns $40,000 is a better man than one who is on welfare.

2. Real men do not show emotion, except perhaps anger, nor are they especially aware of their own emotions and those of others. "Staying cool" is the ideal.

3. Real men are oriented to achievement.

4. It is not enough to attain a moderate success; a man must continually accomplish more.

5. The acquisition of power is the ultimate good, even when it means stepping on others.

6. Women are to be dominated, sexually and otherwise. To allow a woman to be in a superior position—at work or even in bed—is not as satisfying as being in control of her.

7. Being like a woman is to be avoided at all costs. The clearest violation of this standard is to have warm, possibly sexual feelings about another man, but it is also suspect to do "women's work," such as caring for children, keeping house, baking cookies.

8. Real men are decisive. Experiencing difficulty when making decisions is unmasculine.

9. Making mistakes is a serious violation of the male code.

10. Real men do not ask for help.

Women

1. A woman's worth is very much a function of how much money her husband (or boyfriend) earns, how much influence he has on his job or in society. A woman whose husband (or boyfriend) earns $40,000 is more valuable than one whose husband (or boyfriend) is on welfare.

2. Real women are in touch with their feelings and, except for anger, display emotion easily. They are emotionally supportive of others.

3. Real women are not achievement-oriented, except perhaps in maintaining well-run households.

4. True success is obtained vicariously. Women are content to bask in the glory of their husbands' and children's accomplishments and to effect change in society indirectly, for example, by collecting donations for charities.

5. Cooperation rather than the acquisition of power is the ultimate good for women.

6. Being dominant, sexually or otherwise, is eschewed. If a woman is in a superior position—at work or even in bed—she runs the risk of appearing to be emasculating.

7. A woman's femininity is lost through aggression, competitiveness, and other masculine traits. A woman should never appear more intelligent than her male peers.

8. Real women willingly allow their men to make the significant decisions that will shape family and social life.

9. Making mistakes enhances a woman's femininity, for it makes her appear more vulnerable.

10. Real women require assistance from others.

Readers of this book are no doubt familiar with the considerable women's liberation literature. The topics of this literature, which are also explored more personally in women's consciousness-raising groups, are the stereotypes of the female sex role code just summarized. Women support one another as sisters in their resolve to break through the needless constraints they feel are placed on them because they are females.

Closely tied to the women's movement is men's liberation. From what, you might ask, do men need to be liberated? Do they not enjoy most of society's rewards? The women's movement has forced men to question the male role, to ask themselves what are the parameters of masculinity? How "soft," for example, dare a man become before feeling threatened by the loss of his maleness? What are the emotional costs of constantly achieving and competing? What do men, and women, stand to gain if male sex role stereotypes are also challenged (Farrell, 1975)?

In the past few years men have been talking to one another in groups modeled after women's consciousness-raising sessions. In such groups a man is able, often for the first time, to relate to another man in a noncompetitive way. Support is given for expressing weakness and fear. Because displays of affection between men are often regarded as indications of homosexuality, they are usually avoided at all costs; in men's consciousness-raising groups participants must get over such concerns before they feel comfortable indicating that they care for and like other men. Sexist attitudes are exposed—it does not take long for the word "girl" to be stricken from the vocabulary—and the male participants are encouraged to relate to other people in a more emotionally open fashion. The following is excerpted from a statement of purpose issued by one such group.

Both Men and Women suffer the bondage of a tradition of belief that is both discriminating and oppressive. We must walk hand in hand, in common cause [of liberation. Our] essential purpose . . . is to provide insight into what it means to be a male in our society. . . . We have built a society in which we compete with one another, disconnect from each other and ourselves as feeling, responsive men and suffer the consequences of this alienation. We have cut ourselves off from the rich potentials of brotherhood and remain strangers to each other. . . .

Too long have we been estranged from our-selves; too long have we denied ourselves the inherent sensitivities of our sex; too long have we denied others this sensitivity. . . . The threat inherent in exposing our feelings, the fear of expressing emotion, can be overcome if and when we . . . support each other. . . .

Men interacting with men . . . paves the way for a firmer understanding of the way we relate to women. It is conceded that men have built a society, and continue to control it, out of an attitude of dominance. This sexist tradition is firmly ingrained in all males and it dictates the way men bond together. Sexism has been . . . the conditioning of all males since history was first recorded. For us today to question this prerogative . . . demands an undaunted effort at re-educating each and every one of us in the way we develop and implement our attitudes and value systems . . . and introduce them into our social structure. . . . [Men must] support men in their collective efforts to understand just what it really means to be a male in our society.

F. Richard Vanacek

Those active in both the women's and men's liberation movements believe that considerable pain and stress of everyday life can be traced to unnecessary rigid conceptions of sex roles. Learning that women will be considered aggressive if they seek to dominate, that men must not cry or ask for help, can limit the personal growth of men and women and cause needless questioning of an individual's masculinity or femininity. And it may underlie much anxiety and depression.

A source of strain is generally overlooked, however, by those most deeply involved in people's liberation. Behavior does not change easily. An adult cannot turn himself or herself around as quickly and as completely as liberation rhetoric suggests. Habits of thought and action are "overlearned" by the time a person reaches maturity. A twenty-one-year-old woman may realize that she has every right to tell her lover what she desires from him, but her childhood learning that sexuality is suspect may inhibit her. A twenty-one-year-old male may intellectually acknowledge that his feelings of vulnerability are part of the human condition, but awareness alone will not enable him to reveal to his close friends that he lacks confidence in himself. The process of shedding our socially acquired sex roles may itself generate stress and helplessness if changes are expected too quickly and completely.

ture of the project, its results merit careful consideration. They should be compared in turn to outcomes achieved by other institutional efforts to reform youthful offenders. While residing at the school, the residents did "shape up," that is, they became less aggressive as time went on, took care of their living quarters, engaged in the academically relevant activities, and in general acted less like juvenile delinquents and more like young men in their teens without serious police records. Their performance on standardized aptitude tests also improved significantly. After eleven months of the program the average increase in IQ was 12.5 points. But did this improvement carry over to living in the community when they left the training school? After two and a half years a follow-up study was conducted to determine whether the special school project had had beneficial effects after the men returned to normal living. Most of the former residents were located and interviewed; their school and police records were checked. Achievement tests were administered, and the findings indicated that they had retained many of the gains they had made during the CASE II experience. People

in the law enforcement field ask questions about recidivism. Did they again get into trouble with the law? The answer for the CASE II boys is that for two years they had a lower recidivism rate than that of comparable men who had not had the specially designed operant learning program while institutionalized. But by the third year their recidivism was near the norm. Apparently the beneficial effects of the project dissipate with time and other experiences.

Another excellent residential program carefully conceived according to operant principles was established by Montrose Wolf and Ellery Phillips of the University of Kansas (Phillips et al., 1972). Achievement Place, located in the middle-class community of Lawrence, Kansas, is run by a young couple who for nine to twelve months act as surrogate parents for about nine boys of junior high school age referred from the courts for delinquent behavior. At Achievement Place specific prosocial behavior earns the youngsters a set amount of reinforcement and undesirable behavior costs them points (see Table 15.6, page 471). They bring home daily report cards from the community schools they attend. The points they

Residents of Achievement Place, an operantly run treatment home for delinquents, in a group discussion.

earn can be exchanged for snacks, a ride on a bicycle, or a trip downtown. After four consecutive weeks of improvement the youngster has earned himself off the exchange system to the merit system, which means free privileges and praise for good behavior. The next step is the homeward-bound program. With continued good behavior the youngster is able to spend a little more time at home each week. This system has allowed boys to return to their homes and communities without the stigma and deterioration that all too often follow institutionalization in jails or state hospitals. The actual cost to county or state authorities for financing these small facilities is far less than that for traditional hospitals and prisons, and indications are that the program is more effective than reformatories in improving schoolwork and school attendance as well as in reducing recidivism, at least for a time. There are now eighty Achievement Places for boys and girls in twelve states and in Canada. The originators of the program are now trying to maintain formal contact with the youths who have left in order to provide them with continued support and assistance when needed. They hope that thereby the gains made at Achievement Place will become more enduring (Kirigin, Braukmann, and Wolf, 1977).

Halfway houses and aftercare

Another kind of residence for people unable to function on their own is the halfway house. These are protected living units, typically located in large, formerly private residences. Here patients discharged from a mental hospital live, take their meals, and gradually return to ordinary community life by taking a part-time job or going to school. Living arrangements may be relatively unstructured; some houses set up money-making enterprises that help to train and support the residents. Depending on how well funded the halfway house is, the staff may include psychiatrists or clinical psychologists. The most important staff members are paraprofessionals, often graduate students in clinical psychology or social work who live in the house and act as both administrators and as friends to the residents. Group meetings, at which residents talk out their frustrations and learn to relate to others

Aftercare is a crucial component of the mental health system now that so many patients have been released from hospitals. These two residents of a halfway house are preparing dinner. They and the other residents share this and other chores on a rotating basis.

in honest and constructive ways, are often part of the routine.

Many people in mental hospitals neither profit from nor need the unnatural restraints that are intrinsic to closed institutions, yet they are not yet able to return to their families, to their university dormitories, and to their own apartments. The nation's requirements for effective halfway houses for ex-mental patients cannot be underestimated. Properly run residences are scarce. In several states there has been pressure from governors and from legislators to discharge as many hospital patients as possible. In the past twenty years these institutions have released more than half their nearly 600,000 residents. But discharge has all too often been bad for the patients. Some local communities object to the presence of shabbily dressed, often inappropriately behaving ex-patients in their neighborhoods. They have sometimes been exploited by entrepreneurs who, for their federal disability money, house them in unsanitary, poorly administered hotels and motels. Many ex-patients reenter the hospital in what has been termed the "revolving door" syndrome. Clearly, it is not enough merely to discharge mental patients. They must have outpatient services and a protective place to live (see Box 21.4, page 692).

A model of what aftercare can be is provided by the Paul and Lentz (1977) comparative treatment study discussed in Chapter 19 (page 595). When patients were discharged from any of the three wards of the program, social-learning, milieu therapy, or routine custodial-care, they usually went to live in nearby boarding homes. These homes, often converted motels, were staffed by workers who had been trained by the Paul-Lentz project to treat the ex-patients according to social-learning principles. These workers, some of whom had B.A. degrees, attended to the specific problems of the ex-patients, using rewards, including tokens for a time, to encourage more independence and normal functioning. At any time the staff knew how a particular patient was doing, because assessment was careful and ongoing. The mental health center project, and this is of paramount importance, acted as consultant to these community boarding homes in order to help their staff work with the ex-patients in as effective a manner as possible. Some boarding homes for ex-mental patients are supported financially by the state as part of the mental health system, but only rarely have the procedures followed in these homes been carefully planned and monitored by professional mental health staff.

In spite of many practical problems, such as staff layoffs, the results were as positive as had been the impact of the social-learning ward program. Through their training the aftercare staff did succeed in interacting with ex-patients in a manner somewhat consistent with social-learning principles. They positively reinforced appropriate behavior and did not attend much to bizarre behavior, as they had done before their training. The ex-patients seemed to benefit from the aftercare; more than 90 percent of the patients discharged from the social-learning ward were able to remain continuously in the community residences during the year-and-a-half follow-up period. Some had been living in the community residences for over five years. The revolving-

door syndrome in this instance did not take hold. Finally, in a finding rather critical in these days of inflation and diminishing public funds, the social-learning program, the mental health center treatment combined with the aftercare, was much less expensive than the institutional care such patients usually receive.

Overall Evaluation of Community Psychology Work

Primary prevention
It has been suggested that the results of community psychology have not lived up to the rhetoric (Bernstein and Nietzel, 1980). Nowhere are successes more notably lacking than in primary prevention (Cowen, 1977), in keeping disorders from developing in the first place. Community psychologists often argue heatedly that the work of most clinicians in tertiary prevention, or therapy for already existing disorders, is effort in the wrong place and at the wrong time. They claim that too few people can be served at the tertiary level, because therapy requires highly skilled professional helpers, and that little success can be expected because the disorders have been allowed to develop fully and are for this reason very difficult, perhaps impossible, to treat.

These are important criticisms. Evidence is being collected, however, to determine just what measures are effective with which of the disorders. But primary prevention procedures are more problematic. Social activism, "going out into the community" to change social systems and neighborhoods, rests on two assumptions: that the major causes of human psychological suffering are environmental, and that the community interventions now being undertaken are aimed at the correct environmental causes. The review of the major mental disorders in Chapters 5 through 17 gives scant assurance that we know this much about how mental and emotional problems develop. For this reason it can be argued that some community psychology efforts are premature, that what is needed more than social action, or at least in addition to it, is continuing and vigorous research into the causes of the disorders.

Paraprofessionals and ethnicity

Community psychology programs rely on peers, on people who come from the same backgrounds as those receiving services; these paraprofessionals have some training but not the credentials for mental health work. The prevailing belief is that these individuals will better know the life circumstances of those in need and, most importantly, will be more acceptable to them. Extensive research on modeling provides some justification for these assumptions. Subjects in studies of learning through observation are found to acquire information more readily from models who are perceived as credible and relevant to them; similarity of age and background are important determinants of credibility and relevance (Rosenthal and Bandura, 1978). We can therefore expect that individuals unaccustomed to the standard middle-class fare of a professional office and formal appointments will find the activities and advice of helpers similar to themselves more acceptable.

> *Few models seem as plausible or relevant as people who have shared but overcome clients' own problems. This is critical if a client rejects staff members as reference figures because they appear too remote in age, education, status, ethnicity, and so on, for suitable comparisons with self, or are perceived as outsiders, lacking vivid conversation with the client's burdens and viewpoint (Rosenthal and Bandura, 1978, p. 649).*

Several studies have examined the effects of race on the counseling relationship. A review of them suggests that black clients prefer black counselors to white counselors, engage in more self-exploration with counselors of their own race, and in general feel more positively toward black helpers than toward white helpers (Jackson, 1973). At the same time the studies suggest that race differences are *not* insurmountable barriers to understanding between counselor and client. Counselors with considerable empathy are perceived as more helpful by clients, regardless of the racial mix. None of these studies investigated whether the therapy provided to black clients by white and black counselors differed in effectiveness.

What is new in CMHCs?

Problems of community mental health centers were examined a decade ago in a rather controversial critique by Ralph Nader's Center for Study of Responsive Law (Holden, 1972). This report held that the centers are based on a good and commendable set of ideas but that the implementation has been rather poor. Often the problem is one of old wine in new bottles. Nader's group pointed out that centers are usually controlled by psychiatrists whose training and outlook are tied to one-to-one therapy, typically along psychoanalytic lines; the "fit" between treatment and the problems of lower-income people who are the centers' primary constituencies is often loose. Liberman's BAM project, which was examined earlier, was a noteworthy exception.

Only about half the number of community mental health centers envisioned by Congress have been established. A more recent examination of these centers by the President's Commission on Mental Health (1978) found that they are not serving severely disturbed children and adolescents, the aged, and discharged mental patients. Only about 7 percent of ex-patients ever go to a community mental health center.

Social factors in community psychology

Enthusiasm for community psychology must unfortunately be tempered with awareness of social reality—the conditions of deprivation that community psychologists assume produce and maintain disordered behavior. To train a black youngster for a specific vocational slot can have a beneficial long-term outcome for the individual only to the extent that society at large provides the appropriate opportunity to use these skills. Those who work in community psychology are of course aware that racial and social prejudices play a central role in limiting the access of many minority groups to the rewards of the culture at large. Although efforts to improve the sociocultural milieu must of course continue if our society has any commitment to fostering social and mental well-being, programs may raise expectations that will only be dashed by the realities of the larger culture. This is the quandary of any mental health professional who ventures forth from the consulting room into the community.

Community psychology has as its goal the change of large systems and groups of people rather than treating individual problems. And it is in the seeking mode; psychologists take the initiative in serving people, rather than waiting for individuals in need to come to them. On the face of it, this is a tall order. What do we know about the principles that operate to produce change in societal values and institutions? When a community psychologist organizes a rent strike, for example, what are the best ways of doing so, that is, of persuading the greatest number of tenants to work together in the joint effort? Will gentle persuasion be most effective, or does the situation call for strident harangues against the landlord? Furthermore, if the community psychologist hopes to take actions that meet the wishes and needs of the community, how does he or she determine them? It will be recalled from Chapter 3 the difficulties the psychologist has in assessing the needs of an individual client with whom there is extensive direct contact. How much more difficult, then, to assess the needs of thousands of people! Does one talk primarily to their leaders? If so, how do certain people become leaders and spokespersons? And once chosen, how do these individuals stay abreast of what the needs of their constituents are?

Community psychologists necessarily become social activists to some degree, which raises the danger that these well-meaning professionals may *impose* values and goals on their clients. John Kennedy's launching of the community mental health movement proclaimed that the federal government is rightfully concerned about improving the mental health of Americans. But what is mental health? Who is to decide? To what extent do the people being served by community psychologists have a say in how they are to be helped?

These are but a few of the nettlesome questions that must continually be posed if community psychology is to act responsibly and effectively. The focus of this field is on large-scale factors. Many people are involved; many lives, then, will be affected by decisions and actions. Questions of values and questions of effectiveness are inherent in any effort to alter the human condition.

Perhaps a major contribution of the community psychology movement is in sensitizing mental health professionals to the social, political, and ethical factors in human behavior. These "macro" variables are assumed to be critical in influencing behavior, and the attempt is made to manipulate them. The forces impinging on all of us exert their power in sometimes subtle fashion. If we do not look for these forces, we are unlikely, as suggested in our discussion of paradigms in Chapters 1 and 2, to find them.

Somatic Treatment

Many of the therapeutic procedures considered thus far are psychological in nature; improvements in behavior are sought through techniques that provide new learning experiences, raise expectations for help, and facilitate insight. But behavior can also be affected by direct manipulation of the body. The intimate relationship between mind and body was indicated in the discussion of psychophysiological disorders (see page 198). If psyche and soma are only two ways of talking about the same thing, it is reasonable to expect behavior to change when we intervene in certain bodily processes. Moreover, the many theories that blame psychopathology on physiological dysfunctions imply the efficacy of physiological treatments.

In the chapters on specific disorders, we have briefly discussed how various somatic therapies, those that attempt to change behavior by directly manipulating physiological processes, are used in treatment. Here we discuss some of the most widely used procedures in more detail.

There are three major types of somatic treatment for abnormal behavior—drugs, surgical procedures, and convulsion therapies. Evidence indicates that *some* methods are effective in treating *some* psychological problems. But, as we have cautioned many times before, this evidence does not in turn provide support for a physiological explanation of any of these disorders. In fact, somatic therapies have *not* usually been discovered through investigation of the physiology behind a particular disorder. Rather, the majority of the current treatments were discovered by accident, a few, as we shall see, under somewhat astonishing circumstances.

Drug Therapies

Four major categories of drugs have been used for some time in the amelioration of psychological disorders: minor tranquilizers, neuroleptics, stimulants, and antidepressants. Table 20.2 gives examples of several widely used drugs in these categories, indicating the chemical groups that

TABLE 20.2
Several Psychoactive Drugs Categorized by Their Effects on Behavior

Effect group	Chemical group	Generic name	Trade name
Minor tranquilizers	propanediols	meprobamate	Miltown, Equanil
	benzodiazepines	chlordiazepoxide diazepam	Librium Valium
Neuroleptics (antipsychotics)	phenothiazines	chlorpromazine trifluoperazine thioridazine	Thorazine Stelazine Mellaril
	butyrophenones	haloperidol	Haldol
	thioxanthenes	chlorprothixene	Taractan
Stimulants	amphetamines	dextroamphetamine	Dexedrine
	piperidyls	methylphenidate	Ritalin
Antidepressants	tricyclics	imipramine amitriptyline nortriptyline	Tofranil Elavil Aventyl
	monoamine oxidase inhibitors	phenelzine tranylcypromine	Nardil Parnate

they belong to as well as both their generic and brand names. More recently lithium carbonate has become a preferred treatment for bipolar affective disorder.

Although we have reserved our extended discussion of therapeutic drugs for this chapter, the sad truth is that many of them could well have been mentioned in Chapter 10 on drug addiction and drug dependence. Even the minor tranquilizers can be abused, and some of them, like Miltown, are physically addictive over long periods of regular use. Both because of our psychological needs and because of the physiological realities of our bodies, human beings are all too prone to use psychoactive chemicals in self-defeating ways.

Minor tranquilizers

As the name suggests, minor tranquilizers are used to reduce anxiety that is not of major proportions. They are usually prescribed for outpatients who suffer neurotic anxiety and psychosomatic disorders involving tension, and sometimes for the depressed individual who is also anxious. Barbiturates, which have been used to relieve anxiety since the turn of the century, were the first drugs in this category to gain widespread acceptance. But because of hazards such as addiction and undesirable side effects (see page 313), they were supplanted in the 1950s by a number of newly developed minor tranquilizers. The first of these was patented in 1952 by Berger and called meprobamate. Its trade names are Miltown and Equanil. Meprobamate, which operates by reducing muscular tension, belongs to a group of drugs called the propanediols. At present the propanediols have fallen in popularity and have been replaced by another group of minor tranquilizers, the benzodiazepines. Librium and Valium are the most prominent. Indeed, in the mid-1970's Valium was thought to be the most widely prescribed drug of those available to physicians. The tranquilizer business has boomed throughout the years, with numerous entries finding their way to the marketplace. Tranquilizers have become an accepted part of American culture; anxious businesspeople and overtaxed parents are depicted as popping "happy" pills to get them through their trying days.

Because minor tranquilizers are usually pre-scribed for outpatients by general practitioners, arranging controlled research is very difficult. In controlled evaluations of patients with anxiety disorders or anxious depression who take benzodiazepines, these drugs generally produce greater improvement than a placebo (Greenblatt and Shader, 1978). Many people who take benzodiazepines, however, complain of drowsiness and lethargy, sometimes staggering. Like meprobamate, these drugs too can be physically addictive taken in heavy doses over a long period.

Neuroleptics[4]

Phenothiazine, the nucleus of the phenothiazine drugs, was first produced by a German chemist in the late nineteenth century and was used to treat parasitic worm infections of the digestive system of animals. The drug went largely unnoticed until the 1940s, when the antihistamines were discovered by Bovet. The drugs with antihistaminic properties also have a phenothiazine nucleus. Antihistamines were prescribed to treat a variety of conditions ranging from the common cold and asthma to low blood pressure and shock. The French surgeon Laborit pioneered the use of antihistamines to reduce surgical shock. He noticed that they made his patients somewhat sleepy and less fearful about the impending operation. Laborit's work encouraged drug companies to reexamine antihistamines that had previously been rejected because they had stronger tranquilizing than antihistaminic effects. Shortly thereafter a French chemist, Charpentier, prepared a new phenothiazine derivative and called it chlorpromazine. It proved very effective in calming schizophrenics. As indicated earlier (see page 431), phenothiazines are now believed to block impulse transmission in the dopaminergic pathways of the brain, which gives them their therapeutic properties.

Chlorpromazine was first used therapeutically in the United States in 1954 and rapidly became the preferred treatment for schizophrenics. By 1970 over 85 percent of all patients in state mental hospitals were receiving chlorpromazine

---

[4] Neuroleptics are sometimes referred to as antipsychotic drugs, a relatively accurate description of their effects, and as major tranquilizers, a misleading term. The implication of the term major tranquilizer is that drugs in this category are useful for anxiety of greater magnitude than that treated with minor tranquilizers. But this is not the case; neuroleptics are not an effective treatment for anxiety disorders.

or one of the other phenothiazines. In recent years two other neuroleptics have also been given to schizophrenics, butyrophenones and the thioxanthenes. Both seem generally as effective as the phenothiazines.

There is little doubt that the phenothiazines are useful in managing schizophrenic patients, and for this reason they are often referred to as antipsychotic drugs. In one study, conducted by the National Institute of Mental Health, patients newly admitted to nine different hospitals were randomly assigned to take one of four drugs on a double-blind basis (Cole, 1964). Three of the drugs were different types of phenothiazine and the fourth was a placebo. The physicians in charge were allowed to adjust drug dosage to meet each patient's needs. During and after six weeks of treatment, three different measures were made of each patient: daily observations by ward personnel, a comprehensive rating by physician and nurse of severity of mental illness, and a one-hour diagnostic interview.

The ratings of improvement were as follows. None of the patients on any of the phenothiazines was rated as worse, 5 percent were rated as having shown no change, and 95 percent were rated as improved, with 75 percent of them considered much or very much improved. Of the patients on the placebo, 15 percent were rated as worse, 25 percent as having shown no change, and 60 percent as having improved, but only 10 percent of those who improved were in the "very much" category. On the basis of the psychiatric interview and daily observations, measurements on twenty-one variables such as social participation, confusion, and self-care were derived. As can be seen in Table 20.3, on thirteen of the twenty-one measures the drug patients were better than those on the placebo.

Such evidence is impressive. But is phenothiazine medication the preferred treatment when it is compared with other potential treatments a hospitalized schizophrenic patient might receive? In an attempt to answer this question, May (1968) assigned first-admission schizophrenic patients in a psychiatric hospital to one of five treatment groups.

1. Individual psychoanalytic psychotherapy conducted by psychiatric residents.

2. Phenothiazine drugs.

3. Individual psychoanalytic psychotherapy plus phenothiazine medication.

TABLE **20.3**
Superiority of Phenothiazines over a Placebo in Lessening Schizophrenics' Problems
(from Cole, 1964)

Symptom or behavior	Placebo	Drug	Difference
Social participation	0.49*	1.51	1.02
Confusion	0.33	1.11	0.78
Self-care	0.13	0.88	0.75
Hebephrenic symptoms	−0.13	0.58	0.71
Agitation and tension	0.27	0.95	0.68
Slowed speed	−0.07	0.57	0.64
Incoherent speech	−0.17	0.43	0.60
Irritability	−0.20	0.40	0.60
Indifference to environment	−0.05	0.45	0.50
Hostility	0.09	0.54	0.45
Auditory hallucinations	0.18	0.62	0.44
Ideas of persecution	0.36	0.78	0.42
Disorientation	0.16	0.37	0.21

* The higher the score, the greater the improvement. A minus score indicates deterioration.

4. Electroconvulsive therapy (to be discussed later in this chapter).

5. Milieu therapy.

Two classes of dependent variables were analyzed: clinical ratings of the patient's progress made by nurses and therapists, and data on release rate and length of time spent in the hospital. Drugs alone and the psychotherapy-plus-drugs combination were the two best treatments according to all the clinical measures. These two treatments were also superior both in shortening stay and in increasing the number of releases. Indeed, phenothiazines alone were found to be as effective as phenothiazines plus an extensive course of psychotherapy. This pattern of results persisted at a five-year follow-up (May et al., 1976).

One of the unanswered questions about antipsychotic drugs is whether a particular medication is best suited for a particular type of patient. As indicated in Chapters 13 and 14, schizophrenia is believed to be a *group* of mental disorders; although DSM-III states a set of general characteristics, seveal types are generally recognized. The extreme suspiciousness of a paranoid schizophrenic might best be treated with one kind of phenothiazine, for example, the withdrawal of a catatonic schizophrenic by another. Although psychiatrists have developed hunches based on their clinical experiences, there is little actual evidence on differences in responding to one or another antipsychotic drug (Neale and Oltmanns, 1980). In practice, a psychiatrist usually prescribes a given drug at a particular dosage and then observes how it affects the patient. Changes in the drug itself, or its dosage, are made on the basis of how the patient appears to be doing. This approach, seemingly inefficient and haphazard, is nonetheless the best and most rational procedure to follow, given the present state of knowledge.

It is also difficult to predict which schizophrenics will respond favorably to any of the neuroleptic drugs. Experimental research finds the mean improvement score of a group of patients receiving a neuroleptic to be greater than the same score of another group of patients receiving a placebo. But these analyses of mean scores obscure the fact that *some* patients who receive neuroleptics do not improve and some are even harmed by them. Clearly, it would be desirable to be able to predict in advance of treatment which patients will benefit. Many variables, premorbid adjustment and various symptoms, for example, have been assessed in this search to determine which patients will benefit from neuroleptics. Unfortunately, the results have been inconclusive (Neale and Oltmanns, 1980).

Although the phenothiazine regimen reduces symptomatology so that patients can be released from the hospital, it should not be viewed as a cure-all. What, for example, happens to a patient when he or she is discharged? Typically, patients are kept on so-called *maintenance doses* of the drug; they continue to take their medication and return to the hospital on occasion for adjustment of the dose level. But it turns out that released patients being maintained on phenothiazine medication may make only marginal adjustments to the community. The phenothiazines do not turn a socially incompetent schizophrenic with a poor premorbid history into a "pillar of the community." Furthermore, readmissions are frequent. The advent of the "phenothiazine era" reduced long-term institutionalization significantly. But in its place evolved the "revolving door" pattern of admission, discharge, and readmission already remarked on.

Some progress has been made in at least slowing down the revolutions per minute of the door. We know that applying social-learning principles in aftercare homes is one way of helping deinstitutionalized patients remain in the community. There is also some evidence that a maintenance program of drugs plus another form of psychotherapy is effective at preventing relapse (Hogarty et al., 1974). One group of released patients received drugs plus a treatment program called major role therapy. In this therapy ex-patients are helped to assume productive social roles in the community and to reestablish personal relationships through the active help of a counselor. Then gradually they make more and more of their own daily decisions. Members of this group were rated as more adjusted after eighteen months of treatment than three other groups of released patients who received only the drug, only a placebo, and a placebo plus

TABLE 20.4

Nine-Month Relapse Rates of Schizophrenics Discharged, with and without Maintenance Medication, to Low-EE Homes and to High-EE Homes with Little and Much Family Contact

(from Vaughn and Leff, 1976)

Drug status	Family atmosphere and contact		
	Low EE	High EE, little contact	High EE, much contact
Maintenance medication	12%	15%	53%
No drugs	15%	42%	92%

major role therapy. The necessity for maintenance medication also depends on the homes to which the patients are discharged. We have indicated that the level of "expressed emotion" of family members, their criticism and hostility toward ex-schizophrenic patients, figures in whether they relapse. The relation of maintenance medication to expressed emotion and relapse is given in Table 20.4. Maintenance medication is valuable for ex-patients living in high-EE homes but does not affect the rate of relapse of those living in low-EE homes (Vaughn and Leff, 1976).

Finally, the potentially serious side effects of phenothiazines must be noted. Patients generally report that taking the drug is disagreeable, causing dryness of the mouth, blurred vision, grogginess, and constipation. Among the other common side effects are low blood pressure and jaundice. Perhaps this unpleasantness is one of the reasons maintenance programs have proved so difficult. It is a problem to get patients to take these drugs initially and to keep them taking them once they have left the hospital (Van Putten et al., 1981).

Even more disturbing are the extrapyramidal side effects; they stem from dysfunctions of the nerve tracts that descend from the brain to spinal motor neurons. Extrapyramidal side effects resemble symptoms of neurological diseases, which is the reason these drugs are called neuroleptics. These side effects most closely resemble the symptoms of Parkinson's disease. People taking phenothiazines have "pill rolling" tremors of the fingers, a shuffling gait, muscular rigidity, and drooling. Dystonia and dyskinesia are arching of the back and a twisted posture of the neck and body. Akasthesia is an inability to remain still; people pace constantly, fidget, and make chewing movements and other movements of the lips, fingers, and legs. These perturbing symptoms can be treated by drugs used with patients with Parkinson's disease. In a muscular disturbance of older patients, called tardive dyskinesia, the mouth muscles involuntarily make sucking, lip-smacking, and chin-wagging motions. This syndrome affects from 10 to 15 percent of patients treated with phenothiazines for a long period of time. Some improvement comes from treatment with benzodiazepines or phenobarbital (Borbruff et al., 1981).

In spite of the many difficulties, phenothiazines will undoubtedly continue to be the primary treatment for schizophrenics until something better is discovered. They are surely preferable to the straitjackets formerly used to restrain patients.

Stimulants

One form of amphetamine, dextroamphetamine, and a piperidyl derivative, methylphenidate, are currently prescribed for hyperactive children (see page 464). Their use for this purpose became controversial when a 1970 *Washington Post* article reported that between 5 to 10 percent of school children in Omaha, Nebraska, were receiving the stimulants (Maynard, 1970). The public became aroused and investigations followed. It became apparent that the use of stimulants for calming children was widespread, and that prescriptions were being written somewhat indiscriminately. Shortly thereafter the Food and Drug Administration tightened its regulations.

The available evidence indeed indicates that stimulants are an effective treatment for hyperactivity (for example, Conners et al., 1972; Gittelman-Klein et al., 1976). In the Conners study 35 to 40 percent of the children showed dramatic improvement, and another 30 to 40 percent were moderately improved. The most frequent side effects of stimulants are decreased appetite and insomnia, but both are short-lived. Children taking stimulants do look different, however. Their cheeks are sunken, the skin is pale, and there are dark shadows beneath the eyes. People know that they are on medication, which can be upsetting to children.

A closer examination of the actual effects of stimulants reveals that they have differential impact on the many problems of the hyperactive child. Stimulants reduce impulsive and undercontrolled behavior, increase attention, and allow direction and control of motor activity. Yet they may not improve performance of cognitive tasks and ability to do schoolwork (Gittelman-Klein and Klein, 1976; Rie et al., 1976); as indicated earlier, they may even *interfere* with learning when administered in doses strong enough to reduce hyperactive behavior (Sprague and Sleator, 1977). For these reasons, as well as the possibility that undesirable side effects will appear with long-term use, other treatments for hyperactivity should be considered. A study by Gittelman-Klein and her co-workers (1976) indicates that operant programs can be quite effective alone, and that a combination of stimulants and behavior therapy is the best available treatment. Three treatments were compared, behavior therapy plus a placebo, behavior therapy plus a stimulant, and behavior therapy alone. All brought significant improvement, but at the end of eight weeks, children receiving a combination of stimulants and behavior therapy were indistinguishable from their normal classmates.

Antidepressants

The *tricyclics* and the *monoamine oxidase* (MAO) *inhibitors* are two subcategories of anti-

depressants. Both classes of drugs were discovered serendipitously. Imipramine, a tricyclic, has a three-ring molecular structure similar to that of the phenothiazines; hence it was hoped that it might also be an effective treatment for schizophrenics. Early clinical work with the drug showed that it was of little value with schizophrenics, but it did produce an unexpected elevation in mood; for this reason it was subsequently used as an antidepressant. Tricyclics are now assumed to interfere with the reuptake of norepinephrine and serotonin by the nerve cell after it has fired, thus keeping more of the neurotransmitter available at the synapse. The MAO inhibitor iproniazid was originally a treatment for tuberculosis. Because it improved the outlook of tubercular patients, it too was adopted as an antidepressant. The enzyme monoamine oxidase degrades monoamines of the central nervous system. Since a MAO inhibitor prevents this intracellular degradation, excess amounts of free norepinephrine and serotonin collect at the receptor sites (see Box 8.4, page 252). Thus both classes of drugs are considered to produce their therapeutic effects by raising levels of brain amines, facilitating neural transmission.

The available evidence suggests that the tricyclics are effective drugs to combat depression (Davis, Klerman, and Schildkraut, 1967). But it is also clear that tricyclics do not benefit *all* depressives. Thus research directed at determining which depressed patients are most likely to benefit from the drug is important. Some of this research has been carried out on so-called endogenous and exogenous depressives, those who have a very deep depression as opposed to those with a less severe form. The tricyclic drugs were found more effective in relieving endogenous depression than exogenous (Stern, Rush, and Mendels, 1980).

Of current interest is the finding that some tricyclics, for example, imipramine and nortriptyline, work principally to increase levels of norepinephrine, whereas others, for example amitriptyline, increase levels of serotonin. Patients who have low levels of MHPG, the major metabolite of norepinephrine, respond best when treated with nortriptyline, a tricyclic that would be expected to prevent the reuptake of norepinephrine and thus raise its levels at the synapse (Hollister, Davis, and Berger, 1980). Similarly, patients who show low levels of 5-HIAA, serotonin's principal metabolite, respond best to tricyclics that are expected to raise serotonin levels (Stern, Rush, and Mendels, 1980). As was mentioned in Chapter 8, findings such as these suggest that there may be different biochemical deficiencies among depressed patients. Like the phenothiazines, the tricyclics also produce some undesirable side effects. These include dry mouth, constipation, dizziness, palpitations, and blurred vision.

Recent research has examined the combined effects of tricyclics and various forms of psychotherapy. In two studies the combination seemed to offer an optimal treatment (DiMascio et al., 1979; Weissman et al., 1981). The already reported study by Rush, Beck, and their colleagues (1977), comparing Beck's cognitive therapy with administration of imipramine, found the cognitive treatment superior. Clearly more research is needed to determine the most effective combination of antidepressant drugs and psychological treatments with different types of affective disorders.

Although MAO inhibitors are generally more effective than a placebo, they are decidedly less useful than the tricyclics (Klerman, 1975). They continue to be given patients who do not respond to tricyclics, but interest in them has declined because of their severe side effects. MAO inhibitors have greater toxicity than any other drug used for the treatment of psychological disorders; they are harmful to the liver, brain, and cardiovascular system. Moreover, these drugs have even been found to interact with other drugs and foods to cause death. Patients taking MAO inhibitors should avoid foods and beverages high in tyramine. Aromatic cheeses, avocado, beer, broad beans, Chianti wine, chicken livers, cream, game, lox, pickled herring, snails, and yeast extracts (Honigfeld and Howard, 1978) cannot be ingested, even in moderate amounts.

Lithium carbonate

In this decade there has been great interest in the possibility of using lithium carbonate in the treatment of mania. The drug was discovered by Cade in 1949, who noted its sedative effect on guinea pigs. It was not used widely in the United States until more recently, however, for it had been judged dangerous after causing a few deaths. In these instances it had been ingested unrestrictedly as a salt substitute by patients with cardiac disease.

Although lithium carbonate is clearly an effective treatment for mania, whether it is the best somatic treatment available is unclear. For example, in double-bind studies in which lithium is compared with chlorpromazine, or other neuroleptics, the two treatments are about equally useful (for example, Shopsin et al., 1975).

In addition to the claim that lithium subdues mania, it has also been proposed that the drug can lift depression and, when taken regularly, reduces the likelihood of subsequent manic and depressive episodes. Lithium can lift depression in some patients, particularly bipolars. Its greatest benefit, however, is as a prophylactic, forestalling subsequent episodes of mania and depression in bipolar patients (Gerbino, Oleshansky, and Gershon, 1978). Whenever lithium is used, it is important that blood levels be carefully monitored to avoid a potentially fatal overdose.

Psychosurgery

In the last decades of the nineteenth century, Gottlieb Burckhardt, a Swiss physician, reported removing parts of the brains of several very disturbed patients. The rudimentary practice of trephining in prehistoric times, which was occasionally taken up again during the medieval period and in a number of primitive societies, had already established breaching of the skull as a means of correcting behavior. The "modern era" of psychosurgery begins with the work of a Portugese neuropsychiatrist, Antonio de Egas Moniz. He had attended a scientific meeting in London in 1935 and was impressed by a report of Jacobsen and Fulton about brain surgery performed on two chimpanzees. The prefrontal areas of their cerebral cortexes had been removed. Before the operation the animals had been highly emotional and subject to violent temper tantrums when frustrated through experimentation. Afterward they were indifferent.

On the basis of this single case of two chimpanzees whose behavior was calmed through brain surgery, Moniz later persuaded a colleague, Almeida Lima, to operate on the frontal lobes of human patients. Within a few years a hundred lobotomies had been performed, and in 1949 Moniz shared a Nobel prize in medicine for this work. Moniz himself retired in 1944, partly because he had been rendered a hemiplegic by a bullet lodged in his spine. One of his lobotomized patients had shot him (Valenstein, 1973).

Lobotomy was introduced in the United States by Walter Freeman and James Watts; by 1950 they had operated on over a thousand patients. The rate picked up in the early 1950s, and Freeman later claimed that he had performed or supervised over 3500 lobotomies.

The original lobotomy was a very crude surgical procedure. In one of the two methods usually applied, a hole was drilled in each side of the head, and a blunt instrument was then inserted and rotated in an arc, destroying considerable white matter. In the other procedure, the transorbital technique, a surgical needle inserted into the brain through the thin structure separating the eye and the brain was similarly rotated (Figure 20.4). It is estimated that each of these techniques destroys about 120 square centimeters of brain tissue (Shevitz, 1976). The rationale behind both procedures was that the frontal cortex exaggerates the emotional responses produced in lower regions of the brain, in particular the thalamus and hypothalamus. Cutting the

tracts connecting these areas to the frontal cortex was assumed to have a calming effect.

As with most of the treatments we have discussed, there was an initial flurry of interest in psychosurgical procedures coupled with enthusiastic claims for their effectiveness. While the techniques were in relatively widespread use, they were applied to schizophrenics, to depressives, and less frequently to persons with personality and anxiety disorders. Persons plagued by obsessions were more frequently operated on than other neurotics. The results of studies attempting to assess the efficacy of the treatment were unimpressive. For example, Robbin (1958, 1959) compared changes in lobotomy patients and controls. Lobotomy was found to produce a slightly greater discharge rate, but more of these patients were subsequentely readmitted. Similarly, Barahal (1958) did a five-to-ten-year follow-up on 1000 lobotomy cases. His findings compelled him to publicize the high rate of undesirable side effects, such as seizures, extreme listlessness, stupor, and even death. In sum, these surgical procedures have little to recommend them; they lack demonstrated effectiveness and can have serious, *irreversible* consequences. With the advent of the phenothiazines in the mid-1950s, the popularity of lobotomy dropped off dramatically.

But newer surgical procedures have continued to be used in treating abnormal behavior. More precise techniques allow the frontal cortex to be

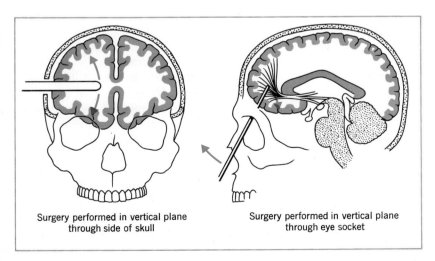

Surgery performed in vertical plane
through side of skull

Surgery performed in vertical plane
through eye socket

FIGURE **20.4**
Psychosurgeons attempt to eliminate especially troublesome behavior, such as violent psychotic episodes, by cutting the connections between the cortex of the frontal lobes and lower centers of the brain.

separated from lower brain areas with a destruction of only 8 square centimeters of brain tissue (Shevitz, 1976). The procedure apparently has beneficial effects for some patients—notably those with severe depression, anxiety, and obsessive-compulsive disorders—and fewer undesirable side effects. Current thinking would limit these operations to patients with very severe, long-lasting problems that have not responded to any other treatment.

Convulsive Therapy

Several people became interested in the therapeutic induction of convulsions, all during the same decade. In 1932 in Vienna, the psychiatrist Manfred Sakel had been experimenting with insulin injections as a means of reducing withdrawal symptoms in morphine addicts. In one patient the low blood sugar level produced by the insulin accidentally elicited a coma, and Sakel observed that afterward the patient's mental state was less confused. He continued to experiment with insulin-produced coma and reported that it could even reduce psychotic symptoms. The technique was soon in rather widespread use, both in Europe and North America. But each treatment took four or five hours, and they went on for several months. Patients gained a great deal of weight through the disruption of their sugar metabolism. The procedure, which was very expensive because of the medical care required, declined in popularity as its health hazards and limited effectiveness came to be appreciated.

At about the same time that Sakel began his work, the clinical experience of a Hungarian physician, Von Meduna, led him to the opinion that an "antagonism" existed between epilepsy and schizophrenia. He leapt from this conclusion to propose that inducing a convulsion might cure schizophrenia. He chose the drug Metrazol for this purpose.

The originators of electroconvulsive shock therapy (ECT) were the Italian physicians U. Cerletti and L. Bini. Cerletti had been interested in epilepsy and was seeking a means by which its seizures could be experimentally induced. The "solution" became apparent during a visit to a slaughterhouse, where Cerletti saw animals rendered unconscious by electric shocks administered to the head. Shortly thereafter he found that by applying electric shocks he could produce full epileptic seizures, rigidity followed by spasms, in his laboratory. Not long after that, in 1938 in Rome, he used the technique on a schizophrenic patient.

The electrical means of inducing a convulsion became the preferred method. The technique has remained essentially the same since its introduction by Cerletti and Bini, at least until recently. Electrodes are placed on each side of the patient's forehead, and a current of between 70 and 130 volts is allowed to pass between them for a fraction of a second, inducing a grand mal seizure (see page 717). A period of electrical silence in the patient's brain follows; then there is a gradual resumption of the preconvulsion pattern. Patients nowadays are typically given a sedative and relaxant beforehand to reduce the incidence of bone fractures and bruises occasionally suffered during ECT. The usual ECT regimen entails about ten treatments given at a rate of about three per week.

Following ECT the patient is often very confused and shows loss of memory both for happenings before the treatment and for whatever transpired within one hour afterward. The confusion and loss of memory generally disappear within several weeks, but sometimes the individual has trouble remembering past events for months, even years.

A new development in ECT is unilateral shock, the application of shock to only one of the cerebral hemispheres, usually the nondominant one. Unilateral ECT causes less confusion and less impairment of memory. In most studies it has been found to be as therapeutically effective as the standard procedure (Inglis, 1969; Abrams, 1975).

Electroconvulsive therapy, although originally applied to both schizophrenics and depressed patients, is now used primarily for profoundly depressed people. As we saw previously when we reviewed the May (1968) study, phenothiazine medication is more effective for schizophrenics than is ECT. For severe depressives, though, ECT is a fast and sure treatment. Indeed, it is sometimes regarded as the optimal treatment for severe depression (for example, Klerman,

1972), even though the mechanism by which it works is unknown, and even though it does not prevent future episodes of depression.

In spite of the promise carefully administered ECT holds for deeply depressed patients, many professionals object to its use; it is applied much less often than it once was. A major problem is the fear that many patients have of ECT. In spite of amnesia for the episode, and even though muscle relaxants are given to prevent bone fractures, patients are often reluctant to undergo, or their families to sanction, such treatments, at least without considerable urging from the medical staff. The procedure is in truth violent in nature; ECT does entail the deliberate induction of a seizure and subsequent unconsciousness. Many people therefore consider the "cure" worse than the "disease." But it is difficult to dismiss ECT, since the evidence does indicate that it is effective in treating depression.

Summary

Group therapy takes advantage of some special properties of the group itself. A group can exert especially strong social pressure for change. Members also benefit from sharing common concerns and aspirations. Sensitivity training and encounter groups enable people to learn how they affect others and are affected by them. Efforts are made to get behind the social facades that people present to the world, so that they may deal honestly and more effectively with one another. Controlled research on outcome and process in group therapy of all kinds is just beginning to be done.

In family therapy the problems of the "identified" patient are considered the manifestation of disturbances within the family unit. Family members learn how their behavior and attitudes affect one another, that flexibility and changing communication patterns can bring greater harmony. Marital therapy helps unhappy couples resolve the conflicts inevitable to any ongoing relationship of two adults living together. One technique consists of caring days; one partner at a time concentrates on giving pleasure to the other, breaking the cycle of bitterness and hostility plaguing them. Marital therapists of all theoretical allegiances try to improve partners' communication of needs and wants to each other. An act may be well intentioned but have a negative impact. Talking openly about this problem appears to ease the tensions of many couples. In one research project schizophrenics discharged from the hospital to their homes manage to remain there because their families learn to reduce the level of hostility and criticism aimed at them. Continuing research in family and marital therapies promises to elucidate the problems for which they are the most appropriate and the processes by which they bring gratifying relief.

Community psychology and the related community mental health movement try to prevent mental disorders from developing, to seek out troubled people, and to find the social conditions that may be causing human problems. Community workers must make their values explicit, for they are often fostering social change rather than helping individuals adjust to what some consider untenable social conditions.

Deinstitutionalization, the policy of having former mental patients live, if at all possible, at home or in small residences is part of this movement. Much work needs to be done, however, in designing and supplying adequate sheltered residences and care that will help them live in the community. Primary prevention is difficult to institute, a reflection of our inadequate knowledge of how disordered behavior develops. We know very little either about how to determine the needs of a community and how to mobilize large groups of people for change.

Somatic treatments attempt to alter abnormal functioning by intervening directly in bodily processes. A variety of psychoactive drugs have proved effective: minor tranquilizers for calming anxious but nonpsychotic people, neuroleptics for lessening the thought disorders and behavioral problems of schizophrenics, stimulants for reducing hyperactivity in children, antidepressants for lifting the mood of depressed individuals, and lithium for controlling the wide swings in affect of bipolar patients. As useful as these different drugs are, they all have side effects, sometimes serious ones, and psychological therapies are usually needed to treat aspects of the disorders that remain untouched by medication. In earlier decades treatments were also tried for seemingly intractable psychotic conditions: psychosurgery, in which connections between the cortex and lower regions of the brain are severed; and convulsive therapies, notably electroconvulsive shock treatment, to induce a grand mal seizure by passing high-voltage shock through the cortex. Psychoactive drugs have virtually eliminated the need for these measures, although ECT remains an apparently effective treatment for profound depression.

chapter 21

LEGAL AND ETHICAL ISSUES

Criminal Commitment
Civil Commitment
Ethical Dilemmas in Therapy and Research

Amendment 1   Congress shall make no law respecting an establishment of religion, or prohibiting the free exercise thereof; or abridging the freedom of speech, or of the press; or the right of the people peaceably to assemble, and to petition the Government for a redress of grievances.

Amendment 4   The right of the people to be secure in their persons, houses, papers, and effects, against unreasonable searches and seizures, shall not be violated. . . .

Amendment 5   No person . . . shall be compelled in any criminal case to be a witness against himself, nor be deprived of life, liberty, or property, without due process of law. . . .

Amendment 6   In all criminal prosecutions, the accused shall enjoy the right to a speedy and public trial . . . ; to be confronted with the witnesses against him; to have compulsory process for obtaining witnesses in his favor, and to have

the Assistance of Counsel for his defense.

Amendment 8   Excessive bail shall not be required, nor excessive fines imposed, nor cruel and unusual punishments inflicted.

Amendment 13   . . . Neither slavery nor involuntary servitude, except as a punishment for crime whereof the party shall have been duly convicted, shall exist within the United States, or any place subject to their jurisdiction. . . .

Amendment 14   . . . No State shall . . . deprive any person of life, liberty, or property, without due process of law; nor deny to any person within its jurisdiction the equal protection of the laws.

Amendment 15   . . . The right of citizens of the United States to vote shall not be denied or abridged by the United States or by any State on account of race, color, or previous condition of servitude.

These elegant statements describe and protect some of the rights of American citizens and others residing in this country. Against what are these rights being protected? Be mindful of the circumstances under which most of these statements were issued. After the Constitutional Convention delegates had delineated the powers of government in 1787, the first Congress saw fit in 1789 to amend what they had framed and to set specific limits on the federal government. Amendments beyond the original ten have been added since that time. The philosophical ideal of American government has always been to allow citizens the maximum degree of liberty consistent with preserving order in the community at large.

We open our final chapter in this way because the legal and mental health systems collaborate continually, although often subtly, to deny a substantial proportion of our population their basic civil rights. With the best of intentions, judges, governing boards of hospitals, bar associations, and professional mental health groups have worked over the years to protect society at large from the actions of people regarded as mentally ill or mentally defective and considered dangerous to themselves or to others. But in so doing they have abrogated the rights of thousands of people in both criminal and civil commitment proceedings. Those who have broken the law, or who are alleged to have done so, can be committed to a prison hospital through *criminal commitment* proceedings. *Civil commitment* is a set of procedures by which a person who has not broken a law can be deprived of his or her liberty and incarcerated in a mental hospital. In effect, both commitments remove individuals from the normal processes of the law.

Criminal Commitment

We shall examine first the role of psychiatry and psychology in the criminal justice system. Almost as early as the concept of a *mens rea* or guilty mind and the rule "No crime without an evil intent" had begun to be accepted in English common law, insanity had to be taken into consideration, for a disordered mind may be regarded as unable to formulate and carry out a criminal purpose. At first insanity was not a trial defense, but the English crown sometimes granted pardons to people who had been convicted of homicide if they were judged completely and totally mad (Morris, 1968). By the reign of Edward I (1272–1307), the concept of insanity had begun to be argued in court and could lessen punishment. Then during the course of the fourteenth century it became the rule of law that a person proved to be wholly and continually mad could be defended against a criminal charge.

In modern times judges and lawyers have called on psychiatrists, and recently clinical psychologists as well, for assistance in dealing with criminal acts thought to have been committed when the accused was suffering extreme emotional upset or anguish. Are such emotionally disturbed perpetrators less criminally responsible than those who are not distraught but commit the same crimes? Should such individuals even be brought to trial for transgressions against society's laws? Although efforts to elicit professional opinions on these issues are undoubtedly well intentioned, injustices are sometimes done those whose emotional states and mental capacities have created doubts about their legal responsibility for their acts and about their competency to stand trial.

Landmark Decisions on the Insanity Defense

A staggering amount of material has been written on the insanity defense. Alan A. Stone[1] (1975), a

---

[1] One of the sources for our treatment of criminal and civil commitment is Stone's excellent monograph *Mental Health and Law: A System in Transition*, published by the National Institute of Mental Health in 1975. It is strongly recommended to those who have special interest in the topic.

professor of law and psychiatry at Harvard, has proposed an intriguing reason for this great interest. Criminal law rests on the assumption that people have free will and that, if they do wrong, they have *chosen* to do so and should therefore be punished. "Our jurisprudence . . . while not oblivious to deterministic components, ultimately rests on a premise of freedom of will" (*United States* v. *Brawner*[2]). Stone suggests that the insanity defense strengthens the concept of free will by pointing to the few people who constitute an exception because they do not have it, namely those judged to be insane. These individuals are assumed to have diminished responsibility for their actions because of a mental defect, an inability to distinguish between right and wrong, or both. They lack the degree of free will that would justify holding them legally accountable for criminal acts. By exclusion, everyone else *has* free will! "The insanity defense is in every sense the exception that proves the rule. It allows the courts to treat every other defendant as someone who chose 'between good and evil' " (Stone, 1975, p. 222).

Historically, in modern Anglo-American criminal law, there have been three important court rulings that bear on the problems of legal responsibility and mental illness. The so-called "irresistible impulse" concept was formulated in 1834 in a case in Ohio wherein it was decided that an insanity defense was legitimate if a pathological impulse or drive that the person could not control had compelled him to commit the criminal act. The irresistible impulse test was confirmed in two subsequent court cases, *Parsons* v. *State* and *Davis* v. *United States*.[3]

The second well-known concept, the McNaghten rule, was announced in the aftermath of a murder trial in England in 1843. The defendant, Daniel McNaghten, had meant to kill the British prime minister but had instead mistaken the secretary of Sir Robert Peel for his employer. McNaghten claimed that he had been instructed to kill Lord Peel by the "voice of God." The judges ruled that

. . . . to establish a defence of insanity, it must be clearly proved that, at the time of the committing of the act, the party accused was labouring under such a defect of reason, from disease of the mind, as not to know the nature and quality of the act he was doing; or if he did know it, that he did not know he was doing what was wrong.

This "right-wrong" concept has been applied in the United States for many years. It is the sole test in just fewer than half the states; in most other jurisdictions it is one of the standards and is often applied in conjunction with irresistible impulse.

The third decision, made in the 1954 case of *Durham* v. *United States*,[4] says that the "accused is not criminally responsible if his unlawful act was the product of mental disease or mental defect." David Bazelon, the presiding justice, believed that by referring simply to mental illness he would leave the profession of psychiatry free to apply its full knowledge. It would no longer be limited to considering impulses or knowledge of right and wrong. Judge Bazelon purposely did not incorporate in what would be called the Durham test any particular symptoms of mental disorder that might later become obsolete. The psychiatrist was accorded great liberty to convey to the court his or her own evaluation of the accused's mental condition. Forcing the jury to rely to this extent on expert testimony did not prove workable courtroom practice, however. The Durham test has been replaced in most of the jurisdictions that had adopted it.

In 1962 the American Law Institute (ALI) proposed its own guidelines, which were intended to be more specific and informative to lay jurors than the "mental disease or mental defect" of the Durham test.

1. A person is not responsible for criminal conduct if at the time of such conduct as a result of mental disease or defect he lacks substantial capacity either to appreciate the criminality (wrongfulness) of his conduct or to conform his conduct to the requirements of law.

---

[2] United States v. Brawner, No. 22,714 (D.C. Cir. June 23, 1972).
[3] Parsons v. State, 2 So. 854, 866-67 (Ala. 1887); Davis v. United States, 165 U.S. 373, 378 (1897).

[4] Durham v. United States, 214 F. 2d 862, 876 (D.C. Cir. 1954).

"BUT YOU JUST CAN'T PLEAD INSANITY DUE TO AN EXTRA Y-CHROMOSOME IN A CASE OF EMBEZZLING."

2. As used in the Article, the terms "mental disease or defect" do not include an abnormality manifested only by repeated criminal or otherwise antisocial conduct (The American Law Institute, 1962, p. 66).

The first of the ALI guidelines in a sense combines the McNaghten rule and the irresistible-impulse concept. According to legal scholars, however, the phrases substantial capacity, appreciate criminality of conduct, and conform conduct to the law broaden these concepts and allow the jurors themselves to decide whether the defendant should be blamed for misconduct. The questions whether there was irresistible impulse and whether there was knowledge of right and wrong are more exacting and require expert opinion. The second ALI guideline concerns those who are repeatedly in trouble with the law; they are not to be deemed mentally ill only because they keep committing crimes. The ALI test is being adopted in more and more states and is already the standard in all federal circuit courts of appeal.

Many issues are raised by the insanity defense, for in its application an abstract principle must be fit to specific life situations. As in all aspects of the law, terms can be defined in a number of ways—by the defendants, defense lawyers, prosecutors, judges, and, of course, jurors—and testimony can be presented in diverse fashion, depending on the skill of the interrogators and the intelligence of the witnesses.

A final point should be stressed. Only the defendant's mental condition *at the time the crime was committed* is in question. Consequently, retrospective, often speculative, judgment on the part of attorneys, judges, jurors, and psychiatrists is required. Moreover, if the defendant is acquitted by reason of insanity, hospitalization may not be automatic, for the acquittal concerns the state of mind at the time the criminal act was committed. By the time a trial has been held, the person may well be considered sane and therefore not in need of treatment (Schwitzgebel and Schwitzgebel, 1980)!

Case Example

To illustrate the problems that may be raised by an insanity plea, let us consider the case of Charles Rouse, as reported in a *New Republic* article by James Ridgeway (1967). Rouse, a twenty-year-old resident of Washington, D.C., was arrested one night while carrying a suitcase containing a .45 Colt automatic pistol, ammunition, two electric drills, and some razor blades. The maximum penalty for carrying such lethal weapons in the District of Columbia is one year, yet Rouse was confined for more than four years. How did this happen?

The Durham decision of 1954 applied in the District of Columbia at that time. During his trial Rouse was examined by court psychiatrists and judged to be suffering from "antisocial reaction," sufficient grounds to be acquitted by reason of insanity according to the Durham test. Rouse received such an acquittal. But this "acquittal" did not lead to freedom. Rather, he was incarcerated in a federal mental hospital, St. Elizabeth's, in Washington, for psychotherapeutic treatment of his personality disorder. He was kept there much longer than he would have been confined had no issues been raised about his sanity.

Those who favor close liaison between mental health workers and the courts argue that it would have been unjust to Rouse to hold him legally responsible for his misdemeanor, and that the most charitable and effective course of action—both for him and for society at large—was to treat the mental disorder that presumably had brought about the arrest in the first place. But how therapeutic was Rouse's forced hospitalization? After two years of confinement in St. Elizabeth's, Rouse had his attorney file a writ of habeas corpus, a procedure which an incarcerated person can institute in order to obtain a court hearing on whether continued detainment is justified. At this hearing Dr. E., Rouse's psychiatrist in the hospital, was asked to report on Rouse's behavior. The doctor cited examples of what he regarded as "poor judgment." Rouse had refused an invitation to leave maximum security and to move to less constricted areas of the prison hospital, preferring instead to seek relief through litigation and a court hearing. He had also left group therapy in a "cavalier manner," evidence, Dr. E. said, of lack of insight and poor judgment and of the continuing mental illness that had been the basis of his acquittal two years earlier.

The doctor also mentioned additional examples of what he considered to be diseased behavior, such as Rouse's reluctance to become involved with the other patients. "And because he does not get together with people I conclude that he is antisocial, antisocial since he cannot tolerate the anxiety that comes with having relationships with people" (p.25). Dr. E. recommended to the judge that Rouse not be released yet, for "In my opinion if Mr. Rouse were placed at liberty at the present time it would be a precipitous thing to do and he would be dangerous to himself and to other people by virtue of his mental illness. I think he needs supervision over the long haul" (p.25). Indeed, Dr. E. stated that, if released, Mr. Rouse would be likely to obtain guns and ammunition and to shoot someone.

In his defense, Rouse's attorney produced testimony by another psychiatrist who felt that further hospitalization would be *detrimental* and that Rouse should therefore be discharged. The judge, however, agreed with Dr. E., saying that Rouse had not taken advantage of the help available at St. Elizabeth's and that he was therefore not ready for release. Rouse was ultimately discharged on grounds that people under criminal commitment have a _right to treatment_ and that

his confinement at St. Elizabeth's amounted only to punishment.[5]

A number of general problems are highlighted by this case.

1. The judgment of psychiatrists and psychologists plays a crucial role in how long a person remains in a mental hospital for treatment of a problem that is said to have caused a criminal act. But professionals frequently *disagree* about the presence of a problem.

2. The hospital psychiatrist may interpret as evidence of continued mental illness any efforts made by the patient to escape from the hospital environment, even if by legal means. In Rouse's case it seemed as though almost everything he did was construed as symptomatic of his assumed illness.

3. Unorthodox behavior, particularly if it breaks a law, can be regarded as evidence of a dangerous mental disorder and can thereby remove the individual from the direct jurisdiction of the courts. It can cause the individual to be incarcerated for longer periods of time than he would have served had he been convicted and sentenced as an ordinary criminal.

Rouse's case is, of course, only one among many that could be discussed. Few others show forensic psychiatry[6] in as unfavorable a light. The record is bad enough, however, that many persons advocate reducing the role played by mental health professionals in the legal process. We discuss some of these issues later in the chapter.

Competency To Stand Trial

The insanity defense concerns the accused's mental state *at the time of the crime*. A second issue, whether the person is competent to stand trial, concerns the defendant's mental condition *at the time of his or her trial*. It is obviously possible for a person to be judged competent to

---

[5] Rouse v. Cameron, 373 F. 2d 451 (D.C. Cir. 1966).
[6] This term refers to the activities of psychiatrists concerned with legal responsibility and criminal commitment. Psychologists have also become involved in legal proceedings.

stand trial yet be acquitted by reason of insanity. By the same token, it is possible for a person to be deemed incompetent to stand trial when no final courtroom consideration has yet been given to his criminal responsibility for the act in question.

Far greater numbers of people are committed to prison hospitals after being judged incompetent to stand trial than are tried and acquitted by reason of insanity. In fact, it has been estimated that as many as ten people are confined in prison hospitals because of incompetency to stand trial for every one ultimately sent there for having been found not guilty by reason of insanity. Our criminal justice system is so organized that the fitness of individuals to stand trial must be decided before their responsibility for the crime of which they are accused can be determined (Schwitzgebel and Schwitzgebel, 1980). Once a trial is held, the defendant may be found guilty and sent to prison, be found not guilty of having performed the illegal act and consequently set free, or be found not guilty by reason of insanity and therefore committed to a prison hospital.

With the Supreme Court case, *Pate* v. *Robinson*,[7] as precedent, the defense attorney, prosecutor, or judge may raise the question of mental illness whenever there is reason to believe that the accused's mental condition might interfere with the upcoming trial. Over the years most jurisdictions in this country have shown concern that the accused may be "presently insane and otherwise so mentally incompetent as to be unable to understand the proceedings against him or properly to assist in his own defense" (Pfeiffer, Eisenstein, and Dabbs, 1967, p. 322). Another way of stating this problem of competency is to say that the courts do not want a person to be brought to trial *in absentia*, which is a basic principle of English common law. A disturbed person can of course by physically present; what is referred to here is his or her mental state. If after examination the person is deemed too mentally ill to participate meaningfully in a trial, the trial is routinely delayed. The accused is incarcerated in a prison hospital with the hope that

means of restoring adequate mental functioning can be found.

Being judged incompetent to stand trial can have severe consequences for the individual. Bail is automatically denied, even though it might be routinely granted if the question of incompetency had not been raised. The accused is incarcerated in a facility for the criminally insane for the pretrial examination; these institutions are typically the worst of hospitals. The accused may well lose employment and undergo the trauma of being separated from family and friends and from familiar surroundings for months or even longer, perhaps making his emotional condition even worse and thereby delaying his fitness to stand trial. Some people have languished in a prison for many years, waiting to be found competent to stand trial.

Many psychiatrists, when asked to render a competency judgment, assume that if they judge the person to be mentally disturbed in any way, it follows that he or she cannot stand trial; thus have many people been deprived of their day in court. Robey (1965) has pointed out, however, that even a psychotic person may sufficiently understand his position in the legal proceedings to participate in them and to talk with his attorney rationally. Robey proposes that a person be allowed to come to trial *even though* he may behave in a bizarre manner before and during the proceedings. The accused may be at a severe disadvantage if, during the trial, he is confused, deluded, hallucinating, and so on, but a somewhat inequitable trial may be preferable to being incarcerated until behavior is judged normal once again. It should be kept in mind that some of the people we are talking about are proved, once they have been brought to trial, *not* to have committed the crimes of which they were accused.

A 1972 Supreme Court case, *Jackson* v. *Indiana*,[8] forced the states to a shorter-term determination of incompetency. The case concerned a mentally retarded deaf-mute man who was deemed not only incompetent to stand trial but unlikely ever to become competent. The Court ruled that the length of pretrial confinement must

[7] Pate v. Robinson, 383 U.S. 375 (1966).

[8] Jackson v. Indiana, 406 U.S. 715 (1972).

be limited to the time it takes to determine whether the defendant is likely to become competent to stand trial in the foreseeable future. If the defendant is unlikely ever to become competent, the state should after this period either institute civil commitment proceedings or release the defendant. Legislation has been drafted in most states to define more precisely the minimal requirements for competency to stand trial, ending the latitude that has deprived thousands of people of their rights to due process (Amendment 14) and a speedy trial (Amendment 6).

The era of modern medicine has also had an impact on the competency issue. The concept of "synthetic sanity" (Schwitzgebel and Schwitzgebel, 1980) has been introduced: if a drug like Thorazine temporarily produces a modicum of rationality in an otherwise deranged defendant, the trial may proceed. The likelihood that the defendant will become incompetent to stand trial if and when the drug is withdrawn will not disqualify him from having his day in court.[9]

Thomas S. Szasz and the Case Against Forensic Psychiatry and Psychology

His polemic

"By codifying acts of violence as expressions of mental illness, we neatly rid ourselves of the task of dealing with criminal offenses as more or less rational, goal-directed acts, or different in principle from other forms of conduct" (Szasz, 1963, p. 141).

This quotation from one of Szasz's most widely read books enunciates the basic theme of his polemic against the weighty role that his own profession of psychiatry plays in the legal system. To understand the view of this outspoken and eloquent critic of forensic psychiatry, we must first of all examine the distinction made between *descriptive* and *ascriptive* responsibility. As Szasz points out, a person may be judged descriptively responsible in the sense that all agree a particular act was, in fact, performed by him. Assigning ascriptive responsibility, however, is a

Thomas S. Szasz, noted psychiatrist who argues strongly against the use of the insanity defense.

social judgment that society should inflict consequences upon someone deemed descriptively responsible. The court verdict of "not guilty by reason of insanity" says, first, that John Doe was descriptively responsible for commiting a crime, but second, that society will not ascribe legal responsibility to him and punish him for what he did. Killing in wartime is another example of this divergence between descriptive and ascriptive responsibilities. To murder the enemy as a member of a nation's armed forces is to be responsible for another person's death. Yet the soldier is not punished for his action and indeed may win honors for it.

To hold a person criminally responsible is to ascribe or attribute legal responsibility to him. A given social group makes the judgment that the person who is descriptively responsible for a criminal act will receive criminal punishment. As Szasz points out, being criminally responsible is not a trait that is inherent in a person and that society uncovers. Rather, society at a given time and for a given criminal act decides that it will hold the perpetrator legally responsible and punish him.

[9] State of Louisiana v. Hamptom, 216 So. 2d 311 (1969); State of Tennessee v. Stacy, No. 446 (Crim. App., Knoxville, TN, August 4, 1977).

Edward Oxford's attempt to assassinate Queen Victoria on June 10, 1840. The artist who drew this did not know that Oxford was not a "gentleman" but a waiter in a tavern.

Szasz goes on to suggest that mental illness began to be used as an explanation for criminal behavior when people acted in a way that was considered particularly irrational and threatening to society. According to Szasz, these exceptional cases all involved violence against people of high social rank. In shooting at a Lord Onslow in 1724, a man named Arnold was believed to have as little understanding of his murderous act as "a wild beast." Another man, James Hadfield, was deemed deranged for attempting to assassinate King George III in 1800 as he sat in a box at the Theatre Royal. And a third, Oxford by name, was regarded as insane for trying to kill Queen Victoria in 1840. The best-known case has already been mentioned, that of Daniel McNaghten (1843), who killed Sir Robert Peel's private secretary after mistaking him for Peel. In all these cases from English law, which forms the basis for all American law, people of low social rank openly attacked their superiors. Szasz believes that ". . . the issue of insanity may have been raised in these trials in order to obscure the social problems which the crimes intended to dramatize" (1963, p. 128).

Other cases here and abroad, such as the assassinations of John and Robert Kennedy, the South African prime minister, Hendrik Verwoerd, Martin Luther King, and John Lennon, and the attempted assassinations of Ronald Reagan and Pope John Paul II, may to a degree reflect the social ills of today. Moreover, court proceedings in the Soviet Union are ominous. In *A Question of Madness*, the well-known Russian biochemist Zhores Medvedev (1972) told how Soviet psychiatrists collaborated with the state in attempting to muzzle his criticism of his government. They diagnosed him as suffering from paranoid delusions, split personality, and other mental ailments that would make it dangerous for him to be at large in society. In the years since, the confinement of political protesters for madness has, if anything, increased in the Soviet Union (see Box 21.1).

But pleas of insanity are made in far more ordinary cases. And of course Szasz does not claim that all these pleas involve some sort of silent conspiracy of the establishment to cover up social problems. Szasz sets forth a polemic much broader in scope. His basic concern is with individual freedom, which includes the right to deviate from prevailing mores. Far from advocating that people be held *less* accountable for antisocial acts, he argues that legal responsibility be extended to *all*, even to those whose actions are so far beyond the limits of convention that some people explain their behavior in terms of mental illness.

Szasz's villain is what he calls "psychoauthoritarianism." He traces all contemporary thought on the matter to Alexander and Staub (1929), who argued that although the usual legal proceedings may be appropriate for "normal criminals," psychoanalysis should form the basis for handling "neurotic" criminals. They presented their position in a forthright manner.

We propose a more consistent application of the principle that not the deed but the doer should be punished. . . . The implementation of this principle requires expert diagnostic judgment which can be expected only from specially trained psychiatric experts. Before any sentence is imposed, a medical-legal diagnosis should be required. This would amount to an official recognition of unconscious motivations in all human behavior. The neurotic criminal obviously has a limited sense of responsibility. Primarily he is a sick person, and his delinquency is the outcome of his emotional disturbances. This fact, however, should not exempt him from the conse-

. . .I was arrested in 1963 for preparing two photocopies of [Milovan] Djilas's book "The New Class" and was placed in solitary confinement at the Lubyanks Prison. I was . . . summoned by General Svetlichny, who was then in charge of the Moscow K.G.B., and was offered [a chance] to repent and tell who gave me the book and who helped me make the photocopies. Then I would be released.

The obvious purpose of [this conversation] was to turn me into an informer and to make me cooperate with the authorities. But when nothing came of this, I was given a psychiatric examination, was declared mentally ill and was sent to Leningrad. I attribute my release to the fact that the Leningrad school [of psychiatry was disputing] with the Moscow school and [refuting] their diagnoses [of schizophrenia]. In February 1965 I was freed.

At the end of 1965, I was again arrested for organizing the first human rights demonstration, which took place on December 5 in defense of [Andrei] Sinyavsky and [Yuli] Daniel. . . . Up to that time, there had been no demonstrations since 1927 and the legislature forgot to foresee the proper measure of punishment for those who should take part in demonstrations. Consequently, there were no legal punitive means of punishment. I was simply dispatched to one of the Moscow psychiatric hospitals with the intention that my old diagnosis be confirmed and then, without a new court hearing or investigation, I would again be sent to Leningrad as a person who had not as yet been fully "cured" from the previous time.

The K.G.B.'s calculations were undermined by honest young doctors at city hospital No. 13, who prepared an extensive report stating that I was not mentally ill. In spite of the doctors' conclusions, I was transferred to another city hospital, in accordance with the K.G.B.'s instructions. In this hospital, the doctors also did not find me to be ill and insisted that I be released. And once again—upon the instructions of the K.G.B.—I was transferred, but this time to the Serbsky Institute. In the face of the well-supported conclusion provided by two hospitals, even the Serbsky Institute did not [dare] to declare me insane. . . . [But at] that very time, when my mother went to see General Svetlichny, he stomped his feet and screamed: "He will never be released! *We* will let him rot in the insane aslyum!"

In the meantime, my case had attracted public attention and became well known in the West, thanks to the pronouncements made by Valery Tarsis and the activities of Amnesty International. Finally, the authorities were forced to appoint a neutral commission. But four professors who were specially summoned could not come to a unified conclusion. Two of them, representing Snezhnevsky's [Moscow] school, declared me to be mentally ill. The other two, opponents of his school, refuted their diagnosis.

I remained confined amid this situation for eight months, six of which were spent at the Serbsky Institute. You need not think that the dispute was strictly scientific: It was a matter of conformity or nonconformity of doctors, and the authorities could not find a sufficient number of conformists for a case which had attracted such publicity.

I was released after a representative of Amnesty International came to Moscow and went straight to Georgy Morozov, the director of the Serbsky Institute, and told him that if I were not immediately released, my case would be raised before the Bertrand Russell tribunal.

By the end of the 1960's, a well-established methodology of psychiatric repression had evolved . . . the K.G.B. provided the ideological direction, giving the instruction that opponents of the regime be declared insane and the psychiatrists worked out an entire system with a diagnostic basis. By this time the Snezhevsky school was in firm command of Soviet psychiatry.

The following categories of individuals were most liable to be declared "insane":

1. Prominent figures, whose trials would prove to be uncomfortable in the propagandistic sense.

2. So-called revisionists—that is, those who criticize the system from Marxist positions.

3. Persons who stood up for their convictions during the period of investigation, used legal means of defense and insisted on their right not to give any evidence whatsover.

4. Believers, including those who faced purely political charges, without any "religious articles."

. . . In the 1970's political prisoners have been sent more and more often to psychiatric prison hospitals before the expiration of their camp sentences. This practice allows the authorities to lengthen their terms for an endless period of time.

Now another new method has emerged: the practice of giving psychiatric diagnoses to political prisoners prior to their release from camp. After being freed with such a diagnosis, a former prisoner always lives under the Damocles sword of compulsory hospitalization.

How do Soviet psychiatrists attempt to justify their complicity in such a widely developed system of psychiatric repression?

The main features of today's psychiatric prisons, of which psychiatrists can no longer claim to be unaware, include treatment (with no regard to harmful effects), indefinite periods of confinement, the necessity of showing repentance in order to be freed, the discreditation of the person and his ideas, constant blackmail after the person's release, and his complete lack of any rights (such tested means of resistance as hunger strikes and the lodging of complaints, which are widely used in camps and prisons, serve only to burden a psychiatric diagnosis).

Under these conditions, every person who is arrested is afraid of being declared insane, and the threat of being sent to a psychiatric prison is used as blackmail during the period of investigation and during the course of the psychiatric examination (Bukovsky, 1977).

Zhores Medvedev (left) and Vladimir Bukovsky (right), Soviet dissidents who were detained in mental hospitals for criticizing the government.

quences of his action. *If he is curable, he should be incarcerated for the duration of psychiatric treatment as long as he still represents a menace to society. If he is incurable, he belongs in a hospital for incurables for life (p. xiii).*

These are strong statements. Some have criticized Szasz for erecting a straw man, the assumption being that nowadays no one really believes the Alexander and Staub position to be well founded. In all likelihood, however, this view—with "psychotic" or "psychopathic" substituted for "neurotic"—still prevails, both in this country and elsewhere, to an extent that we cannot be complacent about its effects.

Of the many problems presented by the Alexander and Staub argument, Szasz suggests that the following are especially important.

1. Disputes in legal proceedings in which insanity is an issue are common; the prosecution and the defense routinely produce "expert" witnesses whose positions are diametrically opposed.

2. In view of the criticisms that have been made of Freud, a proposal for the "official recognition of unconscious motivations in all human behavior" seems an anachronism. To base important social judgments on a poorly tested theory appears almost foolhardy. It should be mentioned in passing that Freud himself recommended that psychological opinions *not* play a role in court.

3. It is *at least* open to question whether enforced psychotherapy can ever be meaningful and effective. Rouse's case is a good example of the undue power that a prison psychiatrist can have over a criminal entrusted to him for "treatment," and of the trouble that the patient can get into if he refuses psychotherapy.

Szasz's overall lament is that

> Instead of recognizing the deviant as an individual different from those who would judge him, but nonetheless worthy of their respect, he is first discredited as a self-responsible human being and then subjected to humiliating punishment defined and disguised as treatment (1963, p. 108).

Evaluation of Szasz's position

As might be expected, Szasz has been answered by many whom he has criticized and by others who sincerely believe that psychiatry and psychology should have an important role in deciding how to deal with people whose criminal acts seem attributable to mental illness. When society acts with great certainty on the basis of "expert scientific opinion," however, particularly when that opinion denies to an individual the rights and respect accorded others in society, it may be well to let Szasz remind us that Sir Thomas Browne, a distinguished British physician, in 1664 testified in a court of law that witches did indeed exist, "as everyone knew."

And yet the abuses documented by Szasz should not blind us to the fact that—for whatever combination of physiological and psychological reasons—some people are, at times, a danger to others and to themselves. Although Szasz and others object to the mental illness metaphor as an explanation, it is difficult to deny that there is, indeed, madness in the world. People *do* occasionally imagine persecutors, whom they sometimes act against with force. Some people *do* hallucinate and on this basis may behave in a dangerous fashion. Our concern for the liberties of one individual has always been tempered with our concern for the rights of others.

But does it help a criminal acquitted by reason of insanity to place him in a prison mental hospital with an indeterminate sentence, pending his rehabilitation? The answer can surely not be an unqualified yes. Should such a person, then, be treated like any other convicted felon and be sent to a penitentiary? Considering the psychic damage that we know may occur in ordinary prisons, a yes to this question cannot be enthusiastic either. But a prison sentence is more often a finite term of incarceration. If we cannot dem-onstrate that people are rehabilitated in hospitals, perhaps it is just as well to rely on our prisons and on the efforts of penologists to improve these institutions and to find ways of helping inmates alter their behavior so that it will not be antisocial after release.[10]

---

[10] The treatment model, however, is being challenged by simple, old-fashioned, retributive justice (Monahan, 1977). Today punishment rather than rehabilitation is likely to be the primary purpose of imprisonment. Prisoners who were given treatment, whether job training or psychotherapy, have no different crime rates after release than inmates who simply sat out their terms in their cells and led a routine prison life. Prisoners themselves have been agitating for finite sentences, rather than the indeterminate sentence that promises early parole depending on "rehabilitation."

Civil Commitment

Civil commitment affects far greater numbers of people than criminal commitment. It is beyond the scope of this book to examine in detail the variety of state civil commitment laws and regulations. Each state has its own, and they are in almost constant flux. Our aim instead is to provide an overview that will give the reader a basic understanding of the issues and of the current directions of change.

In virtually all states of the union, a person can be committed to a mental hospital against his or her will if a judgment is made that he or she (1) is mentally ill and (2) is dangerous or needs treatment. At present, dangerousness to self or others is more often the second criterion, rather than the need for treatment. Indeed, recent court rulings point to *imminent* dangerousness as the principal criterion for civil commitment.[11]

Historically, governments have had the duty of protecting their citizens from harm. We take for granted the right and duty of government to set limits on our freedom for the sake of protecting us. Few drivers, for example, question the limits imposed on them by traffic signals. We usually go along with the Food and Drug Administration when it bans uncontrolled use of drugs that cause cancer in laboratory animals, although some people, to be sure, feel they have the right to decide for themselves what risks to take with their own bodies. Government, then, has a long-established right to protect us both from ourselves—the *parens patriae* power of the state; and from others—the police power of the state. Civil commitment is one further exercise of these powers.

Specific commitment procedures are generally of two types, formal and informal. Formal or judicial commitment is by order of a court. It can be requested by any responsible citizen; usually a relative or friend seeks the commitment. If the judge believes that there is good reason to pursue the matter, he or she will order a mental health examination. The person has the right to object to these attempts to "certify" him, and a court hearing can be scheduled to allow him to present evidence against commitment.

Informal, emergency commitment can be accomplished without initially involving the courts. For example, a hospital administrative board may decide that a voluntary patient requesting discharge is too disturbed and dangerous to be released. They are able to detain the patient with a temporary, informal commitment order. Any person acting wildly may be taken immediately to the state hospital by the police. Perhaps the most common informal commitment procedure is the "2PC" or "two physicians' certificate." In most states two physicians, not necessarily psychiatrists, can sign a certificate that will allow a person to be incarcerated for some period of time, ranging from twenty-four hours to as long as twenty days.[12] Detainment beyond this period requires judicial commitment.

Dangerousness: Problems in Definition and Prediction

The likelihood of committing a dangerous act is central to civil commitment, but is "dangerousness" easily defined? Stone (1975) suggests that, like beauty, it is in the eye of the beholder. Society punishes physical violence in the streets, for example, far more harshly than it punishes a business executive who knowingly neglects to replace defective gasoline tanks in an airplane (Geis and Monahan, 1976). White-collar dangerousness receives much less attention and retribution, even though it hurts more people. Monahan (1981) does mention a ruling of a federal court that writing a bad check was an act sufficiently dangerous to justify commitment because the economy would collapse if everyone did it. This would seem to be an extreme interpretation of dangerousness! The court decision has not been widely applied.

Commitment is necessarily a form of preventive detention: the prediction is made that a person judged mentally ill may in the future behave in a dangerous manner and should therefore be detained. Ordinary prisoners, however, are released from penitentiaries, even though crime

---

[11] Suzuki v. Yuen, 617 F. 2d 173 (1980).

[12] Special issues are involved in the commitment, institutionalization, and treatment of the mentally retarded, juveniles, drug addicts, and the aged. The reader is referred to Stone (1975) and to Schwitzgebel and Schwitzgebel (1980) for an in-depth discussion and for guidance to the burgeoning law and psychology-psychiatry literature.

statistics show that most will commit additional crimes. Moreover, the imprisonment of a criminal and the conviction by a court of law that precedes it are carried out only after a person has done some harm to others. Some may say it is like closing the barn door after the horses have thundered out. But our entire legal and constitutional system is organized to protect people from preventive detention. Even if witnesses have seen a person commit a serious crime, he or she is assumed innocent until proved guilty by the courts. The person who openly threatens to inflict harm on others, such as a man who for an hour each day points a loaded machine gun at a nearby apartment house, is another matter. Does the state have to wait until he fires a round? No. It is here that the civil commitment process can be brought into play, although the person must be deemed not only an imminent danger to others but mentally ill as well (Schwitzgebel and Schwitzgebel, 1980). Claiming mental illness turns out to be a minor problem. Most mental health professionals, in agreement with the lay public, will conclude that a person has to be insane to behave in this way.

Studies have examined how good mental health professionals are at predicting that a person will commit a dangerous act (for example, Kozol, Boucher, and Garofalo, 1972; Stone, 1975; Monahan, 1973, 1976); they were found to be poor at making this judgment. Some workers have even argued that civil commitment for the purposes of preventive detention should be abolished. Monahan (1978), however, carefully scrutinized these studies and concluded that the professional's ability to predict violence is still an open question. Most of the studies conformed to the following methodological pattern.

1. People were institutionalized for mental illness and for being a danger to the community.

2. While these people were in the hospital, some of them were again predicted to be violent if released into the community.

3. After a period of time, these people were released, thus putting together the conditions for "a natural experiment."

4. Checks on the behavior of the released patients over the next several years did not reveal much dangerous behavior.

What is wrong with such research? Monahan points out that little if any consideration was given to changes that institutionalization itself might have effected. In the studies reviewed, the period of incarceration ranged from several months to fifteen years. Prolonged periods of enforced hospitalization might very well make patients more docile, if for no other reason than that they become that much older. Furthermore, the conditions in the open community where the predicted violence would be done can vary widely. We should not expect this kind of prediction to have great validity.

These studies, which have occasioned such pessimism about predicting whether a patient is dangerous, are therefore flawed. Yet they have also been used in arguments against emergency commitment. The fact of the matter is that neither these studies nor any others have examined this specific issue! Monahan, however, has theorized that prediction of dangerousness is probably far easier and surer in true emergency situations than after extended periods of hospitalization. When an emergency commitment is sought, the person may appear out of control and be threatening violence in his or her own living room or, like the man in the street with a machine gun, against people in the nearby apartment house. He or she may also have been violent in the past—a good predictor of future violence—and victims and weapons may be on hand. A dangerous outburst seems imminent. Thus, unlike the danger to society predicted in the studies previously examined, the violence requiring an emergency commitment is expected almost immediately and in a known situation. Common sense tells us that such predictions of violence are likely to be very accurate. To test the validity of these expectations, we would have to leave alone half the people predicted to be immediately violent and later compare their behavior to that of persons hospitalized in such emergency circumstances. Such an experiment would be ethically irresponsible. Mental health professionals must apply logic and make the most prudent judgments possible.

BOX 21.2 Violent Behavior of Former Mental Patients

The association between mental illness and proneness to violence is very strongly embedded in the public's mind. We *assume* that many psychotic people are violent, that violence is often a result of madness, and that therefore society should be very wary about allowing mentally ill people to remain in our midst.

Is there really a cause-effect relationship or even a high correlation between mental disorder and dangerousness? First, it must be appreciated that only the violent ex-mental patient makes the six-o'clock news. Nonviolent, even positive and exemplary behavior on the part of former mental patients is not particularly newsworthy. Our impressions are therefore formed by extremely selective reporting.

Monahan (1981) recently reviewed the prevalence of mental disorder in prison populations and the violent crime rate of people released from mental hospitals. Granted that many violent people manage to avoid prison, and that many mentally ill people have never been in a mental hospital, he did not find a strong relation between violence and mental disorder.

Mental illness of criminals. Several studies (for example, Bolton, 1976; Guze, 1976; Monahan, Caldeira, and Friedlander, 1979) have found the prevalence of psychiatric disorder in prisoners to be in the range of 25 percent. The estimate of emotional disorders in the general population is similar, according to the President's Commission on Mental Health (1978). But people designated as sociopaths by prison clinicians do represent a sizable proportion of the prison population. Is not this particular disorder then associated with crime and perhaps violent crime? Diamond (1974) does not believe so, for prisoners are usually judged to be sociopathic based on a large number of previous arrests, delinquency in schools, poor job records, and "wanderlust," with a history of prostitution added as a criterion for women. Such a broad definition makes most people in prison sociopaths! Prisoners then have not been shown to have higher rates of mental illness than people in the population at large.

Violent behavior of former mental patients. Almost all the studies published in the 1950s and earlier found that released mental patients had a *lower* arrest rate for violent behavior than the general population; studies published in the 1960s and 1970s found them to have a *higher* arrest rate. Does this mean that, somehow, mentally ill people have only in the past twenty years become especially violent? Cocozza, Melick, and Steadman (1978) have concluded rather that a different group of people are now confined for a time in mental hospitals. Figure 21.1 summarizes the arrest records of 1938 patients released from mental hospitals in New York State in 1975. If we consider the total patient sample, their arrest rate for violent and potentially violent crimes is indeed significantly higher than in the general population. But if we divide the patients according to whether they had ever been arrested before their hospitalization, the statistics are more revealing. Released patients who had never been arrested before they entered the hospital had an arrest rate *lower* than in the general population, released patients with one earlier arrest had the same or slightly higher arrest rate, and released patients with two or more earlier arrests had a much higher arrest rate. Monahan concludes, ". . . compared with the general population, the higher rate of violent crime committed by released mental patients can be accounted for entirely by those patients with a record, particularly an extensive record, of criminal activity that predated their hospitalization" (1981, pp. 80-81).

A 1947 sample of patients indicated that 15 percent had a prior arrest record (Brill and Malzberg, 1954) as compared to 26 percent of the 1975 sample. The deinstitutionalization sweeps of the past decades released into the community patients unlikely to cause trouble, but at the same time people who earlier might have been sent to jail or prison were being

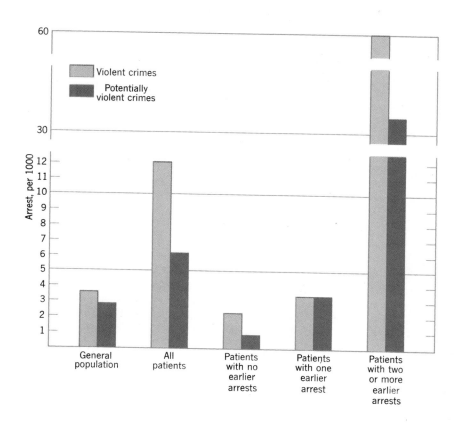

FIGURE **21.1**
Annual arrest rates per 1000 for violent and potentially violent crimes for the general population, for all patients in a 1975 sample, and for patients with no earlier arrests and with one and two or more earlier arrests. After data reported by Cocozza, Melick, and Steadman, 1978.

committed to mental hospitals. In just the past few years it has become more difficult to confine a person in a mental hospital against his or her will. It will be interesting to see what the statistics of the 1980s will look like.

The President's Commission on Mental Health drew the following conclusion.

The sporadic violence of so-called "mentally ill killers" as depicted in stories and dramas is more a device of fiction than a fact of life. Patients with serious psychological disorders are more likely to be withdrawn, apathetic, and fearful. We do not deny that some mentally ill people are violent, but the image of the mentally ill person as essentially a violent person is erroneous (1978, p. 56).

Recent Trends for Greater Protection

The United States Constitution is a remarkable document. It lays down the basic duties of our elected federal officials and guarantees a set of civil rights. But there is often some distance between the abstract delineation of a civil right and its day-to-day implementation. Moreover, judges must *interpret* the Constitution as it bears on specific contemporary problems. Since nowhere in this cornerstone of our democracy is there specific mention of committed mental patients, lawyers and judges interpret various sections of the document to justify what they consider necessary changes in society's treatment of people whose mental health is in question.

In 1972 voluntary admissions to mental hospitals began to outnumber involuntary admissions. But it is still the case that great numbers of people admitted to a state or county mental hospital are there against their wishes. Moreover, it is impossible to know how many of those who admit themselves voluntarily do so under threat of civil commitment. One survey (Gilboy and Schmidt, 1971) revealed that 40 percent of patients who had "voluntarily" admitted themselves to a mental hospital in Chicago had actually been threatened with commitment by the police officers who had brought them there. The issue of enforced mental hospitalization is still very much with us. Even though psychiatrists, psychologists, the courts, and hospital staff are apparently growing more reluctant to commit, tens of thousands of mental patients are in hospitals against their will.

In a democratic society the most grievous wrong that can be suffered by a citizen is loss of liberty. The situation of mental patients is improving, however. The rights accorded to ordinary citizens, and even to criminals, are gradually being extended to those threatened with civil commitment and to those who have already been involuntarily hospitalized. No longer is it assumed that deprivation of liberty for purposes of mental health care is reason to deny to the individual all other rights. For example, a federal court decision in Wisconsin, *Lessard* v. *Schmidt*,[13] gives a person threatened with civil commitment the right to timely, written notice of the proceeding, opportunity for a hearing with counsel, the right to have the hearing decided by jury, Fifth Amendment protection against self-incrimination, and other similar procedural safeguards already accorded defendants in criminal actions. A Supreme Court decision, *Addington* v. *Texas*,[14] further provides that the state must produce "clear and convincing evidence" that a person is mentally ill and dangerous before he can be involuntarily committed to a mental hospital. And recently the Ninth Circuit Court of Appeals ruled that this danger must be "imminent."[15] Clearly the trend is to restrict the power of the state to curtail individual freedoms because of "mental illness." Although protection of the rights of the mentally ill will add tremendously to the burden of both civil courts and state and county mental hospital staffs, it is a price a free society will have to pay.

> *Given the record of past [criminal proceedings and] the tragic parody of legal commitment used to warehouse American citizens, it is . . . important that the individual feel sure that the [present] mental health system [in particular] cannot be so used and abused . . . for while the average citizen may have some confidence that if called by the Grand Inquisitor in the middle of the night and charged with a given robbery, he may have an alibi or be able to prove his innocence, he may be far less certain of his capacity, under the press of fear, to instantly prove his sanity (Stone, 1975, p. 57).*

Least restrictive alternative

Civil commitment rests on presumed dangerousness, but of late dangerousness is being considered not an invarying trait of the individual but behavior occurring in a specific social context. Thus a person may be deemed dangerous if allowed to live by himself in an apartment, but not dangerous if living in a boarding home and taking prescribed psychoactive drugs every day under medical supervision. The "least restrictive al-

[13]Lessard V. Schmidt, 349 F. Supp. 1078 (E.D. Wisc. 1972), *vacated and remanded on other grounds*, 94 S. Ct. 712 (1974), *reinstated* 413 F. Supp. 1318 (E.D. Wisc. 1976).

[14] Addington v. Texas, No. 77-5992, April 30, 1979.
[15] Suzuki v. Yuen, 617 F. 2d 173 (1980).

ternative" to freedom is to be provided when treating disturbed people and protecting them from harming themselves and others. A number of court rulings, for example, *Lake v. Cameron*[16] and *Lessard v. Schmidt*, require that only mental patients who cannot be adequately looked after in less restrictive homes be confined in hospitals. Thus commitment is no longer necessarily in an institution. Rather a patient might well be required to reside in a supervised boarding home or in other sheltered quarters (Schwitzgebel and Schwitzgebel, 1980). Of course, this principle will have meaning only if society provides suitable residences.

Right to treatment

One aspect of civil commitment has come to the attention of the courts, the so-called right to treatment. If a person is deprived of liberty because he or she is mentally ill and is a danger to self or others, is not the state required to provide treatment to alleviate these problems? Is it not unconstitutional (and even indecent) to incarcerate someone without afterward providing the help he or she is supposed to need? This important question has been the subject of several recent court cases.

The right to treatment was first invoked in the criminal case of *Rouse v. Cameron* by Judge David Bazelon, author of the Durham test discussed earlier. The right gained in legal status and was extended to all civilly committed patients in a landmark decision involving the Partlow State School and Hospital for the mentally retarded of Tuscaloosa, Alabama, and two other institutions. In 1971 a class action suit was filed on behalf of a retarded boy at the Partlow school, Ricky Wyatt, against Dr. Stickney, a new Commissioner of Mental Health. Dr. Stickney was a willing defendant, for he wanted very much to modernize the Alabama hospitals and the care they provided. In *Wyatt v. Stickney*[17] an Alabama federal court ruled in 1972 that the only justification for the civil commitment of pa-

tients to a state mental hospital is treatment. As stated by Judge Frank Johnson, "To deprive any citizen of his or her liberty upon the altruistic theory that the confinement is for humane and therapeutic reasons and then fail to provide adequate treatment violates the very fundamentals of due process." Rather, committed mental patients "have a constitutional right to receive such individual treatment as will give each of them a realistic opportunity to be cured or to improve his or her mental condition." This ruling, upheld on appeal, is a milestone in the protection of people confined by civil commitment, at least to this extent: the state cannot simply put them away without meeting minimal standards of care.

The *Wyatt* ruling is significant, for in the past the courts had asserted that it was beyond their competence to pass judgment on the care given to mental patients. The courts had assumed that mental health professionals possess special and exclusive knowledge about psychopathology and its treatment. Repeated reports of abuses, however, gradually prodded the American judicial system to rule on what goes on within the walls of mental institutions (Schwitzgebel and Schwitzgebel, 1980). Although not applied throughout the country, the *Wyatt* decision sets forth very specific requirements, such as dayrooms of at least forty square feet; curtains or screens for privacy in multi-patient bedrooms sleeping no more than five persons; a comfortable bed; one toilet per eight persons; the right to wear any clothing the patient wishes, provided it is not deemed dangerous; opportunities to interact with members of the opposite sex; and no physical restraints, except in emergency situations. It is perhaps wise to bear in mind that, when the *Wyatt* action was taken, Alabama state mental facilities averaged one physician per 2000 patients, an extreme situation indeed.

The *Wyatt* ruling and others like it, however, do not specify that the patient must obtain the *best* treatment, clearly an unrealistic requirement in view of how little is known about treatment. But some meaningful intervention must be attempted. The states were certainly obliged at least to eliminate the snake pits that had too long been an affront both to incarcerated patients and to the general population responsible for their establishment and maintenance.

---

[16] Lake v. Cameron, 364 F. 2d 657 (D.C. Cir. 1966).
[17] Wyatt v. Stickney, 325 F. Supp. 781 (M.D. Ala. 1971), *enforced in* 334 F. Supp. 1341 (M.D. Ala. 1971), 344 F. Supp. 373, 379 (M.D. Ala. 1972), *aff'd sub nom* Wyatt v. Anderholt, 503 F. 2d 1305 (5th Cir. 1974).

BOX **21.3** Obtaining Patients' Rights

One of the realities of life is the chasm that can exist between what is available in principle and what is available in actuality. Once there are laws, people often have to work to make these laws be of benefit to themselves. This may not be the way things should be, but it is indeed the way they are.

The American Civil Liberties Union maintains a compilation of the rights of mental patients which is constantly updated and is available from them (Ennis and Emery, 1978). Moreover, the ACLU informs mental patients of their rights and makes very practical suggestions on how to obtain these rights. Some of the advice may seem ruthless and conniving, but our adversarial legal system requires such an approach. The system may not always be pretty, but it does seem to work better than anything else in protecting innocent parties.

Ennis and Siegel (1973) recommend several techniques to attorneys representing committed patients who wish to be released. To begin with, a patient's lawyer may request a court hearing in the hope that the hospital will simply release the patient. Psychiatrists dislike court appearances; the mere threat of being hauled before a judge may persuade members of a hospital staff to release the patient. If the hearing is held, other strategies are in order, such as challenging the credibility and impartiality of the psychiatrist who has determined that the patient is dangerous. The following exchange is proposed.

Q: Do you think he might even be dangerous to you?

A: Well, possibly. (If he says no, you can ask why he would be dangerous to others but not to the psychiatrist who recommends deprivation of his liberty.)

Q: In other words, you would feel personally safer if he were hospitalized than if he were at liberty, isn't that correct?

A: Well, yes.

Q: Then you are not completely disinterested in the outcome of this proceeding, are you? (pp. 293–294).

In an even more celebrated case,[18] which eventually found its way to the Supreme Court, a civilly committed mental patient sued two state hospital doctors for his release and for money damages, on the grounds that he had been incarcerated against his will for fourteen years without being treated and without being dangerous to himself or to others. In January 1957, at the age of forty-nine, Kenneth Donaldson had been committed to the Florida state hospital at Chattachoochee on petition by his father, who felt that his son was delusional. Donaldson was found at a brief court hearing before a county judge to be a paranoid schizophrenic and was committed for "care, maintenance, and treatment." The Florida statute then in effect allowed for such commitment on the usual grounds of mental illness and dangerousness. "Dangerousness" could then be defined as inability to manage property and to protect oneself from being taken advantage of by others.

In 1971 Donaldson sued Dr. O'Connor, the hospital superintendent, and Dr. Gumanis, a hospital psychiatrist, for release. Evidence presented at the trial in a United States district court in Florida indicated that the hospital staff could have released Donaldson at any time following a determination that he was not a dangerous person. Testimony made it clear that at no time during his hospitalization had Donaldson's conduct posed any real danger to others or to himself. In fact, just before his commitment in 1957, he had been earning a living and taking adequate care of himself (and immediately upon discharge he secured a job in hotel administration). Nonetheless, O'Connor had repeatedly refused the patient's requests for release, feeling it was his duty to determine whether a committed patient could adapt successfully outside the institution. His judgment was that Donaldson could not. In deciding the question of dangerousness on the basis of "adjustment outside the institution," O'Connor continued to apply a more restrictive standard than that on which most current state laws for commitment rested.

Several responsible people had attempted to obtain Donaldson's release by guaranteeing that they would look after him. For example, in 1963

[18] O'Connor v. Donaldson, 95 S. Ct. 2486 (1975).

a halfway house formally requested that Donaldson be released to its care, and between 1964 and 1968 a former college classmate asked more than once that the patient be released to his care. O'Connor refused, saying that the patient could be released only to his parents, who by this time were quite old and infirm.

The evidence indicated that Donaldson received only custodial care during his hospitalization. No treatment that could conceivably alleviate or cure his assumed mental illness was undertaken. The "milieu therapy" that O'Connor claimed Donaldson was undergoing consisted, in actuality, of being kept in a large room with sixty other patients, many of whom were under criminal commitment. Donaldson had been denied privileges to stroll around the hospital grounds or even to discuss his case with Dr. O'Connor.

The original trial and its appeal concluded that Donaldson was not dangerous and had been denied his constitutional right to treatment, a right based on the Fifth Amendment of the Constitution. O'Connor was found liable for a fine of $38,500. Throughout this litigation Donaldson declared that he was neither dangerous nor mentally ill. *But*, went his claim, *even if* he were mentally ill, he should be released because he was not receiving treatment.

On appeal to the Supreme Court, it was ruled, on June 26, 1975, that "a State cannot constitutionally confine . . . a nondangerous individual who is capable of surviving safely in freedom by himself or with the help of willing and responsible family members or friends." In 1977 Donaldson ultimately settled for $20,000 from the estate of O'Connor, who had died during the appeals process, and from Dr. Gumanis. The money settlement was negotiated without any admission that the doctors were at fault. Nonetheless, this case establishes the principle that mental health professionals working for state institutions are no longer immune from personal liability if they violate patients' rights.

The Supreme Court decision on *O'Connor* v. *Donaldson* created a stir when it was issued, and it is certain to give mental health professionals pause in detaining patients. At the same time, the decision says less than some have assumed. Donaldson earned his release by convincing the Court that he was not dangerous to himself or

Kenneth Donaldson, displaying a copy of the Supreme Court opinion stating that nondangerous mental patients cannot be confined against their will under civil commitment.

others, and that he could survive outside the hospital with support from family and friends. But most states already require that patients be, in fact, considered dangerous, in addition to being judged mentally ill, if they are to be detained under civil commitment. Moreover, although this decision is often cited as yet another affirmation of "right to treatment," the Supreme Court did not, in fact, rule on the constitutionality of this doctrine. Chief Justice Warren E. Burger did, however, issue some warnings about the right to treatment.

Given the present state of medical knowledge regarding abnormal human behavior and its treatment, few things would be more fraught with peril than [for] a State's power to protect the mentally ill [to depend on its ability to provide] such treatment as will give them a realistic opportunity to be cured. Nor can I accept the theory that a State may lawfully confine an individual thought to need treatment and justify that deprivation of liberty solely by providing some treatment. Our concepts of due process would not tolerate such a "trade off" (pp. 588-589).

The *Donaldson* decision did say that a committed patient's status must be periodically reviewed, for the grounds on which a patient was initially committed cannot be assumed to continue in effect forever. In other words, people can change while in a mental hospital and may no longer require confinement. This seems straightforward enough! The Court reminded mental hospital officials that they must not forget their patients. It is a sad commentary on the mental hospital system that the Supreme Court of the United States saw the need to caution it about the obvious and routine (see Box 21.4).

Right to refuse treatment

If a committed mental patient has the right to expect appropriate treatment, since he has lost his freedom because he needs help, does he have a right to *refuse* treatment, or a particular kind of treatment? The answer appears to be yes, for a right to obtain treatment does not oblige the patient to *accept* treatment (Schwitzgebel and Schwitzgebel, 1980). But there are qualifications. A state hospital may have adequate staff to provide up-to-date chemotherapy as well as group therapy but lack the professional resources to offer individual therapy. Suppose that patient

X refuses the available modalities and insists on individual therapy. Would he later be able to sue the hospital for not offering the specific services requested? If the patient has the right to refuse certain forms of treatment, how far should the courts go in ensuring this right, remaining at the same time realistic about the state's ability to provide alternatives? When should the judgment of a professional staff override the wishes of a patient, especially one who is grossly psychotic? Are the patient's best interests always served if he or she can veto the plans of those responsible for care (Stone, 1975)?

Electroconvulsive therapy is a form of treatment that patients often resist. Works of fiction, plus personal reports from people who have undergone ECT, generate strong emotional objections to it. State laws generally allow for ECT to be imposed on committed patients against their will, although in many instances the consent of a third party is required. In 1973 Massachusetts developed very strict guidelines for the administration of ECT. Informed written consent is required from *voluntary* patients, and they can at any later time withdraw consent given earlier. So far so good, but Stone (1975) points out some difficulties. What can a hospital do if an acutely suicidal, but voluntary, patient refuses ECT, which his psychiatrist believes is the best treatment for him? What if this patient also refuses the drugs his psychiatrist prescribes in lieu of ECT and goes on to commit suicide in the hospital? Should the hospital have provided close, round-the-clock surveillance of the patient? But what of the rights of the *other* patients, whose care might well have suffered because of the extra attention given the suicidal patient? A citizen may have the right to kill himself, but does he have the right to do it in a hospital?

Does civil commitment imply an incompetency that renders the patient incapable of forming reasonable opinions concerning therapies? The issue is similar to the problem in criminal commitment proceedings, when a judgment that the accused is mentally ill can deny him access to the courts. Stone believes that a civilly committed person may be competent to refuse a given treatment. He wisely proposes, though, that patients be given the right to refuse only certain treatments, those that are hazardous or very

unpleasant, such as psychosurgery, ECT and any other convulsion therapy, aversion therapy, and chemotherapy with highly addictive drugs like methadone. Stone makes the point that these treatments are risky enough that patients should be allowed to refuse them—even patients under criminal commitment—and that refusal should be overridden only under the special scrutiny of the courts. At the same time, however, administration of less risky treatments would remain the option of the professional staff, with the patient having little to say about their use.[19]

Rights to treatment, to refuse treatment, and to be treated in the least restrictive residence—can they be reconciled?

Several legal principles developed over past years guide the courts and mental health professionals in meeting their constitutional obligations to civilly committed mental patients. Actions taken to implement one principle may conflict with another, however. The basic question is whether the right to be treated in the least restrictive residence can be reconciled with both the right to treatment and the right to refuse treatment. A creative proposal was put forth by Paul and Lentz (1977) in their report on the comparative study of social-learning and milieu therapies on wards at a mental health center. They argue that under certain conditions a committed mental patient can and should be coerced into a particular therapy program, even if the patient states that he or she does not wish to participate.

They propose that some hospital treatments have minimal goals and others optimal, and that institutions should have the right and the duty to do whatever is reasonable to move patients toward minimal goals. Achievement of minimal goals—self care, such as getting up in the morn-

---

[19] A resistant patient is able to ward off psychological therapies if he or she wishes, merely by refusing to participate. The high-risk techniques mentioned above are all somatic therapies, requiring little if any cooperation by the patient. What else in the armamentarium of clinical psychology and psychiatry could conceivably be *imposed* on an unwilling patient? The only answer seems to be various psychoactive drugs, such as Thorazine. When patients are given their "meds" in mental hospitals, the drugs are often dissolved in liquid and must be drunk in the presence of a nurse or an aide, to ensure that they are being taken. Still, it is the common experience of those who have worked in mental hospitals that patients can manage to avoid taking their medication. Few treatments, then, can be forced on a patient. Unless staff members are able to enlist at least minimal cooperation, they can do little to help.

BOX **21.4** Releasing Mental Patients—to Their Benefit?

The cumulative impact of court rulings such as *Wyatt* v. *Stickney* and *O'Connor* v. *Donaldson* is to put mental health professionals on notice that they must be more careful about keeping people in mental hospitals against their will, and that they must attend more to the specific treatment needs of committed patients. Pressure is being put both on them and on state governments in particular to upgrade the quality of care in mental institutions. In view of the abuses that have been documented in hospital care, these are surely encouraging trends.

But the picture is not all that rosy. For judges to declare that patient care must meet certain minimal standards does not automatically translate into that praiseworthy goal. There is not an unlimited supply of money. Sadly enough, care of the mentally ill has never been one of government's high priorities. Nor is support of research in the social and behavioral sciences. Many states have instead embarked on deinstitutionalization, discharging as many patients as possible from mental hospitals and also discouraging admissions. In New York State, for example, 126,000 patients were discharged from state hospitals in the New York City area between 1965 and 1977; and many thousands more were refused admission under new and stringent criteria for entry (Office of the Comptroller, 1979, as cited in Baxter and Hopper, 1981). The maxim has become "Treat them in the community," the assumption being that virtually anything is preferable to institutionalization.

But what is this community that former mental patients are supposed to find more helpful to them upon discharge? Facilities outside the hospitals are not prepared to cope with the influx of former mental patients. Some promising programs were described in Chapter 20, but these are very much the exception, not the rule. The state of affairs in many large metropolitan areas is an unrelenting social crisis.

In New York City, in 1973, as estimated 25,000 ex-mental patients were living on disability or welfare in run-down hotels, without medication and other necessary aftercare (Stone, 1975). In the subsequent years the situation, if anything, has worsened. The Community Service Society, an old and respected social agency

in New York, has published a study, *Private Lives/Public Spaces* (Baxter and Hopper, 1981), on people who live on the streets, in train and bus terminals, in abandoned buildings, on subways, in carvernous steam tunnels running north from Grand Central Station in Manhattan, and some of them in shelters operated by public agencies, churches, and charitable organizations. The lives of these homeless are desperate.

[In a train station at 11:00 p.m.] . . . the attendant goes off duty and women rise from separate niches and head for the bathroom. There they disrobe, and wash their clothes and bodies. Depending on the length of [the] line at the hand dryers, they wait to dry their clothes, put them in their bags or wear them wet. One woman cleans and wraps her ulcerated legs with paper towels every night. The most assertive claim toilet cubicles, line them with newspapers for privacy and warmth and sleep curled around the basin. Once they are taken, the rest sleep along the walls, one on a box directly beneath the hand dryer which she pushes for warm air. One of the women regularly cleans up the floors, sinks and toilets so that no traces of their uncustomary use remain (Baxter and Hopper, 1981, p. 77).

It has been estimated that there are about 36,000 homeless individuals in New York City; other major cities such as Washington and Boston harbor proportionately similar numbers. Although not all these people are former mental patients—a "street culture" has existed for hundreds of years in cities all over the world—the State Office of Mental Health's very conservative estimate is that half of them are mentally ill. A three-day screening of residents of one of the city shelters for men indicated a much higher proportion: 14 percent suffered from alcohol or drug abuse, another 10 percent were mildly disturbed, and 60 percent were moderately or severely so. Sixteen men, of 240, were considered in immediate need of hospitalization. To say that their mental health needs are not being met is an understatement.

[In the Men's Shelter] . . . met and talked with Phillip, a twenty-five-year-old man here since May 1977, at which time according to his rec-

ords, he was being treated with Thorazine at a clinic in Brooklyn "to relieve nervous tensions." Plans at that time to help him find his own residence apparently fell through. At some point— he isn't clear on this, nor is his record—he was hospitalized. Says he came here from the hospital. A slight, obviously "distracted" young man. . . . When we asked the standard questions (who is the president, what is the date, etc.), he first says he doesn't know, pauses, then—if you wait for it—blurts out the correct answer. Spends his days "just hanging around," sleeps either in the hotels or on the streets, eats in the Shelter. When asked if he in fact sees a social worker once a month, he says "yes," then adds, "See?" and dropping his pants he examines his genitals. Joe (the staff member) gently advises him to pull up his trousers, he does so and skips off to play a round of hopscotch by himself (Baxter and Hopper, 1981, p. 44-45).

Single-room-occupancy (SRO) hotels have housed more ex-mental patients than any other form of residence. A city tax abatement program exempts developers who convert these low-cost hotels into upper-income residences from paying city property taxes for up to twenty years. At the current rate of conversion, there will be none of these hotels left by 1984. Conditions in SRO hotels are often deplorable. Managers frequently refuse to make plumbing repairs or fix broken locks, to provide heat and hot water, and yet they continue to raise rents. The attitude is "Take it or leave it." Many people do elect to leave, ending up on the streets.

The welfare department referred Jane to a hotel on the Upper West Side. She left, even with a week's rent paid in advance, because she couldn't bear the filth, the strange noises and people running down the hallways all through the night. She said, "I decided no place is better than that place," and went at first to sleep in the train station sitting up. She distrusts any referrals from the welfare department, and is awaiting a job so that she can secure a decent place to live on her own, preferably outside the city. In the meantime, she has found a cardboard box in which to sleep, located in an alleyway along with ten to fifteen others (Baxter and Hopper, 1981, p. 35).

Those who come to the Men's Shelter, run by the city, no longer actually sleep there but are processed and given vouchers to the flophouses on the Bowery. A general air of threat pervades the Shelter. Violence is frequent enough to keep people on edge; lice, tuberculosis, hepatitis, and respiratory ailments are common afflictions. The work is demanding and thankless. More than a few of the staff are demoralized by the knowledge that the problems run too deep for any remedying through their efforts. Admission to the Women's Shelter is very restrictive. Homes run by charities such as the Salvation Army and by churches offer much better accommodations and are staffed by people genuinely committed to serving the disadvantaged. But they cannot help more than a fraction of those in need. Ellen Baxter and Kim Hopper estimate in their Community Service Society report that altogether public and private facilities in New York City have approximately 3200 beds for the population of 36,000 homeless.

A large proportion of those eligible for various governmental benefits—Social Security, pensions from the Veterans Administration, disability through the Supplemental Security Income program, Home Relief, welfare—do not receive them out of ignorance or because, for unknown reasons, monthly checks have just stopped arriving. If these needy people do receive their benefits, they are often maneuvered out of all their funds by unscrupulous hotel managers, or they are mugged by younger homeless individuals. For some people the bewildering bureaucracy of local and federal assistance agencies poses such an obstacle that they cannot manage application and must negotiate survival without the limited benefits to which they are legally entitled. Sometimes social workers are unsuccessful in helping them find their way through the administrative mazes.

Oftentimes the marginal existence that defines the lives of many ex-mental patients is adduced as evidence of their awesome and incurable illness. But, as Baxter and Hopper conclude in their moving and graphic report, to locate the problem solely within the individual is to overlook the state of the medical, psychiatric, and social service systems. They are in disarray and are failing their responsibilities.

ing, bathing, eating meals, and the like; being able to communicate with others on the most basic level; and not being violent or assaultive—will allow patients to move into a less restrictive residence. The elimination of symptomatic behavior would also be regarded as a minimal goal if the local community requires patients to conform, at least to some extent, to community standards.[20] Paul and Lentz go on to argue that if empirical evidence indicates that particular treatments do achieve minimal goals—the Paul and Lentz study does indicate the superiority of social-learning programs—patients might justifiably be forced to participate in them, even if they or their legal guardians will not give consent voluntarily. Protection of their interests would be the responsibility of an institutional review board, a group of professionals and laypeople who would review all therapy and research activities for a given hospital. The board would decide *for* patients what therapy is likely to achieve minimal goals and allow them to leave the hospital.

If the patient is determined to be operating above minimal levels, he should have the right to refuse treatments that have optimal goals, such as acquiring vocational skills, obtaining a high school diploma, and other "luxury" items that can enhance the quality of a patient's life. According to Paul and Lentz, these goals should not be considered so vital that the patient is forced into working toward them.

Ethical Dilemmas in Therapy and Research

In this textbook we have examined a variety of theories and a multitude of data focusing on *what is* and *what is thought to be*. Ethics and values, often embodied in our laws, are a different order of discussion. They concern *what ought to be*, having sometimes little to do with what is. It is extremely important to recognize the difference. Within a given scientific paradigm we are able to examine what we believe is reality. As the study of philosophy and ethics reveals, however, the statements that people have made for thousands of years about what should be are another matter. The Ten Commandments are such statements. They are prescriptions and proscriptions about human conduct. For example, the eighth commandment, "Thou shalt not steal," in no way describes human conduct, for stealing is not uncommon. It is, instead a pronouncement of an ideal that people *should* aspire to. The integrity of an ethical code that proscribes stealing does not depend on any evidence concerning the percentage of people who steal. Morals and data are two separate realms of discourse.

The legal trends reviewed thus far in this chapter place limits on the activities of mental health professionals. These legal constraints are important, for laws are one of society's strongest means of forcing all of us to behave in certain ways. Psychologists and psychiatrists also have professional and ethical constraints. All professional groups promulgate "shoulds" and "should nots," and by guidelines and mandates they limit to some degree what therapists and researchers do with their patients, clients, and subjects. Courts as well have ruled on some of these questions. We examine now the ethics of making psychological interventions into the lives of other human beings. More questions will be asked than can be answered.

Ethical Restraints on Research

It is basic to science that what can be done is likely to be attempted. The most reprehensible ethical insensitivity is documented in the brutal

---

[20] Many therapists are accused of forcing patients to conform to community standards that are themselves open to question. But the issue here is not whether mental patients wear clean pants with a belt to hold them up, but whether they wear pants at all.

experiments conducted by certain German physicians on concentration camp prisoners during the Third Reich. One experiment, for example, investigated how long people lived when their heads were bashed repeatedly with a heavy stick. Even if important information might be obtained from this kind of atrocity, which seems extremely doubtful, such actions cannot be allowed. The Nuremberg trials, conducted by the Allies following the war, brought these and other barbarisms to light and meted our severe punishment to soldiers, physicians, and other Nazi officials who had engaged in or contributed to such actions, even when they claimed that they had merely been following orders.

It would be reassuring to be able to say that such gross violations of human decency take place only during incredible and cruel epochs such as the Third Reich, but unfortunately this is not the case. Spurred on by a blind enthusiasm for their work, researchers in this country have sometimes dealt with human subjects in reproachable ways.[21]

Henry K. Beecher, a research professor at Harvard Medical School, surveyed medical research since 1945 and found that ". . . many of the patients [used as subjects in experiments] never had the risk satisfactorily explained to them, and . . . further hundreds have not known that they were the subjects of an experiment although grave consequences have been suffered as the direct result . . ." (1966, p. 1354). One experiment compared penicillin to a placebo as a treatment to prevent rheumatic fever. Even though penicillin had already been acknowledged as the drug of choice to give people with a streptococcal respiratory infection in order to protect them from later contracting rheumatic fever, placeboes were administered to 109 servicemen without their knowledge or permission. More men received penicillin than the placebo, but three members of the control group contracted serious illnesses—two had rheumatic fever and one acute nephritis, a kidney disease—as compared to none of those who had received penicillin.

---

[21] Researchers who use animals in their experiments have also occasionally dealt with their subjects in gratuitously harsh fashion. The American Psychological Association has guidelines for handling laboratory animals that are intended to minimize their discomfort and danger.

The training of scientists equips them splendidly to pose interesting questions, sometimes even important ones, and to design experiments that are as free as possible of confounds. They have no special qualifications, however, for deciding whether a particular line of inquiry that involves humankind *should* be followed. Society needs knowledge, and a scientist has a right in a democracy to seek that knowledge. The ordinary citizens employed as subjects in experiments must, however, be protected from unnecessary harm, risk, humiliation, and invasion of privacy. There are several international codes of ethics for the conduct of scientific research—the Nuremberg Code formulated in the aftermath of the Nazi war crime trials, the Declaration of Helsinki, and statements from the British Medical Research Council. Closer to home, in the early 1970s the Department of Health, Education and Welfare began to issue guidelines and regulations governing scientific research that employs human subjects. In addition, a blue-ribbon panel, the National Commission for the Protection of Human Subjects of Biomedical and Behavioral Research, conducted hearings and inquiries into restrictions that the federal government might impose on research performed with mental patients, prisoners, and children. And already for several years the proposals of behavioral researchers, many of whom conduct experiments related to psychopathology and therapy, have been reviewed for safety and general ethical propriety by "human subjects committees" and "institutional review boards" in hospitals, universities, and research institutes. Such committees—and this is very significant—are composed not just of behavioral scientists but of citizens of the community, lawyers, students, and specialists in a variety of disciplines, such as professors of English, history, and comparative religion. They are able to block any research proposal or require questionable aspects to be modified if in their collective judgment the research will put participating subjects at too great risk.

Informed Consent

Participation in research brings up the all-important concept of *informed consent*. Just as com-

mitted mental patients are gaining the right to refuse treatment, so may anyone refuse to be a
subject in an experiment. The investigator must
provide enough information to enable subjects to
judge whether they want to take the risks inherent in being a participant (Box 21.5). The prospective subjects must be legally capable of giving consent, and there must be no deceit or
coercion in obtaining it. For example, an experimental psychologist might be interested in determining whether imagery will help college students associate one word with another. One
group of subjects will be asked to associate pairs
of words in their minds by generating a fanciful
image connecting the two, such as "a CAT riding
on a BICYCLE." The consent form will state that
the experiment consists of sitting for half an hour
in front of a screen, watching pairs of words
being projected on it, and trying to learn the
pairs by devising images that can connect them
in memory. A prospective subject might decide,
however, that such a session is likely to be boring and can without penalty, decline to participate. In fact, review committees require that a
subject be at liberty to withdraw from an experiment at any time, without penalty, although it is
understandable that he or she would feel pressure not to do so.[22]

Paired-associates research is relatively innocuous, but what if the experiment poses real risks,
such as ingesting a drug? Or the prospective subject may be a committed mental patient, or a
retarded child, unable to understand fully what
is being asked. Such a subject may not feel free
to refuse participation. And what of the rights of
the researcher, which often are not as carefully
considered as those of subjects, and of the cost
to society of important research left undone?
Will scientists become reluctant to undertake
certain types of work because review committees
make the process of obtaining informed consent
unduly onerous and time-consuming?

[22] It is not easy to demonstrate that a researcher has in fact obtained
informed consent. Epstein and Lasagna (1969) found that only one-
third of subjects volunteering for an experiment really understood
what the experiment entailed. In a more elaborate study Stuart (1978)
discovered that most college students could not accurately describe a
simple experiment, even though it had just been explained to them
and they had agreed to participate. A signature on a consent form is
no assurance that informed consent has really been obtained, which
poses a real challenge to investigators and members of review panels
who are committed to upholding codes of ethics governing participation of human subjects in research.

Davison and Stuart (1975) proposed a scheme
(Table 21.1) that might protect subjects' rights
when they participate in research, without ham-
pering researchers in their quest for knowledge.
In determining how careful the researchers must
be when obtaining informed consent, Davison
and Stuart would ask four questions.

1. What is the level of risk? Little harm is likely
   in a memory experiment, but a study requiring subjects to withstand electric shock applied to the fingers poses some risk.

2. Is the research of potential benefit to the subject or client? A subject might stand to gain a
   great deal from being in the study or to gain
   nothing directly, except the satisfaction of
   having helped a scientist find out something
   new.

3. Is the technique an established one, whose
   risks and benefits are known, or is it new and
   experimental, so that the researcher is unable
   to indicate how beneficial, harmful, or dis-
   comfiting participation might be?

4. Is the subject realistically free to give consent
   or to refuse participation? A college student
   has great freedom to refuse, but a prisoner
   would probably feel considerable coercion to
   participate in an experiment if asked to do
   so.

These four questions are not the only ones that
might be asked, and the numbered consent procedures in Table 21.1 are merely suggestions.
Clearly, the judgment of many other people
would be needed to establish meaningful values
and to work out a set of procedures. The
scheme, however, may help human subjects
committees organize their thinking about the
problem of obtaining informed consent in a variety of circumstances.

Treatment or Research?

What is the difference between treatment and research? This is a question that people attempting
to replace old procedures with newer, possibly
more effective methods must address. Martin
(1975) considered the following example. In
school district A a teacher who has read about

TABLE 21.1

Guidelines for Protecting Subjects' Right To Participate Only in Experiments of Own Choice

(after Davison and Stuart, 1975)

Level of risk	Freedom to give consent	High potential benefit to subject		Low potential benefit to subject, high potential benefit to society	
		Established procedure	Experimental procedure	Established procedure	Experimental procedure
Low risk	Great freedom	2–4*	4	2–4	4–5
	Feels some coercion	5	5	5–6	7
High risk	Great freedom	4	5	5–6	7
	Feels some coercion	6	6	7	8

*The numbers indicate the degree of care that should be exercised in obtaining consent.

1. *No consent by the subject is necessary.* The investigator assures protection of the subject's rights. The nonobtrusive observation of traffic flow in public places or other public behavior might fall into this category. This procedure and the next are permissible only when a review panel has determined that the potential risk of harm to the anonymously observed subjects is nil.

2. *Subject is simply asked to sign a consent form for participation in research as a subject of observations, with no explanation of the nature of the study.* One example would be observing the supermarket shopping of individuals; an explanation of the objectives of the study might change relevant behavior.

3. *Subject is asked to sign a consent form for participation in research, with "debriefing" following participation.* Such a study might examine interpersonal behavior in public places; prior disclosure of the hypotheses could change behavior. A panel of experts would have to determine that subjects risked little in participating, including minimal humiliation following debriefing.

4. *Subject is asked to sign a consent form for participation in a project, after full disclosure of the objectives and methods of the research.* This procedure would be applied in efforts to evaluate treatment by randomly assigning subjects to experimental, to placebo control, and to no-treatment control groups. A review panel must judge that risk of harm to control subjects is equal to or less than it would be were there no experiment.

5. *Subject is asked to sign a consent form for participation in a project, after full disclosure of the objectives and methods of the research and in the presence of at least one witness who is not involved in the research.* This procedure would be appropriate any time a review panel senses that subjects may feel obliged to participate. Research with adjudicated offenders could fall into this category.

6. *Subject is asked to sign a consent form for participation in a project, after full disclosure of the objectives and methods of the research and in the presence of witnesses. The consent is reviewed by an independent human subjects committee within the institution.* This procedure might be applied in the experimental evaluation of a program carrying out an institutional objective, for example, vocational training in prisons and mental hospitals.

7. *Subject is asked to sign a consent form for participation in a project, after full disclosure of the objectives and methods of the research and in the presence of witnesses. The consent is reviewed by an independent human subjects committee within the institution and by a similar committee outside the institution.* The procedure could be applied when the research concerns behavior changes that are not strictly related to institutional objectives, for example, a study of the role of repetition when mental patients are taught phrases in a foreign language.

8. *No consent is possible because the rights of subjects cannot be protected.*

some of the token economy research in classrooms (for example, O'Leary and O'Leary, 1977) has adopted token reinforcement as a means of persuading a group of underachieving and often disruptive students to attend to their lessons. The results have been quite encouraging: the classroom is quieter, the students are in their seats more often, and their academic performance has improved. Moreover, the students themselves like the program. Is this an experiment? Should the teacher have obtained informed consent from the parents? A few miles away in school district B another teacher is also applying a token economy. The project is funded by a federal grant, calls itself experimental, and routinely obtained

the informed consent that is commonplace for research. There is no doubt that *this* program is research, but does the similarity of district A's program to this one make it research as well?

Because of their relative newness, the application of behavioral procedures is likely to be construed as research, even though not so intended, and to be viewed with some apprehension. And yet we often take for granted—in fact, we applaud—an elementary school teacher who finds a novel way of exciting children about the learning process. "She's really a creative teacher. She doesn't content herself with the curriculum and the materials provided by the school board." To be sure, in many instances the difference be-

BOX **21.5** A Contract To Implement Informed Consent for Therapy

Informed consent is now an issue not just for research and for treatment in mental institutions but also for private therapy which individuals seek on their own initiative. Traditionally a person who consults a therapist, in essence hiring the therapist to perform expert services, consents to be treated in a certain way and for a certain purpose. In the past the client's informed consent to be treated was seldom obtained in any explicit or formal way, however.

The spirit of consumerism in the 1970s and a desire to be open and accountable, along with dramatic increases in malpractice suits, prompted therapists to consider whether more explicit arrangements might not be in their own and in their clients' best interests. Richard Stuart, a leading behavior therapist, has suggested an intervention contract. The proposed contract would place great demands on the therapist, on the fields of clinical psychology and psychiatry to provide evidence that particular techniques are effective, and on the client as well. Although not yet widely adopted, such a contract might become so should insurance companies require documentation on how and why a particular program of treatment was undertaken.

Name of Client: Name of Therapist:
   Address: Title:
   Phone: Organization:
                              Highest academic degree:
                              License:

1. I, the above named therapist, certify that I am (circle one) duly licensed to offer the services described below *or* under the supervision of _____ who is so licensed.
      (Name, address)

2. I have assessed the client's behavior change objective(s) in the following manner:
_____
_____

3. I propose to use the following intervention technique(s) in my effort to assist the client to achieve the above objective(s): _____
_____

   a. This (these) technique(s) have been fully described in the following standard professional reference: _____
_____

   b. The most recent comprehensive account of the clinical results achieved with this (these) technique(s) may be found in the following source(s):

4. It is expected that this (these) intervention technique(s) will have the following beneficial effects for the client by the dates specified: _____

5. It is also noted that this (these) intervention technique(s) may be associated with the following undesirable side effect(s): _____
_____

6. Both the progress toward achieving the specified objectives and the potential side effects will be monitored continuously in the following manner(s):

_____
(Date)   (Signature of Therapist)

A. I, the above named client, assert that I have discussed the above named objectives for the change of my behavior and that I consent to work toward the achievement of those objectives.

B. I further assert that I have discussed the above named intervention technique(s) with the therapist and that I consent to apply these techniques.

C. I further assert that I shall provide the above named data in order to determine the effectiveness of the use of the intervention technique(s).

D. I further assert that I shall provide the therapist with the following compensation for his or her efforts in my behalf: _____

E. I further assert that I have freely entered into this contract knowing the therapeutic objectives and both the positive and negative potential effects of the intervention technique(s).

F. I further assert that I have been assured of my right to terminate my participation in treatment at any time, for any reason, and without the need to offer an explanation.

G. I further specifically limit the above named therapist's use of any information which can in any way identify me to others unless I have offered my specific, written permission.

_____
(Date)   (Signature of Client)   (Signature of Witness)

Source: Copyright © 1975, by Richard B. Stuart, Behavior Change Systems.

---

tween treatment and research is clear. For example, the drug Anectine, a paralytic agent often used to relax patients about to receive ECT, was imposed on a prisoner for a different purpose, to produce a frightening "unconditioned response"—inability to breathe—in an aversion therapy endeavor. Although the drug is in routine use to protect ECT patients from physical harm, a judge ruled that employing it in this way without obtaining informed consent appeared to be cruel and unusual punishment.[23]

Confidentiality and Privileged Communication

When an individual consults a physician, a psychiatrist, or a clinical psychologist, he or she ex-

[23] Mackey v. Procunier, 477 F. 2d 877 (9th Cir. 1973).

pects all that goes on in the session to remain confidential. Nothing will be revealed to a third party, excepting only to other professionals and those intimately involved in the treatment, such as a nurse or medical secretary. The ethical codes of the various helping professions dictate this _confidentiality._

A _privileged communication_ is one between parties in a confidential relation that is protected by statute. The recipient cannot be compelled to disclose it as a witness. The right of privileged communication is a major exception to the access that courts have to evidence in judicial proceedings. Society believes that, in the long term, the interests of people are best served if communications to a spouse and to certain professionals remain off limits to the prying eyes and ears of the police, judges, and prosecutors. The husband-wife, doctor-patient, pastor-penitent, and attorney-client relationships are the traditional ones, but in recent years states have extended the right of privileged communication to the clients of licensed psychologists. Some states are more protective of clients of licensed psychologists than they are of clients of psychiatrists.

There are important limits to the client's right of privileged communication, however. According to the current California psychology licensing law, for example, this right is eliminated for any of the following reasons.

1. If the client is accused of a crime and has requested a determination to be made about his sanity.

2. If the client has accused the therapist of malpractice; the therapist, in other words, can divulge information about the therapy in order to defend himself in any legal action initiated by the client.

3. If the client is under sixteen, and the therapist has reason to believe that the child has been a victim of a crime, such as child abuse. In fact, the psychologist is *required* to report to the police within thirty-six hours any suspicion he or she has that the child client has been physically abused, including being sexually molested.

4. If the client initiated therapy in hopes of evading the law for having committed a crime or for planning to do so.

5. If the therapist judges that the client is a danger to himself or to others, and if disclosure of information is necessary to ward off such danger (see Box 21.6).

Who Is the Client?

Is it always clear to the clinician who the client is? In private therapy, when an adult pays a clinician a fee for help with a personal problem that has nothing to do with the legal system, the consulting individual is clearly the client. But an individual may be referred to the clinician for an evaluation of his or her competency to stand trial. Or the clinician may be hired by an individual's family to assist in civil commitment proceedings. Perhaps the clinician is employed by a state mental hospital as a regular staff member

and sees a particular patient about problems in controlling aggressive impulses. It should be clear, although it is alarming how seldom it *is* clear, that in these instances the clinican is serving more than one client. In addition to the patient, he or she is also serving the family or the state, and it is incumbent on the mental health professional to inform the patient that this is so. This dual allegiance does not necessarily indicate that the patient's own interests will be sacrificed, but it does mean that discussions will not inevitably remain secret and that the clinician may act in a way that displeases the individual.

A recent United States Supreme Court ruling held that a psychiatrist who plans to testify for the prosecution must warn a defendant he or she is about to interview that what is said between them will not be held in confidence, that, in other words, the right of privileged communications has been suspended. This ruling—already part of the ethics codes of both the American Psychiatric and the American Psychological Associations—came in the aftermath of a dramatic series of twenty first-degree murder convictions in Texas.

The high court voted unanimously [on May 18, 1981] to throw out the death sentence imposed upon Ernest B. Smith, a convicted Texas murderer. Smith was condemned to die by a jury in Dallas after a psychiatrist who had examined Smith in jail testified for the state that Smith was a dangerous man who, if allowed to live, would commit future acts of violence. Before the prison examination, the psychiatrist told Smith only that he had come to determine whether Smith was mentally competent to stand trial. The justices ruled Monday that the psychiatrist should also have given Smith a "Miranda" warning, advising Smith that whatever he said in the interview might later be used against him in court. [In *Miranda* v. *Arizona,* the] landmark 1966 ruling, the high court held that police may not question a person in custody unless they first warn him he has a right to remain silent and talk with a lawyer, and that whatever he says may be used against him in court. . . .

Protection tightened. The ruling in the Texas case (*Estelle* v. *Smith, 79-1127)* will tighten up the legal protection granted to criminal defendants against being tricked into confessing crimes

BOX 21.6 The Tarasoff Case—The Obligation To Warm

The client's right to privileged communication—the legal right of a client to require that what goes on in therapy remain confidential—is an important protection, but as we have seen, it is not absolute. Society has long stipulated certain conditions in which confidentiality in a relationship should not be maintained because of the harm that can befall others. A famous California court ruling in 1974* described circumstances in which a therapist should breach the sanctity of a client's communication. First, what appear to be the facts of the case.

In the fall of 1968, Prosenjit Poddar, a graduate student from India studying at the University of California at Berkeley, met Tatiana (Tanya) Tarasoff at a folk dancing class. They saw each other weekly during the fall, and on New Year's Eve she kissed him. Poddar interpreted this act as a sign of formal engagement (as it might have been in India where he was a member of the Harijam or "untouchable" caste). Tanya told him that she was involved with other men, and indicated that she did not wish to have an intimate relationship with him.

Poddar became depressed as a result of the rebuff, but he saw Tanya a few times during the spring (occasionally tape recording their conversations in an effort to understand why she did not love him). Tanya left for Brazil in the summer, and Poddar at the urging of a friend went to the student health facility where a psychiatrist referred him to a psychologist for psychotherapy. When Tanya returned in October, 1969, Poddar discontinued therapy. Based in part on Poddar's stated intention to purchase a gun, the psychologist notified the campus police, both orally and in writing, that Poddar was dangerous and should be taken to a community mental health center for psychiatric commitment.

The campus police interviewed Poddar, who seemed rational and promised to stay away from Tanya. They released him, and notified the health service. No further efforts at commitment were made because apparently the supervising psychiatrist decided that such was not needed and, as a matter of confidentiality, requested that the letter to the police as well as certain therapy records be destroyed.

On October 27th, Poddar went to Tanya's home armed with a pellet gun and a kitchen knife. She refused to speak to him. He shot her with the pellet gun. She ran from the house, was pursued, caught, and repeatedly and fatally stabbed. Poddar was found guilty of voluntary manslaughter rather than first or second degree murder. The defense established, with the aid of the expert testimony of three psychiatrists, that Poddar's diminished mental capacity (paranoid schizophrenia) precluded the malice necessary for first or second degree murder. After his prison term, he returned to India where, according to his own report, he is happily married (Schwitzgebel and Schwitzgebel, 1980, p. 205).

It was normal procedure for the counseling center psychologist to suspend the confidentiality of the professional relationship and take steps to have Poddar committed, for he judged him to be an imminent danger. Poddar had stated that he intended to purchase a gun, and by his other words and actions he had convinced the therapist that he was desperate enough to harm Tanya. What the psychologist did not do, and what the court decided he should have done, was to warn the likely victim, Tanya Tarasoff, that her

Tatiana Tarasoff and Prosenjit Poddar, who was convicted
of manslaughter in her death. The court ruled that his therapist, who had become convinced Prosenjit might harm
Tatiana, should have warned her of the impending danger.

former friend had bought a gun and might use it against her. Or, as stated by the California
state supreme court: ''Once a therapist does in fact determine, or under applicable professional standards reasonably should have determined, that a patient poses a serious danger
of violence to others, he bears a duty to exercise reasonable care to protect the foreseeable
victims of that danger.''

This ruling has had a profound impact on psychotherapists, some claim a chilling effect,
for it imposes on them a new obligation. They argue that if clients are informed of this
limitation to the confidentiality of what they say to their therapists—and professional ethics
require therapists to provide this information—clients may become reluctant to express
feelings of anger to therapists, for fear therapists will notify the people at whom they are
angry. Clients may become less open with their therapists, perhaps derive less benefit from
therapy, and even become *more* likely to inflict harm on others for not having disclosed
their anger as a first step toward controlling it. The welfare of the people whom the Tarasoff ruling intends to protect may be endangered by the very ruling itself!

The *Tarasoff* ruling, now being applied in other states as well, necessitates the prediction
of dangerousness. The law now requires clinicians to use this very imperfect predicting
skill in deciding when to violate confidentiality. A survey of over 1200 psychologists and
psychiatrists in California (Wise, 1978) indicates how the *Tarasoff* decision is affecting their
thinking and practices; the effects are not necessarily positive. On the plus side, one-third
reported consulting more often with colleagues concerning cases in which violence was an
issue; this should have a good outcome, since obtaining input from other professionals
may improve the solitary clinician's decision making, presumably to the benefit of the
client. On the minus side, about 20 percent of the respondents indicated that they now
avoid asking their clients questions about violence, an ostrichlike stance which may keep
the clinician from obtaining important information and yet, in a legal sense, reduces his or
her legal liability should the client harm another person. And a substantial number of
therapists keep less detailed records, again in an effort to reduce legal liability.

*Tarasoff v. Regents of the University of California, 529 P. 2d 553 (Cal. 1974), *vac., reheard in bank, and aff'd* 131
Cal. Rptr. 14, 551 P. 2d 334 (1976).

or making damaging statements to psychiatrists who examine them in jail. The decision will also overturn the death sentences of many other inmates who have been condemned on the basis of psychiatric testimony. The effect will be especially severe in Texas, where psychiatrists have routinely testified for the prosecution about the supposed "future dangerousness" of persons convicted of first-degree murder. The psychiatrist who testified against Smith . . . has also been a witness for the state against fifty persons sentenced to die in Texas. [His] presence in Texas death-penalty cases was so commonplace that he became known in the Dallas area as "the hanging psychiatrist."

Many cases threatened. Texas has 140 inmates on death row—more than any other state except Florida. Texas Assistant Attorney General Douglas Becker said Monday that the new court ruling "is going to invalidate so many of these cases. . . . It's frustrating." Becker said twenty is a "conservative estimate" of the number of death sentences that will be thrown out because of the Supreme Court decision. . . . Joel Berger, the attorney for the NAACP Legal Defense Fund who represented Smith, said he thinks the decision will void at least thirty death sentences in Texas and perhaps more. He said the ruling might also affect a few death-row inmates in Virginia and Oklahoma.

The high court emphasized that Smith's murder conviction still stands. Texas prosecutors have the right to try to persuade a jury once again that he should be executed. However, Berger pointed out that under Texas law, the jury that decides whether capital punishment should be imposed on a defendant must be the same jury that decides whether to convict him. Therefore, Berger said, if Texas again wants to seek the death penalty against Smith or any other inmate affected by Monday's decision, the state would have to retry the entire case and run the risk of an acquittal. Otherwise, he said, the sentences could be commuted to life imprisonment.

In his decision for the court, [Chief Justice Warren E. Burger] wrote that by testifying for the prosecutors, [the] psychiatrist became an "agent of the state, recounting unwarned statements (by Smith) made in a post-secret custodial setting." The high court carefully left open the possibility that a defendant could be forced to submit to an examination by a prosecution psychiatrist when defense lawyers are planning to introduce the testimony of a defense psychiatrist at his trial. In cases in which a defendant pleads innocent by reason of insanity, both prosecution and defense commonly call psychiatrists as witnesses to testify about the defendant's state of mind. The justices also emphasized that their ruling does not mean a defense lawyer has the right to be present when a state-appointed psychiatrist examines a defendant. . . .

Smith was convicted of capital murder for his participation in the 1973 murder of a grocery store cashier, William Moon. The state's evidence showed Smith stood by while another man fired the shot that killed Moon. ("Court Backs Suspects' Right To Remain Silent," by Jim Mann. Published May 19, 1981. Copyright © 1981, by Los Angeles Times. Reprinted by permission.)

Choice of Goals

Ideally the client sets the goals for therapy, but in practice it is naive to assume that some are not imposed by the therapist and even go against the wishes of the client. School systems often want to institute programs that will teach children to "be still, be quiet, be docile" (Winett and Winkler, 1972, p. 499). Many behavior therapists have assumed that young children *should* be compliant, not only because the teacher can then run a more orderly class but because children are assumed to learn better when they are so. But do we really know that the most efficient and most enjoyable learning takes place when children are forced to remain quietly in their seats? Some advocates of "open classrooms" believe that curiosity and initiative, even in the youngest elementary school child, are at least as important as the acquisition of academic skills. Furthermore, perhaps the traditional skills of reading and writing are better imparted to youngsters when they have greater freedom to choose where and when they are to study. As is generally the case in psychology, evidence is less plentiful than are strongly held and vehemently defended opinions. But the issue is clear: any professionals consulted by a school system should be mindful of their own personal biases with respect to goals and be prepared to work toward different ones if the parents and school

The open classroom (left) chooses to help youngsters acquire academic skills by encouraging curiosity and initiative, the traditional classroom (right) by maintaining orderliness and undivided attention.

personnel so wish. Any therapist of course retains the option of not working for a client whose goals and proposed means of attaining them are abhorrent in his or her view.

A therapist working in a mental hospital has the quandary of deciding what will benefit patients. One of the *Wyatt* v. *Stickney* rulings states that patients must be paid at least the federal minimum wage for performing the janitorial, gardening, and other chores that have traditionally been assigned mental patients as a form of "occupational therapy." Further, any work must be done voluntarily. The *Wyatt* case revealed that in a particular hospital patients had become a cheap and captive "slave" labor force, responsible for the maintenance of the institution.

It might be argued that schizophrenic patients are better off mowing a lawn than languishing in bed, plagued by their imagined persecutors. And it might be argued further that cajoling or even forcing patients to learn how to sweep a hall, or fry an egg, or change the oil in a car will enhance their chances of ultimately becoming employable outside the institution. David Wexler (1973), a professor of law, wrote a relevant paper, "Token and Taboo," which has received considerable attention from behavior therapists and from those working in the new law-and-behavior field. He pointed out that the *Wyatt* ruling, although intended to protect patients, might eventually work to their disadvantage. Directors of hospitals are always interested in running as

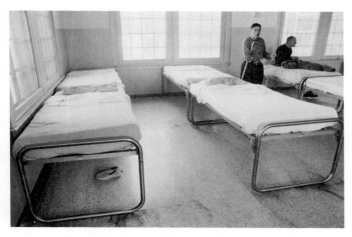

One of the *Wyatt* v. *Stickney* rulings states that patients must be paid for doing chores. Although the ruling was intended to prevent patients from being used as "slave labor," its impact on their rehabilitation was not carefully considered.

efficient and economical an institution as possible, for this is what they are paid to do. Hitherto patient labor was attractive because it was, in fact, cheap. But seldom has it been as effective and efficient as labor that can be bought on the outside and brought into the hospital. If it is necessary to pay a federal minimum wage anyway, hospital administrators may choose to hire efficient employees. Patients may be deprived of valuable opportunities to learn new skills, and hospital life may become even more odious and boring.

In fact, Wexler's concerns were borne out by a 1973 court ruling. In *Souder* v. *Brennen*[24] a federal court decided that mental patients in state and private institutions came under the jurisdiction of the Fair Labor Standards Act and therefore had to be paid the federal minimum wage for any work done. Opportunities for patients to earn money were drastically reduced in most state hospitals across the country. Although the federal court no doubt acted in the best short-term interests of institutionalized patients, how such a decision might in the long term affect the rehabilitation of the very people the ruling intended to protect was not carefully considered. The basis for the *Souder* decision was ruled unconstitutional in a 1976 Supreme Court ruling

[24] Sounder v. Brennen, 367 F. Supp. 808 (D.D.C. 1973).

(Paul and Lentz, 1977); it is unclear whether federal laws can be brought to bear on how much mental patients must be paid for work that helps maintain the institution.

And yet one long-term benefit is possible: mental health professionals will be forced to consider more carefully whether maintenance work is, in fact, helpful in preparing a patient for life outside the hospital. If such work can be shown to be truly rehabilitative, and not just a convenience to the institution, the *Wyatt* ruling might not preclude patients from performing it without pay.[25]

Much of the controversy about the goals of therapy concerns the institutionalized patient, whose freedom is obviously limited. But people who consult therapists voluntarily also operate within constraints on their freedom. The issue has been stated by Seymour Halleck (1971), a psychiatrist, who asserts that the neutrality of the therapist is a myth. In his opinion therapists influence their clients in ways that are subtle yet powerful.

At first glance, a model of psychiatric [or psychological] practice based on the contention that people should just be helped to learn to do the things they want to do seems uncomplicated and desirable. But it is an unobtainable model. Unlike a technician, a psychiatrist [or psychologist] cannot avoid communicating and at times imposing his own values upon his patients. The patient usually has considerable difficulty in finding the way in which he would wish to change his behavior, but as he talks to the psychiatrist his wants and needs become clearer. In the very process of defining his needs in the presence of a figure who is viewed as wise and authoritarian, the patient is profoundly influenced. He ends up wanting some of the things the psychiatrist thinks he should want (p.19).

Psychologists agree, and research (for example, Rosenthal, 1955) supports the contention

[25] On the other hand, once sweeping a floor is construed as treatment, patients who object to the work may be able to invoke the legal right to refuse treatment. It does sometimes appear that the law and the helping professions may be on a collision course.

that patients are profoundly influenced by the values of their therapists. A person not only seeks out a therapist who suits his taste and meets what he believes are his needs but also adopts some of the ideals, sometimes even the mannersims, of the therapist. Most therapists are keenly aware of this modeling after themselves, which surely increases the already heavy responsibilities of their professional role. Perry London (1964), a leading writer on the ethics of therapeutic intervention, has even suggested that therapists are contemporary society's secular priests, purveyors of values and ethics to help clients live "the good life" (see Box 21.7).

Choice of Techniques

The end does not justify the means. Most of us take in this maxim with our mother's milk. It is said to be intrinsic to a free society. In recent years questions concerning behavioral techniques have been debated among professionals and have even been the subject of court rulings. Perhaps because the various insight therapies are restricted to talking and listening, they have seldom been scrutinized as behavior therapy has. The very concreteness and specificity of behavioral techniques have called attention to them, as has their alignment with experimental psychology. Likening people to rats and pigeons and referring to each and every happening as a "stimulus" or "response" are offensive to some.

Token economy

Certain behavioral techniques have been singled out by the courts. The token economy is one. In their efforts to expedite the rehabilitation of mental patients (and prisoners as well), some behavior therapists offer them access to certain amenities as consequences for certain changes in behavior. A patient who wants to sleep in privacy can do so for 100 tokens, which may in turn be earned by attending group therapy every day for two weeks. Setting up such a contingency requires denial of a private room initially. But the *Wyatt* v. *Stickney* rulings suggest that privacy is an *absolute right* of a mental patient, and therefore it cannot be made *contingent* on anything the patient does or does not do. The patient should have it as a constitutional right. Also

guaranteed by the *Wyatt* rulings and other decisions are three meals a day, without delay or deprivation. The residents on Paul and Lentz's social-learning ward had to purchase their meals with tokens.

These limitations on the choice of reinforcers met with a great outcry from some behavior therapists working in hospital settings. Many patients, they argued, are so regressed that the only way to motivate them is to use food as a primary reinforcer, which cannot be done if the Constitution is interpreted as forbidding hospital staff from ever delaying a meal or depriving a patient of food. Wexler (1973) suggests that these legal constraints only require behavior therapists to be more ingenious and inventive than they have been in the past. Staff may have to provide eggs for a patient's breakfast, but if the patient prefers them hard-boiled to soft-boiled, this choice can be made part of a contingency.

Paul and Lentz (1977) provide a detailed account of how their social-learning therapy for chronic schizophrenics would have measured up to the *Wyatt* criteria. Many effective and safe procedures would have been forbidden if *Wyatt* had been strictly applied, which of course it did not have to be, for it was a local decision, applying in Alabama, and the Paul and Lentz project was conducted in Illinois. For example, residents were secluded for more than an hour if their dangerous and assaultive behavior could not be controlled by verbal instructions and by costing them a certain number of already-earned tokens. Paul argues that a technique that creates discomfort and even pain in a mental patient should be considered in the context of an entire program. Theirs had a far greater proportion of positive incentives and reinforcements encouraging prosocial behavior. Paul wonders too whether the *Wyatt* rules, set down because hospitals were not giving residents any treatment, should be applied to a program effectively rehabilitating chronic schizophrenics for release to sheltered residences.

Aversion therapy

To some people the very term behavior therapy conjures up an image of the violent Beethoven-loving protagonist in Kubrick's *Clockwork Orange,* eyes propped open with a torturous appa-

Several psychologists have argued that the social pressures on homosexuals to become heterosexual make it difficult to believe that the small minority of people who consult therapists for help in changing from same-sex to opposite-sex partners act with free choice (Silverstein, 1972; Davison, 1974, 1976; Begelman, 1975). Silverstein's statement about the pressures homosexuals are under to want to become heterosexual was given in Chapter 11 (page 364). It has further been suggested that the mere availability of change-of-orientation programs serves unwittingly to condone the prejudice against homosexuality. Clinicians work to develop procedures and study their effects only if they are concerned about the problem to be dealt with by their techniques. The therapy literature contains scant material on helping homosexuals develop as individuals without changing their sexual orientation, in contrast to the many articles and books on how best to discourage homosexual behavior and substitute for it heterosexual patterns. Aversion therapy has been the most widely used behavioral technique (Davison and Wilson, 1973; Henkel and Lewis-Thomé, 1976). "What are we really saying to our clients when, on the one hand, we assure them that they are not abnormal and on the other hand, present them with an array of techniques, some of them painful, which are aimed at eliminating that set of feelings and behavior that we have just told them is okay?" (Davison, 1976, p. 161).

For these reasons it has been proposed that therapists not help homosexuals become heterosexual even when such treatment is requested. This is obviously a radical proposal, and it has evoked some strong reactions. Gay-activist groups are understandably pleased, considering the suggestion concrete support for the belief that homosexuality per se is not a mental disorder. But many psychologists and psychiatrists are concerned about limiting the choices available to people seeking therapy. Why should a therapist decide for potential clients which options are to be available? Do not therapists have a responsibility to satisfy the needs expressed by their clients (Sturgis and Adams, 1978)? A reply to this important criticism can be that therapists always decide what therapy they will offer by refusing to take clients whose goals they disagree with. Court rulings can also put constraints on the treatments available to patients. In *Kaimowitz* v. *Michigan Department of Mental Health,** for example, a state court held that a committed mental patient could not volunteer for psychosurgery, which he had hoped would eliminate fits of uncontrollable aggression and thereby gain him his release. The judge felt that, living in the coercive environment of a state hospital, the patient could not give informed consent to such an untested procedure. The request of a patient for a certain kind of treatment has never been sufficient justification for providing it (see Davison, 1978).

It has been asserted that continued research will help develop sex reorientation programs that are even more effective than those already available (Sturgis and Adams, 1978). To discourage such work would deprive today's homosexuals of promising therapies and tomorrow's homosexuals of improved treatments. This objection, however, is not relevant. The fact that we *can* do something does not indicate that we *should*. The proposal to deny sexual reorientation therapy is philosophical-ethical in nature, not empirical. The decision whether we should change sexual orientation will have to be made on moral grounds.

* Kaimowitz v. Michigan Department of Mental Health, 42 U.S.L. Week 2063 (Mich. Cit. Ct., Wayne City. July 10, 1973).

Will numbers of people be hurt by eliminating the sex reorientation option? Some have raised the specter of an upsurge in suicides among homosexuals if therapists refuse to help them switch. These are very serious concerns, but they overlook the possibility, some would say the fact, that far greater numbers of people have been hurt over the years by the availability of sex reorientation programs. As already argued, the existence of these treatments is consistent with societal prejudices and discrimination against homosexuals.

The proponents who wish to terminate change-of-orientation programs believe that much good can come of their proposal. Homosexuals would be helped to think better of themselves, and greater efforts could be directed toward the problems homosexuals have, rather than to the problem of homosexuality.

It would be nice if an alcoholic homosexual, for example, could be helped to reduce his or her drinking without having his or her sexual orientation questioned. It would be nice if a homosexual fearful of interpersonal relationships, or incompetent in them, could be helped without the therapist assuming that homosexuality lies at the root of the problem. It would be nice if a nonorgasmic or impotent homosexual could be helped as a heterosexual would be rather than [being guided] to change-of-orientation regimens . . . the hope [is] that therapists will concentrate their efforts on such human problems rather than focusing on the most obvious "maladjustment"—loving members of one's own sex (Davison, 1978, p. 171).

---

ratus, being made nauseous by a drug while scenes of violence flashed on a screen and Beethoven's Ninth Symphony soared in his ears. Aversion therapy programs never really reach this level of coercion and drama, but certainly any such procedure entails making the patient uncomfortable, sometimes extremely so. Making patients vomit or cringe with pain from electric shock applied to the extremities are two aversive techniques worthy of their name. Can there be any circumstances that justify therapists inflicting pain on clients?

Before too glibly exclaiming "No!" consider the following report.

The patient was a nine-month-old baby who had already been hospitalized three times for treatment of vomiting and chronic rumination (regurgitating food and rechewing it in the

mouth). A number of diagnostic tests, including an EEG, plus surgery to remove a cyst on the right kidney, had revealed no organic basis for the problems, and several treatments, including a special diet, had been attempted without success. When referred to Lang and Melamed (1969), two behavior therapists, the child was in critical condition and was being fed by tubes leading from the nose directly into the stomach. The attending physician had stated that the infant's life was in imminent danger if the vomiting could not be halted.

Treatment consisted of delivering a series of one-second-long electric shocks to the infant's calf each time he showed signs of beginning to vomit. Sessions followed feeding and lasted under an hour. After just two sessions, shock was rarely required, for the infant learned quickly to stop vomiting in order to avoid the shock. By the sixth session he was able to fall asleep after eating. Nurses reported that the in-session inhibition of vomiting generalized as the infant progressively reduced his vomiting during the rest of the day and night. About two weeks later the mother began to assume some care of the hospitalized child, and shortly thereafter the patient was discharged with virtually complete elimination of the life-threatening pattern of behavior. Throughout the three weeks of treatment and observation, the child gained weight steadily. One month after discharge the child weighed twenty-one pounds and was rated as fully recovered by the attending physician. Five months later he weighed twenty-six pounds and was regarded as completely normal, both physically and psychologically.

The use of aversion therapy has been subject to an understandably great amount of regulation. An additional reason for administrative and judicial concern is that aversion techniques smack more of research than of standard therapy. The more established a therapeutic procedure, whether it be medical or psychological, the less likely it is to attract the attention of the courts or other governmental agencies. Paul and Lentz (1977) had a few very assaultive patients. Their account of administrative problems demonstrates that patients may be subject to more extreme procedures if special attention is paid only to newer techniques.

> *Some consideration was given to the contingent use of mild electric shock. . . . However, early in the explorations of the necessary safeguards and review procedures to be followed before evaluating such methods, the department director telephoned to explain that aversive conditioning was a politically sensitive issue. Therefore, more than the usual proposal, preparation, documentation, and committee reviews would be required—to the extent that approval would probably take about eighteen months. Instead, it was suggested that convulsive shock (which can cause tissue damage) be employed since "ECT is an accepted medical treatment." With those alternatives, our choice was to abandon either use of shock . . . (p. 499).*

A ruling of the *Wyatt* case forbids the use of aversion therapy except with informed consent after consultation with a lawyer. Mindful that short-term application of electric shock can sometimes keep retarded and autistic children from their self-destructive acts, Martin (1975) proposes that

> *The test should be that aversive therapy might be used where other therapy has not worked, where it can be administered to save the individual from immediate and continuing self-injury, when it allows freedom from physical restraints which would otherwise be continued, when it can be administered for only a few short instances, and when its goal is to make other nonaversive therapy possible. Such an aversive program certainly requires consent from a guardian and immediate review of the results of each separate administration (p. 77).*[26]

Extra precautions such as these are necessary when treatment deliberately inflicts pain on a patient or client; they are especially necessary when the patient cannot realistically be expected to give informed consent. But should we be concerned only with physical pain? The anguish we suffer when a loved one dies is psychologically painful. It is perhaps more painful than an electric shock of 1500 microamperes. Who is to say? Since we allow that pain can be psychological, shall we permit a Gestalt therapist to make a patient cry by confronting him with feelings he has turned away from for years? Shall we forbid a psychoanalyst from guiding a patient to an insight that will likely cause great anguish, all the more so for the conflict's having been repressed for years?

Concluding Comment

An underlying theme of this book concerns the nature of knowing. How do we decide that we understand a phenomenon? The branch of philosophy concerned with the methods and

---

[26] In addition to being humane, Martin's suggestions are consistent with an established legal principle which holds that therapy should begin with the technique that intrudes least on the patient's freedom and exposes him or her to the least possible risk (Morris, 1966).

grounds for knowledge is called epistemology. The rules of the science game that govern our definition of and search for knowledge require theories that can be tested, experiments that can be replicated, and data that are public. But given the complexity of abnormal behavior and given the vast areas of ignorance, far more extensive than the domains that have already been mapped by science as it is currently practiced, we have great respect for theoreticians and clinicians, those inventive souls who make suppositions, offer hypotheses, follow hunches—all based on rather flimsy data but holding some promise that scientific knowledge will be forthcoming.

This final chapter demonstrates again something emphasized at the very beginning of this book, namely that the behavioral scientists and the mental health professionals who give treatment are only human beings. They suffer from the same foibles that sometimes plague nonspecialists. They occasionally act with a certainty their evidence does not justify, and they sometimes fail to anticipate the moral and legal consequences of the ways in which they conduct research and apply the tentative findings of their young discipline.

The authors of this textbook hope that they have communicated in some measure their love for the subject matter and, more importantly, their commitment to the kind of questioning, doubting stance that wrests useful knowledge from nature and will yield more as new generations of scholars build upon the achievements of their predecessors.

Summary

This final chapter dealt with legal and ethical issues in treatment and research. Some of the civil liberties of people are rather routinely set aside when judgments are made by mental health professionals and the courts that mental illness has played a role in determining their behavior. Criminal commitment sends a person to a hospital, either before a trial for an alleged crime, because he is deemed incompetent to stand trial; or after an acquittal by reason of insanity, because a mental defect, the inability to know right from wrong, or both are believed to have played a role in his committing a criminal act. A person who is considered ill and dangerous to himself and to others, though he has not broken a law, can be civilly committed to an institution. Recent court rulings have provided greater protection to all committed mental patients, particularly those under civil commitment: they have the right to written notification, to counsel, to a jury decision concerning their commitment, and to Fifth Amendment protection against self-incrimination; the right to the least restrictive treatment setting; the right to be treated; and even the right to refuse treatment, particularly any procedure that entails considerable risk. A number of moral issues in therapy and research were reviewed: ethical restraints on research, the duty of scientists to obtain informed consent from prospective human subjects, the question whether a program is treatment or research, the right of clients to confidentiality, the setting of therapy goals, and the choice of techniques.

appendix

When the brain becomes dysfunctional, a whole host of impairments, of sensory and motor functions as well as of emotional and psychological ones, are likely. The disorders to be considered here are psychological and behavioral abnormalities that are caused by transient or permanent brain dysfunctions; they are often similar to the psychopathologies considered in earlier chapters.

DSM-III distinguishes two major categories, *organic brain syndromes* and *organic mental disorders* (Table A.1). The several types of organic brain syndromes, for example, organic affective disorder and organic hallucinosis, each have specific groups of psychological and behavioral symptoms that can be produced by several different causes. Each of the organic mental disorders, in contrast, have a specific presumed cause. The symptoms for disorders in the two categories may be similar. For example, halluci-

nations are principal symptoms both of organic hallucinosis and of alcohol withdrawal delirium and alcohol hallucinosis, two of the alcohol organic mental disorders. The difference is that in organic mental disorders a presumed cause of the symptoms is part of the diagnosis itself.

Two major classes of organic mental disorders are distinguished, *Dementias Arising in the Senium and Presenium* and *Substance-Induced Mental Disorders*. Senile dementias have already been discussed in Chapter 17. The substance-induced disorders are the specific effects, such as intoxication, withdrawal, delirium, hallucinations, and memory dysfunctions, brought on by ingesting alcohol, narcotics, barbiturates, amphetamines, cocaine, and the other substances covered in Chapter 10. Therefore what remains to be presented here are the organic brain syndromes and the presenile dementias.

Organic Brain Syndromes

Delirium and Dementia

Delirium and its principal causes in the elderly were discussed in Chapter 17. Although more common in older people, delirium can occur at any age and can be traced to a wide range of conditions—systemic infections; metabolic disorders, such as kidney and liver disease and thiamine deficiency; substance intoxication and withdrawal; seizures; head traumas; and brain lesions in particular areas of the parietal and occipital lobes. As indicated in Chapter 17, in the elderly Alzheimer-type degeneration and vascular diseases are the most frequent causes of dementia. Infectious diseases of the central nervous system are another major cause of dementia.

Encephalitis is a generic term that refers to inflammation of brain tissue. A large number of living and nonliving agents can enter the body by various routes and inflame the brain. Most are living, and the most important are several viruses, usually carried by insects such as mosquitoes and ticks. In other cases, though, infection may have spread from another part of the body, for example, the sinuses and ears. Epidemics of one form, encephalitis lethargica, were widespread in the United States and Europe about the time of World War I. It was referred to as sleep-

TABLE **A.1**
The Categories of Brain Disorders in DSM-III

I. *Organic Brain Syndromes* (symptoms presumed to be caused by a brain dysfunction but with no specific etiology indicated)
   A. Delirium.
   B. Dementia.
   C. Amnestic syndrome.
   D. Organic delusional syndrome.
   E. Organic hallucinosis.
   F. Organic affective syndrome.
   G. Organic personality syndrome.
   H. Intoxication.
   I. Withdrawal.
   J. Atypical or mixed organic brain syndrome.

II. *Organic Mental Disorders* (symptoms linked to specific known or presumed organic causes)
   A. Dementias Arising in the Senium and Presenium
      1. Primary degenerative dementia (for example, Alzheimer-type disease).
      2. Multi-infarct dementia.
   B. Substance-Induced Organic Mental Disorders (diagnosis usually made in conjunction with Substance Use Disorders)
      1. Alcohol organic mental disorders.
      2. Barbiturate or similarly acting sedative or hypnotic organic mental disorders.
      3. Opioid organic mental disorders.
      4. Cocaine organic mental disorder.
      5. Amphetamine or similarly acting sympathomimetic organic mental disorders.
      6. Phencyclidine (PCP) or similarly acting arylcyclohexylamine organic mental disorders.
      7. Hallucinogen organic mental disorders.
      8. Cannabis organic mental disorders.
      9. Tobacco organic mental disorder.
      10. Caffeine organic mental disorder.

ing sickness because those infected were extremely lethargic and slept for prolonged periods, days and weeks at a time. They could, however, be roused from stupor for brief intervals. The epidemics are suspected of having an influenza virus as their cause, one which apparently vanished from the face of the earth, for the epidemics stopped occurring around 1926.

The major symptoms of encephalitis are vomiting, headache, drowsiness and lethargy, a stiff neck and back, fever, tremors, and sometimes convulsive seizures and coma. In the acute phase of the disease patients are delirious and disoriented. Later they may remain depressed and irritable and have dementia, that is, difficulties in concentrating and remembering. Recovery is usually complete, but some patients may have permanent paralysis of an arm or leg, uncontrollable tremors, seizures, deafness, speech disturbances, and dementia. If the disorder occurs in infants, they will often be mentally retarded; their developing brains are particularly susceptible to damage from infection.

The symptoms of meningitis, an inflammation of the meninges (see Box A.1), are quite similar to those of encephalitis. The causes are varied but usually bacterial. The principal epidemic form, meningococcal meningitis, occurs all over the world; epidemics of major proportions happen every eight to twelve years.

The syphilitic spirochete *Treponema pallidum* invades the body through mucous membranes after being contacted during either intercourse or oral-genital contact. The disorder may also be transmitted from an infected mother to her fetus. The first indication of the disorder is a small sore on the site of the infection—lips, genitals, or anus—which appears after ten to twenty days and then in a few weeks disappears. Before the sore disappears, a diffuse, copper-colored rash may cover the body. Fatigue, headache, and fever may accompany the rash, as well as sore throat, inflammation of the eyes, vague pains in bones and joints, and lesions in the mucous membranes of mouth and genitalia.[1] Thereafter

[1] Unfortunately, these early signs do not always appear, making detection of the disease difficult. For this reason blood tests are recommended if there is any suspicion of venereal disease after sexual contact with a highly experienced person or with a relative stranger.

no overt difficulties are evident for many years, but during this period spirochetes may be invading the lymph glands, the bone marrow, and the other tissues and organs of the body. Damage usually becomes observable when the individual is in his or her forties or fifties and the spirochetes have either invaded the walls of the heart, causing a heart attack, or penetrated the neural tissue. About 30 percent of those infected will ultimately have neurological impairment.

The clinical picture depends on the area of the nervous system affected. In some cases the meninges of the brain are infected, in others the motor nerves of the spinal cord. The most severe damage is done when the cerebral cortex, usually that of the frontal areas, is invaded, producing the syndrome called general paresis. The convolutions flatten through atrophy; on autopsy, the shrinkage of the cerebral cortex is obvious. The first symptoms are irritability, fatigue, depression, loss of motivation at work, irresponsibility in personal affairs, and inattention to personal appearance. The individual becomes progressively more callous and forgetful and grossly lacking in judgment. Some become euphorically expansive and have absurd and grandiose delusions of position, power, wealth, and physical prowess. Others are depressed and hopeless.

Loss of tone in the facial muscles and failure of the pupils to contract to light are obvious signs. Tremors of the eyelids, lips, facial muscles, and fingers, mispronunciation and slurring of words, deterioration of handwriting, and a wobbly gait indicate loss of control of the voluntary musculature. Massive confusion gradually replaces psychosis. In the final stages the individual is paralyzed, inarticulate, and subject to convulsions, for the mind and body have all but ceased functioning.

With trauma, or injury to the brain, there is often some degree of hemorrhaging and destruction of brain tissue. If the damage is severe, dementia may result. One of the most frequent traumas causing dementia is the _subdural hematoma_. The skull is fractured and bone tears the arachnoid membrane (see Box A.1), causing blood to fill the subdural space between the dura mater and the arachnoid and to destroy much neural tissue.

BOX A.1 Structure and Function of the Human Brain

The brain is located within the protective covering of the skull and is enveloped with three layers of nonneural tissue, membranes referred to as *meninges*. The three membranes are the outer, tough *dura mater,* the intermediate, web-like *arachnoid,* and the inner, soft *pia mater.* Viewed from the top, the brain is divided by a midline fissure into two mirror-image *cerebral hemispheres;* together they constitute most of the cerebrum. The major connection between the two hemispheres is a band of nerve fibers called the *corpus callosum.* Figure A.1 shows the surface of one of the cerebral hemispheres. The upper, side, and some of the lower surfaces of the hemispheres constitute the *cerebral cortex.* The cortex consists of six layers of tightly packed neuron cell bodies with many short, unsheathed interconnecting processes. These neurons, estimated to be 10 to 15 billion in number, make up a thin outer covering, the so-called gray matter of the brain. The cortex is vastly convoluted; the ridges are called *gyri* and the depressions between them *sulci* or fissures. Deep fissures divide the cerebral hemispheres into several distinct areas, called lobes. The *frontal lobe* lies in front of the central sulcus; the *parietal lobe* is behind it and above the lateral sulcus; the *temporal lobe* is located below the lateral sulcus; and the *occipital lobe* lies behind the parietal and temporal lobes. Different functions tend to be localized in particular areas of the lobes—vision in the occipital; discrimination of sounds in the temporal; reasoning and other higher mental processes, plus the regulation of fine voluntary movements, in the frontal; initiation of movements of the skeletal musculature in a band in front of the central sulcus; in a band behind this sulcus, receipt of sensations of touch, pressure, pain, temperature, and body position from skin, muscles, tendons, and joints.

The two hemispheres of the brain are believed to have different functions. The left hemisphere, which generally controls the right half of the body by a crossing over of motor and sensory fibers, is usually dominant; it is responsible for speech and, according to some neuropsychologists, for analytical thinking in right-handed people and in a fair number of left-handed people as well. The right hemisphere controls the left side of the body and is believed to specialize in discerning spatial relations and patterns and in intuition. But analytical thinking cannot be located exclusively in the left hemisphere or intuitive and even creative thinking in the right; the two hemispheres communicate with each other constantly via the corpus callosum. Localization of apparently different modes of thought is probably not as clear-cut as some would have us believe.

If the brain is sliced in half, separating the two cerebral hemispheres (Figure A.2), additional important features can be seen. The gray matter of the cerebral cortex does not extend throughout the interior of the brain. Much of the interior is *white matter* and is made up of large tracts or bundles of myelinated (sheathed) fibers which connect cell bodies in the cortex with those in the spinal cord and in other centers lower in the brain. These centers are additional pockets of gray matter, referred to as *nuclei.* Some cortical cells project their long fibers or axons to motor neurons in the spinal cord, but others project them only as far as these clusters of interconnecting neuron cell bodies. Four masses are deep within each hemisphere, called collectively the *basal ganglia,* and other important areas and structure of the brain also contain nuclei. The nuclei serve both as way stations, connecting tracts from the cortex with other ascending and descending tracts, and as integrating motor and sensory control centers. Deep within the brain too are cavities, called *ventricles,* which are continuous with the central canal of the spinal cord and which are filled with cerebrospinal fluid.

In Figure A.2 are shown four important functional areas or structures.

1. The *diencephalon,* connected in front with the hemispheres and behind with the midbrain, contains the *thalamus* and the *hypothalamus,* which consist of groups of nuclei. The thalamus is a relay station for all sensory pathways except the olfactory. The nuclei making up the thala-

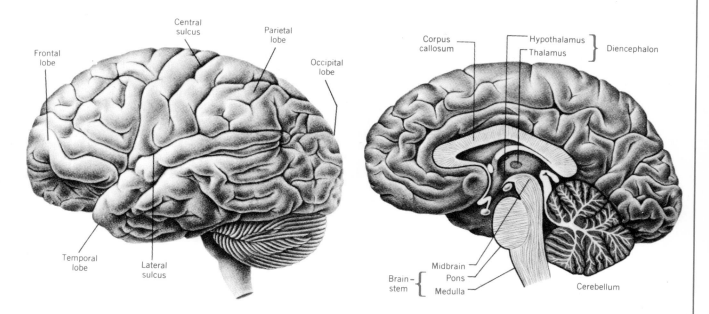

FIGURE **A.1**
Surface of the left cerebral hemisphere, indicating the lobes and the two principal fissures of the cortex.

FIGURE **A.2**
Slice of brain through the medial plane, showing the internal structures.

mus receive nearly all impulses arriving from the different sensory areas of the body before passing them on to the cerebrum, where they are interpreted as conscious sensations. The hypothalamus is the highest center of integration for many visceral processes. Its nuclei regulate metabolism, temperature, water balance, sweating, blood pressure, sleeping, and appetite.

2. The *midbrain* is a mass of nerve fiber tracts connecting the cerebral cortex with the pons, the medulla oblongata, the cerebellum, and the spinal cord.

3. The *brainstem* is made up of the *pons* and *medulla oblongata* and functions primarily as a neural relay station. The pons contains tracts that connect the cerebellum with the spinal cord and the cerebellum with motor areas of the cerebrum. The medulla oblongata serves as the main line of traffic for tracts ascending from the spinal cord and descending from the higher centers of the brain. At the bottom of the medulla, many of the motor fibers cross to the opposite side. The medulla also contains nuclei that

maintain the regular life rhythms of the heartbeat, of the rising and falling diaphragm, and of the constricting and dilating blood vessels. In the core of the brainstem is the *reticular formation,* sometimes called the reticular activating system because of the important role that it plays in arousal and in the maintenance of alertness. The tracts of the pons and medulla send in fibers to connect with the profusely interconnected cells of the reticular formation, which in turn send fibers to the cortex, the basal ganglia, the hypothalamus, the septal area, and the cerebellum.

4. The *cerebellum,* like the cerebrum, is made up for the most part of two deeply convoluted hemispheres with an exterior cortex of gray matter and an interior of white tracts. The cerebellum receives sensory nerves from the vestibular apparatus of the ear and from muscles, tendons, and joints. The information received and integrated relates to balance and posture and equilibrium and to the smooth coordination of the body when in motion.

A fifth important part of the brain, not shown in Figure A.2, is the *limbic system,* structures which are continuous with one another in the lower cerebrum, and which developed earlier than did the mammalian cerebral cortex. This system is made up of cortex that is phylogenetically older than the so-called neocortex, which covers most of the hemispheres. The *juxallocortex,* which consists of four or five layers of neurons, surronds the corpus callosum and the underlying thalamus. The cingulate gyrus stretching above the corpus callosum is an important structure made up of this juxallocortex. The *allocortex,* with only three layers of neurons, makes up the cortex of the septal area, which is anterior to the thalamus; the long, tubelike hippocampus, which stretches from the septal area into the temporal lobe; and the part of the lower temporal lobe that surrounds the under portions of the hippocampus and the amygdala (one of the basal ganglia), which is embedded in its tip. The amygdala and the septal area itself, which also consists of nuclei, are sometimes considered part of the limbic system because of their anatomical and functional connections to its other structures. The limbic system controls the visceral and physical expression of emotion—quickened heartbeat and respiration, trembling, sweating, and alterations in facial expressions—and the expression of appetitive and other primary drives—hunger, thirst, mating, defense, attack, and flight.

Amnestic Syndrome

The principal symptom of *amnestic syndrome* is impairment in both short- and long-term memory when there is no delirium and dementia, no clouding of consciousness and no intellectual deterioration. The person is unable to recall information known in the past and cannot learn new material. The memory problems usually create some disorientation; sometimes the individual resists acknowledging memory difficulties through *confabulation,* filling in gaps with fictions.

Amnestic syndrome is brought on by damage to both sides of the brain, in certain diencephalic and temporal lobe structures. Although there are many possible causes—head trauma, infection, infarction of the posterior cerebral arteries—the most common are chronic alcohol use and thiamine deficiency.

One specific amnestic syndrome, *Wernicke's disease,* is frequent among alcoholics, who often do not eat properly. Symptoms include confusion and drowsiness, partial paralysis of the muscles that control eye movements, and an unsteady gait. Autopsy reveals lesions in the pons and cerebellum and in the mammillary bodies, two small, rounded structures of the hypothalamus that contain nuclei. In addition, there is atrophy in the gray matter surrounding several of the ventricles.

A sizable number of patients with Wernicke's disease also develop *Korsakoff's psychosis.* The primary symptoms are anterograde amnesia, a loss of memory for events that have just occurred, and confabulation. Shortly after dinner a patient with Korsakoff's psychosis may be asked what he had for the evening meal. Unable to recall the details, he quickly provides a description of a imaginary meal. It often happens, however, that such descriptions are patently false and elaborate fabrications. A patient in a mental institution may state that he has just finished a meal of Beef Wellington with a delightful sauce containing truffles, apparently not recognizing the extreme improbability of being served such a meal.

Patients with Korsakoff's psychosis are usually lucid and friendly, yet they lack judgment, being unaware of the implausibility of the stories they tell and only poorly planning other aspects of their lives. They may become apathetic and sometimes grossly confused and severely disoriented. On autopsy, these patients reveal a pattern of brain damage similar to that of Wernicke's disease. But in addition they also have lesions in the thalamus.

Organic Delusional Syndrome

The delusions in *organic delusional syndrome* are caused by physiological factors that do not cloud consciousness or cause any significant loss of intellectual abilities. Mild impairments may be evident, however, and the person's speech may be somewhat incoherent and rambling. The patient may be either hyperactive, pacing and rocking back and forth, or apathetically immobile. Mood is anxious or depressed. Drugs such as amphetamines, marijuana, and, hallucinogens and brain lesions, particularly to the nondominant hemisphere, can cause the syndrome. Some individuals with Huntington's chorea have a paranoid delusional syndrome. Finally, some people with temporal lobe epilepsy have delusions, even between seizures.

There are various forms of *epilepsy,* in all of which consciousness is altered by sudden disruption of the usual rhythmical electric discharge of brain cells.[2] In temporal lobe epilepsy the focus of the abnormal and excessive electric discharge is in the temporal lobes of the brain. The seizures begin with an aura, a signal of the forthcoming attack, which may take the form of dizziness, fear, or unusual sensory experiences such as ringing in the ears or unusual odors. Then the person loses contact with the environment. But during the attack the epileptic appears conscious and engages in some sort of routine or organized activity. The act may be simple and repetitive, such as chewing or moving the limbs in a particular way, or the epileptic may engage in a complex and prolonged series of activities. These seizures may last only a few seconds or minutes but occasionally much longer. After the attack individuals have no memory for their actions. The behavior of these people is often psychotic, even between seizures (Glaser, Newman, and Schafer, 1963).

Organic Hallucinosis

In *organic hallucinosis* the patient experiences persistent and recurrent hallucinations when alert, well oriented, and in a state of full wakefulness. The use of hallucinogens and prolonged heavy drinking of alcohol are the major causes. Hallucinogens generally bring visual hallucinations, long-term alcohol abuse auditory. In the course of the DTs, during withdrawal from alcohol, however, the hallucinations are visual. The sensory deprivations of blindness and deafness may cause hallucinations. Those who are blind have visual ones, the deaf auditory hallucinations. Untreated cataracts and otosclerosis may cause chronic hallucinosis. Finally, seizures localized in the temporal or occipital lobes may also cause hallucinations.

Organic Affective Syndrome

The mood disturbances of *organic affective syndrome* resemble those of either mania or depression and are usually caused by toxic or metabolic factors. As with the other organic syndromes, these affective disturbances must occur without delirium or dementia to warrant the diagnosis. Depressive symptoms may be brought on by drugs such as reserpine, which is used to treat hypertension, and by methyldopa, used in the treatment of Parkinson's disease. Endocrine disturbances are another route to either mania or depression.

Endocrine glands secrete their hormones directly into the bloodstream. Thus these powerful substances are delivered to nearly every cell in the body, including the neurons of the brain. Either oversecretions or undersecretions of the

---

[2] The other major forms of epilepsy are grand mal, petit mal, and Jacksonian or focal epilepsy. *Grand mal* begins with an aura. In the tonic phase the muscles of the body suddenly become rigid. The patient loses consciousness and falls heavily to the ground if he has not been able to prepare for the attack. The arms and trunk are flexed, the legs outstretched and breathing ceases. After about half a minute, in the clonic phase, which lasts another one or several minutes, the muscles alternately contract and relax, producing violent contortions and jerking movements of the limbs. Breathing resumes. The jaws also open and close, and saliva collects on the lips. Eventually, as the convulsive movements dissipate, the epileptic seizure passes from the clonic phase into coma. The individual remains unconscious and the muscles relax. Upon awakening, perhaps almost immediately or only after several hours, the individual has no memory of what happened after the beginning of the tonic phase. *Petit mal,* more frequent in children and rare after twenty years of age, is only a short (15 to 50 seconds) disturbance or alteration of consciousness. The person stops what he is doing and his eyes roll up. There may be a few twitches of the eye and face muscles, but in most instances such seizures are difficult to recognize. The person may be aware only that his mind has gone blank for a few moments. *Jacksonian* or *focal* epilepsy muscle spasms are limited to particular areas of the body. There are several variants, depending on the area of the brain in which the neurons discharge abnormally. A motor seizure may begin with discharge near the lateral sulcus and be manifested as twitches of the thumb and index finger. A discharge beginning in the visual cortex may produce hallucinations. Sometimes these seizures remain localized and there is no loss of consciousness. But they may also spread, perhaps beginning with the thumb and index finger and then extending to the hand, arm, and shoulder, and sometimes ultimately throughout the entire body.

thyroid gland may bring on affective problems. In hyperthyroidism or _Graves' disease,_ described by an Irish physician, Robert Graves, in the first part of the nineteenth century, an oversecretion of the hormone thyroxin speeds up metabolic processes, causing weight loss, sweating, and motor agitation and inducing a state of apprehension, restlessness, and either elated mood or irritability. Thinking proceeds at a rapid pace; persons with Graves' disease may be misdiagnosed as suffering an episode of mania. About 20 percent of hyperthyroid patients may have transitory delusions and hallucinations. Hypothyroidism, which brings on a condition called _myxedema_ in adults, is a deficiency in thyroid hormone. Metabolic processes are slowed down and so too are speech and thinking. The individual has poor emotional control, suffers from fatigue, and gains weight. He or she moves as little as possible and loses interest in activities and surroundings. As the disorder progresses, the skin becomes dry and brittle, and hair is lost from the eyebrows and the genital area. In severe cases depression may be deep enough to be considered psychotic. In children the disorder causes mental retardation. Fortunately, hypothyroidism is a very rare condition today, for the iodine of iodized salt prevents the thyroid deficiency.

The adrenal cortex is centrally involved in the activation of emergency physiological responses and the energy needs of the human organism. A chronic insufficiency of cortisone secretion by the adrenal cortex produces _Addison's disease,_ first described by the English physician Thomas Addison. The patient loses weight, suffers from low blood pressure, and is irritable and easily fatigued; skin and mucuous membranes also darken. The person becomes depressed and less sociable. When abnormal growths on the cortices of the adrenal glands make them secrete too much cortisone, the condition produced is called _Cushing's syndrome._ Harvey Cushing, the American brain surgeon, described this rare disease, which usually affects young women. The afflicted individual has severe mood swings, none of them pleasant. She is most often depressed but may then become anxious, agitated, and irritable. Physical changes, some quite disfiguring ones—obesity, muscle wasting, changes

in skin color and texture, and bone porosity which may bring spinal deformity—can also occur.

Organic Personality Syndrome

In _organic personality syndrome_ the personality undergoes a great change, usually because of damage to the brain. The specific nature of the personality change, although very difficult to predict, depends to some extent on function and location of the brain structures that are altered. Some people become emotionally labile and unable to control themselves. They may have sudden bouts of crying and temper outbursts with little provocation. Or they may be sexually indiscrete, shoplift, and act otherwise inappropriately with little concern for consequences. Others may become apathetic, losing interest in their daily activities, friends, and hobbies. Still others may develop a paranoid suspiciousness.

One cause of these personality changes is a brain _tumor_ or _neoplasm,_ an abnormal growth which can produce a wide variety of psychological as well as physical symptoms. Tumors are either malignant or benign. Malignant growths interfere directly with neural functioning by destroying the original brain tissue from which they started to grow. Benign tumors do not destroy tissue but may, as they grow, increase intracranial pressure and thus disrupt the normal functioning of the brain. Brain tumors usually originate either in glial cells—which support and protect neurons, determine their supply of nutrients and enzymes, and remove dead cells—or in the dura, the outermost membrane covering the brain. Metastatic tumors, though, can invade the brain after being carried by the blood from another area of the body such as the lung.

In addition to causing persistent headaches, vomiting, and sensory and motor impairments—double vision, jerky reflexes and coordination, visual, olfactory, and auditory hallucinations, seizures, and paralysis—tumors in the frontal, temporal, and parietal lobes may first disturb the personality. The individual may be preoccupied and confused, depressed and irritable, and careless about dress, appearance and work. Very occasionally, the person explodes in a sudden and destructive outburst, totally out of character and completely incomprehensible to family, friends, and society at large. After the event it is usually realized, however, that the individual has had earlier warning symptoms and has even communicated them.

If either a benign or a malignant tumor continues to grow, the patient usually dies. Even if the tumor is removed, the functions that have been lost through the destruction of neural tissue do not return because brain cells do not regenerate.

The two lesser brain traumas—the _concussion,_ a brief loss of consciousness caused by a jarring blow to the head; and the _contusion,_ a bruise of neural tissue and coma when a blow shifts the brain and compresses it against the opposite side of the skull—are serious enough but will not usually change the personality.[3] But a _laceration,_ a direct wound to the brain when an object enters the skull and pierces, ruptures, or tears tissue, may. A famous historical case, reported by Dr. J. M. Harlow (1896), illustrates vividly some personality changes following a severe laceration. The patient, Phineas Gage, was working on evacuation of rocks for the roadway of the Rutland and Burlington Railroad in Cavendish, Vermont, when a premature blast sent a tamping iron, three feet, seven inches in length and over an inch in diameter, through his left cheek, upward, and through the top of his skull. Although Gage recovered with no loss of motor or sensory functions, he was a changed person. Dr. Harlow described how the injury later affected Gage's behavior.

> His physical health is good, and I am inclined to say that he has recovered. Has no pain in head, but says it has a queer feeling which he is not able to describe. Applied for his situation as foreman, but is undecided whether to work or travel. His contractors, who regarded him as the most efficient and capable foreman in their employ previous to his injury considered the change in his mind so marked that they could not give him his place again. The equilibrium or balance, so to speak, between his intellectual faculties and animal propensities, seems to have been destroyed. He is fitful, irreverent, indulging at times in the grossest profanity (which was not previously his custom), manifesting but little deference for his fellows, impatient of restraint or advice when it conflicts with his desires, at times pertinaciously obstinate, yet capricios and vascillating, devising many plans for future operations, which are no sooner arranged than they are abandoned in turn for others. . . . his mind is radically changed, so decidedly that his friends and acquaintances said he was "no longer Gage" (pp. 339–340).

---

[3] A series of severe blows to the head, such as a boxer suffers, can eventually lead to a brain syndrome called "punch-drunkenness." Areas of brain tissue become permanently damaged by the accumulation of injuries; the individual cannot pay attention or concentrate, and memory as well as motor functions are groggy and slow. A person speaks as though slightly drunk. Emotions are unstable and poorly controlled; intellectual impairment is sometimes profound.

Presenile Dementias

Rare forms of mental deterioration that begin when the individual is in the forties or fifties are referred to as *presenile dementias.* Alzheimer's disease, Pick's disease, Huntington's chorea, and Parkinson's disease are such disorders.

Alzheimer's disease

In *Alzheimer's disease* the brain tissue deteriorates rather rapidly, death usually occurring four or five years after the onset of symptoms. The disorder is three times more prevalent among women than among men. The disease was first described by the German neurologist Alois Alzheimer in 1860. It commences with difficulties in concentration; the individual appears absent-minded and irritable, shortcomings which soon begin to interfere with the way she leads her life. She blames others for personal failings and has delusions of being persecuted. Memory continues to deteriorate, with the individual becoming increasingly disoriented and agitated.

The primary physiological change in the brain, evident at autopsy, is a general atrophy of the cerebral cortex as neurons are lost. The fissures widen and the ridges become narrower and flatter. Moreover, senile plaques are found scattered throughout the cortex—small round areas in which tissue has degenerated into granular material and filaments—and tangled threadlike structures, neurofibrillary tangles, replace nerve cells in the basal ganglia. Alzheimer's disease is probably *not* simply an early variant of senile dementia. It occurs much more abruptly and is distinguished by symptoms that are not notable in senile dementia, such as speech impairments, involuntary movements in the limbs, hyperactivity and agitation, and occasional convulsions, as well as by a much more rapid mental deterioration.

Pick's disease

Another presenile disorder was first described by Arnold Pick, a Prague physician, in 1892. *Pick's disease* is a degenerative disorder of the central nervous system in which the frontal and temporal lobes atrophy. As the disease progresses, the deterioration becomes more and more pervasive. The total weight of the brain may be reduced to less than 1000 grams from the usual weight of about 1300 grams. As in Alzheimer's disease, the age of onset is generally in the forties and fifties, and symptoms of the two disorders are also similar. The patient has difficulties with memory and in abstract thinking; he or she is confused and unable to concentrate and has transitory speech impairment. But in Pick's disease affect may be blunted, and the patient is likely to become apathetic and inactive. Life expectancy after onset if usually four to seven years.

Huntington's chorea

The degenerative disorder *Huntington's chorea* was first described by the American neurologist George Huntington in 1872, after his father and grandfather, both physicians, had observed the disease in several generations of a family. Symptoms usually begin when the individual is in the thirties, and thereafter deterioration is progressive. The early behavioral signs are slovenliness, disregard for social convention, violent outbursts, depression, irritability, poor memory, euphoria, poor judgment, delusions, suicidal ideas and attempts, and hallucinations. The term chorea was applied to the disorder because of the patient's choreiform movements—involuntary, spasmodic twitching and jerking of the limbs, trunk, and head. These signs of neurological disturbance do not appear until well after behavior has already started to deteriorate. Facial grimaces, a smacking of the lips and tongue, and explosive, often obscene speech are other symptoms. The afflicted individual is likely to have severe problems in speaking, walking, and swallowing. Through the course of the disorder, the suicide rate becomes high, and eventually there is a total loss of bodily control. Death is inevitable, but it may be delayed for ten to twenty years after the onset of illness. The incidence is about 5 cases per 100,000 persons (Boll, Heaton, and Reitan, 1974).

The following excerpts from the biography of the American folksinger Woody Guthrie illustrate the development of the disorder, some of the prominent clinical symptoms, and the personal tragedy of the illness.

[Describing the first signs, Woody's wife, Marjorie, commented] "What confused me, and Woody himself, in the early stage of the illness was that by nature he was a rather moody person. As early as 1948, we began to notice that he was more reflective, and often depressed by trivial things. . . . [Shortly thereafter] the symptoms of the disease had become more obvious. Woody developed a peculiar lopsided walk and his speech became explosive. He would take a deep sigh before breathing out the words. The moods and depressions became more exaggerated and more frequent. . . ." [In 1952 the first serious attack occurred. As his wife described it,] "Woody had a violent outburst and foamed at the mouth." [He was hospitalized for three weeks and diagnosed as an alcoholic. After his release he had another violent seizure which, this time, led to a three-month hospitalization. Later] "the disease was making rapid progress. Woody found it increasingly difficult to control his movements, appearing to be drunk even when he wasn't drinking. Friends watched with apprehension as he dived into traffic, oblivious of danger, Chaplinlike, warding off each car as it sped toward him."

[Finally, in 1956, it was recognized that Guthrie had Huntington's chorea, and he spent his remaining years in hospitals. One incident related by his wife, which occurred shortly after his hospitalization, is especially poignant.] "In the early years of his stay in hospitals, Woody would leave every now and then on his own. One day he took the wrong bus and landed in some town in New Jersey. Noticing his disheveled appearance, his distraught air and halting gait, a policeman picked him up, took him to the local police station, and booked him on a vagrancy charge.

"Woody told the police that he was not a homeless bum but a sick man. He explained that he was staying at a New York hospital and begged them to get him home. 'Well,' they said, 'if you're sick you can stay in our hospital.' Finally, they let him call me and I went tearing out to New Jersey.

"When I arrived I was received by a staff doctor, a Viennese psychiatrist. 'Your husband is a very disturbed man,' he said imperiously, 'with many hallucinations. He says that he has written a thousand songs.'[4]

'It is true,' I said.
'He also says he was written a book.'
'That's also true.'
'He says that a record company has put out nine records of his songs!' The doctor's voice dripped disbelief.
'That is also the truth.' I said" (Yurchenco, 1970, pp. 139–148).

The disorder is a genetically determined one, passed on by a single dominant gene. The offspring of an individual with the disorder have a 50 percent chance of being afflicted. A postmortem examination of the brain of an individual with Huntington's chorea reveals widespread atrophy and scarring. The major pathological change is a loss of neurons in the caudate nucleus, one of the basal ganglia. The cerebral cortex also atrophies, especially the frontal areas. High levels of dopamine in the caudate nucleus appear to be primarily responsible for the choreiform movements.

Parkinson's disease

In 1817 James Parkinson described a slowly progressive degeneration which begins later in life, between the ages of fifty and seventy. The primary symptoms of *Parkinson's disease* are severe and continual muscular tremors, usually occurring at a rate of four to eight movements per second, which rhythmically agitate the limbs, hands, neck, and face. The tremor may begin in one hand or arm, spread to the leg of that side, then to neck, jaw, and face, and finally to the two other limbs. Only muscles that are at rest are subject to tremors, however, not those of the sleeping body or those that are engaged in a coordinated movement. But handwriting becomes small and this and other manual skills may eventually be lost; speech, swallowing, and chewing are laborious. Other physiological effects include muscular rigidity, akinesia—an inability to initiate movements—and defects in balance. The face later becomes masklike and expressionless, the head shakes, the fingers make pill-rolling movements, and the gait is stiff and distinctive, with the upper part of the body moving forward ahead of the legs. The individual may have difficulty concentrating, become apathetic, and withdraw from social contact. About 90 percent of patients with Parkinson's disease are depressed,

---

[4] In addition to misdiagnosing Mr. Guthrie, the physician had confused the concepts of delusion and hallucination.

and in 30 percent intellectual deterioration is evident (DeJong and Sugar, 1971). About one and a half million Americans are afflicted with the disorder (Stang, 1970).

The etiology of Parkinson's disease varies. It is at times attributable to atherosclerosis; other cases are the aftereffects of encephalitis. The basic brain pathology is a loss of the deeply pigmented nerve cells in the substantia nigra, a nucleus within the midbrain which is an important motor relay station. The neurons in the substantia nigra that are destroyed are those that release dopamine. One by-product of dopamine metabolism is melanin, which gives the substantia nigra its characteristic color. A reduced number of these cells means not only that the substantia nigra loses color but that less dopamine is released in the corpus striatum, to which the axons of these neurons normally extend. The corpus striatum consists of the caudate and lenticular nuclei, two of the basal ganglia. Tracts of white matter between them give the mass a striped appearance. With reduced amounts of dopamine in the corpus striatum, the action of the neurotransmitter acetylcholine released by the cholinergic motor neurons in the caudate nucleus is insufficiently opposed. And because the neurotransmitter of the cholinergic tracts is not under the inhibitory control of dopamine, too many of the postsynaptic motor neurons fire, producing the uncontrollable muscular tremors and stiffness of Parkinson's disease. Parkinsonism can be treated either by administering anticholinergic drugs to reduce the action of the cholinergic neurons, or by giving the patient a precursor of dopamine, L-dopa. Encouraging as much movement as possible and speech therapy are also helpful.

■■ ■

REFERENCES

Abel, G. G., Barlow, D. H., Blanchard, E. B., & Guild, D. The components of rapists' sexual arousal. *Archives of General Psychiatry,* 1977, **34,** 895–903.

Abraham, K. Notes on the psychoanalytical investigation and treatment of manic-depressive insanity and allied conditions, 1911. In E. Jones (Ed.), *Selected papers of Karl Abraham, M.D.* London: Hogarth Press, 1927.

Abrams, R. What's new in convulsive therapy? In S. Arieti & G. Chrzanowski (Eds.), *New dimensions in psychiatry.* New York: Wiley, 1975.

Abramson, L. Y., Garber, J., Edwards, N. B., & Seligman, M. E. P. Expectancy changes in depression and schizophrenia. *Journal of Abnormal Psychology,* 1978, **87,** 102–109.

Abramson, L. Y., & Sackeim, H. A. A paradox in depression: Uncontrollability and self-blame. *Psychological Bulletin,* 1977, **84,** 839–851.

Abramson, L. Y., Seligman, M. E. P., & Teasdale, J. D. Learned helplessness in humans: Critique and reformulation. *Journal of Abnormal Psychology,* 1978, **87,** 49–74.

Abse, D. W. *Hysteria and related mental disorders.* Baltimore: Williams and Wilkins, 1966.

Abuzzahab, F. S., & Anderson, F. O. (Eds.) *Gilles de la Tourette's syndrome.* Vol. 1. *International Registry.* St. Paul, Minn.: Mason Publishing Company, 1976.

Achenbach, T. M. *Developmental psychopathology.* New York: Wiley, 1974.

Achenbach, T. M., & Edelbrock, C. S. The classification of child psychopathology: A review of empirical efforts. *Psychological Bulletin,* 1978, **85,** 1275–1301.

Adler, A. Compulsion neurosis, 1931. In H. L. Ansbacher & R. R. Ansbacher (Eds.), *Superiority and social interest.* Evanston, Ill.: Northwestern University Press, 1964.

Agras, S., Sylvester, D., & Oliveau, D. The epidemiology of common fears and phobias. Unpublished manuscript, 1969.

Akhter, S., Wig, N. N., Varma, V. K., Pershad, D., & Verma, S. K. A phenomenological analysis of symptoms in obsessive-compulsive neurosis. *British Journal of Psychiatry,* 1975, **127,** 342–348

Albee, G. W., Lane, E. A., & Reuter, J. M. Childhood intelligence of future schizophrenics and neighborhood peers. *Journal of Psychology,* 1964, **58,** 141–144.

Aldrich, C. K., & Mendkoff, E. Relocation of the aged and disabled: A mortality study. *Journal of the American Geriatrics Society,* 1963, **11,** 185–194.

Alexander, F. *Psychosomatic medicine.* New York: Norton, 1950.

Alexander, F., & French, T. M. *Psychoanalytic therapy.* New York: Ronald Press, 1946.

Alexander, R., & Staub, H. *The criminal, the judge, and the public: A psychological analysis.* Glencoe, Ill.: The Free Press, 1929.

Allderidge, P. Hospitals, mad houses, and asylums: Cycles in the care of the insane. *British Journal of Psychiatry,* 1979, **134,** 321–324.

Allen, M. G. Twin studies of affective illness. *Archives of General Psychiatry,* 1976, **33,** 1476–1478.

Alloy, L. B., & Abramson, L. Y. Judgment of contingency in depressed and nondepressed students: Sadder but wiser? *Journal of Experimental Psychology: General,* 1979, **108,** 441–485.

Allport, G. W. *Pattern and growth in personality.* New York: Holt, Rinehart and Winston, 1961.

American Cancer Society. *Task force on tobacco and cancer—Target 5.* Report to the Board of Directors, American Cancer Society, 1976.

American Law Institute. *Model penal code: Proposed official draft.* Philadelphia: The American Law Institute, 1962.

American Psychiatric Association. *Diagnostic and statistical manual of mental disorders.* First edition, 1952; second edition, 1968; third edition, 1980. Washington, D. C.: American Psychiatric Association.

Anastasi, A. *Psychological testing.* (3rd ed.) New York: Macmillan, 1968.

Anderson, F. O., & Abuzzahab, F. S. Current knowledge of the syndrome. In F. S. Abuzzahab & F. O. Anderson (Eds.), *Gilles de la Tourette's syndrome.* Vol. 1. *International Registry.* St. Paul, Minn.: Mason Publishing Co., 1976.

Andreasen, N. C. Thought, language, and communication disorders: II. Diagnostic significance. *Archives of General Psychiatry,* 1979, **36,** 1325–1330.

Angrist, B., Lee, H. K., & Gershon, S. The antagonism of amphetamine-induced symptomatology by a neuroleptic. *American Journal of Psychiatry,* 1974, **131,** 817–819.

Arieti, S. *Interpretation of schizophrenia.* New York: Basic Books, 1955.

Arieti, S. New views on the psychodynamics of phobias. *American Journal of Psychotherapy,* 1979, **33,** 82–95.

Arkonac, O., & Guze, S. B. A family study of hysteria. *New England Journal of Medicine,* 1963, **268,** 239–242.

Aronson, E. *The social animal.* San Francisco: Freeman, 1972.

Aronson, E., & Carlsmith, J. R. Experimentation in social psychology. In G. Lindzey & E. Aronson (Eds.), *The handbook of social psychology.* Vol. 2. *Research methods.* Menlo Park, Calif.: Addison-Wesley, 1968.

Asarnow, R. F., MacCrimmon, D. J., Cleghorn, J. M., & Steffy, R. A. The McMaster-Waterloo project: An attentional and clinical assessment of foster children at risk for schizophrenia. *Journal of Abnormal Psychology,* 1977, **86,** 267–275.

Ashcroft, G., Crawford, T., & Eccleston, E. 5-Hydroxyindole compounds in the cerebrospinal fluid of patients with psychiatric or neurological disease. *Lancet,* 1966, **2,** 1049–1052.

Atchley, R. A. *The social forces in later life: An introduction to social gerontology.* (2nd ed.) Belmont, Calif.: Wadsworth, 1977.

Atthowe, J. M. Treating the hospitalized person. In W. E. Craighead, A. E. Kazdin, & M. J. Mahoney (Eds.), *Behavior modification: Principles, issues, and applications.* Boston: Houghton Mifflin, 1976.

Ausubel, D. P. Causes and types of narcotic addictions: A psychosocial view. *Psychiatric Quarterly,* 1961, **35,** 523–531. (a)

Ausubel, D. P. Personality disorder is disease. *American Psychologist,* 1961, **16,** 69–74. (b)

Ax, A. F. The physiological differentiation between fear and anger in humans. *Psychosomatic Medicine,* 1953, **15,** 433–442.

Ayllon, T., & Azrin, N. H. The measurement and reinforcement of behavior of psychotics. *Journal of the Experimental Analysis of Behavior,* 1965, **8,** 357–383.

Ayllon, T., & Azrin, N. H. *The token economy: A motivational system for therapy and rehabilitation.* New York: Appleton-Century-Crofts, 1968.

Ayllon, T., & Kelly, K. Effects of reinforcement on standardized test performance. *Journal of Applied Behavior Analysis,* 1972, **4,** 477–484.

Bach, G. R. The marathon group: Intensive practice of intimate interactions. *Psychological Reports,* 1966, **181,** 995–1002.

Bachrach, A. J., Erwin, W. J., & Mohr, J. P. The control of eating behavior in an anorexic by operant conditioning techniques. In L. P. Ullmann & L. Krasner (Eds.), *Case studies in behavior modification.* New York: Holt, Rinehart and Winston, 1965.

Bagby, E. The etiology of phobias. *Journal of Abnormal Psychology,* 1922, **17,** 16–18.

Bahm, A. K., Chandler, C., & Eisenberg, L. *Diagnostic characteristics related to service on psychiatric clinics for children.* Paper presented at the 38th Annual Convention of Orthopsychiatry, Munich, 1961.

Bakwin, H. The genetics of enuresis. In I. Kolvin, R. C. MacKeith, & S. R. Meadow (Eds.), *Enuresis and encopresis.* Philadelphia: Lippincott, 1973.

Baller, W. R. *Bed-wetting: Origin and treatment.* Elmsford, N.Y.: Pergamon Press, 1975.

Bancroft, J. H., Jones, G. H., & Pullan, B. R. A simple transducer for measuring penile erections, with comments on its use in the treatment of sexual disorders. *Behaviour Research and Therapy,* 1966, **4,** 239–241.

Bandura, A. *Principles of behavior modification.* New York: Holt, Rinehart and Winston, 1969.

Bandura, A. Self-efficacy: Toward a unifying theory of behavioral change. *Psychological Review,* 1977, **84,** 191–215.

Bandura, A., Blanchard, E. B., & Ritter, B. Relative efficacy of desensitization and modelling approaches for inducing behavioral, affective, and attitudinal changes. *Journal of Personality and Social Psychology,* 1969, **13,** 173–199.

Bandura, A., Grusec, J. E., & Menlove, F. L. Vicarious extinction of avoidance behavior. *Journal of Personality and Social Psychology,* 1967, **5,** 16–23.

Bandura, A., Jeffrey, R. W., & Bachicha, D. L. Analysis of memory codes and cumulative rehearsal in observational learning. *Journal of Research in Personality,* 1974, **7,** 295–305.

Bandura, A., & Menlove, F. L. Factors determining vicarious extinction of avoidance behavior through symbolic modeling. *Journal of Personality and Social Psychology,* 1968, **8,** 99–108.

Bandura, A., & Perloff, B. Relative efficacy of self-monitored and externally imposed reinforcement systems. *Journal of Personality and Social Psychology,* 1967, **7,** 111–116.

Bandura, A., & Rosenthal, T. L. Vicarious classical conditioning as a function of arousal level. *Journal of Personality and Social Psychology,* 1966, **3,** 54–62.

Bandura, A., & Walters, R. H. *Adolescent aggression.* New York: Ronald Press, 1959.

Bandura, A., & Walters, R. H. *Social learning and personality development.* New York: Holt, Rinehart and Winston, 1963.

Barahal, H. S. 1000 prefrontal lobotomies: Five-to-ten-year follow-up study. *Psychiatric Quarterly,* 1958, **32,** 653–678.

Barbach, L. G. *For yourself.* New York: Doubleday, 1975.

Barber, T. X. *Hypnosis: A scientific approach.* New York: Van Nostrand Reinhold, 1969.

Barber, T. X., & Calverley, D. S. Experimental studies in "hypnotic" behavior: Suggested deafness evaluated by delayed auditory feedback. *British Journal of Psychology,* 1964, **55,** 439–446. (a)

Barber, T. X., & Calverley, D. S. An experimental study of "hypnotic" (auditory and visual) hallucinations. *Journal of Abnormal and Social Psychology,* 1964, **63,** 13–20. (b)

Barber, T. X., & Silver, M. J. Fact, fiction, and the experimenter bias effect. *Psychological Bulletin, Monograph Supplement,* 1968, **70,** 1–29.

Barkley, R. A., & Cunningham, C. E. The effects of methylphenidate on the mother-child interactions of hyperactive children. *Archives of General Psychiatry*, 1979, **36**, 201–208.

Barkley, R. A., Hasting, J. E., Tousel, R. E., & Tousel, S. E. Evaluation of a token system for juvenile delinquents in a residential setting. *Journal of Behavior Therapy and Experimental Psychiatry*, 1976, **7**, 227–230.

Barlow, D. H., Abel, G. G., & Blanchard, E. B. Gender identity change in transsexuals. *Archives of General Psychiatry*, 1979, **36**, 1001–1007.

Barlow, D. H., Reynolds, E. J., & Agras, W. S. Gender identity change in a transsexual. *Archives of General Psychiatry*, 1973, **29**, 569–576.

Baron, R. A., & Byrne, D. *Social psychology: Understanding human interaction.* (2nd ed.) Boston: Allyn and Bacon, 1977.

Barrett, C. L. Systematic desensitization versus implosive therapy. *Journal of Abnormal Psychology*, 1969, **74**, 587–592.

Barrett, C. L., Hampe, E., & Miller, L. Research on psychotherapy with children. In S. L. Garfield & A. E. Bergin (Eds.), *Handbook of psychotherapy and behavior change: An empirical analysis.* (2nd ed.) New York: Wiley, 1978.

Bartak, L., Rutter, M., & Cox, A. A comparative study of infantile autism and specific development language disorders: I. The children. *British Journal of Psychiatry*, 1975, **126**, 127–145.

Basedow, H. *The Australian aboriginal.* London: Adelaide, 1925.

Basmajian, J. V. Learned control of single motor units. In G. E. Schwartz & J. Beatty (Eds.), *Biofeedback: Theory and Research.* New York: Academic Press, 1977.

Bateson, G. Jackson, D. D., Haley, J., & Weakland, J. Toward a theory of schizophrenia. *Behavioral Science*, 1956, **1**, 251–264.

Battle, E. S., & Lacey, B. A. A context for hyperactivity in children, over time. *Child Development*, 1972, **43**, 757–773.

Bauer, D. H. An exploratory study of developmental changes in children's fears. *Journal of Child Psychology and Psychiatry*, 1976, **17**, 69–74.

Baum, A., & Valins, S. Residential environments, group size and crowding. *Proceedings of the 81st Annual Convention of the American Psychological Association.* Washington, D.C.: American Psychological Association, 1973.

Baum, M. Extinction of avoidance responding through response prevention (flooding). *Psychological Bulletin*, 1970, **74**, 276–284.

Baxter, E., & Hopper, K. *Private lives/public places: Homeless adults on the streets of New York City.* New York: Community Service Society, 1981.

Beck, A. T. *Depression: Clinical, experimental and theoretical aspects.* New York: Harper and Row, 1967.

Beck, A. T. The core problem in depression: The cognitive triad. In J. Masserman (Ed.), *Depression: Theories and therapies.* New York: Grune and Stratton, 1970.

Beck, A. T. *Cognitive therapy and the emotional disorders.* New York: International Universities Press, 1976.

Beck, A. T., Kovacs, M., & Weissman, A. Hopelessness and suicidal behavior: An overview. *Journal of the American Medical Association*, 1975, **234**, 1146–1149.

Beck, A. T., Rush, A. J., Shaw, B. F., & Emery, G. *Cognitive therapy of depression.* New York: Guilford Press, 1979.

Beck, A. T., & Ward, C. H. Dreams of depressed patients: Characteristic themes in manifest content. *Archives of General Psychiatry*, 1961, **5**, 462–467.

Beck, A. T., Ward, C. H., Mendelson, M., Mock, J. E., & Erbaugh, J. K. Reliability of psychiatric diagnosis: II. A study of consistency of clinical judgments and ratings. *American Journal of Psychiatry*, 1962, **119**, 351–357.

Beck, A. T., Weissman, A., Lester, D., & Trexler, L. The measurement of pessimism: The hopelessness scale. *Journal of Consulting and Clinical Psychology*, 1974, **42**, 861–865.

Becker, C., & Kronus, S. Sex and drinking patterns: An old relationship revisited in a new way. *Social Problems*, 1977, **24**, 482–497.

Bednar, R. L., & Kaul, T. J. Experiential group research: Current perspectives. In S. L. Garfield & A. E. Bergin (Eds.), *Handbook of psychotherapy and behavior change: An empirical analysis.* (2nd ed.) New York: Wiley, 1978.

Beecher, H. K. Ethics and clinical research. *New England Journal of Medicine*, 1966, **274**, 1354–1360.

Begelman, D. A. Ethical and legal issues of behavior modification. In M. Hersen, R. Eisler, & P. M. Miller (Eds.), *Progress in behavior modification.* New York: Academic Press, 1975.

Behar, M. Prevalence of malnutrition among preschool children of developing countries. In N. W. Scrimshaw & J. E. Gordon (Eds.), *Malnutrition, learning and behavior.* Cambridge, Mass.: M.I.T. Press, 1968.

Beisser, H. R., Glasser, N., & Grant, M. Psychosocial adjustment of children of schizophrenic mothers. *Journal of Nervous and Mental Disease*, 1967, **145**, 429–440.

Beitchman, J. H., Dielman, T. E., Landis, J. R., Benson, R. M., & Kemp, P. L. Reliability of the Group for Advancement of Psychiatry diagnostic categories in child psychiatry. *Archives of General Psychiatry*, 1978, **35**, 1461–1468.

Bell, I. R., & Schwartz, G. E. Voluntary control and reactivity in human heart rate. *Psychophysiology,* 1975, **12,** 339–348.

Bell, J. E. *Family therapy.* New York: Jason Aronson, 1975.

Bellack, A. S., Hersen, M., & Turner, S. M. Generalizatin effects of social skills training in chronic schizophrenics: An experimental analysis. *Behavior Research and Therapy,* 1976, **14,** 391–398.

Bellak, L., Hurvich, M., & Gediman, H. K. *Ego functions in schizophrenics, neurotics, and normals.* New York: Wiley, 1973.

Belliveau, F., & Richter, L. *Understanding "Human Sexual Inadequacy."* New York: Bantam, 1970.

Bem, D. J., & Allen, A. On predicting some of the people some of the time: The search for cross-situational consistencies in behavior. *Psychological Review,* 1974, **81,** 506–520.

Bemis, K. M. Current approaches to the etiology and treatment of anorexia nervosa. *Psychological Bulletin,* 1978, **85,** 593–617.

Benda, C. E., Squires, N. D., Ogonik, M. J., & Wise, R. Personality factors in mild mental retardation: I. Family background and sociocultural patterns, *American Journal of Mental Deficiency,* 1963, **68,** 24–40.

Bennet, I. *Delinquent and neurotic children.* London: Tavistock Publications, 1960.

Bennett, W. The nicotine fix. *Harvard Magazine,* 1980, **82,** 10–14.

Benson, H. *The relaxation response.* New York: Morrow, 1975.

Berger, K. S., & Zarit, S. H. Late life paranoid states: Assessment and treatment. *American Journal of Orthopsychiatry,* 1978, **48,** 528–537.

Bergin, A. E. Some implications of psychotherapy research for therapeutic practice. *Journal of Abnormal Psychology,* 1966, **71,** 235–246.

Bergin, A. E. The evaluation of therapeutic outcomes. In A. E. Bergin & S. L. Garfield (Eds.), *Handbook of psychotherapy and behavior change: An empirical analysis.* New York: Wiley, 1971.

Bergin, A. E., & Lambert, M. J. The evaluation of therapeutic outcomes. In S. L. Garfield & A. E. Bergin (Eds.), *Handbook of psychotherapy and behavior change: An empirical analysis.* (2nd ed.) New York: Wiley, 1978.

Bergler, E. Personality traits of alcohol addicts. *Quarterly Journal of Studies on Alcohol,* 1946, **7,** 356–361.

Berman, E. M., & Lief, H. I. Sex and the aging process. In W. W. Oaks, G. A. Melchiode, & I. Ficher (Eds.), *Sex and the life cycle.* New York: Grune and Stratton, 1976.

Bernard, J. *The future of marriage.* New York: Bantam, 1973.

Bernstein, D. A., & Nietzel, M. T. *Introduction to clinical psychology.* New York: McGraw-Hill, 1980.

Berry, J. C. Antecedents of schizophrenia, impulsive character and alcoholism in males. Paper presented at the 75th Annual Convention of the American Psychological Association, Washington, D.C., 1967.

Bettelheim, B. *The informed heart.* New York: The Free Press, 1960.

Bettelheim, B. *The empty fortress.* New York: The Free Press, 1967.

Bettelheim, B. *Children of the dream.* London: Collier-Macmillan, 1969.

Bettelheim, B. Bringing up children. *Ladies Home Journal,* 1973, **90,** 28.

Bettelheim, B. *A home for the heart.* New York: Knopf, 1974.

Bibring, E. The mechanism of depression. In P. Greenacre (Ed.), *Affective disorders.* New York: International Universities Press, 1953.

Bieber, I., Dain, H. J., Dince P. R., Drellich, M. G., Grand, H. C., Gundlach, R. H., Kremer, M. W. Rifkin, A. H., Wilbur, C. B., & Bieber, T. B. *Homosexuality: A psychoanalytical study.* New York: Random House, 1962.

Bijou, S. W., & Baer, D. M. *Child development.* Vol. 1. *A systematic and empirical theory.* New York: Appleton-Century-Crofts, 1961.

Bild, B. R., & Havighurst, R. J. Senior citizens in great cities: The case of Chicago. *Gerontologist,* 1976, **16,** whole issue.

Bindrim, P. A report on a nude marathon: The effect of physical nudity upon the practice interaction in the marathon group. *Psychotherapy: Theory, Research and Practice,* 1968, **5,** 180–188.

Birren, J. E. Translations in gerontology—From lab to life: Psychophysiology and speed of response. *American Psychologist,* 1974, **11,** 808–815.

Bitterman, M. E. Issues in the comparative psychology of learning. In R. B. Masterson, M. E. Bitterman, C. B. G. Campbell, & N. Hotten (Eds.), *The evolution of brain and behavior in veterbrates.* Hillsdale, N.J.: Lawrence Erlbaum Associates, 1975.

Black, M., Freeman, B. J., & Montgomery, J. Systematic observation of play behavior in autistic children. *Journal of Autism and Childhood Schizophrenia,* 1975, **5,** 363–371.

Blanchard, E. B., & Miller, S. T. Psychological treatment of cardiovascular disease. *Archives of General Psychiatry,* 1977, **34,** 1402–1413.

Blanchard, E. B., Miller, S. T., Abel, G. G., Haynes, M. R., & Wicker, R. Evaluation of biofeedback in the treatment of borderline essential hypertension. *Journal of Applied Behavior Analysis,* 1979, **12,** 99–109.

Blaney, P. H. Contemporary theories of depression: Critique and comparison. *Journal of Abnormal Psychology,* 1977, **86,** 203–223.

Blenker, M. Environmental change and the aging individual. *Gerontologist,* 1967, **7,** 101–105.

Blessed. G., Tomlinson, B. E., & Roth, M. The association between quantitative measures of dementia and of senile change in the cerebral gray matter of elderly subjects. *British Journal of Psychiatry,* 1968, **114,** 797–811.

Bleuler, E. *Lehrbruch der psychiatrie.* (4th ed.) Berlin: Springer, 1923.

Block, J. *Lines through time.* Berkeley, Calif.: Bancroft Books, 1971.

Bloomfield, H. H. Assertive training in an outpatient group of chronic schizophrenics: A preliminary report. *Behavior Therapy,* 1973, **4,** 277–281.

Blum, J. E., Jarvik, L. F., & Clark, E. T. Rate of change on selective tests of intelligence: A twenty year longitudinal study. *Journal of Gerontology,* 1970, **25,** 171–176.

Bobruff, A., Gardos, G., Tarsy, D., Rapkin, R. M., Cole, J. O., & Moore, P. Clonazepan and phenobarbital in tardive dyskinesia. *American Journal of Psychiatry,* 1981, **138,** 189–193.

Bockhoven, J. *Moral treatment in American psychiatry.* New York: Springer, 1963.

Bogdan, R., & Taylor, S. The judged, not the judges: An insider's view of mental retardation. *American Psychologist,* 1976, **31,** 47–52.

Boll, T. J., Heaton, R., & Reitan, R. M. Neuropsychological and emotional correlates of Huntington's chorea. *Journal of Nervous and Mental Disease.,* 1974, **158,** 61–69.

Bolton, A. A study of the need for and availability of mental health services for mentally retarded jail inmates and juveniles in detention facilities. Unpublished report, Arthur Bolton Associates, Boston, 1976. Cited in J. Monahan, *The clinical prediction of violent behavior.* Rockville, Md.: National Institute of Mental Health, 1981.

Bond, I. K., & Hutchison, H. C. Application of reciprocal inhibition therapy to exhibitionism. *Canadian Medical Association Journal,* 1960, **83,** 23–25.

Borkovec, T. D. Investigations of fear and sleep disturbance: Methodological, measurement and theoretical issues in therapy outcome research. In G. E. Schwartz & D. Shapiro (Eds.), *Consciousness and self-regulation: Advances in research.* New York: Plenum Press, 1977.

Borkovec, T. D., & O'Brien, G. T. Methodological and target behavior issues in analogue therapy outcome research. In M. Hersen, R. M. Eisler, & P. M. Miller (Eds.), *Progress in behavior modification,* Vol. 3. New York: Academic Press, 1976.

Bornstein, P. H., Hamilton, P., Miller, D., Quevillon, C., & Spitzform, R. Reliability and validity enhancement: A treatment package for increasing fidelity of self-report. *Journal of Clinical Psychology,* 1977, **33,** 861–866.

Bosch, G. *Infantile autism.* New York: Springer-Verlag, 1970.

Botwinick, J. Intellectual abilities. In J. E. Birren & K. W. Schaie (Eds.), *Handbook of the psychology of aging.* New York: Van Nostrand Reinhold, 1977.

Bourne, P. G., Alford, J. A., & Bowcock, J. Z. Treatment of skid row alcoholics with disulfiram. *Quarterly Journal of Studies on Alcohol,* 1966, **27,** 42–48.

Bower, G. H. Mood and memory. *American Psychologist,* 1981, **36,** 129–148.

Bowers, K. S. Situationism in psychology: An analysis and a critique. *Psychological Review,* 1973, **80,** 307–336.

Bowers, M. B., Jr. Central dopamine turnover in schizophrenic syndromes. *Archives of General Psychiatry,* 1974, **31,** 50–54.

Bowlby, J. *Attachment and loss.* Vol. 2. *Separation.* New York: Basic Books, 1973.

Brady, J. P., & Lind, D. L. Experimental analysis of hysterical blindness. *Archives of General Psychiatry,* 1961, **4,** 331–359.

Braginsky, B. M., Grosse, M., & Ring K. Controlling outcomes through impression management: An experimental study of the manipulative tactics of mental patients. *Journal of Consulting Psychology,* 1966, **30,** 295–300.

Bransford, J. D., & Johnson, M. K. Considerations of some problems of comprehension. In W. G. Chase (Ed.), *Visual information processing.* New York: Academic Press, 1973.

Brecher, E. M., & the Editors of *Consumer Reports. Licit and illicit drugs.* Mount Vernon, N.Y.: Consumers Union, 1972.

Brenner, M. H. *Mental illness and the economy.* Cambridge, Mass.: Harvard University Press, 1973.

Brenner, M. H. Personal stability and economic security. *Social Policy,* 1977, **8,** 2–5.

Bridge, T. P., Cannon, H. E., & Wyatt, R. J. Burned-out schizophrenia: Evidence for age effects on schizophrenic symptomatology. *Journal of Gerontology,* 1978, **33,** 835–839.

Bridger, W. H., & Mandel, I. J. Abolition of the PRE by instructions in GSR conditioning. *Journal of Experimental Psychology,* 1965, **69,** 476–482.

Brill, H., & Malzberg, B. Statistical report on the arrest record of male ex-patients, age 16 and over, released from New York State mental hospitals during the period 1946–48. Unpublished manuscript, New York State Department of Mental Hygiene, 1954. As cited in J. Monahan, *The clinical prediction of violent behavior.* Rockville, Md.: National Institute of Mental Health, 1981.

Brodie, H. K. H., & Leff, M. J. Bipolar depression: A comparative study of patient characteristics. *American Journal of Psychiatry,* 1971, **127,** 1086–1090.

Brotman, H. B. Who are the aging? In E. W. Busse & E. Pfeiffer (Eds.), *Mental illness in later life.* Washington, D.C.: American Psychiatric Association, 1973.

Broverman, I. K., Broverman, D. M., & Clarkson, F. E. Sex-role stereotypes and clinical judgments of mental health. *Journal of Consulting and Clinical Psychology,* 1970, **34,** 1–7.

Brown, G. W., & Birley, J. L. T. Crises and life changes and the onset of schizophrenia. *Journal of Health and Social Behavior,* 1968, **9,** 203–214.

Brown, G. W., Bone, M., Dalison, B., & Wing, J. K. *Schizophrenia and social care.* London: Oxford University Press, 1966.

Brown, W. F. Heredity in the psychoneuroses. *Proceedings of the Royal Society of Medicine,* 1942, **35,** 785–790.

Brownmiller, S. *Against our will: Men, women and rape.* New York: Simon and Schuster, 1975.

Budoff, M., & Gottlieb, J. Special-class EMR children mainstreamed: A study of an aptitude (learning potential) x treatment interaction. *American Journal of Mental Deficiency,* 1976, **81,** 1–11.

Budzynski, T. H., Stoyva, J. M., Adler, C. S., & Mullaney, D. M. EMG biofeedback and tension headache: A controlled outcome study. *Psychosomatic Medicine,* 1973, **35,** 484–496.

Buell, J., Stoddard, P., Harris, F. R., & Baer, D. M. Collateral social development accompanying reinforcement of outdoor play in a preschool child. *Journal of Applied Behavior Analysis,* 1968, **1,** 167–173.

Bukovsky, V. General Svetlichny: "We will let him rot in the insane asylum!" *The New York Times,* May 3, 1977.

Bunney, W. E., Goodwin, F. K., & Murphy, D. L. The "Switch Process" in manic-depressive illness. *Archives of General Psychiatry,* 1972, **27,** 312–317.

Bunney, W. E., Murphy, D. L., Goodwin, F. K., & Borge, G. F. The switch process from depression to mania: Relationship to drugs which alter brain amines. *Lancet,* 1970, **1,** 1022.

Burgess, A. W., & Holmstrom, L. L. *Rape: Victims of crisis.* Bowie, Md.: Robert J. Brady Company, 1974.

Burwen, L. S., & Campbell, D. T. The generality of attitudes toward authority and nonauthority figures. *Journal of Abnormal and Social Psychology,* 1957, **54,** 24–31.

Buss, A. H. *Psychopathology.* New York: Wiley, 1966.

Busse, E. W. Psychoneurotic reactions and defense mechanisms in the aged. In E. Palmore (Ed.), *Normal aging: Reports from the Duke Longitudinal Study.* Durham, N.C.: Duke University Press, 1970.

Butler, R. N., & Lewis, M. *Aging and mental health.* (2nd ed.) St. Louis: Mosby, 1977.

Cadoret, R. J. Evidence for genetic inheritance of primary affective disorder in adoptees. *American Journal of Psychiatry,* 1978, **135,** 463–466.

Cadoret, R. J. Psychopathology in adopted-away offspring of biologic parents with antisocial behavior. *Archives of General Psychiatry,* 1978, **35,** 176–184.

Calhoun, J. B. Space and the strategy of life. *Ekistics,* 1970, **29,** 425–437.

Cameron, N. *Personality development and psychopathology: A dynamic approach.* Boston: Houghton Mifflin, 1963.

Campbell, M., Friedman, E., DeVito, E., Greenspan, L., & Collins, P. J. Blood serotonin in psychotic and brain damaged children. *Journal of Autism and Childhood Schizophrenia,* 1974, **4,** 33–41.

Cannon, W. E. "Voodoo" death. *American Anthropologist,* 1942, **44,** 169–182.

Cantwell, D. P. Genetic studies of hyperactive children. In R. Fieve, D. Rosenthal, & H. Brill (Eds.), *Genetic research in psychiatry.* Baltimore: Johns Hopkins University Press, 1975.

Cantwell, D. P., Baker, L., & Rutter, M. Family factors. In M. Rutter & E. Schopler (Eds.), *Autism: A reappraisal of concepts and treatment.* New York: Plenum Press, 1978.

Cantwell, D. P., & Carlson, G. A. Stimulants. In J. S. Werry (Ed.), *Pediatric psychopharmacology: The use of behavior modifying drugs on children.* New York: Brunner/Mazel, 1978.

Cantwell, D. P., Russell, A. T., Mattison, R., & Will, L. A comparison of DSM-II and DSM-III in the diagnosis of childhood psychiatric disorders. *Archives of General Psychiatry,* 1979, **36,** 1208–1228.

Caplan, G. *Principles of preventive psychiatry.* New York: Basic Books, 1964.

Caporael, L. Ergotism: The satan loosed in Salem? *Science,* 1976, **192,** 21–26.

Cappell, H. An evaluation of tension models of alcohol consumption. In R. J. Gibbins, Y. Israel, H. Kalant, R. E. Popham, W. Schmidt, & R. G. Smart (Eds.), *Research advances in alcohol and drug problems,* Vol. 2. New York: Wiley, 1975.

Carpenter, W. T., Murphy, D. L., & Wyatt, R. J. Platelet monoamine oxidase activity in acute schizophrenia, *American Journal of Psychiatry,* 1975, **132,** 438–441.

Carr, A. T. Compulsive neurosis: Two psychophysiological studies. *Bulletin of the British Psychological Society,* 1971, **24,** 256–257..

Carr, A. T. Compulsive neurosis: A review of the literature. *Psychological Bulletin,* 1974, **81,** 311–319.

Carr, E. G., Schreibman, L., & Lovaas, O. I. Control of echo-lalic speech in psychotic children. *Journal of Abnormal Child Psychology*, 1975, **3**, 331–351.

Cashman, J. A. *The LSD story.* Greenwich, Conn.: Fawcett Publications, 1966.

Casper, R. C., Eckert, E. O., Halmi, K. A., Goldberg, S. C., & Davis, J. M. Bulimia: Its incidence and clinical importance in patients with anorexia nervosa. *Archives of General Psychiatry*, 1980, **37**, 1030–1035.

Cautela, J. R. Treatment of compulsive behavior by covert sensitization. *Psychological Record*, 1966, **16**, 33–41.

Cautela, J. R. Covert extinction. *Behavior Therapy*, 1971, **2**, 192–200.

Chao, R. C., Green, D. E., Forrest, I. S., Kaplan, J. N., Winship-Ball, A., & Braude, M. The passage of ^{14}C-delta^9-tetrahydrocannabinol into the milk of lactating squirrel monkeys. *Research Communications in Chemical Pathology and Pharmacology*, 1976, **15**, 303–317.

Chapman, L. J., & Chapman, J. P. Illusory correlation as an obstacle to the use of valid psychodiagnostic signs. *Journal of Abnormal Psychology*, 1969, **74**, 271–287.

Chapman, L. J., & Chapman, J. P. *Disordered thought in schizophrenia.* New York: Appleton-Century-Crofts, 1973.

Chein, I., Gerard, D. L., Lee, R. S., & Rosenfeld, E. *The road to H: Narcotics, delinquency, and social policy.* New York: Basic Books, 1964.

Chesler, P. *Women and madness.* Garden City, N.Y.: Doubleday, 1972.

Chesno, F. A., & Kilmann, P. R. Effects of stimulation intensity on sociopathic avoidance learning. *Journal of Abnormal Psychology*, 1975, **84**, 144–151.

Chilton, R. J. Continuity in delinquency area research: A comparison of studies for Baltimore, Detroit, and Indianapolis. *American Sociological Review*, 1964, **29**, 73.

Chinn, P. C., Drew, C. J., & Logan, D. R. *Mental retardation: A life cycle approach.* (2nd ed.) St. Louis: C. V. Mosby, 1979.

Churchill, D. W. Psychotic children and behavior modification. *American Journal of Psychiatry*, 1969, **125**, 1585–1590.

Churchill, W. *Homosexual behavior among males: A cross-cultural and cross-species investigation.* Englewood Cliffs, N.J.: Prentice-Hall, 1967.

Clark, R. *Crime in America.* New York: Simon and Schuster, 1970.

Clark, W. B., & Cahalan, D. Changes in drinking behavior over a four-year span. *Addictive Behaviors*, 1976, **1**, 251–259.

Clausen, J. A., & Kohn, M. L. Relation of schizophrenia to the social structure of a small city. In B. Pasamanick (Ed.), *Epidemiology of mental disorder.* Washington, D.C.: American Association for the Advancement of Science, 1959.

Cleckley, H. *The mask of sanity.* (5th ed.) St. Louis, Mo.: Mosby, 1976.

Cloninger, C. R., Reich, T., & Guze, S. B. The multifactorial model of disease transmission: II. Sex differences in the familial transmission of sociopathy (antisocial personality). *British Journal of Psychiatry*, 1975, **127**, 11–22.

Cobb, S., & Rose, R. M. Hypertension, peptic ulcer, and diabetes in air traffic controllers. *Journal of the American Medical Association*, 1973, **224**, 489–493.

Cobbin, D. M., Requin-Blow, B., Williams, L. R., & Williams, W. O. Urinary MHPG levels and tricyclic antidepressant drug selection. *Archives of General Psychiatry*, 1979, **36**, 1111–1115.

Cochrane, R. Hostility and neuroticism among unselected essential hypertensions. *Journal of Psychosomatic Research*, 1973, **17**, 215–218.

Cocozza, J., Melick, M., & Steadman, H. Trends in violent crime among ex-mental patients. *Criminology*, 1978, **16**, 317–334.

Coggins, W. J. The general health status of chronic cannabis smokers in Costa Rica. In S. Szara & M. Braude (Eds.), *Pharmacology of marihuana.* New York: Raven Press, 1976.

Cohen, B. D., Nachmani, G., & Rosenberg, S. Referent communication disturbances in acute schizophrenia. *Journal of Abnormal Psychology*, 1974, **83**, 1–14.

Cohen, H. L., & Filipczak, J. *A new learning environment.* San Francisco: Jossey-Bass, 1971.

Cohen, S. Therapeutic aspects. In *Marijuana research findings: 1980.* Washington, D.C.: U.S. Government Printing Office, 1980.

Cohen, S., Glass, D., & Singer, J. E. Apartment noise, auditory discrimination, and reading ability in children. *Journal of Experimental Social Psychology*, 1973, **9**, 407–422.

Cole, J. O. Phenothiazine treatment in acute schizophrenia: Effectiveness. *Archives of General Psychiatry*, 1964, **10**, 246–261.

Collaborative study of children treated for phenylketonuria, preliminary report 8. Principal investigator: R. Koch. Presented at the Eleventh General Medicine Conference, Stateline, Nevada, February 1975.

Conger, J. J. The effects of alcohol on conflict behavior in the albino rat. *Quarterly Journal of Studies on Alcohol*, 1951, **12**, 1–29.

Conger, J. J., Sawrey, W. L., & Turrell, E. S. The role of social experience in the production of gastric ulcers in hooded rats in a conflict situation. *Journal of Abnormal and Social Psychology*, 1958, **57**, 214–220.

Conn, J. H., & Conn, R. N. Discussion of T. Barber's "Hypnosis as a causal variable in present-day psychology: A critical analysis." *Journal of Clinical and Experimental Hypnosis,* 1967, **15,** 106–110.

Conners, C. K. A teacher rating scale for use in drug studies with children. *American Journal of Psychiatry,* 1969, **126,** 884–888.

Conners, C. K., Taylor, E., Meo, G., Kurtz, M., & Fournier, M. Magnesium pemoline and dextroamphetamine: A controlled study in children with minimal brain dysfunction. *Psychopharmacologia,* 1972, **26,** 321–336.

Cooper, A. F., Kay, D. W. K., Curry, A. R., Garside, R. F., & Roth, M. Hearing loss in paranoid and affective psychoses of the elderly. *Lancet,* 1974, **2,** 851–854.

Cooper, J. E., Kendell, R. E., Gurland, B. J., Sharpe, L., Copeland, J. R M., & Simon, R. *Psychiatric diagnosis in New York and London.* London: Oxford University Press, 1972.

Coppen, A., Prange, A. J., Whybrow, P. C., & Noguera, R. Abnormalities in indoleamines in affective disorders. *Archives of General Psychiatry,* 1972, **26,** 474–478.

Corey, G. *Theory and practice of counseling and psychotherapy.* Belmont, Calif.: Wadsworth, 1977.

Covi, L., Lipman, R. S., Derogatis, L. R., Smith, J. E., & Pattison, J. H. Drugs and group psychotherapy in neurotic depression. *American Journal of Psychiatry,* 1974, **131,** 191–197.

Cowan, P. A., Hoddinott, B. A., & Wright, B. A. Compliance and resistance in the conditioning of autistic children: An exploratory study. *Child Development,* 1965, **36,** 913–923.

Cowen, E. L. Psychologists in primary prevention: Blowing the cover story. An editorial. *American Journal of Community Psychology,* 1977, **5,** 481–490.

Cox, A., Rutter, M., Newman, S., & Bartak, L. A comparative study of infantile autism and specific developmental language disorders: II. Parental characteristics. *British Journal of Psychiatry,* 1975, **126,** 146–159.

Craig, M. M., & Glick, S. J. Ten years' experience with the Glueck social prediction table. *Crime and Delinquency,* 1963, **9,** 249–261.

Craik, F. I. M. Age differences in human memory. In J. E. Birren & K. W. Schaie (Eds.), *Handbook of the psychology of aging.* New York: Van Nostrand Reinhold, 1977.

Crisp, A. H. The possible significance of some behavioural correlates of weight and carbohydrate intake. *Journal of Psychosomatic Research,* 1967, **11,** 117–131.

Crisp, A. H., Palmer, R. L., & Klucy, R. S. How common is anorexia nervosa? A prevalence study. *British Journal of Psychiatry,* 1976, **128,** 529–554.

Crissey, M. S. Mental retardation: Past, present, and future. *American Psychologist,* 1975, **30,** 800–808.

Crowe, R. R. An adoption study of antisocial personality. *Archives of General Psychiatry,* 1974, **31,** 785–791.

Crowne, D. P., & Marlowe, D. *The approval motive: Studies in evaluative dependence.* New York: Wiley, 1964.

Cruickshank, W. M. Myths and realities in learning disabilities. *Journal of Learning Disabilities,* 1977, **10,** 51–63.

Cunningham, C. E., & Barkley, R. A. The interactions of normal and hyperactive children with their mothers in free play and structured tasks. *Child Development,* 1979, **50,** 217–224.

Daneman, E. A. Imipramine in office management of depressive reactions (a double-blind study). *Diseases of the Nervous System,* 1961, **22,** 213–217.

Davis, J. M. Dopamine theory of schizophrenia: A two-factor theory. In L. C. Wynne, R. L. Cromwell, & S. Matthysse (Eds.), *The nature of schizophrenia.* New York: Wiley, 1978.

Davis, J. M. Overview: Maintenance therapy in psychiatry: II. Affective disorders. *American Journal of Psychiatry,* 1976, **133,** 1–13.

Davis, J. M., Klerman, G., & Schildkraut, J. Drugs used in the treatment of depression. In L. Efron, J. O. Cole, D. Levine, & J. R. Wittenborn, *Psychopharmacology, A review of progress.* Washington, D.C.: U.S. Clearinghouse of Mental Health Information, 1967.

Davison, A. N., & Dobbing, J. Myelination as a vulnerable period in brain development. *British Medical Bulletin,* 1966, **22,** 40–44.

Davison, G. C. A social learning therapy programme with an autistic child. *Behaviour Research and Therapy,* 1964, **2,** 146–159.

Davison, G. C. Differential relaxation and cognitive restructuring in therapy with a "paranoid schizophrenic" or "paranoid state." *Proceedings of the 74th Annual Convention of the American Psychological Association.* Washington, D.C.: American Psychological Association, 1966.

Davison, G. C. Elimination of a sadistic fantasy by a client-controlled counterconditioning technique. *Journal of Abnormal Psychology,* 1968, **73,** 84–90. (a)

Davison, G. C. Systematic desensitization as a counterconditioning process. *Journal of Abnormal Psychology,* 1968, **73,** 91–99. (b)

Davison, G. C. Counter control in behavior modification. In L. A. Hamerlynck, L. C. Handy, & E. J. Mash (Eds.), *Behavior change: Methodology, concepts and practice.* Champaign, Ill.: Research Press, 1973.

Davison, G. C. Homosexuality: The ethical challenge. Presidential address to the Eighth Annual Convention of the Association for Advancement of Behavior Therapy, Chicago, 1974.

Davison, G. C. Homosexuality: The ethical challenge. *Journal of Consulting and Clinical Psychology*, 1976, **44,** 157–162.

Davison, G. C. Not can but ought: The treatment of homosexuality. *Journal of Consulting and Clinical Psychology,* 1978, **46,** 170–172.

Davison, G. C. And now for something completely different: Cognition and little r. In M. J. Mahoney (Ed.), *Psychotherapy process: Current issues and future directions.* New York: Plenum Press, 1980.

Davison, G. C., & Goldfried, M. R. Postdoctoral training in clinical behavior therapy. Menninger Clinic Bulletin 17, 1973.

Davison, G. C. & Stuart, R. B. Behavior therapy and civil liberties. *American Psychologist,* 1975, **30,** 755–763.

Davison, G. C., Tsujimoto, R. N., & Glaros, A. G. Attribution and the maintenance of behavior change in falling asleep. *Journal of Abnormal Psychology,* 1973, **82,** 124–133.

Davison, G. C., & Valins, S. Maintenance of self-attributed and drug-attributed behavior change. *Journal of Personality and Social Psychology,* 1969, **11,** 25–33.

Davison, G. C., & Wilson, G. T. Attitudes of behavior therapists toward homosexuality. *Behavior Therapy,* 1973, **4,** 686–696.

DeJong,, R. N., & Sugar, O. *The yearbook of neurology and neurosurgery.* Chicago: Year Book Medical Publishers, 1971.

DeJonge, G. A. Epidemiology of enuresis: A survey of literature. In I. Kolvin, R. C. MacKeith, & S. R. Meadow (Ed.), *Enuresis and encopresis.* Philadelphia: Lippincott, 1973.

Dekker, E., & Groen, J. Reproducible psychogenic attacks of asthma. *Journal of Psychosomatic Research,* 1956, **1,** 58–67.

Dekker, E., Pelser, H. E., & Groen, J. Conditioning as a cause of asthmatic attacks. *Journal of Psychosomatic Research,* 1957, **2,** 97–108.

DeMyer, M. The nature of the neuropsychological disability of autistic children. *Journal of Autism and Childhood Schizophrenia,* 1975, **5,** 109–127.

DeMyer, M., Barton, S., DeMyer, W. E., Norton, J. A., Allen, J., & Sterle, R. Prognosis in autism: A follow-up study. *Journal of Autism and Childhood Schizophrenia,* 1973, **3,** 199–246.

DeMyer, M., Pontius, W., Norton, J.A., Barton, S., Allen, J., & Steele, R. Parental practices and innate activity in autistic and brain-damaged infants. *Journal of Autism and Childhood Schizophrenia,* 1972, **2,** 49–66.

Denhoff, E. The natural history of children with minimal brain dysfunction. *Annals of the New York Academy of Sciences,* 1973, **205,** 188–205.

Depue, R. A., & Monroe, S. M. Learned helplessness in the perspective of the depressive disorders: Conceptual and definitional issues. *Journal of Abnormal Psychology,* 1978, **87,** 3–20.

Deutsch, A. *The mentally ill in America.* New York: Columbia University Press, 1949.

DeVries, H. A. Physiology of exercise and aging, In D. S. Woodruff & J. E. Birren (Eds.), *Aging: Scientific perspectives and social issues.* New York: Van Nostrand Reinhold, 1975.

Diament, C., & Wilson, G. T. An experimental investigation of the effects of covert sensitization in an analogue eating situation. *Behavior Therapy,* 1975, **6,** 499–509.

Diamond, B. The psychiatric prediction of dangerousness. *University of Pennsylvania Law Review,* 1974, **123,** 439–452.

Diamond, S., Baldwin, R., & Diamond, R. *Inhibition and choice.* New York: Harper and Row, 1963.

Didion, J. *The white album.* New York: Simon and Schuster, 1979.

DiMascio, A., Weissman, M. M., Prusoff, B. A., Neu, C., & Zwilling, M. Differential symptom reduction by drugs and psychotherapy in acute depression. *Archives of General Psychiatry,* 1979, **36,** 1450–1456.

Dodson, B. *Liberating masturbation.* New York: Bodysex Designs, 1974.

Dole, V., & Nyswander, M. Methadone maintenance: A report of two years' experience. In *Problems of drug dependence.* Washington, D.C.: National Academy of Science, National Research Council, 1966.

Doleys, D. M. Behavioral treatments for nocturnal enuresis in children: A review of the recent literature. *Psychological Bulletin,* 1977, **8,** 30–54.

Doll, E. A. *Measurement of social competence: A manual for the Vineland Social Maturity Scale.* Circle Pines, Minn.: American Guidance Service, Inc., 1953.

Dollard, J., & Miller, N. E. *Personality and psychotherapy.* New York: McGraw-Hill, 1950.

Domino, E. F., Krause, R. R., & Bowers, J. Various enzymes involved with putative transmitters. *Archives of General Psychiatry,* 1973, **29,** 195–201.

Doppelt, J., & Wallace, W. Standardization of the Wechsler Adult Intelligence Scale for older persons. *Journal of Abnormal and Social Psychology,* 1955, **51,** 312–330.

Doubros, S. G. Behavior therapy with high level, institutionalized, retarded adolescents. *Exceptional Children,* 1966, **33,** 229–233.

Douglas, J. D. *The social meanings of suicide.* Princeton, N.J.: Princeton University Press, 1967.

Drabman, R. S., Spitalnik, R., & O'Leary, K. D. Teaching self-control to disruptive children. *Journal of Abnormal Psychology,* 1973, **82,** 10–16.

Dunham, H. W. *Community and schizophrenia: An epidemiological analysis.* Detroit: Wayne State University Press, 1965.

Durkheim, E. *Suicide,* 1897. (2nd ed., 1930, in French.) English translation by J. A. Spaulding & G. Simpson. New York: The Free Press, 1951.

Dworkin, B. R., Filewich, R. J., Miller, N. E., & Craigmyle, N. Baroreceptor activation reduces reactivity to noxious stimulation: Implications for hypertension. *Science,* 1979, **205,** 1299–1301.

Eastman, C. Behavioral formulations of depression. *Psychological Review,* 1976, **83,** 277–291.

Edwards, A. L. *The social desirability variable in personality, research.* New York: Dryden Press, 1957.

Edwards, G., Hensman, C., Hawker, A., & Williamson, V. Alcoholics Anonymous: The anatomy of a self-help group. *Social Psychiatry,* 1967, **1,** 195–204.

Egan, G. *The skilled helper.* Monterey, Calif.: Brooks/Cole, 1975.

Ehrhardt, A., & Money, J. Progestin-induced hermaphroditism: IQ and psychosexual identity in a study of ten girls. *Journal of Sex Research,* 1967, **3,** 83–100.

Eisdorfer, C., & Cohen, D. The cognitively impaired elderly: Differential diagnosis. In M. Storandt, I. C. Siegler, & M. F. Elias (Eds.), *The clinical psychology of aging.* New York: Plenum Press, 1978.

Eisenberg, L., & Kanner, L. Early infantile autism. *American Journal of Orthopsychiatry,* 1956, **26,** 556–566.

Ellenberger. H. F. The story of ''Anna O'': A critical review with new data. *Journal of the History of the Behavior Sciences,* 1972, **8,** 267–279.

Ellingson, R. J. Incidence of EEG abnormality among patients with mental disorders of apparently nonorganic origin: A criminal review. *American Journal of Psychiatry,* 1954, **111,** 263–275.

Ellis, A. *The folklore of sex.* New York: Grove Press, 1961.

Ellis, A. *Reason and emotion in psychotherapy.* New York: Lyle Stuart, 1962.

Ellis, A. Rational-emotive treatment of impotence, frigidity, and other sexual problems. *Professional Psychology,* 1971, **2,** 346–349.

Ellis, A. The basic clinical theory of rational-emotive therapy. In A. Ellis & R. Grieger (Eds.), *Handbook of rational-emotive therapy.* New York: Springer, 1977.

Ellis, H. *Studies in the psychology of sex.* New York: Random House, 1906.

Elmore, A. M. A comparison of the psychophysiological and clinical response to biofeedback for temporal pulse amplitude reduction and biofeedback for increases in hand temperature in the treatment of migraine. Unpublished doctoral dissertation, State University of New York at Stony Brook, 1979.

Elmore, A. M., & Tursky, B. The biofeedback hypothesis: An idea in search of a theory and method. In A. A. Sugerman & R. E. Tarter (Eds.), *Expanding dimensions of consciousness.* New York: Springer, 1978.

Elmore, J. L., & Sugarman, A. A. Precipitation of psychosis during electroshock therapy. *Diseases of the Nervous System,* 1975, **3,** 115–117.

Emery, R. E., & O'Leary, K. D. Children's perceptions of marital discord and behavior problems of boys and girls. Paper presented at the annual meeting of the Association for Advancement of Behavior Therapy, San Francisco, 1979.

Endicott, J., & Spitzer, R. L. A diagnostic interview: The Schedule for Affective Disorders and Schizophrenia. *Archives of General Psychiatry,* 1978, **35,** 837–844.

Endler, N. S., Hunt, J. McV., & Rosenstein, A. J. An S-R inventory of anxiousness. *Psychological Monographs,* 1962, **76,** No. 536.

Engel, B. T., & Bickford, A. F. Response specificity: Stimulus response and individual response specificity in essential hypertension. *Archives of General Psychiatry,* 1961, **5,** 478–489.

Engel, B. T., & Bleecker, E. R. Application of operant conditioning techniques in the control of cardiac arrhythmias. In P. A. Obrist, A. H. Black, J. Brener, & I. V. DiCara (Eds.), *Cardiovascular psychophysiology.* Chicago: Aldine, 1974.

Englemann, S. *Conceptual learning.* San Rafael, Calif.: Dimensions Publishing Company, 1969.

English, H. B. Three cases of the ''conditioned fear response.'' *Journal of Abnormal and Social Psychology,* 1929, **34,** 221–225.

Ennis, B., & Emery, R. *The rights of mental patients—An American Civil Liberties Union Handbook.* New York: Avon, 1978.

Ennis, B., & Siegel, L. *The rights of mental patients.* American Civil Liberties Union Handbook Series. New York: Avon, 1973.

Enright, J. B. An introduction to Gestalt techniques. In J. Fagan & I. L. Shepherd (Eds.), *Gestalt therapy now: Theory, techniques, applications.* Palo Alto, Calif.: Science and Behavior Books, 1970.

Epstein, L. C., & Lasagna, L. Obtaining informed consent. *Archives of Internal Medicine,* 1969, **123,** 682–688.

Epstein, S. The stability of behavior: On predicting most of the people much of the time. *Journal of Personality and Social Psychology,* 1979, **37,** 1097–1126.

Erikson, E. H. *Childhood and society.* New York: Norton, 1950.

Erlenmeyer-Kimling, L. A prospective study of children at risk for schizophrenia: Methodological considerations and some preliminary findings. In R. D. Wirt, G. Winokur, & M. Roff (Eds.), *Life history research in psychopathology,* Vol. 4. Minneapolis: University of Minnesota Press, 1975.

Erwin, W. J. A 16-year follow-up of a case of severe anorexia nervosa. *Journal of Behavior Therapy and Experimental Psychiatry,* 1977, **8,** 157–160.

Evans, I. M. Classical conditioning. In M. P. Feldman & A. Broadhurst (Eds.), *Theoretical and experimental bases of the behaviour therapies.* New York: Wiley, 1976.

Evans, R. B. Childhood parental relationships of homosexual men. *Journal of Consulting and Clinical Psychology,* 1969, **33,** 129–135.

Evans, R. I., & Henderson, A. Smoking in children and adolescents: Psychosocial determinants and prevention strategies. In N. A. Krasnegor (Ed.), *The behavioral aspects of smoking.* Washington, D.C.: National Institute on Drug Abuse, 1979.

Exner, J. E. *The Rorschach: A comprehensive system.* Vol. 2, *Current research and advanced interpretation.* New York: Wiley, 1978.

Eysenck. H. J. The effects of psychotherapy: An evaluation. *Journal of Consulting Psychology,* 1952, **16,** 319–324.

Eysenck, H. J. *Dynamics of anxiety and hysteria.* London: Routledge and Kegan Paul, 1957.

Eysenck, H. J. Classification and the problem of diagnosis. In H. J. Eysenck (Ed.), *Handbook of abnormal psychology.* London: Pitman, 1960.

Eysenck, H. J. *Fact and fiction in psychology.* Baltimore: Penguin, 1965.

Eysenck, H. J. "Crime as destiny." *New Behaviour,* 1975, **9,** 46–49.

Fagan, J., & Shepherd, I. L. (Eds.) *Gestalt therapy now: Theory, techniques, applications.* Palo Alto, Calif.: Science and Behavior Books, 1970.

Falloon, I. R. H., Boyd, J. L., & McGill, C. W. Behavioral family therapy for relapsing schizophrenics. In J. P. Curran & P. M. Monti (Eds.), *Social skills training: A practical handbook for assessment and treatment.* New York: Guilford Press, 1980.

Farina, A. *Abnormal psychology.* Englewood Cliffs, N.J.: Prentice-Hall, 1976.

Farkas, G., & Rosen, R. C. The effects of alcohol on elicited male sexual response. *Studies in Alcohol,* 1976, **37,** 265–272.

Farrell, W. *The liberated man.* New York: Random House, 1975.

Farris, E. J., Yeakel. E. H., & Medoff, H. Development of hypertension in emotional gray Norway rats after air blasting. *American Journal of Physiology,* 1945, **144,** 331–333.

Federal Bureau of Investigation. *Crime in the United States: Uniform crime reports, 1975.* Washington, D.C.: U.S. Government Printing Office, 1976.

Feinberg, I., & Carlson, V. R. Sleep variations as a function of age in man. *Archives of General Psychiatry,* 1968, **18,** 239–50.

Feingold, B. F. *Introduction to clinical allergy.* Springfield, Ill.: Charles C Thomas, 1973.

Feinsilver, D. B., & Gunderson, J. G. Psychotherapy for schizophrenics—Is it indicated? *Schizophrenia Bulletin,* 1972, **1,** 11–23.

Fenichel. O. *The psychoanalytic theory of neurosis.* New York: Norton, 1945.

Fernando, C. K., & Basmajian, J. V. Biofeedback in physical medicine and rehabilitation. *Biofeedback and Self-regulation,* 1978, **3,** 435–455.

Ferster, C. B. Positive reinforcement and behavioral deficits of autistic children. *Child Development,* 1961, **32,** 437–456.

Ferster, C. B. Classification of behavioral pathology. In L. Krasner & L. P. Ullmann (Eds.), *Research in behavior modification.* New York: Holt, Rinehart and Winston, 1965.

Figley, C. R. Psychosocial adjustment among Vietnam veterans: An overview of the research. In C. R. Figley (Ed.), *Stress disorders among Vietnam veterans.* New York: Brunner/Mazel, 1978.

Fillmore, K. M., & Caetano, R. *Epidemiology of occupational alcoholism.* Paper presented at the National Institute on Alcohol Abuse and Alcoholism's Workshop on Alcoholism in the Workplace, Reston, Va., May 22, 1980.

Fischer, M. Psychoses in the offspring of schizophrenic monozygotic twins and their normal co-twins. *British Journal of Psychiatry,* 1971, **118,** 43–52.

Fletcher, C., & Doll, R. A survey of doctors' attitudes to smoking. *British Journal of Prevention and Social Medicine,* 1969, **23,** 145–153.

Flowers, J. V. Behavioral analysis of group therapy and a model for behavioral group therapy. In S. M. Ross & D. Upper (Eds.), *Behavioral group therapy: An annual review,* Vol. 1. Champaign, Ill.: Research Press, 1979.

Flowers, J. V., Booraem, C. D., & Hartman, K. A. Client improvement on higher and lower intensity problems as a function of group cohesiveness. Paper presented at Western Psychological Association, Seattle, Wash., 1977.

Folstein, S., & Rutter, M. A twin study of individuals with infantile autism. In M. Rutter & E. Schopler (Eds.), *Autism: A reappraisal of concepts and treatment.* New York, Plenum Press, 1978.

Fontana, A. Familial etiology of schizophrenia: Is a scientific methodology possible? *Psychological Bulletin,* 1966, **66,** 214–228.

Ford, C. S., & Beach, F. A. *Patterns of sexual behavior.* New York: Harper, 1951.

Ford, D. H., & Urban, H. B. *Systems of psychotherapy: A comparative study.* New York: Wiley, 1963.

Fordney-Settlage, D. S. Heterosexual dysfunction: Evaluation of treatment procedures. *Archives of Sexual Behavior,* 1975, **4,** 367–388.

Foucault, M. *Madness and civilization.* New York: Mentor Books, 1965.

Foxx, R. M., & Azrin, N. H. *Toilet training the retarded: A rapid program for day and night time independent toileting.* Champaign, Ill.: Research Press, 1973.

Fozard, J. L., Wolf, E., Bell, B., McFarland, R. A., & Podolsky, S. Visual perception and communication. In J. E. Birren & K. W. Schaie (Eds.), *Handbook of the psychology of aging.* New York: Van Nostrand Reinhold, 1977.

Framo, J. L. Personal reflections of a therapist. *Journal of Marriage and Family Counseling,* 1975, **1,** 15–28.

Frank, J. D. *Persuasion and healing.* (2nd ed.) Baltimore: Johns Hopkins University Press, 1973.

Frankl, V. *From death camp to existentialism.* Boston: Beacon Press, 1959.

Frankl, V. *Man's search for meaning.* New York: Washington Square Press, 1963.

Freed, E. X. Anxiety and conflict: Role of drug-dependent learning in the rat. *Quarterly Journal of Studies on Alcohol,* 1971, **32,** 13–29.

Freud, A. *The ego and mechanisms of defense.* New York: International Universities Press, 1946.

Freud, A. *The psychoanalytic treatment of children: Lectures and essays.* London: Imago, 1946.

Freud, S. Three contributions to the theory of sex, 1905. In A. A. Brill (Ed.), *The basic writings of Sigmund Freud.* New York: Modern Library, 1938.

Freud, S. Analysis of a phobia in a five-year-old boy, 1909. In *Collected works of Sigmund Freud.* Vol. 10. London: Hogarth Press, 1955.

Freud. S. A case of paranoia running counter to the psychoanalytical theory of the disease, 1915. In *Collected papers,* Vol. 2. London: Hogarth Press, 1956.

Freud, S. Mourning and melancholia, 1917. In *Collected papers,* Vol. 4. London: Hogarth Press and the Institute of Psychoanalysis, 1950.

Freud, S. Lines of advance in psychoanalytic therapy, 1918. In *The complete psychological works of Sigmund Freud.* Translated by J. Strachey. London: The Hogarth Press, and the Institute of Psychoanalysis, 1955.

Freud, S. *The problem of anxiety,* 1926. New York: Norton, 1936.

Freud, S. Analysis terminable and interminable. *International Journal of Psychoanalysis,* 1937, **18,** 373–391.

Freund, K. A laboratory method for diagnosing predominance of homo- and hetero-erotic interest in the male. *Behaviour Research and Therapy,* 1963, **1,** 85–93.

Friar, L. R., & Beatty, J. Migraine: Management by trained control of vasoconstriction. *Journal of Consulting and Clinical Psychology,* 1976, **44,** 46–53.

Friedberg, C. K. *Diseases of the heart.* (3rd ed.) Philadelphia: Saunders, 1966.

Friedhoff, A. J., & Van Winkle, E. Isolation and characterization of a compound from the urine of schizophrenics. *Nature,* 1962, **194,** 897–898.

Friedman, E., Shopsin, B., Sathananthan, G., & Gershon, S. Blood platelet monoamine oxidase activity in psychiatric patients. *American Journal of Psychiatry,* 1974, **131,** 1392–1394.

Friedman, J. M. Sexual adjustment of the postcoronary male. In J. LoPiccolo & L. LoPiccolo (Eds.), *Handbook of sex therapy.* New York: Plenum Press, 1978.

Friedman, M. *Pathogenesis of coronary artery disease.* New York: McGraw-Hill, 1969.

Friedman, M., & Rosenman, R. H. Association of specific overt behavior pattern with blood and cardiovascular findings. *Journal of the American Medical Association,* 1959, **169,** 1286–1296.

Friedman, R., & Dahl, L. K. The effect of chronic conflict on the blood pressure of rats with a genetic susceptibility to experimental hypertension. *Psychosomatic Medicine,* 1975, **37,** 402–416.

Frohman, C. E., Harmison, C. R., Arthur, R. E., & Gottlieb, J. S. Conformation of a unique plasma protein in schizophrenia. *Biological Psychiatry,* 1971, **3,** 113–121.

Fromm-Reichmann, F. Notes on the development of treatment of schizophrenics by psychoanalytic psychotherapy. *Psychiatry,* 1948, **11,** 263–273.

Fromm-Reichmann, F. Some aspects of psychoanalytic therapy with schizophrenics. In E. Brady & F. C. Bedlich (Eds.), *Psychotherapy with schizophrenics.* New York: International Universities Press, 1952.

Gagnon, J. H. *Human sexualities.* Chicago: Scott, Foresman, 1977.

Gagnon, J. H., & Davison, G. C. Enhancement of sexual responsiveness in behavior therapy. Paper presented at the 82nd Annual Convention of the American Psychological Association, New Orleans, 1974.

Gagnon, J. H., & Davison, G. C. Asylums, the token economy, and the metrics of mental life. *Behavior Therapy,* 1976, **7,** 528–534.

Gagnon, J. H., & Simon, W. *Sexual conduct: The social origins of human sexuality.* Chicago: Aldine, 1973.

Gaines, J. The founder of Gestalt therapy: A sketch of Fritz Perls. *Psychology Today,* November 1974, **8,** 117–118.

Galin, D., Diamond, R., & Braff, D. Lateralization of conversion symptoms: More frequent on the left. *American Journal of Psychiatry,* 1977, **134,** 578–580.

Garcia, J., McGowan, B. K., & Green, K. F. Biological constraints on conditioning. In A. H. Black & W. F. Prokasy (Eds.), *Classical conditioning. II: Current research and theory.* New York: Appleton-Century-Crofts, 1972.

Garfield, S., & Kurtz, R. A survey of clinical psychologists: Characteristics, activities, and orientations. *The Clinical Psychologist,* 1974, **28,** 7–10.

Garfinkel, P. E., Moldofsky, H., & Garner, D. M. The heterogeneity of anorexia nervosa. *Archives of General Psychiatry,* 1980, **37,** 1036–1040.

Garmezy, N. Vulnerability research and the issue of primary prevention. *American Journal of Orthopsychiatry,* 1971, **41,** 101–116.

Gatz, M., Smyer, M. A., & Lawton, M. P. The mental health system and the older adult. In L. W. Poon (Ed.), *Aging in the 1980s.* Washington, D.C.: American Psychological Association, 1981.

Gebhard, P. H., Gagnon, J. H., Pomeroy, W. B., & Christenson, C. V. *Sex offenders.* New York: Harper and Row, 1965.

Geer, J. H., Davison, G. C., & Gatchel, R. I. Reduction of stress in humans through nonveridical perceived control of aversive stimulation. *Journal of Personality and Social Psychology,* 1970, **16,** 731–738.

Geer, J. H., Morokoff, P., & Greenwood, P. Sexual arousal in women: The development of a measuring device for vaginal blood volume. *Archives of Sexual Behavior,* 1974, **3,** 559–566.

Geis, G. Forcible rape: An introduction. In D. Chappell, R. Geis, & G. Geis (Eds.), *Forcible rape: The crime, the victim, and the offender.* New York: Columbia University Press, 1977.

Geis, G., & Monahan, J. The social ecology of violence. In T. Lickona (Ed.), *Moral development and behavior.* New York: Holt, Rinehart and Winston, 1976.

General Register Office, *A glossary of mental disorders.* Studies on Medical and Population Subjects 22, London: General Register Office, 1968.

George, L. K., & Weiler, S. J. Aging and sexual behavior: The myth of declining sexuality. *American Journal of Psychiatry,* in press.

Gerbino, L., Oleshansky, M., & Gershon, S. Clinical use and mode of action of lithium. In M. A. Lipton, A. DiMascio, & F. K. Killam (Eds.), *Psychopharmacology: A generation of progress.* New York: Raven Press, 1978.

Gibbons, D. C. *Delinquent behavior.* Englewood Cliffs, N. J.: Prentice-Hall, 1975.

Gibbs, J. (Ed.) *Suicide.* New York: Harper and Row, 1968.

Gilboy, J. A., & Schmidt, J. R. "Voluntary" hospitalization of the mentally ill. *Northwestern University Law Review,* 1971, **66,** 429–439.

Ginsburg, H. P., & Opper, S. *Piaget's theory of intellectual development: An introduction.* Englewood Cliffs, N.J.: Prentice-Hall, 1969.

Gittelman-Klein, R., & Klein, D. F. Methylphenidate effects in learning disabilities. *Archives of General Psychiatry,* 1976, **33,** 655–664.

Gittelman-Klein, R., Klein, D. F., Abikoff, H., Katz, S., Gloisten, A. C., & Kates, W. Relative efficacy of methylphenidate and behavior modification in hyperkinetic children: An interim report. *Journal of Abnormal Child Psychology,* 1976, **4,** 361–379.

Gittelman-Klein, R., Klein, D. F., Katz, S., Saraf, K., & Pollack, E. Comparative effects of methylphenidate and thioridazine in hyperkinetic children. *Archives of General Psychiatry,* 1976, **33,** 1217–1231.

Glaros, A. G. Expectation effects of subjects undergoing EEG alpha and beta wave feedback training. Unpublished doctoral dissertation, State University of New York at Stony Brook, 1975.

Glass, D. C. *Behavior patterns, stress, and coronary disease.* Hillsdale, N.J.: Lawrence Erlbaum Associates, 1977.

Glass, D. C., & Singer, J. E. *Urban stress: Experiments on noise and social stressors.* New York: Academic Press, 1972.

Glasscote, R., Gudeman, J. E., & Miles, C. D. *Creative mental health services for the elderly.* Washington, D.C.: American Psychiatric Association, 1977.

Glover, E. *On the early development of mind.* New York: International Universities Press, 1956.

Glueck, S., & Glueck, E. *Predicting delinquency and crime.* Cambridge, Mass.: Harvard University Press, 1959.

Goetzl, U., Green, R., Whybrow, P., & Jackson, R. X-linkage revisited. *Archives of General Psychiatry,* 1974, **31,** 665–671.

Goffman, E. *Asylums: Essays on the social situation of mental patients and other inmates.* Chicago: Aldine, 1961.

Goldberg, E. M., & Morrison, S. L. Schizophrenia and social class. *British Journal of Psychiatry,* 1963, **109,** 785–802.

Golden, G. S. Tourette Syndrome: The pediatric perspective. *American Journal of Diseases of Children,* 1977, **131,** 531–534.

Goldenberg. I. I. *Prospectus and guidelines for residential youth centers.* Washington, D.C.: U.S. Department of Labor, Office of Special Manpower Programs, 1969.

Goldfried, M. R., & Davison, G. C. *Clinical behavior therapy.* New York: Holt, Rinehart and Winston, 1976.

Goldfried, M. R., Decenteceo, E. T., & Weinberg, L. Systematic rational restructuring as a self-control technique. *Behavior Therapy,* 1974, **5,** 247–254.

Goldfried, M. R., & Merbaum, M. (Eds.) *Behavior change through self-control.* New York: Holt, Rinehart and Winston, 1973.

Goldfried, M. R., & Sprafkin, J. N. *Behavior personality assessment.* Morristown, N.J.: General Learning Press, 1974.

Goldfried, M. R., Stricker, G., & Weiner, I. B. *Rorschach handbook of clinical and research applications.* Englewood Cliffs, N.J.: Prentice-Hall, 1971.

Goldfried, M. R., & Trier, C. S. Effectiveness of relaxation as an active coping skill. *Journal of Abnormal Psychology,* 1974, **83,** 348–355.

Goldstein, A. Opioid peptides (endorphins) in pituitary and brain. *Science,* 1976, **193,** 1081–1086.

Goldstein, L., Sugarman, A. A., Stolberg, H., Murphee, H. B., & Pfeiffer, C. C. Electrocerebral activity in schizophrenics and non-psychotic subjects. *Electroencephalography and Clinical Neurophysiology,* 1965, **19,** 350–361.

Goldstein, S. E., & Birnbom, F. Hypochondriasis and the elderly. *Journal of the American Geriatrics Society,* 1976, **24,** 150–154.

Goodman, G. An experiment with companionship therapy: College students and troubled boys—Assumptions, selection, and design. In B. G. Guerney (Ed.), *Psychotherapeutic agents: New rules for nonprofessionals, parents, and teachers.* New York: Holt, Rinehart and Winston, 1969.

Goodwin, D. W. Alcoholism and heredity: A review and hypothesis. *Archives of General Psychiatry,* 1979, **36,** 57–61.

Goodwin, D. W., Crane, J. B., & Guze, S. B. Alcoholic "blackouts": A review and clinical study of 100 alcoholics. *American Journal of Psychiatry,* 1969, **126,** 191–198.

Goodwin, D. W., Powell, B., Bremer, D., Hoine, H., & Stern, J. Alcohol and recall: State dependent effects in man. *Science,* 1969, **163,** 1358–1360.

Goodwin, D. W., Schulsinger, F., Hermansen, L., Guze, S. B., & Winokur, G. A. Alcohol problems in adoptees raised apart from alcoholic biological parents. *Archives of General Psychiatry,* 1973, **128,** 239–243.

Goodwin, D. W., Schulsinger, F., Knop, J., Mednick, S. A., & Guze, S. B. Psychopathology in adopted and nonadopted daughters of alcoholics. *Archives of General Psychiatry,* 1977, **34,** 1005–1009.

Gottesman, I. Differential inheritance of the psychoneuroses. *Eugenics Quarterly,* 1962, **9,** 223–227.

Gottesman, I., & Shields, J. *Schizophrenia and genetics: A twin study vantage point.* New York: Academic Press, 1972.

Gottlieb, J., Cohen, L. & Goldstein, L. Social contact and personal adjustment as variables relating to attitudes toward EMR children. *Training School Bulletin,* 1974, **71,** 9–16.

Gottman, J., Notarius, C., Gonso, J., & Markman, H. *A couple's guide to communication.* Champaign, Ill.: Research Press, 1976.

Gottman, J., Notarius, C., Markman, H., Bank, S., Yoppi, B., & Rubin, M. E. Behavior exchange theory and marital decision making. *Journal of Personality and Social Psychology,* 1976, **34,** 14–23.

Gove, W. R. Societal reaction as an explanation of mental illness: An evaluation. *American Sociological Review,* 1970, **35,** 873–884.

Gove, W. R., & Fain, T. The stigma of mental hospitalization. *Archives of General Psychiatry,* 1973, **28,** 494–500.

Gove, W. R., & Tudor, J. Adult sex roles and mental illness. *American Journal of Sociology,* 1973, **78,** 812–835.

Goyette, C. H., & Conners, C. K. Food additives and hyperkinesis. Paper presented at the 85th Annual Convention of the American Psychological Association, 1977.

Grace, W. J., & Graham, D. T. Relationship of specific attitudes and emotions to certain bodily diseases. *Psychosomatic Medicine,* 1952, **14,** 243–251.

Graham, D. T. Health, disease and the mind-body problem: Linguistic parallelism. *Psychosomatic Medicine,* 1967, **29,** 52–71.

Graham, D. T., Kabler, J. D., & Graham, F. K. Physiological responses to the suggestion of attitudes: Specificity of attitude hypothesis in psychosomatic disease. *Psychosomatic Medicine,* 1962, **24,** 159–169.

Graham, D. T., Stern, J. A., & Winokur, G. Experimental investigation of the specificity of attitude hypothesis in psychosomatic disease. *Psychosomatic Medicine,* 1958, **20,** 446–457.

Graham, J. R., & Wolff, H. G. Mechanisms of migraine headache and action of ergotamine tartrate. *Archives of Neurology and Psychiatry,* 1938, **18,** 23–45.

Graham, P. J., Rutter, M. L., Yule, W., & Pless, I. B. Childhood asthma: A psychosomatic disorder? Some epidemiological considerations. *British Journal of Preventive Medicine,* 1967, **21,** 78–85.

Gray, J. *The psychology of fear and stress.* New York: McGraw-Hill, 1971.

Green, R. *Sexual identity conflict in children and adults.* New York: Basic Books, 1974.

Green, R. One hundred ten feminine and masculine boys: Behavioral contrasts and demographic similarities. *Archives of Sexual Behavior,* 1976, **5,** 425–446.

Green, R., & Money, J. *Transsexualism and sex reassignment.* Baltimore: Johns Hopkins University Press, 1969.

Greenblatt, D. J., & Shader, R. I. Pharmacotherapy of anxiety with benzodiazepines and β-adrenergic blockers. In M. A. Lipton, A. DiMascio, & K. F. Killiam (Eds.), *Psychopharmacology: A generation of progress.* New York: Raven Press, 1978.

Greenspan, K., Schildkraut, J. J., Gordon, E. K., Baer, L., Aronoff, M., & Durell, J. Catecholamine metabolism in affective disorders: III. MHPG and other catecholamine metabolites in patients treated with lithium carbonate. *Journal of Psychiatric Research,* 1970, **1,** 7.

Griest, D., Wells, K. C., & Forehand, R. Examination of predictors of maternal perceptions of maladjustment in clinic-referred children. *Journal of Abnormal Psychology,* 1979, **88,** 277–281.

Griffith, J. J., Mednick, S. A., Schulsinger, F., & Diderichsen, B. Verbal associative disturbances in children at high-risk for schizophrenia. *Journal of Abnormal Psychology,* 1980, **89,** 125–131.

Gross, M. B., & Wilson, W. C. *Minimal brain dysfunction.* New York: Brunner/Mazel, 1974.

Grosz, H. J. & Zimmerman, J. A second detailed case study of functional blindness: Further demonstration of the contribution of objective psychological data. *Behavior Therapy,* 1970, **1,** 115–123.

Groth, N. A., & Burgess, A. W. Sexual dysfunction during rape. *The New England Journal of Medicine,* 1977, **297,** 764–766.

Group for Advancement of Psychiatry. *Psychopathological disorders in childhood: Theoretical considerations and a proposed classification.* Report 62. New York: Mental Health Memorials Center, 1966.

Gubbay, S., Lobascher, M., & Kingerlee, P. A neurological appraisal of autistic children: Results of a Western Australia survey. *Developmental Medicine and Child Neurology,* 1970, **12,** 422–429.

Guerney, B. G. (Ed.) *Psychotherapeutic agents: New roles for nonprofessionals, parents and teachers.* New York: Holt, Rinehart and Winston, 1969.

Gunderson, J. G., Autry, J. H., Mosher, L. R., & Buchsbaum, S. Special report: Schizophrenia, 1973. *Schizophrenia Bulletin,* 1974, **2,** 15–54.

Gurland, B. J. The comparative frequency of depression in various adult age groups. *Journal of Gerontology,* 1976, **31,** 283–292.

Gurman, A. S., & Kniskern, D. P. Research on marital and family therapy: Progress, perspective, and prospect. In S. L. Garfield & A. E. Bergin (Eds.), *Handbook of psychotherapy and behavior change: An empirical analysis.* (2nd ed.) New York: Wiley, 1978.

Guze, S. B. The diagnosis of hysteria: What are we trying to do? *American Journal of Psychiatry,* 1967, **124,** 491–498.

Guze, S. B. *Criminality and psychiatric disorders.* New York: Oxford University Press, 1976.

Haggard, E. Some conditions determining adjustment during and readjustment following experimentally induced stress. In S. Tomkins (Ed.), *Contemporary psychopathology.* Cambridge, Mass.: Harvard University Press, 1943.

Hall, C. S. *A primer of Freudian psychology.* New York: New American Library, 1954.

Halleck, S. L. *The politics of therapy.* New York: Science House, 1971.

Hanusa, B. H., & Schulz, R. Attributional mediators of learned helplessness. *Journal of Personality and Social Psychology,* 1977, **35,** 602–611.

Harburg, E., Erfurt, J. C., Hauenstein, L. S., Chape, C., Schull, W. J., & Schork, M. A. Socioecological stress, suppressed hostility, skin color, and black-white male blood pressure: Detroit. *Psychosomatic Medicine,* 1973, **35,** 276–296.

Hare, R. D. *Psychopathy: Theory and research.* New York: Wiley, 1970.

Hare, R. D. Electrodermal and cardiovascular correlates of sociopathy. In R. D. Hare & D. Schalling (Eds.), *Psychopathic behaviour: Approaches to research.* New York: Wiley, 1978.

Harley, J. P. Dietary treatment in behavioral disorders. In B. W. Camp (Ed.), *Advances in behavioral pediatrics.* Greenwich, Conn.: JAI Press, in press.

Harlow, J.M. Recovery from the passage of an iron bar through the head. *Publication of the Massachusetts Medical Society,* 1868, **2,** 327ff.

Harrell, R. F., Woodyard, E., & Gates, A. D. *The effects of mothers' diets on the intelligence of offspring.* New York: Teachers College Press, Columbia University, 1955.

Harrington, A., & Sutton-Simon, K. Rape. In A. P. Goldstein, P. J. Monti, T. J. Sardino, & D. J. Green (Eds.), *Police crisis intervention.* Kalamazoo, Mich.: Behaviordelia, 1977.

Hart, B. M., Reynolds, N. J., Baer, D. M., Brawley, E. R., & Harris, F. R. Effect of contingent and noncontingent social reinforcement on the cooperative play of a preschool child. *Journal of Applied Behavior Analysis,* 1968, **1,** 73–76.

Hartmann, H. *Ego psychology and the problem of adaptation.* New York: International Universities Press, 1958.

Harvey, P., Winters, K. C., Weintraub, S., & Neale, J. M. Distractibility in children vulnerable to psychopathology. *Journal of Abnormal Psychology,* 1981, **90,** 298–304.

Hastings, D. W. *Impotence and frigidity.* Boston: Little, Brown, 1963.

Hawley, C., & Buckley, R. Food dyes and hyperkinetic children. *Academic Therapy*, 1974, **10**, 27–32.

Hayden, A. H., & Haring, N. G. The acceleration and maintenance of developmental gains in Down's syndrome school-age children. In P. Mittler (Ed.), *Research to practice in mental retardation*, Vol. 1. Baltimore: University Park Press, 1977.

Hays, P. Etiological factors in manic-depressive psychoses. *Archives of General Psychiatry*, 1976, **33**, 1187–1188.

Heath, R. G., & Krupp, I. M. Schizophrenia as an immunologic disorder. *Archives of General Psychiatry*, 1967, **16**, 1–33.

Heaton, R. K. Subject expectancy and environmental factors as determinants of psychedelic flashbacks. *Journal of Nervous and Mental Disease*, 1975, **161**, 157–165.

Heaton, R. K., & Victor, R. G. Personality characteristics associated with psychedelic flashbacks in natural and experimental settings. *Journal of Abnormal Psychology*, 1976, **85**, 83–90.

Heber, R. F. *Epidemiology of mental retardation*. Springfield, Ill.: Charles C Thomas, 1970.

Heber, R. F., & Garber, H. The Milwaukee Project: A study of the use of family intervention to prevent cultural-familial mental retardation. In B. Z. Friedlander, G. M. Sterritt, & G. E. Kirk (Eds.), *Exceptional infant*. Vol. 3. *Assessment and intervention*. New York: Brunner/Mazel, 1975.

Heiman, J. R., & LoPiccolo, J. Effectiveness of daily versus weekly therapy in the treatment of sexual dysfunction. Unpublished manuscript, State University of New York at Stony Brook, 1981.

Heiman, N. M. Postdoctoral training in community mental health. *Menninger Clinical Bulletin* 17, 1973.

Heller, J. *Something happened*, 1966. New York: Knopf, 1974.

Hembree, W. C., Nahas, G. G., & Huang, H. F. S. Changes in human spermatozoa associated with high dose marihuana smoking. In G. G. Nahas & W. D. M. Paton (Eds.), *Marihuana: Biological effects*. Elmsford, N.Y.: Pergamon Press, 1979.

Hempel, C. The theoretician's dilemma. In H. Feigl, M. Scriven, & G. Maxwell (Eds.), *Minnesota studies in the philosophy of science*, Vol. 2. Minnneapolis: University of Minnesota Press, 1958.

Henkel, H., & Lewis-Thomé, J. *Verhaltenstherapie bei männlichen Homosexuellen*. Diplomarbeit der Studierenden der Psychologie, University of Marburg, 1976.

Henry, J. P., Ely, D. L., & Stephens, P. M. Changes in catecholamine-controlling enzymes in response to psychosocial activation of defense and alarm reactions. In *Physiology, emotion, and psychosomatic illness*. Ciba Symposium 8. Amsterdam: Associated Scientific Publishers, 1972.

Hepler, R. S., & Frank, I. M. Marijuana smoking and intraocular pressure. *Journal of the American Medical Association*, 1971, **217**, 1392.

Hepler, R. S., Frank, I. M., & Petrus, R. Ocular effects of marijuana smoking. In M. C. Braude & S. Szara (Eds.), *Pharmacology of marijuana*. New York: Raven Press, 1976.

Herbert, J. Personality factors and bronchial asthma. A study of South African Indian children. *Journal of Psychosomatic Research*, 1965, **8**, 353–364.

Herbert, M. *Conduct disorders of childhood and adolescence*. New York: Wiley, 1978.

Hermelin, B., & O'Connor, N. Measures of occipital alpha rhythm in normal, subnormal, and autistic children. *British Journal of Psychiatry*, 1968, **114**, 603–610.

Hernández-Peón, R., Chávez-Ibarra, G., & Aguilar-Figueroa, E. Somatic evoked potentials in one case of hysterical anesthesia. *EEG and Clinical Neurophysiology*, 1963, **15**, 889–892.

Heston, L. L. Psychiatric disorders in foster home reared children of schizophrenic mothers. *British Journal of Psychiatry*, 1966, **112**, 819–825.

Hewett, F. M. Teaching speech to an autistic child through operant conditioning. *American Journal of Orthopsychiatry*, 1965, **33**, 927–936.

Higgins, G. F. Sexuality and the spinal cord injured patient. In J. LoPiccolo & L. LoPiccolo (Eds.), *Handbook of sex therapy*. New York: Plenum Press, 1978.

Hilgard, E. R. *Hypnotic susceptibility*. New York: Harcourt Brace Jovanovich, 1965.

Hill, D. EEG in episodic psychotic and psychopathic behavior: A classification of data. *EEG and Clinical Neurophysiology*, 1952, **4**, 419–442.

Hill, J. H., Liebert, R. M., & Mott, D. E. W. Vicarious extinction of avoidance behavior through films: An initial test. *Psychological Reports*, 1968, **12**, 192.

Hill, S. Y. Introduction: The biological consequences. In *Alcoholism and alcohol abuse among women: Research issues*. Rockville, Md.: National Institute on Alcohol Abuse and Alcoholism, 1980.

Hiroto, D. S., & Seligman, M. E. P. Generality of learned helplessness in man. *Journal of Personality and Social Psychology*, 1975, **31**, 311–327.

Hite, S. *The Hite report*. New York: Macmillan, 1976.

Hoch, P. H., & Dunaif, S. L. Pseudopsychopathic schizophrenia. In P. H. Hoch & J. Zubin (Eds.), *Psychiatry and the law*. New York: Grune and Stratton, 1955.

Hoch, P. H., & Polatin, P. Pseudoneurotic forms of schizophrenia. *Psychiatric Quarterly*, 1949, **23**, 248–276.

Hodapp, V., Weyer, G., & Becker, J. Situational stereotypy in essential hypertension patients. *Journal of Psychosomatic Research*, 1975, **19**, 113–121.

Hodgson, R. J., & Rachman, S. J. The effects of contamination and washing on obsessional patients. *Behaviour Research and Therapy*, 1972, **10**, 111–117.

Hogan, D. The effectiveness of sex therapy: A review of the literature. In J. LoPiccolo & L. LoPiccolo (Eds.), *Handbook of sex therapy*. New York: Plenum Press, 1978.

Hogarty, G. E., Goldberg, S. C., Schooler, N. R., Ulrich, R. F., & The Collaborative Study Group. Drug and sociotherapy in the aftercare of schizophrenic patients: II. Two-year relapse rates. *Archives of General Psychiatry*, 1974, **31**, 603–608.

Hogarty, G. E., Goldberg, S. C., Schooler, N. R., & The Collaborative Study Group. Drug and sociotherapy in the aftercare of schizophrenic patients: III. Adjustment of nonrelapsed patients. *Archives of General Psychiatry*, 1974, **31**, 609–618.

Hokanson. J. E., & Burgess, M. The effects of three types of aggression on vascular processes. *Journal of Abnormal and Social Psychology*, 1962, **65**, 446–449.

Hokanson, J. E., Burgess, M., & Cohen, M. F. Effects of displaced aggression on systolic blood pressure. *Journal of Abnormal and Social Psychology*, 1963, **67**, 214–218.

Hokanson, J. E., DeGood, D. E., Forrest, M. S., & Brittain, T. M. Availability of avoidance behaviors for modulating vascular-stress responses. *Journal of Personality and Social Psychology*, 1971, **19**, 60–68.

Hokanson. J. E., Willers, K. R., & Koropsak. E. Modification of autonomic responses during aggressive interchange. *Journal of Personality*, 1968, **36**, 386–404.

Holden. C. Nader on mental health centers: A movement that got bogged down. *Science*, 1972, **177**, 413–415.

Hollingshead, A. B., & Redlich, F. C. *Social class and mental illness: A community study*. New York: Wiley, 1958.

Hollister, L. E., Davis, K. L., & Berger, P. A. Subtypes of depression based on excretion of MHPG and response to nortriptyline. *Archives of General Psychiatry*, 1980, **37**, 1107–1110.

Hollon, S. D., & Beck, A. T. Cognitive therapy of depression. In P. C. Kendall & S. D. Hollon (Eds.), *Cognitive-behavioral interventions: Theory, research, and procedures*. New York: Academic Press, 1979.

Holmes. T. H., & Rahe, R. H. The social readjustment rating scale. *Journal of Psychosomatic Research*, 1967, **11**, 213–218.

Holmes, T. S., & Holmes, T. H. Short-term intrusions into the life style routine. *Journal of Psychosomatic Research*, 1970, **14**, 121–132.

Honigfeld, G., & Howard, A. *Psychiatric drugs: A desk reference*. (2nd ed.) New York: Academic Press, 1978.

Horan, J. J., Linberg, S. E., & Hackett, G. Nicotine poisoning and rapid smoking. *Journal of Consulting and Clinical Psychology*, 1977, **45**, 344–347.

Horn, A. S., & Snyder, S. H. Chlorpromazine and dopamine: Conformational similarities that correlate with the antischizophrenic activity of phenothiazine drugs. *Proceedings of the National Academy of Sciences*, 1971, **68**, 2325–2328.

Horney, K. *Self-analysis*. New York: Norton, 1942.

Horwitz, L. *Clinical prediction in psychotherapy*. New York: Jason Aronson, 1974.

Houts, P. S., & Serber, M. (Eds.) *After the turn-on, what? Learning perspectives on humanistic groups*. Champaign, Ill.: Research Press, 1972.

Hoy, E., Weiss, G., Minde, K. & Cohen, H. The hyperactive child at adolescence: Cognitive, emotional, and social functioning. *Journal of Abnormal Child Psychology*, 1978, **6**, 311–324.

Hsu, L. K. G. Outcome of anorexia nervosa: A review of the literature (1954 to 1978). *Archives of General Psychiatry*, 1980, **37**, 1041–1046.

Huber, H., Karlin, R., & Nathan, P. E. Blood alcohol discrimination by nonalcoholics: The role of internal and external cues. *Journal of Studies on Alcohol*, 1976, **37**, 27–39.

Huessy, H. R., Metoyer, M., & Townsend, M. 8–10 year follow-up of 84 children treated for behavioral disorder in rural Vermont. *Acta Paedopsychiatrica*, 1974, **40**, 230–235.

Hugdahl, K., Fredrikson, M., & Öhman, A. Preparedness and arousability as determinants of electrodermal conditioning. *Behaviour Research and Therapy*, 1977, **15**, 345–353.

Hunt, W. A., & Bespalec, D. A. An evaluation of current methods of modifying smoking behavior. *Journal of Clinical Psychology*, 1974, **30**, 431–438.

Hurlburt, R. T. Random sampling of cognitions and behavior. *Journal of Research in Personality*, 1979, **13**, 103–111.

Hurley, R. L. *Poverty and mental retardation: A causal relationship*. New York: Random House, 1970.

Hutchings, B., & Mednick, S. A. Registered criminality in the adoptive and biological parents of registered male adoptees. In S. A. Mednick, F. Schulsinger, J. Higgins, & B. Bell (Eds.), *Genetics, environment and psychopathology*. New York: Elsevier, 1974.

Hutt, C., Hutt, S. J., Lee, D., & Ounsted, C. Arousal and childhood autism. *Nature*, 1964, **204**, 908–909.

Hutt, C., & Ounsted, C. The biological significance of gaze aversion with particular reference to the syndrome of infantile autism. *Behavioral Science*, 1966, **11**, 346–356.

Ikard, F. F., Green, D. E., & Horn, D. The development of a scale to differentiate between types of smoking as related to the management of affect. Paper presented at the annual meeting of the Eastern Psychological Association, Washington, D.C., 1968.

Inglis, J. Electrode placement and the effect of ECT on mood and memory in depression. *Canadian Psychiatric Association Journal*, 1969, **14,** 463–471.

Ingram, I. M. The obsessional personality and obsessional illness. *American Journal of Psychiatry,* 1961, **117,** 1016–1019.

Inhelder, B. *The diagnosis of reasoning in the mentally retarded.* (2nd ed.) New York: Chandler Publishing, 1968.

Innes, G., Millar, W. M., & Valentine, M. Emotion and blood pressure. *Journal of Mental Science,* 1959, **105,** 840–851.

Insull, W. (Ed.) *Coronary risk handbook.* New York: American Heart Association, 1973.

Iscoe, I., & Semler, I. J. Paired associates learning in normal and mentally retarded children as a function of four experimental conditions. *Journal of Comparative and Physiological Psychology,* 1964, **57,** 387–392.

Issidorides, M. R. Observations in chronic hashish users: Nuclear aberrations in blood and sperm and abnormal acrosomes in spermatozoa. In G. G. Nahas & W. D. M. Paton (Eds.), *Marihuana: Biological effects.* Elmsford, N.Y.: Pergamon Press, 1979.

Itil, T. M. Summary progress report on Grant MH20801. St. Louis, Mo., 1972.

Jackson, A. M. Psychotherapy: Factors associated with the race of the therapist. *Psychotherapy: Theory, Research, and Practice,* 1973, **10,** 273–277.

Jackson, D. D., & Weakland, J. Conjoint family therapy: Some considerations on theory, technique and results. *Psychiatry,* 1961, **24,** 30–45.

Jacobs, M., Jacobs, A., Gatz, M., & Schaible, T. Credibility and desirability of positive and negative structured feedback in groups. *Journal of Consulting and Clinical Psychology,* 1973, **40,** 244–252.

Jacobson, E. *Progressive relaxation.* Chicago: University of Chicago Press, 1929.

Jacobson, N. S., & Margolin, G. *Marital therapy: Strategies based on social learning.* New York: Brunner/Mazel, 1979.

James, N., & Chapman, J. A genetic study of bipolar affective disorder. *British Journal of Psychiatry,* 1975, **126,** 449–456.

Jarvik, M. E. Biological influences on cigarette smoking. In N. A. Krasnegor (Ed.), *The behavioral aspects of smoking.* Washington, D.C.: National Institute on Drug Abuse, 1979.

Jarvik, M. E., Cullen, J. W., Gritz, E. R., Vogt, T. M., & West, L. J. (Eds.) *Research on smoking behavior.* Washington, D.C.: National Institute on Drug Abuse, 1977.

Jeans, R. F. I. An independently validated case of multiple personality. *Journal of Abnormal Psychology,* 1976, **85,** 249–255.

Jellinek, E. M. Phases of alcohol addiction. *Quarterly Journal of Studies on Alcohol,* 1952, **13,** 673–684.

Jenkins, C. D. Psychologic and social precursors of coronary disease. *New England Journal of Medicine,* 1971, **284,** 244–255, 307–317.

Jenkins, C. D. Recent evidence supporting psychologic and social risk factors for coronary disease. *New England Journal of Medicine,* 1976, **294,** 987–994, 1033–1038.

Jenkins, C. D., Rosenman, R. H., & Zyzanski, S. J. Prediction of clinical coronary heart disease by a test for the coronary-prone behavior pattern. *New England Journal of Medicine,* 1974, **290,** 1271–1275.

Jenkins, C. D., Zyzanski, S. J., & Rosenman, R. H. Coronary-prone behavior: One pattern or several? *Psychosomatic Medicine,* 1978, **40,** 25–43.

Jenkins, R. L., & Fine, B. N. Experience in 20 cases of Tourette's Syndrome. In F. S. Abuzzahab & F. O. Anderson (Eds.), *Gilles de la Tourette's syndrome.* Vol. 1. *International Registry.* St. Paul, Minn.: Mason Publishing Company, 1976.

Jenkins, R. L., & Glickman, S. Patterns of personality organization among delinquents. *Nervous Child,* 1947, **6,** 329–339.

Jersild, A. T., & Holmes, F. B. *Children's fears.* New York: Teachers College Press, Columbia University, 1935.

Jersild, A. T., Markey, F. V., & Jersild, C. L. Children's fears, dreams, wishes, daydreams, likes, dislikes, pleasant and unpleasant memories. In A. T. Jersild (Ed.), *Child psychology.* Englewood Cliffs, N.J.: Prentice-Hall, 1960.

Johnson, A. M., Falstein, E. I., Szurek, S. A., & Svendson, M. School phobia, *American Journal of Orthopsychiatry,* 1941, **11,** 701–702.

Jones, B. M. Memory impairment on the ascending and descending limbs of the blood alcohol curve. *Journal of Abnormal Psychology,* 1973, **82,** 24–32.

Jones, B. M., & Parsons, O. A. Impaired abstracting ability in chronic alcoholics. *Archives of General Psychiatry,* 1971, **24,** 71–75.

Jones, B. M., & Parsons, O. A. Alcohol and consciousness: Getting high, coming down. *Psychology Today,* January 1975, **8,** 53–58.

Jones, E. *The life and work of Sigmund Freud,* Vol. 2. New York: Basic Books, 1955.

Jones, M. *The therapeutic community.* New York: Basic Books, 1953.

Jones, M. C. A laboratory study of fear: The case of Peter. *Pedagogical Seminary,* 1924, **31,** 308–315.

Jones, M. C. Personality correlates and antecedents of drinking patterns in males. *Journal of Consulting and Clinical Psychology,* 1968, **32,** 2–12.

Jones, M. C. Personality antecedents and correlates of drinking patterns in women. *Journal of Consulting and Clinical Psychology,* 1971, **36,** 61–70.

Jones, R. T. Human effects. In R. C. Peterson (Ed.), *Marijuana research findings: 1976.* NIDA Research Monograph 14. Washington, D.C.: U.S. Government Printing Office, 1977.

Jones, R. T. Human effects: An overview. In *Marijuana research findings: 1980.* Washington, D.C.: U.S. Government Printing Office, 1980.

Jones, R. T., & Benowitz, N. The 30-day trip—Clinical studies of cannabis tolerance and dependence. In M. C. Braude & S. Szara (Eds.), *Pharmacology of marijuana.* New York: Raven Press, 1976.

Kagan, J. Reflection-impulsivity and reading ability in primary grade children. *Child Development,* 1965, **36,** 609–628.

Kahn, R. L., Zarit, S. H., Hilbert, N. M., & Niederehe, G. Memory complaint and impairment in the aged. *Archives of General Psychiatry,* 1975, **32,** 1569–1573.

Kamiya, J. Conscious control of brain waves. *Psychology Today,* April 1968, **1,** 56–61.

Kanfer, F. H., & Phillips, J. S. *Learning foundations of behavior therapy.* New York: Wiley, 1970.

Kanner, L. Autistic disturbances of affective contact. *Nervous Child,* 1943, **2,** 217–250.

Kanner, L. Follow-up of eleven autistic children originally reported in 1943. In L. Kanner (Ed.), *Childhood psychosis: Initial studies and new insights.* Washington, D.C.: Winston-Wiley, 1973.

Kanner, L., & Eisenberg, L. Notes on the follow-up studies of autistic children. In P. Hoch & J. Zubin (Eds.), *Psychopathology of childhood.* New York: Grune and Stratton, 1955.

Kanter, N. J., & Goldfried, M. R. Relative effectiveness of rational restructuring and self-control desensitization for the reduction of interpersonal anxiety. *Behavioral Therapy,* 1979, **10,** 472–490.

Kantorovich, N. V. An attempt at associative-reflex therapy in alcoholism. *Psychological Abstracts,* 1930, **4,** 493.

Kaplan, H. S. *The new sex therapy.* New York: Brunner/Mazel, 1974.

Kasanin, J. The acute schizoaffective psychoses. *American Journal of Psychiatry,* 1933, **13,** 97–123.

Kasl, S. V., & Cobb, S. Blood pressure changes in men undergoing job loss: A preliminary report. *Psychosomatic Medicine,* 1970, **6,** 95–106.

Katchadourian, H. A., & Lunde, D. T. *Fundamentals of human sexuality.* New York: Holt, Rinehart and Winston, 1972.

Kay, D. W. K., Beamish, P., & Roth, M. Old age mental disorders in Newcastle upon Tyne. Part I. A study of prevalence. *British Journal of Mental Science,* 1964, **10,** 146–158.

Kazdin, A. E. Covert modelling, imagery assessment, and assertive behavior. *Journal of Consulting and Clinical Psychology,* 1975, **43,** 716–724.

Kazdin, A. E., & Wilson, G. T. *Evaluation of behavior therapy: Issues, evidence, and research strategies.* Cambridge, Mass.: Ballinger, 1978.

Keen, S. Some ludicrous theses about sexuality. *Journal of Humanistic Psychology,* 1979, **19,** 15–22.

Kegel, A. H. Sexual function of the pubococcygeus muscle. *Western Journal of Surgery,* 1952, **60,** 521–524.

Keith, S. J., Gunderson, J. G., Reifman, A., Buchsbaum, S., & Mosher, L. R. Special report: Schizophrenia 1976. *Schizophrenia Bulletin,* 1976, **2,** 509–565.

Kelly, C. New NIDA studies document dramatic rise in drug abuse. *ADAMHA News,* July 11, 1980.

Kelly, E., & Zeller, B. Asthma and the psychiatrist. *Journal of Psychosomatic Research,* 1969, **13,** 377–395.

Kendell, R. E. *The role of diagnosis in psychiatry.* London: Blackwell, 1975.

Kennedy, W. A. School phobia: Rapid treatment of 50 cases. *Journal of Abnormal Psychology,* 1965, **70,** 285–289.

Kent, R. N., O'Leary, K. D., Diament, C., & Dietz, A. Expectation biases in observational evaluation of therapeutic change. *Journal of Consulting and Clinical Psychology,* 1974, **42,** 774–780.

Kernberg, O. F. Summary and conclusion of "Psychotherapy and psychoanalysis: Final report of the Menninger Foundation's Psychotherapy Research Project." *International Journal of Psychiatry,* 1973, **11,** 62–77.

Kessler, J. *Psychopathology of childhood.* Englewood Cliffs, N.J.: Prentice-Hall, 1966.

Kessler, P., & Neale, J. M. Hippocampal damage and schizophrenia: A critique of Mednick's theory. *Journal of Abnormal Psychology,* 1974, **83,** 91–96.

Kety, S. S. From rationalization to reason. *American Journal of Psychiatry,* 1974, **131,** 957–963.

Kety, S. S., Rosenthal, D., Wender, P. H., & Schulsinger, F. The types and prevalence of mental illness in the biological and adoptive families of adopted schizophrenics. In D. Rosenthal & S. S. Kety (Eds.), *The transmission of schizophrenia.* Elmsford, N.Y.: Pergamon Press, 1968.

Kety, S. S., Rosenthal, D., Wender, P. H., Schulsinger, F., & Jacobson, B. Mental illness in the biological and adoptive families of adopted individuals who have become schizophrenic: A preliminary report based on psychiatric interviews. In R. R. Fieve, D. Rosenthal, & H. Brill (Eds.), *Genetic Research in Psychiatry.* Baltimore: Johns Hopkins University Press, 1975.

Keuthen, N. Subjective probability estimation and somatic structures in phobic individuals. Unpublished manuscript, State University of New York at Stony Brook, 1980.

Kidd, K. K., Prusoff, B. A., & Cohen, D. J. Familial pattern of Gilles de la Tourette syndrome. *Archives of General Psychiatry*, 1980, **37**, 1336–1340.

Kimble, G. *Hilgard and Marquis' conditioning and learning.* New York: Appleton-Century-Crofts, 1961.

Kinsey, A. C., Pomeroy, W. B., & Martin, C. E. *Sexual behavior in the human male.* Philadelphia: Saunders, 1948.

Kinsey, A. C., Pomeroy, W. B., Martin, C. E., & Gebhard, P. H. *Sexual behavior in the human female.* Philadelphia: Saunders, 1953.

Kinsman, R. A., Spector, S. L., Shucard, D. W., & Luparello, T. J. Observations on patterns of subjective symptomatology of acute asthma. *Psychosomatic Medicine*, 1974, 36, 129–143.

Kirigin, K. A., Braukmann, C. J., & Wolf, M. M. Consumer and outcome evaluation of community group homes for juvenile offenders. Paper presented to the National Conference on Criminal Justice Evaluation, Washington, D.C., 1977.

Kistin, H., & Morris, R. Alternatives to institutional care for the elderly and disabled. *Gerontologist*, 1972, **12**, 139–142.

Klee, G. D., Bertino, J., Weintraub, W., & Calaway, E. The influence of varying dosage on the effects of lysergic acid diethylamide (LSD-25). *Journal of Nervous and Mental Disease*, 1961, **132**, 404–409.

Klee, G. D., & Weintraub, W. Paranoid reactions following lysergic acid diethylamide (LSD-25). In P. B. Bradley, P. Demicker, & C. Radonco-Thomas (Eds.), *Neuropsychopharmacology.* Amsterdam, Netherlands: Elsevier, 1959.

Kleeman, S. T. Psychiatric contributions in the treatment of asthma. *Annals of Allergy*, 1967, **25**, 611–619.

Klein, D. C., & Seligman, M. E. P. Reversal of performance deficits and perceptual deficits in learned helplessness and depression. *Journal of Abnormal Psychology*, 1976, **85**, 11–26.

Klein, D. F., & Davis, J. M. *Diagnosis and drug treatment of psychiatric disorders.* Baltimore: Williams and Wilkins, 1969.

Klein, M. *The psychoanalysis of children.* London: Hogarth Press, 1932.

Kleinmuntz, B. *Personality measurement: An introduction.* Homewood, Ill.: Dorsey Press, 1967.

Klerman, G. L. Drug therapy of clinical depressions. *Journal of Psychiatric Research*, 1972, **9**, 253–270.

Klerman, G. L. Drug therapy of clinical depressions—Current status and implications for research on neuropharmacology of the affective disorders. In D. F. Klein & R. Gittelman-Klein (Eds.), *Progress in psychiatric drug treatment.* New York: Brunner/Mazel, 1975.

Kluger, J. M. Childhood asthma and the social milieu. *American Academy of Child Psychiatry*, 1969, **8**, 353–366.

Knapp, P. H. The asthmatic and his environment. *Journal of Nervous and Mental Disease*, 1969, **149**, 133–151.

Knight, R. P. The dynamics of chronic alcoholism. *Journal of Nervous and Mental Disease*, 1937, **86**, 538–548.

Koenig, K., & Masters, J. Experimental treatment of habitual smoking. *Behaviour Research and Therapy*, 1965, **3**, 235–243.

Kogan, W. S., Dorpat, T. L., & Holmes, T. H. Semantic problems in evaluating a specificity hypothesis in psychophysiologic reactions. *Psychosomatic Medicine*, 1965, **27**, 1–8.

Kohn, M. L. Social class and schizophrenia: A critical review. In D. Rosenthal & S. S. Kety (Eds.), *The transmission of schizophrenia.* Elmsford, N.Y.: Pergamon Press, 1968.

Kolb, L. C. *Noyes' modern clinical psychiatry.* (7th ed.) Philadelphia: Saunders, 1968.

Kolvin, I., MacKeith, R. C., & Meadow, S. R. *Bladder control and enuresis.* Philadelphia: Lippincott, 1973.

Konig, P., & Godfrey, S. Prevalence of exercise-induced bronchial lability in families of children with asthma. *Archives of Diseases of Childhood*, 1973, **48**, 513.

Kopfstein, J. M., & Neale, J. M. A multivariate study of attention dysfunction in schizophrenia. *Journal of Abnormal Psychology*, 1972, **80**, 294–299.

Kozol, H., Boucher, R., & Garofalo, R. The diagnosis and treatment of dangerousness. *Crime and Delinquency*, 1972, **18**, 371–392.

Kramer, M., Taube, A., & Redick, R. W. Patterns of use of psychiatric facilities by the aged: Past, present and future. In C. Eisdorfer & M. Lawton (Eds.), *The psychology of adult development and aging.* Washington, D.C.: American Psychological Association, 1973.

Kranz, H. *Lebenschicksale krimineller Zwillinge.* Berlin: Springer-Verlag, 1936.

Krasnegor, N. A. Introduction. In N. A. Krasnegor (Ed.), *The behavioral aspects of smoking.* Washington, D.C.: National Institute on Drug Abuse, 1979.

Kringlen, E. Natural history of obsessional neurosis. *Seminars in Psychiatry*, 1970, **2**, 403–419.

Kroll, P., Chamberlain, P., & Halpern, D. The diagnosis of Briquet's syndrome in a male population. *Journal of Nervous and Mental Disease*, 1979, **169**, 171–174.

Kuhlman, W. H., & Kaplan, B. J. Clinical applications of EEG feedback training. In R. J. Gatchel & K. P. Price (Eds.), *Clinical applications of biofeedback: Appraisal and status.* Elmsford, N.Y.: Pergamon Press, 1979.

Kuhn, T. S. *The Copernican revolution*. New York: Random House, 1959.

Kuhn, T. S. *The structure of scientific revolutions*. Chicago: University of Chicago Press, 1962.

Kuriansky, J. B., Deming, W. E., & Gurland, B. J. On trends in the diagnosis of schizophrenia. *American Journal of Psychiatry*, 1974, **131**, 402–407.

Kutchinsky, B. *Studies on pornography and sex crimes in Denmark*. Copenhagen: New Social Science Monographs, 1970.

Lacey, J. I. Somatic response patterning and stress: Some revisions of activation theory. In M. H. Appley & R. Trumball (Eds.), *Psychological stress*. New York: McGraw-Hill, 1967.

Lachman, S. J. *Psychosomatic disorders: A behavioristic interpretation*. New York: Wiley, 1972.

Lahey, B. B., Stempniak, M., Robinson, E. J., & Tyroler, M. J. Hyperactivity and learning disabilities as independent dimensions of child behavior problems. *Journal of Abnormal Psychology*, 1978, **87**, 333–340.

Laing, R. D. Is schizophrenia a disease? *International Journal of Social Psychiatry*, 1964, **10**, 184–193.

Lambert, M. J., Bergin, A. E., & Collins, J. L. Therapist-induced deterioration in psychotherapy. In A. S. Gurman & A. M. Razin (Eds.), *Effective psychotherapy: A handbook of reserach*. Elmsford, N.Y.: Pergamon Press, 1977.

Lando, H. A. Successful treatment of smokers with a broad-spectrum behavioral approach. *Journal of Consulting and Clinical Psychology*, 1977, **45**, 361–366.

Lane, E. A., & Albee, G. W. Childhood intellectual differences between schizophrenic adults and their siblings. *American Journal of Orthopsychiatry*, 1965, **35**, 747–753.

Lang, A. R., Goeckner, D. J., Adessor, V. J., & Marlatt, G. A. Effects of alcohol on aggression in male social drinkers. *Journal of Abnormal Psychology*, 1975, **84**, 508–518.

Lang, P. J. The mechanics of desensitization and the laboratory study of fear. In C. M. Franks (Ed.), *Behavior therapy: Appraisal and status*. New York: McGraw-Hill, 1969.

Lang, P. J. Learned control of human heart rate in a computer directed environment. In P. A. Obrist, A. H. Black, J. Brener, & L. V. DiCara (Eds.), *Cardiovascular psychophysiology*. Chicago: Aldine, 1974.

Lang, P. J., & Lazovik. A. D. Experimental desensitization of a phobia. *Journal of Abnormal and Social Psychology*, 1963, **66**, 519–525.

Lang, P. J., & Melamed, B. G. Case report: Avoidance conditioning therapy of an infant with chronic ruminative vomiting. *Journal of Abnormal Psychology*, 1969, **74**, 1–8.

Lange, A. J., & Jakubowski, P. *Responsible assertive behavior*. Champaign, Ill.: Research Press, 1976.

Lange, J. *Verbrechen als Schicksal*. Leipzig: Georg Thieme Verlag, 1929.

Langer, E. J. Old age: An artifact? In J. McGaugh & S. Kiesler (Eds.), *Aging: Biology and behavior*. New York: Academic Press, 1981.

Langer, E. J., & Abelson, R. P. A patient by any other name . . .: Clinician group difference in labelling bias. *Journal of Consulting and Clinical Psychology*, 1974, **42**, 4–9.

Langer, E. J., & Rodin, J. The effects of choice and enhanced personal responsibility for the aged. *Journal of Personality and Social Psychology*, 1976, **34**, 191–198.

Langevin, R., Paitich, D., Ramsay, G., Anderson, C., Kamrad, J., Pope, S., Geller, G., Pearl, L., & Newman, S. Experimental studies of the etiology of genital exhibitionism. *Archives of Sexual Behavior*, 1979, **8**, 307–331.

Langevin, R., Paitich, D., & Steiner, B. The clinical profile of male transsexuals living as females versus those living as males. *Archives of Sexual Behavior*. 1977, **6**, 143–154.

Lasagna, L., Mosteller, F., Von Felsinger, J. M., & Beecher, H. K. A study of the placebo response. *American Journal of Medicine*, 1954, **16**, 770–779.

Lavelle, T. L., Metalsky, G. I., & Coyne, J. C. Learned helplessness, test anxiety, and acknowledgement of contingencies. *Journal of Abnormal Psychology*, 1979, **88**, 381–387.

Lawton, M. P. Schizophrenia forty-five years later. *Journal of Genetic Psychology*, 1972, **121**, 133–143.

Lazarus, A. A. Group therapy of phobic disorders by systematic desensitization. *Journal of Abnormal and Social Psychology*, 1961, **63**, 504–510.

Lazarus, A. A. Behavior therapy, incomplete treatment, and symptom substitution. *Journal of Nervous and Mental Disease*, 1965, **140**, 80–86.

Lazarus, A. A. Behavior therapy in groups. In G. M. Gazda (Ed.), *Basic approaches to group psychotherapy and counseling*. Springfield, Ill.: Charles C Thomas, 1968.(a)

Lazarus. A. A. Learning theory and the treatment of depression. *Behavior Research and Therapy*, 1968, **6**, 83–89.(b)

Lazarus, A. A. *Behavior therapy and beyond*. New York: McGraw-Hill, 1971.

Lazarus, A. A. Multimodal behavior therapy: Treating the BASIC ID. *Journal of Nervous and Mental Disease*, 1973, **156**, 404–411.

Lazarus, A. A., & Davison, G. C. Clinical innovation in research and practice. In A. E. Bergin & S. L. Garfield (Eds.), *Handbook of psychotherapy and behavior change: An empirical analysis*. New York: Wiley, 1971.

Lazarus, A. A., Davison, G. C., & Polefka, D. Classical and operant factors in the treatment of a school phobia. *Journal of Abnormal Psychology*, 1965, **70**, 225–229.

Lazarus, R. S. Psychological stress and coping in adaptation and illness. *International Journal of Psychiatry in Medicine*, 1974, **5**, 321–333.

Lazovik, A. D., & Lang, P. J. A laboratory demonstration of systematic desensitization psychotherapy. *Journal of Psychological Studies*, 1960, **11**, 238–247.

Lee, T., & Seeman, P. Dopamine receptors in normal and schizophrenic human brains. *Proceedings of the Society of Neurosciences*, 1977, **3**, 443.

Leff, J. P. Schizophrenia and sensitivity to the family environment. *Schizophrenia Bulletin*, 1976, **2**, 566–574.

Lefkowitz, M. M., & Burton, N. Childhood depression: A critique of the concept. *Psychological Bulletin*, 1978, **85**, 716–726.

Leibtag, D. Potent new heroin smoked and snorted. *ADAMHA News*, July 11, 1980.

Leland, H., & Smith, D. *Play therapy with mentally subnormal children.* New York: Grune and Stratton, 1965.

Lemieux, G., Davignon, A., & Genest, J. Depressive states during rauwolfia therapy for arterial hypertension. *Canadian Medical Association Journal*, 1956, **74**, 522–526.

Leonard, C. V. Depression and suicidality. *Journal of Consulting and Clinical Psychology*, 1974, **42**, 98–104.

Levendusky, P., & Pankratz, L. Self-control technique as an alternative pain medication. *Journal of Abnormal Psychology*, 1975, **84**, 165–168.

Levenson, M. Cognitive and perceptual factors in suicidal individuals. Unpublished doctoral dissertation, University of Kansas, 1972.

Levitsky, A., & Perls, F. S. The rules and games of Gestalt therapy. In J. Fagan & I. L. Shepherd (Eds.), *Gestalt therapy now: Theory, techniques, applications.* Palo Alto, Calif.: Science and Behavior books, 1970.

Levitt, E. E. Research on psychotherapy with children. In A. E. Bergin & S. L. Garfield (Eds.), *Handbook of psychotherapy and behavior change: An empirical analysis.* New York: Wiley, 1971.

Levitt, E. E., & Edwards, J. A. A multivariate study of correlative factors in youthful cigarette smoking. *Developmental Psychology*, 1970, **2**, 5–11.

Levy, L. H. *Psychological interpretation.* New York: Holt, Rinehart and Winston, 1963.

Lewinsohn, P. H. A behavioral approach to depression. In R. J. Friedman & M. M. Katz (Eds.), *The psychology of depression: Contemporary theory and research.* Washington, D.C.: Winston-Wiley, 1974.

Lewinsohn, P. H., & Libet, J. M. Pleasant events, activity schedules and depression. *Journal of Abnormal Psychology*, 1972, **79**, 291–295.

Lewinsohn, P. H., Weinstein, M., & Alper, T. A behavioral approach to the group treatment of depressed persons: A

methodological contribution. *Journal of Clinical Psychology*, 1970, **26**, 525–532.

Liberman, R. P., DeRisi, W. J., King, L. W., Eckman, T. A., & Wood, D. W. Behavioral measurement in a community mental health center. In P. O. Davidson, F. W. Clark, & L. A. Hamerlynck (Eds.), *Evaluation of behavioral programs in community, residential, and school settings.* Champaign, Ill.: Research Press, 1974.

Lichtenstein, E., & Danaher, B. G. Modification of smoking behavior: A critical analysis of theory, research, and practice. In M. Hersen, R. M. Eisler, & P. M. Miller (Eds.), *Progress in behavior modification*, Vol. 4. New York: Academic Press, 1977.

Lieber, C. S. The metabolism of alcohol. *Scientific American*, 1976, **234**, 25–34.

Lieberman, M. A., Yalom, I. D., & Miles, M. B. *Encounter groups: First facts.* New York: Basic Books, 1973.

Liebert, R. M., & Baron, R. A. Short-term effects of televised aggression on children's aggressive behavior. In J. P. Murray, E. A. Rubinstein, & G. A. Comstock (Eds.), *Television and social behavior*, Vol. 2. Washington, D.C.: U.S. Government Printing Office, 1972.

Liebert, R. M., Neale, J. M., & Davidson, E. S. *The early window: The effects of television on children and youth.* Elmsford, N.Y.: Pergamon Press, 1973.

Liebson, I. Conversion reaction: A learning theory approach. *Behaviour Research and Therapy*, 1967, **7**, 217–218.

Liem, J. H. Effects of verbal communications of parents and children: A comparison of normal and schizophrenic families. *Journal of Consulting and Clinical Psychology*, 1974, **42**, 438–450.

Linton, H. B., & Langs, R. J. Empirical dimensions of LSD-25 reactions. *Archives of General Psychiatry*, 1964, **10**, 469–485.

Lion, J. R. Outpatient treatment of psychopaths. In W. H. Reid (Ed.), *The psychopath: A comprehensive study of antisocial disorders and behaviors.* New York: Brunner/Mazel, 1978.

Lipinski, D. P., Black, J. L., Nelson, R. O., & Ciminero, A. R. The influence of motivational variables on the reactivity and reliability of self-recording. *Journal of Consulting and Clinical Psychology*, 1975, **43**, 637–646.

Lockyer, L., & Rutter, M. A five-to-fifteen-year follow-up of infantile psychosis: III. Psychological characteristics. *British Journal of Psychiatry*, 1969, **115**, 865–882.

London, P. *The modes and morals of psychotherapy.* New York: Holt, Rinehart and Winston, 1964.

Loney, J., Langborne, J. E., Jr., & Paternite, C. E. An empirical basis for subgrouping the hyperkinetic/minimal brain dysfunction syndrome. *Journal of Abnormal Psychology*, 1978, **87**, 431–441.

LoPiccolo, J. Direct treatment of sexual dysfunction in the

couple. In J. Money & H. Musaph (Eds.), *Handbook of sexology.* New York: Elsevier/North Holland, 1977.

LoPiccolo, J., & Hogan, D. R. Multidimensional treatment of sexual dysfunction. In O. F. Pomerleau & J. P. Brady (Eds.), *Behavioral medicine: Theory and practice.* Baltimore: Williams and Wilkins, 1979.

LoPiccolo, J., & LoPiccolo, L. (Eds.) *Handbook of sex therapy.* New York: Plenum Press, 1978.

Lothstein, L. M. The postsurgical transsexual: Empirical and theoretical considerations. *Archives of Sexual Behavior,* 1980, **9,** 547–564.

Lotter, V. Epidemiology of autistic conditions in young children: I. Prevalence. *Social Psychiatry,* 1966, **1,** 124–137.

Lotter, V. Factors related to outcome in autistic children. *Journal of Autism and Childhood Schizophrenia,* 1974, **4,** 263–277.

Lotter, V. Follow-up studies. In M. Rutter & E. Schopler (Eds.), *Autism: A reappraisal of concepts and treatment.* New York: Plenum Press, 1978.

Lovaas, O. I. The autistic child: Language development through behavior modification. New York: Irvington, 1977.

Lovaas, O. I., Koegel, R., Simmons, J. Q., & Long, J. S. Some generalization and follow-up measures on autistic children in behavior therapy. *Journal of Applied Behavior Analysis,* 1973, **6,** 131–166.

Lovaas, O. I., Schreibman, L., Koegel, R., & Rehm, R. Selective responding by autistic children to multiple sensory input. *Journal of Abnormal Psychology,* 1971, **77,** 211–222.

Lovibond, S. H. *Conditioning and enuresis.* Oxford, England: Pergamon Press, 1964.

Lovibond, S. H., & Caddy, G. Discriminated aversive control in the moderation of alcoholics' drinking. *Behavior Therapy,* 1970, **1,** 437–444.

Lowen, A. *The physical dynamics of character structure.* New York: Grune and Stratton, 1958.

Lowenthal, M. F., Berkman, P., & Associates. *Aging and mental disorder in San Francisco.* San Francisco: Jossey-Bass, 1967.

Lowenthal, M. F., & Haven, C. Interaction and adaptation: Intimacy as a critical variable. *American Sociological Review,* 1968, **33,** 20–30.

Luborsky, L, & Spence, D. P. Quantitative research on psychoanalytic therapy. In S. L. Garfield & A. E. Bergin (Eds.), *Handbook of psychotherapy and behavior change: An empirical analysis.* (2nd ed.) New York: Wiley, 1978.

Luparello, T. J., McFadden, E. R., Lyons, H. A., & Bleecker, E. R. Psychologic factors and bronchial asthma. *New York State Journal of Medicine,* 1971, **71,** 2161–2165.

Luthe, W., & Schultz, J. H. *Autogenic therapy.* Vol. 1. *Autogenic methods.* New York: Grune and Stratton, 1969.

Lyght, C. E. (Ed.) *The Merck manual of diagnosis and therapy.* (11th ed.) Rahway, N.J.: Merck Sharp and Dohme Research Laboratories, 1966.

Lykken, D. T. A study of anxiety in the sociopathic personality. *Journal of Abnormal and Social Psychology,* 1957, **55,** 6–10.

Lystad, M. M. Social mobility among selected groups of schizophrenics. *American Sociological Review,* 1957, **22,** 288–292.

Maccoby, N., & Alexander, J. Use of media in lifestyle programs. In P. O. Davidson & S. M. Davidson (Eds.), *Behavioral medicine: Changing health lifestyles.* New York: Brunner/Mazel, 1980.

Maccoby, N., Farquhar, J. W., Wood, P. D., & Alexander, J. Reducing the risk of cardiovascular disease: Effects of a community-based campaign on knowledge and behavior. *Journal of Community Health,* 1977, **3,** 100–114.

MacCorquodale, K., & Meehl, P. On the distinction between hypothetical constructs and intervening variables. *Psychological Review,* 1948, **55,** 95–107.

MacFarlane, J. W., Allen, L., & Honzik, M. P. *A developmental study of the behavior problems of normal children between 21 months and 14 years.* Berkeley: University of California Press, 1954.

MacPhillamy, D. J., & Lewinsohn, P. H. A scale for the measurement of positive reinforcement. Unpublished manuscript, University of Oregon, 1973.

MacPhillamy, D. J., & Lewinsohn, P. H. Depression as a function of levels of desired and obtained pleasure. *Journal of Abnormal Psychology,* 1974, **83,** 651–657.

Maddi, S. R. The existential neurosis. *Journal of Abnormal Psychology,* 1967, **72,** 311–325.

Maher, B. A. *Principles of psychopathology: An experimental approach.* New York: McGraw-Hill, 1966.

Maher, B. A. *Journal of Consulting and Clinical Psychology,* 1974, **42,** 1–3. (Editorial).

Mahler, M. S. On child psychosis and schizophrenia: Autistic and symbiotic infantile psychoses. In *Psychoanalytic Study of the Child,* Vol. 7. New York: International Univerties Press, 1952.

Mahoney, M. J. Research issues in self-management. *Behavior Therapy,* 1972, **3,** 45–63.

Mahoney, M. J. *Cognition and behavior modification.* Cambridge, Mass.: Ballinger, 1974.

Mahoney, M. J. *Abnormal psychology: Perspectives on human variance.* New York: Harper and Row, 1980.

Main, T. F. Perception and ego-function. *British Journal of Medical Psychology,* 1958, **31,** 1–7.

Mandler, G. Anxiety. In D. L. Sills (Ed.), *International encyclopedia of the social sciences.* New York: Macmillan, 1966.

Mandler, G., & Sarason, S. B. A study of anxiety and learning. *Journal of Abnormal and Social Psychology,* 1952, **47,** 561–565.

Mann, A. U. Psychiatric morbidity and hostility in hypertension. *Psychological Medicine,* 1977, **7,** 653–659.

Mannello, T. A., & Seaman, F. J. Prevalence, costs and handling of drinking problems on seven railroads. Washington, D.C.: University Research Corporation, 1979.

Margolin, G. The relationship among marital assessment procedures: A correlational study. *Journal of Consulting and Clinical Psychology,* 1978, **46,** 1556–1558.

Margolin, G., & Weiss, R. L. Comparative evaluation of therapeutic components associated with behavioral marital treatment. *Journal of Consulting and Clinical Psychology,* 1978, **46,** 1476–1486.

Maricq, H. R., & Edelberg, R. Electrodermal recovery rate in a schizophrenic population. *Psychophysiology,* 1975, **12,** 630–634.

Marijuana research findings: 1980. Washington, D.C.: U.S. Government Printing Office, 1980.

Marks, I. M. *Fears and phobias.* New York: Academic Press, 1969.

Marks, I. M., & Gelder, M. G. Different onset ages in varieties of phobia. *American Journal of psychiatry,* 1966, **123,** 218, 221.

Marks, I. M., & Gelder, M. G., Transvestism and fetishism: Clinical and psychological changes during faradic aversion. *British Journal of Psychiatry,* 1967, **113,** 711–729.

Marks, I. M., Gelder, M. G., & Bancroft, J. Sexual deviants two years after electrical aversion. *British Journal of Psychiatry,* 1970, **117,** 73–85.

Marlatt, G. A., Demming, B., & Reid, J. B. Loss of control drinking in alcoholics: An experimental analogue. *Journal of Abnormal Psychology,* 1973, **81,** 233–241.

Marmor, J. Psychoanalytic therapy as an educational process: Common denominators in the therapeutic approaches of different psychoanalytic schools. In J. H. Masserman (Ed.), *Science and psychoanalysis.* Vol. 5. *Psychoanalytic education.* New York: Grune and Stratton, 1962.

Marshall, J. R. Changes in aged white male suicide: 1948–1972. *Journal of Gerontology,* 1978, **33,** 763–768.

Marshall, W. L., Gauthier, J., & Gordon, A. The current status of flooding therapy. In M. Hersen, R. M. Eisler, & P. M. Miller. *Progress in behavior modification,* Vol. 7. New York: Academic Press, 1979.

Marston, A., & Marston, M. *Comprehensive weight control,* New York: BMA Cassettes, 1980.

Martin, B. The assessment of anxiety by physiological behav-ioral measures. *Psychological Bulletin,* 1961, **58,** 234–255.

Martin, D., & Lyon, P. *Lesbian/woman.* New York: Bantam, 1972.

Martin, R. *Legal challenges to behavior modification: Trends in schools, corrections, and mental health.* Champaign, Ill.: Research Press, 1975.

Maslow, A. H. *Toward a psychology of being.* New York: Van Nostrand Reinhold, 1968.

Massie, H. N., & Beels, C. C. The outcome of family treatment of schizophrenia. *Schizophrenia Bulletin,* 1972, **1,** 24–36.

Masters, W. H., & Johnson, V. E. *Human sexual response.* Boston: Little, Brown, 1966.

Masters, W. H., & Johnson, V. E. *Human sexual inadequacy.* Boston: Little, Brown, 1970.

Matefy, R. E. Role-play theory of psychedelic drug flashbacks. *Journal of Consulting and Clinical Psychology,* 1980, **48,** 551–553.

Mathe, A., & Knapp, P. Emotional and adrenal reactions of stress in bronchial asthma. *Psychosomatic Medicine,* 1971, **33,** 323–329.

Mausner, B. An ecological view of cigarette smoking. *Journal of Abnormal Psychology,* 1973, **81,** 115–126.

May, P. R. A. *Treatment of schizophrenia: A comparative study of five treatment methods.* New York: Science House, 1968.

May, P. R. A. Psychotherapy research in schizophrenia—Another view of present reality. *Schizophrenia Bulletin,* 1974, **1,** 126–132.

May, P. R. A., Tuma, A. H., Yale, C., Potepan, P., & Dixon, W. J. Schizophrenia—A follow-up study of results of treatment: II. Hospital stay over two to five years. *Psychiatry,* 1976, **33,** 481–486.

Maynard, R. Omaha pupils given "behavior" drugs. *Washington Post,* June 29, 1970.

Mays, D. T., & Franks, C. M. Getting worse: Psychotherapy or no treatment—The jury should still be out. *Professional Psychology,* 1980, **11,** 78–92.

McAdoo, W. G., & DeMyer, M. K. Personality characteristics of parents. In M. Rutter & E. Schopler (Eds.), *Autism: A reappraisal of concepts and treatment.* New York: Plenum Press, 1978.

McCary, J. L. *Human sexuality.* (2nd ed.) New York: Van Nostrand Reinhold, 1973.

McClelland, D. C. Sources of hypertension in the drive for power. Paper presented as The Kittay Scientific Foundation Symposium "Psychopathology and Human Adaptation," New York, 1975.

McClelland, D. C., Davis, W. N., Kalin, R., & Wanner, E. *The drinking man.* New York: The Free Press, 1972.

McCord, J., McCord, W., & Thurber, E. Some effects of paternal absence on male children. *Journal of Abnormal and Social Psychology*, 1962, 64, 361–369.

McCord, W., & McCord, J. *The psychopath: An essay on the criminal mind.* New York: Van Nostrand Reinhold, 1964.

McCord, W., McCord, J., & Gudeman, J. Some current theories of alcoholism. *Quarterly Journal of Studies on Alcohol*, 1959, **20**, 727–749.

McCord, W., McCord, J., & Gudeman, J. *Origins of alcoholism.* Stanford, Calif.: Stanford University Press, 1960.

McFall, R. M., & Hammen, C. L. Motivation, structure, and self-monitoring: Role of nonspecific factors in smoking reduction. *Journal of Consulting and Clinical Psychology*, 1971, **37**, 80–86.

McFall, R. M., & Lillesand, D. B. Behavior rehearsal with modelling and coaching in assertion training. *Journal of Abnormal Psychology*, 1971, **77**, 313–323.

McGhie, A., & Chapman, J. S. Disorders of attention and perception in early schizophrenia. *British Journal of Medical Psychology*, 1961, **34**, 103–116.

McGuigan, F. J. Covert oral behavior and auditory hallucinations. *Psychophysiology*, 1966, **3**, 421–428.

McGuire, R. J., Carlisle, J. M., & Young, B. G. Sexual deviations as conditioned behaviour: A hypothesis. *Behaviour Research and Therapy*, 1965, **2**, 185–190.

McMullen, S., & Rosen, R. C. Self-administered masturbation training in the treatment of primary orgasmic dysfunction. *Journal of Consulting and Clinical Psychology*, 1979, **47**, 912–918.

McNeil, E. *The quiet furies.* Englewood Cliffs, N.J.: Prentice-Hall, 1967.

Mednick, B. R. Breakdown in high-risk subjects: Familial and early environmental factors. *Journal of Abnormal Psychology*, 1973, **82**, 469–475.

Mednick, S. A. A learning theory approach to research in schizophrenia. *Psychological Bulletin*, 1958, **55**, 316–327.

Mednick, S. A. A longitudinal study of children with high-risk for schizophrenia, *Mental Hygiene*, 1966, **50**, 522–535.

Mednick, S. A. Breakdown in individuals at high-risk for schizophrenia: Possible predispositional perinatal factors. *Mental Hygiene*, 1970, **54**, 50–63.

Mednick. S. A. Berkson's fallacy and high-risk research. In L. C. Wynne, R. L. Cromwell, & S. Matthysse (Eds.), *The nature of schizophrenia.* New York: Wiley, 1978.

Mednick, S. A., & Hutchings, B. Genetic and psychophysiological factors in psychopathic behaviour. In R. D. Hare & D. Schalling (Eds.), *Psychopathic behaviour: Approaches to research.* New York: Wiley, 1978.

Mednick, S. A., & Schulsinger, F. Some premorbid characteristics related to breakdown in children with schizophrenic mothers. In D. Rosenthal & S. S. Kety (Eds.), *The transmission of schizophrenia.* Elmsford, N.Y.: Pergamon Press, 1968.

Medvedev, Z. *A question of madness.* New York: Knopf, 1972.

Meehl, P. E. Schizotaxia, schizotypy, schizophrenia. *American Psychologist*, 1962, **17**, 827–838.

Meichenbaum, D. H. Cognitive modification of test-anxious college students. *Journal of Consulting and Clinical Psychology*, 1972, **39**, 370–380.

Meichenbaum, D. H. *Cognitive-behavior modification.* New York: Plenum Press, 1977.

Meichenbaum, D. H., Gilmore, J. B., & Fedoravicius, A. Group insight vs. group desensitization in treating speech anxiety. *Journal of Consulting and Clinical Psychology*, 1971, **36**, 410–421.

Meichenbaum, D. H., & Goodman, J. Training impulsive children to talk to themselves: A means of developing self-control. *Journal of Abnormal Psychology*, 1971, **77**, 115–126.

Melamed, B. G., Hawes, R. R., Heiby, E., & Glick, J. Use of filmed modelling to reduce uncooperative behavior of children during dental treatment. *Journal of Dental Research*, 1975, **54**, 797–801.

Melamed, B. G., & Siegel, L. J. Reduction of anxiety in children facing hospitalization and surgery by use of filmed modeling. *Journal of Consulting and Clinical Psychology*, 1975, **43**, 511–521.

Mello, N. K., & Mendelson, J. H. Experimentally induced intoxication in alcoholics: A comparison between programmed and spontaneous drinking. *Journal of Pharmacology and Experimental Therapy*, 1970, **173**, 101.

Mellor, C. S. First rank symptoms of schizophrenia. *British Journal of Psychiatry*, 1970, **117**, 15–23.

Meltzer, H. Y., Sachar, E. J., & Frantz, A. G. Serum prolactin levels in acutely psychotic patients: An indirect measurement of central dopaminergic activity. In E. Usdin (Ed.), *Neuropsychopharmacology of monoamines and their regulatory enzymes.* New York: Raven Press, 1974.

Mendels, J., & Cochrane, C. The nosology of depression. The endogenous-receptive concept. *American Journal of Psychiatry*, 1968, **124**, 1–11.

Mendels, J., Fieve, A., Fitzgerand, R. G., Ramsey, T. A., & Stokes, J. W. Biogenic amine metabolites in cerebrospinal fluid of depressed and manic patients. *Science*, 1972, **175**, 1380–1382.

Mendels, J., Stinnett, J. L., Burns, D., & Frazer, A. Amine precursors and depression. *Archives of General Psychiatry*, 1975, **32**, 22–30.

Mendelson, J. H. Experimentally induced chronic intoxication and withdrawal in alcoholics. *Quarterly Journal of Studies on Alcohol*, Supplement 2, 1964.

Mendelson, J. H., Rossi, A. M., & Meyer, R. E. (Eds.) *The use of marijuana, A psychological and physiological inquiry.* New York: Plenum Press, 1974.

Mendelson, W.., Johnson, N., & Stewart, M. A. Hyperactive children as teenagers: A follow-up study. *Journal of Nervous and Mental Disease,* 1971, **153,** 273–279.

Mendlewicz, J., & Rainer, J. D. Adoption study supporting genetic transmission in manic-depressive illness. *Nature,* 1977, **268,** 327–329.

Metalsky, G. I., Abramson, L. V., Seligman, M. E. P., Semmel, A., Peterson, C., & Von Baeyer, C. Attributional styles and affective reactions to life events in the classroom: A test of the reformulated model of learned helplessness and depression. *Journal of Personality and Social Psychology,* in press.

Metzner, R., Litwin, G., & Weil, G. M. The relation of expectation and mood to psilocybin reactions. *Psychedelic Review,* 1965, **5,** 3–39.

Meyer, A. The aims and meaning of psychiatric diagnosis. *American Journal of Insanity,* 1917, **74,** 163–168.

Meyer, A. Genetic-dynamic psychology versus nosology, 1926. In E. E. Winters (Ed.), *The collected papers of Adolph Meyer,* Vol. 3. Baltimore: Johns Hopkins University Press, 1951.

Meyer, J., & Reter, D. J. Sex reassignment follow-up. *Archives of General Psychiatry,* 1979, **36,** 1010–1015.

Meyer, V. Modification of expectations in cases with obsessional rituals. *Behaviour Research and Therapy,* 1966, **4,** 273–280.

Meyer, V., & Chesser, E. S. *Behavior therapy in clinical psychiatry.* Baltimore: Penguin, 1970.

Meyer, V., Robertson, J., & Tatlow, A. Home treatment of an obsessive-compulsive disorder by response prevention. *Journal of Behavior Therapy and Experimental Psychiatry,* 1975, **6,** 37–38.

Meyer-Bahlburg, H. Sex hormones and female homosexuality: A critical examiation. *Archives of Sexual Behavior,* 1979, **8,** 101–119.

Miklich, D. R., Rewey, H. H., Weiss, J. H., & Kolton, S. A preliminary investigation of psychophysiological responses to stress among different subgroups of asthmatic children. *Journal of Psychosomatic Research,* 1973, **17,** 1–8.

Milgram, N. A. Cognition and language in mental retardation: Directions and implications. In D. K. Routh (Ed.), *The experimental psychology of mental retardation.* Chicago: Aldine, 1973.

Miller, I. W., & Norman, W. H. Learned helplessness in humans: A review and attribution theory model. *Psychological Bulletin,* 1979, **86,** 93–118.

Miller, M. Geriatric suicide: The Arizona study. *The Gerontologist,* 1978, **18,** 488–495.

Miller, N. E. The influence of past experience upon the transfer of subsequent training. Unpublished doctoral dissertation, Yale University, 1935.

Miller, N. E. Studies of fear as an acquirable drive: I. Fear as motivation and fear-reduction as reinforcement in the learning of new responses. *Journal of Experimental Psychology,* 1948, **38,** 89–101.

Miller, N. E. Liberalization of basic S-R concepts: Extensions to conflict behavior, motivation, and social learning. In S. Koch (Ed.), *Psychology: A study of a science,* Vol. 2. New York: McGraw-Hill, 1959.

Miller, R. G., Palkes, H. S., & Stewart, M. A. Hyperactive children in suburban elementary schools. *Child Psychiatry and Human Development,* 1973, **4,** 121–127.

Miller, W. R., Seligman, M. E. P., & Kurlander, H. M. Learned helplessness, depression, and anxiety. *Journal of Nervous and Mental Disease,* 1975, **161,** 347–357.

Milton, O., & Wahler, R. G. (Eds.) *Behavior disorders: Perspectives and trends.* (2nd ed.) Philadelphia: Lippincott, 1969.

Mintz, E. Time-extended marathon groups. *Psychotherapy,* 1967, **4,** 65–70.

Mintz, R. S. Psychotherapy of the suicidal patient. In H. L. P. Resnik (Ed.), *Suicidal behaviors.* Boston: Little, Brown, 1968.

Mintz, S., & Alpert, M. Imagery vividness, reality testing, and schizophrenic hallucinations. *Journal of Abnormal Psychology,* 1972, **79,** 310–316.

Minuchin, S., Baker, L., Rosman, B. L., Liebman, R., Milman, L., & Todd, T. C. A conceptual model of psychosomatic illness in children: Family organization and family therapy. *Archives of General Psychiatry,* 1975, **32,** 1031–1038.

Mirsky, I. A. Physiologic, psychologic, and social determinants in the etiology of duodenal ulcer. *American Journal of Digestive Diseases,* 1958, **3,** 285–314.

Mischel, W. *Personality and assessment.* New York: Wiley, 1968.

Mischel, W. Toward a cognitive social learning reconceptualization of personality. *Psychological Review,* 1973, **80,** 252–283.

Mischel, W. On the future of personality assessment. *American Psychologist,* 1977, **32,** 246–254.

Mishler, E. G., & Waxler, N. E. *Interaction in families: An experimental study of family processes and schizophrenia.* New York: Wiley, 1968.

Mohr, J. W., Turner, R. E., & Jerry, M. B. *Pedophilia and exhibitionism.* Toronto: University of Toronto Press, 1964.

Monahan, J. The psychiatrization of criminal behavior. *Hospital and Community Psychiatry,* 1973, **24,** 105–107.

Monahan, J. The prevention of violence. In J. Monahan (Ed.),

Community mental health and the criminal justice system. Elmsford, N.Y.: Pergamon Press, 1976.

Monahan, J. Prisons: A wary verdict on rehabilitation. *Washington Post,* April 30, 1977, A13.

Monahan, J. Prediction research and the emergency commitment of dangerous mentally ill persons: A reconsideration. *American Journal of Psychiatry,* 1978, **135,** 198–201.

Monahan, J. *The clinical prediction of violent behavior.* Rockville, Md.: National Institute of Mental Health, 1981.

Monahan, J., Caldeira, C., & Friedlander, H. The police and the mentally ill: A comparison of arrested and committed persons. *International Journal of Law and Psychiatry,* 1979, **2,** 509–518.

Money, J., & Ehrhardt, A. *Man and woman, boy and girl.* Baltimore: Johns Hopkins University Press, 1972.

Money, J., Hampson, J. G., & Hampson, J. L. An examination of some basic sexual concepts: The evidence of human hermaphroditism. *Johns Hopkins Hospital Bulletin,* 1955, **97,** 301–319.

Moniz, E. *Tentatives opératoires dans le traitement de certaines psychoses.* Paris: Masson, 1936.

Monroe, J. L. Psychological and physiological differences between good and poor sleepers. *Journal of Abnormal Psychology,* 1968, **72,** 255–264.

Moos, R. H. *Evaluating treatment environments.* New York: Wiley, 1974.

Moreno, J. L., & Kipper, D. A. Group psychodrama and community-centered counseling. In G. M. Gazda (Ed.), *Basic approaches to group psychotherapy and group counseling.* Springfield, Ill.: Charles C Thomas, 1968.

Morganstern, K. P. Implosive therapy and flooding procedures: A critical review. *Psychological Bulletin,* 1973, **79,** 318–334.

Morris, A. A. Criminal insanity. *Washington Review,* 1968, **43,** 583–622.

Morris, J. *Conundrum.* New York: Harcourt Brace Jovanovitch, 1974.

Morris, J. B., & Beck, A. T. The efficacy of antidepressant drugs. *Archives of General Psychiatry,* 1974, **30,** 667–674.

Morris, N. Impediments to legal reform. *University of Chicago Law Review,* 1966, **33,** 627–656.

Morrison, J. R., & Stewart, M. A. A family study of the hyperactive child syndrome. *Biological Psychiatry,* 1971, **3,** 189–195.

Morrison, J. R., & Stewart, M. A. The psychiatric status of the legal families of adopted hyperactive children. *Archives of General Psychiatry,* 1973, **28,** 888–891.

Mowrer, O. H. A stimulus-response analysis of anxiety and its role as a reinforcing agent. *Psychological Review,* 1939, **46,** 553–565.

Mowrer, O. H. On the dual nature of learning—a reinterpretation of "conditioning" and "problem-solving." *Harvard Educational Review,* 1947, **17,** 102–148.

Mowrer, O. H. *Learning theory and personality dynamics.* New York: Ronald Press, 1950.

Mowrer, O. H., & Mowrer, W. M. Enuresis: A method for its study and treatment. *American Journal of Orthopsychiatry,* 1938, **8,** 436–459.

Mowrer, O. H., & Viek, P. An experimental analogue of fear from a sense of helplessness. *Journal of Abnormal and Social Psychology,* 1948, **43,** 193–200.

Munjack, D. J., & Kanno, P. H. Retarded ejaculation: A review. *Archives of Sexual Behavior,* 1979, **8,** 139–150.

Murphy, D. L., & Wyatt, R. J. Reduced MAO activity in blood platelets from schizophrenic patients. *Nature,* 1972, **238,** 225–226.

Naranjo, C. Present-centeredness: Technique, prescription, and ideal. In J. Fagan & I. L. Shepherd (Eds.), *Gestalt therapy now: Theory, techniques, applications.* Palo Alto, Calif.: Science and Behavior Books, 1970.

Nathan, P. E., & Goldman, M. S. Problem drinking and alcoholism. In O. F. Pomerleau & J. P. Brady (Eds.), *Behavioral medicine: Therapy and practice.* Baltimore: Williams and Wilkins, 1979.

Nathan, P. E., & Harris, S. L. *Psychopathology and society.* (2nd ed.) New York: McGraw-Hill, 1980.

Nathan, P. E., Samaraweera, A., Andberg, M. M., & Patch, V. D. Syndromes of psychosis and psychoneurosis. *Archives of General Psychiatry,* 1968, **19,** 704–716.

Nathan, P. E., Titler, N. A., Lowenstein, L. W., Solomon, P., & Rossi, A. M. Behavioral analysis of chronic alcoholism. *Archives of General Psychiatry,* 1970, **22,** 419–430.

National Cancer Institute. *The smoking digest: Progress report on a nation kicking the habit.* Washington, D.C.: U.S. Department of Health, Education and Welfare, October 1977.

National Institutes of Health. *Teenage smoking, national patterns of cigarette smoking, ages 12 through 18.* Washington, D.C.: U.S. Department of Health, Education and Welfare, 1976.

National Survey on Drug Abuse, 1979. Washington, D.C.: National Institute on Drug Abuse, 1979.

Nawas, M. M., Fishman, S. T., & Pucel, J. C. The standardized desensitization program applicable to group and individual treatment. *Behaviour Research and Therapy,* 1970, **6,** 63–68.

Neale, J. M. Perceptual span in schizophrenia. *Journal of Abnormal Psychology,* 1971, **77,** 196–204.

Neale, J. M., & Katahn, M. Anxiety, choice and stimulus uncertainty. *Journal of Personality,* 1968, **36,** 238–245.

Neale, J. M., & Liebert, R. M. Reinforcement therapy using aides and patients as behavioral technicians: A case report of a mute psychotic. *Perceptual and Motor Skills,* 1969, **28,** 835–839.

Neale, J. M., & Liebert, R. M. *Science and behavior: An introduction to methods of research.* Englewood Cliffs, N.J.: Prentice-Hall, 1973.

Neale, J. M., & Oltmanns, T. F. *Schizophrenia.* New York: Wiley, 1980.

Nelson, J. C., & Bowers, M. B. Delusional unipolar depression. *Archives of General Psychiatry,* 1978, **35,** 1321–1328.

Nelson, R. E. Irrational beliefs in depression. *Journal of Consulting and Clinical Psychology,* 1977, **45,** 1190–1191.

Nelson, R. E., & Craighead, W. E. Selective recall of positive and negative feedback, self-control behaviors, and depression. *Journal of Abnormal Psychology,* 1977, **86,** 379–388.

Nelson, R. O. Assessment and therapeutic functions of self-monitoring, In M. Hersen, R. M. Eisler, & P. M. Miller (Eds.), *Progress in behavior modification.* New York: Academic Press, 1977.

Nelson, R. O., Lipinski, D. P., & Black, J. L. The effects of expectancy on the reactivity of self-recording. *Behavior Therapy,* 1975, **6,** 337–349.

Nelson, R. O., Lipinski, D. P., & Black, J. L. The reactivity of adult retardates' self-monitoring: A comparison among behaviors of difference valences, and a comparison with token reinforcement. *Psychological Record,* 1976, **26,** 189–201.

Nelson, R. O., Lipinski, D. P., & Boykin, R. A. The effects of self-recorders' training and the obtrusiveness of the self-recording device on the accuracy and reactivity of self-monitoring. *Behavior Therapy,* 1978, **9,** 200–208.

Nemetz, G. H., Craig, K. D., & Reith, G. Treatment of female sexual dysfunction through symbolic modeling. *Journal of Consulting and Clinical Psychology,* 1978, **46,** 62–73.

Nesbitt, P. D. Smoking, physiological arousal, and emotional response. *Journal of Personality and Social Psychology,* 1973, **25,** 137–144.

Neugarten, B. L. Personality and aging. In J. E. Birren & K. W. Schaie (Eds.), *Handbook of the psychology of aging.* New York: Van Nostrand Reinhold, 1977.

Neugebauer, R. Mediaeval and early modern theories of mental illness. *Archives of General Psychiatry,* 1979, **36,** 477–484.

Neuhaus, E. C. A personality study of asthmatic and cardiac children. *Psychosomatic Medicine,* 1958, **20,** 181–186.

Neuringer, C. Rigid thinking in suicidal individuals. *Journal of Consulting Psychology,* 1964, **28,** 54–58.

Newmark, C. S., Frerking, R. A., Cook, L., & Newmark, L. Endorsement of Ellis' irrational beliefs as a function of psychopathology. *Journal of Clinical Psychology,* 1973, **29,** 300–302.

Nisbett, R. E., & Wilson, T. D. Telling more than we can know: Verbal reports on mental processes. *Psychological Review,* 1977, **84,** 231–259.

Nowlan, R., & Cohen, S. Tolerance to marijuana: Heart rate and subjective "high." *Clinical Pharmacology Therapeutics,* 1977, **22,** 550–556.

Nowlis, D. P., & Kamiya, J. The control of electroencephalographic alpha rhythms through auditory feedback and the associated mental activity. *Psychophysiology,* 1970, **6,** 476–484.

Noyes, R., Clancy, J., Crowe, R., Hoenk, P. R., & Slymen, D. J. The familial prevalence of anxiety neurosis. *Archives of General Psychiatry,* 1978, **35,** 1057–1059.

Nunnally, J. C. *Psychometric theory.* New York: McGraw-Hill, 1967.

Nyhan, W. L. Disorders of nucleic acid metabolism. In G. E. Gaull (Ed.), *Biology of brain dysfunction.* New York: Plenum Press, 1973.

O'Connor, R. D. Modification of social withdrawal through symbolic modeling. *Journal of Applied Behavior Analysis,* 1969, **2,** 15–22.

Office of the Comptroller, The City of New York. Performance analysis of programs of New York State assistance to New York City agencies serving deinstitutionalized psychiatric patients. September 21, 1979. As cited in E. Baxter & K. Hopper, *Private lives/public spaces: Homeless adults on the streets of New York City.* New York: Community Service Society, 1981.

Öhman, A., Erixon, G., & Löfberg, I. Phobias and preparedness: Phobic versus neutral pictures as conditioned stimuli for human autonomic responses. *Journal of Abnormal Psychology,* 1975; **84,** 41–45.

O'Leary, K. D. Pills or skills for hyperactive children. *Journal of Applied Behavior Analysis,* 1980, **13,** 191–204.

O'Leary, K. D., & O'Leary, S. G. (Eds.) *Classroom management.* (2nd ed.) Elmsford, N.Y.: Pergamon Press, 1977.

O'Leary, K. D., Pelham, W. E., Rosenbaum, A., & Price, G. H. Behavioral treatment of hyperkinetic children: An experimental evaluation of its usefulness. *Clinical Pediatrics,* 1976, **15,** 510–515.

O'Leary, K. D., & Turkewitz, H. Marital therapy from a behavioral perspective. In T. J. Paolino, Jr., & B. S. McCrady (Eds.), *Marriage and marital therapy.* New York: Brunner/Mazel, 1978.

O'Leary, K. D., Turkewitz, H., & Taffel, S. J. Parent and therapist evaluation of behavior therapy in a child psychological clinic. *Journal of Consulting and Clinical Psychology,* 1973, **41,** 289–293.

O'Leary, K. D., & Wilson, G. T. *Behavior therapy: Application and outcome.* Englewood Cliffs, N.J.: Prentice-Hall, 1975.

Oltmanns, T. F., Broderick, J. E., & O'Leary, K. D. Marital adjustment and the efficacy of behavior therapy with children. Paper presented at the Association for the Advancement of Behavior Therapy, New York City, December 1976.

Oltmanns, T. F., O'Hayon, J., & Neale, J. M. The effects of anti-psychotic medication and diagnostic criteria on distractibility in schizophrenia. *Journal of Psychiatric Research,* 1978, **14,** 81–92.

Oltmanns, T. F., Weintraub, S., & Neale, J. M. Cognitive slippage in children vulnerable to schizophrenia. Paper presented at the 84th Annual Convention of the American Psychological Association, 1976.

Orenstein, H., & Carr, J. Implosive therapy by tape-recording. *Behaviour Research and Therapy,* 1975, **13,** 177–182.

Orne, M. T. The nature of hypnosis: Artifact and essence. *Journal of Abnormal and Social Psychology,* 1959, **58,** 277–299.

Orris, J. B. Visual monitoring performance in three subgroups of male delinquents. Unpublished M.A. thesis, University of Illinois, 1967.

Osgood, C. E., Luria, Z., & Smith, S. W. II. A blind analysis of another case of multiple personality using the semantic personality technique. *Journal of Abnormal Psychology,* 1976, **85,** 256–270.

Osgood, C. E., Suci, G. J., & Tannenbaum, P. H. *The measurement of meaning.* Urbana: University of Illinois Press, 1957.

Overton, D. A. State-dependent learning produced by depressant and atropine-like drugs. *Psychopharmacologia,* 1966, **10,** 6–31.

Page, E. P. Miracle in Milwaukee: Raising the IQ. In B. Z. Friedlander, G. M. Sterritt, & G. E. Kirk (Eds.), *Exceptional infant.* Vol. 3. *Assessment and intervention.* New York: Brunner/Mazel, 1975.

Pahnke, W. N. Drugs and mysticism. Unpublished doctoral dissertation, Harvard University, 1963.

Parloff, M. B., Waskow, I. E., & Wolfe, B. E. Research on therapist variables in relation to process and outcome. In S. L. Garfield & A. E. Bergin (Eds.), *Handbook of psychotherapy and behavior change: An empirical analysis,* (2nd ed.) New York: Wiley, 1978.

Parsons, O. A. Brain damage in alcoholics: Altered states of consciousness. In M. M. Gross (Ed.), *Alcohol intoxication and withdrawal.* New York: Plenum Press, 1975.

Pasamanick, B., Rogers, M., & Lilienfeld, M. A. Pregnancy experience and the development of behavior disorder in children. *American Journal of Psychiatry,* 1956, **112,** 613–617.

Paskewitz, D. A., & Orne, M. T. Visual effects on alpha feedback training. *Science,* 1973, **181,** 360–363.

Patsiokas, A. T., Clum, G. A., & Luscomb, R. L. Cognitive characteristics of suicide attempters. *Journal of Consulting and Clinical Psychology,* 1979, **47,** 478–484.

Patterson, G. R. A basis for identifying stimuli which control behaviors in natural settings. *Child Development,* 1974, **45,** 900–911. (a)

Patterson, G. R. Interventions for boys with conduct problems: Multiple settings, treatments, and criteria. *Journal of Consulting and Clinical Psychology,* 1974, **42,** 471–481. (b)

Patterson, G. R., Cobb, J. A., & Ray, R. S. A social engineering technology for retraining families of aggressive boys. In H. E. Adams & I. P. Unikel (Eds.), *Issues and trends in behavior therapy.* Springfield, Ill.: Charles C Thomas, 1973.

Patterson, G. R., Ray, R. S., Shaw, D. A., & Cobb, J. A. *Manual for coding of family interactions.* New York: ASIS/NAPS, Microfiche Publications, 1969.

Patterson, G. R., & Reid, J. B. Reciprocity and coercion: Two facets of social systems. In C. Neuringer & J. Michael (Eds.), *Behavior modification in clinical psychology.* New York: Appleton-Century-Crofts, 1970.

Paul, G. L. *Insight vs. desensitization in psychotherapy.* Stanford, Calif.: Stanford University Press, 1966.

Paul, G. L. Insight versus desensitization in psychotherapy two years after termination. *Journal of Consulting Psychology,* 1967, **31,** 333–348.

Paul, G. L. Chronic mental patient: Current status—future directions. *Psychological Bulletin,* 1969, **71,** 81–94.

Paul, G. L., & Lentz, R. J. *Psychosocial treatment of chronic mental patients: Milieu versus social learning programs.* Cambridge, Mass.: Harvard University Press, 1977.

Paul, G. L., & Shannon, D. T. Treatment of anxiety through systematic desensitization in therapy groups. *Journal of Abnormal Psychology,* 1966, **71,** 124–135.

Pavlov, I. P. *Lecture on conditioned reflexes.* New York: International Publishers, 1928.

Paykel, E. S. Recent life events and clinical depression. In E. K. E. Gunderson & R. H. Rahe (Eds.), *Life stress and illness.* Springfield, Ill.: Charles C Thomas, 1974.

Pearson, C., & Gatz, M. Health and mental health in older adults: First steps in the study of a pedestrian complaint. *Rehabilitation Psychology,* in press.

Pechacek, T. F. Modification of smoking behavior. In N. A. Krasnegor (Ed.), *The behavioral aspects of smoking.* Washington, D.C.: National Institute on Drug Abuse, 1979.

Pentoney, P. Value change in psychotherapy. *Human Relations,* 1966, **19,** 39–46.

Perley, M. J., & Guze, S. B. Hysteria—the stability and usefulness of clinical criteria. *New England Journal of Medicine,* 1962, **266,** 421–426.

Perlmutter, M. What is memory aging the aging of? *Developmental Psychology,* 1978, **14,** 330–345.

Perls, F. S. *Ego, hunger, and aggression.* New York: Vintage, 1947.

Perls, F. S. *Gestalt therapy verbatim.* Moab, Utah: Real People Press, 1969.

Perls, F. S. Four lectures. In J. Fagan & I. L. Shepherd (Eds.), *Gestalt therapy now: Therapy, techniques, applications.* Palo Alto, Calif.: Science and Behavior Books. 1970.

Perls, F. S., Hefferline, R. F., & Goodman, P. *Gestalt therapy: Excitement and growth in the human personality.* New York: Julian Press, 1951.

Perris, L. The separation of bipolar (manic-depressive) from unipolar recurrent depressive psychoses. *Behavioral Neuropsychiatry,* 1969, **1,** 17–25.

Pervin, L. A. The need to predict and control under conditions of threat. *Journal of Personality,* 1963, **31,** 570–585.

Peters, J. E., & Stern, R. M. Specificity of attitude hypothesis in psychosomatic medicine: A reexamination. *Journal of Psychosomatic Research,* 1971, **15,** 129–135.

Peters, J. J. The Philadelphia rape victim project. In D. Chappell, R. Geis, & G. Geis. (Eds.), *Forcible rape: The crime, the victim, and the offender.* New York: Columbia University Press, 1977.

Peters, M. Hypertension and the nature of stress. *Science,* 1977, **198,** 80.

Pfeiffer, E. Psychopathology and social pathology. In J. E. Birren & K. W. Schaie, (Eds.), *Handbook of psychology and aging.* New York: Van Nostrand Reinhold, 1977.

Pfeiffer, E., & Busse, E. W. Mental disorders in later life—Affective disorders: Paranoid, neurotic and situational reactions. In E. W. Busse & E. Pfeiffer (Eds.), *Mental illness in later life.* Washington D.C.: American Psychiatric Association, 1973.

Pfeiffer, E., Eisenstein, R. B., & Dabbs, G. E. Mental competency evaluation for the federal courts: I. Methods and results. *Journal of Nervous and Mental Disease,* 1967, **144,** 320–328.

Pfeiffer, E., Verwoerdt, A., & Wang, H. S. Sexual behavior in aged men and women: I. Observations on 254 community volunteers. *Archives of General Psychiatry,* 1968, **19,** 753–758.

Pfeiffer, E., Verwoerdt, A., & Wang, H. S. The natural history of sexual behavior in a biologically advantaged group of aged individuals. *Journal of Gerontology,* 1969, **24,** 193–198.

Phares, J. *Clinical psychology: Concepts, methods, and professions.* Homewood, Ill.: Dorsey Press, 1979.

Phillips, E. L., Phillips, E. A., Fixsen, D. L., & Wolf, M. M. *The teaching-family handbook.* Lawrence, Kans.: Kansas Printing Service, 1972.

Phillips, L. Case history data and prognosis in schizophrenia. *Journal of Nervous and Mental Disease,* 1953, **117,** 515–525.

Piaget, J. *The origins of intelligence in children.* (2nd ed.) New York: International Universities Press, 1952.

Pilowsky, I. Primary and secondary hypochondriasis. *Acta Psychiatrica Scandinavica,* 1970, **46,** 273–285.

Pinel, P. *A treatise on insanity,* 1801. English translation by D. D. Davis. New York: Hafner, 1962.

Pinney, J. M. Preface. In N. A. Krasnegor (Ed.), *Cigarette smoking as a dependence process.* Washington, D.C.: National Institute on Drug Abuse, 1979.

Pirsig, R. M. *Zen and the art of motorcycle maintenance: An inquiry into values.* New York: Morrow, 1974.

Plummer, S., Baer, D. M., & LeBlanc, J. M. Functional considerations in the use of time out and an effective alternative. *Journal of Applied Behavior Analysis,* 1977, **10,** 689–706.

Pokorny, A. D. Myths about suicide. In H. L. P. Resnik (Ed.), *Suicidal behaviors.* Boston: Little, Brown, 1968.

Pope, L. Motor activity in brain-injured children. *American Journal of Orthopsychiatry,* 1970, **40,** 761–770.

Post, F. *The significance of affective symptoms in old age.* London: Oxford University Press, 1962.

Post, F. Dementia, depression, and pseudodementia. In D. F. Benson & D. Blumer (Eds.), *Psychiatric aspects of neurologic disease.* New York: Grune and Stratton, 1975.

Post, R. M., Fink, E., Carpenter, W. T., & Goodwin, F. K. Cerebrospinal fluid amine metabolites in acute schizophrenia. *Archives of General Psychiatry,* 1975, **32,** 1063–1069.

Post, R. M., Kotin, J., Goodwin, F. K., & Gordon, E. K. Psychomotor activity and cerebrospinal fluid metabolites in affective illness. *American Journal of Psychiatry,* 1973, **129,** 67–72.

Prange, A. J., Wilson, I. C., Lynn, C. W., Alltop, L. B., Stikeleather, R. A., & Raleigh, N.C. L-Tryptophan in mania. *Archives of General Psychiatry,* 1974, **30,** 56–62.

President's Commission on Mental Health. Report to the President. Washington, D.C.: Superintendent of Documents, U.S. Government Printing Office, 1978.

Price, R. H. *Abnormal behavior. Perspectives in conflict.* New York: Holt, Rinehart and Winston, 1972. (a)

Price. R. H. Psychological deficit versus impression management in schizophrenic word association performance. *Journal of Abnormal Psychology,* 1972, **79,** 123–137. (b)

Preble, E., & Casey, J. J. Taking care of business—The heroin user's life in the street. *International Journal of the Addictions,* 1969, **4,** 1–24.

Prochaska, J. O. *Systems of psychotherapy.* Homewood, Ill.: Dorsey Press, 1979.

Proctor, J. T. Hysteria in childhood. *American Journal of Orthopsychiatry,* 1958, **28,** 394–407.

Proshansky, H. M., Ittelson, W. M., & Rivlin, L. (Eds.) *Theory and research in environmental psychology.* New York: Holt, Rinehart and Winston, 1972.

Purcell, K., Brady, K., Chai, H., Muser, J., Molk, L., Gordon, N., & Means, J. The effect on asthma in children of experimental separation from the family. *Psychosomatic Medicine,* 1969, **31,** 144–164.

Purcell, K., & Weiss, J. H. Asthma. In C. G. Costello (Ed.), *Symptoms of psychopathology: A handbook.* New York: Wiley, 1970.

Quay, H. C. Personality dimensions in delinquent males as inferred from the factor analysis of behavior ratings. *Journal of Research in Crime and Delinquency,* 1964, **1,** 33–37.

Quay, H. C. Psychopathic personality as pathological stimulus seeking. *American Journal of Psychiatry,* 1965, **122,** 180–183.

Rachman, S. J. Sexual fetishism: An experimental analogue. *Psychological Record,* 1966, **16,** 293–296.

Rachman, S. J., & Hodgson, R. *Obsessions and compulsions.* Englewood Cliffs, N.J.: Prentice-Hall, 1978.

Rachman, S. J., & Wilson, G. T. *The effects of psychological therapy.* (2nd ed.) Elmsford, N.Y.: Pergamon Press, 1980.

Radloff, L. Sex differences in depression: The effects of occupation and marital status. *Sex Roles,* 1975, **1,** 249–265.

Rahe, R. H., & Holmes, T. H. Life crises and disease onset: A prospective study of life crises and health changes. Unpublished manuscript.

Rahe, R. H., & Lind, E. Psychosocial factors and sudden cardiac death: A pilot study. *Journal of Psychomatic Research,* 1971, **15,** 19–24.

Rank, O. *Will therapy.* New York: Knopf, 1936.

Rapaport, D. *The organization and pathology of thought.* New York: Columbia University Press, 1951.

Rapoport, J. L., Buchsbaum, M. S., Zahn, T. P., Weingartner, H., Ludlow, D., & Mikkelson, E. J. Dextroamphetamine: Cognitive and behavioral effects in normal prepubertal boys. *Science,* 1978, **199,** 560–563.

Rappaport, J. *Community psychology: Values, research, and action.* New York: Holt, Rinehart and Winston, 1977.

Rappaport, J., & Chinsky, J. M. Models for delivery of service from a historical and conceptual perspective. *Professional Psychology,* 1974, **5,** 42–50.

Rappaport, M. Competing voice messages: Effects of message load and drugs on the ability of acute schizophrenics to attend. *Archives of General Psychiatry,* 1967, **17,** 97–103.

Raskin, A., Schulterbrandt, J., Boothe, J., Reating, N., & McKeon, J. Treatment, social and psychiatric variables related to symptom reduction in hospitalized depressives. In J. R. Wittenborn, S. Goldberg, & P. May (Eds.), *Psychopharmacology and the individual patient.* New York: Raven Press, 1970.

Rees, J., & Botwinick, J. Detection and decision factors in auditory behavior of the elderly. *Journal of Gerontology,* 1971, **26,** 133–136.

Rees, L. The significance of parental attitudes in childhood asthma. *Journal of Psychosomatic Research,* 1963, **7,** 181–190.

Rees, L. The importance of psychological, allergic and infective factors in childhood asthma. *Journal of Psychosomatic Research,* 1964, **7,** 253–262.

Reeve, V. C. Incidence of marijuana in a California impaired driver population. Sacramento: State of California, Department of Justice, Division of Law Enforcement Investigative Services, 1979.

Reich, W. *The function of the orgasm.* New York: Noonday Press, 1942.

Reid, E. C. Autopsychology of the manic-depressive. *Journal of Nervous and Mental Disease,* 1910, **37,** 606–620.

Reinhold, R. Leveling off of drug use found among students. *The New York Times,* February 19, 1981.

Reitan, R. M. Psychological deficits resulting from cerebral lesions in man. In J. M. Warren & K. Akert (Eds.), *The frontal granular cortex and behavior.* New York: McGraw-Hill, 1964.

Rekers, G. A., & Lovaas, O. I. Behavioral treatment of deviant sex role behaviors in a male child. *Journal of Applied Behavioral Analysis,* 1974, **7,** 173–190.

Rescorla, R. A., & Solomon, R. L. Two-process learning theory: Relationships between Pavlovian conditioning and instrumental learning. *Psychological Review,* 1967, **74,** 151–182.

Resnik, H. L. P. (Ed.) *Suicidal behaviors.* Boston: Little, Brown, 1968.

Richards, P., Berk, R. A., & Forster, B. *Crime as play: Delinquency in a middle class suburb.* Cambridge, Mass.: Ballinger, 1979.

Richter, C. P. On the phenomenon of sudden death in animals and man. *Psychosomatic Medicine,* 1957, **19,** 191–198.

Ricks, D. M. The beginning of vocal communication in infants and autistic children. Unpublished dissertation, University of London, 1972.

Ridgeway, J. R. Who's fit to be free? *The New Republic,* 1967, **156,** 24–26.

Rie, H. E., Rie, E. D., Stewart, S., & Ambuel, F. P. The effects of methylphenidate on underachieving children. *Journal of Consulting and Clinical Psychology,* 1976, **44,** 250–260.

Riegel, K. F., & Riegel, R. M. Development, drop, and death. *Developmental Psychology,* 1972, **6,** 306–319.

Rimland, B. *Infantile autism.* New York: Appleton-Century-Crofts, 1964.

Rimland, B. Psychogenesis versus biogenesis: The issues and the evidence. In S. C. Plog & R. B. Edgerton (Eds.), *Changing perspectives in mental illness.* New York: Holt, Rinehart and Winston, 1969.

Rimm, D. C., & Masters, J. C. *Behavior therapy: Techniques and empirical findings.* (2nd ed.) New York: Academic Press, 1979.

Ringuette, E. L., & Kennedy, T. An experimental study of the double-bind hypothesis. *Journal of Abnormal Psychology,* 1966, **71,** 136–142.

Ritter, B. The group treatment of children's snake phobias, using vicarious and contact desensitization procedures. *Behaviour Research and Therapy,* 1968, **6,** 1–6.

Ritvo, E. R., Rabin, E., Yuwiler, A., Freeman, B. J., & Geller, E. Biochemical and hematologic studies: A critical review. In M. Rutter & E. Schopler (Eds.), *Autism: A reappraisal of concepts and treatment.* New York: Plenum Press, 1978.

Rivera, G. *Willowbrook.* New York: Random House, 1972.

Robbin, A. A. A controlled study of the effects of leuctomy. *Journal of Neurology, Neurosurgery, and Psychiatry,* 1958, **21,** 262–269.

Robbin, A. A. The value of leucotomy in relation to diagnosis. *Journal of Neurology, Neurosurgery, and Psychiatry.* 1959, **22,** 132–136.

Robey, A. Criteria for competency to stand trail: A checklist for psychiatrists. *American Journal of Pscyhiatry,* 1965, **122,** 616–622.

Robins, E., & Guze, S. Establishment of diagnostic validity in psychiatric illness: Its application to schizophrenia. *American Journal of Psychiatry,* 1970, **126,** 983–987.

Robins, L. N. *Deviant children grown up.* Baltimore, Md.: Williams and Wilkins, 1966.

Robins, L. N. Follow-up studies of behavior disorders in children. In H. C. Quay & J. S. Werry (Eds.), *Psychopathological disorders of childhood.* New York: Wiley, 1972.

Robinson, N. M., & Robinson, H. B. *The mentally retarded child.* (2nd ed.) New York: McGraw-Hill, 1976.

Rochester, S. R., Martin, J. R., & Thurston, S. Thought-process disorder in schizophrenia: The listener's task: *Brain and Language,* 1977, **4,** 95–114.

Rodin, J., & Langer, E. J., Long-term effects of a control-relevant intervention with the institutionalized aged. *Journal of Personality and Social Psychology,* 1977, **35,** 897–902.

Rogers, C. R. *Counseling and psychotherapy: New concepts in practice.* Boston: Houghton Mifflin, 1942.

Rogers, C. R. *Client-centered therapy.* Boston: Houghton Mifflin, 1951.

Rogers, C. R. *On becoming a person: A therapist's view of psychotherapy.* Boston: Houghton Mifflin, 1961.

Rogers, C. R. *Carl Rogers on encounter groups.* New York: Harper and Row, 1970.

Rogers, C. R., Gendlin, G. T., Kiesler, D. V., & Truax, C. B. *The therapeutic relationship and its impact: A study of psychotherapy with schizophrenics.* Madison: University of Wisconsin Press, 1967.

Rolf, J. E. The social and academic competence of children vulnerable to schizophrenia and other behavior disorders. *Journal of Abnormal Psychology,* 1972, **80,** 225–243.

Romanczyk, R. G., Diament, C., Goren, E. R., Trunell, G., & Harris, S. L. Increasing isolate and social play in severely disturbed children: Intervention and postintervention effectiveness. *Journal of Autism and Childhood Schizophrenia,* 1975, **43,** 730–739.

Romanczyk, R. G., Kent, R. N., Diament, C., & O'Leary, K. D. Measuring the reliability of observational data: A reactive process. *Journal of Applied Behavior Analysis,* 1973, **6,** 175–184.

Rose, R. M., Jenkins, C. D., & Hurst, M. W. *Air traffic controller health change study.* Report to the Federal Aviation Administration, 1978.

Rosen, E., Fox, R., & Gregory, I. *Abnormal psychology.* (2nd ed.) Philadelphia: Saunders, 1972.

Rosen, J. N. A method of resolving acute catatonic excitement. *Psychiatric Quaterly,* 1946, **20,** 183–198.

Rosen, R. C., & Rosen, L. *Human sexuality.* New York: Knopf, 1981.

Rosenhan, D. L. On being sane in insane places. *Science,* 1973, **179,** 250–258.

Rosenman, R. H., Brand, R. J., Jenkins, C. D., Friedman, M., Straus, R., & Wurm, M. Coronary heart disease in the Western Collaborative Group Study: Final follow-up experience of 8½ years. *Journal of the American Medical Association,* 1975, **233,** 872–877.

Rosenman, R. H., Friedman, M., Straus, R., Wurm, M., Kositichek, R., Hahn, W., & Werthessen, N. T. A predictive study of coronary heart disease. *Journal of the American Medical Association,* 1964, **189,** 103–110.

Rosenthal, D. Changes in some moral values following psychotherapy. *Journal of Consulting Psychology,* 1955, **19,** 431–436.

Rosenthal, D. *Genetic theory and abnormal behavior.* New York: McGraw-Hill, 1970.

Rosenthal, R. *Experimenter bias in behavioral research.* New York: Appleton-Century-Crofts, 1966.

Rosenthal, R. Covert communication in the psychological experiment. *Psychological Bulletin,* 1967, **67,** 356–367.

Rosenthal, T. L., & Bandura, A. Psychological modeling: Theory and practice. In S. L. Garfield & A. E. Bergin (Eds.), *Handbook of psychotherapy and behavior change: An empirical analysis.* (2nd ed.) New York: Wiley, 1978.

Rosman, B. L., Minuchin, S., & Liebman, R. Family lunch session: An introduction to family therapy in anorexia nervosa. *American Journal of Orthopsychiatry,* 1975, **45,** 846–852.

Rosman, B. L., Minuchin, S., & Liebman, R. Input and outcome of family therapy of anorexia nervosa. In J. L. Claghorn (Ed.), *Successful psychotherapy.* New York: Brunner/Mazel, 1976.

Ross, A. O. *Psychological disorders of childhood: A behavioral approach to theory, research, and practice.* (2nd ed.) New York: McGraw-Hill, 1981.

Ross, D. M. Case study of a hyperactive four-year-old. Unpublished manuscript. Stanford University, 1961.

Ross, D. M., & Ross, S. A. Storage and utilization of previously formulated mediators in educable mentally retarded children. *Journal of Educational Psychology,* 1973, **65,** 205–210.

Ross, D. M., & Ross, S. A. *Hyperactivity: Research, theory, and action.* New York: Wiley, 1976.

Ross, J. L. Anorexia nervosa: An overview. *Bulletin of the Menninger Clinic,* 1977, **41,** 418–436.

Roth, S., & Kubal, L. The effects of noncontingent reinforcement on tasks of differing importance: Facilitation and learned helplessness effects. *Journal of Personality and Social Psychology,* 1975, **32,** 680–691.

Rothman, D. *The discovery of the asylum.* New York: Harper and Row, 1971.

Rubin, V., & Comitas, L. *Ganja in Jamaica: A medical anthropological study of chronic marihuana use.* The Hague: Mouton, 1976.

Runck, B. *Biofeedback—Issues in treatment assessment.* Rockville, Md.: National Institute of Mental Health, 1980.

Rush, A. J., Beck, A. T., Kovacs, M., & Hollon, S. D. Comparative efficacy of cognitive therapy and pharmacotherapy in the treatment of depressed outpatients. *Cognitive Therapy and Research,* 1977, **1,** 17–39.

Ruskin, A., Board, O. W., & Schaffer, R. L. Blast hypertension: Elevated arterial pressure in victims of the Texas City disaster. *American Journal of Medicine,* 1948, **4,** 228–236.

Rutter, M. Prognosis: Psychotic children in adolescence and early adult life. In J. K. Wing (Ed.), *Childhood autism: Clinical, educational, and social aspects.* Elmsford, N.Y.: Pergamon Press, 1966.

Rutter, M. Psychotic disorders in early childhood. In A. J. Cooper (Ed.), *Recent developments in schizophrenia. British Journal of Psychiatry,* Special Publication 1, 1967.

Rutter, M. Parent-child separation: Psychological effects on the children. *Journal of Child Psychology and Psychiatry,* 1971, **12,** 233–260.

Rutter, M. The development of infantile autism. *Psychological Medicine,* 1974, **4,** 147–163.

Rutter, M. Maternal deprivation, 1972–1978: New findings, new concepts, new approaches. *Child Development,* 1979, **50,** 283–305.

Rutter, M., & Lockyer, L. A five to fifteen year follow-up of infantile psychosis: I. Description of sample. *British Journal of Psychiatry,* 1967, **113,** 1169–1182.

Rutter, M., Tizard, J., & Whitmore, K. *Education, health, and behavior.* London: Longmans, 1970.

Ryan, D. V., & Neale, J. M. Test taking sets and the performance of schizophrenics on laboratory tasks. *Journal of Abnormal Psychology,* 1973, **82,** 207–211.

Ryan, W. *Blaming the victim.* New York: Random House, 1971.

Sackeim, H. A., Nordlie, J. W., & Gur, R. C. A model of hysterical and hypnotic blindness: Cognition, motivation and awareness. *Journal of Abnormal Psychology,* 1979, **88,** 474–489.

Sakel, M. The pharmacological shock treatment of schizophrenia. *Nervous and Mental Disease Monograph 62,* 1938.

Sallan, S. E., Zinberg, N. E., & Frei, E. Antiemetic effect of delta-9-THC in patients receiving cancer chemotherapy. *New England Journal of Medicine,* 1975, **293,** 795–797.

Salter, A. *Conditioned reflex therapy.* New York: Farrar, Straus, 1949.

Sarbin, T. R. Contributions to role-taking theory: I. Hypnotic behavior. *Psychological Review,* 1950, **57,** 255–270.

Sargent, J. D., Green, E. E., & Walters, E. D. Preliminary report on the use of autogenic feedback techniques in the treatment of migraine headaches. *Headache,* 1972, **12,** 120-124.

Sargent, J. D., Green, E. E., & Walters, E. D. The use of autogenic feedback training in a pilot study of migraine and tension headaches. *Psychosomatic Medicine,* 1973, **35,** 129–135.

Sartorius, N., Shapiro, R., & Jablonsky, A. The international pilot study of schizophrenia. *Schizophrenia Bulletin,* 1974, **2,** 21–35.

Sassenrath, E. N., Chapman, L. F., & Goo, G. P. Reproduction in rhesus monkeys chronically exposed to moderate amounts of delta-9-tetrahydrocannabinol. In G. G. Nahas & W. D. M. Paton (Eds.), *Marihuana: Biological effects.* Elmsford, N.Y.: Pergamon Press, 1979.

Satir, V. *Conjoint family therapy.* Palo Alto, Calif.: Science and Behavior Books, 1967.

Satterfield, J. H., Cantwell, D. P., Lesser, L. I., & Podosin, R. L. Physiological studies of the hyperactive child. *American Journal of Psychiatry,* 1972, **128,** 1418–1424.

Sawrey, W. L., & Weisz, J. D. An experimental method of producing gastric ulcers: Role of psychological factors in the production of gastric ulcers in the rat. *Journal of Comparative and Physiological Psychology,* 1956, **49,** 457–461.

Scarlett, W. A. Social isolation from agemates among nursery school children. *Journal of Child Psychology and Psychiatry,* 1980, **21,** 231–240.

Schachter, S. Nicotine regulation in heavy and light smokers. *Journal of Experimental Psychology: General,* 1977, **106,** 5–12.

Schachter, S. Pharmacological and psychological determinants of smoking. *Annals of Internal Medicine,* 1978, **88,** 104–114.

Schachter, S., Kozlowski, L. T., & Silverstein, B. Effects of urinary pH on cigarette smoking. *Journal of Experimental Psychology: General,* 1977, **106,** 13–19.

Schachter, S., & Latané, B. Crime, cognition, and the autonomic nervous system. In D. Levine (Ed.), *Nebraska symposium on motivation,* Vol. 12. Lincoln: University of Nebraska Press, 1964.

Schachter, S., Silverstein, B., Kozlowski, L. T., Herman C. P., & Liebling, B. Effects of stress on cigarette smoking and urinary pH. *Journal of Experimental Psychology: General,* 1977, **106,** 24–30.

Schachter, S., Silverstein, B., & Perlik, D. Psychological and pharmacological explanations of smoking under stress. *Journal of Experimental Psychology: General,* 1977, **106,** 31–40.

Schaefer, C. E. *Childhood encopresis and enuresis.* New York: Van Nostrand Reinhold, 1979.

Schaie, K. W. Quasi-experimental research designs in the psychology of aging. In J. E. Birren & K. W. Schaie (Eds.), *Handbook of the psychology of aging.* New York: Van Nostrand Reinhold, 1977.

Schain, R. J., & Reynard, C. L. Effects of a central stimulant drug (methylphenidate) in children with hyperactive behavior. *Pediatrics,* 1975, **55,** 709–716.

Scheerer, M., Rothman, E., & Goldstein, K. A case of "idiot savant": An experimental study of personality organization. *Psychological Monographs,* 1945, **58,** whole issue No. 269.

Scheff, T. J. *Being mentally ill: A sociological theory.* Chicago: Aldine, 1966.

Schildkraut, J. J. The catecholamine hypothesis of affective disorders. *American Journal of Psychiatry,* 1965, **122,** 509–522.

Schmauk, F. J. Punishment, arousal, and avoidance learning in sociopaths. *Journal of Abnormal Psychology,* 1970, **76,** 443–453.

Schneider, K. *Clinical psychopathology.* New York: Grune and Stratton, 1959.

Schoeneman, T. J. The role of mental illness in the European witchhunts of the sixteenth and seventeenth centuries: An assessment. *Journal of the History of the Behavioral Sciences,* 1977, **13,** 337–351.

Schofield, W. *Psychotherapy: The purchase of friendship.* Englewood Cliffs, N.J.: Prentice-Hall, 1964.

Schulsinger, F. Psychopathy: Heredity and environment. *International Journal of Mental Health,* 1972, **1,** 190–206.

Schulsinger, H. A ten-year follow-up of children with schizophrenic mothers. *Acta Psychiatrica Scandinavica,* 1976, **63,** 371–386.

Schulz, J. H. Income distribution and the aging. In R. H. Binstock & E. Shanas (Eds.), *Handbook of aging and the social sciences.* New York: Von Nostrand Reinhold, 1976.

Schulz, R., & Brenner, G. Relocation of the aged: A review and theoretical analysis. *Journal of Gerontology,* 1977, **32,** 323–333.

Schur, E. M. Drug addiction in England and America. In D. Wakefield (Ed.), *The Addict.* Greenwich, Conn.: Fawcett Publications, 1965.

Schutz, W. C. *Joy.* New York: Grove Press, 1967.

Schuyler, D., & Katz, M. M. *The depressive illnesses: A major public health problem.* Washington, D.C.: U.S. Government Printing Office, 1973.

Schwab, J. J., Fennell, E. B., & Warheit, G. J. The epidemiology of psychosomatic disorders. *Psychosomatics,* 1974, **15,** 88–93.

Schwartz, G. E. Biofeedback as therapy: Some theoretical and practical issues. *American Psychologist,* 1973, **28,** 666–673.

Schwartz, G. J. College students as contingency managers for adolescents in a program to develop reading skills. *Journal of Applied Behavior Analysis,* 1977, **10,** 645–655.

Schwartz, L. S. Hers column. *The New York Times,* October 9, 1980, C2.

Schwartz, M. A., Wyatt, R. J., Yang, H., & Neff, N. Multiple forms of monoamine oxidase in brain: A comparison of enzymatic activity in mentally normal and chronic schizophrenic individuals. *Archives of General Psychiatry,* 1974, **31,** 557–560.

Schwartz, M. S. The economic and spatial mobility of paranoid schizophrenics. Unpublished M.A. thesis, University of Chicago, 1946.

Schwartz, R., & Schwartz, L. J. *Becoming a couple.* Englewood Cliffs, N.J.: Prentice-Hall, 1980.

Schwartz, R. M., & Gottman, J. M. Toward a task analysis of assertive behavior. *Journal of Consulting and Clinical Psychology,* 1976, **44,** 910–920.

Schwitzgebel, R. L., & Schwitzgebel, R. K. *Law and psychological practice.* New York: Wiley, 1980.

Segovia-Riquelma, N., Varela, A., & Mardones, J. Appetite for alcohol. In Y. Israel & J. Mardones (Eds.), *Biological basis of alcoholism.* New York: Wiley, 1971.

Seiden, R. H. Suicide: Preventable death. *Public Affairs Report,* 1974, **15,** 1–5.

Seligman, M. E. P. Phobias and preparedness. *Behavior Therapy,* 1971, **2,** 307–320.

Seligman, M. E. P. Fall into helplessness. *Psychology Today,* June 1973, **7,** 43–48.

Seligman, M. E. P. Depression and learned helplessness. In R. J. Friedman & M. M. Katz (Eds.), *The psychology of depression: Contemporary theory and research.* Washington, D.C.: Winston-Wiley, 1974.

Seligman, M. E. P. Comment and integration. *Journal of Abnormal Psychology,* 1978, **87,** 165–179.

Seligman, M. E. P., Abramson, L. V., Semmel, A., & Von Baeyer, C. Depressive attributional style. *Journal of Abnormal Psychology,* 1979, **88,** 242–247.

Seligman, M. E. P., & Hager, M. (Eds.) *Biological boundaries of learning.* New York: Appleton-Century-Crofts, 1972.

Selling, L. S. *Men against madness.* New York: Greenberg, Publisher, 1940.

Selye, H. A syndrome produced by diverse nocuous agents. *Nature,* 1936, **138,** 32.

Shader, R. I., & DiMascio, A. *Psychotropic drug side-effects: Clinical and theoretical perspectives.* Baltimore: Williams and Wilkins, 1970.

Shapiro, A. K. A contribution to a history of the placebo effect. *Behavioral Science,* 1960, **5,** 109–135.

Shapiro, A. P. An experimental study of comparative responses of blood pressure to different noxious stimuli. *Journal of Chronic Diseases,* 1961, **13,** 293–311.

Shapiro, D., & Surwit, R. S. Learned control of physiological function and disease. In H. Leitenberg (Ed.), *Handbook of behavior modification and behavior therapy.* Englewood Cliffs, N.J.: Prentice-Hall, 1976.

Shapiro, D., & Surwit, R. S. Biofeedback, In O. F. Pomerleau & J. P. Brady (Eds.), *Behavioral medicine: Theory and practice.* Baltimore: Williams and Wilkins, 1979.

Shapiro, D., Tursky, B., & Schwartz, G. E. Control of blood pressure in man by operant conditioning. *Circulation Research,* 1970, **26,** 127–132.

Shaw, B. F. Comparison of cognitive therapy and behavior therapy in the treatment of depression. *Journal of Consulting and Clinical Psychology,* 1977, **45,** 543–551.

Sheppard, H. L. Work and retirement. In R. H. Binstock & E. Shanas (Eds.), *Handbook of aging and the social sciences.* New York: Van Nostrand Reinhold, 1976.

Sherman, A. R. Real-life exposures as a primary therapeutic factor in the desensitization treatment of fear. *Journal of Abnormal Psychology,* 1972, **79,** 19–28.

Shevitz, S. A. Psychosurgery: Some current observations. *American Journal of Psychiatry,* 1976, **133,** 266–270.

Shneidman, E. S. Suicide. In *Encyclopedia Britannica.* Chicago: Encyclopedia Britannica, 1973.

Shneidman, E. S., & Farberow, N. L. A psychological approach to the study of suicide notes. In E. S. Shneidman, N. L. Farberow, & R. E. Litman (Eds.), *The psychology of suicide.* New York: Jason Aronson, 1970.

Shneidman, E. S., Farberow, N. L., & Litman, R. E. (Eds.) *The psychology of suicide.* New York: Jason Aronson, 1970.

Shopsin, B., Friedman, E., & Gershon, S. Parachlorophenylalanine reversal of tranylcypromine effects in depressed patients. *Archives of General Psychiatry,* 1976, **33,** 811–819.

Shopsin, B., Gershon, S., Thompson, H., & Collins, P. Psychoactive drugs in mania. *Archives of General Psychiatry,* 1975, **32,** 34–42.

Short, J. F., & Nye, F. I. Extent of unrecorded juvenile delinquency: Tentative conclusions. *Journal of Criminal Law, Criminology, and Police Science,* 1958, **49,** 296–302.

Siegel, R. A. Probability of punishment and suppression of behavior in psychopathic and nonpsychopathic offenders. *Journal of Abnormal Psychology,* 1978, **87,** 514–522.

Siemens, A. J. Effects of cannabis in combinations with ethanol and other drugs. In *Marijuana research findings: 1980.* Washington, D.C.: U.S. Government Printing Office, 1980.

Silverstein, B. An addiction explanation of cigarette-induced relaxation. *Dissertation Abstracts International,* 1976, **37,** 1929.

Silverstein, B., Kozlowski, L. T., & Schachter, S. Social life, cigarette smoking, and urinary pH. *Journal of Experimental Psychology: General,* 1977, **106,** 20–23.

Silverstein, C. Behavior modification and the gay community. Paper presented at the annual convention of the Association for Advancement of Behavior Therapy, New York City, 1972.

Silverstein, C. *A family matter: A parent's guide to homosexuality.* New York: McGraw-Hill, 1977.

Simeons, A. T. W. *Man's presumptuous brain: An evolutionary interpretation of psychosomatic disease.* New York: Dutton, 1961.

Simpson, M. T., Olewine, D. A., Jenkins, F. H., Ramsey, S. J., Zyzanski, S. J., Thomas, G., & Hames, C. G. Exercise-induced catecholomines and platelet aggregation in the coronary-prone behavior pattern. *Psychosomatic Medicine,* 1974, **36,** 476–487.

Sines, J. O. Physiological and behavioral characteristics of rats selectively bred for susceptibility to stomach ulcer development. *Journal of Neuropsychiatry,* 1963, **4,** 396–398.

Singer, M., & Wynne, L. C. Differentiating characteristics of the parents of childhood schizophrenics, childhood neurotics, and young adult schizophrenics. *American Journal of Psychiatry,* 1963, **120,** 234–243.

Sintchak, G. H., & Geer, J. H. A vaginal plethysmograph system. *Psychophysiology,* 1975, **12,** 113–115.

Sizemore, C. C., & Pittillo, E. S. *I'm Eve.* Garden City, N.Y.: Doubleday, 1977.

Skinner, B. F. "Superstition" in the pigeon. *Journal of Experimental Psychology,* 1948, **38,** 168–172.

Skinner, B. F. *Science and human behavior.* New York: Macmillan, 1953.

Skinner, H. A., Jackson, D. N., & Hoffman, H. Alcoholic personality types: Identification and correlates. *Journal of Abnormal Psychology,* 1974, **83,** 658–666.

Sklar, L. A., & Anisman, H. Stress and coping factors influence tumor growth. *Science,* 1979, **205,** 513–515.

Skrzypek, G. J. The effects of perceptual isolation and arousal on anxiety, complexity preference and novelty preference in psychopathic and neurotic delinquents. *Journal of Abnormal Psychology,* 1969, **74,** 321–329.

Slater, E. Erbpathologie des manisch-depressiven irreseins, Die Eltern und Kinder von Manisch-Depressiven. *Zeitschrift für die gesarnte Neurologie und Psychiatrie,* 1938, **163,** 1–47.

Slater, E. The thirty-fifth Maudsley lecture: Hysteria 311. *Journal of Mental Science,* 1961, **107,** 358–381.

Slater, E., & Glithero, E. A follow-up of patients diagnosed as suffering from hysteria. *Journal of Psychosomatic Research,* 1965, **9,** 9–13.

Slater, E., & Shields, J. Genetic aspects of anxiety. In M. H. Lader (Ed.), *Studies of anxiety.* Ashford, England: Headley Brothers, 1969.

Slavson, S. R. *Analytic group psychotherapy with children, adolescents and adults.* New York: Columbia University Press, 1950.

Sloane, R. B., Staples, F. R., Cristol, A. H., Yorkston, N. J., & Whipple, K. *Psychotherapy versus behavior therapy.* Cambridge: Harvard University Press, 1975.

Smith, P. B. Controlled studies of the outcome of sensitivity training. *Psychological Bulletin,* 1975, **82,** 597–622.

Snyder, S. H. *Madness and the brain.* New York: McGraw-Hill, 1974.

Snyder, S. H., Banerjee, S. P., Yamamura, H. I., & Greenberg D. Drugs, neurotransmitters, and schizophrenia. *Science,* 1974, **184,** 1243–1253.

Sobell, M. B., & Sobell, L. C. Second-year treatment outcome of alcoholics treated by individualized behavior therapy: Results. *Behaviour Research and Therapy,* 1976, **14,** 195–215.

Solnick, J. V., Rincover, A., & Peterson, C. R. Some determinants of the reinforcing and punishing effects of time-out. *Journal of Applied Behavior Analysis,* 1977, **10,** 415–424.

Sommer, R. *Personal space: The behavioral basis of design.* Englewood Cliffs, N.J.: Prentice-Hall, 1969.

Soueif, M. I. Some determinants of psychological deficits associated with chronic cannabis consumption. *Bulletin of Narcotics,* 1976, **28,** 25–42.

Spanos, N. P. Barber's reconceptualization of hypnosis: An evaluation of criticisms. *Journal of Experimental Research in Personality,* 1970, **4,** 241–258.

Spanos, N. P. Witchcraft in histories of psychiatry: A critical appraisal and an alternative conceptualization. *Psychological Bulletin,* 1978, **35,** 417–439.

Speer, D. C. Rate of caller re-use of a telephone crisis service. *Crisis Intervention,* 1971, **3,** 83–86.

Speer, D. C. An evaluation of a telephone crisis service. Paper presented at the Midwestern Psychological Association meeting, Cleveland, Ohio, 1972.

Spiess, W. F. S. The psychophysiology of premature ejaculation. Unpublished doctoral dissertation, State University of New York at Stony Brook, 1977.

Sperling, M. Conversion hysteria and conversion symptoms: A revision of classification and concepts. *Journal of the American Psychoanalytic Association,* 1973, **21,** 745–771.

Spitzer, R. L. On pseudoscience in science, logic in remission, and psychiatric diagnosis: A critique of Rosenhan's "On being sane in insane places." *Journal of Abnormal Psychology,* 1975, **84,** 442–452.

Spitzer, R. L., Endicott, J., & Robins, E. *Research diagnostic criteria.* New York: Biometrics Research, 1975.

Spitzer, R. L., Forman, J. B. W., & Nee, J. DSM-III field trials: I. Initial interrater diagnostic reliability. *American Journal of Psychiatry,* 1979, **136,** 815–817.

Sprague, R. L., & Gadow, K. D. The role of the teacher in drug treatment. *School Review,* 1976, **85,** 109–140.

Sprague, R. L., & Sleator, E. K. Methylphenidate in hyperkinetic children: Differences in dose effects on learning and social behavior. *Science,* 1977, **198,** 1274–1276.

Srole, L., Langner, T. S., Michael, S. T., Opler, M. K., & Rennie, T. A. C. *Mental health in the metropolis: The midtown Manhattan study.* New York: McGraw-Hill, 1962.

Sroufe, L. A. Drug treatment of children with behavior problems. In F. Horowitz (Ed.), *Review of child development research.* Chicago: University of Chicago Press, 1975.

Staats, A. W., & Butterfield, W. H. Treatment of nonreading in a culturally deprived juvenile delinquent: An application of learning principles. *Child Development,* 1965, **36,** 925–942.

Staats, A. W., & Staats, C. K. *Complex human behavior.* New York: Holt, Rinehart and Winston, 1963.

Stampfl, T. C., & Levis, D. J. Essentials of implosive therapy: A learning-therapy-based psychodynamic behavior therapy. *Journal of Abnormal Psychology,* 1967, **72,** 496–503.

Stang, R. R. The etiology of Parkinson's disease. *Diseases of the Nervous System,* 1970, **31,** 381–390.

Stanton, A. H., & Schwartz, M. S. *The mental hospital.* New York: Basic Books, 1954.

Stanton, M. D., & Bardoni, A. Drug flashbacks: Reported frequency in a military population. *American Journal of Psychiatry,* 1972, **129,** 751–755.

Starfield, B. Enuresis: Its pathogenesis and management. *Clinical Pediatrics,* 1972, **11,** 343–350.

Staub, E., Tursky, B., & Schwartz, G. E. Self-control and predictability: Their effects on reactions to aversive stimulation. *Journal of Personality and Social Psychology,* 1971, **18,** 157–162.

Steele, R. S. The physiological concomitants of psychogenic motive arousal in college males. Unpublished doctoral dissertation, Harvard University, 1973.

Stefanis, C., Boulougouris, J., & Liakos, A. Clinical and physiological effects of cannabis in long-term users. In M. C. Braude & S. Szara (Eds.), *Pharmacology of marijuana,* Vol. 2. New York: Raven Press, 1976.

Stephens, J. H., & Kamp, M. On some aspects of hysteria: A clinical study. *Journal of Nervous and Mental Disease,* 1962, **134,** 305–315.

Sterman, H. B. Neurophysiologic and clinical studies of sensorimotor EEG biofeedback training: Some effects on epilepsy. *Seminars in Psychiatry,* 1973, **5,** 507–525.

Stern, D. B. Handedness and the lateral distribution of conversion reactions. *Journal of Nervous and Mental Disease,* 1977, **164,** 122–128.

Stern, R. S., & Cobb, J. P. Phenomenology of obsessive-compulsive neurosis. *British Journal of Psychiatry,* 1978, **132,** 233–234.

Stern, S. L. Rush, J., & Mendels, J. Toward a rational pharmacotherapy of depression. *American Journal of Psychiatry,* 1980, **137,** 545–552.

Sternbach, R. A. *Principles of psychophysiology.* New York: Academic Press, 1966.

Stevenson, J., & Jones, I. H. Behavior therapy technique for exhibitionism: A preliminary report. *Archives of General Psychiatry,* 1972, **27,** 839–841.

Stewart, M. A., Pitts, F. N., Craig, A. G., & Dieruf, W. The hyperactive child syndrome. *American Journal of Orthopsychiatry,* 1966, **36,** 861–867.

Stoller, F. H. Accelerated interaction: A time-limited approach based on the brief intensive group. *International Journal of Group Psychotherapy,* 1968, **18,** 220–235.

Stone, A. A. *Mental health and law: A system in transition.* Rockville, Md.: National Institute of Mental Health, 1975.

Stone, L. J., & Hokanson, J. E. Arousal reduction via self-punitive behavior. *Journal of Personality and Social Psychology,* 1969, **12,** 72–79.

Strupp, H. H., Hadley, S. W., & Gomes-Schwartz, B. *Psychotherapy for better or worse: An analysis of the problem of negative effects.* New York: Jason Aronson, 1977.

Stuart, R. B. An operant interpersonal program for couples. In D. H. L. Olson (Ed.), *Treating relationships.* Lake Mills, Iowa: Graphic Publishing Company, 1976.

Stuart, R. B. Protection of the right to informed consent to participate in research. *Behavior Therapy,* 1978, **9,** 73–82.

Stuart, R. B. *Helping couples change: A social learning approach to marital therapy.* New York: Guilford Press, 1980.

Sturgis, E. T., & Adams, H. E. The right to treatment: Issues in the treatment of homosexuality. *Journal of Consulting and Clinical Psychology,* 1978, **46,** 165–169.

Sullivan, H. S. Research in schizophrenia. *American Journal of Psychiatry,* 1929, **9,** 553–567.

Sullivan, H. S. *The interpersonal theory of psychiatry.* New York: Norton, 1953.

Surwit, R. S., Shapiro, D., & Good, M. I. A comparison of cardiovascular biofeedback, neuromuscular biofeedback, and meditation in the treatment of borderline essential hypertension. *Journal of Consulting and Clinical Psychology,* 1978, **46,** 252–263.

Sutherland, S., & Scheri, D. J. Crisis intervention with victims in rape. In D. Chappell, R. Geis, & G. Geis (Eds.), *Forcible rape: The crime, the victim and the offender.* New York: Columbia University Press, 1977.

Syndulko, K. Electrocortical investigations of sociopathy. In R. D. Hare & D. Schalling (Eds.), *Psychopathic behaviour: Approaches to research.* New York: Wiley, 1978.

Szasz, T. S. The myth of mental illness. *American Psychologist,* 1960, **15,** 113–118.

Szasz, T. S. *Law, liberty, and psychiatry.* New York: Macmillan, 1963.

Szasz, T. S. (Ed.) *The age of madness: The history of involuntary hospitalization.* New York: Jason Aronson, 1974.

Tashkin, D. P., Calvarese, B., & Simmons, M. Respiratory status of 75 chronic marijuana smokers: Comparison with matched controls. University of California at Los Angeles School of Medicine. Abstract in *American Review of Respiratory Diseases,* 1978, **117,** 261.

Tate, B. G., & Baroff, G. S. Aversive control of self-injurious behavior in a psychotic boy. *Behaviour Research and Therapy,* 1966, **4,** 281–287.

Taylor, J. A. A personality scale of manifest anxiety. *Journal of Abnormal and Social Psychology,* 1953, **48,** 285–290.

Taylor, J. K., & Hirt, M. Irrelevance of retention interval length and distractor-task similarity in schizophrenic cognitive interference. *Journal of Consulting and Clinical Psychology,* 1975, **43,** 281–285.

Terry, R. D., & Wisniewski, H. M. Sans teeth, sans eyes, sans taste, sans everything. *Behavior Today,* March 25, 1974, **5,** 84.

Terry, R. D., & Wisniewski, H. M. Structural aspects of aging of the brain. In C. Eisdorfer & R. O. Friedel (Eds.), *Cognitive and emotional disturbances in the elderly.* Chicago: Year Book Medical Publishers, 1977.

Theodor, L. H., & Mandelcorn, M. S. Hysterical blindness: A case report and study using a modern psychophysical technique. *Journal of Abnormal Psychology,* 1973, **82,** 552–553.

Thibaut, J. W., & Kelley, H. H. *The social psychology of groups.* New York: Wiley, 1959.

Thigpen, C. H., & Cleckley, H. *The three faces of Eve.* Kingsport, Tenn.: Kingsport Press, 1954.

Thorndike, E. L. *The psychology of wants, interests and attitudes.* New York: Appleton, Century, 1935.

Tollefson, D. J. The relationship between the occurrence of fractures and life crisis events. Unpublished master of nursing thesis, University of Washington, Seattle, 1972.

Tomlinson, B. E., & Henderson, G. Some quantitative findings in normal and demented old people. In R. D. Terry & S. Gershon (Eds.), *Neurobiology of aging.* New York: Raven Press, 1976.

Tramontana, J., & Stimbert, V. Some techniques of behavior modification with an autistic child. *Psychological Reports,* 1970, **27,** 498.

Treffert, D. A., McAndrew, J. B., & Dreifuerst, P. An inpatient treatment program and outcome for 57 autistic and schizophrenic children. *Journal of Autism and Childhood Schizophrenia,* 1973, **3,** 138–153.

Truett, J., Cornfield, J., & Kannel, W. Multivariate analysis of the risk of coronary heart disease in Framingham. *Journal of Chronic Disease,* 1967, **20,** 511–524.

Tuckman, J., Kleiner, R. J., & Lavell, M. Emotional content of suicide notes. *American Journal of Psychiatry,* 1959, **116,** 59–63,

Turkewitz, H., & O'Leary, K. D. A comparison of communication and behavioral marital therapy. Paper presented at the Eleventh Annual Convention of the Association for Advancement of Behavior Therapy, Atlanta, December 1977.

Turner, R. J., & Wagonfeld, M. O. Occupational mobility and schizophrenia. *American Sociological Review,* 1967, **32,** 104–113.

Twain, M. *The adventures of Tom Sawyer,* 1976, In L. Teacher (Ed.), *The unabridged Mark Twain.* Philadelphia: Running Press, 1976.

Ullmann, L., & Krasner, L. *A psychological approach to abnormal behavior.* (2nd ed.) Englewood Cliffs, N.J.: Prentice-Hall, 1975.

Umbarger, C. C., Dalsimer, J. S., Morrison, A. P., & Breggin, P. R. *College students in a mental hospital.* New York: Grune and Stratton, 1962.

United States Department of Health, Education and Welfare. *Smoking and health.* Public Health Service Publication 1103. Washington, D.C.: U.S. Government Printing Office, 1964.

United States Department of Health, Education and Welfare. *Smoking and health, a report of the Surgeon General.* Washington, D.C.: DHEW Publication, 1979.

United States Public Health Service. *Vital Statistics of the United States, 1970.* Vol. 11. *Mortality.* Rockville, Md.: 1974.

Upper, D., & Ross, S. M. (Eds.) *Behavioral group therapy 1980: An annual review.* Champaign, Ill.: Research Press, 1980.

Valenstein, E. S. *Brain control.* New York: Wiley, 1973.

Van Praag, H., Korf, J., & Schut, D. Cerebral monamines and depression: An investigation with the probenecid technique. *Archives of General Psychiatry,* 1973, **28,** 827–831.

Van Putten, T., May, P. R. A., Marder, S. R., & Wittman, L. A. Subjective response to antipsychotic drugs. *Archives of General Psychiatry,* 1981, **38,** 187–190.

Vardaris, R. M., Weisz, D. J., Fazel, A., & Rawitch, A. B. Chronic administration of delta-9-tetrahydrocannabinol to pregnant rats: Studies of pup behavior and placental transfer. *Pharmacology and Biochemistry of Behavior,* 1976, **4,** 249–254.

Vaughn, C. E., & Leff, J. P. The influence of family and social factors on the course of psychiatric illness: A comparison of schizophrenic and depressed neurotic patients. *British Journal of Psychiatry,* 1976, **129,** 125–137.

Von Felsinger, J. M., Lasagna, L., & Beecher, H. K. The response of normal men to lysergic acid derivatives. *Journal of Clinical and Experimental Psychopathology,* 1956, **17,** 414–428.

Von Wright, J. M., Pekanmaki, L., & Malin, S. Effects of conflict and stress on alcohol intake in rats. *Quarterly Journal of Studies on Alcohol,* 1971, **32,** 420–441.

Wachtel, P. *Psychoanalysis and behavior therapy: Toward an integration.* New York: Basic Books, 1977.

Waldfogel, S. Emotional crisis in a child. In A. Burton (Ed.), *Case studies in counseling and psychotherapy,* Englewood Cliffs, N.J.: Prentice-Hall, 1959.

Waldron, I. The coronary-prone behavior pattern, blood pressure, employment and socio-economic status in women. *Journal of Psychosomatic Research,* 1978, **22,** 79–87.

Walen, S., Hauserman, N. M., & Lavin, P. J. *Clinical guide to behavior therapy.* Baltimore: William and Wilkins, 1977.

Walton, D. The application of learning theory to the treatment of a case of somnambulism. *Journal of Clinical Psychology,* 1961, **17,** 96–99.

Ward, C. H., Beck, A. T., Mendelson, M., Mock, J. E., & Erbaugh, J. K. The psychiatric nomenclature: Reasons for diagnostic disagreement, *Archives of General Psychiatry,* 1962, **7,** 198–205.

Warner, K. E. The effects of the antismoking campaign on cigarette consumption. *American Journal of Public Health,* 1977, **67,** 645–650.

Watson, G. C., & Buranen, C. The frequency and identification of false positive conversion reactions. *Journal of Nervous and Mental Disease,* 1979, **167,** 243–247.

Watson, J. B. Psychology as the behaviorist views it. *Psychological Review,* 1913, **20,** 158–177.

Watson, J. B., & Rayner, R. Conditioned emotional reactions. *Journal of Experimental Psychology,* 1920, **3,** 1–14.

Watson, L. S. *Child behavior modification: A manual for teachers, nurses, and parents.* Elmsford, N.Y.: Pergamon Press, 1973.

Watt, N. F. Childhood and adolescent roots of schizophrenia. In D. Ricks, A. Thomas, & M. Roff (Eds.), *Life history research in psychopathology,* Vol. 3. Minneapolis: University of Minnesota Press, 1974.

Watt, N. F., Stolorow, R. D., Lubensky, A. W., & McClelland, D. C. School adjustment and behavior of children hospitalized for schizophrenia as adults. *American Journal of Orthopsychiatry,* 1970, **40,** 637–657.

Weinberg, G. *Society and the healthy homosexual.* New York: St. Martin's Press, 1972.

Weinberg, W. A., Rutman, J., Sullivan, L., Penick, E. C., & Dietz, S. G. Depression in children referred to an educational diagnostic center. *Journal of Pediatrics,* 1973, **83,** 1065–1072.

Weinberger, D. A., Schwartz, G. E., & Davidson, R. J. Low-anxious, high-anxious and repressive coping styles: Psychometric patterns and behavioral and physiological responses to stress. *Journal of Abnormal Psychology,* 1979, **88,** 369–380.

Weiner, B., Frieze, I., Kukla, A., Reed, L., Rest, S., & Rosenbaum, R. M. *Perceiving the causes of success and failure.* New York: General Learning Press, 1971.

Weiner, H., Thaler, M., Reiser, M. F., & Mirsky, I. A. Etiology of duodenal ulcer: I. Relation of specific psychological characteristics to rate of gastric secretion. *Psychosomatic Medicine,* 1957, **17,** 1–10.

Weiner, J. W. The effectiveness of a suicide prevention program. *Mental Hygiene,* 1969, **53,** 357–363.

Weintraub, S., Liebert, D., & Neale, J. M. Teacher ratings of children vulnerable to psychopathology. *American Journal of Orthopsychiatry,* 1975, **45,** 838–845.

Weisman, R. Cocaine paraphrenalia sales up more than 50%. *ADAMHA News,* February 22, 1980.

Weiss, G., Hechtman, L., Perlman, T., Hopkins, J., & Wener, A. Hyperactives as young adults. *Archives of General Psychiatry,* 1979, **36,** 675–681.

Weiss, G., Kluger, E., Danielson, E., & Elman, M. Effect of long-term treatment of hyperactive children with methylphenidate. *Canadian Medical Association Journal,* 1975, **112,** 159–165.

Weiss, G., Minde, K., Werry, J.S., Douglas, V., & Nemeth, E. Studies on the hyperactive child: VII. Five-year follow-up. *Archives of General Psychiatry,* 1971, **24,** 409–414.

Weiss, J. M. Effects of coping responses on stress. *Journal of Comparative and Physiological Psychology,* 1968, **24,** 409–414.

Weiss, J. M. Somatic effects of predictable and unpredictable shock. *Psychosomatic Medicine,* 1970, **32,** 397–408.

Weiss, J. M. Psychological and behavioral influences on gastrointestinal lesions in animal models. In J. D. Maser & M. E. P. Seligman (Eds.), *Psychopathology: Experimental models.* San Francisco: Freeman, 1977.

Weiss, R. L., Hops, H., & Patterson, G. R. A framework for conceptualizing marital conflict, a technology for altering it, some data for evaluating it. In L. A. Hamerlynck, L. C. Handy, & E. J. Mash (Eds.), *Behavior change: Methodology, concepts, and practice.* Champaign, Ill.: Research Press, 1973.

Weiss, T., & Engel, B. T. Operant conditioning of heart rate in patients with premature ventricular contractions. *Psychophysiology,* 1975, **12,** 310–312.

Weissman, M. M., Klerman, G. L., & Paykel, E. S. Clinical evaluation of hostility in depression. *American Journal of Psychiatry,* 1971, **128,** 261–266.

Weissman, M. M., Klerman, G. L., Prusoff, B. A., Sholom-skas, D., & Padian, N. Depressed outpatients. Results one year after treatment with drugs and/or interpersonal psychotherapy. *Archives of General Psychiatry,* 1981, **38,** 51–56.

Weissman, M. M., & Myers, J. K. Affective disorders in a U.S. urban community. *Archives of General Psychiatry,* 1978, **35,** 1304–1310.

Weitzenhoffer, A. M., & Hilgard, E. R. *Stanford hypnotic susceptibility scale, Forms A and B.* Palo Alto, Calif.: Consulting Psychologists Press, 1959.

Wender, P. H., Rosenthal, R., Kety, S. S., Schulsinger, F., & Welner, J. Cross-fostering: A research strategy for clarifying the role of genetic and experiential factors in the etiology of schizophrenia. *Archives of General Psychiatry,* 1974, **30,** 121–128.

Werry, J. S., Sprague, R. L., & Cohen, M. N. Conners' Teacher Rating Scale for use in drug studies with children—An empirical study. *Journal of Abnormal Child Psychology,* 1975, **3,** 217–229.

Werry, J. S., Weiss, G., & Douglas, V. Studies on the hyperactive child: I. Some preliminary findings. *Canadian Psychiatric Association Journal,* 1964, **9,** 120–130.

Wexler, D. B. Token and taboo: Behavior modification, token economies, and the law. *California Law Review,* 1973, **61,** 81–109.

White, W. A. *Outlines of psychiatry,.* (13th ed.) New York: Nervous and Mental Disease Publishing Company, 1932.

Whitlock, F. A. The aetiology of hysteria. *Acta Psychiatrica Scandinavica,* 1967, **43,** 144–162.

Wickens, D. D., Allen, C. K., & Hill, F. A. Effects of instruction on extinction of the conditioned GSR. *Journal of Experimental Psychology,* 1963, **66,** 235–240.

Widom, C. S. A methodology for studying noninstitutionalized psychopaths. *Journal of Consulting and Clinical Psychology,* 1977, **45,** 674–683.

Wiener, G. Varying psychological sequelae of lead ingestion in children. *Public Health Reports,* 1970, **85,** 19–24.

Wig, N. N., & Varma, V. K. Patterns of long-term heavy cannabis use in North India and its effects on cognitive functions: A preliminary report. *Drug and Alcohol Dependence,* 1977, **2,** 211–219.

Wiggins, J. Inconsistent socialization. *Psychological Reports,* 1968, **23,** 303–336.

Wilder, C. S. *Chronic conditions and limitations of activity and mobility: United States, July 1965 to June 1967.* Vital and Health Statistics, 1971, Series 10, No. 61. Washington, D.C.: Department of Health, Education and Welfare, 1971.

Wilkins, L. T. *Evaluation of penal measures.* New York: Random House, 1969.

Williams, H., & McNicol, K. N. Prevalence, natural history and relationship of wheezy bronchitis and asthma in children: An epidemiological study. *British Medical Journal,* 1969, **4,** 321–325.

Williams, L., Martin, G. L., McDonald, S., Hardy, L., & Lambert, L., Sr. Effects of a backscratch contingency of reinforcement for table serving on social interaction with severely retarded girls. *Behavior Therapy,* 1975, **6,** 220–229.

Wilson, G. T., & Abrams, D. Effects of alcohol on social anxiety and physiological arousal: Cognitive versus pharmacological processes. *Cognitive Therapy and Research,* 1977, **1,** 195–210.

Wilson, G. T., & Davison, G. C. Aversion techniques in behavior therapy: Some theoretical and metatheoretical considerations. *Journal of Consulting and Clinical Psychology,* 1969, **33,** 327–329.

Wilson, G. T., & Davison G. C. Processes of fear reduction in systematic desensitization: Animal studies. *Psychological Bulletin,* 1971, **76,** 1–14.

Wilson, G. T., & Lawson, D.M. The effects of alcohol on sexual arousal in women. *Journal of Abnormal Psychology,* 1976, **85,** 489–497.

Wilson, G. T., & O'Leary, K. D. *Principles of behavior therapy.* Englewood Cliffs, N.J.: Prentice-Hall, 1980.

Wilson, R. C., Christensen, P. R., Merrifield, P. R., & Guilford, J. P. *Alternate uses test.* Beverly Hills, Calif.: Sheridan Psychological Company, 1975.

Wilson, W. R. Unobtrusive induction of positive attitudes. Unpublished doctoral dissertation, University of Michigan, 1975.

Wiltz, N. A., & Patterson, G. R. An evaluation of parent training procedures designed to alter inappropriate aggressive behavior in boys. *Behavior Therapy,* 1974, **5,** 215–221.

Winett, R. A., & Winkler, R. C. Current behavior modification in the classroom: Be still, be quiet, be docile. *Journal of Applied Behavior Analysis,* 1972, **5,** 499–504.

Wing, J., Birley, J. L. T., Cooper, J. C., Graham, P., & Isaacs, A. D. Reliability of a procedure for measuring and classifying "present psychiatric state." *British Journal of Psychiatry,* 1967, **113,** 499–506.

Winick, M., Rosso, P., & Waterlow, J. Cellular growth of cerebrum, cerebellum, and brain stem in normal and marasmic children. *Experimental Neurology,* 1970, **26,** 393–400.

Winkler, R. What types of sex-role behavior should behavior modifiers promote? *Journal of Applied Behavior Analysis,* 1977, **10,** 549–552.

Winokur, G. Sexual behavior: Its relationship to certain effects and psychiatric diseases. In G. Winokur (Ed.), *Determinants of human sexual behavior.* Springfield, Ill.: Charles C Thomas, 1963.

Winokur, G. Unipolar depression. *Archives of General Psychiatry,* 1979, **36,** 47–52.

Winokur, G., & Clayton, P. J. Family history studies: I. Two types of affective disorders separated according to genetic and clinical factors. In J. Wortis (Ed.), *Recent advances in biological psychiatry,* Vol. 9. New York: Plenum Press, 1967.

Winokur, G., Clayton, P. J., & Reich, T. *Manic-depressive illness.* St. Louis: Mosby, 1969.

Winters, K. C., Weintraub, S., & Neale, J. M. Validity of MMPI codetypes in identifying DSM-III schizophrenics, unipolars and bipolars. *Journal of Consulting and Clinical Psychology,* 1981, **49,** 486–487.

Wise, T. Where the public peril begins: A survey of psychotherapists to determine the effects of Tarasoff. *Stanford Law Review,* 1978, **31,** 165–190.

Witkin, H. A., Mednick S. A., Schulsinger, F., Bakkestrom, E., Christiansen, K. O., Goodenough, D. R., Hirschhorn, K., Lundsteen, C., Owen, D. R., Philip, J., Rubin, D. B., & Stocking, M. Criminality in XYY and XXY men. *Science,* 1976, **193,** 547–555.

Wolberg, L. R. *The technique of psychotherapy.* New York: Grune and Stratton, 1954.

Wold, D. A. The adjustment of siblings to childhood leukemia. Unpublished medical thesis, University of Washington, Seattle, 1968.

Wolf, A. The psychoanalysis of group. *American Journal of Psychotherapy,* 1949, **3,** 16–50.

Wolf, M., Risley, T., & Mees, H. Application of operant conditioning procedures to the behavior problems of an autistic child. *Behaviour Research and Therapy,* 1964, **1,** 305–312.

Wolin, S. J. Introduction: Psychosocial consequences. In *Alcoholism and alcohol abuse among women: Research issues.* Rockville, Md.: National Institute on Alcohol Abuse and Alcoholism, 1980.

Wollersheim, J. P. Effectiveness of group therapy based upon learning principles in the treatment of overweight women. *Journal of Abnormal Psychology,* 1970, **76,** 462–474.

Wolpe, J. *Psychotherapy by reciprocal inhibition.* Stanford, Calif.: Stanford University Press, 1958.

Wolpe, J. Cognitive behavior and its roles in psychotherapy: An integrative account. In M. J. Mahoney (Ed.), *Psychotherapy process: Current issues and future directions.* New York: Plenum Press, 1980.

Wolpe, J., & Rachman, S. J. Psychoanalytic "evidence," a critique based on Freud's case of Little Hans. *Journal of Nervous and Mental Disease,* 1960, **131,** 135–147.

Wong, B. The role of theory in learning disabilities research: I. An analysis of problems. *Journal of Learning Disabilities,* 1979, **12,** 19–29.

Woodruff, R. A., Goodwin, D. W., & Guze, S. B. *Psychiatric diagnosis.* New York: Oxford University Press, 1974.

Woodruff, R. A., & Pitts, F. M. Monozygotic twins with obsessional illness. *American Journal of Psychiatry,* 1964, **120,** 1075–1080.

World Health Organization. *Manual of the international statistical classification of diseases, injuries and causes of death.* Geneva: WHO, 1948.

Yablonsky, L. The anti-criminal society: Synanon. *Federal Probation,* 1962, **26,** 50–57.

Yablonsky, L. *Synanon: The tunnel back.* Baltimore: Penguin, 1967.

Yalom, I. D. *The theory and practice of group psychotherapy.* (2nd ed.) New York: Basic Books, 1975.

Yalom, I. D., Green, R., & Fisk, N. Prenatal exposure to female hormones: Effect on psychosexual development in boys. *Archives of General Psychiatry,* 1973, **28,** 554–561.

Yalom, I. D., & Lieberman, M. A. A study of encounter group casualties. *Archives of General Psychiatry,* 1971, **25,** 16–30.

Yates, A. J. *Behavior therapy.* New York: Wiley, 1970.

Young, G. C. The aetiology of enuresis in terms of learning theory. *Medical Officer,* 1965, **113,** 19–22.

Young, M., Benjamin, B., & Wallis, C. Mortality of widowers. *Lancet,* 1963, **2,** 454.

Yurchenco, H. *A mighty hard road: The Woody Guthrie Story.* New York: McGraw-Hill, 1970.

Yuwiler, A., Ritvo, E., Geller, E., Glousman, R., Scheiderman, G., & Matsuno, D. Uptake and efflux of serotonin from platelets and autistic and nonautistic children. *Journal of Autism and Childhood Schizophrenia,* 1975, **5,** 83–98.

Zarit, S. H. *Aging and mental disorders: Psychological approaches to assessment and treatment.* New York: The Free Press, 1980.

Zeigob, L. E., Arnold, S., & Forehand, R. An examination of observer effects in parent-child interactions. *Child Development,* 1975, **46,** 509–512.

Zerbin-Rüdin, E. Genetic research and the theory of schizophrenia. *International Journal of Mental Health,* 1972, **1,** 42–62.

Ziegler, F. J., Imboden, J. B., & Meyer, E. Contemporary converion reactions: A clinical study. *American Journal of Psychiatry,* 1960, **116,** 901–910.

Zigler, E. Mental retardation. In P. London & D. Rosenhan (Eds.), *Foundations of abnormal psychology.* New York: Holt, Rinehart and Winston, 1968.

Zigler, E. Development versus difference theories of mental retardation and the problem of motivation. *American Journal of Mental Deficiency,* 1969, **73,** 536–556.

Zigler, E., Butterfield, E. C., & Capobianco, F. Institutionalization and the effectiveness of social reinforcement: A five- and eight-year follow-up study. *Developmental Psychology,* 1970, **3,** 255–263.

Zigler, E., & Phillips, L. Psychiatric diagnosis and symptomatology. *Journal of Abnormal and Social Pathology,* 1961, **63,** 69–75.

Zilbergeld, B., & Evans, M. The inadequacy of Masters and Johnson. *Psychology Today,* 1980, **14,** 28–43.

Zilboorg, G., & Henry, G. W. *A history of medical psychology.* New York: Norton, 1941.

Zimbardo, P. G., Andersen, S. M., & Kabat, L. G. Paranoia and deafness: An experimental investigation. *Science,* 1981, in press.

Zung, W. W. K. A self-rating depression scale. *Archives of General Psychiatry,* 1965, **12,** 63–70.

■ ■

GLOSSARY

Acetylcholine. A *neurotransmitter*[1] of the central, somatomotor, and *parasympathetic* nervous systems and in the ganglia and the *neuron*—sweat gland junctions of the *sympathetic*.

Acute brain syndrome. See *delirium*.

Addiction. See *substance dependence*.

Addison's disease. An endocrine disorder produced by *cortisone* insufficiency and marked by weight loss, fatigue, and a darkening of the skin.

Adrenal glands. Two small areas of tissue, located just above the kidneys; the inner core of each gland, the medulla, secretes *epinephrine* and *norepinephrine*, the outer cortex, *cortisone* and other steroid hormones.

Adrenaline. A hormone which is secreted by the *adrenal glands*; also called *epinephrine*.

Adrenergic system. All the nerve cells for which *norepinephrine* and *epinephrine* (and more broadly, other *monoamines, dopamine* and *serotonin*) are the transmitter substances, as opposed to the *cholinergic,* which consists of the nerve cells activated by *acetylcholine*.

Advanced accurate empathy. A form of *empathy* in which the therapist infers concerns and feelings that lie behind what the client is saying; represents an *interpretation*. Compare with *primary empathy*.

Affect. A subjective feeling or emotional tone often accompanied by bodily expressions noticeable to others.

Affective disorder. A disorder in which there are disabling mood disturbances.

Affirming the consequent. An error in logic by which, if A causes B on one occasion, it is assumed that A is the cause when B is observed on any other occasion.

Age effects. Consequences of being a given chronological age; compare with *cohort effects*.

Ageism. Prejudicial attitudes toward old people.

Agoraphobia. A cluster of fears centering around being in open spaces and leaving the home.

Alcoholism. A behavioral disorder in which consumption of alcoholic beverages is continuous and excessive and impairs health and social and occupational functioning; a physiological dependence on alcohol. See *substance dependence*.

Alkaloid. Organic base found in seed plants, usually in mixture with a number of similar alkaloids; alkaloids are the active chemicals giving many drugs their medicinal properties and other powerful physiologic effects.

Alpha rhythm. A dominant pattern (8 to 13 cps) of the *brain waves* of a resting but awake adult.

Altruistic suicide. As defined by Durkheim, self-annihilation that the person feels will serve a social purpose, such as the self-immolations practiced by Buddhist monks during the Vietnam war.

Alzheimer's disease. A *presenile dementia* involving a progressive atrophy of cortical tissue and marked by speech impairment, involuntary movements of limbs, occasional *convulsions,* intellectual deterioration, and psychotic behavior.

Ambivalence. The simultaneous holding of strong positive and negative emotional attitudes toward the same situation or person.

American Law Institute Guidelines. Rules proposing insanity to be a legitimate defense plea if during criminal conduct individual could not judge right from wrong or control his behavior as required by law. Repetitive criminal acts are disavowed as a sole criterion. Compare *McNaghten rule* and *irresistible impulse*.

Amino acid. One of a large class of organic compounds, important as the building blocks of proteins.

Amnesia. Total or partial loss of memory which can be associated with a *dissociative disorder,* an *organic brain syndrome,* or *hypnosis.* **Anterograde,** loss of memory for events that have just occurred. **Retrograde,** loss of memory for events immediately preceding a traumatic incident; and sometimes for events extending far back in time. See *psychogenic amnesia*.

Amphetamines. A group of stimulating drugs which produce heightened levels of energy and, in large doses, nervousness, sleeplessness, and paranoid *delusions*.

Anaclitic depression. Profound sadness of an infant when separated from its mother for a prolonged period.

Anal personality. An adult who, when anal retentive, is found by psychoanalytic theory to be stingy and sometimes obsessively clean; when anal expulsive, to be aggressive. Such traits are assumed to be caused by *fixation* through either excessive or inadequate gratification of id impulses during the *anal stage* of *psychosexual* development.

Anal state. In psychoanalytic theory, the second *psychosexual stage,* occurring during the second year of life, during which the anus is considered to be the principal *erogenous zone*.

Analgesia. Insensitivity to pain without loss of consciousness; sometimes found in *conversion disorder*.

Analogue experiment. Experimental study of a phenomenon different from but related to the actual interests of the investigator.

Analysand. A person being psychoanalyzed.

Analyst. See *psychoanalyst*.

Anesthesia. Impairment or loss of sensation, usually of touch but sometimes of the other senses; often part of *conversion disorder*.

---

[1] Italicized words or variants of these terms are themselves defined elsewhere in the glossary.

Animal phobias. Fear and avoidance of small animals.

Anomic suicide. As defined by Durkheim, self-annihilation triggered by the person's inability to cope with sudden and unfavorable change in social situation.

Anorexia nervosa. Disorder in which a person is unable to eat or to retain any food or suffers a prolonged and severe diminution of appetite. The individual has an intense fear of becoming obese, feels fat even when emaciated, and, refusing to maintain a minimal body weight, loses at least 25 percent of original weight.

Anoxia. Deficiency in oxygen reaching the tissues severe enough to damage the brain permanently.

Antabuse (disulfiram). A drug which makes the drinking of alcohol produce nausea and other unpleasant effects.

Anterograde amnesia. Inability to form new memories after the brain has been damaged.

Antidepressant. A drug which alleviates *depression,* usually by energizing the patient and thus elevating mood.

Antisocial personality. Also called a psychopath or a sociopath, this person is superficially charming and a habitual liar, has no regard for others, shows no remorse after hurting them, has no shame for behaving in an outrageously objectionable manner, is unable to form relationships and take responsibility, and does not learn from punishment.

Anxiety. An unpleasant feeling of fear and apprehension accompanied by increased physiological arousal. In learning theory considered a drive which mediates between a threatening situation and avoidance behavior. Anxiety can be assessed by self-report, by measuring physiological arousal, and by observing overt behavior.

Anxiety disorders. Disorders in which fear or tension is overriding and the primary disturbance: *phobic disorders;* the *anxiety states,* which are *panic disorder, generalized anxiety disorder,* and *obsessive-compulsive disorder;* and *posttraumatic stress disorder.* Major category of DSM-III covering most of what used to be referred to as the *neuroses.*

Anxiety neurosis. DSM-II term for what are now diagnosed as *panic disorder* and *generalized anxiety disorder.*

Aphasia. Loss or impairment of the ability to use language because of lesions in the brain. **Executive,** difficulties in speaking or writing the words intended. **Receptive,** difficulties in understanding written or spoken language.

Arousal. A state of activation, either behavioral or physiological.

Ascriptive responsibility. The social judgment assigned to someone who has committed an illegal act and who, it is decided, should be punished for it; contrast with *descriptive responsibility.*

Assertion training. *Behavior therapy* procedures which attempt to help a person express more easily thoughts,

wishes, and beliefs and legitimate feelings of resentment or approval.

Asthma. A *psychophysiological disorder* characterized by narrowing of the airways and increased secretion of mucus, which often cause breathing to be extremely labored and wheezy.

Asylum. Refuge established in western Europe in the fifteenth century as a place to confine and provide for the mentally ill; forerunner of the mental hospital.

Attention. Maintenance of a readiness to respond; or focusing on relevant information.

Attention deficit disorder. Developmentally inappropriate inattention and impulsiveness. New DSM-III term for *hyperactivity,* reflecting the belief that hyperactive children suffer from a diminished ability to attend to the task at hand.

Attribution. The explanation a person has for his or her behavior.

Aura. Signal or warning of an impending epileptic *convulsion,* taking the form of dizziness or an unusual sensory experience.

Autism. Absorption in self or fantasy as a means of avoiding communication and escaping objective reality. See also *infantile autism.*

Autonomic nervous system. Division of the nervous system which regulates involuntary functions; innervates *endocrine glands, smooth muscle,* and heart muscle; initiates the physiological changes that are part of expression of emotion. See *sympathetic* amd *parasympathetic nervous system.*

Aversion therapy. A *behavior therapy* procedure which pairs a noxious stimulus, such as a shock, with situations that are undesirably attractive.

Aversive stimulus. A stimulus that elicits pain, fear, or avoidance.

Avoidance learning. An experimental procedure in which a neutral stimulus is paired with a noxious one so that the organism learns to avoid the previously neutral stimulus.

Avoidant disorder of childhood or adolescence. Persistent shrinking from strangers and from peers, despite a clear desire for affection, to the extent that social functioning is impaired; relations with family members are warm. New DSM-III diagnosis.

Avoidant personality. Thinking poorly of themselves, individuals with an avoidant personality are extremely sensitive to potential rejection and remain aloof from others, even though they very much desire affiliation and affection.

Barbiturate. A class of synthetic *sedative* drugs which are addictive and in large doses can cause death because the diaphragm relaxes almost completely.

Basal ganglia. Clusters of nerve cell bodies (*nuclei*) deep within the *cerebral hemispheres.* They are the lenticular nucleus, the caudate nucleus (collectively, the corpus striatum), the claustrum, and the amygdala.

Baseline. The state of a phenomenon before the *independent variable* is introduced, providing a standard against which the effects of the variable can be measured.

Behavior genetics. The study of individual differences in behavior that are attributable in part to differences in genetic makeup.

Behavior modification. A term sometimes used interchangeably with *behavior therapy*.

Behavior rehearsal. A *behavior therapy* technique in which a client practices new behavior in the consulting room, often aided by demonstrations of the therapist.

Behavior therapy. A branch of psychotherapy narrowly conceived as the application of *classical* and *operant conditioning* to the alteration of clinical problems, but more broadly conceived as applied experimental psychology.

Behavioral assessment. Sampling of ongoing conditions, feelings, and overt behavior in their situational context, to be contrasted with the *projective test* and *personality inventory*.

Behavioral medicine. *Behavioral therapy* procedures which apply to *psychophysiological disorders*; a new area of specialization.

Behaviorism. School of psychology associated with John B. Watson, who proposed that observable behavior, not consciousness, is the proper subject matter of psychology. Currently, some who consider themselves behaviorists do use *mediational* concepts, provided they are firmly anchored to observables.

Bell and pad. *Behavior therapy* technique for eliminating nocturnal *enuresis*; if the child wets, an electric circuit is closed and a bell sounds, waking the child.

Beta rhythm. The dominant pattern (14 to 25 cps) of *brain waves* found in an alert adult responding to a stimulus. See also *alpha rhythm*.

Biofeedback. A term referring to procedures that provide an individual immediate information of even minute changes in muscle activity, skin temperature, heart rate, blood pressure, and other somatic functions. It is assumed that voluntary control over these bodily processes can be achieved through this knowledge, thereby ameliorating to some extent certain *psychophysiological disorders*.

Bioenergetics. Therapy based on Wilhelm Reich's unorthodox analytic theory that all psychological distress is caused by problems in achieving full sexual satisfaction.

Biophysical system. As applied by Masters and Johnson, the part of the sexual response system that includes the genitalia and hormones.

Bipolar disorder. A term applied to the disorder of people who have experienced episodes of both *mania* and *depression* or of mania alone.

Bisexual. One who engages in both *heterosexual* and *homosexual* relations.

Borderline personality. This impulsive and unpredictable person has an uncertain self-image, intense and unstable social relationships, and extreme swings of mood; he or she may appear psychotic under stress.

Brain wave. Rhythmic fluctuations in voltage between parts of the brain produced by the spontaneous firings of its *neurons*; recorded by the *electroencephalograph*.

Brainstem. The part of the brain connecting the spinal cord with the *cerebrum*; contains the *pons* and *medulla oblongata* and functions as a neural relay station.

Brief reactive psychosis. Disorder in which the person has a sudden onset of psychotic symptoms—*incoherence, loosening of associations, delusions, hallucinations*—immediately after a severely disturbing event; the symptoms last more than a few hours but for no more than two weeks. New DSM-III diagnosis; see *schizophreniform disorder*.

Briquet's syndrome. See *somatization disorder*.

Bulimia. Episodic binge eating, often associated with induced vomiting.

Cardiovascular disorders. Medical problems involving the heart and blood circulation system, such as *hypertension* and *coronary heart disease*.

Case study. The collection of historical or biographical information on a single individual, often including experiences in therapy.

Castration. Surgical removal of the *testes* or ovaries.

Castration anxiety. Fear of having the genitals removed or injured.

CAT scan. Computerized axial tomography, a new method of diagnosis employing X-rays taken from different angles and then analyzed by computer to produce a representation of the part of the body in cross section. It can be used on the brain.

Catatonic immobility (catatonia). Fixity of posture, sometimes grotesque, maintained for long periods with accompanying muscular rigidity, trancelike state of consciousness, and *waxy flexibility*.

Catatonic schizophrenic. Psychotic patient whose primary symptoms alternate between stuporous immobility and excited agitation.

Catecholamines. *Monoamine* compounds (NH_2), each having a catechol portion (C_6H_6). Catecholamines known to be *neurotransmitters* of the central nervous system are *norepinephrine* and *dopamine*; another, *epinephrine*, is principally a hormone.

Catechol-O-methyltransferase (COMT). An enzyme which deactivates *catecholamines* in the *synapse*.

Cathartic method. Therapeutic procedure introduced by Breuer in late nineteenth century whereby a patient recalls and relives an earlier emotional catastrophe and reexperiences the tension and unhappiness.

Central nervous system. The part of the nervous system which in vertebrates consists of the brain and spinal cord and to which all sensory impulses are transmitted and from which motor impulses pass out; also supervises and coordinates the activities of the entire nervous system.

Central sulcus. A major fissure transversing the middle of the top and lateral surfaces of each *cerebral hemisphere,* dividing the *frontal lobe* from the *parietal.*

Cerebellum. An area of the hindbrain concerned with balance, posture, and motor coordination.

Cerebral atherosclerosis. A chronic disease impairing intellectual and emotional life and caused by a reduction in the brain's blood supply through a buildup of fatty deposits in the arteries.

Cerebral cortex. Thin outer covering of each of the *cerebral hemispheres,* highly convoluted, and made up of nerve cell bodies, which constitute the *gray matter* of the brain.

Cerebral hemisphere. Either of the two halves which make up the *cerebrum.*

Cerebral hemorrhage. Bleeding onto brain tissue from ruptured blood vessel.

Cerebral thrombosis. Formation of blood clot in cerebral artery, blocking circulation in that area of brain tissue and producing paralysis, loss of sensory functions, and even death.

Cerebrovascular diseases. Illnesses that disrupt blood supply to the brain, as in *stroke.*

Cerebrum. Two-lobed structure extending from the *brainstem* and constituting anterior part of brain. Largest and most recently developed portion of the human brain; coordinates sensory and motor activities as well as being seat of higher cognitive processes.

Childhood onset pervasive developmental disorder. Disorder of children older than thirty months but younger than twelve who indicate little empathy or emotional responsiveness to their peers, cling to their parents, take peculiar postures or make stereotyped movements, resist any change, have sudden anxieties and unexplained rages, and may occasionally be self-injurious. New DSM-III diagnosis replacing the earlier *childhood schizophrenia.*

Childhood schizophrenia. A childhood disorder, usually distinguished from *infantile autism,* in which emotions are grossly impaired, perceptions distorted, and body movements peculiar. Onset is after five years of age. DSM-II diagnosis replaced by *childhood onset pervasive developmental disorder.*

Chlorpromazine. Generic term for one of the most widely prescribed antipsychotic drugs, sold under the name *Thorazine.*

Cholinergic system. All the nerve cells for which *acetylcholine* is the transmitter substance, in contrast to the *adrenergic,* or more precisely the *monoaminergic.*

Choreiform. Pertaining to the involuntary, spasmodic, jerking movements of the limbs and head found in *Huntington's chorea* and other nervous disorders.

Chromosomes. Threadlike bodies within the nucleus of the cell, DNA being the principal constituent; regarded as carrying the *genes.*

Chronic. Of lengthy duration or recurring frequently, often with progressing seriousness.

Chronic brain syndrome. See *senile dementia.*

Chronic schizophrenic. Psychotic patient who had earlier deteriorated over a long period of time before diagnosis and who has usually been hospitalized for more than two years.

Civil commitment. Procedure whereby a person can be legally certified as mentally ill and hospitalized, even against his will.

Clang association. A stringing together of words because they are similar in sound, with no attention paid to their meaning, for example, ''How are you Don, pawn, gone?''

Classical conditioning. A basic form of learning, sometimes referred to as Pavlovian conditioning, in which a neutral stimulus is repeatedly paired with another stimulus (called the *unconditioned stimulus,* UCS) that naturally elicits a certain desired response (UCR). After repeated trials the neutral stimulus becomes a *conditioned stimulus* (CS) and evokes the same or similar response, called now the *conditioned response* (CR).

Classificatory variables. Characteristics which subjects bring with them into scientific investigations, such as sex, age, and mental status; studied by *correlational* research and *mixed designs.*

Client-centered therapy. A *humanistic-existential insight therapy,* developed by Carl Rogers, which emphasizes the importance of the therapist's understanding of the client's subjective experiences and assisting him or her to gain more awareness of the current motivations for behavior; the goal is not only to reduce anxieties but also to foster actualization of the client's potential.

Climacteric. The period in middle age when for the female menstruation ceases and for the male sexual activity and competence may be reduced.

Clinical psychologist. An individual who has usually earned a Ph.D degree in psychology or a Psy.D. and whose training has included an internship in a mental hospital or clinic.

Clinical psychology. Special area of psychology concerned with the study of psychopathology, its causes, prevention, and treatment.

Clitoris. Small heavily innervated erectile structure located above the vaginal opening; primary site of female responsiveness to sexual stimulation.

Clonic phase. Stage of violent contortions and jerking of limbs in a *grand mal epileptic* attack.

Cocaine. A pain-reducing and stimulating *alkaloid* obtained from coca leaves; increases mental powers, produces euphoria, heightens sexual desire, and in large doses causes *paranoia* and *hallucinations.*

Cognition. The process of knowing; the thinking, judging, reasoning, planning activities of the human mind. Behavior is now often explained as depending on the course these *symbolic processes* take.

Cognitive restructuring. Any *behavior therapy* procedure which attempts to alter the manner in which clients think about life so that they change their overt behavior and emotions.

Cohort effects. Consequences of having been born in a given year and having grown up during a particular time period with its own unique pressures, problems, challenges, opportunities; to be distinguished from *age effects.*

Coitus. Sexual intercourse.

Colic. A condition found in infants in which gas collects in the stomach and produces distress.

Community mental health. Delivery of services to needy, underserved groups through centers that offer outpatient therapy, short-term inpatient care, day hospitalization, twenty-four-hour emergency services, and consultation and education to other community agencies such as the police.

Community psychology. An approach to therapy which emphasizes prevention and the seeking out of potential difficulties rather than waiting for troubled individuals to initiate consultation. The location for professional activities tends to be in the persons' natural surroundings rather than in the therapist's office. See *prevention.*

Competency to stand trial. Legal decision whether a person can participate meaningfully in his or her own defense.

Compulsion. Irresistible impulse to repeat an irrational act over and over again.

Compulsive personality. Perfectionistic and work- rather than pleasure-oriented, people with a compulsive personality have inordinate difficulty making decisions, are overconcerned with details and efficiency, and relate poorly to others because they demand that things be done their way and are unduly conventional, serious, formal, and stingy with their emotions.

Concordance. As applied in *behavior genetics,* the similarity in psychiatric diagnosis or in other traits in a pair of twins.

Concrete operations stage. Third period of intellectual development, ages seven to eleven, according to Piaget; the child has acquired well-organized cognitive systems, such as notions of time, space, and number.

Concrete reasoning. A pattern of thinking in which abstractions and generalizations cannot be made and terms and details of conversation are interpreted literally.

Concurrent validity. See *validity.*

Concussion. A jarring injury to the brain produced by a blow to the head; usually involves a momentary loss of consciousness followed by transient disorientation and memory loss.

Conditioned response (CR). Response elicited by a given neutral stimulus (CS), after it has become conditioned by repeated contingent pairings with another stimulus (UCS) that naturally elicits this same or a similar response.

Conditioned stimulus (CS). A neutral stimulus which, after repeated contingent pairings with another stimulus (UCS) that naturally elicits a certain response (UCR), comes to elicit the same or a similar response, called the *conditioned response* (CR).

Conduct disorders. Patterns of extreme disobedience in youngsters, including theft, vandalism, lying, and early drug use; may be precursors of *antisocial personality* disorder.

Confabulation. Filling in gaps in memory caused by brain dysfunction with made-up and often improbable stories which the subject accepts as true.

Confidentiality. A principle observed by lawyers, doctors, and pastors, by psychologists and psychiatrists that the goings-on in a professional and confidential relationship are not divulged to anyone else. See *privileged communication.*

Conflict. A state of being torn between competing forces.

Confounds. Variables whose effects are so intermixed that they cannot be measured separately, making the design of the *experiment* internally invalid and its results impossible to interpret.

Congenital. Existing at or before birth but not acquired through heredity.

Construct. An entity inferred by a scientist to explain observed phenomena. See also *mediator.*

Contingency. A close relationship, especially of a causal nature, between two events, one of which regularly follows the other.

Control group. Subjects in an *experiment* for whom the *independent variable* is not manipulated, thus forming a *baseline* against which the effects of the manipulation can be evaluated.

Controlled drinking. A pattern of alcohol consumption that is moderate and avoids the extremes of total abstinence and of inebriation.

Contusion, cerebral. A bruising of neural tissue marked by swelling and hemorrhage and resulting in coma; may permanently impair intellectual functioning.

Conversion disorder. A *somatoform disorder* in which sensory or muscular functions are impaired, usually suggesting neurological disease, even though the bodily organs themselves are sound; *anesthesias* and paralyses of limbs are examples. The symptom appears suddenly when the person is in a state of stress, or it allows him or her to avoid responsibility or gain needed attention.

Convulsion. Violent and extensive twitching of the body caused by involuntary pathological muscle contractions.

Convulsive therapy. A biological therapy which induces *convulsions* by drugs or electric shock in hopes of effecting beneficial behavior change. See *electroconvulsive therapy.*

Coronary heart disease. Angina pectoris, chest pains caused by insufficient supply of blood and thus oxygen to the heart; and myocardial infarction, or heart attack, in which the blood and oxygen supply is reduced so much that heart muscles are damaged.

Corpus callosum. Large band of nerve fibers connecting the two *cerebral hemispheres.*

Correlational method. Research strategy used to establish whether two or more variables are related. Such relationships may be positive—as values for one variable increase, those for the other do also; or negative—as values for one variable increase, those for the other decrease.

Cortisone. A hormone secreted by the adrenal cortices.

Co-twin. In *behavior genetics* research using the *twin method,* the member of the pair who is tested later to determine whether he has the same diagnosis or trait discovered earlier in his birth partner, the *index case.*

Counterconditioning. Relearning achieved by eliciting a new response in the presence of a particular stimulus.

Countertransference. Feelings which the *analyst* unconsciously directs to the *analysand* but which come from his or her own emotional vulnerabilities and unresolved *conflicts.*

Covert sensitization. A form of *aversion therapy* in which the subject is told to imagine the undesirably attractive situations and activities at the same time that unpleasant feelings are also induced by imagery.

Cretinism. Condition beginning in prenatal or early life characterized by *mental retardation* and physical deformities; caused by severe deficiency in the output of the *thyroid gland.*

Criminal commitment. Procedure whereby a person is confined in a mental institution either for determination of *competency to stand trial* or after acquittal by reason of insanity.

Critical period. Stage of early development in which organism needs certain inputs and during which important irreversible patterns of behavior are acquired. See *imprinting.*

Cultural-familial retardation. Mild backwardness in mental development with no indication of brain pathology but evidence of similar limitation in at least one of the parents or siblings.

Cunnilingus. Oral stimulation of female genitalia.

Cushing's syndrome. An endocrine disorder usually affecting young women; produced by oversecretion of *cortisone* and marked by mood swings, irritability, agitation, and physical disfigurement.

Defect theorist. In the study of *mental retardation,* a person who believes that the cognitive processes of retardates are qualitatively different from those of normal individuals; contrast with *developmental theorist.*

Defense mechanism. In psychoanalytic theory, a reality-distorting strategy unconsciously adopted to protect the ego from anxiety.

Delay of reward gradient. Learning theory term for the finding that rewards and punishments lose their effectiveness the farther in time they are removed from the response in question.

Delirium. A state of great mental confusion in which consciousness is clouded, attention cannot be sustained, and the stream of thought and speech is incoherent. The person is probably disoriented, emotionally erratic, restless or lethargic, and often has *illusions, delusions,* and *hallucinations.*

Delirium tremens (DTs). One of the *withdrawal symptoms* when a period of heavy alcohol consumption is terminated; marked by fever, sweating, trembling, cognitive impairment, and *hallucinations.*

Delta rhythm. See *slow brain waves.*

Delusion. A belief contrary to reality, firmly held in spite of evidence to the contrary; common in paranoid disorders. **Of control,** belief that one is being manipulated by some external force such as radar, TV, or a creature from outer space. **Of grandeur,** belief that one is an especially important or powerful person. **Of persecution,** belief that one is being plotted against or oppressed by others.

Delusional jealousy. The unfounded conviction that one's mate is unfaithful. The individual may collect small bits of "evidence" to justify the *delusion.*

Dementia. Progressive deterioration of mental faculties—of memory, judgment, abstract thought, control of impulses, intellectual ability—that impairs social and occupational functioning and eventually changes the personality.

Dementia praecox. An older term for *schizophrenia,* chosen to describe what was believed to be an incurable and progressive deterioration of mental functioning beginning in adolescence.

Demographic variable. Varying characteristic which is a vital or social statistic of an individual, sample group, or population, for example, age, sex, *socioeconomic status*, racial origin, education and the like.

Demonology. The doctrine that a person's abnormal behavior is caused by an autonomous evil spirit dwelling within.

Dependent personality. Lacking in self-confidence, people with a dependent personality passively allow others to run their lives and make no demands on them, lest they endanger these protective relationships.

Dependent variable. In a psychological *experiment*, the behavior that is measured and is expected to change with manipulation of the *independent variable*.

Depersonalization. An alteration in perception of the self in which the individual loses a sense of reality and feels estranged from the self and perhaps separated from the body; may be a temporary reaction to stress and fatigue or part of *panic disorder, depersonalization disorder,* and *schizophrenia.*

Depersonalization disorder. A *dissociative disorder* in which the individual feels unreal and estranged from the self and surroundings, enough to disrupt functioning. The patient may feel that the extremities have changed in size or that he or she watches the self from a distance.

Depression. Emotional state marked by great sadness and apprehension, feelings of worthlessness and guilt; withdrawal from others, loss of sleep, appetite, and sexual desire, or interest and pleasure in usual activities; and either lethargy or agitation. Called *major depression* in DSM-III and by others *unipolar depression,* it can be an associated symptom of other disorders.

Derealization. Loss of the sense that the surroundings are real; present in several psychological disorders, such as *panic disorder, depersonalization disorder,* and *schizophrenia.*

Descriptive responsibility. In legal proceedings, the judgment that the accused performed an illegal act; contrast with *ascriptive responsibility.*

Deterioration effect. In abnormal psychology, harmful outcome from being in psychotherapy.

Detumescence. Flow of blood out of the genital area.

Developmental theorist. In the study of *mental retardation,* a person who believes that the cognitive development of retardates has simply been slower than that of normal individuals, not qualitatively different; contrast with *defect theorist.*

Diagnosis. The determination that the set of symptoms or problems of a patient indicate a particular disorder.

Diathesis. *Predisposition* toward a disease or abnormality.

Diathesis-stress paradigm. View which, as applied in psychopathology, assumes that individuals predisposed toward a particular mental disorder will be particularly affected by stress and will then manifest abnormal behavior.

Dichotic listening. Experimental procedure in which a subject hears two taped messages simultaneously through earphones, one in each ear, usually with the instruction to attend to only one of the messages.

Diencephalon. Lower area of the forebrain containing the *thalamus* and *hypothalamus.*

Directionality problem. A difficulty in *correlational* research whereby it is known that two variables are related but it is unclear which is causing the other.

Disease. The medical concept that distinguishes an impairment of the normal state of the organism by its particular group of symptoms and its specific cause.

Disease model. See *medical model.*

Disorganized schizophrenic. A person with *schizophrenia* who has rather diffuse and regressive symptoms; the individual is given to silliness, facial grimaces, and inconsequential rituals and has constantly changeable moods and poor hygiene. There are few significant remissions and eventually considerable deterioration. This form of schizophrenia was formerly called hebephrenia.

Disorientation. A state of mental confusion with respect to time, place, and identity of self, other persons, and objects.

Displacement. A *defense mechanism* whereby an emotional response is unconsciously redirected from a perhaps dangerous object or concept to a substitute less threatening to the ego.

Dissociation. A process whereby a group of mental processes is split off from the mainstream of consciousness, or behavior loses its relationship with the rest of the personality.

Dissociative disorders. Disorders in which the normal integration of consciousness, memory, or identity is suddently and temporarily altered: *psychogenic amnesia, psychogenic fugue, multiple personality,* and *depersonalization disorder.* New DSM-III category.

Dizygotic (fraternal) twins. Birth partners who have developed from separate fertilized eggs and who are only 50 percent alike genetically, no more so than siblings born from different pregnancies.

Dominant gene. One of a pair of *genes* which predominates over the other and determines that the *trait* it fosters will prevail in the *phenotype.*

Dopamine. A *catecholamine* which is both a precursor of *norepinephrine* and itself a *neurotransmitter* of the central nervous system. Disturbances in certain of its tracts apparently figure in *schizophrenia* and *Parkinson's disease.*

Double bind. An interpersonal situation in which an individual is confronted, over long periods of time, by mutually inconsistent messages to which he or her must respond. Believed by some theorists to cause *schizophrenia.*

Double-blind procedure. A method for reducing the biasing effects of the expectations of subject and experimenter; neither is allowed to know whether the *independent variable* of the *experiment* is being applied to the particular subject.

Down's syndrome (mongolism). A form of *mental retardation* generally caused by an extra *chromosome*. The child's IQ is usually less than 50, and his or her physical characteristics are distinctive, the one most often noted being slanted eyes.

Dream analysis. A key psychoanalytic technique in which the unconscious meanings of dream material are uncovered.

Drive. A *construct* explaining the motivation of behavior; or an internal physiological tension impelling an organism to activity.

Drug addiction. Physiological reliance on a drug developed through continual use; characterized by *tolerance* and *withdrawal symptoms.*

Drug dependence. Habitual use of a drug out of psychological but not physiological need; contrast with *drug addiction.*

DSM-III. The current diagnostic and statistical manual of the American Psychiatric Association.

Dualism. Philosophical doctrine that a human being is both mental and physical and that these two aspects are separate but interacting; advanced in its most definitive statement by Descartes. Contrast with *monism.*

Durham decision. A 1954 American court ruling that an accused person is not *ascriptively* responsible if his or her crime is judged attributable to mental disease or defect.

Dysfunction. Impairment or disturbance in the functioning of an organ, organ system, behavior or cognition.

Dyslexia. Disturbance in the ability to read; one of the *learning disabilities* or *specific developmental disorders.*

Dyspareunia. Painful or difficult sexual intercourse, the pain or difficulty usually being caused by infection or a physical injury such as torn ligaments in the pelvic region.

Echolalia. The immediate and sometimes pathological repetition of the words of others; a speech problem often found in autistic children. In **delayed echolalia** this inappropriate echoing takes place hours or weeks later.

Eclecticism. In psychology, the view that more is to be gained by employing concepts from various theoretical systems than by restricting oneself to a single theory.

Ego. In psychoanalytic theory, the predominantly conscious part of the personality, responsible for decision making and for dealing with reality.

Ego-alien. Foreign to the self, such as a *compulsion.*

Ego analysis. An important set of modifications of classical *psychoanalysis,* based on a conception of the human being as having a stronger, more autonomous *ego* with gratifications independent of *id* satisfactions. Sometimes called ego psychology.

Ego-dystonic homosexuality. Disorder of people who are persistently dissatisfied with their *homosexuality* and wish instead to be attracted to members of the opposite sex. New DSM-III diagnosis.

Egoistic suicide. As defined by Durkheim, self-annihilation committed because the individual feels extreme alienation from others and from society.

Ejaculate. To expel semen, typically during male orgasm.

Elective mutism. Pattern of continuously refusing to speak in almost all social situations, including school, even though the child understands spoken language and is able to speak.

Electra complex. See *Oedipus complex.*

Electrocardiograph. Device for recording the electrical activity that occurs during the heartbeat.

Electroconvulsive therapy (ECT). Treatment which produces a *convulsion* by passing electric current through the brain; useful in alleviating profound *depression,* although typically an unpleasant and occasionally dangerous procedure.

Electroencephalogram (EEG). A graphic recording of electrical activity of the brain, usually that of the *cerebral cortex,* but sometimes the electrical activity of lower areas.

Empathy. Awareness and understanding of another's feelings and thoughts; see *primary empathy* and *advanced accurate empathy.*

Empty-chair technique. *Gestalt therapy* procedure for helping the client become more aware of denied feelings; the client talks to important people or to feelings as though they were present and seated in a nearby vacant chair.

Encephalitis. Inflammation of brain tissue caused by a number of agents, the most important being several viruses carried by insects.

Encephalitis lethargica. Known as sleeping sickness. Form of encephalitis which occurred earlier in this century and was characterized by lethargy and prolonged periods of sleeping.

Encopresis. Disorder in which, through faulty control of the sphincters, the person repeatedly defecates in his or her clothing after an age at which continence is expected.

Encounter group. See *sensitivity group.*

Endocrine gland. Any of a number of ductless glands which release *hormones* directly into the blood or lymph. The secretions of some endocrine glands increase during emotional arousal.

Endogenous. Attributable to internal causes.

Endogenous depression. Profound sadness assumed to be caused by a biochemical malfunction in contrast to an environmental event; more recently regarded simply as having a more severe set of *symptoms*.

Endorphins. *Opiates* produced within the body; they may have an important role in the processes by which it builds up *tolerance* to drugs and is distressed by their withdrawal.

Enuresis. Disorder in which, through faulty control of the bladder, the person wets repeatedly during the night (nocturnal enuresis) or during the day after an age at which continence is expected.

Environmental psychology. A recent community-oriented psychology which assumes that people's feelings and behavior are importantly a function of their physical setting.

Enzyme. A complex protein produced by the cells to act as a catalyst in regulating metabolic activities.

Epilepsy. An altered state of consciousness accompanied by sudden changes in the usual rhythmical electrical activity of the brain. See also *grand mal, petit mal, Jacksonian*, and *psychomotor epilepsy*.

Epinephrine. Hormone (a *catecholamine*) secreted by the medulla of the *adrenal gland;* its effects are similar, but not identical, to those of stimulating the *sympathetic* nerves; causes an increase in blood pressure, inhibits peristaltic movements, and liberates glucose from the liver. Also called *adrenaline.*

Ergot. See *LSD.*

Erogenous. Capable of giving sexual pleasure when stimulated.

Eros (libido). Freud's term for the life-integrating instinct or force of the *id*, sometimes equated with sexual drive; compare *Thanatos.*

Essential hypertension. A *psychophysiological disorder* characterized by high blood pressure that cannot be traced to an organic cause; causes enlargement and degeneration of small arteries, enlargement of the heart, and kidney damage.

Estrogen. Female sex hormone produced especially in the ovaries; stimulates the development of and maintains the secondary sex characteristics, such as breast enlargement.

Etiological validity. See *validity.*

Etiology. All the factors that contribute to the development of an illness or disorder.

Eugenics. Science concerned with improving the hereditary qualities of the human race through social control of mating and reproduction.

Ex post facto analysis. In *correlational research*, an attempt to reduce the *third-variable problem* by picking subjects who are matched on characteristics that may be *confounds.*

Excitement phase. As applied by Masters and Johnson, the first stage of sexual arousal which is initiated by any appropriate stimulus.

Exhibitionism. Marked preference for obtaining sexual gratification by exposing one's genitals to an unwilling observer.

Existential analysis. See *humanistic-existential therapy.*

Existential neurosis. Disorder in which patient feels alienation, considers life meaningless, and finds no activity worth selecting and pursuing. See also *premorbid personality.*

Exogenous. Attributable to external causes.

Exogenous depression. Profound sadness assumed to be caused by an environmental event.

Exorcism. Casting out of evil spirits by ritualistic chanting or torture.

Experiment. The most powerful research technique for determining causal relationships, requiring the manipulation of an *independent variable*, the measurement of a *dependent variable*, and the *random assignment* of subjects to the several different conditions being investigated.

Experimental hypothesis. What the investigator assumes will happen in a scientific investigation if certain conditions are met or particular variables are manipulated.

Expressed emotion. In the literature on *schizophrenia*, the amount of hostility and criticism directed from one person to another, usually within a family.

External validity. See *validity.*

Extinction. Elimination of a classically *conditioned response* by the omission of the *unconditioned stimulus*. In *operant conditioning*, the elimination of the conditioned response by the omission of *reinforcement.*

Extradural hematoma. Hemorrhage and swelling between the skull and dura mater when a *meningeal* artery is ruptured by a fractured bone of the skull.

Extroversion. See *introversion-extroversion.*

Factitious disorder. Disorder in which the individual's physical or psychological symptoms appear under voluntary control and are adopted merely to assume the role of a sick person. This goal is not voluntary, however, and implies a severe disturbance. New DSM-III diagnosis; compare with *malingering.*

Falsifiability. See *testability.*

Familiar. A supernatural spirit often embodied in an animal and at the service of a person.

Family interaction method. A procedure for studying family behavior by observing their interaction in a structured laboratory situation.

Family method. Research strategy in *behavior genetics* in which the frequency of a *trait* or of abnormal behavior is determined in relatives who have varying percentages of shared genetic background.

Family therapy. A form of *group therapy* in which members of a family are helped to relate better to one another.

Fear-drive. In the Mowrer-Miller theory, an unpleasant internal state which impels avoidance. The necessity to reduce a fear-drive can form the basis for new learning.

Fear-response. In the Mowrer-Miller theory, a response to a threatening or noxious situation which is covert and unobservable but which is assumed to function as a stimulus to produce measurable physiological changes in the body and observable overt behavior.

Fellatio. Oral stimulation of the *penis.*

Fetal alcohol syndrome. Retarded growth of the developing fetus and infant; cranial, facial, and limb anomalies, and mental retardation caused by heavy consumption of alcohol by the future mother during pregnancy.

Fetishism. Reliance on an inanimate object or a part of the body for sexual arousal.

First-rank symptoms. In *schizophrenia,* specific *delusions* and *hallucinations* proposed by Schneider as particularly important for its more exact diagnosis.

Fixation. In psychoanalytic theory, the arrest of *psychosexual* development at a particular stage through too much or too little gratification at that stage.

Flashback. Unpredictable recurrence of *psychedelic* experiences from an earlier drug trip.

Flat affect. A deviation in emotional response wherein virtually no emotion is expressed whatever the stimuli, or emotional expressiveness is blunted; or a lack of expression and muscle tone in the face.

Flight of ideas. Rapid shift from one subject to another in conversation, with only superficial associative connections; a symptom of *mania.*

Flooding therapy. A *behavior therapy* procedure in which a fearful person exposes himself or herself to what is frightening, in reality or in the imagination, for extended periods of time and without opportunity for escape.

Follow-up study. A research procedure whereby individuals observed in an earlier investigation are contacted at a later time.

Forced-choice selection. Format of a *personality inventory* in which the response alternatives for each item are equated for social desirability.

Forensic psychiatry. The branch of psychiatry that deals with the legal questions raised by disordered behavior.

Formal operations stage. Final stage of intellectual development, eleven years and older, according to Piaget; the child becomes able to deal with the hypothetical; thinking is not tied to concrete external objects.

Free association. A key psychoanalytic procedure, in which the *analysand* is encouraged to give free rein to his or her thoughts and feelings, verbalizing whatever comes into the mind without monitoring its content; the assumption is that, over time, hitherto repressed material will come forth for examination by the analysand and *analyst.*

Free-floating anxiety. Continual anxiety not attributable to any specific situation or reasonable danger; see *generalized anxiety disorder.*

Frontal lobe. The forward or upper half of each *cerebral hemisphere,* in front of the *central sulcus;* active in reasoning and other higher mental processes.

Fugue. See *psychogenic fugue.*

Functional psychosis. A condition in which thought, behavior, and emotion are disturbed without known pathological changes in tissues or the conditions of the brain.

Galvanic skin response (GSR). Change in electric conductivity of the skin caused by increase in activity of sweat glands when the *sympathetic nervous system* is active, in particular when the organism is anxious.

Gay. A colloquial term for a homosexual; now often adopted by homosexuals who have openly announced their sexual orientation.

Gay liberation. The often militant movement seeking to achieve civil rights for homosexuals and recognition of the normality of *homosexuality.*

Gender identity. The deeply ingrained sense a person has of being either a man or woman.

Gender identity disorders. Disorders in which there is a deeply felt incongruence between anatomic sex and the sensed gender: *transsexualism* and *gender identity disorder of childhood.* New DSM-III category.

Gene. An ultramicroscopic area of the *chromosome;* the smallest physical unit of the DNA molecule that carries a piece of the information of heredity.

General paresis. See *neurosyphilis.*

Generalized anxiety disorder. One of the *anxiety disorders;* anxiety is so chronic, persistent, and pervasive that it seems *free-floating.* The individual is jittery and strained, distractible and apprehensive that something bad is about to happen. A pounding heart, fast pulse and breathing, sweating, flushing, muscle aches, a lump in the throat, and an upset gastrointestinal tract are some of the bodily indications of this extreme anxiety.

Genetic disease. An abnormality determined at the moment of conception.

Genital stage. In psychoanalytic theory, the final *psychosexual stage* reached in adulthood, in which heterosexual interests predominate.

Genotype. An individual's unobservable, physiological genetic constitution; the totality of *genes* possessed by an individual. Compare *phenotype*.

Germ theory. General view in medicine that disease is caused by infection of the body by minute organisms and viruses.

Gerontology. Interdisciplinary study of aging and of the special problems of the aged.

Gestalt therapy. A *humanistic therapy*, developed by Fritz Perls, which encourages clients to satisfy emerging needs so that their innate goodness can be expressed, to increase their awareness of unacknowledged feelings, and to reclaim parts of the personality that have been denied or disowned.

Gestation period. The length of time, normally nine months in human beings, during which a fertilized egg develops into an infant ready to be born.

Gilles de la Tourette's syndrome. Extremely rare disorder in which the person involuntarily grimaces, twitches, makes strange sounds—clicks, grunts, yelps, barking—and utters profanities.

Glans. The heavily innervated tip of the *penis*.

Glove anesthesia. An hysterical lack of sensation in the part of the hand that would usually be covered by a glove.

Going in drag. Dressing in female attire, usually with extensive makeup, by a male homosexual.

Grand mal epilepsy. The most severe form of *epilepsy*, involving loss of consciousness and violent *convulsions*.

Grandiosity. An inflated appraisal of one's worth, power, knowledge, importance, or identity.

Graves' disease. An endocrine disorder resulting from oversecretion of the hormone *thyroxin;* metabolic processes are speeded up, producing apprehension, restlessness, and irritability.

Gray matter. Neural tissue made up largely of nerve cell bodies; constitutes the cortex covering the *cerebral hemisphere,* the *nuclei* in lower brain areas, columns of the spinal cord, and the ganglia of the *autonomic nervous system*.

Grimace. Distorted facial expression, often a symptom of *schizophrenia*.

Group therapy. Method of treating psychological disorders whereby several persons are seen simultaneously by a single therapist.

Gyrus. A ridge or convolution of the *cerebral cortex*.

Habituation. In physiology, a process whereby an organism's response to the same stimulus temporarily lessens with repeated presentations.

Halfway house. A homelike residence for people who are considered too disturbed to remain in their accustomed surroundings but do not require the total care of a mental institution.

Hallucination. A perception in any sensory modality without relevant and adequate external stimuli.

Hallucinogen. A drug or chemical whose effects include *hallucinations*. Hallucinogenic drugs such as *LSD, psilocybin,* and *mescaline* are often called *psychedelic*.

Hashish. The dried resin of the *Cannabis* plant, stronger in its effects than the dried leaves and stems which constitute *marijuana*.

Hebephrenia. See *disorganized schizophrenic*.

Helplessness. A *construct* referring to the sense of having no control over important events; considered by many theorists to play a central role in *anxiety* and *depression*. See *learned helplessness*.

Hermaphrodite. A person with parts of both male and female genitalia.

Heroin. An extremely addictive *narcotic* drug derived from *morphine*.

Heterosexual. One who desires or engages in sexual relations with members of the opposite sex.

High-risk method. A research technique, used especially in the study of *schizophrenia,* involving the intensive examination of people who have a high probability of later becoming abnormal.

Histrionic personality. This person is overly dramatic and given to emotional excess, impatient with minor annoyances, immature, dependent on others, and often sexually seductive, without taking responsibility for flirtations. Formerly called hysterical personality.

Hives. A transient skin condition characterized by slightly raised, itching patches; often considered a *psychophysiological disorder*.

Homophobia. Fear of *homosexuality*.

Homosexuality. Sexual desire or activity directed toward a member of one's own sex.

Homovanillic acid. A major metabolite of *dopamine*.

Hormone. A chemical substance produced by an *endocrine gland* and released into the blood or lymph for the purpose of controlling the function of a distant organ or organ system. Metabolism, growth, and development of secondary sexual characteristics are among the functions so controlled.

Humanistic-existential therapy. *Insight* psychotherapy which emphasizes the individual's subjective experiences, free will, and ever-present ability to decide on a new life course.

Huntington's chorea. A fatal *presenile dementia*, passed on by a single *dominant* gene. The symptoms include spasmodic jerking of the limbs, psychotic behavior, and mental deterioration.

Hurler's syndrome (gargoylism). An inherited physical and mental deterioration in which monopolysaccharides accumulate in the cells. Survival past the age of twenty is unusual.

5-Hydroxyindoleacetic acid (5-HIAA). The major metabolite of *serotonin* that is present in the cerebrospinal fluid.

Hyperactivity. A childhood disorder marked by an inability to inhibit movement and to concentrate in situations that call for it; problems in learning, in listening and finishing things, and in relating to others are also common. Called *attention deficit disorder* with hyperactivity in DSM-III.

Hypertension. Abnormally high arterial blood pressure, with or without known organic causes. See *essential hypertension*.

Hyperventilation. Very rapid and deep breathing associated with high levels of anxiety; causes level of carbon dioxide in blood to be lowered, with possible loss of consciousness.

Hypnosis. A trancelike state or behavior resembling sleep, characterized primarily by increased suggestibility and induced by suggestion.

Hypochondriasis. A *somatoform disorder* in which the person, misinterpreting rather ordinary physical sensations, is preoccupied with fears of having a serious disease and is not dissuaded by medical opinion. Difficult to distinguish from *somatization disorder*.

Hypothalamus. A collection of *nuclei* and fibers in the lower part of the *diencephalon*; concerned with the regulation of many visceral processes, such as metabolism, temperature, water balance, and so on.

Hysteria (hysterical state). Disorder, known to the ancient Greeks, in which a physical incapacity, a paralysis, an anesthesia, or an analgesia, makes no anatomical sense, for example, *glove anesthesia*; an older term for *conversion disorder*. In the late nineteenth century *dissociative disorders* were identified as such and considered hysterical states.

Hysterical neurosis. DSM-II category for *dissociative* and *somatoform disorders*.

Id. In psychoanalytic theory, that part of the personality present at birth, composed of all the energy of the *psyche* and expressed as biological urges which strive continually for gratification.

Ideas of reference. *Delusional* thinking which reads personal significance into seemingly trivial remarks and activities of others and completely unrelated events.

Idiographic. In psychology, relating to investigative procedures that consider the unique characteristics of a single person, studying them in depth, as in the *case study*; contrast with *nomothetic*.

Idiot savant. An individual with a rare form of *mental retardation*, being extraordinarily talented in one or a few limited areas of intellectual achievement.

Illusion. A misperception of a real external stimulus, such as hearing the slapping of waves as footsteps.

Imipramine. An *antidepressant* drug, one of the *tricyclic* group.

Implosion therapy. A *behavior therapy* technique for reducing neurotic fears; the client is encouraged to imagine himself in the most frightening of situations and to visualize bizarre images, the assumption being that adult fears are traceable to *psychodynamic* themes of sex and aggression which must be confronted.

Impotence—primary. The physical or psychological condition of a male who has never had an erection sufficient for either heterosexual or homosexual intercourse. **Secondary,** inability of the male to have an erection sufficient for intercourse, although he has a history of at least one successful *intromission*. Replaced in DSM-III by *inhibited sexual excitement*.

Imprinting. The irreversible acquisition of behavior by a neonate of a social species during a *critical period* of development. The neonate is attracted to and mimics the first moving object seen, thereby acquiring specific patterns of behavior.

In absentia. Literally, "in one's absence." Courts are concerned that a person be able to participate personally and meaningfully in his own trial and not be tried *in absentia* because of a distracting mental disorder.

In vivo. As applied in psychology, taking place in a real-life situation.

Inappropriate affect. Emotional responses which are out of context, such as laughter when hearing sad news.

Incest. Sexual relations between close relatives for whom marriage is forbidden, most often between daughter and father or between brother and sister.

Incidence. In community studies of a particular disorder, the rate at which new cases occur in a given place at a given time; compare with *prevalence*.

Incoherence. In *schizophrenia*, an aspect of *thought disorder* wherein verbal expression is marked by disconnectedness, fragmented thoughts, jumbled phrases, and *neologisms*.

Independent variable. In a psychological *experiment*, the factor, experience, or treatment which is under the control of the experimenter and which is expected to have an effect on the subjects as assessed by changes in the *dependent variable*.

Index case. The person who in a genetic investigation bears the diagnosis or *trait* that the investigator is interested in. Same as *proband*.

Indoleamines. *Monoamine* compounds (NH_2), each containing an indole portion (C_8H_7N); indoleamines believed to act in neurotransmission are *serotonin* and tryptamine.

Infantile autism. A childhood disorder marked by early and profound aloneness, a hedged inner world fended from all encroachments; *mustism* or *echolalic* speech; and intolerance of any change in routine or surroundings.

Infectious disease. Illness caused when a microorganism, such as a bacterium or a virus, invades the body, multiplies, and attacks a specific organ or organ system; pneumonia is an example.

Informed consent. Agreement of a person to serve as a research subject or to enter therapy after being told the possible outcomes, both benefits and risks.

Inhibited female orgasm. Recurrent and persistent delay or absence of orgasm in a woman during sexual activity adequate in focus, intensity, and duration; in many instances the woman may experience considerable sexual excitement nonetheless. New DSM-III term.

Inhibited male orgasm. Recurrent and persistent delay or absence of ejaculation after an adequate phase of sexual excitement. New DSM-III term.

Inhibited sexual desire. Sexual interest which is less than the individual, the partner, or both regard as suitable. New DSM-III diagnosis.

Inhibited sexual excitement. Recurrent and persistent lack of sexual excitement during sexual activity. New term for *impotence* in men, frigidity in women; see also *inhibited female orgasm*.

Insanity defense. Legal argument that a defendant should not be held *ascriptively responsible* for an illegal act if the conduct is attributable to mental illness.

Insight therapy. General term for any *psychotherapy* which attempts to impart to a patient greater awareness of what motivates his or her behavior, the assumption being that disordered behavior is caused by *repression* or other unconscious *conflicts*.

Instrumental learning. See *operant conditioning*.

Intelligence quotient (IQ). Technically now a deviation IQ, indicating how far an individual's raw score on an *intelligence test* falls away from the average raw score of his or her chronological age group.

Intelligence test. Standardized means of assessing a person's current mental abilities, for example, the Stanford-Binet test and the Wechsler Adult Intelligence Scale.

Internal validity. See *validity*.

Interpretation. In *psychoanalysis*, a key procedure in which the *analyst* points out to the *analysand* where *resistances* exist and what certain dreams and verbalizations reveal about impulses repressed in the *unconscious;* more generally, any statement by a therapist that construes the client's problem in a new way.

Introjection. In psychoanalytic theory, the unconscious incorporation of the values, attitudes, and qualities of another person into the individual's own ego structure.

Intromission. Insertion of *penis* into *vagina* or anus.

Introspective method. A procedure whereby trained subjects are asked to report on their conscious experiences; the principal method of study in early-twentieth-century psychology.

Introversion-extroversion. In Eysenck's theory of personality, a dimension referring for the most part to conditionability. Extroverts are said to acquire *conditioned responses* slowly and lose them rapidly; the reverse is true of introverts.

Involutional melancholia. An *affective disorder* characterized by profound sadness and occurring at a person's *climacteric* in late middle age; does not appear in DSM-III.

Irrational beliefs. Self-defeating assumptions which are assumed by *rational-emotive* therapists to underlie psychological distress.

Irresistible impulse. The term used in an 1834 Ohio court ruling on criminal responsibility in which it was decided that an *insanity defense* can be established by proving that the accused had an uncontrollable urge to perform the act.

Jacksonian epilepsy. A form of *epilepsy* in which muscle spasms are limited to a particular part of the body.

Juvenile paresis. A form of syphilis which is congenital and is similar to the adult disorder; the onset of deterioration is at twelve to fourteen years, after a symptom-free childhood.

Klinefelter's syndrome. A disorder of males in which an extra X *chromosome* usually keeps the testes small at puberty, may produce *mental retardation,* and may cause secondary female sex characteristics to develop.

Korsakoff's psychosis. A chronic brain disorder associated with *Wernicke's disease;* marked by loss of recent memories and associated *confabulation* and by additional lesions in the *thalamus.*

La belle indifférence. The blasé attitude people with *conversion disorder* have toward their symptoms.

Labile. Easily moved or changed; quickly shifting from one emotion to another or easily aroused.

Laceration. A jagged wound; in the brain, a tearing of tissue by an object entering the skull, often causing paralysis, change in personality, intellectual impairment, and even death.

Latency period. In psychoanalytic theory, the years between ages six and twelve during which id impulses play a minor role in motivation.

Lateral sulcus. A major horizontal fissure along the side of each *cerebral hemisphere,* separating the *frontal* and *parietal lobes* from the *temporal lobe.*

Learned helplessness. An individual's passivity and sense of being unable to act and to control his or her life, acquired through unpleasant experiences and traumas in which efforts made were ineffective; according to Martin Seligman, brings on *depression*.

Learning disabilities. Problems in mastering reading, arithmetic, or speech that are not caused by *mental retardation*, impairment of visual or auditory functions, other psychological disorders, or cultural disadvantage. Called *specific developmental disorders* in DSM-III.

Learning paradigm. As applied in abnormal psychology, a set of assumptions that abnormal behavior is learned in the same way as other human behavior.

Least restrictive alternative. Legal principle according to which a committed mental patient must be treated in a setting that imposes as few restrictions as possible on his or her freedom.

Lesbian. Female homosexual.

Lesch-Nyhan syndrome. A serious kidney disease and *mental retardation* of male infants who receive a defective *gene* on the X *chromosome* from the mother. They become irritable after a few months, lose motor control, are self-mutilative by the second year, and die very young of renal and neurological damage.

Lesion. Any localized abnormal structural change in organ or tissue caused by disease or injury.

Libido. See *Eros*.

Life Change Unit (LCU) **score.** A score produced by totaling ratings of the stressfulness of recently experienced life events; high scores are found to be related to the contracting of a number of physical illnesses.

Limbic system. Lower parts of the *cerebrum* made up of primitive cortex; controls visceral and bodily changes associated with emotion and regulates drive-motivated behavior.

Lithium carbonate. A drug useful in treating both *mania* and *depression* in *bipolar disorder*.

Lobotomy. A brain operation in which the nerve pathways between the *frontal lobes* of the brain and the *thalamus* and *hypothalamus* are cut in hopes of effecting beneficial behavioral change.

Logotherapy. Existential *psychotherapy* developed by Viktor Frankl, aimed at helping the demoralized client restore meaning to life by placing his or her suffering in a larger spiritual and philosophical context. The individual assumes responsibility for his or her existence and for pursuing the values inherent in life.

Longitudinal research. Investigation which collects information on the same individuals repeatedly over time, perhaps many years, in an effort to determine how phenomena change.

Long-term memory. Material stored in memory longer ago than a few minutes.

Loose association. In *schizophrenia*, an aspect of *thought disorder* wherein the patient has difficulty sticking to one topic and drifts off on a train of associations evoked by an idea from the past.

LSD (*d*-lysergic acid diethylamide). A drug synthesized in 1938 and discovered to be a *hallucinogen* in 1943; derived from lysergic acid, the principal constituent of the *alkaloids* of ergot, a grain fungus which in earlier centuries brought on epidemics of spasmodic ergotism, a nervous disorder sometimes marked by psychotic symptoms.

Magical thinking. The conviction of the individual that his or her thoughts, words, and actions may in some manner cause or prevent outcomes in a way that defies the normal laws of cause and effect.

Mainstreaming. Policy of placing handicapped children in regular classrooms; special classes are provided them as needed, but they share as much as possible in the opportunities and ambience afforded normal youngsters.

Major depression. Disorder of individuals who have experienced episodes of *depression* but not of *mania*; DSM-III term. Also called *unipolar depression*.

Malingering. Faking a physical or psychological incapacity in order to avoid a responsibility or gain an end; the goal is readily recognized from the individual's circumstances. To be distinguished from *conversion disorder*, in which the incapacity is assumed to be beyond voluntary control.

Malleus Maleficarum ("the witches' hammer"). A manual written by two Dominican monks in the fifteenth century to provide rules for identifying and trying witches; regarded as a legal document.

Mammillary body. Either of two small rounded structures located in the *hypothalamus* and consisting of *nuclei*.

Mania. Emotional state of intense but unfounded elation evidenced in talkativeness, *flight of ideas* and distractibility, in grandiose plans and spurts of purposeless activity. Called *bipolar disorder* in DSM-III.

Manic-depressive illness, manic-depressive psychosis. Originally described by Kraepelin; an *affective disorder* characterized by alternating moods of euphoria and profound sadness or by one of these moods. Called *bipolar disorder* in DSM-III.

Maple Syrup Urine disease. An inherited defect in *amino acid* metabolism causing *mental retardation* and death usually within first year.

Marathon group. A group session run continuously for a day or even longer, typically for *sensitivity training*, the assumption being that defenses can be worn down by the physical and psychological fatigue generated through intensive and continuous group interaction.

Marijuana. A *psychedelic* drug derived from the dried and ground leaves and stems of the female hemp plant, *Cannabis sativa*.

Marital therapy. Any professional intervention which treats relationship problems of a couple.

Masochism. Marked preference for obtaining or increasing sexual gratification through subjection to pain.

Masturbation. Self-stimulation of the genitals, typically to *orgasm*.

McNaghten rule. A British court decision of 1843 which stated that an *insanity defense* can be established by proving that the defendant did not know what he was doing or did not realize that it was wrong.

Mediation theory. In psychology, the general view that certain stimuli do not directly initiate an overt response but activate an intervening process, which in turn initiates the response; an explanation of thinking, drives, emotions, and beliefs in terms of stimulus and response.

Mediator. In psychology, an inferred state invervening between the observable stimulus and response, being activated by the stimulus and in turn initiating the response; in more general terms, a thought, drive, emotion, or belief. Also called a *construct*.

Medical model (disease model). As applied in abnormal psychology, a set of assumptions that conceptualizes abnormal behavior as being similar to physical diseases.

Medulla oblongata. An area in the *brainstem* through which nerve fiber tracts ascend to or descend from higher brain centers.

Megalomania. Paranoid *delusion of grandeur* in which an individual believes himself to be an important person or to be carrying out great plans.

Melancholia. Vernacular diagnosis of several millenniums' standing for profound sadness and depression. In *major depression* with melancholia the individual is unable to feel better even momentarily when something good happens, regularly feels worse in the morning and awakens early, and suffers a deepening of other symptoms of depression.

Meninges. The three layers of nonneural tissue that envelop the brain and spinal cord. They are the dura mater, the arachnoid, and the pia mater.

Meningitis. An inflammation of the *meninges* through infection, usually by a bacterium, or through irritation. **Meningococcal,** the epidemic form of the disease caused by *Neisseria meningitidis;* takes the life of 10 percent who contract it and causes cerebral palsy, hearing loss, speech defects, and other forms of permanent brain damage in one of four who recover.

Mental age. The numerical index of an individual's cognitive development determined by standardized *intelligence tests.*

Mental retardation. Subnormal intellectual functioning associated with impairment in social adjustment and beginning before age eighteen, usually long before.

Meprobamate. Generic term for *Miltown,* a minor *tranquil-izer,* the first introduced and for a time one of the most widely used.

Mescaline. An *hallucinogen* and *alkaloid* which is the active ingredient of *peyote.*

Mesmerize. First term for hypnotize, after Franz Anton Mesmer, an Austrian physician who in the late eighteenth century treated, and cured, hysterical or *conversion disorders* by what he considered the animal magnetism emanating from his body and permeating the universe.

Metabolism. The sum of the intracellular processes by which large molecules are broken down into smaller ones, releasing energy and wastes, and by which small molecules are built up into new living matter, consuming energy.

Methadone. A synthetic addictive *narcotic* for treating *heroin* addicts; acts as a substitute for heroin by eliminating its effects and the craving for it.

Methedrine. A very strong *amphetamine,* sometimes shot directly into the veins.

3-Methoxy-4-hydroxyphenylethylene glycol (MHPG). A major metabolite of *norepinephrine.*

Midbrain. The middle part of the brain which consists of a mass of nerve fiber tracts connecting the spinal cord and *pons, medulla,* and *cerebellum* to the *cerebral cortex.*

Migraine headache. Extremely debilitating headache caused by sustained dilation of the extracranial arteries, the temporal artery in particular; the dilated arteries trigger pain-sensitive nerve fibers in the scalp.

Mild mental retardation. A limitation in mental development measured on IQ tests at between 50 and 70; children with such a limitation are considered the educable mentally retarded and are placed in special classes.

Milieu therapy. Treatment procedure which attempts to make the total environment and all personnel and patients of the hospital a *therapeutic community,* conducive to psychological improvement; the staff conveys to the patients the expectation that they can and will behave more normally and responsibly.

Miltown. Trade name for *meprobamate,* one of the principal *minor tranquilizers.*

Minimal brain damage. Term sometimes applied to *hyperactive* children, reflecting the belief that at least some of these youngsters suffer from minor brain defects.

Minnesota Multiphasic Personality Inventory (MMPI). A lengthy *personality inventory* by which an individual is diagnosed through his true-false replies to groups of statements indicating *anxiety, depression,* masculinity-femininity, and paranoia.

Minor tranquilizer. A drug which reduces moderate to low levels of *anxiety;* most often used with anxiety disorders.

Mirroring. A *psychodrama* technique in which an individual sees himself portrayed by another person, thereby acquiring a better idea of how he is viewed by others.

Mixed design. A research strategy in which both *classificatory* and *experimental* variables are used; assigning subjects from discrete populations to two experimental conditions is an example.

Model. A set of concepts from one domain applied to another by analogy. For example, in trying to understand the brain we may assume that it functions like a computer.

Modeling. Learning by observing and imitating the behavior of others.

Moderate mental retardation. A limitation in mental development measured on IQ tests at between 35 and 49; children with this degree of retardation are often institutionalized, and their training is focused on self-care rather than development of intellectual skills.

Mongolism. See *Down's syndrome.*

Monism. Philosophical doctrine that ultimate reality is a unitary organic whole and that therefore mental and physical are one and the same. Contrast with *dualism.*

Monoamine. An organic compound containing nitrogen in one amino group (NH_2). Some of the known *neurotransmitters* of the central nervous system, called collectively brain amines, are *catecholamines* and *indoleamines,* which are monoamines.

Monoamine oxidase (MAO). An enzyme which deactivates *catecholamines* and *indoleamines* within the presynaptic *neuron,* indoleamines in the *synapse.*

Monoamine oxidase inhibitors. A group of *antidepressant* drugs which keep the enzyme *monoamine oxidase* from deactivating *neurotransmitters* of the central nervous system. With more *norepinephrine* and *serotonin* available in the *synapse,* mood is elevated.

Monozygotic twins. Genetically identical siblings who have developed from a single fertilized egg.

Moral anxiety. In psychoanalytic theory, the *ego's* fear of punishment for failure to adhere to the *superego's* standards of proper conduct.

Moral treatment. A therapeutic regimen, introduced by Philippe Pinel during the French Revolution, whereby mental patients were released from their restraints and were treated with compassion and dignity rather than with contempt and denigration; *milieu therapy* gives patients similar encouraging attention.

Morbidity risk. The probability that an individual will develop a particular disorder.

Morphine. An addictive narcotic *alkaloid* extracted from *opium;* used primarily as an analgesic and as a *sedative.*

Mourning work. In Freud's theory of *depression,* the recall by a depressed person of memories associated with a lost

one, serving to separate the individual from the deceased.

Multiaxial. Having several dimensions, each of which is employed in categorizing; the DSM-III is an example.

Multifactorial. Referring to the operation of several variables influencing in complex fashion the development or maintenance of a phenomenon.

Multimodal therapy. Therapy introduced by Arnold Lazarus to encompass the seven modalities in which a client may experience difficulties—behavior, *affect,* sensation, imagery, *cognition,* interpersonal relations, and drugs—and to treat them through a variety of techniques drawn from different schools of therapy.

Multiple-baseline design. An experimental design in which two behaviors of a single subject are selected for study and a treatment is applied to one of them; the behavior that is not treated serves as a baseline against which the effects of the treatment can be determined. Common design in operant research.

Multiple personality. Very rare *dissociative disorder* in which two or more fairly distinct and separate personalities are present within the same individual, each of them with its own memories, relationships, and behavior patterns and only one of them dominant at any given time.

Mutism. The inability or refusal to speak.

Myxedema. An endocrine disorder of adults produced by thyroid deficiency; metabolic processes are slowed, and the patient becomes lethargic, slow-thinking, and depressed.

Narcissistic personality. Extremely selfish and self-centered, people with a narcissistic personality have a grandiose view of their uniqueness, achievements, and talents and an insatiable craving for admiration and approval from others. They are exploitative to achieve their own goals and expect much more from others than they themselves are willing to give.

Narcotic. One of the addictive *sedative* drugs, for example, *morphine* and *heroin;* in moderate doses relieves pain and induces sleep.

Negativism. A tendency to behave in a manner opposite to the desires of others or to what is expected or requested.

Neo-Freudian. A person who has contributed to the modification and extension of Freudian theory.

Neologism. A word made up by the speaker that is usually meaningless to a listener.

Neoplasm. See *tumor.*

Neurodermatitis. Chronic disorder in which patches of the skin become inflamed; a *psychophysiological disorder.*

Neuroleptic. A *psychoactive drug,* such as *Thorazine,* which reduces psychotic symptoms but has side effects resembling symptoms of neurological diseases.

Neurology. The scientific study of the nervous system and especially its structure, functions, and abnormalities.

Neuron. A single nerve cell.

Neurosis. One of a large group of nonpsychotic disorders characterized by unrealistic *anxiety* and other associated problems, for example, phobic avoidances, *obsessions,* and *compulsions.*

Neurosyphilis (general paresis). Infection of the central nervous system by the spirochete *Treponema pallidum,* which destroys brain tissue; marked by eye disturbances, tremors, and disordered speech as well as severe intellectual deterioration and psychotic symptoms.

Neurotic anxiety. In psychoanalytic theory, fear of the consequences of expressing previously punished and repressed id impulses; more generally, unrealistic fear.

Neuroticism. In Eysenck's theory of personality, a dimension referring to the ease with which people can become autonomically aroused.

Neurotransmitter. Chemical substance important in transferring a nerve impulse from one *neuron* to another.

Niacin. One of the complex of B vitamins.

Nicotine. The principal *alkaloid* of tobacco and its addicting agent.

Niemann-Pick disease. An inherited disorder of lipid (fat) metabolism, producing *mental retardation* and paralysis and bringing early death.

Nomothetic. Relating to the abstract, recurrent, universal, to the formulation of general laws that explain a range of phenomena. Contrast with *idiographic.*

Nomenclature. A system or set of names or designations used in a particular discipline, such as the DSM-III.

Norepinephrine. A *catecholamine* which is a *neurotransmitter* of the central nervous system. Disturbances in its tracts apparently figure in *depression* and *mania.* It is also a neurotransmitter secreted at the nerve endings of the *sympathetic nervous system;* and a hormone, liberated with *epinephrine* in the adrenal medulla and similar to it in action; and a strong vasoconstrictor.

Normal curve. As applied in psychology, the bell-shaped distribution of a measurable *trait* depicting most people in the middle and few at the extremes; see *statistical paradigm.*

Nosology. A systematic classification of diseases.

Nucleus. In anatomy, a mass of nerve cell bodies (*gray matter*) within the brain or spinal cord by which descending nerve fibers connect with ascending nerve fibers.

Object choice. In the psychology of sex, the type of person or thing selected as a focus for sexual activity.

Objective anxiety. In psychoanalytic theory, the *ego's* reaction to danger in the external world; same as realistic fear.

Observer drift. The tendency of two raters of behavior to begin to agree with each other, achieving unusually high levels of *reliability;* their way of coding behavior differentiates their scores from those of another pair of raters. Regarded as a threat to reliable and valid *behavioral assessment.*

Obsession. Intrusive and recurring thought which seems irrational and uncontrollable to the person experiencing it.

Obsessive-compulsive disorder. An *anxiety disorder* in which the mind is flooded with persistent and uncontrollable thoughts or the individual is compelled to repeat certain acts again and again, causing significant distress and interference of everyday functioning.

Occipital lobe. The posterior area of each *cerebral hemisphere,* situated behind the *parietal* and above the *temporal lobes;* responsible for reception and analysis of visual information and for some visual memory.

Occupational drinking. The considerable consumption of alcohol which is associated with particular vocations, very often on the job, such as uncommonly heavy drinking of bartenders.

Oedipus complex. In Freudian theory, the desire and conflict of the four-year-old male child who wants to possess his mother sexually and to eliminate the father rival. The threat of punishment from the father makes the boy *repress* these id impulses. Girls have a similar sexual desire for the father, which is repressed in analogous fashion and is called the Electra complex.

Operant behavior. A response which is supposedly voluntary and operates on the environment, modifying it so that a reward or goal is attained.

Operant conditioning. The acquisition or elimination of a response as a function of the environmental contingencies of *reward* and *punishment.*

Operational definition. A definition of a theoretical concept which equates it with a set of observable operations that can be measured.

Operationism. A school of thought in science which holds that a given concept must be defined in terms of a single set of identifiable and repeatable operations that can be measured.

Opium. The dried milky juice obtained from the immature fruit of the opium poppy. This addictive *narcotic* produces euphoria and drowsiness and reduces pain.

Oral stage. In psychoanalytic theory, the first *psychosexual stage* which extends into the second year, during which the mouth is the principal *erogenous zone.*

Organic brain syndrome. A mental disorder in which intellectual or emotional functioning or both are impaired through a *pathology* or dysfunction of the brain.

Organismic variable. Physiological or psychological factor assumed to be operating "under the skin"; these variables are one of the foci of *behavioral assessment.*

Orgasm (climax). The involuntary, intensely pleasurable, climactic phase in sexual arousal, lasting a number of seconds and usually involving muscular contractions and *ejaculation* in the male and similar contractions in the genitalia of the female.

Orgasmic reorientation. A *behavior therapy* technique for altering classes of stimuli to which people are sexually attracted; individuals are confronted by a conventionally arousing stimulus while experiencing *orgasm* for another, undesirable reason.

Outcome research. Research on the effectiveness of *psychotherapy*; contrast with *process research*.

Overcontrolled. In reference to childhood disorders, problems which create distress for the child, such as *anxiety* and *social withdrawal*.

Paired-associate learning. Memorizing words in pairs.

Panic disorder. An *anxiety disorder* in which the individual has sudden and inexplicable attacks of jarring symptoms, such as difficulty breathing, heart palpitations, dizziness, trembling, terror, and feelings of impending doom.

Paradigm. A set of basic assumptions that outline the universe of scientific inquiry, specifying both the concepts regarded as legitimate and the methods to be used in collecting and interpreting data.

Paradigm clash. The conflict created when a basically different set of assumptions threatens to replace a prevailing *paradigm*, for example, Copernicus' proposal that the sun—not the earth—is the center of the solar system.

Paralinguistic. Relating to audible components of speech, such as tone of voice, which communicate meaning beyond the content of the words spoken.

Paranoia. General term for *delusions* of persecution, *grandiosity,* or both; found in several pathological conditions, *paranoid disorders, paranoid schizophrenia,* and *paranoid personality* disorder. Can be produced as well by large doses of certain drugs, such as cocaine and alcohol.

Paranoid disorder. Disorder in which the individual has persistent persecutory *delusions* or *delusional jealousy*—an unfounded conviction that his or her mate is unfaithful—is very often contentious, but has no thought disorder and does not hallucinate.

Paranoid personality. This person, expecting to be mistreated by others, becomes suspicious, secretive, jealous, and argumentative. He or she will not accept blame and appears cold and unemotional.

Paranoid schizophrenic. Psychotic patient who has numerous systematized *delusions* as well as *hallucinations* and *ideas of reference.* He or she may also be agitated, angry, argumentative, and sometimes violent.

Paraphilias. Sexual attractions to unusual objects and sexual activities unusual in nature. New DSM-III category.

Paraprofessional. In clinical psychology, an individual lacking a doctoral degree but trained to perform certain functions usually reserved for clinicians, for example, a college student trained and supervised by a behavioral therapist to shape the behavior of autistic children through contingent reinforcers.

Parasympathetic nervous system. The division of the *autonomic nervous system* which is involved with maintenance; it controls many of the internal organs and is active primarily when the organism is not aroused.

Parataxic distortion. According to the ego analyst Harry Stack Sullivan, an unconscious misperception of reality stemming from a childhood disorganization in interpersonal relationships and extended to all later relationships.

Parietal lobe. The middle division of each *cerebral hemisphere,* situated behind the *central sulcus* and above the *lateral sulcus;* receiving center for sensations of the skin and of bodily positions.

Parkinson's disease. A *presenile dementia* characterized by uncontrollable and severe muscle tremors, a stiff gait, a masklike, expressionlike face, and withdrawal.

Passive-aggressive personality. People with a passive-agressive personality indirectly resist the demands of others by such exasperating behavior as being late, missing appointments, not answering calls, and making foolish mistakes; their dawdling is considered a hostile way to control others without assuming responsibility for their own anger.

Pathology. The anatomical, physiological, and psychological deviations of a disease or disorder; and the study of these abnormalities.

PCP. See *phencyclidine.*

Pearson product moment correlation coefficient (r). A statistic, ranging in value from -1.00 to $+1.00$; the most common means of denoting a correlational relationship. The sign indicates whether the relationship is positive or negative; the magnitude indicates the strength of the relationship.

Pedophilia. Preference for obtaining sexual gratification through contact with youngsters defined legally as underage.

Penile plethysmograph. Device for recording changes in penile size and thus for detecting blood flow and erection.

Penis. The male organ of copulation.

Pepsinogen. Substance secreted by the peptic cells of the gastric glands in the stomach; if amounts are excessive, can contribute to the development of an *ulcer.*

Perseveration. The persistent repetition of words and ideas, often found in *schizophrenics.*

Personality disorders. A heterogeneous group of disorders, listed separately on axis II; regarded as long-standing, inflexible, and maladaptive traits which impair social and occupational functioning but not contact with reality.

Personality inventory. Self-report questionnaire by which examinee indicates whether statements assessing habitual behavioral tendencies apply to him.

Personality structure. See *trait.*

Petit mal epilepsy. A form of *epilepsy* involving a momentary alteration in consciousness, more frequent in children than adults.

Peyote. A *hallucinogen* obtained from the root of the peyote cactus, the active ingredient being the *alkaloid mescaline.*

Phallic stage. In psychoanalytic theory, the third *psychosexual stage,* extending from ages three to six, during which maximal gratification is obtained from genital stimulation.

Phencyclidine. Known as angel dust, PeaCe Pill, zombie, and other street names, this very powerful and hazardous drug causes profound disorientation, agitated and often violent behavior, and even seizures, coma, and death.

Phenomenology. As applied in psychology, the view that the phenomena of subjective experience should be studied because behavior is considered to be determined by how people perceive themselves and the world rather than by objectively described reality.

Phenothiazine. Class name for a group of nonaddictive drugs which relieve psychotic symptoms and which are considered *neuroleptics;* their molecular structure, like that of the *tricyclic drugs,* consists of three fused rings.

Phenotype. The totality of observable characteristics of a person; compare with *genotype.*

Phenylketonuria (PKU). A genetic disorder which, through a deficiency in a liver enzyme, phenylalanine hydroxylase, causes severe *mental retardation* unless phenylalanine can be largely restricted from diet until the age of six.

Phillips Scale. Series of questions which is filled out by the researcher from the case history of a schizophrenic and is used to assess his *premorbid adjustment.*

Phobic disorder. An *anxiety disorder* in which there is intense fear and avoidance of specific objects and situations, recognized as irrational by the individual.

Physiological paradigm. A broad theoretical point of view holding that mental disorders are caused by aberrant *somatic* processes.

Physiology. Study of the functions and activities of living cells, tissues, and organs and of the physical and chemical phenomena involved.

Pick's disease. A *presenile dementia* involving diffuse atrophy of *frontal* and *temporal lobes,* impairing memory, concentration, and ability to think abstractly; eventually results in psychosis and death.

Placebo. Any therapy or inactive chemical agent, or any attribute or component of such a therapy or chemical, which affects a person's behavior for reasons having to do with his or her expectation of change.

Placebo effect. The action of a drug or psychological treatment that is not attributable to any specific operations of the agent. For example, a tranquilizer can reduce anxiety both because of its special biochemical action and because the recipient expects relief. See *placebo.*

Plateau phase. According to Masters and Johnson, the second stage in sexual arousal during which excitement and tension have reached a stable high level before *orgasm.*

Play therapy. The use of play as a means of uncovering what is troubling a child and of establishing *rapport.*

Pleasure principle. In psychoanalytic theory, the demanding manner by which the *id* operates, seeking immediate gratification of its needs.

Plethysmograph. An instrument for determining and registering variations in the size of an organ or limb and in the amount of blood present or passing through it.

Polydrug abuse. The misuse of more than one drug at a time, such as drinking heavily and taking heroin.

Pons. An area in the *brainstem* containing nerve fiber tracts connecting the *cerebellum* with the spinal cord and with motor areas of the *cerebrum.*

Positive spikes. An EEG pattern recorded from the *temporal lobe* of the brain, with frequencies of 6 to 8 cps and 14 to 16 cps; often found in impulsive and aggressive people.

Posttraumatic stress disorder. An *anxiety disorder* in which a particularly stressful event, such as military combat or a natural disaster, brings in its aftermath intrusive reexperiencings of the trauma, a numbing of responsiveness to the outside world, estrangement from others, a tendency to be easily startled, nightmares, recurrent dreams, and otherwise disturbed sleep.

Predictive validity. See *validity.*

Predisposition. An inclination or tendency to respond in a certain way, either inborn or acquired; in abnormal psychology, a factor which lowers the ability to withstand stress and inclines the individual toward *pathology.*

Premature ejaculation. Inability of the male to inhibit his *orgasm* long enough for mutually satisfying sexual relations.

Premorbid adjustment. In research on *schizophrenia,* the social and sexual adjustment of the individual before the onset or diagnosis of his symptoms; patients with good premorbid adjustment are those found to have been relatively normal earlier, but those with poor premorbid adjustment had inadequate interpersonal and sexual relations.

Premorbid personality. Maddi's term for a person who plays social roles well and satisfies his biological needs and yet has a feeling of emptiness and lack of fulfillment; he is regarded as a candidate for *existential neurosis.*

Preoperational stage. Second period of intellectual development, ages two to seven, according to Piaget; the child develops an internal representation of the external world but still is unable to manipulate ideas in an abstract fashion.

Preparedness. In *classical conditioning* theory, a biological *predisposition* to be especially sensitive to particular stimuli and to associate them readily with the *unconditioned stimulus.*

Presenile dementia. A degeneration of brain tissue occurring when the individual is in his forties or fifties and causing progressive mental deterioration.

Prevalence. In community studies of a disorder, the percent of a population that has it at a given time; compare with *incidence.*

Prevention. Primary, efforts in *community psychology* to reduce the incidence of new cases of psychological disorder by such means as altering stressful living conditions and genetic counseling. **Secondary,** efforts to detect disorders early, so that they will not develop into full-blown, perhaps chronic disabilities. **Tertiary,** efforts to reduce the long-term consequences of having a disorder, equivalent in most respects to therapy.

Primary empathy. A form of *empathy* in which the therapist understands the content and feeling of what the client is saying and expressing, from the client's *phenomenological* point of view; compare with *advanced accurate empathy.*

Primary impotence. See *impotence.*

Primary narcissism. In psychoanalytic theory, the part of the *oral stage* of *psychosexual* development during which the *ego* has not yet differentiated from the *id.*

Primary process. In psychoanalytic theory, one of the *id's* means of reducing tension, by imagining what it desires.

Privileged communication. One between parties in a confidential relation that is protected by statute. A spouse, doctor, lawyer, pastor, psychologist, or psychiatrist cannot be forced, except under unusual circumstances, to disclose it as a witness.

Proband. The person who in a genetic investigation bears the diagnosis or *trait* that the investigator is interested in. Same as *index case.*

Process-reactive. A dimension used to distinguish schizophrenics; process schizophrenics suffer long-term and gradual deterioration before the onset of their illness, whereas reactive schizophrenics have a better premorbid history and a later rapid onset of symptoms. See *premorbid adjustment.*

Process research. Research on the psychological mechanisms by which a therapy may bring improvement. Compare *outcome research.*

Profound mental retardation. A limitation in mental development measured on IQ tests at less than 20; children with this degree of retardation require total supervision of all their activities.

Progestins. Steroid progestational hormones which are regarded as the biological precursors of androgens, the male sex hormones.

Prognosis. A prediction of the likely course and outcome of an illness.

Projection. A *defense mechanism* whereby characteristics or desires unacceptable to the *ego* are attributed to someone else.

Projective test. A psychological assessment device employing a set of standard but vague stimuli, on the assumption that unstructured material will allow unconscious motivations and fears to be uncovered. The Rorschach series of inkblots is an example.

Pronoun reversal. A speech problem in which the child refers to himself as "he" or "you" and uses "I" or "me" in referring to others; often found in the speech of children with *infantile autism.*

Psilocybin. A *psychedelic* drug extracted from the mushroom *Psilocybe mexicana.*

Psyche. The soul, spirit, or mind as distinguished from the body; in psychoanalytic theory, the totality of the *id, ego,* and *superego* including both conscious and unconscious components.

Psychedelic. A drug which expands consciousness; see also *hallucinogen.*

Psychiatrist. A physician (M.D. degree) who has taken specialized postdoctoral training, called a residency, in the diagnosis, treatment, and prevention of mental and emotional disorders.

Psychoactive drug. A chemical compound having a psychological effect, altering mood or thought processes; a *tranquilizer* is an example.

Psychoanalysis. A term applied primarily to the therapy procedures pioneered by Freud, entailing *free association, dream interpretation,* and working through of the *transference neurosis.* More recently the term has come to encompass the numerous variations on basic Freudian therapy.

Psychoanalyst (analyst). A therapist who has taken specialized postdoctoral training in psychoanalysis, after earning either an M.D. or a Ph.D.

Psychodrama. A kind of group psychotherapy, introduced by Moreno, in which patients play out, in theatrical settings, their feelings toward important figures and situations in their lives.

Psychodynamic. In psychoanalytic theory, relating to the mental and emotional forces and processes that develop in early childhood and their effects on behavior and mental states.

Psychogenesis. Development from psychological origins as distinguished from somatic origins; contrast with *somatogenesis*.

Psychogenic amnesia. A *dissociative disorder* in which the person suddenly becomes unable to recall important personal information, to an extent that cannot be explained by ordinary forgetfulness.

Psychogenic fugue. A *dissociative disorder* in which the person, totally amnesic and unable to recall the past, suddenly moves to a new location and assumes a new identity.

Psychogenic pain disorder. A *somatoform disorder* in which the person complains of severe and prolonged pain, which is not accounted for by organic pathology but which does follow stress or permits the patient to avoid a hated activity or to gain attention and sympathy.

Psychological autopsy. Analysis of an individual's *suicide* through the examination of his letters and through interviews with friends and relatives in the hope of discovering why he took his life.

Psychological deficit. Term used to indicate that performance of a pertinent psychological process is below that expected of the normal person.

Psychological dependency. Term sometimes applied to the reason for *substance abuse;* reliance on a drug because its effects make stressful situations more bearable, without physiological addiction to it.

Psychological test. Standardized procedure designed to measure subject's performance of a particular task or to assess his personality.

Psychomotor epilepsy. Form of epileptic seizure in which the individual loses contact with the environment but appears conscious and performs some routine, repetitive act or engages in more complex activity.

Psychopath. See *antisocial personality.*

Psychopathologist. Mental health professional who conducts research into the nature and development of mental and emotional disorders; academic backgrounds can differ, some having been trained as experimental psychologists, others as psychiatrists, still others as biochemists.

Psychophysiological disorder. A disorder with physical symptoms that may involve actual tissue damage, usually in one organ system, and that are produced in part by continued mobilization of the *autonomic nervous system* under stress. *Hives* and *ulcers* are examples. No longer listed in DSM-III in a separate category, such disorders are now diagnosed on axis I as psychological factor influencing a physical condition; on axis III is given the specific physical condition.

Psychophysiology. The discipline concerned with the bodily changes that accompany psychological events.

Psychosexual disorders. Disorders of sexual functioning in which psychological factors are assumed to be of major etiological significance: *gender identity disorders, paraphilias,* and *psychosexual dysfunctions.* New major DSM-III category.

Psychosexual dysfunctions. Dysfunctions in which the appetitive or psychophysiological changes of the normal sexual response cycle are inhibited. New DSM-III diagnoses.

Psychosexual stages. In psychoanalytic theory, critical developmental phases which the individual passes through, each stage characterized by the body area providing maximal erotic gratification. The adult personality is formed by the pattern and intensity of instinctual gratification at each stage.

Psychosexual trauma. As applied by Masters and Johnson, earlier frightening or degrading sexual experience which is related to present *psychosexual dysfunction.*

Psychosis. A severe mental disorder in which thinking and emotion are so impaired that the individual is seriously out of contact with reality.

Psychosocial system. As applied by Masters and Johnson, the social, psychological, and cultural attitudes toward sexual responding.

Psychosomatic disorder. See *psychophysiological disorder.*

Psychosurgery. Any surgical technique in which neural pathways in the brain are cut in order to change behavior. See *lobotomy.*

Psychotherapy. Primarily verbal means of helping troubled individuals change their thoughts, feelings, and behavior to reduce distress and to achieve greater life satisfaction; see *insight therapy* and *behavior therapy.*

Psychotic depression. Profound sadness and unjustified feelings of unworthiness in which there are also *delusions.*

Psychoticism. In Eysenck's theory of personality, a dimension referring to degree of contact with reality.

Punishment. In psychological experiments, any noxious stimulus imposed on the animal to reduce the probability that it will behave in the way deemed by the experimenter to be incorrect.

Q-sort. A personality test in which the respondent sorts a number of descriptive statements into categories ranging from "very characteristic" to "very uncharacteristic," depending on how they apply to him. Often used in research on *client-centered therapy.*

Random assignment. A method of assigning subjects to groups in an *experiment* that gives each subject an equal chance of being in each group. The procedure helps to ensure that groups are comparable before the experimental manipulation begins.

Rape. To force sexual intercourse or other sexual activity on another person. **Forcible rape** is the legal term. **Statutory rape** is sexual intercourse between an adult male and a female who is under the age of consent.

Rapid-smoking treatment. A *behavior therapy* technique for reducing cigarette smoking in which the person is instructed to puff much more quickly than usual, in an effort to make the whole experience an aversive one.

Rapport. A close, trusting relationship.

Rational-emotive therapy. A *cognitive-restructuring behavior therapy* introduced by Albert Ellis and based on the assumption that much disordered behavior is rooted in what people tell themselves. The therapy aims to alter the unrealistic goals individuals set for themselves, such as ''I must be universally loved.''

Rationalization. A *defense mechanism* in which a plausible reason is unconsciously invented by the *ego* to protect itself from confronting the real reason for an action, thought, or emotion.

Raynaud's disease. A *psychophysiological disorder* in which capillaries, especially of the fingers and toes, are subject to spasm; characterized by cold, moist hands, commonly accompanied by pain; may progress to local gangrene.

Reaction formation. A *defense mechanism* whereby an unconscious and unacceptable impulse or feeling which would cause anxiety is converted into its opposite so that it can become conscious and be expressed.

Reaction time test. A procedure for determining the interval between the application of a stimulus and the beginning of the subject's response.

Reactivity. The phenomenon whereby the object of observation is changed by the very fact that it is being observed.

Recessive gene. A *gene* which must be paired with one identical to it in order to determine a *trait* in the *phenotype*.

Recovery time. The period it takes for a physiological process to return to *baseline* after the body has responded to a stimulus.

Refractory phase. Brief period after stimulation of a nerve, muscle, or other irritable element during which it is unresponsive to a second stimulus; or period after intercourse during which the male cannot have another orgasm.

Regression. A *defense mechanism* in which anxiety is avoided by retreating to the behavior patterns of an earlier *psychosexual stage*.

Reinforcement. In *operant conditioning,* increasing the probability that a response will recur either by presenting a contingent positive event or by removing a negative one.

Reliability. The extent to which a test, measurement, or classification system produces the same scientific observation each time it is applied.

Repression. A *defense mechanism* whereby impulses and thoughts unacceptable to the *ego* are pushed into the *unconscious.*

Resistance. During *psychoanalysis,* the defensive tendency of the unconscious part of the *ego* to ward off from consciousness particularly threatening repressed material.

Resistance to extinction. The tendency of a *conditioned response* to persist in the absence of any *reinforcement.*

Resolution phase. In the sexual arousal cycle, the last stage, during which sexual tensions abate.

Response acquiescence. A ''yea''-saying *response set,* or agreeing with a question regardless of its content.

Response cost. An *operant conditioning* punishment procedure in which the misbehaving person is fined already earned reinforcers.

Response deviation. A tendency to answer questionnaire items in an uncommon way, regardless of their content.

Response hierarchy. The ordering of a series of responses according to the likelihood of their being elicited by a particular stimulus.

Response prevention. A *behavior therapy* technique in which the person is discouraged from making an accustomed response; used primarily with *compulsive* rituals.

Response set. The tendency of an individual to respond in a particular way to questions or statements on a test—for example, with a ''False''—regardless of the content of each query or statement.

Reticular formation. Network of *nuclei* and fibers in the central core of the *brainstem;* important in arousing the cortex and maintaining alertness, in the processing of incoming sensory stimulation, and in adjusting spinal reflexes.

Retrograde amnesia. Loss of memory for events immediately preceding a traumatic incident; and sometimes, after brain damage, for events extending far back in time.

Retrospective report. A recollection by an individual of a past event.

Revealed-differences technique. A procedure for studying family behavior by observing its members in a laboratory as they try to agree on an answer to a particular question.

Reversal design (ABAB design). An experimental design in which behavior is measured during a baseline period (A), during a period when a treatment is introduced (B), during the reinstatement of the conditions that prevailed in the baseline period (A), and finally during a reintroduction of the treatment (B). Common in operant research to isolate cause-effect relationships.

Reward. In psychological experiments, any satisfying event or stimulus which, by being contingent with a response, reinforces this response which it follows and increases the probability that the subject will so respond again.

Rh factor. Substances present in the red blood cells of most people. If Rh factors are present in the blood of a fetus but not in that of the mother, her system produces antibodies which may enter the bloodstream of the fetus and indirectly damage the brain.

Right to refuse treatment. Legal principle according to which a committed mental patient may decline to participate in unconventional or risky treatments.

Right to treatment. Legal principle according to which a committed mental patient must be provided some minimal amount and quality of professional intervention, enough to provide a realistic opportunity for meaningful improvement.

Rorschach test. A *projective test* in which the examinee is instructed to interpret a series of ten inkblots reproduced on cards.

Role playing. See *behavior rehearsal.*

Rosenthal effect. The tendency for results to conform to experimenters' expectations unless stringent safeguards are instituted to minimize human bias; named after Robert Rosenthal, who performed many of the original experiments revealing the problem.

Rubella (German measles). An infectious disease which if contracted by the mother during the first three months of pregnancy has a high risk of causing *mental retardation* and physical deformity in the child.

Sadism. Marked preference for obtaining or increasing sexual gratification by inflicting pain on another person.

Schemata. Ways of perceiving or construing the world.

Schizoaffective disorder. Diagnosis to be applied when it is difficult to determine whether patient has an *affective disorder* or either *schizophreniform disorder* or *schizophrenia.* First suggested as a type of schizophrenia, it is retained in DSM-III without diagnostic criteria.

Schizoid personality. This person, emotionally aloof and indifferent to the praise, criticism, and feelings of others, is usually a "loner" with few, if any, close friends and with solitary interests.

Schizophrenia. A group of psychotic disorders characterized by major disturbances in thought, emotion, and behavior—disordered thinking in which ideas are not logically related; perception and attention are faulty; bizarre disturbances in motor activity; flat or inappropriate emotion; reduced tolerance for stress of interpersonal relations, causing patient to withdraw from people and reality, often into a fantasy life of *delusions* and *hallucinations.* The problems must last at least six months at some time during the person's life; see *schizoaffective disorder, schizophreniform disorder,* and *brief reactive psychosis.*

Schizophreniform disorder. Diagnosis for people who have all the symptoms of *schizophrenia,* except that the disorder lasts more than two weeks and less than six months. Emotional turmoil, fear, and confusion are evident, and *hallucinations* are particularly vivid, but the disorder does not appear to be precipitated by stress. New DSM-III diagnosis; see *brief reactive psychosis.*

Schizophrenogenic. Causing or contributing to the development of *schizophrenia;* often applied to the cold, conflict-inducing mother who is alleged to make her children schizophrenic.

Schizotypal personality. This eccentric individual has oddities of thought and perception—*magical thinking, illusions, depersonalization, derealization*—speaks digressively and with overelaborations, and is usually socially isolated. Under stress he or she may appear psychotic.

School phobia. An acute, irrational dread of attending school, usually accompanied by somatic complaints; the most common *phobia* of childhood.

Secondary impotence. See *impotence.*

Secondary process. The reality-based decision-making and problem-solving activities of the *ego;* compare with *primary process.*

Sedative. A drug which slows bodily activities, especially those of the central nervous system; used to reduce pain and tension and to induce relaxation and sleep.

Self-actualization. Fulfilling one's potential as an always growing human being; believed by *client-centered therapists* to be the master motive.

Self-monitoring. In *behavioral assessment,* a procedure whereby the individual observes and reports certain aspects of his or her own behavior, thoughts, or emotions.

Semantic Differential. A self-report inventory requiring the respondent to rate each concept, such as mother, in one of seven positions between a number of polar adjectives, such as clean–dirty, strong–weak.

Senile dementia. Disorder brought on by progressive deterioration of the brain caused in part by aging; marked by memory impairment, inability to think abstractly, loss of standards and control of impulses, poor personal hygiene, great *disorientation,* and eventually obliviousness.

Senile plaques. Small areas of tissue degeneration in the brain, made up of granular material and filaments.

Sensate focus. Term applied to exercises prescribed at the beginning of the Masters and Johnson sex therapy program; partners are instructed to fondle each other to give pleasure but to refrain from intercourse, thus reducing anxiety about sexual performance.

Sensitivity (encounter) group. A small group of people who spend a period of time together both for therapy and for educational purposes; participants are encouraged or forced to examine their interpersonal functioning and their often-overlooked feelings about themselves and others.

Sensorimotor stage. First period of intellectual development, from birth to two years, according to Piaget; the child essentially knows by doing and has no internal representation of the world in symbols.

Sensory-awareness procedures. Techniques which help clients tune into their feelings and sensations, as in *sensate-focus* exercises, and be open to new ways of experiencing and feeling.

Separation anxiety disorder. Disorder in which the child feels intense fear and distress when away from someone on whom he or she is very dependent; said to be an important cause of *school phobia*.

Serotonin. An *indoleamine* which is a *neurotransmitter* of the central nervous system. Disturbances in its tracts apparently figure in *depression* and *mania*.

Severe mental retardation. A limitation in mental development measured in IQ tests at between 20 and 34; individuals so afflicted often cannot care for themselves, communicate only briefly, and are listless and inactive.

Sex-change surgery. Operation removing existing genitalia of a *transsexual* and constructing a substitute for the genitals of the opposite sex.

Sexual orientation disturbance. Earlier term for DSM-III's *ego-dystonic homosexuality*.

Sexual response cycle. The general pattern of sexual physical processes and feelings, building to an orgasm by stimulation; as proposed by Masters and Johnson, made up of four phases: *excitement, plateau, orgasm,* and *resolution*.

Sexual script. Rules people have for guiding their actions in sexual situations.

Sexual value system. As applied by Masters and Johnson, the activities that an individual holds to be acceptable and necessary in a sexual relationship.

Shaping. In *operant conditioning*, reinforcing responses that are successively closer approximations of the desired behavior.

Shell shock. A confused, disoriented state appearing in soldiers exposed to the strains of modern warfare.

Sibling. One of two or more persons having the same parents.

Sidestream smoke. The smoke from the burning end of a cigarette, containing higher concentrations of ammonia, carbon monoxide, nicotine, and tar than that inhaled by the smoker.

Significant difference. See *statistical significance*.

Single-subject experimental designs. Designs for experiments conducted with a single subject; procedures include the *reversal* and *multiple-baseline* designs in operant research.

Situational determinants. The environmental conditions that precede and follow a particular piece of behavior, being a primary focus of *behavior assessment*.

Situational orgasmic dysfunction. Inability of a woman to have an *orgasm* in particular situations.

Skeletal (voluntary) muscle. One of the muscles which clothe the skeleton of the vertebrate, being attached to bone, and which are under voluntary control.

Skinner box. A laboratory apparatus in which an animal is placed for an *operant conditioning* experiment; contains a lever or other device which the animal must manipulate to obtain a reward or avoid punishment.

Sleeping sickness. See *encephalitis lethargica*.

Slow brain waves. The theta rhythm (4 to 7 cps) usually recorded by EEG from subcortical parts of the brain and the delta rhythm (less than 4 cps) normally recorded during deep sleep; sometimes recorded in awake sociopaths.

Smooth (involuntary) muscle. Thin sheets of muscle cells associated with *viscera* and walls of blood vessels; performs functions not usually under direct voluntary control.

Social desirability. In completion of *personality inventories*, the tendency of the responder to give what he or she considers the socially acceptable answer, whether or not it is an accurate description.

Social phobia. Collection of fears linked to the presence of other people.

Social-skills training. *Behavior therapy* procedures for teaching socially unknowledgeable individuals how to meet others, to talk to them and maintain eye contact, to give and receive criticism, offer and accept compliments, to make requests and express feelings, to approach members of the opposite sex, and how otherwise to improve their relations with other people. *Modeling* and *behavioral rehearsal* are two such procedures.

Social-withdrawal disorder. Disorder of extremely shy children who never "warm up" to new people both young and old, even after prolonged exposure to them. They have loving relations within the family, but they do not join in group play, and in crowded rooms they cling to their parents or hide.

Socioeconomic status. Relative position in the community as determined by occupation, income, and amount of education.

Sociopath. See *antisocial personality*.

Sodomy. Originally, penetration of the male organ into the anus of another male; broadened in English law to include heterosexual anal intercourse and by some state statutes to cover unconventional sex generally.

Soma. The totality of an organism's physical makeup.

Somatic weakness. Vulnerability of a particular organ or organ system to psychological stress and thereby to a particular *psychophysiological disorder*.

Somatization disorder. A *somatoform disorder* in which the person continually seeks medical help for recurrent and multiple physical symptoms that have no discoverable physical cause. The medical history is complicated and dramatically presented. Also called Briquet's syndrome; compare *hypochondriasis.*

Somatoform disorders. Disorders in which physical symptoms suggest physical problem but have no known physiological cause; they are therefore believed to be linked to psychological conflicts and needs but not voluntarily assumed: *somatization disorder* (Briquet's syndrome), *conversion disorder, psychogenic pain disorder, hypochondriasis.* New DSM-III category.

Somatogenesis. Development from bodily origins as distinguished from psychological origins; compare with *psychogenesis.*

SORC. An acronym for the four sets of variables that are the focus of behavioral assessment: situational determinants, organismic variables, overt responses, and reinforcement contingencies.

Specific-attitudes theory. Hypothesis that certain attitudes are associated with certain *psychophysiological disorders,* for example, that a person who feels mistreated may develop *hives.*

Specific developmental disorders. Delays in the development of language and articulation, in being able to read and do arithmetic, skills which are related to maturation. Some signs of the disturbances are often evident in adulthood. New DSM-III category listed on axis II.

Specific-reaction theory. Hypothesis that an individual develops a given *psychophysiological disorder* because of the innate tendency of the autonomic system to respond in a particular way to stress, for example, by increasing heart rate or developing tension in the forehead.

Spectator role. As applied by Masters and Johnson, a pattern of behavior in which the individual's focus on and concern for sexual performance impedes his or her natural sexual responses.

Stability-lability. A dimension of classifying the responsiveness of the *autonomic nervous system.* Labile individuals are those in whom a wide range of stimuli can elicit autonomic *arousal.* Stable individuals are not so easily aroused.

State-dependent learning. The phenomenon whereby an organism shows the effects of learning that took place in a special condition such as intoxication better in that condition than in the ordinary state.

State-dependent memory. The phenomenon whereby people are better able to remember an event if they are in the same state as when it happened. If they are in a greatly different state when they try to remember, happy now, and sad then, memory is poor.

Statistical paradigm. As applied in abnormal psychology, a set of assumptions by which a substantial deviation from the average is considered to be abnormal.

Statistical significance. A magnitude of difference that has a low probability of occurring by chance alone and is by convention regarded as important.

Statutory rape. Sexual intercourse, whether forced or not, with a female who is below an age fixed by local statute as that of consent.

Stimulant. A drug which increases alertness and motor activity and at the same time reduces fatigue, allowing an individual to remain awake for an extended period of time.

Stress. A stimulus which strains the physiological or psychological capacities of an organism.

Stroke. Sudden loss of consciousness and control followed by paralysis; caused by sudden anemia of a portion of the brain when a blood clot obstructs an artery or by hemorrhage into the brain when an artery ruptures.

Subdural hematoma. Hemorrhage and swelling of the arachnoid torn by a fractured bone of the skull.

Substance abuse. Use of a drug for at least a month to such an extent that the person is often intoxicated throughout the day and fails in important obligations and in attempts to abstain, but there is no physiological dependence. See *psychological dependency.*

Substance dependence. Abuse of a drug accompanied by a physiological dependence on it, made evident by *tolerance* and *withdrawal symptoms;* also called addiction.

Substance use disorders. Disorders in which drugs like alcohol and cocaine are abused to such an extent that behavior becomes maladaptive; social and occupational functioning is impaired, and control or abstinence becomes impossible. Reliance on the drug may be either psychological, as in *substance abuse,* or physiological, as in *substance dependence* or addiction.

Successive approximations. Responses which closer and closer resemble the desired response in *operant conditioning;* see *shaping.*

Suicide. Taking of one's own life intentionally.

Sulcus (fissure). A shallow furrow in the *cerebral cortex* separating adjacent convolutions or *gyri.*

Superego. In psychoanalytic theory, the part of the personality that acts as the conscience and reflects society's moral standards as they have been learned from parents and teachers.

Symbiotic psychosis. Disorder of childhood marked by extreme reluctance of the child to be separated from his or her mother and by agitated panic attacks.

Symbolic loss. In psychoanalytic theory, the unconscious interpretation by the *ego* of an event like rejection as a total loss such as suffered in the death of a loved one.

Symbolic process. In behavioral analysis, an activity utilizing symbols.

Sympathetic nervous system. The division of the *autonomic nervous system* which acts on bodily systems—for example, speeding up the contractions of the blood vessels, slowing those of the intestines, and increasing the heartbeat—to prepare the organism for exertion, emotional stress, and extreme cold.

Symptom. An observable physiological or psychological manifestation of a disease, often occurring in a patterned group of symptoms to constitute a *syndrome.*

Synanon. A residential mutual-help community, primarily for drug addicts, in which participants are held responsible for their behavior and encouraged, through harsh and direct feedback, to change their behavior.

Synapse. A small gap between two *neurons* where the nerve impulse passes from the axon of the first to the dendrites or cell body of the second.

Syndrome. A group or pattern of *symptoms* which tend to occur together in a particular *disease.*

Systematic desensitization. A major *behavior therapy* procedure which requires a fearful person, while deeply relaxed, to imagine a series of progressively more fearsome situations. The two responses of relaxation and fear are incompatible and fear is dispelled. Useful for treating psychological problems in which *anxiety* is the principal difficulty.

Systematic rational restructuring. A variant of *rational-emotive therapy* in which the client imagines a series of increasingly anxiety-provoking situations while attempting to reduce distress by talking about them to the self in a more realistic, defusing fashion.

Systematized delusion. A highly organized set of mistaken beliefs which has become the dominant focus of the paranoid patient's life.

Tachycardia. Racing of the heart, often associated with high levels of anxiety.

Tarantism. Wild dancing mania, prevalent in the thirteenth century in western Europe; supposedly incited by the bite of a tarantula.

Taraxein. A protein (a gamma globulin) in the blood serum of schizophrenics, asserted by Heath to be responsible for their psychosis.

Tardive dyskinesia. A muscular disturbance of older patients who have used *phenothiazines* for a very long time, marked by involuntary lip-smacking and chin-wagging.

Tay-Sachs disease. A disorder of lipid (fat) metabolism causing severe *mental retardation,* muscular weakness, eventual blindness, and death in about the third year.

Taylor Manifest Anxiety Scale. Fifty items drawn from the MMPI as a self-report questionnaire to assess anxiety.

Temporal lobe. A large area of each *cerebral hemisphere* situated below the *lateral sulcus* and in front of the *occipi-*

tal lobe; contains primary auditory projection and association areas and general association areas.

Testability. The extent to which a scientific assertion is amenable to systematic probes, any one of which could negate the scientist's expectations.

Testes. Male reproductive glands or gonads; the site where sperm develop and are stored.

Testosterone. Male sex hormone secreted by the *testes;* responsible for the development of sex characteristics such as enlargement of the testes and growth of facial hair.

Tetrahydrocannabinol (THC). The major active chemical in *marijuana* and *hashish.*

Thalamus. A major brain relay station consisting of two egg-shaped lobes located in the *diencephalon;* receives impulses from all sensory areas except for the olfactory and transmits them to the *cerebrum.*

Thanatos. In psychoanalytic theory, the death instinct, which is the second of the two basic instincts within the *id,* the other being *Eros.*

Thematic Apperception Test (TAT). A *projective test* consisting of a set of black and white pictures reproduced on cards, each depicting a potentially emotion-laden situation. The examinee, presented with the cards one at a time, is instructed to make up a story about each situation.

Theory. A formally stated and coherent set of propositions that purport to explain a range of phenomena, order them in a logical way, and suggest what additional information might be gleaned under certain conditions.

Therapeutic community. A concept in mental health care that views the total environment as contributing to prevention or treatment, such as *Synanon* for drug addicts.

Theta rhythm. See *slow brain waves.*

Thiamine. One of the complex of B vitamins.

Third-variable problem. The difficulty in *correlational research* on two variables whereby their relationship may be attributable to a third factor.

Thorazine. Trade name for *chlorpromazine,* one of the *neuroleptics* and a member of the *phenothiazine* group of drugs.

Thought disorder. A symptom of *schizophrenia;* evidenced by problems such as *incoherence, loose associations,* and *concrete reasoning* and speech marked by *neologisms* and *clang associations.*

Thyroid gland. Endocrine structure whose two lobes are located on either side of the windpipe; secretes *thyroxin.*

Thyroxin. Iodine-containing hormone secreted by the *thyroid gland;* participates in regulation of carbohydrate *metabolism,* thus determining the level of activity and in infants growth, development, and intelligence.

Time-out. An *operant conditioning* punishment procedure in which for bad behavior the person is temporarily removed from a setting where reinforcers can be obtained and put in a boring room.

Token economy. A *behavior therapy* procedure, based on *operant conditioning* principles, in which institutionalized patients are given scrip rewards such as poker chips for socially constructive behavior. The tokens themselves can be exchanged for desirable items and activities such as cigarettes and extra time away from the ward.

Tolerance. A physiological condition in which greater and greater amounts of an addictive drug are required to produce the same effect. See *substance dependence.*

Tonic phase. State of rigid muscular tension and suspended breathing in a *grand mal epileptic* attack.

Trait. A somatic characteristic or an enduring *predisposition* to respond in a particular way, distinguishing one individual from another.

Trance logic. A way of thinking during *hypnosis* that allows a person to entertain as real phenomena that are inherently contradictory, such as seeing two people in place of one.

Tranquilizer. A drug which reduces anxiety and agitation, such as *Valium.*

Transference. The venting of the *analysand's* emotions, either positive or negative, by his treating the *analyst* as the symbolic representative of someone important in his past. An example is the analysand's becoming angry with the analyst to release emotions actually felt toward his father.

Transference neurosis. A crucial phase of *psychoanalysis* during which *analysand* reacts emotionally toward the *analyst,* treating him as a parent and reliving childhood experiences in his presence; enables both analyst and analysand to examine hitherto repressed conflicts in the light of present-day reality.

Transsexual. A person who believes he is opposite in sex to his biological endowment and often desires *sex-change surgery.*

Transvestism. The practice of dressing in the clothing of the opposite sex, usually for the purpose of sexual arousal.

Trauma. A severe physical injury or wound to the body caused by an external force; or a psychological shock having a lasting effect on mental life.

Traumatic disease. Illness produced by external assault such as poison, a blow, or stress, for example, a broken leg.

Tremor. An involuntary quivering of voluntary muscle, usually limited to small musculature of particular areas.

Trephining. A crude surgical practice of the Stone Age, whereby a hole was chipped in the skull of a person who was behaving peculiarly, presumably to allow the escape of evil spirits.

Tricyclic drug. One of a group of *antidepressants* so-called because the molecular structure of each is characterized by three fused rings; tricyclics are assumed to interfere with the reuptake of *norepinephrine* and *serotonin* by a neuron after it has fired.

Trisomy. A condition wherein there are three rather than the usual pair of *chromosomes* within the cell nucleus.

Tumescence. Flow of blood into the genitals.

Tumor (neoplasm). Abnormal growth which when located in the brain can be either malignant and directly destroy brain tissue, or benign and disrupt functioning by increasing intracranial pressure.

Twin method. Research strategy in *behavior genetics* in which *concordance* rates of *monozygotic* and *dizygotic* twins are compared.

Two-factor theory. Mowrer's theory of avoidance learning according to which (1) fear is attached to a neutral stimulus by pairing it with a noxious *unconditioned stimulus,* and (2) a person learns to escape the fear elicited by the *conditioned stimulus,* thereby avoiding the UCS. See *fear-drive.*

Type A and type B. Two contrasting behavior patterns revealed through studies seeking the causes of *coronary heart disease.* Type A people are competitive, rushed, aggressive, and overcommitted to their work, type Bs more relaxed and relatively free of pressure. Type As are at risk for heart disease.

Ulcer. A break in skin or mucous membrane accompanied by tissue disintegration; in the stomach or duodenum, a lesion in the lining caused by excessive secretion of hydrochloric acid; generally regarded as a *psychophysiological disorder.*

Unconditional positive regard. According to Rogers, a crucial attitude for the *client-centered* therapist to adopt toward the client, who needs to feel accepted totally as a person in order to evaluate the extent to which his current behavior contributes to his self-actualization.

Unconditioned stimulus (UCS). A stimulus which elicits an instinctual, *unconditional response;* meat powder producing salivation is an example.

Unconscious. A state of unawareness without sensation or thought; in psychoanalytic theory, the part of the personality, in particular the *id* impulses, or id energy, of which the *ego* is unaware.

Undercontrolled. In reference to childhood disorders, problem behavior of the child that creates trouble for others, such as his or her disobedience and aggressiveness.

Unipolar depression. A term applied to the disorder of individuals who have experienced episodes of *depression* but not of *mania;* referred to as *major depression* in DSM-III.

Vagina. The sheathlike female genital organ which leads from the uterus to the external opening.

Vaginal barrel. The passageway of the vaginal canal leading from the external opening to the uterus.

Vaginal orgasm. Sexual climax experienced through stimulation of the *vagina*.

Vaginal plethysmograph. Device for recording the amount of blood in the walls of the *vagina* and thus for measuring arousal.

Vaginismus. Painful, spasmodic contractions of the outer third of the *vaginal barrel*, making insertion of the *penis* impossible or extremely difficult.

Validity—internal. The extent to which experimental results can be confidently attributed to the manipulation of the *independent variable*. **External,** the extent to which research results may be generalized to other populations and settings. As applied to psychiatric diagnoses, **concurrent,** the extent to which previously undiscovered features are found among patients with the same diagnosis; **predictive,** the extent to which predictions can be made about the future behavior of patients with the same diagnosis; **etiological,** the extent to which a disorder in a number of patients is found to have the same cause or causes.

Valium. A *minor tranquilizer,* believed to be the most widely prescribed drug of those available to physicians.

Variable. A characteristic or aspect in which people, objects, events, or conditions vary.

Vasoconstriction. Narrowing of the lumen of a blood vessel, implicated in diseases such as *hypertension*.

Vicarious conditioning. Learning by observing the reactions of others to stimuli or through listening to what they say.

Vineland Social Maturity Scale. An instrument for assessing how many age-appropriate, socially adaptive behaviors a child engages in.

Viscera. The internal organs of the body located in the great cavity of the trunk proper.

Vitamin. Any of various organic substances which are as far as is known essential to the nutrition of many animals, acting usually in minute quantities to regulate various metabolic processes.

Voodoo death. The demise of a member of a primitive culture after breaking a tribal law or being cursed by the witch doctor.

Voyeurism (peeping). Marked preference for obtaining sexual gratification by watching others in a state of undress or having sexual relations.

Waxy flexibility. An aspect of *catatonia* in which the patient's limbs can be moved into a variety of positions, thereafter maintained for unusually long periods of time.

Wernicke's disease. A chronic brain disorder produced by a deficiency of B-complex vitamins; marked by confusion, drowsiness, partial paralysis of eye muscles, and unsteady gait and by lesions in the *pons, cerebellum,* and *mammillary bodies.* Chronic alcoholics are especially susceptible.

White matter. Neural tissue, particularly of the brain and spinal cord, consisting of tracts or bundles of myelinated (sheathed) nerve fibers.

Withdrawal symptoms. Negative physiological and psychological reactions evidenced when a person suddenly stops taking an addictive drug; cramps, restlessness, and even death are examples. See *substance dependence.*

Woolly mammoth. A metaphor for the way the repressed conflicts of psychoanalytic theory are encapsulated in the *unconscious,* making them inaccessible to examination and alteration; thus maintained they cause disorders in adulthood.

Word association test. Experimental procedure in which a list of words is read to the subject who has been instructed to respond to each with the first word that comes to mind.

Working through. In *psychoanalysis,* the arduous, time-consuming process through which the *analysand* confronts repressed conflicts again and again and faces up to the validity of the analyst's *interpretations* until problems are satisfactorily solved.

XYY. The sex *chromosome* designation of men with an extra male chromosome; a *genotype* thought at one time to predispose for violence but now considered less determinative in this regard.

Zeitgeist. German word for the trends of thought and feeling, of culture and taste of a particular time period.

Zygote. The fertilized egg cell formed when the male sperm and female ovum unite.

PHOTO CREDITS

Photo of John Neale by Jerry Bushart.
Photo of Gerald Davison by Conrad Johnson.

Chapter 1

Page 6: David Mangurian. Pages 7 and 9: The Bettmann Archive. Page 10: The New York Public Library. Page 11: The Bettmann Archive. Page 12: (left) Radio Times Hulton Picture Library (top right) Bildarchiv Preussicher Kulturbesitz (bottom right) H. Roger-Viollet. Page 13: (left) Radio Times Hulton Picture Library (right) H. Roger-Viollet. Page 14: The Bettmann Archive. Page 15: Courtesy Commonwealth of Massachusetts. Page 16: P. Boyer and S. Nissenbaum, ''Ergotism: The Satan Loosed In Salem?'', Caporal, L.R., *Science* Volume 192, pp. 21–26, Figure 1, 2 April 1976. Copyright 1976 by the American Association for the Advancement of Science. Page 17: The Bettmann Archive. Page 18: The Trustees of Sir John Soane's Museum. Page 19: Radio Times Hulton Picture Library. Page 20: (left) The Historical Society of Pennsylvania (top right) Brown Brothers (bottom right) H. Roger-Viollet. Page 21: (top left and top center) The New York Public Library-Picture Collection. (top right) © Inge Morath/Magnum (bottom) Bulloz/Art Reference Bureau. Page 22: Historical Pictures Service, Inc. Page 24: H. Roger-Viollet. Page 26: News and Publication Service, Stanford University. Page 27: The Bettmann Archive. Page 29: Courtesy of American Museum of Natural History.

Chapter 2

Page 41: (top and bottom left) Photo by Edmund Engelman (right) Culver Pictures. Page 42: © Erika Stone 1979/Peter Arnold. Page 46: Collection, The Museum of Modern Art, New York. Oil on Canvas 9½ × 13 inches. Given anonymously. Page 49: Culver Pictures. Page 52: Courtesy B.F. Skinner, Photo by Kathy Bendo. Page 61: The Bettmann Archive. Pages 62 and 63: Sidney Harris.

Chapter 3

Page 71: (top left) © Ian Berry/Magnum (bottom left) Leonard Freed/Magnum (top right) © Linda Ferrer 1981/Woodfin Camp. Page 86: © Menschenfreund. Page 90: Copyright 1943 by the President and Fellows of Harvard College; Copyright © 1971 by Henry A. Murray. Page 92: Courtesy Dr. Henri F. Ellenberger. Page 101: © Bohdan Hrynewych/Stock, Boston. Page 106: Michal Heron/Woodfin Camp. Page 114: Courtesy Dan O'Leary, Photo by Stella Kupferberg. Page 115: Photography by Charlyce Jones.

Chapter 4

Page 121: Joel Gordon. Page 125: Sidney Harris. Page 127: Staff photo by Gerald Martineau/The Washington Post. Page 132: Jean-Marie Simon/Taurus Photos. Page 133: George Roos/Peter Arnold. Page 138: Sybil Shelton/Peter Arnold.

Chapter 5

Page 151: (top left) Michael Weisbrot and Family (right) Emilio Mercado/Jeroboam (bottom left) Elizabeth Hamlin/Stock, Boston. Page 161: Peter Menzel/Stock, Boston. Page 163: (top left and top right) Kathy Bendo (bottom left) Rita Freed/Nancy Palmer. Page 167: The Bettmann Archive. Page 691: Henri Bureau/Sygma. Page 171: © Baron Wolman 1980/Woodfin Camp. Page 173: (top) Billy Rose Theater Collection. The New York Public Library at Lincoln Center. Astor, Lenox & Tilden Foundation (bottom) Teri Leigh Stratford and John Ioan Gotman.

Chapter 6

Page 183: © Menschenfreund. Page 187: © Van Bucher 1970/Photo Researchers. Page 192: (top) © Joan Liftin 1978/Woodfin Camp (bottom) Donald McCullin/Magnum. Page 193: © Menschenfreund.

Chapter 7

Page 199: Courtesy Central Museum der Gemeente, Utrecht. Page 203: (top left) Michael Weisbrot and Family (top right) Rose Skytta/Jeroboam (bottom left) Michael Weisbrot and Family (bottom right) Randy Matusow. Page 205: Courtesy David C. McClelland. Page 209: Dr. Jeanne M. Riddle, Department of Pathology, Wayne State University-School of Medicine, Detroit, Michigan. Page 210: Sidney Harris. Page 211: Fred Ward/Black Star. Page 215: Sepp Seitz, 1980/Woodfin Camp. Page 217: American Heart Association, Dallas, Texas. Page 225: Ray Ellis/Photo Researchers.

Chapter 8

Page 231: Bruce Davidson/Magnum. Page 236: Courtesy Aaron T. Beck. Page 244: Marion Bernstein. Page 257: © 1980 Hazel Hankin. Page 260: Paul Fusco/Magnum. Page 262: United Press International. Page 264: The New York Times. Page 267: Reprinted with permission of Concern for Dying, New York City.

Chapter 9

Page 273: Ken Graves/Jeroboam. Page 274: © Menschenfreund. Page 283: United Press International. Page 285: Joel Gordon. Page 288: Courtesy S. Schachter, by Robert M. Krauss.

Chapter 10

Page 297: Charles Gatewood/Stock, Boston. Page 300: Culver Pictures (left) Anne Dorfman (right) Charles Gatewood. Page 312: The Bettmann Archive. Page 313: Cary Wolinsky/Stock, Boston. Page 316: (top) Courtesy of The New York Historical Society, New York City. (bottom) Anne Dorfman Page 317: © Ken Robert Buck/The Picture Cube. Page 328: Culver Pictures. Page 334: Patrick Chauvel/Sygma.

Chapter 11

Page 345: Courtesy Jude Patton. Page 346: United Press International. Page 351: Giancarlo Botti/Sygma. Page 354: Mary Stuart Lang. Page 363: Sybil Shelton/ Peter Arnold.

Chapter 12

Page 370: The Bettmann Archive. Page 371: Ira Wyman/Sygma. Page 380: © Hella Hammid/Rapho-Photo Researchers. Page 385: © Andrew Brilliant/The Picture Cube.

Chapter 13

Page 393: (left) Radio Times Hulton Picture Library (right) The Bettmann Archive. Page 400: Courtesy Mrs. Heidi Schneider. Page 401: Reprinted by permission from *Schizophrenia Bulliten* (Issue No. 7), 1973. Page 403: Benyas/Black Star. Page 405: Bill Bridges/Globe Photos.

Chapter 14

Page 419: James Gelvin/Black Star. Page 426: Courtesy David Rosenthal. Page 430: Christopher S. Johnson. Page 434: P. Schön Jensen. Page 440: Burk Uzzle/Magnum. Page 441: © Marcia Keegan 1981/ Woodfin Camp.

Chapter 15

Page 458: © Teri Leigh Stratford/Photo Researchers. Page 465: Eileen Christelow/Jeroboam. Page 469: United Press International. Page 474: Elizabeth Barry/ The Picture Cube. Page 476: Michael Weisbrot & Family. Page 479: From "The Control of Eating Behavior in an Anorexic by Operant Conditioning Techniques" by A.J. Bachrach, W.J. Erwin and J.P. Mohr, from *Case Studies in Behavior Modification* edited by Leonard P. Ullmann & Leonard Krasner. Copyright © 1965 by Holt, Rinehart & Winston, Inc. Reprinted by permission of Holt, Rinehart & Winston.

Chapter 16

Page 495: © Lester Sloan 1980/Woodfin Camp. Page 496: © Bruce Roberts/Photo Researchers. Page 497: © Bruce Roberts/Rapho-Photo Researchers. Page 502: © Bob Adelman/Magnum. Page 504: Ken Heyman. Page 505: © Rick Friedman/The Picture Cube. Page 511: Steve Potter/Stock, Boston. Page 518: © Andrew Skoinick 1978 Benhaven from *Science News* Volume 119 No. 10. Page 519: Photograph © 1981 by Jill Krementz.

Chapter 17

Page 524: (top left) © 1981 Ira Berger (top right) Frank Siteman/Stock, Boston (bottom left) Ginger Chih/Peter Arnold (bottom right) © Susan Petty 1981/Woodfin Camp. Page 526: Conald C. Deitz/Stock, Boston. Page 527: Alan Carey. Page 528: Michael Weisbrot. Page 532: Mariette Pathy Allen. Page 549: (left) © Joel Gordon 1979 (right) From "Senile Psychosis" by Armando Ferraro in *American Handbook of Psychiatry* Volume 2 by Silvano Arieti. © 1959 by Basic Books, Inc. By permission of Basic Books, Inc., Publishers, New York.

Chapter 18

Page 560: James R. Holland/Stock, Boston. Page 561: © H.W. Silvester/Rapho-Photo Researchers. Page 562: Stella Kupferberg. Page 577: (top) Courtesy W.W. Norton and Company (bottom) The Bettmann Archive. Page 579: © Paul Fusco/Magnum. Page 580: Courtesy Gestalt Institute of Cleveland.

Chapter 19

Page 588: Courtesy Joseph Wolpe. Page 589: Don Hogan Charles/The New York Times. Pages 592 and 593: Sidney Harris. Page 595: © Joel Gordon 1978. Page 596: Courtesy Gordon Paul. Page 607: Courtesy Albert Bandura. Page 609: Courtesy Albert Ellis. Page 614: Courtesy Andrew Salter, Photo by Stella Kupferberg. Page 618: © 1980 Susan Joffe.

Chapter 20

Page 625: © 1981 Ira Berger. Page 626: Michael Weisbrot. Page 629: Hap Stewart/Jeroboam. Page 641: © 1981 Hazel Hankin. Page 644: Vicki Lawrence/ Stock, Boston. Page 647: Philip Jon Baily/Jeroboam. Page 654: Courtesy Achievement Place, Photo by Tom Plambeck. Page 655: © Suzanne Wu 1981/Jeroboam.

Chapter 21

Page 673: Sidney Harris. Page 676: Courtesy Thomas Szasz, Photo by G. Szilasi. Page 677: The New York Public Library-Picture Collection. Page 680: (left) The New York Times (right) Melloul/Sygma. Pages 690 and 702: Wide World. Page 704: (left) Frank Siteman/ Stock, Boston (right) Elizabeth Crews/Stock, Boston. Page 705: Jeff Albertson/Stock, Boston.

QUOTATION CREDITS

Page 28, second column, line 3: Copyright © 1974, by Robert M. Pirsig. Reprinted by permission of William Morrow and Company.

Pages 104, 105, Table 3.10: Copyright © 1976, by Holt, Rinehart and Winston. Reprinted by permission of Holt, Rinehart and Winston.

Page 146, first column, quotation: Copyright © 1966, 1974, by Scapegoat Productions.

Page 239, Table 8.1: From Aaron T. Beck, *Depression: Causes and Treatment.* Philadelphia: University of Pennsylvania Press, 1970. (Originally published as *Depression: Clinical, Experimental and Theoretical Aspects.* New York: Harper & Row, 1967.) Copyright © 1978, by Aaron T. Beck, M.D.

Pages 276, 277, case of Dan: Copyright © 1967, by Prentice-Hall. Reprinted by permission.

Page 284, Table 9.1: Copyright © 1976, by the American Association of the Advancement of Science.

Page 309, Table 10.2: From *Twelve Steps, Twelve Traditions.* Copyright © 1952, by Alcoholics Anonymous World Services, Inc. Reprinted by permission of Alcoholics Anonymous World Services, Inc.

Page 340, case history: Copyright © 1981, by Raymond C. Rosen and Linda J. Rosen. Reprinted by permission of Random House, Inc.

Pages 370, 371, quotation: Copyright © 1970, by Fred Belliveau and Lin Richter. Reprinted by permission of Little, Brown and Company.

Page 443, second column, quotation: Copyright © 1946, by Human Sciences Press.

Pages 485, 486, case history: Copyright © 1976, by the American Psychological Association. Reprinted by permission.

Pages 534, 535, case history: Copyright © 1980, by The Free Press, a Division of Macmillan Publishing Company. Reprinted by permission of Macmillan Publishing Company.

Page 571, Table 18.1: Reprinted by permission of Harvard University Press.

Pages 609–611, dialogues: Copyright © 1976, by Holt, Rinehart and Winston. Reprinted by permission of Holt, Rinehart and Winston.

Pages 692, second column, quotations: 693, first column, quotation: Copyright © 1981, by Community Service Society, Institute for Social Welfare Research. Reprinted by permission of Ellen Baxter, Kim Hopper, and Community Service Society.

Page 709, first column, quotation: Reprinted by permission of Harvard University Press.

Page 721, case history: Copyright © 1970, by Henrietta Yurchenco and The Guthrie Children's Trust Fund. Reprinted by permission of McGraw-Hill Book Company.

Denhoff, E., 462
Depue, R. A., 233, 247
Descartes, R., 199
Deutsch, A., 19
DeVries, H. A., 549
Diament, C., 592
Diamond, B., 684
Diamond, R., 188, 512
Diamond, S., 512
Didion, J., 226
DiMascio, A., 633, 665
Djilas, M., 678
Dobbing, J., 501
Dodson, B., 387
Dole, V. D., 319
Doleys, D. M., 455, 456, 457
Doll, E. A., 489
Doll, R., 324
Dollard, J., 303–304
Domino, E. F., 432
Donaldson, K., 689
Doppelt, J., 523
Dorpat, T. L., 208
Doubros, S. G., 597
Douglas, J. D., 261
Douglas, V., 462
Down, L., 494
Drabman, R. S., 603
Dreifuerst, P., 512, 514
Drew, C. J., 507
Dunaif, S. L., 395
Dunham, H. W., 420
Durkheim, E., 262, 264
Dworkin, B. R., 208

Eastman, C., 237
Eccleston, E., 254
Edelberg, R., 437n
Edelbrock, C. S., 451
Edward, I., 671
Edwards, A. L., 96
Edwards, G., 308
Edwards, J. A., 321
Egan, G., 574
Ehrhardt, A., 343, 344
Eisdorfer, C., 533
Eisenberg, L., 512, 516
Eisenstein, R. B., 675
Ellenberger, H. F., 27n
Ellingson, R. J., 283
Ellis, A., 58–59, 103, 164, 170, 373, 384,
     608–610, 611, 612, 613
Ellis, H., 370, 371
Elmore, A. M., 225, 226–227, 601, 602
Elmore, J. L., 633
Ely, D. L., 215
Emery, R., 688
Emery, R. E., 468
Endicott, J., 87, 410

Endler, N. S., 117
Engel, B. T., 215, 600
Englemann, S., 458
English, H. B., 156
Ennis, B., 688
Enright, J. B., 582
Epictetus, 616
Epstein, L. C., 696n
Epstein, S., 116
Erikson, E. H., 565
Erixon, G., 158
Erlenmeyer-Kimling, L., 436n
Erwin, W. J., 479
Evans, I. M., 158
Evans, M., 386
Evans, R. B., 367
Evans, R. I., 321
Exner, J. E., 93n
Eysenck, H. J., 36, 37n, 159, 221, 468, 569,
     641

Faberow, N. L., 266
Fagan, J., 580
Fain, T., 75
Falloon, I. R. H., 637
Farina, A., 19
Farkas, G., 299
Farrell, W., 653
Farris, E. J., 215
Fedora vicius, A., 613
Feinberg, I., 544
Feingold, B. F., 463
Feinsilver, D. B., 444
Fenichel, O., 303
Fennell, E. B., 200
Fernando, C. K., 601
Ferster, C. B., 237, 515–516
Figley, C. R., 148
Filipczak, J. A., 471, 651, 654
Fillmore, K. M., 306
Fine, B. N., 481
Fischer, M., 428
Fishman, S. T., 629
Fisk, N., 343
Fletcher, C., 324
Flowers, J. V., 634
Folstein, S., 515
Fontana, A., 422
Ford, C. S., 352
Ford, D. H., 562, 566, 572, 577
Fordney-Settlage, D. S., 387
Forehand, R., 113, 453
Forman, J. B. W., 83
Forster, B., 470n
Foucault, M., 15
Fox, R., 299, 313–314
Foxx, R. M., 507
Fozard, J. L., 523
Framo, J. L., 636

Frank, I. M., 332
Frank, J. D., 560
Frankl, V., 258–259, 576
Franks, C. M., 633n
Frantz, A. G., 432
Fredrikson, M., 158
Freed, E. X., 303
Freeman, B. J., 511
Freeman, W., 666
Frei, E., 332
French, T. M., 162
Freud, A., 477, 565
Freud, S., 5, 27, 40–48, 63, 126, 147, 150,
     152–153, 154–155, 158, 162, 175, 180, 184,
     186, 195, 234–235, 237, 262, 315, 322, 367,
     373, 380, 414–415, 416–417, 439, 563, 565,
     566, 568, 572, 585, 680
Freund, K. A., 348
Friar, L. R., 227
Friedberg, C. K., 216
Friedhoff, A. J., 431
Friedlander, H., 684
Friedman, E., 254, 432
Friedman, J. M., 547
Friedman, M., 217
Friedman, R., 215
Frohman, C. E., 431
Fromm-Reichmann, F., 421, 443, 444
Fulton, C. F., 665

Gadow, K. D., 464
Gage, P., 719
Gagnon, J. H., 342, 352, 353, 357, 365, 367,
     370n, 371, 373, 387, 598
Gaines, J., 580
Galen, 9
Galin, D., 188
Garber, H., 506
Garcia, J., 157
Garfield, S., 63
Garfinkel, P. E., 479
Garmezy, N., 281
Garner, D. M., 479
Garofalo, R., 683
Gatchel, R. I., 168–170, 237
Gates, A. D., 501
Gatz, M., 526, 553
Gauthier, J., 591
Gebhard, D., 352, 357, 365
Gediman, H. K., 415
Geer, J. H., 168–170, 237, 348
Geis, G., 355n, 682
Gelder, M. G., 154, 360
Genest, J., 254
George III, 677
George, L. K., 546
Gerbino, L., 665
Gershon, S., 254, 432, 665
Gibbons, D. C., 469

801

SUBJECT INDEX